Platinum Edition

Using

Visual Basic 5

que®

Loren Eidahl et al.

Platinum Edition Using Visual Basic 5

Library of Congress Catalog No.: 97-68766

ISBN: 0-7897-1412-4

99 98 97   6 5 4 3 2 1

Interpretation of the printing code: the rightmost double-digit number is the year of the book's printing; the rightmost single-digit number, the number of the book's printing. For example, a printing code of 97-1 shows that the first printing of the book occurred in 1997.

Screen reproductions in this book were created using Collage Plus from Inner Media, Inc., Hollis, NH.

Contents at a Glance

Table of Contents

I | Visual Basic Fundamentals

1 Introduction to Visual Basic 5   15

V | ActiveX Controls and Documents

23 Using Microsoft's Object Technologies   625

VI | **Database Programming**

28   Building Database Applications   773

31   Improving Data Access with Data Access Objects (DAO)   845

VII   Web Programming

VIII | Distributed Client/Server Environment Programming

41 Using Visual Basic in a Client/Server Environment   1163

Credits

PRESIDENT
Roland Elgey

SENIOR VICE PRESIDENT/PUBLISHING
Don Fowley

GENERAL MANAGER
Joe Muldoon

MANAGER OF PUBLISHING OPERATIONS
Linda H. Buehler

PUBLISHING MANAGER
Fred Slone

TITLE MANAGER
Brad Jones

EDITORIAL SERVICES DIRECTOR
Carla Hall

MANAGING EDITOR
Caroline D. Roop

ACQUISITIONS MANAGER
Cheryl D. Willoughby

ACQUISITIONS EDITOR
Kelly Marshall

PRODUCT DIRECTOR
Chris Nelson

SENIOR EDITOR
Susan Ross Moore

PRODUCTION EDITOR
Leah D. Williams

EDITORS
Kelli M. Brooks
Matthew B. Cox
Sean Dixon
Susan Shaw Dunn
Patricia Kinyon
Bill McManus

COORDINATOR OF EDITORIAL SERVICES
Maureen A. McDaniel

WEBMASTER
Thomas H. Bennett

PRODUCT MARKETING MANAGER
Kourtnaye Sturgeon

ASSISTANT PRODUCT MARKETING MANAGER
Gretchen Schlesinger

TECHNICAL EDITORS
Lowell Mauer
Timothy Monk

SOFTWARE SPECIALIST
Brandon K. Penticuff

ACQUISITIONS COORDINATOR
Carmen Krikorian

SOFTWARE RELATIONS COORDINATOR
Susan D. Gallagher

SOFTWARE COORDINATOR
Andrea Duvall

EDITORIAL ASSISTANTS
Travis Bartlett
Jennifer L. Chisholm

BOOK DESIGNER
Ruth Harvey

COVER DESIGNER
Sandra Schroeder

PRODUCTION TEAM
Christy M. Lemasters
Timothy S. Neville I
Julie Searls
Sossity Smith
Lisa Stumpf

INDEXER
Charlotte Clapp
Becky Hornyak

Composed in *Century Old Style* and *ITC Franklin Gothic* by Que Corporation.

This book is dedicated to the loving memory of Alex and Erin. Although you will never read this, know that you will be in my thoughts always.

—Love, Dad

About the Authors

Loren D. Eidahl is the President of Cornerstone Technology Systems (CTS), an Internet consulting firm specializing in providing complete Internet business solutions, ranging from Internet access to total integrated solutions. CTS has developed several successful professional business applications, including the *Gallery* point of sale application and the *NetSuite* Internet business toolkit. Currently, CTS is developing products to assist business owners who want to perform secure electronic commerce over the Internet.

Loren has been involved with computers since the early days of the PC when 16K was a lot of RAM, and BASIC was definitely not Visual. Over the past ten years he has been a consultant to a wide range of industries, including a national retail chain and several large financial institutions. When not hacking code, writing computer books, or speaking about business on the Internet, he can be found somewhere in Northern Minnesota trout fishing. Loren can be reached via e-mail at **leidahl@cornerstonetech.com** or on the Web at **http:// www.cornerstonetech.com**.

Brian Siler has spent the past two years working as a programmer analyst for a major hotel corporation, developing their executive information system in Visual Basic. Brian is a graduate of the University of Memphis with a Bachelor of Science degree in Computer Science. He has developed applications using Visual Basic, C, HTML, and SQL on a variety of platforms, including PCs, AS/400, Unix, and Vax. Brian may be contacted via e-mail at **bsiler@bigfoot.com**.

Jeff Spotts is a programmer analyst for a major hotel corporation by day; by night, he teaches Visual Basic programming courses at Memphis State Technical Institute. He also creates miscellaneous custom-designed software systems for individuals and businesses. His specialty is creating database applications using Visual Basic as a front-end interface to a variety of database engines. He has been involved with computer hardware and software since the late 1970s and has been programming in Visual Basic since just after its introduction. Jeff may be contacted via e-mail at **jspotts@pobox.com**.

Francesco Balena is the editor-in-chief of *Visual Basic Journal*, the only Italian magazine entirely devoted to Visual Basic. He is a contributing editor of *Computer Programming,* the leading Italian magazine for programmers, and a contributing editor as well as licensee of *Visual Basic Programmer's Journal.* Francesco has used BASIC for 15 years. He has written five books in Italian on DOS, QuickBasic, and VB, in addition to several shareware tools for VB. He is a speaker at VBITS conferences, as well as many Italian conferences, and he offers teaching and consulting services in Italy and abroad. When he has enough of computers and programming, he plays alto saxophone with his jazz combo and likes to spend as much time as possible with his wife Adriana and the little Andrea baby.

Jeff Gainer owns Arrowhead Systems Consulting, Limited, a software management consulting firm based in Hamilton, Montana. He has been a commercial software developer since 1986 and has published numerous works of fiction and nonfiction since 1975. He is a contributor to Que's *Web Development with Visual Basic 5.* Jeff became involved with software in graduate school while using a variety of prehistoric computers to perform textual analysis on the works of various English and American authors. Jeff and his wife, Colly, make their home in the Bitterroot Valley of Western Montana with their Bichon Frise puppies, "Menton" and "Tiny Boo." You can visit Jeff's company on the Web at **http://www.montana.com/asc/**.

Nelson Howell is a veteran of the computer industry. Starting with IBM Mainframes in 1967, he has survived the changes from mainframes to minis to microcomputers. He has had the opportunity to meet computer founders, including J Presper Eckert and Admiral Grace Hooper. In addition to writing, he is now engaged in providing support to software users for Integra Technology International. Now at home in Tucson, Arizona, he is surrounded by his family of four sons and a very tolerant wife.

Duncan Mackenzie is a Microsoft Certified Solution Developer for Online Business Systems, a full-service consulting firm with offices in Winnipeg, Minneapolis, and Calgary. Duncan's experience in the Microsoft toolset, especially in Win32 and COM development, comes from years of working on leading edge projects for Online's clients. His most recent focus has been leading Online in the move from traditional client/server development to intranet/Internet development. Duncan can be reached at **duncanm@online.mb.ca**.

Lowell Mauer has been a programmer and instructor for 18 years. He has taught programming at Montclair State College in New Jersey and has developed and marketed a Visual Basic application for airplane pilots. He is involved in creating several corporate Web site applications. As a manager of technical support, he has attended seminars and training sessions in several countries, and he is an expert in more than six computer languages. Currently, he is a Senior Business Analyst at Cognos Corporation in New York City, N.Y., where he is a consultant for several PC-based computer products.

Brad Shannon has been developing applications in the Hospitality industry for the past eight years. He has worked on both Mid Range and PC Platforms using a variety of programming languages and databases. He can be contacted at **100576.1474@compuserve.com**.

Mike Mckelvy is owner and president of McKelvy Software Systems, a software consulting Firm in Birmingham, Alabama. He specializes in the development of database applications. Mike has been developing software for business and engineering applications for over 15 years and has written a variety of engineering and financial analysis programs for a number of businesses. Mike is also the author of *Using Visual Basic 4* and the co-author of Que's *Special Edition Using Visual Basic 4* and *Visual Basic Expert Solutions*.

Acknowledgments

To fully acknowledge everyone who had a part in this work would take more space than I have been allotted. With that in mind, I would like to mention a few people who were key.

First, I would like to thank my wife Melissa, who provided me with encouragement when I needed it the most.

A very special thank you to Kelly Marshall, who gave me the chance to be a part of this project. I also enjoyed working with Chris Nelson and Susan Moore, whose insightful comments and suggestions helped to bring out the finer points in the manuscript. I would also like to thank all of the co-authors and technical editors that I had a chance to work with on this project.

I would like to thank my two children, Breanna and Derek, for being understanding when Daddy couldn't play with them. Finally, I would like to thank God for giving me the talent, wisdom, and patience needed to accomplish this project.

We'd Like to Hear from You!

As part of our continuing effort to produce books of the highest possible quality, Que would like to hear your comments. To stay competitive, we *really* want you to let us know what you like or dislike most about this book or other Que products.

Please send your comments, ideas, and suggestions for improvement to:

The Expert User Team

E-mail: **euteam@que.mcp.com**

CompuServe: 105527,745

Fax: (317) 581-4663

Our mailing address is:

Expert User Team

Que Corporation

201 West 103rd Street

Indianapolis, IN 46290-1097

You can also visit our Team's home page on the World Wide Web at:

http://www.mcp.com/que/developer_expert

Thank you in advance. Your comments will help us to continue publishing the best books available in today's market.

Thank You,

The Expert User Team

Introduction

Over the past five years we have witnessed the birth of a development tool that has made as permanent a mark in the world of application development as BASIC did. That tool is Visual Basic. Visual Basic 5 (VB5) represents the latest version of this remarkable tool that is destined to change the way we view Windows application development. With the introduction of a compiler and its enhanced controls, VB5 applications can hold their own against C++ applications for speed and extensibility.

Even though VB5 can create blazing fast applications, VB5 is best known for its ability to create Internet and client/server applications very quickly. In this book, you learn how to use VB5 to create every type of application from stand-alone to client/server, including Internet applications. ■

Why You Need This Book

This book was written for the intermediate to advanced Visual Basic programmer who wants to build cutting-edge applications. The intentions behind this book are to explain the various aspects of Visual Basic programming and how these skills can be used to create exciting and creative applications.

Although there are some new and tricky aspects of Visual Basic programming, this book is not intended to be a general programming tome. If you are new to Visual Basic 5, you would be better off purchasing Que's *Special Edition, Using Visual Basic 5.*

This book is actually several types of books in one. The first is a tutorial. The first few sections of this book are designed to get you up to speed quickly with Visual Basic 5. A solid foundation of coding principles and Visual Basic syntax is covered early on, providing the proper ground-work for solid growth.

This book is also designed to be a Visual Basic 5 reference manual. This book provides a good reference to the Visual Basic language and structure, should you want to refresh your knowl-edge in a particular area.

Probably the most compelling reasons why you need this book are the real-world examples. This book provides examples for every major concept explored in this book. What this does is provide you with code that can be used as templates for your own development projects, saving you large amounts of time and energy in the process.

This book is also designed to provide the necessary hands-on experience you need to create ActiveX controls and ActiveX-based applications that are both useful and stable in Web and non-Web situations. Visual Basic 5 contains a complete suite of tools designed to enable you to take full advantage of the Internet. There are tools that let you easily connect your programs to the Internet and include browser capabilities in your programs. In addition, you now can create ActiveX documents and ActiveX controls from Visual Basic. Because ActiveX is the corner-stone of Microsoft's Internet strategy, this puts you right in the middle of the action. And the really good news is that all of your ActiveX pieces can be used in non-Internet programs as well, extending the usefulness of any ActiveX components you create.

A Word About Code Examples

As every programmer knows, a good program is virtually crash-proof. Error-checking must be done for every action that may fail, and appropriate error messages must be given to the user. Unfortunately, good error checking requires a lot of extra program code. For the programmer working on his next magnum opus, this is all just part of the game. But for an author writing a programming book, this extra code has different implications.

A programming book should present its topics in as clear a manner as possible. This means featuring programs whose source code is not obscured by a lot of details that don't apply di-rectly to the topic at hand. For this reason, the programs in this book do not always employ proper error checking. For example, user input may go unverified and control properties may be assumed to be valid.

In short, if you use any of the code in this book in your own project or controls, it's up to you to add whatever error checking may have been left out. Never assume anything in your programs. Any place in your code that you can't be 100 percent sure of your program's state, you must add error checking to ensure that the program doesn't come crashing down on your user. Just because this book's author may have been lax in his error checking (for good reasons) does not let you off the hook.

What Software Do You Need?

The software needed for building the examples in this book depends a great deal on which examples you want to build. At the very least, you need Visual Basic 5 and a copy of Internet Explorer 3, running on Windows 95.

NOTE Internet Explorer can be found on the CD-ROM included with this book. ■

For the examples on integrating Visual Basic and other technologies, you might also need a copy of the specific tools being discussed in those chapters. When building Internet-enabled Visual Basic applications, you may need to have Microsoft's Inet DLLs to provide the API functions being used in the examples. For the examples on ActiveX controls, the ActiveX Software Development Kit (SDK) is needed. For the chapters on Active Server Pages, you need a copy of Microsoft's InterDev.

How This Book Is Organized

This book is divided into 10 major parts including the appendixes. These parts enable you to read only those areas that you have an interest in at the time.

Throughout this book, you will find references to other chapters and sections where specific material is either introduced or explained in greater detail. This way, you can avoid reading those sections that are not of interest, or you can benefit from a more detailed discussion.

What follows is an overview of topics you'll find in each section of this book.

Part I—Visual Basic Fundamentals

This section covers the basics to get you started on your programming adventure. This section starts by taking you on a tour of forms and controls, which are the building blocks of every program you create in Visual Basic. You can see how forms and controls are manipulated by their properties and perform tasks with their methods.

Chapter 1, "Introduction to Visual Basic 5," discusses some of the new features that have been added to VB.

Chapter 2, "Introduction to the Development Environment," takes you on a tour of the newly enhanced Integrated Development Environment (IDE). Even if you are not new to VB, make sure you read this section to learn about the new IDE.

In Chapter 3, "Creating Your First Program," we instruct you step-by-step on how to build an application in Visual Basic.

In Chapter 4, "Working with Forms and Controls," you learn how to effectively use Form and Control Collections. This chapter also shows you how to position your form on-screen.

Chapter 5, "Adding Menus and Toolbars to Your Program," steps you through the process of creating Windows-style toolbars. You also learn how to create pop-up menus by using the menu editor.

Chapter 6, "Using Dialogs to Get Information," discusses when message boxes come in handy. While forms provide the main interface with your users, sometimes you just need to display a bit of information.

Chapter 7, "Responding to the User," discusses how Event-driven programs let your users execute tasks in almost any order. This lets them process information in the way they find most comfortable.

In Chapter 8, "Programming Visual Basic," you learn how to use variables to store and retrieve information while your programs are running.

Part II—More on Visual Basic Controls

Controls are the backbone of every program that you create in Visual Basic. Part II, "More on Visual Basic Controls," teaches you about a few of the more advanced controls that Visual Basic 5 has to offer.

Chapter 9, "Using the Windows Standard Controls," teaches you about the standard controls that have been a part of Visual Basic since the beginning. These controls are the ones that are most often used in your programs. The discussion shows you some of the basics of the controls, some advanced techniques, and the new features of some of these controls.

Chapter 10, "Using the Windows Common Controls," shows you how to create a status bar for your applications. You also learn how to use the TreeView and ListView controls. These two controls provide the capability to implement Windows Explorer-style interfaces for working with lists.

Chapter 11, "Exploring New Visual Basic 5 Controls," discusses some of the new controls that Visual Basic now includes, such as the FlexGrid, a new grid control that enables you to create spreadsheet-type applications or to provide browse capabilities for database programs.

Chapter 12, "Using Control Arrays," teaches you about the control arrays and how you can effectively use them in your Visual Basic applications.

Chapter 13, "Using Containers," discusses how to group the various types of controls for better functionality.

Part III—Outputting and Displaying Information

This sections covers the ways that you can present your information to the end user. This section starts by looking at how text, fonts, and colors can determine how the message is perceived. You also discover how to use features within Crystal Reports to produce reports created from within your application.

In Chapter 14, "Working with Text, Fonts, and Colors," you learn how to display text on-screen through the use of the TextBox and Masked Edit controls. You also learn how to use the RichTextBox control to create a simple word processor that enables your users to control the appearance of the text that they enter.

Chapter 15, "Displaying and Printing Reports," shows you how to send text to the printer and how to line up the information in columns using print zones and formatting functions.

Chapter 16, "Using Crystal Reports," provides you with the information you need to add Crystal Reports' capabilities to your Visual Basic application by using the Crystal Reports Custom Control.

Part IV—Professional Visual Basic Programming

After you have learned some of the basics of creating programs, you are ready for more detailed material. Part IV, "Professional Visual Basic Programming," introduces you to some of the concepts of program design.

In Chapter 17, "Managing Your Projects," you learn how to use the same form in multiple programs. You will also learn how to create a form template to make it easier to create similar forms.

Chapter 18, "Introduction to Classes," shows you how to create a class from scratch and how to use the Class Builder to create new classes from existing ones.

Chapter 19, "Designing User Interfaces," discusses why it is important to design your program before you start writing code. You also see some of the things that make a bad user interface and learn how to avoid some common design mistakes.

In Chapter 20, "Building a Multiple Document Interface," you learn how to create a multiple document interface (MDI) program. You see how this type of program differs from those created with single forms.

Chapter 21, "Creating Online Help," takes a look at the Help Workshop that comes with Visual Basic 5, as well as the new features of Help. You also see how to access the Help file from several different areas within a Visual Basic program.

Chapter 22, "Packaging Your Visual Basic Applications," discusses an application package, which includes many different elements that can be included in a Visual Basic application. Understanding each component and knowing when and how to create them makes your job much easier.

Part V—ActiveX Controls and Documents

ActiveX controls can be used in Visual Basic programs, Internet applications, or other ActiveX-enabled programs. If you have never worked with ActiveX controls or want to find new and creative ways to use them, this section should be of great interest to you. This section deals exclusively with ActiveX controls—how to build, enhance, and debug them.

Chapter 23, "Using Microsoft's Object Technologies," gives you a broad overview of the object technology foundation that Microsoft has made available to you for developing Windows applications using Visual Basic.

Chapter 24, "Creating ActiveX Controls," discusses how ActiveX controls have grown and changed as well as how to create your first control. There are two basic approaches to building ActiveX controls by using Visual Basic 5. Take a look at what each approach involves and some of the issues you need to consider when choosing between the two approaches.

In Chapter 25, "Extending ActiveX Controls," you learn how to create property sheets that provide you with the greatest flexibility at design time. You also will be using the Application Setup Wizard to package your ActiveX control for use in Web pages. This chapter shows you how to prepare your control so that it can be used in Web pages and automatically downloaded by users of Microsoft's Internet Explorer Web browser.

In Chapter 26, "Creating a User-Drawn Control," you learn how to create the user interface, as well as events that respond to user actions. You also learn how to change the appearance of your control based on user events.

Chapter 27, "Creating ActiveX Documents," shows you the differences between and similarities of ActiveX documents and standard Visual Basic applications.

Part VI—Database Programming

Database programs make up a large percentage of all programs in use in the business world today. These programs range in complexity from a simple program for managing a mailing list to a program to handle the power bills for all the customers of a major utility. Part VI, "Database Programming," takes you through the process of building database applications to meet a variety of needs.

Chapter 28, "Building Database Applications," walks you through the process of designing and creating a sample database.

Chapter 29, "Using the Visual Basic Data Control," covers the Data control, which allows you to easily build simple database programs or create database management and report systems for existing databases. You also can use the Data control to quickly start a more complex database that you can build on.

Chapter 30, "Doing More With Bound Controls," enhances those skills that you learned in the previous chapters.

Chapter 31, "Improving Data Access with Data Access Objects (DAO)," shows you how much programming power is available for creating database applications.

In Chapter 32, "Using Remote Data Objects (RDO)," you learn how your Visual Basic programs can easily access data stored in a variety of remote locations through the use of Remote Data Objects (RDO). You see how the recent addition of RDO to Visual Basic's repertoire makes short work of writing applications that need to work with remote data.

Chapter 33, "Database Access with ActiveX Data Objects (ADO)," shows you how to use the ADO object model. This chapter also shows you how to build Web-based and no-Web examples.

Chapter 34, "Multiuser Databases," shows you the steps needed to make your database accessible in multiuser applications safely. This chapter will also show how data replication can be used in your applications.

Part VII—Web Programming

The Internet presents an opportunity like no other for the Visual Basic programmer. Visual Basic 5 enables you create programs specifically to be used and deployed over the Internet. One of the new tools available to Visual Basic programmers is Active Server Pages.

Chapter 35, "Internet Programming with VBScript," shows you how HTML elements combined with VBScript allow users to extend the scope and functionality of Web pages. You learn how to change a static Web page into an interactive, dynamic page by using VBScript and the Internet Explorer Object Model.

Chapter 36, "Programming Web Pages," provides an in-depth look at how to create Web pages by using ActiveX controls. This chapter shows you how to include ActiveX controls in your Web pages with the help of the HTML tag <OBJECT>.

In Chapter 37, "Creating Active Server Pages," you'll learn how you can create Web sites that do almost anything by using Active Server Pages (ASP). This chapter shows you how you can use ASP to create dynamic Web sites very quickly.

Chapter 38, "Working with Active Server Page Objects," continues where the previous chapter left off. You learn what objects are available in ASP and how and when to use them. You also learn how to share information between pages for one visitor to your site, or for all of your visitors.

In Chapter 39, "Using the Web, Databases, and Visual Basic," you will be able to combine your knowledge of ASP, databases, and Web design to create a Web database application. You create a sample Web application that connects to a database; although simple in scope, it can be used as a template for your own applications.

Chapter 40, "Programming Web Functionality into Your Applications," takes you on a tour explaining the Web controls available with Visual Basic 5.0. You further enhance your knowledge of the controls by building a sample application.

Part VIII—Distributed Client/Server Environment Programming

While single-user, PC-based database applications are important, they are not the only database applications you want to build. Chapter 43 discusses some of the considerations required when implementing client/server applications. You also learn how to connect your programs to databases through Open Database Connectivity (ODBC). This gives you access to a wide range of PC, mini-computer, and mainframe databases.

In Chapter 41, "Using Visual Basic in a Client/Server Environment," you learn how to create powerful client/server database applications by using Microsoft's SQL server 6.5 and Visual Basic 5.0.

In Chapter 42, "Using Visual Basic with Microsoft Transaction Server," you see how Transaction Server works and how it uses Microsoft's Distributed Common Object Model (DCOM) technology to provide a transparent platform for building distributed applications.

Part IX—Advanced Topics

Part IX, "Advanced Topics," expands on the fundamentals covered earlier in the book.

In Chapter 43, "Creating a Visual Basic Add-In," you discover how easy it is to create an add-in for Visual Basic. This chapter shows you how to create an add-in that is both fun and can be used as a template for your own efforts.

In Chapter 44, "Building a Wizard," you create your own Visual Basic Wizard. The fundamentals taught in this chapter can be used by you on your own projects.

Chapter 45, "Accessing the Windows Registry and INI Files," provides you with detailed coverage on accessing and manipulating information contained in INI files using the Windows 95 API. It also shows you how to manipulate Registry information using the functions contained in Visual Basic and those contained in the Windows 95 API.

Chapter 46, "Accessing the External Functions: The Windows API," explains how to use some of the more useful API functions. Calling the API enables you to write more advanced applications that are not possible with pure VB programming.

Part X—Appendixes

Appendix A, "Visual Basic Resources," provides you with information on where to find help for your Visual Basic 5 questions.

Appendix B, "What's on the CD," gives you a quick synopsis of the individual items that have been included on the CD-ROM.

The Companion CD-ROM

The CD-ROM included with this book contains the source code and reference materials referred to throughout the book. This source code can easily be cut and pasted right into your own application, saving you time in coding and debugging.

The CD-ROM also contains a huge array of software, including the add-ins, viewers, utilities, and other software packages. These utilities can easily be installed right from the CD-ROM. For a complete listing of the CD-ROM's contents, to turn to Appendix B, "What's on the CD."

Conventions Used in This Book

To make the text easier to understand, this book adopts several style conventions. For example, you'll notice that variable names, function names, and other types of program code that are part of a text paragraph are printed in computer type (monospaced) to set the code off from the surrounding text.

This book presents a variety of code, message and HTML text, commands, and response codes. To distinguish these elements clearly from the rest of this book's text, the code, message text, commands, and response codes appear in a special monospaced font. For example, when this book displays a few lines of code, it looks similar to the following:

```
Function AddTwoNumbers(x As Integer, y As Integer) As Integer
    AddTwoNumbers = x + y
End Function
```

However, a more extensive code listing is presented in a formal listing, such as Listing 0.1.

Listing 0.1   INTRO.BAS—A Sample Code Listing

```
Function CalculatePercentChange(X As Integer, Y As Integer) As Double
    Dim OnePercent As Double

    OnePercent = X / 100#
    If (OnePercent > 0) Then
        CalculatePercentChange = Y / OnePercent
    Else
        CalculatePercentChange = 0#
    End If
End Function
```

Even though this book contains a large amount of code, you don't have to type it all. The CD that accompanies this book provides all demonstrated code (along with the pieces that aren't shown in the text).

Also, occasionally code lines are too long to be printed on one line of this book. In this case, you see the "code continuation character," represented by the symbol ➥, which shows you that the line on which it appears should be typed as a continuation of the preceding line. Here's an example of the code continuation character in use:

```
Public Function ChangeInv(aiPrdID As Long,
➥aiChange As Integer, _
                            ByRef aiBackOrder
➥As Integer, _
Dim ctxObject As ObjectContext
    Dim rdoConn As rdoConnection
    Dim strSQL As String
    Dim rdoRS As rdoResultset
```

Several type and font conventions are used in this book to help make reading it easier:

- *Italic type* is used to emphasize the author's points or to introduce new terms.
- Screen messages, code listings, and command samples appear in `monospace typeface`.
- URLs, newsgroups, Internet addresses, and anything you are asked to type appears in **boldface**.
- Keyboard hotkeys are indicated with <u>underlining</u>. For example, if you see the command <u>T</u>ools, <u>O</u>ptions, pressing Alt and T causes the Tools menu to appear, and then pressing O takes you to the Options dialog box.

As you read this book, you will come across icons and boxes that mark off separated sections of text. These are Notes, Tips, and Cautions which are not necessarily part of the subject under discussion, but related pieces of important information. Some examples of these elements follow.

CAUTION

Cautions present information that you want to be aware of to avoid any disastrous results.

N O T E Notes provide additional information about the subject that you are reading about.

T I P Tips provide unique information that may be based on the author's own unique experiences. In some cases a Tip might provide information that is not available anyplace else.

Cross-references point to sections in other chapters where you can find additional information about the topic being discussed. They look like this:

▶ **See** "Creating a Toolbar with Code," **p. xxx**
▶ **See** "Creating Classes that Contain Collections," **p. xxx**

Sidebar

Longer discussions not integral to the flow of the chapter are set aside as sidebars. Look for these sidebars to find out even more information.

Troubleshooting sections anticipate common problems in the form of a problem and its solution. The response provides you with practical suggestions for solving these problems. A typical example would be:

◆ **TROUBLESHOOTING**

I can't save my file to a floppy disk. Make sure that you've placed a disk in the proper drive. If you know that you have the disk properly placed, make sure it's formatted and ready to receive information.

Sometimes the code listing is too big to comfortably fit into the allotted space in the book. In these cases a special "On the CD-ROM" symbol appears beside the listing, as it appears beside this paragraph. This symbol indicates that the complete listing has been included on the CD-ROM in the folder specified for your convenience.

ON THE WEB

http://www.quecorp.com   On the Web elements refer you to useful Web pages.

Contacting the Author

I welcome your comments and feedback and will certainly do my best to clarify any points presented in this book. Please understand that it's not possible to answer specific questions or provide code examples, but I will do my best to make sure you are able to get started in the right direction.

Good code, like good food, should be enjoyed with close friends. If you have created an exciting application or a unique solution to a problem, I would like to hear about it. On any code submissions please indicate whether you would liked it placed on my Web site for general viewing by the Visual Basic community. Feel free to drop me a note at **leidahl@cornerstonetech.com** any time.

It's difficult to cover every conceivable solution to a given problem; it seems that there is always a better solution just around the corner! If you have ideas to be included "next time," I'd be more than happy to hear them. Until then, enjoy the power that Visual Basic 5 gives you.

- Loren D. Eidahl, Minneapolis MN, 1997

Visual Basic Fundamentals

Introduction to Visual Basic 5

If you have visited a local computer store lately, you've seen that there is an overwhelming number of software packages that you can purchase for your computer. In fact, there are literally thousands of programs available that run under Windows 95, not including those written by companies and individuals for their own use. Looking through the software titles, you can find game programs, productivity programs (such as word processors and spreadsheets), communications programs, databases, and many others. And if you have surfed the Internet, you've seen even more types of programs there.

In addition to all these commercial or publicly available programs, many companies need custom programs to handle their business. These programs can range from custom report writers that prepare expense statements to complex client/server programs that handle billing by using the information stored on a mainframe. Whatever the case may be, one thing these programs probably have in common is a Windows "look-and-feel." Visual Basic makes this easy.

What kinds of programs can you write in Visual Basic?

Visual Basic makes it easy for you to create simple and complex Windows programs, as well as your own customized ActiveX documents, ActiveX Controls, and Visual Basic Add-ins.

What are the new features of Visual Basic 5?

Visual Basic 5 is full of new and improved features and controls that make it possible for you to create more powerful programs faster than ever.

What is object-oriented programming?

You learn how Visual Basic uses object-oriented techniques to create programs that are powerful, robust, and efficient.

Not content just to use available "off-the-shelf" software, you have decided to embark on the adventure of creating your own programs. Well, you've come to the right place and chosen the right programming language. Visual Basic is capable of producing almost any program that your imagination can come up with, including the following:

- Simple single-purpose applications
- Games
- Point-of-sale systems
- Internationally distributed database applications

And while another programming language might be better suited to a particular specialized situation, Visual Basic is perhaps the most versatile and easy-to-use programming language available. ■

Exploring the New Features of Visual Basic 5

As with a new version of any product, Visual Basic 5 incorporates a number of new and enhanced features that make it more powerful and easier to use than previous versions. In addition to a new and improved development environment (IDE), VB version 5.0 includes some performance enhancements. One of the most requested features for Visual Basic was the capability to compile a program to *native code*, or code that is optimized specifically for the microprocessor on which it runs. Microsoft has finally granted this wish. VB5's native code compiler allows your programs to run much faster than before. Also, a faster forms engine greatly enhances the speed of loading forms, adding to the improved performance of applications created with VB5.

In addition to these two performance features, there are a number of other major features that were added to version 5 of Visual Basic. These features are covered in functional groups in the next few sections.

- A native code compiler and improved forms engine make your programs run faster.
- The development environment has been enhanced to make entering code and designing forms easier.
- A variety of program types—other than just the standard EXE, such as DLLs and OCXs—can be created.
- A slew of new controls has been added, including several specifically designed for using the Internet.

Native Code Compiler and Other General Features

One of the key general features of Visual Basic is the capability to compile your programs to native code, much as you can do with C++. As stated previously, this gives you faster programs.

However, don't confuse native code with code that doesn't require the Visual Basic runtime library. Native-code compiled programs are optimized for the microprocessor(s) that they run on; however, the Visual Basic runtime library is still required to provide a fully functional program.

N O T E The Visual Basic *runtime library* contains functions needed to operate your program. For example, the library includes the code for drawing a window on the screen. As a programmer you may not be aware of such functions, so distributing your program may involve including some additional files. ■

Visual Basic also gives you some new design capabilities. As always, you can create programs that use a series of independent forms to display and handle information, or you can create Multiple Document Interface (MDI) programs (which have one main "parent" form and one or more internal "child" forms). Visual Basic 5 also has added the capability to create programs that will run inside a Web browser, either on your local machine or anywhere in the world via the Internet!

▶ **See** "Introducing MDI Applications," **p. 542**

Another new feature is the capability to edit multiple projects in a single Visual Basic session. You'll find this to be a very convenient tool when you use such other new features as custom-created ActiveX controls and Dynamic Link Libraries (DLLs). These types of programs typically involve interaction among multiple VB projects. Therefore, the capability to switch between related projects or compile several projects at a time is very useful.

Development Environment Features

If you have used previous versions of Visual Basic, you will notice an entirely new interface the first time you start the program (see Figure 1.1). The interface has been redesigned to be more compatible with Microsoft's other programming languages—Visual C++, Visual J++, and so on. This makes it easier for programmers who work in multiple environments to move back and forth between them. In fact, the default installations of many of Microsoft's development products now share a common "parent" directory (usually C:\Program Files\DevStudio\).

All of the various windows that make up the Visual Basic development environment are now set up in an MDI-style interface contained within a parent Microsoft Visual Basic form (see Figure 1.2). This makes it easier to manage all the pieces of your program. Many of the windows, such as the Toolbox, Properties window, and Debug window are *dockable*, meaning that they can be placed in a fixed position that remains consistent as you work in the environment. A handy new Form Layout window shows you at a glance how all of your application's forms will be placed on the screen at run time.

FIG. 1.1
Visual Basic version 5.0 sports a totally new user interface.

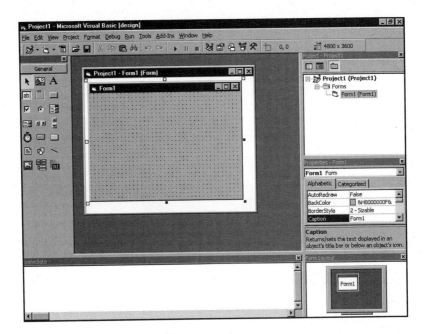

FIG. 1.2
In the new development environment, all windows are contained within the Visual Basic "parent" window.

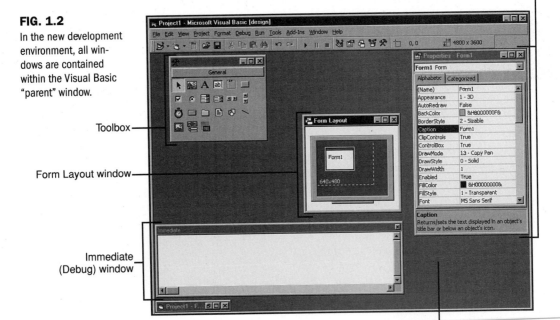

Properties window

Toolbox

Form Layout window

Immediate (Debug) window

Visual Basic parent window

Other great features of the development environment include the following:

- The capability to edit multiple projects simultaneously
- Dockable toolbars and development windows
- Code editor enhancements, including a more robust, context-sensitive right-click menu
- A richer debugging environment
- Pop-up lists to help you remember the syntax of available functions, methods, and properties.

Of course, if you're resistant to change or just don't like the new development environment, Visual Basic 5 has an option to enable you to return to the "classic" Single Document Interface (SDI) environment.

▶ **See** "Understanding the Environment's Key Features," **p. 30**

Enhancements to the Code Editor

Because a great deal of the work done in creating programs takes place in the code editor, Microsoft has added some new features that make it easier to use. These features include the following:

- *Drop-down properties list*   Displays a dynamic list of the properties and methods available for an object. You can select the property or method by typing only the first couple of characters instead of having to type out the entire word. Pressing Enter or the spacebar selects the desired entry in the list. This saves time and cuts down on typographical errors.

- *Quick Info*   Provides you with the syntax of a function, statement, or method. This information appears in the form of an oversized ToolTip. Having this information appear on-screen saves you the trouble of looking it up in the Help file.

- *Parameter Info*   Displays the parameters that are required for a particular function or method. This is similar to Quick Info.

- *The Data Tips window*   While in Break mode, displays as a ToolTip the value of a variable over which the mouse pointer is placed.

- *Block Comment commands*   Allow you to comment out an entire section of code simply by selecting the code and invoking the command. Similarly, you can remove the comment character from the block of code. This makes it easier to enable and disable sections of code for debugging or other reasons.

New Database Features

Since version 3, Visual Basic has been able to access a native database—the Jet database engine that it shares with Microsoft Access. With each new version of Visual Basic, more and more powerful database features have been added. Version 5 is no exception. Also, the new ODBCDirect functionality provides a truly efficient mechanism for dealing directly with Open Database Connectivity (ODBC)-compliant database engines.

N O T E   Most database features are available only in the Professional and Enterprise editions of Visual Basic. ▓

A nice new database feature is the Visual Data Manager application that is automatically installed as an add-in to the Visual Basic environment (see Figure 1.3). This add-in makes it easy for you to create and edit the structure of a database, as well as to input and edit the actual data. Additionally, the Visual Data Manager lets you create, test, and save SQL statements for use in your programs. As a bonus, the full source code for the Visual Data Manager add-in is included so you can study and utilize its data management techniques. (If you're a user of an earlier version of Visual Basic and used the old Data Manager add-in, give Visual Data Manager a try. It's a lot better!)

FIG. 1.3

The Visual Data Manager is a powerful new add-in for working with databases.

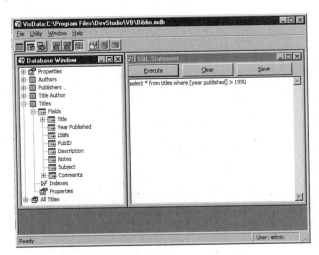

Version 3 of the Jet engine, which appeared in Visual Basic 4 and Microsoft Access 95, added the capability to replicate databases. This was a great feature for allowing multiple locations to work on the data and then combining all the changes into a central master database. Version 5 of Visual Basic takes this a step further with version 3.5 of the Jet engine. Now you can do *partial* replication of a database, meaning that you can provide copies of portions of the database instead of the entire thing. This will cut down on network traffic for updating the master database, as well as prevent people from seeing parts of the database that they don't need to see.

Internet Features

Whether you are a seasoned Internet developer or a neophyte, there are several features in Visual Basic that will help you write programs for the Internet. The first of these is the capability to create ActiveX controls, which was formerly the domain of C++ programmers. Now you can quickly write controls from within Visual Basic. You can use these controls in your Visual Basic programs (just like regular OCXs), place them on a Web page, or deploy them as part of an ActiveX document. These controls can work with any browser that supports ActiveX.

Another major feature gives you the capability to create ActiveX documents. These are applications that run inside of Internet Explorer. You can also use ActiveX documents (whether created by Visual Basic or other products) within Visual Basic. This allows you to run programs such as an icon editor or HTML editor from within Visual Basic as if it were part of the development environment.

Finally, there are new controls that make it easier for you to create Internet-enabled applications. The WebBrowser control lets you incorporate browser features into your application. With a few lines of code, you can add a fully functional Microsoft Internet Explorer Window to your program. The Winsock control makes it easier to connect your application to the Internet. Finally, the Internet Transfer control helps manage the sometimes mundane task of transferring files via two widely-used Internet transport mechanisms: HyperText Transfer Protocol (HTTP) and File Transfer Protocol (FTP).

Control Features

What new version would be complete without new controls? A couple of the Internet controls have already been mentioned, but there are a few other noteworthy additions.

The new MSChart control enables you to create many types of business charts in your programs. This control can create bar, pie, line, area, and scatter charts, just to name a few. The new MSFlexGrid control works like a regular grid but allows formatting of individual cells. The MSFlexGrid also gives you other advanced features such as sorting, cell grouping, pivoting, multiple selections, and in-cell pictures.

A couple of other new controls also deserve mentioning:

- *Animation control*   This allows you to display silent AVI (Audio Video Interleaved) clips. AVI clips are a series of bitmaps that are viewed like a movie. With this control, you can add a continuous animation much like the "flying paper" displayed as Windows 95 copies files from one folder to another.

- *UpDown control*   This is a pair of arrow buttons that the user can click with the mouse to modify the value of a number in a "buddy" control. For example, without writing any code you can combine a TextBox control with arrow buttons that modify its contents.

- *Internet Transfer control*   This allows you to send and retrieve files on HTTP and FTP servers.

In addition to the new controls, several of the old controls have been enhanced to provide greater functionality. For example, the PictureBox and Image controls now have the capability to display GIF or JPEG files, formats that are commonly used on the Internet. Also, most controls now have a `ToolTipText` property, which allows you to specify text that appears when the mouse pointer is rested on the control.

Finally, if you haven't found what you need among the provided controls, Visual Basic gives you the capability to create your own ActiveX controls and Dynamic Link Libraries (DLLs).

Checking Out the Wizards

Visual Basic has had a Setup Wizard for a number of versions. This made it easy to create the distribution disks that you needed in order to pass your program on to your users. The Setup Wizard is still present in version 5, but with some nice enhancements. Now you can create setup programs to handle installations from floppy disks or CDs, across a network, or even from the Internet. In addition to the Setup Wizard, Visual Basic includes several other wizards to make it easier for you to develop programs. These include the following:

- *Application Wizard* Creates a fully functional application that includes a toolbar and status bar on the main form. It can include such specialized forms as a splash screen, a login screen, an options dialog, and an About box. You can then customize the code created by the wizard to meet your programming needs.

- *ActiveX Control Interface Wizard* Helps you create the public code interface of an ActiveX control.

- *ActiveX Document Migration Wizard* Helps you create an ActiveX document from your existing forms. ActiveX documents can be run in Internet Explorer and other ActiveX-enabled programs.

- *Data Form Wizard* Creates a basic data entry form based on the structure of a table in a database. This fully functional form can be used as-is or modified to handle more complex database programming.

- *PropertyPage Wizard* Helps you build property pages for the ActiveX controls you create.

Types of Programs You Can Create in Visual Basic

Visual Basic's version 5 lets you create many different types of 32-bit programs for the Windows operating systems. (A few of these types of programs are listed in the Introduction.)

N O T E Programs created with Visual Basic 5.0 are 32-bit applications and can only be run on either the Windows NT or Windows 95 operating systems. They cannot be run on 16-bit Windows systems. ■

While you will most likely create stand-alone programs that are used directly by end users, Visual Basic 5 also gives you the ability to create libraries of functions that can be compiled into DLL files. These functions can be used by other programs to handle specialized tasks. In addition, Visual Basic 5 allows you to create your own ActiveX components, which can be used by your programs, other programs, and even accessed over the Internet.

Checking Out Visual Basic's Background

Before diving into the details of Visual Basic, let's take a brief look at the history of programming and some of the basic concepts that apply to programming in any language. This understanding of program basics will make it easier for you to write better and more efficient programs.

What Is a Program?

To begin, you need to know the answer to the question, "Just what is a program?" A *computer program* is simply a set of instructions that tells the computer how to perform a specific task.

Computers need explicit instructions for every single task they perform. They even need instructions for the simplest tasks, such as how to get a keystroke, place a letter on the screen, or store information to a disk. Fortunately, many of these instructions are contained on the processor chip or are built into the operating system, so you don't have to worry about them.

Even with less advanced programming languages, you must still be concerned with mundane tasks such as drawing command buttons, repainting screens, and so on. Visual Basic takes care of much of this detail work for you. Instead, you'd rather concentrate on providing instructions for the tasks, such as calculating employee payroll, creating the mailing list for your neighborhood, or formatting text to display the information in the latest annual report. Visual Basic 5 and the Rapid Application Development (RAD) concept make this possible.

N O T E   Rapid Application Development means exactly what it sounds like: an environment that lets you develop applications rapidly! Visual Basic makes it easy to spend your programming time creating a good program without having to worry about mundane "behind-the-scenes" details.

For example, if you want to use a command button in a program, all you have to do is draw one on a form (screen) as you're designing the program. You then set its properties to define how it looks and acts; you could also write small pieces of program code to tell it what to do when it's clicked. You don't have to be concerned with how the button is actually painted on the screen; for example, the button looks like it's pushed down. Visual Basic takes care of these lower-level tasks for you. ■

A Few Definitions

Now for a few technical terms. You will hear these terms often in discussions of Visual Basic, so a general understanding of the following terms should be helpful to you:

- *Controls*   Reusable objects that provide the pieces of the visual interface of a program. Examples of controls are a text box, a label, or a command button.
- *Event*   An action initiated by the user, the operating system, or the program itself. Examples of events are a keystroke, a mouse click, the expiration of a specified amount of time, or the receipt of data from a port.
- *Methods*   Predefined actions that can be performed by an object. For example, a form has a Hide method that makes it invisible to the user.

- *Object*   A basic element of a program, which contains properties to define its characteristics, contains methods to define its tasks, and recognizes events to which it can respond. Controls and forms are examples of the objects used in Visual Basic.
- *Procedures*   Segments of code that you write to accomplish a task. Procedures are often written to respond to a specific event. Types of procedures include Sub procedures, which consist of a sequence of statements; and Functions, which return a value.
- *Properties*   The characteristics of an object, such as its size, position, color, or text font. Properties determine the appearance and sometimes the behavior of an object. Properties are also used to provide data to an object and to retrieve information from the object.

Event-Driven Programming

Visual Basic lets you create programs that respond to user actions and system events. This type of programming is known as *event-driven programming*. To get some insight into how event-driven programming works, let's take a look at how programs ran in the past and how things are different in the Windows environment.

▶ **See** "Handling Events in Your Programs," **p. 157**

Before the advent of Windows (back in the old days of DOS and the "prehistoric times"— before PCs), programs were written to be run in a *sequential* fashion. That is, when the program started, it proceeded, instruction by instruction, until it reached the end of the program or a fatal error occurred. The general steps for running a program that processed a data file were as follows:

1. Create an input file.
2. Start the program.
3. Wait until the program finishes—often overnight for large programs.
4. Examine the output file or printed report.
5. Check the output for errors and, if necessary, repeat the entire process.

As software matured, we saw the gradual introduction of a limited form of *interactive processing*, in which the user had some control over the sequence of events. Such improvements as menu systems and hot-key commands allowed a little more flexibility to the user, but the program itself still retained much control over its flow.

Even programs that most people take for granted, such as word processing packages, worked this way. For the early word processors, you would create your file with formatting codes embedded in the actual document (much like RTF or HTML codes today), and then run the file through a formatter to be printed. These programs got the job done, but they weren't nearly as easy to use as today's programs. They were, however, easier to write. This is because each program had a clearly defined task and little or no user interaction. The programmer had nearly complete control over the sequence of events required to complete a task.

Then came Windows. Windows programs (and many later-generation DOS programs) provided the user with the ability to interact with the objects that made up the program's interface to a much greater extent. Programs would now respond to occurrences such as mouse movements and clicks, and would respond differently depending upon where the mouse pointer was located. Because this sequential programming structure would no longer work in such a wide-open environment, a new model was needed: the *event model*.

In the event model, each user interaction—such as a mouse click or a keystroke—is known as an *event*. Therefore, programs that respond to these events are known as *event-driven programs*. These programs provide almost immediate feedback to the users and give them greater control over the programs' activity. For example, an order-taking program written in a sequential processing style might ask the users for information about the items they are ordering one line at a time. They must follow the sequence of events determined by the programmer; if they were to make an error, they would have to start over. An event-driven application, on the other hand, might present the users with a visual form to fill out, as well as several processing options. Controls such as command buttons, menus, and text boxes would allow the users to determine the order in which they input the data and when the program processes the data. Correcting an error would be as simple as retyping the erroneous information. Figure 1.4 shows the interface for a typical event-driven program.

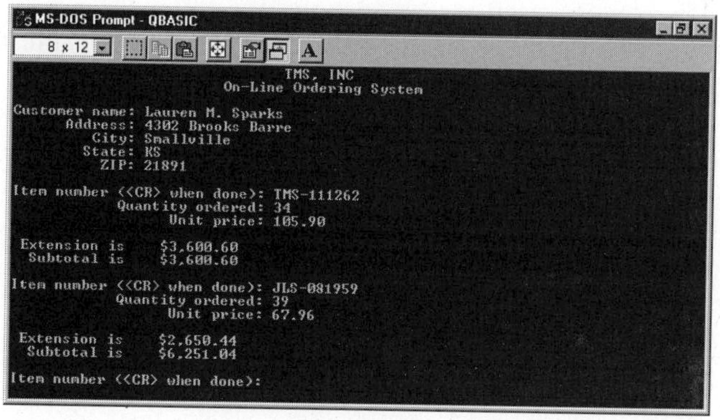

FIG. 1.4
In an event-driven program, the user might have several options governing the flow of events.

```
MS-DOS Prompt - QBASIC
  8 x 12
                         TMS, INC
                   On-Line Ordering System
Customer name: Lauren M. Sparks
       Address: 4302 Brooks Barre
          City: Smallville
         State: KS
           ZIP: 21891

Item number <<CR> when done): TMS-111262
           Quantity ordered: 34
                 Unit price: 105.90

Extension is    $3,600.60
Subtotal is     $3,600.60

Item number <<CR> when done): JLS-081959
           Quantity ordered: 39
                 Unit price: 67.96

Extension is    $2,650.44
Subtotal is     $6,251.04

Item number <<CR> when done):
```

While event-driven programs are great for users, they were very difficult for developers to write until the introduction of advanced programming languages like Visual Basic. Visual Basic was designed with the event model in mind, making it much easier for people to create Windows applications.

Object-Oriented Programming

One key concept that makes it easier to create Windows programs is *object-oriented programming*, or *OOP*. This technology makes it possible to create reusable components that become the building blocks of programs.

Figure 1.5 shows the interface for a typical object-oriented program.

What Is Object-Oriented Programming?   The OOP model provides support for three basic principles—*encapsulation*, *inheritance*, and *polymorphism*. Let's take a brief look at each of these terms.

FIG. 1.5

In an object-oriented program, the user has an interactive order form.

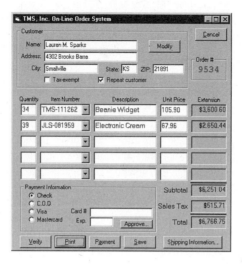

Encapsulation means that the information about an object (its *properties*) and the processes that are performed by the object (its *methods*) are all contained within the definition of the object. A real-world example of an object is a car. You describe a car by its properties, such as a red convertible or a black four-door sedan. Each characteristic—color, number of doors, convertible, or hardtop—is a property of the car. As for the methods, these are the things that a car does in response to an event. For example, you initiate an event when you turn the key to start the car. The car's "start method" takes over at that point, providing instructions such as "engage the starter gear, turn the starter, start fuel flow, initiate power to spark plugs, and disengage the starter." You don't have to tell the car *how* to start because it was taught how to start when it was designed.

Inheritance means that one object can be based upon the description of another object. Continuing with the car example, I can define a car as something that has four wheels, an engine, and passenger seats. I can then define a convertible as a car that has a retractable top. The convertible inherits the properties of the car and adds a new property, the retractable top. I don't have to redefine the car's properties for the convertible. Therefore, the convertible is said to inherit the properties of the car. In addition to properties, objects can also inherit methods and events from other objects.

N O T E This discussion of inheritance is included for the purpose of fully describing OOP. Visual Basic does not directly support inheritance in its implementation of object-oriented programming. ■

Polymorphism means that many objects can have the same method and that the appropriate action is taken for the specific object calling the method. For example, in your programs, you display text to the screen and output text to the printer. Each of these objects (the screen and the printer) can have a print or display method that tells the object to place text in a certain location. The method knows what to do, based on the object calling the method.

What OOP Does for You The key element of OOP with which you will be working is reusable components, known as *controls*. The controls that you will use in building your programs are objects that have properties and methods and respond to events. You control the appearance and behavior of a control through its properties. For example, you specify how the text in a TextBox control will look by setting its `Font` and `Color` properties. The controls you use have methods built into them that shield you from many of the tedious tasks of programming. Again look at the TextBox control as an example. It knows how to retrieve a keystroke and display it in the edit region of the box in the proper format. You don't have to supply the details.

Each control also recognizes specific events. Most controls know if the mouse has been moved over them or if a mouse button has been clicked. They even know which button was clicked. Components that handle text know when a key was pressed and which one it was. And, for most events, you can write code that will take specific action when the event occurs.

The Parts of a Program

As you begin to create a program, there are three basic parts of the program that you need to consider—the *user interface*, the *processing of information*, and the *storage of information*.

The user interface is the part of the program that your users see and with which they interact. This user interface is composed of the screens you design by using Visual Basic's forms and controls. A few key objectives for a good user interface are the following:

- Present information in a neat manner.
- Make instructions clear.
- Make the appropriate parts of the interface (such as menus) consistent with corresponding parts of other programs.
- Make key tasks easily accessible by providing menu shortcuts and/or toolbars.

The processing of information is handled by the code that you write to respond to events in the program. One of your objectives here is to make the code as efficient as possible, thereby providing good response time for your users. It's also important to make the code easy to maintain so that future modifications or updates to the code can be made with relative ease. Key components in making code easy to maintain include making it easy to read and using code modules to keep individual tasks small and simple. Making your code easy to read is done by properly formatting the lines of code and providing comments within the code to describe what it does.

From Here...

Now that you have been introduced to some of Visual Basic's capabilities, you are probably ready to jump right in and get started creating programs. A few chapters you might want to explore include the following:

- See Chapter 2, "Introduction to the Development Environment," to learn more about Visual Basic 5's IDE (Integrated Development Environment).

- See Chapter 3, "Creating Your First Program," to get started creating program interfaces.
- See Chapter 8, "Programming Visual Basic," for more information about writing program code to have your programs perform their assigned tasks.

Introduction to the Development Environment

As old-timers will note, the development environment is completely different from the one in previous versions of Visual Basic. The environment is, however, consistent with the development environments of Microsoft's other programming languages. We'll look closely at the development environment in the section "Exploring the Visual Basic Interface," but first let's take a brief look at the key features of the new environment. ∎

A completely new development environment

If you have used previous versions of Visual Basic, you will discover that almost everything about the interface has changed. I found that, after an initial adjustment period, these changes added a lot of flexibility to the development environment.

Working in multiple windows

The form and code windows are now set up as MDI child windows. The new style allows you to easily switch from one window to another, keeping your toolbar and menus available at all times.

Most windows are dockable

This means that you can have the Properties window, Project window, and toolbox docked against the edge of your screen or floating somewhere in the middle.

Toolbars for everything

Visual Basic 5 has new and improved toolbars that make it easier to accomplish many of your programming tasks, such as lining up controls precisely on a form.

Help is available

In addition to detailed help files with context-sensitive links, Visual Basic 5 includes many detailed VB articles in the Books Online.

Understanding the Environment's Key Features

A significant change in VB5 is its use of a Multiple-Document Interface (MDI). If you are unfamiliar with MDI, you can compare it to having multiple documents open in Microsoft Word. Each document is contained in a child window which is, in turn, contained within the main parent window. As with other MDI applications, such as Word or Excel, you can choose to have the child document fill the whole window or have multiple windows visible simultaneously.

 If you are not already using a large monitor (17" or greater) at high resolution, get one! While the new interface is great, you need a lot of screen space to use it most effectively. I recommend a screen resolution of 800 × 600 as a minimum or 1024 × 768 if your video card (and eyes) can support it.

Next, you can edit more than one project in the same Visual Basic session. This means you don't have to close one project in order to open and make changes to another. This is very convenient if you are developing projects that interact with each other, because you can save and compile all projects in a group with a single menu option.

Another new feature is dockable toolbars and windows. This means that a window can be floating in the middle of the screen or docked along one of the edges. Dockable windows include the toolbars and windows with small title bars, such as the toolbox.

In addition to the window management enhancements, Visual Basic has some useful tools to make code entry easier. Microsoft calls them *Auto List Member* and *Auto Quick Info*; you will call them fantastic. If you have trouble remembering MessageBox constants, control properties, or even the parameters to your own functions, the code editor now presents the information automatically while you type! For example, as soon as you press the spacebar after a MsgBox function call, you are presented with the parameters in a ToolTip-like format with a drop-down box of the available constants.

 When you are presented with the drop-down box mentioned in the preceding paragraph, you don't have to use the mouse to select an item. Just keep typing (or use the arrow keys) until the list item you want is highlighted; then press the spacebar, comma (,), Enter, or Tab, and continue with your program!

Starting Up

When you start Visual Basic, you see the New Project dialog box, shown in Figure 2.1. This dialog box has the following three tabs:

- *New*   Lets you choose one of several types of projects to create
- *Existing*   Allows you to browse for a project that's already been created and saved
- *Recent*   Presents you with a list of projects that have been previously worked on. The most recent projects are listed first

FIG. 2.1

The New Project dialog box's New tab lets you select from several types of projects to create.

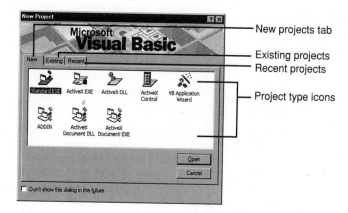

New projects tab

Existing projects

Recent projects

Project type icons

If you choose to create a new project, Visual Basic creates the appropriate project template for you based on your selection from the New Project dialog box. You can choose to create one of these project types:

- *Standard EXE*   This is the type of project you would use to create a standard Windows program (.EXE file). You will probably use this type of project most often.

- *ActiveX EXE*   This is an automation server that performs tasks as part of a multiple-tier application. The end result is a program that contains public classes that can be accessed by other programs or can run by itself. This used to be known as an *OLE automation server*.

- *ActiveX DLL*   This is a remote automation program created as a DLL. ActiveX DLLs cannot run alone; however, because an ActiveX DLL runs in-process, it is faster than an out-of-process ActiveX EXE.

- *ActiveX Control*   With this option, you can create your own custom controls (OCXs). These can be used in your Visual Basic programs or in any ActiveX-capable application.

- *VB Application Wizard*   If you want something quick and generic, this option builds the skeleton of an application (similar to a word processor template). You can then customize the application to suit your needs.

- *Addin*   This type of program is used to provide additional functionality to Visual Basic itself. An example of an add-in is the Visual Data Manager.

- *ActiveX Document DLL*   This type of project creates a DLL that can be utilized by applications running within Microsoft Internet Explorer.

- *ActiveX Document EXE*   This type of project creates an application that can run inside Microsoft Internet Explorer.

The Visual Basic Work Area

After you select the project type from the New Project dialog box, you are presented with the design environment. This is where you do the work of actually creating your masterpiece application. The basic design environment is shown in Figure 2.2. This is probably what Visual Basic 5 looked like when you started it for the first time.

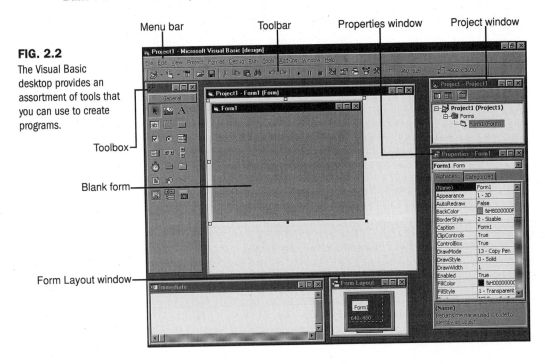

FIG. 2.2
The Visual Basic desktop provides an assortment of tools that you can use to create programs.

As you can see, Visual Basic shares a lot of elements with other Windows programs. The toolbars and menus look similar to those in Office 97. A few of the menu items are the same: File, Edit, Help, and others.

Using the Menu Bar

Many programmers want to find quick keyboard shortcuts for frequently used tasks. As with other Windows programs, the menus at the top of the Visual Basic screen can be displayed by holding down the Alt key while pressing the appropriate underlined character in the menu bar. After the initial menu is displayed, simply press the underlined character of a menu item to select it. For example, press Alt+F to open the File menu, and then press P to choose the Print command.

Visual Basic also utilizes several shortcut keys that let you bypass the menu entirely. Most of these are listed to the right of their respective menu items. For example, in the View menu you might notice F2 to the right of Object Browser. This means that you can see the Object Browser by pressing F2. Although some quick shortcuts are listed in Table 2.1, a quick perusal of the menus would definitely be worth your while.

Table 2.1 Shortcut Keys

Menu Item	Shortcut Key	Description
Edit, Cut	Ctrl+X	Removes the selected text or control from its current location and copies it to the Clipboard.
Edit, Copy	Ctrl+C	Makes a copy of the selected text or control on the Clipboard, but does not remove it from its original location.
Edit, Paste	Ctrl+V	Pastes the contents of the Clipboard to the active form or code window.
Edit, Undo	Ctrl+Z	Undoes the last change.
Edit, Find	Ctrl+F	Finds a piece of text. (You must be in an edit window to use this.)
File, Open	Ctrl+O	Opens a project.
File, Save	Ctrl+S	Saves the current file.
File, Print	Ctrl+P	Displays the Print dialog box, from which you can print the current form or module or the entire application.
View, Project	Ctrl+R	Shows the Project Explorer window Explorer (if it's not already displayed).
View, Properties	F4	Shows the Properties window (if it's not already Window displayed).

 TIP Experimentation is encouraged! In addition to the preceding list, Visual Basic includes some not-so-obvious tricks such as Ctrl+Y (delete a line of code), which is apparently an homage to WordStar.

Examining the Changes in Familiar Menus   The File menu is basically the same as it was in previous versions of Visual Basic (see Figure 2.3). However, because Visual Basic 5.0 allows multiple projects on the desktop, some project management functions have been moved to the new Project menu.

The Edit menu has the standard features you would expect, such as Cut, Copy, and Paste, but also has quite a few new features that are associated with the new capabilities of the code editor (see Figure 2.4). These features give you the following capabilities:

- *Indent/Outdent*   You can indent and outdent (un-indent) selected blocks of code.
- *List Properties/Methods*   You can call up a list of properties and methods of an object.
- *List Constants*   You can list Visual Basic constants that you would use in a statement.
- *Parameter Info*   You can get information about the parameters required for a function, such as the message box.
- *Complete Word*   Visual Basic fills in the rest of partially completed code words for you, which saves you typing.

■ *Bookmarks* You can set and use bookmarks to make it easier to move back and forth between sections of your code. (Bookmarks are indicated by blue squares in the left margin of the code window.)

FIG. 2.3
Visual Basic's File menu assists you in managing the files that make up your projects.

FIG. 2.4
The Edit menu offers quite a few commands to help you write code.

The View menu provides you with access to all the parts of the Visual Basic interface. From the View menu, you can display and hide various parts of the design environment. These can include toolbars, design windows, and windows containing program code.

The Project menu contains many of the functions you need to manage an individual project. From this menu, you can add and remove project elements—such as forms, modules, and user controls. The Project menu also provides you with access to the Components dialog box, where you select the controls to be used in the project, and to the Project Properties dialog box, where you select things like the startup form and compiler options.

The other familiar menus—Run, Tools, Add-Ins, and Help—are all similar to their counterparts in earlier versions of Visual Basic.

Checking Out the New Menus Three new menus have been added to Visual Basic 5: Format, Debug, and Window. While the Window menu is new to Visual Basic, it should be familiar to you if you have worked with other Windows programs. This menu lets you arrange and select multiple form and code windows.

The Debug menu contains tools that help you track down problems in your code (see Figure 2.5). From here, you can set breakpoints and watches, as well as control how the code is executed in debug mode. It is interesting to note that the Debug window from previous versions is now called the Immediate window and commands can be executed here even when the program is *not* running.

FIG. 2.5

The Debug menu provides numerous commands to aid in troubleshooting your code.

The final new menu is the Format menu, shown in Figure 2.6. This menu provides you with a number of features for working with groups of controls on your form. These features make it easy to align multiple controls, set the height or width of multiple controls to make them consistent, center a group of controls, or adjust the spacing between controls. If you have worked in previous versions of Visual Basic (and even if you haven't), you will really appreciate the power of these features.

▶ **See** "Using Controls," **p. 91**

FIG. 2.6

The Format menu helps you with the placement and sizing of controls on your forms.

Accessing Functions with the Toolbars

Visual Basic's toolbars provide you with quick access to some of the functions you will use most often. There are four toolbars available (see Figure 2.7):

- ■ *Standard*   The Standard toolbar is displayed by default and offers quick access to frequently used functions.
- ■ *Debug*   The Debug toolbar has buttons for use when you're debugging your programs.
- ■ *Edit*   The Edit toolbar's buttons are handy when you're writing code.
- ■ *Form Editor*   The Form Editor toolbar contains buttons that help you tweak the appearance of controls on your forms.

Standard toolbar

FIG. 2.7

Visual Basic's Standard toolbar is docked below the menu bar; the other toolbars are floating on the desktop. The toolbars can be modified from the Customize dialog box.

Edit toolbar

Debug toolbar

Form Editor toolbar

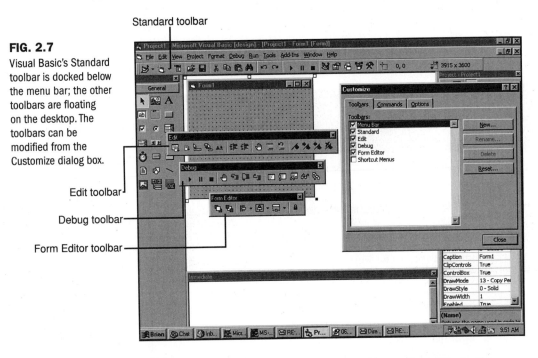

The Standard toolbar is the only one displayed the first time you start Visual Basic. You can specify which toolbars are displayed by choosing Toolbars from the View menu or by right-clicking any visible toolbar. Any of them can be free-floating or "docked" just below the menu bar; their startup positions will be the same as the last time you exited Visual Basic. Selecting View, Toolbars, Customize enables you to modify the existing toolbars or even create your own.

Visual Basic's toolbars follow the standard used by the latest generation of programs in that they provide you with ToolTips. A ToolTip is a little yellow box that pops up if you let the mouse pointer hover over a button for a few seconds; it contains a description of the underlying button's function.

Part

I

Ch

2

T I P Starting with version 5.0, ToolTips also display the value of a variable in a code window. Use this feature by letting the mouse pointer hover over a variable name while in break mode. This is a real time-saver if you are used to setting up a watch or printing values in the Immediate window.

Display all the toolbars as explained in the preceding paragraph and move the pointer over the buttons to familiarize yourself with them. Remember that you can always use the ToolTip feature when you're unsure which button is which.

Two of these buttons require special attention. The Add Project button and the Add Form button both invoke drop-down lists of items (see Figure 2.8). If you select one of these items, the default item for the button changes to the type of item that you selected.

FIG. 2.8

Drop-down buttons enable you to specify the type of project or file to be added.

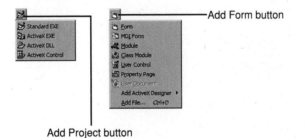

The Add Project button enables you to add a project to the desktop. This can be one of the following four types:

- Standard EXE
- ActiveX EXE
- ActiveX DLL
- ActiveX Control

The Add Form button lets you add any of the following pieces to your current project:

- Form
- MDI form
- Module
- Class module
- User control
- Property page
- Existing files

We address most of the other buttons on the toolbar a little later. However, two special areas on the toolbar deserve mentioning. At the far right of the toolbar are two blocks with a pair of numbers in each block. These two blocks show the position and size of the form or control with which you are working. The two numbers in the first block indicate the horizontal and vertical positions, respectively, of the upper-left corner of the current object, as measured from the upper-left corner of the screen (if the current object is a form), or of the current form (if the current object is a control). The two numbers in the second block show the horizontal and vertical dimensions, respectively, of the current object. These numbers are not visible, however, when editing in a code window.

N O T E   Both the position and dimension information are given in *twips*. A twip is a unit of measure that Visual Basic uses to ensure that placement and sizing of objects is consistent on different types of screens. A twip is equal to 1/20 of a printer's point; there are approximately 1,440 twips in a logical inch (the amount of screen space that would take up one inch when printed). ■

One final note about the toolbars. If you don't like having them located at the top of the screen, you can move any of them by clicking the double bars at the left edge and dragging to a new location. You can park a toolbar against any other edge of the desktop or leave them floating in the middle as shown in Figure 2.9.

FIG. 2.9
Even the Standard toolbar can float freely on the desktop.

Standard toolbar floating—

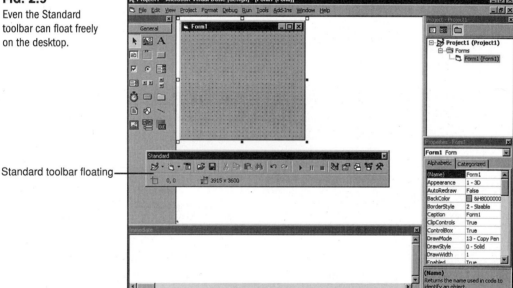

Organizing Visual Basic's Controls

The controls that are used in Visual Basic are the heart and soul of the programs that you create. The controls enable you to add functionality to your program quickly and easily. There are controls that enable you to edit text, connect to a database, retrieve file information from a user, or display and edit pictures.

Obviously, with all these controls available, you need a way to keep them organized. This is the function of the toolbox (see Figure 2.10). This toolbox contains buttons representing the controls that are available for use in your program. (A list of the basic set of Visual Basic 5 controls is contained in Table 2.2.) Clicking one of the control "tools" enables you to draw a control of that type on a form. Double-clicking a tool places a default-sized control of that type in the center of the current form. Clicking the Pointer tool in the upper-left of the toolbox cancels a pending control-drawing function and restores the mouse pointer's normal functionality.

FIG. 2.10
The basic control set that is available when you first start Visual Basic The toolbox can be moved around on-screen to a location that is convenient for you.

Pointer tool

Table 2.2 Standard Visual Basic Controls

Control Button	Control Name	Function
	PictureBox	Displays a graphic image.
	Label	Displays text that the user cannot directly modify.
	TextBox	Displays text that the user can edit.
	Frame	Provides a method for grouping controls. (To group controls in a frame, select the frame with a single-click first, then draw a control in it.)
	CommandButton	Enables the user to initiate a program action. Can include an icon, caption, and ToolTips.
	CheckBox	Displays or enables input of a two-part choice, such as Yes/No or True/False.
	OptionButton	Displays or enables a choice among multiple items. (Also known as a radio button.)
	ComboBox	Enables the user to select an entry from a list or enter a new value.
	ListBox	Displays a list of items from which the user can select one or more entries.
	HscrollBar (Horizontal Scroll bar)	Produces a numerical value based on the scroll bar's horizontal position.
	VscrollBar (Vertical Scroll bar)	Same as above but vertical. Note the scrollbars behave like standard Windows scrollbars.

continues

Table 2.2 Continued

Control Button	Control Name	Function
	Timer	Provides a means for an action to be taken after passage of a certain amount of time.
	DriveListBox	Displays and enables a user to choose from available disk drives on the computer.
	Dir ListBox	Displays and enables a user to choose from available subdirectories on a drive.
	FileListBox	Displays and enables a user to choose from available files in a directory.
	Shape	Displays geometric shapes on the form.
	Line	Displays lines on the form.
	Image	Displays a graphic image. Similar in appearance to the picture control but with different functionality.
	Data	Provides a link to database files.
	OLE	Provides you with a way to link to OLE servers.

You can add other controls to the toolbox by selecting the Components item from the Project menu. This brings up the Components dialog box (see Figure 2.11). This dialog box enables you to choose any additional controls (OCXs) that have been installed on your system. If you choose to add a control to the toolbox, it appears in the toolbox after you choose the OK or Apply button.

FIG. 2.11

Controls are added to the toolbox with the Components dialog box.

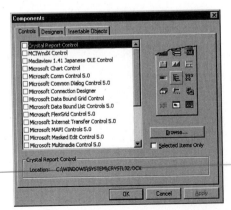

TIP You can also access the Components dialog box by right-clicking the mouse on the toolbox and then selecting the Components item from the pop-up menu.

By default, all the components for your project will appear in the toolbox in one big group. However, if you use a lot of controls, this can make it very difficult to manage all of them. To help with this problem, Visual Basic enables you to add tabs to the toolbox. (It has one tab, General, by default.) To add a tab, right-click the toolbox, select Add Tab from the pop-up menu, and give the new tab a name. You can then move controls from one tab to another and group your controls in the way that is most convenient to you. Figure 2.12 shows the toolbox with a Data Access tab added to it.

FIG. 2.12

A new feature in Visual Basic 5 gives you the ability to group control tools using custom tabs in the toolbox.

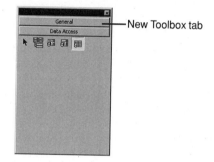

New Toolbox tab

The Canvas of Your Programs

The windows you design in your Visual Basic programs are known as *forms*. The form can be thought of like an artist's canvas. You use elements in the toolbox to "draw" your user interface on a form.

The form is part of the desktop and is your primary work area for creating the user interface. If you look closely at the form in Figure 2.13, you might notice that the form has dots on it. These dots form a grid whose purpose is to help you position controls on the form; it is invisible when your program is running. You can control the spacing of the grid dots from the Tools, Options, General dialog box. You can also choose not to display the grid at all.

FIG. 2.13

When designing a form in Visual Basic, a grid is available to help you easily line up controls.

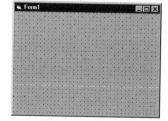

Controlling Your Forms and Controls

The Properties window is an important part of the Visual Basic desktop. It shows all the available properties for the currently selected form, control, or module (see Figure 2.14). If the Properties window isn't visible, first select the object(s) whose properties you want to view or change and then press F4. It can also be viewed by selecting Properties Windows from the View menu or by right-clicking an object and choosing Properties from the context-sensitive menu that pops up.

FIG. 2.14

The Properties window provides an easy way to change the properties that govern the appearance and behavior of controls.

Selected property

Property description

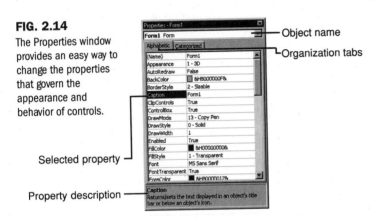

Object name

Organization tabs

Properties determine how a form or control looks and how it behaves in a program. The Properties window lists all of the currently selected object's properties that can be changed at *design time,* as opposed to *runtime* properties, which can be changed only during program execution. Many properties can be changed either at design time or at runtime.

An example of a property is the Caption property of a Label control. It can be changed by simply typing **Hello World** into the Caption field in the Properties window (a design time change) or with a statement in your code like Form1.Label1.Caption = "Hello World" (a runtime change).

The Properties window has two tabs on it. These tabs enable you to group the properties either alphabetically or by logical categories. Another improvement to the Properties window is that it now includes a description of the selected property in a pane at the bottom. This avoids much of the need to look up properties in the Help system.

N O T E In a change from previous versions of Visual Basic, the Name property of any object appears at the top of the list of properties, rather than in its proper alphabetical order. ■

N O T E Many controls have an entry in the Properties window labeled (Custom). This brings up a special Property Page dialog box containing all of the design-time properties for that control in an easy-to-modify format. ■

Using the Project Window

Another window on the desktop is the Project window. This window shows a list of all the forms and code modules that are used in your program. Figure 2.15 shows an example of a Project window. If you want to view a form or code module, double-click it here during design time, or click it once and click the View Form or View Code button.

FIG. 2.15

The Project window shows the files that make up the open project(s).

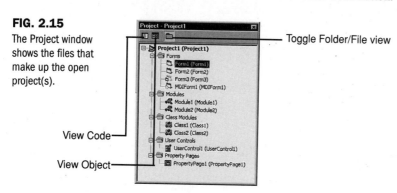

Toggle Folder/File view

View Code

View Object

Par
I

Ch

2

> **N O T E** One way to think of a project is as a group of related files. The Project brings together all the files needed to create your program. ■

When you save a project, you're basically saving a list of the various files that make up a project. The project file itself is stored with a default extension of .VBP (Visual Basic Project). Several other types of files make up the components of the projects. Some of the more common types are listed in Table 2.3.

Table 2.3   Visual Basic File Types

File Type	Extension
Visual Basic Form	.FRM
Code Module	.BAS
Class Module	.cLS
User-Created Control	.CTL
ActiveX Document Form File	.DOB

The Project window uses an outline list to show you not only the Forms and Code modules in the open project(s) but also any Class modules, User-defined controls, or Property pages. There are two ways to view your project. The folder view, accessible by clicking the left button, displays the parts of your project organized by category. On the other hand, clicking the rightmost button lists the elements of your project based on their associated file names.

Where Work Gets Done

The final piece of the desktop is one or more Code windows. Code windows are where you do all the entry and editing of program code that enables your programs to actually perform tasks (see Figure 2.16). Each form has its own associated Code window. A project can also contain a couple of types of stand-alone Code windows known as *modules*. To access a Code window, you can double-click a form or one of its objects, or you can click the View Code button in the Project window while the appropriate object is highlighted.

Form name

FIG. 2.16

The Code window is where you enter and edit the instructions that perform the work of your program.

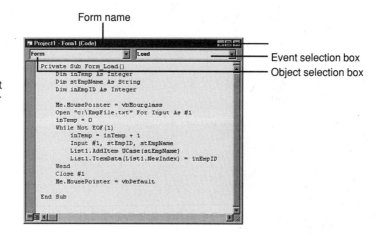

Event selection box

Object selection box

```
Private Sub Form_Load()
    Dim inTemp As Integer
    Dim stEmpName As String
    Dim inEmpID As Integer

    Me.MousePointer = vbHourglass
    Open "c:\EmpFile.txt" For Input As #1
    inTemp = 0
    While Not EOF(1)
        inTemp = inTemp + 1
        Input #1, stEmpID, stEmpName
        List1.AddItem UCase(stEmpName)
        List1.ItemData(List1.NewIndex) = inEmpID
    Wend
    Close #1
    Me.MousePointer = vbDefault

End Sub
```

Customizing Your Environment

As we've discussed, the Visual Basic development environment is highly customizable. Most of the windows and toolbars in Visual Basic can be placed at the edges of the main program window, or they can float anywhere on the screen. You can position and resize the windows to fit your preferences; the next time you start Visual Basic, the environment will be as you left it. Figure 2.17 shows you one way the development environment can be rearranged.

FIG. 2.17
The various pieces
of Visual Basic's
development environ-
ment can be arranged
in many ways.

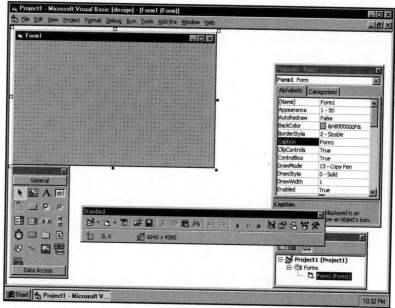

Getting Help When You Need It

As you work with the many features of Visual Basic, you may need more information about a particular command or object than is provided in this book. Fortunately, Microsoft has included a great online help system with Visual Basic 5. In addition to a searchable index, context-sensitive help is available from the development environment. This means you can highlight a word or object and press the F1 key to bring up related information.

The Basic Help System

The easiest way to access the Help system is through the Help menu. There are several choices available on the menu for Visual Basic help:

- Microsoft Visual Basic Help Topics
- Books Online
- Obtaining Technical Support
- Microsoft On the Web
- About Microsoft Visual Basic

Select <u>M</u>icrosoft Visual Basic Help Topics to enter the main online Help system. The Contents tab you find there displays the main table of contents for the Help system, as shown in Figure 2.18. From here, you can choose topics of interest and navigate through the other parts of the Help system. You choose a topic by clicking one of the *hypertext links* (similar to those you find when browsing the World Wide Web).

FIG. 2.18

The Help system's Contents page displays a road map of the topics available.

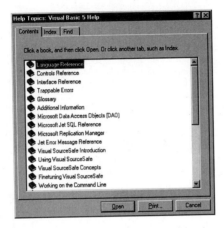

Clicking the Help system's Index tab displays an extensive listing of help topics available (see Figure 2.19). To find a specific item, type part of the name of the item in the window's text box until the desired topic appears in the list and then click the topic in the list. You can also use the scroll bar in the list box to locate a specific topic.

FIG. 2.19

The Help system's Index page helps you locate specific topics.

While the Index page allows a quick selection based on topic name, the Find page goes one step further. It has the additional capability of searching for a specific word or words within all of the available topics. The first time you use the Find option, a Word List will be created. Then you can type in a word or phrase and list the help topics that contain it. The Find screen is shown in Figure 2.20.

FIG. 2.20

From the online Help system's Find tab, you can search the help file for specific words.

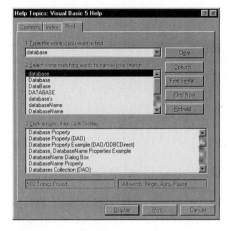

Context-Sensitive Help

In addition to letting you look up information in the Contents, Index, and Find pages, Visual Basic provides you with context-sensitive help. This enables you to directly get the help you need for a particular control or code keyword while you're working with that object or in the Code window. To get help for any control, simply select the control on your form and then press the F1 key. The Help system displays information about the control. This help page, an example of which is shown in Figure 2.21, also provides links to detailed descriptions of the properties, methods, and events of the control.

FIG. 2.21

The Help page for a control provides a description of the control as well as links to related pages.

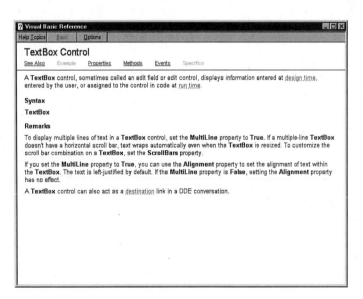

For code keywords, simply place the cursor in the word in the Code window and then press F1. The Help system goes directly to the page for that command and provides you with the syntax of the command, as well as other information about it. In addition, for most commands, a link is provided that gives you an example of how the command is used.

TIP When you find the help topic for a command you're working with, you can copy sample code from the help screen to the Clipboard and then paste it directly into your application's Code window. Use Ctrl+C and Ctrl+V, respectively, to copy and paste the text.

From Here...

This chapter introduced you to Visual Basic's development environment. You now know the basic methods for manipulating code and forms. As with any skill, the best way to learn is to practice. Think of some ideas for example programs and try writing them. Sample programs with varying levels of complexity are presented in this book; you can also find some in Visual Basic's Samples folder. On the other hand, if you would like to learn even more about the design environment, there are more chapters that explore it extensively. A couple of good places to go next are:

- Chapter 3, "Creating Your First Program," takes you step-by-step through creating a working VB program.
- Chapter 4, "Working with Forms and Controls," explains forms and controls.
- Chapter 8, "Programming Basics," teaches you all about the programming language of Visual Basic.

Creating Your First Program

If you're like me, the first thing you want to do with a new programming language is to jump in and start programming. Well, that's exactly what we're going to do in this chapter. You will learn some of the fundamentals of Visual Basic programming by creating a working program. The program you create will be one that should be useful—a loan payment calculator. ■

What are the basic steps in creating a program?

Learn how program creation progresses from design to implementation to distribution.

How you create the interface of a program

The interface of a Visual Basic program consists of its forms and controls (the parts that the user sees and interacts with). In this chapter we explore how to use these tools effectively as you design your applications.

How to make the program perform tasks

Because a program must do more than just look good, you should design it to perform useful functions.

How to test a program

Obviously, as you are creating a program, you need to test it to make sure that it does what you want it to do. Read this chapter to find out about Visual Basic's extensive debugging tools.

Where and how to save your work

In order to save you hours of frustration over lost work, we will explain how to save a project and its associated files.

Designing Your Program

A college English professor of mine was once describing different types of novelists: "A traditionalist author usually orders his story beginning-middle-end, a modernist might reverse that order, and a post-modernist would only include two of the three parts."

Unfortunately, authors of computer programs do not have that luxury. Due to the structured nature of computing, designing before coding is crucial to a project's success. New programmers have a tendency to resist this, but even with small programs you need to get into the habit of planning. If you do nothing else, sit down with a blank sheet of paper and make some notes about what you want the program to accomplish, and sketch out what the interface should look like.

N O T E Please keep in mind that the strategy presented in this chapter is by no means the only approach to programming, but rather one set of guidelines. ■

The key steps in creating a computer program are the following:

1. Design the program's tasks (how it works).
2. Design the user interface (how it looks).
3. Actually write the code (implement Steps 1 and 2).
4. Test and debug the program (beta testing).
5. Document and distribute the program (put it in use).

These steps are very generalized and definitely not all-inclusive. As we discuss the following sample program, we'll list some Visual Basic-specific steps.

N O T E If you are tackling a large project, breaking it down into smaller pieces will make it much more manageable. Many of Visual Basic's features (such as custom controls) can be used for dividing up a large project in a team environment. A structured, object-oriented approach is also worth investigating. ■

The Importance of Design

When starting a new project, it is tempting to just sit down and start hacking out code. After all, drawing the interface and writing the program code are the most fun and creative aspects of programming. However, a good program starts with a solid design. An in-depth flowchart might not be necessary for very small-scale projects, but on the other hand, it is never a good idea to start without a plan.

The design process should produce the following results:

■ A concise list of tasks to be performed by the program

■ Deadlines for when particular tasks need to be completed

■ Clarification of the dependence of one part of the program on another

■ The criteria for testing the program

For a program like the sample in this chapter, the design can be a simple statement of what the program should accomplish. For more complex programs, the design might include written criteria, data diagrams, flowcharts, a milestone document, and a test and acceptance plan. It is up to you and your client (the program's user) to determine the right level of documentation that is necessary for a given project. However, you should always make sure that the design is clearly spelled out, and you should always write it down.

The Sample Program Design

Now let's specify the design of the sample program. In this chapter, you create a simple program that calculates the monthly payment of a loan. The program allows the user to input values for the amount of the loan (principal), the annual interest rate, and the length (term) of the loan. The program provides the user with a way of starting the calculation. Finally, the program verifies that the necessary information was entered, performs the calculation, and then displays the results to the user.

As you can see, in one short paragraph, I specified what the program would do, what information was required to perform the task, and provided some information about how the interface should be designed. That wasn't so bad, was it?

Creating the Interface of Your Program

Now that we have specified the design of the program, it's time to get started with the actual creation of the program. (Note that I'm combining interface design and creation because our program is so simple.) Developing the user interface requires several Visual Basic controls from the Toolbox. You start out using just three controls. In the section "Enhancing Your Program," you learn how to use additional controls to make the loan calculator even better.

Starting at the Beginning

To start working on the sample program, you need to start Visual Basic; or if you are already in Visual Basic, you should start a new project by selecting File, New Project. Whichever you do, you are presented with the New Project dialog box (see Figures 3.1 and 3.2).

FIG. 3.1
The New Project dialog box that appears when you first start Visual Basic 5.

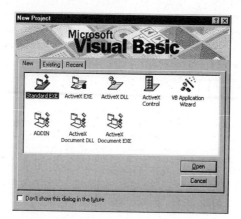

FIG. 3.2

The New Project dialog box that opens when you choose File, New Project from within Visual Basic 5.

This dialog box provides you with a choice of application types that you can create. Because the first program is nothing fancy, choose to create a Standard EXE. This choice presents you with the design environment of Visual Basic, displayed in Figure 3.3.

▶ **See** "Starting Up," **p. 30**

FIG. 3.3

After starting Visual Basic's design environment, you are ready to begin creating your first program.

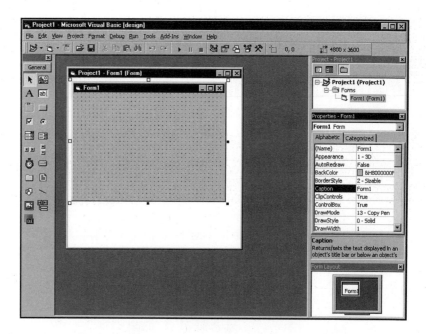

N O T E Because the design environment is customizable, your screen might not look exactly like the one shown in Figure 3.3. ■

Saving Your Work

As you are working on your program, you need to save it so you can use it again. In fact, you should save your work often in case of a power failure or other problem. It's very good practice to save your projects as soon as you start working on them, and then save regularly as the work progresses. At the very least, you should save your program before the first time you run it. This way, if it causes your system to crash (yes, it happens to the best of us), you won't lose your work.

You can save your project by choosing File, Save Project from Visual Basic's menu system, or by clicking the Save Project button on the toolbar. The process of saving a project is a little more complex than you might expect; however, with a little practice you'll have no problem. In order to save a project, you must save each *component* of your project (each form, code module, and so on) into its own file and then save the *project* itself into its project file.

Look at the Project window on your Visual Basic desktop. It consists of a list of the components that make up the current project. The Forms folder under Project1 (the default name of a new project) contains exactly one entry—Form1, which is the one and only form in this application. Each form in a project is saved into its own file; the project (list) itself is saved into a separate file.

When you choose to save the project, Visual Basic first wants you to save the components (forms, for example) into their own files before saving the actual project file. The first time you save the project, you are led through a series of Save File As dialog boxes so you can specify the name and location of each file that makes up your project. Subsequent project save operations simply resave the components using the same file names as before, unless new components have been added to the project since the last save. In this case, the Save File As dialog box is presented for each new component (see Figure 3.4).

Part

I

Ch

3

 On my hard drive, I have created a VBCODE subdirectory. Underneath that I create a subdirectory, (for example, LOANCALC) for each new Visual Basic project. This makes it easy to keep your project files organized in one place.

FIG. 3.4
The Save File As dialog box allows you to specify the name and location of your program files.

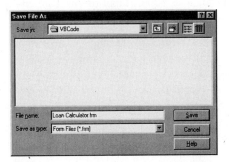

 You can have Visual Basic automatically save your program before you run it by setting the option in the Environment Options dialog box. You can choose to have Visual Basic save your program, prompt you to save changes, or not save the changes before running the program.

How You Get User Input

Most programs need a way for users to enter information. There are a number of Visual Basic controls that you can use for input. The first thing to do is look in the Toolbox and see which controls you need. The user interface for your loan calculator is responsible for accepting input, displaying output, and calling functions that perform the loan calculations. So, the three controls that you use initially are the TextBox, the Label, and the CommandButton. These controls are part of the basic set of controls that you find in the Toolbox when you start Visual Basic (see Figure 3.5).

FIG. 3.5
Visual Basic's controls are the building blocks of your programs.

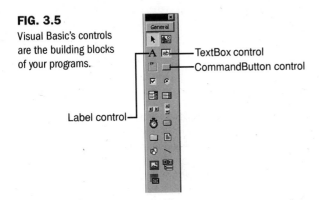

TextBox control
CommandButton control
Label control

The most commonly used control is the TextBox control, also known simply as a *text box*. The name text box is, in this case, self-explanatory (it's a *box* that accepts and displays *text*). An analogy would be boxes you see when filling out a job application or a survey. You might find a box called First Name. It can both accept user input (from a pen) and display information. This real-world box is very similar to a Visual Basic TextBox.

Without something like a TextBox control, displaying a piece of information on the screen would be quite complicated. In olden days, your program would have to determine where to position the information on the screen, determine the size of the display area, and then print the information to the desired spot. With a text box, you only are concerned with what to display, and the control takes care of the rest. If you don't like where the information is displayed, you simply reposition your text box on the form. No coding is required. Similarly, if you don't like the appearance of the text box, you can easily change the text font or the colors.

Accepting user input works the same way. Although the TextBox control sounds simple, it does a lot of work behind the scenes:

- It picks out the character that corresponds to the key pressed by the user.
- It places the character at the appropriate position in the display.
- It handles cursor movement, delete, and backspace key functions.
- It handles text insertion or overwrite functions.
- It stores the information in the computer's memory so your program can retrieve it.

Adding a Control to Your Form   To use a control in your program, you must first put it on a form. The first control we'll add for the loan calculator is a TextBox control. To do this, follow these steps:

1. Select the TextBox control in the Toolbox by clicking it.

2. Move the mouse to the form and place the cursor at one corner of the area where you want the control. Note that the mouse cursor is a cross while you are in drawing mode.

3. Click and hold the left mouse button.

4. Drag the mouse to the opposite corner of the area where you want the control. As you drag the mouse, you might notice a "rubber band" box that shows you the area that will be occupied by the control. If you stop moving the mouse, a ToolTip appears telling you the actual dimensions of the control (see Figure 3.6).

5. Release the mouse button, and the control is drawn on your form (see Figure 3.7).

FIG. 3.6

You place controls on your form by using the mouse to set their position and size.

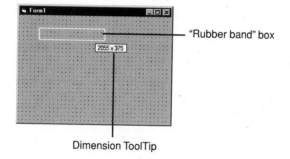

"Rubber band" box

Dimension ToolTip

FIG. 3.7

The completed text box appears on the form and is selected (notice the selection/resizing handles).

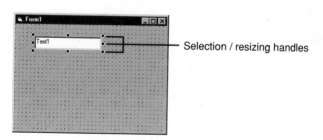

Selection / resizing handles

   You can also add a control to a form by double-clicking the control's icon in the Toolbox. This places a control of a default size in the center of the form. You can then move and resize the control to your liking with the selection/resizing handles, as described in the upcoming section, "Moving and Resizing a Text Box."

Setting the Properties of the Control   After you have added a text box to your form, you need to set some of its properties. Remember, properties control the appearance and behavior of an object. The two properties you need to set for your text box are the Name and Text properties.

The Name property is very important, because it is used in your program code to identify the control. If you don't know a control's name, you cannot write code to communicate with it. Just in case you forget to assign a name to a text box, Visual Basic initially assigns one for you. For the first text box on the form, this default name is Text1. For the second text box, the name is Text2, and so on. You could just use the default names, but that would not be a good programming practice. Remember that you will use these names to identify the text boxes in your code. A descriptive name makes it easier to maintain your program when you need to make the inevitable changes. For instance, if you have text boxes for first name, last name, and address, it is easier to remember which text box is which if they are named txtLname, txtFname, and txtAddress rather than Text1, Text2, and Text3.

N O T E   The text box names I suggested begin with the prefix *txt*. A three-character prefix is commonly used to identify the type of control, in this case a text box. Other prefixes that are often used to name controls include *lbl* for labels and *cmd* for command buttons. ■

▶ **See** "Referencing Forms and Controls from Your Code," **p. 77**

To change the name of your text box, go to the Name property in the Properties window and type in a new name in the edit area for the property. For the first text box in the sample program, use the name txtPrincipal (see Figure 3.8).

FIG. 3.8

Use the Properties window to set the various properties of the controls in your project.

The other property that you need to set for the text box is its Text property. At any given point in time, the Text property contains the actual text (characters) that appears in the text box. You might notice that, by default, the text box displays the name *originally* assigned to the control by Visual Basic (even if you have subsequently changed the Name property). Typically, you will want different text displayed when your form is shown; and quite often, you will want the text box to appear blank. To clear the text box, go to the Text property in the Properties window, highlight the text in the edit area, and press the Delete key. If you want any other text to appear in the text box, simply type in the desired text in the edit area.

N O T E Keep in mind that right now you are in design mode; once the program is running you can only change properties with code. ▪

Adding the Remaining Text Boxes
Now that you have added one text box to the form, it should be a simple matter to add the other text boxes that are needed for the sample program. Go ahead and add three more text boxes and name them `txtTerm`, `txtInterest`, and `txtPayment`. Go ahead and remove the default value from the `Text` property of each text box, as well. When you have finished adding the text boxes, your form should look similar to the one in Figure 3.9.

FIG. 3.9
The Loan Calculator program requires four text boxes.

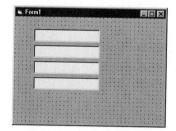

 To draw multiple controls of the same type, hold down the Ctrl key when you select the control in the Toolbox. This keeps the Toolbox from switching back to the mouse pointer and allows you to draw multiple instances of the control.

If your form does not look like the one in the figure, no problem. The great thing about a visual design environment is that you can easily change the appearance of an object on the form.

Moving and Resizing a Text Box
You can move the text box to a new location or change its size with just mouse movements. To move a control, simply click it with the mouse and then drag it to a new location. If you pause while you are dragging the control, a ToolTip is displayed showing you the position of the upper-left corner of the control.

To change the size of a control, select the control on the form (again by clicking it) and then click and drag one of the eight *sizing handles* (small squares positioned on each edge and each corner) on the control to make it a different size. This is similar to resizing a window in any other program. A control's sizing handles are illustrated in Figure 3.10.

Now that you have created four text boxes to accept input, you need to label them so the user knows what information to enter. To make room for the labels, let's move the four text boxes to the right side of the form. Rather than moving them one at a time, we can select all of them and move the group. To do this, first hold down the Ctrl key. Next, single-click each of the text boxes with the mouse so the selection handles are visible. Finally, while holding the mouse button down, drag the group of controls to the right side of the form. When finished, your form should look similar to Figure 3.11.

Part
I
Ch
3

FIG. 3.10

A control's sizing handles let you use the mouse to change its size.

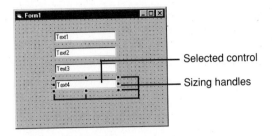

FIG. 3.11

Selecting a group of controls, as in the example pictured here, allows you to move them all at once.

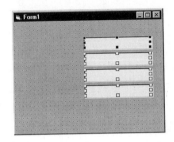

Identifying the Inputs

As we mentioned earlier, you need some type of on-screen indication of what information the text boxes hold (the names that you gave the controls previously are for use within the code and are not displayed on the screen). The easiest way to do this is to place a Label control next to each text box. The label's caption can contain a description of the data to be entered.

In many respects, a label control is very similar to a text box. It can contain letters, numbers, or dates. It can contain a single word or an entire paragraph. Figure 3.12 shows several label controls that illustrate the diversity of appearances you can get. Using the earlier analogy of a job application, the labels are like the words printed on the form to tell you where to write your name or other information.

FIG. 3.12

Labels can take on many sizes and appearances.

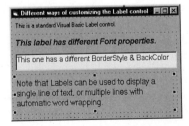

The key difference between a label control and a text box is that *the information in a Label control can't be edited by the user.* Also, the Label control does not have a `Text` property. Instead, the information you see in the Label control is stored in its `Caption` property.

To add a label control to your program, follow these steps:

1. Select the Label control from the Toolbox.
2. Draw a Label control to the left of the top-most text box.
3. Change the label's Name property to lblPrincipal.
4. Change the label's Caption property to Principal: (be sure to include the colon at the end).

By adding this label, you have now made the program easier to use by telling the users where to enter the amount of the loan. As you did with the text boxes for the program, go ahead and create the rest of the labels. You need to create one label to go along with each of the text boxes. Table 3.1 lists the recommended Name and Caption property settings. When you have finished, your form should resemble Figure 3.13.

Table 3.1   Labels that Identify the Program's Input

Label Name	Caption
lblPrincipal	Principal:
lblTerm	Term (Years):
lblInterest	Interest Rate (%):
lblPayment	Monthly Payment:

FIG. 3.13
Labels in the program tell the user what information to enter.

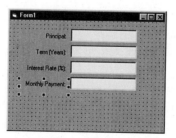

 TIP To get your labels to right-align near the text boxes like they do in Figure 3.13, select the label controls and change the Alignment property to 1 - Right Justify. The Alignment property field in the Properties window has a drop-down list of alignment choices.

Adding a Command Button

The last controls that you need for the sample program are CommandButton controls. While the TextBox and Label controls are designed for input and display, the CommandButton control is used to initiate a task, similar to a real-life pushbutton. You add a command button to your form the same way that you add the text boxes and labels—by drawing it on the form with the mouse.

First, click the CommandButton control in the Toolbox; then draw the first command button on the form and give it a unique name, just like you did for the other controls. The name used in the sample project is cmdCalculate. Also, command buttons, like labels, have a caption. The caption appears on the button's face and typically describes what the button does. For the sample program, change the Caption property to Calculate Payment. Draw a second command button, cmdExit, and set its Caption property to Exit. Your form should now look like the one in Figure 3.14.

FIG. 3.14
CommandButton controls allow the user to initiate actions in the program.

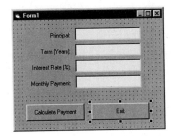

> **N O T E**   In Visual Basic 5, the CommandButton control has undergone a big improvement: you can add a graphic to it with the Style and Picture properties. In previous versions of Visual Basic, you couldn't do this with a standard CommandButton control. ▪

Performing Tasks

At this point, the interface portion of our sample program is complete. However, if you were to run the program, it wouldn't really do anything. Sure, you could type some numbers into the text boxes, but the program would not perform any calculations on them—which is why you were writing it in the first place.

In order to make your program perform a task, you need to write some code. And in order for the program to perform the task(s), you must have a way of telling the program *when* to perform *which* task. You do this by creating *event procedures*, which are segments of code that are executed when a particular event (the Click event, for example) occurs to a particular object (the cmdExit command button, for example). We discuss event procedures in more detail a little later.

Let's start with the easiest code, the Exit button. Double-click the button to bring up the form's Code window, and you might notice a subroutine template, which consists of two lines. These lines, illustrated in Figure 3.15, define the beginning and the end of the event procedure. The default event for command buttons is the Mouse click, so you see the cmdExit_Click subroutine.

Any code you place in this procedure (or sub) is executed whenever the user clicks the CommandButton control. Press Tab to indent the code (that makes it easier to read) and then type the word **End** into the subroutine so that it looks like this code:

```
Private Sub cmdExit_Click()
    End
End Sub
```

At this point, you can run the program (by clicking the Start button, by selecting Run, Start from Visual Basic's menu system, or by pressing F5); then click the Exit button to stop it.

FIG. 3.15

Visual Basic provides a skeleton procedure, or template, for each event.

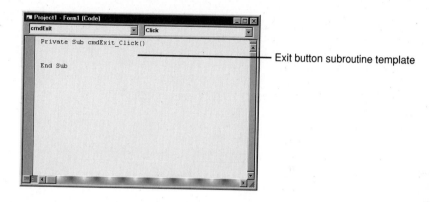

Exit button subroutine template

Activating an Event

In Visual Basic, a program typically takes actions in response to an event. In the preceding, you defined the Click event procedure for cmdExit. An *event* is something that happens to an object either as the result of a user action, an action instigated by another part of the program, or some action from the operating system. Examples of events are the user's pressing a key, the user's moving a mouse, the value of a control being changed, or a specified amount of time elapsing. Whenever the user initiates the Click event for cmdExit, the program executes cmdExit's Click event procedure, which simply consists of the End statement.

▶ **See** "Handling Events in Your Programs," **p. 157**

Each control you use in your programs has been set up to recognize certain types of events. Some controls can respond to mouse clicks, while other controls can respond to changes in their values. If you want a control in your program to respond to a specific event, you must place code in the appropriate event procedure for that control. Otherwise, your program ignores the event.

Look near the top of the Code window, and you will notice two drop-down boxes. The box on the left lists all of the objects that have been placed on the form (as well as the form itself); the one on the right lists the available events for the object that is currently selected in the leftmost box. If you browse through the right-hand list, you'll see that the CommandButton control can respond to more events than just a mouse click. One helpful way to think of your form code is like a long text file, and the Code window is a navigation tool to quickly jump between different procedures.

The easiest way to begin entering code is to double-click the control that you want to have respond to an event. Double-clicking the control opens the form's Code window, automatically selecting the appropriate object, as shown in Figure 3.16.

N O T E Double-clicking a control is a shortcut to the code for the control's default event, or whichever event has code in it. For example, the logical main purpose of a CommandButton control is the Click event. However, if there is no code in a command button's Click event procedure, but there is code in the MouseMove event, double-clicking the control would display the MouseMove event procedure. ▦

FIG. 3.16

Double-clicking the cmdCalculate command button opens the Code window and places the cursor in cmdCalculate's Click event procedure.

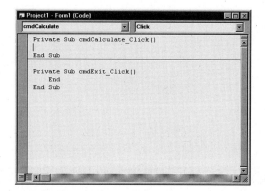

```
Private Sub cmdCalculate_Click()

End Sub

Private Sub cmdExit_Click()
    End
End Sub
```

T I P You can also open the Code window by pressing the F7 key, by clicking the View Code button in the Project window, or by selecting View, Code from the menu system.

The next event procedure code to write is for the cmdCalculate command button, because this is the control the user uses to start the calculation:

```
Private Sub cmdCalculate_Click()

End Sub
```

You place the code to calculate the loan payment between the two lines marking the beginning and end of the procedure. (Notice that the procedure name, cmdCalculate_Click, is created from the name of the control and the name of the event.)

Writing Program Code

The actual code that is used in this event procedure consists of two parts—the *variable declarations* and the *procedure code*. This section explains the code you need to enter for the Calculate Payment button.

Variable Declarations   The variable declarations area is where you tell Visual Basic the names of the variables that you will be using in the procedure and what type of information each variable will store. Although Visual Basic does not require you to declare your variables, it's good practice to do so and will save you a number of headaches.

T I P Always declare your variables! In the Tools, Options menu item, under the Editor tab, make sure Require Variable Declaration is checked. This causes Visual Basic to report an error if you attempt to use a variable that hasn't been declared (for example, if you inadvertently misspell the variable's name).

The declarations for the sample code are shown in the following code segment. Figure 3.17 shows the variable declarations as they should appear in the subroutine for the Calculate Payment button.

```
Dim crPrincipal As Currency, sgInterest As Single
    Dim crPayment As Currency, inTerm As Integer
    Dim sgFctr As Single
```

FIG. 3.17
The first code entered in cmdCalculate's Click event procedure should be the variable declarations, as pictured here.

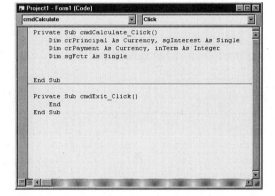

As you might notice in the preceding example, the general format for variable declarations is the word Dim, followed by a variable name of your choosing, followed by As, and the variable's type. Variables can be declared on separate lines or together on the same line.

As with object names, you should follow a naming standard. The naming standard I use for variables uses the first two characters of the variable name as a prefix designating its type; the rest of the name describes its purpose. The variable named crPrincipal, for example, is a Currency type variable that stores the principal amount; sgInterest is a Single type variable storing the interest rate. We discuss variable naming conventions more thoroughly in Chapter 8, "Programming Basics."

T I P A common beginner mistake is a statement like Dim x, y, z As Integer. In this case, only z would be an Integer, while x and y would be a special type called a Variant. The Variant data type is a special type discussed later in the book. The correct syntax would be to place the declarations on a separate line or place the words As Integer after each variable name.

▶ **See** "Variable Declarations," **p. 172**

Procedure Code The procedure code is the part of the subroutine that does the actual work. In the case of the sample program, the code retrieves the input values from the text boxes, performs the calculation, and inserts the monthly payment value into the appropriate text box. This code is shown in Listing 3.1. Figure 3.18 shows how the procedure code actually appears in the subroutine.

On the CD

Listing 3.1 LOANCALC.FRM—Calculates the Monthly Payments Using Procedure Code

```
crPrincipal = txtPrincipal.Text
sgInterest = txtInterest.Text / 1200
inTerm = txtTerm.Text
sgFctr = (1 + sgInterest) ^ (inTerm * 12)
crPayment = sgInterest * sgFctr * crPrincipal / (sgFctr - 1)
txtPayment.Text = Format(crPayment, "Fixed")
```

FIG. 3.18

Entering the calculation code completes the Click event procedure for cmdCalculate.

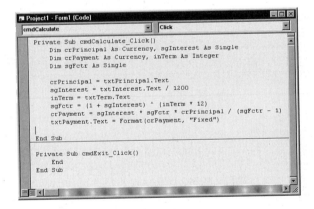

Now that we have created the event procedure, let's briefly review what it does:

- The input values are retrieved from the text boxes and stored in variables.
- The actual calculation is performed using math operators.
- The value of the crPayment variable, which contains the result, is formatted and placed in a text box.

N O T E In the example code we referred to the text boxes by specifying both the name of the control and the name of the property, separated by a dot (or period). This gives rise to the term *dot notation.* Using dot notation, you can retrieve or set the value of almost any property of a control. Both our code and descriptions of the controls we've drawn are located within the same form. If we needed our code to access one of the controls from another form or module, the form name would be added to the beginning of the dot notation, as in Form1.txtPrincipal.Text. ■

N O T E　The Text property of a text box is known as its "default" property. This means that if you do not specify a property name, the Text property is assumed for the text box; therefore, the last statement in Listing 3.1 could have been written txtPayment = Format(crPayment, "Fixed"). ▨

▶ **See** "Referencing Forms and Controls from Your Code," **p. 77**

Running Your Program

Now let's run the program and see if it works. To run the program, click the Start button on the Visual Basic toolbar; alternatively, choose <u>R</u>un, <u>S</u>tart from the menu system, or press the F5 key. Visual Basic then compiles your program to check for errors, and, if none are found, your program runs. You can now enter values for the principal, term, and interest rate of the loan. Use the following values:

Principal	**75,000**
Term	**30**
Interest	**8.5**

Then click the Calculate Payment button, and the monthly payment is displayed. The payment amount should be 576.69.

After you have finished testing the program and trying various combinations of values, you can return to the design environment by clicking the Exit button, or clicking the End button on Visual Basic's toolbar.

The loan payment calculator is contained in the file LOANCALC.VBP.

Sharing Your Program

If the program will be used outside of the VB design environment, you need to compile the program. You can compile your program by choosing <u>F</u>ile, Ma<u>k</u>e LOANCALC.EXE. Choosing this item causes Visual Basic to check your program for errors and then create an executable file that can be used by double-clicking it from Windows Explorer or a shortcut.

▶ **See** "Compiling Your Program," **p. 481**

Enhancing Your Program

A loan payment calculator is a useful tool, but there are several things that you can do to the program to make it even more useful. Let's look at two enhancements that will help you learn a little more about Visual Basic programming techniques.

Exploring Properties

While forms and controls are typically thought of as just what the user sees on the screen, their appearance and behavior are controlled by three basic elements: *properties*, *methods*, and *events*. This section explains these elements in terms of how they define a form, but the principles discussed here apply to all controls that you might use in Visual Basic.

▶ **See** "Handling Events in Your Programs," **p. 157**

When you look at a form, you see a rectangular window on the screen, like the one shown in Figure 4.1. But in reality, this window is defined by a series of properties. For example, the position of the form on the screen is controlled by the Left and Top properties, while the form's size is controlled by its Height and Width properties. The form title that you see in the title bar displays the contents of the form's Caption property. By setting properties, you can even determine which control buttons appear on the form.

FIG. 4.1

The basic elements of a form are defined by its properties.

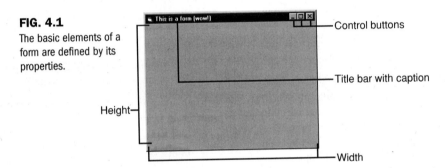

You can use a text editor such as Notepad to open the .FRM file that is created for each of your forms. This text file stores the form's property settings as well as the event code. Figure 4.2 shows a portion of an .FRM file.

> **CAUTION**
>
> For most forms, Visual Basic also creates a file with an .FRX extension. This file stores graphics and other binary elements that cannot be defined by text. It is important when moving forms to another subdirectory to copy the .FRX files as well.

You can think of the properties of a form or control as descriptions of the object's characteristics. This is similar to describing a person. For example, how would you describe yourself? You would probably cite such characteristics as height, weight, hair color, and eye color. Each element of your description could be considered a property.

FIG. 4.2

The properties of a form
are stored in text format
in an .FRM file.

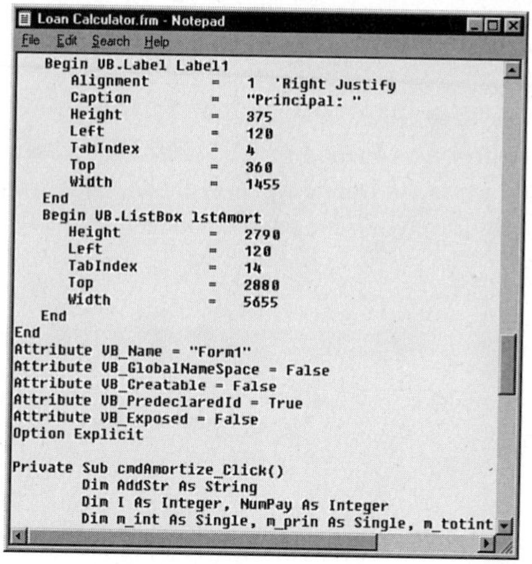

```
Loan Calculator.frm - Notepad
File  Edit  Search  Help
   Begin VB.Label Label1
      Alignment        =    1  'Right Justify
      Caption          =    "Principal: "
      Height           =    375
      Left             =    120
      TabIndex         =    4
      Top              =    360
      Width            =    1455
   End
   Begin VB.ListBox lstAmort
      Height           =    2790
      Left             =    120
      TabIndex         =    14
      Top              =    2880
      Width            =    5655
   End
End
Attribute VB_Name = "Form1"
Attribute VB_GlobalNameSpace = False
Attribute VB_Creatable = False
Attribute VB_PredeclaredId = True
Attribute VB_Exposed = False
Option Explicit

Private Sub cmdAmortize_Click()
   Dim AddStr As String
   Dim I As Integer, NumPay As Integer
   Dim m_int As Single, m_prin As Single, m_totint
```

N O T E   The term "object" in this chapter refers to *visual* objects such as forms and custom
controls. In later chapters we will further discuss objects and object-type variables, and
how they relate to Visual Basic program code. ■

What Properties Do Most Objects Have in Common?

All objects in Visual Basic do not have the same set of properties. However, there are several
properties that are common to most objects. Some important, common properties are:

- Left
- Top
- Height
- Width
- Name
- Enabled
- Visible
- Index

Controlling Form Size

You can control a form's size by selecting it and dragging its sizing handles at design time, or
by changing the values of its Height and Width properties at either design time or runtime. If
you do this at design time, you will see a corresponding change in the Height and Width properties in the Properties window. During program execution, you can use code to respond to or
initiate a change in size. Try it now:

1. Create a new Standard EXE project and press F5 to run it.

2. Press Ctrl+Break (or click the Break button) to enter Break mode.

3. Press Ctrl+G to bring up the Immediate window.

4. In the Immediate window, type **Print Form1.Width** and press Enter. (The Immediate window, formerly known as the Debug window, enables you to type and execute program statements while in Break mode.) The current value of the Width property is printed (see Figure 4.3).

FIG. 4.3

You can print many properties of a form, such as the Width property, in the Immediate window.

5. In the Immediate window, type **form1.Width = form1.Width * 2** and press Enter.

6. Press F5 (or click the Start button), and notice that Form1's width has doubled (see Figure 4.4).

FIG. 4.4

Setting a new value for the Width property in the Immediate window causes the form's width to change immediately.

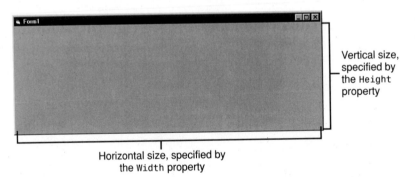

Vertical size, specified by the Height property

Horizontal size, specified by the Width property

You can see the value of the new width by returning to Break mode and again entering **Print Form1.Width** in the Immediate window.

Measurements in Visual Basic 5

By default, all distances are measured in *twips*. A twip is a unit of measure for objects. The actual physical size of a twip varies depending on screen resolution. You can specify another unit of measure for objects within a container using the container's ScaleMode property. However, the screen's scale mode cannot be changed, so a form's Left, Top, Height, and Width properties are always measured in twips.

Adjusting Form Position

In addition to controlling a form's size, you can control its position with the Left and Top properties (see Figure 4.5). The Left property specifies the distance of the left side of the object from the left side of the object's container. The Top property specifies the distance of the top edge of the object from the top of its container. In the case of a standard form, the container is the entire screen. If you draw a control on a form, the form is the control's container. It is also necessary to mention that some controls themselves, such as PictureBox and Frame controls, can act as containers for other controls.

FIG. 4.5
This TextBox's position is measured relative to the form.

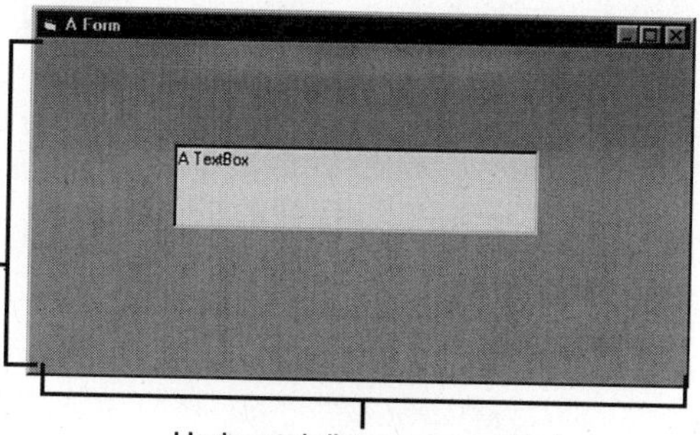

Vertical distance, specified by the Top property

Horizontal distance, specified by the Left property

> **N O T E** An object's Top and Left properties can actually have a negative value! For example, a Label control whose Left property value is –1440 would be positioned so that its left edge is approximately one inch to the left of its container; therefore, some or all of it would not be seen. ■

While the position of most forms is measured in relation to the upper-left corner of the screen, a form that is part of a Multiple Document Interface (MDI) or browser application is positioned relative to the upper-left corner of the client area (see Figure 4.6).

Controlling User Interaction

Even if your application includes many forms and controls, you probably do not want the user to have access to all of them at the same time. For example, suppose you are writing a word processor. You might have Save File and Load File buttons, but you would not want the user to press Save File until after a file has been loaded. Two properties, the Visible property and the Enabled property, allow you to manage this process.

The Visible property determines if an object can be seen on the screen. The Enabled property determines whether the user can interact with an object. Both properties can be set to either True or False.

FIG. 4.6

MDI child forms and
ActiveX documents are
positioned relative to
the parent form.

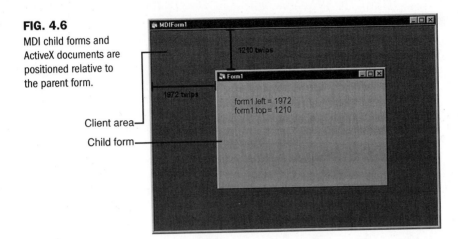

Client area

Child form

If the Visible property is set to False, the object is not shown, and the user will not know that
the object is even there. If the Enabled property is set to False, the object is visible (provided
that the Visible property is True), but the user cannot interact with it. Typically, if an object is
disabled, it is shown on the screen in a *grayed-out*, or *dimmed*, mode. This provides a visual
indication that the object is unavailable.

A good example of objects that are variably available and unavailable occurs in the wizard
interface in some Windows programs. A Wizard organizes a task into several logical steps, with
three navigation buttons (typically labeled Back, Next, and Finish) that are used to move between steps. Depending on which step the user is currently working on, all of these buttons
may not be enabled, as in Figure 4.7.

FIG. 4.7

Because the user is on
step 1 of 4, the
Enabled property of
the Back button is set
to False, causing it to
be grayed out.

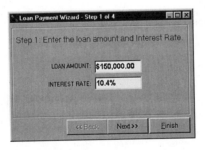

 If you are implementing a wizard interface in Visual Basic, one option is to draw the controls for each
step in a frame. The Visual Basic Frame control acts as a container, so setting its own Visible
property relevant to the user's current step affects all the controls within it. For more information, see
Chapter 13, "Using Containers."

Referencing Forms and Controls from Your Code

One other key property of every Visual Basic object is the Name property. The Name property defines a unique identifier by which you can refer to the object in code. Each form, text box, label, and so on must have a unique name.

> **N O T E** All forms in a project must have different names. However, control names have to be unique only for the form on which they are located. That is, you can have a "Text1" control on each form in your project, but you can't have two "Form1" forms in your project. ▪

Visual Basic provides a default name when an object is first created. For example, Form1 is the name given to the first form created for your project, and Text1 is the name given to the first text box that you place on a form. However, the first thing you should do after drawing a control or form is to provide it with a name that has some meaning. For example, I always use frmMain as the name of the main interface form in my applications.

As you are naming your objects, it's good programming practice to use the first three characters of the object's name as a prefix to identify the type of object to which the name refers. As in the frmMain form that we just discussed, the prefix frm indicates that the object is a form. Table 4.1 lists suggested prefixes for many of Visual Basic's objects (forms and controls).

Part

I

Ch

4

Table 4.1 Prefixes that Identify the Object Type

Object Type	Prefix	Object Type	Prefix
CheckBox	chk	Horizontal ScrollBar	hsb
ComboBox	cbo	Image	img
Command Button	cmd	Label	lbl
Common Dialog	cdl	Line	lin
Data Control	dat	ListBox	lst
Data Bound ComboBox	dbc	Menu	mnu
Data Bound Grid	dbg	OLE Container	ole
Data Bound ListBox	dbl	Option Button	opt
Directory ListBox	dir	Picture Box	pic
Drive ListBox	drv	Shape	shp
File ListBox	fil	TextBox	txt
Form	frm	Timer	tmr
Frame	fra	Vertical ScrollBar	vsb
Grid	grd		

Remember that the names you assign will be used in code, so avoid carpal tunnel syndrome by keeping them short!

To set the Name property for an object, select the object, view the Properties window (by clicking the Properties button, by selecting View, Properties Window, or by pressing the F4 key), and click the Name property. You can then type a new value.

FIG. 4.8

The Name property is located at the top of the list on the Alphabetic page and is the first property listed under the Misc group on the Categorized page.

T I P To quickly go to a specific property while in the Properties window, hold down the Ctrl and Shift keys and press the first letter of the property name. This takes you to the first property starting with that letter. Additional key presses take you to the next property with the same letter.

A First Look at Methods and Events

So far in this chapter, we have concentrated on properties, showing how they can control an object's appearance. However, forms and controls in Visual Basic are not just idle components that sit and look pretty. In addition to properties, an object can have *methods*, which define tasks that it can perform. The tasks can be simple, such as moving the object to another location, or they can be more complex, such as updating information in a database.

Taking Action with Methods

A method is really just a program function that is built into the object. Using its embedded methods, the object knows how to perform the task; you don't have to provide any additional instructions. For example, forms have a PrintForm method that prints them to the current printer. The statement Form1.PrintForm prints an exact duplicate of Form1. Because the low-level details for the PrintForm method are encapsulated within the form object, a Visual Basic programmer does not have to be concerned with them.

As you may have guessed, methods, like properties, use *dot notation*. When typing code, Visual Basic uses the Auto List Member feature to list an object's methods and properties when you type the object's name followed by a period. While there are different methods for different objects, many objects have the following methods in common:

- `Drag`   Handles the operation of the user's dragging and dropping the object within its container
- `Move`   Changes the position of an object
- `SetFocus`   Gives focus to the specified control
- `ZOrder`   Determines whether an object appears in front of or behind other objects in its container

N O T E   *Focus* refers to the *current* control that receives user actions, such as keystrokes. Only one control on any form can have the focus at any given time. Focus is usually indicated by the position of the edit cursor (for text boxes) or a dotted rectangle around the control (for check boxes, option buttons, and command buttons). ■

Responding to Actions with Events

In addition to performing tasks, the objects in your program can respond to actions, whether generated by the user or externally. These actions are handled through the use of *events*. For example, when a user clicks a command button, he causes a `Click` event to occur to that command button. Part of the definition of an object determines to which events it responds.

Examples of events are clicking a command button, selecting an item in a list box, or changing the contents of a text box. Events also occur when the user exits a form or switches to another form. When an event happens to an object, the object executes an *event procedure* for that specific event. To respond to events, you have to place program code in the object's event procedures. For example, in Chapter 3 you placed code in the `Click` event of a command button for the Loan Calculator program.

▶ **See** "Performing Tasks," **p. 60**

Chapter 7, "Responding to the User," delves into all the intricacies of events. In that chapter, you learn how to write code to handle events and how multiple events are related.

▶ **See** "Handling Events in Your Programs," **p. 157**

How Properties and Methods Are Related

By now, you know that objects have properties to define their appearance, methods that let them perform tasks, and events that let them respond to user actions. You might think that all these things happen independently of one another, but that is not always the case. Sometimes, the properties and methods of an object are related. That is, as you invoke a method of an object, the properties of the object are changed. Also, most times that you use the methods of an object or change its properties with code, you do so in response to an event.

N O T E Some property changes can trigger events. For example, changing the Height or Width property of a form in code triggers the form's Resize event. ■

You can see one example of the interdependence of methods and properties of an object when the Move method is used and the Left and Top properties are set. You can cause an object to change position either by using the Move method or by setting the Left and Top properties to new values. For example, the following two code segments accomplish the same task of changing a text box control's position to 100 twips from the left and 200 twips from the top of its container:

```
'CODE SEGMENT 1 - Move the text box by setting its properties
txtName.Left = 100
```

```
'CODE SEGMENT 2 - Move the text box using the Move method
txtName.Move 100, 200
```

You should notice two things about these code segments. First, code lines beginning with a single quote (') are considered comments; that is, Visual Basic ignores anything after the single quote. You can use comments to describe or explain your code. Second, if you type the code segments, you'll notice that the Move method has two additional arguments available. These optional arguments can change the size of the object. This has the same effect as setting the Height and Width properties to new values.

Similarly, the Show and Hide methods of a form have the same effect as changing the form's Visible property. When you invoke the form's Hide method, the effect is the same as setting its Visible property to False. (The effect, of course, is that the form disappears from the screen.) Likewise, the form's Show method produces the same effect as setting its Visible property to True.

Forms

So far, most of our examples have used the Form object. A form is a container that holds all the other controls (such as labels, text boxes, and pictures) that make up the user interface. Most of your programs will use a number of forms.

N O T E It is possible to create a Visual Basic program that contains no forms at all! One example might be a command-line program that processes files and requires no user interface. ■

Parts of a Form

When you start a new Standard EXE project, you are presented with the *default project*, which normally includes a single standard form (see Figure 4.9). Because this form is where you start work on your user interface, let's take a look at the different parts of it.

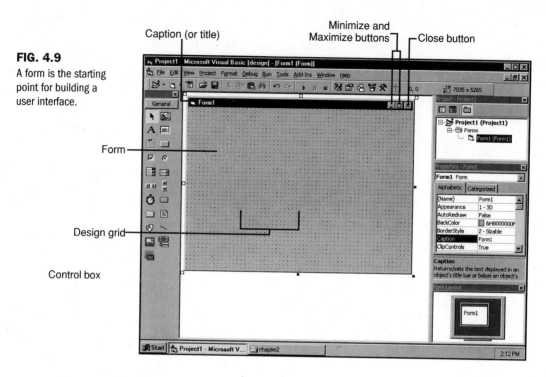

Caption (or title)

Minimize and
Maximize buttons

Close button

FIG. 4.9
A form is the starting
point for building a
user interface.

Form

Design grid

Control box

As you can see in Figure 4.9, a Visual Basic form contains all the elements you would expect to find as part of a window in a program. It contains a title bar, a control menu, and a set of Minimize, Maximize/Restore, and Close buttons. Note that many of these elements, such as the Close button, are always present at design time even if the properties are set in such a way that they are not visible at runtime.

Another design-time feature is a grid that allows you to easily line up controls as you are designing your interface. You can control the behavior of the design grid through the Options dialog box, accessible by choosing Tools, Options. In this dialog box, you can change the size of the grid or even turn it off completely. You can also choose whether or not controls are automatically aligned to the grid. If this option is on (the default setting), the upper-left corner of each control is aligned with the grid point that's closest to the corner. Using the default setting makes it easy to line up controls. In fact, I set the grid to be smaller than the default, which allows more precise control alignment.

Form Properties Revisited

Forms, like most of the objects used in Visual Basic, have a series of properties that control their behavior and appearance. In the earlier section "Controlling User Interaction," you learned about some of the properties that apply to forms. In this section, you learn about several additional key properties of forms. You also learn how these properties can be controlled during program design and execution. Table 4.2 lists several of the key properties of a form and provides a brief description of each. The table also identifies whether the value of the property can be changed while the program is running.

Table 4.2 Key Properties for Controlling a Form

Property Name	Description	Changeable at Run Time
BorderStyle	Sets the type of border that is used for the form	No
ControlBox	Determines whether the control box (containing the Move and Close menus) is visible when the program is running	No
Font	Determines the font used to display text on the form	Yes
Icon	Determines the icon that is shown in the form's title bar and that appears when the form is minimized	Yes
MaxButton	Determines whether the Maximize button is displayed on the form when the program is running	No
MDIChild	Determines whether the form is a child form for an MDI application	No
MinButton	Determines whether the Minimize button is displayed on the form when the program is running	No
StartUp Position	Determines the initial position of a form when it is first shown	Yes
WindowState	Determines whether the form is shown maximized, minimized, or in its normal state	Yes

Now let's take a closer look at some of these properties. The BorderStyle property has six possible settings that control the type of border displayed for the form (see Table 4.3). These settings control whether the form is sizable by clicking and dragging the border; they control the buttons that are shown on the form; and they even control the height of the form's title bar (see Figure 4.10).

Table 4.3 Possible *BorderStyle* Property Settings that Control the Type of Window Displayed

Setting	Effect
0 - None	No border is displayed for the form. The form also does not display the title bar or any control buttons.
1 - Fixed Single	A single-line border is used. The title bar and control buttons are displayed for the form. The form is not resizable by the user.
2 - Sizable border	The border appearance indicates that the form can be resized. The title bar and control buttons are displayed. The form can be resized by the user by clicking and dragging the border. This is the default setting.
3 - Fixed Dialog	The form shows a fixed border. The title bar, control box, and Close button are shown on the form. Minimize and Maximize buttons are not displayed. The form cannot be resized.
4 - Fixed ToolWindow	The form has a single-line border and displays only the title bar and Close button. These are shown in a reduced font size (approximately half height).
5 - Sizable ToolWindow	This is the same as the Fixed ToolWindow, except that the form has a sizable border.

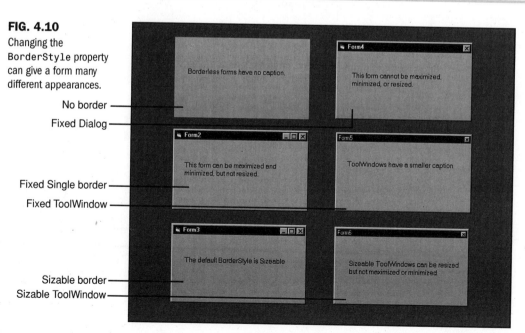

FIG. 4.10

Changing the BorderStyle property can give a form many different appearances.

No border
Fixed Dialog

Fixed Single border
Fixed ToolWindow

Sizable border
Sizable ToolWindow

Part

I

Ch

4

N O T E Setting the `BorderStyle` property to prevent resizing does not affect the form's appearance in the design environment; it affects it only at run time. ■

The default setting provides a border that enables the user to resize the form while the program is running. This is the type of form that you find in most of the programs you use, such as Microsoft Word or Microsoft Money. However, you can change the `BorderStyle` setting to make the form look like almost any type of window that you would see in a program, including toolboxes and dialog boxes. You can even remove the form's border altogether.

In Table 4.3, several of the `BorderStyle` definitions indicate that a control box and the Close, Minimize, and Maximize buttons would be displayed in the title bar of the form. This is the default behavior. But even with these border styles, you can individually control whether these elements appear on the form. The `ControlBox`, `MaxButton`, and `MinButton` properties each have a `True` or `False` setting that determines whether the particular element appears on the form. The default setting for each of these properties is `True`. If you set a property to `False`, the corresponding element is not displayed on the form. These properties can be changed only at design time.

The `Font` property lets you set the base font and font characteristics for any text displayed directly on the form by using the form's `Print` method.

N O T E The `Font` property of a form is actually an object itself with its own properties. For example, to change the size of a form's font, you would enter **Form1.Font.Size = 10** in a Code window (or the Immediate window, for that matter) to change the size to 10 points. ■

In addition, setting the form's `Font` property sets the font for all controls subsequently added to the form.

TROUBLESHOOTING

I set the `Font` property of the form, but the font in the title of the form did not change. The `Font` property of the form has no effect on the form's title; it affects only on its internal area. Windows itself controls the font for a window title. This can be changed in the Windows 95 Control Panel.

When I use a form's `Print` method, sometimes I can't see my text. If you do not set the form's `AutoRedraw` property to `True` or use the `Refresh` method, your text can be erased when another window is stacked on top of the form. Also, you need to look at the `CurrentX` and `CurrentY` properties to make sure that the text is displayed within the visible area of the form.

One final form property of note is the `StartupPosition` property. As you might guess, this property controls where the form is located when it is first displayed. There are four possible settings for the `StartupPosition` property. These settings are summarized in Table 4.4.

Table 4.4 Possible *StartupPosition* Property Settings that Control Where the Form Is Initially Displayed

Setting	Effect
0 - Manual	The initial position is set by the Top and Left properties of the form.
1 - CenterOwner	The form is centered in the Windows desktop unless it is an MDI child form, in which case it is centered within its parent window.
2 - CenterScreen	The form is centered in the Windows desktop.
3 - Windows Default	The form is placed in a position determined by Windows based upon the number and position of other windows open at that time.

N O T E This feature is a godsend to longtime Visual Basic programmers. In previous versions of Visual Basic, you had to write code to center the form by setting the Top and Left properties or by using the Move method. With the StartupPosition property, this is all handled for you. ■

Part

I

Ch

4

Although the StartupPosition property can center your form for you when the form first loads, it does not keep the form centered. For example, if you resize the form, it does not remain centered. If you want to have the form centered after it has been resized, you still need to write code to perform the task. This code (see Listing 4.1) should be placed in the form's Resize event procedure.

On the CD

Listing 4.1 *FORMDEMO.FRM*—Using Code to Keep a Form Centered After Its Size Is Changed

```
If Me.Height >= Screen.Height Then
    Me.Top = 0
Else
    Me.Top = (Screen.Height - Me.Height) / 2
End If
If Me.Width >= Screen.Width Then
    Me.Left = 0
Else
    Me.Left = (Screen.Width - Me.Width) / 2
End If
```

Note in the preceding listing the use of the Me keyword, instead of the form name (such as Form1). When used in a form's code, Me represents the form itself without having to refer to it by name, much as a pronoun can refer to a person without having to use his or her name. This means that the same block of code could be inserted into several forms without any changes. Also, if a form is ever renamed, Me ensures that the changed name doesn't affect procedures that act upon the form.

TIP Visual Basic's new Form Layout window is useful if you are working in a higher resolution than that in which your users will be running your program. Right-click the Window and check the Resolution Guides option to see form sizes relative to standard screen resolutions.

Displaying a Form

If you write a program with just a single form, you needn't worry about displaying the form or hiding it. This is done automatically for you as the program starts and exits. This single form is known as the *Startup Object* or *Startup Form*. When you run your program, Visual Basic loads your Startup form into memory and displays it. As long as this form remains loaded, your program keeps running and responding to events. When you press the Close button on the form (or execute the End statement), the program stops.

N O T E   You can select a Startup form in the Project Properties dialog box. It is also possible to have a program start from a Sub procedure named Main in a code module rather than from a form. ▧

However, if you have multiple forms—as most of your programs do—you need to understand how to manage them. The state of a form is controlled by Visual Basic's Load and Unload statements, as well as the form's Show and Hide methods.

The Load statement places a form in memory, but does not display it. The following line of code shows how the statement is used:

```
Load frmMember
```

By using this, you are *explicitly* loading the form. However, the form is loaded automatically if you access a property, method, or control on it.

Because the load operation is performed automatically, it is not really necessary to use the Load statement with a form. However, it is important to be aware when a form is being loaded, because the code in the Form_Load event will be executed at that time.

 TIP There are some cases where you would want to use the Load statement (see the "Using *Load* to Enhance Performance" sidebar later in this section).

To display the form, you must use the Show method. The Show method works, whether or not the form was loaded previously into memory. If the form was not loaded, the Show method *implicitly* loads the form and then displays it. The Show method is used as follows:

```
frmMember.Show
```

The Show method also has an optional argument that determines whether the form is shown as a *modal* or *modeless* form. If a form is shown modally, then no other forms or code outside that form are executed until the modal form is closed. Think of the program code as being paused as long as a modal form is displayed. An example of a modal form is the Windows 95 Shut Down screen. You cannot put the focus on another window while the Shut Down Windows form is displayed.

If a form is shown modeless, you can move at will between the current form and other forms in the program. The preceding statement displayed a form as modeless. To create a modal form, you simply set the optional argument of the Show method to vbModal, as shown here:

```
frmMember.Show vbModal
```

> **N O T E** A modal form is typically used when you want the user to complete the actions on the form before working on any other part of the program. For example, if a critical error occurs, you do not want the user to switch to another form and ignore it. ▧

After a form is displayed, you have two choices for getting rid of it. The Hide method removes the form from the screen but does not remove it from memory. Use Hide when you need to temporarily remove the form from view but still need information in it, as in the following code example:

```
frmSelect.Show vbModal

frmResults.Print "The date you entered was: " & frmSelect.txtDate
```

In the preceding example, the purpose is to display a form and then retrieve a value from a text box on it. Because the form is shown modally, the second statement is not executed until the form is removed from the screen. Presumably, the user would enter the information and then press a button that executed frmSelect's Hide method.

If you are finished with a form and the information contained on it, you can remove it from both the screen and memory with the Unload statement. The Unload statement uses basically the same syntax as the Load statement, as shown here:

```
Unload frmMember
```

> **TIP** If you are using the Unload statement from within the form you are removing, you can use the keyword Me to specify the form. This prevents errors if you later rename your form. In this case, the statement would be the following:
>
> ```
> Unload Me
> ```

When you are using a control's property in code, you can use it just like you would a variable or constant. You can use the properties in comparison statements to make decisions, and you can use them in assignment statements to set the value of a variable. You can also use an assignment statement to set the value of a property. The following code shows how the Text property of a text box is used to retrieve a name entered by the user, convert it to all capitals, and put the modified text back in the text box:

```
Sub cmdCapitalize_Click()
  Dim sName As String
  sName = txtName.Text
  sName = Ucase$(sName)
  txtName.Text = sName
End Sub
```

To reference an object's property in code, you must specify the name of the object (the text box named txtName in the preceding code) and the name of the property (the Text property in this example), using a dot (or period) to separate them. Be aware, however, that some properties are read-only at run time, and some only exist at run time. An object can have more properties than those listed in the Properties window. To find a complete list, look up the control in the Help system and follow the *Properties* hyperlink.

N O T E   If you are referring to a control on a form other than the current form, you also need to specify the name of the form. The form name precedes the control name and is separated from it by a dot (.). A generalized syntax for changing property values that always works is *formname.objectname.propertyname = value*. For example:

frmMember.txtName.Text = "Smith, John" ■

It is good programming practice to always specify the name of the property, but many controls have what is known as a *default property*. A default property can be referenced simply by specifying the name of the control. For example, the Text property is the default property of the TextBox control. Therefore, the following two statements work exactly the same:

```
'************************************
'Property name specifically referenced
'************************************
txtName.Text = "Mike"


'****************************************************
'Property name omitted, utilizing default property
'****************************************************
txtName = "Mike"
```

Table 4.6 shows the default property of a number of controls.

Table 4.6   Default Properties of Common Controls

Control Type	Value Property
Check box	Value
Combo box	Text
Directory list box	Path
Drive list box	Drive
File list box	FileName
Horizontal scroll bar	Value
Image	Picture
Label	Caption
Option button	Value
Picture box	Picture
Text box	Text
Vertical scroll bar	Value

Part

I

Ch

4

Finding Out What Controls Can Do

In the previous sections, you learned what controls are and how to use them in your programs. You also learned a little about their properties, methods, and events. In this section, you find out more details about some of the most frequently used controls. You learn about other controls in Part II, "Visual Basic Controls."

Working with Text

One of the most common tasks in programming is working with text. Now, *text* here does not just mean paragraphs and sentences like those you handle with a word processor. When you deal with text in a program, you also might want to display or retrieve a single word, a number, or even a date. For example, in a data-entry program, you might need to handle the name, address, telephone number, date of birth, and other information about a member. Text information can easily be handled using Visual Basic's TextBox control. Figure 4.12 shows a data-entry screen for a membership application.

Visual Basic provides several controls for handling text. The major controls included with VB are the Label, TextBox, Masked Edit, and RichTextBox controls. These controls can handle most of your program's text editing and display needs.

FIG. 4.12

You can handle all types of information with text controls.

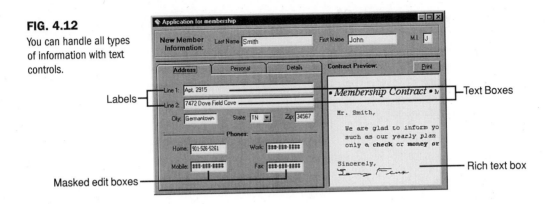

NOTE In this chapter, only the Label and TextBox controls are covered. The RichTextBox and Masked Edit controls are covered in detail in Chapter 14, "Working with Text, Fonts, and Colors." ▪

Using a Label Control to Display Text The simplest control that displays text is the Label control. The most common use of the Label control is identifying different items on a form, such as the data-entry form shown in Figure 4.12. Each label identifies the information in the edit field next to it. Used in this way, each label typically is set up at design time, and the necessary text is assigned to the label's Caption property in the Properties dialog box.

However, you are not limited to using the Label control in this manner. In fact, you can use the Label control to display any type of information to the user. A label can display a date, a number, a single word, or even an entire paragraph of information.

While the Caption property of the Label control contains the text to be displayed, there are other properties of the control that influence *how* the text is displayed. The most obvious of these properties are the Font and ForeColor properties, which determine the typeface and text color of the control, respectively. However, if you are going to use the label to display more than a small amount of text, the AutoSize and WordWrap properties are the ones that will be most important to you.

If you know in advance what text is going to be displayed in a label's Caption property, you can set the size of the label to accommodate the text. However, if different text will be displayed in the label at different times (for instance, in a database application), it needs to be able to adjust to the length of its current contents. The AutoSize property of the Label control determines whether or not the size of the control automatically adjusts to fit the text being displayed. When AutoSize is False (the default), the label's size remains unchanged regardless of the length of its caption. If a caption is too long for the label, some of it will not be visible.

Setting AutoSize to True causes a label to automatically adjust its size to fit its caption. If the caption is longer than the label's original size allows, the method of resizing depends upon the value of the WordWrap property. If the WordWrap property is False (the default), the label expands horizontally to allow the caption to fit, even if the label grows so large that it runs past the right edge of the screen. If the WordWrap property is set to True, the label expands vertically to allow enough lines of text to accommodate the caption, even if the label runs off the bottom edge of the screen. (The *words wrap* to new lines, hence the property name WordWrap.) In either case, the Caption property contains the entire caption, even if some of the text "spills off" of the form. The effects of the different settings of the AutoSize and WordWrap properties are shown in Figure 4.13.

 T I P When assigning a label's Caption property, you can force a new line by including a *carriage return* and *line feed* combination. This technique is a throwback to the ancient days of manual typewriters. When a manual typewriter user reached the end of a line, he had to manually move the paper up to the next line (a line feed) and return the carriage to the beginning of that line (a carriage return). In Visual Basic, you can insert a carriage return/line feed combination by inserting ASCII characters 13 and 10 into the caption at the point where the line should break. Visual Basic supplies a predefined constant, vbCrLf, to help you accomplish this task:

```
Label1.caption = "First Line" & vbCrLf & "Second Line"
```

FIG. 4.13
These four labels have the same long caption; their AutoSize and WordWrap properties determine if and how they resize to fit the caption.

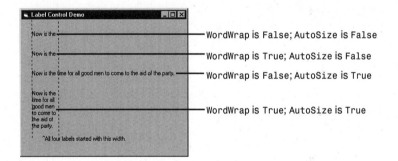

CAUTION
To preserve the original width of your Label control, you must set the WordWrap property to True before setting the AutoSize property. Otherwise, when you set the AutoSize property to True, the Label control adjusts horizontally to fit the current contents of the Caption property.

There are three other properties that, from time to time, you might need to use with the Label control. These are the Alignment property, the Appearance property, and the BorderStyle property. The Alignment property determines how the text is aligned within the Label control. The possible options are Left-Justified, Right-Justified, and Centered. The Appearance can be set to Flat or 3-D to govern whether the label appears raised from the form. The BorderStyle property determines whether the Label control has no border or a single-line border around the label. With BorderStyle set to Fixed Single, the Label control takes on the appearance of a noneditable text box. The effects of the Alignment, Appearance, and BorderStyle properties are shown in Figure 4.14.

Part
I
Ch
4

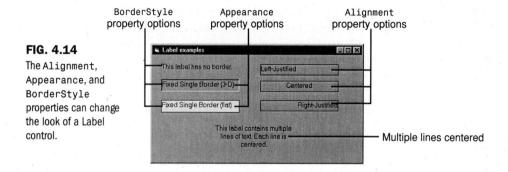

FIG. 4.14

The Alignment, Appearance, and BorderStyle properties can change the look of a Label control.

> **N O T E**   The Alignment property also affects the text when the label is used to display multiple lines. The control aligns each line according to the setting of the Alignment property (refer to Figure 4.14).

Entering Text with a Text Box   Because much of what programs do is to retrieve, process, and display text, you might guess (and you would be correct) that the major workhorse of many programs is the TextBox control. The text box enables you to display text; more importantly, however, it also provides an easy way for your users to enter and edit text and for your program to retrieve the information that was entered.

In most cases, you use the text box to handle a single piece of information, such as a name or address. But the text box is capable of handling thousands of characters of text. A TextBox control's contents are stored in its Text property—the main property with which your programs will interact. You can also limit the number of characters a user can enter with the MaxLength property.

By default, the text box is set up to handle a single line of information. This is adequate for most purposes, but occasionally your program needs to handle a larger amount of text. The text box has two properties that are useful for handling larger amounts of text—the MultiLine and ScrollBar properties.

The MultiLine property determines whether the information in a text box is displayed on a single line or multiple lines. If the MultiLine property is set to True, information is displayed on multiple lines, and word-wrapping is handled automatically. The user can press Enter to force a new line. The ScrollBar property determines whether or not scroll bars are displayed in a text box, and if so, what type of scroll bars (None, Horizontal, Vertical, or Both). The scroll bars are useful if more text is stored in the Text property than fits in the text box. The ScrollBar property has an effect on the text box only if its MultiLine property is set to True. Figure 4.15 shows the effects of the MultiLine and ScrollBar properties.

FIG. 4.15

You can use a text box to enter single lines of text or entire paragraphs.

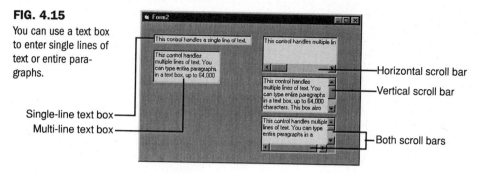

Horizontal scroll bar

Vertical scroll bar

Both scroll bars

Single-line text box

Multi-line text box

◆ **TROUBLESHOOTING**

The text box in my program will handle only about 32,000 characters instead of the 64,000 specified in the documentation. When you use the default value of zero for the MaxLength property, this corresponds to a limit of 32 kilobytes (about 32,766 characters). To allow more characters, set the MaxLength property to the desired value, but don't exceed 64 kilobytes (about 65,535 characters).

T I P When a text box is activated (known as *receiving the focus*) by the user tabbing to it or clicking in it, a common practice is to select (or highlight) its contents. While there's no automatic way to accomplish this, it can be done pretty easily. One method that I recently discovered has quickly become my favorite. Enter this line of code in the text box's GotFocus event procedure:

```
SendKeys  "{Home}+{End}"
```

The SendKeys statement sends a string of characters to the active form at run time just as if the user typed them at the keyboard. In this case, we're acting as if the user pressed the Home key, then a shifted End key (the plus sign before {End} represents Shift). This causes the text to be highlighted, so the user can begin entering new text without having to delete what is already there.

Actions

Another control important to practically every application that you will develop is the CommandButton control. Typically, this control is used to let the user initiate actions by clicking the button. Setting up a CommandButton control is quite simple. You draw the button on the form and then set the Caption property of the button to the text that you want displayed on the button's face. To activate the button, just place code in the button's Click event procedure. As any other event procedure, this code can consist of any number of valid Visual Basic programming statements.

While users most often use command buttons by clicking them, some users prefer accessing commands through the keyboard versus using the mouse. This is often the case for data-entry intensive programs. To accommodate these users, you want your program to trigger command button events when certain keys are pressed. You accomplish this by assigning an *access key* to

Part

I

Ch

4

the command button. When an access key is defined, the user holds down the Alt key and presses the access key to trigger the Click event of the CommandButton control.

You assign an access key when you set the CommandButton control's Caption property. Simply place an ampersand (&) in front of the letter of the key you want to use. For example, if you want the user to be able to press Alt+P to run a print command button, you set the Caption property to &Print. The ampersand does not show up on the button, but the letter for the access key is underlined. The caption Print then appears on the command button.

> **N O T E** If, for some reason, you need to display an ampersand in a CommandButton caption, simply use two of them in a row in the Caption property—for example, Save && Exit. ▪

In addition to captions, your command buttons can have pictures. Simply set the Style property to Graphical, and use the Picture property to select a picture file. Figure 4.16 shows several options for creating command buttons.

FIG. 4.16
Command buttons can communicate their functions to the user in many ways.

One command button on a form can be designated as the *default button*. This means the user can simply press Enter while the focus is on any control (except another command button or a text box whose MultiLine property is True) to trigger the default button. This activates the default button's Click event, just as if the user had clicked it with the mouse. To set up a button as the default button, set its Default property to True. Only one button on a form can be the default button.

You can also designate one button as the *cancel button*, which is similar to the default button but works with the Esc key. To make a command button into a cancel button, set its Cancel property to True. As with default buttons, only one button on a form can be a cancel button. As you set the value of the Default or Cancel property of one button to True, the same property of all other buttons on the form is set to False.

Working with Multiple Controls in the Design Environment

So far, you have seen how to add controls to your forms and how to set the properties of a single control at a time. But sometimes you need to be able to work with multiple controls at the same time. For example, if you have a bunch of label controls on a form and decide to change their font, you don't want to have to select and change each label control individually. That would be a real hassle. Fortunately, you don't have to handle controls one at a time; you can work with them in groups.

The first step in working with multiple controls is to select the controls you need to move or modify. You can select a group of controls by clicking the mouse on your form and dragging it. As you drag the mouse, you see a dashed-line box appear on the form as shown in Figure 4.17. Use this box to enclose the controls you want to select.

FIG. 4.17

You can easily select multiple controls with the mouse.

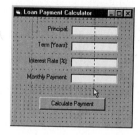

When you release the mouse button, any controls that are inside the box or touching it are selected. The selected controls are indicated by small boxes at each corner and in the center of each side of the control (see Figure 4.18).

FIG. 4.18

Selection points (boxes) indicate that a control is selected.

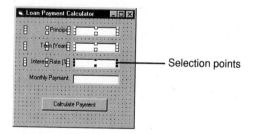

Selection points

N O T E You can also select multiple controls by holding down the Ctrl key while you click them individually. If you need to select a group of controls that are contained within a frame or picture box, you *must* Ctrl+click them because the dashed-line box technique won't work. ■

You can add controls to a group or remove them by clicking the control while holding down the Shift or Ctrl key. You can even do this after making an initial selection with a mouse drag, so you can refine your selection to exactly the group of controls you want to work with.

After the group of controls has been selected, you can move the group as a whole by clicking one of the controls in the group and dragging the group to a new location. The controls retain their relative positions within the group as you move them. You can also use editing operations such as Delete, Cut, Copy, and Paste on the group as a whole.

Using the Properties Window

In addition to the ability to move, cut, copy, paste, and delete a group of controls, you can also work with their properties as a group. For example, if you want to change the font of a group of Label controls, simply select the group of controls and access the Font property in the

Properties window. When you change the property, all the selected controls are affected. This is a great tool for making changes to many controls at once. I use this technique frequently to change the alignment of all the Label controls on my form.

While it is obvious that this works for a group of controls of the same type (such as a group of labels or a group of text boxes), you might be wondering what happens when your group includes controls of several different types. In this case, Visual Basic displays the properties that are common to all the controls in the group. These properties typically include Top, Left, Height, Width, Font, ForeColor, Visible, and Enabled. You can only edit the properties that are common to all the controls. However, this is very useful if you want to align the left or top edges of a group of controls. To do this, simply select the group and set the Left property of the group (or the Top property). Figure 4.19 shows a selected group of different controls and the Properties window containing their common properties.

FIG. 4.19
Common properties of different controls can be modified as a group.

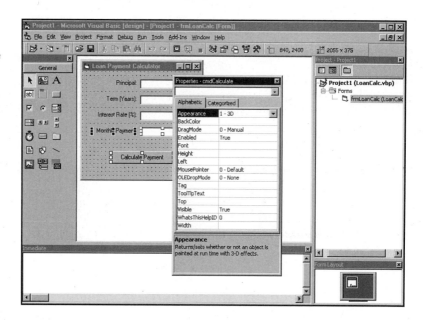

Using the Form Editor Toolbar

Editing common properties is not the only way to work with a group of controls. Visual Basic 5 adds a great tool to the development environment. This tool is the Form Editor toolbar (see Figure 4.20), which is accessible by selecting View, Toolbars, Form Editor. Table 4.7 shows and explains each of the toolbar buttons.

FIG. 4.20
The Form Editor toolbar makes it easy to align and size multiple controls.

Table 4.7   The Form Editor Toolbar Buttons

Button	Name	Function
	Bring to Front	Move selected control in front of other controls on the same part of the form.
	Send to Back	Move selected control behind other controls on the same part of the form.
	Align	Lines up a group of controls
	Center	Centers a group of controls
	Make Width Same Size	Resizes a group of controls to match
	Lock Controls Toggle	Prevents movement or resizing of controls with the mouse (however, the controls can still be modified with the Properties window)

The Form Editor toolbar allows you to manipulate the position and size of a group of controls. The Align button allows you to align the left, right, top, or bottom edges of a group of controls. While you can align the left and top edges of a group by setting the Left or Top properties directly, there is no direct way to align the right or bottom edges. The Align button also enables you to line up the vertical or horizontal centers of the controls. This cannot be done directly with the properties. To choose which type of alignment to use, click the arrow button to the right of the Align button. This displays a menu that allows you to pick the alignment. You can also choose to align all the selected controls to the grid. This causes the upper-left corner of each control to be moved so that it is touching the grid point nearest its current location.

Another task that was tedious in previous versions of Visual Basic was centering controls on the form. This has also been made easy using the Form Editor toolbar. Next to the Align button is the Center button. This button allows you to center the group of controls horizontally or vertically within the form. The entire group is centered as if it were a single control; the relative position of each control in the group remains the same. As with the alignment options, you select the type of centering you want from a pop-up menu that appears when you click the arrow button next to the Center button.

The last button on the Form Editor is the Make Same Size button. This button allows you to make the height or width of all the controls in the group the same. While you can do this by setting the appropriate properties, the Form Editor makes it much more convenient.

Figure 4.21 shows a group of controls that has been made the same size as well as centered horizontally within the form.

Part

I

Ch

4

FIG. 4.21

With the Form Editor toolbar, centering and resizing controls is a snap!

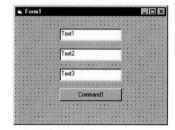

 T I P If you press the wrong button on the Form Editor toolbar, you can undo the changes by clicking the toolbar's Undo button, or by pressing Ctrl+Z.

Using the Format Menu

Just when you thought you had seen every possible way to manipulate multiple controls, you find out that there is one more option available to you—Visual Basic's Format menu (see Figure 4.22). The Format menu contains all of the same functions as the Form Editor toolbar, but also has three other options for working with multiple controls—Horizontal Spacing, Vertical Spacing, and Size to Grid.

FIG. 4.22

The Format menu offers a number of tools for fine-tuning the appearance of controls on your forms.

The Horizontal Spacing option allows you to make the spacing between controls equal. This gives you a clean look for groups of controls such as command buttons. If you think the controls are too close together, you can choose to increase the spacing. The spacing is increased by one grid point. You can also choose to decrease the spacing between controls, or remove the spacing altogether. Choosing Vertical Spacing allows you to perform the same tasks in the vertical direction. Figure 4.23 shows a "before" and "after" look at a group of command buttons. The "after" portion shows the effect of setting the horizontal spacing equal.

FIG. 4.23

Equal horizontal spacing makes this group of buttons look orderly.

The final item on the Format menu is the Size to Grid item. Selecting this option sets the Height and Width properties of each selected control so that it exactly matches the grid spacing.

Working with the Controls Collection

By now, you're probably thinking, "All this is great when I am in the design environment, but what about while my program is running?" Well, as you know, you can change the properties of any single control by specifying the control name, the property name, and the new property value. But does this mean that you have to set each control individually? No way!

Each form contains a collection called the Controls collection. This collection identifies each control that is on the form. Using this collection and a special form of the For loop, you can change a specific property of every control on your form.

Changing All Controls

As an example, you might want to give your users a way to select the font they want to use for the controls on the form. Trying to set each form in code would be a real pain. But, with the For Each loop, you can set the font of every control on the form with just three lines of code (see Listing 4.4).

On the CD

Listing 4.4   COLLECT.FRM—Collections Enable You to Set Properties for Multiple Controls in Code

```
For Each Control In Form1.Controls
    Control.Font = "Times New Roman"
Next Control
```

You can do the same thing with any other properties that are supported by all the controls on the form.

Changing Selected Controls

But what if you want to set a property that is not supported by all the form's controls? For example, if you want to change the text color of your controls, the command button doesn't have a ForeColor property, although other types of controls do. For this problem, you use another code statement, the TypeOf statement. This statement allows you to determine the type of any object. This way, you can set up a routine that changes the ForeColor property of all controls that are not command buttons. This is shown in Listing 4.5.

Modifying the Menu After creating your menu, you will probably find that you need to make some changes to the menu's structure. This also is easily accomplished with the Menu Editor. Table 5.1 lists some common editing needs and how they are accomplished.

Table 5.1 Editing a Menu with a Few Mouse Clicks

Editing Function	How to Do It
Move an item	Select the item and then click one of the Move arrows to move the item up or down in the list. The indentation level of the menu does not change as you move the item.
Add an item to the middle of the list	Select the item that should appear below the new item in the list and then click the Insert button. A blank item appears; you can then enter the Caption and Name properties for the item. The new item is indented at the same level as the item below it.
Remove an item	Select the item and then click the Delete button. The item is immediately deleted, without any confirmation. (There is no Undo feature in the Menu Editor; whatever you delete is gone.)

TIP When moving menu items, you can use the Alt+U key combination instead of the Up button, or you can use the Alt+B keys instead of the Down button.

Adding Access Keys and Shortcut Keys for Quick Access If you have been working in Windows for a while, you have probably noticed that many menu items can be accessed by using a combination of keystrokes. You can let users access your menu items in the same way. There are two types of key combinations that can be used this way: *access keys* and *shortcut keys*.

What is the access key for a menu item? The access key (sometimes called a *mnemonic* key) is indicated by an underscore beneath the letter in the item's caption (for example, the F in File). You create an access key by placing an ampersand (&) in front of the appropriate letter in the Caption property. For the File menu, the Caption property would be &File. You can create an access key for any or all of the items in your menu.

NOTE While it is typical to use the first letter of the caption as the access key, this is not a good idea if that letter is already in use. For example, Visual Basic's Format menu uses the second letter as the access key to avoid conflict with the File menu. It is possible to assign the same access key to multiple menu items. If you do that, Visual Basic just cycles through the items with each press of the access key. However, this is not standard practice because having to press an access key multiple times defeats its purpose. In addition, many users don't know that they can cycle through the items in this manner, and become frustrated when they see no apparent way to select the desired choice.

When you have access keys defined for your menu, the user can select a top-level menu item (the ones in the menu bar) by holding down the Alt key and then pressing the access key. This causes the submenu for that item to drop down, showing the items for that group. The user can then start the desired task by pressing the access key defined for the menu item. For example, for the <u>N</u>ew item of the <u>F</u>ile menu, the user could press Alt+F and then press N.

N O T E   Instead of holding down Alt and pressing an access key, you can just press Alt (or F10) first, and then use the arrow keys to navigate the menus. ■

To create an effective set of access keys, you must specify a different key for each of the top-level menu items. Then specify a different key for each of the items in the submenu. Conceivably, you can have up to 36 access keys, one for each letter of the alphabet and one for each of the ten digits, but you will run out of screen space for the choices before running out of letters.

TIP   If possible, use the first letter of the menu item as the access key, because typically the user expects this.

In addition to the access keys just discussed, you can assign shortcut keys to some of the more commonly used functions in your program. Shortcut keys provide direct access to a function through a single key (such as Delete) or key combination (such as Ctrl+S), without having to navigate the menu system. Users can take advantage of shortcut keys to perform tasks quickly.

To assign a shortcut key to one of your functions, enter the Menu Editor, select the menu item for which you want a shortcut key, and then select the desired key from the <u>S</u>hortcut list. The key is assigned to that function, and the shortcut-key information appears next to the menu item in the menu (see Figure 5.7). There are 79 shortcut keys that you can use.

Part

I

Ch

5

FIG. 5.7

Ctrl+O has been assigned as the shortcut key for the <u>F</u>ile, <u>O</u>pen menu function.

<u>F</u>ile, <u>O</u>pen menu item   Ctrl+O shortcut

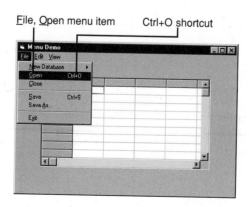

You can assign any unused shortcut key to any menu item, but be aware that there are a few "standard" keys used in many Windows programs. Some of these keys are listed in Table 5.2. As examples, the "Description" column explains what these keys do when you're working within Visual Basic itself.

Table 5.2   Shortcut Keys Speed Access to Program Tasks

Menu Item	Shortcut Key	Description
Edit, Cut	Ctrl+X	Removes selected text or control(s) from its current location and copies it to the Clipboard.
Edit, Copy	Ctrl+C	Makes a copy of the selected text or control(s) in the Clipboard.
Edit, Paste	Ctrl+V	Pastes the contents of the Clipboard to the active form or Code window.
Edit, Undo	Ctrl+Z	Undoes the last change.
Edit, Find	Ctrl+F	Opens the Find dialog box to allow the user to search for text.
File, New	Ctrl+N	Creates a new Visual Basic project.
File, Open	Ctrl+O	Opens the Open Project dialog box to allow the user to select a project to open.
File, Save	Ctrl+S	Saves the current file.
File, Print	Ctrl+P	Opens the Print dialog box to allow selection of items to be printed.

TIP As with access keys, try to have the shortcut key correspond to the first letter of the item name; for example, Ctrl+P for Print. This makes it easier for users to remember the shortcuts. To avoid confusing your users, use the standard shortcut keys listed in Table 5.2 whenever possible.

TROUBLESHOOTING

When I try to save the changes to my menu, I get the error message `Shortcut key already defined`. **What happened?** If you got this message, you inadvertently gave the same shortcut key to two or more functions. You need to look through the menu-item selection area to find the duplicate definition, and then assign another key to one of your items.

Code for the Menu Items

After creating the menu's structure, you need to write code to let the menu items actually perform tasks. As with a form or other controls, you do this by writing code in an event procedure. A menu item handles only one event—the `Click` event. This event is triggered when the user clicks the menu item, or when he selects the item and presses Enter.

N O T E A menu item's `Click` event is also triggered when the user uses an access key or shortcut key to access an item. ■

To add code to a menu item's `Click` event, first select the menu item on the form by clicking the item. This starts the Code Editor and sets up the `Event` procedure for the selected item. Then simply type in the code to handle the task. The following sample code could be used to create a new database in response to a menu selection:

```
Private Sub mnuNewDb_Click()
  Dim sFileName As String

  dlgGetFile.ShowOpen
  sFileName = dlgGetFile.FileName
  Set dbMain = DBEngine.WorkSpaces(0).CreateDatabase(sFileName,dbLangGeneral)
  MsgBox "New database created."
End Sub
```

The preceding code uses a CommonDialog control named `dlgGetFile` to obtain a file name from the user. It then uses this file name to create a new database.

▶ **See** "Using Built-In Dialog Boxes," **p. 139**

Optional Settings

In addition to the required `Caption` and `Name` properties, each menu item has several optional properties that you can set either to control the behavior of the menu or to indicate the status of a program option. Three of these properties are `Visible`, `Enabled`, and `Checked`. The menu item's `Visible` and `Enabled` properties work just like their counterparts on a form or control. When the `Visible` property is set to `True`, the menu item is visible to the user. If the `Visible` property is set to `False`, the item and any associated submenus are hidden from the user. You have probably seen the `Enabled` and `Visible` properties used in a word processing program (though you might not have been aware of how it was accomplished), where only the File and Help menus are visible until a document is selected for editing. After a document is open, the other menu items are shown. Changing the setting of the `Visible` property allows you to control what menu items are available to the user at a given point in your program. Controlling the menu this way lets you restrict the user's access to menu items that might cause errors if certain conditions are not met. (You wouldn't want the user to access edit functions if there was nothing to edit, right?)

The `Enabled` property serves a function similar to that of the `Visible` property. The key difference is that when the `Enabled` property is set to `False`, the menu item is *grayed out*. This means that the menu item still can be seen by the user but cannot be accessed. For example, the standard <u>E</u>dit, Cu<u>t</u> and <u>E</u>dit, <u>C</u>opy functions should not be available if there is no text or object selected, but there's nothing wrong with letting the user see that they exist (see Figure 5.8).

FIG. 5.8

Disabled menu items are visible to the user but are shown in gray tones, indicating that the items are unavailable at the present time.

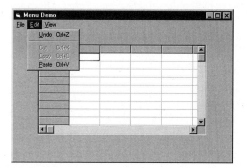

Both the `Visible` and `Enabled` properties can be set in the Menu Editor at design time, and from your program code at runtime. In the Menu Editor, the properties are set by using check boxes. The default value of the properties is `True`. In code, you set the property value by specifying the name of the menu item (from the `Name` property), the name of the property, and the value you want to set. This is shown in the following line of code for the Edit menu:

```
Mnu_Edit.Visible = False
```

The `Checked` property of the menu item determines whether or not a check mark is displayed to the left of the item in the menu, as shown in Figure 5.9. The `Checked` property is typically used to indicate the status of a program item or option; for example, whether a toolbar or particular window is visible. The menu item is then used to toggle back and forth between two program states. The following code causes the menu's check mark to toggle on and off every time it is clicked:

```
Private Sub mnuShowSorted_Click()
  mnuShowSorted.Checked = Not(mnuShowSorted.Checked)
End Sub
```

Because the `Checked` property can only be `True` or `False`, the preceding code makes nice use of some Boolean logic with the `Not()` function. At any point in the program code, the state of the `Checked` property indicates whether or not the user wants something to be displayed in sorted order.

CAUTION

You cannot set the `Checked` property to `True` for an item on the menu bar (top menu level). Doing so results in an error.

Check mark

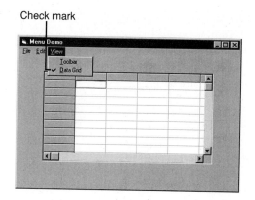

FIG. 5.9

The *Checked* property controls whether or not a check mark is placed to the left of a submenu item.

You might have also noticed two other items in the Menu Editor. These items specify the value of the `NegotiatePosition` and `WindowList` properties of the menu item. The `NegotiatePosition` property specifies whether and where the menu item of your application is displayed when an embedded object on a form is active and its menu is shown (for example, if your application has an instance of Word embedded for modifying a document). If the `NegotiatePosition` property is 0, your menu is not displayed while the object is active. If the property is not 0, your menu item is displayed to the left of, in the middle of, or to the right of the object's menu (property settings of 1, 2, or 3, respectively).

The `WindowList` property specifies whether the current item will contain a list of MDI child forms that are open within the MDI parent. When this property is set to `True`, the menu automatically adds items as child forms are opened and removes the items when the corresponding child form is closed.

▶ **See** "Maintaining a Window List," **p. 554**

▶ **See** "Maintaining a Window List," **p. 554**

Part

I

Ch

5

Creating Pop-Up Menus

So far, the discussion of menus has looked at the menu bar that appears along the top of the form. Visual Basic also supports *pop-up menus* in your programs. A pop-up menu is a small menu that appears somewhere on your form in response to a program event.

Pop-up menus often are used to handle operations or options related to a specific area of the form (see Figure 5.10)—for example, a format pop-up menu for a text field that lets you change the font or font attributes of the field. You can find this menu type in many of the latest generation of Windows programs, including Visual Basic itself.

When a pop-up menu is invoked, usually with by right-clicking the mouse, it appears on-screen near the current mouse pointer location. The user then makes a selection from the menu. After the selection is processed, the menu disappears from the screen.

FIG. 5.10

This grid's pop-up menu provides a convenient way to initiate program functions specifically related to the grid.

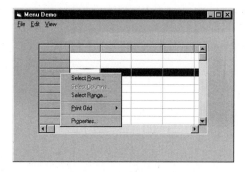

Creating the Menu to Be Displayed

You create a pop-up menu in the same way that you created the main menu for your program—from the Menu Editor. There is, however, one extra step. The pop-up menu should be hidden, so that it does not appear on the menu bar. To do this, set the `Visible` property of the top-level menu item to `False`.

N O T E   Typically, you will hide the menu item that is used as a pop-up menu, but you can use any of the top-level items of a menu bar as a pop-up menu. That is, a particular menu can appear both as a pop-up menu and as a part of the main menu of a form. █

Creating a pop-up menu is easy. The following four steps tell you how to create a pop-up menu to handle text formatting:

1. Create a top-level menu item with `Format` as its `Caption` property and `popFormat` as its `Name` property.

2. Set the `Visible` property of the menu item to `False` by clearing the <u>V</u>isible check box in the Menu Editor.

3. Create three submenu items under `popFormat`, with the `Caption` properties `Bold`, `Italic`, and `Underline` and the `Name` properties `popBold`, `popItalic`, and `popUnder`, respectively.

4. Click the OK button to accept the menu changes.

Notice that the Format menu does not appear on your form's menu bar. However, the menu is present and can be modified in the Menu Editor.

The technique you must use to add code to the `Click` event of the items in a pop-up menu is also a little different. Because the menu is not visible on the form, you cannot just click the item to bring up the code-editing window. Instead, bring up the code-editing window by selecting the View Code button in the Project window, or double-clicking the form. Then, select the desired menu item in the Code window's Object list at the upper-left corner. This enables you to enter code for the hidden items.

Activating a Pop-Up Menu

To have the pop-up menu appear on your screen, you must invoke the form's PopUpMenu method. You do this by specifying the name of the form where the menu will be displayed, the PopUpMenu method, and the name of the menu to be shown.

While you can use this method from anywhere in your code, pop-up menus are used most often in response to mouse clicks, usually those using the right mouse button. The following code shows how the Format menu created in the last section would be called up by clicking the right mouse button anywhere on your form:

```
Private Sub Form_MouseUp(Button As Integer, Shift As Integer,  X As Single,
➥Y As Single)
  If Button = vbRightButton Then
     frmMain.PopUpMenu popFormat
  End If
End Sub
```

In this code segment, the MouseUp event is used to take an action whenever a mouse button is pressed. The event passes a parameter, the Button parameter, that tells you which of the mouse buttons was pressed. Because you want the menu to appear in response to only a right button click, you check for the value of the Button parameter. If it is equal to vbRightButton (an intrinsic constant for the right mouse button), the pop-up menu is displayed.

NOTE   You can create multiple pop-up menus and have them displayed in response to different mouse buttons or in different areas of the screen. The X and Y parameters passed in to the MouseUp event procedure report the location of the mouse cursor at the time the event occurred. ■

Part
I
Ch
5

Creating a Toolbar for Your Application

You have probably noticed that many Windows programs now have one or more toolbars in addition to the menu. These toolbars provide the user with an easy way to access the most commonly used functions of the program. Some programs also use toolbars to help with specific tasks, such as the Drawing toolbar that is in Microsoft Word. Because toolbars are becoming so common, users have come to expect to find them in all programs.

Fortunately, it is easy for you to set up a toolbar in Visual Basic. To create a toolbar, you only need to use two controls—the Toolbar control and the ImageList control. The Toolbar control sets up the buttons of the actual toolbar displayed to the user and handles the user's actions. The ImageList control contains a collection of bitmaps for use by other controls. In this case, our Toolbar control will display images from the ImageList on its buttons.

Setting Up the Toolbar Control

To set up a toolbar on your form, you need to add the Toolbar and ImageList controls to the Toolbox. These two controls are part of the Windows Common Controls group. This group of controls is included with VB, but is not in the Toolbox by default. To add them to the Toolbox, use the Components dialog box, which you access by selecting Project, Components; then select the check box for Microsoft Windows Common Controls 5.0.

Getting the Images for Your Toolbar   After these controls have been added to the Toolbox, you can begin the creation of your toolbar. Follow these steps to create a toolbar:

1. Draw an ImageList control on your form and give it a unique name. Because the ImageList control is not visible to the user, its size is set by Visual Basic. No matter what size you draw it on the form, it always appears as a little box.

2. To add bitmap images to the control, open its Property Pages dialog box by either pressing the ellipsis (…) button of the Custom property in the Properties window, or by right-clicking the ImageList control and selecting Properties. From this dialog box, shown in Figure 5.11, you can add images from graphics files (icons and bitmaps) stored on your hard drive.

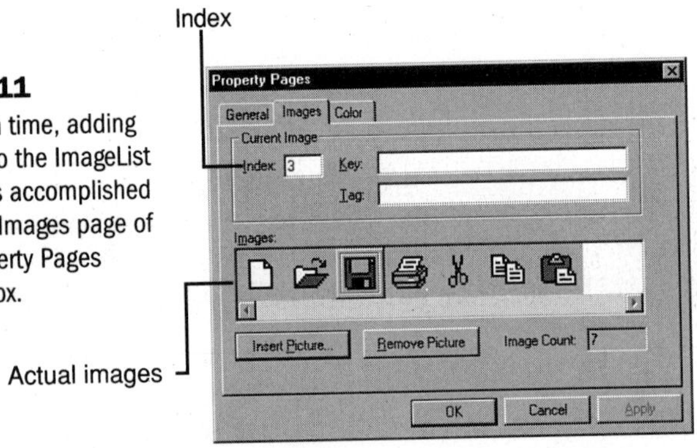

FIG. 5.11
At design time, adding images to the ImageList control is accomplished with the Images page of the Property Pages dialog box.

3. To add an image to the ImageList control, click the Insert Picture button. This presents you with the Select Picture dialog box, from which you can choose the bitmap or icon you want. As you select the picture, it is added to the control and displayed in the Images area.

4. When you have added all the pictures you might need, click the OK button to close the dialog box.

After completing these steps, your ImageList control will be ready to use for supplying images to your toolbar.

Creating the Toolbar   Next, you need to set up the toolbar itself by following these steps:

1. Select the toolbar icon in the Toolbox, and draw the Toolbar control on your form. Visual Basic positions the toolbar at the top of the form, and the control spans the width of the form.

2. A toolbar can be aligned along any of the four edges of its form. If, for example, you want to position it along the bottom of your form, set its Align property to 2 - vbAlignBottom. You can align it to the left or right edge of the form by setting the Align property to 3 - vbAlignLeft or 4 - vbAlignRight, respectively; in these cases, you should adjust

the Width property to keep it from filling the form completely. If you want a free-floating toolbar, set its align property to 0 - vbAlignNone; you can then adjust its position and size by setting the Left, Top, Width, and Height properties.

3. To continue setting up the Toolbar control, bring up its Property Pages dialog box by right-clicking the control and choosing Properties. Figure 5.12 shows the first page of the Toolbar control's Property Pages.

FIG. 5.12

You can assign an ImageList control to your toolbar in the General tab of the toolbar's Property Pages dialog box.

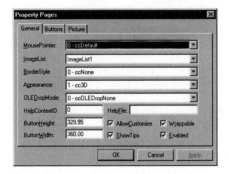

4. Next, set the Toolbar control's ImageList property to the name of the ImageList control that you already set up to provide images. Clicking the arrow to the right of the ImageList property provides you with a list of all ImageList controls on the current form.

There are several other properties on the Property Pages' General tab that control the appearance and behavior of the toolbar. These properties are summarized in Table 5.3.

Table 5.3 Toolbar Properties that Control Its Appearance and Behavior

Property Name	Description
BorderStyle	Determines whether a single-line border is displayed around the toolbar or no border is used.
ButtonHeight	Specifies the height (in twips) of the buttons in the toolbar.
ButtonWidth	Specifies the width (in twips) of the buttons in the toolbar.
AllowCustomize	Determines whether the user is allowed to customize the toolbar by adding, deleting, or moving buttons.
ShowTips	Determines whether ToolTips are shown if the mouse is rested on one of the buttons.
Wrappable	Determines whether the toolbar wraps around to a second row of buttons if there are more buttons than fit on a single row.

Creating the Buttons of the Toolbar The next step in creating your toolbar is to create the buttons that will be placed on the toolbar. For this, you move to the Buttons page of the Property Pages (see Figure 5.13).

FIG. 5.13

You assign images, captions, and identifiers to toolbar buttons in the Buttons page.

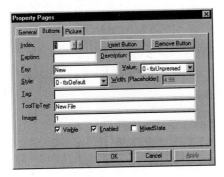

To add a button to the toolbar, click Insert Button. This adds a new button after the current button. For each button that you add, you need to specify several properties—the Key property, the Style property, and the Image property. These three are the minimum required to set up a button.

The Key property specifies a string that is used to identify the button in code. You see how this is used in the following section, "Enabling the Buttons with Code." The Key property for each button must be unique, and you should assign a string that is meaningful to you. This makes it easier to remember when you are writing your code. The Image property specifies the index of the picture that you want to appear on the face of the button. The index corresponds to the Index of the picture in the ImageList control. You can specify a value of zero for the Image property if you do not want a picture to appear on the button.

The Style property determines the type of button that you create. Table 5.4 summarizes the various settings of the Style property. Each of the button styles is shown in Figure 5.14.

Table 5.4 *Style* **Property Settings that Control the Behavior of Toolbar Buttons**

Setting	VB Constant	Description of Behavior	Example
0	tbrDefault	The button is a standard pushbutton.	The Save Project button in VB.
1	tbrCheck	The button indicates that an option is on or off by its state.	The Bold button in Word.

Setting	VB Constant	Description of Behavior	Example
2	tbrButtonGroup	The button is part of a group. Only one button of the group can be depressed at a time.	The alignment buttons in Word.
3	tbrSeparator	The button is used to provide space between other buttons. The button has a width of eight pixels.	N/A
4	tbrPlaceHolder	This button is used to hold a space in the toolbar for other controls such as a combo box.	The font combo box in Word.

FIG. 5.14
Examples of the different toolbar button styles. Note that the placeholder and separators are not really buttons.

In addition to these three key properties, there are several other properties that can be set for each button on the toolbar (see Table 5.5).

Part
I

Ch
5

Table 5.5   Optional Properties that Provide Further Control over a Button Toolbar

Property	Description
Caption	This is text that is displayed beneath the picture on a button.
Description	This is text that describes the button to the user when he invokes the Customize Toolbar dialog box.
ToolTipText	This text appears when the mouse is rested on the button. This text is only displayed if the ShowTips property of the toolbar is set to True (which is the default).
Value	Sets or returns the current state of the button. A value of 0 indicates that the button is not pressed. A value of 1 indicates that the button is pressed. You typically set the value of a single button in a button group to 1. You can then use the Value property in your code to determine which button is pressed.

> **T I P** Unless the images on your buttons are self-explanatory, you should make sure to include ToolTips. Otherwise, there is no way for the user to know what the button does unless he presses it. ToolTips give your program a professional appearance and are easy to add.

After setting up the buttons on the toolbar, you can exit the Property Pages dialog box by clicking the OK button. Your toolbar is now set up and ready for use—almost.

Enabling the Buttons with Code

You have seen how to set up the toolbar, but until you add code to the toolbar's events, it cannot perform any functions. The buttons of the toolbar do not have events of their own. Instead, you actually write your code for the `ButtonClick` event of the toolbar itself. This event passes a Button object, representing the button that was pressed, as a parameter to the event procedure. In your code, you use the value of the Button object's `Key` property to determine which button was actually pressed. Listing 5.1 shows a typical event procedure for taking actions based on the button pressed.

On the CD

Listing 5.1 *TOOLBAR.FRM*—Using the *Key* Property of the Button to Determine What Action to Take

```
Private Sub Toolbar1_ButtonClick(ByVal Button As ComctlLib.Button)

    Select Case Button.Key
        Case "New"
                mnuNew_Click
        Case "Open"
                mnuOpen_Click
        Case "Save"
                mnuSave_Click
    End Select
End Sub
```

In Listing 5.1, the procedures being called are actually the `Click` event procedures of menu items. This allows you to code an action once and then call it from either the menu or the toolbar. Doing this makes it easier to maintain your code because changes or corrections only have to be made in a single location. Also, note the introduction of the `Select Case` statement, which is more readable than a nested `If` statement. We'll discuss it in more detail in a later chapter.

The project TOOLBAR.VBP contains the sample program used in this chapter. The program shows a standard menu, a pop-up menu, and a toolbar.

Allowing the User to Customize the Toolbar

One of the really great features of the Toolbar control is that you can allow your users to customize the toolbar to their liking. When the `AllowCustomize` property of the toolbar is set to `True`, the user can access the Customize Toolbar dialog box by double-clicking the toolbar. This dialog box, shown in Figure 5.15, allows the user to add buttons to the toolbar, remove buttons, or move the buttons to a different location.

FIG. 5.15

The `AllowCustomize` property lets users customize the toolbar to their liking, without the need for additional code.

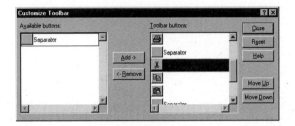

Other Methods of Creating a Toolbar

Although using the Toolbar control is the easiest method of creating a toolbar for your application, there are other ways of accomplishing the task. You can use a picture box as a container and Image controls to represent the buttons. One advantage of this method is that you can use the picture box to display other images besides the buttons. You can also use graphics methods and print methods to display other information. Another advantage is that the toolbar created with a picture box can be located anywhere on your form. You see how to create a toolbar using a picture box in Chapter 13, "Using Containers."

There are also several third-party controls that allow you to create toolbars for your forms. Some of these controls even allow you to create floating toolbars like Visual Basic's Form Editor toolbar.

Part
I

Ch
5

From Here...

This chapter has shown you the advantages of creating menus and toolbars for your programs. Hopefully, you have also seen how easy it is to create these items. You were also exposed to several other topics in this chapter. To learn more about them, refer to the following chapters:

■ To learn more about the Windows common controls, including the Toolbar and ImageList controls, see Chapter 10, "Using the Windows Common Controls."

■ To learn more about MDI child forms, see Chapter 20, "Building a Multiple Document Interface."

CHAPTER 6

Using Dialogs to Get Information

A *dialog box* is a small window used to display or accept information. Its name comes from the fact that it is, in essence, a *dialog* (or conversation) with the user. A dialog box is usually shown *modally*, which means the user must close it (or "answer the dialog") before continuing with any other part of the program. This chapter looks at two dialog boxes built in to the Visual Basic language: the message box and the input box. Next, you use the CommonDialog custom control, which allows you to place four types of standard dialog boxes in your program. Finally, you see some guidelines for creating your own form-based dialog box. ■

Providing user information with a message box

While forms provide the main interface with your users, sometimes you just need to display a bit of information. This is where message boxes come in handy.

Getting user decisions with the message box

A message box can also be used for basic Yes/No decision making.

Using the input box

Just need one piece of information? The input box might be just the thing you are looking for.

Working with dialog boxes your users will know

With the CommonDialog control, you can use some of the same dialog boxes as other Windows programs.

What do you do if the built-in dialog boxes don't meet your needs? Build your own.

You learn how to create your own dialog boxes that provide an enhanced message box or input box.

Keeping the User Informed

A big part of any programming project is providing information to users about the program's progress and status. While the forms and controls of your program provide the main interface to the user, they are not necessarily the best vehicles for providing bits of information that require immediate attention, such as warnings or error messages. For providing this type of information, the message box is the way to go.

The *message box* is a simple form that displays a message and at least one command button. The button is used to acknowledge the message and close the form. Because message boxes are built in to the Visual Basic language, you do not have to worry about creating or showing a form. To see a simple message box, type the following line of code into Visual Basic's Immediate window (choose <u>V</u>iew, <u>I</u>mmediate Window to open the window) and press Enter:

```
MsgBox "Hello World!"
```

Optionally, the message box can display an icon or use multiple buttons to let the user make a decision. This is done with the use of optional parameters. For example, the following code line produces the message box shown in Figure 6.1:

```
MsgBox "Delete record?", vbYesNo + vbExclamation, "Confirm Delete"
```

N O T E You can try it yourself. Just type the code in the Immediate window and press Enter. ▓

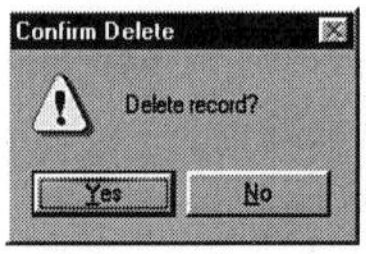

FIG. 6.1

A message box commu-
nicates with the user.

Message boxes can be used in either of two ways, depending on your needs. You can use the message box to simply display information, or you can use it to get a decision from the user. In either case, you will use some form of the MsgBox function.

N O T E Although this chapter refers to them interchangeably, there is a conceptual difference between using MsgBox as a function and a statement. By definition, a *function* returns a value, whereas a *statement* does not. Also, the syntax for parameters is slightly different—a function's parameters must be enclosed in parentheses. For example, if you wanted to see the return value from the MsgBox function, you could type the following line in the Immediate window:

```
Print MsgBox ("Delete record?", vbYesNo + vbExclamation, "Confirm Delete") ▓
```

While the message box is very useful, it does have a few limitations:

- The message box cannot accept text input from the user. It can only display information and handle the selection of a limited number of choices.
- You can use only one of four predefined icons and one of six predefined command button sets in the message box. You cannot define your own icons or buttons.

■ By design, the message box requires a user to respond to the message before the program can continue. This means that the message box cannot be used to provide continuous status monitoring of the program, since no other part of the program can be executing while the message box is waiting for the user's response.

Displaying a Message

The simplest way to create a message box in your program is to use the MsgBox function as a statement, without returning a value. When using the MsgBox function this way, you simply specify the message text that you want to appear in the message box and then call the function. For the simplest message, only the OK button is shown in the message box. This allows the user to acknowledge the message:

```
MsgBox "Please insert a disk in Drive A:"
```

When you specify the message text, you can use a *literal constant* (a string of text enclosed in quotes, as shown above) or a string *variable*, as in this example:

```
Dim stMyText as String

stMyText = "Hello," & vbCrLf & "World"
MsgBox stMyText
```

Note the use of the intrinsic (predefined) constant vbCrLf (which you learned about in Chapter 4, "Working with Forms and Controls"), representing a carriage return/line feed combination, to make "Hello" and "World" appear on separate lines.

▶ **See** "Working with Text," **p. 95**

The default message box uses the project name for its caption and has only an OK button. You can dress up your messages a little bit with two optional parameters—the *buttons* argument and the *title* argument. The *buttons* argument is an integer number that can specify the icon to display in the message box, the command button set to display, and which of the command buttons is the default. The *title* argument is a text string that specifies custom text to be shown in the title bar of the message box. The full syntax of the MsgBox function is as follows:

```
MsgBox(prompt[, buttons] [, title] [, helpfile, context])
```

If you choose to display an icon in the message box, you have a choice of four icons. These icons and their purposes are summarized in Table 6.1.

Part

I

Ch

6

Table 6.1 Icons Indicate the Type of Message Being Shown

Icon	Icon Name	Purpose
⊗	Critical Message	Indicates that a severe error has occurred. Often a program is shut down after this message.
⚠	Warning Message	Indicates that a program error has occurred that requires user correction or that may lead to undesirable results.

continues

Table 6.1   Continued

Icon	Icon Name	Purpose
	Query Message	Indicates that the program requires additional information from the user before processing can continue.
	Information Message	Informs the user of the status of the program. Often used to notify the user of the completion of a task.

To tell Visual Basic that you want to use an icon in the message box, you set a value for the *buttons* argument of the MsgBox function. The *buttons* argument can be set to one of four values, as defined in the following table. You can use either the numerical value or the constant from the table:

Options

Message Type	Argument Value	Constant
Critical	16	vbCritical
Query	32	vbQuestion
Warning	48	vbExclamation
Information	64	vbInformation

TIP Good programming practice dictates that you use the appropriate constant to represent the integer value. This makes your programs more readable and will not require any conversion should Microsoft change the integer values.

N O T E The constants listed in the preceding table not only affect the icon that is displayed, but also the sound produced by Windows when a message appears. You can set sounds for different message types in the Windows Control Panel. ■

To illustrate how icons and titles can be used in your message boxes, the following code produces the message box shown in Figure 6.2:

```
MsgBox "This message box contains an icon.", vbInformation, "Icon Demo"
```

FIG. 6.2
Use titles and icons to give the user visual cues to the nature of the message.

If you are wondering how you are going to remember the syntax of the MsgBox function and the constants to be used for the options, don't worry. The new statement completion capabilities of Visual Basic's Code Editor help tremendously with this. When you type the space after the

MsgBox function name in a Code window (or the Immediate window, for that matter), a pop-up appears that shows you the syntax of the command (see Figure 6.3).

FIG. 6.3
Syntax help assists you in setting up the message box.

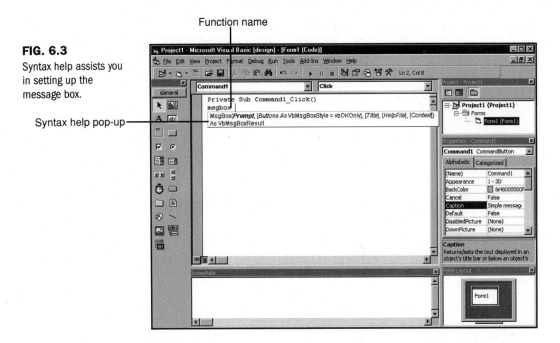

Then, after you enter the message to be displayed and enter a comma, Visual Basic pops up a list of constants that can be used to add an icon to the message box or to specify the button set to be used. You can select one of the constants from the list or type it in yourself. This is one of the really great new features in the editor. Figure 6.4 shows the constants list in action.

Returning a Value from the *MsgBox* Function

The MsgBox function, as described previously, works fine for informing users of a problem or prompting them to take an action. However, to get a decision from the user, you need to use the MsgBox function's return value. There are two key differences to using the MsgBox function this way—you (usually) assign the function's return value to a variable, and you must enclose the arguments of the function in parentheses. This value reports which command button was clicked by the user. The following line of code shows how the value returned by the function can be assigned to a variable for further processing:

```
inResult = MsgBox("The printer is not responding", vbRetryCancel,
➡"Printer Error!")
```

Additional statements after the preceding code could check the value of the variable inResult with, for example, an If statement, and take appropriate action.

FIG. 6.4

You no longer have to remember the options' constants with the pop-ups available in the editor.

Constants list ——

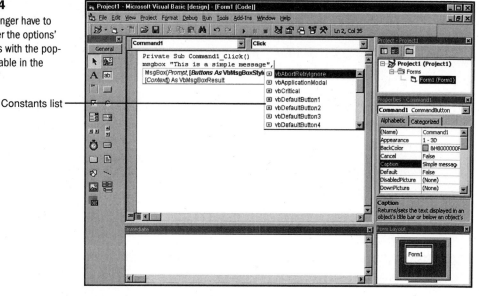

Six sets of command buttons can be used in the `MsgBox` function:

- *OK*   Displays a single button with the caption OK. This simply asks the user to acknowl-edge receipt of the message before continuing.

- *OK, Cancel*   Displays two buttons in the message box, letting the user choose between accepting the message and requesting a cancellation of the operation.

- *Abort, Retry, Ignore*   Displays three buttons, usually along with an error message. The user can choose to abort the operation, retry it, or ignore the error and attempt to continue with program execution.

- *Yes, No, Cancel*   Displays three buttons, typically with a question. The user can answer yes or no to the question, or choose to cancel the operation.

- *Yes, No*   Displays two buttons for a simple yes or no choice.

- *Retry, Cancel*   Displays the two buttons that allow the user to retry the operation or cancel it. A typical use is reporting that the printer is not responding. The user can either retry after fixing the printer or cancel the printout.

To specify the command buttons that will appear in the message box, you need to specify a value for the *buttons* argument of the `MsgBox` function. The values for each of the command button sets are listed in Table 6.2.

Table 6.2 Set the *buttons* Argument to One of the Following Values to Specify Which Set of Buttons to Use

Button Set	Value	Constant
OK	0	vbOKOnly
OK, Cancel	1	vbOKCancel
Abort, Retry, Ignore	2	VBAbortRetryIgnore
Yes, No, Cancel	3	vbYesNoCancel
Yes, No	4	vbYesNo
Retry, Cancel	5	vbRetryCancel

Because the *buttons* argument controls both the icon and the command-button set for a message box, you might wonder how you can specify both at the same time. You do this by adding the values of the constants together. The MsgBox function is designed so that any combination of the icon constant and the command-button constant creates a unique value. This value is then broken down by the function to specify the individual pieces. The following code combines an icon constant and command button constant to create a warning message that allows the user to choose an action. The results of the code are illustrated in Figure 6.5.

```
inOptVal = vbExclamation + vbAbortRetryIgnore
inRetVal = MsgBox("File does not exist.", inOptVal, "My Application")
```

 T I P When you are using the pop-up constants list, you can select a second constant for the options parameter by entering a plus sign (+) after selecting the first constant.

N O T E If you want your message box to display a Help button, add the constant vbMsgBoxHelpButton, which has a value of 16384, to whichever button set constant you choose. ■

FIG. 6.5

The *buttons* argument controls both the icon and the command buttons displayed by the MsgBox function.

If you are using more than one command button in the message box, you can also specify which button is the default. The *default button* is the one that has focus when the message box is displayed. This button is the one that the user is most likely to choose so that he can just press the Enter key. For example, if you display a message box to have the user confirm the deletion of the record, you probably should set up the default button so that the record would not be deleted. This way, the user must make a conscious choice to delete the record.

Part
I

Ch
6

To specify which button is the default, you need to add another constant to the *buttons* argument of the MsgBox function. The four possible default button values are identified in the following table:

Default Button	Value	Constant
First	0	vbDefaultButton1
Second	256	vbDefaultButton2
Third	512	vbDefaultButton3
Fourth	768	vbDefaultButton4

A user might choose from seven buttons, with the selection depending on the button set used in the message box. Each button returns a different value to identify the button to your program (see Table 6.3).

Table 6.3   Return Values Indicate the User's Choice

Button	Value	Constant
OK	1	vbOK
Cancel	2	vbCancel
Abort	3	vbAbort
Retry	4	vbRetry
Ignore	5	vbIgnore
Yes	6	vbYes
No	7	vbNo

As always, it is preferable to use the constant in your code rather than the actual integer value. After you know which button the user selected, you can use that information in your program. The following code is used to confirm the deletion of a file:

```
Dim stFileName As String
Dim stMsgTitle As String
Dim stMsgText As String
Dim inReturn As Integer
Dim inOptions As Integer

stFileName = "C:\MYDIR\MYFILE.TXT"
stMsgText = "Do you really want to delete '" & stFileName & "'?"
inOptions = vbQuestion + vbYesNo + vbDefaultButton2
stMsgTitle = "Delete Confirmation"
inReturn = MsgBox(stMsgText, inOptions, stMsgTitle)

If inReturn = vbYes Then
    Kill stFileName
    MsgBox stFileName & " has been deleted.",vbInformation,"File deleted"
End If
```

For completeness, one final setting can be applied to the *buttons* argument of the MsgBox function. You can choose to have the message box be modal for your application or for the entire system. Remember from earlier chapters that when a *modal* window is shown, it must be closed before continuing with the program. If you specify that the message box is modal to the system, the user must respond to the message box before he can do any further work on the computer at all. The system modal option should be used with extreme care. The default behavior is application modal, which means the user could continue to work in other applications.

To use the default of application modal, you do not have to add anything to the *buttons* argument, or you can add the vbApplicationModal constant, which has a value of 0. To make the message box system modal, you need to add the constant vbSystemModal, which has a value of 4096, to the *buttons* argument.

Getting Information from the User

Many times in a program, you need to get a single piece of information from the user. You might need the user to enter a person's name, the name of a file, or a number for various purposes. Although the message box lets your users make choices, it does not allow them to enter any information in response to the message. Therefore, you have to use some other means to get the information. Visual Basic provides a built-in dialog box for exactly this purpose: the *input box*.

The input box displays a message to tell the user what to enter, a text box where the user can enter the requested information, and two command buttons—OK and Cancel—that can be used to either accept or abort the input data. A sample input box is shown in Figure 6.6.

FIG. 6.6

An input box lets the user enter a single piece of data in response to a message.

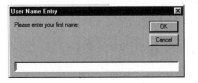

Setting Up the Input Dialog Box

Programmatically, the input box works very much like the message box with a return value. You can specify a variable to receive the information returned from the input box and then supply the input box's message (prompt) and, optionally, a title and default value. An example of the InputBox function is the following:

```
Dim stMsg as String, stUserName As String
stMsg = "Please type your name below:"
stUserName = InputBox(stMsg, "Enter user name", "Anonymous")
```

In this statement, the information returned by the InputBox function will be stored in the variable stUserName. The first argument, the *prompt* parameter, represents the message that is displayed to the user to indicate what should be entered in the box. Like the message in the message box, the prompt can be up to 1,024 characters. Word-wrapping is automatically performed on the text in the prompt so that it fits inside the box. Also, as with the message box, you can insert a carriage return/line-feed combination (vbCrLf) to force the prompt to show multiple lines or to separate lines for emphasis.

After the prompt comes the *title* argument, which specifies the text in the input box's title bar. The other argument in the preceding example is the *default* argument. If included, it appears as an initial value in the input box. This value can be accepted by the user, modified, or it can be erased and a completely new value entered.

The minimum requirement for the InputBox function is a prompt parameter, as in the statement

```
stReturnVal = InputBox("How's the weather?")
```

In addition to the input box's optional parameters to specify a window title and default value, other optional parameters allow you to set its initial screen position, as well as the help file to be used if the user needs assistance. Refer to the complete syntax of the InputBox function in Visual Basic's help system.

N O T E   Unlike the MsgBox function, there is no option in the InputBox function to specify any command buttons other than the defaults of OK and Cancel. ▪

Values Returned by *InputBox*

When the input box is used, the user can enter up to 254 characters of text in the input box's entry area, which resembles a text box. If he types more text than will fit in the displayed entry area, the text he's already typed will scroll to the left. Once he's done, he can choose the OK or Cancel button. If he chooses the OK button, the input box returns whatever is in the text box, whether it is new text or the default text. If the user clicked the Cancel button, the input box returns an empty string, regardless of what is in the text box.

To be able to use the information entered by the user, you must determine if the data meets your needs. First, you probably want to make sure that the user actually entered some information and chose the OK button. You can do this by using the Len function to determine the length of the returned string. If the length is zero, the user pressed the Cancel button or left the input field blank. If the length of the string is greater than zero, you know that the user entered something. To see how the Len function works, enter each of these lines in the Immediate window and note the different results:

```
Print Len("Hello")
```

```
Print Len("")
```

You may also need to check the returned value to make sure it is of the proper type. If you are expecting a number that will subsequently be compared to another number in an If statement, your program should present an error message if the user enters letters. To make sure that you have a numerical value with which to work, you can use the Val function, which returns the numerical value of a string. If the string contains or starts with numbers, the function returns the number. If the string does not start with a number, the function returns zero. To understand the Val function, enter these lines in the Immediate window to see what each returns:

```
Print Val("Hello")

Print Val("50 ways to leave your lover")

Print Val("100 and 1 make 101")
```

The following code illustrates additional processing of the returned value of the input box with Val and Len:

```
Dim stInputVal As String
stInputVal = InputBox("Enter your age")
If Len(stInputVal) = 0 Then
    MsgBox "No age was selected"
Else
    If Val(stInputVal) = 0 Then
        MsgBox "You entered an invalid age."
    Else
        MsgBox "Congratulations for surviving this long!"
    End If
End If
```

Using Built-In Dialog Boxes

In earlier sections, you learned what a dialog box is and how to use two simple dialog boxes. In this section, you learn about the Microsoft CommonDialog control, which allows you to use standard Windows dialog boxes to specify file names, select fonts and colors, and control the printer. And while the ease of setup is a great benefit, an even bigger bonus is that these dialog boxes are already familiar to the user. This is because they are the same dialog boxes used by Windows itself.

General Usage of the CommonDialog Control

When using a single CommonDialog control, you have access to the following standard Windows dialog boxes:

- *Open* Lets the user select the name and location of a file to open.
- *Save As* Lets the user specify a file name and location in which to save information.
- *Font* Lets the user choose a base font and set any font attributes that are desired.
- *Color* Lets the user choose from a standard color or create a custom color for use in the program.

■ *Print*   Lets the user select a printer and set some of the printer parameters.

■ *Help*   Takes the user into the Windows Help system.

Although the CommonDialog control is included with Visual Basic, it's not one of the controls included in the Toolbox by default. To access the CommonDialog control, you might first have to add it to your project (and to the Toolbox) by selecting it from the Components dialog box. This dialog box is accessible by choosing Project, Components. From there, select Microsoft Common Dialog Control 5.0 in the Controls list and click OK.

After the CommonDialog control is added to the Toolbox, you can add the control to a form by clicking the control and drawing it on the form just like any other control. The CommonDialog control appears on your form as an icon, as the control itself is not visible when your application is running.

The following sections discuss each type of dialog box that can be created with the CommonDialog control. For each of these dialog boxes, you need to set some of the control's properties. You can do this through the Properties window, or you can use the CommonDialog control's Property Pages dialog box. The Property Pages dialog box provides you easy access to the specific properties that are necessary for each of the common dialog box types (see Figure 6.7). You can access the Property Pages dialog box by clicking the ellipsis (...) button in the Custom property of the CommonDialog control, or by right-clicking the control and selecting Properties.

FIG. 6.7
The Property Pages
dialog box makes it
easy to set up the
CommonDialog control.

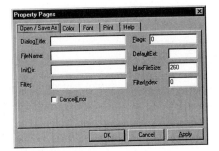

The File Dialog Boxes

One of the key uses of the CommonDialog control is to obtain file names from the user. The CommonDialog control's File dialog box can be used in either of two modes: Open and Save As. Open mode lets the user specify the name and location of a file to be retrieved and used by your program. Save As mode lets the user specify the name and location of a file to be saved.

The dialog boxes for the Open and Save As functions are very similar. Figure 6.8 shows the Open dialog box.

Button to use file list mode

Button to create a new folder

Button to move up one folder level

Drive/Folder list box

FIG. 6.8
The Open and Save
dialog boxes share
many components.

Selected file

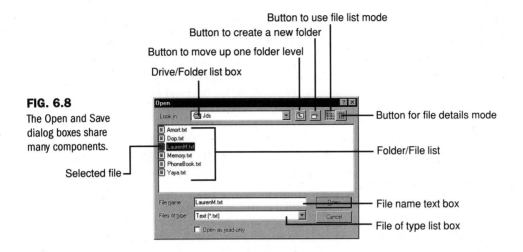

Button for file details mode

Folder/File list

File name text box

File of type list box

These are the dialog box's major components:

- *Drive/Folder list*   The current folder is listed here. If the current folder is the root (\), the current drive is listed here. You can use the combo box and navigation buttons to move up folder levels, similar to the way you would in the Windows Explorer.

- *File/Folder selection list*   The names indicated in this area are the folders and files one level beneath the item in the Drive/Folder list. An item in this area can be opened either by double-clicking it, or by highlighting it and pressing Enter. If the item you open is a folder, the display is updated to show the contents of the new current folder. If the item you open is a file, the dialog box closes.

- *File Name text box*   This text box can be used by the user for manual file name entry and folder navigation. If he enters a file name, the dialog box closes. If he enters a path like `C:\Data\Word` and presses Enter, the dialog box is updated to show that folder. Also, if a user single-clicks a file name in the file/folder selection area, it appears here.

- *File Type list box*   Here, the user selects the type of files to display. These types are determined by the extension portion of the file name; the available types are controlled by the `Filter` property of the CommonDialog control.

- *Toolbar buttons and Command buttons*   The buttons in the upper-right corner let the user move up one folder level, create a new folder, or switch the file display area between the list mode and the file details mode. The buttons at the lower-right let the user process the selection or cancel the dialog box.

Opening and Saving Files   To open an existing file, use the `ShowOpen` method of the CommonDialog control. (This method displays the dialog box in Figure 6.8.) You use this method by specifying the name of the CommonDialog control and the method name, as shown in the following lines of code:

```
cdlGetFile.ShowOpen
Msgbox "You Selected " & cdlGetFile.FileName
```

Part

I

Ch

6

FIG. 6.11

The Print dialog box provides a consistent way for your users to set printer options.

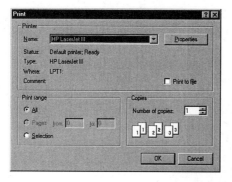

If users want to change any printer-specific parameters (such as paper size and margins), they can click the Properties button on the Print dialog box. This brings up the Properties dialog box for the selected printer, as shown in Figure 6.12. This dialog box lets you control all the settings of the printer, just as with the Windows Control Panel.

FIG. 6.12

The Properties dialog box for the printer lets you control paper size, margins, and other printer attributes.

The Print dialog box returns the information provided by the user in the dialog box's properties. The FromPage and ToPage properties tell you the starting and ending pages of the printout as selected by the user. The Copies property tells you how many copies the user wants printed.

This is provided only as information. The Print dialog box does not automatically create the desired printout. As with other CommonDialogs, your program must complete the task, as in this example:

```
cdlPrint.Flags = cdlPDDisablePrintToFile
cdlPrint.Copies = 3
cdlPrint.PrinterDefault = True
cdlPrint.ShowPrinter
MsgBox "The default printer is:" & Printer.DeviceName
```

In this sample code, properties and flags are used to disable the Print to File option and set the default number of copies to 3. In addition, the `PrinterDefault` property means that the dialog box will use the control's properties to modify the default system printer.

The Help Dialog Box

This usage of the CommonDialog control invokes the Windows Help engine by running WINHLP32.EXE. To use this dialog box, you must set the CommonDialog control's `HelpFile` property to the name and location of a properly formatted Windows help (.hlp) file and set the `HelpCommand` property to tell the Help engine what type of help to offer. After setting these properties, use the CommonDialog control's `ShowHelp` method to initiate the Help system. The user can then navigate the Help system by using your program's Help file.

Creating Your Own Dialog Boxes

Although the CommonDialog control provides you with a number of dialog boxes to use in your programs, sometimes some things just can't be accomplished with these built-in tools. For example, if you want to set your own captions for the command buttons in a dialog box, you can't do this with the message box, nor can the message box handle more than three buttons. Also, consider the built-in input box. This dialog box cannot display an icon, nor can it handle more than one input item. So what are you supposed to do? Build your own, of course.

In this section, you see how to build a simple, but flexible, dialog box to display a message and a set of custom command buttons. Your dialog box will allow you to choose to have from one to three buttons displayed and will be able to display any of four icons. From this example, you will be able to see how you can build more complex dialog boxes.

Setting Up the Dialog Box Form

The first thing you have to do in creating a dialog box is to create the form itself. To do this, follow these steps:

1. Create a new Standard EXE project.
2. Add a new form to the project (making a total of two forms).
3. Give the new (second) form a unique name, such as `frmDialog`. It will become your dialog box.
4. Set `frmDialog`'s `Caption` property to Custom Dialog Box.
5. Set the `BorderStyle` property to `3 - Fixed Dialog`.
6. Set the `ControlBox` property to `False`.
7. Set the `StartUpPosition` property to `2 - CenterScreen`.

With these property settings, your dialog box will start up in the center of the screen and will have a border that, like standard Windows dialog boxes, doesn't allow the user to resize it. In addition, it won't have the Control Menu icon at the left-hand side of the title bar.

N O T E   The Project window now contains two files, one for each of the two forms. When you save the project, you need to supply file names for both form (.FRM) files, as well as a file name for the overall project (.VBP) file. ▨

Adding Controls to the Form

Now that you have created a dialog-style form, the next step is to add a Label control to display your message to the user.

Next, you will want to add Image controls that will display the icon in the dialog box. You'll be using five Image controls—the one that the user actually sees, and four other (invisible) Image controls that will hold the four icons that could possibly be displayed in the visible control. The ImageList control technique discussed in Chapter 5, "Adding Menus and Toolbars to Your Program," could also have been used here.

▶ **See** "Getting the Images for Your Toolbar," **p. 122**

Continue building the dialog box form as follows:

1. Place one Label control on the form. Size it to the width that you want. Name the label `lblMessage` so it can be referenced from code.

2. Set the label's `WordWrap` and `AutoSize` properties to `True`. (Note that the `WordWrap` property must be set first.)

3. Place one Image control near the Label control. This Image control will actually display the icon to the user. Change its name to `imgShow`.

4. Create four other Image controls to hold the other possible icons for display. Use the default names of `Image1`, `Image2`, `Image3`, and `Image4`.

5. For the last four Image controls, set the `Picture` property to the desired icon and set the `Visible` property to `False`.

6. Finally, create three command buttons on the form. Name them `cmdMessage1`, `cmdMessage2`, and `cmdMessage3`. The last two of these buttons need to have the `Visible` property set to `False`.

This technique allows your program to display only the requested number of buttons when the dialog box is called. Make sure that all the command buttons are the same size. When you have finished, your form should look something like the one in Figure 6.13.

FIG. 6.13
Your custom dialog box will have several command buttons and images to allow choices.

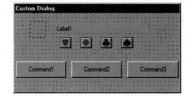

Telling Your Dialog What to Display

While placing the controls on the form is a critical part of creating a custom dialog box, the main work of the dialog box is done with code.

First, you need to have a way for the user to set the dialog box's options before showing it. This is accomplished with *public variables*. Chapter 8, "Programming Basics" discusses public variables more fully; for now, think of a public variable as something that acts much like a property that applies to the form in which it is declared. It can be accessed from any part of your application by using the form name, a dot, and the variable name (for example, `frmMain.stFileName`).

▶ **See** "Variable Declarations," **p. 172**

You declare public variables in the form's General Declarations section:

1. Open frmDialog's Code window by double-clicking any empty part of it. (You can also select frmDialog in the Project window and click the View Code button.)

2. In the code window's upper-left drop-down box, select (General). Make sure that (Declarations) is showing in the upper-right drop-down box.

3. Enter the following code to create the public variables:

```
Option Explicit
Public inNumCmd as Integer
Public inImageID as Integer
Public stCmdCaption1 as String
Public stCmdCaption2 as String
Public stCmdCaption3 as String
Public inBtnPressed As Integer
```

The main part of your code will be located in the form's `Activate` event procedure. The `Activate` event occurs when the form becomes the "active" form. Your code controls which image and command buttons are visible to the user and properly positions them on the form. The code, shown in Listing 6.1, assumes that all the command buttons are the same size. By setting the `Top`, `Left`, and `Visible` properties of the buttons, the visible command buttons are shown near the bottom of the label control that displays the message. The `Left` property of each button is set so that the button group is centered in the form. And the height of the form itself is adjusted so that there is not a lot of empty space showing.

Listing 6.1   DIALOG.FRM—Using the Form's *Activate* Event to Adjust the Position of the Controls

```
Private Sub Form_Activate()
  Dim inCtlTop As Integer
  Dim inCmdWidth As Integer

'First, select an image based
'on the ImageID public variable:
  Select Case inImageID
    Case 1
```

Part

I

Ch

6

continues

Listing 6.1 Continued

```
        imgShow.Picture = Image1.Picture
    Case 2
        imgShow.Picture = Image2.Picture
    Case 3
        imgShow.Picture = Image3.Picture
    Case 4
        imgShow.Picture = Image4.Picture
  End Select

'The tops of the controls will be
'240 twips below the message label:
  inCtlTop = lblMessage.Top + lblMessage.Height + 240
  cmdMessage1.Top = inCtlTop
  cmdMessage2.Top = inCtlTop
  cmdMessage3.Top = inCtlTop

'The form will be sized 500 twips below the buttons
  Me.Height = cmdMessage1.Top + cmdMessage1.Height + 500

'Set the CommandButton captions
  cmdMessage1.Caption = stCmdCaption1
  cmdMessage2.Caption = stCmdCaption2
  cmdMessage3.Caption = stCmdCaption3

'Set the CommandButton visible properties
  Select Case inNumCmd
    Case 2
        cmdMessage2.Visible = True
    Case 3
        cmdMessage2.Visible = True
        cmdMessage3.Visible = True
  End Select


'Finally, center the buttons on the form
  Select Case inNumCmd
    Case 1
        inCmdWidth = cmdMessage1.Width
        cmdMessage1.Left = (frmDialog.ScaleWidth - inCmdWidth) / 2
    Case 2
        inCmdWidth = 2 * cmdMessage1.Width + 105
        cmdMessage1.Left = (frmDialog.ScaleWidth - inCmdWidth) / 2
        cmdMessage2.Left = cmdMessage1.Left + cmdMessage1.Width + 105
    Case 3
        inCmdWidth = 3 * cmdMessage1.Width + 2 * 105
        cmdMessage1.Left = (frmDialog.ScaleWidth - inCmdWidth) / 2
        cmdMessage2.Left = cmdMessage1.Left + cmdMessage1.Width + 105
        cmdMessage3.Left = cmdMessage2.Left + cmdMessage2.Width + 105
  End Select
End Sub
```

Another thing that you want your dialog box to be able to do is to tell the calling program which button was pressed. You handle this by using the Public variable inBtnPressed that was declared in frmDialog's General Declarations section. The dialog box will set a different value of the variable for each command button (see Listing 6.2). You will also want to unload the form when any command button has been pressed. This ensures that the dialog box is reset when it is reloaded (causing the Load event to occur again).

On the CD

Listing 6.2   DIALOG.FRM—Using the *Click* Event to Set the Variable Indicating Which Button Was Pressed

```
Private Sub cmdMessage1_Click()
  inBtnPressed = 1
  Unload Me
End Sub

Private Sub cmdMessage2_Click()
  inBtnPressed = 2
  Unload Me
End Sub

Private Sub cmdMessage3_Click()
  inBtnPressed = 3
  Unload Me
End Sub
```

Calling the Dialog from a Program

Now that you have entered all the code, you are ready to use it! This involves three basic steps:

1. Set the public variables that the dialog box is expecting.

2. Show the dialog box as a modal form.

3. After the dialog box has been unloaded, have the calling program use the returned result.

To test the dialog box, put a command button on the other form in your project and enter the sample code in Listing 6.3.

On the CD

Listing 6.3   DEMO.FRM—Setting the Variables of the Dialog Box Before Showing It

```
Private Sub Command1_Click()
  Dim stMsg as string
  stMsg = "This is a dialog with a custom set of buttons. This is something that"
  stMsg = stMsg & "cannot be achieved with a normal message box."
  With frmDialog
    .lblMessage.Caption = stMsg
```

continues

Part

I

Ch

6

Table 8.1 Continued

Type	Stores	Memory Requirement	Range of Values
Double	Decimal numbers	Eight bytes	+/– 5E-324 to 1.8E308
Currency	Numbers with up to 15 digits left of the decimal and four digits right of the decimal	Eight bytes	+/– 9E14
String	Text information	One byte per character	Up to 65,400 characters for fixed-length string and up to two billion characters for dynamic strings
Byte	Whole numbers	One byte	0 to 255
Boolean	Logical values	Two bytes	`True` or `False`
Date	Date and time information	Eight bytes	1/1/100 to 12/31/9999
Object	Instances of classes; OLE objects	Four bytes	N/A
Variant	Any of the preceding data types	16 bytes + 1 byte per character	N/A

In addition to the preceding variable types, there are specialized types to deal with databases (Database, Field, and Recordset). Visual Basic knows about these other data types when you add a reference to a *type library*. It is also possible to create *user-defined types* to meet your needs.

Variable Declarations

In the section "Working with Variables" earlier in this chapter, you saw an example of the `Dim` statement, which is used to tell Visual Basic the name and type of your variable. However, Visual Basic does not require you to specifically declare a variable before it is used. If a variable is not declared, Visual Basic creates the variable by using a default data type known as a *variant.* A variant can contain any type of information. Using a variant for general information has two major drawbacks—it can waste memory resources, and the variable type might be invalid for use with some data-manipulation functions that expect a specific variable type.

It is good programming practice to declare your variables before they are used, so take a look at the two ways to declare a variable in Visual Basic—explicit and implicit declaration.

Explicit Declaration   *Explicit declaration* means that you use a statement to define the type of a variable. These statements do not assign a value to the variable but merely tell Visual Basic what the variable can contain.

Each of the following statements can be used to explicitly declare a variable's type:

```
Dim varname [As vartype][, varname2 [As vartype2]]

Private varname [As vartype][, varname2 [As vartype2]]

Static varname [As vartype][, varname2 [As vartype2]]

Public varname [As vartype][, varname2 [As vartype2]]
```

Dim, Private, Static, and Public are Visual Basic keywords that define how and where the variable can be used. *varname* and *varname2* represent the names of two variables that you want to declare. As indicated in the syntax, you can specify multiple variables in the same statement as long as you separate the variables with commas. Note that the syntax shows only two variables on one line, but you can specify several. In fact, over a thousand characters will fit on one line in the Code window. From a practical standpoint, however, you should refrain from writing lines of code that are wider than the displayed Code window. This will make your code much easier to read, as you don't have to scroll left and right when looking at it.

vartype and *vartype2* represent the type definitions of the respective variables. The *type definition* is a keyword that tells Visual Basic what kind of information will be stored in the variable. As indicated, the variable type is an optional property. If you include the variable type, you must include the keyword As. If you do not include a variable type, the Variant type (which is the default) is used.

The following code shows the use of these declaration statements for actual variables:

```
Private inNumVal As Integer
Private inAvgVal As Integer, varInptVal As Variant
Static sgClcAverage As Single
Dim stInptMsg As String
```

Implicit Declaration   It is best to declare your variables using the Dim or other statements shown in the section "Working with Variables" earlier in this chapter, but in many cases you also can assign a type to a variable using an *implicit declaration*. With this type of declaration, a special character is used at the end of the variable name when the variable is first assigned a value. The characters for each variable type are shown in Table 8.2.

Table 8.2   Special Characters at the End of a Variable Name that Can Identify the Type of Data Stored by the Variable

Variable Type	Character
Integer	%
Long	&
Single	!
Double	#
Currency	@
String	$
Byte	None
Boolean	None
Date	None
Object	None
Variant	None

The variables that were declared using the code in the preceding section could have been used as implicitly declared variables, without having to declare their types with Dim statements, as follows:

```
inNumVal% = 0
inAvgVal% = 1
varInptVal = 5
sgClcAverage! = 10.1
stInptMsg$ = "Mike"
```

You might have noticed that the variable varInptVal didn't have a declaration character. This means that InptVal will be of the Variant type.

Fixed-Length Strings   Most strings that you use in your programs will be of the type known as *variable-length strings*. These strings can contain any amount of text, up to approximately two billion characters. As information is stored in the variable, the size of the variable adjusts to accommodate the length of the string. Both the implicit and explicit declarations shown earlier created variable-length strings. There is, however, a second type of string in Visual Basic—the *fixed-length string*.

As the name implies, a fixed-length string remains the same size, regardless of the information assigned to it. If a fixed-length string variable is assigned an expression shorter than the defined length of the variable, the remaining length of the variable is filled with the space character. If the expression is longer than the variable, only the characters that fit in the variable are stored; the rest are truncated.

A fixed-length string variable can only be declared by using an explicit declaration of the form, like the following:

```
Dim varname As String*strlength
```

Notice that this declaration is slightly different from the previous declaration of a string variable. The declaration of a fixed-length string variable contains an asterisk (*) to tell Visual Basic that the string will be of a fixed length. The final parameter, *strlength*, tells the program the maximum number of characters that the variable can contain.

Variable Arrays

All the variables you've worked with so far have been single-instance variables. Often, however, you'll find it very useful to work with *variable arrays*. An array is a group of variables of the same type, sharing the same name. This makes it easy to process groups of related areas. For example, you might want to have a group of variables that tracks the sales in each of your company's four regions. You could declare a currency variable for each region, plus one for the total sales across all regions, like this:

```
Dim crRegSales1 As Currency, crRegSales2 As Currency
Dim crRegSales3 As Currency, crRegSales4 As Currency
Dim crTotalSales As Currency
```

Then, if you wanted to calculate the total sales for all regions, you might use this code:

```
crTotalSales = crRegSales1 + crRegSales2 + crRegSales3 + crRegSales4
```

This isn't all that cumbersome. However, what if you had 20 regions? Or several hundred? You can see how working with large numbers of related variables could get messy very quickly.

You can greatly enhance this example by using a variable array. We'll create an array of variables named crRegSales; the array will contain as many elements (instances of variables) as we have regions. We could rewrite our previous example for 20 regions like this:

```
Dim crRegSales(1 To 20) As Currency
Dim crTotalSales As Currency
Dim inCounter As Integer
Dim stTemp As String

    crTotalSales = 0
    For inCounter = 1 To 20
        crTotalSales = crTotalSales + crRegSales(inCounter)
    Next inCounter
    stTemp = "Total sales for all regions = "
    stTemp = stTemp & Format(crTotalSales, "currency")
        MsgBox stTemp, vbInformation, "Sales Analysis"
```

Note this example's use of a *repetition loop*. The block of code beginning with the For instruction and ending with the Next instruction defines a group of program statements that will be repeated a certain number of times (in this case, 20). Using loops makes short work of processing variable arrays. We cover loops in the section "Working with Loops" a little later in this chapter.

As you progress through this book, you'll see several cases where variable arrays can make your coding much simpler.

Determining Where a Variable Can Be Used

In addition to telling Visual Basic what you want to be able to store in a variable, a declaration statement tells Visual Basic where the variable can be used. This area of usage is called the *scope* of the variable. This is analogous to the coverage area of a paging system. When you purchase a pager, you make a decision whether you want local service, regional service, or nationwide service. This is then programmed into your pager when you buy it. If you go outside the service area, your pager does not work. In a similar manner, you can declare variables to work in only one procedure, work in any procedure of a form, or work throughout your program.

By default, a variable that is implicitly declared is local to the procedure in which it is created. If you don't specify any kind of declaration, explicit or implicit, you create a local variable of the variant type. Therefore, to create variables that have a scope other than local, you must use a declaration statement.

N O T E The scope of a variable is determined not only by the type of declaration, but by the location of the declaration as well. For instance, the `Dim` and `Private` keywords assume different meanings in different parts of a form's code. ■

Creating Variables that Are Available Everywhere   In most programs, unless you have only one form and no code modules, you will find that you need some variables that can be accessed from anywhere in the code. These are called `Public` variables. (Other languages, as well as earlier versions of Visual Basic, might refer to these as `Global` variables. In fact, Visual Basic still recognizes the `Global` keyword.) These variables are typically used to hold information such as the name of the program's user, or to reference a database that is used throughout the program. They might also be used as flags to indicate various conditions in the program.

To create a `Public` variable, you simply place a declaration statement with the `Public` keyword in the declarations section of a module of your program. The following line shows the `Public` declaration of a variable used for referencing a database:

```
Public dbMemDB As Database
```

▶ **See** "Determining the Scope of Procedures and Functions," **p. 472**

In a form or a class module, the `Public` keyword has a special meaning. Variables defined as `Public` act like a property of the form or class that is available anywhere in the program. These properties are referenced like the built-in properties of a form or control instead of like a variable. The `Public` properties are used to pass information between forms and other parts of your program.

Keeping a Variable Local If you do not need to access a variable from everywhere in your program, you do not want to use the `Public` keyword in a declaration. Instead, you should use the `Dim` or `Private` keywords. These keywords tell Visual Basic to define the variable within the scope of the current procedure or form. With these declarations, the location of the statement determines the actual scope of the variable. If the variable is defined in the General Declarations section of a form or module, the variable is available to every procedure in that form or module. This is known as a *form-level* or *module-level variable*. If the variable is declared inside a procedure, it can be used only within that procedure. This is typically known as a *local variable*.

Using Static Variables Most variables that are created inside a procedure are discarded by Visual Basic when the procedure is finished. There are times, however, when you might want to preserve the value of a variable even after the procedure has run. This is often the case when you call the procedure multiple times, and the value of a variable for one call to the procedure is dependent on the value left over from previous calls.

To create a variable that retains its value, you use the `Static` keyword in the variable declaration. This tells Visual Basic that the variable can be referenced only within the procedure, but to remember the value because it might be needed again. Here's an example of a variable declared using the `Static` keyword:

```
Static inPageNumber As Integer
```

N O T E   If you use the `Static` keyword to declare a procedure, all variables in the procedure are treated as static. ▧

Using the *Option Explicit* Statement

You learned in the earlier section, "Variable Declarations," that it's good programming practice to declare your program's variables before they are used. You can ensure that you do this by setting one of the environment options of Visual Basic. To do this, access Visual Basic's Options dialog box by choosing Tools, Options. In this dialog box's Editor tab, you find the Require Variable Declaration option (see Figure 8.1). Selecting this box forces you to declare each variable before you use it.

FIG. 8.1
The Require Variable Declaration option helps prevent you from mistyping variable names.

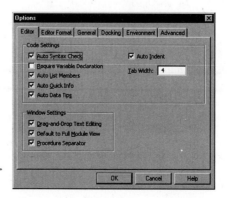

Setting the <u>R</u>equire Variable Declaration option causes the `Option Explicit` statement to be placed in the General Declarations section of each new module or form that is added to your project, as shown in Figure 8.2.

FIG. 8.2

The *Option Explicit* statement is added to your program.

```
Option Explicit

Private Sub Form_Load()

End Sub
```

If you have invoked `Option Explicit` and you fail to declare a variable, you will receive the error message `Variable not defined` when you try to run your code. The integrated debugger highlights the offending variable and pauses the execution of your program. The benefit of this is that it helps you avoid errors in your code that might be caused by typographical errors. For example, you might declare a variable using the following statement:

```
Dim stMyName As String
```

If in a later statement, you mistyped the variable name, Visual Basic would catch the error for you, rather than continue with unpredictable results. For example, the following statement would cause an error:

```
stMyNme = "Tina Marie"
```

> **CAUTION**
> If you set the <u>R</u>equire Variable Declaration option after starting to create a program, the option has no effect on any forms or modules that have already been created. In this case, you can add the `Option Explicit` statement as the first line of code in the General Declarations section of any existing forms or modules.

TIP If you use some capital letters in your variable declarations, then enter your code in all lowercase letters. Visual Basic automatically sets the capitalization of your variable to match the declaration. This gives you an immediate visual indication that you typed the name correctly.

What's Different About Constants

Variables are just one way of storing information in the memory of a computer. Another way is to use *constants*. Constants in a program are treated a special way. After you define them (or they are defined for you by Visual Basic), you cannot change them later in the program by using an assignment statement. If you try, Visual Basic generates an error when you run your program.

Constants are most often used to replace a value that is hard to remember, such as the color value for the Windows title bar. It is easier to remember the constant `vbActiveTitleBar` than the value 2147483646. You can also use a constant to avoid typing long strings if they are used in a number of places. For example, you could set a constant such as FileFoundError containing the string "The requested file was not found."

Constants are also used a lot for conversion factors, such as 12 inches per foot or 3.3 feet per meter. The following code example shows how constants and variables are used:

```
Const MetersToFeet = 3.3
inDistMeters = InputBox("Enter a distance in meters")
inDistFeet = inDistMeters * MetersToFeet
MsgBox "The distance in feet is: " & Str(inDistFeet)
```

Another common use for constants is to minimize changes to your code for reasons such as changing your program's name, version number, and so forth. You can define constants at the beginning of your program and use the predefined constants throughout the program. Then, when a version number changes, all you need to do is change the declaration of the constant. The following example illustrates this technique:

```
Public Const ProgTitle = "My Application Name"
Public Const ProgVersion = "3.1"
```

Note the use of the Public keyword, which makes these constants available throughout the application (assuming that their declaration is in a module).

Constants that Visual Basic Supplies   Visual Basic supplies a number of built-in constants for various activities. These are known as *intrinsic constants*. There are color-definition constants, data-access constants, keycode constants, and shape constants, among many others. Especially useful are constants correlating to a command's parameter information, such as the vbExclamation constant that we've used for a MessageBox statement in previous chapters.

 The constants that you need for most functions are defined in the help topic for the function. If you want to know the value of a particular constant, you can use the Object Browser (see Figure 8.3). Access the Object Browser by clicking its icon in the Visual Basic toolbar, by selecting View, Object Browser from the menu system, or simply by pressing F7. You can use the list to find the constant that you want. When you select it, its value and function are displayed in the text area at the bottom of the dialog box.

Creating Your Own Constants   While Visual Basic defines a large number of constants for many activities, there will be times when you need to define your own constants. Constants are defined using the Const statement to give the constant a name and a value, as illustrated in the following syntax:

```
Const constantname [As constanttype] = value
```

If you think this statement looks similar to the declaration of a variable, you are right. As with declaring a variable, you provide a name for the constant and, optionally, specify the type of data it will hold. The Const keyword at the beginning of the statement tells Visual Basic that this statement defines a constant. This distinguishes the statement from one that just assigns a value to a variable. In declaring the type of a constant, you use the same types as you did for defining variables. (These types are defined in Table 8.1.) Finally, to define a constant, you must include the equal sign (=) and the value to be assigned. If you are defining a string constant or date constant, remember to enclose the value in either quotes (" ") or the pound sign (#), respectively.

FIG. 8.3
The Object Browser shows you the value and function of most of Visual Basic's internal constants.

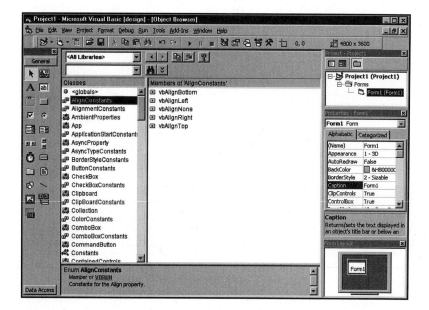

A constant's scope is also important. The same rules for the scope of variables, which were discussed in the earlier section, "Determining Where a Variable Can Be Used," apply to constants as well.

Writing Simple Statements

Now you know a little about variables and constants. You know what data they can store and how to initially set them up. But that is just the beginning of working with information in a program. You also need to be able to assign information to the variable and manipulate that information. Stay tuned—it's covered in the next section.

Using the Assignment Statement

After setting up a variable, the first thing you need to do to use the variable is to store information in the variable. This is the job of the *assignment statement*. The assignment statement is quite simple; you specify a variable whose value you want to set, place an equal sign after the variable name, and then follow this with the expression that represents the value you want stored. The expression can be a literal value, an expression or equation using some combination of other variables and constants, or even a function that returns a value. There is no limit on the complexity of the expression you can use. The only restriction is that the expression must yield a value of the same type as the variable to which it is assigned. The following statements illustrate different assignment statements:

```
inNumStudents = 25
inSumScores = 2276
sgAvgScore = SumScores / NumStudents
stTopStudent = "Janet Simon"
inISpace = InStr(TopStudent," ")
stFirstName = Left(TopStudent,ISpace)
```

You might have noticed that these statements look very similar to the ones used to set the properties of forms and controls in the section "Setting and Retrieving Property Values" in Chapter 4, "Working with Forms and Controls." Actually, they are the same. Most properties of forms and controls act like variables. They can be set at design time, but can also be changed at runtime using an assignment statement. You can also use a property on the right side of a statement to assign its value to a variable for further processing. For example, you use this assignment statement to read the top student name from a text box:

```
stTopStudent = txtTop.Text
```

Using Math Operators

Processing numerical data is one of the key activities of many computer programs. Mathematical operations are used to determine customer bills, interest due on savings or credit card balances, average scores for a class test, and many other bits of information. Visual Basic supports a number of different math operators that can be used in program statements. These operations and the Visual Basic symbol for each operation are summarized in Table 8.3. The operations are then described in detail.

Table 8.3   Math Operations and the Corresponding Visual Basic Symbol

Operation	Operator
Addition	+
Subtraction	−
Multiplication	*
Division	/
Integer division	\
Modulus	mod
Exponentiation	^

Addition and Subtraction   The two simplest math operations are addition and subtraction. You use these operations in such everyday chores as balancing your checkbook or determining how much change you should get back from a sales clerk. If you have ever used a calculator to do addition and subtraction, you already have a good idea how these operations are performed in a line of computer code.

A computer program, however, gives you greater flexibility than a calculator in the operations you can perform. Your programs are not limited to working with literal numbers (for example, 1, 15, 37.63, –105.2). Your program can add or subtract two or more literal numbers, numeric variables, or any functions that return a numeric value. Also, as with a calculator, you can perform addition and subtraction operations in any combination. Now let's take a look at exactly how you perform these operations in your program.

As indicated in Table 8.3, the operator for addition in Visual Basic is the plus sign (+). The general use of this operator is shown in the following syntax line:

```
result = number1 + number2 [+ number3]
```

result is a variable (or control property) that will contain the sum of the numbers. The equal sign indicates the assignment of a value to the variable. number1, number2, and number3 are the literal numbers, numeric variables, or functions that are to be added together. You can add as many numbers together as you like, but each number pair must be separated by a plus sign.

The operator for subtraction is the minus sign (–). The syntax is basically the same as for addition:

```
result = number1 - number2 [- number3]
```

While the order does not matter in addition, in subtraction, the number to the right of the minus sign is subtracted from the number to the left of the sign. If you have multiple numbers, the second number is subtracted from the first, then the third number is subtracted from that result, and so on, moving from left to right. For example, consider the following equation:

```
result = 15 - 6 - 3
```

The computer first subtracts 6 from 15 to yield 9. It then subtracts 3 from 9 to yield 6, which is the final answer stored in the variable result.

You can create assignment statements that consist solely of addition operators or solely of subtraction operators. You can also use the operators in combination with one another or other math operators. The following code lines show a few valid math operations:

```
val1 = 1.25 + 3.17
val2 = 3.21 - 1
val3 = val2 + val1
val4 = val3 + 3.75 - 2.1 + 12 - 3
val4 = val4 + 1
```

If you are not familiar with computer programming, the last line might look a little funny to you. In fact, that line is not allowed in some programming languages. However, in Visual Basic, you can enter a line of code that tells the program to take the current value of a variable, add another number to it, and then store the resulting value back in the same variable.

Multiplication and Division   Two other major mathematical operations with which you should be familiar are multiplication and division. Like addition and subtraction, these operations are used frequently in everyday life.

Multiplication in Visual Basic is very straightforward, just like addition and subtraction. You simply use the multiplication operator—the asterisk (*) operator—to multiply two or more numbers. The syntax of a multiplication statement is almost identical to the ones for addition and subtraction, as follows:

```
result = number1 * number2 [* number3]
```

As before, `result` is the name of a variable used to contain the product of the numbers being multiplied, and `number1`, `number2`, and `number3` are the literal numbers, numeric variables, or functions.

As a demonstration of how multiplication and division might be used in a program, consider the example of a program to determine the amount of paint needed to paint a room. Such a program could contain a form that lets the painter enter the length and width of the room, the height of the ceiling, and the coverage and cost of a single can of paint. Your program could then calculate the number of gallons of paint required and the cost of the paint. An example of the form for such a program is shown in Figure 8.4. The actual code to perform the calculations is shown in Listing 8.1.

FIG. 8.4
Multiplication and
division are used to
determine the amount
of paint needed for a
room.

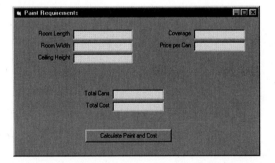

On the CD

Listing 8.1   COSTEST.FRM—Cost Estimation Using Multiplication and Division Operators

```
sgRmLength = Val(txtLength.Text)
slRmWidth = Val(txtWidth.Text)
sgRmHeight = Val(txtHeight.Text)
sgCanCoverage = Val(txtCoverage.Text)
crCanCost = val(txtCost.Text)
sgRmPerimeter = 2 * sgRmLength + 2 * sgRmWidth
sgWallArea = sgRmPerimeter * sgRmHeight
sgNumGallons = sgWallArea / sgCanCoverage
crProjCost = sgNumGallons * crCanCost
txtGallons.Text = sgNumGallons
txtTotalCost.Text = crProjCost
```

Division in Visual Basic is a little more complicated than multiplication. In Listing 8.1, you saw one type of division used. This division is what you are most familiar with and what you will find on your calculator. This type of division returns a number with its decimal portion, if one is present.

However, Visual Basic supports three different ways to divide numbers. These are known as *floating-point division* (the normal type of division, with which you are familiar); *integer division*; and *modulus*, or *remainder*, *division*.

Floating-point division is the typical division that you learned in school. You divide one number by another, and the result is a decimal number. The floating-point division operator is the forward slash (/):

```
result = number1 / number2 [/ number3]
'The following line returns 1.333333
Print 4 / 3
```

Integer division divides one number into another and then returns only the integer portion of the result. The operator for integer division is the backward slash (\):

```
result = number1 \ number2 [\ number3]
'The following line returns 1
Print 4 \ 3
```

Modulus, or remainder, division divides one number into another and returns what is left over after you have obtained the largest integer quotient possible. The modulus operator is the word mod:

```
result = number1 mod number2 [mod number3]
'The following line returns 2, the remainder when dividing 20 by 3
Print 20 mod 3
```

As with the case of addition, subtraction, and multiplication, if you divide more than two numbers, each number pair must be separated by a division operator. Also, like the other operations, multiple operators are handled by reading the equation from left to right.

Figure 8.5 shows a simple form that is used to illustrate the differences between the various division operators. The code for the command button of the form is shown as follows:

```
inpt1 = Text1.Text
inpt2 = Text2.Text
Text3.Text = inpt1 / inpt2
Text4.Text = inpt1 \ inpt2
Text5.Text = inpt1 Mod inpt2
```

The project CALULAT.VBP on the CD-ROM contains a calculator program that demonstrates the various math th operations.

FIG. 8.5

This program demonstrates the difference between Visual Basic's three types of division operators.

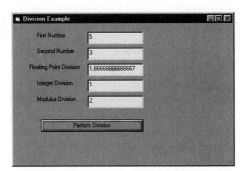

After setting up the form, run the program, enter **5** in the first text box and **3** in the second text box, and then click the command button. Notice that different numbers appear in each of the text boxes used to display the results. You can try this with other number combinations as well.

Exponents Exponents are also known as powers of a number. For example, 2 raised to the third power (2^3) is equivalent to 2×2×2, or 8. Exponents are used quite a lot in computer operations, where many things are represented as powers of two. Exponents are also used extensively in scientific and engineering work, where many things are represented as powers of ten or as natural logarithms. Simpler exponents are used in statistics, where many calculations depend on the squares and the square roots of numbers.

To raise a number to a power, you use the *exponential operator*, which is a caret (^). Exponents greater than one indicate a number raised to a power. Fractional exponents indicate a root, and negative exponents indicate a fraction. The following is the syntax for using the exponential operator:

```
answer = number1 ^ exponent
```

The equations in the following table show several common uses of exponents. The operation performed by each equation is also indicated:

Sample Exponent	Function Performed
3 ^ 2 = 9	This is the square of the number.
9 ^ 0.5 = 3	This is the square root of the number.
2 ^ –2 = 0.25	A fraction is obtained by using a negative exponent.

Operator Precedence Many expressions contain some combination of the operators we've just discussed. In such cases, it's important to know in what order Visual Basic processes the various types of operators. For example, what's the value of the expression 4 * 3 + 6 / 2 ? You might think that the calculations would be performed from left to right. In this case, 4 * 3 is 12; 12 + 6 is 18; 18 / 2 is 9. However, Visual Basic doesn't necessarily process expressions straight through from left to right. It follows a distinct order of processing known as *operator precedence*.

Simply put, Visual Basic performs subsets of a complex expression according to the operators involved, in this order:

- Exponentiation (^)
- Negation (-)
- Multiplication and division (*; /)
- Integer division (\)
- Modulus arithmetic (Mod)
- Addition and subtraction (+, -)

Within a subset of an expression, the components are processed from left to right. When all subset groups have been calculated, the remainder of the expression is calculated from left to right.

In the previous example (4 * 3 + 6 / 2), the multiplication and division portions (4 * 3, which is 12, and 6 / 2, which is 3) would be calculated first, leaving a simpler expression of 12 + 3, for a total of 15.

An important note is that normal operator precedence can be overridden by using parentheses to group sub-expressions that you want to be evaluated first. Multiple nested levels of parentheses can be used. Visual Basic calculates sub-expressions within parentheses first, innermost set to outermost set, and then applies the normal operator precedence.

CAUTION

Understanding operator precedence is crucial to making sure your programs evaluate expressions the way that you expect. For example, if you wanted to calculate the average of two test scores, you might write this line of code:

```
sgAvgScore = inTest1 + inTest2 / 2
```

This line of code might look right, but Visual Basic's calculation won't be correct. Because the division operator has a higher precedence than the addition operator, the sub-expression `inTest2 / 2` will be calculated first and then added to `inTest1`. This is obviously incorrect. You can avoid this problem by using parentheses to control the flow of evaluation:

```
sgAvgScore = (inTest1 + inTest2) / 2
```

This expression will be calculated properly by evaluating the sum of `inTest1 + inTest2` first and then dividing the sum by 2. If `inTest1`'s value was 97 and `inTest2`'s value was 88, the expression would be evaluated as (97 + 88) / 2, or 185 / 2, which would store the correct result of 92.5 in sgAvgScore. Leaving out the parentheses would have resulted in an undesired answer (following the rules of operator precedence) of 97 + 88 / 2, or 97 + 44, or 141!

Visual Basic's *Operator Precedence* help screen has a very good discussion of the topic, including how the precedence extends to comparison operators and logical operators.

Working with Strings

Visual Basic supports only one string operator, the *concatenation operator.* This operator is used to combine two or more strings of text, similar to the way the addition operator is used to combine two or more numbers. The concatenation operator is the ampersand symbol (&). When you combine two strings with the concatenation operator, the second string is added directly to the end of the first string. The result is a longer string containing the full contents of both source strings.

The concatenation operator is used in an assignment statement as follows:

```
newstring = stringexpr1 & stringexpr2 [& stringexpr3]
```

In this syntax, `newstring` represents the variable that will contain the result of the concatenation operation. `stringexpr1`, `stringexpr2`, and `stringexpr3` all represent string expressions. These can be any valid strings, including string variables, literal expressions (enclosed in quotes), or functions that return a string. The ampersand between a pair of string expressions tells Visual Basic to concatenate the two expressions. The ampersand must be preceded and followed by a space. The syntax shows an optional second ampersand and a third string expression. You can combine any number of strings with a single statement. Just remember to separate each pair of expressions with an ampersand.

N O T E If you are working on converting programs from an older version of Visual Basic, you might find strings combined using the plus sign operator. This was prevalent in versions of Visual Basic prior to version 4, as well as in older BASIC languages. While Visual Basic still supports the plus sign operator, in case this operator is present in older code that you are modifying, I recommend that you use the ampersand for any work that you do to avoid confusion with the mathematical addition operation. ■

Listing 8.2 shows how the concatenation of strings would be used in a simple program to generate mailing labels. The fields from the different text boxes are combined to create the different lines of the mailing label. The form for this program is shown in Figure 8.6.

On the CD

Listing 8.2 Mailing.Frm—String Concatenation Used in Mailing Labels

```
stFirst$ = txtFirst.Text
stLast$ = txtLast.Text
stAddr$ = txtAddress.Text
stCity$ = txtCity.Text
stState$ = txtState.Text
stZip$ = txtZip.Text
If optTitle1.Value Then stTitle$ = "Mr. "
If optTitle2.Value Then stTitle$ = "Mrs. "
If optTitle3.Value Then stTitle$ = "Miss "
If optTitle4.Value Then stTitle$ = "Ms. "
stLine1$ = stTitle$ & stFirst$ & " " & stLast$
stLine3$ = stCity$ & ", " & stState$ & "  " & stZip$
picOutput.Print stLine1$
picOutput.Print stAddr$
picOutput.Print stLine3$
```

FIG. 8.6
The mailing label
application shows how
strings are combined for
display or printing.

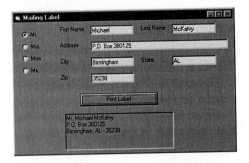

Making Decisions in Your Program

Many of the statements in your programs will be assignment statements, but there are other statements that are important for handling more complex tasks. These statements are known collectively as *control statements*. Without control statements, your program would start at the first line of code and proceed line by line until the last line was reached. At that point, the program would stop.

One type of control statement is the *decision statement*. These statements are used to control the execution of parts of your program, based on conditions that exist at the time the statement is encountered. There are two basic types of decision statements: If statements and Select Case statements. Each is covered in this section.

Using the *If* Statement

For many decisions, you will want to execute a statement (or group of statements) only if a condition is True. There are two forms of the If statement for handling True conditions—the *single line* If statement and the *multiple line* If statement. Each uses the If statement to check a condition. If the condition is True, the program runs the commands associated with the If statement. If the condition is False, the commands are skipped, and any Else portion of the If statement block is executed.

The Single Line *If* Statement   The single line If statement is used to perform a single task when the condition in the statement is True. The task can be a single command, or you can perform multiple commands by calling a procedure. The following is the syntax of the single line If statement:

If *condition* Then *command*

The argument *condition* represents any type of logical condition, which can be any of the following:

- Comparison of a variable to a literal, another variable, or a function
- A variable or database field that contains a True or False value
- Any function or expression that returns a True or False value

The argument *command* represents the task to be performed if the condition is True. This can be any valid Visual Basic statement, including a procedure call. The following code shows how an If statement would be used to print a person's name if his or her fortieth birthday occurred during a particular year. This code is retrieving information from a database to perform the comparison and get the names (Figure 8.7 shows the output list that might be generated):

```
inCompYear = Val(txtYear.Text) - 40
inBirthYear = Year(Members("BirthDate"))
If inBirthYear = inCompYear Then Picture1.Print Members("FullName")
```

FIG. 8.7

You can use comparisons to print the names of 40-year-olds.

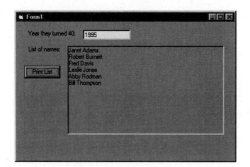

Multiple Commands for the Condition   If you need to execute more than one command in response to a condition, you can use the multiple line form of the If statement. This is also known as a *block* If statement. This form bounds a range of statements between the If statement and an End If statement. If the condition in the If statement is True, all the commands between the If and End If statements are run. If the condition is False, the program skips to the first line after the End If statement. Listing 8.3 shows how a block If statement is used to credit an invoice in a membership program. The program asks the user if a credit should be issued and executes the block of code if the user answers yes.

On the CD

Listing 8.3   CREDIT.TXT—Making Decisions in Code

```
If Retval = vbYes Then
   OrgCanc.Close
   Set OrgCanc = MemDb.OpenRecordset("Dues", dbOpenTable)
   OrgCanc.Index = "InvoiceID"
   OrgCanc.Seek "=", InvcID
   TotDues = OrgCanc("AmountDue") - TotDues
   If TotDues < 0 Then
      TotDues = 0
      OrgCanc.Edit
      OrgCanc("AmountDue") = TotDues
      OrgCanc("LastUpdate") = Date
      OrgCanc("UpdateBy") = UserID
      OrgCanc.Update
   End If
End If
```

TIP If you have a lot of commands between the `If` and `End If` statements, you might want to repeat the condition as a comment in the `End If` statement, as in this example:

```
If crTotalSales > crProjectedSales Then

    ' A bunch of lines of code

Else

    ' Another bunch of lines of code

End If 'crTotalSales > crProjectedSales
```

This makes your code easier to read.

Working with the *False* Condition

Of course, if a condition can be `True`, it can also be `False`; and there may be times when you want code to execute only on a `False` condition. There may be other times when you want to take one action if a condition is `True` and another action if the condition is `False`. This section looks at handling the `False` side of a condition.

Using the *Not* Operator   One way to execute a statement, or group of statements, for a `False` condition is to use the `Not` operator. The `Not` operator inverts the actual condition that follows it. If the condition is `True`, the `Not` operator makes the overall expression `False`, and vice versa. Listing 8.4 uses the operator to invert the value of the `NoMatch` property of a recordset. `NoMatch` is `True` if a record is not found in a search operation, and it is `False` if the search succeeds. Because the program can operate on a record only if it is found, the `Not` operator and `NoMatch` property are used as the condition of the `If` statement.

On the CD

Listing 8.4   FALSEIF.TXT—Handling a False Condition

```
If Not OrgCanc.NoMatch Then
    OrgCanc.Edit
    OrgCanc("Renewed") = False
    OrgCanc("LastUpdate") = Date
    OrgCanc("UpdateBy") = UserID
    OrgCanc.Update
End If
```

Handling *True* and *False* Conditions   The other way of handling `False` conditions allows you to process different sets of instructions for the `True` or `False` condition. You can handle this "fork in the road" in Visual Basic with the `Else` part of the `If` statement block.

To handle both the `True` and `False` conditions, you start with the block `If` statement and add the `Else` statement, as follows:

```
If condition Then
    statements to process if condition is True
Else
    statements to process if condition is False
End If
```

The `If` and `End If` statements of this block are the same as before. The condition is still any logical expression or variable that yields a `True` or `False` value. The key element of this set of statements is the `Else` statement. This statement is placed after the last statement to be executed if the condition is `True`, and before the first statement to be executed if the condition is `False`. For a `True` condition, the program processes the statements up to the `Else` statement and then skips to the first statement after the `End If`. If the condition is `False`, the program skips the statements prior to the `Else` statement and starts processing with the first statement after the `Else`.

N O T E If you want to execute code for only the `False` portion of the statement, you can just place code statements between the `Else` and `End If` statements. You are not required to place any statements between the `If` and `Else` statements. ■

Listing 8.5 shows how both parts of an `If` statement are used to handle different handicap calculations for men and women in a golf handicap program.

On the CD

Listing 8.5   HANDICAP.TXT—Handicap Calculation Using Conditional Statements

```
If slope = 1 Then
    avgdif! = totdif! / bstscr
    hcidx! = Int(avgdif! * 0.96 * 10) / 10
    hcp% = Int(hcidx! + 0.5)
Else
    hcidx! = 0!
    avgdif! = Int(totdif! / bstscr * 100) / 10
    hcp% = 0
    Call Hcpchrt(avgdif!, hcp%)
End If
' Get member record
Get #1, pnt, mmbr
' Set maximum handicap for gender
If mmbr.gendr = "M" Then
    If hcp% > 36 Then hcp% = 36
Else
    If hcp% > 40 Then hcp% = 40
End If
```

Working with Multiple *If* Statements

In the previous sections, you saw the simple block If statements, which evaluate one condition and can execute commands for either a True or a False condition. You can also evaluate multiple conditions with an additional statement in the block If. The ElseIf statement lets you specify another condition to evaluate whether or not the first condition is False. Using the ElseIf statement, you can evaluate any number of conditions with one If statement block. Listing 8.6 shows how a series of ElseIf conditions could be used to determine the grade distribution in a class.

On the CD

Listing 8.6   GRADESIF.TXT—Grade Distribution with Multiple *If* Statements

```
For I = 0 To numstd
    If inpGrades(I) >= 90 Then
        GradeDist(4) = GradeDist(4) + 1
    ElseIf inpGrades(I) >= 80 Then
        GradeDist(3) = GradeDist(3) + 1
    ElseIf inpGrades(I) >= 70 Then
        GradeDist(2) = GradeDist(2) + 1
    ElseIf inpGrades(I) >= 60 Then
        GradeDist(1) = GradeDist(1) + 1
    Else
        GradeDist(0) = GradeDist(0) + 1
    End If
Next I
```

The preceding code works by first evaluating the condition in the If statement. If the condition is True, the statement (or statements) immediately following the If statement is executed; and then the program skips to the first statement after the End If statement.

If the first condition is False, the program skips to the first ElseIf statement and evaluates its condition. If this condition is True, the statements following the ElseIf are executed, and control again passes to the statement after the End If. This process continues for as many ElseIf statements as are in the block.

If all the conditions are False, the program skips to the Else statement and processes the commands between the Else and the End If statements. The Else statement is not required.

Using *Select Case*

Another way to handle decisions in a program is to use the Select Case statement. This allows you to conditionally execute any of a series of statement groups based on the value of a test expression, which can be a single variable or a complex expression. The Select Case statement identifies the test expression to be evaluated. Then a series of Case statements specifies the possible values. If the value of the test expression matches the value (or values) indicated in the Case statement, the commands after the Case statement are executed. If the value does not match, the program proceeds to the next `Case` statement. The `Select Case` structure is similar to a series of `If/Then/ElseIf` statements. The following lines of code show the syntax of the `Select Case` block:

```
Select Case testvalue
    Case value1
        statement group 1
    Case value2
        statement group 2
End Select
```

The first statement of the `Select Case` block is the `Select Case` statement itself. This statement identifies the value to be tested against possible results. This value, represented by the `testvalue` argument, can be any valid numeric or string expression, including literals, variables, or functions.

Each conditional group of commands (those that are run if the condition is met) is started by a `Case` statement. The `Case` statement identifies the expression to which the `testvalue` is compared. If the `testvalue` is equal to the expression, the commands after the `Case` statement are run. The program runs the commands between the current `Case` statement and the next `Case` statement or the `End Select` statement. If the `testvalue` is not equal to the value expression, the program proceeds to the next `Case` statement.

The `End Select` statement identifies the end of the `Select Case` block.

N O T E Only one case in the `Select Case` block is executed for a given value of `testvalue`, even if more than one of the `Case` statements match the value of the test expression. ■

CAUTION

The `testvalue` and `value` expressions must represent the same data type. For example, if the `testvalue` is a number, the values in the `Case` statements also must be numbers.

The simplest form of the `Select Case` block uses only a single value for the comparison expression. You might use this type of statement to handle a payroll calculation where you have a single pay rate for each job grade. Figure 8.8 shows a form that could be used to calculate pay for hourly employees with various job classifications. The code to perform the calculation is shown in Listing 8.7.

On the CD

Listing 8.7   PAYROLL.FRM—Payroll Calculation with the *Select Case* Statement

```
totpay = 0.0
paygrd = Val(txtGrade.Text)
payhrs = Val(txtHours.Text)
```

continues

Listing 8.7   Continued

```
Select Case paygrd
    Case 1
        totpay = payhrs * 4.35
    Case 2
        totpay = payhrs * 4.85
    Case 3
        totpay = payhrs * 5.35
    Case 4
        totpay = payhrs * 5.85
End Select
txtPay.Text = totpay
```

FIG. 8.8

A payroll calculator can use a *Select Case* structure to handle different wages for different classes of employees.

Case statements within a Select Case structure can also handle *lists*, *ranges*, and *comparisons* of values in addition to discrete values. Note the use of Case Is < 0, Case 1 to 9, and Case Is > 50 in this example:

```
inQtyOrdered = Val(txtQuantity)
Select Case inQtyOrdered
    Case Is < 0 'note use of comparison
        MsgBox "Order quantity cannot be negative!", vbExclamation
        Exit Sub
    Case 1, 2, 3 'note use of list
        sgDiscount = 0
    Case 4 To 9 'note use of range
        sgDiscount = 0.03
    Case 10 To 49
        sgDiscount = 0.08
    Case Is > 50
        sgDiscount = 0.1
End    Select
```

The preceding examples work fine if your test variable matches one of the conditions in a Case statement. But how do you handle other values that are outside the ones for which you tested? You can have your code do something for all other possible values of the test expression by adding a Case Else statement to your program. The Case Else statement follows the last command of the last Case statement in the block. You then place the commands that you want executed between the Case Else and the End Select statements.

You can use the Case Else statement to perform calculations for values not specifically called out in the Case statements. Or you can use the Case Else statement to let users know that they entered an invalid value. Listing 8.8 shows how to add a message to let the user know that an invalid code was entered in the payroll program shown earlier.

Listing 8.8   PAYROLL.FRM—Handling Invalid Input with the *Case Else* Statement

```
totpay = 0#
paygrd = Val(txtGrade.Text)
payhrs = Val(txtHours.Text)
Select Case paygrd
    Case 1
        totpay = payhrs * 4.35
    Case 2
        totpay = payhrs * 4.85
    Case 3
        totpay = payhrs * 5.35
    Case 4
        totpay = payhrs * 5.85
    Case Else
        MsgBox Str(paygrd) & " is an invalid pay code."
End Select
txtPay.Text = totpay
```

Working with Loops

The other major type of control statement is the *loop*. Loops are used to perform repetitive tasks in your program. There are two main types of loops that are supported by Visual Basic—counter loops and conditional loops. *Counter loops* are used to perform a task a set number of times. *Conditional loops* are used to perform a task while a specified condition exists or until a specified condition exists. Each of these types of loops is discussed in this section.

For Loops

A counter loop is also known as a For loop, or a For/Next loop. This is because the ends of the loop are defined by the For statement and the Next statement. At the beginning of a For loop, you define a counter variable, as well as the beginning and end points of the variable's value, and optionally the Step value, or the amount it is to be increased or decreased after each pass through the loop. The first time the loop is run, the counter variable is set to the value of the beginning point. Then after each time the program runs through the loop, the value of the counter is incremented by the Step value and checked against the value of the end point. If the counter is larger than the end point, the program skips to the first statement following the loop's Next statement.

FIG. 8.9
A series of *For* l
used to initialize
arrays.

Typi
Howe
place
Exit

List

Pri
txt
For

Next
End

This c
neces
is use

N O T

of an a

Do Loops

The ke
sion th

CAU

If the b

except

numbe

T I P   For ease

statemer

CAU

Althou

types.

executi

Listing

membe

new me

Listin

Dim I

'Clea

For I

t:

Next

'Set

For I

cl

Next

'Clea

For I

m:

Next

'Clea

For I

ms

Next

CAU

Never re

FIG. 8.10
The list was set up by using a *Do Until* loop to read through database records until the end of the data was reached.

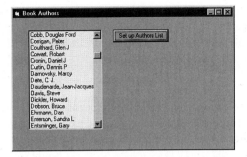

Making Your Program Bug-Free

No matter how long you have been developing programs or how good you are at what you do, you'll still have errors crop up in your program. It's easy to make mistakes. All it takes is a simple typo to make your program refuse to run. This is called a *syntax error*. There are also *logic errors*, where your program runs but it just doesn't do what you want it to do.

Because you will make errors, one of the keys to successful program development is the ability to track down these errors, or *bugs* as they are often known, and fix them. Visual Basic provides you with a number of tools to help you find and eliminate bugs. These tools provide you with the following capabilities:

- Syntax checking, which makes sure you enter commands correctly
- Watches for variables, which let you see the changing value of variables as your program runs
- Code tracing, which lets you see which program lines are being executed
- Procedure call listing, which tells you how your program got to a certain point

How to Avoid Syntax Errors

One of the best ways to eliminate bugs is to prevent them in the first place. Visual Basic provides you with a syntax checker that checks each line of code as you enter it. If you have an error in the code, the checker alerts you to the problem as soon as you move to another line. The syntax checker looks for misspelled keywords and missing items in a statement, such as a parenthesis or a keyword. When you have a syntax error, Visual Basic shows the erroneous line in red and displays a message telling you the cause of the problem. Figure 8.11 shows how the syntax checker can alert you to a missing part of an If statement.

The syntax checker is turned on when you first install Visual Basic. However, if for some reason it has been turned off, you can activate it by checking the Auto Syntax Check box in the Editor Options dialog box (see Figure 8.12). Access this dialog box by choosing Tools, Options.

FIG. 8.11

The syntax checker is reporting an incomplete statement.

Invalid statement ———

Error message ———

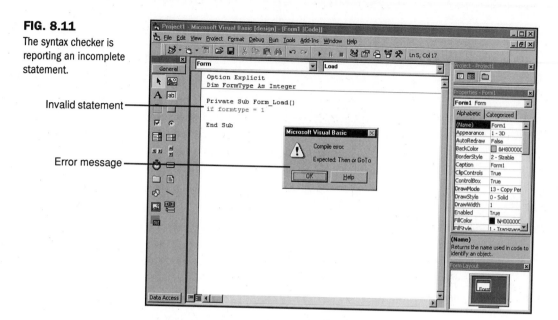

FIG. 8.12

Automatic Syntax Checking is one of many options that can be selected for Visual Basic's editor.

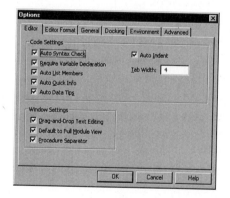

Another great feature of Visual Basic is the new Auto List Members code-completion assistant. This assistant helps you by popping up the syntax of Visual Basic functions and by providing you with property lists for any object used in the code. While this feature is designed to help speed your coding, it also helps cut down on errors. Figure 8.13 shows how a property list for a form is displayed after you enter a dot after the form's name in the code line.

Another thing that Visual Basic does for you in the Code window is properly capitalizes keywords and displays them using blue text. This gives you another visual indication that you have correctly entered a command.

FIG. 8.13

The code-completion assistant helps eliminate programming errors.

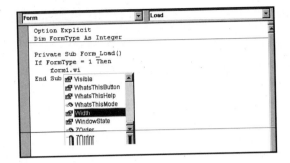

 TIP If you enter all your control names and properties in lowercase and spell them correctly, Visual Basic capitalizes them. This indicates that you didn't make any typos.

 TIP If you don't like the default colors that are used in the Code Editor, you can change them by using the Editor Format tab on the Options dialog box.

What Happens When an Error Occurs

While you are running your code from the Visual Basic development environment, you might encounter errors in your program. These errors can be the runtime errors listed in the Help files or the program manuals. When you encounter an error, you are shown an error message like the one in Figure 8.14. The error message gives you the error number and a text description of the problem.

FIG. 8.14

A missing file leads to a runtime error.

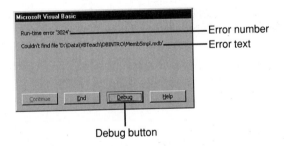

Notice that the message box has several command buttons on it. One of these buttons, the Debug button, provides you with the first line of assistance in tracking down errors in your code. If you choose the Debug button, you are shown the code-editing window with the offending line highlighted by a yellow highlight bar and arrow (see Figure 8.15).

Sometimes the error is obvious, such as mistyping a variable name or declaring a variable as the wrong type. Other times, though, you need to dig deeper to find the source of the error.

FIG. 8.15
By choosing Debug from the error message box, you can attempt to pinpoint the cause of the error.

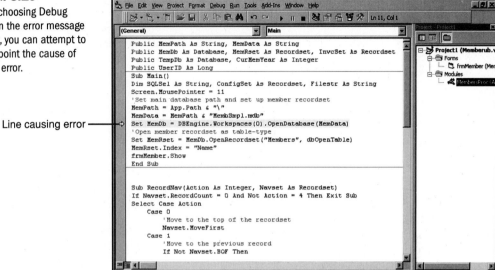

Line causing error ⟶

How the Debugging Environment Works

Visual Basic's debugging environment provides you with the tools you need to locate and eliminate errors in your program. These tools are easily accessible from the Debug toolbar. This toolbar, shown in Figure 8.16, provides you with quick access to all the information windows of the debug environment and all of the functions for stepping through your code. Table 8.4 describes each of the Debug toolbar buttons. The Debug toolbar is accessible by choosing View, Toolbars, Debug; or by right-clicking any visible toolbar and selecting Debug from the toolbar list.

FIG. 8.16
The Debug toolbar organizes the debug functions in a convenient location.

Table 8.4   Debug Toolbar Buttons

Button	Name	Function
▶	Start	Begins program execution, or continues if program has been paused.
‖	Break	Pauses program execution by placing the program in "break mode."

continues

Table 8.4 Continued

Button	Name	Function
■	End	Stops a running program.
🖐	Toggle Breakpoint	Toggles the current code line as a "breakpoint;" the program will pause and enter break mode before the line is executed.
▣	Step Into	When in break mode, causes the next line of code to be executed, even if it means stepping into another procedure or function.
☝	Step Over	When in break mode, causes the next line of code to be executed; if the next line is a procedure or function call, the entire procedure or function will be executed before the program is paused again.
⮌	Step Out	When in break mode, causes the remainder of the current procedure or function to be executed before the program is paused again.
▦	Locals Window	Displays the Locals window, which lists all variables that have been defined in the active procedure, along with their current values.
▤	Immediate Window	Displays the Immediate window, which allow you to manually execute lines of code while in break mode.
▨	Watch Window	Displays the Watch window, where can add "watches" to allow you to keep an eye on how the values of your program's variables change as the program runs.
👓	Quick Watch	Displays the Quick Watch dialog box, which shows you the current value of the selected variable or expression. You can add the expression to the Watch window from here.
⬚	Call Stack	Displays the Calls dialog box, which contains a list of all procedures and functions that are currently running but have not yet finished executing.

Let's take a closer look at the tools at your disposal.

How to Determine the Value of a Variable

Often when you encounter an error, it is because a variable contains a value that you did not expect. It might be that a variable had a zero value and was then used in a division operation. Or a variable that was supposed to contain the name of a file somehow had a number stored in it. You can also see how a variable changes as the program runs. Watching the change in a variable's value, or the lack of a change, is one of the major factors in finding many program errors, including infinite loops.

To debug your program, you have to be able to determine the values of the variables that are used in the program at different points in the execution. Visual Basic provides you with several basic methods of checking the values of variables, including the Watch window, the Locals window, Quick Watches, and Auto Data Tips.

 Using the Watch Window   One way to view the value of variables is with the Watch window. This window shows you the expression you are watching, the value of the expression, the type of watch, and the procedure where the expression is being evaluated (see Figure 8.17). By using the Watch window, you can look at only the variables or expressions that interest you. You can access the Watch window from the Debug toolbar or by choosing View, Watch Window.

FIG. 8.17

The Watch window shows the value of variables and expressions you define.

To set up a variable or expression for viewing, you have to add it to the Watch window. To do this, choose Debug, Add Watch. This brings up the Add Watch dialog box (see Figure 8.18). This dialog box allows you to enter the name of the variable to observe in the Expression field.

FIG. 8.18

The Add Watch dialog box lets you set up variables to observe during program execution.

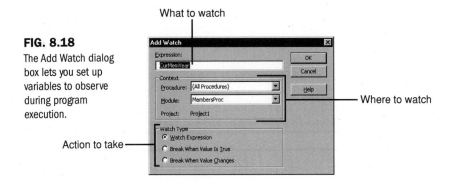

The Add Watch dialog box also allows you to specify where you want to observe the variable. These context settings let you observe the value of the variable during the entire program or just during a specific procedure.

The Watch Type options let you decide whether to just look at the value of the variable or to break (pause the execution of the code) when a specific condition exists. You can choose to have the program pause every time a variable changes or when the watch expression is True. This way, you can determine when a variable reaches or exceeds a specific value. To use this type of watch, the expression must be a Boolean variable or a logical expression.

If at a later time you want to edit the watch expression, you can right-click the mouse in the Watch window and select the Edit Watch item from the pop-up window. This brings up the Edit Watch dialog box, which is basically the same as the Add Watch dialog box, but adds a command button that allows you to delete the watch.

 Using the Locals Window   Sometimes it is easier to just check the values of all the variables in a procedure than it is to try to guess which variable has the problem. This is easily done with the Locals window, which is viewed by clicking the Locals Window button on the Debug toolbar, or by choosing View, Locals Window. This window, shown in Figure 8.19, lists all the variables declared in the current procedure along with their current values. Variables that are declared outside the current procedure are not shown.

FIG. 8.19

The Locals window lets you look at all the declared variables in a procedure.

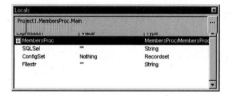

Using Quick Watches and Auto Data Tips   If you only need to find out the current value of a variable, but do not need to track its value as the program progresses, you can use a quick watch. A quick watch displays a dialog box that shows the name of the variable, its current value, and the procedure in which it is currently being used (see Figure 8.20).

FIG. 8.20

A quick watch provides a snapshot look at a variable.

Current value

Variable
Module

 To use a quick watch, highlight a variable in the Code window while the program is paused. Then you can click the Quick Watch button on the Debug toolbar or choose Debug, Quick Watch to show the dialog box. You can also run a quick watch by pressing Shift+F9. Note that the Quick Watch dialog box has an option to add the watch to the Watch window that we described previously.

Another way to quickly view the value of a variable or an object property is to rest the mouse pointer on the variable in the Code window. After the mouse is still for a second or two, the value pops up in a little box similar to a ToolTip (see Figure 8.21). This handy tool is known as Auto Data Tips. You can also select an entire expression and rest the mouse pointer on it to see the evaluated value of the expression.

FIG. 8.21

Resting the mouse pointer on App.Path in break mode causes Auto Data Tips to display its value in a ToolTip.

```
Sub Main()
Dim SQLSel As String, ConfigSet As Recordset, Filestr As String
Screen.MousePointer = 11
'Set main database path and set up member recordset
MemPath = App.Path & "\"
App.Path = "D:\Data\VBTeach\DBINTRO" 1.mdb"
Set MemDb = DBEngine.Workspaces(0).OpenDatabase(MemData)
'Open member recordset as table-type
Set MemRset = MemDb.OpenRecordset("Members", dbOpenTable)
MemRset.Index = "Name"
frmMember.Show
End Sub
```

Running Commands

Another part of the Debug environment is the *Immediate window*. This window allows you to enter program commands, which will be executed as soon as you press Enter. From this window, you can print or even change the value of a variable using an assignment statement. You can also use commands to change the environment of your program, such as the fonts on a form or the color of text in a text box.

 The Immediate window allows you to enter any single-line command. Loops and block statements (If blocks and Select Case blocks) are not allowed. If you issue the print command from the Immediate window, the results are printed on the line following the command. This provides another way to view the contents of a variable. Figure 8.22 shows how the Immediate window can be used to find the value of a variable or set a variable. If the Immediate window is not open, you can access it by clicking the Immediate Window button on the Debug toolbar, or by choosing View, Immediate Window.

FIG. 8.22

You can execute many types of statements in the Immediate window.

```
Immediate                          ×
memdata = app.Path & "\membsamp.mdb"
```

Another Debugging Tool

 One final item you might need in debugging is the *Call Stack window* (see Figure 8.23), which can be viewed by clicking the Call Stack button on the Debug toolbar, by choosing View, Call Stack, or by pressing Ctrl+L. This window tells you which procedure is currently executing. It also shows the entire string of procedure calls from the initial procedure to the current one. These calls are listed from the most recent procedure (at the top of the list) to the initial calling procedure (at the bottom of the list). This list helps you determine how you got to the current point. This way, you will know if a procedure is being accessed from an area that you don't want.

FIG. 8.23
The Call Stack shows you the procedures that led up to the current procedure.

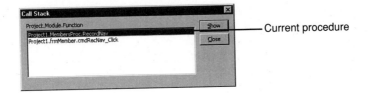

Current procedure

Pausing the Program's Execution

Whenever Visual Basic encounters an error, it automatically pauses the execution of the program by placing it in *break mode*. There also might be times that you want to pause a program when there is no error. You would do this to check the value of variables at a specific point.

There are several ways to pause a program without an error having occurred:

- Set a watch to pause the program, either when a variable changes value or when an expression is True.
- Press Ctrl+Break on the keyboard.
- Click the Break button on either the Standard or Debug toolbar.
- Set a breakpoint in code to pause at a particular line.

Setting a watch point to pause the program was discussed previously in the "Using the Watch Window" section; clicking the Break button and pressing Ctrl+Break are self-explanatory. Therefore, let's concentrate on setting a breakpoint in the code.

A breakpoint in code is set while you are in design mode. To set the breakpoint, you must have the Code window open and be in the procedure containing the statement where you want the break to occur. At this point, you can set the breakpoint in one of these ways:

- Click the mouse in the gray margin to the left of the statement.
- Select the statement on which to break and click the Toggle Breakpoint icon from the Debug toolbar.
- Select the statement on which to break and choose Debug, Toggle Breakpoint.
- Select the statement on which to break and press F9.
- Add the Stop statement to your code at the point where you want the program to pause.

When a breakpoint is set, the code statement is highlighted as shown in Figure 8.24.

Each of the methods for setting the breakpoint actually toggles the breakpoint status of the line. This means that if the statement is not a breakpoint, it becomes one. Conversely, if it is already a breakpoint, the breakpoint is removed.

Tracing Through Your Code

In the previous sections, you learned how to pause the code; but for debugging to be effective, you have to be able to execute program statements and watch their effects.

FIG. 8.24

A breakpoint enables you to pause the code at a specific statement.

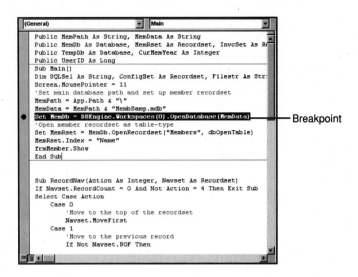

Part

I

Ch

8

Breakpoint

After the execution of the program has stopped, you have several options for continuing the execution. You can do any of the following:

- Execute a single statement
- Execute a group of statements
- Resume normal execution of the code

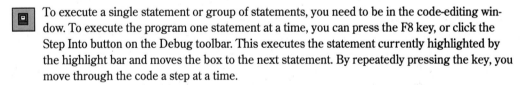

To execute a single statement or group of statements, you need to be in the code-editing window. To execute the program one statement at a time, you can press the F8 key, or click the Step Into button on the Debug toolbar. This executes the statement currently highlighted by the highlight bar and moves the box to the next statement. By repeatedly pressing the key, you move through the code a step at a time.

This method is extremely useful for determining which part of a conditional statement is being accessed. When the program encounters an `If` or `Select Case` statement, it evaluates the condition and moves immediately to the proper part of the block for the condition. For example, if the condition in an `If` statement is `False`, execution of the program immediately moves to the `Else` portion of the `If` block.

If the current statement contains a procedure call, pressing F8 or clicking the Step Into button causes you to go to the first step of the procedure. If you want to run the entire procedure and return to the next line in the current program, press Shift+F8 or click the Debug toolbar's Step Over button. Also, if you have stepped into the procedure and want to run the rest of the procedure, you can click the Debug toolbar's Step Out button or press Ctrl+Shift+F8. This runs the remaining lines of code in the procedure and pauses again at the statement after the procedure call.

If you're fairly certain that a block of statements is error-free, you might want to execute the entire block at once instead of executing each statement individually. You can accomplish this by placing the cursor on the statement where you next want to pause the program execution and pressing Ctrl+F8. This method is useful for executing an entire loop after you have determined that the loop is not part of the problem.

 Finally, when you think you have resolved the problem and want to finish executing the program, you can press the F5 key to allow the program to continue running normally. You can also do this by pressing the Continue button (which is the break-mode version of the Run button) on the Standard or Debug toolbar.

From Here...

This chapter has provided you with an overview of programming in Visual Basic. You have learned how to handle mathematical operations, string manipulations, decisions, and loops in your code. You have also seen how to use the debugging environment to eliminate errors in your code. For some more material on programming, refer to the following chapters:

- To learn how to create procedures and functions, see Chapter 17, "Managing Your Projects."
- Read about database programming in Chapter 28, "Building Database Applications."

More on Visual Basic Controls

Using the Windows Standard Controls

In the first part of the book, you learned some of the fundamentals of writing programs in Visual Basic. Along the way, you were exposed to some of the basics of working with controls. Part II of the book takes you deeper into the world of Visual Basic controls. In this first chapter, you will look at some of the standard controls, most of which have been a part of Visual Basic since version 1. You will see some of the basic operations of these controls, as well as see some of the new features that have been incorporated into Visual Basic 5. ■

Most of your programs will require users to make choices

You will see how option buttons and check boxes enable you to control with ease the choices available to the user.

For many applications, you will have a large number of available choices

You will see how the ListBox and ComboBox controls make quick work out of creating and managing lists of choices.

Scroll bar—another way to enter numbers

While you will use a text box for many types of numeric input, you will often find that a scroll bar is easier for the user to work with and for you to handle in your program.

Keeping time with a control

If you need to have certain activities occur at specific intervals, the Timer control is the right tool for the job.

Recapping the Basics

Because several of the standard controls have been covered earlier in the book, they will not be covered in this chapter. These controls and the chapters that cover them are summarized in Table 9.1.

Table 9.1 Controls Covered in Previous Chapters

Control Name	Chapter
TextBox	Chapter 14, "Working with Text, Fonts, and Colors"
Label	Chapter 14, "Working with Text, Fonts, and Colors"
Command Button	Chapter 4, "Working with Forms and Controls"
PictureBox	"Doing Graphics," on the companion CD-ROM
Image	"Doing Graphics," on the companion CD-ROM
Shape	"Doing Graphics," on the companion CD-ROM
Line	"Doing Graphics," on the companion CD-ROM

Recall from these previous chapters that there are several properties, methods, and events that are common to almost all controls. Most controls have Name, Top, Left, Height, Width, Enabled, and Visible properties. There are also several other common properties that have yet to be discussed—until now.

Maintaining Order

The first of these properties is the TabIndex property. This property determines the order in which controls are accessed as the user presses the Tab key while the form on which the controls reside is active. The TabIndex property starts with zero for the first control you add to a form. As you add more controls, each control is given a TabIndex property that is one greater than the last control. If you design your form perfectly the first time, your controls will be accessed in the proper order and you will never have to worry about this property. However, changes to your form are inevitable and the order can get messed up. When this happens, you will have to reset the Tab order of the controls by setting the TabIndex properties.

Figure 9.1 shows a typical form used in a program. Since it is not possible to show the effects of good and bad tab orders in print, two programs are included on the companion CD to illustrate the concept. The form in Figure 9.1 is used in both programs. The two programs are BadTab.Vbp and GoodTab.Vbp. A user reasonably might expect to move from field to field in a logical order, which, in this case, would be First Name, Middle Initial, Last Name, Address, and so on. You should make sure the TabIndex property of your forms' controls causes the focus to flow correctly.

On the CD

Since it is not possible to show the effects of good and bad tab orders in print, two programs are available on the CD-ROM to illustrate the concept. The form in Figure 9.1 is used in both programs. The two programs are BADTAB.VBP and GOODTAB.VBP.

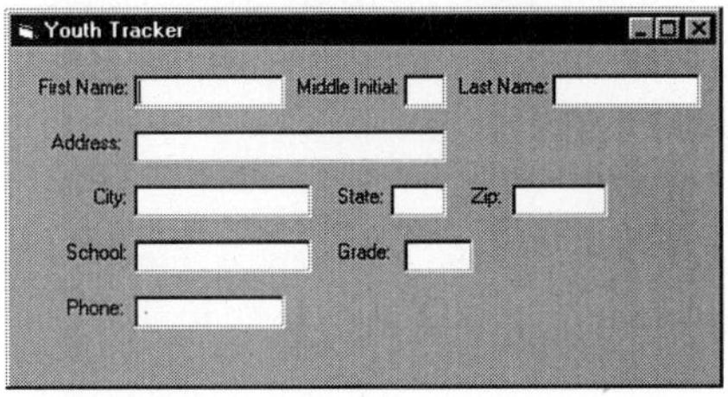

FIG. 9.1
Users expect a form's focus to flow logically.

The only way to change the tab order of the controls on your form is to set the TabIndex property of each control that you need to shift. As you set a new value for the TabIndex property of a control, Visual Basic automatically adjusts the property values for all controls that have higher TabIndex property values than the new value.

N O T E Even though Label controls can't receive the focus, they still have a TabIndex property. This is to aid in creating keyboard-friendly programs. TabIndex comes into play if a Label control's Caption property includes an access key; for example, a Label control whose Caption property is &Name will show the "N" to be an access key (Name). If the user presses the access key (in this case, Alt+N), the focus moves to the control with the next-higher TabIndex (assuming that it's a control that can receive the focus). If our Label control has a TabIndex property of 9, for example, you might have an associated TextBox control whose TabIndex property is 10. Then, when the user presses Alt+N, the focus moves to the "Name" TextBox, which is probably positioned next to the label. This technique, in effect, lets a Label control act as a caption for a text box. ■

Another property related to the TabIndex property is the TabStop property. TabStop is a property of any control that can receive the focus in a program. The value of the TabStop property determines whether the user can move the focus to the control by pressing the Tab key. The default value of True allows the user to use the Tab key. Setting the TabStop property to False means that the control won't receive the focus as the user presses Tab; however, it can still be accessed with the mouse.

Exploring Other Common Properties

Another useful property of many controls is the ToolTipText property, which enables you to display text in a ToolTip when the user pauses the mouse pointer over a control. ToolTips are used to help the user determine which controls will perform a desired action. A ToolTip is enabled if any text is entered for the ToolTip property. Figure 9.2 shows a ToolTip at work.

FIG. 9.2

ToolTips provide a clue to the function of a control.

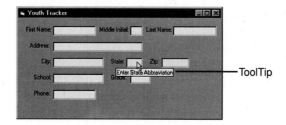

Another common property of note is the Index property. If this property has a value (0 or greater), this indicates that the control is part of a control array.

Working with User Choices

Previously, you have seen how to acquire input from a user through the use of a text box. This works well for a number of data-gathering needs. But what if you just want a simple piece of information, such as "Do you own a car?" or "What is your marital status?" In these cases, the choice of answers you want to provide is limited to two or, at most, a few choices.

Although a text box works for getting this information, what is the user supposed to enter? For a "yes" or "no" choice, do you want the user to type out the entire word or just use the first letter? Or would you prefer *true* or *false* responses? By the same token, what should a person enter for marital status? Are you looking just for married or single, or do you want to include divorced and widowed?

These differences may not seem like much on the surface, but they can have a critical difference in how you write a program. If you set up a program to handle only the words *yes* and *no*, your program will have a problem if users type in "Maybe," or if they mistype a word.

You can eliminate this problem and provide the user with more direction to the responses you seek by giving them a specific set of choices from which to select. This can be accomplished through the use of check boxes and option buttons.

Check boxes and option buttons are great for small numbers of options, but sometimes you need the capability to handle a large number of options. For example, you might want to allow your users to pick the state in which they live instead of having to type it in a text box. Trying to cram 50 option buttons onto a form would be difficult and would make for a poorly designed form. Fortunately, there is another solution to the problem: lists.

Visual Basic provides two basic types of lists to handle large numbers of choices—list boxes and combo boxes. Lists can support a single choice or multiple choices. Some lists even allow the user to enter values that are not on the list.

Each of these controls used for obtaining user input will be discussed in the remainder of this chapter. We'll also look at scroll bars, which give the user an easy way to specify a value within a controlled range.

Checking for Yes or No

Visual Basic's CheckBox control is used to get an answer of either "yes" or "no" from the user. It works like a light switch. Either it is on or it is off; there is no in between. When a check box is on, a check mark (✓) is displayed in the box. This indicates that the answer to the check box's corresponding question is "Yes." When the check box is off, or unchecked, the box is empty, indicating an answer of "No." Figure 9.3 shows a selected (on) and deselected (off) box.

Part
II
Ch
9

N O T E The check mark or empty box format is characteristic of the standard-form check box. If you set the check box's Style property to 1-Graphical, pictures are used to indicate checked and unchecked.

FIG. 9.3

A check box can indicate a "Yes" or "No" response to a question.

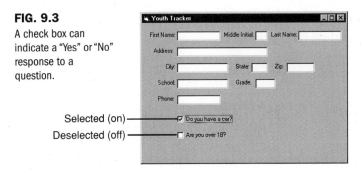

The prompts used in a check box do not necessarily have to be in the form of a question. If you have looked at some of the option dialog boxes used for programs, you have seen check boxes used to specify which options should be turned on. The prompt for the check box is simply the option name, instead of a question. Figure 9.4 shows the Environment Options dialog box for Visual Basic, which shows this type of use.

FIG. 9.4

In the Environment tab of Visual Basic's Options dialog box, users can choose the templates they want to be shown by selecting check boxes.

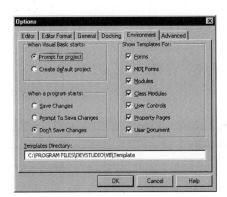

Creating a Check Box

Although the check box has been around for a while, Visual Basic 5 has added a new twist to the old standard. When a check box's Style property is set to 1-Standard or 2-Graphical, your check box will appear in one of the following ways:

- *Standard* check boxes use the familiar box that either is empty or contains a check mark.
- *Graphical* check boxes look like command buttons. When the check box is "unchecked," it appears in the up position. When it is "checked," it appears in the down position.

The appearance of each of these check box styles is shown in Figure 9.5.

FIG. 9.5

Graphical-style check boxes can give a new appearance to your programs.

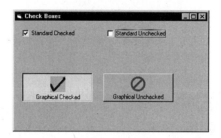

 To create a check box, select CheckBox control from the Toolbox and draw one (or more) on your form. When you first draw the check box, it has the default caption (prompt) of Check1. Since this will have absolutely no meaning to a user, you need to change the caption to something more descriptive. Select the Caption property from the Properties window and change it to something meaningful. At this point, what you do to control the appearance of the check box depends on the style of check box you select.

Controlling the Appearance of a Standard Check Box   If you are creating a standard check box, leave the Style property in its default setting of 0-Standard. After you have selected the standard style, there are several things you can do to change the appearance of the check box:

- Change the font used for the control's prompt.
- Modify the ForeColor and BackColor properties to change the control's colors.
- Change the Appearance property to create either a Flat or 3-D appearance.
- Change the Alignment property to determine on which side of the box the prompt is placed.

The effects of the Appearance and Alignment properties are shown in Figure 9.6. The default value of the Appearance property is 3-D and the default value of the Alignment property is left-justified. Both the Alignment and the Appearance properties are read-only at runtime; this means that they can only be set while you are in the design environment. You cannot change these properties with program code.

Flat appearance   3-D appearance

FIG. 9.6
By modifying properties
of your check boxes,
you can produce a wide
variety of visual effects.

Left-justified text⌐

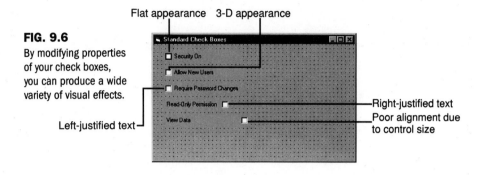

──Right-justified text
──Poor alignment due
to control size

CAUTION

If you use right justification for the check box, make sure that the control is sized so that the box is next to the prompt. Otherwise, a misalignment (like the one in Figure 9.6) can cause confusion for the user.

Controlling the Appearance of a Graphical Check Box   If you are creating a graphical check box, set the Style property to 1–Graphical. Several of the properties that you can set for the Standard check box also can influence the appearance of the graphical check box. Specifically, you can set the font used for the prompt, and you can set the colors of the check box. Also, the Appearance property can be used to give the control a flat or 3-D appearance. The Alignment property has no effect on the graphical check box.

However, these properties are not the really great feature of the graphical check box—the greatest feature is that you can include pictures on the check box. In fact, you can assign three different pictures to the check box, one for each of the three different states. The properties used to set the pictures, and the check box states they represent, are summarized in Table 9.2.

Table 9.2   Picture Used to Indicate the State of the Check Box

Property	State	Description
DisabledPicture	Disabled	The Enabled property of the check box has been set to False. This indicates that the user cannot access this check box.
DownPicture	Checked	This indicates that the user has selected the option represented by the check box.
Picture	Unchecked	The user has not selected this check box.

To set any one of these picture properties, you can enter the file name (including path) of a bitmap or other graphics file. You also can use the Load Picture dialog box to select a picture to be loaded. This is the easier of the two methods for selecting a picture. Figure 9.7 shows the various states of a graphical check box.

Setting the Initial Value   No matter which style of check box you choose to create, one final thing that you need to do is set the initial state for the control, either checked or unchecked. Whether the check box is checked or not is controlled by the Value property. If you want the check box to be checked when the program starts, set the Value property to 1–Checked; otherwise leave the property with a setting of 0–Unchecked, which is the default value.

> **N O T E**   There is a third setting possible for the check box's Value property. The setting is 2–Grayed. When set to this value, the check box will show a gray check mark in the box. This usually indicates that the choice represented by the check box *must* be True, and, thus, the user cannot change it. The user cannot set the check box to this value. ■

Determining the User's Choice

When a check box is shown on a form, the user can change the value of the check box by clicking it (unless it's gray). The user also can use the Tab key to move the focus to the check box and then press the spacebar to change its value. One click of the mouse or one press of the spacebar toggles (changes) the value from checked to unchecked, or vice versa. A second click returns the check box to its original setting.

For most programs, you will want to determine in your code whether the check box is checked. You do this by looking at the Value property. The code in Listing 9.1 shows how you would set the global options in a program using an Options dialog box comprised of check boxes. Note the use of the intrinsic constant vbChecked, which represents a Value property setting of 1. The intrinsic constants vbUnchecked and vbGrayed also are available to represent the other possible values. The form used for this dialog box is shown in Figure 9.8.

Listing 9.1   OPTIONS.FRM—Setting Global Options Using a Series of Check Boxes

```
glbSecurity = False
glbAddUser = False
glbPassChange = False
If chkSecurity.Value = vbChecked Then glbSecurity = True
If chkAddUser.Value = vbChecked Then glbAddUser = True
If chkPassChange.Value = vbChecked Then glbPassChange = True
```

```
'************************
' Alternate coding
'************************
If chkSecurity = vbChecked Then glbSecurity = True
If chkAddUser = vbChecked Then glbAddUser = True
If chkPassChange = vbChecked Then glbPassChange = True
```

N O T E While specifying the Value property makes reading the code easier, Value is the default property of the check box. Therefore, the code could be written the way it is shown in the last three lines of Listing 9.1. ■

FIG. 9.8

A user may select any number of check boxes, such as those contained in a typical Options dialog box.

N O T E You can provide an access key for check boxes by specifying an ampersand (&) in the Caption property immediately before the desired access key character. For example, if a check box's Caption property is &Registered Voter, the user can check or uncheck it by pressing Alt+R, rather than clicking the mouse. The same concept applies to option buttons, which are discussed in the following section. ■

Picking One Option Out of Many

Another way to allow users to make choices is through the use of option buttons. Option buttons let the user select a single item out of a group of items. This is the equivalent of a multiple-choice test. You can choose one, and only one, option button from a group. A typical option button group is shown in Figure 9.9.

FIG. 9.9

Option buttons provide a "pick one" capability for your programs.

Option buttons work like the speed selection buttons on a blender. If you press down one button, all the other buttons come up. The option buttons work the same way insofar as that, when you select one button, whichever other button was currently selected becomes deselected.

Creating a Set of Buttons

To use option buttons, you need to create a button for each possible choice the user can select. For instance, you might have the user select eye color from the choices blue, hazel, green, or brown. For this, you would need four option buttons.

 Placing the Buttons on the Form To create the set of option buttons, you draw each button on the form and set its properties. Like the check box, the prompt for the option button is contained in the `Caption` property. To create the form shown in Figure 9.9, draw four buttons on the form and set the `Caption` of each button to one of the four eye color choices—blue, hazel, green, and brown. For other programs, you might have more or fewer options than four. You can create as many option buttons as are needed to allow for all the choices you want to present to your user.

TIP If you need to include the possibility of an option other than the ones you have presented, you can use an option button labeled "Other" and have a text box next to it to accept the user's entry. The text box would be enabled only when the user selected the "Other" button.

Setting the Appearance of the Buttons Option buttons have the same capabilities for controlling the appearance of an individual button as a check box. You can, of course, choose different fonts for the prompts, and different colors, too. As with the check box, you also can change the `Alignment` property of the option buttons to place the circle to the right or left of the prompt; however, if you use right-justification, make sure that the control isn't so large that the caption is too far from the button.

The arrangement of individual buttons within the group is an additional factor in the appearance of option buttons. You can arrange buttons either horizontally or vertically, as shown in Figure 9.10. My personal preference is to use vertical groups when using standard-style buttons so that all the circles in the buttons are aligned. If you are using Graphical-style buttons, the arrangement is less important.

FIG. 9.10

Option buttons may be arranged in either horizontal or vertical groups, depending on your preference.

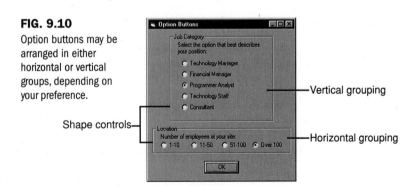

Like the check box, option buttons in Visual Basic 5 can be created in either of two styles—standard or graphical. To choose the type of button, you set the `Style` property of the button. For the graphical-style button, you then set the pictures that will be displayed for each of the button states. The different styles of option buttons are shown in Figure 9.11.

FIG. 9.11

Your choice of standard or graphical option buttons can profoundly affect your program's appearance.

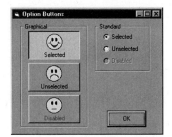

N O T E Although it isn't required that you use the same style for all the option buttons on your form, it is a good idea to use a consistent style to avoid confusing the user. This will also help prevent forms that look too cluttered with unnecessary graphics. ■

Choosing the Initial Button   Once you have placed all the required buttons on the form, you probably will want to designate one of the buttons as the initial choice. To do this, select the button you want to be the initial choice and set its `Value` property to `True`. The circle associated with this button becomes a filled circle (or the graphical button displays the picture in the `DownPicture` property). All the other buttons on the form change to empty circles, or display the picture in the `Picture` property. (Remember, only one button can be selected at a time.)

Determining the User's Selection

When the option buttons are displayed in your program, the user can choose one by clicking it. A button also may be selected by using the cursor keys. Whichever option button has the focus is the one that has the filled circle. The filled circle indicates the choice on-screen.

Since your program can't see the screen to tell which option button is selected, it needs another means to ascertain which button the user picked. The `Value` property of each option button tells your program whether that particular button is selected. The property is set to `True` for the selected option button and `False` for all others. Therefore, you need to examine the `Value` property of each option button to find the one that is `True`.

Looking at the eye color example, the code in Listing 9.2 examines the `Value` property of the option buttons and prints out the appropriate eye color on the form. To be able to run this code, we added a command button (which we named `cmdColorChoice`) to the form. The code is contained in the `Click` event procedure for the command button.

Listing 9.2 EYECOLOR.FRM—Checking for the Selected Button Using a Series of If Statements

```
Private Sub cmdColorChoice_Click()
    Form1.Cls
    If BlueEyes.Value Then
        Form1.Print "Your eyes are blue"
    ElseIf GreenEyes.Value Then
        Form1.Print "Your eyes are green"
    ElseIf HazelEyes.Value Then
        Form1.Print "Your eyes are hazel"
    ElseIf BrownEyes.Value Then
        Form1.Print "Your eyes are brown"
    End If
End Sub
```

Creating Multiple Groups of Option Buttons

Although only one option button placed *directly* on a form can be selected at a time, there is a way to give your users choices from several groups of buttons at the same time. Grouping your buttons allows users to select items cafeteria-style, like one entree, one vegetable, one dessert, and one drink. When the buttons are grouped properly, the user can select one, but only one, button from each group of buttons. The cafeteria example is shown in Figure 9.12.

FIG. 9.12

You can create multiple option-button groups that enable the user to select one button from each group.

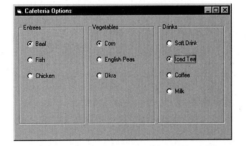

The secret to creating button groups is the use of a *container* control, which is a control that can hold other controls within its borders. There are several controls that can be used for this purpose, including the Frame control, the Picture control, the SSTab control, and the Shape control (refer to Figure 9.10). Each of these controls can hold other controls within its borders. Any controls placed within a container control are treated as a part of the container. This means that when a container is moved, all the controls within it move, too. Likewise, if a container is disabled, none of the controls in it are accessible.

The purpose of using a container with option buttons is to segregate the buttons within the container from buttons that are on the form or in another container. This means that the user can select one button from each container, in addition to one button that is on the form itself.

You can create as many containers as you need. Refer to Chapter 13, "Using Containers," for more detailed information about working with containers.

▶ **See** "Creating Groups of Option Buttons," **p. 341**

Because your users now can select a button from each group, you need a set of statements, such as the ones in Listing 9.2, for each group of buttons.

> **N O T E** While check boxes and option buttons may appear to be very similar, the fact that only one option button (within a group) may be selected makes them quite different functionally. For example, if you offer the user a group of check boxes, you can obtain multiple on/off responses at once that you couldn't get with option buttons. This is handy when a question you ask the user might have more than one valid response (the responses aren't mutually exclusive). Also, if you have a group of option buttons, the user can't deselect all options if one option has been selected. The user can select and deselect check boxes at will. This is an important consideration if you want your user to be able to select none of your choices. ▪

Working with Lists

Often, you may want to give your user a greater number of choices than might be feasible with check boxes and option buttons. Visual Basic supplies two controls that allow you to present your user with a list of choices. Each of these controls has the capability of presenting your user with a list that can get rather lengthy if necessary.

The most straightforward control of this type is the ListBox control. We'll discuss the other one, the ComboBox control, a little later in the section "Using Combo Boxes to Handle Choices."

Making a List

The simplest control that can be used to present a list of choices is the ListBox control. Figure 9.13 shows a simple list used to pick a state abbreviation for use on a mailing label. This simple list shows all the components that make up the list box.

FIG. 9.13
A simple list box contains a series of choices for the user.

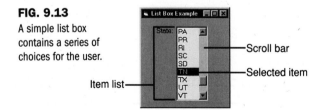

Item list—

Scroll bar

Selected item

The key parts of the list box are the following:

- *Item list*   This is the list of items from which the user can select. These items are added to the list in the design environment or by your program as it is running.

- *Selected item*   This is the item that is chosen by the user. Depending on the style of list you choose, a selected item is indicated by a highlight bar or by a check in the box next to the item.

- *Scroll bar*   This indicates that there are more items on the list than fit in the box and provides the user with an easy way to view the additional items.

To the user, the simple list box is similar to choosing channels on their TV. The cable company decides which channels to put on the selection list. The customer then can pick any of these channels, but can't add one to the list if they don't like any of the choices provided. With the list box, the choices are set up by you, the programmer; the user can select only from the items you decide should be available.

 Setting Up the List Box   When you first draw a list box on the form, it shows only the border of the box and the text List1 (for the first list box). There is no scroll bar present and, of course, there are no list items. A vertical scroll bar is added to the list box when you have listed more items than fit in the box. This is done automatically by the control.

After you draw the list box, the next step in setting it up is to add items to the list. These will be the choices available to the user. The list items are stored in a string array in the List property of the list box. Each list item is an element in this array. To add items to the list at design time, select the List property from the Properties dialog box. You will see the text (List) and a down arrow in the property field. Click the down arrow to access the list item input area, as shown in Figure 9.14.

FIG. 9.14

You add items to a list box by using the item input area of the *List* property.

ListBox control—

List item input area—

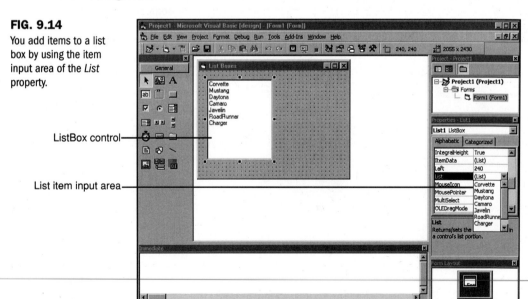

You add items to the list by typing in the text that you want to appear in the list box. Each line in the List property corresponds to a selection that is presented to the user. After you add an item to the list, press Ctrl+Enter to move to the next line of the list.

After you have added all the items you need, press Enter to accept the list. At this point, the list box displays all the items you have entered and, if necessary, includes a vertical scroll bar at the right of the list. Note that the list box doesn't have a horizontal scroll bar if the choices are too wide for the control, so you should make sure that the list box is wide enough to display all of its entries. It's also a good idea to keep the items' textual names as short as possible to help avoid this problem.

Part
II
Ch
9

Modifying the Item List from Your Program   There may be situations at runtime where you want to modify the list of items displayed in the list. For example, if you are using a list box to display food items, you might want to set up the list so that meat items are not displayed for a vegetarian user.

To accommodate these types of situations, the list box allows you to use code to add items to or remove items from the list box as the program is running. If you want, you even can place code in the Load event procedure of your form to set up the initial list, instead of typing the entries in through the Properties window. To manipulate items in the list, use the AddItem and RemoveItem methods.

Using the AddItem method is very straightforward. You simply specify the name of the ListBox control, the name of the method, and specify a string that you want added to the list. This is shown in the following line of code:

```
lstAvailable.AddItem "Corvette"
```

The list item can be a string of text or a number (though numbers are not typically handled by lists), and can be in the form of a literal value or a variable. Remember, if you are using a literal string, you need to enclose it within double quotes. There is an optional parameter, Index, that may be used with the AddItem method. This parameter specifies the location within the list where you want the new item to appear. You will specify the index value of the item in front of which you want to add your item. For example, if there are five items in the list and you want your item to appear ahead of the third item, you use code like the following:

```
lstAvailable.AddItem "Corvette", 2
```

N O T E   The Index of the list items is zero-based. This means that the first item on the list has an index of 0, the second item has an index of 1, and so on. ■

If you include an index value, it must be separated from the list item by a comma. Including the index causes the item to be placed exactly where you want it. If you omit the index, the item is placed at the end of the list, or in alphabetic order if the Sorted property is set to True.

> **CAUTION**
>
> If you specify an index value that is outside the range of indexes in the list box, an error will be generated. You can avoid this by checking the `ListCount` property, which reports the number of items currently in the list, to make sure this doesn't occur. Also, specifying an index less than `0` will cause an error.

Deleting an item from the list is a little trickier than adding an item because you need to know the index of the item to be deleted. If you know in advance what the index is, you can simply delete the item by using the `RemoveItem` method. For example, the following code deletes the first item in the list:

```
lstAvailable.RemoveItem 0
```

In a more typical situation, you will want to delete an item that the user has selected. You will learn about determining the user's selection in the section "Determining the User's Choice" a little later in the chapter. For now, you can look at the code in Listing 9.3 to see how to delete the selected item.

Listing 9.3   *LISTDEMO.FRM*—Removing a Selected Item by Using the *RemoveItem* Method

```
Dim LstIdx As Integer
LstIdx = lstAvailable.ListIndex
If LstIdx >= 0 Then lstAvailable.RemoveItem LstIdx
```

In another situation, you might want to remove a specific item based on the item's text. This involves searching the list to find the item and then using the `RemoveItem` method to delete the item (see Listing 9.4).

Listing 9.4   *LISTDEMO.FRM*—Searching the Items to Find the One to Be Deleted

```
Dim I, LstIdx As Integer
LstIdx = -1
For I = 0 To lstAvailable.ListCount - 1
    If lstAvailable.List(I) = "Mustang" Then
        LstIdx = I
        Exit For
    End If
Next I
If LstIdx >= 0 Then lstAvailable.RemoveItem LstIdx
```

 TIP If you want to remove all the items in a list, use the `Clear` method (for example, `lstAvailable.Clear`). Essentially, this method throws away your entire list.

Sorting the List In the preceding section, you saw how to modify the list by adding and removing items. You also saw that you can add an item to a specific location by specifying an index. But what do you do if you want your entire list sorted in alphabetic order?

Fortunately, this is a very simple task. To sort the list, you simply set the Sorted property to True. Then, no matter in which order you enter your items, they appear to the user in alphabetic order. The indexes of the list items are adjusted as they are added so that they remain in proper order.

Setting the Appearance of the List In previous versions of Visual Basic, lists like the one shown in Figure 9.13 were the only available styles—In Visual Basic 5, you now have a choice. You can use a standard list, or you can make your list look like a series of check boxes. You handle the selection of the list type by setting the Style property. The two settings of the property are 0–Standard and 1–Checkbox (see Figure 9.15). This property also can be changed at run time by setting its value to one of the intrinsic constants vbListBoxStandard or vbListBoxCheckBox, respectively.

FIG. 9.15
Checkbox-style list boxes provide the user with an intuitive way to select multiple items.

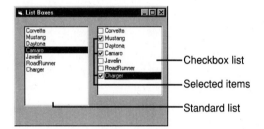

Checkbox list
Selected items
Standard list

Another way to change the list's appearance is to use the Columns property. The default value of the property is 0. This results in the standard list box previously discussed. Setting the property to 1 causes the list to be presented one column at a time, but to scroll horizontally instead of vertically. Setting the property to greater than 1 causes the list to display in the number of columns specified by the property (for example, a value of 2 displays the list in two columns). When the list is displayed in multiple columns, the list scrolls horizontally. The Columns property can be used with either the Standard or Checkbox styles of lists. These styles are shown in Figure 9.16.

FIG. 9.16
You also can create multicolumn lists.

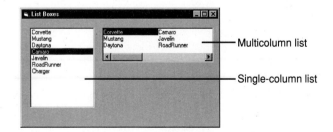

Multicolumn list
Single-column list

The list works the same way no matter how many columns you use.

Part
II
Ch
9

Determining the User's Choice

For most programs, you will want to retrieve the user's selection and do something with it. To find out what the user selected, you need to work with two properties of the list box: the `ListIndex` and `List` properties.

The `ListIndex` property reports the index number of the item that was selected. You then can retrieve the actual item from the `List` property by using the index number. The following code displays the selected item in a text box:

```
idx = Fruits.ListIndex
ChosenFruit.Text = Fruits.List(idx)
```

Handling Multiple Choices   There are occasions when you need to let the user select more than one item from a list. The list box supports this with the `MultiSelect` property. This property has three possible settings: `0-None`, `1-Simple`, and `2-Extended`.

A setting of `0-None` means that multiple selections are not permitted, and the list box can accept only one selection at a time. This is the default setting. The other two settings both permit multiple selections; the difference is in how they let the user make selections. This will be explained through the example that follows.

One great use of multiple item selections is in an order-entry system. When a person places an order with a company, they usually are buying more than one item. A multiple-selection list allows the salesperson to select all the items for the order and then to process the entire order at once.

With a setting of `1-Simple`, users can click an item with the mouse to select it, or click a selected item to deselect it. If they is use the keyboard to make the selection, they can use the cursor keys to move the focus (the dotted line border) to an item, then press the spacebar to select or deselect it. Figure 9.17 shows a list with multiple items selected.

FIG. 9.17

You can select multiple items from a list with the proper setting of the `MultiSelect` property.

The other setting of the `MultiSelect` property, `2-Extended`, is more complex. In this mode, users quickly can select a range of items by clicking the first item in the range and then, while holding down the Shift key, click the last item in the range—all items in between the first and last item are selected. To add or delete a single item to or from this selection, the user holds down the Ctrl key while clicking the item.

Getting All the Selections   Getting the selections from a multiple-selection list box is a little different than getting them for a single selection. Since the ListIndex works only for a single selection, you can't use it. Instead, you have to examine each item in the list to determine whether it is selected.

Whether an item is selected or not is indicated by the list box's Selected property. This property is an array that has an element for each item in the list. The value of the Selected property for each item is either True (the item is selected) or False (the item is not selected).

You also need to know how many items are in the list so that you can set up the loop to check all the selections. This information is contained in the ListCount property. The following code prints onto the form the name of each list item that is selected:

```
numitm = Fruits.ListCount
For I = 0 to numitm - 1
   If Fruits.Selected(I) Then Form1.Print Fruits.List(I)
Next I
```

Keeping Other Data in the List

What if you want the user to see a meaningful list, such as a list of names, but you also want to have the list remember a number that's associated with each name? The ItemData property of a list box is, in essence, an array of long integers, one for each item that has been added to the list box. No matter what position an item occupies in the list box, the ItemData array remembers the number associated with that particular element. This happens even if the list box's Sorted property is True, meaning that items won't necessarily be listed in the order that they're added. For example, the ItemData array element associated with the first item in a list box named List1 can be accessed as List1.ItemData(0). The array element for the currently selected list box entry can be accessed with List1.ItemData(List1.ListIndex) (recall that the ListIndex property reports which item is currently selected).

As items are added to a list box, an associated element is created in the ItemData array. Of course, it's your job to place the appropriate value into the proper position of the ItemData array. So how can your program know into which list box position a newly added item went, especially if the list box is sorted? Visual Basic makes this easy. A list box's NewIndex property contains the index number of the most recently added item in the list. The following code adds a new customer to a sorted list box and then adds that customer's account number to the correct element of the associated ItemData array:

```
lstCustomers.AddItem "Thomas, June"
lstCustomers.ItemData(lstCustomers.NewIndex) = "21472301"
```

Now, our program can allow the user to select from a list box containing meaningful elements (names), but the background processing can be done with an associated number, which is easier for the computer. This is illustrated in the Click event procedure of the list box:

```
Private Sub lstCustomers_Click()
    Dim lgThisCust As Long
    lgThisCust = lstCustomers.ItemData(lstCustomers.ListIndex)
    Call LookUpAccount(lgThisCust)
End Sub
```

Creating a Two-Column Pick List

One of the best ways to demonstrate the use of the methods for modifying a list is to create what is known as a two-column pick list. You probably have seen these pick lists used in a number of applications. A form contains two lists; one list contains the available choices and the other list contains the user's selections. As the user selects an item from the available list, the item is removed from that list and is added to the selected list. If the user removes a selection, the process is reversed. These lists also give the user the capability to select all items, or remove all items. Figure 9.18 shows the list created by the following example.

FIG. 9.18

Two-column pick lists clearly show the user's choices.

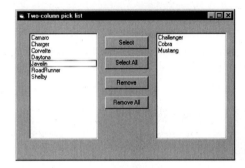

To start creating the list, follow these steps:

1. Place two ListBox controls on your form. For aesthetic purposes, these two controls should be the same size and should be lined up vertically with each other.

2. To match the sample code, name one of the ListBox controls lstAvailable and the other lstSelected.

3. Set the Sorted property of each ListBox control to True. This makes it easier for your users to find individual items.

4. Next, create an array of four control buttons in between the lists. These buttons will handle the user options of Select, Select All, Remove, and Remove All.

5. The key to the pick list is the code for the command buttons:

   - For the buttons that remove or add a single selection, you need to determine the index of the selection, remove it from one list, and add it to the other.

   - For the buttons that process all items, you need a loop that runs through all the items on the list, adding them to the other list and then clearing the source list.

   The code for all this is shown in Listing 9.5.

Listing 9.5   *TWOCOLUMN.FRM*—Two-Column Pick Lists Make Use of the *AddItem*, *RemoveItem*, and *Clear* Methods

```
Private Sub cmdSelect_Click(Index As Integer)
Dim I, LstIdx As Integer, MovItm As String
Select Case Index
    Case 0
        'Single selection
        LstIdx = lstAvailable.ListIndex
        If LstIdx < 0 Then Exit Sub
        MovItm = lstAvailable.List(LstIdx)
        lstSelected.AddItem MovItm
        lstAvailable.RemoveItem LstIdx
    Case 1
        'Select all
        If lstAvailable.ListCount = 0 Then Exit Sub
        For I = 0 To lstAvailable.ListCount - 1
            MovItm = lstAvailable.List(I)
            lstSelected.AddItem MovItm
        Next I
        lstAvailable.Clear
    Case 2
        'Single removal
        LstIdx = lstSelected.ListIndex
        If LstIdx < 0 Then Exit Sub
        MovItm = lstSelected.List(LstIdx)
        lstAvailable.AddItem MovItm
        lstSelected.RemoveItem LstIdx
    Case 3
        'Remove all
        If lstSelected.ListCount = 0 Then Exit Sub
        For I = 0 To lstSelected.ListCount - 1
            MovItm = lstSelected.List(I)
            lstAvailable.AddItem MovItm
        Next I
        lstSelected.Clear
End Select
End Sub
```

Part
II

Ch
9

As shown in Listing 9.5, the code works only when the user clicks the command button. You would probably also want your users to be able to select items directly from the list. You can do this by placing code to call the command button procedure in the Db1Click event procedure of each list (see Listing 9.6).

Listing 9.6 *TWOCOLUMN.FRM*—**Using the *DblClick* Event to Allow the User to Pick with the Mouse**

```
Private Sub lstAvailable_DblClick()
cmdSelect_Click 0
End Sub

Private Sub lstSelected_DblClick()
cmdSelect_Click 2
End Sub
```

As an exercise, you can modify this pick list to handle multiple selections by the user in each list.

Using Combo Boxes to Handle Choices

Another control that enables you to present lists to the user is the ComboBox control. The combo box can be used in three different forms.

- ■ *The drop-down combo box* Presents the user with a text box combined with a drop-down list. The user can either select an item from the list portion or type an item in the text box portion.

- ■ *The simple combo box* Displays a text box and a list that doesn't drop down. As with the drop-down combo box, the user can either select an item from the list portion or type an item in the text box portion.

- ■ *The drop-down list* Displays a drop-down list box from which the user can make a choice. He cannot enter an item that is not in the list.

The combo box has many things in common with the list box. Both use the AddItem, RemoveItem, and Clear methods to modify the contents of the list. Both can present a sorted or an unsorted list. Both support the ItemData array and NewIndex property, mentioned earlier. However, there are some things that one box can do but the other cannot.

The main thing the combo box lacks is support for multiple selections. The key advantage of the combo box, though, is that it allows the user to enter a choice that is not on the list. This works like an election ballot, where you can choose a candidate from the list of those running, or write in your own.

N O T E The drop-down list does not support the user entering choices that are not on the list. ■

FIG. 9.19
Each of the three styles of combo boxes behaves differently when the user selects his choice.

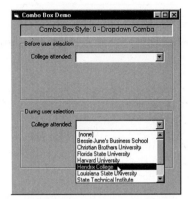

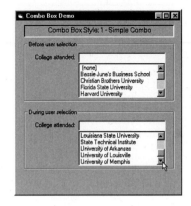

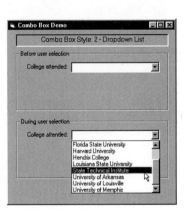

This section explains how to use the different forms of the combo box. The drop-down list is examined first because it is the simplest of the combo box styles.

Creating a Drop-Down List

A drop-down list functions exactly like a list box. The key difference is that the drop-down list takes up less room on your form. When users want to select an item from the list, they click the down arrow, located to the right of the box, to extend the list. After the drop-down list appears, they then make a selection by clicking the item they want to choose. After the selection is made, the list retracts like a window shade, and the selection appears in the box.

You create a drop-down list by drawing a combo box on the form, and then setting the Style property to 2-Dropdown List. You then can begin adding items to the list by using the List property, just like you did for the list box. However, keep in mind that the user can't add an item that's not in the list.

Working with Choices that Are Not on the List

The drop-down list is very useful for presenting a number of choices in a small amount of space. However, the real power of the combo box is its capability to allow users to enter choices other than those on the list. This capability is available with the other two styles of combo box—the simple combo box and the drop-down combo box. Both styles provide a list of items from which you can select and both allow you to enter other values. The difference between the two styles is the way in which you access items already in the list.

 A simple combo box is set up by drawing the control on the form, and then setting the `Style` property to `1–Simple Combo`. With the simple combo box, the user can access the items in the list using the mouse or the arrow keys. If the user doesn't find what he wants on the list, he can type in a new choice.

The drop-down combo box works like a combination of the drop-down list and the simple combo box. You select an item from the list the same way you would for a drop-down list, but you also can enter a value that is not on the list. The drop-down combo box is created by setting the `Style` property to `0–Dropdown Combo`. The drop-down combo box is the default setting of the `Style` property.

As with the list box and the drop-down list, you can use the `List` property to add items to the list of selections. You also can modify the list for any of the combo box styles while your program is running. As with the list box control, you modify the list by using the `AddItem`, `RemoveItem`, and `Clear` methods.

Setting the Initial Choice

Depending on your application, you might want to set the initial item for a combo box. An example of setting the choice is in a program that needs to know your citizenship. You can provide a list of choices, but set the initial value to "U.S. citizen" because that would be the selection of most people in this country.

You set the initial value by using the `ListIndex` property, as shown in the following code:

```
Fruits.ListIndex = 3
```

This statement causes the fourth item in the list to be displayed when the combo box is first shown. (Remember, the list indexes start at `0`.) Setting the initial choice will work with any of the three combo box styles. You also can set the initial choice of the combo box by setting the `Text` property to the desired value. If you do not set an initial choice by setting the index, the text contained in the `Text` property will be displayed.

> **CAUTION**
>
> The initial value of the `Text` property is the name of the combo box. If you do not want this to appear in your combo box on start up, set either the `ListIndex` property or the `Text` property in code.

TIP If you want your combo box to be blank when the form is first shown, simply delete the contents of the Text property while you are in the design environment.

Retrieving the User's Choice

Getting the user's choice from a combo box is different than getting it from a list box. With a combo box, you need the capability to handle users entering a value that is not on the list. You can retrieve the user's choice with the Text property of the combo box. The Text property holds any value that is typed in by the user, or holds the item selected from the list. The following line of code prints the user's selection:

```
Form1.Print cboFruits.Text
```

Adding a User-Created Item to the List

If you include a combo box as part of a data entry form, you may want the capability to take any new items entered by the user and add them to the list of choices. That way, when the user enters another record, they won't have to type the same choice again.

The combo box does not have a specific method to handle this function, nor does the addition of a new item trigger a particular event. However, you can take advantage of the fact that there will be more than one control on the form into which the user must enter data. A typical data entry form for a personnel application is shown in Figure 9.20. The combo box to which you want to add choices is the one for College Attended. As users enter colleges not on the list, those colleges are added to the list so that they only have to be entered one time.

FIG. 9.20
This typical application uses a combo box to obtain college information.

Combo box

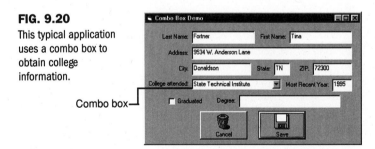

Handling this enhancement makes one assumption—in almost all cases, after users enter the college name, they will move to the next field to enter more information, or click a command button to execute a task. Either way, the focus moves from the combo box to another control. This triggers the LostFocus event. Therefore, you can use this event as the trigger to add new items to the list. When the user moves the focus, your code first needs to retrieve the value of the Text property as the new item. Next, you need to scan the list of items to make sure that the item does not exist already. Then, if the item is, in fact, new, you can add the item to the list. Listing 9.7 illustrates how this can be accomplished.

Listing 9.7   *COMBODEMO.FRM*—Adding User Entries to the List

```
Dim NewItm As String, I As Integer, AddNewItm As Boolean
AddNewItm = True
With cboCountry
    NewItm = cboCountry.Text
    For I = 0 To .ListCount - 1
        If .List(I) = NewItm Then
            AddNewItm = False
            Exit For
        End If
    Next I
    If AddNewItm Then
        .AddItem NewItm
    End If
End With
```

Inputting Data with the Scroll Bars

You have seen scroll bars used in a text box for multiple line editing and in lists to access long lists of items. While they look basically the same, these scroll bars are different from the scroll bar controls in Visual Basic.

Scroll bars work like the volume control on your stereo system. Your stereo has minimum and maximum volume settings. The volume knob, or slider bar, enables you to set any volume in between the minimum and maximum ranges. Scroll bars also have minimum and maximum settings and let you use a slider to set a value anywhere within the range.

Visual Basic provides two types of scroll bars for entering numerical data: the vertical scroll bar and the horizontal scroll bar. These two controls are shown in Figure 9.21. The two scroll bars are referred to in the documentation as the VScrollBar and HscrollBar controls, respectively.

FIG. 9.21

The VScrollBar and HScrollBar controls can be used to enter or display numerical data.

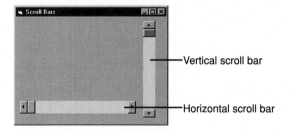

Vertical scroll bar

Horizontal scroll bar

The only difference between these two controls is the orientation of the bar on the form. All the methods, events, and properties of the controls are the same. The following discussion examines the HScrollBar control, but it applies equally to the VScrollBar.

Setting Up the Bar

The scroll bar is capable of accepting whole numbers (integers) anywhere in the range of –32,768 to 32,767. One typical range is from 0 to 100, where the user enters a number as a percentage. Another possible use of scroll bars is to control the speaker volumes in a multimedia application. Also, if you have experimented with the colors in Windows, you have seen the scroll bars that enable you to enter the relative amounts of red, green, and blue that will appear in a color. These bars have a range of 0 to 255, the possible values of the color settings.

Setting the Upper and Lower Boundaries   The range of values that can be entered with the scroll bars is determined by the settings of the Min and Max properties. The Min property sets the lower boundary of the value range and has a default setting of 0. The Max property sets the upper boundary of the range and has a default value of 32,767. You can change the settings of these properties from the Properties window, or through the use of code statements, as shown in the following example. For this example, use the Properties window to set the Min property to 0 and the Max property to 100.

```
hsbPercent.Min = 0
hsbPercent.Max = 100
```

Controlling the Size of the Value Changes   If you have used a scroll bar in a word processor or other program, you know that clicking the arrow at either end of the bar moves you only a short distance, but clicking in between an arrow and the position button moves you a greater distance. The scroll bar controls work the same way, and you get to set how much the numbers will change with each kind of move. The number entered in a scroll bar is contained in the Value property. This property changes every time the user clicks the scroll bar or drags the position button, as indicated in Figure 9.22.

FIG. 9.22

Clicking various parts of the scroll bar changes its value by different amounts.

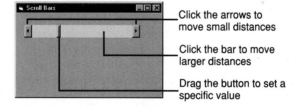

Click the arrows to move small distances

Click the bar to move larger distances

Drag the button to set a specific value

The amount that the Value property increases or decreases when an arrow is clicked is controlled by the SmallChange property, which gives you very fine control over the numbers being entered. Its default value is 1, which probably is a good number to use for most purposes.

When you click between the arrow and the position button, the Value property can change by a different amount than if you click an arrow. The amount of this change is set by the LargeChange property. The default setting of the LargeChange property is 1. The setting you use depends on your application. For example, a value of 10 is a good number if you are setting percentages.

T I P A good rule of thumb is to set the LargeChange property to a number about 5 to 10 percent of the total range (for example, a value of 50 for a 0 to 1000 range).

How to Show the User the Numbers

A scroll bar, by itself, is not all that useful. The user cannot determine the range of numbers. Without knowing the number range, making a guess at the actual value of the scroll bar is fruitless. There are several ways to display additional information about the scroll bar value that will make them easier for the user to work with. These options are discussed next.

First, you can tell the user the minimum and maximum values. You can do this by adding label controls above (or beside) each end of the scroll bar. Although these labels help users to see what is the approximate value, they still cannot see the exact value. The only way to know the actual value of the scroll bar is to display it in another control, such as a text box or label. Figure 9.23 shows these enhancements.

FIG. 9.23

Associating labels or text boxes with the scroll bar shows users the range and actual value.

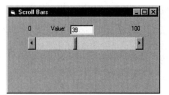

Assigning the value of the scroll bar to a text box is easy. You use a code statement like the following:

```
txtActValue.Text = hsbPercent.Value
```

The statement itself is the easy part. What's tricky is knowing where to put the statement. To show the value at all times, you actually have to place this statement in three events:

- *Load event*   The first event is the Load event for your form. Placing the assignment statement in this event displays the initial value of the scroll bar.

- *Change event*   The second location for the statement is the Change event of the scroll bar. This event is triggered each time the user clicks one of the arrows or clicks the bar. The Change event is triggered also when you release the mouse button after dragging the position button to a new location.

- *Scroll event*   Unfortunately, the Change event is not triggered while the position button is being dragged. If you want the user to be able to see the changes in the Value property while dragging the button, you need to place the code statement in a third location, the Scroll event of the scroll bar.

If you use a text box to display the actual value of the scroll bar, you can let the user enter a value directly in the text box. Then, using the Change event of the text box, you can update the value of the scroll bar accordingly. The code for this process is shown in Listing 9.8.

Listing 9.8 *SCROLLDEMO.FRM*—Updating the Scroll Bar from a Text Box

```
Dim ValSet As Integer
ValSet = Val(txtValue.Text)
If ValSet > hsbPercentage.Max Then ValSet = hsbPercentage.Max
If ValSet < hsbPercentage.Min Then ValSet = hsbPercentage.Min
hsbPercentage.Value = ValSet
```

Counting Time

Another control that comes in handy on occasion is the Timer control. This control works like the cooking timer on your microwave oven. It counts down a specified amount of time and then fires the Timer event. You can specify the action that should occur by writing code for the Timer control's Timer event procedure.

The timer works by counting the number of milliseconds (thousandths of a second) that have elapsed since the form containing the control was loaded, or since the Timer event was last fired. When the count reaches the amount set by the Interval property, the control triggers the Timer event and runs whatever code is present.

Setting Up the Timer

 You set up a Timer control by first drawing it on the form. At design time, the Timer control shows up as an icon on the form, no matter how large you draw it to begin with (see Figure 9.24). The Timer control is not visible on the form when your program is running.

FIG. 9.24

The Timer control is visible only at design time.

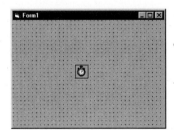

To make the control work, the Interval property is the only property that you need to set. You can set the Interval property for any value between 0 and 65,535. A setting of 0 disables the Timer control. Any other setting specifies the number of milliseconds that should elapse before the Timer event is triggered. The minimum setting, 1, is shorter than the blink of an eye. The maximum setting is just a little longer than a minute. If you want 10 seconds to elapse, set the Interval property to a value of 10,000.

Since the maximum value of the Interval property corresponds to about a minute, how can you set up longer time intervals? You set up code within the Timer event that tracks how many times the Interval has elapsed, as shown in Listing 9.9.

Listing 9.9   TIMERDEMO.FRM—Using a *Static* Variable to Track Multiple Minutes Elapsing

```
Private Sub tmr_Timer()
    Static ElTime
    If ElTime >= 20 Then
        MsgBox "Time's Up!"
        ElTime = 0
    Else
        ElTime = ElTime + 1
    End If
End Sub
```

The first line of the code defines the variable that tracks the number of times the interval has elapsed. The keyword Static means that the value of the variable is maintained even after the event procedure is ended, so it will be intact the next time the event procedure is executed. (For more information about Static variables, see Chapter 8, "Programming Visual Basic.")

▶ **See** "Determining Where a Variable Can Be Used," **p. 176**

The conditional statement determines whether the timer has elapsed 20 or more times. If so, a message box displays, informing the user. The number of times then is reset to 0 to start the cycle over again. If the number of times is less than 20, one is added to the ElTime variable and the procedure is exited.

By adjusting the Interval property of the timer and the number of times it elapses, you can make the Timer control count any amount of time.

Creating a Screen Blanker

A useful function for the Timer control is to blank the screen after a specified period of time. Screen-blanking routines were originally used to prevent damage to the screen from having the same image displayed for long periods of time. The more current usage is for security reasons. Many times, people are in the middle of an application and have to leave their desk for a few minutes to attend to other tasks. If the users are not careful, sensitive information can be left on-screen for anyone to see. Screen blankers provide a way to hide this information if there is no program activity for a specified period of time. Of course, this security measure would reasonably need to be enhanced with some type of password protection before the original screen is restored.

 The Timer control can be used to create a simple screen blanker for use with your programs. To start, add a Timer control to your main form. Set the Interval property of the timer to the desired amount of time. (For demonstration purposes, set the timer to 10 seconds, or an Interval value of 10,000.)

Next, add a second form to your program. You now need to change the `BackColor` property of the new form to black and change the `BorderStyle` property to `0-None`. This will give you a black form with no borders, captions, or buttons when the program is run. You then need to add the following line of code to the form's `Load` event:

```
frmScreenBlank.WindowState = vbMaximized
```

This code causes the form to be maximized as it is loaded, covering the entire screen.

Now all you need is code to activate the blank form and to deactivate it. The code to activate the form is placed in the `Timer` event of the Timer control on the first form. The code is as follows:

```
frmScreenBlank.Show
```

This causes the form to be loaded and displayed when the Timer event is triggered. Finally, to deactivate the blank form, place the following line in both the `Click` and `KeyPress` events of `frmScreenBlank`:

```
frmScreenBlank.Hide
```

This code causes the blank form to be hidden when a key is pressed or the mouse is clicked while the blank form is displayed. When the form is hidden, the original form and the rest of the screen once again displays. Now, run the code and try it for yourself.

To add to the security of the screen blanker, you can add a password routine to the code that hides the form. This way, the user has to enter a password before the screen displays again. You also might want to have the application terminate after a set period of time instead of just having the screen go blank.

From Here...

This chapter discussed the use of a number of standard controls that are included with Visual Basic. You have seen examples of how to use each one. You can enhance your understanding of these controls by practicing! Try using them in a variety of applications to see how they behave in different situations. For more information about using these controls and others with which they may interact, refer to the following chapters:

- To learn about using the Windows controls that can be accessed from a Visual Basic program, see Chapter 10, "Using the Windows Common Controls."
- For a discussion of the controls that have been recently added to Visual Basic, see Chapter 11, "Exploring New Visual Basic 5 Controls."
- To see how to arrange these and other controls in functional groups, see Chapter 13, "Using Containers."

Part II
Ch 9

CHAPTER 10

Using the Windows Common Controls

Visual Basic includes a group of common controls that enable you to develop programs with many of the same features as programs from Microsoft and other vendors. These controls let you create toolbars to supplement your menus, status bars to keep your users informed, progress bars to indicate the completion level of a task, and other neat controls. This chapter continues the in-depth discussion of controls that began in Chapter 9, "Using the Windows Standard Controls," by covering the capabilities of the Windows Common Controls. ■

Adding Toolbars to your program

With a little bit of programming, you can make your toolbars respond to changes in your program.

Keeping the user informed

A status bar allows you to inform users of program operations in a manner with which they are familiar.

Following a program's progress

When users run a task, they want to see action. A progress bar lets users know that a task is running and gives them an approximation of the time remaining until completion.

Making input easier for the user

Make numerical input simple with the Slider control.

Working with lists of objects

The TreeView and ListView controls provide the capability to implement Windows Explorer-style interfaces for working with lists.

Giving your application pages

The TabStrip control enables you to create multiple pages and allows your user to navigate among them.

Working with the Windows Common Controls

To use the controls described in this chapter, you must first make them available in your Toolbox. From the Visual Basic menu, choose Project, Components. When the Components dialog box appears, place a check mark next to Microsoft Windows Common Controls 5.0 and click OK. Your Toolbox will then be updated with the new controls.

Creating Toolbars

Toolbars, such as the one shown in Figure 10.1, are an integral part of Windows interface standards, so much so that Microsoft has packaged them into the COMCTL32.OCX custom control. Applications that don't have toolbars are becoming the exception to the rule for an obvious reason: Toolbars provide a convenient place on-screen for users to look for frequently used functions. Because the toolbar is normally near the top of the window, it provides a familiar place for the user to look in almost any application.

FIG. 10.1

A Visual Basic program can include the Toolbar control.

Toolbar ⏐

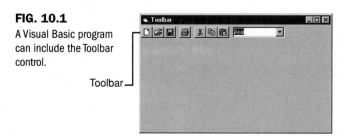

The Toolbar control works with an ImageList control, which holds all the button images. Visual Basic includes a number of images in the Graphics subdirectory. Icon and bitmap files can be stored in an ImageList control; the size of these pictures will influence the size of the toolbar buttons. Before you can design an effective toolbar, you need to pick out your images and add them to an image list.

Reviewing the Basics

Toolbars were first discussed in Chapter 5, "Adding Menus and Toolbars to Your Program," in which you saw how toolbars were used to supplement the menus of a program by placing commonly used functions where the user could get to them easily.

The Toolbar control enables you to create five different types of buttons:

- Push buttons that work like command buttons
- Check buttons that work in an on/off mode, like a check box
- Button groups that work like option buttons
- Separator buttons that create spaces in the toolbar
- Placeholder buttons that create empty space, allowing you to place other controls, such as combo boxes, on the toolbar

The ImageList control is used to hold the images that are placed on the toolbar buttons. The Toolbar and the ImageList controls can be set up through the Properties window and through the Property Pages of the controls.

▶ **See** "Creating a Toolbar for Your Application," **p. 121**

Creating a Toolbar with Code

Although you can set up a toolbar in the design environment, you can also set up and change a toolbar at runtime with program code. To use the Toolbar and other common controls successfully, you need to understand the concept of collections.

Understanding Collections   A *collection* is a group of objects. In the case of the ImageList control, there is a collection called `ListImages`. The objects stored in this particular collection are the images in the ImageList control. By manipulating the `ListImages` collection from code, you can add, remove, and change images.

Think of a collection as being similar to, but not exactly like, an array. You can access it like an array, as in the following line of code, which sets a form's picture to the first image in an ImageList control:

```
Set form1.Picture = ImageList1.ListImages(1).Picture
```

Notice that a specific object is referred to with its *index*—in this case, 1. Remember, a collection stores objects, unlike an array, which stores values. These objects have their own set of properties.

One special property that objects in a collection have is the `Key` property. An object's key is a text string that can be used in the same manner as an index:

```
Set form1.Picture = ImageList1.ListImages("Smiley Face").Picture
```

Of course, you have to set the key first, usually when an object is added to a collection. Each type of collection has `Add` and `Remove` methods defined that include `Key` and `Index` as parameters. If omitted, the index is supplied by Visual Basic. The key, however, is optional.

Setting Up the Toolbar   To set up a Toolbar control in code, you have to first set up an ImageList control (either in design mode or with code). Then, you can assign ImageList to the toolbar with the following statement:

```
Set ToolBar.ImageList = ImageList1
```

Next, you manipulate the toolbar's `Buttons` collection to create toolbar buttons. In the example below, a separator and standard button are added to a toolbar control, `tbrMain`:

```
tbrMain.Buttons.Add 1, "Sep1",, tbrSeparator, 0
tbrMain.Buttons.Add 2, "open","Open File" , tbrDefault, 1
```

In the example above, two additional `Button` objects are created in the `Buttons` collection by using the `Add` method. The first two parameters are the button's index and key, each of which must be unique. The third parameter is the button caption. The fourth parameter (`tbrSeparator` and `tbrDefault`) is a constant representing the type of button. Finally, an index value from the associated image list tells the toolbar which picture to use.

Part
II

Ch
10

The Add method can also work as a function. If used in this manner, it returns a pointer to the Button object just created. The preceding code could be rewritten like this:

```
Dim btn As Button

Set btn = tbrMain.Buttons.Add(, "Sep1", , tbrSeparator, 0)

Set btn = tbrMain.Buttons.Add(,"open", , tbrDefault)
btn.ToolTipText = "Click to open a file"
btn.Caption = "Open File"
btn.Image = 1
```

Note that the ToolTipText property must be defined from a Button object because it is not in the Add method's parameters. Also, in the preceding example, the Index properties will be defined automatically because they were not specified. This is generally the preferred way of doing things because, as objects are added and deleted from a collection, the index of a particular object will change. The Key, however, will always be associated with a specific object.

Your code can use the Key to determine which button was pressed. For example, consider the following code in the toolbar's ButtonClick event:

```
Private Sub Toolbar1_ButtonClick(ByVal Button As ComctlLib.Button)

    Select Case Button.Key
        Case "open"
            'Insert open file code here
        Case "save"
            'Insert save file code here
        Case "exit"
            'Insert code to end the program
    End Select

End Sub
```

The preceding code works great for buttons of type tbrDefault. However, if you have any tbrCheck buttons, you should have your code also check the Value property to see what the state of the button is:

```
        Case "boldface"
            If Button.value = tbrUnpressed then
                'Button is "Up" - Turn bold off
            Else
                'Button is "down" - Turn bold on
            End If
```

If you set the MixedState property of a button to True, it will always look grayed out—no matter what the value.

Monitoring the Status of Your Program

One of the most important aspects of any program is keeping the user informed about what is going on in the program at any given time. Users like to know whether a database is open, how many records there are in a set, and how many records have been processed so far in the current task. For a program such as a word processor, the users like to know what's the current page and what's the current position on that page. This type of information is called *status information*, which is usually displayed on-screen all the time, rather than in a message box.

Before the StatusBar control, Visual Basic programmers often used "fake" status bars made from panels and Label controls. These worked quite well (and still do today). However, the StatusBar control introduced in Visual Basic 4 provides a much better alternative. You don't have to worry about extra overhead, because it is likely that you probably already are using one of the other Common Controls in the same OCX.

Figure 10.2 shows a typical status bar from a Visual Basic program.

FIG. 10.2

Status bars display current information about a program.

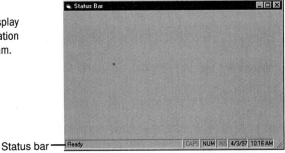

Status bar —— Ready   CAPS NUM INS 4/3/97 10:16 AM

Creating a Status Bar

 You start the creation of the status bar by selecting the control and drawing it on your form. When it is first drawn, the status bar will span the width of its parent form and will contain a single panel, as shown in Figure 10.3. You will also notice that no matter where on your form you draw the status bar, it moves to the bottom of the form automatically. This is the typical location for a program's status bar.

FIG. 10.3

A status bar placed on a form is configured automatically.

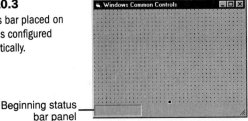

Beginning status ___
bar panel

After you have drawn the status bar, you are ready to start setting the properties to control its appearance and to create any additional panels that you will need for to display information. As you saw when you first drew the status bar control, it sizes itself to fit across the entire form. This is an automatic action, and you have no control over it. You can, however, control the height of the status bar either by setting its Height property or by clicking and dragging one

FIG. 10.8

You can create flat, inset, or raised panels.

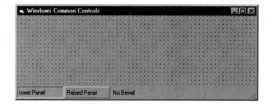

Managing Your Panels   You have seen how to set the properties of an individual panel, but you also need to know how to add and remove panels. Within the Property Pages, this is very easy. To add a new panel, you simply click the Insert Panel button on the Panel page. This sets up a blank set of properties for the new panel. To remove a panel, click the Remove Panel button. This instantly removes the panel from the status bar, without requesting verification. Finally, if you want to move from panel to panel, click the arrow buttons on the Panel page.

The status bar also gives you the capability to add and remove panels from code. This is handled by the methods of the `Panels` collection. There are three methods of the `Panels` collection:

- `Add`   Creates a new panel for the status bar.
- `Remove`   Deletes a specific panel from the status bar.
- `Clear`   Removes all the panels of the status bar.

Listing 10.1 shows how to add a new date panel to the status bar and how to delete the first panel in the bar. This listing also uses the `Count` property of the `Panels` collection, which tells you how many panels are present in the status bar.

Listing 10.1   STATUS.FRM—Use the Methods of the *Panels* Collection to Manage Panels in Code

```
Dim NewIdx
StatusBar1.Panels.Add
NewIdx = StatusBar1.Panels.Count
With StatusBar1.Panels(NewIdx)
    .Style = sbrDate
    .Bevel = sbrRaised
    .ToolTipText = Format(Date, "Long Date")
End With
StatusBar1.Panels.Remove 1
```

N O T E   Unlike most other collections, the `Panels` collection starts with an index of 1 and the index values run up to the `Count` property. ■

Running the Status Bar from Code

Now that you know how to set up the status bar, you are ready to see how it is used in code. You have seen that the key status and date/time panels handle their tasks automatically. These things are great, but the real power of the status bar is its capability to change the text that appears in the text-style panel(s) as your program is running. These text panels tell the user the actual status of operations in your program.

To update the status of an item in your program, you assign a text string to the Text property of the Panel object, as shown in the following line of code:

```
StatusBar1.Panels(1).Text = "Viewing record 1 of 10"
```

You can, of course, set other properties of the panels the same way. You can even set up your entire status bar from code by using the methods of the Panels collection and the properties of the Panel objects. As an example, Listing 10.2 shows how to set up the status bar shown in Figure 10.9.

Listing 10.2   STATUS.FRM—You Can Set Up Your Entire Status Bar from Code

```
Private Sub Form_Load()
With StatusBar1
    .Panels(1).AutoSize = sbrSpring
    .Panels(1).Text = "Ready"
    .Panels.Add
    .Panels(2).Style = sbrCaps
    .Panels(2).AutoSize = sbrContents
    .Panels(2).MinWidth = 100
End With
End Sub
```

T I P As with the Toolbar control, you also can reference a specific panel with its key:

```
sbrMain.Panels("page").Text = "Page 1 of 14"
```

FIG. 10.9
Control your status bar by setting the properties of the Panel objects.

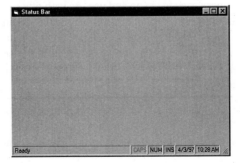

Part
II

Ch
10

Sliding into Numbers

Another Windows Common Control is the Slider control. The Slider control provides another means for the user to enter numeric data into a program. The slider works like the slider switches you might find on your stereo system's graphic equalizer or in a manner similar to the scroll bars that you have in the standard control set of Visual Basic. However, the slider has one advantage over the scroll bars. With the slider, you can also select a range of values, not just a single value by specifying minimum and maximum desired values.

Setting Up the Slider Control

 You start creating the slider by drawing it on your form. There then are four main properties that control the appearance of the slider. These properties are summarized in Table 10.2. The effects of these properties are shown in Figure 10.11.

Table 10.2   Properties of the Slider Control

Property	Settings
BorderStyle	Set to 0 for no border or 1 for a single line border.
Orientation	Set this property to 0 for a horizontal slider or 1 for a vertical slider.
TickStyle	This property controls the placement of the tick marks on the slider. Set this to 0 to display tick marks below or to the right of the slider, set it to 1 to place tick marks above or to the left of the slider, set it to 2 to place tick marks on both sides, or set it to 3 to show no tick marks.
TickFrequency	Determines how many tick marks are displayed. This can be set to any positive number.

FIG. 10.11

The slider lets you select numeric information.

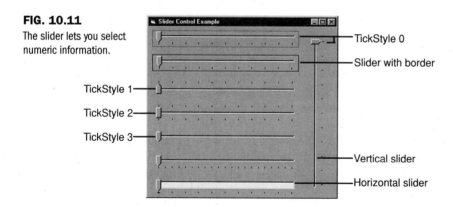

After you have set up the appearance of the slider, you will need to set several properties that control its operation. The first two properties are the Min and Max properties, which control the range of values that can be handled by the slider control. The other two properties are the LargeChange and SmallChange properties. The LargeChange property controls how much the value of the slider will change if the user presses the Page Up or Page Down keys or clicks the mouse to either side of the slide bar. The SmallChange property controls how much the value of the slider will change if the user presses the right or left arrow keys. SelectRange is the final property affecting the operation of the slider. This property determines whether the slider can select only a single value or possibly select a range of values.

Using the Slider Control

When your users encounter the Slider control in your program, they can click the slide bar and drag it to set a value. They can also use the Page Up, Page Down, and right and left arrow keys to change the value. The information entered by the user is contained in the Value property of the slider.

Part
II

Ch
10

N O T E The keyboard keys work on a Slider control only if it has the focus.

If the SelectRange property is set to True, the user also can select a range of values by holding down Shift while clicking and dragging the slider bar. Unfortunately, this technique is not automatic; it must be managed by your code. You'll need to add code to the slider's MouseDown event procedure to determine whether the user has held down Shift while dragging the slider. If so, your code can set the slider's SelStart property, which defines the starting value of the range, and the SelLength property, which defines the extent of the range. Visual Basic's help system contains a very good example under the topic "SelLength, SelStart Properties (Slider control)."

Creating a Project with the Slider Control

To really demonstrate the use of the Slider control, you now will build a "color blender" project that uses an array of Slider controls to set the BackColor property of a form.

Setting Up the Interface of the Project To create the color blender, start a new project in Visual Basic and save it as ColorBld.Vbp. Next, rename the form to frmBlend and save it as frmBlend.Frm.

N O T E At this point, you need to add the Windows Common Controls to the Toolbox, if they are not already present (refer to "Working with the Windows Common Controls" earlier in this chapter). Now you can start creating the interface of the program by adding controls.

Follow these steps to add the controls for the color blender project:

1. Place a check box on the form and name it ckGray. Set the Caption property of the check box to Only Shades Of Gray.

2. Place a Slider control on the form and name it sldColor.

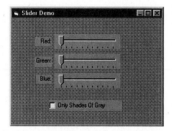

3. Place a label on the form to the left of the slider and name it lblColor.

4. Make a set of control arrays for lblColor and sldColor. To do this, hold down the Ctrl key and click both lblColor and sldColor. Go to the Edit menu and click Copy. Paste the copied controls onto the form. You will be presented with a dialog box asking if you want to create a control array. Click Yes.

5. Add a third element to each control array by choosing Paste again.

6. Using the Properties window, set the caption of lblColor(0) to Red:, the caption of lblColor(1) to Green:, and lblColor(2) to Blue:.

7. Place the lblColor() and sldColor() control arrays as shown in Figure 10.12.

FIG. 10.12

The main form of the color blender project contains an array of Slider controls.

Setting Up the Code of the Project   After you set up the interface of the program, you need to add some code to a couple of events to make the program work. The first event is the Load event of the form, which sets the initial condition of the program. The code for the Load event is shown in Listing 10.5.

Listing 10.5   COLORBLD.VBP—Initialize the Program in the *Load* Event of the Form

```
Private Sub Form_Load()

    Dim nCount As Integer
    Dim lRed As Long, lGreen As Long, lBlue As Long

'Set up the sliders
    For  nCount = 0 To 2
        sldColor(nCount ).Min = 0
        sldColor(nCount ).Max = 255

        sldColor(nCount ).TickFrequency = 4
```

```
      Next  nCount

      'Initialize the color of the form
      'control. (This will set the color to black. RGB(0,0,0))
      frmBlend.BackColor = RGB(lRed, lGreen, lBlue)

   End Sub
```

Next, you will need to add the code that actually changes the colors in response to movements of the Slider control. This code will be placed in the `Scroll` event of the Slider controls. The code is shown in Listing 10.6.

Listing 10.6   COLORBLD.VBP—Moving the Slider Changes the Color in the Color Blender

```
Private Sub sldColor_Scroll(Index As Integer)
   Dim nCount As Integer
   Dim lRed As Long, lGreen As Long, lBlue As Long


   'Gray is equal values of Red, Green and Blue
   If ckGray Then
      'move all the sliders


      For nCount = 0 to 2
         sldColor(nCount).Value = sldColor(Index).Value
      Next nCount
   End If

   'Set the RGB value
   lRed = sldColor(0).Value
   lGreen = sldColor(1).Value
   lBlue = sldColor(2).Value

   'Assign the resultant RGB value to the backcolor

   frmBlend.BackColor = RGB(lRed, lGreen, lBlue)

End Sub
```

Running the Project   After you have entered the code, you are ready to run the program. Click the Start button or press F5 to compile and run the program. Then try setting different combinations of the color sliders to see the effect on the color blender.

The `ColorBld.Vbp` project works like this: After an initialization process in the `Form_Load` event, most of the work takes place in the `sldColor_Scroll` event. As the user moves a slider from the array of Slider controls, the moved slider's index is passed into the `sldColor_Scroll` event. The application checks the value of the ckGray check box. If it is checked (True), the value of the moved slider is assigned to all the controls in the slider control array. This causes all the sliders to move to the same position before any other code is executed.

Part
II

Ch
10

On the CD

Listing 10.8 FRMLISTV.FRM—The Menu *click* Events for FRMLISTV.FRM

```
Private Sub mnuLarge_Click()
    lvMain.View = lvwIcon
End Sub

Private Sub mnuSmall_Click()
    lvMain.View = lvwSmallIcon
End Sub

Private Sub mnuList_Click()
    lvMain.View = lvwList
End Sub

Private Sub mnuDetail_Click()
    lvMain.View = lvwReport
End Sub

Private Sub mnuExit_Click()
    End
End Sub
```

▶ **See** "Creating a Menu Bar," **p. 108**

 Running the Program You now can run the program by clicking the Start button or by pressing F5. Figure 10.18 shows two different views of the same list.

FIG. 10.18
While the report view displays detailed information with column headings, the large icons view simply shows a picture above the item text.

In the Form_Load event, the ListItem objects (baseball teams) for the ListView's ListItem collection are created and added. As each ListItem is added to the ListItems collection, values are assigned to SubItems(1) (the "Win" column) and SubItems(2) (the "Loss" column) of the ListItem, itmX.

The menu has six menu items with the captions Large Icons, Small Icons, List, Details, a separator bar, and Exit. The Click event handlers of the first four menu items set the View property of the ListView control. The views are lvwIcons, lvwSmallIcons, lvwList, and lvwReport, respectively. The itmExit_Click event terminates the application.

You have just seen a sample project that demonstrates the ListView's ability to display items. Like the ListBox, however, the ListView control has many events and properties, such as the ItemClick event discussed below, designed to select and manipulate item(s).

The `ItemClick` event passes an object to your program, so you can take appropriate action:

```
Private Sub ListView1_ItemClick(ByVal Item As ComctlLib.ListItem)
    If Item.Text = "Magic Item" Then MsgBox "You clicked the magic item!"
End Sub
```

The ListView control has properties to sort the report view based on a column header. By using the `ColumnClick` event, it would be very easy to change the sort order to the selected column:

```
Private Sub lvMain_ColumnClick(ByVal ColumnHeader As ComctlLib.ColumnHeader)
        lvMain.SortKey = ColumnHeader.Index - 1
        lvMain.Sorted = True
End Sub
```

As you may have noticed, items in a ListView can be renamed by single-clicking the text. Two events, `BeforeLabelEdit` and `AfterLabelEdit`, lets your program know which item the user is changing.

As stated at the beginning of the chapter, the ListView and TreeView are fairly complex controls. To discover all the features, I suggest creating several sample programs to test all the properties and methods.

Using the TreeView Control

The TreeView control is similar to a ListView in that it can display items with a combination of text and graphics. However, the TreeView does so by showing items within a tree hierarchy. If you have taken a math or computer science class, you already may have discussed the "tree hierarchy." An example of a tree you might have seen in math class is shown in Figure 10.19.

FIG. 10.19
In this tree structure, each node of the tree is represented by a circle.

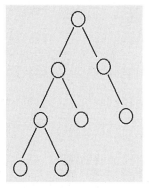

If you are unfamiliar with tree hierarchies, study the next few sections carefully, as this concept will make understanding the TreeView control a lot easier.

N O T E If you have used the OutLine control in previous versions of Visual Basic, you'll find that the TreeView control is a more robust alternative. ■

Given the hierarchical nature of the TreeView control, *root, parent,* and *child* are fundamental concepts that must be understood for you to work effectively with the control. Also, the TreeView uses the `Node` object extensively. This being the case, mastery of the `Node` object is also a requirement for effective use of the TreeView. The most common example of the TreeView is the left pane of the Windows Explorer (refer to Figure 10.13).

Understanding Nodes A *hierarchy* is an organization in which each part has a defined relationship with the other parts. For example, take your family tree. Your parents and their parents are "above" you in the hierarchy; your children and their children are "below" you.

In the family tree example, each person is considered to be a *node* on the tree. Relationships between nodes are indicated by *branches*. A node's branches can connect it to other nodes (for example, lines on the family tree connecting you to your parents), or it can simply exist by itself (if you don't have any children).

Like the family tree or a real-life tree, all TreeView controls have nodes. `Nodes` is (notice the use of the singular verb) both a property of a TreeView control and an object in itself. If you have followed the discussion up to now regarding collections, this concept probably makes some sense to you. (If you're unclear about collections, review the "Understanding Collections" section earlier in this chapter.) Like the Toolbar control's `Buttons` collection, the TreeView's `Nodes` collection has properties and methods, including an `Add` method used to create new nodes:

```
tv1.Nodes.Add , , "mykey", "Test Node", 1, 2
```

And, like the other `Add` methods discussed so far, it can return a reference to the object just created:

```
Dim tempNode As Node
Set tempNode = tv1.Nodes.Add(, , "mykey", "Test Node")
tempNode.Image = 1
tempNode.SelectedImage = 2
tempNode.ExpandedImage = 3
```

The TreeView control presents a "collapsible" view of the tree structure, as seen in Figure 10.20.

FIG. 10.20

A simple tree structure created in a TreeView control.

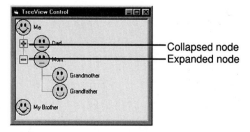

Collapsed node
Expanded node

In this figure, notice the use of plus, minus, lines, and images to indicate which parts of the tree are "expanded" and which are "collapsed."

Understanding the *Root* Property   At the very top (or bottom, depending on how you look at it) of a tree structure is its root. A *root* is the node from which all other nodes descend. A tree has only one root node. In the tree pictured in Figure 10.20, the node called "Me" is the root node, simply because it was the first one added to the TreeView control.

Part of what defines a node is its root. Therefore, each node in the Nodes collection has a Root property that refers to the tree's root node. For the tree pictured in Figure 10.20, the following code would verify that "Me" is the root of every node:

```
Dim tempNode As Node
For Each tempNode in tv1.Nodes
        Print tempNode.Text & "'s root is " & tempnode.Root.Text
Next tempNode
```

Note that Root is both a property of a node and a node itself.

Working with the *Parent* Property   You have just seen that every node in the Nodes collection can access the root. However, just knowing the root of a node is not enough to define a position in the tree hierarchy. Look at, for example, Figure 10.21, which is a company organizational chart.

FIG. 10.21

Note in this particular TreeView control that the images for each node have been disabled.

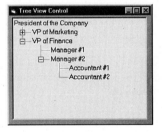

If you want to know where you are in this structure, you need to know more than just where the root (President) is. This brings us to the first of several tree relationships, the *Parent relationship*. To be a parent, a node must have children. In Figure 10.21, the president of the company is a parent to both of the vice president nodes. Both managers shown in the figure also have the same parent, VP of Finance.

Suppose you were an ambitious little node trying to climb the corporate ladder. You could use this code to check your progress:

```
Dim MyNode As Node

Set MyNode = tv1.Nodes("Me")

If MyNode = MyNode.Root Then
    MsgBox "You're the boss!"
Else
    MsgBox "Try getting promoted to " & MyNode.Parent.Text
End If
```

As you can see from the example, each node object has a `Parent` property that refers to its parent node. The only exception is the root node, whose `Parent` property does not refer to anything.

Working with the *Children* Property   To be a parent, a node must have children. To find out if a node is a parent, you query the `Children` property by using code like this:

```
Private Sub TreeView1_NodeClick(ByVal MyNode As Node)
    If MyNode.Children = 0 Then
        MsgBox "I am not a parent"
    End If
End Sub
```

As you can see, the `Children` property returns an integer value that represents the number of children a given node has. To be considered a child, a node has to have a direct connection. In other words, as shown in Figure 10.21, the president of the company has two children—the two VPs.

Working with the *Child* Property   Whereas the `Children` property simply returns the count of child nodes, the `Child` property returns an actual node (just like the `Root` and `Parent` properties). However, even if a parent has multiple children, the `Child` property returns only the first of the given parent node's descendants. If a given node doesn't have a child, its `Child` property will contain an invalid reference. Therefore, you should not try to access it if the `Children` property is `0`. In Figure 10.21, Manager #2's `Child` property is Accountant #1.

The immediate question that comes to mind is how to access child nodes other than the first one. Well, each node has several properties that are used to determine who its "brothers and sisters" are, as demonstrated in the following code:

```
Sub PrintAllChildren()

    Dim anyNode As Node
    Dim kidNode As Node
    Dim inCounter As Integer

    For Each anyNode In tv1.Nodes

      If anyNode.Children <> 0 Then 'this node is a parent

          Print anyNode.Text & "'s children are: "
          Set kidNode = anyNode.child
          Print kidNode.Text

          inCounter = kidNode.FirstSibling.Index
          While inCounter <> kidNode.LastSibling.Index
             Print tv1.Nodes(inCounter).Next.Text
             inCounter = tv1.Nodes(inCounter).Next.Index
          Wend

      End If

    Next anyNode
End Sub
```

Remember, for a given node, there is only one child. All the other nodes that share the child's parent are considered Next or Previous nodes. However, among all the nodes that share the same value for the Parent property, there is a FirstSibling and a LastSibling.

N O T E Nodes are tricky; there's no question about it. One of the best ways to get a grasp of nodes is to see the node code (no poetry intended) in action. The online help file examples that Microsoft provides with your version of VB are pretty good once you get a basic understanding of the hierarchy concepts. It is suggested that you create several test programs until you are comfortable using the TreeView control. ■

To learn more about the TreeView control, keep reading. This section focused on accessing nodes already in the TreeView control. The next section will add nodes to a TreeView control as part of a sample project.

Using the TabStrip Control

The last control that will be covered is the TabStrip control. The TabStrip, shown in Figure 10.22, adds a whole new dimension to form organization and information presentation. Of all the controls in the Common Controls group, it probably has attained the most prominence in the Windows interface arsenal.

N O T E The TabStrip control is different from the tabbed dialog box. Aside from the visual difference, the most important distinction is that the TabStrip is not a container. Containers are discussed in Chapter 13, "Using Containers." ■

▶ **See** "Using Tabbed Dialogs," **p. 348**

FIG. 10.22

A Property Pages dialog box is an example of using a TabStrip control.

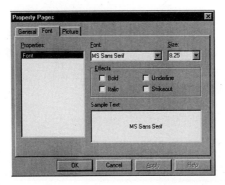

Next, a sample project will be created to illustrate the capabilities of the TabStrip. In this sample project, the purpose of the TabStrip control will be to switch between two lists of information. The lists will be baseball teams displayed in a TreeView control. The TabStrip will enable you to select which league to display.

Starting the Project

To begin the TreeTab project, start a new project in Visual Basic. Next, rename the default form "Form1" to frmTreTb. Then follow these steps:

1. Add a TabStrip control and name it something short and meaningful, like tsMain.

2. Next, add a TreeView control to the form and name it tv1. Now you are ready to start setting the properties of the controls.

CAUTION

The TabStrip control is *not* a container. This means that controls placed in a TabStrip control do not assume the `Visible`, `Enabled`, and relative `Top` and `Left` properties of the TabStrip, as they would if you were to draw a control into a selected Frame control. Thus, clicking a TabStrip will bring it to the front, covering other controls that are before it.

To manipulate how controls appear in relation to a TabStrip, pay particular attention to the `ZOrder` method of the TabStrip and the affected controls. During design mode, you can right-click the TabStrip control and choose Send to Back.

Setting Up the TabStrip

The next step in creating the project is to create the tabs in the TabStrip. Because two leagues need to be shown, two tabs are needed in the TabStrip. To set up the TabStrip control, follow these steps:

1. Start by right-clicking tsMain. This will bring up the TabStrip context menu.
2. Click the Properties menu item at the bottom of the context menu to display the Property Pages dialog box for tsMain.
3. Click the Tabs tab and type **American League** in the Caption field (see Figure 10.23).

FIG. 10.23

The Property Pages dialog box makes it easy to insert tabs into a TabStrip control.

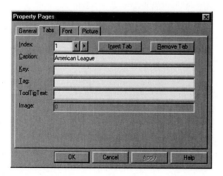

4. Click the Insert Tab button. A tab will be added.

5. In the Caption field, type **National League**.

6. Click OK. You will see that the captions have appeared in the TabStrip control.

Creating the Code to Set Up the TreeView Control

As was the case in the ListView project, the setup of the TreeView control is easier to accomplish through code. In the case of your sample project, you want to display a hierarchical organization of a selected baseball league. Each league has three divisions: East, West, and Central. The divisions have five, five, and four teams, respectively.

To take advantage of this common structure, put the data into two text files, ALEAGUE.TXT and NLEAGUE.TXT. These files will contain a list of the 14 teams in each league. They can be created in Notepad or any other text editor, as shown in Figure 10.24.

Part

II

Ch

10

FIG. 10.24

In the sample program, the TreeView will be filed with items from the two text files pictured here.

Create the subroutine shown in Listing 10.9 to load information from the text files into the TreeView control.

Listing 10.9   FRMTRETB.FRM—*DisplayLeague* Procedure Displays League Information in the TreeView Control

```
Public Sub DisplayLeague(sLeague As String)

    Dim tempNode As Node
    Dim nCounter As Integer
    Dim sTemp As String

    tv1.Nodes.Clear

    'Add the League
    Set tempNode = tv1.Nodes.Add(, , "R", sLeague)

    'Add the Divisions
    Set tempNode = tv1.Nodes.Add("R", tvwChild, "E", "East Division")
    Set tempNode = tv1.Nodes.Add("R", tvwChild, "C", "Central Division")
    Set tempNode = tv1.Nodes.Add("R", tvwChild, "W", "West Division")
```

continues

Listing 10.9   Continued

```
'Open the text file with team names
If sLeague = "National League" Then
Open "C:\NLEAGUE.TXT" For Input As #1
Else
Open "C:\ALEAGUE.TXT" For Input As #1
End If

'Add the 5 EAST teams
For nCounter = 1 To 5
    Line Input #1, sTemp
    Set tempNode = tv1.Nodes.Add("E", tvwChild, "E" & nCounter, sTemp)
Next nCounter
tempNode.EnsureVisible

'Add the 5 CENTRAL teams
For nCounter = 1 To 5
    Line Input #1, sTemp
    Set tempNode = tv1.Nodes.Add("C", tvwChild, "C" & nCounter, sTemp)
Next nCounter
tempNode.EnsureVisible

'Add the 4 WEST teams
For nCounter = 1 To 4
    Line Input #1, sTemp
    Set tempNode = tv1.Nodes.Add("W", tvwChild, "W" & nCounter, sTemp)
Next nCounter
tempNode.EnsureVisible

'Close the Input file
Close #1

'Set the Desired style
tv1.Style = tvwTreelinesText
tv1.BorderStyle = vbFixedSingle

'Set the TreeView control on top
tv1.ZOrder 0

End Sub
```

Notice that the relationships in the tree view are defined as a node is added. The Add method's first parameter lists a "relative" node and the second parameter lists the relationship to that relative. The constant tvwChild indicates the new node is a child of the relative node.

Taking Action in the Program

Now, return to the topic of the TabStrip control and set up the form's Load event. When the form first appears, you probably want it to show something, so call the DisplayLeague procedure to display the American League teams. The code for the Load event is shown in Listing 10.10.

Listing 10.10 FRMTRETB.FRM—Use the *Load* Event to Initialize the Program

```
Private Sub Form_Load()

    'Put the tree view on top of the tab
    tv1.ZOrder 0

    'Call our procedure
    DisplayLeague "American League"
End Sub
```

At this point, you can run your program and the American League teams will be displayed. However, clicking the TabStrip will have no effect on the TreeView because you have not yet added the necessary code to the TabStrip's Click event. This code, shown in Listing 10.11, calls the DisplayLeague procedure with the name of the desired league.

Listing 10.11 FRMTRETB.FRM—Switch Leagues by Clicking the Appropriate Tab

```
Private Sub tsMain_Click()
    Dim nTemp As Integer

    nTemp = tsMain.SelectedItem.Index
    DisplayLeague tsMain.Tabs(nTemp).Caption

End Sub
```

Now your sample program is done. Figure 10.25 shows how the program looks.

FIG. 10.25

The sample application displays a list of base-ball teams when a tab is clicked.

Understanding How the Application Works

The crux of the project is the DisplayLeague procedure. First, this procedure creates a node for the League divisions:

```
Set tempNode = tv1.Nodes.Add("R", tvwChild, "E", "East Division")
```

The constant tvwChild tells the application to make this new node a child of the node, "R".

Then, to each Division node, several team nodes are added:

```
Set tempNode = tv1.Nodes.Add("E", tvwChild, "E" & nCounter, sTemp)
```

Notice that the first argument in the Add method is now "E", which is the unique key of the Node of the Eastern Division. This is how the "E1" node (which displays Yankees) knows that it is a child of the Eastern Division.

Next, the entire Division node and its children are told to remain expanded (TreeView nodes can be expanded and collapsed) in the line:

```
MyNode.EnsureVisible
```

(You also could have set each Division node's Expanded property to True.)

The last thing that deserves attention is the way the TabStrip reports back which tab has been clicked. In the TabStrip control, tabs are an array of, well, tabs. So, when you click a tab, you are actually selecting a tab, like selecting a ListIndex in a ListBox control. In light of this, to find out which tab is being clicked, the following line makes a bit more sense:

```
nTemp = tsMain.SelectedItem.Index
```

From Here...

The Windows Common Controls covered in this chapter can enhance your programs in many ways. Each has its own special capabilities that can improve the interface of your applications. The best way to learn about them is to put them in your programs and try them out. Some of the topics mentioned here are covered in more detail in other chapters:

- To learn more about creating toolbars and menus for your programs, see Chapter 5, "Adding Menus and Toolbars to Your Programs."
- For a discussion of some additional new controls, see Chapter 11, "Exploring New Visual Basic 5 Controls."

CHAPTER 11

Exploring New Visual Basic 5 Controls

Displaying information in a grid

Learn how to present data to your users in a grid format with the MSFlexGrid control.

Playing video clips

Add AVI animations to your programs with the Animation control.

Making data entry easier

The UpDown Control can be used with a TextBox or other control to aid in entering numeric values.

In some of the previous chapters, you learned about many of the controls that you can use in Visual Basic. These controls are the heart and soul of most programs that you create. In Chapter 9, "Using the Windows Standard Controls," you learned about many of the controls that have been a part of Visual Basic since its inception. These controls let you work with text, handle choices, work with lists, and initiate program actions. In Chapter 10, "Using the Windows Common Controls," you learned about the controls that are used in many Windows 95/Windows NT programs. ■

If you have followed the progress of Visual Basic, you know that each new version brings with it new and enhanced controls. In version 5 of Visual Basic, Microsoft did not disappoint us. Visual Basic 5 contains some new controls that give you greater capabilities in your programs. Three of these controls are the subject of this chapter:

- *MSFlexGrid*   Displays information in a tabular form like a spreadsheet or the grid display of a database program
- *Animation*   Enables you to display animation sequences with no sound
- *UpDown*   Works with other controls to enable you to increment the value of a control such as a text box or label

N O T E   The controls discussed in this chapter are available only in the Professional and Enterprise Editions of Visual Basic. If you are using the Learning Edition, you won't be able to re-create the examples. ■

Using the MSFlexGrid Control

Much of the information that computer programs deal with is presented in the form of columns and rows. The most common example of a program which deals with this type of information display is a spreadsheet. Since spreadsheets were among the first successful commercial PC programs, and spreadsheet software is one of the two most widely used program categories in the world (word processors being the other), it is safe to assume that people have become very comfortable seeing data displayed in rows and columns. In fact, for many people, and many types of data, this is the preferred method of viewing information.

Figure 11.1 shows a typical table view of data.

FIG. 11.1

A table view allows users to quickly view and process a large amount of data.

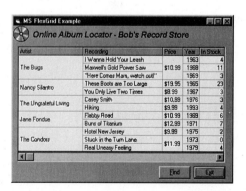

Visual Basic has two separate controls for working with rows and columns of information: the DBGrid control for displaying and editing the contents of a database, and the new MSFlexGrid control for handling many other grid display needs. The DBGrid control is covered in Chapter 30, "Doing More with Bound Controls."

N O T E   The MSFlexGrid control can be bound to a data control to display information from a
database. However, the information is displayed as read-only and therefore cannot be
modified as it can with the DBGrid control. ▦

The MSFlexGrid control is capable of displaying text or pictures in any of its cells. Moreover,
you can use the grid to sort information in the tables and format the information for easier
viewing. The FlexGrid, as it's also known, is capable of fixing (or freezing) rows and columns
along the top and left edges of the grid. This lets you provide labels for the items that are always displayed to the user. Sounds great, right? Then let's take a look at how this grid works.

Setting Up the MSFlexGrid Control

The first step to using the MSFlexGrid control is to add it to the Toolbox. You do this by choosing Project, Components. This brings up the Components dialog box, which allows you to add
and remove controls and other components from your project. To add the MSFlexGrid, select
the check box next to the control name and click OK. The control is listed as *Microsoft
FlexGrid Control 5.0* and is contained in the Msflxrd.ocx file, usually in your
\Windows\system directory. When you close the Components dialog box, the FlexGrid is
added to the Toolbox. It appears as a yellow grid with a cylinder attached.

 After adding the control to the Toolbox, you are ready to add a FlexGrid to your form. Do this
by clicking the control and then drawing it on the form. The FlexGrid is initially drawn with
two rows and two columns as shown in Figure 11.2.

Part

II

Ch

11

FIG. 11.2
Resizing the FlexGrid in
the design environment
does not change the
number of rows or
columns.

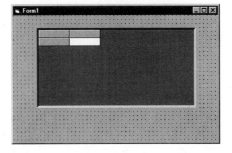

After drawing the control on the form, you first want to specify a unique name for the control.
Then you are ready to begin setting the properties that will control its appearance and behavior.

Controlling the FlexGrid's Appearance   There are several properties that affect the appearance of the FlexGrid control. The FlexGrid control is much more customizable than the standard grid included with previous versions of Visual Basic. Properties can be used to control the
headers of the grid, the colors that are used to indicate the various states of cells, and of course
the fonts used to display information.

The Rows and Cols properties of the FlexGrid determine how many total rows and columns display in the grid. If the number of rows and columns is greater than can fit on-screen, the FlexGrid automatically provides scrollbars. Some of the displayed rows and columns can set as *fixed* (non-scrolling), which creates Excel-style headers. The headers are controlled by the FixedRows and FixedCols properties. The default value of these properties is 1, but you can set them to anything from 0 up to the value of the Rows and Cols properties respectively. These four properties are illustrated in Figure 11.3.

FIG. 11.3

Use fixed rows and columns for the headers of the grid.

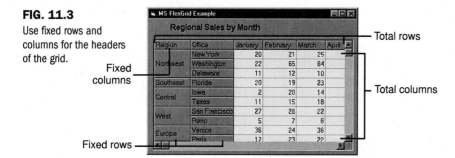

To control the colors displayed, the FlexGrid control has five major sets of color properties. These properties are summarized in Table 11.1.

Table 11.1   Color Properties

Background Color Property	Foreground Color Property	Color Use
BackColor	ForeColor	Controls the colors of any standard cells in the grid. A standard cell is one that is not part of the fixed rows or columns and is not selected.
BackColorFixed	ForeColorFixed	Controls the colors of the "header" cells in the fixed rows and columns.
BackColorSel	ForeColorSel	Controls the colors in cells that are selected.
BackColorBkg	N/A	Controls the color of the "empty space" in the FlexGrid control that is not occupied by any cells.
CellBackColor	CellForeColor	Controls the color of an individual cell. Can only be used during runtime.

The font information for most cells in the grid is controlled by the Font property of the grid itself. This property has the same effect as the Font property in other controls. However, you can format individual cells with different fonts using the properties listed next:

- `CellFontName` Specifies the name of the font for the given cell.
- `CellFontSize` Specifies the size of the font for the cell.
- `CellFontBold` Determines whether the font appears in boldface.
- `CellFontItalic` Determines whether italic fonts are used.
- `CellFontUnderline` Determines whether text in the cell appears underlined.

When the settings of the `CellFont` properties are changed, the properties will affect only the current cell, unless a group of cells is selected. If multiple cells are selected, the property change affects all the selected cells.

To change the appearance of an individual cell, you can use the `Color` and `Font` properties in conjunction with the `Row` and `Col` properties. For example, the following code selects the cell in row 3, column 4, and then changes it to a Bold Red font:

```
fgMain.Row = 3
fgMain.Col = 4
fgMain.Text = "Bold Font"
fgMain.CellFontBold = True
fgMain.CellForeColor = vbRed
```

In addition to handling the cells' colors, the FlexGrid control gives you control over the lines that make up the grid. These lines are controlled by the following properties:

- `GridColor` Sets the color of the grid lines in all standard cells.
- `GridColorFixed` Sets the color of the grid lines in the fixed cells.
- `GridLines` Sets the appearance of the grid lines for the standard cells. This property can have one of these settings:

  0 - `flexGridNone` (no grid lines)

  1 - `flexGridFlat` (flat grid lines)

  2 - `flexGridInset` (inset grid lines)

  3 - `flexGridRaised` (raised grid lines)

- `GridLinesFixed` Sets the appearance of the grid lines in the fixed cells. This property has the same possible settings as the `GridLines` property.
- `GridLineWidth` Sets the width of the lines use to make up the grid.

Controlling the FlexGrid's Behavior As you know, the properties of a control affect not only its appearance, but its behavior as well. The FlexGrid is no exception. The FlexGrid has several unique properties that control how it behaves while running in your program. These properties include:

- `AllowBigSelection` Determines whether the user can select a row or column by clicking the header (fixed cell) of the row or column. The default value of this property is `True`.
- `AllowUserResizing` Determines whether the user can change the size of the rows or columns in the grid. The property has four possible settings:

    0 - `flexResizeNone` (no resizing allowed, the default)

    1 - `flexResizeColumns` (the user can resize columns only)

    2 - `flexResizeRows` (the user can resize rows only)

    3 - `flexResizeBoth` (the user can resize rows and columns)

When allowed, the user can resize a row or column by clicking the mouse on the grid line to the right or below a cell and then dragging the mouse to set the new size.

■ `FillStyle` Determines whether setting the value of a cell property will affect only the current cell or all selected cells. The default value (0 - `flexFillSingle`) allows only the current cell's properties to be set. Changing the `FillStyle` property's value to 1 - `flexFillRepeat` causes setting a cell property (such as `CellFontName` or `Text`) to set the value for all selected cells.

■ `MergeCells` Determines whether adjacent cells with the same contents will be merged to be shown in the grid as a single cell. This feature is useful in presenting information such as sales data where you might have multiple sales people in the same region. The property's default value is 0 for no merging. You can change the value to 1 to allow merging of anywhere in the grid, 2 to allow merging across columns but not across rows, or 3 to allow merging across rows but not across columns. Figures 11.4 through 11.6 show the effects of the `MergeCells` property.

■ `SelectionMode` Determines how the user can select cells in the grid. The default value (0) allows the user to select cells individually, just like you would in a spreadsheet. Setting the `SelectionMode` property to 1 forces selections to cover entire rows, while setting the property to 2 forces the selections to cover entire columns.

■ `WordWrap` Determines whether the text in a cell will wrap to multiple lines (property set to True) or will only show the text that will fit on a single line in a cell (False).

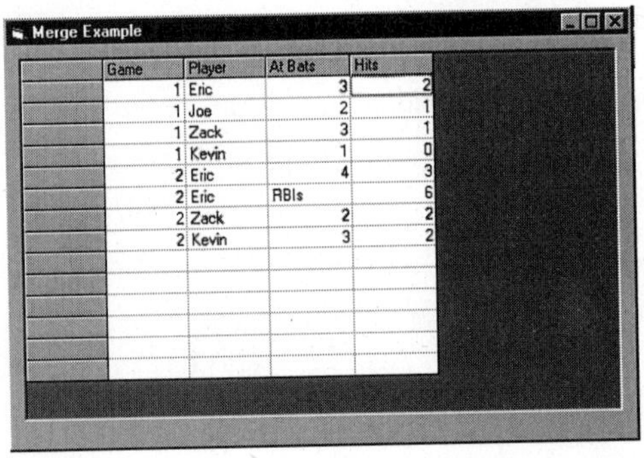

FIG. 11.4

No merging keeps all cells separate regardless of their contents.

FIG. 11.5
Free merging allows cells to automatically combine if their contents are the same.

Free merging

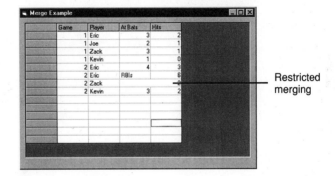

Free merging

FIG. 11.6
Restricted merging allows merging in a single direction.

Restricted merging

Binding the FlexGrid to Data

One use of the FlexGrid is to display the contents of a database table or the results of a query. The FlexGrid is can be bound to a data source, but can only display the data from the source; you cannot update via the attached Data control.

To use the FlexGrid to display data, follow these steps:

1. Start a new project and add the FlexGrid to your Toolbox (refer to "Setting Up the MSFlexGrid Control" earlier in the FlexGrid coverage).

2. Place a Data control on your form.

3. Set the DatabaseName property of the Data control to the database containing the desired information.

4. Set the RecordSource property to the name of the table or query that you want displayed. You can also set the property to a valid SQL statement.

5. Add a FlexGrid control to your form.

6. Set the DataSource property of the FlexGrid to the name of the data control you just created.

N O T E   Chapter 30, "Using the Visual Basic Data Control," contains detailed coverage of setting up and using data controls. ▓

▶ **See** "Understanding the Data Control," **p. 804**

Figure 11.7 shows a FlexGrid being used to display information from biblio.mdb, a sample database included with Visual Basic. The RecordSource property of the data control has been set to the following SQL statement:

```
Select PubID, Name, [Company Name] from Publishers
```

As you can see, the column headings default to the field names in the query results.

FIG. 11.7

You can display information from a database in the FlexGrid control.

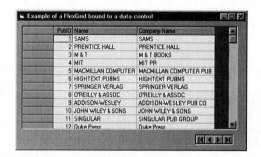

Working with the MSFlexGrid Control in Code

Obviously, the FlexGrid would be of limited value if you could only make changes to it at design time or use it only to display database information. You can, of course, work with the grid and its contents from your program code. Most of the properties that you can set at design time can also be set from program code. In addition, there are other properties that enable you to set and retrieve the contents of individual cells. There are also several methods and events that are specific to the FlexGrid control. You take a look at these features in this section.

Working with Cells   The most common task that you will perform in working with a grid is setting or retrieving the value of a cell. In the FlexGrid, the contents of all cells are treated as text strings. This means that you have to perform the appropriate checks and conversions if you need to retrieve numerical values or dates from the cells.

There are three properties that you can use to set or retrieve the value of a cell in the FlexGrid: Text, TextArray, and TextMatrix. You can use each of these properties to retrieve or set the value of a single cell.

When used to retrieve a value, the Text property returns the value of the current cell. This cell is defined by the settings of the Row and Col properties. The following code shows how you would retrieve the value of the cell in the second row and second column of the grid:

```
fgMain.Row = 1
fgMain.Col = 1
txtReturn = fgMain.Text
```

N O T E The row and column numbers are zero based, meaning that the first row is row 0, the second row is row 1, and so forth. ■

When using the Text property to set a value, the cell(s) that are affected depend on the setting of the FillStyle property and the current user selection. If only a single cell is selected, the Text property only sets the value of the selected cell. If multiple cells are selected, the Text property will set the value of the current cell if the FillStyle property is set to 0, or will set the value of all the selected cells if the FillStyle property is set to 1. The Text property has one disadvantage in its use: You can only retrieve or set the value of the current cell. This means if you want to process multiple cells, you will have to set the Row and Col properties for each cell's value you want to retrieve:

```
fgMain.Row = 1
fgMain.Col = 1
fgMain.Text = "One Cell"
fgMain.Col = 2
fgMain.Text = "Another Cell"
```

The TextArray property provides another means of setting and retrieving the value of a cell. The TextArray property can be used to retrieve the value of any cell, not just the current cell. This makes it a little easier to use than the Text property for working with multiple cells. The TextArray property uses a single index to specify the cell to be retrieved. This index is determined by multiplying the desired row number by the number of columns in the grid and then adding the desired column number. This index numbering system is shown in Figure 11.8. The following code shows how to retrieve the value from the cell in the third column of the second row:

```
inDesiredCol = 2
inDesiredRow = 1
txtRet = fgMain.TextArray(inDesiredRow * fgMain.Cols + inDesiredCol)
```

FIG. 11.8

TextArray indexes go across each row sequentially.

The final property for setting and retrieving the value of a cell is the TextMatrix property, which requires two arguments: the index of the row and the index of the column to be retrieved. This is probably the easiest of the value properties to use. The following code shows how the TextMatrix property would be used to retrieve the value from the cell in the third column of the second row:

```
txtReturn = fgMain.TextMatrix(1,2)
```

Notice in Figure 11.8 that the row and column numbers start with 0. Therefore, code example row 1 is actually the second row in the grid, and column 2 is the third column.

Adding and Deleting Rows   There are two ways that you can change the number of rows that are contained in the FlexGrid: You can change the Rows property of the grid, or you can use the AddItem and RemoveItem methods. Whereas changing the Rows property adds or removes items from the bottom of the grid, the FlexGrid's methods let you control the insertion and deletion points.

N O T E   The only way to change the number of columns is by setting the Cols property of the grid. ▪

The AddItem method enables you to add a new row to the FlexGrid control. By default, the row is added to the bottom of the grid. You can, however, specify an index value for the method to insert the row somewhere else in the grid. This method works the same way as a list box's AddItem method. When using the AddItem method, you must specify the text to insert in at least the first column of the grid. The following lines of code show how the AddItem method can be used:

```
fgMain.AddItem "NewRow"
fgMain.AddItem "NewRow",2
fgMain.AddItem "NewRow" & Chr(9) & "NewRow"
```

N O T E   To specify the values for multiple cells, create a text string containing the values of all the input cells, in column order. Between each pair of values, insert the Tab character by using the Chr(9) function. ▪

To delete a specific row from the grid, you use the RemoveItem method, which requires you to specify the row number of the row to be removed. This method works in a similar manner to the RemoveItem method of the ListBox control. The following code shows you how to remove the second row of the grid. (Remember that row numbers are zero based.)

```
fgMain.RemoveItem 1
```

N O T E   The AddItem and RemoveItem methods do not work with fixed rows. ▪

To clear the entire grid, you use the Clear method, as shown in the following line:

```
MSFlexGrid1.Clear
```

Understanding the Unique Events of the FlexGrid   The FlexGrid control responds to many of the same events as other controls. There are, however, several unique events that you will find useful as you program the grid:

- **EnterCell** Fires each time the focus moves into a cell. This is similar to a control's **GotFocus** event. The event procedure does not pass the index of the cell as a parameter. Therefore, you have to use the **Row** and **Col** properties of the grid to determine the cell.
- **LeaveCell** Fires when the focus moves out of a cell. This is similar to the **LostFocus** event of a control.
- **RowColChange** Fires when the focus is moved from one cell to another.
- **SelChange** Occurs when the selection of cells changes to a different cell or range of cells.

A possible use of these events is updating another control when a user chooses a new cell. For example, you could have report detail information displayed when a user clicks a particular cell.

Using Video in Your Programs

The Animation control provides you an easy way to get animation in your programs. You use the Animation control to play silent AVI (Audio Video Interleaved) clips. The AVI file format is basically aseries of bitmaps that are shown in sequence to create the animation effect, similar to the individual drawings in a cartoon. You would typically use the Animation control to indicate that a task is in progress, such as the File Copy routine of Windows 95, shown in Figure 11.9. These animations run in the background while other tasks are performed.

FIG. 11.9
A copy in progress is indicated by a simple animation.

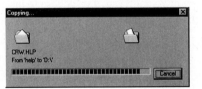

> **NOTE** Another way to create simple animation effects might be to use a Timer control to change the position of an Image control at a specified interval. Although this method requires a little more coding than is necessary with the Animation control, you do not need to have your animation already saved in an AVI file. The Timer control is covered in Chapter 9, "Using the Windows Standard Controls."
>
> You can find additional information about creating your own animation in "Creating Multimedia Programs," on this book's CD-ROM.

▶ **See** "Counting Time," **p. 241**

Setting Up the Animation Control

The Animation control is one of the two controls contained in the Windows Common Controls 2 set. The other control is the UpDown control discussed in the later section called "Using the UpDown Control." These controls are contained in the file Comct232.ocx. To use the Animation control, you have to first add "Microsoft Windows Common Controls-2 5.0" to your

Part
II

Ch
11

Control arrays are very handy on many occasions. Not only do they simplify the implementation of common functionality among multiple controls, but they also permit you to dynamically create new controls at run time, which is not otherwise possible in Visual Basic. ■

Creating a Control Array

You can create a control array in a number of ways. As different as they may appear, they ultimately deliver identical results. Therefore, you can freely choose any of the following approaches, according to your preferences and mood.

Changing the *Name* Property

Say you have two TextBox controls on your form, Text1 and Text2. You realize that they should be part of the same control array, named txtArray. Simply go to the Properties window and type the txtArray string for the Name property of both of them.

> **N O T E** If you're not sure whether you want or need to use control arrays, skip ahead to the "The Benefits of Control Arrays" section later in the chapter. Convinced, you then can return to this material and get about the business of creating your arrays. ▨

As soon as you confirm the string for the second control, Visual Basic realizes that you might want to create a control array and shows the message box in Figure 12.1. Just press **Y** to confirm, and you'll have a brand new array of controls.

FIG. 12.1

This message box informs that you are about to create a control array.

This procedure is most appropriate when you are creating a control array that includes two or more controls that already exist on the form. If you know in advance that you want to create a control array, other procedures might be preferable.

> **CAUTION**
> You should always make your decisions about control arrays before writing the code that references the controls themselves. In fact, you must use a different syntax when referring to an item of a control array; therefore, if you gather two or more existing controls into an array, you are forced to revise all the code that references them before you are able to run the program without syntax errors. You could do some of this work by using a simple Search-and-Replace command, but you would have to rewrite all the relevant event procedures.

Worse yet, even if the program runs without any syntax errors, it probably still conceals a number of subtle bugs that will not appear until later in the development stage. Therefore, you are compelled to re-test every single block of statements that reference the controls.

You can avoid these troubles if you create your control arrays before writing the code that uses the individual controls.

Using the Clipboard

Using the Clipboard is the most common way to create control arrays. Say you place a text box on your form. If you want it to be the first item of your brand new control array, you can just follow this simple procedure:

1. Select the control by using the mouse.

2. Choose Edit, Copy; click the Copy button; or press Ctrl+C.

3. Choose Edit, Paste; click the Paste button; or press Ctrl+V.

4. Press **Y** to confirm the message box that appears in Figure 12.1.

When you copy a control to the Clipboard and then paste it back to the form, you are implicitly asking Visual Basic to create a replica of the original control. The new control inherits all the properties of the original one, including its name. When Visual Basic detects an attempt to create a control with the same name as another control on the same form, it assumes that you mean to create a control array and asks for a confirmation.

CAUTION

After you press Ctrl+C to copy the selected control to the Clipboard, the control is no longer selected. The selection handles move to the parent form instead. This happens because VB anticipates your intention to paste the copy on the form surface, which is exactly what you mean to do most of the time. In fact, the control in the Clipboard is pasted on the object—form or control—that is currently selected.

However, if you need to place the new control within another container control—a PictureBox or Frame control, for example—you need to select the container before pressing Ctrl+V.

If you reply No to the message box, VB creates a new control of the same type as the original; the new control inherits all the original properties except the name. Two controls may share a common name only if they belong to the same control array.

TIP Experienced Visual Basic programmers often take advantage of this feature to create controls that are of the same type and share similar attributes, even if they don't belong to a control array. For instance, suppose that you must create several multi-lined TextBox controls of the same size, with their Text property set to a null string and their ScrollBars property set to 3 - Both. You may save a lot of typing and mouse activity by creating the "prototype" TextBox control, setting its properties as required,

continues

Part
II

Ch
12

More Concise Code

You have already seen that control arrays tend to reduce the amount of code that you must write to manage a group of homogeneous controls. Let me show what I mean with another example.

Many programmers like to highlight the contents of a text box as soon as the field gets the input focus. Besides offering a visual clue, this approach lets the user edit the current value by pressing a cursor key or replace it with a new string by pressing an alphanumerical key. If all of the text boxes on the form are grouped in one control array, you only have to write one line in their common GotFocus event procedure:

```
Private Sub Text1_GotFocus(index As Integer)
    ' highlight the field contents when it gets the input focus
    Text1(index).SelStart = 0
    Text1(index).SelLength = Len(Text1(index).Text)
End Sub
```

 Here is another little, but useful, example. If you use a lot of ComboBox controls and want to automatically open the controls' list portion when they get the input focus (thus saving your users the trouble to do this activity themselves), just gather the controls in a control array and add this simple procedure:

```
Private Sub Combo1_GotFocus(index As Integer)
    ' send an Alt-Down key combination
    SendKeys "%{DOWN}"
End Sub
```

Reduced File Size and Memory Overhead

Although it may not be immediately apparent, control arrays also enable you to build shorter executable files and save memory during execution. To prove this point, I built a form with 11 text boxes on it and no code at all. I then compiled this form to native code, and obtained an EXE file of 10,752 bytes. I replaced the controls with a control array of 11 text boxes, recompiled the program, and the file shortened to 9,216 bytes. That's about 1.5K less then the original EXE, or 140 fewer bytes for each control. Not really impressive, I admit, when the average system now has 16 or 32 megabytes of RAM.

But what happens if you add some code in the event procedures related to the controls? Suppose that you wish to convert each key to uppercase. If you are dealing with regular TextBox controls, you have to write 11 distinct KeyPress event routines, such as the following:

```
Private Sub Text1_KeyPress(KeyAscii As Integer)
    KeyAscii = Asc(UCase$(Chr$(KeyAscii)))
End Sub
```

Of course, if you adopt the control array approach, you only need a single event routine. When compiled to native code, the program based on control arrays is about 5K shorter than the program that uses regular controls (9,728 versus 14,848 bytes), which is about 500 bytes per control.

With a real-world program consisting of dozens of forms and hundreds of controls, you can reasonably expect to save several hundreds of kilobytes, or even more, depending on how complex the code in shared event procedures is. Saving these kilobytes means fewer installation disks, faster download from the Internet, and—above all—more free memory at run time. If your application has a smaller memory footprint, it usually runs faster, especially on lowly machines that only have 8 or 16 megabytes of RAM. The reduced size of your memory footprint means that your application has a larger market—you may sell more of them and make more money.

OK, I got carried away. You probably won't get rich just because you decided to use control arrays. But I think you get the point: control arrays help you deliver smaller and more efficient applications—a fact that you should never overlook.

Readable and Elegant Code

Because they can help you gather in a few places the code associated with multiple controls, control arrays are a very useful means to reduce the huge number of event procedures often necessary in complex Visual Basic programs. Fewer procedures mean easier navigation through the program code, allowing the whole application to be more comfortably maintained.

Many programmers, especially beginners, tend to underestimate the importance of elegance in code and do not put any effort into adding a good amount of remarks, correctly indenting If blocks and loops, and so on. While the "quick and dirty" approach works well for prototypes and small-sized programs and utilities, you should not follow it for commercial quality applications, especially if you plan to maintain and update them for a number of years.

Control arrays give you cleaner code with fewer procedures, so they indirectly increase the readability of your listings. Of course, you still need a disciplined approach to code writing. You are requested to follow a (relatively small) number of guidelines and conventions, but at least you don't have to struggle with hundreds of distinct event procedures.

On the other hand, control arrays do have a readability defect, which is explained in the next section.

A Defect of Control Arrays

This is probably the wrong section for this discussion, but I thought it would be fair to balance the many advantages of control arrays with at least one defect. After all, nothing is perfect, and control arrays are no exception.

Meaningless Names for Controls   If you gather more unrelated controls in one control array, you obviously lose the opportunity to assign a meaningful name to each individual control. This trait reduces the overall readability of the program because names like txtQuantity and txtUnitPrice are clearly more descriptive than, say, Text1(1) and Text(2).

If you are experiencing this kind of problem, you may reduce its extent by using symbolic constants for indexes, as in:

Part
II

Ch
12

```
Const QUANTITY = 1
Const UNITPRICE = 2
Const TOTAL = 3
Private Sub Text1_Change(index As Integer)
    If Text1(QUANTITY).Text <> "" And Text1(UNITPRICE).Text <> "" Then
        Text1(TOTAL).Text = Format$(Val(Text1(QUANTITY).Text) * _
            Val(Text1(UNITPRICE).Text))
    End If
End Sub
```

Experienced VB programmers know how to write concise code that relies on control arrays and still give controls meaningful names. To fully understand the technique they use, you need to know about object variables.

▶ **See** "Implementing OOP with Classes in Visual Basic," **p. 493** for more information about object variables. If object variables are new to you, you should probably jump over the remainder of this section and come back after reading that chapter.

Improve the Readability of Code   Among their many capabilities, object variables let you access controls—either regular controls or members of a control array—by using different, more descriptive names. In the previous example, you might declare three form-level object variables of type TextBox:

```
Dim txtQuantity As TextBox
Dim txtUnitPrice As TextBox
Dim txtTotal As TextBox
```

You could then assign the three text boxes to these variables. Be sure to perform the assignments before you reference the variables. The Form_Load event is a good place to do them:

```
Private Sub Form_Load()
    Set txtQuantity = Text1(0)
    Set txtUnitPrice = Text1(1)
    Set txtTotal = Text1(2)
End Sub
```

At this point, txtQuantity and Text1(0) actually point to the same control, so you can use them interchangeably:

```
Private Sub Text1_Change(index As Integer)
    If txtQuantity.Text <> "" And txtUnitPrice.Text <> "" Then
        txtTotal.Text = Format$(Val(txtQuantity.Text) * _
            Val(txtUnitPrice.Text))
    End If
End Sub
```

Using the numerical index is still more convenient in certain cases—when writing generic validation code, for instance:

```
Private Sub Text1_KeyPress(Index As Integer, KeyAscii As Integer)
    ' reject a decimal point if the field already has one
    If Chr$(KeyAscii) = "." Then
        If Instr(Text1(Index).Text, ".") > 0 Then KeyAscii = 0
    End If
End Sub
```

Using Static Control Arrays

This section shows you a number of interesting uses for *static* control arrays.

N O T E Please note that I use the terms *Static* and *Dynamic* control arrays only for didactical purposes, and to introduce advanced features in a gradual manner. Regardless of the method you use to create a control array and its elements, you use the same code to manipulate items created at design time and items created dynamically at run time. ▪

Groups of Option Buttons

Option buttons—also known as radio buttons—are used for mutually exclusive choices. Say you have seven option buttons —optSunday, optMonday,...optSaturday. The user can select one button and store the corresponding value into a database. Somewhere in your program you presumably have the following procedure:

```
Function SelectedWeekDay()
    If optSunday.Value = True Then
        SelectedWeekDay = 0
    ElseIf optMonday.Value = True Then
        SelectedWeekDay = 1
    ' ...
    ' .. all the way down to ...
    ' ...
    ElseIf optSaturday.Value = True Then
        SelectedWeekDay = 6
    End If
End Function
```

The only good thing you can say about this approach is that it works. It is neither concise nor efficient. You can save some typing if you group all the seven option buttons into an optWeekday control array:

```
Function SelectedWeekDay() As Integer
    Dim i As Integer
    For i = 0 To 6
        If optWeekday(i).Value = True Then
            SelectedWeekDay = i
            Exit For
        End If
    Next
End Function
```

You can even use a single routine for all the arrays of option buttons used in your program, saving even more code, as shown in Listing 12.3.

Listing 12.3   A Reusable Routine to Determine which Button is Selected in an Array of Option Buttons

```
Function SelectedOption(optArray As Object) As Integer
    Dim opt As OptionButton
```

continues

Listing 12.9   Continued

```
        fnum = FreeFile()
        Open RecentFilePath For Output As #fnum
        fileIsOpened = True
        For Index = 1 To RECENTFILES_MAX
            ' only store non-blank items
            If recentFiles(Index) <> "" Then
                Print #fnum, recentFiles(Index)
            End If
        Next
WriteRecentFiles_Err:
    If fileIsOpened Then Close #fnum
End Sub

Private Function RecentFilePath() As String
        ' return the path of the text file that holds the list
        ' of most recently opened files
        RecentFilePath = App.Path & IIf(Right$(App.Path, 1) <> _
            "\", "\", "") & App.EXEName & ".mru"
End Function

Private Sub UpdateRecentFileMenu()
        ' update the menu with the list of recent files
        Dim Index As Integer
        ' unload any loaded items
        ' except the first one (index=0) that is a static element
        Do While mnuFileList.UBound > 0
            Unload mnuFileList(mnuFileList.UBound)
        Loop
        ' temporarily hide the separator at the
        ' beginning of the list
        mnuFileList(0).Visible = False

        ' load filenames into the menu array
        For Index = 1 To RECENTFILES_MAX
            ' take only non-null items into account
            If recentFiles(Index) = "" Then Exit For

            ' load the array item
            Load mnuFileList(Index)
            ' set its caption and hotkey
            mnuFileList(Index).Caption = "&" & Format$(Index) & _
                ". " + recentFiles(Index)
            ' make it visible
            mnuFileList(Index).Visible = True
            ' if at least one item is visible, also the separator
            ' at the beginning of the list should be visible
            mnuFileList(0).Visible = True
        Next
    End Sub

Private Sub AddToRecentFileList(ByVal filename As String)
        ' add a new file to the list of the recently opened files
        Dim found As Integer
```

```
        Dim Index As Integer
        Dim ercode As Integer
        ' do nothing if the file is already on top of the list
        If filename <> recentFiles(1) Then
            ' check if the file is already in the list
            ' if not found, use the last item of the list
            found = RECENTFILES_MAX
            For Index = 1 To RECENTFILES_MAX - 1
                If recentFiles(Index) = filename Or _
                    recentFiles(Index) = "" Then
                        found = Index
                        Exit For
                End If
            Next
            ' move all items in the range [1, found] one
            ' position toward higher indexes
            For Index = found To 2 Step -1
                recentFiles(Index) = recentFiles(Index - 1)
            Next
            ' store the file in the first position
            recentFiles(1) = filename
            ' update the menu
            UpdateRecentFileMenu
        End If
End Sub
```

When working with files, you should always add an error handler because many things could go wrong: another application or user might be reading the file, or the file might have been deleted or corrupted. If an error occurs while reading the individual lines of the file, the error handling routine should close the opened file. If the open command itself has failed, the file does not need to be closed. The two routines ReadRecentFiles and WriteRecentFiles use the fileIsOpened variable to differentiate between the two cases. Note that even if no error occurs, the execution flows into the error handling routine and correctly closes the file.

Both the ReadRecentFiles and the WriteRecentFiles routines call the RecentFilePath function that returns the location of the file that holds the names of recently opened images. In a fully Windows 95-compliant application, you would probably store this information in the system Registry. Because this point is not central to our discussion, I have simply used a text file stored in the same directory as the main application.

N O T E The code in the RecentFilePath function shows how to avoid a common error that can be made when building file paths. Many programmers, in fact, believe that they could build a complete file path using a simpler statement:

```
RecentFilePath = App.Path & "\" & App.EXEName & ".mru"
```

Unfortunately, the previous line of code won't work if the application was installed or copied to the root directory. In that case, the string returned by the App.Path property contains a trailing backslash. Therefore, you end up with *two* consecutive backslashes, and your file name is not valid. ■

Part

II

Ch

12

Listing 12.12   Continued

```
End Sub

Private Sub chkBackorder_GotFocus(Index As Integer)
    NewCurrentLine Index
End Sub

Private Sub NewCurrentLine(newLine As Integer)
    ' set a yellow background for the controls on the
    ' current line, and white for all the others
    Dim Index As Integer
    Dim foColor As Long, bkColor As Long

    currentLine = newLine

    For Index = txtQty.LBound To txtQty.UBound
        If Index = currentLine Then
            foColor = vbHighlightText
            bkColor = vbHighlight
        Else
            foColor = vbWindowText
            bkColor = vbWindowBackground
        End If
        txtQty(Index).ForeColor = foColor
        txtQty(Index).BackColor = bkColor
        cboProductID(Index).ForeColor = foColor
        cboProductID(Index).BackColor = bkColor
        txtDescription(Index).ForeColor = foColor
        txtDescription(Index).BackColor = bkColor
        txtUnitPrice(Index).ForeColor = foColor
        txtUnitPrice(Index).BackColor = bkColor
        lblTotal(Index).ForeColor = foColor
        lblTotal(Index).BackColor = bkColor
        ' don't touch checkbox's colors
    Next
End Sub
```

The NewCurrentLine procedure, as shown in Listing 12.12, does more than simply update the currentLine variable. It quickly scans all of the cells in the grid and sets their foreground and background colors so that they highlight the current line.

N O T E   The preceding code uses VB color constants instead of numerical values. vbHighlight is usually blue, and vbHighlightText is usually white. The default value for vbWindowsBackground is white, and the default value for vbWindowsText is black.

The advantage of this approach is that it delivers coherent results even if the user changes the system color scheme, and the grid continues to be perceived as well integrated in the user interface. You should always use system colors when possible. ▪

Adding and Removing Grid Lines   The core routine of this sample program is the cmdAddItem_Click event procedure that adds a new line of invoice details (see Listing 12.13).

Listing 12.13   INVOICES.FRM—The Routine that Adds a New Line of Controls to the Grid

```
Private Sub cmdAddItem_Click()
    ' add a new line for Invoice details
    Dim newLine As Integer
    Dim lineTop As Single
    Dim i As Integer

    newLine = txtQty.UBound + 1
    ' exit if too many lines
    If newLine > LINES_MAX Then Exit Sub

    ' load all the controls that make up the row
    ' it is preferable to load all controls *before* acting
    ' on their properties, because otherwise a change event might
    ' rise an error since it would refer to a non existing control
    Load txtQty(newLine)
    Load cboProductID(newLine)
    Load txtDescription(newLine)
    Load txtUnitPrice(newLine)
    Load lblTotal(newLine)
    Load chkBackorder(newLine)

    ' then move controls in the correct position, make
    ' them visible and clear them
    lineTop = txtQty(newLine - 1).top + txtQty(newLine - 1).Height

    ' we don't need to modify the Left property, whose
    ' value is inherited by the control in the above line
    txtQty(newLine).top = lineTop
    txtQty(newLine).Visible = True
    txtQty(newLine).text = ""

    cboProductID(newLine).top = lineTop
    cboProductID(newLine).Visible = True
    cboProductID(newLine).text = ""

    txtDescription(newLine).top = lineTop
    txtDescription(newLine).Visible = True
    txtDescription(newLine).text = ""

    txtUnitPrice(newLine).top = lineTop
    txtUnitPrice(newLine).Visible = True
    txtUnitPrice(newLine).text = ""

    lblTotal(newLine).top = lineTop
    lblTotal(newLine).Visible = True
    lblTotal(newLine).Caption = ""

    chkBackorder(newLine).top = lineTop
    chkBackorder(newLine).Visible = True
    chkBackorder(newLine).Value = 0
```

Part
II

Ch
12

continues

Listing 12.13 Continued

```
' load product IDs into the combo box
cboProductID(newLine).Clear
For i = 1 To PRODUCT_NUM
        cboProductID(newLine).AddItem ProductInfo(i).ID
Next

' set input focus to the Qty textbox
DoEvents
txtQty(newLine).SetFocus

End Sub
```

It is worth noting that the routine loads all the control arrays' items *before* acting on their properties. This order is necessary because as soon as you touch the Text property of the txtQty or
txtUnitPrice controls, that control's Change event tries to update the contents of the lblTotal
field on the same line. Of course, if the lblTotal control hasn't been created yet, a runtime error
occurs.

Deleting the current line is a bit tricky because you have to move the contents of all the subsequent lines one position upward first. Only then you can use a set of Unload commands to
safely delete the last line of controls, as shown in Listing 12.14. Note that you cannot delete the
first line of the grid: it cannot be unloaded because it contains controls that were created at
design time:

**Listing 12.14 INVOICES.FRM—The Routine that Deletes One Row of
Controls in the Grid**

```
Private Sub cmdDeleteItem_Click()
        ' delete the current line
        Dim Index As Integer
        Dim lastLine As Integer

        lastLine = txtQty.UBound

        ' exit if the cursor is not on an invoice item or if there
        ' is only one line (these controls are created at design time
        ' and cannot be unloaded)
        If currentLine = 0 Or lastLine = 1 Then Exit Sub

        ' move all values up one row
        For Index = currentLine To lastLine - 1
            txtQty(Index).text = txtQty(Index + 1).text
            cboProductID(Index).text = cboProductID(Index + 1).text
            txtDescription(Index).text = txtDescription(Index + 1).text
            txtUnitPrice(Index).text = txtUnitPrice(Index + 1).text
            lblTotal(Index).Caption = lblTotal(Index + 1).Caption
            chkBackorder(Index).Value = chkBackorder(Index + 1).Value
        Next

        ' clear the lblTotal value for the last line
```

```
'  (this forces the evaluation of grand total)
lblTotal(lastLine).Caption = ""

' if we are about to delete the control that has the
' input focus, move the focus elsewhere
If currentLine = lastLine Then
    txtQty(lastLine - 1).SetFocus
End If

' unload the last line of controls
Unload txtQty(lastLine)
Unload cboProductID(lastLine)
Unload txtDescription(lastLine)
Unload txtUnitPrice(lastLine)
Unload lblTotal(lastLine)
Unload chkBackorder(lastLine)
End Sub
```

Customizing the Grid's Behavior   The event routines that customize the behavior of your grid are next. As soon as the user selects a Product ID, the Description and Unit Price fields are filled with corresponding data, as illustrated in Listing 12.15.

Listing 12.15   INVOICES.FRM—The Routine that Fires when the User Selects a Product ID

```
Private Sub cboProductID_Click(Index As Integer)
    ' the user has selected a product
    Dim i As Integer

    i = cboProductID(Index).ListIndex
    If i >= 0 Then
        txtDescription(Index).text = _
            ProductInfo(i + 1).Description
        txtUnitPrice(Index).text = _
            Format$(ProductInfo(i + 1).UnitPrice, "###.00")
    End If
End Sub
```

Similarly, when the user modifies the value in the Q.ty or Unit Price fields, the Total field is immediately updated to reflect the total value for that line. The code that implements this behavior is shown in Listing 12.16.

Listing 12.16   INVOICES.FRM—The Code that Evaluates the Total for the Current Line in the Invoice and the Grand Total in the Right Corner of the Form

```
Private Sub txtQty_Change(Index As Integer)
    UpdateLineTotal Index
End Sub
```

continues

Part

II

Ch

12

Listing 12.16   Continued

```
Private Sub txtUnitPrice_Change(Index As Integer)
    UpdateLineTotal Index
End Sub

Private Sub UpdateLineTotal(Index As Integer)
    ' update the total value of current line
    If txtQty(Index).text <> "" And txtUnitPrice(Index).text <> "" Then
        lblTotal(Index).Caption = Format$(CCur(txtQty(Index).text) * _
        CCur(txtUnitPrice(Index).text), "###,###.00")
    Else
        lblTotal(Index).Caption = ""
    End If
End Sub

Private Sub lblTotal_Change(Index As Integer)
    ' update the grand total
    Dim i As Integer, result As Currency

    For i = lblTotal.LBound To lblTotal.UBound
        If lblTotal(i).Caption <> "" Then
            result = result + CCur(lblTotal(i).Caption)
        End If
    Next
    lblGrandTotal.Caption = Format$(result, "###,###.00")
End Sub
```

Whenever one of the Total fields is modified, its Change event updates the Grand Total field in the bottom-right corner of the form.

Listing 12.17 shows the routine that is executed when the user clicks the column headers:

Listing 12.17   INVOICES.FRM—This Routine Asks for a Label for the Column Header when the User Clicks the *lblColumn* Label Controls

```
Private Sub lblColumn_Click(Index As Integer)
    ' change the header of this column
    Dim newCaption As String
    newCaption = InputBox$ _
        ("Enter a new label for this column", "My Grid", _
        lblColumn(Index).Caption)
    If newCaption <> "" Then
        lblColumn(Index).Caption = newCaption
    End If
End Sub
```

Validating the Data Entered by the User   The last group of routines implements a limited form of data validation on the many fields on the form, both within and outside the grid. Again, this is a rather simple task, thanks to control arrays (see Listing 12.18).

Listing 12.18   INVOICES.FRM—This Code Rejects Invalid Keys in a Few Fields in the Invoice Header

```
Private Sub txtHeader_KeyPress(Index As Integer, KeyAscii As Integer)
    ' ensure that numeric fields only get numeric keys
    If KeyAscii < 32 Then Exit Sub
    Select Case Index
        Case 0, 5    ' Invoice number & ZIP code
            If KeyAscii < 48 Or KeyAscii > 57 Then
                KeyAscii = 0
            End If
        Case 1       ' invoice date
            If (KeyAscii < 48 Or KeyAscii > 57) Then
                If KeyAscii <> Asc("/") Then KeyAscii = 0
            End If
    End Select
    ' protest loudly if necessary
    If KeyAscii = 0 Then Beep
End Sub

Private Sub txtQty_KeyPress(Index As Integer, KeyAscii As Integer)
    ' ignore non-numeric input
    If (KeyAscii < 48 Or KeyAscii > 57) And KeyAscii >= 32 Then
        KeyAscii = 0
        Beep
    End If
End Sub

Private Sub txtUnitPrice_KeyPress(Index As Integer, KeyAscii As Integer)
    ' ignore non-numeric input, but accept decimal separator
    If (KeyAscii < 48 Or KeyAscii > 57) And KeyAscii >= 32 _
        And KeyAscii <> Asc(".") Then
            KeyAscii = 0
            Beep
    End If
End Sub
```

Note that you need more robust routines for data validation in a commercial-quality program. For instance, you should check that the date of the invoice is valid, that the State name is correct, and so on. Now that you have the necessary tools, you can create routines that are more robust than the ones used in this example.

From Here...

This chapter has shown you what control arrays are and you have seen a few possible control array applications. However, as you continue to read this book, you will surely find other ways to put them to good use. Here's a short list of chapters you might refer to for inspiration:

- See Chapter 11, " Exploring New Visual Basic 5 Controls," to learn what a commercial-grade grid can do and try to enhance the simulated grid introduced in this chapter to match those advanced features.

- In Chapter 20, "Building a Multiple Document Interface," you revise the Notepad-like application and add a list of recently opened files, using the material in this chapter as a guideline.

CHAPTER 13

Using Containers

So far, you've learned a good bit about designing programs. You know by now that your programs must not only function properly, they must look good as well. No matter how hard you work to make your program perform its assigned tasks as efficiently as possible, a bland or poorly designed interface can cause your users to have the perception, however unfounded, that your program is junk.

Chapter 20, "Designing User Interfaces," discusses several techniques for enhancing the part of your program that your user sees. You've also seen several different types of controls that you can use in your programs. This chapter takes this knowledge a step further. You will see how to use containers to organize the controls that your application uses. Proper use of containers to group your programs' controls often means the difference between a "functional" program and a really nice one. ■

Using frames to create button groups

By placing option buttons in different containers, you can create multiple groups and allow multiple selections.

Increase your available screen space

The amount of space on a form is limited. By using containers to hold other controls, you can create multiple pages on a single form.

Control the functions accessible to the user

By placing command buttons or toolbars in containers, you can show only the buttons that a user needs at any given time. This can help the user work with the program and make the programming easier.

Create professional-looking dialog boxes

You can use containers, including the tabbed dialog box control, to create dialog boxes that strengthen your program's user interface.

Create wizards for your programs

Many programs today contain wizards to help users with difficult tasks. By using containers, you can create your own wizard to help users with your program.

Exploring the Uses of Containers

Containers are a special type of control that is available in Visual Basic. The primary function of containers is to help you organize other controls on your forms. Containers can help you show or hide controls as a group, respond to changes in the program, or respond to user actions. Containers are also used to create functional groups of option buttons so that you can select more than one button at a time on a form. This extends what you can do with option buttons in your programs.

Creating Multiple Pages on a Form

When you develop a simple program, one form might provide sufficient space for your entire application. But as you develop more complex programs, you will find that the available space on a form is one of the most limiting factors in program design. You can only place so many controls on a single form before you either run out of room or, more often, before your form starts looking very cluttered. A cluttered form looks unprofessional and is hard to use. Figure 13.1 shows a membership information form that tries to handle too much information.

FIG. 13.1

Cluttered forms are a poor design choice.

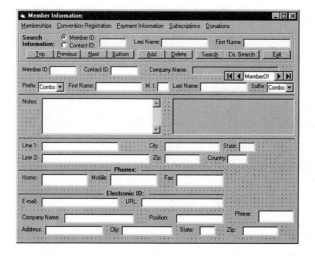

You could solve the problem by using multiple forms. This way, you can place some of the controls on a second or third form and show the supplemental forms only when necessary. For many applications, this is the best solution to the problem, especially if the data on the different forms is not closely related.

However, many applications (like the membership program shown in Figure 13.1) contain a large amount of related data. For these types of applications, moving between multiple forms to enter data is very inconvenient. Another solution is to go ahead and add all the controls you need to the form, but selectively hide and show certain controls by using their `Visible` properties. However, this method requires an unwieldy amount of code if you have more than a few controls, and it makes positioning them in design mode almost impossible.

Fortunately, there is an alternative. Several container controls in Visual Basic allow you to show, hide, and position groups of controls. They are known as *container controls* because you can draw other controls inside of them. For example, you could draw a TextBox on a PictureBox similar to the way you draw it on a form. The PictureBox then "contains" the TextBox.

> **N O T E**   Container controls create a different visual relationship between the form and the controls they contain. The code events and scope of variables on the form remain unaffected. ■

Containers enable you to place all the controls on one form but display only the ones that you need to work with at the moment. You can use command buttons, toolbar buttons, or the container's own tabs to switch back and forth between groups of controls. Three container controls come with Visual Basic:

- ■ Frame control
- ■ PictureBox control
- ■ Tabbed Dialog control

> **N O T E**   The Tabbed Dialog is one of the Custom Controls in Visual Basic. To use it, you must first add it to the Toolbox from the Components dialog box (choose Project, Components). ■

> **CAUTION**
> Even when using containers, you should still limit the number of controls that you place on a single form. Remember, they are still on the form even if they are not currently visible. Too many controls use a lot of memory and make your forms load much slower. A good limit is 200 controls on a single form.

Creating Groups of Option Buttons

In addition to using containers to place more controls on a single form, you will find that containers are useful for creating groups of option buttons. In Chapter 9, "Using the Windows Standard Controls," you saw that you could select only a single option button on a form. Let's now revise that rule to read "you can select only a single option button within a container." Placing container controls on the form allows you to create multiple groups of option buttons. This lets you create applications with groups of multiple choice questions, such as the survey form shown in Figure 13.2.

Using Frames

The Frame control is the simplest of all the container controls. The only function of the Frame control is to hold other controls. In contrast, the PictureBox control can display graphics in addition to holding other controls, and the Tabbed Dialog control has built-in page navigation features.

Part

II

Ch

13

FIG. 13.2

Survey forms use containers to create multiple button groups.

The Frame control is quite simple and performs its job very well. In fact, it has one key advantage over the other container controls: It uses fewer of your system's resources than the other controls. Therefore, if you do not need to display pictures in the background of your container and do not need the built-in navigation features, the Frame control is the best choice for the job. You will almost always use the frame for creating button groups.

Setting Up a Frame

As with all other controls, the first step in setting up the Frame control is to draw it on your form in the size that you want. Then, of course, you need to set the Name property to a unique name. At this point, there are several properties you can set that control the appearance of the frame: Caption, Appearance, and BorderStyle. Figure 13.3 shows a variety of frames that display different effects of these properties.

▶ **See** "Exploring Properties," **p. 72**

FIG. 13.3

You control the frame's appearance through the Appearance, BorderStyle, and Caption properties.

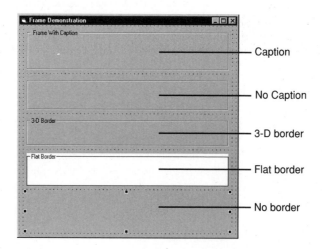

The first property of note is the Caption property. If you enter a value in the Caption property, the text you enter appears in the upper-left corner of the frame. This caption can be used to identify the contents of the frame or provide other descriptive information. If you don't want a caption and simply want an unbroken border around the frame, delete the text in the Caption property.

TIP To avoid having the lines of the border touch the text of the caption, insert a space before and after the text when you set the Caption property.

The second property is the Appearance property. This property controls whether the border of the frame is shown as a single-line, single-color border, which gives the control a flat look, or is shown using lines, which give the control a 3-D effect.

The final property is the BorderStyle property. This property determines whether the border around the frame is displayed. If the BorderStyle property is set to None (using a value of 0), no border is displayed, and the caption is not displayed because it is also part of the border.

TIP If you want the frame to appear without a border, leave the border turned on while you are in design mode, but then set the BorderStyle property to 0 when your form loads. Having the border displayed in the design environment makes it easier to see the boundaries of the frame.

Working with Controls in a Frame

After you have set the properties of the frame, you are ready to start placing controls in the frame. You can place any controls you like in the frame (or any other container). You can even place containers within containers.

To place controls in a frame, first highlight the frame with a single click (it's important that the frame is selected before drawing the control). Then draw controls in the frame just like you would draw them on the form. You need to make sure that the cursor is inside the frame when you start drawing the control. Otherwise, the control will not be contained by the frame. Figure 13.4 shows several controls for a personnel application drawn in a frame.

▶ **See** "Adding Controls to the Form," **p. 93**

Part
II
Ch
13

FIG. 13.4
Make sure that your cursor is inside the frame before you start to draw a control.

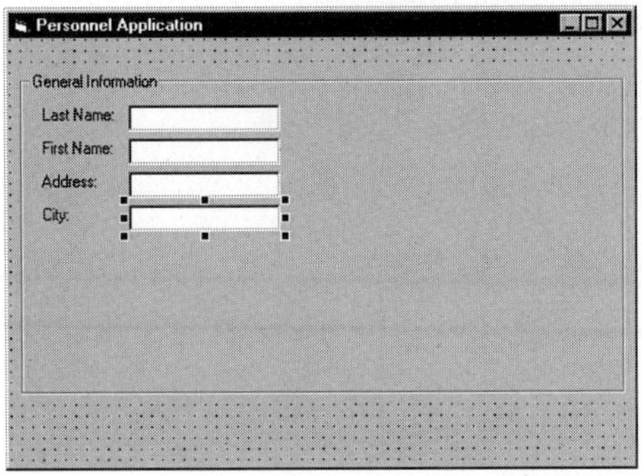

Personnel Application

General Information
Last Name:
First Name:
Address:
City:

Here are a couple of points about controls and frames. First, any controls already on the form will not be contained by the frame, even if you draw the frame over the control. Second, unlike moving controls around on the form, you cannot move a control into or out of a frame by dragging and dropping the control. You can drag a control over the frame and the control will look like it is contained within the frame, but it really isn't. The only way to move a control from other parts of the form into the frame is to use cut and paste. You first cut the control from the form by selecting the control and then pressing Ctrl+X or choosing Edit, Cut. The next step is to paste the control into the frame by selecting the frame and then pressing Ctrl+V or choosing Edit, Paste. The control is initially placed in the upper-left corner of the frame, but after the control is in the frame, you can use drag and drop to move the control. You can use the same technique to move a control out of the frame. You can, of course, move multiple controls at the same time.

 T I P If you want to make sure that a control is in the frame, try moving the frame. If the control moves with it, the control is part of the frame. If the control does not move with the frame, you can use cut and paste to move it into the frame.

In Chapter 4, "Working with Forms and Controls," you saw how you could select multiple controls on a form to work with their common properties or to handle alignment and sizing tasks. You can do the same thing with controls inside a frame. The only difference is in the way you select the controls. To select a group of controls, you first need to click the form so that no controls are selected. Then hold down the Shift or Ctrl key while you click and drag the mouse around the controls in the frame. This selects the group of controls, as shown in Figure 13.5. You can still select or deselect other controls by holding down the Ctrl key while you click the controls.

FIG. 13.5

You can work with multiple controls inside a container.

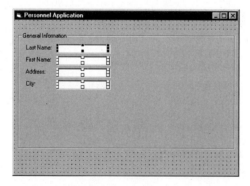

N O T E When selecting a group of controls, the selected controls must either be all inside or all outside a container. Also, control selection cannot span containers. ■

After the multiple controls are selected, you can work with their common properties or use the Format menu's commands to position and size the controls.

CAUTION

The Format menu's Center in Form command centers the selected controls in the form, not within the frame or other container control that they might reside in. This, in effect, renders the Center in Form command useless for controls placed inside a container.

Swapping Pages on a Form

In the section "Creating Multiple Pages on a Form" earlier in this chapter, you read that one of the uses of frames and other containers is to create multiple "pages" on a form. This technique refers to alternately showing different controls in the same location, much like turning the pages in a book. Now you get to see how this is done. The first step of the process is to determine what data will be placed in each frame to create the pages of the form. After you have determined what data will fit into each frame, you can start creating the frames themselves. You create the first frame in the manner that was discussed in the last two sections—that is, draw the frame on the form and then add the controls to the frame. Figure 13.6 shows the frame used to create the first page of a personnel application.

FIG. 13.6

The first page of a sample personnel application contains general information.

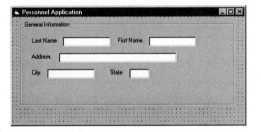

If you're going to use a series of "pages" on a form, including several frames, frames within frames, and so forth, it's a good idea to create a "storyboard" to help stay organized. This involves sketching out each frame and the controls it will contain, as well as tracking the navigation order between the various frames, much like a story editor might sketch out the various scenes of a cartoon to keep track of how it flows.

Part
II

Ch
13

Creating the second page of the form is only slightly trickier than the first page. The key thing that you have to watch is that you start drawing the second frame outside the bounds of the first frame. If you don't do this, the second frame will be contained within the first frame, which defeats the purpose of multiple frames. The easiest way to handle this is to start the second frame below and to the right of the bottom right corner of the first frame. After you draw the second frame, you can add the control of the "page" to the frame. Figure 13.7 shows the second page of the personnel application.

You will probably want to have both frames sized the same. The easiest way to do this is to set the Height and Width properties of the frames to the same value. You might notice in Figure 13.7 that the first frame is hidden by the second frame. If you need to work with the first frame again, select it and press Ctrl+J to bring it to the front of the form. (Ctrl+K moves it to the back of the display order.)

FIG. 13.7

The second page of the sample application contains education information.

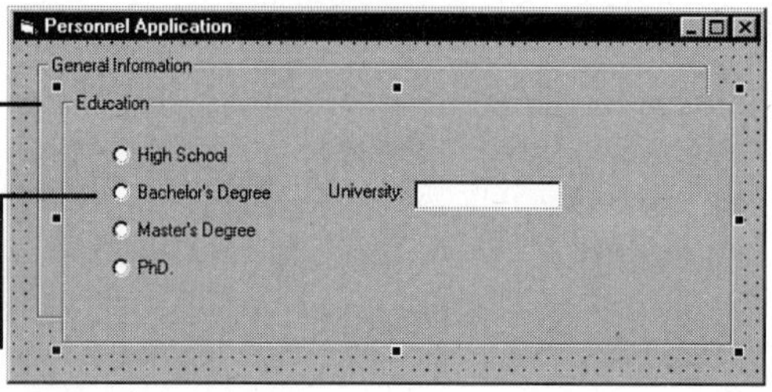

TIP Use code at the beginning of your program to align and size frames. This makes them easier to select in the design environment, and it means you don't have to realign them before running the program.

Now that the frames are set up, you need a way to switch back and forth between them in your program. You switch between the frames by setting the Visible property of one to True while setting the Visible property of the other to False. When the Visible property of a container is set to False, the container and all its associated controls disappear from view. When the Visible property is set to True, the container and controls reappear.

The actual switch takes place in code that you write for the program. You can place the code in any event you want. However, the most typical location is in the Click event of command buttons. The code in Listing 13.1 shows how the second frame would be hidden and the first frame displayed.

Listing 13.1 *FRAMES.FRM*—Use a Command Button to Switch Between Frames

```
fraEducation.Visible = False
fraGeneral.Visible = True
fraGeneral.Top = 240
fraGeneral.Left = 240
```

Similar code would be used to display the second form and hide the first form. You would also want to place the code from Listing 13.1 in the Load event of the form to set up the initial page of the application. Figure 13.8 shows how the form would look with the first frame displayed.

Another approach to handling two pages is to use the same command button for both pages and to change the Caption property of the command button to identify which frame it will display. Listing 13.2 shows how to accomplish this.

FIG. 13.8
You can use one
command button for
each page of the
application.

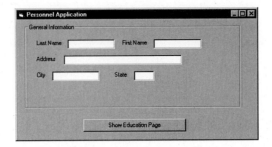

Listing 13.2   FRAMES.FRM—Use a Single Button to Switch Between Two Frames

```
If fraGeneral.Visible Then
    fraGeneral.Visible = False
    fraEducation.Visible = True
    fraEducation.Top = 240
    fraEducation.Left = 240
    cmdGeneral.Caption = "General Information"
Else
    fraEducation.Visible = False
    fraGeneral.Visible = True
    fraGeneral.Top = 240
    fraGeneral.Left = 240
    cmdGeneral.Caption = "Education Information"
End If
```

You can obviously extend this discussion of using two frames to handle more frames or other containers. In fact, you'll do this when you look at creating a wizard in the section "Creating Your Own Wizard" later in this chapter.

Using Picture Boxes

Like the Frame control, the PictureBox control can also be used as a container for other controls. When used as a container, the picture box holds other controls and allows you to hide and display the controls as a group. Setting up the picture box is very similar to setting up a frame. Simply draw the picture box on your form and then add the controls that you want the picture box to contain.

The PictureBox control has two key advantages over the Frame control: The picture box can display a picture as the background for the other controls, and you can use the Print method and graphics methods to display information directly in the picture box. The only drawback to using the picture box is that it requires more resources than the frame does. Figure 13.9 shows a children's software sign-in screen in which a picture box with a background is used as a container for other controls.

Part
II

Ch
13

FIG. 13.9

Use the picture box if you want a background behind your other controls.

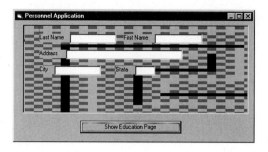

Picture boxes are extremely versatile and can greatly enhance your application's interface. You can, for example, use one or more picture boxes within other containers to precisely place graphic images or to have multiple graphics within one frame. You can also print text to picture boxes instead of a printer, in effect creating a "print preview" for your reports.

▶ **See** "Outputting Reports to Familiar Controls," **p. 398**,

▶ **See** "Using the PictureBox Control," found in "Doing Graphics" on this book's CD-ROM, for more information about setting up a picture box.

Using Tabbed Dialogs

Another way to display large amounts of information on a single form is to use a tabbed dialog, also known as an SSTab control. Tabbed dialogs are used in many of the programs with which you are already familiar. For example, the Options dialog box of Visual Basic (shown in Figure 13.10) and the Options dialog box of Word both use tabbed dialogs to organize and present the various program options.

FIG. 13.10

Tabs enable you to place a lot of information on a form and allow your users easy access to the information.

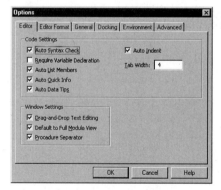

The tabbed dialog can best be compared to the use of file tabs or index tabs in a notebook. Each tab can have a label on it to indicate its contents. Each of the tab pages functions like a Frame control to separate the controls on the current page from the controls on other pages. The tabbed dialog is one of the custom controls that comes with Visual Basic. To be able to use it, you must first select Microsoft Tabbed Dialog Control 5.0 from the Components dialog box (choose Project, Components). After you have selected it, the SSTab control is added to the Toolbox.

N O T E There are two minor differences between the functionality of a tab in the tabbed dialog and a frame. First, you cannot create groups of option buttons directly on a tab. (If you need to place separate groups of option buttons on a tab, you need to place them within a frame on the tab.) Second, tabs have hiding, showing, and alignment built in, while frames must be controlled more with code. ▓

Creating the Tabbed Dialog

Setting up the tabbed dialog begins like the setup of any other control—you draw it on the form. When you first draw the control, it is displayed with three tabs in a single row as shown in Figure 13.11. You can change the total number of tabs and the number of tabs on each row by setting the Tabs and TabsPerRow properties. Changing the setting of the Tabs property increases or decreases the number of tabs from the initial value of three. The TabsPerRow property tells the control how many tabs to display on each row of the SSTab control. If the number of tabs is greater than the number per row, additional rows are added to accommodate all the requested tabs.

FIG. 13.11

The tabbed dialog is initially drawn with three tabs.

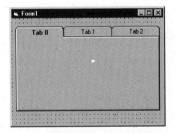

After you have created the tabbed dialog on your form, you can begin adding controls to the tabs. To do this, select the tab where you want the controls to be, and begin drawing controls directly on the tab. To work with another tab, simply select it by clicking the tab with the mouse. As with the frame or picture box, you can place any controls you want on each tab of the tabbed dialog. (See the note earlier in this section about grouping option buttons.) Figure 13.12 shows a completed tabbed dialog.

N O T E Unless you set the Tab property in your startup code, the initial tab displayed will be the last one selected in the design environment. ▓

Part
II

Ch
13

Customizing the Dialog

In addition to controlling the number of tabs in the tabbed dialog, you can control its overall appearance by using a number of properties. Two properties are also available for each tab that allow you to customize the individual tabs.

FIG. 13.12

Place controls on each page of the tabbed dialog to create multiple pages of an application.

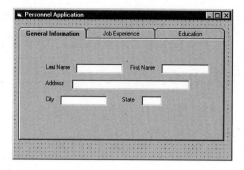

Changing the Appearance of the Dialog

Five key properties of the tabbed dialog control its overall appearance: Style, TabHeight, TabMaxWidth, TabOrientation, and WordWrap.

The Style property controls whether the tabs look like those in Microsoft Office for Windows 3.1 or the property page tabs of Windows 95 applications. The Office-style tabs are the default setting of the property. With the Office-style tabs, each tab is the same width, and the width is set by the TabMaxWidth property. If you choose Windows 95-style tabs, the TabMaxWidth property is ignored, and the tabs are sized to fit the caption of the tab. Figure 13.13 shows both styles of tabs.

FIG. 13.13

The two styles of SSTab controls illustrate how different-length tab captions are treated.

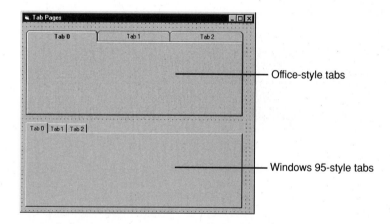

Office-style tabs

Windows 95-style tabs

The TabHeight property controls the height (in twips) of the tab portion of each page. The TabMaxWidth property sets the maximum width (in twips) of each tab. Setting this property to 0 causes the tabs to be sized to fit all the way across the control. Remember, the TabMaxWidth property has no effect on Windows 95-style tabs.

The TabOrientation property controls the placement of the tabs in relation to the body of the control. You can choose to have the tabs placed at the top of the control (the default setting), the bottom of the control, or on the right or left side of the control. Figure 13.14 shows the placement of tabs at the top and right of the control.

FIG. 13.14

You can choose where to position the tabs on the control.

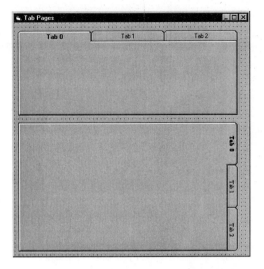

> **T I P** If you are placing the tabs at the side of the control, be sure to use a TrueType font that can be rotated to be displayed vertically.

The final property to look at is the WordWrap property. This property controls whether multiple lines of text will be printed in the tab. If WordWrap is set to True, the text of the Caption property will be placed on multiple lines, if necessary. If there are more lines than will fit within the height of the tab, some of the caption will be lost. If the WordWrap property is set to False, only one line will be shown in the tab. If the Caption is larger than the tab can accommodate, only the center portion of the caption will be visible.

Customizing the Individual Tabs   While the previous section dealt with the appearance of the tabbed dialog as a whole, you can also customize the individual tabs of the control. There are two properties for customizing each tab: the TabCaption property and the TabPicture property. These properties allow you to specify a custom caption and a picture for each tab in the control. While you are working with the tabbed dialog in the design mode, you do not see these properties listed in the Properties window. Instead, you see the Caption and Picture properties. As you work with each tab, the TabCaption and TabPicture properties for that tab are displayed in the Caption and Picture properties.

Setting the Caption property has the same effect on a tab as it does on a label or command button. The contents of the Caption property are displayed on the tab. Unless you are using long captions, each caption will probably appear as a single line of text on the tab. If the caption is long, its appearance will be controlled by the setting of the WordWrap property.

If you want to include a picture on the tab, you simply set the Picture property of the tab to the image that you want displayed. If a picture is used, the SSTab control places as much of the picture on the tab as possible. The picture is centered vertically and horizontally on the tab. If the picture is taller than the tab height, both the top and bottom of the picture are cropped.

Part

II

Ch

13

From side to side, the picture and the caption are centered together. This means that the caption text appears to the right of the picture, and the total width of of the picture and the caption are centered. The picture is not cropped on the sides unless it is wider than the width of the tab. For pictures smaller than the width of the tab, the full width of the picture is shown and the caption is given the remaining space. Figure 13.15 shows a SSTab control with pictures and captions set for each tab.

FIG. 13.15

Pictures on the tabs can indicate the information they contain.

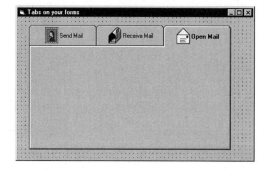

Using the Property Pages   Although you can set all the properties of the Tabbed Dialog control from the Properties window, you might find it easier to use the Property Pages. You access the Property Pages by clicking the ellipsis (...) button next to the `Custom` property in the Properties window. The Property Pages give you access to all the properties of the tabbed dialog and make it easy for you to set the caption and picture of the individual tabs. Figure 13.16 shows the Property Pages for the tabbed dialog.

FIG. 13.16

Access all properties of the tabbed dialog by using the Property Pages.

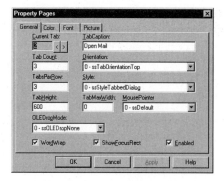

Controlling the Dialog from Code

You can set up all the pages of the tabbed dialog from design mode, but sometimes you might want to change some parts of the dialog while your program is running. The most common thing to do in code is to disable or hide particular tabs in the control. You might do this for a personnel application where you would want only managers to have access to information about employee compensation or evaluations. Most of the properties of the tabbed dialog are handled through the use of simple assignment statements. However, changing the properties of individual tabs requires special treatment.

Previously, you saw that the caption and picture displayed on each tab were contained in the `TabCaption` and `TabPicture` properties, respectively. These properties are actually property arrays, with one element for each tab in the control. The index of the array runs from 0 to one less than the total number of tabs in the control. For example, if you want to change the caption of the first tab in the tabbed dialog, you would use the following code:

```
tbdPersonnel.TabCaption(0) = "Employee"
```

In a similar manner, you could change the picture displayed on the tab by setting the `TabPicture` property. In this case, you would use the `LoadPicture` statement to get a picture from a file, or you could use a picture contained in the `Picture` property of another control.

To handle the personnel application, you would want to either disable or hide any tabs that contained confidential information. To disable a tab, you would set its `TabEnabled` property to `False`. When the tab is disabled, its caption is grayed to indicate that the tab cannot be accessed. This is shown in Figure 13.17. If you want to hide the tab altogether, you can set the `TabVisible` property to `False` keep to the user from even knowing that the tab exists.

FIG. 13.17

Disabled tabs cannot be accessed by the user.

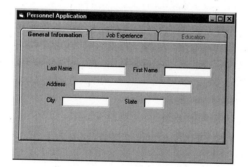

One other thing that you might want to do in your application is to show a specific tab in response to a user action. You might want to have a data validation routine that checks the value of all entered data before saving it to a database. If the user failed to enter a value or entered an improper value, you will want to display the tab that contains the control with the invalid data. To show a specific tab, you simply set the `Tab` property of the tabbed dialog. For example, the following code displays the second tab of a dialog:

```
tbdPersonnel.Tab = 1
```

Putting Containers to Work

Now that you have seen how to create the various types of containers for your programs, look at how you might use a few of these in real-life situations. Look at several relatively simple situations and then move on to creating a wizard that you could use in your applications.

Part

II

Ch

13

Displaying the Proper Buttons

You saw that one use of frames was to create multiple pages of information on a single form. However, you can also use frames to provide the user with only the command buttons that are appropriate to a specific task. I have used several variations of this method in my own programs.

The first use of this technique is in data-entry applications. In a typical application, you have buttons that allow you to move from record to record within a table. This lets the user display data and search for a particular record. Figure 13.18 shows a typical set of buttons.

FIG. 13.18
One set of buttons shown is for record navigation.

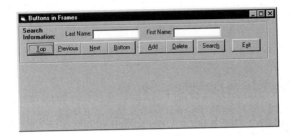

However, as soon as users start editing the record, you would want to display buttons that allow them to either save the changes or cancel the changes and return the original values to the display. Also, it is a good idea to avoid any problems that might be associated with moving to other records while editing is in progress. How can you handle this? Frames to the rescue!

By placing the record navigation buttons in one frame and the Save and Cancel buttons in another frame, you can easily switch between the two buttons sets. To make the switch, you simply set the Visible property of one frame to True and set the other one to False. This is handled by code similar to that shown in Listing 13.3. The code also changes the ForeColor property of the controls to give a visual indication to users that they're in edit mode. You can call this code from the Change event of your text boxes so that it is invoked whenever users make a change. Figure 13.19 shows the same form after the button switch.

On the CD

Listing 13.3   *SWITCH.FRM*—Use Multiple Frames to Handle Command Button Sets

```
Dim I As Integer

' For the sake of this example, we have an array of 8 text boxes
For I = 0 To 8
    txtOrg(I).ForeColor = vbRed
Next I

'Here we hide one frame and then show another
fraRecNav.Visible = False
fraSave.Visible = True
```

FIG. 13.19
A second set of buttons is used to handle Save and Cancel functions.

A second use of frames for containing buttons is to display only the functions that a user is allowed to see. In one of my applications, different sets of command buttons were available to users with different security levels. By grouping the buttons in frames, it was easy to show only those buttons that corresponded to the user's security level.

Creating Browse and Detail Pages

One use of the two-page form is to create a browse and detail page for information in a database. The browse page would use a grid control to display selected information from a number of records. The detail page would then display all the information for the record currently selected in the grid. A single command button could be used to make the switch between the two pages. Figures 13.20 and 13.21 show the two views of the data.

FIG. 13.20
Browse multiple records to get an overall view of data.

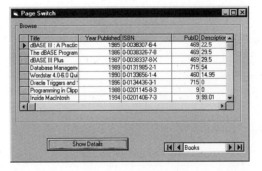

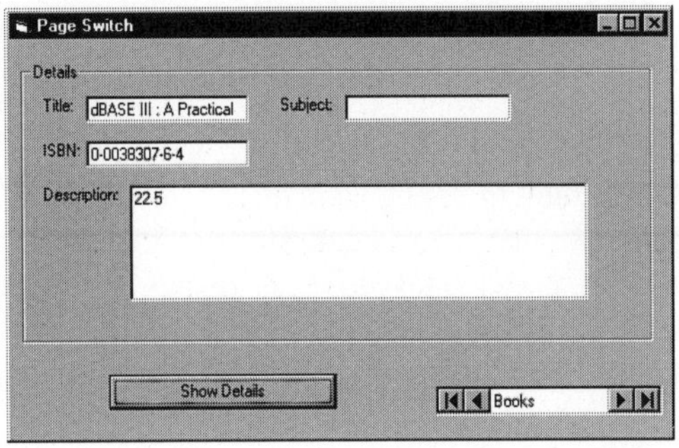

FIG. 13.21
Switch to detail view to get more information or to edit the data.

Part
II

Ch
13

Creating Your Own Wizard

You have probably come across *wizards* in several of the applications that you use. Wizards are actually miniature programs that help you perform a specific task step by step. For example, Word has a wizard that helps you perform a mail merge, and Visual Basic has a wizard that helps you set up a data access form. You can create your own wizard by using a series of frame controls. To make the wizard that you create really flexible, you will use control arrays for the frames and the command buttons. This makes the wizard easier to set up and easier to program.

The first step in creating a wizard is to set up a frame template. To do this, start with a clean form and draw a frame that is the size you need for all the pages of your wizard. Next, check the Height and Width properties of the form and place code in the Load event of the form to set these properties to their initial values. You will see why this is necessary in a moment. After drawing the frame, set its Name property to a unique name. Next, delete the text in the Caption property so that you have an unbroken border on the frame. Finally, create the first element of the frame array by setting the Index property to 0.

After you have set up the frame, you need to set up three command button arrays. Within each frame we will place command buttons with captions set to Exit, Previous, and Next. To create a command button array, draw a command button on the frame and set its Name and Caption properties. Then set its Index property to 0. As with the frame array, this creates the first element of each button array. After you have added the command buttons, your form should look like Figure 13.22.

FIG. 13.22

Start the wizard by creating a template frame as the first element of a control array.

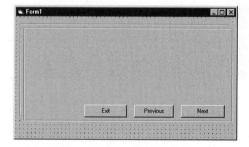

The reason for using control arrays will now become obvious. Before you place any other control on the frame, make a copy on the form. You do this by clicking the frame, pressing Ctrl+C to make a copy, and then pressing Ctrl+V to paste the copy on the form. As you make the copy of the frame, you also create copies of all the controls in the frame. This makes it easy to create multiple pages that have the same basic look. Also, by using command button arrays, you have to enter code in only one place to handle the navigation between pages. Listing 13.4 shows the code that would be used to move to the next page in the wizard. This code also sets the Top and Left properties of the next frame to assure that it is in the same position as the previous frame. Similar code would be used to move to the previous page. Also, if you had processing that needed to occur between pages, you could use a `Select` statement and check the `Index` argument to determine which page you are on.

On the CD

Listing 13.4 WIZARD.FRM—Use a Control Array to Facilitate the Programming of the Wizard

```
Private Sub cmdNext_Click(Index As Integer)
 fraWizard(Index).Visible = False
 fraWizard(Index + 1).Visible = True
 fraWizard(Index + 1).Top = 240
 fraWizard(Index + 1).Left = 240

 Select Case Index + 1
    Case 1
            'Code to process first page goes here
    Case 2
            'Code to process second page goes here
 End Select
End Sub
```

After you have created all the pages you need, you need to place a Finish button on the last page. Also, on the last page, you need to disable or hide the Next button because there is no next page. Similarly, you should disable the Previous button on the first page of the wizard. At this point, the shell of your wizard has been created and you can begin setting up the other controls for the individual pages.

From Here...

Containers provide a number of useful functions in your programs. They allow you to place more information on your forms, create groups of options, and even create your own wizards. To learn more about some of the other topics mentioned in this chapter, take a look at the following chapters:

- ■ To learn more about option buttons, see Chapter 9, "Using the Windows Standard Controls."

- ■ To learn more about using picture boxes, see "Doing Graphics" on the companion CD-ROM.

Part

II

Ch

13

Outputting and Displaying Information

CHAPTER 14

Working with Text, Fonts, and Colors

The vast majority of your programs will use text as the primary means of communicating information to the users. "Text" refers not only to text displayed on-screen in controls, but also to text that is stored and created in your program code. To write almost any program in Visual Basic, you need to know how to work with text. In earlier chapters, you learned about displaying text in labels and text boxes. This chapter expands on that knowledge by showing you how properties and functions are used to manipulate text. You also see how to change the appearance of your text by using fonts and colors in your programs. ■

Using controls to work with text

You will see how to display text on-screen through the use of the TextBox and Masked Edit controls.

Manipulating text in Visual Basic

You will learn about some of the many functions available in Visual Basic for working with text.

Controlling the appearance of your text with fonts

You will explore the use of the Font object's properties in your programs.

Letting users control text formatting

You will see how to use the RichTextBox control to create a simple word processor that enables your users to control the appearance of the text that they enter.

Using colors to enhance your interface

You can use a variety of colors to display text and other objects on-screen and on color printers. You will see how the color of the text is controlled.

Getting and Displaying Text

Two of the primary tasks of any program are to retrieve information from the user and to display information to the user. This information is often in the form of text and can be something as simple as the names in a membership list, or something as complex as developing a specialized word processor for a particular industry. Visual Basic provides a number of ways to input and display information. For input, the primary control is the text box, but there are several other controls covered in this chapter. For output, you can display information on-screen by using the TextBox and Label controls, or you can print information directly on a Form object or to the Printer object. This chapter sticks with using the controls; printing is covered in Chapter 15, "Displaying and Printing Reports."

Reviewing the Basic Controls

In Chapter 4, "Working with Forms and Controls," you were introduced to the TextBox and Label controls. As you probably remember, the label can display text to the user, whether the text was entered into the label at design time or assigned with code to the label's Caption property at runtime. The Label control can display a single line of text or multiple lines easily, but it does not allow the user to input text or scroll through the text if there is more than would fit in the control.

The text box, on the other hand, can do everything a label can do—and it allows editing and scrolling. Using a text box, users can enter anything they want, and your program can retrieve this information through the Text property. Your program can also set the Text property to display information back to the user.

Using Other Features of the TextBox Control

In addition to the text box's standard properties, there are several other properties and features of the text box that make it even more versatile. Some key additional properties are the following:

- Locked   This prevents the user from entering information in the text box.
- MaxLength   This limits the number of characters that the text box can display.
- PasswordChar   This causes the textbox to hide the information typed by the user.
- SelLength, SelStart, and SelText   These enable the user to manipulate only the selected (highlighted) part of the text in the text box.

Locking Out the User   First, take a look at the Locked property. Its purpose is to enable you to use the TextBox control for display only. When this property is set to True, no editing can be performed in the text box. One example of using the Locked property is the display of a large amount of text in a text box with scroll bars. This permits users to scroll through the information, but prevents them from changing it. Even when a text box is locked, however, the user can select text and copy it to the Windows Clipboard by right-clicking it and selecting Copy from the context menu that appears.

N O T E Do not confuse the `Locked` property with the `Enabled` property. Setting the `Locked`
property to `True` does not create the "grayed-out" effect. It prevents users from modifying
your text, but it still allows them to select and copy text from the text box to the Windows Clipboard.
Text in text boxes whose `Enabled` property is set to `False` cannot be selected; therefore, it cannot be
copied to the Windows Clipboard. ■

There is nothing special involved in using the `Locked` property; it can be set to `True` or `False` in
code, as follows:

```
txtTest.Locked = True
txtTest.Text = "You can't edit this!"
```

One obvious use of the `Locked` property is to prevent a user from accidentally changing the
information in a text box. In this case, you could place a command button on the form that the
user must click to be allowed to edit the information on the screen. For example, suppose your
Personnel department frequently needs to look up information on employees. A locked text
box will prevent accidental editing of this information. This example is shown in Figure 14.1.

FIG. 14.1

Using the `Locked`
property prevents
inadvertent editing of
text. Notice in the pop-
up menu (automatically
implemented by
Windows), only the
Copy option is available
for a locked text box.

One way to process a bunch of text boxes as a group is to use a control array, which enables
you to use a `For` loop rather than list each text box individually. In this case, code could be
written in the command button's `Click` event procedure to change the `Locked` property from
`True` to `False` as follows:

```
Private Sub cmdEdit_Click()

    Dim I As Integer
    For I = 0 To 5
     txtInfo(I).Locked = False
    Next I

End Sub
```

Another way to change the `Locked` property on a bunch of text boxes is to use a `For Each` loop.
This works even when your text boxes are not in a control array:

Part
III

Ch
14

```
Private Sub cmdEdit_Click()

    Dim objControl As Control

    For Each objControl In Me.Controls
        If TypeOf objControl Is TextBox Then objControl.Locked = True
    Next objControl

End Sub
```

Notice that the For Each structure in this code works with any property or control, not just the Locked property. Also notice that a real-life version of the program probably would check the security level of the user before allowing the edit.

Placing a Limit on Characters   Although typically you think of the text box as handling any amount of text, there are times when you will want to limit the amount of text that a user can enter. You can handle this by using the MaxLength property of the text box control. The purpose of this property is to restrict the number of characters that the user can enter.

There are a number of reasons that you might want to limit the number of characters a user can enter. In many programs, you will be dealing with IDs that are a fixed length. For example, an inventory program might use numbers that are 10 characters long for their parts, or a personnel information system might use social security numbers, which are, by definition, nine digits long.

Another need to limit the length of a text field occurs when working with database files. Most fields in a database file have a specific length. If you allow your user to enter more characters than can be stored in the field, information may be lost, or an error may be generated.

Setting the maximum number of characters is quite easy. Just select the MaxLength property of the text box and type in a number. If you want to permit the user to enter an unlimited number of characters, then enter 0 (the default setting) for the value.

N O T E   The amount of text that the user can enter is not really unlimited. A text box whose MultiLine property is set to True can handle a maximum of about 32,000 characters; single-line text boxes are limited by system memory constraints. ▪

So what happens when the user is entering data and gets to the maximum number of characters? At that point, the text box stops accepting additional characters and beeps each time another character is typed. You can try this for yourself. Place a text box on a form and set the MaxLength property to 10. Then, run the program and start typing in the letters of the alphabet. You will see that A–J are accepted, but when you try to type in the k, the text box does not accept it. This occurs even if you have sized the control so that there is plenty of additional space to the right of the text you entered.

Hiding the Contents If you are using a text box as part of a login form, you will want the ability to hide the password that is entered by the user. To do this, simply enter a character in the `PasswordChar` property of the text box. This changes the text box's display behavior so that the password character is substituted for each character in the `Text` property. You may have seen this effect many times when logging in to Windows or to your company's network.

Note that the contents of the `Text` property still reflect what is actually typed by the user, and your code always sees the "real" text. Although you can enter any character, it is customary to use the asterisk (*) character for hiding text (see Figure 14.2).

FIG. 14.2

Avoid prying eyes by using the PasswordChar property.

Editing Text in a Text Box Thus far, you have looked at how to create various types of text boxes, but how can users edit what they've entered? Are they limited just to typing information? Fortunately, no.

If you have used any Windows word processor, you are already familiar with how to edit the text in a text box. Just as with a word processor, users can use ordinary keys, such as Delete and Backspace, and they can highlight text with the mouse or by using Shift with the cursor keys. They then can cut (Ctrl+X), copy (Ctrl+C), or paste (Ctrl+V) text and even undo their last change by pressing Ctrl+Z. Using these techniques, they can remove or change text and move text around within a text box or between text boxes (see Figure 14.3).

FIG. 14.3

Your users can copy text from one text box and paste it into another.

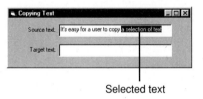
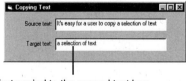

Selected text   Text copied to the second text box

 To select a single word in a text box, double-click the word. You can also use a combination of Shift, Ctrl, and the arrow keys to highlight a word at a time.

Part
III

Ch
14

Windows also provides a pop-up menu for editing use. The user can simply highlight some text in a text box and right-click the text box. A pop-up menu opens containing the Cut, Copy, Paste, and Delete commands, as well as a Select All option. This menu also has an Undo command users can employ to reverse a change, though it's active only when no text is selected.

You already know that the Text property contains all the text in a text box. Suppose a user has selected some text in a text box, and you want to manipulate only that text. The selected text is identified by three properties:

- SelStart   Identifies the starting position of the selected text.
- SelLength   Identifies the length of the selected text.
- SelText   Contains the contents of the selection.

You can use these properties to work with a selected piece of text in your program. Look at the example in Figure 14.3. In this case, the SelText property would contain just the phrase "a selection of text." The SelLength property would contain the integer value 19, which is the length of that string. And the SelStart property would contain the integer value 29, which means the selected phrase starts with the 29th character in the text box.

In addition to determining what has been selected, you can also set the properties from code to alter the selection. Every time you set the SelStart property, you must set the SelLength property to highlight some characters. To select the first three characters, you could use this code:

```
txtTest.SelStart = 0
txtTest.SelLength = 3
```

The SelLength property can be changed multiple times. This will cause the selection to increase or decrease in size, automatically updating the SelText property. Setting the SelText property from code causes the currently selected text to be replaced with a new string, for example:

```
txtTest.SelText = "jumped into oncoming traffic."
```

One use of these properties is to highlight the entire contents of a text box. Suppose, for example, that you have populated some text boxes for a user to edit. When the user presses the Tab key to move to a text box, you might want to highlight whatever is in the text box automatically (this is a Windows standard). This way, the user can start typing immediately, automatically deleting the existing text. This is illustrated in the following code for a text box's GotFocus event:

```
Private Sub txtSelect_GotFocus()
  With txtSelect
    .SelStart = 0
    .SelLength = Len(.Text)
  End With
End Sub
```

N O T E   The first character in a text box has an index value of 0. ▪

Although the text box is great, you can't perform the drag-and-drop editing that you find in some newer word processors. You are also limited to one font and one color of text within each text box. If you require formatting capabilities that are more advanced, you'll probably find what you're looking for in the Masked Edit control described in the next section.

Limiting Text with the Masked Edit Control

Although limiting the number of characters that a user can enter is one way of controlling the input, it often is also necessary to control the type of characters that can be entered (such as letters, digits, or punctuation marks). In addition, there may be times when you want to change the appearance of the text box to include familiar placeholders for data entry, such as parentheses in a phone number or hyphens in a social security number. You could use a standard text box and program code to accomplish this, but there is an easier way.

Visual Basic provides a number of custom controls that are not among the standard set present when you start Visual Basic. Among these is the Masked Edit control. This control enables you to specify the number, type, and position of characters in the data entry field. It also enables you to use placeholder characters within the field. Figure 14.4 illustrates two examples of the Masked Edit control after the user has entered text. Note that they look like ordinary text boxes; however, the masked edit capability of the controls have helped ensure that the data entered conforms to the program's needs.

FIG. 14.4
The Masked Edit control provides considerable control over the number, type, and position of characters in a text field, although it looks to the user just like a normal text box.

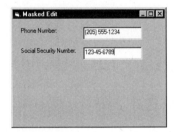

Adding the Masked Edit Control to Your Project   Because the Masked Edit control is not part of the standard control Toolbox, the first step in using the control is to instruct Visual Basic to make the control available to you. Choose Project, Components to open the Components dialog box. After you are in the dialog box, click the box next to Microsoft Masked Edit Control 5.0 and click Apply or OK to add the control to the Toolbox (see Figure 14.5).

 TIP   You can also access the Components dialog box by pressing Ctrl+T or by right-clicking the Toolbox.

    Now that you have added the Masked Edit control to the Toolbox, you are ready to work with it in your program. As with any other control, to add a Masked Edit control to your form, you select its tool in the Toolbox and then draw it on the form where you want it to appear. A Masked Edit control supports only one line of input, so you need to draw it wide enough to contain all the characters to be entered.

N O T E   The Masked Edit control is capable of handling a maximum of 64 characters. Although this is quite sufficient for most needs, if your program requires a larger field, you have to use a standard text box and control the formatting with code. ▪

Part
III

Ch
14

FIG. 14.5

Any control that displays a check mark next to its name will appear in the Toolbox.

The Masked Edit control added to the Toolbox

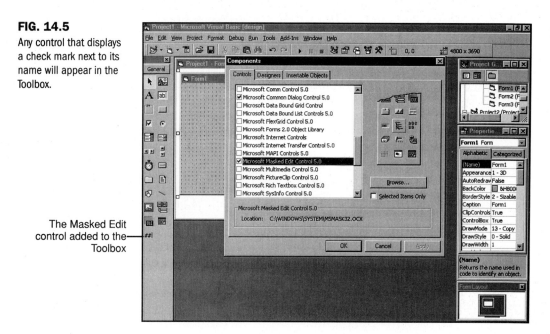

Allowing Only Certain Characters   The purpose of the Masked Edit control is to make sure data is entered in a specific format. Suppose, for example, you put a text box on a form and ask the user to enter a date. One user might use a date format with slashes—12/7/41, for example—whereas another might spell it out—Dec. 7, 1941. The same type of inconsistent input could occur with phone numbers or dollar amounts, among others. You could handle this in code by validating the information before processing it. However, using the Masked Edit control is a cleaner way to do this because it requires no code. With this control, you can specify which characters are allowable and where they are placed in a field.

The Masked Edit control has a Mask property that allows you to tell the control where you want specific characters placed. The Mask property is a string that represents a template of what the text input should look like; for example, ###-#### represents seven numbers with a dash after the third number. The # is a special *character code*, which means only an integer (0–9) can be entered at this location.

The character codes also specify how many characters can be entered in the field. If you put only five character codes in the mask, then no more than five characters can be entered by the user. Table 14.1 shows some of the different character codes that can be used in the Masked Edit control.

Table 14.1 Specify the Characters to Be Entered Using the Mask Property

Mask Code	Allowable Characters
#	Any digit 0–9, space, plus or minus (+ or –) signs
?	Any letter a–z or A–Z
A	Any letter or digit
&	Any character or space

If the Mask property is blank (which is the default setting), then the Masked Edit control behaves like a simple text box.

N O T E A complete list of allowable character codes is listed in Visual Basic's help system under "Mask property." Take a moment to go over this list, which includes number placeholders and optional masks. ▪

By using the Mask property, you can develop input masks for almost any type of data. For example, the mask for a five-digit ZIP code would be #####, or a ZIP+4 code would be entered as #####-####. If you wanted a mask for two-letter state abbreviations, you would use ??. The great thing about this control is that it relieves the developer from some extra coding.

If the user "violates" the mask rules, then the Masked Edit box beeps; the user cannot continue entering text unless it is correct. For example, if the mask is ####, no characters will be displayed until a number is entered. Optional masks, such as 9 for optional numbers, produce a different effect. For example, the mask ?9? would accept either two letters in a row or a number surrounded by two letters.

Keeping Your Place in the Field   Character codes are not the only things that you can enter in the Mask property. You can also place any other characters in the mask for use as placeholders. These characters include (but are not limited to) asterisks (*), dollar signs ($), parentheses, hyphens, and commas. For example, the typical notation for a phone number is (212) 555-1234. Within this notation, the parentheses, space, and hyphen are all placeholders. To represent this in an input mask, you would set the Mask property to (###) ###-####. As a user types a phone number, the first three numbers are entered between the parentheses; then the input skips to the third location in front of the hyphen. In other words, the masked input control automatically skips the placeholders.

By using the character codes and placeholders, you can create many kinds of custom input fields. A few examples are shown in Table 14.2.

Part
III

Ch
14

Table 14.2   Create Many Types of Input Masks with Character Codes and Placeholders

Desired Input	Mask	Example
ZIP Code	#####	35242
Phone Number	(###) ###-####	(205) 555-7575
Social Security Number	###-##-####	123-45-6789
Month-Day-Year	AAA ##, ####	Feb 18, 1998
Date	##/##/##	02/18/98
Time	##:## AA	02:31 pm

Figure 14.6 shows how the Masked Edit control appears before the user types any text in it. Notice that there are underscore (_) characters in every location that you had entered a character code in the Mask property. This tells you, or the user, what locations are available for typing. The character used to indicate these input positions is contained in the PromptChar property. The default value of this property is the underscore, but you can change it to any other character you want, for example, # for a phone number.

FIG. 14.6

Use the PromptChar property to specify which character to use to indicate input positions.

Getting the Information from the Masked Edit Control

Like the text box, the Masked Edit control supports both the Text and SelText properties. This lets you access the entire contents of the field, or just a selected portion.

There are a few differences in the behavior of these properties of which you should be aware. The Text property contains all the information that the user entered, plus any placeholder characters that were in the Mask property. For example, the phone number mask that was used earlier contained parentheses, a space, and a hyphen ((###) ###-####). When a user enters a phone number, only the digits are entered, but the Text property contains all the digits and the placeholders. That is, if the user entered 2055550770, the Text property would contain (205) 555-0770.

There is also another property that can be used to reference the information in the Masked Edit control. This property is the ClipText property. This property, in conjunction with the ClipMode property, enables you to retrieve only the information that the user typed, with or without the placeholder characters. The ClipMode property has two settings, 0–mskIncludeLiterals and 1–mskExcludeLiterals. By setting this property to mskExcludeLiterals, you can retrieve just the user information, with no placeholder characters. Figure 14.7 shows the difference between the information retrieved with the Text and ClipText properties.

FIG. 14.7

The Text and ClipText properties return different parts of the entered information.

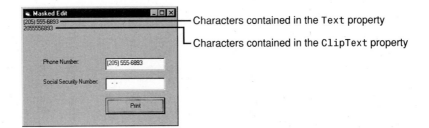

Characters contained in the Text property

Characters contained in the ClipText property

Why is the ClipText property important? Because with many types of numerical entries, such as dates, times, and phone numbers, you want to provide the placeholders for easy data entry by users, but you do not want to store the numbers with all the placeholders. Also, the Mask property can display numbers with commas separating the thousands, millions, and other groups (such as 1,000,000). When the number is used for calculations, you cannot have the commas present.

 T I P The Masked Edit box's beep may not be informative enough for users to correct invalid keystrokes, in which case you might want to use the control's ValidationError event. For example, if the mask is ## and the user types an A, then the ValidationError event occurs. You could add code to this event to inform the user of the proper formatting.

Modifying Text with a Program

Although the text box allows the user to enter and edit text, you will also have many occasions in which you need to modify text strings within your program. Visual Basic provides a number of functions that are useful in modifying text. These functions are as follows:

- ■ UCase and LCase   Changes the case of text to all uppercase or all lowercase, respectively.
- ■ InStr   Finds the location of one string contained within another.
- ■ Left and Right   Retrieves a selected number of characters from one end of a string.
- ■ Mid   Retrieves or replaces a selected number of characters in a string.
- ■ LTrim, RTrim, and Trim   Removes spaces from one or both end(s) of a string.
- ■ Len   Returns the length of a string.

Part

III

Ch

14

N O T E All of the functions in this list (except `Len`) return a `Variant` data type. For each of them, there is an identical function with a dollar sign ($) at the end of the function's name to indicate a String type return value. I recommend using the $ versions (such as `Left$`) whenever possible because they are more efficient. For the sake of readability, the `Variant` versions are used in this chapter. ■

In addition, Visual Basic has the concatenation operator and the ampersand (&), which enables you to combine strings. This section explains how to use these various functions in your program. The concatenation operator was covered in Chapter 8, "Programming Basics." If you need to refresh your memory about its use, please refer to that chapter.

▶ **See** "Working with Strings," **p. 187**

Changing the Case of Letters

There are two functions that can modify the case of letters in a string: `UCase` and `LCase`. The `UCase` function returns a string with all the letters converted to uppercase (capital) letters. The `LCase` function does just the opposite, converting the entire string to lowercase letters.

Although these may appear to be somewhat trivial functions, they actually are quite useful for a number of tasks. First, you can use the functions to properly capitalize names or other words that a user may enter. The code in Listing 14.1 capitalizes the first letter of a word and makes the rest of the word lowercase.

Listing 14.1   CASES.FRM—Using *UCase* and *LCase* to Properly Capitalize a Word

```
Dim lcWord, as String, ProperWord as String, WordLen As Integer
lcWord = LCase(lcWord)
WordLen = Len(lcWord)
ProperWord = UCase(Left(lcWord, 1)) & Right(lcWord, WordLen - 1)
```

These functions are useful, for example, when comparing user input to a predefined value or a range of values. If we convert the user's input to uppercase, we can compare it to an uppercase test string, as in the following example:

```
Select Case UCase(txtOperation.Text)

   Case "WASH"
      ' Do Something
   Case "RINSE"
      ' Do Something Else
   Case "SPIN"
      ' Do Something Else Yet
   Case Else
      MsgBox "Invalid Entry!"

End Select
```

In the code above, if the UCase function had not been used, then the user would receive the Invalid Entry message even if he had entered a "correct" choice in lowercase or mixed case ("Rinse", for example).

Another Visual Basic function, StrConv, performs special conversions of strings. Most of the conversions it can perform are either redundant (converting to all uppercase or all lowercase, for example) or beyond the scope of this book (converting between different types of Japanese characters), but one of its conversion types is worth mentioning here. StrConv can convert a string to *proper case*, where the first letter of each word is capitalized. The following code sample demonstrates this technique:

```
lblHeadline = StrConv(stHeadline, vbProperCase)
```

Examples of using UCase and LCase, as well as StrConv, are illustrated in Figure 14.8.

FIG. 14.8

LCase, UCase, and StrConv can be used to modify the case of the letters in a string of text.

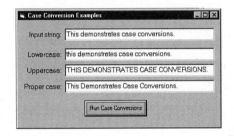

Chapter 10, "Managing Your Project," provides more information on functions and their uses.

▶ **See** "Using Procedures and Functions," **p. 464**

Getting Pieces of a String

Look at the following code from Listing 14.1 again. In addition to using just the UCase and LCase functions, it also uses several functions to extract pieces of text from the original string. This illustrates one of the more important tasks involved in manipulating strings—the capability to add, remove, or change single characters, words, or sections of a string.

```
Dim lcWord, as String, ProperWord as String, WordLen As Integer
lcWord = LCase(lcWord)
WordLen = Len(lcWord)
ProperWord = UCase(Left(lcWord, 1)) & Right(lcWord, WordLen - 1)
```

Visual Basic provides a number of functions that are designed for string manipulations. There are functions that add and remove spaces, a function for determining the length of a string, a function for performing a search, and a function for exchanging one piece of a string for another string.

Determining What Is in the String For many string-related tasks, the first programming requirement is to determine if a word, phrase, or other group of characters exists in a string, and if so, where. The capability to find one string within another enables you to perform word searches within text. This can be used to perform a global replacement of a string, such as replacing the word "text" with the word "string" throughout a word-processing document.

Part

III

Ch

14

Another, more common, reason for searching within a string is *parsing* the string. For example, suppose you have an input string that contains a person's name in this format: "Dr. Stirling P. Williams, Jr." If you have a file of a hundred such strings, putting this information into a database with separate first and last name fields would be a little difficult. However, you could use a string search function along with a little program logic to parse the string into smaller pieces. The function that enables you to search a string for a character or group of characters is the InStr function. This function has two required and two optional parameters. The required parameters are the string to be searched and the text to search for. If the search text appears in the string being searched, InStr returns the index of the character where the search string starts. If the search text is not present, InStr returns 0. The simple syntax of the InStr function is shown here:

```
chrpos = InStr(sourcestr, searchstr)
```

For example, the function call

```
Print Instr("I'll see you next Tuesday.","you")
```

would print a result of 10 because that is the position where the word "you" begins.

The first optional parameter of the InStr function tells the function the character position from which to start the search. This position must be a positive integer. If the starting position is greater than the length of the string, InStr will return 0. This syntax of the InStr function is as follows:

```
chrpos = InStr(StartPos, sourcestr, searchstr)
```

For example, the function call

```
Print Instr(7,"Pride cometh before a fall","e")
```

would return the value of 10, even though the first "e" in the string is at position 5, because the search starts from position 7.

The other optional parameter determines whether the search to be performed is case-sensitive (uppercase and lowercase letters do not match) or case-insensitive. Setting the value of the comparison parameter to 0, its default value, performs a case-sensitive search. Setting the value to 1 performs a case-insensitive search. This syntax is shown here:

```
chrpos = InStr(StartPos, sourcestr, searchstr, 1)
```

Note that with the optional parameters, you can write code that will find each successive search string in your text. The code in Listing 14.2 will print the words in a string that are separated by spaces. It works by taking the result of the InStr function and passing it back in to the StartPos parameter.

Listing 14.2 PARSESTR.FRM—Using the *InStr* Function to Divide a String into Words

```
Sub PrintWords(stInput As String)
    Dim inCounter As Integer
    Dim inFoundPos As Integer

    Const PARSECHAR = " "  'Space

    'If string is blank then do nothing
    If Len(stInput) = 0 Then Exit Sub

    'Start at the first character
    inCounter = 1

    'Search for a space
    inFoundPos = InStr(inCounter, stInput, PARSECHAR)

    'If a space is found print the word and keep searching
    While inFoundPos <> 0
      Debug.Print Mid$(stInput, inCounter, inFoundPos - inCounter)
      inCounter = inFoundPos + 1
      inFoundPos = InStr(inCounter, stInput, PARSECHAR)
    Wend

    'Print the remainder of the string
    If inCounter < Len(stInput) Then
        Debug.Print Mid$(stInput, inCounter)
    End If
End Sub
```

The input and results of this code appear in Figure 14.9.

FIG. 14.9
Use InStr to find all
the spaces in a string.

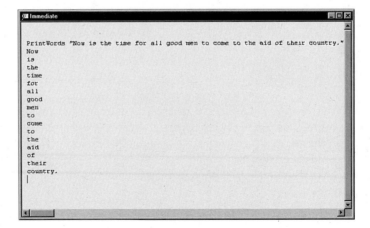

Determining the Length of the String   For many operations, you may need to know how many characters are in a string. You might need this information to know whether the string with which you are working will fit in a fixed-length database field. Or, if you are working with big strings, you may want to make sure that the combined size of the two strings does not exceed the capacity of the string variable. In any case, to determine the length of any string, the Len function is used, as illustrated in the following code line:

```
result = Len(inputstr)
```

You can use the Len function in a number of applications. In many cases, it is used to determine whether there are any characters in a string. If there are no characters, you may want to issue an error message, or at least bypass any further processing. In Listing 14.1, you saw how the Len function was used to find the number of characters so that you could use the Right function to get the remainder of a string.

> **CAUTION**
>
> The Len function reports only the number of characters that are present in a string. It does not report whether a string will fit within a control or on a line of a printout. For these purposes, you need to use the TextWidth and TextHeight methods of the object to which the string is being written. These methods are discussed in Chapter 16, "Displaying and Printing Reports."
>
> ▶ **See** "Using *TextHeight* and *TextWidth*," **p. 416**

Getting Rid of Spaces   Long strings typically contain spaces in the middle of the string, which are necessary for proper spacing of words, paragraphs, and so on. However, you also may end up with spaces at the beginning or end of your strings, which often are unwanted spaces. These spaces typically occur when the user accidentally types a space at the beginning or end of a text field. They also show up when you are using a fixed-length string and the number of characters in the string do not fill the available space.

For example, the following calls to the Len() function would each return a different number:

```
Print Len("Hello, world!")
Print Len("   Hello, world!")
Print Len("Hello, world!   ")
```

Most of the time, spaces don't do any harm except take up a little memory. However, when you combine strings, or try to take action based on their content, unwanted spaces can cause all kinds of problems. For example, suppose you had two 30-character text boxes for first and last names. The user could inadvertently type three characters of text and then a bunch of spaces. If you needed to concatenate the first and last name for a mailing label, the extra spaces would be included. However, Visual Basic provides some string "trimming" functions to eliminate the trailing spaces.

To get rid of the spaces at the end of a string, you can use one of these Visual Basic functions:

- **LTrim**   Removes the spaces from the beginning of a string.
- **RTrim**   Removes the spaces from the end of string.
- **Trim**   Removes the spaces from both the beginning and end of a string.

Each of these functions use a similar syntax. The code in the following lines shows how the Trim function would be used to remove the spaces in the mailing label example (the results of these trimmed strings are shown in Figure 14.10):

```
picMail.Print Trim(FirstName) & " " & Trim(LastName)
picMail.Print Trim(Address)
picMail.Print Trim(City) & ", " & Trim(State) & "   " & Trim(Zip)
```

FIG. 14.10

This user typed extraneous spaces (that we can't see) after the words "Joe" and "Smallville," but Visual Basic's Trim function removed them.

Extracting Pieces of a String   Okay, you have the capitalization of the string right and you have removed all the spaces that you don't need at the ends of the string, but now you find you need to work with only a part of the string. Can Visual Basic help with this problem too? Of course it can.

You will find many situations in which you need to work with only part of a string. Perhaps you'll need to extract the first name of a person from her full name, or maybe you'll need to make sure that the information with which you are working will fit in the database field in which it needs to be stored. This is easy to accomplish by using one of the following Visual Basic functions:

- **Left**   Retrieves a specified number of characters from the left end of a string.
- **Right**   Retrieves a specified number of characters from the right end of a string.
- **Mid**   Retrieves characters from the middle of a string.

First, look at the Left and Right functions, as these are slightly easier to use. (By the way, none of these functions is hard to use.) To use these functions, you specify the input string and the number of characters to be retrieved. The syntax of these two statements is shown in the following lines:

```
OutStr = Left(InptStr, NumChars)
OutStr = Right(InptStr, NumChars)
```

Part
III

Ch
14

When you use these functions, the number of characters specified must be a number greater than or equal to 0. If you enter **0**, a 0 length string is returned. If the number of characters is greater than the length of the input string, the entire string is returned. You will find, as you write programs that manipulate strings, that the Left and Right functions are often used in conjunction with the other string functions.

This is illustrated in Listing 14.3, which retrieves the first name of a person from the full name. This function is used to print name tags for an organization's events. Figure 14.11 shows how this code is used. The function assumes that the person's first and last names will be separated by a space. The function then looks for a space in the input text and, upon finding the space, it extracts the characters preceding the space and supplies those characters as the first name. If there are not any spaces in the input string, the function assumes that only a first name was entered.

Listing 14.3 NAMETAG.FRM—Using the *InStr* and *Left* Functions to Extract a Person's First Name

```
BasString = Trim(txtName.Text)
I = InStr(BasString, " ")
If I > 0 Then
    ScndString = Trim(Left(BasString, I))
Else
    ScndString = BasString
End If
PrtLine1 = ScndString
PrtLine2 = BasString
```

FIG. 14.11

Print name tags using the Left and InStr functions.

Mid is another function that is used to retrieve a substring from a string, and it works in a similar manner to the Left and Right functions, but it has one additional argument. The Mid function is used to retrieve a letter, word, or phrase from the middle of a string.

The Mid function contains two required arguments and one optional argument, as shown in the following syntax:

```
newstr = Mid(sourcestr, startpos[, numchars])
```

Startpos represents the character position at which the retrieved string will begin. If startpos is greater than the length of the string, an empty string is returned. The optional argument numchars represents the number of characters that will be returned from the sourcestr. If numchars is omitted, the function will return all characters in the source string, from the starting position, on to the end. The following are some examples of the Mid function:

```
Print Mid("Robert Allen",8)    'Returns "Allen"
Print Mid("Robert Allen",8,2)  'Returns "Al"
```

Replacing Characters in a String   Now to add a little confusion to your life. You just saw how the Mid function retrieves a piece of a string from the middle of a source string. The same keyword, Mid, is used to replace a part of a string. However, the syntax is quite different, in that we're using the function on the left-hand side of an assignment statement in this case. When used to replace characters in a string, it is referred to as the Mid statement.

The Mid statement replaces part of one string with another string by using the following syntax:

```
Mid(sourcestr, startpos[, numchars]) = replstr
```

The sourcestr in this case is the string that will receive the replacement characters. Sourcestr must be a string variable; it cannot be a literal string or string function. Startpos is the character position at which the replacement will start. This must be an integer number greater than zero. Numchars is an optional argument that specifies the number of characters from the replacement string being used by the function. Replstr represents the string containing the replacement characters. This string can be a string variable, a literal string, or a string function.

The Mid statement preserves the original length of the string. In other words, if the space remaining between the starting position and the end of the string is less than the length of the replacement string, only the leftmost characters will be used from the replacement string.

There are a number of uses for the Mid statement in your programs. Remember the capitalization example in Listing 14.1? Using the Mid statement, you can perform the same function with the following code:

```
inptstr = Trim(txtInput.Text)
frstLtr = UCase(Left(inptstr,1))
Mid(inptstr, 1) = frstLtr
txtOutput.Text = inptstr
```

In another program, I needed to eliminate any carriage return or line feed characters that were embedded in a string to keep them from causing printing problems. I used the Mid statement to replace these characters with a space. This is shown in Listing 14.4.

Part
III

Ch

> **Listing 14.4   NAMETAG.FRM—Using the *Mid* Statement to Eliminate Specific Characters in a String**
>
> ```
> 'Replace Line feeds with spaces
>     nFindPos = 0
>     Do
>       nFindPos = InStr(sInput, Chr$(10))
>       If nFindPos > 0 Then Mid(sInput, nFindPos) = " "
>     Loop Until nFindPos = 0
>
> 'Replace Carriage returns with spaces
>     nFindPos = 0
>     Do
>       nFindPos = InStr(sInput, Chr$(13))
>       If nFindPos > 0 Then Mid(sInput, nFindPos) = " "
>     Loop Until nFindPos = 0
> ```

Working with Specific Characters

Listing 14.4 shows the use of a function that you have not seen before—the Chr function. This function is used to return a character that corresponds to a specific ASCII code. For example, the following two statements both print "HELLO":

```
Print "HELLO"
Print Chr$(65) & Chr$(69) & Chr$(76) & Chr$(76) & chr$(79)
```

N O T E   As with other functions mentioned earlier in this chapter, Chr has two forms: Chr() returns a Variant; Chr$() returns a string. ▪

In the previous example, typing **HELLO** is a lot simpler. However, there are some characters you can't type, like line feeds and carriage returns, so you have to use the Chr function:

```
Print "Line 1" & Chr$(13) & Chr$(10) & "Line 2"
```

The Carriage return/line feed combination deserves special mention. Frequently, you will find yourself using this combination to force a new line in a string, text box, or message box. For this purpose, Visual Basic has included an intrinsic constant, vbCrlf, so that the preceding line of code could be rewritten as follows:

```
Print "Line 1" & vbCrLf & "Line 2"
```

The Chr function can also be used to include quotes:

```
Print Chr$(34) & "This will be printed with quotes" & Chr$(34)
Print "this will not have quotes"
```

You can also use the Chr function to return any letter or number character. Table 14.3 lists some commonly used ASCII character codes.

Table 14.3   ASCII Codes for Some Commonly Used Characters

Code	Represents
8	BackSpace
9	Tab
10	Line feed
13	Carriage Return
32	Space
34	Double quote (")
48	0 (the character for zero)
65	A
97	a

Asc is the companion function to the Chr function. Asc returns the ASCII code of the input character. The following code shows how Asc is used:

```
Print Asc("A") 'Returns 65
```

Working with Strings and Numbers

Another thing to consider is the relationship between strings and numbers. You may already know that some numbers are often treated as character strings. ZIP codes and phone numbers are two such examples. However, there are times when you need to convert a number to a string variable to use it in a string function, or to print it in combination with another string. Likewise, there are times when you need to use numbers contained in a string variable in a mathematical equation or a numeric function.

Visual Basic provides the Str function to convert a number to a string, and the Val function to convert a string to a number. To convert a number to a string, you can do the following:

```
numstr = Str(inptnum)
```

numstr represents a string variable that contains the output of the function. inptnum represents the number to be converted. This can be a number, a numeric variable, or a numeric function. If inptnum is a positive number, Str will return a space in front of the number because Str reserves one character to contain a negative sign, if necessary.

To convert a string to a number, the Val function is used, as follows:

```
numvar = Val(inptstr)
```

numvar represents a numeric variable that stores the output of the function. inptstr can be a literal string, a string variable, or a string function. The Val function first strips out any spaces from the string and then starts reading the numbers in the string. If the first character in the

Part
III

Ch
14

string is not a number (or minus sign), Val returns 0. Otherwise, Val reads the string until it encounters a non-numeric character. At this point, it stops reading and converts the digits it has read into a number.

A Closing Note on Working with Strings

In the preceding few sections, you have read a lot of information about string functions. Make sure, before continuing, that you have learned the concept of what each function is doing. More importantly, understand that string functions return values, but they *do not* modify the input. Consider the following example with the UCase function:

```
Dim s1 As String
Dim s2 As String
s1 = "which case am i"
s2 = UCase$(s1)
```

After this code is executed, the variable s2 will appear in all uppercase letters, whereas s1 will remain unchanged.

Also note that it is common practice to nest string functions within statements rather than using an extra variable. For example, consider the following Select Case statement, which uses a bunch of nested string functions to help with input validation. Users can come up with any capitalization they want to, but it will be handled by the code.

```
stUserInput = InputBox$("Type Yes or No, please!")
Select Case Left$(Trim$(Ucase$(stUserInput)),1)
    Case "Y"
      MsgBox "Yes"
    Case "N"
      MsgBox "No"
    Case Else
      MsgBox "type YES or NO please!"
End Select
```

Controlling the Appearance of Your Text

Being able to manipulate the text in a string is only part of working with text. After manipulating the text within your program, you probably will also want the capacity to control how the text appears to the user. This is the function of *fonts*. If you have worked with a word processor at all, you probably have done some work with fonts. A font describes how the letters and numbers that you use will look. Figure 14.12 shows several different fonts in different sizes. Fonts are like different styles of handwriting—some people print in block capital letters, other people write in script, and some people produce beautiful calligraphy.

FIG. 14.12

Fonts control the appearance of the text on-screen.

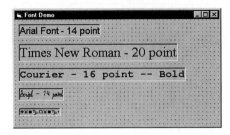

Properties of the Font Object

You may remember from earlier chapters that the Font property is actually an object that has its own properties. The following font object properties control the appearance of the fonts in your program:

- **Name**   Identifies one of the fonts installed on your system. This is a descriptive name in the form of a string, such as "Arial" or "Times New Roman."

- **Bold**   Determines whether or not the font is presented in boldface. Boldface increases the thickness of the lines used to draw the letter, making the letters appear darker and heavier than non-bold characters.

- **Italic**   Controls whether letters are italicized. An italicized character is slanted, with the top of the letter more to the right than the bottom of the letter.

- **Underline**   Controls whether the text is displayed with a thin line under each letter that is printed.

- **Size**   Controls the point size of the font. A font's size is measured in the traditional printer's measure of points. One point is 1/72 of an inch; therefore, capital letters in a 72-point font would be approximately one inch high.

- **Strikethrough**   Controls whether the text is displayed with a thin line through the middle of each letter.

- **Weight**   Controls the width of the line that is used to draw each letter. There are two settings for Weight 400 or 700. These correspond to normal and bold text, respectively.

Recall that the Font property can be accessed in code with dot notation:

```
TxtName.Font.Name="Arial"
TxtName.Font.Size = 10
```

The Font property that you probably will use most often is the Size property. Typically, the default font size is in the range of 8 to 12 points. If desired, though, you can set the font size anywhere from 1 to over 2,000 points, though I wouldn't recommend either extreme. A point size below 8 becomes difficult to read, and a point size of 250 will cause just a few characters to fill the entire screen. Figure 14.13 gives you an idea of the different point sizes.

Part

III

Ch

14

FIG. 14.13

Fonts can range in size
from tiny to jumbo.

4-point font

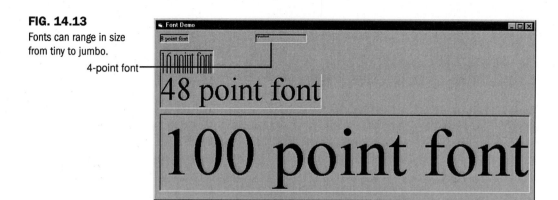

N O T E   A *point* defines the height of the character cell used to draw a character. It is equivalent to
1/72 of an inch. Therefore, when using a 12-point font, approximately six lines of text fit in
a vertical inch. ▪

The idea behind using different fonts and font attributes is to increase the readability of the
information on the screen or to add emphasis to a particular piece of information. The proper
use of fonts can greatly enhance the programs you create.

CAUTION

It is easy to get carried away using different fonts, and this can cause some problems. Too many different
fonts on a single screen can make it look disorganized and confusing. It is best to choose one or two fonts
and then use the fonts' attributes to achieve effects. This will give your programs a cleaner look. However, try
not to get carried away with the other attributes!

Making Life Easier for Portable Computer Users

One big advantage of being able to control font size is that you can make text more readable on
portable computers by increasing the font size. Portable (laptop) PC users probably already know this
well. The 10- or 12-point font that looks great on a 17-inch desktop monitor can be difficult to read
on the 10-inch screen of a portable computer. Therefore, keep in mind the users' screen resolution.
While developers and other "techies" might have 1024×768 or higher screen resolution, the general
public usually uses a much lower resolution, such as 800×600, or even 640×480.

As you may have noticed already, to set a particular font, you have to know its name. It's important to account for the fact that not all systems have the same fonts installed. The `Screen` and
`Printer` objects have properties that let you determine the available fonts for display and printing, as demonstrated in the following code:

```
Dim inCount As Integer
For inCount = 0 To Screen.FontCount - 1
   Print Screen.Fonts(inCount)
Next inCount
```

Of course, you also could use a Font dialog box (from the Common Dialog control) to let the user select from a list of available fonts.

▶ **See** "Form Properties Revisited," **p. 81**

▶ **See** "The Font Dialog Box," **p. 143**

Controlling Fonts in Your Program

Visual Basic lets you control all the attributes of the fonts in your programs. You can specify a font for an entire form or for individual controls. You can even control the fonts used by the printer. Visual Basic enables you to set up fonts during the design phase of your program. It also gives you the ability to actually change them while the program is running. This means that you can allow your user to select fonts for certain parts of the program. Or, you can set up the program so that the fonts change in response to some event in the program, such as a change in the value of a text box.

Setting an Initial Font   The default font for Visual Basic programs is called *MS Sans Serif*. This is the font used in the title bars of most Windows programs. Unless you change the font for a control, this font will be used in every control that you add to your program.

If you want to use a single font for all the components on a form, you can set that font as the form's *base font* before you place any controls on the form. When you change a form's font before adding any controls, all its controls will use that same font (assuming you don't change it for any subsequent controls).

 To set the base font for your form, click the form, and then open the Properties window by pressing F4 or clicking the Properties Window button. Click the ellipsis button next to the Font property to open the Font dialog box. This dialog box, shown in Figure 14.14, enables you to choose the base font, as well as any other attributes you want to set for the form's Font object. Once you have set a particular font, it will be used for all controls added to the form.

N O T E   Changing the font used for the form will not affect any controls already on the form, only new controls that are added to the form. Also, the font setting does not affect the font used for the form's caption (the text in the title bar). This font is controlled from the Windows Control Panel setting. ■

FIG. 14.14

You can change the font for a form by using the Font dialog box.

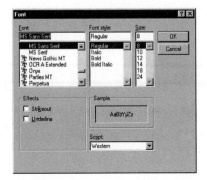

Part

III

Ch

14

CAUTION

If you are creating programs for others to use on their machines, be careful choosing fonts. Others using your program may not have the same fonts as you do. Windows will attempt to substitute a similar font on the user's machine, but the resulting display may be unacceptable.

Setting the Font for Individual Controls   In addition to setting the font for the form, you may want to set a different font, or different attributes, for a single control or group of controls. For example, you may want to give all of your labels one font and all your text boxes a different font. Or, you may decide to use one font for controls containing numbers and another font for those containing letters. (For more information about working with multiple controls, see Chapter 4, "Working with Forms and Controls.")

▶ **See** "Working with Multiple Controls in the Design Environment," **p. 100**

Fonts for individual controls can be changed the same way they are changed for the form. This is done in the design environment by using the Font dialog box. Each control has a Font property. In fact, you could use a different font for each control on your form, though this would lead to a very confusing form.

Changing Fonts While the Program Is Running   Changing fonts in the design environment is great, but if you want your users to be able to set the fonts in your program, you have to provide a way to change your fonts in code. Fortunately, this is easy to do with assignment statements. Each of the properties of the font object can be set from code, as well as from the design environment. Take a brief look at how each property is handled in code; Figure 14.15 shows a program that illustrates the different font properties.

FIG. 14.15

Fonts can be controlled from code.

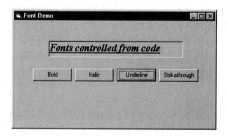

Changing the Base Font   To change the base font of an object, you use an assignment statement that specifies the Name property of the object's Font property. While you can specify the name of a font in a variable or constant, typically you will use the Font dialog box of the CommonDialog control to ask the user for the desired base font. This makes it easy for your users to choose a font. (For more information about the Font dialog box, see Chapter 6, "Using Dialogs to Get Information.")

▶ **See** "The Font Dialog Box," **p. 143**

The following line of code shows how you would change the base font of an object:

```
txtFontDemo.Font.Name = "Times New Roman"
```

Changing the Size of a Font   To set the size of a font, you specify an integer value for the Size property of the Font object. As stated earlier, this value can range from 1 to over 2,000, although values of 8 to 48 are the ones most often used. The following line shows how a font's size is set:

```
txtFontDemo.Font.Size = 16
```

> **CAUTION**
>
> When changing the font size in code, the control using the font may not be able to adjust to accommodate the new size. Therefore, part of the text in the control may not be visible to the user.

Recall from earlier chapters that setting Font properties of a text box causes all existing text to change, whereas setting Font properties of a form or printer does not.

Setting the Other Properties of the Font Object   The other four key properties of the Font object (Bold, Italic, Underline, and StrikeThrough) all have possible values of either True or False. To turn on a property, set its value to True; to turn off a property, set its value to False. The following lines of code illustrate this:

```
txtFontDemo.Font.Bold = True
txtFontDemo.Font.Italic = True
txtFontDemo.Font.StrikeThrough = True
txtFontDemo.Font.Underline = True
```

Working with Formatted Text

Thus far, you have learned how the user can enter text and how you can display text by using the TextBox and Label controls. You also have learned how to manipulate text in your program. Finally, you have seen how fonts can be used to change the appearance of text. But, even with all these capabilities, you haven't learned how to give your users the capability to format text like they can do with a word processor.

Starting with version 4, Visual Basic includes the RichTextBox control. This control enables the user to apply different fonts, font attributes, and colors to different sections of the text being edited. The user can also control the justification of text and create such effects as indention and bulleted lists. The RichTextBox control accomplishes all these functions by providing support for the Rich Text Format (RTF) language. The control interprets RTF codes and applies the proper formatting to the text. The control also has the capability of importing and exporting RTF files. Figure 14.16 shows how text appears in a RichTextBox control and which RTF codes are used to create the effects.

Part
III

Ch
14

FIG. 14.16

RTF codes allow formatting information to be stored in a text file.

RTF text—

RTF codes—

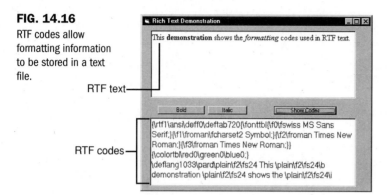

N O T E   The RichTextBox control is also discussed in Chapter 15, "Displaying and Printing Reports." ▪

▶ **See** "Using the RichTextBox Control," **p. 399**

RTF versus HTML

You might think that because both RTF and HTML use codes to store formatting information in a text file, they can be used together, or interchangeably. Unfortunately, that is not true. RTF codes originally were designed as a means for different word processors to exchange information through the use of text files. This means that you can work in one word processor, save the information to an RTF file, and then send the information to another person with a different word processor. The other person can then see the formatting of the text when the file is opened. HTML, on the other hand, is designed to pass formatting information across the Internet so that it can be interpreted and displayed by a browser. While both formats use the same concept of tags to embed formatting information, the tags used are not the same.

Using the RichTextBox Control

In many ways, the RichTextBox control works the same way as the standard text box. It shares many properties with the TextBox control, including the Text property, which works in the same way. In fact, the rich text box supports all properties that are supported by the text box. This makes it easy to substitute rich text boxes for any text boxes in your program. Simply delete a text box and insert a rich text box with the same name in its place. You do not need to change any of your program code to accomplish this. You will, however, want to add new code to take advantage of the additional capabilities of the rich text box.

Like the TextBox control, the RichTextBox control supports single- and multiple-line display and editing of text. Both controls can be locked (by setting the Locked property to True) to provide a read-only display of information. Both controls support cut, copy, and paste operations for editing. And finally, both can be bound to a Data control for use in database applications.

The discussion in this section focuses on the unique capabilities of the RichTextBox control. To learn about the basic capabilities that it shares with the text box, refer to the section "Getting and Displaying Text," earlier in this chapter.

Understanding Text Formatting The RichTextBox control enables the user to select a portion of the text in the control and apply special formatting to it. The user can change the font of the selection, make the selection bold or italic, or underline the selection. When the user applies any or all of these formats to the selection, the new formatting is shown on-screen. In addition, formatting codes (which are not shown on the screen) are placed in the text of the control. These codes allow the formatting information to be stored and then used by other programs that support RTF format codes. This means that you can export your formatted text to a word processor or other program and retain the formatting.

Setting Up the RichTextBox Control The RichTextBox control is one of the custom controls that comes with Visual Basic. You must add it to the Toolbox by using the Components dialog box, which is accessible by choosing the Components item from the Project menu.

 Once you have added the control to the Toolbox, you can use it just like any other control. Simply select it from the Toolbox and draw it on your form. As you can see in Figure 14.17, a rich text box looks just like a standard text box on the form. But remember—looks can be deceiving.

FIG. 14.17
The RichTextBox control looks like a standard text box when drawn on the form.

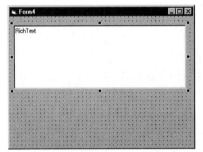

Working with the Font Options

The rich text box is a very powerful tool for creating programs that edit text because it provides tremendous control over the formatting of the text it contains. This section will cover many of the effects that are possible with the rich text box.

A common denominator of all the formatting options is the manner in which they affect the text that is displayed in the control. If you set a format property while some text is selected, only the selected text is affected by the new property value. However, if you set a new format value with no text selected, the property affects all text typed from the point at which it is inserted, until the property value is again changed. This works exactly like the formatting options in a word processing program.

Part
III

Ch
14

Setting the Initial Font   After placing a rich text box on your form, probably the first thing you will want to do is set the properties of the Font object. You do this by following the guidelines described earlier in this chapter in the section "Controlling Fonts in Your Program." Setting the font in the design environment does two things—it sets the initial font the user sees and it sets the initial values of the SelFontName, SelFontSize, SelBold, SelItalic, SelUnderline, and SelStrikeThru properties. These properties control the appearance of selected text.

> **N O T E**   If you change the value of the Font property or any of its attributes, it will affect all text that
> has not had any special formatting applied. ▓

In a similar manner, setting the ForeColor property of the RichTextBox control sets the initial value of the SelColor property.

Changing the Appearance of Words   After the font has been set and the user begins entering text, formatting individual words and phrases can be accomplished by setting one or more of the following properties:

- ▓ SelFontName   Changes the font of the selection.
- ▓ SelBold   Makes the selection bold.
- ▓ SelItalic   Makes the selection italic.
- ▓ SelFontSize   Changes the size of the selection's type.
- ▓ SelUnderline   Underlines the selection.
- ▓ SelStrikethru   Shows the selection in strikethrough mode.

Each of these properties can be set by using an assignment statement. Some of these properties can be applied through the use of buttons in a toolbar that will set the properties. Figure 14.18 shows the main form of an example project. This project contains a RichTextBox control and a toolbar that enables the user to turn on the SelBold, SelItalic, SelUnderline, and SelStrikethru properties of the selected text. The form also contains drop-down lists that enable users to change the font and font size of the selection.

▶ **See** "Creating a Toolbar for Your Application," **p. 121**

Figure 14.19 shows the form after modifying the font for portions of the text.

FIG. 14.18

You can set the font properties of text by using a toolbar and the proper code.

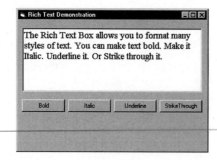

FIG. 14.19

You can change the appearance of a single word or a phrase with the RichTextBox control.

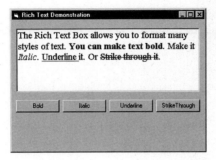

Working with Paragraphs

With the RichTextBox control, you also can change the alignment of individual paragraphs in your text. You can align paragraphs along the left edge of the RichTextBox (the default), or along the right edge, or centered in the box. The SelAlignment property controls the alignment of the paragraph and can have one of three values, which are set forth in Table 14.4. Figure 14.20 shows three RichTextBox controls that contain the same paragraph but with different alignment settings.

Table 14.4   The *SelAlignment* Property Values and Their Effects

Property Value	Effect
rtfLeft (0)	Sets the beginning of each line flush with the left side of the box.
rtfRight (1)	Sets the end of each line flush with the right side of the box.
rtfCenter (2)	Centers each line between the edges of the box.

FIG. 14.20

Setting the SelAlignment property controls how the selected paragraphs appear in the control.

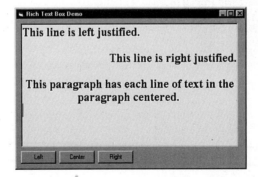

Searching the Text

Another feature of the RichTextBox control is that you can search its contents for a string of text. You can choose to have the search confined to the selected text or to a specific section of the text. You can also have the search look through the entire contents of the rich text box.

Another available search option is the choice of whether to match the case of the search string. If case matching is not required, the strings "The" and "the" are considered a match. If case matching is required, the strings do not match because one contains a capital letter and the other does not.

This sounds very similar to the Instr function; as a matter of fact, you could use the Instr function with the RichTextBox control's Text property. However, the RichTextBox control has a special function of its own: the Find Method. This method specifies the string for which to search, the starting and ending points of the search, and any optional parameters. An advantage to using this instead of Instr is that Find causes the text it finds to be selected, so that font properties can be applied. The Find method uses the following syntax:

```
rtbname.Find(searchstr, start, end, options)
```

In this method, the searchstr parameter identifies the string that you want to find. This can be a literal string, a variable, or a string function. Start and end specify the scope of the search. If both parameters are included, the search is performed on all text between the two points. If end is omitted, the entire contents of the RichTextBox are searched. If both parameters are omitted, only the selected text is searched.

Adding a Splash of Color

Using different fonts is one way to change the appearance of information in your programs. Another method is to use color, which can grab a user's attention, convey important information, or simply make an application more visually appealing.

Setting the Color of Controls at Design Time

As with fonts, you can set color properties for your form and for individual controls at design time. In fact, most controls allow you to set two colors. You can set the background color by using the BackColor property and you can set the foreground or text color by using the ForeColor property.

> **N O T E**   Unlike font settings, the color settings for a form do not carry forward to controls placed on the form. ■

The default setting for each of the color properties is based on the Windows system color settings. The default setting of the BackColor property is the window background color, usually white. The default setting of the ForeColor property is the color of the text in Windows menus, usually black.

> **N O T E**   If you use the default color settings, changing the Windows system colors will make the colors in your program change too. This is an important point to consider when distributing programs. ■

There are two ways to set the colors of your form and controls at design time. You can either use the color palette or select colors from a list from the Properties window. You can also, of course, set color properties by using code.

Using the Color Palette   The color palette is one of the tools available to you at design time. The color palette is accessed by choosing Color Palette from the View menu. The color palette is shown in Figure 14.21.

FIG. 14.21
The color palette enables you to easily choose the foreground and background colors of your controls.

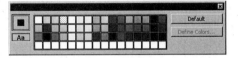

The color palette consists of a property selection area (two concentric squares), a series of color indicators, and two command buttons. To change the color properties of one of your controls, first select the control with a single-click. Then, using the mouse, choose either the foreground (click the inner box) or background (click the outer box). Next, click the color that you want in the color indicator boxes. As you choose the colors, you immediately will see the results both in the color palette and in your control. If you want to return your control's colors to their default values, just click the default button.

Using the Color List   The other way to set the colors of a control at design time is to modify the individual properties from the Properties window. To set a color, select the property (ForeColor, BackColor, or one of the other color properties); then click the arrow button at the right of the property value. This opens the color list (see Figure 14.22). This color list contains two tabs. The first tab shows the system colors for Window Text, Desktop, Window Background, and so on. You can choose to use one of these colors by clicking the appropriate color block. The other tab contains a series of color squares from the color palette. On this tab, you can choose the color you want by clicking the appropriate square.

FIG. 14.22
You can set the color of the ForeColor or BackColor property from the color list.

Part
III

Ch
14

Changing Colors with Code

As with most everything else, the ForeColor and BackColor properties can be changed with code in your program. You do with an assignment statement in which you tell the program what control and property to change, and what the new value is for the property. But what are the values? Can you just say, "Make this red?" Well, almost.

In the computer world, every color is a combination of some amount of red, green, and blue; the color number used as the property setting represents the amounts of blue, green, and red, respectively, in the desired color. The number is often represented in hexadecimal format; for example, blue is represented by &H00FF0000&.

If you are a glutton for punishment, you can figure out how much red, green, and blue go into a particular shade and then convert that information into the right numerical value. Fortunately, it is much easier than that. Visual Basic provides a set of constants for several common colors. These constants represent the numerical value needed for the color. Table 14.5 shows the names of the constants and the color they represent.

Table 14.5   Color Constants Provide the Numerical Values for Many Common Colors

Color	Constant	Numerical Value (Decimal)
Black	vbBlack	0
Red	vbRed	255
Green	vbGreen	65280
Yellow	vbYellow	65535
Blue	vbBlue	16711680
Magenta	vbMagenta	16711935
Cyan	vbCyan	16776960
White	vbWhite	16777215

To use one of these color constants, simply enter its name in the assignment statement. The following code displays yellow text on a blue background:

```
ColorDemo.ForeColor = vbYellow
ColorDemo.BackColor = vbBlue
```

In addition to the predefined color constants, you can use Visual Basic's RGB function, which accepts parameters for the amounts of red, green, and blue (each expressed in the range of 0–255) and returns the appropriate color number. For example,

```
frmTestForm.BackColor = RGB(0, 255, 0)
```

sets a form's background color to green.

TIP If you want to use a color that does not have a constant, the Common Dialog control's Color dialog box can be used to find out the numeric value.

Remember, the colors you select may be affected by the color scheme on an individual PC. This means selecting colors that change with the system will make your application better suited for an individual's color preferences. On the other hand, it is not unusual for the user to "mess up" his color scheme. For example, he might pick the right color combination so that highlighted text looks the same as other text. Therefore, in some instances, it might be beneficial for a program to choose a specific color. The determining factor should be how important colors are to the usefulness of your program.

From Here...

In this chapter, you learned about manipulating text—both from code and in the design environment. You saw how the Masked Edit control can make input validation easier, and how the RichTextBox control can be the foundation of a simple word processor. The code examples in the chapter also provided some examples of what you can do with string functions. Finally, some additional properties of the font object were introduced and you learned how to set colors in an application.

- To find out about other controls you can use to display text information, see Chapter 10, "Using the Windows Common Controls."

- To learn more about using the RichTextBox in code, see Chapter 15, "Displaying and Printing Reports."

- To apply what you have learned to interface design, see Chapter 19, "Designing User Interfaces."

Part
III

Ch
14

Displaying and Printing Reports

Alot of your programming effort, and a lot of the material in this book, is geared toward getting information into your program and processing it. However, all the input and processing isn't much good if you can't get the results back out to the user. In this chapter, we focus on basic reporting and information display. When we use the term "reporting" we are not only referring to printed reports, but also on-screen information. The techniques discussed in this chapter can be used to produce both types of reports. You can also write report functions that are generic enough to be used for both the screen and printer. ■

Creating on-screen reports with controls

With the right formatting, the TextBox, RichTextBox, and ListBox controls are well-suited to display large amounts of information.

Print information while you are developing a program

Print to the Immediate (or Debug) window to get values of variables and expressions.

Simple reports with the Printer Object

Send text to the printer and line up information in columns using print zones and formatting functions.

Control every aspect of your printing

Use fonts and colors to spice up your printout, add graphics, and precisely position each element of a report.

Printing to on-screen objects

Print to a form and to a picture box to display reports on the screen.

Send information to a file.

Use the Print statement to send information to a file for storage or for transfer to another program.

Outputting Reports to Familiar Controls

If a paper report is not necessary, you can create fairly sophisticated-looking reports on-screen with some of Visual Basic's custom controls. In this section, we look at three controls suitable for doing this: the text box, the rich text box, and the list box.

Using the Text Box

You already know from earlier chapters that the Label and TextBox controls can display multiple lines of information in a variety of fonts and colors. If your report is mainly paragraphs of text, a TextBox control might be ideal. The MultiLine and ScrollBars properties allow the user to view more text than will fit on the screen at a time. By using the intrinsic constants vbCrLf to force a new line and vbTab to hit the tab stops, you can easily format a text box like the one in Figure 15.1.

FIG. 15.1

Simple reports can be created by using the TextBox control.

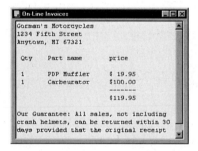

In Figure 15.1, all the formatting "logic" is in the text itself, not the text box. The way to code something like this is to fill the Text property incrementally:

```
Text1.Text = Text1.Text & "New Text"
```

However, rather than repeatedly accessing the Text property, it is more efficient to build your string in a local variable first and then assign it to the text box:

```
Dim stHeader As String

stHeader = "Gorman's Motorcycles" & vbCrLf
stHeader = stHeader & "1234 Fifth Street" & vbCrLf
stHeader = stHeader & "Anytown, MI 67321" & vbCrLf
txtRpt.Text = txtRpt.Text & stHeader & vbCrLf
```

Note in the preceding example the use of the constant vbCrLf to insert a special new line character. In addition, the tab character (vbTab) can be used to create a column effect:

```
stTemp = stTemp & " 1" & vbTab & "Carburetor" & vbTab & "$100.00" & vbCrLf
```

If each item in a column has a different length, you might want to use spaces instead of tab characters:

```
'This code inserts one column
inPadSpaces = COLWIDTH - Len(stNewText)
```

```
If inPadSpaces < 0 then inPadSpaces = 1
txtRpt.Text = txtRpt.Text & stNewText & Space(inPadSpaces)
```

Note the use of the `Space()` function, which creates a string with the specified number of space characters.

Text boxes can also be assigned large strings without any formatting, like the bottom (Guarantee) section in Figure 15.1. If no special characters are included and the `Multiline` property is set to `True`, the text box simply wraps words automatically.

▶ **See** "Modifying Text with a Program," **p. 371**

 T I P   To make sure your columns line up properly, use a nonproportional font, such as Courier.

Using the RichTextBox Control

A big drawback of using the TextBox control is that color and font options can only be applied to the entire text box. A rich text box, on the other hand, has no such limitations. It allows sections of text to be formatted individually and includes additional options such as bulleted lists and embedded objects.

The RichTextBox control is designed to work with the Rich Text File Format (RTF). RTF is a standard file format for documents, similar to DOC or HTML. Both WordPad and Microsoft Word have the capability to read and write RTF files. As a matter of fact, this feature is also built in to the RichTextBox control with the `LoadFile` and `SaveFile` methods:

```
Private Sub cmdLoad_Click()
  Rtb1.LoadFile "C:\MYFILE.RTF"
End Sub

Private Sub cmdSave_Click()
  Rtb1.SaveFile "C:\MYFILE.RTF"
End Sub
```

In addition to loading and saving files, the text in a rich text box can also be manipulated with code. You probably can already imagine some useful applications. For example, you could generate reports from a database, save them to RTF format, and e-mail them to your users—all from within a Visual Basic program.

The real strength of a RichTextBox control is in the formatting, which enables you programmatically to create sharp-looking documents like the one shown in Figure 15.2.

If you browse through the RichTextBox control's properties, you'll notice options for underlining, color, and font characteristics. The `Sel` prefix on many of them indicates that they affect only the selected (or highlighted) text. For example, the following code makes the selected text bold:

```
RichTextBox1.SelBold = True
```

FIG. 15.2

A rich text box allows you to use multiple formatting options within the same text box.

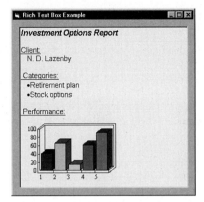

As with the text box, you can assign text using the Text property. Every time you set this property, the RichTextBox converts it to RTF format. You can view the RTF codes (similar to viewing HTML source) in the TextRTF property or by opening an RTF file with a text editor.

Let's look at the code used to create the report in Figure 15.2. First, I added all the information using the Text property:

```
Dim s As String
s = "Investment Options Report" & vbCrLf & vbCrLf
s = s & "Client" & vbCrLf & "N. D. Lazenby" & vbCrLf & vbCrLf
s = s & "Categories" & vbCrLf
s = s & "Retirement plan" & vbCrLf
s = s & "Stock options" & vbCrLf
s = s & vbCrLf & "Profits" & vbCrLf
rtb1.Text = s
```

Next, I formatted the first line, so I selected it with the SelStart and SelLength properties:

```
rtb1.SelStart = 0
rtb1.SelLength = Len("Investment Options Report")
rtb1.SelFontSize = 12
rtb1.SelItalic = True
rtb1.SelBold = True
```

A quicker way to highlight some text is the built-in Find method:

```
rtb1.Find "Client", 0
rtb1.SelUnderline = True
rtb1.SelFontSize = 11
```

When used as a function, Find returns the search string's starting position:

```
Dim nPos1 As Integer, nPos2 As Integer
nPos1 = rtb1.Find("retire", 0)
nPos2 = rtb1.Find("options", 20) + Len("options")
rtb1.SelStart = nPos1
rtb1.SelLength = nPos2 - nPos1
rtb1.SelBullet = True
rtb1.SelBold = False
rtb1.SelIndent = 200
```

Rich Text boxes also support embedded OLE objects, such as bitmaps:

```
Dim obj as OLEObject
Set obj = rtb1.OLEObjects.Add (, , "C:\graph.bmp","Paint.Picture")_
```

Using the ListBox Control

Another way to present lists of information is to use the ListBox control. This control enables you to add items to a list; the user can then scroll through them. While list boxes are used primarily for presenting choices to the user and allowing him to pick one or more items, they can also be used for simple reports. Listing 15.1 shows how a list box might be used to display a list of students and grades.

Listing 15.1 LISTREPORT.FRM—Using a List Control for Simple Tables

```
'This code assumes the students and grades
'have already been stored in variable arrays

Dim I As Integer
Dim inPadSpaces As Integer
Const NUMSTUDENTS = 10
Const COLWIDTH = 20

lstGrades.Font.Name = "Courier New" 'Non-proportional font
lstGrades.Clear
For I = 1 To NUMSTUDENTS
    inPadSpaces = COLWIDTH - Len(Student(I))
    If inPadSpaces < 0 Then nPadSpaces = 1
    lstGrades.AddItem Student(I) & Space(inPadSpaces) & CStr(Grade(I))
Next I
```

Figure 15.3 shows what a list box would look like after executing the code in Listing 15.1.

N O T E   Although you cannot tell from looking at it, the student names in Figure 15.3 were not added in alphabetical order. Setting a list box's Sorted property to True at design time keeps your list sorted as you add items to it. ▪

FIG. 15.3

Tabular reports can be created in a list box.

The list box has the added benefit of knowing if the user has selected an item. The items of a list box are stored in its List array, and the selected item's array index is stored in the ListIndex property. You can determine which item is selected by placing some code in the list box's Click event:

```
Private Sub lstGrades_Click()

  Dim stStudent As String
  Const COLWIDTH = 20

  stStudent = lstGrades.List(lstGrades.ListIndex)
  stStudent = left$(stStudent,COLWIDTH)
  Msgbox "You clicked on " & stStudent

End Sub
```

Instead of just using the MsgBox statement, your example could be expanded to display more information about the selected student. Note that in the preceding code you pull the student name directly from the list. The ListBox control also has a property called ItemData that can be used to store an integer value that is not displayed—for example, student ID number.

▶ **See** "Working with Lists," **p. 225**

The list box concludes the discussion of simple reports with custom controls. However, it is important to note that if you do any serious on-screen reporting, you will probably rely on a grid control more than any of the controls discussed in this chapter. There are a number of third-party grid controls available. In a later chapter, we discuss the Flex Grid, which is included with Visual Basic.

▶ **See** "Using the MSFlexGrid control," **p. 280**

Printing Reports

For many tasks, it is convenient to display information on the screen; however, sometimes there is just no substitute for the printed page. Printed reports are simply more convenient to carry with you to read on the plane, in a meeting, or during the commercials in your favorite TV program. The reports you create can be simple, containing plain text and some columns of numbers; or the reports can be very elaborate, containing font and color effects, tables, and even graphs. You can create any type and complexity of report in Visual Basic using the techniques in this chapter. The key is in the layout and testing of the report. Unfortunately, Visual Basic does not ship with a visual report designer for general-purpose printing. Therefore, you must work with the old-fashioned method of "code and test." After you get a little experience, however, most printing tasks become relatively easy.

N O T E   Visual Basic ships with Crystal Reports, which is a visual report designer mainly used for database reports. This designer and its associated control are covered in Chapter 29, "Using the Visual Basic Data Control." ■

Printable Objects

The primary means of printing text is the Print method. An object's Print method is used just like any other method. For example, place the following line of code in a form's Click event:

```
Form1.Print "Hello, World!"
```

Every time you click the form, a new line of text appears. While we will primarily discuss printing information to paper using the Printer object, the Print method works with the following four objects in Visual Basic:

- *Forms* You can print information to the background of a form. All printing will appear behind any controls that are on the form.

- *Printer* You can send information to the default printer or specify a particular printer. The information is sent to the Print Manager and then to the printer when you complete a page or document.

- *PictureBox controls* You can print to the background of a PictureBox control, superimposing text on the picture (if there is one present). This is similar to printing to a form.

- *Immediate window* During program development, you can print text to the Immediate window (formerly known as the Debug window) to help check on the progress of your program. You can also print contents of variables to help with bug hunting.

The code statements you use to create your printout work the same way no matter which of these output objects you specify. In fact, you can use a class to create a generic print routine that will work with any output object.

Printing Simple Reports

In its simplest form, the Print method specifies the object where you want to print, the Print method itself, and the information you want to have printed. For example, the following statement prints a string of text to the printer:

```
Printer.Print "This prints a single line of text."
```

Used in this way, the Print method prints a single piece of information and then advances to the next line of the printer. The information you print is not limited to text. You can print text, numbers, or dates by using the Print method. Also, as you might expect, you can specify the information to be printed using either literals or variables. The following lines show several print examples:

```
Dim stVariable As String, inVariable As Integer
stVariable = "This is text information"
inVariable = 500
Printer.Print "Print a single string"
Printer.Print stVariable
Printer.Print 25
Printer.Print inVariable
```

The Print method would be of limited usefulness if you could only print a single item at a time. In fact, you can send multiple pieces of information to the printer (or other object) using the Print method. To print more than one item, simply place multiple items in the print list, and separate each item with a comma or a semicolon. If you separate two items with a comma, the second item is printed in the next *print zone*. This usually places some space between the items, as each print zone is 14 characters wide. If you separate the items with a semicolon, the second item is printed immediately after the first item, with no intervening spaces.

The following code sample (see Listing 15.2) shows how separators make a difference in where information is printed. The output from this code is shown in Figure 15.4.

Listing 15.2   PRINTDEMO.FRM—Commas and Semicolons Affect the Location of a Printed Item

```
Dim s1 As String
Dim s2 As String

s1 = "String 1"
s2 = "String 2"

'Print s1 and s2 on the same line with no spaces
picTest.Print s1; s2
'Print a blank line
picTest.Print

'Print s1 and s2 separated by some spaces
picTest.Print s1;
picTest.Print "    "; s2

'Print a blank line, then s1 and s2 in separate print zones
picTest.Print vbCrLf & s1, s2
```

FIG. 15.4

The separators between items in a print statement determine the amount of space between them.

You can, of course, include a lot more than two or three items in the `Print` method's expression list. These items can be a mix of text and numbers, as long as each is separated by a comma or semicolon. You can even mix separators within the list.

One other item of note: The `Print` method typically starts a new line each time it is invoked. You can change this behavior by including a comma or semicolon after the last item in the expression list. This indicates to the next print statement that it should continue on the same line. Using a comma starts the next item in the next print zone, and using a semicolon starts the next item immediately after the preceding one.

> **CAUTION**
>
> Because the `Print` method does not automatically handle word wrapping, printing a lot of items or several large items can result in printing some information off the edge of the page. See the later sections "Using *TextHeight* and *TextWidth*" and "Using Word Wrapping in Your Printouts" to learn about preventing this.

Controlling Spacing in Your Reports

Specifying only a list of information to be printed leaves much to be desired in controlling the placement and appearance of any reports you are creating. Fortunately, you can position text by embedding spaces and tabs, just like the earlier examples with the TextBox control. Two special functions that are used with the `Print` method are the `Spc` and `Tab` functions.

The `Spc` function places a specified number of spaces in the printout. This is used to create a specific amount of space between two items in the expression list. You use the `Spc` function by placing it in the expression list of the `Print` method as shown in the following line of code:

```
Printer.Print "First Field"; Spc(10); "Second Field"
```

When using the `Spc` function, you should always use a semicolon as the separator. Otherwise, the spaces created by the `Spc` function will not start immediately after the preceding item, but will start in the next print zone. This will most likely give you more space than you want.

```
'Not a good way to use the Spc Function
Print "First Field", Spc(10), "Second Field"
```

The `Spc` function is most useful when you deal with information of a known length (such as five characters, ten characters, and so on) and with a fixed font. However, if you are trying to create columns in a report, the `Tab` function is usually the better choice. The `Tab` function causes subsequently printed characters to start at a specific location. You use the `Tab` function in a manner similar to the `Spc` function, but instead of specifying the number of spaces, you specify the character position where you want the printing to start. The following line of code causes the second item to be printed in column 30 of the printout:

```
Printer.Print "First Field"; Tab(30); "Second Field"
```

Figure 15.5 shows the effects of using the `Spc` and `Tab` functions to create columns in a report. Notice that the report using the `Tab` function produces more consistent results than the `Spc` function.

FIG. 15.5

The Spc function inserts a specified number of spaces, while the Tab function moves to a specific position.

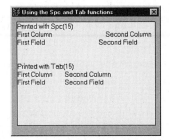

Using the Spc and Tab functions

Printed with Spc(15)
First Column   Second Column
First Field   Second Field

Printed with Tab(15)
First Column Second Column
First Field   Second Field

> **CAUTION**
>
> If the position specified by the Tab function is further to the left on the page than the end of the last printed item, the Tab function causes the printout to move to that character position on the next line on the page.

Using Functions to Control the Appearance of Your Text

In addition to using the Spc and Tab functions to handle the spacing of your reports, there are other functions that are extremely useful in creating reports for your programs. The String function works like the Spc function, except that you can specify any character you want to fill the spaces. The Format function lets you apply special formatting to strings, numbers, and dates to make them more readable for your users.

Using the *String* Function   You have probably seen the Table of Contents of a book where a series of dots (a *dot leader*) separates the title of a chapter from the page number where it starts. If you want to do this in your reports, use the String function. The String function requires two arguments—the character to use and the number of times to repeat the character. For example, the following line of code would place a series of 20 periods on the printout after the first data item:

```
Printer.Print "Chapter 1"; String(20, "."); "15"
```

In the String function, you can either specify the literal character to use or the ASCII code of the character. The following code has the same effect as the preceding line:

```
Printer.Print "Chapter 1"; String(20, 46); "15"
```

Figure 15.6 shows an example of dot leaders embedded by using the String function.

FIG. 15.6

Use the String function to embed characters in your printout.

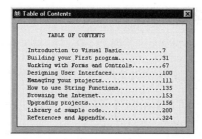

```
TABLE OF CONTENTS

Introduction to Visual Basic...........7
Building your First program...........31
Working with Forms and Controls.......67
Designing User Interfaces............100
Managing your projects...............111
How to use String Functions..........135
Browsing the Internet................153
Upgrading projects...................156
Library of sample code...............200
References and Appendix..............324
```

Another use of the String function would be in printing checks, where you want to be sure that the amount line of the check is filled to avoid tampering. In this case, the typical character to use is the asterisk (*).

Using the *Format* Function   There are several types of information that require special handling. Two, in particular, are numbers and dates. When you tell the Print method to print a number, it prints it using the least number of digits possible. There are two problems with this. First, users might be accustomed to seeing numbers in a particular format, such as two decimal places for currency numbers. Second, if all your numbers are not the same size, it makes it difficult to line them up in columns. Similar problems apply to printed dates. For example, you may want only two digits in the year or to print the full name of the month instead of an abbreviation.

The Format function makes it easy for you to apply custom formatting to any text that you want to print. You can choose from some of the built-in formats or create your own by specifying format strings.

Formatting Numbers   The most common use of the Format function is to place numbers in a particular format to make them easier for the users to read. To use the Format function, you specify the input value and the format as shown in the following line of code:

```
Printer.Print Format(crGrossSales, "Currency")
```

For working with numbers, there are several named formats that you can use. Table 15.1 shows the named formats for numbers that are available with the Format function. Figure 15.7 shows the various format types for a group of numbers. In all cases, you must enclose the name of the format in double quotes.

Table 15.1   Named Formats Make It Easy to Display Numbers

Named Format	Description
General Number	Displays the number with no special formatting.
Currency	Displays the number with a thousands separator, and two digits to the right of the decimal.
Fixed	Displays at least one digit to the left and two digits to the right of the decimal.
Standard	Displays the number with the thousands separator, and at least one digit to the left and two digits to the right of the decimal.
Percent	Multiplies the number by 100 and displays the number followed by the percent (%) sign.
Scientific	Displays the number in standard scientific notation.
Yes/No	Displays Yes for a non-zero value and No for zero.
True/False	Displays True for a non-zero value and False for zero.
On/Off	Displays On for a non-zero value and Off for zero.

If the named formats in Visual Basic don't meet your needs, you can define your own formats. (See Table 15.2 for the codes needed to define formats.) You specify a format by creating a "template" string indicating where the digits of the number will be placed, if thousands and decimal separators will be used, and any special characters that you want printed. For example, the following line of code prints a number with four decimal places and a thousands separator:

```
Printer.Print Format(TotalDistance, "##,##0.0000")
```

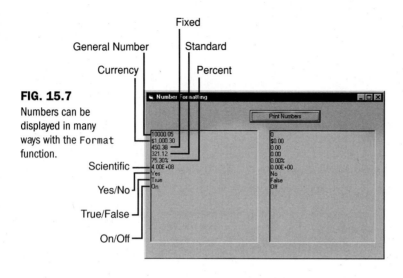

FIG. 15.7
Numbers can be displayed in many ways with the Format function.

Table 15.2 Codes for Defining Numeric Formats

Symbol	Purpose	Meaning
0	Digit placeholder	Displays the digit or displays 0 if there is no digit in that location.
#	Digit placeholder	Displays the digit or displays nothing if there is no digit in that location. This causes leading and trailing zeros to be omitted.
.	Decimal Separator	Indicates where the decimal point will be displayed.
,	Thousands Separator	Indicates where the separators will be displayed.
%	Percentage Indicator	Indicates where a percent sign will be displayed. Also causes the number to be multiplied by 100.
E-, E+, e-, e+	Scientific Notation	Using E- or e- displays a minus sign next to negative exponents, but displays no sign for positive exponents. Using E+ or e+ displays a sign for any exponent.

Formatting Dates   Another form of data that is often a chore to print is dates. If you specify the Print method with a date, it is displayed in the default format for your system—typically something like 2/18/98. If you want to display the date in another manner (for example, February 18, 1998), you need to use the Format function. Table 15.3 lists some predefined date and time formats (see Figure 15.8). If they do not suit your needs, you can create a custom format. The codes for creating user-defined date and time formats are listed in Visual Basic's Help system.

object to which you will be printing. These [...]
in Figure 15.10. (Also see the "What Is the [...]
sidebar.)

FIG. 15.10

You can determine the interior dimensions of an object with its *ScaleHeight* and *ScaleWidth* properties.

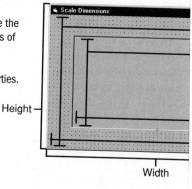

What Is the Difference Between Scal[...]

You might be wondering why we just don't use the [...]
determine its size. The reason is that the `Height` a[...]
dimensions of an object. For example, on a form, th[...]
title bar, the borders on the form, and any menu ba[...]
forms, the `Height` property can be as much as 69[...]
almost half an inch larger. You can see how this cou[...]
printable area of a form. The relation of the `Width`[...]
specifies the external dimensions of the object whil[...]

To use the `ScaleHeight` and `ScaleWidth` prop[...]
values. The easiest way to do this is to store t[...]
just before your report generation routine. Th[...]

```
inPicWid = picOutput.ScaleWidth
inPicHgt = picOutput.ScaleHeight
```

After you have established the dimensions of [...]
positions on the object. For example, the follc[...]
middle of the object:

```
picOutput.CurrentX = inPicWid *.5
picOutput.CurrentY = inPicHgt *.5
picOutput.Print "Hello!"
```

Note the use of the `CurrentX` and `CurrentY` pr[...]
box before printing.

■ *Und*[...]

■ *Str*[...]

▶ **S**[...]

These pro[...]
ture boxes[...]
are in desi[...]
Print Man[...]

As an exan[...]
gross sales[...]
names and[...]
specified a[...]
minimum. [...]
code in List[...]
Figure 15.9[...]

**Listing 1[...]
Figures**

```
Dim I As [...]
Dim Gross[...]
Dim SalesF[...]

'Note: the[...]

picOutput.[...]
picOutput.[...]
picOutput.[...]
picOutput.[...]

For I = 1 [...]
   If Gros[...]
   If Gros[...]
   picOutp[...]
   picOutp[...]
   picOutp[...]
   picOutp[...]
Next I
```

Note that you a[...]
fonts in the mi[...]
followed by a so[...]
time to print the[...]
only the numbe[...]

```
For I = 1 To [...]
   picOutput.F[...]
   If GrossSal[...]
```

TIP To include the current date and/or time on your report, you can use the Now function:

```
Form1.Print Format(Now,"mm/dd/yyyy")
```

Table 15.3   Named Date Formats

Named Format	Description
General Date	Shows the date and time if the expression contains both portions. Otherwise, displays either the date or the time.
Long Date	Prints the day of the week, the day of the month, the month, and the year.
Medium Date	Prints the day of the month, a three letter abbreviation for the month, and the year.
Short Date	Prints the day, month, and year as 3/5/97.
Long Time	Prints hours, minutes, and seconds along with the A.M./P.M. indication.
Medium Time	Prints hours and minutes along with A.M. or P.M.
Short Time	Prints hours and minutes in military time.

FIG. 15.8

By Using named formats, you can enhance the appearance of date information.

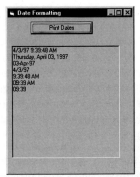

TIP User-defined formats can be useful for making decisions in your program. The expression

```
Format(stMyDate,"w")
```

returns a number representing the day of the week. You could use the result of the expression to skip printing reports on the weekend, for example.

Creating Sp

The Print me
reports visual
ready aware o
report headin
change the co
add lines, box

All of these op
can turn your
reporting tool:
the functions o

Working with F

The first step i
mation. The Pr
it prints inform
tribute, you mu
example, place

```
Private Sub C
    Form1.Font.
    Form1.Print
    Form1.Font.I
    Form1.Font.:
    Form1.Print
End Sub
```

Note how the Fo
boxes. When us
think of this is tl
settings, whatev
Font object to *al*

The three main o
the various attril
each object.

We cover fonts ir
list shows you th
your printouts:

- ■ *Name* Det
- ■ *Size* Det
- ■ *Bold* Det
- ■ *Italic* D

N O T E These drawing functions are discussed in de
each of them in "Doing Graphics," found on t

Positioning the Parts of Your

So far, we have only looked at printing informati
method itself. For many situations, you will wan
and graphical objects on the screen and the prin

Naturally, there are properties that allow you to
tion anywhere in your print area. Using these pr
layout of your reports. However, with the added
determine the size of the object you are printing
print. Then you need to make sure all the pieces
ever arranged furniture in a room, you have son

Visual Basic has several functions that help you
ous pieces with which you are working. Printab
specify exact placement text.

Finding an Object's Printable Area

In most instances, you probably think of the pri
However, Visual Basic doesn't typically work wi
Visual Basic works with units of measure called
1440 twips in an inch.) This makes measuremei
more accurate. Also, when you are determining
consider whether the printer is working in port
is some size other than the standard 8.5 × 11. (I
inches.)

▶ **See** "Accessing Functions with the Toolbars,"

If you are working with the Printer object, the o
primarily by the Windows Print Manager and tl
changes to the printer settings in the section "C
forms and picture boxes, the printable area is c
any resizing that has been done by the user. Be
cases, other objects), you cannot assume that tl
ones available when your printing process start

The best way to determine the available space i
ScaleWidth properties of the object. These pro

Using *TextHeight* and *TextWidth*

Now that you can determine the size of an object's printable area, you need to determine the
size of the text you are placing on that object. The Print method is very simple-minded. It does
not check to see whether the text is wider than the area where it is to be printed. Therefore,
if the text is too wide, it simply disappears off the right edge of the print area, as shown in
Figure 15.11.

▶ **See** "Using Word Wrapping in Your Printouts," **p. 429**

FIG. 15.11
Word wrapping would
be useful here.

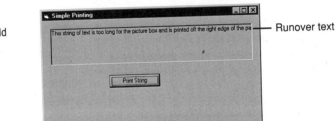

— Runover text

Each of the objects that support the Print method also has two other methods that allow
you to determine the size of the text to be printed. These methods are the TextHeight and
TextWidth methods. As you can probably guess, the TextHeight method tells you the vertical
dimensions (in twips) of a piece of text, and the TextWidth method tells you how much of an
area the text will cover horizontally. The following lines of code demonstrate the use of the
two methods:

```
Dim sgHeight As Single
Dim sgWidth As Single
Dim stUserName As String

stUserName = "STEVE BAKER"

sgHeight = Printer.TextHeight(stUsername)
sgWidth = Printer.TextWidth(stUsername)
```

When using the TextHeight and TextWidth methods, you must supply a string in the form of a
literal string, a string variable, or a string function. If you try to use a number or numeric variable, you get an error. Therefore, if you need to print a number, use the Str, CStr, or Format
functions to convert the number to a string. You should also remember that literal strings must
be enclosed within quotation marks.

▶ **See** "Working with Strings and Numbers," **p. 381**

When determining the size of a piece of text, the TextHeight and TextWidth methods take into
account the font used by the target of the output, as well as the font attributes such as size,
bold, and italic. One use of the value returned is to adjust the font size to be sure that a piece of
text fits in a specified area or to make sure the maximum possible font size is used. Listing 15.5

shows how you would check the size of the text and then reduce the font if necessary to make it fit in the available space. The results are shown in Figure 15.12.

Listing 15.5 PRINTSIZE.FRM—Using *TextHeight* and *TextWidth* to Determine Whether the Font Size Needs to Be Changed

```
Private Sub CmdSizetext_Click()

    Const MINIMUM_SIZE = 8
    Dim stInput As String
    Dim inWidth As Integer
    Dim inHeight As Integer
    Dim inFontSize As Integer
    Dim blTooBig As Boolean

    picOutput.Cls
    stInput = InputBox$("Enter some text")
    If Len(stInput) = 0 Then Exit Sub
    inFontSize = Val(InputBox$("Enter initial font size", , "12"))
    lblInitial = "Initial Size: " & inFontSize
    inWidth = picOutput.ScaleWidth
    inHeight = picOutput.ScaleHeight
    picOutput.Font.Size = inFontSize
    blTooBig = True

    Do While blTooBig And inFontSize > MINIMUM_SIZE
        If picOutput.TextWidth(stInput) < inWidth And_
            ➥picOutput.TextHeight(stInput) < inHeight Then
            blTooBig = False
        Else
            inFontSize = inFontSize - 1
            picOutput.Font.Size = inFontSize
        End If
    Loop
    picOutput.Print stInput
    lblActual = "Actual size: " & inFontSize
End Sub
```

FIG. 15.12

The text had to be resized because it would not have fit at the requested font size.

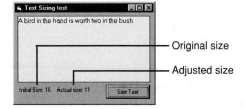

Original size

Adjusted size

Placing the Elements of the Report

In our examples so far, we have controlled the position of printed text by adding spaces or tabs. However, there are two properties that can set the position of a piece of text within the print area. These properties are the `CurrentX` and `CurrentY` properties. Setting these properties is like positioning your drawing pencil on the form. For text, the `CurrentX` and `CurrentY` properties define the upper-left corner of the print position. When the `Print` method is issued, the text is printed down and to the right of this position. In other words, if the text you are about to print had a box around it, the coordinates (`CurrentX`, `CurrentY`) would represent the upper-left corner of the box, as measured from the upper-left corner of the screen.

▶ **See** "Controlling Form Size," **p. 73**

The primary use of these two properties is to set the current position before printing the next piece of text in your report. If you do not modify the values of these properties, each time the `Print` method is invoked, the printout will start at the far left of the next available line (unless the previous `Print` method ended with a semicolon or comma). You can use the `CurrentX` and `CurrentY` properties to create indented areas on your report, or to handle centering and right-justifying the text. To see how the `CurrentX` and `CurrentY` properties are used, take a look at Listing 15.6 and its resulting output in Figure 15.13.

Listing 15.6   PRINTSIZE.FRM—Using *CurrentX* and *CurrentY* to Position Text on a Page

```
Private Sub cmd_Center_Click()
    Dim stTest As String
    Dim inWidth As Integer
    Dim inHeight As Integer

    stTest = "This text is centered"
    With picOutput
        inWidth = .ScaleWidth
        inHeight = .ScaleHeight
        .Font.Name = "Times New Roman"
        .Font.Size = 14
        .Font.Bold = True
        .CurrentX = (inWidth - .TextWidth(stTest)) / 2
        .CurrentY = (inHeight - .TextHeight(stTest)) / 2
    End With
    picOutput.Print stTest

End Sub
```

FIG. 15.13

Center text by using *CurrentX* and *CurrentY*.

You look at more ways to handle text positioning later in the chapter in "Exploring Printer Functions You Can Create."

Controlling the Printer

In our discussions so far, we have assumed that the printer was set up and ready to print, and that it would just print whatever we sent to it. For the most part, this is correct. However, there are a number of properties and methods that are used to set up the printer and then control it while your report is being created. Some of the things you can do include the following:

- Set the orientation of the printer.
- Set the number of copies to be printed.
- Start a new page.
- End a print job in progress.

This section shows you how to set up the printer and how to control it.

Setting the Properties of the Printer

Although the default settings of the printer are usually sufficient for most jobs, you do have quite a bit of control over the way the printer is set up. As with most everything else in Visual Basic, you control the printer by setting properties. These properties are part of the `Printer` object and can be set with simple assignment statements. Table 15.4 summarizes these properties and the effects that they have on your printouts. Keep in mind that some of the properties listed in the table (such as `Duplex`) do not apply to every printer.

Table 15.4 Properties that Control a Printer

Property Name	Description
Copies	Tells the printer how many copies of each page to make.
DeviceName	Returns the name of the printer—for example, HP DeskJet 660C.
DriverName	Returns the name of the printer driver—for example, HPFDJC04.
Duplex	Determines whether the printout will be on one side of a page or both sides. If the printout is on both sides of the page, this property also determines whether the second side assumes a horizontal or vertical flip of the page.
FontTransparent	Determines whether background text and graphics will show through text printed on the page.
Orientation	Determines whether the page is in portrait or landscape mode.
Page	Tells your program the current page number.

continues

FIG. 15.16
The form on the left shows what you see on-screen, and the one on the right shows which parts of a form are omitted by the *PrintForm* method.

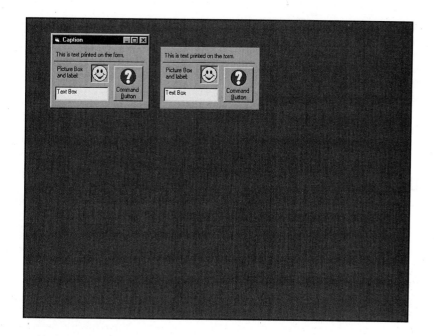

Aligning the Text on a Page

One of the most commonly used techniques is to align the text on the page. If you use word processors, you are probably familiar with the concept of text justification. The three main types of justification are left-justified, right-justified, and centered. These all refer to the horizontal position of the text within the line. In addition, we will look at aligning text vertically with the top or bottom of the page and at centering the text vertically in the page.

Moving to the Left   Left-justifying text is the simplest way to align text. If left alone, the Print method will start at the left edge of the output object and print from left to right. The routine shown in Listing 15.9 shows the function for left-justifying text and the routine that calls the function. The call to the procedure specifies the output object, the starting CurrentX and CurrentY properties for the printout, the size of the print region, and the text to be printed.

Listing 15.9   TEXTFUNC.FRM—Setting the *CurrentX* Property to Left-Justify Text

```
Dim txStr As String
Dim objWid As Integer
Dim  objHgt As Integer

txStr = Text1.Text
objWid = Picture1.ScaleWidth
objHgt = Picture1.ScaleHeight
Picture1.Cls
LeftJustify Picture1, 5, 5, objWid, objHgt, txStr
```

```
Private Sub LeftJustify(objOut As Object, LMarg, TMarg, RgWid, RgHgt _
        As Integer, InptStr As String)

    objOut.CurrentX = LMarg
    objOut.CurrentY = TMarg
    objOut.Print InptStr
End Sub
```

This same routine could be used to align text at the top of the specified region.

Moving to the Right　Right-justifying text is a little trickier than handling left-justified text. To align text with the right edge of a region, you must know the size of the text and the size of the region. As with the procedure for left-justifying text, the size and position of the region are passed to the procedure to right-justify the text. Therefore, the key task involved is to determine the size of the text to be printed. As you know, this can be accomplished with the TextWidth method. Listing 15.10 shows how the right-justification is accomplished. The results of the procedure are displayed in Figure 15.17.

Listing 15.10　TEXTFUNC.FRM—Using the *TextWidth* Function to Determine Where to Print Right-Justified Text

```
Private Sub RightJustify(objOut As Object, LMarg, TMarg, RgWid, RgHgt _
        As Integer, InptStr As String)

    Dim txMarg As Integer

    txMarg = RgWid - objOut.TextWidth(InptStr) - 10
    If txMarg < 0 Then txMarg = 0
    objOut.CurrentX = LMarg + txMarg
    objOut.CurrentY = TMarg
    objOut.Print InptStr

End Sub
```

FIG. 15.17

A sample program demonstrates a technique for right-justification of text.

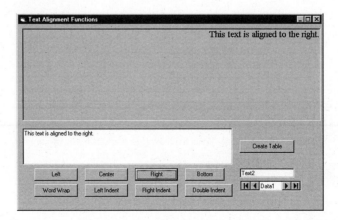

Text can be aligned along the bottom of the object as well. This is handled by the routine in Listing 15.11, which uses the TextHeight method to determine the position of the text.

Listing 15.11   TEXTFUNC.FRM—Using *TextHeight* to Handle Alignment Along the Bottom of the Object

```
Private Sub BottomAlign(objOut As Object, LMarg, TMarg, RgWid, RgHgt _
        As Integer, InptStr As String)

    Dim txMarg As Integer

    txMarg = RgHgt - objOut.TextHeight(InptStr) - 10
    If txMarg < 0 Then txMarg = 0
    objOut.CurrentX = LMarg
    objOut.CurrentY = TMarg + txMarg
    objOut.Print InptStr
End Sub
```

Staying in the Middle   The final alignment function is centering. Centering is accomplished by determining the blank space available on the line and placing an equal amount of the space on both sides of the text to be printed. This is again accomplished using the CurrentX property and the TextWidth method. Listing 15.12 shows the procedure for centering text horizontally on the page. A similar method can be used to center the text vertically on the page, or to center the text in both directions. Figure 15.18 shows the results of the centering operation.

FIG. 15.18

Center text on the page either horizontally, vertically, or both.

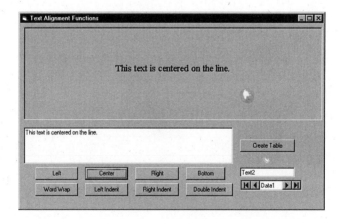

Only horizontal centering is shown in the listing, but all three routines are included in the sample project TextFunc.Vbp. You can load this project from the accompanying CD-ROM.

Listing 15.12   TEXTFUNC.FRM—The Custom *CenterText* Function

```
Private Sub CenterText(objOut As Object, LMarg, TMarg, RgWid, RgHgt _
        As Integer, InptStr As String)

    Dim txMarg As Integer

    txMarg = (RgWid - objOut.TextWidth(InptStr)) / 2
    If txMarg < 0 Then txMarg = 0
    objOut.CurrentX = LMarg + txMarg
    objOut.CurrentY = TMarg
    objOut.Print InptStr

End Sub
```

Using Word Wrapping in Your Printouts

One of the most useful functions that you can create is word wrapping. Word wrapping breaks up a line of text (usually at a space) and places additional text on the following lines of the printout. This prevents the information in the report from being printed off the edge of the page. To handle its task, the word wrapping function performs the following steps:

1. Finds the first/next word in the text using the InStr function to look for a space
2. Adds the word to a variable containing the line to be printed
3. Determines whether the text in the variable will fit on the current line
4. Repeats Steps 1 through 3 until the maximum number of words are included for the line
5. Prints the line of text
6. Removes the printed text from the input string
7. Repeats these steps until the entire input string has been printed

The procedure to handle word wrapping is shown in Listing 15.13. Figure 15.19 shows the input text in the text box and the word wrapped text in the picture box

Listing 15.13   TEXTFUNC.FRM—Word Wrapping Ensures that Information Is Not Printed Past the End of the Line

```
Private Sub WordWrap(objOut As Object, LMarg, TMarg, RgWid, RgHgt _
        As Integer, InptStr As String)

    Dim StrtPos As Integer
    Dim EndPos As Integer
    Dim TxtLen As Integer
    Dim PrntLn As String
    Dim PrntIn As String

    PrntIn = InptStr
    objOut.CurrentY = TMarg
```

continues

Listing 15.13   Continued

```
Do
    EndPos = 0
    TxtLen = 0
    PrntLn = ""
    Do
        StrtPos = EndPos + 1
        EndPos = InStr(StrtPos, PrntIn, " ")
        PrntLn = Left(PrntIn, EndPos)
        TxtLen = objOut.TextWidth(PrntLn)
    Loop Until TxtLen > RgWid - 10 Or EndPos = 0
    If EndPos = 0 Then
        PrntLn = PrntIn
        PrntIn = ""
    Else
        PrntLn = Left(PrntIn, StrtPos - 1)
        PrntIn = LTrim(Mid(PrntIn, StrtPos))
    End If
    objOut.CurrentX = LMarg
    objOut.Print PrntLn
Loop While Len(PrntIn) > 0

End Sub
```

FIG. 15.19

Word wrapping makes
your report look more
professional.

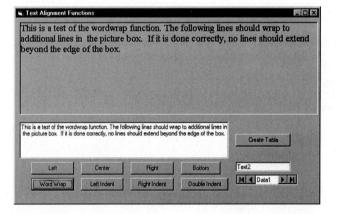

As with the other procedures, the WordWrap procedure allows you to specify the starting
position and print region size for the output. This gives you much greater flexibility in what you
can accomplish with the procedure. By varying the starting position and region size, you can
handle left, right, and double indents for your paragraphs. The results of these techniques are
shown in Figures 15.20 through 15.22. The actual code is contained in the sample project.

FIG. 15.20

Left Indent is handled by changing the starting position of the word wrapping.

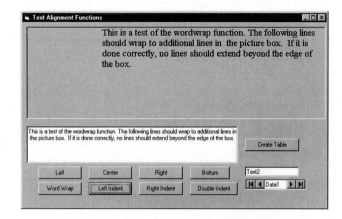

FIG. 15.21

Right Indent is handled by changing the print region width for the word wrapping.

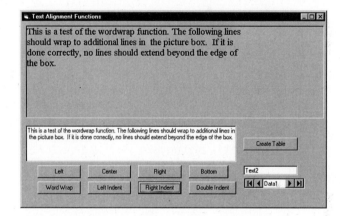

FIG. 15.22

Double Indent is handled by changing both the starting position and the region width.

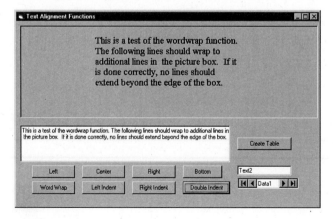

Part
III

Ch
15

Creating a Table with a Display Grid

The final technique we want to show you is how to create a table. The table uses several of the functions that we just created. Specifically, it uses the CenterText function to center the table headers within each column. It also uses the WordWrap function to handle word wrapping within a cell. Finally, the table uses the graphics methods to draw the lines of the table. The example presented in Listing 15.14 shows how you would print a table of book titles, ISBN numbers, and comments from the Biblio database. The table is shown in Figure 15.23.

Listing 15.14 TEXTFUNC.FRM—Using Text Functions and Line Methods to Create a Table

```
Dim txStr As String
Dim LineY As Integer
Dim  I As Integer
Dim  objWid As Integer
Dim  objHgt As Integer    Dim ColLft(1 To 3) As Integer, ColWid(1 To 3) As_
    Integer

Printer.Font.Name = "Times New Roman"
Printer.Font.Size = 14
Printer.Orientation = vbPRORLandscape
objWid = Printer.ScaleWidth - 20
objHgt = Printer.ScaleHeight - 10
ColLft(1) = 10
ColWid(1) = objWid / 3
ColLft(2) = ColLft(1) + ColWid(1)
ColWid(2) = objWid / 3
ColLft(3) = ColLft(2) + ColWid(2)
ColWid(3) = objWid - ColWid(1) - ColWid(2)
LineY = 10
Printer.Line (ColLft(1), LineY)-(ColLft(1) + objWid, LineY)
CenterText Printer, ColLft(1), LineY + 5, ColWid(1), objHgt, "Title"
CenterText Printer, ColLft(2), LineY + 5, ColWid(2), objHgt, "ISBN"
CenterText Printer, ColLft(3), LineY + 5, ColWid(3), objHgt, "Comments"
Printer.Font.Size = 10

For I = 1 To 2
    LineY = Printer.CurrentY + 10
    Printer.Line (ColLft(1), LineY)-(ColLft(1) + objWid, LineY)
    txStr = Data1.Recordset!Title & ""
    LeftJustify Printer, ColLft(1), LineY + 5, ColWid(1), objHgt, txStr
    t xStr = Data1.Recordset!ISBN & ""
    LeftJustify Printer, ColLft(2), LineY + 5, ColWid(2), objHgt, txStr
    txStr = Data1.Recordset!Comments & ""
    WordWrap Printer, ColLft(3), LineY + 5, ColWid(3), objHgt, txStr
    Data1.Recordset.MoveNext
Next I

LineY = Printer.CurrentY + 10
Printer.Line (ColLft(1), LineY)-(ColLft(1) + objWid, LineY)
Printer.Line (ColLft(1), 10)-(ColLft(1), LineY)
Printer.Line (ColLft(2), 10)-(ColLft(2), LineY)
```

```
Printer.Line (ColLft(3), 10)-(ColLft(3), LineY)
Printer.Line (ColLft(1) + objWid, 10)-(ColLft(1) + objWid, LineY)

Printer.EndDoc
```

FIG. 15.23

You can create tables
using text functions.

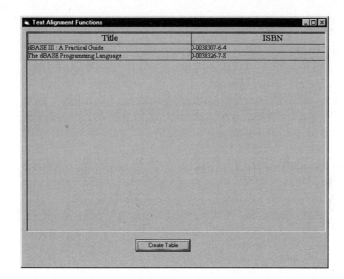

From Here...

In this chapter, you have seen how you can display reports on the screen and print them on
paper. You also saw that while the Print method is fairly simple, you can use code to create a
number of text effects in your printouts. You even saw how graphics could be used to enhance
your reports. To learn more about some of the topics covered in this chapter, refer to the following:

- To learn more about the options available for displaying text and fonts, see Chapter 14,
  "Working with Text, Fonts, and Colors."

- To learn more about the Picturebox and drawing functions, see "Doing Graphics," found
  on this book's CD-ROM.

CHAPTER 16

Using Crystal Reports

Chapter 15, "Displaying and Printing Reports," explains how to send information to a printer from within a Visual Basic application. However, creating great looking reports requires a unique program designed specifically for that purpose. Crystal Reports is a complete reporting tool from Seagate Software Company. A single-use copy of the Crystal Reports product, Version 4.6, is included on the CD-ROM that comes with Visual Basic 5. By using this reporting tool, you can create professional looking reports to display on-screen with your application or send to a printer.

In this chapter, you learn how to use the Crystal Reports application to produce usuable, professional looking reports with very little effort. In addition, you are going to see how to add Crystal Reports to your Visual Basic application by making use of the OCX control that comes with it. ■

▪ **Take a short tour of the Crystal Reports interface**

Before learning how to create reports using this product, take a quick look at some of the functions and features included with Crystal Reports.

▪ **Use Crystal Reports to create a report**

Use the sample database (NWIND.MDB) that comes with Visual Basic 5 to create a professional-looking report.

▪ **Use the Crystal Reports Control with Visual Basic**

Add Crystal Reports' capabilities to your Visual Basic application by using the Crystal Reports Custom Control.

▪ **Add a Report Selection Form**

See how to give the user the capability to select the report they want to see.

Taking a Short Tour of Crystal Reports

This section describes Crystal Reports and then takes you on a quick tour of the tools, facilities, and options available through Crystal Reports. Crystal Reports is a powerful yet easy-to-use program for creating custom reports, lists, and labels from data in your existing databases. Crystal Reports works by connecting to one or more of your databases. Using these connections, Crystal Reports draws in the values from database fields you select and uses them in the report, either in their original form or as part of a formula that generates more complex values. Crystal Reports is designed to work with all kinds of data, such as the following:

- Numbers
- Currency
- Text
- Dates
- Boolean

There is a wide range of built-in tools that you can use to manipulate data to fit the requirements of the report. These tools enable you to:

- Create calculations
- Calculate subtotals and grand totals
- Convert data from one type to another
- Calculate averages
- Count the total number of records in a query
- Test for the presence of specific values
- Filter database records
- Perform date calculations

The data from your database can be placed wherever you need it on the report and can be highlighted with special fonts and font sizes. Using Crystal Reports, your reports can be as simple or as complex as your needs require. Once you have designed a report for your application, you can use it within the application or as a template to create other similar reports. Crystal Reports was created to enable technical and non-technical users to create customized reports quickly and easily by using a variety of databases. While most database programs include their own report generators, they are usually too difficult for non-technical people to use, and they generally require a good understanding of how that database program works.

N O T E   No matter how much you modify the data in a report, Crystal Reports does not write any
data back into your original database. ■

What Databases Crystal Report Can Work With

Crystal Reports connects to almost any database available on the market. There are actually two methods of connecting to a database, Data File and SQL/ODBC. The first method is designed for the simpler, PC-based databases, such as dBASE and Microsoft Access. The other method is to use ODBC (Open DataBase Connectivity) to connect to any database that has an ODBC connection. Some of the databases in this group are Microsoft Access, Oracle, Sybase, and Microsoft SQL Server.

A Close Look at the Crystal Reports Interface

When you start Crystal Reports, you see the plain application window shown in Figure 16.1. After you begin working with a report, Crystal Reports contains two separate tabbed windows that you use to design and test your reports: the Design window and the Preview window. Neither of these windows has its own menus. Instead, they use the commands from the main menu. They also have scroll bars at the bottom and right side of the window. Most of the Crystal Reports workspace is used by the Design and Preview windows (see Figure 16.2). These windows have their own unique features and functions, which are discussed in the following sections.

Part
III

Ch
16

FIG. 16.1

The Crystal Reports main window is used to control all reporting features in the product.

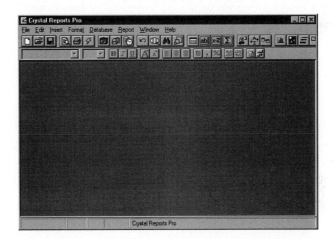

The Design Window   The Design window is divided into two separate sections that provide on-screen information that aids in the designing of the report. The Edit box is the large white area of the Design window. This is where you actually build your report. The horizontal lines in the edit box separate the report into sections. As you add new groupings to your report, more sections will appear in the edit box. The gray area to the left of the Edit box provides additional information to assist you in placing the data and other objects into the report. The horizontal lines just mentioned extend into the gray area, enabling you to identify which section is which.

As with most Windows-based development tools, Crystal Reports has several tools incorporated into the interface. The Edit box has a ruler that can be displayed. It also has a Snap-to-Grid feature that assists in lining up objects on the report. Access to the Crystal Reports functions and features are via the toolbar at the top of the main window, the main menu, or by using the right-click pop-up menus directly on the report. Depending on what you are doing, Crystal Reports provides a wizard to help you in the process of creating:

- Column Totals
- Selection Conditions
- Data Groups
- Formulas (calculated fields)
- Sort Criteria

FIG. 16.2

The Design tab displays the report in the development mode. No data is displayed on this tab.

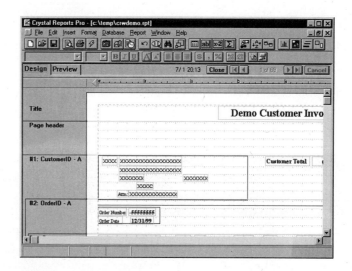

In addition, the right-click pop-up menus provide access to the related functions for a selected object. Some of these options are:

- Changing font styles
- Formatting the data
- Adding borders
- Changing colors
- Browsing the data from the database
- Adding conditions

This chapter only touches on some of these options. To see how to make use of them, see the section "Using Crystal Reports to Create a Report."

After you select your database, the Design window is displayed. You then use this window to insert and format the data that you need in your report. When you start a new report, five sections are created automatically in the Design window (see Table 16.1).

Table 16.1   Design Windows Working Sections

Section Name	Description
Title	Displays the report title, data, and any other information that needs to appear at the top of the report. Information displayed here is shown only once.
Page Header	Similar to the Title section; this information is displayed at the top of every page.
Details	Displays the detail information from the query.
Page Footer	Usually displays the page number and any other information that you want at the bottom of each page.
Summary	Displays information only on the last page of your report.

Reports are built by inserting data fields, formulas, and other information (record counts, record numbers, and so forth) into the Details section of the Design window. You use the Insert menu to select or create the fields you want to insert on the report. Subtotals and other group values are added by selecting a field and then building the conditions to generate the new subtotal or group value (in other words, change of customer number, change of state, and so forth). These group sections are created as needed, and the values are placed in that section. If you want the value to be some other place on the report, you simply select it and drag it to where you want it located.

Although you are not really adding any totals using the Formula Editor, the Total tab that is covered in "Defining Totals in the Report" later in this chapter take you through the process of selecting fields to sum or total on the report.

The Preview Window   To see how your report will look when printed, switch over to the Preview window. Whenever you select this option, Crystal Reports gathers the data, performs any defined calculations, and then displays the report (see Figure 16.3). Once the data is displayed, you can review the positioning and formatting of all information on the report. Additionally, you can see the results of all summaries, calculations, and record and group selections. In effect, this is what the final report looks like.

A nice feature of the Preview window is that you can still modify the format of your report without having to return to the Design window.

The Preview Window's Look and Feel   Working in the Preview window does have a different look and feel than working in the Design window. Each field in the database can contain hundreds of values, depending on the number of records in the database. When you place a field in the report on the Design window, a single field box is displayed that represents all of those values. When you select this field, sizing handles appear and the border changes color (see Figure 16.4).

FIG. 16.3
Use the Preview window to see how a report will look printed, without actually printing it.

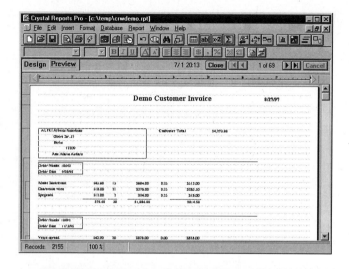

FIG. 16.4
Although the new border color doesn't show up in this figure, it is yellow when you see it on-screen.

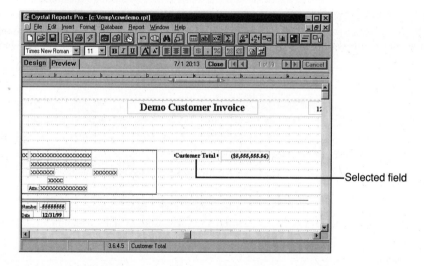

Selected field

In the Preview window, on the other hand, you are working with the actual data. Instead of a field box, the values themselves are displayed. When you select a field, a sizing box appears around every value from the selected field. Despite the difference in look and feel, however, the process of building and modifying the report is the same in both windows.

The Experts of Crystal Reports

Crystal Reports contains experts that assist you with the process of creating reports. When you choose File, New, the Create New Report dialog box displays, as shown in Figure 16.5.

FIG. 16.5

This dialog box is also referred to as the standard Report Gallery, and it shows each Report Expert you can choose from.

The Report Gallery displays a series of icons representing the different types of experts that are at your disposal. Each report expert takes you through the steps needed to build a report. If you simply want to build a new report based on one that already exists, click the Another Report button. The program will make a duplicate of the original report. You then can modify it as needed to create the new report. If you want to build a report from scratch, click the Custom button. Several Report Type and Data Type buttons appear at the bottom of the Report Gallery (see Figure 16.6).

FIG. 16.6

The Custom Report buttons enable you to create a report from scratch.

Depending on the type of report you want to create, click the corresponding button and follow the instructions if you selected an expert, or simply build the report if you choose to start from scratch.

Adding Calculations Crystal Reports uses formulas and functions to help you create reports more quickly and easily. By using these formulas and functions, you can do the kind of number crunching and data manipulation that is needed for an advanced database report. To create a calculated field, use the Edit Formula dialog box, shown in Figure 16.7.

The Formula Editor enables you to work with both formulas and functions. A *formula* is a set of instructions that are used to calculate information you can't get directly from the database. If a database record has two fields, Unit Price and Quantity Sold, but does not have a field that multiplies both fields to calculate Sales Price, then you need a formula to perform this function to display it in a report. This type of formula is called a simple formula, which uses the standard arithmetic operators. However, not all of your calculations can be reduced to simple formulas. Some will require complex calculations or manipulations of the database fields.

FIG. 16.7

Use the Formula Editor to build simple and complex calculations.

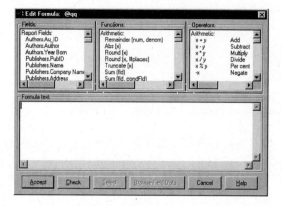

If you want to display the average monthly unit sales for the previous year, rounded to the nearest unit, you need a mathematical formula. The functions required to perform these activities involve a fair amount of data manipulation. While some of this can be done by using Crystal Reports operators alone, many of them can't be done without the use of functions. In fact, even those that can be done with Crystal Reports can be done more quickly and efficiently by using functions.

A *function* is a predefined procedure or subroutine that is used to evaluate, calculate, or transform data from the database. An example of a function is the use of the UpperCase function to transform all characters in a string to uppercase characters. When you use a function, Crystal Reports performs the set of instructions that are built into the function, without your having to specify each operation separately. By performing multiple operations with a single command, this kind of function is similar to shorthand writing in that it makes it easier to create reports.

The Formula Editor is divided into four sub-windows that can be used to build the calculation (refer to Figure 16.7). The Fields window lists all of the database fields that are available to you, based on the tables you have previously attached to the report. The Functions window lists all of the functions that Crystal Reports has available for you to use in a calculated field. The Operators window lists all of the operators that you can use when creating a calculation. The largest and last window is the Formula Text window, where the calculation is actually built. You can choose to use the different windows to select items or you can type directly into the formula text area.

N O T E   You can select an item from the Formula Editor windows (Fields, Functions, or Operators) by double-clicking it, or by selecting it and then clicking the Select button at the bottom of the editor to add it to the calculation. ■

You can combine fields, functions, and operators to create complex calculations from database fields. This enables you to create a very complex calculation in pieces of the final calculation and then combine them together to form the finished calculation.

Filtering Your Data   When you select a field to appear on your report, Crystal Reports prints field values from every record in the selected database. However, in many cases, you may want to include only a specific group of rows from the database rather than including all the rows. For example, you may want only a specific group of customers from the database, or you may want to include only rows from invoices that fall within a particular range of dates. With Crystal Reports, this filtering process is easy. The program includes four options, listed in Table 16.2, on the Report menu for restricting or filtering your report to specific records or groups of records.

Table 16.2   Crystal Reports Options for Filtering the Data

Menu Option	Description
Select Records	Enables you to limit the number of records in your report based on a condition or conditions specified using a selection formula dialog box.
Edit Record Selection Formula	Uses the Formula Editor to enable you to modify the selection condition.
Select Groups	Enables you to limit your report to a specific group or groups, based on a condition or conditions specified using a selection formula dialog box.
Edit Group Selection Formula	Uses the Formula Editor to enable you to modify the selection condition.

Even though you will be able to create professional-looking reports after completing this chapter, there are many more features included in Crystal Reports. In the next section, you see how to create a report by using the Crystal Reports program, and then learn how to access the report from a Visual Basic application.

Using Crystal Reports to Create a Report

The first step in designing your reports is to start up Crystal Reports. You can run Crystal Reports in either of two ways. First, you can select the program from the Visual Basic folder on the Start menu of Windows 95. By using this option, you don't even need to have Visual Basic loaded to work on your reports. The second method of starting Crystal Reports is to choose Visual Basic's Add-Ins, Report Designer. Either method starts Crystal Reports and places you in the startup screen that appeared earlier in Figure 16.1.

Choosing the Report Template

After you start Crystal Reports, you can create a new report by choosing New, File or by clicking the New Report button on the toolbar. In the New Report dialog box that opens, you can specify the type of report that you want to produce (see Figure 16.8).

FIG. 16.8

In the Create New Report dialog box, you can select options for your report.

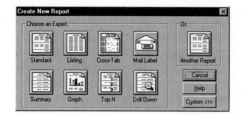

Crystal Reports supports the creation of the following basic report types:

- *Standard* Creates a standard report with rows and columns. It often has summary information at the bottom of the columns.

- *Listing* Creates a simple row and column listing of the information in a recordset.

- *Cross-Tab* Inverts the order of a standard columnar report. It is often used to obtain a quick summary view of a more complex set of data.

- *Mail Label* Create items such as mailing labels or name tags from the information in your database.

- *Summary* Presents summary information about the data, such as total and average sales, or the number of attendees.

- *Graph* Shows the information in a graphical form.

- *Top N* Shows only a specified number of the top records in the recordset. For example, this report can be used to show the top five salespeople in the company.

- *Drill Down* Shows the supporting information, or detail information, for each record.

When you select the type of report you want to create, the Report Expert automatically starts. The report type that is used in this example is the Standard report type. The Standard Report Expert has seven steps to create the report. Each of these steps is shown on a tab in the Create Report Expert dialog box, shown in Figure 16.9.

FIG. 16.9

The Create Report Expert guides you through the steps of creating a report.

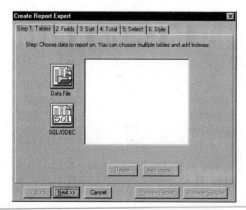

The first step in creating the report is to select the type of data source to use for the report. Crystal Reports supports the following two data sources for the reports (and a third one, also listed here, if you buy the full retail product):

- *Data File*   A table or query in a database. This option is used for xBase, MS Access, and Paradox databases.

- *SQL/ODBC*   With this data source, you can retrieve data from any SQL-based database. This option is generally used to access larger databases that can be located anywhere on the network.

- *Data Dictionary*   The *data dictionary* is used to allow an end-user to access a database without knowing anything about how the database is designed.

N O T E   The Data Dictionary feature of Crystal Reports is only available by purchasing the professional edition of Crystal Reports. ■

To select the data source for the demo report, select the Data File button to display the Choose Database File dialog box, as shown in Figure 16.10.

FIG. 16.10

Choose the database with which to work.

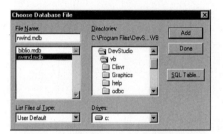

For this report, you will be using the Northwind database (.../Devstudio/vb/nwind.mdb) that comes with Visual Basic 5. After the database file is selected, all of the tables and queries in the database are added to the report. If you see the expert in the background, you will see the tables and queries listed. Click the Done button to return to the expert. You are then automatically taken to the dialog box's second tab.

The second tab of the Expert enables you to review and modify the relation information that is already present in the database. Because the Northwind database already has the relationship information defined, you will see the relationships, as shown in Figure 16.11. When this tab is first displayed, the message about Tables is to allow you to add additional tables to the relationship diagram.

Click the OK button on the message displayed and then click the Next button to continue to the third tab.

N O T E   Some databases, such as Access, enable you to define the table relationships within the database itself. ■

Part III

Ch

16

FIG. 16.11
Crystal Reports accesses the relationships from the database.

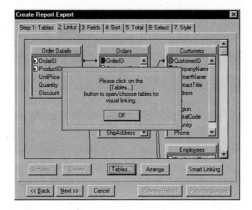

Selecting the Data Fields

The next step in the Create Report Expert is to select the individual fields that you want to have appear on the report. This tab of the dialog box is shown in Figure 16.12.

FIG. 16.12
Select the data fields to include from a list of available fields.

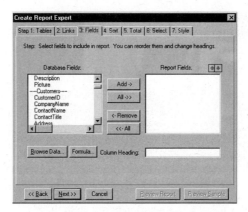

Fields are added by double-clicking the individual fields in the Database Fields list or by highlighting the fields that you want to select and then clicking the Add button. The Fields tab of the dialog box also enables you to set the order of the fields in the report. For each field in the Report Fields list, you can also specify a custom column heading in the text box below the list. Select the fields listed in Table 16.3 and add them to the fields list.

Table 16.3   Database Fields to Be Added to the Report

Table	Field
Customers	CustomerID
	CompanyName
	ContactName

Table	Field
	Address
	City
	Region
	PostalCode
Orders	OrderID
	OrderDate
Order Details	ProductID
	Quantity
	UnitPrice
	Discount
Products	ProductName

There also may be times when you will want to combine fields or use them in a calculation. The Fields page also has a button that enables you to enter formulas for calculated fields. The report that you are creating needs two calculated fields, so click the Formula button to add the fields included in Table 16.4.

Table 16.4   Calculated Fields to Be Added to the Report

Field Name	Calculation
Extended Price	Order Details.Quantity * Order Details.UnitPrice
Discounted Price	Extended Price - Extended Price * Order Details.Discount

Notice that each calculated field name has a "@" added to the beginning of the name. This denotes that the field is a calculated field. You will also see that they are listed in a new section called Report Fields in the Database Fields window. They still need to be added to the report like any other field.

N O T E   Each calculated field must be added to the list separately. ▪

Report Creation Tabs

After you have specified all of the fields required for the report, you can preview the report or continue to set other options. Before you preview the report, the other available options on the other tabs of the Create Report Expert will be explained. These options are summarized in the following list:

Tab	Purpose
Sort	Specifies an order by which the lines of the report are sorted.
Total	Determines whether subtotals and grand totals of numerical data are included on the report.

Select	Specifies a selection criteria for the report. Choose it to produce only a subset of the recordset that is the source of the data. Use of a subset greatly increases the speed of your report.
Style	Specifies a specific style of the report, such as placing lines after each record, or making the entire report appear as a table; also enables you to add pictures to the report.

Next, you will add a few sorts and totals to the sample report. To specify the sorts needed, click the Next button.

Using the Sort Tab   The Sort tab enables you to select the fields to sort, the order in which they are sorted, and in which direction they are sorted (see Figure 16.13).

FIG. 16.13
Set the sort fields and their properties.

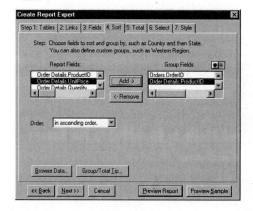

Select the following fields to sort in the listed order:

- Customers.CustomerID
- Orders.OrderID
- Orders.ProductID

Click Next to add the subtotals to the report.

Defining Totals in the Report   The Total tab displays a tab for every field that you select to be sorted (see Figure 16.14).

Create the following totals, listed in Table 16.5, by removing any unwanted fields from the Total Fields list.

Table 16.5   Picking the Correct Fields to Total

Tab Name	Field to Sum
Customers.CustomerID	@Discounted Price

Tab Name	Field to Sum
Orders.OrderID	Order Details.Quantity @Discounted Price
Order Details.ProductID	None

Click the <u>N</u>ext button twice to go to the Style tab.

FIG. 16.14
Specify the totals for a report.

Narrowing Down Your Report Criteria

Although the Select tab is not used in this example, there are a couple of significant things to mention about this tab for the time when you do need it.

The Select tab enables to you to easily set up conditions that Crystal Reports will use when retrieving data from the database. By using this tab, you can build standard conditions. However, if you need more complex conditions, you should create your own selection formulas.

Using the Style Tab   The Style tab enables you to select a style for the report and enter a Title that is displayed at the top of the report. Select the Standard style and then enter **Demo Customer Invoice** as the Title (see Figure 16.15).

You are now finished with the initial setup of the report.

Previewing the Report

After you have selected the report fields and any other information needed for the report, you can preview the report to see how the actual data will look. Click the <u>P</u>review Report button on the Expert to display the initial report, which is shown in Figure 16.16.

As you can see from this preview, the report needs some formatting to make it look more professional. Some of the numeric fields need to be formatted and the following items need to be added to the report:

- A page header
- A system date
- Page numbering

FIG. 16.15

Select the style for the report from a list of available templates.

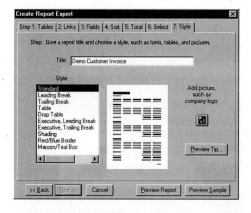

FIG. 16.16

Display a preview of the report you just created.

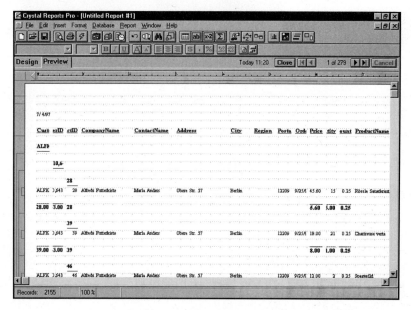

These fields can be added to the report by using the Special Fields option on the Insert menu. Right-clicking any field or label gives you a pop-up menu that lists all of the editing options available for the selected object. In addition to these changes, you probably want to move the fields around to arrange them in the style of an invoice. After all of these changes are completed, the report should resemble the one shown in Figure 16.17.

Saving the Report

 After you have completed the design of the report, you need to save the report file so that you can access the report from your Visual Basic program. Saving the report can be done either by clicking the Save button on the toolbar or by choosing File, Save or Save As. Any of these actions display the Save dialog box so that you can enter a filename for the report, as shown in Figure 16.17.

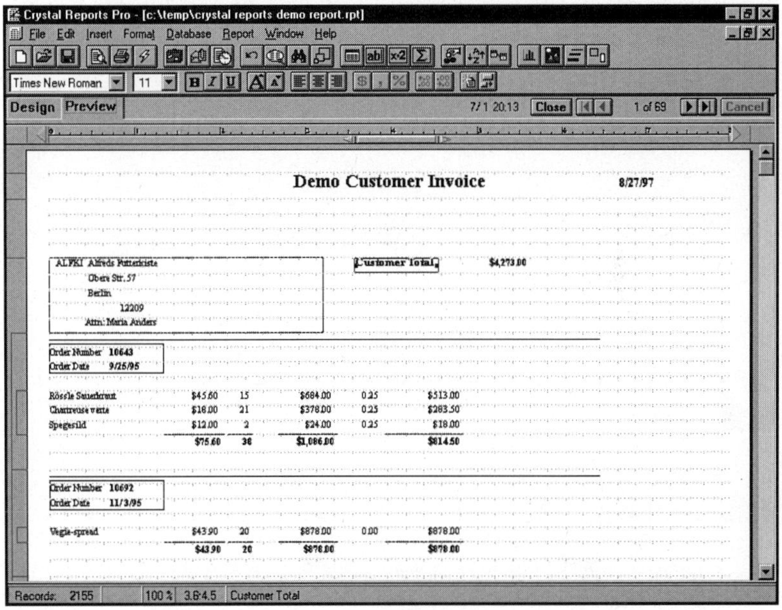

Part

III

Ch

16

FIG. 16.17

Here is the completed
Customer Invoice
report, which can be
saved by using a long
filename instead of an
old eight-character
name.

NOTE Because Crystal Reports is Windows 95/Windows NT 4.0-compliant, you can use a long file name to name the report. ■

Running a Report

Although you can run the reports you create from within Crystal Reports, you'll probably want to access them from within your Visual Basic program. You can do so by using the Crystal Reports custom control, which is one of the controls installed with Crystal Reports. The Crystal Reports control provides a link between the Crystal Reports engine and the reports you create with the report designer.

Using the Crystal Reports Control with Visual Basic

The first step in accessing Crystal Reports is to make the control available to your program. If Visual Basic is not started, start it and then create a new project. Now you need to add the

Crystal Reports control to your Visual Basic Toolbox. To do so, choose Components from the Project menu of Visual Basic. The Components dialog box appears, which is shown in Figure 16.18. In this dialog box, you can specify which custom controls are available in your project.

FIG. 16.18

You must make the Crystal Reports control available to your project by selecting it in the Components dialog box.

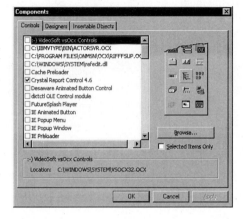

 TIP You also can access the Components dialog box by clicking the right mouse button on the Toolbox and then choosing Components from the pop-up menu, or by pressing Ctrl+T.

TROUBLESHOOTING

I Can't find the Crystal Reports custom control in the Components dialog box. What happened to it? If you elected to perform a custom setup of Visual Basic, you may have left Crystal Reports out of the setup process. You need to rerun the Visual Basic setup program and install Crystal Reports.

Setting Up the Control

 After the Crystal Reports control is available in your toolbox, you can use it in your program. To gain access to the control, simply select it from the toolbox and place it on the form where you will access the reports from. Because the Crystal Reports control is not visible at runtime, it appears only as an icon on your form. After the control is on the form, you can set the properties that access the reports you create with the report designer.

Specifying the Report to Run   The key property that you need to specify is the `ReportFileName` property. This property specifies the actual report that you will run from your program. You can easily set this property by clicking the ellipsis button that appears to the right of the property in the Properties window. The Crystal Reports Property Pages, shown in Figure 16.19, then appears. From this page, you can specify the name of the report and whether the report should go to the printer, a preview window, a file, or to a message through the MAPI interface.

FIG. 16.19

Select the report name and destination from the Property Pages of Crystal Reports.

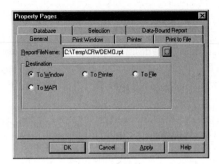

Part

III

Ch

16

On the General tab of the Property Pages, either type the name of the report into the field for the ReportFileName property, or select the report from a file dialog box by clicking the ellipsis button on the Property Pages.

Selecting the ReportFileName is the minimum setup for Crystal Reports. The other tabs on the properties page enable you to customize the report to specific requirements. These tabs are:

Print Window	Sets the properties of the Print display window
Printer	Sets the number of copies to print
Print to File	Sets the file name and file type when printing a report to the printer
Database	Enables you to enter the UserId and connection info for a database
Selection	Enables entry of the SelectionFormula and GroupSelectionFormula
Data-Bound Report	Sets Heading for a database report

At this point, you can write the line of code necessary to run the report and test it by running your program.

Setting Optional Properties   Although only the ReportFileName is required for a report, you may want to use several optional properties with the report. The first of these properties is the SelectionFormula property. This property enables you to limit the number of records that will be included in the report. The SelectionFormula property is similar to the Where clause of an SQL statement but it uses its own particular format to enter the information. To specify the SelectionFormula, you must specify the name of the recordset and the field to be compared. You must express this recordset/field combination in dot notation and enclose it in curly brackets. After specifying the recordset and field, you must specify the comparison operator and the value to be compared. The final result is an expression like the following:

```
{MemberShipList.OrgCode}=1
```

You also can use multiple expressions by including the And or Or operators.

FIG. 17.2

The *End Sub* statement is automatically added when you define a new procedure.

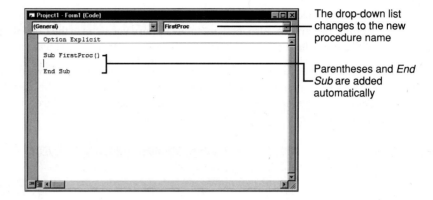

The drop-down list changes to the new procedure name

Parentheses and *End Sub* are added automatically

The full syntax of a Sub procedure includes the Sub statement, the End Sub statement, and the procedure commands:

```
[Public ¦ Private] [Static] Sub procname([arguments])
statements_to_be_run
End Sub
```

The Public, Private, and Static keywords in the Sub statement are optional parameters that affect the locations that the procedure might be called from. These keywords indicate the scope of the procedure in the same way that they indicated the scope of a variable.

▶ **See** " Determining Where a Variable Can Be Used," **p. 176**

The other method of creating a procedure is to use the Add Procedure dialog box (see Figure 17.3). You access this dialog box by choosing Tools, Add Procedure.

FIG. 17.3

Although typing it in by hand is faster, you can also create a new procedure in the current module or form by using the Add Procedure dialog box.

After you are in the dialog box, perform the following steps to create the shell of your procedure:

1. Enter the name of the procedure in the Name text box.
2. Choose the type of procedure (Sub, Function, Property, or Event).
3. Choose the scope of the procedure (Public or Private).
4. Choose whether to treat All Local Variables as Statics.

To create a procedure, you need to choose the Sub procedure type. This is the same as the procedures that are used in handling events in your code. A *function type of procedure* is one that returns a specific value. These procedures are covered later in this chapter. A *property procedure* is one used to set or retrieve the value of a property in a form or class module. An *event procedure* is one that is used to respond to an event in a form or class module.

After you have entered the necessary information, choose OK. Visual Basic then creates the framework of a procedure in the Code window.

Running the Procedure After a procedure has been developed, you need a way to run it from other parts of your program. There are two methods for running a procedure—use the `Call` statement or use just the procedure name. With either method, you simply specify the procedure name and any arguments that are required by the procedure. (The arguments are the ones specified in the `Sub` statement when you defined the procedure.)

The syntax for running a procedure is as follows:

```
Call procname([arguments])
```

or

```
procname arguments
```

Part
IV

Ch
17

In either syntax, `procname` refers to the name of the procedure. This is the name that is specified in the `Sub` statement that defined the procedure. `Arguments` refers to the parameters passed to the procedure. In the calling statement, the arguments can be literal values, variables, or functions that return the proper data type. This is different from the `Sub` statement where all the arguments have to be variable names. All parameters must be separated by commas.

Let's look at a brief example of a procedure that uses parameters. Suppose your program needs to log all of its operations and errors to a text file. A procedure that handled writing messages to the log file, along with a date and time, could be very useful:

```
Sub LogPrint(stMessage As String)
Dim inFileNum As Integer
    inFileNum = FreeFile
    Open "C:\EVENTLOG.TXT" for append as #inFileNum
    Print #inFileNum, Now & " - " & stMessage
    Close #inFileNum
End Sub
```

The following line of code calls the procedure. When calling a procedure, you can supply values for its arguments using either a variable, a literal string, or a combination of the two:

```
LogPrint "Error Opening the file " & stUserFile
```

The `LogPrint` procedure is very simple, yet it saves a lot of time in the long run. It makes the calling code shorter and more readable. In addition, if you ever want to change the output of the log file from a text file to a database, printer, or pager, you only have to change the `LogPrint` function itself.

> **CAUTION**
>
> Typically, you must include the same number of parameters in the calling statement as are present in the definition of the procedure. Also, the values supplied by the calling statement must match the data types expected by the procedure. Violating either of these conditions results in an error when you run your program.

At the start of this section, I listed two methods of calling a procedure. The following line of code calls the `LogPrint` procedure using the other syntax:

```
Call LogPrint ("The server was rebooted")
```

As you can see, the `Call` keyword can either be included or omitted in running the procedure. However, the `Call` keyword and parentheses go together. If you use the `Call` keyword, you must include the parameters in a set of parentheses. I recommend using the syntax that does not use `Call`. As you will see after looking at the examples in the next section, this makes it easier to distinguish between procedure calls and function calls.

Passing Data to the Procedure   There are two ways to get information into a procedure for processing—you can define the variables as public variables that are available everywhere in your program, or you can pass the variables directly to the procedure in the calling statement.

For example, you could add a second argument to the `LogPrint` procedure that allows it to work with multiple files:

```
Sub LogPrint(stLogFile As String, stMessage As String)
Dim inFileNum As Integer
    inFileNum = FreeFile
    Open stLogFile for append as #inFileNum
    Print #inFileNum, Now & " - " & stMessage
    Close #inFileNum
End Sub
```

However, this means that if you only wanted to use one log file, you still would have to pass the file name to the procedure each time you called it:

```
LogPrint "C:\LOGFILE.TXT", "Error Opening the file " & stUserFile
```

For this particular procedure, the `stLogFile` argument probably does not change much throughout the program. However, hard-coding it into the `LogPrint` procedure does not make much sense either, so a public variable would be the logical choice:

```
Public stLogFileName As String
Sub LogPrint(stMessage As String)
    Dim inFileNum As Integer
```

```
        inFileNum = FreeFile
        Open stLogFileName for append as #inFileNum
        Print #inFileNum, Now & " - " & stMessage
        Close #inFileNum
End Sub
```

Before calling the procedure, your program would need to set the value of stLogFileName. The Public keyword makes it visible to all the other procedures in your program. The variable inFileNum, on the other hand, can only be used within the LogPrint procedure, as it should be.

If you are going to use the variables in a number of procedures and the procedure is specific to the current program, it is better to set up the variables as public variables. However, for the sake of reusability among projects, it is a good idea to keep procedures as independent as possible. To do this, you should define all the necessary parameters to be passed to the procedure in the Sub statement and pass the parameters in the calling statement.

The parameters used by a procedure can provide two-way communication between the procedure and the calling program. The procedure can use information in the parameters to perform a calculation and then pass the results back to the calling program in another parameter.

For example, the following procedure gets the height and width of a rectangle from the parameters list and then calculates the area and perimeter of the rectangle. These values are returned through the parameters list:

```
Sub CalcRectangle(rcWidth as Integer, rcHeight as Integer,
    ➥rcArea as Integer, rcPerimeter as Integer)
        rcArea = rcWidth * rcHeight
        rcPerimeter = 2 * (rcWidth + rcHeight)
End Sub
```

The procedure can be called by either of the following code segments in Listing 17.1.

Listing 17.1 PROCCALL.TXT—Two Ways of Calling a Procedure

```
'********************************
'This code can call the procedure
'********************************

sqWid = 5
sqHgt = 5
sqArea = 0
sqPerm = 0
Call CalcRectangle(sqWid, sqHgt, sqArea, sqPerm)

'************************************
'This code can also call the procedure
'************************************

newArea = 0
newPerm = 0
CalcRectangle 4, 10, newArea, newPerm
```

Part
IV

Ch
17

TIP This example has a single output value, which makes it more suited to a function than a sub, but we discuss that shortly in the section entitled "Working with Functions."

Passing parameters to a procedure this way is known as *passing by reference*. In this case, the variable name passed to the procedure and the variable name used in the procedure both refer to (reference) the same location in memory. This is what enables the procedure to modify the value that is then passed back to the calling code. You can also pass a parameter to a procedure *by value*. This causes the procedure to use a *copy* of the information that was passed to it, which prevents the procedure code from modifying the value used by the calling program.

By default, when you declare a parameter for a procedure, passing by reference is used. To modify this behavior, you must explicitly tell Visual Basic to pass the parameter by value. Do this by placing the ByVal keyword in the parameter list before each variable that is to be passed by value. This is illustrated in the following lines of code:

```
Sub CalcRectangle(ByVal rcWidth As Integer, ByVal rcHeight As Integer, _
    ➥_rcArea, rcPerimeter As Integer)
```

> **CAUTION**
>
> If you are passing parameters by reference, you need to explicitly declare the variable in the calling program and in the procedure, and you need to be sure that the variable types are the same.

Exiting a Procedure Early   As your programs, and therefore procedures, grow in complexity, there might be times when you don't need to execute all the commands in the procedure. If you need to exit the procedure before all the commands have been executed, you can use the Exit Sub statement.

One way that we often use the Exit Sub statement is in the beginning of the procedure in a routine that checks parameters for proper values. If any of the parameters passed to procedure are the wrong type or have values that could cause a problem for the procedure, we use Exit Sub to terminate the procedure before the error occurs. This is a type of *data validation*. The following code modifies the previous area calculation code to perform this check:

```
Sub CalcRectangle(rcWidth as Integer, rcHeight as Integer, rcArea as Integer,
rcPerimeter as Integer)
If rcWidth <= 0 Or rcHeight <= 0 Then
    Exit Sub
  End If
  rcArea = rcWidth * rcHeight
  rcPerimeter = 2 * (rcWidth + rcHeight)
End Sub
```

Working with Functions

Functions are very similar to procedures, with one key difference—they return a value. This value can be assigned to a variable or used in expressions. Visual Basic has a variety of built-in functions that you can use, such as Abs which returns the absolute value of a number, or Left which returns a specified number of characters from the left end of a string. You can build your own functions, as well.

To build a function, you have the same two choices you had in building a procedure—start from scratch or use the Add Procedure dialog box. To start from scratch, select the point in the Code window where you want the function to start and then enter the keyword Function followed by the name of the function. The naming conventions for functions are the same as those for procedures. To use the Add Procedure dialog box, just select the Function Type on the dialog box. Either method will create the shell of the function just as it did for a procedure. This shell is shown in the following lines of code:

```
Public Function NumAverage()

End Function
```

Although the first line is an acceptable function declaration, most of the time you will define the type of value that will be returned by the function. You define this function type like you define variable types in a Dim statement—by using the As keyword followed by the variable type. This function type declaration follows the parentheses that enclose the parameter declaration. In addition, you will typically declare the parameters that are passed to the function in the declaration statement. A more complete declaration statement is shown in the following line:

```
Public Function NumAverage(inpt1 As Single, inpt2 As Single) As Single
```

The other key difference between building a function and a procedure is that you will assign a value to the function somewhere within the code of the function. This value must be of the same type as specified in the function declaration. This is shown in the second line of the following code:

```
Public Function NumAverage(inpt1 As Single, inpt2 As Single) As Single
    NumAverage = (inpt1 + inpt2) / 2
End Function
```

NOTE Although your function code can assign a value to the function multiple times, only the last value assigned before the end (or exit) of the function is returned. ■

When you call a function, you typically assign its return value to a variable in your program, or use the value in a conditional statement as shown here:

```
'Assigning a function to a variable
AvgNum = NumAverage(25, 15)

'Using a function in a conditional expression
If NumAverage(num1, num2) > 20 Then Msgbox "What an average!"
```

NOTE If you need your function to simply perform a task (opening a database, for example), you can call the function the same way that you would call a procedure, throwing away the return value. ■

There are a number of functions built and demonstrated in the FUNCDEMO.VBP project, which you can download from **www.quecorp.com/...** is on the companion CD-ROM.

Determining the Scope of Procedures and Functions

When you create a procedure (or function), you might want to limit where it can be used, and how resources are allocated to make its code available to other parts of your program. Where a procedure can be called from is referred to as the *scope* of the procedure.

Procedures can be defined in either of two ways: *public procedures* or *private procedures.* Which of these keywords you use in the Sub statement determines which other procedures or programs have access to your procedure.

> **N O T E**   The scope of procedures and functions is related to the scope of variables, which is
> discussed in the section entitled "Determining Where a Variable Can Be Used" in Chapter 8,
> "Programming Basics." ▓

▶ **See** "Determining Where a Variable Can Be Used," **p. 176**

Going Public   If you want to have your procedure or function available throughout your program, you need to use the Public keyword when you define the procedure. Using the Public keyword allows a procedure defined in one form or module to be called from another form or module. However, you have to be more careful with the names of public procedures because each public procedure must have a unique name.

If you omit the keywords Public and Private from the Sub statement, the procedure is set up by default as a public procedure.

Keeping It Private   Using the Private keyword in the Sub statement lets the procedure be accessed from only the form or module in which it is defined. There are, of course, advantages and disadvantages to this approach. The advantage is that you can have private procedures of the same name in separate modules. The disadvantage is that the procedure is not accessible from other modules.

One thing you might have noticed in working with event procedures in other chapters is that they are, by default, private procedures. This is because, typically, controls are not accessed outside of the form on which they reside. This is an example of *information hiding*, or *encapsulation,* a technique used in object-oriented programming. If you are sharing a module with a team of developers, you could define the functions they call as public, while the internal procedures they don't need to know about remain private.

Preserving Variables   Typically, when a procedure is executed, the variables it uses are created, used in the procedure, and then destroyed when the procedure is terminated. However, there might be times when you want to preserve the value of the variables for future calls to the procedure. You can handle this by using the Static keyword. This keyword can be applied to the declaration of the variables in the procedure or in the declaration of the procedure itself.

When `Static` is used in a variable declaration, only the variables included in the `Static` statement are preserved. If you use the `Static` keyword in the procedure declaration, all the variables in the procedure are preserved. In the following example, `inCurrentCount` is a static variable:

```
Public Function AddItUp(inNew As Integer) As Integer

    Static inCurrentCount As Integer
    inCurrentCount = inCurrentCount + inNew
    AddItUp = inCurrentCount

End Function
```

> **TIP** For efficiency's sake, it's important to place your procedures in the appropriate scope. Giving a procedure too broad of a scope (for example, making a procedure public when it only needs to be private) wastes valuable system resources. If you create a public procedure, Visual Basic must allocate appropriate resources to make it available to all parts of your program. Using the `Static` keyword to force a procedure to "remember" its local variables causes an extra allocation of resources as well. In general, you should make procedures private if possible, and avoid the use of static variables as well. This allows Visual Basic to manage memory more efficiently, since it is free to unload the various sections of code as needed.

Reusing Functions and Procedures

You can create a procedure in either of two places—a form or a module. Where you place the procedure depends upon where you need to use it and what its purpose is. If the procedure is specific to a form or modifies the properties of the form or its associated controls, you should probably place the procedure in the form itself.

If, on the other hand, you are using the procedure with multiple forms in your program or have a generic procedure used by multiple programs, you should place it in a module. The storage location of your procedure is determined by where you create it. If you want, you can move a procedure from a form to a module or vice versa by using cut-and-paste editing.

 Storing a Procedure in a Form File   To create a procedure in a form file, you just need to choose the form from the Project window and then access the code for the form. This is done by either double-clicking the form itself (or any control) or choosing the View Code button in the project window (see Figure 17.4). After the Code window appears, you create a procedure as described in the earlier section "Creating a Procedure."

Using a Module File for Procedures   A module file contains only code, no form elements or events. If you already have a module file in your project, you can create a new procedure by selecting the file, opening the Code window, and then using the previous steps to build the procedure.

> **TIP** Double-clicking the module name in the Project window automatically opens the Code window for the module.

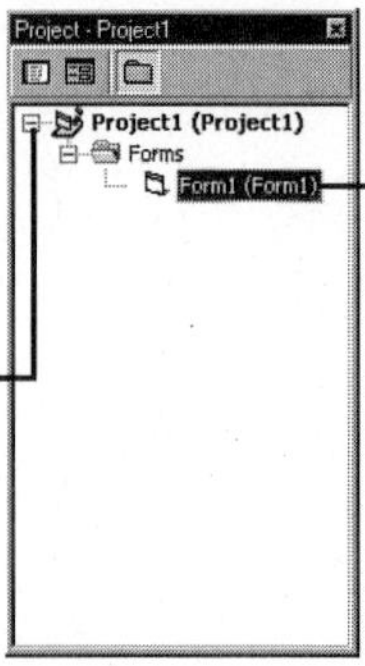

FIG. 17.4
You can select a form
for your procedure from
the Project window.

Selected form

Button used to open
the Code window

If you don't have a module file in your project, or if you want to use a new module, you can create a module by selecting Project, Add Module. You can also create a new module by clicking the arrow on the Add Form button in the toolbar and then choosing Module from the drop-down menu. Either way, a new module is created and the Code window appears for you to begin editing. When you save your project or exit Visual Basic, you are asked for a file name for the module file.

> **N O T E**   The toolbar button for adding new forms and modules is a drop-down button, which means clicking the arrow will give you a list of items. Once an item has been selected, the icon on the button changes. ▪

Working with Multiple Forms

Although some programs you write will be simple enough that you can use a single form, most will be made up of multiple forms. One reason for this is the limitation of the amount of space on a single form. Another more important reason is that you will want to use multiple forms in your program to logically separate program tasks. For example, if you have a task in your program that is not performed often, it makes more sense to put it on a separate form than try to squeeze it on a single form with everything else. Also, loading and unloading forms as you need them saves system resources. In other words, your program takes up as little space as possible while running.

Adding New Forms to Your Program

When Visual Basic first starts a new project, typically it loads one blank form, as shown in Figure 17.5. As you design your program, you add controls to this form and write code to handle events that occur on the form.

At some point in your design, you will decide that you need one or more additional forms to handle a new task or provide space to relieve the crowding on the initial form. Adding a new form is simple. You can either click the Add Form button or select Project, Add Form. This places a new blank form on the screen. This form looks just like your first form initially did.

If you did not rename your first form from the default of Form1, the new form is named Form2 (or Form3, Form4, and so on). Otherwise, the new form is named Form1.

FIG. 17.5
Visual Basic starts a new project with a single blank form.

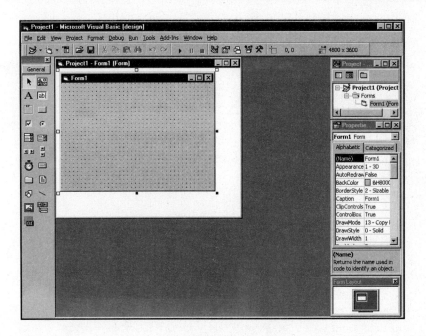

 TIP You can add files, forms, or modules from a pop-up menu by right-clicking within the Project window.

After you have added a new form, you can place controls on it and write code for its events, just like for the initial form. You also need to be able to access the new form from other forms in your program. This is handled through the Load and Unload statements and the Show and Hide methods of the form object.

▶ **See** "Displaying a Form," **p. 86**

Adding Code Modules to a Project

As you write more code to handle more events and more tasks, you will often find that you need to access the same procedure from a number of different places on a form or from multiple forms. If this is the case, it makes sense to store the procedure in a module file.

 TIP If you have a library of common functions, such as printing routines, keep them in a separate module file so you can easily add the library to different projects.

 A module file contains only Visual Basic code. It does not contain any controls, pictures, or other visual information. When the time comes to add a module file to hold your procedures, you can do this either by clicking the arrow on the Add Form button and choosing <u>M</u>odule from the drop-down menu, or by choosing Project, Add Module. Either of these actions adds a new module to your project and places you in the Code window for the module (see Figure 17.6).

FIG. 17.6
You can open the Code window by double-clicking the module name in the Project window.

Module name

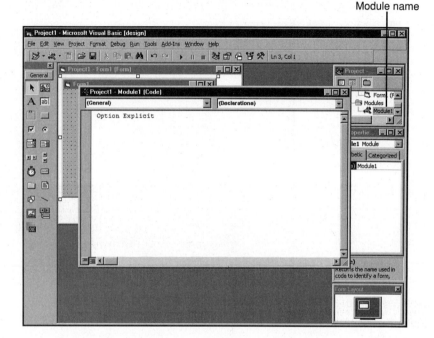

When you first open a new module, Visual Basic gives it the default name of Module1 (or Module2 for a second module, and so on). Like your forms and controls, it is a good idea to give the module a unique name. The module has a Name property, just as a form does. To change the name of the module, simply change the value of the Name property in the Property window.

Accessing the Forms and Modules of a Project

As you add forms and modules to your program, they are added to the Project window. This window allows you to easily access any of the pieces of your program (see Figure 17.7). You simply select a form or module by clicking its name in the Project window. For a form, you can then click the View Object button to work on the design of the form, or click the View Code button to edit the code associated with the form. For a module, only the View Code button is enabled because a module has no visual elements. Double-clicking the name of a form has the same effect as clicking the View Object button. Double-clicking a module name has the same effect as clicking the View Code button.

FIG. 17.7

The Project window gives you easy access to all your forms and modules.

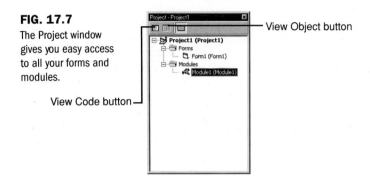

View Object button

View Code button

Managing Components in Your Project

Forms and modules are just two of the types of components that you can add to your project. In addition, you can also add *custom controls* and *class modules*. Some of these components, such as forms and modules, are editable code. Others, such as third-party controls and DLLs, are usually already compiled. While these types of items are part of your project, they do not show up in the Project window and are added by means of some special dialog boxes.

Managing Program References

One of the things that you have to manage is your program's *references*. The references point to different library routines that enable your code to perform specific tasks. For example, if you will be accessing databases with your programs, you need to specify the Data Access Object library as one that is used by your code. Controlling references is quite easy in Visual Basic. The References dialog box lets you select the references required by your program by marking the check box to the side of the reference (see Figure 17.8). Mark the ones you need and unmark the ones you don't need. You access the References dialog box by selecting Project, References.

FIG. 17.8

The References dialog box lets you choose which libraries are used by your program.

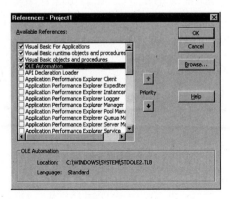

TIP After adding a reference to your project, its public constants and functions can be viewed in the Object Browser, which is displayed by clicking the Object Browser button or by pressing F2.

Controlling Your Controls

In a manner similar to library references, you can add and remove custom controls from your project. When you loaded Visual Basic, a number of custom controls were loaded into the Toolbox window automatically. However, you will usually need controls designed to perform specific tasks that are beyond the capabilities of the standard controls. You manage the custom controls in your project by using the Components dialog box (see Figure 17.9). Select Project, Components to access this dialog box. As with the References dialog box, you choose the custom controls to add to your program by marking the check box next to the control name. After you exit the dialog box, your control toolbox is modified to display the new controls.

FIG. 17.9
The Components dialog box lets you add controls to your project.

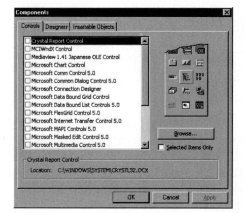

Adding Forms, Modules, and Classes to the Project

As you develop more programs, you might find that you have standard procedures or forms that can be used in many of your projects. You also might have developed custom procedures for getting the names and passwords of users, for opening files, or for any number of other tasks that are used in almost every program.

You could rebuild the form or rewrite the procedure for each program, but that would be a very inefficient way to do your program development. A better way is to reuse modules and forms that have been previously developed and fully tested.

Getting these modules and forms into your current project is a simple process. By selecting Project, Add File, you bring up the Add File dialog box (see Figure 17.10). This dialog box lets you locate and select files to be added to your current project. Unfortunately, the Add File dialog box lets you add only a single file at a time. Therefore, if you have multiple files to add, you must repeat the operation several times.

CAUTION

If you add the same form or module to separate projects, remember that changing functions in the module will affect all projects that use it. If you are about to radically change a shared module, use the Save *modulename* As option in the File menu or copy the module to another subdirectory first.

FIG. 17.10

The Add File dialog box can be accessed from the menu system, standard toolbar, by right-clicking in the Project window, or by pressing Ctrl+D.

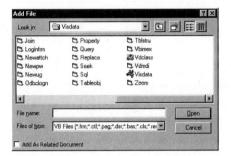

N O T E Files with the .FRM and .FRX extensions are form files. Files with the .BAS extension are module files.

You also might want to use one of Visual Basic's form templates in your project. These templates are predefined forms that are set up for a specific function, such as an About Box, a Splash Screen, a DataGrid form, or a Tip of the Day form. The advantage of using these templates is that the skeleton of the form is already created for you. You simply add your own graphics, label captions, and minimal code to customize the form to your needs. As an example, Figure 17.11 shows the About Box form template.

FIG. 17.11

Form templates make it easy to develop common pieces of a program.

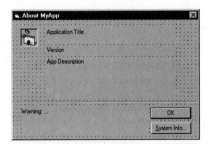

  To access one of the form templates, bring up the Add Form dialog box by clicking the Add Form button on the toolbar or selecting Project, Add Form (see Figure 17.12). You can then choose one of the form types from the New tab of the dialog box.

If you create a form that you think you will use in a number of programs, you can make a template out of it as well. Simply save the form in the form template folder of Visual Basic. Then the next time you want to add a new form, your template will appear in the Add Form dialog box as well.

FIG. 17.12

Form templates are "canned" templates that can be quickly customized and used in your project.

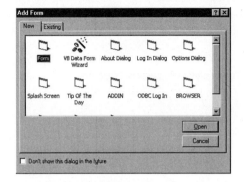

N O T E If you let Visual Basic install to the default directory, the forms templates are stored in the `\Program Files\DevStudio\Vb\Template\Forms` folder. This folder might be different on your machine, depending on where you installed Visual Basic. ▪

Removing Pieces

To remove a module or form from your project, simply select the form or module in the Project window and choose Project, Remove *filename*. Visual Basic asks you to confirm that you want to remove the file and then removes it from your project.

Controlling How Your Program Starts

When you first start a programming project, Visual Basic assumes that the first form created is the one that will be displayed as soon as the program starts. Although this will be the case for many programs, for others you will want to start with one of the forms you create later in the development process. For some programs, you might not want to start with a form at all.

Setting the Startup Form

If the first form is not the one you want to use to start your program, Visual Basic lets you choose which of your forms is shown initially by the program. This selection is made in the *Projectname* – Project Properties dialog box, as shown in Figure 17.13. You access this dialog box by selecting Project, Project Properties.

FIG. 17.13
The Startup Object list lets you choose which form is loaded when your program starts.

Part
IV
Ch
17

Using *Sub Main*

You might have noticed that, in addition to listing all the forms contained in your project, the Startup Object list includes the entry Sub Main. This is a reserved procedure name that lets your program start without an initial form. If you choose this option, one of your module files must include a procedure called Main.

One reason to start your program with the Sub Main option might be that you need to perform some initialization routines before loading any forms. Another reason might be if you are developing a command-line utility that requires no user interaction.

Creating Distributable Programs

When you complete your program, it is time to move it out of the VB development environment so others can use it. The first step is to compile the source code. The objective here is to create an .EXE file (or .DLL, depending upon the project type) that can be distributed to other machines. After compiling, you create installation files for the program by using the Application Setup Wizard. The purpose of the Setup Wizard is to package your program and all necessary support files, so it will run on a machine that does not have Visual Basic installed.

Compiling Your Program

When you are ready to compile your program, all you have to do is select File, Make. This menu item lists the project name and the proper file extension for the type of program you are creating. For a Standard EXE or ActiveX EXE, the file extension is .EXE. For an ActiveX DLL, the file extension is .DLL, and for the ActiveX Control, the file extension is .OCX. After selecting the Make item, you are shown the Make Project dialog box, which allows you to specify the name and location of the executable file. Visual Basic then does the rest of the work.

While Visual Basic handles the actual compilation with no intervention, there are a few decisions you need to make in the Compile tab of the *Projectname* – Project Properties dialog box. The first choice to make is whether to compile to P-code or native code. P-code is the way Visual Basic programs have been compiled since version 1, while compiling to native code is a new option to Visual Basic 5.0. Native code is optimized for the processor chip and runs faster than P-code, but produces a significantly larger executable file. If you choose to compile to native code, you also need to make a decision about compiler optimization. You can choose to have the compiler try to create the smallest possible code, the fastest possible code, or not perform any optimization. You also have the option of compiling your program specifically for the Pentium Pro processor.

To choose the compiler options, you need to click the Compile tab of the Project Properties dialog box (see Figure 17.14). To squeeze every last bit of speed out of VB, you might want to also look at the Advanced Optimizations dialog box, also shown in Figure 17.14. As you can see, Microsoft put these options in here with a "use at your own risk" warning. However, I usually check Remove Array Bounds Checks, because the program code itself should do this, and Remove Safe Pentium FDIV Checks, which turns off software correction for the infamous Pentium chip bug. If you want to play it safe, the Advanced Options dialog box should probably be the last thing you do.

FIG. 17.14

In Visual Basic 5, there are several options for optimizing the compiled program.

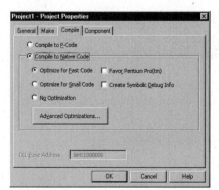
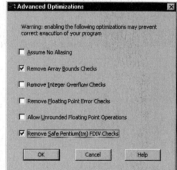

Using the Setup Wizard

Even though you might have just compiled your code into an executable file, that executable file cannot run on its own. Users of your program must have some Visual Basic runtime files (that is, DLLs) properly installed first. I would be lying if I said that each new release of Visual Basic has made it simpler to distribute your application to other PCs; on the contrary, just the opposite has occurred. In the days of Visual Basic 3.0, sometimes copying the 400K file VBRUN300.DLL and your EXE were the only steps required. Today, the equivalent Visual Basic 5.0 DLL file is over 1 megabyte in size. Additionally, the mere presence of a required DLL file is usually not enough; more often than not it must also be *registered* in the Windows Registry. On the bright side, the Application Setup Wizard included with Visual Basic 5.0 is much better than previous versions. The Application Setup Wizard is used to "package" your program with the required support files, so that it can be installed from a disk, directory, or the Internet—just like any off-the-shelf program. In this section, we focus on the setup steps for a Standard EXE project.

Using the Setup Wizard with a Standard EXE Project   A shortcut to the Application Setup Wizard should have been installed with VB. If you run the Setup Wizard, after you get past the introductory message you see a screen like the one in Figure 17.15.

FIG. 17.15

The first step in the Application Setup Wizard is to choose a project and select the type of installation.

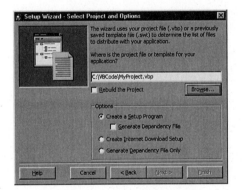

The purpose of this screen is to tell the Setup Wizard which project you want to work with, as well as what kind of installation to create. As you might guess, the Internet Download option is for distribution over the Internet. For a Standard EXE project, you should choose the default Create a Setup Program option. If you check Rebuild the Project, the Setup Wizard attempts to launch VB and compiles your EXE before adding it to the installation. I usually do not do this, because it adds an extra step. Note that you can choose Generate a Dependency File either as part of the standard setup or by itself. A dependency file holds information about all the files required by your program, for the purpose of combining the installation of your project with another one. After you press Next, you are presented with the Distribution Method screen, shown in Figure 17.16.

The screen in Figure 17.16 lets you select how to group the installation files. Unless you are distributing your application on floppy disks (which is becoming less and less common these days), you will probably want to choose one of the directory options. Single Directory means all the setup files will be placed in a single subdirectory on your hard drive. Disk Directories divides the files into floppy-size subdirectories, should you ever need to manually copy them to

Part
IV
Ch
17

disk. If you know your application will always be installed from a network server or CD-ROM, Single Directory is the best choice. Depending on your choice, the next screen (not pictured here) asks you to select an installation directory or floppy disk size.

FIG. 17.16

The Application Setup Wizard can create install files on disks, a single subdirectory, or multiple subdirectories.

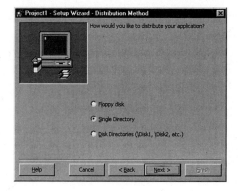

Now that you have told the Application Setup Wizard where to create the install files, it presents a series of screens as it determines what files are necessary. The first screen, ActiveX Server Components, is shown in Figure 17.17. (ActiveX server components are ActiveX DLLs or EXEs that your main project uses.) Although the setup wizard automatically scans your project's references for these items, you still have the option of adding and removing them here.

FIG. 17.17

The check box indicates an item (and its dependent files, if known) will be included in the installation package.

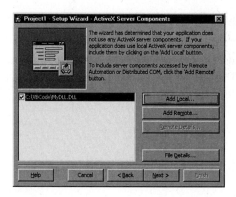

When you move on from the screen in Figure 17.17, the Setup Wizard scans your project and displays the File Summary, as shown in Figure 17.18. The File Summary lists all the files that the Setup Wizard thinks your application needs. If you have additional files to distribute, such as .INI or .BMP files used by your program, you can add them with the Add... button. You can also find out more information about individual files (such as the destination directory) by pressing the File Details button.

Suppose you want to add another EXE, DLL, or OCX file to your project. One reason might be because you have separated your application into multiple projects; for example, you might have created an "Administration module" for managing login IDs. If you have not already run the Setup Wizard for the other project, you might see the warning shown in Figure 17.19. Do not panic, however, as this simply means that the dependency information for the new file is not available.

FIG. 17.18

The File Summary screen allows you to add or remove files from the installation.

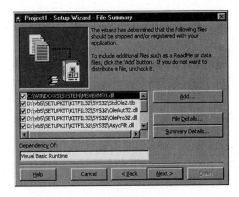

FIG. 17.19

This warning message indicates that the Setup Wizard could not find a dependency (.DEP) file for the selected item.

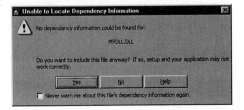

The reason for this message is to make sure your installation works. For example, if you decide to include additional EXEs, you also need the DLLs and OCXs required by those EXEs. You can either generate the dependency information with the Setup Wizard or skip this step if you know that no special files are required. After the File Summary screen, you are given the option to save your setup template so that you can create an install for this project without answering all these questions again.

Finally, now that the Setup Wizard has all the information it needs, your installation files will be copied to the location specified earlier. After this is complete, you should be able to test your install by running SETUP.EXE.

N O T E The setup wizard compresses installation files to save space. Compressed files are indicated by an underscore (_) in the last character of the file name, as in MYPROGRAM.EX_. If you need to compress files manually, the utility COMPRESS.EXE is included with Visual Basic. ■

When creating a setup for a bunch of different users, test your installation thoroughly to make sure all the necessary components are included. Testing on your own PC is not sufficient, because you already have the required DLLs and OCXs.

TIP A method of ensuring that your installation includes all the right parts is to try it on a test machine that contains nothing but the operating system. This can be a tricky situation, because each test of the install changes the test machine. I suggest getting software that allows you to restore a PC from an image file, so that you can test with a variety of software configurations.

A Closer Look at the Setup Process You've just seen what goes into creating a set of setup files. It is probably a safe bet to assume that most computer users are already familiar with the concept of installing, or setting up, an application. Who hasn't spent 30 minutes feeding their PCs floppy disks to install some new software? From the user's viewpoint, the setup program performs a very simple function. However, for troubleshooting purposes, the developer needs to realize that there is a lot more going on than just copying files to the destination PC. One of the files created by the setup wizard, SETUP.LST, is the controlling "script" for the entire setup process. You can view SETUP.LST in a text editor, as shown in Figure 17.20.

FIG. 17.20

A typical SETUP.LST created by the Setup Wizard.

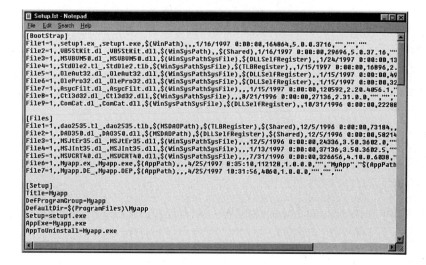

Don't let the cryptic lines of text intimidate you; the structure of the file is actually fairly straightforward. It contains all the information necessary to control the entire installation. Let's take a brief step-by-step look at how SETUP.LST is used:

1. When SETUP.EXE is executed, the files in the [BootStrap] section of SETUP.LST are copied, uncompressed, and registered on the destination machine. Because the Visual Basic runtime files might not be present, SETUP.EXE must be written in a language capable of running without them (such as C).

   The files in the [BootStrap] section are necessary to run a Visual Basic 5.0 program, specifically SETUP1.EXE, which does most of the work in setting up your application. This is the main purpose for SETUP.EXE, basically a "wrapper" for SETUP1.EXE.

2. SETUP1.EXE displays a welcome screen and asks the user to choose a destination directory for the application, as seen in Figure 17.21.

FIG. 17.21

Installations created by the Setup Wizard default to the Program Files directory.

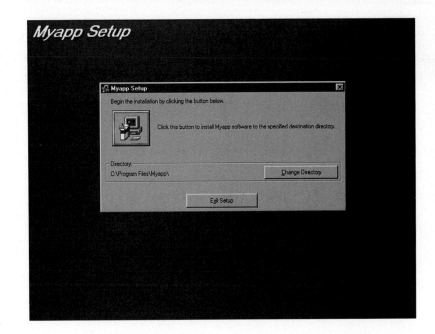

Part
IV

Ch
17

3. If you choose to continue, the program creates the application directory and begins copying files. The files to be copied are listed in the [Files] section of SETUP.LST. You might notice that for each file in the [Files] section there is a long list of parameters. Parameters 3, 4, and 5 represent the compressed file name, destination file name, and destination directory, respectively.

4. When SETUP1.EXE finishes copying files, it attempts to register some of them. Typically, a message like Updating your system is displayed during this process. Whether a file needs to be registered or not is determined by the 6th parameter, typically $(DLLSelfRegister) or $(EXESelfRegister).

N O T E If you need to manually register a file, use the REGSVR32 utility included with Visual Basic. ActiveX EXEs can be registered with Windows by running them with the command line parameter /REGSERVER. ▪

5. Finally, SETUP1.EXE creates the shortcut icons for your program. The last two file parameters determine the icon's description and command line. The default program group name is listed in the [Setup] section.

Customizing Setup   Now that you are familiar with what the installation process actually does, you can modify it to meet your needs. Although tampering with an "official" SETUP.LST files is probably not a supported activity, I have had success with the customizations listed in Table 17.1.

Table 17.1   Editing the SETUP.LST File

Customization	How To
Adding Files	Copy an existing `Filexx=` line and increment the number. Make sure to supply the copy and registration parameters mentioned in the last section, as well as the file date, size, and version number, all of which can be obtained from the Windows Explorer.
Default directory	The suggested install directory is usually a subdirectory of the \Program Files directory on the user's PC. To specify a different default directory, change the `DefaultDir` line in the `[Setup]` section—for example, `DefaultDir=C:\MYAPPDIR`.
Forcing a directory	If you want to take away a user's option to choose the destination directory, set the `DefaultDir` option as previously described above. Then add the line `ForceUseDefDir=1` to the `[Setup]` section.
Background description	By default, the message displayed on the screen will be the project name. You can modify the `Title=` line in the `[Setup]` section to make it a bit more descriptive, as in `Title="On-Line Reporting System"`.
The setup program itself	If you want to run a setup program other than SETUP1.EXE, you can still use Microsoft's SETUP.EXE to install the VB5 runtime DLLs. To do this, change the Setup line in the `[Setup]` section to point to your program—for example, `Setup=MySetup.exe`. You can also remove the `[Files]` section entirely if your setup program doesn't need it.
Annoying messages	Although it is not the intended purpose, setting the 7th file parameter to `$(Shared)` removes two warning messages regarding replacing an existing file. The messages are contradictory, like `Cancel Setup?` followed by `Continue Setup?`, and probably would confuse some users. By marking the file as a Shared component, you are telling the setup program that the user does not need to be prompted before overwriting it.

N O T E   Microsoft includes the source code for SETUP1.EXE with Visual Basic. If you want to make changes to it, open the project SETUP1.VBP in the \kitfiles\setup1 directory. ■

Even though you can customize SETUP.LST to a great extent, a standard Setup Wizard install still might not be suitable for your needs. For example, you might want to create your own "wrapper" program around SETUP.EXE. This program could be very useful in a corporate environment. For example, you could temporarily map a network drive to the install server, run SETUP.EXE, and then disconnect the drive after installation. If you e-mailed this program to the users, they would not have to worry about connecting to the right network drive. Another possibility would be storing each user's date of installation in a database. As with SETUP.EXE, you might have to write this program so it would run without the VB5 runtime files. Fortunately, Microsoft includes VBRUN300.DLL with Windows 95, so you don't have to resort to C.

> **CAUTION**
> When using the Setup Wizard, the version number of your program is very important. If you do not increment the version number in the Project Properties dialog box, SETUP assumes a previous user already has the correct version; therefore, it does not need to copy over it. After an install is complete, view the ST5UNST.LOG file to see which files the Setup Wizard actually copied.

From Here...

This chapter has given you a look at how you manage the various parts of your programs. You've seen several techniques for making your programming more efficient. You've also been exposed to many of the assorted components that comprise a complete program. For more information on creating and using the various parts, see the following chapters:

- To learn more about how forms work with controls to enhance your Visual Basic programs, see Chapter 4, "Working with Forms and Controls."
- To learn more about specific controls, see Chapter 10, "Using the Windows Common Controls," and Chapter 11, "Exploring New VB5 Controls."

Part
IV
Ch
17

Building a Class in Visual Basic

Classes in Visual Basic are developed by using the Class Module. This module contains only variable declarations and procedure code. There is no user-interface component of a class module. However, a class can take action using a form that is in the program. In the case of an ActiveX DLL or EXE, the forms can be included with the project.

N O T E You can add properties to forms and code modules using the same principals as those for adding classes. ■

A class module is a fairly simple program object. A class module has only three built-in properties and two native events. It has no methods of its own. After a class module is created, you can add properties, methods, and events to the class by declaring variables and by programming procedures and functions in the class module.

Creating a New Class Module

You start the process of creating a new class module by selecting Add Class Module from Visual Basic's Project menu. This starts a new class module with the default name of Class1 and opens the Code window for the class, as shown in Figure 18.1.

FIG. 18.1

When creating a new class module, you use the Code window the same way you did when creating a standard module.

After the new class is created for your project, you need to set the values of some key properties that define the class. These properties are Instancing and Name.

Choosing a Name   You want to give each of your classes a unique name that is descriptive of the function it will perform. In addition, many developers like to preface the class name with the letter *c* to indicate in the programs that this is the name of a class. Using this convention, a class that provided improved printer functionality might be named cPrinter.

Creating a Public Class   When you add a class module to a Standard EXE project, your class module can be used from other modules or forms in the current project only. It cannot be seen from another program. In other words, it is a private class.

To create a public class that can be made available to other programs, you need to use either an ActiveX EXE or an ActiveX DLL project. After it is created, you then register your DLL (or EXE) with Windows. Your ActiveX project then shows up in the References dialog box of Visual Basic. To use the class, you simply add a reference to it in another project.

The way instances of your class are created depends on whether you created a DLL or EXE, as well as the setting of the Instancing property, described in the next section. An ActiveX EXE can be executed like a standard program, but in general is less efficient than a DLL.

N O T E   In Visual Basic version 5.0, ActiveX EXEs and DLLs replace the concept of OLE Automation servers. These new types of projects can still be thought of as servers, because they "serve" up objects to client programs. ■

Setting the *Instancing* Property   The final property of the class module is the Instancing property. The Instancing property defines the way instances of your class are created. The valid property values vary depending on what type of VB project you are working with. The Instancing property should only concern you if you plan on creating a public class module. If you are working in a Standard EXE project, the Instancing property is not even available. While learning the basics of classes and OOP, you can just forget about this property and use a Standard EXE project. However, this property is usually set during the creation of a class, so I mention the property values here. Table 18.1 describes the possible settings for the Instancing property.

Table 18.1   Controlling Access to Your Class with *Instancing* Property

Value	Name	Description
1	Private	The class cannot be accessed outside the current project.
2	Public Not Creatable	Instances of the class can be created only within the project that defines the class. However, other applications can control the class after it is created.
3	SingleUse	Other applications can create instances of the class. However, each time another instance of the class is created, a new copy of the program containing the class is started. (This setting is not available for an ActiveX DLL project.)
4	Global SingleUse	Like SingleUse, but makes the class act like a global variable in the client program.

continues

```
        Printer.Print InText
        Printer.Font.Bold = curBold
End Sub
```

Adding Events to Your Class

In Chapter 4, "Working with Forms and Controls," you learned what events were and how to handle them in your code. An event is triggered when the user takes an action, such as a keystroke, or when a change has taken place, such as having a specific amount of time elapsing. Your classes can also initiate events as they are running. This is a new feature of Visual Basic 5 that enhances the capability of your classes.

▶ **See** "A First Look at Methods and Events," **p. 78**

To create an event in your class, you need to do two things:

1. Declare the event in the class.
2. Use the RaiseEvent statement to trigger the event.

To declare an event, you simply supply the name of the event and the variable passed by the event in a statement like the following:

```
Public Event QueryStatus(ByVal Completion As Single, _
ByRef Cancel As Boolean)
```

This statement is placed in the declarations section of the class in which you want the event. The Public keyword is necessary to allow programs using the objects created from the class to respond to the event. The variables allow the event to pass information to the program using the class and to receive information back from the program. The event declared in the preceding code could be used to keep the user informed of the status of a long query and to allow the user to cancel the query prior to completion.

After the event is declared, you can use the RaiseEvent statement to trigger the event anywhere in the code of your class. For the QueryStatus event, you might want to trigger the event after every 100 records that have been processed as shown in Listing 18.1.

Listing 18.1 TRIGGER.FRM—Triggering an Event in Your Class

```
Public Sub ProcessData()
Dim MaxRecords As Long, RecordsProcessed As Long
Dim blnCancel As Boolean
If ClsRset.RecordCount = 0 Then Exit Sub
ClsRset.MoveLast
MaxRecords = ClsRset.RecordCount
RecordsProcessed = 0
blnCancel = False
ClsRset.MoveFirst
Do While Not ClsRset.EOF
    If RecordsProcessed Mod 100 = 0 Then
        RaiseEvent QueryStatus(RecordsProcessed / MaxRecords, blnCancel)
```

```
        If blnCancel Then Exit Sub
    End If
    ClsRset.MoveNext
    RecordsProcessed = RecordsProcessed + 1
Loop
End Sub
```

To write code for an object event in your program, see the section titled "Handling an Object's Events" later in this chapter.

Creating Public Constants as Enumerations

You can't declare public constants in a public class module, so how do you make constants available to other applications through a class? You use an *enumeration,* or, in Visual Basic, Enum.

Public enumerations in a public class are available to other applications and viewable through the Object Browser. In the following code, which shows the definition for an enumeration, you need only assign the actual value of the first member (in this case, One). The remaining members are automatically assigned their values sequentially.

```
Public Enum Numbers
    One = 1
    Two = 2
    Three = 3
    Four = 4
    Five = 5
End Enum
```

After including this declaration in your program, you can refer to the constants One, Two, Three, Four, and Five, which will return the values 1, 2, 3, 4, and 5, respectively. Figure 18.4 shows how Enum looks in the Object Browser from another application.

Part
IV

Ch
18

FIG. 18.4

The Enum name appears in the Classes list, and the items appear in the Members list of the Object Browser.

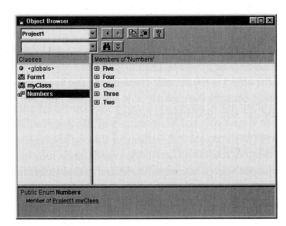

A

Listing 18.6   Continued

```
Public Property Set OutputDev(inDev As Object)
    Set OutputTo = inDev
    objhit = OutputTo.Height - m_tmarg - m_bmarg
    objwid = OutputTo.Width - m_lmarg - m_rmarg
End Property
```

Notice that to set the output-device property, a `Property Set` procedure must be used. This is because the output device is an object.

Supplying an Output Method   Next, because the object needs to be able to perform some function, a method must be created for the class. You can do this by creating a `Public` procedure in the class module. The method for the `cPrint` class performs the word-wrapping of the input text. This method is defined by the code in Listing 18.7.

Listing 18.7   PRNTWRP.FRM—A *Public* Procedure Defines the *Output* Method of the *cPrint* Class

```
Public Sub Output(prntvar As String)
txtht = OutputTo.TextHeight("AbgWq")
    Do
        endpos = 0
        txtlen = 0
        prntln = ""
        Do
            strtpos = endpos + 1
            endpos = InStr(strtpos, prntvar, " ")
            prntln = Left$(prntvar, endpos)
            txtlen = OutputTo.TextWidth(prntln)
        Loop Until txtlen > objwid Or endpos = 0
        If endpos = 0 Then
            prntln = prntvar
            endps2 = InStr(1, prntln, vbCrLf)
            If endps2 > 0 Then
                prntln = Left$(prntvar, endps2 - 1)
                prntvar = LTrim$(Mid$(prntvar, endps2 + 2))
            Else
                prntvar = ""
            End If
        Else
            prntln = Left$(prntvar, strtpos - 1)
            endps2 = InStr(1, prntln, vbCrLf)
            If endps2 > 0 Then
                prntln = Left$(prntvar, endps2 - 1)
                prntvar = LTrim$(Mid$(prntvar, endps2 + 2))
            Else
                prntvar = LTrim$(Mid$(prntvar, strtpos))
            End If
        End If
```

```
        OutputTo.CurrentX = m_lmarg
        OutputTo.Print prntln
    Loop While Len(prntvar) > 0
End Sub
```

Initializing the Class Finally, because the user might call the method without first setting the properties of the class, it's a good idea to set initial values for the internal variables. This is done in the `Initialize` event of the class, as shown in Listing 18.8.

Listing 18.8   Setting the Initial Value of Variables

```
Private Sub Class_Initialize()
    m_lmarg = 0
    m_rmarg = 0
    m_tmarg = 0
    m_bmarg = 0
    Set OutputTo = Printer
End Sub
```

Using the Class As I said earlier, to use a class in a program, you must create an instance of the object defined by the class and then set the properties of the object and use its methods. For the `cPrint` class example, this is all done in the form that supplies the user interface for the example code.

Part IV

Ch

18

First, the object is defined in the Declarations section of the form using a declaration statement, as shown here:

```
Dim EhnPrint As New cPrint
```

If the user chooses to set page margins for the output, values can be entered in the text boxes for the appropriate margins. The text-box values are then assigned to the properties of the object, using the code in the `Click` event of the Set Margins command button. This code is shown in Listing 18.9.

Listing 18.9   Setting the Margins of the Output Device

```
Private Sub cmdSetMargin_Click()
    EhnPrint.LMargin = Val(txtMargin(0).Text)
    EhnPrint.RMargin = Val(txtMargin(1).Text)
    EhnPrint.TMargin = Val(txtMargin(2).Text)
    EhnPrint.BMargin = Val(txtMargin(3).Text)
End Sub
```

As you can see, the properties are set using simple assignment statements. The `Val` function is used in the event that the user accidentally enters a text string instead of a number in the text box.

Finally, after the user has entered some text to be printed, the `Output` method of the object can be used to print the text. The following code shows how this is done to print the text to the picture box:

```
Private Sub cmdPicture_Click()
   Set EhnPrint.OutputDev = picPrint
   PrntStr = txtInput.Text
   EhnPrint.Output (PrntStr)
End Sub
```

The code first uses the `Set` statement to tell the `EhnPrint` object to direct the output to the `picPrint` picture box. Next, the text to be printed is retrieved from the text box. Finally, the text string is passed to the object's `Output` method. The results of this operation are shown in Figure 18.9.

FIG. 18.9

The cPrint class can be used to output text to different output devices.

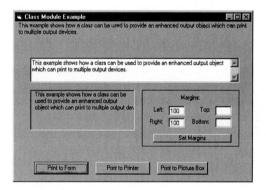

Database Access

Another use of classes is in database access. The sample class shown in this section is used to simply open a database and return the database object to the calling program. You're probably wondering why you wouldn't just use the database objects directly to perform this operation. The answer is that using a class lets you encapsulate the `OpenDatabase` method and all the associated error-handling code that is required for it.

By using a class, you don't have to repeat this code multiple places in your program or in multiple programs. You simply create it once in a class module and then create an instance of the class any time that you need to open the database in your program. You can also easily create an ActiveX DLL from the class module, which keeps you from having to add the class module to other programs. The final advantage is that if you find additional things that you need your open database routine to handle, you have to change the code in only one place—the class module. Then all your programs have the benefit of the changes. The example case is contained in the file CLSDBEX.VBP.

The *cDataAccess* Class   The `cDataAccess` class is fairly simple. The class consists of one method and one read-only property. To use the class, the name of a database is passed to the

OpenDb method, and then the database object is retrieved using the OpenData property. The code for the class is shown in Listing 18.10.

Listing 18.10   DATAACC.FRM—The *cDataAccess* Class Property and Method

```
Private m_ClsDb As Database

Public Property Get OpenData() As Database
Set OpenData = m_ClsDb
End Property
Public Sub OpenDb(dbName As String)
On Error GoTo DBErrHandle
Set m_ClsDb = DBEngine.Workspaces(0).OpenDatabase(dbName, _
False, False)
On Error GoTo 0
Exit Sub

DBErrHandle:

errnum = Err
Select Case errnum
    Case 3049
        'Corrupt database, attempt to repair
        msgstr = "Your database has been damaged.  Do you wish the "
        msgstr = msgstr & "program to attempt to repair it?"
        msgrtn = MsgBox(msgstr, vbYesNo + vbExclamation, "Database Problem")
        If msgrtn = vbNo Then Exit Sub
        RepairDatabase (dbName)
        Resume
    Case 3056
        'Couldn't repair database
        msgstr = "Your database could not be repaired.  You will "
        msgstr = msgstr & "need to restore the database from your "
        msgstr = msgstr & " latest backup!"
        MsgBox msgstr, vbExclamation, "Database Problem"
        Exit Sub
    Case Else
        'Show any other messages
        msgstr = "The following error occurred while trying to open "
        msgstr = msgstr & "the database: "
        msgstr = msgstr & Error$(errnum)
        MsgBox msgstr, vbExclamation, "Database Problem"
        Exit Sub
End Select
End Sub
```

Part
IV

Ch
18

Notice that in the Property Get procedure, the property is defined as a Database object. This is to match the object that will receive the value of the property.

Using *cDataAccess*   The case used as a sample calls the object to open the BIBLIO.MDB database that comes with Visual Basic. The code then opens the Authors table of the database and displays a list of authors in a list box. The code for the example is shown in Listing 18.11.

Listing 18.11   ACCOBJ.FRM—Accessing the *cDataAccess* Object

```
Dim db As Database
Dim rs As Recordset
Dim objData As Object

Private Sub cmdAuthors_Click()
    Set objData = New cDataAccess
objData.OpenDb "C:\VB5\BIBLIO.MDB"
    Set db = objData.OpenData
    Set objData = Nothing
    Set rs = db.OpenRecordset("Authors", dbOpenDynaset)
    Do Until OldRc.EOF
       lstAuthors.AddItem rs("Author")
       rs.MoveNext
     Loop
     Db.Close
End Sub
```

Figure 18.10 shows the results of the sample program.

FIG. 18.10

The cDataAccess object is used to handle the opening of the database.

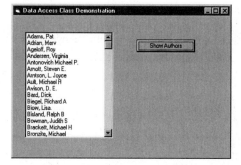

Documenting Objects, Properties, and Methods

One great advantage of using classes is that you can easily distribute them to other programmers. However, unless there is some type of documentation included, understanding how to use your objects could be a major challenge. For example, the programmer needs to know the purpose of each parameter in a function. Fortunately, you can document your objects, properties, and methods at two levels:

■ In the Description line of the Object Browser

■ In a help file that accompanies your application

To document the object's properties and methods in a project, follow these steps:

1. From the Project menu, choose Project Properties. Visual Basic displays the Project Properties dialog box.

2. Enter the name of the project's help file in the <u>H</u>elp File Name text box. The user interface items in your project share the same help file with the project's more technical aspects, such as programming with objects, properties, and methods.

3. From the <u>T</u>ools menu, choose Procedure <u>A</u>ttributes. Visual Basic displays the Procedure Attributes dialog box.

4. Select the method or property that you want to document. Type the description that you want to appear in the Object Browser in the <u>D</u>escription text box. Type the help context ID for the method or property in the Help <u>C</u>ontext ID text box.

5. Repeat Step 4 for each item that you want to document.

Help for a project's objects, properties, and methods resides in the same help file as for the rest of the project. When designing your help file, be careful not to confuse users by including highly technical programming topics in the same table of contents used by people seeking help on your application's user interface.

TROUBLESHOOTING

If you have the Professional Edition of Visual Basic but get an error message when you try to create a `Public` class module, your installation might be corrupt. Try reinstalling the Visual Basic development environment.

If your ActiveX object doesn't recognize methods and properties that you've just defined, check to make sure that you are running the correct version of the object. When debugging, it is easy to accidentally load the compiled DLL or EXE rather than the new version that hasn't yet been compiled. To avoid this, be sure to start the ActiveX application in the other instance of Visual Basic *before* calling it from the client application. Also, make sure the client application's reference points to the correct class in the References dialog box.

If you encounter a `Duplicate Definition` error when trying to add an object to a collection, make sure that the key argument is unique within the collection.

Part
IV

Ch

18

From Here...

This chapter provided you with an introduction to the creation of class modules, which allow you to implement the principles of object-oriented programming. Class modules, when compiled into a separate ActiveX DLL or EXE, provide a powerful tool for encapsulating program functions. In this chapter, we created a sample class and used objects from it in a program. To learn more about some of the topics covered in this chapter, see the following chapters:

- To learn more about writing functions and procedures for use in a class module or other modules, see Chapter 17, "Managing Your Projects."

- You can learn how the techniques applied to classes can be used in creating your own ActiveX controls by referring to Chapters 24, "Creating ActiveX Controls," 25, "Extending ActiveX Controls," and 26, "Creating a User-Drawn Control."

CHAPTER 19

Designing User Interfaces

Visual Basic was created to allow programmers to write real applications, real fast. Prior to the release of Visual Basic 1, writing a Windows application was hard work, requiring a lot of very low-level programming knowledge just to get a simple window to appear. Visual Basic removed this level of "under-the-hood" complexity by automating a good deal of the difficult nuts-and-bolts programming that was required to be able to write even the simplest of Windows applications. Procedures such as creating and placing windows, selecting fonts by which to output text to a control, or defining an event such as a button click—though very difficult things to do in a low-level language such as C—are relatively simple in Visual Basic. However, although VB frees the programmer from the more mundane chores of Windows programming, it does not relieve the programmer from the responsibility to follow good software design and programming practices. ■

A good computer program should be designed to work the way a user does

You will learn what a user-centered design process is and how to implement it.

Graphical user interfaces should be intuitive for the user

Learn how to create consistent and effective interfaces. Also discover how to incorporate standard Graphical User Interface (GUI) design without stifling your creativity.

Perception is reality

You will see how to improve the user's perception of your programs.

While there are easy design traps to fall into, they can be avoided

Learn how to avoid some common programming pitfalls.

Implementing a User-Centered Software Development Process

An analogy can be drawn here: A programmer is to Visual Basic as a cabinetmaker is to power tools. While a power tool can make the labor of cabinetmaking easier, mere use of the tool does not guarantee that the cabinetmaker will make a good cabinet. The use of the tool is only as good as the cabinetmaker's ability to make and follow a schematic, select the appropriate materials, and execute the fundamental skills of cabinetmaking.

The same can be said of writing programs in Visual Basic. Although Visual Basic is a very powerful and easy-to-learn tool, programs created with Visual Basic are only as good as the design and implementation skills of the programmer. Visual Basic makes programming easier, but it does not necessarily make programmers better. Being an effective software developer means having a clear idea of *what* program you want to write, *who* you want to write it for, and *how* you want to do it. Many times, paying attention to the needs, expectations, and habits of the user of your software is a trivial afterthought in the software development process. This tendency is self-defeating because, in most cases, intrinsic ease of use determines the long-term success of your code.

The process of software development can be broken up into three phases (see Table 19.1).

Table 19.1   The Three Phases of Software Development

Phase	Activities
Pre-production	Identify your users Analyze their needs and skills Determine the features they require Prioritize features Create a program specification Create a schematic of the program
Production	Divide the work among developers Write code and build objects Debug and test your code Perform usability tests Correct bugs and address usability issues
Post-production	Prepare online help and end user manuals Document program for future maintenance Prepare program for deployment Evaluate program and process for future versions

Understanding the activities and dynamics of each of these phases is important to the overall efficiency of your development effort and the quality of your end product.

The Pre-Production Phase

The pre-production phase of developing a Windows application is where your product is defined and specified. In pre-production, you draw up the blueprint upon which your product will be built. In this phase, you decide what is the purpose of the product, what are its features, and—of those determined features—which version of your product will implement a given feature set.

In pre-production, you create a *user profile*. The purpose here is to gather as much information as possible about the users of your program. For instance, you determine whether your intended users are comfortable with Windows, thus requiring little elementary support. If your users have never used a computer before, your program will require a good deal of on-screen instruction.

Localization issues are also identified during this phase. Will your product be released only in the U.S. version of English? Will it eventually require other languages? Additionally, consider where and when the customer will run your program. Will it be a point-of-sale system that handles thousands of daily transactions, or will it be used only once a month?

For example, suppose you are writing an Internet application with a Login page. If you are expecting a large number of hits (or hackers), loading your entire program into memory for every login attempt is probably not a good idea. One solution would be to design a fast and small Login object, so you don't bog down the server. It is best to address issues like these at the beginning of the development process where change is cheap, rather than at the end of the process where change is very, very expensive.

 TIP It is always most cost effective to correct a mistake or make a change to a program feature in the pre-production phase. Making a change at a later point in the development process is costly in terms of time and money. This is because the program must be re-specified, re-coded, re-tested, and re-documented.

The Production Phase

The production phase of the development process is where you take the product specification prepared in pre-production and turn it into code. In addition, you create media and other resources that your code might require. In this phase, you determine the optimal language in which to code. (Since this is a book on Visual Basic, for all intents and purposes the optimal language *is* Visual Basic. However, keep in mind that this might not always be the case. Even VB has its limitations and misapplications.)

If you are working within a group of programmers, production is where you divide up the work and do *build* (or version) *control*. A *build* is the process of taking all the pieces of code that each developer is working on and compiling the software. Depending on the testing requirements of your project, you might want to have a daily build scheduled. Because there can be several builds during the development process, there must be a system in place so that each programmer can submit the latest version of his or her code. There is a variety of version control software available to do this, including Microsoft Visual SourceSafe, which is included with the Enterprise Edition of Visual Basic 5.0.

System testing is the process of testing code for bugs, usability, and compliance to specifications. The testing process is also done within the Production phase. There are two major schools of thought concerning testing methods, and both are worth mentioning here.

One method of testing is called *waterfall testing* (see Figure 19.1). In the waterfall method, the testing process is considered to be separate from the programming part of the software development process. Waterfall testing requires that, prior to testing, all the code is written to specifications. Then that code is sent to the tester for testing. After the testing is completed, the results are sent back to the developers to make the necessary code corrections and modifications.

FIG. 19.1
Waterfall testing requires that most testing take place at the end of the production phase.

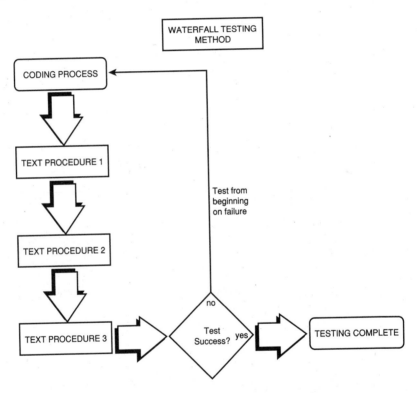

Another testing method is called *iterative testing* (see Figure 19.2). In this method, testing is considered to be part of the programming process. As the programmer completes a discrete set of procedures, he is continually sending his completed work to the tester for inspection and response. While the iterative method might seem like nothing more then a lot of little waterfall tests, it is not. In the iterative testing method, the tester is included in and consulted about the development process from as early as the pre-production phase. In the waterfall method, the tester is brought in well toward the end of the production phase.

Both methods work, and both have their virtues and shortcomings. The waterfall method enables programmers to quickly move from task to task, concentrating on code. However, bugs that the developer overlooks can create their own waterfall of problems when testing finally occurs, especially if the bug happens to be at an early point of the program. And although an iterative approach can provide quicker feedback, requiring the developer to spend a lot of time testing can slow the entire process. One important thing to remember is that any given testing method does not excuse the programmer from testing his own procedures and functions.

FIG. 19.2

Iterative testing requires that testing take place throughout the production phase.

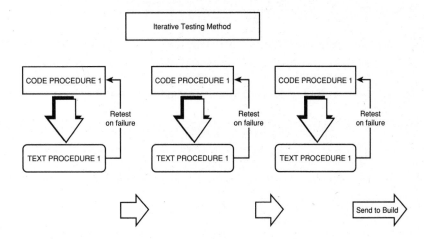

The Post-Production Phase

The post-production phase of software development is where built software is documented, prepared for deployment, and evaluated for future version releases. This process involves all the steps necessary before releasing the software to the public. In the post-production phase, you create both user and programmer documentation, as well as installation media. Beta testing and user feedback can occur during and after this process.

Documentation   After your code is acceptably bug-free and compliant to specifications, you must write the documentation for it. The scope of the documentation includes not only the online help and manuals for the end user, but also the blood-and-guts manuals for the people who will be maintaining your code in following versions. The section "Avoiding Programming Pitfalls" later in this chapter discusses some techniques that you can use to make your code easier to document.

Part IV
Ch 19

> **CAUTION**
>
> Unfortunately, documentation is one area that people often skimp on. This is never a good idea. Just remember, it might be you who has to maintain the code—and your memory might not be as reliable as you think!

Deployment   As your program is being documented, you can also prepare it for deployment. *Deployment* is the act of distributing your program to others. Whether you use a modest floppy disk in an envelope or a more extravagant shrink-wrapped CD-ROM release, you want to put as much effort into your deployment as you did with programming.

> **N O T E**   Visual Basic programs can be deployed several ways, including CD-ROM, floppy disks, or a network. Distribution via the Internet is now a reality as well. See Chapter 17, "Managing Your Projects" for a detailed discussion on creating Setup programs. ▪

▶ **See** "Using the Setup Wizard," **p. 482**

First, you need to use the Setup Wizard or another setup utility to create an installation process for your program. After you have created this installation process, you must thoroughly test it on as many different systems as possible. You might write the most sophisticated piece of software in the world, but if its setup program doesn't install your program properly, your labor is lost.

If you are shipping your program on floppy disks, you should label each disk clearly, avoiding handwritten labels in favor of ones printed on a laser printer or by a professional printer. Using Disk *X* of *Y* tagging on the labels is a good practice to follow. For an end user, there are few things more frustrating than trying to install a piece of software only to find out that you are missing a disk.

However, due to the increasing size of Windows applications, it would not be too bold a prediction to say floppy disk installations are going the way of the dinosaur. Program setup can be an incredibly time-consuming process if the install files must be broken into a large number of 1.44M disk-sized chunks. On the other hand, a blank CD can hold about 650 megabytes of data, and the cost of CD recorders and media has decreased considerably in recent years.

Whatever media you use, label it with clear and brief instructions. If your application is built around components that require their own setup (such as ODBC), try to integrate the setup programs as much as possible. Users will appreciate setups that are simple, with a single icon or command. If distributing via CD-ROM, you might want to include an AUTORUN.INF file, which allows your setup program to start automatically. Also, offer a clear, noticeable message in the deployment package informing the user what to do in the event of difficulty. These things are important and have definite impact on how the quality of your work is perceived.

CAUTION

Files copied from CD-ROM to hard disk have the default file attribute of read-only. You cannot write to them. This can cause problems if your program is deployed with files to which it must write—for example, .INI files or database files. When testing your deployment, check to make sure that your setup program removes the read-only file attribute from the files it copies from CD-ROM.

Evaluation and Future Versions   At the end of every software development process is a period where you look over what you have done to determine how to do it better on the next version. Next version? That's right, because most software gets revised, no matter how small the project. As an example, take the Internet browser market, which releases new browser versions with an almost nauseating frequency. As you were developing your project, without a doubt you came across problems. And, as you solved these problems, you probably said to yourself that the next time you did this, you would do so and so, in such and such a way. Mistakes are things from which we learn, and you would do well to anticipate applying what you have learned from your errors to a future version. Make sure to document your thoughts as you get them, for easy "memory retrieval" later.

Most software is developed under strict time constraints. No person or enterprise can afford to take forever to produce a functional piece of code. As a result, it is often not possible to implement every specified feature in a given release. Therefore, planning to implement features over progressive versions is a viable development strategy.

 As you program, keep notes of ideas you have for future versions. Remember also (although it might make you snarl) that part of a programmer's job is being a salesperson. The decision to upgrade to a new version of Visual Basic is a perfect example. While the developer sees a cool and exciting programming tool, his boss might just see an expense. Do not be afraid to write small prototype programs or mocked-up forms to show others what is possible. This is sometimes known as a *proof-of-concept*.

The evaluation of real-life use of your code happens in the post-production period. The true test of a software product's effectiveness and usability is the test of time. No laboratory condition can ever adequately anticipate every nuance of user interaction. It is only by deploying your program, supporting your program, and eliciting the end users' responses that you can accurately evaluate what works and what doesn't.

Creating Consistent and Effective Graphical Interfaces

Software programs are like cars: the more predictable and sensible they are to use, the easier it is to get where you want to go.

Although the Windows operating system has set some standards regarding graphical user interface design—and VB has made programming for Windows a whole lot simpler—there is still a good deal of unpredictable and improper use of Windows components (menus, buttons, list boxes, combo boxes, and so on). This inconsistency defeats the fundamental purpose of the graphical user interface idea—to make operating a computer a more productive, enjoyable, and less frustrating experience for the user.

Do not think that providing a consistent, predictable graphical interface for your program requires you to forego creativity in any way. Take the active toolbar (or coolbar) used first in Microsoft Internet Explorer. Although it broke standards regarding the look of Windows toolbar buttons, it was a great idea and set the standard for the Office 97 toolbars.

Making a Well-Designed Form

Although designing a form in Visual Basic is a simple thing to do, doing it *well* is not that easy. Good form design involves more than just inserting controls and programming events. To make a well-designed form, you should understand the form's purpose, how it is going to be used, when it is going to be used, and its relationship with the rest of the program.

Let's take a look at the form `frmSettings` (FRMESET.FRM) in Figure 19.3. The purpose of this form is to set the display attributes for another form. This form suffers from a number of poor design choices that prevent it from effectively achieving its full functionality.

This form is in the project EVIL.JOT.VBP, which somes on the CD-ROM accompanying this book.

FIG. 19.3

The code behind the pictured form might work flawlessly, but it leaves much to be desired in terms of layout.

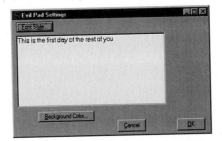

The first item for correction is the choice of setting the form's `BorderStyle` property to `Sizable`. Should the user resize the form either by intention or mistake (double-clicking the title bar is not an uncommon accident), the form does not resize or reposition the controls to accommodate the new form size (see Figure 19.4). Forms that are sizable are generally used in instances where the user needs a window of varying size to accomplish something—for example, Word's document windows or Paint's drawing window. To correct this problem, set the form's `BorderStyle` property to `Fixed Single` or `Fixed Dialog`.

▶ **See** "Form Properties Revisited," **p. 81**

TIP To provide basic re-sizing capabilities, you can place code to move controls around on a form and alter their dimensions in the form's `Resize` event. For example, the line

```
If frmMain.Width > 300 Then lstUserList.Width = frmMain.Width - 300
```

could be used to always keep a list box sized to 300 twips less than the form width, as long as it doesn't result in a negative width.

FIG. 19.4

The controls are not resized or repositioned when the form is resized. The form's *BorderStyle* property should be set to *Fixed Single* or *Fixed Dialog.*

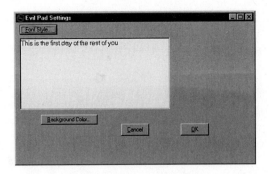

Another mistake is the initial size and location of the form. It completely covers the form whose attributes are to be set (refer to Figure 19.3, in which the primary form is completely hidden behind the settings form). An analogy would be if Microsoft Word's Find window covered up your entire document. To remedy this flaw, the form should be repositioned so that when it appears, at least a portion of the form to be affected is still showing.

Notice too that the form suffers from poor labeling. The designer is assuming that the user intuitively knows what this form is about, what the function of the label control is, and how each button affects the overall program.

Probably the biggest cause for concern with regard to this form's design is the almost arbitrary use of space and the inconsistent placement of buttons and labels on the form. When it comes to the size of a fixed size form (a.k.a. a dialog box), the rule of thumb is "less is best." You want to allow the form to take up no more real estate than it needs, but not to make it so small that controls are congested and text is illegible.

▶ **See** "Setting Up the Dialog Box Form," **p. 147**

You should also organize the placement of controls according to functionality. In the frmSettings form, separating the <u>F</u>ont Style button from the <u>B</u>ackground Color button is confusing and causes a lot of unnecessary mouse movement activity. Positioning the <u>F</u>ont Style and <u>B</u>ackground Color buttons together in one group and the <u>O</u>K and <u>C</u>ancel buttons in another wouldcreate distinct areas of functionality that the user would find more organized and memorable.

Taking into account the pitfalls discussed here, look at Figure 19.5. This is an illustration of the improved form, frmSettngs (FRMSET.FRM), which is part of the Visual Basic project

GOODJOT.VBP. Notice the reduced size of the form, the change of the form's BorderStyle property, the reorganization of the form's buttons, and the inclusion of a frame to provide a sense of functional unity and descriptive labeling.

FIG. 19.5

Notice that in the improved form pictured here, controls have been grouped according to their functionality.

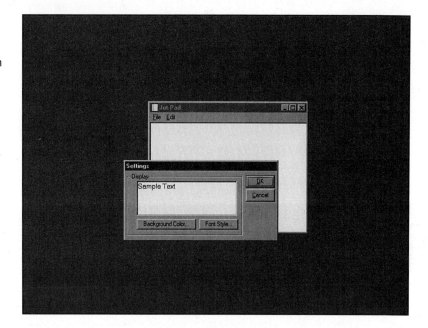

Designing Menus

Another important part of form design is creating consistent, effective menus. This means following some straightforward design guidelines and organizing your menus consistently and concisely. Here are a few guidelines and suggestions that enable you to make professional looking menus that meet the users' expectations:

- Follow standard Windows menu conventions: File, Edit, View, and so on.
- Group menu items logically and concisely.
- Use separator bars to group related items in a drop-down menu.
- Avoid redundant menu entries.
- Avoid menu bar items without drop-down menus.
- Don't forget to use the ellipsis(...) to denote menu entries that activate dialog boxes.

Follow Standard Windows Menu Conventions   Windows has been around for a long enough period of time that its users have developed certain expectations about how Windows applications should work and look. One of the areas where user expectations are fairly specific is the layout of the menu bar.

Take a look at Figure 19.6. In this example, the designer of this menu has chosen to breach the standard Windows menu bar layout convention. Users expect that the menu bar item File comes first, followed by Edit. This design changes the menu bar item order to be Edit, followed by File. The unconventional reordering of the menu bar will probably cause the user to experience initial confusion. In this case, reordering the menu really adds no value to the program, so it is better to stick with the *de facto* Windows convention.

FIG. 19.6

There is no reason to re-order the standard Windows menu bar; it will only confuse the users.

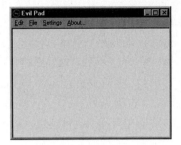

Group Menu Items Logically and Concisely

Figure 19.7 shows another problem with the example menus. Notice that the illustrated Settings menu has only two submenus, Show Settings and Always on Top. These two submenus should be moved to the File menu. Doing this condenses the menu bar without affecting the functionality or accessibility of the moved items.

FIG. 19.7

Since there are only two items in the Settings menu, a better choice would be to move them to the File menu.

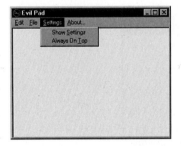

Part
IV

Ch
19

Use Separator Bars to Group Related Items in a Drop-Down Menu

Separator bars provide a level of grouping within a top-level menu. Take Visual Basic's Edit menu for example—related functions such as Copy and Paste are set apart from other items because they logically go together. The separator bars create a visual break in a long menu, allowing the user to quickly know if he or she is looking at the right area. In our example, after the Show Settings and Always on Top drop-down menu items have been moved to the File menu, they can be grouped together by putting a separator bar before and after the items (see Figure 19.8).

▶ **See** "Controlling a Program with a Menu Bar," **p. 108**

FIG. 19.8

This menu system has been simplified by grouping similar functions.

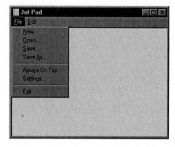

Avoid Redundant Menu Entries   Although it is always a good idea to offer the user multiple ways of performing the same tasks within your program—for example, selecting Edit, Copy or pressing Ctrl+C to copy selected data to the Clipboard—it is not good practice to have a given functionality appear in more than one place within your program's menu system. Nor is it a good idea to have the same menu caption appear in more than one place in your program and perform two entirely different actions.

In Figure 19.9, notice that the caption Settings appears both in the File menu and as a menu item. When you select File, Settings, the Settings dialog box appears. However, when you click the Settings menu bar item, the Settings drop-down menu appears. This is poor practice. Not only will having this caption in two different areas of the program's menu confuse the user, having two different behaviors attached to each caption will absolutely confound him.

FIG. 19.9

In this example, the Settings menu item appears in two places: in the File drop-down menu and the menu bar. This is a confusing design choice. Avoid redundant menu items.

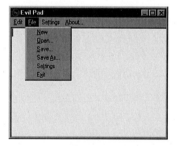

Avoid Menu Bar Items Without Drop-Down Menus   Avoid the situation in which you have a menu bar item that does not have a drop-down menu of selections. In Figure 19.10, you see the About dialog box that appears when you choose About..., which has no menu items under it. A lone top-level item, or *orphan*, has the same behavior as a command button or drop-down menu item. If that sort of behavior is what you want, a CommandButton control could be used to achieve the same effect. The better solution, however, is to move the orphan menu bar item to another menu with a similar set of functions. This is the same principle discussed earlier in "Group Menu Items Logically and Concisely."

FIG. 19.10

A menu bar item that doesn't invoke drop-down menus might confuse users.

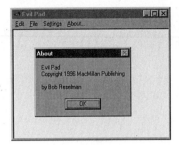

Use the Ellipsis to Denote Menu Entries that Activate Dialog Boxes

When an ellipsis (...) appears next to an item in a drop-down menu, it lets users know that selecting this item does not have any immediate results, but rather brings up a dialog box with more options (as you saw with the About... item in the preceding section). Many people unfamiliar with designing Windows applications frequently forget to use it. Using the ellipsis when the situation warrants adds to the professionalism of your application.

Offering Choices

When it comes time for a user to make a decision within your program, it is usually more efficient to provide a set of choices from which to select (see Figure 19.11) than requiring typed input. Providing the user with choices reduces the risk of error due to typing mistakes. It also makes input validation much easier, as well as shows the user the range of possible choices in many cases.

FIG. 19.11

Selecting a typeface from a list of available fonts is easier for the user than typing in a selection.

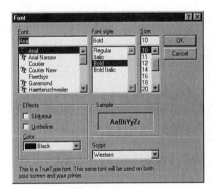

▶ **See** "Working with User Choices," **p. 216**

List Boxes versus Combo Boxes

Two useful controls for offering choices to the user are the list box and the combo box. The ListBox control allows the user to view a list of all available choices before, during, and after a selection is made. The ListBox control allows no typed input; the user can select one (or sometimes more) item from the list. This can be a drawback should the user need to input data that the program does not provide. Another drawback of the list box is that it requires a good deal of window space to be useful. A list box that shows only two or three items can appear cramped and awkward.

N O T E Windows standards dictate that when you use a list box, you let the user select an item in one of two ways: selecting it and pressing a button or double-clicking. An example of this behavior (which uses the ListView control) is a File dialog box. ■

When window space is at a premium, using the ComboBox control might be a better design choice than a list box. The ComboBox control has three styles:

- *DropDown Combo* Displays a drop-down list of selections and also permits users to type input.

- *Simple Combo* Shows an input box above a list, just like a list box with a text box above it.

- *DrowpDown List* Similar to the Simple Combo but does not allow typed input.

The drawback of using the Simple Combo style is that, like the ListBox control, it requires a good deal of window space to be effective.

FIG. 19.12
Depending on the style setting of a combo box, typed user input may or may not be allowed.

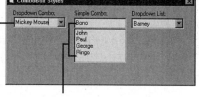

The DropDown ComboBox style enables user input

The Simple Combo style requires more window space

The DropDown List style doesn't permit typed-in user input

 T I P A DropDown List style combo box is a useful control for online report viewing. It allows the user to both select a report parameter (for example, Month-to-Date versus Quarter-to-Date) and, at the same time, shows the currently selected item.

Overusing list boxes and combo boxes can also harm an application's performance. If a list box or combo box lists too many items, the control can increase the form's load time. You can reduce the number of items in a list by finding out what the actual limits are. Does a user need all the states in the United States or only the ten with which the company normally does business?

Option Buttons versus Check Boxes To present a fixed number of choices, use the CheckBox and OptionButton controls. A check box gives the user two choices only: on or off. For example, the Windows Explorer Options dialog box (accessed through the View menu) uses a check box to indicate whether to Display the Full MS-DOS path in the title bar or not (see Figure 20.13). Selecting or deselecting a check box has no effect on any other check boxes on a form.

Option buttons present the user with a fixed list of mutually exclusive choices. Option buttons are usually grouped by placing related buttons in a frame. Only one option button in a group can be selected at any time; selecting one button in a group automatically deselects the other

FIG. 19.16
This splash screen appears when the application first loads to give the user something to look at while program initialization takes place.

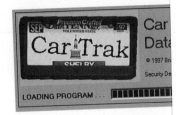

You can also update information in a splash scre
done in setting up the program. A similar techn
modifying a large number of database records.

Avoiding Programming Pitfal

Regardless of whether you are a member of a l
shop, your code will have to be maintained by s
coding and debugging to get a function workin,
a time to improve and enhance it. Even maintai
you have not seen it in six months (or, in my ca
to be horrendous. If you take certain precautio
time needed to maintain your code reasonable

Programming Readable Code

The most important thing that you can do towა
make it readable, not only to yourself but also t
your code, he or she must waste precious time
how. Readable code gives others a quick, intui
readability has a definite impact as to how your
munity. Depending on how you write code, oth
curse your name or admire your skill.

Using Visual Basic Constants

Many Visual Basic code statements utilize nur
should behave. This capability makes writing (
wards difficult. The solution is to use global cc
Code that uses constants is much easier to rea

To use built-in constants, you no longer have t
versions of Visual Basic prior to version 4. Vis
stants in the language. By using these intrinsic
to all programmers, even those who have not

buttons in that group. The Background tab in Windows' Display Properties dialog box uses option buttons to set the background wallpaper to the exclusive states of Tile or Center (see Figure 19.14).

FIG. 19.13
A good use of check boxes is shown in the lower section of the Windows Explorer dialog box, which uses two check boxes to present the user with independent on/off options.

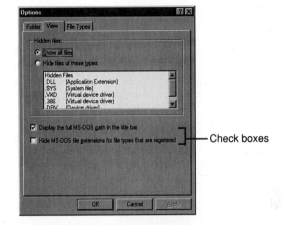

Check boxes

FIG. 19.14
In this dialog box, option buttons are used within a frame to represent a choice between two mutually exclusive states, Tile or Center.

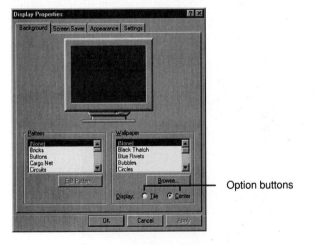

Option buttons

Improving User Perceptions of Your Programs

Perception is reality. No, I'm not having flashback to the 1960s, I am merely referring to how users' *observations* can influence their like or dislike of your program, regardless of its actual functionality. Application speed is a prime example. You might have written the fastest Visual Basic code ever, but it matters little if the user thinks it runs slow. Visual Basic programmers tend to get defensive when users complain about speed, because "the users don't know what the program is doing." However, there are a few tricks you can use to make your program *seem* to run faster.

The key to a program's perceived speed is the fact t[...] *thing needs to happen* right away. Users are more w[...] working as fast as it can. Booting Windows 95 is a g[...] time. However, all the graphics, beeps, and hard dr[...] make it an acceptable wait. The techniques discuss[...] creating "faster" Visual Basic applications.

Load Time If you load all of a program's forms at [...] application needs to show them. Although this slo[...] startup, overall runtime performance is much faste[...] application by using the Load method. This method [...] invisible to the user until the Show method is execu[...]

This technique works well for applications with a s[...] with more forms, you might use this technique for [...] accounting payroll application might load all the fo[...] information during an employee data-entry sessior[...]

The *Sub Main* Subroutine The General tab of th[...] display by choosing *projectname* Properties from t[...] startup form or Sub Main (see Figure 19.15). To ta[...] module with a subroutine named Main. This frees [...] within a form's Load event.

FIG. 19.15
After setting your startup object to *Sub Main*, you can consolidate your program's initialization tasks into a single procedure.

The Sub Main subroutine is an excellent place for [...] time. For example, the Sub Main subroutine migh[...] checking the application's path, and connecting t[...] procedures are very long, you might want to disp[...]

Splash Screens One way to deal with lengthy [...] during load time. A splash screen is a form that [...] its designer (see Figure 19.16). Many commercia[...] Excel, and Visual Basic itself, display splash scre[...] status bar provides the user with visible proof th[...]

---

can also help you, especially if you tend to forget what you have done and why. For example, which of the following code lines is more readily understandable?

```
MsgBox "This is a warning", 64
```

```
MsgBox "This is a warning", vbExclamation
```

When you read code that uses the intrinsic constants, you do not have to remember what each value means.

Commented Code

Writing commented code is a pain, but reading uncommented code—even code that you wrote just yesterday—can be an even greater pain. Trying to figure out the logic of a code segment can be time-consuming. Taking the time on the front end to put in comments, on the other hand, saves you time in the long run. There's an old saying among programmers, "You can never comment too much!" Imagine trying to read and understand the meaning and use of the code in Listing 19.1 without the comments.

Listing 19.1   11LIST01.TXT—Searching the *Tag* Property of Each Control and Displaying the Appropriate Database Field Information in Each Control

```
' The following routine searches through all the controls
' on a form and checks each control's TAG property.
' If the tag property is a field name, this routine loads
' the current field's value into that control

Sub LoadFormData (WndName As Form, dyn As Dynaset)
Dim Cntl%, FieldName$, Result$, N%, i%

Screen.MousePointer = vbHOURGLASS

'Search through all the controls on the indicated form
For Cntl% = 0 To WndName.Controls.Count - 1
  FieldName$ = WndName.Controls(Cntl%).Tag
  If TypeOf WndName.Controls(Cntl%) Is OptionButton Then

    ' Find the value of this field and store in the appropriate
    ' option button control
    N% = Abs(dyn(FieldName$))
    If WndName.Controls(Cntl%).Caption = "YES" Then
        WndName.Controls(Cntl%).Value = N%
    ElseIf WndName.Controls(Cntl%).Caption = "NO" Then
        WndName.Controls(Cntl%).Value = Abs(N% - 1)
    End If

  ElseIf TypeOf WndName.Controls(Cntl%) Is ComboBox Then

    If dyn(FieldName$) <> Null Then
```

```
    ' Format the current field's value
    Result$ = dyn.Fields(FieldName$)
    ' Find the field's value in the current combo box
    For N% = 0 To (WndName.Controls(Cntl%).ListCount - 1)
      i% = WndName.Controls(Cntl%).ListIndex + 1
      WndName.Controls(Cntl%).ListIndex = i%
      If Len(WndName.Controls(Cntl%).Text) <> 0 Then
        Exit For
      End If
    Next N%
  End If

  ' If the control is a text box
  ElseIf TypeOf WndName.Controls(Cntl%) Is TextBox Then

    ' If the current field's value is blank then skip
    If dyn(FieldName$) <> Null Then

      ' Store the formatted value in the text box
      WndName.Controls(Cntl%).Text = dyn.Fields(FieldName$)
    End If
  End If
Next Cntl%

Screen.MousePointer = vbDEFAULT

End Sub
```

Listing 20.1 contains the subroutine `LoadFormData`. You could reference this subroutine in the `Load` event of any form. Simply provide the name of the recordset containing the data, position, and the table at the appropriate record; place the names of the fields that you want in the appropriate control's `Tag` property; and run this routine. In instances where you cannot use Bound controls, this routine works amazingly well. Notice that the use of `vbHourGlass` and `vbDefault` makes it clear what the program is doing to `MousePointer`.

Use Descriptive Naming

Visual Basic allows you to use up to 255 characters to name a variable, sub, or function; it allows 40 characters for a control name. You can take advantage of this feature by giving your variables, functions, and controls names that reflect their identity, purpose, or position. In addition, as we discussed in Chapter 8, it's a good idea to use a naming convention for your objects and variables that helps you determine their type at a glance.

Listing 19.2 shows an example of using descriptive object naming to make your code more readable.

Part

IV

Ch

19

Listing 19.2   11LIST02.TXT—Using Descriptive Naming for Variables and Controls

```
Private Sub cmdChoices_MouseDown(Index As Integer, Button As Integer,
Shift As Integer, X As Single, Y As Single)
    Dim i%
    '"The pressed button typeface will be set according to the option,
opFontFace
    'value set

    'Set the old font (the gf prefix denotes global to form) so it can
    'reset on MouseUp
    gfOldFontFace$ = cmdChoices(Index).Font
    'Adjust for the new font setting
    If opFontFace(0) = True Then
        cmdChoices(Index).Font = opFontFace(0).Caption
    Else
        cmdChoices(Index).Font = opFontFace(1).Caption
    End If

    'Query to option buttons and set the caption case for the button depressed
    For i% = 0 To 2
        Select Case i%
        Case 0
            If optFontCase(i%).Value = True Then cmdChoices(Index).Caption =
UCase(cmdChoices(Index).Caption)
        Case 1
            If optFontCase(i%).Value = True Then cmdChoices(Index).Caption =
LCase(cmdChoices(Index).Caption)
        Case 2
            If optFontCase(i%).Value = True Then cmdChoices(Index).Caption =
gfOldFontCase$(Index)
        End Select
    Next i%
End Sub
```

Notice in the example that you do not even need to look at the form to know `optFontCase` is an option button used to select upper- or lowercase. This would have been a little harder to determine if its default name of `Option1` had been kept.

From Here...

Designing an effective Windows application requires a bit more understanding and planning than just putting controls on a form. Implementing a user-centered software development process helps you design cost-effective, user-friendly applications that work well and are easy to deploy and revise.

An application's appearance is as important as what the application does. A poorly thought-out application interface detracts from the application's usefulness because users focus on the bad interface rather than what it does. Be careful how you organize controls and menus. Also be careful to ensure that your program complies with and responds to the user's expectations.

To find information on related topics, see the following chapters:

- For more information on using the toolbar in Visual Basic, see Chapter 5, "Adding Menus and Toolbars to Your Program."

- To find out more about the use of common Windows components in your programs, see Chapter 10, "Using the Windows Common Controls."

- To see more on making your interface esthetically pleasing, see Chapter 14, "Working with Text, Fonts and Colors."

- For a treasure trove of styles for different kinds of screens and designs, see *Look for the Windows Interface* (Microsoft Press, 1992). Use this book in conjunction with the *Visual Design Guide*.

Part
IV

Ch
19

CHAPTER 20

Building a Multiple Document Interface

As you begin to write more advanced Visual Basic applications, at some point you will probably want to use Windows' Multiple Document Interface (MDI). The MDI allows your programs to work with multiple forms contained within a parent form. This makes your interface cleaner than one that has forms scattered about the screen.

The MDI standard can enhance your programs in two ways. First, you can have one container form that acts as the background for your overall application. If the user moves the container form, the child forms contained inside move as well. This helps keep your application's interface organized and self-contained. Second, and perhaps even more powerful, your users can work on multiple documents at one time. MDI applications allow the use of multiple instances of the same form, which can add much power and flexibility to your programs. ■

MDI applications provide a different user interface than standard forms

You will see how to create a Multiple Document Interface (MDI) application and manage all of the child forms of the application.

Object variables let you create a number of similar forms

You will see how to create instances of forms on-the-fly. This will allow you to create applications similar to Word that handle multiple files at the same time.

Both MDI parent and MDI child forms can have menus

You will learn how the menus interact and how to control the behavior of the child menus.

MDI applications provide the user with easy access to all the forms of the application

In an MDI application, you can automatically arrange all the open windows and keep a list of the windows in the menu. You will see how to apply these techniques to your MDI programs.

Introducing MDI Applications

Many of the applications that you create in Visual Basic will consist of a series of independent forms, like the ones shown in Figure 20.1. Each of these forms is displayed separately on the screen and is moved, maximized, or minimized separately from any other form. With this type of interface, there is no easy way to organize the forms or to deal with them as a group. Even with this limitation, this is a good interface to use for many programs and is probably the most prevalent interface design.

FIG. 20.1

This program's user interface consists of two forms that appear to have no visual relationship to each other.

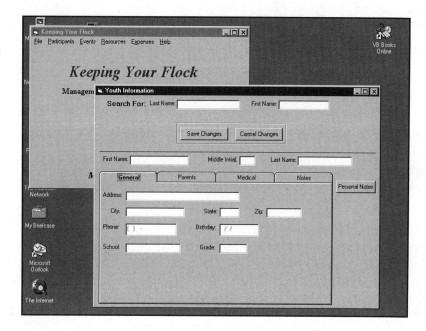

An alternative to this standard interface is the Multiple Document Interface, or MDI. This type of application has one *parent form* that contains most of the other forms in the program. Other forms can be *child forms*, which are contained within the parent, or *standard forms*, which are not. With an MDI application, you can easily organize all the child forms, or minimize the entire group of forms just by minimizing the parent form. Programs such as Microsoft Word and Excel are examples of MDI applications. If you have worked with these programs, you know that you can open multiple windows in the program, access them easily from the menu, and minimize the whole thing with a single click of the mouse. In version 5, even Visual Basic has gone to a true MDI interface style. Figure 20.2 shows three blank workbooks opened simultaneously in Excel as an example of a typical MDI application.

FIG. 20.2
MDI applications let you manage multiple document windows with ease.

Parent window —

Child windows —

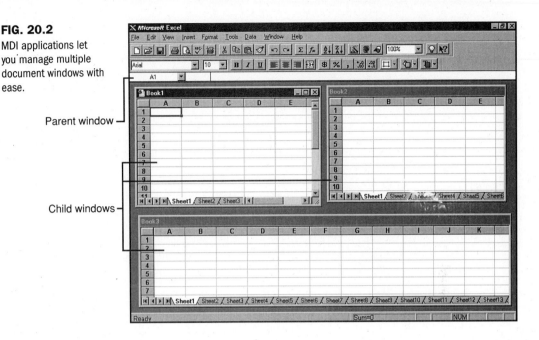

Characteristics of MDI Parent Forms

The MDI form, also known as the parent form, is the container for all the child forms of the application. The MDI form has a number of characteristics that define its behavior. These are:

- An application can only have one MDI form.

- The only controls that the MDI form can contain are those that support the Align property, such as the PictureBox or Toolbar controls. You cannot place other controls on the MDI form.

- You cannot use the Print method or any of the graphics methods to display information on the MDI form.

- When the MDI parent form is minimized, the parent window and all child windows are represented by a single icon on the Windows taskbar. When the parent form is restored, all the child forms are returned to the same layout as they had before the application was minimized.

- If a menu is defined for a child form, the menu will be displayed in the *parent form's* menu bar. If a menu is defined for the parent form, it is not shown at all unless there are no child forms present.

Characteristics of MDI Child Forms

Just as the MDI form has characteristics of its behavior, the MDI child forms also behave in a certain way. The characteristics of an MDI child form are:

Part
IV
Ch
20

- Each child form is displayed within the confines of the parent form. A child form cannot be moved outside the boundaries of the MDI parent form.

- When a child window is minimized, its icon is displayed in the parent window, not on the taskbar.

- When a child form is maximized, it fills the entire work area of the parent form. Also, the parent form's title bar will contain both the name of the parent form and the name of the child form.

- When one child form is maximized, all other child forms are maximized as well.

Creating a Simple MDI Program

As with many programming concepts, the best way to understand how MDI applications work is to create a simple MDI program. This section walks you through the process of setting up a "shell" of an MDI program. It will contain an MDI form and a single child form. You can then use this program as the basis for a fully functional MDI application.

The first step is to start a new project in Visual Basic by choosing the New Project item from the File menu.

Setting Up the Parent Form

After you have started the new project, the next step is to create the MDI parent form. To create the MDI form for your project, select the Add MDI Form item from the Project menu, or choose MDI Form from the Add Object button's drop-down menu. Then, from the Add MDI Form dialog box, select the MDI Form icon and click Open. When the MDI Form is added to your project, it will look like the one in Figure 20.3.

FIG. 20.3
The MDI form has a darker background than a standard form.

You might also notice that the MDI Form is added to the Forms folder of your project. However, if you look closely, you might notice that the MDI form is displayed in the Project window with a different icon than a standard form. The icons help you to easily identify the type of form that you have. Figure 20.4 illustrates the difference between normal and MDI form icons.

After you have added the form to your project, you should specify a descriptive name for the form and set any of the other properties that you need. Most of the properties of the MDI form are the same ones that you set to control the appearance of a standard form.

FIG. 20.4

Icons show the form
type in the Project
window.

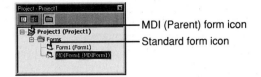

— MDI (Parent) form icon
— Standard form icon

▶ **See** "Parts of a Form," **p. 80**

There are, however, two properties that are unique to the MDI form and deserve special note—the AutoShowChildren property and the ScrollBars property. The AutoShowChildren property determines whether child forms are shown automatically as they are loaded. If the AutoShowChildren property is set to True (the default value), then child forms are shown as soon as they are loaded. This means that the Load statement and the Show method have the same effect on the form.

The ScrollBars property determines whether the MDI form shows scroll bars when necessary. When this property is set to True (the default value), scroll bars are shown on the MDI form if one or more of the child forms extend beyond the boundary of the MDI form, as shown in Figure 20.5. If the property is set to False, scroll bars are not shown under any conditions.

One other property of note is the Picture property. While the MDI form does not support the Print method and graphics methods like a standard form, you can still include a picture as the background of the form.

FIG. 20.5

Scroll bars let you view
portions of child forms
that extend beyond the
boundary of the parent
form.

Part

IV

Ch

20

Setting Up a Child Form

Setting up a child form in an MDI application is even easier than setting up the parent form. A child form is basically a standard form that has the MDIChild property set to True. Therefore, everything you know about creating standard forms applies to creating the child forms of an MDI application.

For the sample application, all you need to do is set the MDIChild property of the form that was first created for the project. To do this, select the form in the Project window, select the MDIChild property in the Properties window, and change its value to True. You might notice that the icon for the form in the Project window changes from a standard icon to an MDI child icon. This is the only change that you will notice in the form while you are in the design window (see Figure 20.6).

FIG. 20.6

Notice how the two child forms' icons differ from those for standard and parent forms.

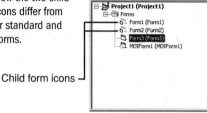

Child form icons ┘

TIP As with other properties with predefined values, you can double-click the MDIChild property in the Properties window to toggle back and forth between the True and False values.

After setting the MDIChild property, all that is left to complete the form is to add the controls you need for your program. You can, of course, design the form first and change the MDIChild property later. The order of the operation has no effect on the behavior of the form. A typical MDI child form is shown in Figure 20.7.

FIG. 20.7

MDI child forms look just like standard forms.

Running the Program

After you have finished setting up both the parent and child forms, you are ready to run the program to see how a child form behaves inside the parent form. First, as always, you should save your work. Then click the Start button on the toolbar or press F5 to run the program. When the program runs, the form layout should resemble Figure 20.8.

There are several things that you should try so that you fully understand the behavior of the parent and child forms. Try the following tasks:

- Minimize the child form and note the location of its icon.
- Move the child form around. It does not move beyond the parent form's boundaries.
- Maximize the child form.
- Minimize and maximize the parent form.

FIG. 20.8

This simple MDI application shows a parent form and two child forms. Note that the child forms are two instances of the same form.

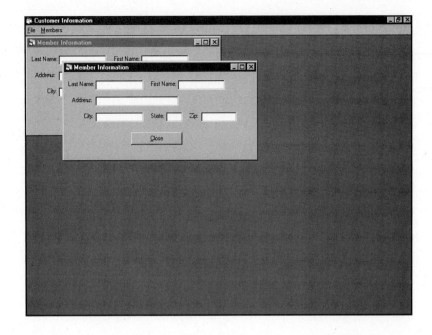

One thing that you might have noticed when you started the program was that the child form was shown automatically when the program started. In the simple example, this is because the child form (the one first created when you started the project) was designated as the startup form. If you would like to have the empty MDI parent form shown when you start the program, you need to change the Startup Object setting in the Project Properties dialog box as shown in Figure 20.9. You access the project properties by choosing the Project Properties item from the Project menu.

FIG. 20.9

Set the startup form and other properties of the project from this dialog box.

Part

IV

Ch

20

Creating Multiple Instances of a Form

You can use the MDI form just to make your application neater and its forms easier to manage. However, if that's all you use MDI forms for, you're missing out on the real power of MDI applications. The most powerful feature of an MDI application is its capability to create and handle *multiple instances of a form* at the same time. For example, if you are working in Microsoft Word, each document you open or each new document that you create is a new instance of the same basic form. In fact, many MDI applications are made up of only two forms: the MDI parent form and the template form for all the child forms in the application.

> **N O T E**   You can have more than one type of template child form in your application. For example, Visual Basic has two basic types of MDI child forms: the Form design child form and the Code child form. You can create as many of each of these types of forms as you need, within the constraints of your system. ▪

Creating an MDI application of this type requires a little more work than was required in the sample application. You first have to define the basic MDI child form at design time and then use object variables to create instances of the form at run time.

To start the process of creating an MDI application with multiple instances of a form, you need to start a new project and then add an MDI form to the project as described in the section "Creating a Simple MDI Program." Next, be sure to set up the MDI form as the startup object using the Project Properties dialog box.

Setting Up the Basic Form

As was the case in "Creating a Simple MDI Program," creating the form template is the same as creating a standard form. You add all the controls to the form that you need for the user interface. Also, you need to write any necessary code for the controls to perform their intended functions. You also need to set the MDIChild property of the form to True.

> **N O T E**   To optimize your application, you might need to write some code for the form in the MDI parent form or a separate module. See the section "Optimizing Your MDI Application" for more details on this subject. ▪

One thing you might notice as you first create an MDI application is that the child form, when first shown at run time, is probably sized differently than it was when you created it. This is illustrated in Figure 20.10. The reason is because an MDI application, by default, assigns a certain size and position to each child form that is shown.

If the default size and position are not acceptable to you, you need to place code in the Load event procedure of the child form to position and size it the way you want. To determine the desired size of the child form, check the Height and Width properties of the form while you are in design mode, and then add code to the form's Load event procedure to set the Height and Width properties to their original values. The same concept applies to the position of the form.

You can set the `Top` and `Left` properties of the child form to set its position. The code in Listing 20.1 shows how to set the size of a child form and center it within the parent form. Figure 20.11 shows the effect of this code.

FIG. 20.10

MDI applications automatically size and position their child forms.

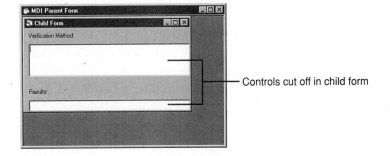

Controls cut off in child form

> **N O T E** If a child window's size becomes too large for its parent, whether by user action or through code, the parent's size is not changed automatically. The parent does, however, automatically show scroll bars when needed, as mentioned in the section "Setting Up the Parent Form" earlier in this chapter. ▪

Listing 20.1   MDIDEMO2.FRM—Use Code to Size and Position the Child Form

```
Private Sub Form_Load()
    Me.Height = 4545
    Me.Width = 6810
    Me.Top = (mdiMain.ScaleHeight - Me.Height) / 2
    Me.Left = (mdiMain.ScaleWidth - Me.Width) / 2
End Sub
```

FIG. 20.11

You can use code to override the default size and position of an MDI child form.

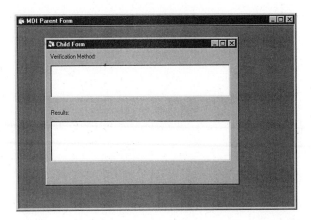

> **N O T E**   You cannot use the StartUpPosition property to set the initial position of a child form
> in an MDI window. In fact, you cannot change the setting of the property from its default
> value of 0 - Manual. ▧

Creating Forms Using Object Variables

After you have created the basic child form, you need a means to create an instance of the form
(at run time) and display it in the MDI application. Doing this requires all of two code lines.
First, you use a Dim statement to create an *object variable* (a variable of Object type) that will
contain an instance of the form. In the Dim statement, you need to use the New keyword to tell
Visual Basic to create a *new instance* of the form. Otherwise, the statement just creates a new
handle to the existing form. After you create the object variable, you use the Show method to
display the form. However, *instead of using the form name, you specify the name of the variable.*
The two required lines of code are shown here:

```
Dim NewFrm As New frmText
NewFrm.Show
```

To see how this code works, place the lines of code in the Click event procedure of the MDI
form, and then run the program. Each time you click the MDI form, a new instance of the child
form is displayed.

Using the Keywords *Me* and *ActiveForm*

Because all the child forms are the same and you use the same variable to create each of them,
how can you know which form to specify when running code? Especially code that is generic
and can work with any of the forms?

There are two particular keywords that you will use extensively in working with MDI applications: Me and ActiveForm. These two keywords let you create generic code routines that will
work with any child form that you create.

Me is a keyword that can be used in any form to refer to itself, just as you can use the word *me*
to refer to yourself without having to use your name. You saw how this keyword was used in
Listing 20.1 to size and position the child form on startup. If you write all code in the child form
using Me to refer to the form name, your code will work for whichever instance of the form is
active at the time.

ActiveForm is actually a property of the MDI form. Its purpose is similar to the Me keyword.
ActiveForm refers to whichever MDI child form is currently active. By using the ActiveForm
property in all code that resides in the MDI form, the code operates only on the active form
and on no other. The following line of code provides a simple example of the ActiveForm
property:

```
mdiMain.ActiveForm.Print "This form is currently active."
```

> **N O T E**   Notice, here and in Listing 20.1, the use of the prefix mdi that was used when naming the
> MDI parent form. ▧

Using the `ActiveForm` property, you can reference any property, method, or event of the currently active child form without having to know its name.

Working with Menus

In Chapter 5, "Adding Menus and Toolbars to Your Program," you saw how to create a menu for your application. You also found out that you can have a different menu for each form in your program, if you so desire. MDI forms can also have menus. You create a menu for your MDI form the same way that you create a menu for a standard form, using the Menu Editor. The menu for the MDI form is usually the primary means by which you access the capabilities of an MDI application.

▶ **See** "Creating a Menu Bar," **p. 108**

In an MDI application, the child forms can also have menus. Like the menu for the MDI form itself, you create child form menus using the Menu Editor. However, when a child form is displayed, its menu is not displayed as part of the child form but on the menu bar of the MDI form. This behavior presents a problem in your MDI applications, because the MDI child form's menu actually *replaces* the MDI parent form's menu when the child is active. This problem is that you cannot access the functions of the parent form while the child is active.

There are two solutions to the problems associated with the replacement of menus. First, you can duplicate all the necessary parent form functions on each child form. Unfortunately, this can lead to a bloated and hard-to-maintain program if you have several child forms with menus.

An alternative solution is to include in the parent window's menu all the menus that are necessary for all child windows. Then you can place code in the `Activate` and `Deactivate` events of the child form to show the parent's menus that are applicable to that child form. For example, in a word processing program, you want the File and Help menus to be available all the time, but you only want the Edit and Format menus available when you are working on a document. You could use code similar to Listing 20.2 to show the menus when a document is active and to hide the menus when the document is inactive. As an alternative, you could show and hide the menus as the form opens and closes using the `Load` and `Unload` events.

Listing 20.2   MDIDEMO.FRM—Use Code to Show and Hide Child Menus

```
Private Sub Form_Activate()
    mnuEdit.Visible = True
    mnuFormat.Visible = True
End Sub

Private Sub Form_Deactivate()
    mnuEdit.Visible = False
    mnuFormat.Visible = False
End Sub
```

Part
IV

Ch
20

To make sure that any menu code in the parent form acts upon the proper child form, use the parent form's `ActiveForm` property as described in the preceding section.

Managing the Children

One of the other benefits of working with MDI applications is that it is easy to manage all the child forms of the application. Visual Basic has a number of tools that make it easy for your users to access the multiple forms that are open inside the MDI form. Your program can provide the user with the means to automatically arrange the child windows. You can even provide a menu item that keeps up with all the open child windows and lets the user access one of them by selecting it from the menu. These capabilities are particularly useful if the user will be switching back and forth between multiple tasks or multiple files in the application.

Using Automatic Organization

One way the user can access multiple forms is by displaying each form on the screen in a particular organizational style. This provides the user with access to each form with just a click of a mouse button. The key to this functionality is the Arrange method of the MDI form. The Arrange method organizes all the child forms of the application in a particular pattern. Each of these patterns results in at least a portion of each form's being visible to the user, and they are commonly used by MDI-compliant Windows applications. To use the Arrange method, you specify the name of the MDI form, the method itself, and a constant representing the pattern that you want to use for the arrangement of the forms. The following line of code illustrates the use of the method:

```
mdiMain.Arrange vbCascade
```

There are four possible window arrangement patterns that you can create with the Arrange method. Each of these patterns is represented by an intrinsic constant. Table 20.1 summarizes the patterns. The four patterns are illustrated in Figures 20.12 through 20.15.

Table 20.1 Arrangements of MDI Child Windows

Constant	Description
vbCascade	Arranges the non-minimized forms in a pattern where each form is offset slightly from the others.
vbTileHorizontal	Each non-minimized child form occupies the full width of the parent form and the child forms are displayed on top of one another. If there are many child forms, they can occupy multiple columns when tiled.
vbTileVertical	Each non-minimized child form occupies the full height of the parent form and the child forms are displayed side-by-side. If there are many child forms, they can occupy multiple rows when tiled.
vbArrangeIcons	Arranges the icons of all minimized child forms near the bottom of the parent.

FIG. 20.12

These child forms have been arranged in a cascade pattern.

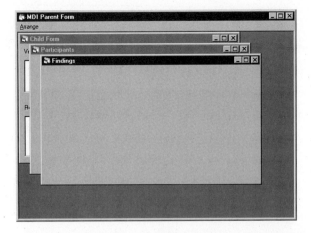

FIG. 20.13

These child forms have been arranged in a vertically tiled pattern.

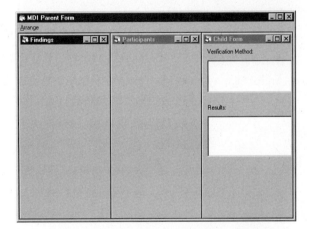

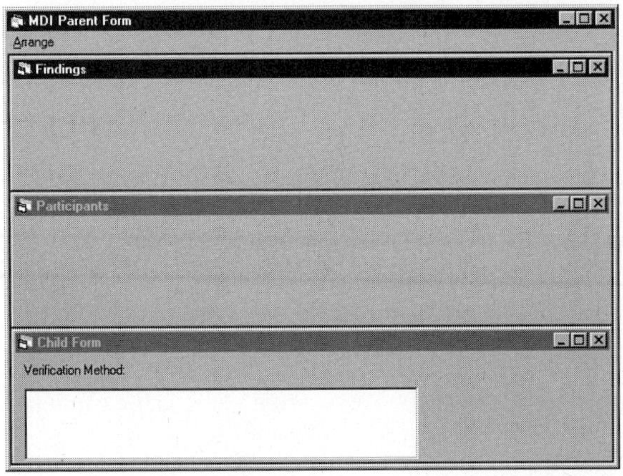

FIG. 20.14

These child forms have been arranged in a horizontally tiled pattern.

Part

IV

Ch

20

FIG. 20.15

Minimized child forms are represented by icons arranged at the bottom of the MDI form.

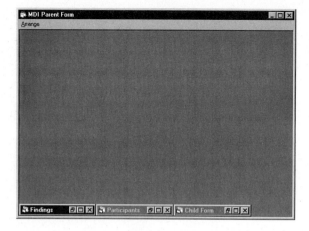

Typically, you place the arrangement options in a <u>W</u>indow menu on the MDI form. Each arrangement option that you want to support is a separate menu item.

Maintaining a Window List

The other way of providing easy access to the child forms of your application is to maintain a list of the open child forms. Fortunately, this is an easy task. You create a window list while you are creating the menu for the MDI parent form. You determine which menu will contain the list and then set that menu item's WindowList property to True in the Menu Editor, as shown in Figure 20.16.

N O T E You can also change the setting of the WindowList property from code. ▓

FIG. 20.16

Check the <u>W</u>indowList box to create a list of open child windows in your MDI menu.

As you add child forms to the application, the window list menu item is automatically updated to include the new form. The caption of the menu item is the caption that is given to the form that you create. The active form in the window list is indicated by a check mark. Figure 20.17 shows a window list for an MDI application.

FIG. 20.17

The window list lets the user select the form with which to work.

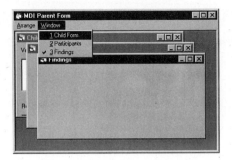

Creating a Sample Application—an MDI Contact Manager

Obviously, the best way to demonstrate the techniques of MDI applications is to build an application that you might actually use. This program uses multiple instances of a template form to become an MDI application.

If part of your job is keeping up with customer contacts, you probably use some kind of contact manager. These programs let you keep up with information about each of your customers, such as their name, address, phone numbers, the date you last contacted them, and so forth. One of the disadvantages of some contact managers is that you can only work with a single contact at a time. This can be very inconvenient if you are working on an order for one customer and another telephones to discuss a new service. In this case, you have to close the client information for the current customer and open the information for the second customer. Wouldn't it be great if you could just open the information for the second customer in a new window? Well, with an MDI contact manager, you can.

This section shows you how to build a very simple MDI contact manager. The program displays only name and address information for a client and is basically an illustration of the concept. To create a full-fledged contact manager, you have to add additional database code. The program uses a Microsoft Access database and the Jet engine to retrieve the data.

▶ **See** "Using Tables," on **p. 848**

Creating the MDI Form

The setup of the MDI form is the same as you have seen in previous sections. You first need to add an MDI form to your project and then set the `AutoShowChildren` property to `False`. You also should set the `Name` and `Caption` properties of the MDI form to something other than the defaults.

After setting the properties of the form, you need to create a menu that displays the customer information in the appropriate child form. The menu items that you need to add are shown in Figure 20.18.

▶ **See** "Creating a Menu Bar," **p. 108**

Part

IV

Ch

20

FIG. 20.18

Our sample MDI
Contact Manager
application has these
menu items.

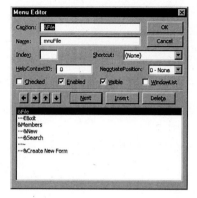

One menu item of note is the Create New Form item. The user can use this option to tell the
program whether to display a selected customer in the existing child form or to create a new
form for each new customer. The Checked property of the item is set to show the status of the
user choice.

Of course, after you create the menu, you need to add code to make the menu options work.
Listing 20.3 shows the code for the menu items shown in Figure 20.18.

**Listing 20.3   MAINMDI.FRM—Use Menu Code to Handle the Tasks of the
Contact Manager**

```
Private Sub filExit_Click()
    Unload Me
End Sub

Private Sub MDIForm_Load()
    Me.WindowState = vbMaximized
End Sub

Private Sub MDIForm_Unload(Cancel As Integer)
    CustDb.Close
End Sub

Private Sub memCreate_Click()
Dim CheckSet As Boolean
    CheckSet = Not memCreate.Checked
    memCreate.Checked = CheckSet
    CreateForm = CheckSet
End Sub

Private Sub memNew_Click()
    If CreateForm Then
        Dim frmMem As New frmMember
        frmMem.Show
    End If
    ClearCust
End Sub
```

```
Private Sub memSearch_Click()
    frmSearch.Show vbModal
    If CreateForm Then
        Dim frmMem As New frmMember
        frmMem.Show
    End If
    ShowCust
End Sub
```

Setting Up the Customer Child Form

The next step in creating the contact manager is setting up the child form that will display a customer's information. To set up the customer form, add a form to your project (or use the initial form that was created) and then set its MDIChild property to True. You probably also need to change the Name and Caption properties of the form. (Set the name of the form to frmMember to match the code in the menu items.) After setting the properties of the form, you need to add controls to the form to display the data. The completed form is shown in Figure 20.19.

FIG. 20.19

Customer information is displayed in a child form.

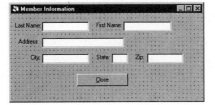

Creating the Search Form

As you look up customer records, you need a search form to allow the user to enter a name to find. The search form can be very simple, consisting of a label, a text box to enter the name, and two command buttons to perform or cancel the search. The code for the form is also very simple; if you proceed with the search, the code uses the FindFirst method of the recordset that contains the contact information to locate the first name corresponding to the desired search information. The complete search form is shown in Figure 20.20, and the code for the form is shown in Listing 20.4.

Part IV
Ch
20

N O T E A *recordset* is a special type of object that acts as a link between a Visual Basic program and information stored in a database. You learn about recordsets in Chapter 31. ■

▶ **See** "Deciding Which Recordset Type to Use," **p. 848**

FIG. 20.20

You can make the search form more complex by adding a First Name search as well.

Listing 20.4   SEARCH.FRM—Use the *FindFirst* Method to Locate the Desired Customer

```
Private Sub cmdCancel_Click()
    Unload Me
End Sub

Private Sub cmdSearch_Click()
Dim SrchStr As String
    SrchStr = txtSearch.Text
    CustRset.FindFirst "LastName = '" & SrchStr & "'"
    Unload Me
End Sub
```

Creating the Heart of the Program

The forms provide the interface of the program, but the real heart of the program is a group of procedures that actually display the data and set the program up. To create the procedures, you first need to add a module to your program. You can do this by selecting the Add Module item from the Project menu, or by selecting Module from the Add Object button's drop-down menu.

▶ **See** "Determining the Scope of Procedures and Functions," **p. 472**

After the module is added to the project, you need to define a couple of Public variables and create the procedure that sets up the program. The public variables are used to provide your entire program with access to the database object. After you define the variables, you need to create a Sub Main procedure to set up the database information and display the MDI parent form. The Public variable declarations and the Sub Main procedure are shown in Listing 20.5.

Listing 20.5   MDIPROCS.BAS—Use *Sub Main* to Set Up the Database and Load the Main Form

```
Public CustDb As Database, CustRset As Recordset
Public CreateForm As Boolean

Sub Main()
    Set CustDb = DBEngine.Workspaces(0).OpenDatabase("D:\VB5Book\NewDb.mdb")
    Set CustRset = CustDb.OpenRecordset("Customers", dbOpenDynaset)
```

```
    mdiMain.Show
    CreateForm = True
End Sub
```

After you create the Sub Main procedure, you need to change the project options to make Sub Main the startup object of the program.

The next two procedures are the ones which either display information about a current customer or set up the information form for you to enter a new customer. These procedures are called by the appropriate menu items of the MDI form. The key feature to note in these procedures is that the ActiveForm property of the MDI form is used to designate which child form will receive the data being sent. The ClearCust and ShowCust procedures are shown in Listing 20.6.

Listing 20.6   MDIPROCS.BAS—Use the *ActiveForm* Property to Send the Output of the Procedure to the Proper Location

```
Public Sub ClearCust()
Dim I As Integer
    For I = 0 To 5
        mdiMain.ActiveForm.txtMember(I).Text = ""
    Next I
End Sub

Public Sub ShowCust()
    With mdiMain.ActiveForm
        .txtMember(0).Text = CustRset!LastName & ""
        .txtMember(1).Text = CustRset!FirstName & ""
        .txtMember(2).Text = CustRset!Address1 & ""
        .txtMember(3).Text = CustRset!City & ""
        .txtMember(4).Text = CustRset!State & ""
        .txtMember(5).Text = CustRset!Zip & ""
    End With
End Sub
```

Running the Program

As you run the program, you can create new windows for each customer that you add, or change the status of the Create New Form menu item to display each customer in the same window. Try it out. As stated before, this example is merely an illustration of the concept, so feel free to add your own enhancements to the program. The MDI contact manager is shown in Figure 20.21.

Part
IV

Ch
20

FIG. 20.21

You can display multiple clients at the same time.

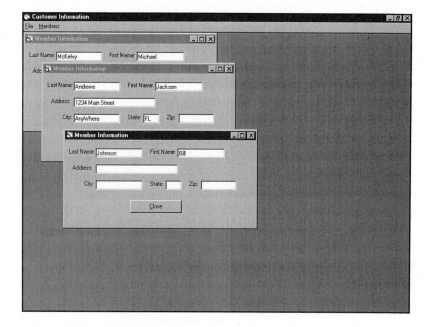

Optimizing Your MDI Application

This chapter has demonstrated a number of techniques that you can use to create MDI applications. As you can see, the MDI form can be a powerful tool for creating programs. However, there are several considerations to keep in mind to optimize your MDI applications. These considerations help keep the performance of your programs as crisp as possible and help keep your users from running into problems. The considerations are:

- Each new child window that is loaded consumes memory. Having memory-intensive child windows causes your application to drain memory quickly, so keep the amount of code and the number of controls in your child windows to a minimum.

- If your child and parent windows have the same menu commands (such as File Open or File Exit), keep the code in the parent. This means your child form's menu Click event procedures should simply call the parent menu's Click event procedure for all shared code.

- Change all of your menu Click event procedures from Private to Public so your child and parent windows can share these events.

- Avoid using the Name property of your child form. Instead, your child forms should use Me (or nothing at all), and your parent form should use ActiveForm.

- Put *all* invisible controls (such as a common dialog control or image list) on the MDI parent form. This allows all of your child windows to share these controls, without consuming extra memory.

Adhering to these concepts both simplifies your code and improves the performance of your MDI application.

Creating an MDI Application Framework

The code shown in this section is designed to provide a basic skeleton for any MDI applications that you create. The skeleton code can be modified to suit your specific needs. Then you can use the skeleton project as a template for your other MDI applications. The completed application is shown in Figure 20.22.

FIG. 20.22

Creating a template project can simplify your future MDI work.

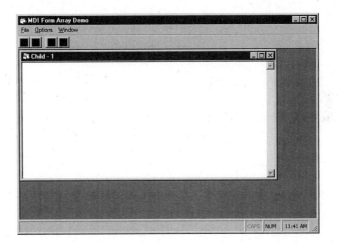

Creating the MDI Parent Template

The MDI parent form is the keeper (or container) of the child windows, so it is responsible for creating new children. With this duty, it is common for the parent to also keep track of the number of child windows it has created. In addition, the parent usually holds shared user interface elements like a toolbar, status bar, and so on.

The following code in Listing 20.7 shows the code used to maintain and expose the window count. WindowCreate and WindowDestroyed are called by the child windows in their Form_Load and Form_Unload event procedures, respectively. ChildWindowCount is a Public property that allows the child windows to find out how many children are loaded.

> **Listing 20.7   MDIPARENT.FRM—Use the Parent to Contain Common Code for All the Child Forms**

```
'*******************************************************************
' MDIParent.frm - Demonstrates some basic concepts on how a MDI parent
'   form should behave in an MDI application.
'*******************************************************************
```

continues

Part

IV

Ch

20

Listing 20.7   Continued

```
Option Explicit
Private mintChildWinCount As Integer
'*********************************************************************
' Returns how many child windows have been created
'*********************************************************************
Public Property Get ChildWindowCount() As Integer
    ChildWindowCount = mintChildWinCount
End Property
'*********************************************************************
' Called when a window is created to increment the window counter
'*********************************************************************
Public Sub WindowCreated()
    mintChildWinCount = mintChildWinCount + 1
    UpdateButtons True
End Sub
'*********************************************************************
' Called when a window is created to decrement the window counter
'*********************************************************************
Public Sub WindowDestroyed()
    mintChildWinCount = mintChildWinCount - 1
    UpdateButtons mintChildWinCount
End Sub
```

You also might notice a call to UpdateButtons in Listing 20.7. This private helper routine enables and disables toolbar buttons. If children exist, then the toolbar buttons are enabled. When the last child is unloaded, WindowDestroyed decrements the variable mintChildWinCount to 0, which causes UpdateButtons to disable the toolbar buttons.

The most important code in MDIPARENT.FRM is the File menu's Click event procedure. This code is responsible for creating windows, opening files, and terminating the application. Because all of these actions on the MDI parent file menu are also on the child form's file menu, you make this event public as shown in Listing 20.8.

Listing 20.8   MDIPARENT.FRM—Handling Menu *Click* Events

```
'*********************************************************************
' File menu handler for the MDI form when no windows are displayed.
' In this demo the child windows will have a menu just like this,
' so we will make this Public so the children can call this event.
'*********************************************************************
Public Sub mnuFileItems_Click(Index As Integer)
    Select Case Index
        '*********************************************************************
        ' File New - Create a new child form, then display it.
        '*********************************************************************
        Case 1
            Dim frmNew As New frmChild
            frmNew.Visible = True
        '*********************************************************************
```

```
        ' File Open - Prompt the user for a filename, then load
        '    it into the child window (in OpenFile) if the user didn't
        '    press cancel in the dialog.
        '**************************************************************
        Case 2
            On Error Resume Next
            With cdlg
                .Flags = cdlOFNFileMustExist
                .Filter = "Text Files (*.txt)¦*.txt¦All Files (*.*)¦*.*"
                .ShowOpen
            End With
            If Err <> cdlg.cdlCancel Then OpenFile cdlg.filename
        '**************************************************************
        ' Index 3 is the separator, so don't do anything.
        '**************************************************************
        'Case 3
        '**************************************************************
        ' File Exit - Terminate the application
        '**************************************************************
        Case 4
            Unload Me
    End Select
End Sub
```

When the File New menu item is clicked (Index = 1), the Dim frmNew As New frmChild line creates a new instance of your child form. However, this doesn't really create the new form. The form is actually created as soon as you access one if its properties or methods. This means that the frmNew.Visible = True line is the line of code that creates the form. After the form is created, the Visible property is set to True, which displays your form.

TIP

Forms created using New are hidden by default, so remember to display them by setting Visible = True.

The File Open (Index = 2) code in Listing 20.8 simply displays an Open dialog box so the user can supply a file name. If the user doesn't click Cancel, then the file is opened using the OpenFile routine, as presented in Listing 20.9. The last item in the select statement is Index 4, which represents the File Exit case. This is an easy one because the proper way to terminate an MDI application is to unload the MDI form.

As mentioned earlier, the OpenFile code is responsible for opening a text file and loading it into a text box on your child form. This code is very simplistic and includes no basic error handling for such cases as testing for files greater than 44K under Windows 95. However, it does provide a basic example of how to load a file into a text box, which is sufficient for this example.

CAUTION

Avoid using the End statement to terminate your applications. End terminates your application immediately, which prevents your Form_Unload events from being executed. The best way to end an MDI application is to unload the MDI form.

Part
IV

Ch
20

Listing 20.9   MDIPARENT.FRM—Shared Code

```
'****************************************************************
' Code shared among the child windows should be put in either a
' module or the MDI parent form.  This OpenFile code will be used
' by all of the children, so we will keep it in the MDI parent form.
'****************************************************************
Public Sub OpenFile(strFileName As String)
    Dim strFileContents As String
    Dim intFileNum As Integer
    '****************************************************************
    ' Get a free file handle
    '****************************************************************
    intFileNum = FreeFile
    '****************************************************************
    ' Open the file
    '****************************************************************
    Open strFileName For Input As intFileNum
        '****************************************************************
        ' Put the contents of the file into the txtData control of
        ' the child form. This code will fail if the file is too
        ' large to fit in the textbox, so you should include
        ' additional error handling in your own code.
        '****************************************************************
        With ActiveForm
            .txtData.Text = Input$(LOF(intFileNum), intFileNum)
            '****************************************************************
            ' Set the caption of the child form to the filename
            '****************************************************************
            .Caption = strFileName
        End With
    '****************************************************************
    ' Always close files you open as soon as you are done with them
    '****************************************************************
    Close intFileNum
End Sub
```

You might notice that the OpenFile routine simply loads the file into the text box on the active window by referencing the ActiveForm property. This is a valid assumption to make, because the active menu will always refer to the active form. Because the user can open a file via the menu (even if he is using the toolbar), you can always assume that any actions you perform in your menu event handlers should be applied to the active form.

The MDI Child

Now that you have had a chance to understand what your MDI parent form is responsible for, let's take a look at how the child should behave in this parent/child relationship.

As mentioned earlier, child forms are responsible for calling the WindowCreated and WindowDestroyed methods of the MDI parent form. Listing 20.10 demonstrates how this is done from the `Form_Load` and `Form_Unload` events. In addition, your child window sets its initial caption based on the MDI parent `ChildWindowCount` property. Although this technique is good for this sample, you might want to make your algorithm for setting your initial caption a little more complex. What do you think would happen if you had three windows, closed the second window, and then created a new window? How could you avoid this problem?

Listing 20.10   MDICHILD.FRM—Use the Child Form for Code Specific to Each Child

```
'*********************************************************************
' MDIChild.frm - Demonstrates some basic techniques on how a MDI child
'    window should behave.
'*********************************************************************
Option Explicit
'*********************************************************************
' When a new form is created it should call the WindowCreated function
' in the MDI parent form (which increments the window count in this
' case). It should also set its caption to distinguish it from other
' child windows.
'*********************************************************************
Private Sub Form_Load()
    MDIParent.WindowCreated
    '*********************************************************************
    ' This works, but it has a fatal flaw.
    '*********************************************************************
    Caption = Caption & " - " & MDIParent.ChildWindowCount
End Sub
'*********************************************************************
' Make sure txtData always fills the client area of the form.
'*********************************************************************
Private Sub Form_Resize()
    txtData.Move 0, 0, ScaleWidth, ScaleHeight
End Sub
'*********************************************************************
' Let the MDI parent know that this window is being destroyed.
'*********************************************************************
Private Sub Form_Unload(Cancel As Integer)
    MDIParent.WindowDestroyed
End Sub
```

One other minor detail you might have noticed in this code is the `Form_Resize` event. This code makes sure your TextBox control always covers the entire client area of the form. This code works with any control, so keep this in mind for your own applications.

Another important concept mentioned previously is that your child forms should use event handlers of the parent menu whenever possible (and vice versa). Listing 20.11 contains the event handlers for all of the menus used by MDICHILD.FRM.

Listing 20.11 MDICHILD.FRM—Handling the Menu Code for the Application

```
'********************************************************************
' Since the child File menu is identical to the MDI parent File menu,
' we should avoid duplicate code by calling the parent's mnuFileItems
' click event.
'********************************************************************
Private Sub mnuFileItems_Click(Index As Integer)
    MDIParent.mnuFileItems_Click Index
End Sub
'********************************************************************
' The options menu is unique to the child forms, so the code should
' be in the child form or separate BAS module.
'********************************************************************
Public Sub mnuOptionsItems_Click(Index As Integer)
    '********************************************************************
    ' Don't stop for errors
    '********************************************************************
    On Error Resume Next
    '********************************************************************
    ' Show the color dialog (since all menu items here need it)
    '********************************************************************
    MDIParent.cdlg.ShowColor
    '********************************************************************
    ' If the use selected cancel, then exit
    '********************************************************************
    If Err = cdlCancel Then Exit Sub
    '********************************************************************
    ' Otherwise set the color based on the value returned from the dlg
    '********************************************************************
    Select Case Index
        Case 1 'Backcolor...
            txtData.BackColor = MDIParent.cdlg.Color
        Case 2 'Forecolor...
            txtData.ForeColor = MDIParent.cdlg.Color
    End Select
End Sub
'********************************************************************
' If you set your indexes of your Window menu properly, you can save
' yourself some code. I was careful to make sure my Window menu items
' indices were equivalent to the possible values for the Arrange
' method.
'********************************************************************
Private Sub mnuWindowItems_Click(Index As Integer)
    MDIParent.Arrange Index
End Sub
```

The first menu is the File menu, which is identical to the parent form, so you simply call the mnuFileItems_Click event in the parent for default processing. The second menu is the Options menu, which only appears in the child form, so you write your implementation code here. However, you make this event handler public so it could be accessed by your Toolbar control, which resides on the parent form. In addition, you use the CommonDialog control on the parent for your code, which displays the color dialog box.

Creating Online Help

Almost every Windows application provides its own Help system. If you think that adding custom Help to your application is as hard as creating your application, you are wrong. In fact, most applications use the built-in Windows Help system and provide only a Help file (.HLP) that the Windows system can use. Deciding what to put into the Help file is the hardest part of the process.

While this chapter cannot answer the question of what should be in the Help file, it will show you how to build, compile, and test the Help files you need to add to your Visual Basic application. In addition, you will see the different techniques you can use to include Help in your application. ■

 T I P If any menu item on your child form requires greater than 12 lines or so of code (excluding `Dims`, comments, and white space), you should move that code to a shared module or into the parent form. That prevents this code from consuming too much free memory every time a new form is added.

Finally, you have your <u>W</u>indow menu that only applies to child forms (although it is the parent form that is responsible for this menu). By carefully creating your menu control array indexes, you are able to write the implementation code for this menu using only one line of code.

From Here...

This chapter has provided you with an introduction to creating MDI applications using Visual Basic. For more information about some of the related topics covered in this chapter, see the following chapters:

- To learn more about setting up forms, see Chapter 4, "Working with Forms and Controls."

- To learn more about creating menus and toolbars, see Chapter 5, "Adding Menus and Toolbars to Your Program."

- To learn more about property procedures, see Chapter 18, "Introduction to Classes."

- To learn more about creating database programs, see Chapter 31, "Improving Data Access with Data Access Objects (DAO)."

Part
IV

Ch
20

Listing 21.1 CONSTITUTION.TXT—Topic Text for the Constitution of the United States

```
The Constitution of the United States has been
the supreme law of the nation since 1789. Drafted
at the Constitutional Convention in Philadephia,
it calls for a government of limited and delegated
powers. Fifty-five delegates representing twelve
states drafted the document; all 13 states had
ratified it by May 29, 1790. The First U.S. Congress
drafted 12 amendments, from which the states ratified
10. Those 10 amendments became known as the Bill
of Rights.
```

Now, insert a page break into the file and then enter the text shown in Listing 21.2. Repeat this process for the remaining text in Listings 21.3, 21.4, and 21.5.

Listing 21.2 PREAMBLE.TXT— Text for the Pop-Up Window Shown from the Constitution Topic

```
We the People of the United States, in Order to
form a more perfect Union, establish Justice,
insure domestic Tranquility, provide for the common
defence, promote the general Welfare, and secure the
Blessings of Liberty to ourselves and our Posterity, do
ordain and establish this Constitution for the United
States of America.
```

Listing 21.3 MAIN.TXT—Description of the Declaration of Independence

```
The Declaration of Independence is the document in
which American colonists proclaimed their freedom from
British rule. The Second Continental Congress, with
representatives of the 13 British colonies in America,
adopted the declaration on July 4, 1776. The document
included an expression of the colonists' grievances and
their reasons for declaring freedom from Britain. The
Declaration of Independence's eloquent rhetoric and political
significance rank it as one of the great historical documents.
```

Listing 21.4 DECLARATION.TXT—Opening Text from the Declaration of Independence

```
When in the Course of human events, it becomes necessary
for one people to dissolve the political bands which have
connected them with another, and to assume among the Powers
of the earth, the separate and equal station to which the
```

Laws of Nature and of Nature's God entitle them, a decent
respect to the opinions of mankind requires that they should
declare the causes which impel them to the separation.

On the CD

Listing 21.5   FLAG.TXT—Text Describing the United States Flag

The American flag contains 13 stripes to signify the
original 13 colonies and the stars on the blue background
represents the states of the union.

When completed, your document should look like the one displayed in Figure 21.10. These separate pages of text will become your final Help file, with a little formatting.

FIG. 21.10

The Word document shows the text that was entered onto different pages.

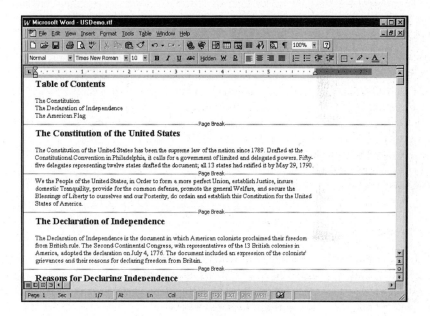

Labeling the Different Topics   Now that you have five topics, you need to identify each one by assigning a *topic ID*, which makes it possible for WinHelp to find them. Footnotes are used to create these topic IDs. You will use three symbols in the footnote area to set up the important features of the Help system. Table 21.1 lists each of these symbols and their functions.

Part

IV

Ch

21

Table 21.1	Custom Footnote Symbols for the Help Text File
Symbol	**Description**
#	Connects a jump page to its jump word or phrase by referencing the jump tag
$	References the jump page title, which will appear in the Help system's Search list box
K	Defines a keyword that the user can then search for in the Index tab

In the footnote section, the # symbol is used to connect a topic page with its jump tag. This identifies each topic in the Help system. Each tag must be unique within the Help system. Although the compiler can successfully compile topics that do not have jump tags, the user of the Help system will be unable to view these topics unless they contain keywords for which to search.

The $ is used to define the title for each Help topic in the file. Titles usually appear at the beginning of the topic, and in the Bookmark menu and Search list box, if the topic contains keywords.

The final symbol, K, is used to specify the topic keywords that may be used to search for related topics. The WinHelp system lists matching topics by their titles in the Search dialog box. This symbol is the only one of the three that allows listing of multiple words or phrases. The following footnote example shows a keyword list for the topic titled "aligning," which is found in the Microsoft Word Help system.

```
K drawing object;graphics;tables;text
```

The custom footnote symbol(s) must be the first items that appear on the jump page, followed by the Help topic title, if any, and then by any text that you want in the topic. To insert a footnote in Word, position the cursor at the beginning of the page and then select Footnote from the Insert menu. This displays the Footnote and Endnote dialog box (see Figure 21.11). You want to use the Custom Mark selection on the form.

FIG. 21.11

Inserting footnotes is easy by using the Footnote and Endnote dialog box.

Click the Custom Mark option button and then enter one of the three symbols previously described. When you click the OK button, the screen splits into two windows, one showing the jump page, and the other showing the footnotes (see Figure 21.12).

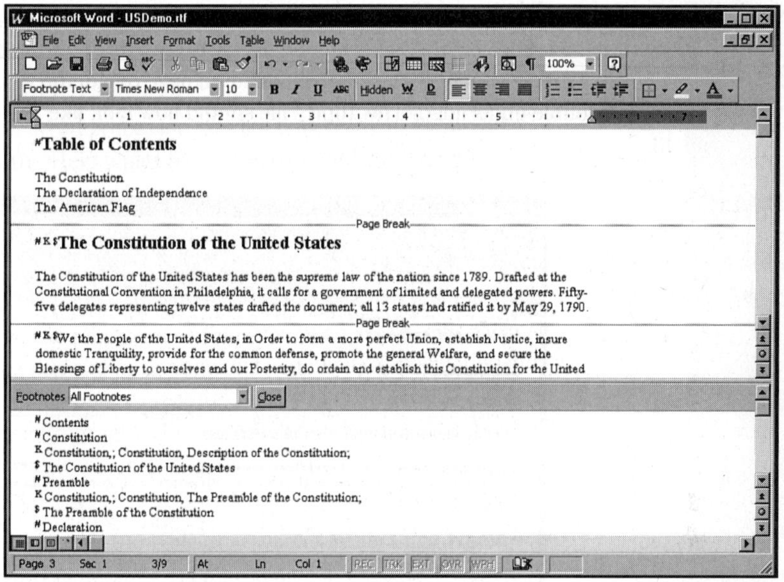

FIG. 21.12
The Word document shows the footnotes that were added.

Set the footnotes in Table 21.2 for each of the pages in the topic file. The custom footnote symbol that you should use is the #.

FIG. 21
When cre
Project fil
options a
to you.

F
S
e
u
s
w

Table 21.2   Footnote Settings for the Demo Help File

Page	Footnote Text
1	Contents
2	Constitution
3	Preamble
4	Declaration
5	Main
6	Flag

By setting these footnotes, you can now set the hyperlinks within each topic to allow the user to jump between topics. To set a link on a topic, you need to format the word or phrases that you want as the links. On the first page of the Help topic file, place the cursor at the end of the word *Constitution* and enter the topic ID phrase **Preamble**. Now, select the word *Constitution* and single-underline it. Next, select the word *Preamble* following the period and format it as Hidden text. This instructs the WinHelp system to display a pop-up window showing the text on the Preamble topic page. Notice that the hidden text that was entered matches the topic ID for the page to jump to.

Part
IV

Ch
21

N
ju
Fi
sh
21

FIG. 21.13
The topics file
hyperlinks an
for each topic

T
fl
v
l

{

F

Ad

FIG
Add
Help
the V
dialc

Adding Macros to the Help File

Help macros enable you to add more functionality to your Help system, which can be used to customize the way WinHelp works with your Help files. You can use more than 50 available macros.

T I P   For more information about Help macros, search for "Macro Quick Reference" in the Help index for the Help Workshop.

Help macros are routines built into the WinHelp program that give you the capability to add and remove custom buttons and menus, change the functions for buttons and menu items, and execute applications from within Help. In this demo, you will see how to add a macro that will execute Notepad so that users can take notes about what they are reading in the Help file.

The macro that you will use is the ExecProgram macro. This macro launches a Windows-based application from within your custom Help system. The syntax of this macro is as follows:

```
ExecProgram("CommandLine", DisplayState)
```

The "Commandline" is the command line for the application that you want to execute. This command must appear in quotes. WinHelp searches for this application in the following paths:

- Current directory
- Windows directory
- The user's path
- The directory of the currently displayed Help file

The $DisplayState$ parameter is a value that indicates how the application is to display when it is executed. The values of this parameter are:

Value	Description
0	Normal window
1	Minimized window
2	Maximized window

To add this macro as a button on each of the windows that you have defined, you need to use a second macro called CreateButton. The CreateButton macro is used to define a new button and to display it in your Help system's button bar. The syntax of this macro is as follows:

```
CreateButton(ButtonId, Caption, Macro)
```

The $ButtonId$ is a name that WinHelp uses to identify the button. This is a string and must be enclosed in quotes. This is also the value that you use in a DisableButton or DestroyButton macro to remove or disable the button.

The second parameter, *Caption*, is the text that appears to the user on the Button. To give the user Alt Key access, place an ampersand (&) before the correct letter in the string.

The last parameter, *Macro*, is the macro string that you want to execute when this button is clicked. This information must also be enclosed in quotes. The final macro that you add to your Help windows is:

```
CreateButton("Take_Note", "&Take Notes", "ExecProgram('notepad.exe', 0)")
```

Single quotes in the ExecProgram macro distinguish between the quotes for the CreateButton and the ExecProgram strings. Add the above macro to the macro tab of each window that is defined in your Help project.

To complete the process, recompile the Help file and then open it. You should see a new button on the button bar (see Figure 21.31). When you click this button, Windows Notepad should open.

FIG. 21.31
The demo Help system shows a new button that opens the Notepad application.

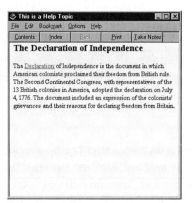

Accessing Help from a Visual Basic Application

In this section, you will learn how to access the Help system from within a Visual Basic application. There are several different methods for accessing the WinHelp system in Visual Basic. To learn how to use these methods, you will create a small Visual Basic application and add the different functions to the program. In this application, you will include a single form that will have several objects on it.

On this one form, you will add the different control objects and the program code to execute the various commands needed to display different topics from your Help file. From within Visual Basic, there are only three unique methods of calling Help. These methods are the following:

- The Windows 95 CommonDialog control
- Built-in Visual Basic Help Context features
- API calls to the WinHelp program

Part
IV

Ch
21

The

and the speed at which it executes to become more important issues to the programmer. You always want your application to run as fast and as efficiently as possible. Before the advent of Windows, a program was contained in one executable file, and if that file became too large, the program would not work very well. It relied on the programmers' skill to create compact code that would execute quickly.

Once Windows programming became commonplace, it was easier to control the size of an application. Applications now can be broken into smaller pieces that are executed only when needed. If you have been using Visual Basic for any length of time, you know that controls (.ocx) are one way of breaking the application into smaller pieces. With Visual Basic version 5, you have the capability to create not only your own custom controls, but also your own Dynamic Link Libraries (.dll) for your application to use. In addition to these methods for enhancing the performance of your application, there are some features of Visual Basic that you can use to minimize memory usage or to maximize the speed at which the program executes. As you probably know already, performance is very subjective. If the user thinks there is a problem in the application, then there *is* a problem, even if one doesn't exist.

When discussing performance, most people think of cars, not computers. However, in today's world of Pentium Pro processors and MMX technology, the computer's processing speed is closing in on the 300MHz range. This means that the users will expect better performance out of every application they install on their computers. However, as computers get faster, applications get larger in an effort to take advantage of the additional speed, so the overall performance doesn't necessarily change. To make your application as quick as possible requires some tuning or optimizing. One of the problems with tuning your application is that the changes you make may not always benefit you in the long run. Changes that you make to the application to improve its performance can cause the code to become more difficult to maintain or to change in the future. Sometimes a change can actually decrease an application's performance.

The user's first impression of your application is very important. This impression begins to form when the user first starts the application. If the application runs for a while before anything is displayed, the user starts to become impatient and assumes that the application does not perform well. The larger and more complex the first form is, the longer it will take to load and display. One of the simplest things that you can add to your application to give the impression of increased performance at startup time is the Splash dialog. If you use the Application Wizard that comes with Visual Basic 5, you will receive the option to include a Splash dialog in your application. If you did not use the Application Wizard, you can always add the Splash dialog later. A Splash dialog is nothing more than a small form that is displayed to the user while the more complex work is being done in the background. A good example of this is Visual Basic itself. When you start Visual Basic, first you see the Splash dialog and then you see the development environment. A example of a Splash dialog is shown in Figure 22.1.

In addition to using the Splash dialog to give the user a good first impression, you can improve your application by using more efficient calculations, variable types, and variable usage. When performing calculations, every data type that is available has its own drawbacks. If you use the *Variant* data type in your application, be aware that even though it is very useful, it is also the

FIG. :
Right-
Comm
to ope
Pages
contro

slowest data type for the computer to process. Each time you reference a Variant data type, the computer must check the data in the variable and create a temporary variable with the correct data type for the data used in the calculation. By using the correct data types for the data you will be accessing in the application, you will increase the performance of the application.

FIG. 22.1

Visual Basic displays this Splash dialog while it initializes the development environment.

The Professional or Enterprise edition of Visual Basic 5 now comes with a method of enhancing the application's performance that was never before available. You now can choose to compile your code either in standard Visual Basic p-code format or in native code format.

P-code, or *pseudocode*, is an intermediate step between the high-level instructions in your Basic program and the low-level *native code* your computer's processor executes. At run time, Visual Basic translates each p-code statement into native code. This takes some time when running an application. However, by compiling the application directly into native code format, you eliminate the intermediate p-code step and runtime compile. If you want more information about optimizing your application, check out the section "Designing for Performance and Compatibility," which can be found in Visual Basic Books Online that comes with the Visual Basic 5 product CD-ROM.

Error Handling

In a perfect world, the applications you create would not need any error handling at all. Unfortunately, you live in an imperfect world where users make mistakes, files are sometimes accidentally deleted, and disk drives run out of space. When designing and creating your application, you need to anticipate the types of errors that might occur in your application and how you can deal with them. If you create your application with no error handling in it, then you are giving Visual Basic the job of trapping any errors that occur and dealing with them on its own.

However, Visual Basic is not very forgiving when it comes to errors. If an application error occurs, Visual Basic displays the default message for that error and then closes the application. This usually occurs after the user has spent a large amount of time entering data but hasn't saved it yet. If the error is not one that Visual Basic can detect, then the application might continue without any messages being displayed and with unpredictable results.

To prevent this from happening, consider the issue of error handling and design it into your application from the beginning. This will also help you test the application because if something doesn't work and an error occurs, you will get messages from the application instead of Visual Basic closing the application.

Error handling is not limited to program and logic type errors. Error handling is needed when databases are accessed to prevent unwanted results. However, data-access errors are corrected in a different way than normal program errors. When you access the database, the method for handling any errors that might occur is different because these errors are caused by some problem with the database itself or the data being manipulated within the database. Because of this difference, data can be damaged if the error is handled incorrectly. You have to decide what action you want to perform when the error occurs. The action you choose depends on what was being done on the database when the error occurred. You might only need to tell the users that the data they are inputting is incorrect, or you might need to reverse an entire group of modifications done to the database.

If you have designed the application correctly and considered every error or problem that might occur, then you have done a good job. However, as someone once said a long time ago, "There will always be one more bug." This is why you need to supply technical support to users of your application.

▶ **See** "Working with Procedures," **p. 464**

▶ **See** "Database Access," **p. 514**

Support

When you call a software company for support, do you like the service you get? What would make it better? Providing customer support has to be one of the hardest things in the world to do. No matter how hard you try, you will never satisfy everyone. Most users will not call unless they have problems they cannot resolve on their own. Unfortunately, by that time they are annoyed with the product and you are starting behind the eight ball with an unhappy customer.

There is more to the support issue than just answering phones. You must consider the following issues and have a definite plan in place before distributing your application:

- Ease of contact
- Questions/Problems
- Upgrades
- Version support

You need to plan for each of these issues when you decide how to provide support. If you plan correctly, then your product will be well-received by the people who use it.

Ease of Contact   When you consider the issue of contact, think of the different means users have available to contact you for help. Some companies make it difficult for the user to get help by limiting the support to certain times of day. Decide how much or how little you want to support the application that you intend to sell. The following are the available options for providing customer support:

- Direct phone number
- Toll-free phone support
- Fax machine to accept requests
- E-mail
- Internet Web site

Each of these options has its own unique problems and expenses. The best way to offer support is over the phone. However, unless you plan to be available 24 hours a day, 7 days a week to answer the phone, you will need to either hire someone to answer the phone or use an answering machine. The first option is expensive to maintain, and many people have difficulty talking to an answering machine. Another way to handle customer support is to allow the user to fax in questions or problems. In both the phone and the fax options, you need to determine how long the response time will be to return a call or a fax. In my experience, if you try to get back to the user within 24 hours, then the user perceives that your support and your efforts to solve their problems are good.

The newest and hottest way to supply support is to make use of the World Wide Web. Many companies are creating Web sites that not only tell users about the company and its products, but also allow users to send questions and report problems to the company. Additionally, the Web makes it very easy for the user to download fixes to problems they might have.

Deciding which way you want to support your application is up to you and your budget. However, you must pick one or more of these options and then implement them before you start selling the application.

Questions/Problems Now that you have users calling, faxing, or e-mailing problems and questions to you, how are you going to handle them? You should develop a good way of tracking both the users who are calling and their questions or problems. This not only helps you keep track of who your users are, but it also helps you pinpoint the questions that are being repeated. This will help you update the application with better technical support or with new features that enhance the application's functionality. In addition, if you have a Web site, you can create a Frequently Asked Questions (FAQ) page.

Dealing with problems is a little different than dealing with questions. You can usually answer questions that deal with how your application works easily enough. However, you need to obtain more information to resolve a specific problem. When you take a problem report, ask the user for every shred of information that you might need to figure out the problem. The following list contains some of the information you should request from a user reporting a problem:

- The version of the application being used
- The type and speed of the user's computer
- The amount of memory on the user's computer
- The content of the error message that was displayed

- Exactly what the user was doing when the error occurred
- Any changes that might have been made to the PC (hardware or software)

Of all these items, the last one is the most difficult—getting enough specificity from the user. You often will hear that the user started the application and then it "blew up." Now, this is not very descriptive of what really happened. You need to know what the user typed, which function keys the user pressed, or which command buttons the user clicked. These bits of information are very important when trying to narrow down the possible problem(s).

Sometimes, when a problem is very hard to figure out, you can come up with a way around the problem. This is called a *workaround*—it doesn't fix the problem, but the user can continue working with the application while you attempt to solve the problem. Workarounds are important because there will be times that a problem takes a long time to fix or cannot be fixed without major changes to the application. You then need to decide if you want to start on the next version of the application or the same version that includes the fixes.

Upgrades   After you decide to create a new version of the application, you have to figure out how the current users of the application can upgrade to this version. If you design the next version without taking this into consideration, users of your current version will be annoyed if you ask them to start from scratch with a new release of the product. Think of how you would feel if you had an application that you spent months learning and entering information into, only to receive a new release that provides no way of moving your preexisting data into it. Keep this in mind or you will soon start losing customers to other products that support this type of upgrade.

Another thing to consider with upgrades is how they will be distributed. Has everything in the application changed or just a few things? You need to have two separate sets of distribution disks—one for new users and the other for current users who are upgrading to the new release. Generally, upgrades should contain fixes to problems that have popped up, as well as any new features and functions. This gives the current users a reason to buy the upgrade and new users a reason to try out the application.

Creating the Package Components

Putting all of the components together takes some time. After you have designed, built, and tested your application, you need to bring it all together into a complete package. There are two main areas that you need to deal with when pulling the package together. The easier of the two areas is the actual creation of the distribution disks for the product. The other area is dealing with all of the legal issues that protect you and your software from theft and liability.

Dealing with the Legal Issues

Dealing with legal issues might sound intimidating; however, legal issues are not all that mysterious. The different issues that must be considered are:

- Product registration
- Software theft

- Product copyright
- Product name trademark

Product registration and software theft involve two sides of the same issue. There is no inexpensive way to prevent someone from copying your distribution disks after you send them to a user. However, if you have your users register when they purchase the product, you can track who the legal owners of your software are. The incentive to register a new product is the availability of support and the receipt of notification for any upgrades or new versions. By assigning a serial number to each copy of your software, you can keep an accurate record of which user has which copy. When providing support to a user, one of the first questions that you should ask is, "What is the serial number of the product?" Then, if the name of the user does not match your records, you have caught someone using your software without paying for it. If you do catch someone doing this, you need to decide the course of action you will take.

You need to protect yourself from the possible theft of your idea, design, or the implementation of your product. By copyrighting your software, you protect your software from unauthorized copying.

N O T E The amount of protection provided by a copyright is proportionate to your desire to take legal action against someone who has used your idea.

CAUTION

Although you can copyright the source code, Help files, and manual for your application, you *cannot* copyright the actual idea or screen design. If you intend to copyright your software, you should do it before you start selling the application. For information about how to apply for a copyright, call or write to:

Publications Section
LM-455
Copyright Office
Library of Congress
Washington D.C. 20559
(202) 707-3000

N O T E A copyright registration is considered effective on the date the copyright office receives all of the required elements in an acceptable format. You should use some type of return receipt to know when it gets to the copyright office.

Whether to trademark the name you choose for your application is the next decision you need to make. Having a trademark for your product prevents someone else from legally using the name. For example, Microsoft would sue another company who tried to use the name Windows for its PC operating system. However, trademarks take time and money. Some developers choose not to spend the time or money and instead take their chances on the name that they choose. Unfortunately, if someone else trademarks the name that they are using, developers without the trademark have to change the name of their product at their own expense. A copyright costs about $50 and a trademark submission costs approximately $200.

> **CAUTION**
>
> If your trademark is rejected, you do not get a refund of your application fee.

There are many other rules and regulations concerning the submission and acceptance of a trademark. You should get the information from the Trademark Office as soon as you can. It can take from 3–9 months to get a trademark approved. If you choose a name and create the documentation before the trademark is approved, you stand the risk of having to redo everything if the name is denied. For more information about trademarks, call or write to:

U.S. Department of Commerce
Patent and Trademark Office
Washington D.C. 20231
(703) 308-4357

Using the Setup Wizard

The Setup Wizard program helps you create a professional-looking installation program for your application. In addition to the standard install process, the Setup Wizard includes the files and programs needed by the users to uninstall your application if they want. Visual Basic also comes with the source code that is used to create the setup program. This Toolkit can be used to add additional code that displays customized forms to the user. An example of a custom form can be seen when installing Visual Basic 5 (see Figure 22.2).

FIG. 22.2

Example Options form displayed during the setup process.

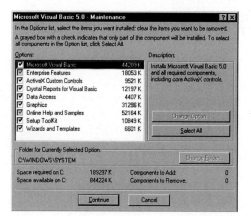

The Setup Wizard takes you through several steps that prompt you for the information needed to create the final setup program. Following are the steps you have to follow to create the final setup program:

N
a
p
s

E
o
f

E
pa
pr
ac
of

From

Th
se
ch
ca
sh
me

If the directo
the directory
ard lets you s
also specify t

The differenc

- *Jet* (db
- *ODBC*
  setup.

N O T E You
proc

In the next se
items that you

- ActiveX
- Applica
- Configu

After making
you can comp
save all of the
enables you tc
entering all of

FIG. 22.5
Saving the template
before completing the
setup creation.

Setup Wizard
Remember, if
ready to use.

After you have
reason for test

1. Select the project and options.
2. Choose the distribution method.
3. Specify the installation destination.
4. Add any ActiveX Server Components.
5. Include any application-specific files.
6. Save the template and build the setup program.

The Setup Wizard then compresses all of the selected files. Depending on which installation setup option you choose, the Setup Wizard asks for disks or simply copies the files to the specified hard drive directory. The Setup Wizard will display several dialog boxes that ask you to either enter required information or confirm the information the Setup Wizard has found. When you start the Application Setup Wizard, you will see an introduction form display. Then, when you click Next, you are prompted to enter the path and file name for your application's project .VBP file (see Figure 22.3).

FIG. 22.3
The Setup Wizard form showing the Project File and Action Options Selection.

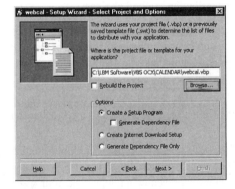

Besides the obvious information that is needed on the first dialog box, you will need to select which type of installation program you want to create. The default action is to create a setup program. This is what you normally choose for a standard Visual Basic application. However, if you are creating an ActiveX control for use on the Internet, you select the second action option. Finally, you can choose to create a dependency file along with the setup program, or by itself.

N O T E A dependency file is used by the Setup Wizard to determine the files that are required by any object of an .ocx, .dll, or .exe ActiveX component, or a project that can be used as a component in other projects. ▪

If you are using components that you have created, you should run the Setup Wizard for those components to create a dependency file for each of them. Setup Wizard looks for these files and uses them to include any other related files that are needed for these components to work. The Setup Wizard displays a list of components for which it can't find the associated dependency files. For any components listed, you should go back and create the needed dependency file before continuing the Setup Wizard process for your application.

After you selec
tion (see Figur

FIG. 22.4
Selecting the distribu-
tion method for your
application.

The following a

- *Floppy D*
  intend to
  required
- *Single D*
  directory
  from whi
  for distri
- *Disk Dir*
  example,
  ries as if
  program
  disks fro

Depending on
displayed. The
for the installat
path to copy the
directory path.
the disk image

TIP You should delete
The Setup Wizard

CAUTION
You cannot choc

---

be
PC
app
exi
sur
use

N C

all

Tes
trat

Distribu

Wh
link
righ
lice
type

▶ S

If yc
cen

Sharev

Whe
proc
into
proc
ucts
softv
shar
rece
shar

The
user
shou
seco
the p

Object technologies need an underlying framework that can enable complex and interrelated programs to work together in harmony. The object architecture Microsoft created is called the Component Object Model, or simply COM. COM is the foundation underlying OLE and ActiveX technologies and is Microsoft's solution for providing object-to-object communication. With the enhancements of the Distributed Component Object Model (DCOM), this technology even provides communication services across networks to objects physically located on differ-ent machines. ■

Object Technology Basics

A basic understanding of COM, OLE, and ActiveX is vital for your success in programming with Visual Basic. You can still use straight programming language to create procedural code, and sometimes that's necessary and appropriate, but doing so can limit the benefits of using an object-oriented design. This chapter focuses on object-oriented foundations.

Benefits of Object-Oriented Programming

Users of custom corporate computer applications continue to demand more functionality from their aging systems, and they are becoming less patient about waiting for new functions to be implemented. Because legacy computer systems tend to be monolithic collections of original code, maintenance code, integration code, and lingering "quick fix" code, these applications have become dramatically more difficult and costly to maintain. Changing key sections of these fragile constructions to add new features is fraught with peril, especially if these applications are part of a mission-critical system. To make matters worse, such applications might be only sparsely documented (if at all), and only rarely are any members of the original programming team still working for the company. If you've ever been faced with the task of extending the life of such an application, you know there must be a better way to build and maintain enterprise-wide computer systems. Fortunately, there is.

Suppose your company, like many companies, has a legacy application that might give unpredict-able results for dates beyond the year 1999. Suppose that instead of being a single, massive col-lection of procedural code, this application was built from functional modules. Each module has a very specific purpose, and calling that module is the only way for the application to perform that specific task. Thus, in this scenario, one dedicated code module has the task of performing all date calculations, and any other module in the entire application relies on that module for any and all date calculations. To test the capability of this program to handle dates beyond the year 2000, you only have to test that date-calculation module to see what happens. If it needs repair, you can change the implementation inside of that module, test it, and then plug it back into the program to complete your task. If the date storage and retrieval module also poses a problem, you can use a similar procedure to test, repair, and restore that module. Instead of this scenario, however, most companies are paying staggering costs to update hundreds of thousands of lines of legacy code, in some cases line-by-line.

With the pace of change in today's business world, companies can no longer afford to create systems that cannot be updated easily. This modular approach exists and is available now.

These magic little modules are known abstractly as *Objects*. Computer-modeled objects can be implemented in software as discrete components that can be created, modified, or reused as building blocks for complex, enterprise-wide applications. Rebuilding existing functionality from scratch is admittedly quite costly and time-consuming. However, after the foundation is in place, you no longer have to start over repeatedly from scratch to create each new application because a large portion of your desired functionality can be constructed from previously built components.

Part

V

Ch

23

Imagine how long it would take for new computers to be developed if computer hardware manufacturers had to start from scratch every time they wanted to build a new computer. Many of the components of a new computer don't require changes since the last model was released, so existing components (such as power supply, video card, network interface card, or modem) are simply reused. Eventually, when new designs are implemented, the new item can easily replace the previous model, with perhaps a modification of that particular interface, but without having to redesign the entire computer.

After the computer is sold to a user, upgrading a component is also simplified by this modular approach. For example, suppose you want to upgrade to a faster modem. You can select your new modem from a variety of vendors, and any modem supported by your operating system will work just fine. You don't need to worry if the modem will work because modems have become a commodity by using standard interfaces and communication protocols.

Software developers are now seeking the tremendous advantages of component architecture that hardware developers have enjoyed for years. By using component-based software architectures, you can implement object-oriented designs, yet maintain a large degree of language neutrality. This enables corporations to make use of existing programming talent in any language supported by the object model implemented on their computer platform. This language neutrality is accomplished by using programming tools that create components that are compatible at the binary level. This process enables programmers around the globe to independently develop components or entire applications that will properly communicate together, as long as the interfaces defined between them remain consistent. These components might originally be created for internal applications, but they can then be shared within the company or even marketed to other companies who have similar needs.

If you are not already familiar with object-oriented programming, you will likely need to invest some time to learn how to implement this new technology effectively. The effort you spend now to become proficient with this technology will reward you with increased productivity, job satisfaction, and job security.

After your development team invests the initial time and energy required to implement object oriented development, the advantages to your company are also worth noting:

- Many of the objects representing standard business functions can be reused, reducing the time required to build new programs and the overall cost of maintaining them.
- When maintenance is required, new versions of individual objects can replace older versions easily, without breaking the application.

■ As needs change, new objects can be relocated transparently to new platforms and even to other computers across the network, still without breaking the applications.

■ Large and complex programming projects that would seem nearly impossible when using other techniques can now be conquered much more easily.

■ The time and expense required to integrate existing application with new applications and to perform emergency repairs on applications will gradually decline as more objects are implemented.

■ The recovered programmer hours can be redirected toward backlogged projects and new initiatives.

You might be wondering if your favorite programming language is able to support object-based application development. A major benefit of COM is that it defines a common binary standard. This means that COM defines an interface as a low-level binary API based on a table of memory pointers, which then enables code modules from different COM-compliant compilers to operate together. Theoretically, a COM-compatible compiler can be built for any programming language that can create memory structures using pointers and can call functions through pointers. Visual Basic includes a COM-compatible compiler.

The result is that client objects implemented in Visual Basic can call on the services of server objects written Visual C++, and vice versa. Each language has certain advantages when creating COM objects, but when used together, they are a powerful combination with which you can tackle nearly any programming challenge you encounter.

A Quick Review of Object-Oriented Programming Terms and Notation

Object-Oriented Programming (OOP) presents a revolutionary improvement in the architecture and tools used to build and maintain computer applications. There are a variety of object-oriented methodologies to choose from, and most are named after the individuals who proposed them. If you want to investigate them in detail, today's leading object-oriented methodologies include Booch, Coad-Yourdon, Jacobsen, Martin-Odell, Rumbaugh, Shalaer-Mellor, and Wirfs-Brock. Despite this wide variety of methodologies, the underlying OOP concepts are essentially the same. To preclude any confusion over the meaning of the OOP terms used in this book, this section provides a brief review of common terms and notation used in object-oriented programming.

Understanding Objects   An OOP *object* can be thought of as a programming entity that in many ways resembles a physical object. OOP objects typically have properties that describe their attributes, and methods that specify their behavior. *Properties* of OOP objects can be much like properties of physical objects, describing attributes such as color, cost, or size. The programmer can set and lock these properties when designing the program or can make them available to the user to change during run time. *Methods* are the named functions an object is programmed to accomplish when called. Methods are invoked by referencing the object and the method's name. When called, the object behaves as defined by the method to obtain, manipulate, or destroy program data, without any requirement to reveal how these tasks are accomplished.

Objects are *portable*, which is to say they can be used without modification in any environment where they are supported. Objects are *reusable* because you can use the same object to perform the same task in different programs. Better yet, you can use objects other people have created if you want to quickly add a standard service or function to one of your own programming projects.

For the purpose of object-oriented programming, an individual object is a particular *instance* created from a particular *class* of objects. A class is a set of objects that you define to have the same attributes and behavior. Classes can be very specific or very general, depending on your needs. For example, you could define a class that encompasses all writing implements, or you could define a class that only represents wooden yellow pencils with number two lead. The *class structure* defines a generic blueprint or model of a new object of that class. Every OOP object belongs to a class, and is completely defined by its class structure.

To actually bring an object to life in the computer, a specific *instance* of the object must be *instantiated*, which is to say a new member of the class is created in memory.

When you define a class in code, you must define all of the object's methods, data structures, and interfaces. By default, the methods and data are reserved for the object's exclusive use and are declared as *private*. If you want to make methods and data available for direct manipulation by other objects, you can declare them as *public* when you define them in the class structure. Typically, you would define any methods and data you wish exposed for clients or used by the user interface as public, and define the internal elements that implement those services as private.

N O T E   C++ programmers have been programming by using object classes for years, but the class structure is a relatively new addition to the Visual Basic language. Support for object classes began with Visual Basic 4 and is further expanded in Visual Basic 5. As more wizards, integration options, and powerful C++ features (such as classes) have been added to Visual Basic, the stigma against using early versions of VB for anything but simple projects has vanished. Visual Basic is now quite suitable for creating robust and reliable enterprise-wide applications. ■

The OOP purists remind us that for an object to qualify as a "true" OOP object, it must support the characteristics of *encapsulation*, *polymorphism*, and *inheritance*. These distinctions are discussed in detail during the examination of the differences between object-*based* and object-*oriented* programming later in this chapter (see "Object-Oriented versus Object-Based Programming").

An object that provides services to another object is acting as a *server*. The object using those services is referred to as the *client*. An object can be both a client and a server at the same time; that is, it can request the services of one object while providing services to yet another object. For clarity, it usually is best to focus on a single relationship between two objects at a time, and denote one as the client and the other as the server.

Object Relationships When trying to design objects, it is handy to have a common method for representing these programming objects graphically. The syntax <object>.<method> can be used to denote invoking a particular method of the server object. There are many variations, but the typical way to represent an object graphically is represented in Figure 23.1.

FIG. 23.1

A COM object contains all the methods, properties, and data required by that object.

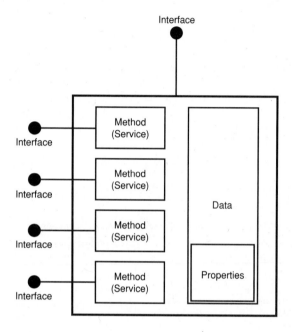

In Figure 23.1, the object and its contents are depicted as rectangles. The interface nodes as shown as circles connected to the object by a straight line extending from the object. Connections to the interfaces are implemented by using memory pointers, which can be drawn as arrows extending from the client object to the interface node of the server object.

When the client and server are operating in the same process space in the computer, the server is referred to as being *in process*, or as an *in-process server*. In-process servers provide the fastest possible service to the client. In-process servers are typically objects in the same program, or objects loaded into the same process space ahead of time from an external source such as a Dynamic Link Library (DLL) file. The relationship between a client and an in-process server is shown in Figure 23.2.

It is also possible for the server object to operate on the same computer as the client object but in a separate process space. In this situation, the server is called a *cross-process* or *out-of-process server*. Because there are two ways to have an out-of-process server, however, it is more specific to refer to this as a *local server*. For example, your spreadsheet becomes a local server to your word processor when you copy a table of numbers from the spreadsheet and paste it into your word processor. This relationship is depicted in Figure 23.3.

FIG. 23.2

This client object has obtained the services of a server object on the same computer and in the same process space. In this relationship, this server is a local, in-process server.

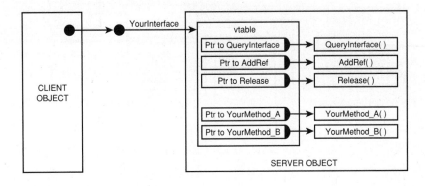

FIG. 23.3

This client object has obtained the services of a server object on the same computer, but outside of its process space. In this relationship, this server is a local, out-of-process server.

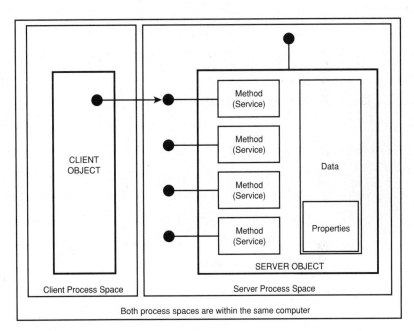

Part
V

Ch
23

The other way an out-of-process server occurs is when the client and server are on different computers. This once-rare situation is rapidly gaining in popularity as objects are distributed across computer networks. The out-of-process object providing the service in this case is called a *remote server*. Performance is typically slower than with in-process or local servers, but the gains in functionality and scalability can be revolutionary, as will be highlighted later when discussing distributed computing. The remote server relationship is depicted in Figure 23.4.

Objects that perform very specific tasks can be conveniently grouped together in a variety of ways. These object-grouping techniques are an effective way to reuse objects and minimize maintenance.

FIG. 23.4

This client object has obtained the services of a server object on another computer on the network. In this relationship, this server is a remote, out-of-process server.

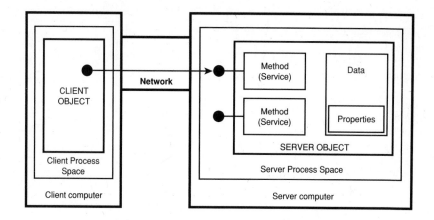

Perhaps the most straightforward way is to create a new object to act as a container in which you place the reused objects. This is referred to as *object containment*, because the outer object completely contains the inner objects. The interfaces of the inner objects are only visible to the outer object and cannot be accessed directly by external objects. This relationship is depicted in Figure 23.5.

FIG. 23.5

This outer object completely contains the interfaces and services of the inner objects. The inner objects are a collection of re-used and new objects that clients can access via communication with the new outer object

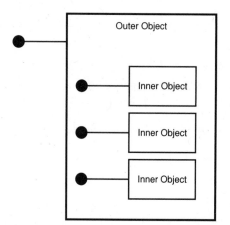

A related grouping method is created by starting with a containment relationship but allowing the outer object to pass along or *delegate* the connecting pointer from the client object directly to the inner object needed to implement the desired function. This is referred to as *object delegation* and is illustrated in Figure 23.6.

Finally, objects can be collected together, or *aggregated*, by an outer object that allows the inner objects to directly expose their interfaces to client objects. This is perhaps the most complicated case to implement, because the clients of the inner objects do not directly see the relationships between the inner and outer objects. This is referred to as *object aggregation* and is described in Figure 23.7.

FIG. 23.6
With object delegation, the client object first obtains a pointer to the external interface of the server. The server then provides the address of the inner object that can provide the requested service, and the client connects directly to the inner object.

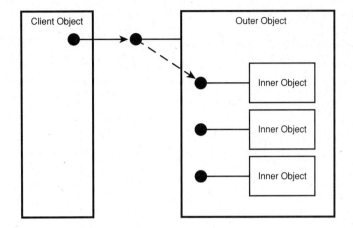

Part
V

Ch
23

FIG. 23.7
With object aggregation, the client object can directly access the exposed interfaces of each inner object in the server's collection.

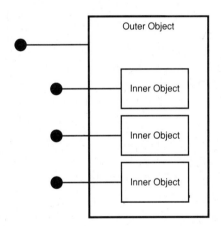

Object-Oriented versus Procedural Programming

Procedural programming is an approach where you determine the steps needed to solve a problem and implement them by creating the algorithms in code that act upon the data and store the resulting output separately from the algorithms. Object-Oriented Programming (OOP) is an approach where you can group a code module's related data and implementation code together into a unified structure, and it acts together in response to requests from other objects. SmallTalk and C-based software development languages have provided this OOP capability for years but are extremely cumbersome for all but dedicated experts. Today you can use Visual Basic (and Visual C++ and Visual J++, either separately or in combination) to create robust, enterprise-wide, object-oriented applications.

OOP Advanced Topics

In object-oriented programming, a discrete combination of code and data must represent each programming object. OOP also requires a way for client objects to dynamically create new instances of objects based on a given class, and to create and destroy server objects as needed, while the application is operating. In comparison, although object-based languages enable you to create object-like structures in code, creating another similar object means you must create it at design time, perhaps cutting and pasting code from the first object.

Furthermore, to qualify as a true OOP object, the programming structure must also support the characteristics of encapsulation, polymorphism, and inheritance. Entire books have been devoted to this, but for the purposes of this chapter, a brief explanation and some simple examples will suffice to illustrate the basic concepts.

Encapsulation

Encapsulation occurs when the desired services and data associated with an object are made available to the client through a predefined interface without revealing how those services are implemented. The client uses the server object's interfaces to request desired services, and the object performs on command without further assistance. For example, suppose you are developing a Domestic Simulator application. You might want to create a "spouse" object class where you define methods for common household tasks, such as methods called "WashDishes" and "MowTheLawn." If a client object (perhaps even another spouse object) determines it is time to invoke WashDishes, it can make that request via the interface you have appropriately named IWashDishes. The desired result might be that any instantiated "Dishes" object with a "Clean" property value currently set to False would be cleaned and set to True.

How this method is accomplished is irrelevant to the client. The WashDishes method can be performed with the time-honored "Wash in Sink" procedure or with any version of the popular "Automatic Dishwasher" procedure, but the end result will be the same. Similarly, the interface IMowTheLawn would be used to invoke the MowTheLawn method. In this case, the server object might be programmed to trim all "Grass" objects with a length property of greater than 3 inches down to an even 3 inches. This MowTheLawn method can use the slow but reliable "Rotary Mower" procedure, the faster "Power Mower" procedure, or the coveted "Riding Mower" procedure, but the end result will be the same. In each case, the simulated grass will be an acceptable length, and the client will have no need or desire to know how it got that way.

Objects can even encapsulate their own data from all other objects. By default, an object's data is considered *private*, and clients must call one of the object's methods to manipulate data or report data values. It is sometimes practical or necessary to expose the data to for direct manipulation by client objects, and this is accomplished by adding the *public* declaration when you define the object's class structure.

COM fully supports encapsulation, as COM permits a client object to access a server object only through its well-defined interfaces.

Polymorphism

Polymorphism is the capability for different kinds of objects to respond appropriately and differently to the same stimulus. In OOP, polymorphism can be seen as the capability for client objects to access the services of different server objects in the same syntactic manner, even when dealing with different types of objects. An illustration should help clarify this concept.

Returning to the Domestic Simulator program, suppose that to make the program more realistic, in addition to the "Spouse" class of objects, you also define object classes representing "Child" and "Dog." Suppose you have your program instantiate a Spouse object called "Katarina," a Child object called "BabyAlex," and a Dog object called "Rover." Still trying to make it realistic, you can individually define methods for each of these objects to appropriately simulate the behaviors of walking, eating, sleeping, and speaking. You can then have your program make a call to Rover.Speak and compare that result with a call to Rover.Eat to see if Rover's bark is worse than his bite. However, asking the spouse object to "Speak" by making a call to Katarina.Speak should give you a dramatically different result than the one produced when you call the Dog object to Speak. Asking the child object to Speak by using BabyAlex.Speak might give little or no result until the Domestic Simulator has run for a sufficient amount of time. Although all these requests are made in exactly the same way—by using the syntax <ObjectName>.Speak—the request produces different results, depending on the type of object. This is polymorphism in action.

COM supports polymorphism by allowing different classes of objects to support interfaces with the same name, while allowing these objects to implement the interfaces differently.

Inheritance

Inheritance is the capability to define increasingly more specific objects, starting with the existing characteristic definitions of general objects. Thus, when a more specific class of objects is desired, you can begin the definition by first inheriting all the characteristics of another defined class and then adding to them. Again, an example is useful to help explain this concept.

Again returning to the Domestic Simulator program, you can first define a class of objects called "Animal" to represent the common attributes of all animals in your simulation. Suppose the Animal class includes characteristics such as breathing and eating. From the Animal class, you can create sub-classes for "Wild_Animal" and "Pet_Animal." Both Wild_Animal and Pet_Animal objects automatically knows how to eat, but now you can define that Pet_Animal objects will eat only from their food bowls, whereas Wild_Animal objects will eat food wherever they find it, including your simulated garden and simulated trash containers. By adding specific characteristics in addition to the common characteristics of the Pet_Animal class, you can create classes for "PetDog," "PetCat," and any other kind of pet you want to share the house with in your simulation. With all this additional behavior defined in higher level classes, your previously mentioned polymorphic pet Rover can now be instantiated from the "PetDog" class, having completely inherited all the common characteristics you defined for a Pet_Animal and for Animals in general.

COM supports *interface inheritance*, which is the capability for one interface definition to inherit characteristics from another interface. COM, however, does not support *implementation inheritance*, which is the capability for one object to inherit the actual implementation code from another object. Implementation inheritance makes sense when an entire application is compiled in the same language. Because COM is standardized at the binary level, and not the language level, passing the actual implementation code between objects would produce unpredictable and potentially disastrous results. This subtle but important difference has sparked an ongoing debate about whether COM truly supports inheritance. For comparison, the CORBA specification does not require implementation inheritance either, but some CORBA implementations have supported it for certain special cases. In practice, being able to integrate objects created from different development languages is extremely useful, and greatly outweighs this one concession to theoretical OOP purity.

In the long run, the debate over whether a language is truly object-oriented becomes merely an academic exercise. What matters to you, the programmer, is which characteristics you need for a particular programming project, and what language or combination of languages provides the easiest, fastest, and most efficient way to implement them.

Progressive Development of Microsoft Object Technologies

In recent years, there has been incredibly rapid progress made in advancing the techniques and technologies used for Object-Oriented Programming and modular program communication. These new and improved technologies with all their new names and integration requirements have also brought their share of confusion to the programming community. A brief look at the most recent steps should help clear away some of that lingering confusion.

COM and OLE 2.0

In 1993, Microsoft created the Component Object Model (COM) and laid the technical foundation that has dramatically improved object communication in the Windows environment. COM provided both the technical specifications for creating compatible objects and the communication "plumbing" in the Windows operating system required to make it work. The first use of this new programming model came when Microsoft completely rebuilt OLE functionality using the new COM architecture. Instead of using a messaging protocol built on top of the operating system (like DDE or OLE 1.0 before it), COM provided interprocess communication (IPC) directly as a service of the operating system. Although it was a very different product and approach, Microsoft kept the OLE name, dubbing it OLE version 2.0.

With the COM communication architecture, OLE 2.0 was able to connect objects outside the process boundaries of an application and could instantly support new versions of objects without changing the source code of the applications that used them. This approach connected binary components actively running in various process spaces. To differentiate this new technology, Microsoft stopped proclaiming that, "OLE stands for Object Linking and Embedding" and declared that OLE was no longer an abbreviation, the word "OLE" was the entire name for the technology. OLE is still spelled out with all capital letters, but is commonly pronounced "Oh-LAY" instead of "Oh-el-E."

With the framework in place to create reusable designs independent of the implementations, any new features and technologies can be accommodated by COM and OLE 2.0 architecture without changing the architecture itself. Many subsequent developments have been built under the OLE banner, but because of the extensible nature of the OLE 2.0 architecture, there is theoretically no technical reason for Microsoft to develop a technology that could properly be named OLE 3.0. For that reason, any subsequent mention of OLE in this book without a version number will refer to the OLE 2.0 set of technologies.

OCX Components

Visual Basic advanced from version 3 to version 4, and the 16-bit VBX components were succeeded by OLE-based 32-bit components called *OLE Controls*. Naturally, OLE Controls needed a new name to distinguish them from their 16-bit VBX predecessors. Microsoft assigned OLE Controls with the .OCX filename extension, and these components became known as "OCXs." OCX components provided modular, 32-bit functionality to all of the popular visual programming languages, including Microsoft Visual C++ and Microsoft Visual Basic. OCXs are full-fledged COM objects.

The Expanding World of OLE

OLE Controls was one member of a whole family of COM-based technologies renamed under the OLE banner. Here are the highlights:

- *OLE Clipboard* The OLE technology that provides the cut, copy, and paste editor functions in the Windows clipboard.

- *OLE Visual Editing* The OLE technology that enables you to edit, while remaining in your current compound document, an object originally created in a different application using the interface and services of that different application. This concept was first know as *In-Place Editing* and later called *In-Place Activation*, before Microsoft renamed it *Visual Editing* and obtained a trademark for the term.

- *OLE Drag-and-Drop* The OLE technology that enables you to select an object from one application in the Windows environment and use the mouse to drag it over another object and then drop it onto that object. Depending on the behavior defined for the target object, the dropped object can be copied, moved, linked, or discarded by using this technique.

- *OLE Automation* The Microsoft technology that enables one component to control or *automate* another application or control. Thus, instead of a component receiving input through the user interface, the component is programmatically operated by another code module. One typical example is enabling your component to access predefined mathematical functions available from an OLE enabled spreadsheet program such as Microsoft Excel, instead of programming them yourself. As do the rest of the OLE components, OLE automation uses the COM architecture to communicate. Of course, the helper program must be installed and available on the user's PC for the OLE Automation in your program to function properly.

■ *OLE Remote Automation*   An interim solution for extending OLE automation capability so it can control objects across machine boundaries. OLE Remote Automation has been encompassed by DCOM.

■ *Network OLE and Distributed OLE*   The names given to the OLE technology that enabled OLE-compatible software components to communicate directly over a network. You could have used Distributed OLE to perform time-consuming or processor-intensive functions on a network server to relieve the burden on a user's PC. Extensive searches against large databases or complex calculation problems were good candidates for this technology. The idea remains today, but these names and technologies have been encompassed by DCOM.

The confusion over the OLE names was beginning to diminish, just about the same time Microsoft realized that the I-net was a much bigger phenomenon than it had anticipated. Microsoft decided to realign its naming conventions once again and return OLE to its roots. The OLE banner was officially removed from all but the original set of technologies related to the linking and embedding of objects into OLE container documents. These three technologies are now grouped into a category called *OLE Documents* and are individually named *Linking*, *Embedding*, and *In-Place Activation*.

Microsoft Embraces the Internet: OCX to ActiveX

In 1995, the Internet revolution spurred Microsoft's technical (and marketing) ingenuity into high gear. Microsoft originally underestimated the importance of the Internet revolution, but within about a 90-day period in late 1995, Bill Gates completely realigned the Microsoft corporate strategy to include Internet support into almost everything they were producing.

To boldly signal their entry into the booming I-net revolution, Microsoft created a new high-tech "Active" brand name for present and future I-Net-related technologies. They decided to market the remaining OLE technologies as "ActiveX," which is easier than OLE to pronounce but much harder to define. Because ActiveX is essentially a brand name, expect the collection of technologies in this category to mutate over time. Microsoft further marked their Internet intentions by declaring their new Internet architecture for the PC would be named the "Active Platform." At present, the following technologies are included under the Active Platform umbrella:

■ *Active Desktop*   Enables the PC desktop to act as an integrated COM container that can hold COM objects such as ActiveX components, can provide all the functionality currently associated with web browsers, and can connect to Internet broadcast channels. The goal is to completely integrate local PC resources with Internet-based resources into a single, unified user interface. This capability will be available in Internet Explorer version 4, and will become a standard part of the operating system with the release of Windows 98.

- *Active Server*   Provides a consistent server-side component programming environment.
- *ActiveX technologies*   COM-based technologies that enable components written in different languages on different operating systems to communicate in a consistent and robust manner.

All of the ActiveX technologies are all built to use COM. However, not all COM-based technologies fit under the ActiveX umbrella. For example, MS Office software and MS Windows operating systems are COM-enabled, but are not considered part of ActiveX.

Today there is probably more confusion than ever among developers over the various names for Microsoft produced technologies. At this point, understanding the underlying concepts is far more important than keeping up with the current naming conventions. If you are curious what the names were in late 1997 when this chapter was written, Figure 23.8 diagrams the relationship of some of these OLE/ActiveX technologies to the COM foundation.

Part
V
Ch
23

FIG. 23.8
The ActiveX and OLE technologies all have a common foundation in COM.

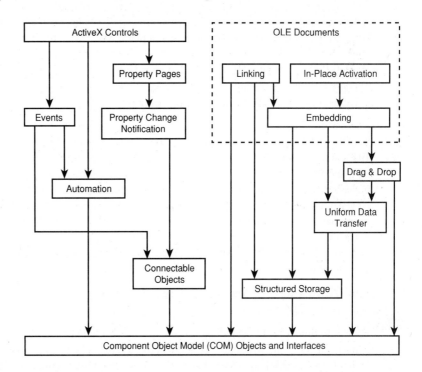

The proud tradition of naming confusion with OLE Controls was continued in March of 1996, when Microsoft used the Active brand to rename these components as "ActiveX Controls," enabled them to operate as COM-compliant components, and dedicated their use to the Internet. Sure, you can still use these controls as widgets in the design-time toolbox of your development language, but now all the promotion and commotion revolves around using ActiveX Controls to make spectacular Web pages and Web-enabled applications.

Although this appeared to be a positive step toward opening the architecture to the rest of the industry, the track record suggests that Microsoft will retain the deciding vote on any significant changes proposed for COM.

The industry track record also indicates, however, that Microsoft is an extremely tough contender in any market it enters. Microsoft can be counted on to be particularly aggressive in promoting and implementing its object technology, because this area is absolutely critical to the advancement of personal computing. In cooperation with Microsoft, Software AG has ported COM and ActiveX support to the Sun Solaris and UNIX family of operating systems with a product called DCOM for the Enterprise (DCOM FTE). Microsoft is working diligently to ensure that every major operating system will soon have COM support. Hence, using Visual Basic to create COM-compliant objects for Windows and UNIX platforms is a safe bet now, and COM objects will have even more utility in the future as COM support spreads to other platforms.

http://www.sagus.com   For more information on COM and ActiveX support for UNIX-based operating systems, visit Software AG's Web site.

There is still a great debate over which object model is best to use: COM or CORBA. Despite all the hype, choices must be based on what is better in a given context. If you're creating applications for the PC desktop, the Object Request Broker de facto standard for Windows-based development is COM, and COM is built right into the operating system. Similarly, COM is the clear choice for homogeneous Windows-based programs used across Windows NT-based computer networks. If, however, your programs need to operate in a network environment that contains a mix of operating systems, including various flavors of UNIX, you might need to integrate your programs by using CORBA-compliant ORB software. Other ORBs may find niche markets where they can survive, but for enterprises where most users have PCs on their desks, the initial stand-off between COM and CORBA will likely give way to integration and then finally to assimilation by COM.

http://www.omg.org/new/corbkmk.htm   Object Management Group maintains a concise set of links to CORBA-related web sites.

Perhaps you are wondering if programs created in Visual Basic (which uses COM) are compatible with CORBA. Such integration is not yet available out of the box, but there are now third-party tools to help you with this integration.

Visigenic is a growing provider of CORBA-compliant technology, and has licensed its VisiBroker ORB product to an increasing number of companies, including Netscape, Novell, Oracle, Sybase, and Silicon Graphics. Visigenic also offers a product called VisiBridge, which provides technology that enables COM objects on Windows platforms to communicate with CORBA objects on UNIX and mainframe operating systems.

http://www.visigenic.com   For more information on VisiBroker, VisiBridge, and other Visigenic products, visit their Web site.

Another popular CORBA-compliant object broker is Orbix from Iona. Orbix also provides a bridging technology that allows application integration between COM-based Windows platforms and CORBA-based UNIX platforms.

http://www.iona.com   For more on Orbix and other Iona products, visit their Web site.

These and other products to bridge the compatibility gap between COM and CORBA are very useful, and will be necessary until the two competing standards can either communicate directly, or are merged into a unified standard. Bridging technology provides valuable integration capability, but unfortunately, as you increase the number of communication layers, the complexity of your programs and the risk for functionality and performance problems also increases. Because COM is quickly being ported to nearly every major computing platform, it might not be long before native COM support is available in all common platforms and Visual Basic programmers will have much less need for a COM-to-CORBA interface layer.

The battle between CORBA and COM to become the generally accepted ORB standard is nowhere near over. Netscape Communications Corporation is including a CORBA-compliant object request broker and support for the Internet Inter-Orb Protocol (IIOP)—the CORBA-compliant Internet protocol from OMG—in their Enterprise 3.0 server and Communicator 4.0 browser. This means Netscape's browsers can use IIOP to connect with remote objects across the I-net. The incompatibility gap between Microsoft's Internet Explorer and Netscape Navigator/Communicator is widening, but Microsoft is trying to make this a moot point by using Active Desktop as a preemptive strike to essentially eliminate the need for—and ultimately even the existence of—all competing browsers. Microsoft's Active Desktop concept integrates all the functions of traditional browser technology directly into the desktop of all future Windows operating systems. Hence, if the PC using public embraces this new version of Windows, the PC browser battle will essentially be over and Microsoft's COM-based technologies will be the de facto standard.

http://www.microsoft.com/oledev   Microsoft maintains a Web page dedicated to OLE and COM topics. You can find a wealth of additional information there.

COM/OLE versus OpenDoc

Assimilation has also begun under the market pressure of the COM/OLE technologies. In late 1993, a coalition of technology companies—including Apple, IBM, Novell, Oracle, SunSoft, Taligent, and Xerox—backed a compound document architecture standard called *OpenDoc* from Component Integration Laboratories (CILabs). This technology provided some promising competition for Microsoft's COM/OLE technology and prompted a great deal of interest and discussion from the industry, but generated only a meager amount of market share. Being both "open" and "standard" was just not enough for the OpenDoc alliance to overcome the growing market success of COM-based technologies. OpenDoc's battle to survive amid the growing dominance of OLE technologies was short lived. The battle concluded in May of 1997, when CILabs essentially surrendered by announcing they were discontinuing support of the OpenDoc architecture.

CILabs has since been dissolved by its board of directors. At the date of this writing, their farewell greetings were posted at the following Web address: **http://www.cilabs.com**.

The Scoop on Java-Based Technologies

Still another battleground for Microsoft's object technologies is in the I-net (Internet and intranet) arena. This battle has become more intense as a result of the explosive increase in

I-net usage and the increasing desire to use I-net for mission-critical, distributed corporate applications.

Sun Microsystems has created a phenomenon of its own with the creation of the Java programming language. Originally created to be a small but powerful means to program applications for small computing devices, it found popularity as a means to create quickly downloadable applets for I-net Web pages. As Java's popularity expanded, so has the scope of what developers are attempting to create using Java and Java related technologies.

Microsoft's mixed position on this situation is easily misunderstood. Microsoft considers Java to be a great *object-oriented programming language* (and has delivered Visual J++ to provide Java programmers a rich development environment). However, Microsoft considers Java related technologies to be a very poor choice as an *operating system*. On all but the smallest computing platforms, the Java Virtual Machine (JVM) that contains and executes the Java applets is essentially an operating system built on top of the native operating system.

Since Java and Java-related technologies are attempting to be a cross-platform solution, the Java language and the JVM must limit itself to the lowest common denominator in terms of platform specific features. Thus, important capabilities available from operating systems (such as Windows) are essentially unavailable to programmers writing "Pure" Java code. The platform-specific implementations of the JVM also introduce the opportunity for incompatibilities, as does the variety of Java development environments. Even if you think you have developed the most "pure" Java applets or even full-fledged Java applications, you should still test them extensively to be sure they work correctly on all desired platforms.

JavaBeans is another Java-related technology that is not popular with Microsoft. JavaBeans is a technology that Sun and IBM have developed to give Java applications the same compound document capabilities that ActiveX provides. JavaBeans can be visual components that you can add to forms in visual development tools, or they can be non-visual components that accomplish background tasks. JavaBeans are also designed to be cross-platform compatible, but the current reality is that you still need to test your Java and your JavaBeans on each combination of platform and Java Virtual Machine that is represented in your user community.

Looking further into Java's relationship to the I-net, Sun actively supports the CORBA specification and has pledged to integrate Java with IIOP, the CORBA-compliant Internet protocol from OMG. Java's existing Remote Method Invocation (RMI) protocol will be integrated to use IIOP across the I-net. Hence, Sun has joined other industry powerhouses such as Netscape, Oracle, and IBM in support of IIOP. Despite such a powerful alliance among giants in the industry, they can still be considered underdogs when compared to Microsoft and its rapidly growing ActiveX/COM/DCOM strategy for I-net development.

Microsoft is hoping that as COM gains further acceptance and use throughout the industry, the importance of CORBA and other architectures will diminish along with their market share. If that happens quickly, Microsoft will have assimilated another major layer of the desktop computing architecture. If not, CORBA will remain as a viable, competing distributed object architecture, both for the desktop and the I-net, and will need to be accounted for when you are integrating and supporting enterprise-wide systems.

On the Web

http://www.microsoft.com   Microsoft provides a variety of information about their positions on these technologies. Simply do a keyword search at their Web site.

http://www.omg.org   A good starting point to locate more information on CORBA is the Object Management Group's Web site.

COM Outside the Windows

Although COM is currently a Windows-based technology, Microsoft and its partners are porting it to every other major computing platform and operating system, including Solaris, MVS, Macintosh, and UNIX. This time the integration rumors are backed by dollars, because in addition to their internal efforts, Microsoft has negotiated outside contracts to port COM and DCOM to some of these other platforms, including UNIX-based machines. As was mentioned previously, COM is native to Windows, and Software AG has already ported COM and ActiveX to Solaris and the UNIX family of operating systems. If COM is not yet supported on your computer system of preference, you probably won't have to wait long until it is.

COM/DCOM Architecture Basics

While still maintaining language neutrality, take a closer look at the common implementation requirements of Microsoft's object technologies. This section provides a quick introduction to COM-related terms and concepts, explained in greater depth in subsequent chapters with language-specific implementation guidance.

Interfaces

The COM infrastructure is built to support communication through object interfaces. In COM, an *interface* can be thought of as the communications link between two different objects, and the set of functions available through that link. Interface names conventionally begin with a capital I to denote their status as an interface, and the remaining text describes the function or service being exposed. For example, in the Domestic Simulator program mentioned earlier, you might name an interface "ISpeak," which would be read as either "I-Speak" or "Interface Speak."

A COM interface is actually implemented as a memory structure called a *VTable*, which contains an array of function pointers. Each element of the VTable array contains the address of a specific function implemented by the object. It is conventional to say that a COM object *exposes its interfaces* to make its functions available to clients. The object also can contain the data manipulated by the methods, and you can choose to keep this data hidden from the client object. This structure is illustrated in Figure 23.9.

Unknown   One of the most basic rules of the COM specification is that all COM objects must support a specific interface named *IUnknown*. The IUnknown interface is the standard starting point for referencing any other interface that the COM object might contain. The COM specification arbitrarily dictates this structure, but it makes sense if you consider that a client object doesn't know what other interfaces are exposed by a server object until the client requests this information using the predefined interface designed to reveal what interfaces are "Unknown."

A more technical way of stating the relationship is that an object's interfaces must either directly or indirectly inherit from IUnknown to be valid under the COM specification. You, the programmer, are responsible for implementing the IUnknown interface for your objects; however, because this is such a routine operation, Microsoft programming tools either accomplish most of this work in the background or allow you to customize some basic example code. Figure 23.9 also shows how a client must request a pointer from Iunknown to access an object's interfaces.

FIG. 23.9

You could define a COM interface called ISample, which is implemented in memory with pointers to the standard COM methods and to your custom-defined methods.

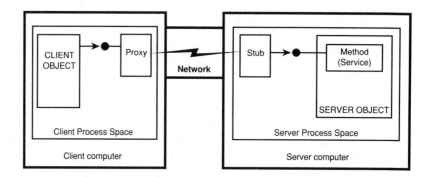

QueryInterface The object's *IUnknown* interface must also implement a function named *QueryInterface*, which reports back to the client whether a requested interface is supported and, if so, provides a means to access it. A successful call to QueryInterface provides the client with a pointer to the requested interface.

Globally Unique Identifiers (GUID)

Every COM component class and interface must be uniquely identified. This is accomplished by providing a means for you, the programmer, to generate and assign a unique number called the *Globally Unique Identifier* (GUID). A GUID (pronounced "goo-id") is a 128-bit integer virtually guaranteed to be unique across space and time until about 3400 AD, because of the algorithm used to create it. To create a new GUID, the algorithm uses the current date and time, a clock sequence, an incremented counter, and the IEEE machine identifier. The odds against any two people ever creating the same GUID are astronomical. After you have created a GUID, you can used it to identify your programming objects and interfaces uniquely. When used to identify an interface, this GUID number is referred to as an *Interface Identifier* (IID). When used to identify an object, the GUID number is called a *Class Identifier* (CLSID).

After a particular interface has been defined, numbered with a unique IID, and published, it must not be changed; thus the interface is said to be *immutable*. When you want to update the features of an interface, you must define, number, and publish an additional interface to supplement the older version, retaining any previous versions within the component. If you don't include these previous versions, you will create version incompatibility problems for your users. You will see an example of this presented in the section on version control.

Registering Your Components

After you have a GUID to identify your new object, you must register it with the host system. For machines running Windows, you do this by adding the appropriate information to the Windows Registry, a special system file containing that machine's hardware and software configuration information. When you create and distribute components, you should build your installation program to update the Registry without requiring manual assistance from the user. After a component is registered, the operating system will know how and where to access that particular object.

Part
V

Ch
23

> **N O T E** According to the current definition, any self-registering OLE component that fully implements IUnknown can be correctly called an ActiveX control. This means that both OLE Automation servers and most of the widget-type controls from a visual development toolbox are included under the ActiveX controls banner. ▦

Binary Compatibility and Version Control

With the ability for developers around the globe to create objects that must work together, you need to be able to update your objects without causing the failure of existing objects that still depend on your previous version. COM requires that client objects specify the exact server interface they want by using that interface's assigned globally unique identifier (described further in the next section). Each version must have a different identifier, and QueryInterface returns a pointer to version the client specifically asks for. COM enables objects to have multiple interfaces, so any number of versions can be supported simultaneously. When all versions are retained by an object and made available to clients, both the old and new clients always work appropriately. When you create a new version of an interface, it is a good practice to change the name as well to avoid confusion. One simple convention is to add a version number to the end of the existing interface name, incrementing it for each new version. With this versioning process, you can safely support both old and new objects on either side of the client-server relationship. Figure 23.10 illustrates this concept, using objects from the Domestic Simulator example.

FIG. 23.10
Mower objects from different vendors will still get the grass cut as long as COM versioning rules are followed.

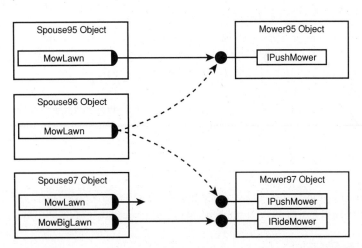

Figure 23.10 depicts the following situation of the COM versioning rules being followed:

■ Original release from both vendors—no problems.

■ LawnSoft releases an upgraded mower object (RideMower). Spouse 95 software was never programmed to look for this new object, but the lawn still gets cut because LawnSoft correctly provided backward compatibility by retaining the old interface as well as the new one.

■ SimSoft releases an upgrade to the Spouse object that enables support for either of LawnSoft's mower objects. If it didn't support both mowers, Spouse 97 objects that only had access to the older Mower95 object could not cut the lawn.

Suppose that purchased the Domestic Simulator described earlier. Spouse95 objects created by SimWare are designed to call the PushMower interface (IpushMower) in the Mower95 object when the simulated lawn needs to be cut. Eventually, LawnSoft releases a new version of their mower object called Mower97 that is the envy of the simulated neighborhood. Some people buy it to upgrade their simulation, but since it's more expensive and not that much better than the mower object everybody started with, most don't buy it. Furthermore, for your simulator to take advantage of this new type of mower, your Spouse object must know that the new mower exists and must know the identifier of the new interface to access it. To enable spouses to use this new variety of mowers, SimWare upgrades their Spouse object and releases the Spouse97 version. The Spouse97 object now has two ways to mow the lawn: use the MowLawn object to call the old PushMower interface, or use the new MowBigLawn object to call the new RideMower interface.

The whole point of this exercise is that since the versioning was done correctly and each object supported prior interfaces, any combination of spouse and mower objects was able to successfully mow the lawn. If not, when you drop in a replacement object, you risk breaking the existing object relationships and your application no longer functions correctly. Make it a habit to ensure that your objects fully support your prior interface definitions as well as any new interface definitions in a given object, and your objects will always work together properly.

Creating COM Objects

A client can create a new instance of an object by making an appropriate call to the object creation services provided by the COM Library. How this is accomplished depends on the language, but the call always needs to provide the GUID for the class identifier (CLSID) of the desired object.

At the completion of the creation process, the client gets a memory pointer to the new object. It can then use that pointer to ask the object directly for pointers to any other services provided by the object.

COM Library Services

Each platform that supports COM provides a COM Library. The COM Library implements a group of functions that supply basic COM services to objects and their clients. The first and foremost service is the means to create a COM object upon request. One way to accomplish this occurs as follows:

- The client asks the COM Library to create an object of a specific CLSID.
- The COM Library uses a system utility called the Service Control Manager (SCM) to find the CLSID information in the system registry, locate the correct server for this class of object, and start it.
- The COM Library uses the server to create a generic instance of the object and passes an interface pointer to the client.
- The client asks the object to initialize itself, thus loading any persistent data associated with the object.

Class Factories

If you want to create more than one object at a time, you could repeat the previous creation process, but a more efficient way is to implement and use a class factory. A class factory is a service component whose only purpose is to create new components of a particular type, as defined by a single CLSID. The standard interface used for this purpose is appropriately called *IClassFactory*. It is up to the component programmer to provide the class factory for each class but, fortunately, implementing the IClassFactory interface is simple and straightforward. If you want to add licensing capabilities to your class factory, you can opt to use Microsoft's newly defined IClassFactory2 interface, which requires the client object to pass the correct key or license to the class factory before it will create the new instance of the desired class.

Monikers

Another way to accomplish the creation of an object is by using a moniker. A *moniker* is a special type of COM object built to know how and where to instantiate another specific object and to initialize that object with its persistent data. Each moniker can identify exactly one instance of an object. If you want more than one instance of a given class of objects, you need to use a different moniker for each object, because each object might have its own unique data. For example, suppose that in the human resources application at your firm, employees and their histories are stored as COM objects. If you use monikers, a separate moniker would be needed for each employee in the company. If your employee object, for example, were needed by the system, the system would call up your particular moniker. Your moniker would then create your employee object in memory, load your history information from the persistent data storage, hand the pointer for the employee object back to the requester, and then unload itself from memory.

You can also create a *composite moniker* that activates a group of other monikers. *Absolute monikers* point to OLE documents instead of objects.

Where COM Objects Live

After it is created, a COM object requires a place in memory where it can exist, deliver the services requested by clients, and then unload itself from memory when all the clients report that they are finished with it. To have this existence, a computer object must live within a *process* or *process space* with a defined area in the system memory, some instruction code, perhaps some associated data, and some resources for interacting with the system. A *thread* is the name given to the action of serially executing a specific set of machine code instructions within a particular process space. Computers with processors and operating systems that can execute more than one thread in each process are said to be *multi-threaded*. A process capable of multi-threading must always have at least one main thread, called the *primary thread*, but can also have many others. In Windows, *user-interface threads* are associated with each window and have message loops that keep the screen display active and responsive to new user input. Meanwhile, Windows uses *worker threads* to accomplish other computing tasks in the background. After a thread is initiated, it executes its code until it finishes, is terminated by the system, or is interrupted by a thread with higher priority.

COM supports multi-threading by putting objects in the same process space into their own groups, referred to as *apartments*. The purpose and function of *apartment threads* are comparable to those of the user-interface threads described above. Similarly, COM uses the term *free threads* to describe what were previously called worker threads. Regardless of the terminology, COM makes multi-threaded development easier by handling the communication between these threads and between the various objects.

COM Objects Communicating Together

COM objects must be designed to be well-behaved neighbors. You want to ensure that any COM objects you create correctly implement the rules that enable consistent behavior and reliable communication with other objects. Following are the most basic rules your COM objects must live by.

Reference Counting

After an object is created, it can take on a life of its own. Because more than one client might be using its services at any one time, each object needs to keep track of its clients so that it doesn't close itself down before all the clients are finished with it. When a client begins using the services of an object, it has the responsibility to call the AddRef method to increment the server object's reference counter. Similarly, when the client has finished, it has the responsibility to notify the server object by calling the Release method to decrement the reference counter. When all clients have released themselves from the object, the reference counter goes to zero. The object then knows its work is completed and can safely save any persistent data and self-destruct by unloading itself from memory. If a client subsequently needs the object, the object is created again and the reference counting process is repeated.

You must implement the methods for AddRef and Release as part of the IUnknown interface. Because all interfaces inherit from IUnknown, the AddRef and Release methods are then automatically available through any interfaces you define for your object.

COM Objects Across Process and Network Boundaries

COM objects need to be able to communicate with their local neighbors on the same machine, as well with distant COM objects residing on machines located on the other side of the world. There is considerably more complexity involved with the latter process, but you need to understand both processes to create objects that comply with the COM specification.

Remote COM Servers   Remote COM servers (also known as *cross-process* or *out-of-process servers*) are COM objects providing service from a physically separate computer that is usually connected via a network. Both computers must be operating with COM-enabled operating systems for this process to work correctly. Remote COM servers typically provide slower performance than their in-process cousins, but they can deliver all the advantages explained earlier for generic OOP remote servers, and COM remote servers can provide compatibility between 16-bit and 32-bit clients.

Transparent Connections: Marshaling, Proxies, and Stubs   In COM, a *proxy* is a small binary component activated in the client's process space, which acts as an in-process connector to the server interface, regardless of the server's physical location. A *stub* is a small binary component activated in the server's process space, which acts as an in-process connector to the proxy in the client (see Figure 23.11). With this arrangement, the COM client doesn't need to know where the server object is located, because COM insulates by creating a proxy or stub as needed, making all servers appear to be in the same process space.

FIG. 23.11

COM proxies and stubs provide each remote objects with an in-process communication link to other objects across a network.

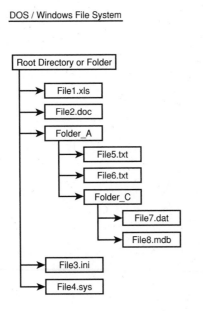

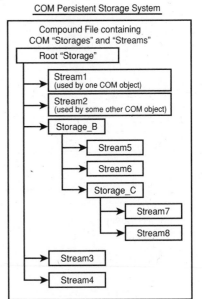

While a great deal more overhead is necessary to communicate with out-of-process objects than in-process objects, no additional effort is necessary for the client. With this architecture, all objects are made available to clients in a uniform, transparent fashion.

Some extra work needs to happen behind the scenes to make this communication process transparent to the objects. For an in-process server, the client can simply use a pointer to the server, but out-of-process clients only have a pointer to the proxy, and COM must support inter-process communication such as Remote Procedure Calls (RPC) to reach the stub, which then communicates through a pointer to reach the server. *Marshaling* is the name given to this process of packaging interface data into an appropriate format for delivery across process or network boundaries. The code module that performs these tasks is called a *marshaler*. For the return trip back to the client, the process to unpackage this data is called *unmarshaling*.

Object Automation   If you want to create an object that can be programmed or automated by another object, your object will expose this capability through a specially defined standard interface called *IDispatch*. The IDispatch interface, also called a *dispatch interface* or *Dispinterface*, must implement a standard method called *Invoke* that acts as a channel to receive automation commands from clients. Dispatch interfaces enable you to expose functions and data as methods and properties, which are combined in logical units called *automation objects*. An application or component that exposes automation objects is called an *OLE automation server*. An application or component that uses the services of an automation server is called an *OLE automation client*. The IDispatch interface is used by OLE Automation servers and is generic across programming languages.

COM Object Data

COM objects, much like traditional applications, need to be able to store their data. A COM object can store its data in the following ways:

- Persistent storage of object data
- Uniform data transfer
- Connectable objects

A COM object that can store its data by using a fairly permanent medium (such as a disk drive) is said to have *persistent* data. Persistent storage is accomplished in COM by means of a structure formerly called *OLE structured storage* and now called *Compound Storage*. This structure essentially implements its own independent file system, and the whole thing is stored within a single traditional file on the host machine.

In comparison to the traditional file structures, the directories are called *storages,* and the data is stored in file-like structures called *streams.* In much the same way that files contain data specially formatted for the program that created it, streams can hold data in any format designated by the object that creates it. The *Root Storage* can contain any number of additional storages, also called *substorages,* and any number of streams. Each substorage can also contain any number of additional substorages and streams, with the only limit being the amount of space available on the disk. This entire structure is then physically stored as a single conventional file on the system's disk drive. The familiar DOS/Windows file structure and the COM Compound Storage system are compared in Figure 23.12.

FIG. 23.12
The COM Structured Storage architecture closely resembles the DOS/Windows file system architecture, but is stored on a single file on the host system.

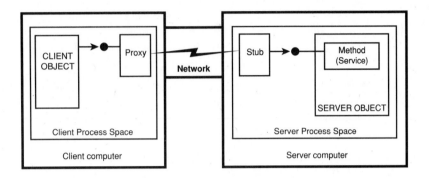

Historically, there have been many ways to exchange data between programs. You could import a data file or copy and paste from the Clipboard, or perhaps a program might read an initialization file. COM has defined a common approach for moving data between objects called *Uniform Data Transfer*. Again, a standard interface is defined to accomplish this functionality, and it is called *IDataObject*. By calling the IDataObject interface, one COM object (an ActiveX control, for instance) can quickly and easily request data from another object any time new data is needed.

When one object needs data from another object based on data changes, timers, or other spontaneous events, a better technology called *Connectable Objects* can be used to pass the data between objects. The idea behind connectable objects is to set up dedicated incoming and outgoing interfaces used exclusively for inter-object communication. Each connection is instantiated with its own *Connection Point* object within the server object. The client instantiates an internal object called a *sink*, which receives the incoming communication. Standard interfaces defined for this purpose are named IConnectionPointContainer and IConnectionPoint.

Strategies for Using Object Technology with Legacy Applications

For most large organizations, the issue is no longer *whether* your firm should move to client-server, object-oriented, and distributed computing models, but *when* and *how*.

Most organizations would like to begin this transition immediately, especially for any new applications, since the benefits of building applications by using object technology are compelling. However, creating new OOP systems of significant size and complexity typically requires additional training for the programming staff, a large investment of funds, and months or years to complete. During that time, all the existing applications built with traditional methods still need to be maintained and updated. Furthermore, new and old systems will usually have to interoperate during the transition, since instant transitions involving multiple systems are rarely possible. This is indeed a daunting task, but the sooner your organization determines their strategy for making the transition, the better prepared you can be for implementing it.

Once committed to begin the transition, the issue is then how you can economically and sensibly accomplish it. Because aging systems still provide a great deal of functionality, and changing them is getting more expensive every day, many businesses have focused on more urgent problems and secretly hoped for some technical breakthrough to come along and save them before it's too late. Object technologies are no magic bullet, but they can help you solve many of the challenges in creating new systems and updating old ones while maximizing your existing investment in your company's legacy code base.

For most large companies it isn't wise, practical, or even possible to simply discard the existing mission-critical applications and quickly rebuild them, using object technologies. If this is your situation, you need an incremental strategy that allows you to selectively redevelop, reengineer, and repackage your legacy systems, blending the old processing models with new ones that can all share the same communication framework. COM object technologies can provide that framework.

Each corporate situation presents unique challenges that must be addressed individually, but when dealing with these challenges, some common themes emerge. Although there are many variations and combinations, this section explores four basic strategies for applying object technology to the challenge of supporting your legacy computer systems:

- Keep your old systems, and interoperate with newly created systems.
- Create new objects around old code to wrap or encapsulate the functions of legacy applications.
- Re-engineer legacy applications, using objects to create new multi-tiered, distributed applications.
- Create object-oriented browser-based interfaces to your legacy data.

Interoperating with Legacy Systems

There are many mission-critical legacy systems that are stable, reliably do exactly what they are supposed to, and require very little maintenance. Perhaps this claim sounds amazing, but these are the applications that allow your business to continue another day while you and your teammates diligently resolve the most recent crisis or create that "rush job" application desperately required by your more vocal users.

Sometimes there is a compelling reason to change the status quo: the business process changes dramatically, the cost for support becomes unacceptable, the program could no longer be supported if a serious modification were required or if the language or platform were no longer supported by your company. In such a case, you will want to start planning the transition and focus on the new system. Because this process will require a great deal of your already scarce programming resources, why not hedge your bets and make use of the legacy system as long as it is practical?

Situations involving this approach would include:

- You have a legacy system that is not yet obsolete, but you anticipate it will be within the next 18 months. Or perhaps you are planning a change to your business processes, for which the change will require a completely different system. Instead of continuing to implement short-term fixes on the old system, spend your time and energy to adequately and completely prepare for and implement the new system. The users might accept this approach more readily if you involve them in the requirements, development, and delivery process. Keep the user community updated on your progress in implementing the new system, ask some key users to help test it, and then offer training sessions as soon as practical to ease anxiety about transitioning to the new system.

- You have a legacy system that manipulates a separate database. In this case, the old system and the new system can be designed to operate safely while simultaneously using the shared database, and the phaseout can happen gradually as functionality is added to the new system. Users can use either system safely during the transition period.

- You have a mission-critical system that simply cannot go down until a replacement system has proven itself. In this case, a completely separate system must be implemented and tested extensively over time to ensure it performs up to corporate expectations. Both systems must be operated independently until the users are fully trained and the new system is trusted. Then a simple and well-publicized transition plan should be implemented to coordinate the movement of all live data and all users to the new system.

- You have a monolithic system that is extremely costly to modify, and complete replacement would be so cost prohibitive that it isn't even an option. This situation is perhaps the most difficult to deal with, as the old system must be maintained in its legacy state for the foreseeable future. Perhaps your best move here would be to encourage your company to take all reasonable steps to retain the legacy programmers. Additionally, you might want to start a divide-and-conquer plan, in which you explore business-reengineering options to begin to move separable business functions onto new systems and away from the great monolithic system.

Object Wrappers for Legacy Code

Another approach is to take existing code modules and imbed them inside a new object that acts as a wrapper, completely isolating the legacy code while retaining its functions. This wrapper can encapsulate any or all of the old interfaces, including screen displays, API calls, database interactions, and any other communication elements, exposing them as appropriate COM interfaces. As time, funding, and priorities permit, you can then progressively design and implement new objects to replace the wrapped modules from the legacy application.

There are several specific ways to use this wrapper approach. A *database wrapper* accesses and encapsulates just the legacy data, completely bypassing legacy code. A *service wrapper* encapsulates legacy system services, such as printers and communications devices. An *application wrapper* encapsulates both the code and data of a legacy system application. Application wrappers can provide the object-oriented equivalent of traditional "screen-scraping" programs, which emulate the interaction of a user on a character-based terminal and provide that data through a new graphical user interface. Although Visual C++ is probably the most common choice for creating these wrappers, you can also use Visual Basic.

Although wrappers can be a fantastic method for leveraging your legacy programming investments, this approach has a major downside because the old, inflexible legacy code is still hiding inside the object wrapper. The effort to replace the wrapped legacy code with a newly constructed, reverse-engineered object is likely going to be seen as a very low priority among the users, because they have already received the new functionality and now feel comfortable with it. From their point of view, maintaining the new functionality is your problem, not their problem. Replacing a functioning wrapper object might also be a tough sell to management, who probably have a huge list of higher priority new initiatives and maintenance projects that need your immediate attention. With this in mind, it is usually wise to build object wrappers with great care and attention to detail, as they might need to last until the underlying function is obsolete to the business, or until a completely new system replaces it.

Reengineering with Objects to Create Multi-Tiered, Distributed Applications

Functions performed by existing monolithic architectures can be reengineered or broken down into a multi-tiered, object-oriented architecture that is more maintainable, scalable, flexible, and reusable.

The first step is to divide functions into three logical groups representing user services, business services, and data services. This analysis can be more challenging than it sounds.

The user services group includes all the functions that support interaction with the user, such as forms, menus, controls, and other visual displays. User interfaces on the old system might be simple text-based screens, whereas the new system probably needs a considerably more elaborate graphical user interface.

The business services group includes the functions that implement the business tasks and rules of the organization. If your company is typical, many of the business rules are undocumented, yet still buried deep within the legacy applications, and must be derived by analyzing procedures and even individual lines of legacy code. When you have discovered them, the business rules contained in the old system must be compared to the rules you want for the new system and adjusted accordingly.

The data services group includes all the functions related to the storage and manipulation of data. Legacy data storage might be implemented with a flat-file data structure, whereas the new system might need to use a relational database.

This logical design might need to be revised as the business needs change, but after the initial implementation is accomplished, subsequent iterations of this cycle are much faster and easier. After this logical division of tasks is accomplished, you can design the physical location of the components.

In most organizations, the legacy system cannot be shut down while the new system is under construction. Where possible, use an incremental development process to allow the programming team to deliver a series of small victories instead of an ever-more-anxious period of waiting (and hoping) for the success of one enormous project release.

The first components to build are the ones that support the lowest level functions of the system. Resist the urge to start with the user interface, because you will quickly become frustrated trying to design interfaces for functions that are not yet implemented. These low-level functions include such things as data access components, networking services, and services for hardware and peripherals. Because these functions are potentially needed by any application on the system, migration of these services to reusable components will provide the fastest benefit for other projects that also require these services.

The next components to build are those that support time-consuming computer processes that can be more efficiently accomplished in a separate process space. The main system's performance can be greatly enhanced by implementing these slower processes as components that can operate in a separate process on the same machine or on a separate, more specialized machine. Functions that fit this category might include fax processing, database report generation, credit card validation, and computing of numeric solutions by using complex algorithms. When these components are moved onto a separate processor, asynchronous processing can be utilized by any application on the system modified to take advantage of it.

After these two groups of components are built, tested, and operational, you have formed the foundation that can support a cycle of continuous improvement. Each of the following projects should provide the remaining components to one major subsystem of the legacy application. Attempting to complete all the remaining components at one time is a risky endeavor that should be avoided if possible for two reasons. First, the users and management of most organizations like to see steady progress for all the money they are investing in your programming projects. The smaller the scope of the project, the less likely you are to encounter problems that require significant schedule delays. Second, because this technology is still relatively new, it is likely that your programming team will be gaining valuable experience during this process, and schedules are rarely built to accommodate many "experience-building" mistakes. By taking the path of incremental improvement, your team can gain experience as they deliver a steady stream of system enhancement on time and on budget.

Browser-Based Interfaces for Legacy Data

One of the fastest and most exciting approaches capitalizes on the recent explosion in the use of I-net technology. You can create object-oriented interfaces for your legacy data by porting the functionality of your legacy applications to a browser-based implementation. The larger your organization, the more promising the benefits, as long as your company already has the equipment and infrastructure in place to facilitate it. If access to Local Area Networks, Wide Area Networks, and the Internet from each desktop is commonplace at your organization, this might be your fastest, least expensive, and most flexible option for transitioning away from your legacy systems.

If your company does not yet have the infrastructure in place, the benefits of this approach can be so compelling as to become a cost-justifiable reason to start investing in the infrastructure.

This I-net approach relies on the browser on each user's desktop to act as the client container for your interfaces and data. The browser and an I-net connection to the company I-net server computers are the only additions required at the user's computer. With this approach, as soon as you change the content delivered by the central server computer, everyone can use the most recent version.

Part

V

Ch

23

For an example, suppose that your firm's existing inventory database resides on a legacy main-frame computer and is accessed from PCs by using a terminal emulator. Replacement with new browser-based graphical user interfaces can be implemented by incrementally creating active server pages to suit the needs of each user group (sales, order fulfillment, finance, and so on). These pages can be delivered from an internal I-net server that was also connected across the network to the legacy mainframe. COM objects created to run on the server provide services by making database calls to the legacy database, and delivering the results to the objects oper-ating in the user's browser container. Both the legacy system and your net I-Net system can operate simultaneously until all the user groups were provided new interfaces. When the legacy database is migrated to a new system, the calls to the legacy database can be modified and redirected to any standard Structure Query Language (SQL) enterprise database product. If your database product is COM-compatible (such as Microsoft's SQL Server), your task is even easier.

The benefits of this I-net approach can be downright exciting to an IS department trying to support a large user base. Gone are the hassles of software version control, trying to physically install or upgrade individual copies of your corporate software on hundreds or thousands of geographically separated computers, or trying to use network install utilities to accomplish these tasks. You can at least expect the following benefits from this I-net approach:

- The programming tools enable much greater flexibility and much faster delivery of minor changes than conventional software development cycles.

- As the users become more familiar with the browser interface, training can become less of a challenge, compared to teaching a new interface with every program.

- Specialized hardware connections and leased circuits to mainframe computers can be redirected just to corporate I-net servers, or the mainframes can be modified to become I-net servers themselves, thus facilitating the standardization of the communication infrastructure.

- The data shared and services provided within the company can be easily and selectively extended to business partners and existing customers, and advertised online to new customers.

The list of benefits goes on, but even these few things are enough to illustrate the advantages to large organizations with a geographically dispersed user base.

Although this approach has numerous benefits, it does have some significant drawbacks that need to be considered before you commit to it. As with any centralized system, if the network goes down, the entire user community might suddenly lose their service. This can be some-what mitigated by operating mirrored servers at separate locations, so if one server cannot be accessed by a given user, that user might be able to establish a connection to the alternate server. Even with mirrored servers, the fragile state of the global I-net communication back-bone does pose a significant risk to mission-critical systems. If this risk is unacceptable, you need to stick with more traditional approaches.

Security is also a factor when considering any I-net based approach. Secure protocols are now available, but they have yet to gain universal trust. However, many corporate information systems can be operated safely with the minor degree of risk currently associated with I-net communication methods.

Strategies for Implementing Object Technologies for New Applications

The first order of business for creating new applications is to gather and document as many of the project requirements as you can. This step cannot be overemphasized. Object-oriented programming allows a great deal of flexibility in designing and adjusting the solution to a given programming problem, but an entire project design might have to be scrapped if a critical requirement is omitted during design and then discovered during user testing. Use every resource at your disposal to ensure that you have captured all the requirements of the user's business process. Rapid prototyping is especially helpful when you're trying to present a new graphical user interface paradigm. By presenting a live demonstration of a sample graphical user interface option for a business process solution, you can often unlock creativity and inno-vation from the users during the design phase before formal development begins. This is a dual edged sword, however, as user expectations and requirements may also rise significantly. The risk is worth it, since you should be able to reveal and solve any existing problems with the business processes that are only rooted in limits imposed by a previous automation system. After you have documented a comprehensive set of business requirements, you can begin creating an object-oriented design.

When designing an application from scratch, the procedural programming strategy typically uses a mixture of two related approaches:

- Divide large tasks into smaller tasks, until each task is simple enough to be implemented directly. This is the *top-down approach* to programming.

- Write procedures that implement basic tasks, and combine them into progressively more complicated structures until you have created the desired functionality. This is the *bottom-up approach* to programming.

The suggested approach for OOP design draws on both the top-down and bottom-up approaches. First, examine your problem description from the top, and look for the items, descriptions, and actions described. The nouns are going to become the object classes, the adjectives are going to become the properties, and the verbs are going to become the methods. Then you can start the design process by establishing the classes and associating each method with the class that is most responsible for that action. From this starting point, you can concentrate on the bottom-level tasks, adding the properties and further refining your design. When your preliminary de-sign is acceptable to you and your colleagues, repackage it as a presentation and walk through it with your most supportive user representatives. Even the most elegant object-oriented designs are worthless if they don't satisfy the needs of the users. Rapid prototyping is also a valuable tool for testing ideas, to ensure that the programmers and the users are communicating effectively and to reveal and facilitate the discussion of any hidden assumptions buried in the individual requirements.

When your most supportive users are happy, test a basic prototype with your least supportive users. Working with these users might not be comfortable, but it will likely yield two very important benefits. First, these more hostile users will tend to make a more determined effort to find the flaws in your project and your logic. Although some portion of this feedback might simply be frivolous griping, many of the comments will reveal places for significantly improving the project. Making peace with hostile users early in the process by negotiating these improvements into the initial design of the project is a much better strategy than avoiding these users and their opinions until you are forced to face them during full-scale user testing. The secondary benefit is that after these initially hostile users become part of the development process, they might join you in feeling some personal ownership in the project, subsequently defending the project to ensure "their" project becomes a success. Requirements definition and preliminary design are critical phases of the development process where changes can be made easily and cheaply, so don't waste the opportunity to capture as many changes as you can while fostering a positive spirit of support among the users.

After you and your users have agreed upon a preliminary object design, resist the urge to immediately begin coding. As a rule, it is cheaper and faster to *buy* an object than it is to *write it yourself*, so this is the time to start looking for pre-built objects. The first place to look is in your own organization. If your organization doesn't have a well-organized object repository, now is the time to start one. Next, look outside your organization for objects that can be obtained from other parts of the same company or from commercial sources. Remember that ActiveX components are COM objects, and there are thousands of commercially distributed ActiveX components to choose from. Only after you have truly exhausted your options for reuse should you pass out the coding assignments.

After your objects are developed, tested, and put into production, you need to determine who is going to support them. The project team that originally created the objects for a specific project will likely move on to other tasks, but the objects they put into the corporate inventory will (eventually) need maintenance. As many other projects reuse your objects, the responsibility for maintenance of a given object can become quite diluted. To avoid inadvertently abandoning these valuable objects, the objects themselves and the repository should be assigned to a project-neutral focal point or team. Perhaps some of the resources saved by reusing objects can be applied to the task of maintaining the object inventory, budgeted independently from the budget lines of the projects that created them. One final caution: Invest the time needed to prevent the nearly universal problem of poorly documented applications. Properly and fully document your objects, and then include that documentation and the objects in the corporate object repository. You may even need to reuse or maintain some of these objects yourself someday, so take the time to document them appropriately the first time around.

From Here...

This chapter has provided an overview of Microsoft's object technologies and general issues involved with Object-Oriented Programming. Now that you have a general understanding of OOP and Microsoft's object technologies, its time to get some instructions on how to create a few of those versatile COM objects known as ActiveX components:

■ To learn about creating ActiveX controls from components, see Chapter 24, "Creating ActiveX Controls."

■ To learn how to expand an existing ActiveX control, see Chapter 25, "Extending ActiveX Controls."

■ To learn how to create your own ActiveX control from scratch, see Chapter 26, "Creating a User-Drawn Control."

■ To learn how to create ActiveX documents, see Chapter 27, "Creating ActiveX Documents."

Part

V

Ch

23

CHAPTER 24

Creating ActiveX Controls

One of the most exciting features of Visual Basic 5 is the ability to create your own ActiveX controls. No longer are you limited to using the controls created by C/C++ programmers; if you can dream up a great control, you can build it yourself by using Visual Basic. What's even better is that you are not limited to using the controls you create only in Visual Basic. You can use your controls in any application or development tool that can use ActiveX controls. This means that you can turn the tables and begin building ActiveX controls in Visual Basic that C++ programmers will be using in their applications. It's a brave new world for the Visual Basic developer.

This chapter discusses building your own controls by using the latest version of Visual Basic. It covers the various approaches that you can take and some of the issues that you need to take into consideration. The information contained in this chapter is then built upon in later sections, as you learn how to build your own ActiveX controls by enhancing an existing control that "almost" does what you need your control to do. ▪

ActiveX control evolution

ActiveX controls have gone through quite an evolution over the past few years; see how ActiveX controls have grown and changed from their earliest incarnation as Visual Basic controls.

Options for building ActiveX controls

There are two basic approaches to building ActiveX controls by using Visual Basic 5. Take a look at what each approach involves, and some of the issues you need to consider when choosing between the two approaches.

Building an ActiveX control

You build a simple ActiveX control, learning how to expose the control's properties, methods, and events.

Enhancing ActiveX controls

Learn how you can take an existing control that almost does what you want and transform it into your own special creation.

ActiveX Basics

ActiveX is a technology that was introduced by the Microsoft Corporation in March, 1996. It was not really a new technology, but a renaming of Microsoft's existing OLE technologies. These technologies include the OLE Controls that were introduced with Visual Basic 4 during the previous year. It was the OLE/ActiveX controls that introduced a way to build component objects that can be placed in various applications, including Web pages. This enhanced the ability of programmers to build robust applications quickly with prebuilt components.

N O T E ActiveX isn't just a new name slapped on an old technology. Along with the new name, Microsoft significantly re-engineered its OLE technologies to make them more "network-friendly." In part, Microsoft removed from the OLE Control (OCX) specification most of the implementation requirements that had added unnecessary overhead to the controls by making them larger and slower than necessary. Along with these changes, Microsoft introduced several new technologies that were aimed specifically for use on the Web, including its Authenticode technology for signing controls and applications. In short, Microsoft put a lot of work into making the evolution of OLE into ActiveX a lot more than just a new name on an old technology. ■

ActiveX controls can be used in Web pages to add functionality and to greatly improve appearance. As HTML and scripting languages are fairly limited, ActiveX controls have no limitations. Web page designers can interact with the ActiveX controls on their pages with scripting languages such as VBScript.

ActiveX is the next step of the Visual Basic component technology. Visual Basic component technology was started with VBXs, which were used in 16-bit implementations, and were followed by OCXs, which were used in both 16- and 32-bit implementations.

With Visual Basic 5, you can create an ActiveX control as an ActiveX control project. These controls can be used with any container application that supports ActiveX controls. To use an ActiveX control on a Web page, the user's browser must support ActiveX. Microsoft Internet Explorer 3.0 and 4.0 support ActiveX controls. A typical ActiveX control as viewed by IE 3.0 is shown in Figure 24.1.

N O T E Netscape Communicator, the latest version of Netscape's popular Web browser, now supports ActiveX controls. Previous versions of Netscape's browser still require special plug-ins to accept ActiveX controls. ■

Building and Implementing an ActiveX Control: An Overview

The basic process of building an ActiveX control is simply a matter of following these steps:

1. Determine what you want your ActiveX control to do.
2. Determine what you want your ActiveX control to look like, if you want it to have any appearance at all.
3. Determine what properties, methods, and events your control will provide.

FIG. 24.1
The ActiveX control on this page allows users to select a specific html page based upon contents of the combobox.

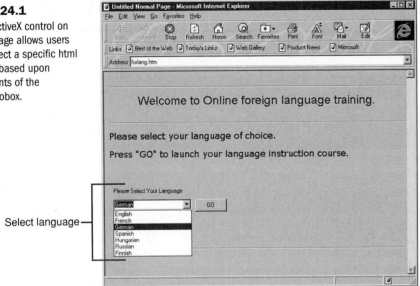

Select language

4. Determine whether you want to build your control by using the constituent (built-in) controls or by using other controls as building blocks for your control. When considering other controls, consider licensing and distribution issues.

5. Start a Visual Basic ActiveX control project and draw your control.

6. Add code to enable all the properties, methods, and events you want your control to have. Consider whether your control will still be safe for initialization and scripting with the enabling of properties and methods.

7. Create a storage location for your control and all of its supporting files. If you are using a project management system, such as Visual SourceSafe, register your project in it.

8. Build a test project and test your control. Make sure to use all the properties, methods, and events that you gave your control.

9. Compile your control into an OCX.

10. Use the Setup Wizard to build a distributable version, including all the supporting files.

11. If you plan on a Web-based control, test your control on an HTML form. Use the one the Setup Wizard made as a starting point. Test all properties, methods, and events from scripting code.

Two Ways to Build an ActiveX Control

Building a Visual Basic ActiveX control can be as easy or as difficult as you choose. It all depends on whether you can use existing controls in your design, how sophisticated your control's user interface will be, and of course, how much program code you have to write to implement the control's functionality. In any case, there are two basic ways to go about building a control:

Part
V

Ch
24

■ *Assemble the control from existing controls* This is also know as using *Constituent Controls*. This is the easier of the two choices, requiring only that you have ActiveX controls.

■ *Enhance an existing control* You can use an existing control as a starting point for your own creative efforts by modifying properties. This is a good way to get the exact functionality that you need in your control.

These two methods of building a control are listed in the order of general difficulty, although, again, how difficult a control is to create depends on several other factors, as well.

This chapter looks at how to create ActiveX controls from existing controls. The next chapter, "Extending ActiveX Controls," explains how you can add additional functionality to your ActiveX controls.

N O T E Before you begin building an ActiveX control, you need to decide what type of control it will be. Will your control perform all of its functions without using any nonconstituent controls? Does the control need another control? Will the control be a visual or nonvisual control? These decisions all have to be made before beginning your ActiveX control project. ■

Advantages of Using Constituent Controls

There are many advantages to assembling an ActiveX control from existing controls. The first is obvious: Because your control's user interface consists of existing controls, you don't have to draw the interface yourself. Another advantage is that your control's users will probably already be familiar with the controls that make up your new control. This familiarity makes your new control easier to use.

Still another advantage is that, when you add an existing control to your new custom control, you get the existing control's complete functionality, too; an important consideration when you consider how many event procedures, methods, and properties are supported by a standard control.

You can often use third-party controls as constituent controls, but usually you'll use Visual Basic's standard controls or intrinsic controls. The Visual Basic *intrinsic controls* are shown in Table 24.1.

Table 24.1 The Visual Basic Intrinsic Controls

Icon	Name	Description
☑	CheckBox	A small button-like control that the user can check or uncheck.
▣	ComboBox	A control that is comprised of a scrollable list containing valid selections and an edit box into which the user can type selections. The user can also use the mouse to choose selections from the list.

Icon	Name	Description
	CommandButton	A typical push-button type of control.
	Data	A control that you can link to database fields.
	DirListBox	A control that displays the directories on the current drive.
	DriveListBox	A control that displays the drives on the system.
	FileListBox	A FileListBox displays the files in the current directory.
	Frame	A control that enables you to place controls into a group, by providing an outline to enclose the group and a caption to identify the group.
	HScrollBar	A control that represents a horizontal scroll bar.
	Image	A control that displays an image.
	Label	A control that holds a static (unchangeable) line of text.
	Line	A control that enables you to draw lines on a form or control.
	ListBox	A control that features a scrollable list from which the user can make a selection. Similar to a ComboBox, but without the edit box.
	OptionButton	A small, circular, button-like control that the user can use to toggle options on or off.
	PictureBox	A control that's similar to an Image control, but which features more methods.
	Shape	A control you can use to draw various types of shapes on a form or control.
	TextBox	A control that represents an editable line of text.
	Timer	A control that's used in Visual Basic projects to access and control Windows timers.
	VScrollBar	A control that represents a vertical scroll bar.

Part

V

Ch

24

A big advantage of using the intrinsic controls as constituent controls is that you don't need to acquire additional licenses to distribute the controls with your programs. The intrinsic controls are built in to the Visual Basic runtime files that you always need to distribute. If you use third-party controls, you almost certainly have to pay licensing fees. (For more information on licensing, see Chapter 25, "Extending ActiveX Controls.")

Using Constituent Controls

The following sections take a look at how you can use constituent controls to build an entirely new control. The address control that you create can itself become a constituent control for future ActiveX controls; in this way, a complete library of controls can be built up quite rapidly and without a lot of coding.

Creating the Address Control

Now that you have some background information on using constituent controls, you can get started creating your first full-fledged ActiveX control. The control that you'll build in the following sections enables users to enter their name and address into a predefined form. To create the control, you'll use Visual Basic Label and TextBox controls as constituent controls. To build this control, follow these steps:

1. Start Visual Basic 5. If it is already running, choose File, New Project.

2. In the New Project dialog box, select ActiveX Control Project. A new project should start with a UserControl object named UserControl1, as shown in Figure 24.2.

FIG. 24.2
ActiveX controls can contain all of the controls that a regular application has.

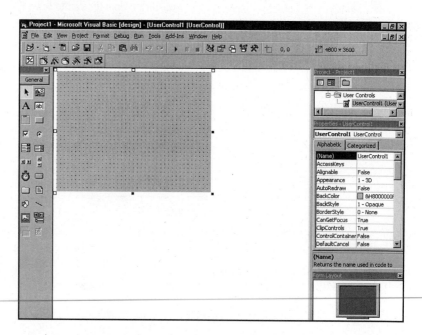

3. Change the `Name` property of the `UserControl` to `AddressPrj`. If the Properties window is not visible, choose <u>V</u>iew, Properties <u>W</u>indow or click the Properties Window button. Find the `Name` property and change it by typing **Address**.

4. Add five Labels to the form and give them the following properties:

Name	`lblName`
Caption	"Name:"
Name	`lblStreet`
Caption	"Street:"
Name	`lblCity`
Caption	"City:"
Name	`lblState`
Caption	"State:"
Name	`lblZip`
Caption	"Zip:"

5. Add five Text boxes to the form with the following properties.

Name	`txtName`
Name	`txtStreet`
Name	`txtCity`
Name	`txtState`
Name	`txtZip`

6. Click the `UserControl` object and resize it so that the constituent controls fit neatly inside. You can resize the control by using the sizing handles or by changing the `Height` and `Width` properties in the Properties window to 3090 and 3810, respectively. The completed form will now look like that shown in Figure 24.3.

FIG. 24.3
The full set of constituent controls should look like this.

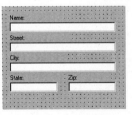

7. Save your project to its own folder, which you should name ..\Samples\Address. Save the `UserControl` with the name **Address.ctl**. Save the project with the name **Address.vbp**.

Adding Program Code to the Control

The next step is to add code that responds to the `Resize` event, which occurs whenever a control is created or resized.

To add program code for the Resize event, first double-click the UserControl object
to display the control's code window. When the window pops up, it displays the
UserControl_Initialize() event procedure. In the Procedures box, select Resize, and the
UserControl_Resize() event procedure appears in the code window. Add the lines shown in
Listing 24.1 to the UserControl_Resize() event procedure.

**Listing 24.1   LSTz_01.TXT—Code for the *UserControl_Resize()* Event
Procedure**

```
' Don't let the developer make the
' height of the control too small.
If UserControl.Height < 3090 _
    Then UserControl.Height = 3090

' Don't let the developer make the
' width of the control too small.
If UserControl.Width < 1500 _
    Then UserControl.Width = 1500

' Change the width of the controls
' to fit into the resized UserControl.
txtName.Width = ScaleWidth - 500
txtStreet.Width = ScaleWidth - 500
txtCity.Width = ScaleWidth - 500
txtState.Width = ScaleWidth / 2 - 400
txtZip.Width = ScaleWidth / 2 - 400

' Reposition the Zip Code controls.
lblZip.Move ScaleWidth / 2 + 160
txtZip.Move ScaleWidth / 2 + 160
```

After adding the previous lines to the UserControl_Resize() event procedure, be sure to save
your changes by clicking the Save Project Group button on VB5's toolbar or by choosing File,
Save Project Group.

Understanding *UserControl_Resize()*

When a developer (who uses the control to create an application or Web page) resizes the
Address control, be sure that the control's interface still looks okay. For this reason, you don't
want the height of the Address control to get smaller because then there won't be room for all
the Label and TextBox constituent controls. (Okay, if you really want to, you can use smaller
fonts, but who wants to go to all that trouble?) So, the first thing UserControl_Resize() does
is make sure that the control's height doesn't get set to less than 3090:

```
If UserControl.Height < 3090 _
    Then UserControl.Height = 3090
```

N O T E   The height of 3090 is an arbitrary number. For the sake of this example, a height of 3090
was chosen. Your control height may be less than or greater than this size. ∎

Now, if the developer tries to make the control too small, UserControl_Resize() will set the height back to where it belongs. The developer can make the control taller, but he can't make it shorter.

N O T E Notice how you can change the value of a property with a line of code such as *Object.Property* = *Value*, where *Object* is the object whose property you want to change, *Property* is the name of the property to change, and *Value* is the value to which you set the property. Notice also that you separate the object and property names with a period. ▪

Although you have to be careful about how the developer changes the control's height, the control's width has a little more flexibility. Because TextBox controls can scroll text, the TextBox doesn't necessarily have to be wide enough to hold the entire line that the user types in. So, your new control can allow the developer to change the width of the Address control. Still, you want to limit the width to a sensible amount. In Listing 24.1, that limit is 1500, which is enforced like this:

Part
V
Ch
24

```
If UserControl.Width < 1500 _
    Then UserControl.Width = 1500
```

N O T E As with the height, the width of 1500 is an arbitrary number. For the sake of this example. a width of 1500 was chosen. Your control width may be less than or greater than this size. ▪

Because you can never know how the developer has set the Address control's size, you need to size and position the constituent controls every time a Resize event occurs. The first step in this task is to set the constituent controls' widths, like this:

```
txtName.Width = ScaleWidth - 500
txtStreet.Width = ScaleWidth - 500
txtCity.Width = ScaleWidth - 500
txtState.Width = ScaleWidth / 2 - 400
txtZip.Width = ScaleWidth / 2 - 400
```

ScaleWidth and ScaleHeight hold the width and height of the UserControl object's visible area. In the first three lines of the previous code segment, the code sets the width of the constituent controls to 500 twips less than the width of the UserControl object's visible width. The width of the txtState and txtZip controls is a little trickier to set because these controls are on the same line. To fit these TextBoxes properly, the code first divides ScaleWidth by 2, giving the total amount of space each TextBox can have. Then the code subtracts 400 twips to put a little space between the controls.

Because the controls for the State and Zip fields are on the same line, when the UserControl object changes width, the Zip controls (lblZip and txtZip) have to be repositioned. The UserControl_Resize() event procedure takes care of that little detail like this:

```
lblZip.Move ScaleWidth / 2 + 160
txtZip.Move ScaleWidth / 2 + 160
```

NOTE You can use an object's Move() method to reposition the object. A call to Move() looks like object.Move left, top, width, height, where object is the object to move, left is the position of the object's left edge, top is the position of the top edge, width is the object's new width, and height is the new height. Only the left argument is required; that is, top, width, and height are optional arguments. ■

Testing the Address Control

You've created your control's interface and added code to handle one important event. You're now ready to see Address in action, by opening the test application's designer window and adding an instance of the Address control. At this point, you'll be playing the role of an application or Web page developer. In this role, you want to see how the control will act when another developer gets his hands on it.

After you have entered all the code for the control, you are ready to test the control. A good way to test your ActiveX control is in a control project. To test the Address control, follow these steps:

1. Remember to save your code.
2. Add a Standard EXE project to the project group.
3. Close the design and Code windows for the User Control. Notice an icon for your control appears in the Toolbox.
4. Add an instance of the Address control to Form1.
5. Set the properties of the control.
6. Run the test program and try out the control.

If you have problems with the control, you can use the same debugging techniques to find problems in controls that you used to find problems in standard programs. You can set break points and step through the code line by line, whether in the ActiveX Control project or in the Standard EXE project. (See Chapter 25, "Extending ActiveX Controls," for more information on debugging your code.)

As you can see, the Address control looks exactly as you designed it. That's because the first time the instance appears in the test application's form, it uses the width and height of the control as you set it when you designed the control. The sizes and positions of the constituent controls are handled in the UserControl_Resize() event procedure, based on the current size of the Address control.

To really see UserControl_Resize() in action, reduce the width of the Address control. When you do, the constituent controls automatically resize themselves according to the new Address size. If you try to reduce the height of the Address control, the control springs back to its minimum size. You can, however, enlarge the control as much as you like. If you reduce the width of the control as far as it'll go, you end up with something like Figure 24.4. No matter how narrow you try to make the control, it'll always stay at least at its minimum size.

FIG. 24.4
This is the test application when the Address control is at its minimum width.

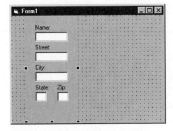

Compiling the Address Control

After you've created and tested your control, you need to compile it into an .OCX file, which is the stand-alone binary version of the control that you can distribute. When you compile your control into an .OCX file, developers can install the control on their systems and then use the control in their own projects, regardless of whether they're working with a programming language, a Web-page authoring application, or some other development tool.

Part
V
Ch
24

To create a stand-alone. OCX file for the Address control, perform the following steps:

1. Double-click Address in the Project Group window. The control's designer window appears.

2. Choose File, Make ADDRESS.OCX. The Make Project dialog box appears.

3. Change the control's file name to **Address.ocx** (you may also need to set the directory to where you want the file to be saved), and click OK. VB5 compiles the new control and writes the .OCX file out to your disk.

4. Choose File, Remove Project. When Visual Basic asks whether you want to remove the project, click Yes. (If you're asked to save files, also choose Yes.)

After completing the previous steps, your project group will contain only the test application, AddressTestApp. However, if you look at Visual Basic's Toolbox, you'll see that the Address control is again available. Now, however, Visual Basic will use the compiled control rather than the version that was originally part of your project group.

> **N O T E** If you need to, you can easily add the Address control project back to the control group from which you deleted it. Just select the File, Add Project command from VB5's menu bar, and then select the project from the Existing page of the Add Project property sheet. ▪

The Address control is one of those controls that can easily be used as the basis for other ActiveX controls. One possible use for the Address control is to provide a consistent look and feel to all of your applications that require user data entry. Another possible use is in a Web page to collect data in a guest book control.

The Address control is by no means a complete and robust control. The next few sections examine how methods and events can be added to your control. Chapter 25, "Extending ActiveX Controls," provides some ways to make your control more robust and bulletproof.

▶ **See** "Control Error Handling," **p. 727**

A Quick Example: Build the AXYesNo

In the previous example, you built an ActiveX control out of constituent controls. You added some code to one of the events and successfully tested the control in a test project. However, you did not add any additional methods or events. You used only those methods and events that were supported by your constituent controls. In the present example, you build an ActiveX control and provide some methods and events.

This ActiveX control has three constituent controls: two command buttons and one label. In this example, you toggle the caption of the label by clicking the two command buttons. To build this control, follow these steps:

1. Start Visual Basic 5. If it is already running, choose File, New Project.

2. In the New Project dialog box, select ActiveX Control Project. A new project should start with a UserControl object named UserControl1.

3. Change the Name property of the UserControl to **AXYesNo**. If the Properties window is not visible, choose View, Properties Window or click the Properties Window button. Find the Name property and change it by typing **AXYesNo**.

4. Add two command buttons to your UserControl. To add controls to the UserControl, click the CommandButton control in the Toolbox, and then draw the buttons, as in Figure 24.5.

FIG. 24.5

Draw two command buttons on the control drawing area by selecting the CommandButton icon and then clicking and dragging on the drawing area.

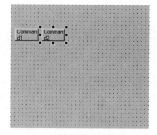

5. Position the two CommandButtons so that you can see both of them. To move a CommandButton, click and drag it across your UserControl. You can also resize it by dragging the sizing blocks located on each of its corners.

6. Name one of the command buttons **cmdYes** and the other **cmdNo**.

7. Set the caption of cmdYes to Yes and the caption of cmdNo to No.

8. Add a Label control to the UserControl object and name it **lblDisplay**.

9. Add code to the Click event of cmdYes to have lblDisplay's Caption property say Yes. To go to the Code window, click cmdYes twice or click the View Code button. The cursor should be set in the Private Sub cmdYes_Click() event. Add the code shown in Listing 24.2.

Listing 24.2   AXYESNO\AXYESNO.CTL—*cmdYes* Code

```
Private Sub cmdYes_Click()
    lblDisplay.Caption = "Yes"
End Sub
```

10. Add code to the Click event of the cmdNo button to have it change lblDisplay's Caption property to No. To navigate between object events inside of the code window, go to the object list and select the cmdNo object. Verify that the event you are looking at in the procedure list is the Click event. Add the code shown in Listing 24.3.

Listing 24.3   AXYESNO\AXYESNO.CTL—cmdNo Code

```
Private Sub cmdNo_Click()
    lblDisplay.Caption = "No"
End Sub
```

Part

V

Ch

24

11. Choose Project, Project1 Properties to open the Project Properties dialog box, and then name the project **AXEYesNo** and provide a project description.

12. Build your control by selecting the File, Make AXYesNo.ocx menu entries.

13. Save your project to its own folder, which you should name ..\Samples\AXYesNo. Save the UserControl with the name **AXYesNo.ctl**. Save the project with the name **AXYesNo.vbp**.

14. Test the control in a test project. Choose File, Add Project. From the Add Project dialog box, select Standard EXE. Inside Visual Basic, close the UserControl object window. Notice that the user control object you made AXYesNo is now available in the Toolbox. Add a AXYesNo to Form1, as in Figure 24.6. Now, test your control by choosing Run, Start, or by clicking the Start button. Click each of the command buttons and verify that they work correctly, as in Figure 24.7. Stop the project by choosing Run, End, or by clicking the End button.

FIG. 24.6

Once you close the window containing the control you are developing, it becomes available in the Toolbox for use in any other Visual Basic application.

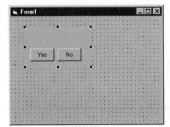

15. Test your ActiveX control from an HTML container by using the Setup Wizard. Close Visual Basic. From the Visual Basic program group on the Start menu, select Application Setup Wizard. On the Select Project dialog box, select ...\AXYesNo\AXYesNo.vbp and check Create Internet Download Setup, as in Figure 24.8.

FIG. 24.7

When you run the standard Visual Basic project, you can verify that your control works correctly.

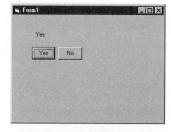

FIG. 24.8

To build the necessary files for use in an HTML document, you need to use the Application Setup Wizard to create an Internet Download Setup.

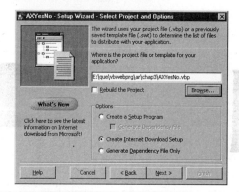

16. On the Internet Distribution Location dialog box, pick a location where you want your distribution files to become available.

17. On the Internet Package dialog box, pick Use Alternate Location for runtime components, but do not give a location, as in Figure 24.9. A blank location will put the files with the other runtime files.

FIG. 24.9

You can specify whether the Visual Basic runtime files (and other necessary files) will be downloaded from the Microsoft Web site, the same Web site as your control, or a third Web site.

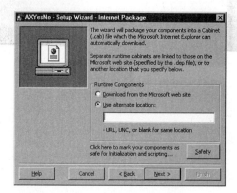

18. On the Internet Package dialog box, click the Safety button. On the Safety dialog box, specify that your control is Safe for Initialization and Safe for Scripting (these settings will be discussed in greater detail in Chapter 25, "Extending ActiveX Controls"), as in Figure 24.10.

FIG. 24.10

By marking your control as safe for initialization and scripting, you place your guarantee that your control can't harm the user's computer, even if used in HTML documents that you didn't build.

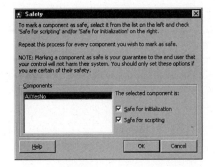

19. Move forward through the ActiveX Server Components dialog box. In the File Summary dialog box, the Setup Wizard shows you a summary of the files that will be included in the package, as in Figure 24.11.

FIG. 24.11

The File Summary dialog box shows which files will be included in the Internet download files that will be packaged for inclusion on a Web site.

20. After the Setup Wizard has completed building the Internet Download files, open the AXYesNo.HTM document in Internet Explorer to test your control in a Web browser, as in Figure 24.12.

Exposing Properties, Methods, and Events

You can make properties, methods, and events of your ActiveX controls available to Web designers to increase your controls' flexibility. After properties, methods, and events are exposed, they are available to be manipulated from script code on an HTML page, such as VBScript. You can make the native properties, methods, and events of your constituent controls available, or you can make up your own properties, methods, and events for the special functionality that you are trying to achieve with your control. You need to be careful in what you enable, as it might make your control unsafe.

▶ **See** "Marking Your Controls Safe for Scripting and Initialization," **p. 735**

FIG. 24.12

After the Setup Wizard has completed building the download files, it creates a simple HTML file you can open in Internet Explorer to test your control.

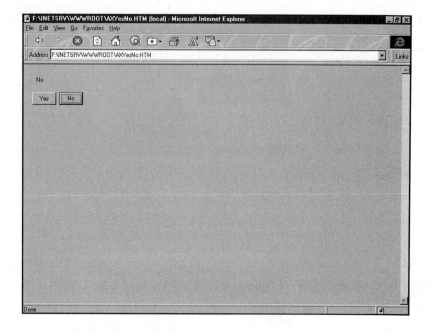

Exposing Properties of ActiveX Controls

Properties are characteristics of your controls. By changing properties, you can change the appearance and behavior of ActiveX controls. By exposing your ActiveX control's properties, you allow Web developers to manipulate your control. The availability of your ActiveX control's properties is controlled by property procedures. A *property procedure* is a public procedure that makes your property available to the outside world. Property procedures allow you to make properties read, write, or read *and* write.

You need to implement two property procedures for all properties that you want to make available to the user of your control. These two property procedures are the Get and Let procedures. The property Get procedure allows the current value of the property to be read by programming code or script, whereas the property Let procedure allows the current value of the property to be changed by the code. These methods also allow the property to appear in the Properties window when using the control in a Visual Basic application.

In the following example, you make the UserControl object that you made in the first example have a public property named BackColor, which will be available for read and write. To make a property of your control available to be read from script, make a property Get procedure. The name of the procedure is BackColor, and it is of type OLE_Color. It returns the value of the UserControl, as seen in Listing 24.4.

Listing 24.4 AXYESNO\AXYESNO.CTL—Reading the *BackColor* Property

```
Public Property Get BackColor() As OLE_COLOR
    BackColor = UserControl.BackColor
End Property
```

To make a property available to be changed from script, use a property Let statement, as in Listing 24.5.

Listing 24.5 AXYESNO\AXYESNO.CTL—Setting the *BackColor* Property

```
Public Property Let BackColor(ByVal New_BackColor As OLE_COLOR)
    UserControl.BackColor() = New_BackColor
    PropertyChanged "BackColor"
End Property
```

To the Web designer, your ActiveX control should look like one object, although it might be made of many constituent controls. For that reason, a Web designer should have to change only one property to change one attribute—for example, there should be only one BackColor property. You can change multiple objects on your control's properties with one property procedure. For example, if you want the BackColor of the UserControl and the label to have the same BackColor, use one property procedure and have it modify two properties, as in Listing 24.6. This enables you to change both BackColor properties with the single property.

Listing 24.6 AXYESNO\AXYESNO.CTL—Setting the *BackColor* Property of Both the *UserControl* and the Label

```
Public Property Let BackColor(ByVal New_BackColor As OLE_COLOR)
    UserControl.BackColor() = New_BackColor
    lblDisplay.BackColor() = New_BackColor
    PropertyChanged "BackColor"
End Property
```

Exposing Methods of ActiveX Controls

Methods give Web designers the ability to perform actions on the objects of their ActiveX controls. A method is just a function or sub that is declared as public. The function or sub's name associates with the name of a method of an object. For instance, you can use the code in Listing 24.7 to add a method to the AXYesNo control, which can then be used to set the label.

Listing 24.7 AXYESNO\AXYESNO.CTL—*SetText* Method

```
Public Sub SetText(Item As String)
    lblDisplay.Caption = Item
End Sub
```

Exposing Events of ActiveX Controls

By exposing events, you give Web designers the ability to call the code that is associated with those events.

To expose an event, you first declare the event's name in the General Declarations section of your UserControl object. Use the keyword Event and then the events name, followed by parentheses—for example, Event Click() declares there will be a Click event.

Second, create a procedure that uses your new event by using the code in Listing 24.8.

Listing 24.8 AXYESNO\AXYESNO.CTL—Exposing the cmdNo's *Click* Event

```
Private Sub cmdNo_Click()
    'Change the caption
    lblDisplay.Caption = "No"
    'Raise the Click event
    RaiseEvent Click
End Sub
```

Enhancing ActiveX Controls

The previous sections introduced the concepts involved in creating ActiveX controls, including how to place controls on a User Control Window, and how to create an entirely new control by adding properties, methods, and events. However, you can also create "new" controls simply by adding capabilities to an existing control. This means you will be working with a single base control, but adding properties, methods, and events to provide additional capabilities to the user. For example, you might want a text box that accepts only certain characters, or perhaps a scroll bar that works with a range of letters rather than numbers. Placing the code that performs these tasks into an ActiveX control makes it easier to use the code in future programs. For example, rather than adding special code to every TextBox control in your program, you simply use your "enhanced" control in place of the text box.

To create these enhanced controls, you use many of the same techniques that you have already learned. However, you also can use a Visual Basic Wizard to make quicker work out of the process, which is explained later in the chapter.

Adding Capabilities to a Control

To create an enhanced control, follow these five basic steps:

1. Start a new ActiveX control project.
2. Add the base control to the User Control Window.
3. Add the properties and methods to the control.
4. Test the control in a test application.
5. Compile your control so that others can use it.

The following sections walk you through these steps, using a text box as the base control. Your "enhanced" text box will have a property that allows the programmer to choose a set of acceptable characters that the user can enter. This control will be called TxtCharLimit (short for "Limited Character TextBox"). It will be just like the standard TextBox but with one additional property, CharAccept, which will allow the user to choose either all characters, just letters, or just numbers.

Creating the Basic Control

The steps to create the enhanced text control are very similar to the steps you used to create the Address and AXYesNo controls. For the enhanced text control, these steps are as follows:

1. Start a new ActiveX control project.

2. Add a text box to the User Control Window with the upper-left corner of the text box in position 0, 0.

3. Name the text box **txtCharSet** and clear its Text property

4. Set the properties of the ActiveX project and the User Control to the values specified in Table 24.2.

   To set the first three values in the table, use the *projectname* Properties dialog box. To set the remaining values, highlight the UserControl object and press F4 to show the Properties window.

Table 24.2 Project and Property Settings for the Enhanced Text Custom Control

Item	Setting
Project Type	ActiveX Control
Project Name	TextLimited
Project Description	Text Box for Limited Character Set
User control Name property	TxtCharLimit
User control Public property	True

When you have completed setting up the user interface of the enhanced text control, it should look like the one in Figure 24.13.

You also need to set up the Resize event procedure of the User Control to make the text box fit the space that is drawn by the developer when using your control. This Resize event procedure is shown in Listing 24.9.

Part
V

Ch
24

FIG. 24.13

A simple text control can be enhanced with other capabilities.

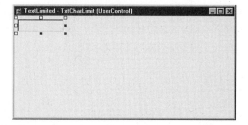

Listing 24.9   *TXTCHARLIMIT.CTL*—Using the *Resize* Event to Make Sure the Text Control Fills the Space

```
Private Sub UserControl_Resize()
  txtCharSet.Height = UserControl.ScaleHeight
  txtCharSet.Width = UserControl.ScaleWidth
End Sub
```

The simple two-line `Resize` event procedure is all the code necessary for the user interface of your sample control. Its purpose is to keep the text box the same size as the `UserControl` object. Before moving on, test it by performing the following steps:

1. Save your project.
2. Close the UserControl window. If you have the Toolbox open, you will notice a new icon appear for your control.
3. Choose File, Add Project. Add a Standard EXE project.
4. Draw your control on Form1 and try resizing it.

The purpose of jumping the gun like that is to get you used to the idea that the code in your ActiveX control does not have to be explicitly executed. Remember, when developing an ActiveX control, the code you write is used at design time in the host program.

For now, remove the Standard EXE project by right-clicking it in the Project Explorer Window and then choosing Remove Project1. Now it is time to work on the enhancements to the control.

Creating the Additional Capabilities

The enhancement you are going to make to the TextBox control is to tell it whether it should accept any characters, just letters, or just numbers. You accomplish this by adding your own property, called `CharAccept`, which can have one of the following three values:

- `0`—Accept any character
- `1`—Accept only numbers
- `2`—Accept only letters

The first thing you need is a private variable to store the property value internally. To do this, create the variable in the General Declarations section of the UserControl object:

```
Private mCharAccept As Integer
```

Next, you need to create the new property, called CharAccept. You can do this either by typing in the Let and Get procedures by hand, or by choosing Tools, Add Procedure, Property. The code for the CharAccept property is fairly easy to understand. When the developer needs the value of the CharAccept property, the Property Get procedure simply passes what is stored in the private variable. When the value of the CharAccept property is set, the Property Let procedure assigns one of the valid values to the private variable. The following is the code for both Property procedures:

```
Public Property Get CharAccept() As Integer
    CharAccept = mCharAccept
End Property

Public Property Let CharAccept(ByVal nNewValue As Integer)

        Select Case nNewValue
         Case 1 To 2
             mCharAccept = nNewValue
         Case Else
             mCharAccept = 0
        End Select

        PropertyChanged "CharAccept"

End Property
```

Part

V

Ch

24

Notice the use of the PropertyChanged method. This method works with the ReadProperties and WriteProperties events, which you see in the next few paragraphs.

You now need to use the InitProperties event of the user control to specify an initial value of the property, as follows:

```
Private Sub UserControl_InitProperties()
    mCharAccept = 0
End Sub
```

This code makes sure that a value is set, even if the developer does not set it.

You also need to create the code for the WriteProperties and ReadProperties events to preserve the design time settings of CharAccept. These two events use the PropertyBag object to save and retrieve the value of the CharAccept property. The PropertyBag object enables you to maintain the design environment value of CharAccept. The code for these two events, shown in Listing 24.10, is not hard to understand. What is important, however, is why you need the code.

Listing 24.10 *TXTCHARLIMIT.CTL*—Holding the Property Value

```
Private Sub UserControl_ReadProperties(PropBag As PropertyBag)
    mCharAccept = PropBag.ReadProperty("CharAccept", 0)
End Sub

Private Sub UserControl_WriteProperties(PropBag As PropertyBag)
    PropBag.WriteProperty "CharAccept", mCharAccept, 0
End Sub
```

Remember that an ActiveX control's code starts executing the moment you draw it on a form. Suppose you set the value of a property during design time. In your sample control, assume you set the value of CharAccept to 1. You also may change it several times while your program is running. The normal behavior for a control is to revert to its original design-time values when the program ends, thus adding the requirement of maintaining two separate *states* of the property.

More simply put, if you change a property at design time, the control has to know to get this new value rather than use the default. Conversely, if the property's value is changed during program execution, the control has to retrieve the value when it returns to the design state.

The PropertyBag object allows your ActiveX control to store properties about itself, making this behavior possible. The PropertyChanged method provides notification that the user has changed a property. By knowing the state of the program and whether the PropertyChange method has been invoked, VB can fire the WriteProperties and ReadProperties events.

The next step in your sample project is to create the code that makes it do something different than a normal text box. In this case, you use the text box's KeyPress event to scan each character as it is entered. Visual Basic will pass the ASCII code of the characters through the event's KeyAscii parameter. Depending on the ASCII code and setting of CharAccept property, you will either accept the character or set KeyAscii to 0, which causes the text box to not display the character.

In addition to not displaying the character, you want to inform the host program that the user has entered an invalid character. You do this by creating an event called UserError. To create this event, add the following line of code to the General Declarations section of the UserControl object:

```
Public Event UserError()
```

This event works like an event in any other control; someone using your control can place code in it. The only thing you have to do is fire the event by using the RaiseEvent method.

Because there are three sets of acceptable characters, you can use a Select statement to handle the choices. One other item of note—you need to enable the backspace key (ASCII code 8) in any of the character sets that you use. Otherwise, the user won't be able to delete the previous character. The code for the KeyPress event is shown in Listing 24.11.

On the CD

Listing 24.11   TXTCHARLIMIT.CTL—Using the *KeyPress* Event to Handle Screening the Keys Entered by the User

```
Private Sub txtCharSet_KeyPress(KeyAscii As Integer)
    If KeyAscii = 8 Then Exit Sub

    Select Case mCharAccept
        Case 0 'Any character is acceptable
            Exit Sub
        Case 1 'Only numbers may be entered
            If KeyAscii >= 48 And KeyAscii <= 57 Then
                Exit Sub
            Else
                KeyAscii = 0
                Beep
                RaiseEvent UserError
            End If
        Case 2 'Only letters may be entered
            If KeyAscii >= 65 And KeyAscii <= 90 Then
                Exit Sub
            ElseIf KeyAscii >= 97 And KeyAscii <= 122 Then
                Exit Sub
            Else
                KeyAscii = 0
                Beep
                RaiseEvent UserError
            End If
    End Select

End Sub
```

The code in this listing is fairly simple. KeyAscii represents the typed character, which is checked for validity by Select Case and If statements. If the character falls outside an acceptable range, the control beeps and raises the UserError event.

Testing the Capabilities

After you have entered all of the code for the control, you are ready to test the control. To test the TxtCharLimit control, follow these steps:

1. Remember to save your code.
2. Add a Standard EXE project to the project group.
3. Close the design and Code windows for the User Control.

   Notice that an icon for your control appears in the Toolbox.
4. Add an instance of the TxtCharLimit control to the form in the test application.
5. Set the properties of the control.
6. Run the test program and try out the control. Try setting the CharAccept property to different values to verify that it accepts only the keystrokes you want.

Part
V

Ch
24

If you have problems with the control, you can use the same debugging techniques to find problems in a control as you do for finding problems in standard programs. You can set break points and step through the code line by line, whether in the ActiveX Control project or in the Standard EXE project. (See Chapter 8, "Programming Visual Basic," for more information on debugging your code.)

Choosing a Toolbox Icon

One thing you may have noticed by now is that all the custom controls you create have the same symbol in the Toolbox. This can cause a lot of confusion if you are working with multiple controls. Although the ToolTips provide a description of the control, it is better to have a custom icon to identify each control. You can do this by setting the value of the `ToolboxBitmap` property of the user control. This property determines what is displayed in the Toolbox for your control. If the property is set to `None`, the default icon is used. You can set the property to any bitmap, but be aware that the Toolbox icon is only 16 × 15 pixels. Therefore, you should use custom bitmaps that are created in that size.

Using the ActiveX Control Interface Wizard

When you created the `CharAccept` property of the enhanced text box, you created one piece of the public interface of the control. However, your users probably will also want to be able to access most of the standard properties, methods, and events of the text box. For example, you may have noticed that the `Text` property was not accessible from your custom control. This makes sense because you did not add any code for it. The section "Exposing Properties of ActiveX Controls" exposed properties with the same name as the component property to allow the user to access these properties. Because there were only a few properties, each property was created by hand. However, you can imagine that handling this for the dozens of properties of a control could get very tedious.

Fortunately, Visual Basic provides a tool to make this process much easier—the ActiveX Control Interface Wizard. First you tell the Wizard the names of all the properties that you want to have for your control. It then enables you to "bind" the properties of your control to the properties of a component of your control. The end result is that the Wizard generates the appropriate code for you.

Adding the Wizard to Visual Basic

The first step to using the VB ActiveX Control Interface Wizard is adding it to your design environment. For this purpose, Visual Basic includes the Add-In Manager. To start the Add-In Manager, choose Add-Ins, Add-In Manager. This opens the Add-In Manager dialog box

To add the VB ActiveX Control Interface Wizard, click the box next to the name of the Wizard. This places a check mark in the box, indicating that the Wizard will be part of your desktop. Next, click the OK button to exit the Add-In Manager and add the Wizard to Visual Basic.

Next, you need to re-create the Limited text control by using the Wizard. To begin, start a new ActiveX Control project and draw a text box on the UserControl window. Set up the names and sizes the same way you did in the previous example. Next, start the Wizard by choosing the ActiveX Control Interface Wizard item from the Add-Ins menu. The Wizard will start by displaying the initial screen, shown in Figure 24.14. You then click the Next button to start the actual work of setting up your properties.

FIG. 24.14

The ActiveX Control Interface Wizard simplifies the process of creating properties by creating much of the code for you.

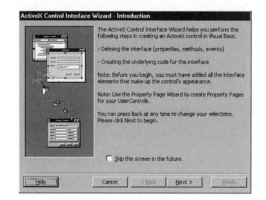

Part
V
Ch
24

N O T E For the Wizard to work most effectively, you must add all the required components to the user control before starting the Wizard. ■

Selecting and Creating Properties

The next step in using the Wizard is to select the properties, methods, and events that you want to make available to your control. Collectively, properties, methods, and events are referred to as *members*. On page two, shown in Figure 24.15, the Wizard contains a list of the names of just about every item that you could find in any control in Visual Basic. To select a property or method to create, highlight the name of the item in the Available names list, and then click the right arrow button to select the item. For your sample control, highlight the Text property on the left and click the right arrow button.

FIG. 24.15

Select properties, methods, and events for your control from the Available names list.

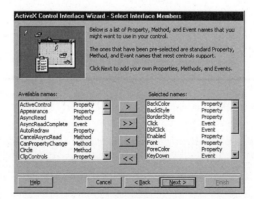

TIP You can also select an item by double-clicking it in the list.

After you add the Text property to the Selected Names list, click the Next button to move to the next page of the Wizard.

NOTE You may have noticed that the selection of properties works just like the two-column pick list control that was created in Chapter 9, "Using the Windows Standard Controls." ◼

After selecting the predefined properties, methods, and events for your control, you are taken to the page of the Wizard where you can enter the new custom items for your control. The Create Custom Interface Members page of the Wizard contains a list of all the custom members that will be created for your control.

If you have previously defined public properties or other members, they will appear in this list when you first access the page. From this page of the Wizard, you can add new members, or edit or delete existing ones. To add a new member, click the New button of the Wizard. This opens the Add Custom Member dialog box. In this dialog box, specify the name of the member and its type. Create the CharAccept property by typing **CharAccept** in the Name field, and then clicking OK.

While you are on this step, create the UserError event. Then click the Next button to move on.

> **CAUTION**
>
> It is advisable not to edit members of the control that you previously defined with code alone. This is because the Wizard works by analyzing comments it places in the code. The Wizard may or may not be able to correctly interpret your hand-typed code.

Assigning Properties

The next step in the Wizard is to assign the public members of the custom control to members of the constituent controls. This process is referred to as *mapping the members*. For example, rather than creating your own Text property, you can simply *map* the Text property of your custom control to the Text property of txtCharSet. The Set Mapping page of the Wizard, shown in Figure 24.16, contains a list of all the properties, methods, and events that you identified as being part of the public interface of the custom control.

The Set Mapping page contains two combo boxes for identifying the control and the control's member to which a public member should be mapped. To map a single public member of the custom control, first select the member in the Public Name list. Go ahead and highlight the Text property on the left. Next, select txtCharSet from the Control drop-down list. (This list contains the names of all the components in your custom control.) After selecting the component, you can select the member of the component from the Member drop-down list. In this case, the Text property will be selected automatically for you. This process is illustrated in Figure 24.17 for the Text property of the TxtCharLimit control.

FIG. 24.16
Mapping the public members of the control gives you a direct link to items in the constituent controls.

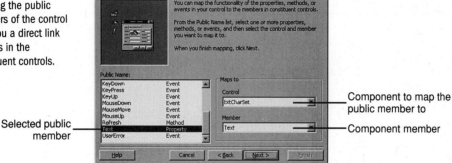

Selected public member

Component to map the public member to

Component member

FIG. 24.17
Select all the public members for the TxtCharLimit control and let the mapping occur automatically.

Note that with this screen, you can map more than one public member at a time. The list of public names supports multiple selections. You can select multiple members from the list, then select a component to which to map the members. Each public member will be mapped to the property or method of the component that bears the same name. For example, the Text property of the custom control would automatically map to the Text property of a text or combo box.

After you have mapped the Text property, click the Next button to proceed to the final page of the Wizard. This final page, shown in Figure 24.18, lets you set the attributes of each public member that is not mapped to a constituent control.

Depending on the type of member you are creating, the Wizard allows you to specify different attributes. For a property, you can specify the type of data the property will hold, the default value of the property, and what type of access the user has to the property at design time and run time. The access type determines if a Property Let, Property Get, or both procedures are created for the property. For Run Time access, you can choose Read/Write, Read Only, Write Only, or none. For Design Time access, you can choose Read/Write, Read Only, or none.

For your sample control, set the Data Type of the CharAccept property to Integer and set the default value to 0. You can also type an optional description in the Description box. Property descriptions appear at the bottom of the Properties window during design time. Because this is the final step of the Wizard, you now are ready to click the Finish button.

FIG. 24.18

Set the attributes for properties and methods before completing the code for the control.

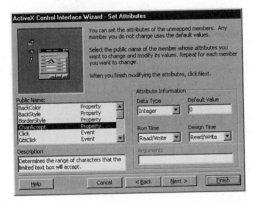

Finishing the Code

After you click the Finish button, the ActiveX Control Interface Wizard creates a number of code modules in your control. The Wizard also displays a summary page, providing you with details of the steps remaining to finish your control.

After reviewing the information on the summary page, you can take a look at the code that was generated by the Wizard. You can view the code by clicking the user control in the Project window and then clicking the View Code button. This opens the Code window containing the code that the Wizard created for you.

Take a look at some of the pieces of the code that is generated. First, in the General Declarations section, you will find that the Wizard has created constants for the default values of any unmapped properties. The CharAccept property has been given a default value of 0. In addition, the Wizard has automatically created the private property variable CharAccept. This is followed by the declaration of any events that you requested to be included in the control. A sample of this code is shown in Listing 24.12. If you mapped any events, you will notice that the Wizard places comments in the code that indicate how events are mapped to component events.

On the CD

Listing 24.12   TEXTLIMITED.CTL—Declarations Code Generated by the Wizard

```
Option Explicit

'Default Property Values:
Const m_def_BackColor = 0
Const m_def_ForeColor = 0
```

```
Const m_def_CharAccept = 0

'Property Variables:
Dim m_BackColor As Long
Dim m_ForeColor As Long
Dim m_CharAccept As Integer

'Event Declarations:
Event Click() 'MappingInfo=txtCharset,txtCharset,-1,Click
Event DblClick()
Event UserError()
Event KeyPress(KeyAscii As Integer)
```

The declarations of variables and events are followed by the property procedures. These procedures are created for properties that are mapped to a component property and those that are custom properties. As seen in Listing 24.13, the code for the Text property is complete, whereas the CharAccept property has a skeleton function ready for you to finish.

Listing 24.13 TEXTLIMITED.CTL—Property Procedures Provide the Means to Set and Retrieve Property Values

```
'WARNING! DO NOT REMOVE OR MODIFY THE FOLLOWING COMMENTED LINES!
'MappingInfo=txtCharset,txtCharset,-1,Text
Public Property Get Text() As String
    Text = txtCharset.Text
End Property

Public Property Let Text(ByVal New_Text As String)
    txtCharset.Text() = New_Text
    PropertyChanged "Text"
End Property

Public Property Get CharAccept() As Integer
    CharAccept = m_CharAccept
End Property

Public Property Let CharAccept(ByVal New_CharAccept As Integer)
    m_CharAccept = New_CharAccept
    PropertyChanged "CharAccept"
End Property
```

Note that if you had requested any methods, the Wizard would create them as Functions, instead of Sub procedures.

Finally, the code to read and write property values to the PropertyBag object is generated automatically. This code is illustrated in Listing 24.14.

Part
V

Ch
24

> **Listing 24.14   TEXTLIMITED.CTL—*UserControl* Events Set Up the Control as Changes Are Made and Saved**

```
'Load property values from storage
Private Sub UserControl_ReadProperties(PropBag As PropertyBag)

    m_BackColor = PropBag.ReadProperty("BackColor", m_def_BackColor)
    m_ForeColor = PropBag.ReadProperty("ForeColor", m_def_ForeColor)
    txtCharset.Text = PropBag.ReadProperty("Text", "")
    m_CharAccept = PropBag.ReadProperty("CharAccept", m_def_CharAccept)
End Sub

'Write property values to storage
Private Sub UserControl_WriteProperties(PropBag As PropertyBag)

    Call PropBag.WriteProperty("BackColor", m_BackColor, m_def_BackColor)
    Call PropBag.WriteProperty("ForeColor", m_ForeColor, m_def_ForeColor)
    Call PropBag.WriteProperty("Text", txtCharset.Text, "")
    Call PropBag.WriteProperty("CharAccept", m_CharAccept, m_def_CharAccept)
End Sub
```

To complete the coding of your control, you need to add the custom code that is required for the CharAccept property and KeyPress event because the Wizard created only a skeleton for these items. After all, if the Wizard could do everything, then you would be out of a job!

Using the Property Pages Wizard

You have seen Property Pages used for some of the controls that come with Visual Basic. These dialog boxes make it easy for you to set the properties of a control by organizing them into groups. You can create property pages for your own custom controls by using the Property Pages Wizard. Like the ActiveX Control Interface Wizard, you have to add the Property Pages Wizard to the desktop by using the Add-In Manager. After this is done, you can access the Wizard from the Add-Ins menu of Visual Basic. As you start the Property Pages Wizard, you are shown an introductory screen that explains the purpose of the Wizard. Clicking the Next button on this page takes you to the first page, where the real work is done.

Creating the Pages

The first page of the Wizard lets you define the pages of the Property Pages dialog box (see Figure 24.19). If you have included Font and Color properties in your control, the Wizard starts out with two default pages—StandardColor and StandardFont. If you do not need these pages, just click the box next to the name to remove them from your Property Pages.

In addition to the default pages, you can add new pages to the dialog box. Clicking the Add button brings up the Property Page Name dialog box, which is an input box where you can enter the name of the page to create. As you add a page name, it is placed in the list of available pages and is automatically checked. The order of the page names in the list is the order in which the tabs will appear in your Property Pages dialog box. You can change the order by selecting a page and using the arrow keys to move it within the list.

FIG. 24.19
Create new pages or rename old ones in the Property Pages Wizard.

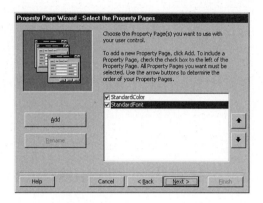

When you have finished adding pages to the dialog box, click the Next button to move to the next page of the Wizard.

Adding Properties to the Pages

The next step in creating your Property Pages is to add the appropriate properties to each page of the dialog box. The Add Properties page of the Property Pages Wizard is shown in Figure 24.20.

FIG. 24.20
The Add Properties page displays a list of available properties and shows the defined pages of the dialog box.

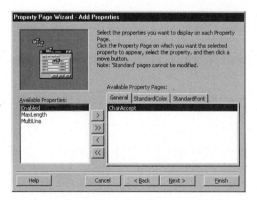

To add a property to a page, click the tab corresponding to the page where you want the property placed, and then select the property from the Available Properties list and click the right arrow button. Notice in Figure 24.20 the addition of a General property page and the inclusion of the CharAccept property. In addition, if you have the default pages of StandardColor and StandardFont, you will notice that the appropriate properties have already been added to these pages.

Part

V

Ch

24

TIP You can drag and drop a property onto a tab to place it on the corresponding page of the Property Pages.

When you have finished adding properties to the pages, click the Finish button to complete the creation of your Property Pages. As with the ActiveX Control Interface Wizard, the Property Pages Wizard shows you a summary page that provides additional information to complete your custom control.

Using the Property Pages in Your Applications

To use the Property Pages you created, you need to add an instance of your custom control to a project. Then, in the Properties window, click the ellipsis button next to the Custom property. Then, just like the Property Pages of other controls, your Property Pages dialog box appears to allow the user to customize the control. A sample of a custom control's Property Pages is shown in Figure 24.21.

FIG. 24.21

Your Property Pages help users set up your custom control.

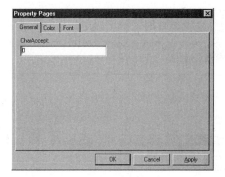

 TIP You can also access the Property Pages by right-clicking the control and then selecting the Properties item from the context menu.

Creating Other Enhanced Controls

Now that you have seen the general concepts for enhancing controls, you are ready to begin creating your own enhanced controls. One idea to get you started is a scroll bar that lets you select letters rather than numbers. This scroll bar lets the user set the upper and lower range of letters for the bar, and to set whether the letters returned by the Value property are upper-case or lowercase. Figure 24.22 shows the use of the scroll bar in a program, and Listing 24.15 shows the code required to make the scroll bar work.

FIG. 24.22

Use a scroll bar to enter letters.

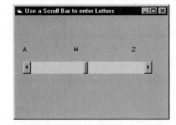

Listing 24.15 LTRSCROLL.CTL—Code to Make the LtrScroll Control Work

```
'Default Property Values:
Const m_def_Max = 26
Const m_def_Min = 1
Const m_def_Value = 0
Const m_def_ReturnCase = 0

'Property Variables:
Dim m_Max As Integer
Dim m_Min As Integer
Dim m_Value As Integer
Dim m_ReturnCase As Integer

Private Sub hsbLetter_Change()
    RaiseEvent Change
End Sub

Public Property Get Max() As String
    m_Max = hsbLetter.Max
    Max = Chr(m_Max + 64)
End Property

Public Property Let Max(ByVal New_Max As String)
    m_Max = Asc(UCase(New_Max)) - 64
    hsbLetter.Max = m_Max
    PropertyChanged "Max"
End Property

Public Property Get Min() As String
    m_Min = hsbLetter.Min
    Min = Chr(m_Min + 64)
End Property

Public Property Let Min(ByVal New_Min As String)
    m_Min = Asc(UCase(New_Min)) - 64
    hsbLetter.Min = m_Min
    PropertyChanged "Min"
End Property
```

continues

Part

V

Ch

24

Listing 24.15   Continued

```
Private Sub hsbLetter_Scroll()
    RaiseEvent Scroll
End Sub

Public Property Get Value() As String
    m_Value = hsbLetter.Value
    If m_ReturnCase = 0 Then
        Value = Chr(m_Value + 64)
    Else
        Value = Chr(m_Value + 96)
    End If
End Property

Public Property Let Value(ByVal New_Value As String)
    m_Value = New_Value
    m_Value = Asc(UCase(New_Value)) - 64
    hsbLetter.Value = m_Value
    PropertyChanged "Value"
End Property

Public Property Get ReturnCase() As Integer
    ReturnCase = m_ReturnCase
End Property

Public Property Let ReturnCase(ByVal New_ReturnCase As Integer)
    If New_ReturnCase > 1 Then New_ReturnCase = 1
    If New_ReturnCase < 0 Then New_ReturnCase = 0
    m_ReturnCase = New_ReturnCase
    PropertyChanged "ReturnCase"
End Property

'Initialize Properties for User Control
Private Sub UserControl_InitProperties()
    m_Max = m_def_Max
    m_Min = m_def_Min
    m_Value = m_def_Value
    m_ReturnCase = m_def_ReturnCase
End Sub
```

Another idea for an enhanced control is a type-ahead combo box. This type of combo box keeps the items in the drop-down list sorted and then performs a search on the item as the user types letters in the edit portion of the box. This type of feature makes the combo box easier to use for data entry.

From Here...

This chapter has shown you how to enhance existing controls to create new controls, and how to use the ActiveX Control Interface Wizard and Property Pages Wizard to make your control-creation work easier. To learn more about other topics covered in this chapter, see the following:

- ■ To learn more about COM, see Chapter 23, "Using Microsoft's Object Technologies."
- ■ To learn more about creating robust ActiveX controls, see Chapter 25, "Extending ActiveX Controls."
- ■ To learn more about creating ActiveX controls , refer to Chapter 26, "Creating a User-Drawn Control."
- ■ To learn more about creating ActiveX documents, see Chapter 27, "Creating ActiveX Documents."

Part
V

Ch
24

Extending ActiveX Controls

In the previous chapter, you received an introduction to the creation of Visual Basic ActiveX controls. In this chapter, you learn how to enhance already existing controls in order to create a new version of the control. In addition, you will learn how to create a control that is able to function without risk of failure. ▪

Learn how to use the *Extender* objects

There's a special relationship between a control and its container. Specifically, a Visual Basic ActiveX control provides Extender and Ambient objects through which the control can communicate with its container.

Learn how to create property pages for your control

You can use standard coding techniques to create property sheets that provide you the greatest flexibility at design time.

Discover how to trap for errors and handle exceptions in your control

Properly debugging and handling errors and exceptions can mean the difference between a usable control and one that is a major security risk to the users of the control.

Package the control for Web use

Using the Application Setup Wizard, you can package your ActiveX control for use in Web pages. Learn how to prepare your control so that it can be used in Web pages and automatically downloaded by users of Microsoft's Internet Explorer Web browser.

Introducing the *Extender* Object

A Visual Basic control's Extender object provides a number of properties, called *extender properties*, that at first glance may appear to be a part of a control instance. Extender properties, though, are in reality part of the Extender object. You can see extender properties when you place an instance of a control on a Visual Basic form.

For example, start a new ActiveX Control project. Then, in the Project Group window, double-click UserControl1 to open the control's designer window, and display the control's properties in the Property Window. Reduce the size of the control by setting its Height property to 1275 and setting its Width property to 1800.

Take a look at the properties listed in the Properties window. These are your control's properties. What's special about these properties is that only you, the control programmer, can change them. The only way a developer can manipulate the properties currently displayed in the Properties window is if you expose the properties in your control's code.

When you used the ActiveX Control Interface Wizard in the previous chapter, you saw one way to expose control properties to the developer. Figure 25.1 shows the Wizard's Select Interface Members dialog box. The control members in the right box are the properties, events, and methods that the Wizard is exposing to developers. That is, only the members in the Selected Names box can be accessed by a developer after you've completed the control.

FIG. 25.1

The ActiveX Control Interface Wizard's Select Interface Members dialog box is one place you can expose properties, events, and methods to a developer.

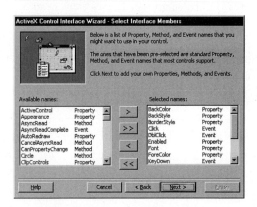

Close the designer window so that the control is available on VB5's Toolbox. Now, double-click Form1 in the Project Group window. The test application's designer window appears. Double-click the control's icon in the toolbox to add an instance of the control to the test application's form. When the control instance appears, its properties appear in the Properties window. Because you haven't exposed any of the control's own properties yet, the properties in the Properties window are all extender properties, supplied by the Extender object.

Although you can manipulate extender properties from your control, you usually won't want to, because extender properties are meant to be used by a developer. The developer is the person who will decide things such as where the control is located in its container (determined by the

Left and Top extender properties), and how big the control will be (determined by the Height and Width extender properties).

If you do want to manipulate extender properties, you can do so through the control's Extender object. For example, suppose, for some reason, that you want your control to always start off set to a specific size. You could write the control's InitProperties() event procedure, as shown in Listing 25.1. Now, whenever an instance of the control is first created (not when it's recreated), it'll be set to a height of 300 twips and a width of 4000 twips.

Listing 25.1 LSTAA_01.TXT—Setting the Starting Size of a Control

```
Private Sub UserControl_InitProperties()
    Extender.Height = 300
    Extender.Width = 4000
End Sub
```

N O T E   Because the InitProperties() event procedure is called only when a control instance is first created, developers can easily resize the control however they like. When the developer reloads the control instance, InitProperties() is not called, so the Height and Width properties don't get reset to their default values. Of course, you can set the starting height and width of a control simply by resizing the control in its designer window. There's no need to write code for setting the Height and Width extender properties. ■

N O T E   A control's Extender object is not available until the control has been sited on its container. This makes sense because the extender properties are based on the container's properties. Until the control is placed on the container, there is no way to determine what the container is or what properties it'll support. For this reason, you can't access the Extender object in a control's Initialize() event procedure, which is called before the control is completely sited on its container. You can, however, access the Extender object in InitProperties() and ReadProperties(). ■

The *Ambient* Object

Of greater interest to a control programmer is the control's Ambient object, which enables a control to respond to changes in the container. The capability of the control to respond to its container provides for the seamless integration of a control. This also increases the control's inherent value through its capability to dynamically adjust itself, in some cases, to the environment of the container.

The Ambient object features many properties, but only a few are especially important to a control programmer. These important ambient properties are listed in Table 25.1 along with their descriptions.

Table 25.1   Important Ambient Properties

Property	Description
BackColor	Holds the container's background color.
DisplayAsDefault	Indicates whether a user-drawn control is the default control in the container.
DisplayName	Holds the control instance's name. You can use DisplayName to identify the control in messages presented to the developer at design time.
Font	Represents the container's currently selected font.
ForeColor	Represents the container's foreground color.
LocaleID	Indicates the locale in which the control is being used. You use this property to set things such as the language of the text and the formats of dates and times for different parts of the world.
TextAlign	Represents the container's text-alignment setting.
UserMode	Indicates whether the control is running at design time or run time. A UserMode value of False indicates design time, and a value of True indicates runtime.

One important reason to use your control's Ambient object is to ensure that the control's colors match those of its container. Imagine what it would look like if your control's background was gray and it was placed into a white spreadsheet. Most likely, the control would work properly, but the color difference would be a distraction to the users and would present an unprofessional appearance. To adjust the colors of your control to match that of its container, you use the BackColor and ForeColor properties. To see how this works, you'll create the AmbientDemo control in the next few sections.

AmbientDemo Control, Example 1

Now that you have the basic control project created, you can experiment to see why ambient properties are so important. To do this, first set the control's Height property to 1125, and set its Width property to 1950. Close the control's designer window so that the control's icon becomes available on VB5's toolbox. Now, in the Project Group window, double-click frmAmbientDemoTestApp. When you do so, the test application's form designer window appears. In the form's Properties window, change the background color to purple.

When you select the new background color, the form's background immediately changes to the selected color. Now, double-click the AmbientDemo control's icon on the toolbox. An instance of the control appears on the form. However, because the control doesn't pay attention to ambient properties, the control's background color is different from the form's background color, as shown in Figure 25.2.

FIG. 25.2
The control's and form's background colors don't match.

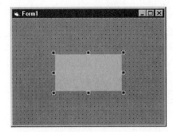

AmbientDemo Control, Example 2

To fix this problem with the AmbientDemo control, you have to set the control's colors to match those of its container. This is where the `Ambient` object enters. First, press your keyboard's Delete key to remove the control instance from the test application's designer window. Then, close the designer window. Double-click AmbientDemo in the Project Group window to open the control's designer window. Double-click the control to display its code window. Next, use the Properties box to find and display the `InitProperties()` event procedure. Finally, add the following two program lines to the procedure:

```
BackColor = Ambient.BackColor
ForeColor = Ambient.ForeColor
```

Your control can now match itself to the container's colors. To prove this, close the control's designer window so that it becomes available in the toolbox. Then, double-click `frmAmbientDemoTestApp` in the Project Group window to reopen the test application's designer window. Finally, double-click the control's icon in the toolbox. *Presto!* When the new control instance appears, it's the same color as the container (see Figure 25.3).

FIG. 25.3
Now the control is the same color as the container.

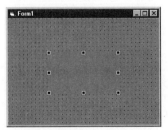

AmbientDemo Control, Example 3

What happens, though, if the designer now changes the form's background color again? Go ahead and try it. Set the form's `BackColor` property to another color. When you do, the form in the designer window immediately changes color to match your selection. The control, however, remains purple. That's because the control doesn't respond to the all-important `AmbientChanged` event.

You can fix that little problem now. First, double-click `AmbientDemo` in the Project Group window to open the control's designer window, and double-click the control to open its code window. In the Properties box, select the `AmbientChanged` event. The `AmbientChanged()` event procedure appears in the code window. Add the following two lines to the procedure:

```
BackColor = Ambient.BackColor
ForeColor = Ambient.ForeColor
```

Close the control's designer window so that the control is again available on VB5's toolbox. Reselect the test application's form, and again change its `BackColor` property. This time, the control keeps up by also changing its background color to match. As you have probably guessed, the `AmbientChanged()` event procedure is called whenever the developer changes an ambient property. The procedure's single parameter is the name of the property that changed.

Building the Calculator Control

In this section, you learn more about methods and events as you use the Calculator control, located on this book's CD-ROM. The Calculator control is designed to build upon what you have already learned. As a result, the Calculator control will be used as the basis for the majority of the topics presented in this chapter.

The Calculator control enables the user to enter two values that are either summed or multiplied, depending on the setting of a control property, when the user clicks the control's button (see Figure 25.4).

The Calculator control can be found on the CD-ROM included with this book. The calculator control can be found in the controls\calculator\ folder on the CD-ROM.

FIG. 25.4
Here's the Calculator control with its constituent controls in place.

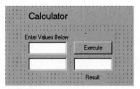

Creating the Interface

The next step, after all the controls are in place, is to create the control interface. As you might recall from the previous chapter, the ActiveX Control Interface Wizard enables you to expose properties, methods, and events of your control. The Calculator control that you are using has a number of properties that can be exposed through this wizard.

▶ **See** "Using the ActiveX Control Interface Wizard," **p. 686**

Briefly, the Calculator control enables the developer to set the control's main caption, as well as the label shown on the CommandButton control. The `Caption` property, which handles the main caption, will be delegated to the constituent lblCaption control, whereas the new

ButtonCaption property will be delegated to the constituent btnExecute control. Also, the control will need a MultValues property that, when set to True, indicates that the calculator should multiply the entries rather than add them. Finally, the control will need a ValidateEntries() method, which validates user input, and a BadEntries event, which is triggered when ValidateEntries() returns False. Figure 25.5 show the Create Custom Interface Members dialog box with the new members.

FIG. 25.5
The Calculator control needs four new control members.

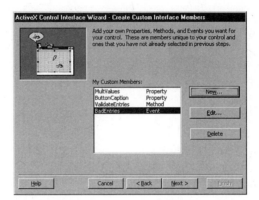

After using the ActiveX Control Interface Wizard on the Calculator control, the Wizard creates additional source code for your control. Listing 25.2 shows the source code created for the Calculator control. As you can see, the code includes not only all the needed constant, variable, and event declarations, but also all of the property procedures, as well as ready-to-go InitProperties(), ReadProperties(), and WriteProperties() events. Now all you have to do is write the program code that completes the control. You do that in the next section.

Listing 25.2   LSTV_02.TXT—Code Created by ActiveX Control Interface Wizard

```
'Default Property Values:
Const m_def_BackColor = 0
Const m_def_ForeColor = 0
Const m_def_Enabled = 0
Const m_def_BackStyle = 0
Const m_def_BorderStyle = 0
Const m_def_MultValues = False
'Property Variables:
Dim m_BackColor As Long
Dim m_ForeColor As Long
Dim m_Enabled As Boolean
Dim m_Font As Font
Dim m_BackStyle As Integer
Dim m_BorderStyle As Integer
Dim m_MultValues As Boolean
```

continues

Part
V

Ch

25

Listing 25.2 Continued

```
'Event Declarations:
Event Click()
Event DblClick()
Event KeyDown(KeyCode As Integer, Shift As Integer)
Event KeyPress(KeyAscii As Integer)
Event KeyUp(KeyCode As Integer, Shift As Integer)
Event MouseDown(Button As Integer, Shift As Integer, _
    X As Single, Y As Single)
Event MouseMove(Button As Integer, Shift As Integer, _
    X As Single, Y As Single)
Event MouseUp(Button As Integer, Shift As Integer, _
    X As Single, Y As Single)
Event BadEntries()

Public Property Get BackColor() As Long
    BackColor = m_BackColor
End Property

Public Property Let BackColor(ByVal New_BackColor As Long)
    m_BackColor = New_BackColor
    PropertyChanged "BackColor"
End Property

Public Property Get ForeColor() As Long
    ForeColor = m_ForeColor
End Property

Public Property Let ForeColor(ByVal New_ForeColor As Long)
    m_ForeColor = New_ForeColor
    PropertyChanged "ForeColor"
End Property

Public Property Get Enabled() As Boolean
    Enabled = m_Enabled
End Property

Public Property Let Enabled(ByVal New_Enabled As Boolean)
    m_Enabled = New_Enabled
    PropertyChanged "Enabled"
End Property

Public Property Get Font() As Font
    Set Font = m_Font
End Property

Public Property Set Font(ByVal New_Font As Font)
    Set m_Font = New_Font
    PropertyChanged "Font"
End Property

Public Property Get BackStyle() As Integer
    BackStyle = m_BackStyle
End Property
```

```
Public Property Let BackStyle(ByVal New_BackStyle As Integer)
    m_BackStyle = New_BackStyle
    PropertyChanged "BackStyle"
End Property

Public Property Get BorderStyle() As Integer
    BorderStyle = m_BorderStyle
End Property

Public Property Let BorderStyle(ByVal New_BorderStyle As Integer)
    m_BorderStyle = New_BorderStyle
    PropertyChanged "BorderStyle"
End Property

Public Sub Refresh()

End Sub

'WARNING! DO NOT REMOVE OR MODIFY THE FOLLOWING COMMENTED LINES!
'MappingInfo=lblCaption,lblCaption,-1,Caption
Public Property Get Caption() As String
    Caption = lblCaption.Caption
End Property

Public Property Let Caption(ByVal New_Caption As String)
    lblCaption.Caption() = New_Caption
    PropertyChanged "Caption"
End Property

Public Property Get MultValues() As Boolean
    MultValues = m_MultValues
End Property

Public Property Let MultValues(ByVal New_MultValues As Boolean)
    m_MultValues = New_MultValues
    PropertyChanged "MultValues"
End Property

'WARNING! DO NOT REMOVE OR MODIFY THE FOLLOWING COMMENTED LINES!
'MappingInfo=btnExecute,btnExecute,-1,Caption
Public Property Get ButtonCaption() As String
    ButtonCaption = btnExecute.Caption
End Property

Public Property Let ButtonCaption(ByVal New_ButtonCaption As String)
    btnExecute.Caption() = New_ButtonCaption
    PropertyChanged "ButtonCaption"
End Property

Public Function ValidateEntries() As Boolean

End Function
```

continues

Listing 25.2 Continued

```
'Initialize Properties for User Control
Private Sub UserControl_InitProperties()
    m_BackColor = m_def_BackColor
    m_ForeColor = m_def_ForeColor
    m_Enabled = m_def_Enabled
    Set m_Font = Ambient.Font
    m_BackStyle = m_def_BackStyle
    m_BorderStyle = m_def_BorderStyle
    m_MultValues = m_def_MultValues
End Sub

'Load property values from storage
Private Sub UserControl_ReadProperties(PropBag As PropertyBag)

    m_BackColor = PropBag.ReadProperty("BackColor", m_def_BackColor)
    m_ForeColor = PropBag.ReadProperty("ForeColor", m_def_ForeColor)
    m_Enabled = PropBag.ReadProperty("Enabled", m_def_Enabled)
    Set Font = PropBag.ReadProperty("Font", Ambient.Font)
    m_BackStyle = PropBag.ReadProperty("BackStyle", m_def_BackStyle)
    m_BorderStyle = PropBag.ReadProperty("BorderStyle", _
        m_def_BorderStyle)
    lblCaption.Caption = PropBag.ReadProperty("Caption", "Calculator")
    m_MultValues = PropBag.ReadProperty("MultValues", _
        m_def_MultValues)
    btnExecute.Caption = PropBag.ReadProperty("ButtonCaption", _
        "Execute")
End Sub

'Write property values to storage
Private Sub UserControl_WriteProperties(PropBag As PropertyBag)

    Call PropBag.WriteProperty("BackColor", m_BackColor, _
        m_def_BackColor)
    Call PropBag.WriteProperty("ForeColor", m_ForeColor, _
        m_def_ForeColor)
    Call PropBag.WriteProperty("Enabled", m_Enabled, m_def_Enabled)
    Call PropBag.WriteProperty("Font", Font, Ambient.Font)
    Call PropBag.WriteProperty("BackStyle", m_BackStyle, _
        m_def_BackStyle)
    Call PropBag.WriteProperty("BorderStyle", m_BorderStyle, _
        m_def_BorderStyle)
    Call PropBag.WriteProperty("Caption", lblCaption.Caption, _
        "Calculator")
    Call PropBag.WriteProperty("MultValues", m_MultValues, _
        m_def_MultValues)
    Call PropBag.WriteProperty("ButtonCaption", btnExecute.Caption, _
        "Execute")
End Sub
```

Testing the Interface

To see the interface in action, close the new control's design window by clicking its close box in the window's upper-right corner. After you close the design window, the control's icon becomes available in VB5's toolbox. Now, double-click `frmCalculatorTestApp` in the Project Group window. The test application's form designer window appears. Double-click the new control's icon in the toolbox. An instance of the control appears on the test application's form.

To test the control from the developer's point of view, click the control instance to display its properties in the Properties window. You see that the `ButtonCaption`, `Caption`, and `MultValues` properties are now available in this window (see Figure 25.6).

FIG. 25.6
Your control's custom properties appear in the same window as the default properties.

Custom properties

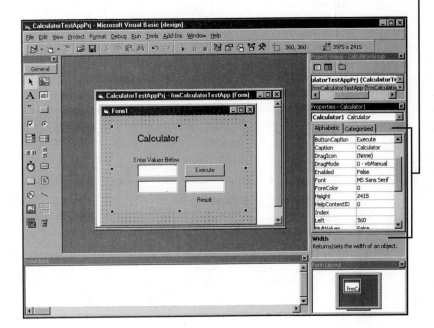

You're now going to use the Calculator control instance to create a simple adding machine. In the Properties window, change the `ButtonCaption` property to **Add**, change the `Caption` property to **Adding Machine**, and leave the `MultValues` property set to `False`.

Now, close the test application's designer window, and save your files. When you do, the `WriteProperties()` event procedure saves your new property settings to the form's source code. Listing 25.3 shows the newly updated source code. About three quarters of the way down the listing, you can see the settings for the Calculator control instance's properties. Notice that the `MultValues` property is not listed in the source code. This is because that

Part
V

Ch
25

particular property is still set to its default value. WriteProperties() saves only modified properties, assuming that you've supplied the correct default value to the PropBag.WriteProperty() method. In this case, the ActiveX Control Interface Wizard supplies the code for you.

Listing 25.3 frmCalculatorTestApp.frm—Source Code Containing the Control's Saved Properties

```
Object = "*\ACalculatorPrj.vbp"
Begin VB.Form frmCalculatorTestApp
   Caption         =   "Form1"
   ClientHeight    =   3195
   ClientLeft      =   60
   ClientTop       =   345
   ClientWidth     =   4680
   LinkTopic       =   "Form1"
   ScaleHeight     =   3195
   ScaleWidth      =   4680
   StartUpPosition =   3   'Windows Default
   Begin CalculatorPrj.Calculator Calculator1
      Height       =   2415
      Left         =   360
      TabIndex     =   0
      Top          =   360
      Width        =   3975
      _ExtentX     =   7011
      _ExtentY     =   4260
      Caption      =   "Adding Machine"
      ButtonCaption =  "Add"
   End
End
Attribute VB_Name = "frmCalculatorTestApp"
Attribute VB_GlobalNameSpace = False
Attribute VB_Creatable = False
Attribute VB_PredeclaredId = True
Attribute VB_Exposed = False
Private Sub Calculator1_Click()

End Sub
```

Go ahead and reopen the test application. Visual Basic now loads the source code and calls the ReadProperties() event procedure to read the property settings back in to the control. As a result, the test application's form reappears exactly as you left it.

Now run the test application. When you do so, the application's window appears. Type two numbers into the left text boxes and then click the Add button. The result of the addition appears in the Result text box.

What happens, though, if you enter an invalid value or leave one of the text boxes blank, and then click the Add button? As the application stands now, the result box will show the word "Undefined."

The developer can, however, add more error handling to the program by responding to the BadEntries event that you defined when you programmed the control. Whenever the user tries to perform a calculation with invalid entries, the control generates the BadEntries event. To see how the developer can supply additional error handling, close the test application. Then, double-click the control in the test application's form designer window. The code window appears. In the Procedures box, select BadEntries. The Calculator1_BadEntries() event procedure appears in the code window. Add the following line to that event procedure:

```
MsgBox "Please enter valid numerical values."
```

Now, rerun the application and enter invalid values into the text boxes. When you click the Add button, not only does the "Undefined" result appear, but a message box also appears, telling the user how to fix the problem (see Figure 25.7).

FIG. 25.7
By responding to the BadEntries event, the control can display error messages.

As a final experiment, close the test application and then click the control in the test application's form designer window. In the Properties window, change ButtonCaption to **Multiply**, set Caption to **Multiplying Machine**, and set MultValues to True. Now, when you run the application, the Calculator will multiply the given values, rather than add them.

Understanding the *btnExecute_Click()* Procedure

When the user clicks the btnExecute CommandButton control, Calculator must perform the requested operation, whether it be addition or multiplication. The program lines that handle this task are found in the btnExecute_Click() event procedure, which responds to the button click. That procedure first declares the local variables it'll use, as shown in Listing 25.4.

Listing 25.4   LSTV_04.TXT—Declaring Local Variables

```
Dim EntriesOK As Boolean
Dim s As String
Dim value1 As Integer
Dim value2 As Integer
Dim result As Integer
```

The procedure then calls the ValidateEntries() method to ensure that the text boxes contain numeric values:

```
EntriesOK = ValidateEntries
```

If EntriesOK gets set to False, there are invalid values in the text boxes. In this case, the procedure triggers the BadEntries event and sets the Result text box to "Undefined":

```
If Not EntriesOK Then
    RaiseEvent BadEntries
    txtResult.Text = "Undefined"
```

If the text boxes do contain valid values, the procedure can do the requested processing. In this case, the procedure first extracts the strings from the text boxes and converts the strings to integers, as shown in Listing 25.5:

Listing 25.5   LSTV_05.TXT—Converting Strings to Integers

```
s = txtValue(0).Text
value1 = Val(s)
s = txtValue(1).Text
value2 = Val(s)
```

After converting the strings, the procedure can perform the requested operation, which is controlled by the MultValues property, as shown in Listing 25.6:

Listing 25.6   LSTV_06.TXT—Performing the Requested Operation

```
If MultValues Then
    result = value1 * value2
Else
    result = value1 + value2
```

Finally, the procedure converts the result to a string and displays the string in the Result text box:

```
s = str(result)
txtResult.Text = s
```

Understanding the *ValidateEntries()* Method

As you just saw, before the btnExecute_Click() event procedure can perform its addition or multiplication, it must be sure that the given values are valid. It does this by calling the ValidateEntries() method, which returns True if the entered values are valid, and returns False if they're not valid. This method first declares the local variables it uses, as shown in Listing 25.7.

Listing 25.7   LSTAA_07.TXT—Declaring *ValidateEntries()*'s Local Variables

```
Dim str As String
Dim asciiValue As Integer
Dim x As Integer
Dim EntriesOK As Boolean
```

The Boolean value `EntriesOK` will hold the result of the validation. The method initializes this value to `True`:

```
EntriesOK = True
```

The method then starts a `For` loop that will iterate through the control array:

```
For x = 0 To 1
```

In this case, there are only two controls in the control array, so the loop goes from 0 to 1.

Inside the loop, the method first extracts the string from the indexed text box:

```
str = txtValue(x).Text
```

If it's not an empty string (the text box isn't empty), the method gets the ASCII code for the first character in the string. Otherwise, if the text box is empty, the method sets the ASCII value to `0`, as shown in Listing 25.8.

Listing 25.8   LSTV_08.TXT—Getting the ASCII Value of the First Character in the String

```
If str <> "" Then
    asciiValue = Asc(str)
Else
    asciiValue = 0
End If
```

The method then compares the returned ASCII code with the ASCII codes for the digits 0 and 9. To be valid, the value being tested must lie within that range. If it doesn't, the method sets `EntriesOK` to False:

```
If (asciiValue < 48) Or (asciiValue > 57) The EntriesOK = False
```

After the For loop completes, the method returns the value of EntriesOK:

```
ValidateEntries = EntriesOK
```

In the next section, you take the newly created Calculator control and create property pages.

Using Property Pages

While using Visual Basic, you may have noticed that when you select a Windows 95 control in a project, the Properties window displays not only all the control's properties but also a selection called Custom. This custom selection contains an ellipsis button that, when clicked, displays a property sheet for the control. The property sheet contains all the control's custom properties, and a developer can use the property sheet to set properties even when not working under Visual Basic.

For example, suppose you add a property sheet to the Calculator control that you created earlier in this chapter. After you've added the property sheet, Visual Basic displays the Custom ellipsis button in the properties section for the control. When you click the ellipsis button, the control's property sheet pops up. When working in Visual Basic on a project containing the control, you can set the control's custom properties from Visual Basic's Property window or from the control's property pages. Figure 25.8 shows what such a property sheet might look like.

FIG. 25.8

A control's property sheet often contains several pages of properties.

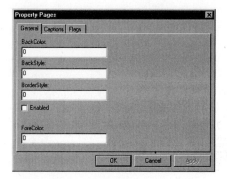

Creating Property Page Objects

The previous chapter taught how to create property pages by using the Property Page Wizard. The property sheet created with the Wizard in that chapter was easy to construct and required very little additional code to be functional. The Property Page Wizard is designed to provide you with a quick way of completing a property sheet; however, the Wizard does not provide many options from which to choose for your own modifications. In this section, you will create property sheets the old-fashioned way, with code. The advantage to this method is that you are able to make design and feature choices that otherwise would be unavailable through the Property Page Wizard.

The first step in creating your custom control's property sheet is to create property page objects for each group of properties. How you organize your properties into groups is up to you, although you'll want to use common sense. If your control has only a few properties, you can probably get away with representing them on a single property page. If the control has many properties, though, you should group related properties onto their own property pages. The typical steps involved in creating a property page for a control are as follows:

1. Create property page objects for each page you want in the property sheet.

2. On the property pages, place controls that the developer will use to edit each of the properties. (For example, you might use a TextBox control to represent a control's Caption property.)

3. Implement the SelectionChanged() event procedure for each property page. This event procedure is called when a developer opens the property page or selects one or more controls in the current project. The SelectionChanged() event procedure is responsible for reading in the current values of each controls' properties.

4. Implement the `Change()` event procedure (or sometimes `Click()`) for each control in each property page. This event procedure is called whenever the developer changes the contents of one of a property page's controls. The `Change()` event procedure notifies Visual Basic of the change, so that Visual Basic can enable the property sheet's Apply button.

5. Implement the `ApplyChanges()` event procedure for each property page. This event procedure is called when the developer closes a property page or when the developer clicks the property sheet's Apply button. Its task is to copy the new property values from the property page's controls to the custom control's properties.

6. Connect the property pages to the custom control.

For the calculator project, you'll create three property pages called General, Captions, and Flags. Follow these steps to create these property page objects:

1. Choose File, Open Project to load the Calculator project into VB5.

2. Select Calculator in the Project Group Window.

3. Choose Project, Add Property Page from the menu bar. The Add Property Page property sheet appears.

4. On the Add Property Page property sheet's New page, double-click the Property Page icon to add a property page object to the project. The property page's designer window appears on the screen.

5. Double-click the Name property in the property page's Properties window and type **CalculatorGeneral**.

6. Also in the Properties window, double-click the Caption property and type **General**.

   A property page's tab uses the Caption property as its label. Because the page's tab is provided by the property sheet that contains the pages, the caption doesn't appear in the designer window.

7. Create two more property sheet objects named CalculatorCaptions and CalculatorFlags, with Caption properties of Captions and Flags, respectively.

Part
V

Ch

25

Placing Controls on the Property Pages

Now that you have created the property page objects, you can add the control you need to represent the properties of the custom control to which the property sheet will be attached. The types of controls to use are up to you. Usually, though, you'll use TextBoxes to represent text properties, CheckBoxes to represent *Boolean properties* (properties that can be set to `True` or `False`), ListBoxes to represent properties with multiple settings, and so on. Follow these steps to add controls to the property pages you created in the previous section:

1. Double-click `CalculatorGeneral` in the Project Group window. The `CalculatorGeneral` property page's designer window appears.

2. Add four Label controls to the property pages, using the following properties:

Name	Caption
lblBackColor	Backcolor
lblBackStyle	BackStyle
lblBorderStyle	BorderStyle
lblForeColor	ForeColor

3. Add four TextBox controls to the property page, using the following properties:

Name	Height	Left	Top	Width
txtBackColor	330	90	370	3700
txtBackStyle	330	90	1020	2700
txtBorderStyle	330	90	1670	2700
txtForeColor	330	90	2970	2700

4. Add a CheckBox control to the property page, using the following properties. When complete, the CalculatorGeneral property page should look like Figure 25.9.

Name	chkEnabled
Caption	"Enabled"

FIG. 25.9

Here's the CalculatorGeneral property page with all of its controls.

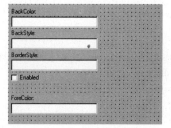

5. Double-click CalculatorCaptions in the Project Group window. The CalculatorCaptions property page's designer window appears.

6. Add two Label controls to the property pages, using the following properties:

Name	Caption
lblButtonCaption	"ButtonCaption:"
lblCaption	"Caption:"

7. Add two TextBox controls to the property page, using the following properties. When complete, the CalculatorCaptions property page should look like Figure 25.10.

Name	txtButtonCaption
Name	txtCaption

FIG. 25.10

Here's the CalculatorCaptions property page with all its controls.

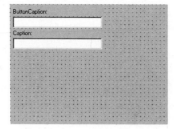

8. Double-click CalculatorFlags in the Project Group window. The CalculatorFlags property page's designer window appears.

9. Add a CheckBox control to the property page (see Figure 25.11), using the following properties:

Name	chkMultValues
Caption	"MultValues"

FIG. 25.11

Place the CheckBox control as shown here.

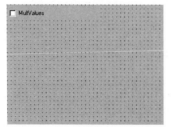

Part
V

Ch
25

Implementing the *SelectionChanged()* Event Procedure

Imagine for a moment that a developer is using the Calculator control as part of an application. The developer has placed two Calculator controls in the application's window. One Calculator control will perform addition and the other will perform multiplication. Now the developer wants to set the controls' properties and therefore calls up the controls' property sheet. When this happens, each property page's SelectionChanged() event procedure gets called, so that each control's current property settings can be loaded into the property pages' controls, where the developer can change them.

Of course, at this point, all you've done is create the property page objects and position Label, TextBox, and CheckBox controls on them. Now you need to write the code for the SelectionChanged() event procedure. To do that, follow these steps:

1. Double-click CalculatorGeneral in the Project Group window to display the CalculatorGeneral property page's designer window.

2. Double-click the property page to display its code window. The window appears, showing the SelectionChanged() event procedure.

3. Add the program lines shown in Listing 25.9 to the SelectionChanged() event procedure.

**Listing 25.9   LSTV_9.TXT—Program Lines for the *SelectionChanged()* Event
Procedure**

```
txtForeColor.Text = SelectedControls(0).ForeColor
chkEnabled.Value = (SelectedControls(0).Enabled And vbChecked)
txtBorderStyle.Text = SelectedControls(0).BorderStyle
txtBackStyle.Text = SelectedControls(0).BackStyle
txtBackColor.Text = SelectedControls(0).BackColor
```

4. Double-click `CalculatorCaptions` in the Project Group window to display the
   `CalculatorCaptions` property page's designer window.

5. Double-click the property page to display its code window. The window appears, showing
   the `SelectionChanged()` event procedure.

6. Add the following program lines to the `SelectionChanged()` event procedure:

   ```
   txtButtonCaption.Text = SelectedControls(0).ButtonCaption
   txtCaption.Text = SelectedControls(0).Caption
   ```

7. Double-click `CalculatorFlags` in the Project Group window to display the
   `CalculatorFlags` property page's designer window.

8. Double-click the property page to display its code window. The window appears, showing
   the `SelectionChanged()` event procedure.

9. Add the following program line to the `SelectionChanged()` event procedure:

   ```
   chkMultValues.Value = (SelectedControls(0).MultValues And vbChecked)
   ```

If you examine the program lines you added to the `SelectionChanged()` event procedures,
you'll see that each control in each property page copies a value from the control into the property page's control. For example, the Calculator control's `Caption` property is represented in
`SelectionChanged()` by the following program line:

```
txtCaption.Text = SelectedControls(0).Caption
```

Recall from the previous section that the developer placed two Calculator controls on
the application's window. If the developer selects both controls before displaying the controls'
property sheet, the property sheet represents a multiple selection. In the previous code line,
you can see that the `SelectedControls` collection object represents the selected controls.
`SelectedControls(0)` is the first selected control and `SelectedControls(1)` is the second.

Currently, the property page can handle only single control selections because it processes
only `SelectedControls(0)`, copying the selected control's Caption property into the property
page's `txtCaption` TextBox control. You'll learn about multiply selected controls later in this
chapter in the section titled "Handling Multiple Control Selection."

Understand that when the property page first appears, its `SelectionChanged()` event procedure copies the current property values into the property page's controls. This enables the
property page to display the current settings to the developer. Each control in each property
page must be represented by a line in `SelectionChanged()`.

Implementing the *Change()* Event Procedure

When the developer changes the contents of a TextBox (or other similar Visual Basic controls), the control's Change() event procedure is called. In the case of a property page, this gives you a chance to notify Visual Basic that the contents of a property have changed, allowing Visual Basic to enable the property sheet's Apply button. All you have to do to tell Visual Basic about this change is to set the control's Changed property to True.

> **N O T E** Some controls, such as CheckBoxes, use their Click() event procedure instead of Change() to handle the change notification. ∎

To handle this important event in the CalculatorGeneral property page, bring up the property page's code window and add the lines shown in Listing 25.10 to the window, outside of any other methods or event procedures. Add the procedures shown in Listing 25.11 to the CalculatorCaptions property page's code window. Finally, add the following procedure to the CalculatorFlags property page's code window.

```
Private Sub chkMultValues_Click()
    Changed = True
End Sub
```

Listing 25.10   LSTV_10.TXT—New Event Procedures for the *CalculatorGeneral* Property Page

```
Private Sub txtForeColor_Change()
    Changed = True
End Sub

Private Sub chkEnabled_Click()
    Changed = True
End Sub

Private Sub txtBorderStyle_Change()
    Changed = True
End Sub

Private Sub txtBackStyle_Change()
    Changed = True
End Sub

Private Sub txtBackColor_Change()
    Changed = True
End Sub
```

Part
V

Ch
25

> **Listing 25.11 LSTV_11.TXT—New Procedures for the *CalculatorCaptions*
> Property Page**

```
Private Sub txtCaption_Change()
    Changed = True
End Sub

Private Sub txtButtonCaption_Change()
    Changed = True
End Sub
```

Implementing the *ApplyChanges()* Event Procedure

The ApplyChanges() event procedure is the opposite of SelectionChanged(). Whereas
SelectionChanged() copies the custom control's current properties into the property page, the
ApplyChanges() event procedure copies the property page's contents back into the custom
control's properties. This happens when the developer clicks the property sheet's Apply button
or when the developer closes a property page.

To add program code for the ApplyChanges event, add the procedure shown in Listing 25.12 to
the CalculatorGeneral property page's code window. Then, add the procedure shown in Listing
25.13 to the CalculatorCaptions property page's code window. Finally, add the following procedure to the CalculatorFlags property page's code window.

```
Private Sub PropertyPage_ApplyChanges()
    SelectedControls(0).MultValues = (chkMultValues.Value = vbChecked)
End Sub
```

> **Listing 25.12 LSTV_12.TXT—The *ApplyChanges()* Event Procedure for the
> *CalculatorGeneral* Property Page**

```
Private Sub PropertyPage_ApplyChanges()
    SelectedControls(0).ForeColor = txtForeColor.Text
    SelectedControls(0).Enabled = (chkEnabled.Value = vbChecked)
    SelectedControls(0).BorderStyle = txtBorderStyle.Text
    SelectedControls(0).BackStyle = txtBackStyle.Text
    SelectedControls(0).BackColor = txtBackColor.Text
End Sub
```

> **Listing 25.13 LSTV_13.TXT—The *ApplyChanges()* Event Procedure for the
> *CalculatorCaptions* Property Page**

```
Private Sub PropertyPage_ApplyChanges()
    SelectedControls(0).ButtonCaption = txtButtonCaption.Text
    SelectedControls(0).Caption = txtCaption.Text
End Sub
```

Connecting the Property Pages to the Control

The property pages you've been building are now complete. All you have to do now is connect the property pages to the control whose properties they represent. To perform that task, follow these steps:

1. Double-click `Calculator` in the Project Group window. The control's designer window appears.

2. In the control's Properties window, double-click the `PropertyPages` property. The Connect Property Pages dialog box appears.

3. Place check marks in the `CalculatorGeneral`, `CalculatorCaptions`, and `CalculatorFlags` check boxes (see Figure 25.12).

FIG. 25.12
The checked property pages will be attached to the control.

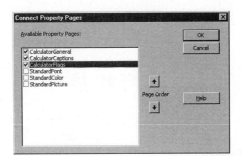

Part
V

Ch
25

4. Click OK in the Connect Property Pages dialog box to associate the selected property pages with the `Calculator` control.

Using the Property Sheet

You've completed the creation of your Calculator control's property sheet. When you're working on an application that contains the control, you can set the control's properties from Visual Basic's Properties window or from the control's property sheet. To see this in action, first make sure that you have closed all of your control's design forms. After you have done this, double-click `frmCalculatorTestApp` in the Project Group window. When the test application's designer window appears, click the Calculator control to select it. When you do, the control's properties appear in the Properties window. If you look closely, you'll see a new property entry called `Custom`.

This new `Custom` property entry is your gateway (under Visual Basic) to the control's property sheet. To see the property sheet, double-click the Custom entry. You also can display the property sheet by clicking Custom and then clicking the ellipsis button. When you do, the property sheet appears. Using this property sheet, you can set the properties of the selected control (see Figure 25.13). Notice that, as soon as you start typing in one of the `TextBoxes`, or when you click on a `CheckBox`, the property sheet's Apply button becomes enabled.

FIG. 25.13

Here's your finished property sheet showing the Caption page.

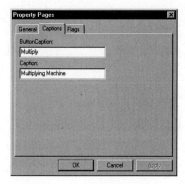

N O T E Remember to save the changes you've made to the Calculator project. Notice that when you do save the changes, the property page files are stored with .PAG file extensions. ■

Handling Multiple Control Selections

You may recall that the `SelectedControls` collection object represents all the controls that a developer has selected when he calls up the property sheet. You use the `SelectedControls` object in the `SelectionChanged()` and `ApplyChanges()` event procedures to access the selected controls' properties. For example, suppose the developer has two Calculator controls selected. Then, in the appropriate property page, `SelectedControls(0).ButtonCaption` represents the `ButtonCaption` property of the first control and `SelectedControls(1).ButtonCaption` represents the `ButtonCaption` property of the second control. The developer can set both controls' button captions to the same value by selecting both controls and then setting the `ButtonCaption` property in the property page that displays that property.

This brings up an important point. Not all properties should be set the same in multiple controls. Suppose that the developer selects two Calculator controls and uses the property sheet to change `ButtonCaption` to "Add." In this case, both instances of the control will have a button labeled "Add," which may be what the developer wants. However, it's not likely that two Calculator controls will have the same `Caption` property because it is the caption that labels the control for the user. So, when dealing with multiple control selections, you have two types of properties:

- Properties that may be set to the same value for multiple controls.
- Properties that should be unique in each control of a multiple control selection.

You can tell how many controls are selected by examining the `SelectedControls` object's `Count` property. If `Count` is greater than 1, you're dealing with a multiple selection. You also can simply code `ApplyChanges()` such that only the properties of the first control in the control collection get assigned properties that should be unique, whereas all controls get assigned properties that can logically be the same from one control to another. Listing 25.14 shows a version of `ApplyChanges()` that takes this latter approach.

Listing 25.14   LSTV_14.TXT—An *ApplyChanges()* Event Procedure That Can Handle Multiple Controls

```
Private Sub PropertyPage_ApplyChanges()
    Dim control As Calculator

    ' Set only the first control's caption.
    SelectedControls(0).ButtonCaption = txtButtonCaption.Text

    ' Set every control's button caption.
    For Each control In SelectedControls
        control.Caption = txtCaption.Text
    Next control
End Sub
```

The special For Each loop enables the program to iterate through the control collection, without dealing with indexes and without needing to know how many controls the collection contains.

Visual Basic's Debugger

As the developer changes property settings, Visual Basic calls the properties' Get and Let property procedures. Event procedures may also be called if the developer does something such as resize the control instance. The important thing to notice is that none of the control's methods or procedures that implement its runtime functionality are called at design time. Therefore, you have to test the control's design time and runtime features separately.

To test design time features, you must act as a developer, placing the control on a test application's form and manipulating it as a developer would, changing property values and resizing the control. To test your control's runtime features, you must run the test application and manipulate the control as the user would.

One very effective way to fully test a control is to create a test project. The test project should call out to all the properties, methods, and events that your control uses. The test project should also test the validation routines that you have in place by providing values outside of the accepted range. The test project should be an .exe program; this way, it can be fully compiled into a stand-alone program.

The Calculator control that you just completed is a good example of a control that needs a test project to fully test its functionality. The test project should try to invoke the Add method when there is no data or the multiply method when the value is a negative number. What you learn from your test application will help to produce better exception and error handling routines for your control.

Your test project should be capable of locating most of the errors that could occur in your control. It is especially important to test out any error handling that you have in your control. This will verify that your control will not cause damage to the user's machine and that you have properly handled the error.

N O T E   The test project can detect a lot of potential problems; however, it can't trap all of the errors that may occur. This can be done only through the use of good code design and solid unit-level testing of each component of the control. ■

To make the testing and debugging task a little easier, Visual Basic includes a built-in debugger. You can use the debugger to set breakpoints in a control's code or to step through program code one line at a time. As you're stepping through program lines, you can watch how the values of variables change. Visual Basic 5 provides you with the debugging commands shown in Table 25.2.

Table 25.2   Visual Basic Debugger Commands

Command	Description
Step Into	Steps into the procedure being called
Step Over	Executes the procedure being called without stepping into the procedure
Step Out	Executes the remaining lines in a procedure
Run to Cursor	Executes all lines up to the current position of the cursor
Add Watch	Adds a variable to the Watch window
Edit Watch	Edits an entry in the Watch window
Quick Watch	Displays the value of the expression at the mouse cursor position
Toggle Breakpoints	Turns a breakpoint on or off
Clear All Breakpoints	Removes all breakpoints that were set
Set Next Statement	Sets the next statement to execute
Show Next Statement	Shows the next statement to execute

To get some practice with Visual Basic's 5 debugger, first create a folder called Calculator2 and copy all the files from the section exercise to the new Calculator2 folder. Then, follow these steps to see Visual Basic's debugger in action:

1. Load the CalculatorGroup.vbg project group from the new Calculator2 folder.

2. In the Project Group window, double-click `Calculator`. The Calculator control's designer window appears.

3. Double-click the designer window. The Calculator control's code window appears, showing the `InitProperties()` event procedure.

4. Click the gray bar to the left of the text cursor. Visual Basic sets a breakpoint on the selected line. This line is marked as a red bar in the code window. You also can turn on

the breakpoint by selecting Debug, Toggle Breakpoint from the menu bar or by pressing F9 on your keyboard.

When the control's code is running, Visual Basic stops program execution when it reaches a breakpoint. This enables you to examine a procedure more carefully, as you'll soon see.

5. Close the code and designer windows. The Calculator control becomes available on VB5's toolbox.

6. In the Project Group window, double-click `frmCalculatorTestApp`. The test application's designer window appears.

7. In the designer window, click the instance of the Calculator control to select it. Then, press your keyboard's delete key to remove the instance from the test application.

8. Double-click the Calculator control's icon in VB5's toolbox. Visual Basic creates an instance of the control, but stops the control's initialization on the first line of the `InitProperties()` event procedure. The line is marked with a red and yellow bar.

Visual Basic stopped execution on this line because that's where you set the breakpoint in Step 4. Now that the control's code execution has stopped, you can use other debugger commands to examine the event procedure line by line. The red part of the bar tells you that there's a breakpoint set on this line. The yellow portion of the bar indicates that this is the next line that will execute.

9. Place the mouse cursor over `m_BackColor` in the code window. The value of the `m_BackColor` variable appears in a small tip box (see Figure 25.14).

Part

V

Ch

25

FIG. 25.14
You can examine the contents of variables just by placing the mouse cursor over the variable's name in the code window.

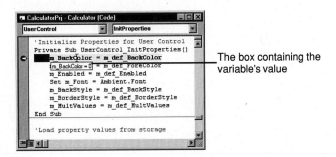

The box containing the variable's value

10. Press F8 (Step Into) a few times. Each time you do, Visual Basic executes the current program line and moves the yellow bar to the next line (see Figure 25.15). This line-by-line execution enables you to examine variables that may have been set or how the program flow is progressing. This knowledge can help you to determine if certain code is being executed, or if your variables have the expected values.

11. Scroll the code window up until you can see the `Get Caption()` property procedure. Set a breakpoint on the `Caption = lblCaption.Caption` line.

12. Press F5 (Start) to continue the program execution. When you do so, the program runs until it hits the breakpoint you set in the `Get Caption()` property procedure.

FIG. 25.15

The yellow bar moves to always indicate the next line to execute.

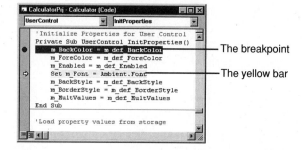

The breakpoint

The yellow bar

13. Select Debug, Add Watch from VB5's menu bar. The Add Watch dialog box appears (see Figure 25.16).

FIG. 25.16

You use the Add Watch dialog box to add expressions to the Watch window.

14. Type **Caption** in the Expression box, and click OK. The Watch Window appears at the bottom of VB5's main window, showing the variable's name, current value, data type, and the context in which you're viewing the expression.

15. Press F8 to execute the current program line. Visual Basic assigns a new value to the Caption variable.

    Many program bugs can be traced to bad values being assigned to variables. By using the Watch Window, you can quickly locate these kinds of problems.

16. Select Debug, Clear All Breakpoints from the menu bar. Visual Basic removes all the breakpoints you set.

17. Select Run, End to end the debugging session. Then, close the open code window, and delete the Calculator control instance from the test application's designer window.

The VB5 debugging tools can be a powerful way to look inside your code while it is executing. The previous example enabled you to walk through the process of debugging your code. If you used the code contained on the CD-ROM, you probably found that there were no errors in the source code. To fully experience the power of the debugger, you need to use it on code that has bugs in it. To help you, Listings 25.15 and 25.16, which have typical programming bugs included in them, provide sample code segments from the Calculator.ctl project.

Listing 25.15   LSTV.15—The Entry Validation Function

```
Public Function ValidateEntries() As Boolean
    Dim str As String
    Dim asciiValue As Integer
    Dim x As Integer

    EntriesOK = True
    For x = 0 To I
        str = txtValue(x)Text
        If str <> "" Then
            asciiValue = Asc(str)
        Else
            asciiValue = 0
        End If
        If (asciiValue < 48) Or (asciiValue > 57) Then
            Entries = False
    Next x

    ValidateEntries = EntriesOK
End Function
```

Listing 25.16   LSTV.16—Read Properties Subroutine

```
'Load property values from storage
Private Sub UserControl_ReadProperties(PropBag As PropertyBag)

    m_BackColor = PropBag.ReadProperty("BackColor", m_def_BackColor)
    m_ForeColor = PropBag.ReadProperty("ForeColor", m_def_ForeColor)
    m_Enabled = PropBag.ReadProperty("Enabled", m_def_Enabled)
    Set Font = PropBag.ReadProperty("Font" Ambient.Font)
    m_BackStyle = PropBag.ReadProperty("BackStyle", m_def_BackStyle)
    m_BorderStyle = PropBag.ReadProperty("BorderStyle", m_def_BorderStyle)
    lblCaption.Caption = PropBag.Property("Caption", "Calculator")
    m_MultValues = PropBag.ReadProperty("MultValues", m_def_MultValues)
    btnExecute.Caption = PropBag.writeProperty("ButtonCaption", "Execute")
End Sub
```

Control Error Handling

The importance of controls running correctly cannot be overstated. Developers and users are depending on you to create a product that they can use with confidence. If a developer incorporates your control into an application and the application then fails for the user because of your control, it's the developer who'll take the blame. It'll appear to the user that the developer's application is at fault. (Of course, in this situation, both you and the developer would have to share the blame. The developer is responsible for testing that his application runs correctly with your control.) There are a few things you should do, and a few things you should not do, to help ensure that your controls won't present developers and users with nasty surprises.

First, use plenty of error handling, especially in event procedures. If an error occurs in an event procedure, and your program code doesn't handle it, the control will crash—bringing down the container in which the control is sited. Notice that you are advised to provide plenty of error handling. Do not *raise* your own errors in event procedures. If you do, your application will surely crash and take everything down with it.

N O T E One way of generating errors is through the `Raise` method. You can use this method if you want more information than generally is available using the Error statement. One of the bits of information that the `Raise` method provides is the source of the error. Additional help related information can also be provided The information that the `Raise` method provides can be useful during the creation of classes in VB. ▒

N O T E Any `Raise` methods that are executed within your ActiveX during run time will cause your control to escape beyond the boundaries of the control. ▒

Typically, all events that have any code attached to them should be error handled. There are some key areas that need special attention:

- File handling
- Input/output connectivity
- Screen control
- User resource checks
- Interaction with other controls
- Boundary conditions

CAUTION

Do not be tempted into taking the easy way out of error handling with the "on error resume next" method. This method enables your program or ActiveX control to continue working even if there was a error, serious or otherwise. This method of error handling does not provide any method of gracefully handling errors.

Properly error handling your procedures and functions takes only a few lines that can easily be cut and pasted where they are needed. In Listing 25.17 you see one example of how to trap for the "No Current Record" error during database activity.

Listing 25.17 errordemo.bas—Proper Error Handling

```
on error goto errhandler

'Write property values to storage
Private Sub UserControl_WriteProperties(PropBag As PropertyBag)

    Call PropBag.WriteProperty("BackColor", m_BackColor, m_def_BackColor)
    Call PropBag.WriteProperty("ForeColor", m_ForeColor, _
        m_def_ForeColor)
```

```
    Call PropBag.WriteProperty("Enabled", m_Enabled, _
        m_def_Enabled)
    Call PropBag.WriteProperty("Font", Font, Ambient.Font)
    Call PropBag.WriteProperty("BackStyle", m_BackStyle, _
        m_def_BackStyle)
    Call PropBag.WriteProperty("BorderStyle", m_BorderStyle, _
        m_def_BorderStyle)
    Call PropBag.WriteProperty("Caption", lblCaption.Caption, _
        "Calculator")
    Call PropBag.WriteProperty("MultValues", m_MultValues, _
        m_def_MultValues)
    Call PropBag.WriteProperty("ButtonCaption", btnExecute.Caption, _
        "Execute")

exit sub
errhandler:

' Here is where you would put your error handling routines
' such as this:
' if err = 3021 then
'   msgbox("There are no records in the database")
' endif

' Note: You may find it more appropriate to use a CASE
' construct rather than a If..Then..Else.

End Sub
```

In Listing 25.17 you saw how to trap for a specific type of error in a procedure. Notice that the first line of code:

```
on error goto errhandler
```

refers to the `errhandler` routine. This routine, located at the end to the parent procedure, actually looks for and traps the error as shown in the following lines of code:

```
errhandler:

' Here is where you would put your error handling
' routines such as this:
' if err = 3021 then
'   msgbox("There are no records in the database")
' endif
```

Although these lines only trap one error, they could easily be modified to trap more than one or to call out to a global error handling procedure. The following code examples shown how a global error handling procedure might be constructed. They are meant to illustrate a point only, your actual code will need to be tailored to the specific needs of the application.

The following code segment would be placed the procedures that you want to trap for errors. The `errortrap()` function is passed the value contained in `err object`.

```
Errhandler:
errortrap(err)
```

The following code segment would be placed in a .BAS file or a .CLS file. The purpose is to assign a message to a global variable based upon the error number passed to it.

```
Function errortrap(err as integer)

Select Case err
    Case 3021
        gError_Msg = "A problem has occurred with your database."
    Case 13
        gError_Msg = "A System error has occurred"

... (more error handling code)

    Case Else
        gError_Msg = "An unexplained error has occurred"
End Select
... (any additional code)
```

Another tip is to always use Get and Let property procedures for a control's properties. Don't create properties by adding public variables to a control. If you use the Get and Let mechanism, you can validate a property's value once, in the property's Let procedure. The property is then guaranteed to be valid in the rest of the program.

If you use public variables for properties, the developer has complete access to the properties' values and can change them behind your program's back. This means that you must check the properties' values every time they're used. Not only is such a practice a pain, it's also a good way to crash a program. You can't raise errors in event procedures, should that be where you discover that a property has been assigned an invalid value.

In general, wherever the developer can change values of data in your control, be sure that the changes are valid. Any such values should be implemented as properties, giving your control the capability to verify the values in the property's Let procedure. Similarly, at run time, be sure that any values that the control accepts from the user are valid. A good example is the Calculator control you worked with in this chapter. When the user enters values into the control's test boxes, you want to be sure that those values can be added or multiplied. The ValidateEntries() method of the Calculator control handles that little detail as described in the "Understanding the ValidateEntries() Method" section.

Distributing ActiveX Controls by Using Setup Wizard

On the CD

The Setup Wizard is a tool used with the Visual Basic Setup Toolkit that aids you in the creation of application setup and distribution. The Setup Wizard sets up distribution of your application across the Internet using automatic code download from Microsoft Internet Explorer, versions 3.0 and 4.0. The Setup Wizard enables automatic downloading of your object with the initialization of the page that contains it with cabinet (.cab) files. Also, the Setup Wizard analyzes your project and determines what supporting files need to be included with your control.

N O T E Cabinet files are specially formatted files that contain ActiveX controls along with all of the necessary support files. These files contain information about the control and the necessary support files that tell the Web browser what files need to be downloaded. The Web browser takes the information from the cabinet file and compares it to the files already on the computer to determine whether any of the files need to be downloaded. This enables the Web browser to avoid downloading any unnecessary files. ▪

You can start the Setup Wizard by choosing Application Setup Wizard from your Start menu or Setupwiz.exe from the \Setupkit\Kitfil32 directory where you installed Visual Basic.

Then you choose to build an Internet Download package with the Application Setup Wizard, and you'll be presented with a series of dialog boxes.

Introduction Dialog Box The Introduction dialog box makes you aware of the capabilities of the Setup Wizard. The first time you run the Setup Wizard, read the description and then select the Skip the Screen in the Future check box, shown in Figure 25.17. Choose Next to go to the next dialog box.

FIG. 25.17
The Setup Wizard Introduction dialog window provides you with some basic information about using the Wizard to build application distribution files.

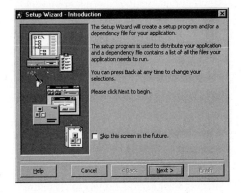

Part
V
Ch
25

Select Project and Options Dialog Box Type the name of the project file or use the Browse button to find the project file. For the distribution options, select Create Internet Download Setup, as seen in Figure 25.18. Choose Next to go to the next dialog box.

FIG. 25.18
To build the necessary files for use in an HTML document, you need to use the Application Setup Wizard to create an Internet Download Setup.

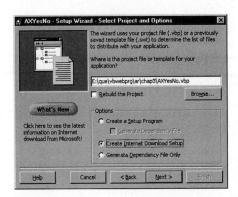

Internet Distribution Location Dialog Box   Use the file browser to specify where you want your ActiveX control to be placed for Internet download, as shown in Figure 25.19. Choose Next to go to the next dialog box.

FIG. 19.19

You need to specify a location for the Setup Wizard to build the Internet Download files.

Internet Package Dialog Box   You must decide where you want to locate the runtime components of your applications. You can either select your own location on one of your own servers or download runtime components from the Microsoft Web site. Specifying a location on an internal server might be better if you don't have a fast connection to the Internet. On the other hand, by specifying the Microsoft Web site at **http://www.microsoft.com/vbasic/ icompdown,** you guarantee that your users always get the latest copies of the runtime components.

Click the Safety command button to set safety levels for each ActiveX control in your project. If your control is safe for initialization, check Safe for Initialization. If your control is safe for scripting, check Safe for Scripting, as in Figure 25.20. (See the later section "Making Your Controls Safe for Scripting and Initialization" for more information.) Choose OK on the Safety dialog box, and Next on the Internet Package dialog box to go to the next dialog box.

FIG. 25.20

By marking your control as safe for initialization and scripting, you are placing your guarantee in your control that it cannot harm the user's computer, even if being used in HTML documents that you did not build.

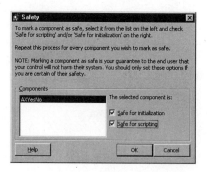

ActiveX Server Components Dialog Box   The Setup Wizard analyzes your project and looks for any ActiveX controls that you might be using as server-side controls. If your control uses any server-side components, either as local or remote components, add them with this dialog box. Choose Next to go to the next dialog box.

If your control will be distributed to other developers for use in building Web pages, you need to include the Property Page DLL with your file distribution. This provides developers with the ability to specify property settings for the control in other, non-Visual Basic development environments. The Setup Wizard stops and asks you if you want to include this DLL with the setup files, as seen in Figure 25.21.

FIG. 25.21
The Setup Wizard asks you if you want to include the Property Pages DLL with your file distribution package.

File Summary Dialog Box

The File Summary dialog box lists all of the files that are distributed with your ActiveX control, as shown in Figure 25.22. If there are any other files you want to include with your file distribution, including readme and licensing files, this is where you add them. Use the Add button to add additional files. Choose Next to complete the Setup Wizard.

FIG. 25.22
The File Summary dialog box shows you what files will be included in the Internet download files that will be packaged for including on a Web site.

Finally, the Setup Wizard provides you with the opportunity to save the information you have specified as a template to be used every time you run the Setup Wizard on this same project. Click the Finish button to build your distribution package.

Viewing Your ActiveX Control in a Web Browser

The Setup Wizard creates a default Web page that has your ActiveX control inserted on it. This Web page is located where you decide to place your ActiveX control. Open this page with a Web browser that supports ActiveX, such as Internet Explorer 3.0, as seen in Figure 25.23. If you view the source code of the page, you see a simple HTML document that contains the <OBJECT> element, specifying the Class ID of your control, as seen in Listing 25.18.

FIG. 25.23

Once you have finished building your Internet distribution files, you can open the HTML file that was generated by the Setup Wizard in Internet Explorer to test your control.

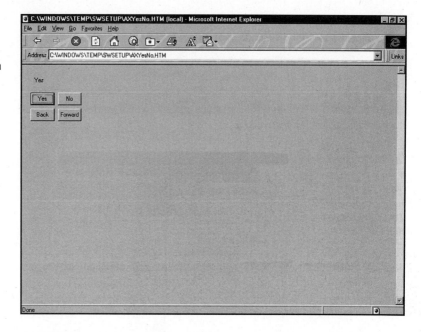

Listing 25.18   AXYESNO.HTM—Source of AXYesNo.HTM

```
<HTML>
<!--     If any of the controls on this page require licensing,
 you must create a license package file.
     Run LPK_TOOL.EXE in the tools directory to create the
required LPK file.
<OBJECT CLASSID="clsid:5220cb21-c88d-11cf-b347-00aa00a28331">
     <PARAM NAME="LPKPath" VALUE="LPKfilename.LPK">
</OBJECT>
-->
<OBJECT
     classid="clsid:B7C523AE-6500-11D0-AB01-444553540000"
     id=AXYesNo
     codebase="AXYesNo.CAB#version=1,0,0,0">
</OBJECT>
</HTML>
```

N O T E   The Class ID included in the HTML in Listing 25.18 will be different from the Class ID generated in your HTML document. This Class ID is a globally unique identifier automatically generated by Visual Basic when you build your control. You will never generate two matching Class IDs, and the Class IDs generated by Visual Basic to identify your controls will never be the same as any other Class IDs generated by anyone else to identify anyone else's control. This Class ID is automatically registered with your system Registry database and is used by the operating system to determine whether the control needs to be downloaded from the Web site, or whether you already have the control on your system. ■

All object information is defined between the `<Object>` and the `</Object>` tags. The following lists some important tags you should be familiar with:

ClassID	The unique ID for this object
ID	The name that you use to specify this control in script
Codebase	Location of distribution files for your ActiveX control

N O T E For information about accessing your ActiveX control from HTML using VBScript, see Chapters 35, "Internet Programming with VBScript," and 36, "Programming Web Pages." ■

Responsible ActiveX Creation and Distribution

ActiveX controls give the control programmer a new tool that can be used responsibly or otherwise. We as ActiveX programmers have a obligation to provide controls that are safe to use and instill a high level confidence in the developers who use our controls. This type of responsible creation encompasses the following ideas which you look at in detail in this section.

- Marking controls safe for initialization and scripting
- Licensing issues
- Versioning of controls

Marking Your Controls Safe for Scripting and Initialization

Safe for Scripting means that there is no way to harm a user's computer or obtain information about the user's computer without permission, no matter what commands are scripted to the control. *Safe for Initialization* means that there is no way to harm a user's computer or obtain information about a user's computer by just executing the control.

If you have not marked your control as safe for scripting and safe for snitialization, then the user's Web browser warns the user that the control is not safe and does not load the control. Only if the user has set the security level on his or her browser to its lowest and least safe setting does the browser download and run your control.

Marking Your ActiveX Controls Safe for Initialization By marking your control safe for initialization, you guarantee users that there is no way to harm their computer or steal information about their computer by loading your control, regardless of the initialization parameters specified in the HTML file. If a user can specify parameters in the `<PARAM>` tags that accompany the `<OBJECT>` element that could cause your control to damage or alter the user's system in any way, you should not mark your control as safe for initialization.

An ActiveX control's initial state is defined by the PARAM statement on the HTML page that calls the object. If your control is safe for initialization, you must verify all properties given in PARAM statements in the controls InitProperties and ReadProperites events.

To mark your control safe for initialization, select the Safe for Initialization check box on the Setup Wizard Safety dialog box. Keep in mind that you are specifying that your control is safe

Part
V

Ch
25

Testing the Button

You now can test your control by pressing F5 to run the test program. Try clicking the ColorBtn to make sure that the events work correctly. If things are not working right, use the normal debugging techniques to find the errors in the control. After you have finished testing and debugging the control, you are ready to compile your control and make it available for use in other projects.

▶ **See** "Making Your Program Bug-Free," **p. 200**

Trying Other Button Styles

After you have created a rectangular button, you may want to try your hand at creating other shapes. For example, you could draw a button that looks like a circle or ellipse. Or, you could draw a triangular button. In fact, you can use any shape that you can create with the graphics methods. The code in Listing 26.6 could be the basis for a circular button. Figure 26.6 shows you how this button would look on a form.

Listing 26.6   CIRCBTN.CTL—Other Button Shapes Can Be Achieved with the Appropriate Code

```
Dim inHeight As Integer
    Dim inWidth As Integer
    Dim CircDim As Integer

    With UserControl
        inHeight = .Height - 10
        inWidth = .Width - 10
        If inHeight > inWidth Then
            CircDim = inWidth / 2
        Else
            CircDim = inHeight / 2
        End If

        .FillColor = mBackColor
        .FillStyle = 0
        UserControl.Circle (CircDim, CircDim), CircDim

        'Print caption
        .ForeColor = mForeColor

        .CurrentX = CircDim - .TextWidth(m_Caption) / 2
        If .CurrentX < 5 Then .CurrentX = 5

        .CurrentY = CircDim - .TextHeight(m_Caption) / 2
        If .CurrentY < 5 Then .CurrentY = 5

        UserControl.Print m_Caption

    End With
```

FIG. 26.6
You can draw other button shapes such as a circle.

From Here...

This chapter has shown you the basics of creating a user-drawn control. While user-drawn controls involve a lot of work, they are very flexible because the programmer is in charge of everything. This chapter demonstrated how to use a programmer-defined `Paint` event to change the appearance of your control. You also learned that modifying the output from the ActiveX Control Interface Wizard is an easy way to produce the effects desired. To find out more about the other aspects of creating controls, see the following chapters:

- To learn more about creating properties, methods, and events, see Chapter 24, "Creating ActiveX controls."
- To learn more about using the wizards, see Chapter 25, "Extending ActiveX Controls."
- To learn more about graphics methods, see "Doing Graphics" on the companion CD-ROM.

Part
V

Ch
26

CHAPTER 27

Creating ActiveX Documents

You probably are aware that there are a lot of things happening with the Internet these days. In particular, the World Wide Web has gained enormous popularity. It seems that everywhere you turn, everyone has a Web site—from car manufacturers to charitable organizations to the guy next door. Internet stuff is everywhere. And although it used to be acceptable to just have a static Web page, more and more people and organizations are providing dynamic content on their pages. These interactive Web pages do a lot more than just display fixed information. It is commonplace to see Web pages that act like applications, and a variety of tools are available to let you create such pages.

When you first take a look at creating interactive content, it can appear very daunting—I know it did for me. More often than not, the concern I hear is not "Can I do this?" but "What's the best way to do this?" When you try to think of ways to program for the Web, dozens of terms may come to mind: PERL, CGI, Active Server Pages, VBScript, and Java, to name a few. The ActiveX documents discussed in this chapter are not necessarily the best choice for all occasions, but they do make Internet programming very accessible to VB programmers. ■

What is an ActiveX document?

You will learn the differences and similarities between ActiveX documents and standard Visual Basic applications.

Creating an ActiveX document

You will see how to use the Visual Basic design environment to create ActiveX documents.

What is a UserDocument object?

You will see how a UserDocument object compares with a standard form and how it differs. You also will see how to add properties to a UserDocument.

Working with multiple documents

You will see how to use the Hyperlink object to move back and forth between the multiple documents of a project.

Testing and running a document-based application

You will see that, although you have to use a second program such as Internet Explorer to test your documents, all of Visual Basic's debugging tools are available to you.

Understanding ActiveX Documents

Since ActiveX documents are perfect for use on the World Wide Web, this chapter will begin with a quick refresher course. You probably have become familiar enough with Web pages to know that they are basically just document files. Web files are very similar to Word documents except they are written in a special format: HTML (which stands for Hypertext Markup Language). Just as Word is the viewer for .doc files, a Web browser (such as Netscape or Internet Explorer) is used to view HTML files. HTML files on the Internet have an address, or *URL* (Universal Resource Locator), that is used to locate a specific document.

That's how the Web began, just a bunch of linked documents. But a static document cannot produce the level of interactivity we see today. Two things about the Web have made this possible:

- The way in which Web pages are retrieved
- Browser enhancements

The Hypertext Transfer Protocol, or HTTP, is the means by which your browser and the Web server communicate. The browser simply requests an URL, and then displays the returned HTML stream.

Notice that I use the word "requests"—this is an important concept. Requesting a file is very different from opening one on your hard drive; hence the need to have a protocol. Think of this process as being similar to you asking a friend to send you a document via e-mail. Unlike opening a document on your hard drive, your friend could edit the document before sending it, or send you a completely different document. In a similar manner, logic can be placed on the Web server to modify the returned document based on any number of things.

On the browser side, the returned HTML stream has evolved quite a bit since the Web's first days. In addition to formatted text and graphics, Web pages can include script code and Java applets. These advances were made possible by the increasing complexity of the Internet browser, which has evolved to support all of these embedded objects. ActiveX documents, discussed in this chapter, take browser enhancements to a new level.

What Is an ActiveX Document?

Put in simplest terms, an ActiveX document is an application that runs inside a container, such as Internet Explorer, instead of running as a stand-alone program. An example of such an application is shown in Figure 27.1.

The "document" portion of the name comes from the analogy to word processing documents or spreadsheets. These files contain data, but must be accessed by a program in order to be viewed or edited. For example, you can create a document in Word and store it in a file. If you pass the file along to another user, that user can't do anything with it unless they have a copy of Word. An ActiveX document works much the same way. You can create an ActiveX document and store it in a file. If you pass the file to someone else, they must have a program capable of supporting ActiveX documents before they can use the file.

FIG. 27.1

A simple ActiveX document running in Internet Explorer.

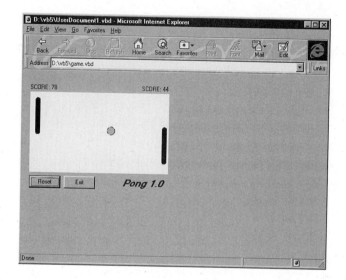

Fortunately, there are many containers that support ActiveX documents, including Internet Explorer, Microsoft Office 97 binders, and the Visual Basic IDE. Your users will run your program inside one of these container applications.

What Are the Advantages of ActiveX Documents?

The primary reason to use ActiveX documents in Visual Basic is to create Internet-enabled applications. Creating ActiveX documents provides a number of advantages over creating Internet applications by other means. Some of these advantages include:

- You do not have to learn another programming language to create the documents. All of your Visual Basic expertise can be applied to ActiveX documents.
- You can design your Internet application by using the Visual Basic design environment. This is a much simpler process than the code-and-test method that you have to use with some other languages.
- You also have access to Visual Basic's rich debugging environment for testing your code and fixing any problems that arise.
- Use of the Hyperlink object makes it easy to navigate to other pages from the browser. These pages can be other ActiveX documents, or any Web address.

So, Visual Basic makes it easy to create an ActiveX document, but why would you want to create one in the first place? Why not just create a standard application? The answer, in a word, is "Internet." ActiveX frees you of the complications involved with the older means of distributing an application. If your program is a standard EXE, then you must send install disk to all of the users. ActiveX documents, on the other hand, can be set up on a Web server so that they are downloaded automatically when a user opens the Web page. Codes embedded in the Web page tell Internet Explorer to download a cabinet (CAB) file containing your application and all necessary components. This Web-based approach makes it simpler to maintain your code and to keep everyone running the same version.

Part
V

Ch
27

Creating Your First ActiveX Document

Creating an ActiveX document is very similar to creating standard applications in Visual Basic. In this chapter, we re-create the loan payment calculator example from Chapter 3, "Creating Your First Program," but this time as an ActiveX document. To create a document, we will follow this basic sequence of events:

1. Start a new ActiveX document project.
2. Create the user interface of the application.
3. Write the code to perform the application's tasks.
4. Test and debug the application.
5. Use the Setup Wizard to create an Internet download setup.

Obviously, there are a number of details involved in each of these steps, but you can see that the process is something with which you are familiar. To walk through the process of creating an ActiveX document, you will create a mortgage calculator like the one you created in Chapter 3. Using this same application will illustrate the similarities between creating an ActiveX document and a standard Visual Basic program.

N O T E The preceding steps refer to creating an *application*. Since an ActiveX document is an interactive application, as opposed to a static file, such as word processing documents, the term *application* will often be used to refer to an ActiveX document. ■

Starting an ActiveX Document Project

The first step toward creating an ActiveX document is to start your project. You do this by selecting the New Project item from the File menu. This opens the New Project dialog box (see Figure 27.2). From this dialog box, select the option to create an ActiveX Document EXE by double-clicking the icon. This starts the new project and displays a blank UserDocument form on the screen, as shown in Figure 27.3.

FIG. 27.2
Select the project type to create from the New Project dialog box.

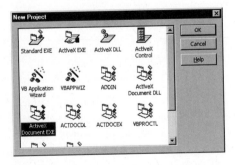

N O T E If the UserDocument is not displayed automatically, double-click the UserDocument object in the Project window to display it. ■

FIG. 27.3
A UserDocument object looks very much like a form.

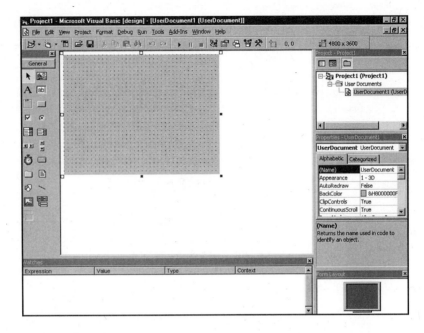

Notice that the UserDocument looks a lot like a form without a border. As a matter of fact, it is exactly like the UserControl object that you will use to create ActiveX controls. You will create the user interface for the ActiveX document here, just like with a form. (For more information about creating ActiveX controls, see Chapter 24, "Creating ActiveX Controls.")

After you have created the project, change the properties of the project and the UserDocument to descriptive names, as listed in Table 27.1. To access the properties of the project, choose *projectname* Properties from the Project menu. The properties of the UserDocument are accessible from the Properties window (View, Properties Window). After setting the properties, save the files of the project by clicking the Save button on the toolbar. You then specify names for each of the new files.

Table 27.1   Project and UserDocument Properties

Property	Setting
Project Type	ActiveX EXE
Project Name	ActXCalc
Project Description	ActiveX Document Loan Calculator
UserDocument Name	CalcDoc

Document File Names

The source code of ActiveX documents is saved in a text file, much the same way a form is saved. The description of the UserDocument object and any controls is stored along with the code of the document in a file with the extension .dob. This is similar to the .frm file of a form. If there are any graphical components of the interface, these are stored in a .dox file, similar to the .frx file for forms. When you compile your ActiveX document, you create either an .exe or .dll file, along with a .vbd file. The .vbd file is the one accessed by Internet Explorer. This .vbd file is the "document" part of the file, similar to a .doc file from Microsoft Word.

Creating the Interface of the Document

The interface of your ActiveX document is created by drawing controls on the UserDocument object, just as you would draw them on the form of a standard program. You can use almost any Visual Basic control in the creation of your document. The only exception to this statement is that you cannot use the OLE Container control as part of an ActiveX document. Another restriction is that an ActiveX document cannot contain embedded objects, such as Word or Excel documents.

> **CAUTION**
>
> If you use custom controls in your document, you need to check licensing and royalty requirements before distributing the controls.

To create the interface of the sample application, you need to add four Label controls, four TextBox controls, and one CommandButton to the UserDocument.

 The Label controls should have the following settings for the Name and Caption properties:

Name	Caption
lblPrincipal	Principal:
lblTerm	Term (Years):
lblInterest	Interest Rate (%):
lblPayment	Monthly Payment:

 All four text boxes should have their Text properties deleted so that the text boxes appear empty when the document is first shown. The text boxes should be named txtInterest, txtPayment, txtPrincipal, and txtTerm.

 The command button of the document should have the Name property set to cmdCalculate and the Caption property set to Calculate Payment.

When you have completed adding the controls to the document, your UserDocument should look like the one in Figure 27.4.

FIG. 27.4

The Document calculator looks similar to the LoanCalc program created earlier.

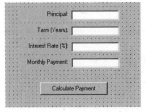

Adding Code to the Document

After you create the interface of the document by using Visual Basic controls, you are ready to write the code that makes the document perform a task. As with the forms in a standard program, you will write code for events of the controls in the document. All code work is done in the Code window. You can access the Code window by double-clicking a control or by clicking the View Code button in the Project window. For the sample application, you need to enter the code from Listing 27.1 in the Click event of the command button.

Listing 27.1   CALCDOC.DOB—Placing Code in the *Click* Event to Run the Calculation

```
Private Sub cmdCalculate_Click()

    Dim m_Principal As Single, m_Interest As Single
    Dim m_Payment As Single, m_Term As Integer
    Dim m_fctr As Single

    m_Principal = txtPrincipal.Text
    m_Interest = txtInterest.Text / 1200
    m_Term = txtTerm.Text
    m_fctr = (1 + m_Interest) ^ (m_Term * 12)
    m_Payment = m_Interest * m_fctr * m_Principal / (m_fctr - 1)
    txtPayment.Text = Format(m_Payment, "Fixed")

End Sub
```

Testing Your ActiveX Document

After entering the code and saving your document, you are ready to test the code. Testing an ActiveX document is a little different than testing a standard program because the document must run inside another application. To test your code, follow these steps:

1. Run your document by pressing F5 or clicking the Start button on the toolbar. (Note that Visual Basic will not display the user interface of your program.)

2. Minimize Visual Basic and start Internet Explorer.

3. From IE's File menu, choose the Open item. This will present an Open dialog box in which you can enter the name of the file to be opened by IE.

Part
V

Ch
27

4. Specify the path and name of your ActiveX document and the name. The name will be the value of the Name property of the UserDocument object, followed by a .vbd extension. If you are running your document within VB, the file is located in the same folder as Visual Basic. For a typical installation, this is C:\Program Files\DevStudio\VB.

5. Click the OK button in the Open dialog box to load your document. The CalcDoc document is shown running in Internet Explorer in Figure 27.5.

N O T E   If you click the Browse button of the Open dialog box to find the file, remember to change the Files of Type selection from HTML files to All Files. ▪

FIG. 27.5
Internet Explorer can host an ActiveX document.

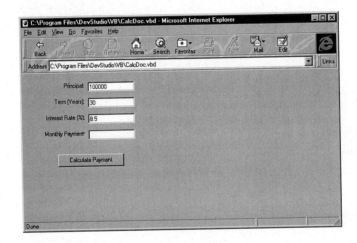

If your code doesn't perform like it should, you can use all of Visual Basic's debugging tools to track down and eliminate errors. (Debugging is discussed in detail in Chapter 8, "Programming Basics.") You can set breakpoints in your code, set "watches" to observe the values of variables, and step through the code line by line to locate an error. Figure 27.6 shows a typical debugging session.

▶ **See** "Making Your Program Bug-Free," **p. 200**

CAUTION
Terminating your program without closing Internet Explorer may cause errors in IE. Therefore, you should close and restart IE each time you run your document.

Compiling Your Document

After you have finished testing and debugging your document, you are ready to compile the document for distribution. To start the compilation process, select the Make item from the File menu of Visual Basic. This opens the Make dialog box, in which you specify the name and location of the EXE or DLL file. The name of the .vbd file is based on the Name property of the UserDocument object. This file is placed in the same folder that you specified for the EXE file.

FIG. 27.6

Debugging tools make it easy to find and correct errors.

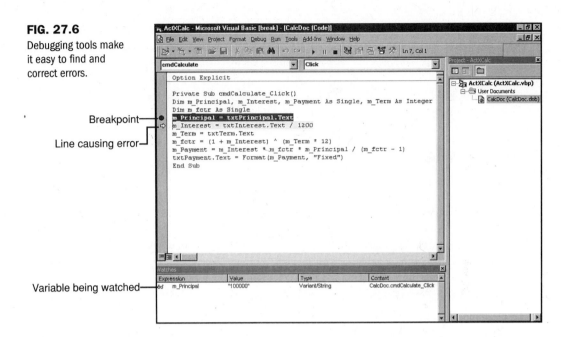

Breakpoint

Line causing error

Variable being watched

After compilation, your document can be used in any of the programs that handle ActiveX documents. As you learned previously, Internet Explorer is one such program. The Office 97 Binder is another. To access an ActiveX document with the Binder, start the Binder and then select the Add from File item in the Section menu. This opens a dialog box that enables you to specify the file to be loaded. You specify the name and location of your .vbd file and then click the OK button to load the document. Figure 27.7 shows the CalcDoc document running inside the Office 97 binder.

FIG. 27.7

The Office 97 Binder provides another means with which to run your ActiveX documents.

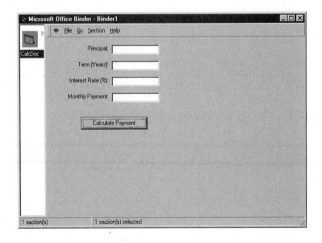

Part

V

Ch

27

If you want to put your ActiveX document on the Internet, you first need to run the Setup Wizard with the Internet Download Setup option. The Wizard will create a CAB file that contains the required components, as well as sample HTML that shows you how to include your document on a Web page. It also creates a SUPPORT directory with the components in the CAB file, should you need to modify anything.

▶ **See** "Distributing ActiveX Controls by Using Setup Wizard," **p. 730**

Exploring the UserDocument Object

Just as a form is the main part of a standard program, the UserDocument object is the key part of an ActiveX document. The UserDocument provides the container for all the controls that make up the user interface of the document. Like a form, you can place controls on the UserDocument or you can use graphics methods and the Print method to display other information directly on the document. This provides great flexibility in the design of your documents and the manner in which you present information to the user.

Understanding the Key Events of a UserDocument

Although the UserDocument is similar to a form in many respects, there are also some key differences. For example, there are several key properties, methods, and events that are supported by a UserDocument but are not supported by a form, and vice versa.

The main events of a form that are not supported by the UserDocument object are the Activate, Deactivate, Load, and Unload events. The UserDocument, on the other hand, supports the following events that are not supported by a form:

- AsycReadComplete   Occurs when the container holding the document has finished an asynchronous read request.

- EnterFocus   Occurs when the ActiveX document receives focus.

- ExitFocus   Occurs when the ActiveX document loses focus.

- Hide   Occurs when the user navigates from the current ActiveX document to another document.

- InitProperties   Occurs when the document is first loaded. However, if any properties have been saved by using the PropertyBag object, the ReadProperties event will occur instead.

- ReadProperties   Occurs in place of the InitProperties event if items are stored in a PropertyBag object. This event also occurs as the document is first loaded.

- Scroll   Occurs when the user uses the scrollbar of the container in which the ActiveX document is running.

- Show   Occurs when the user navigates from another document to the ActiveX document.

- WriteProperties   Occurs as the program is about to be terminated. This event happens right before the Terminate event, but only occurs if the PropertyChanged statement has been used to indicate that a change has occurred in a property's value.

Creating and Storing Properties for a UserDocument

Despite the similarities between the UserDocument and a form, there are some ways in which the UserDocument is much more similar to a UserControl than a form. All three objects—the form, the UserControl, and the UserDocument—enable you to create properties and methods to extend their capabilities. However, only the UserControl and the UserDocument have the capability to use the PropertyBag object. The PropertyBag object, along with some special events, is used to store values of public properties so that settings are preserved between sessions.

Since the process for creating and saving properties was discussed in detail in the coverage of ActiveX controls, the details won't be repeated here (see Chapters 24, "Creating ActiveX Controls" and 26, "Creating a User-Drawn Control"). However, a quick recap will help you remember the steps involved. To create and store properties for the UserDocument, you need to do the following:

1. Create a property by using the Property Let and Property Get procedures. You can create the shell of the property by using the Add Procedure dialog box, accessible from the Tools menu of Visual Basic.

2. To indicate that the value of a property has changed, place the PropertyChanged statement in the Property Let procedure of each property whose value you want to store.

3. To store the values of the property, use the WriteProperty method of the PropertyBag object to output the values of the changed properties. The code for this is placed in the WriteProperties event of the UserDocument.

4. To retrieve the values of the property, use the ReadProperty method of the PropertyBag object to output the values of the changed properties. The code for this is placed in the ReadProperties event of the UserDocument.

   ▶ **See** "Creating the Properties of the Button," **p. 743**

The result of the code for handling these tasks in a sample document is shown in Figure 27.8.

FIG. 27.8
Use the ReadProperty and WriteProperty methods to retrieve and store public properties of the UserDocument.

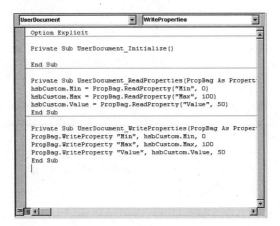

```
UserDocument                    WriteProperties

    Option Explicit

    Private Sub UserDocument_Initialize()

    End Sub

    Private Sub UserDocument_ReadProperties(PropBag As Propert
    hsbCustom.Min = PropBag.ReadProperty("Min", 0)
    hsbCustom.Max = PropBag.ReadProperty("Max", 100)
    hsbCustom.Value = PropBag.ReadProperty("Value", 50)
    End Sub

    Private Sub UserDocument_WriteProperties(PropBag As Proper
    PropBag.WriteProperty "Min", hsbCustom.Min, 0
    PropBag.WriteProperty "Max", hsbCustom.Max, 100
    PropBag.WriteProperty "Value", hsbCustom.Value, 50
    End Sub
```

Working with the Methods of the UserDocument

In addition to the different events that are supported by the UserDocument, there are also two key methods that the UserDocument supports but a form does not: `AsyncRead` and `CancelAsyncRead`. The `AsyncRead` method enables the document to request that its container read in data from a file or URL. As the name implies, the read is performed asynchronously. The `AsyncRead` method requires that you specify the file (or information) to be read and the type of information that is being read. There are three supported data types, as summarized in Table 27.2. The following line of code shows how the method can be used:

```
AsyncRead "C:\Vb\Default.Htm", vbAsyncTypeFile
```

As you can imagine, reading a file asynchronously comes in very handy when working with the Internet. For example, you might write a data viewer application that retrieves information from a server.

Table 27.2 Types of Data Supported by the *AsyncRead* Method

Constant	Description
vbAsyncTypeFile	The data is contained in a file created by Visual Basic.
vbAsyncTypeByteArray	The data is a byte array containing retrieved data.
vbAsyncTypePicture	The data is stored in a picture object.

The `CancelAsyncRead` method is used to terminate an asynchronous read prior to its completion.

Using the Hyperlink Object in Your Document

One object of extreme importance in ActiveX documents is the Hyperlink object. This object has no properties and only three methods. However, the Hyperlink object is what enables an ActiveX document to call another ActiveX document, or to navigate to a Web site. The three methods of the Hyperlink object are the following:

- ■ `NavigateTo` This method causes the container that holds the ActiveX document to jump to a file or URL specified in the method. This is the method to use to move from one ActiveX document to another.

- ■ `GoBack` This method performs a hyperlink jump to the previous document in the history list of a container. If the container does not support hyperlinking or there are no items in the history list, an error occurs.

- ■ `GoForward` This method is the counterpart of the `GoBack` method. `GoForward` causes the container to move to the next document in the history list. If there is no next document, an error occurs.

N O T E A container such as Internet Explorer, which supports hyperlinking, will execute on its own the jump specified in a `NavigateTo` method. A container such as Office 97 Binder, which does not support hyperlinking, will start a hyperlink-capable program to process the jump. ▣

Using the ActiveX Document Migration Wizard

So far, you have learned how to create an ActiveX document from scratch. But, if you are like me, you have a lot of time and effort invested in creating standard Visual Basic applications. Is there any way that you can capitalize on the work you have already done, short of using cut and paste to bring in pieces of a program?

Fortunately, the answer is yes. Visual Basic provides a tool called the ActiveX Document Migration Wizard that can *help* you convert forms from an existing application to UserDocument objects for an ActiveX document. The key word here is "Help." The Wizard does not create a complete ActiveX document directly from your standard application. Instead, the Wizard does the following:

- Copies the properties of the form to a new user document.
- Copies menu items from the source form to the new user document.
- Copies all controls from the source form and retains their relative positions on the form. All control properties are retained. Note that OLE container controls and embedded OLE objects are not copied.
- Copies the code from the form event procedures to the corresponding procedures in the user document. This includes all event procedures associated with the component controls.
- Comments out code statements that are not supported by ActiveX documents, such as `Load`, `Unload`, and `End`.

Although the ActiveX Document Migration Wizard can do a lot of the work of converting a document for you, there are some things that it cannot handle. Therefore, you have to do some coding work before you can compile and distribute your document.

First, you need to remove unsupported events, such as `Load` and `Unload`. Although the Wizard will comment out the `Load` and `Unload` statements, it will not do anything with the event procedures code. If you use these events to initialize the properties of a form or its controls, you may want to move some of the code from the `Load` event to the `Initialize` event of the UserDocument. Likewise, you may want to move some of the code from the `Unload` event to the `Terminate` event of the UserDocument.

You also need to make sure that you do not reference any non-existent objects. For example, if you migrate a form to a UserDocument, any references to the form by name (such as "Form1") would be invalid.

Running the ActiveX Document Migration Wizard

To run the ActiveX Document Migration Wizard, you need to make sure that it is available in Visual Basic. You make the Wizard available by selecting it from the Add-In Manager dialog box, which is accessible by choosing the Add-In Manager item from the Add-Ins menu. After you have added the Wizard to your desktop, you can run it by choosing the ActiveX Document Migration Wizard item from the Add-Ins menu.

To begin converting the forms of a project into ActiveX documents, you first must open the project's forms that you want to convert. The Wizard will work correctly only from within the project. Next, start the ActiveX Document Migration Wizard. This presents the introductory screen, which explains a little of what the Wizard will and will not do for you. Click the Next button on the Wizard to proceed to the second screen—where the work begins.

The second screen of the Wizard, shown in Figure 27.9, enables you to select the forms from the current project that you want to convert to ActiveX documents. All the forms of the current project are shown in the forms list. You can select any form by clicking the check box next to the form name. Multiple selections are allowed. After you have made your selections, click the Next button to proceed to the next step of the process.

FIG. 27.9

Select your forms from the list in the Wizard.

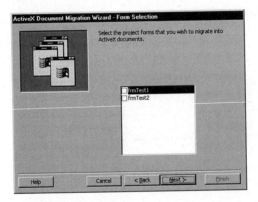

The Options page of the ActiveX Document Migration Wizard, shown in Figure 27.10, lets you control how the Wizard will process the forms you have selected. The three options enable you to do the following:

- Choose to comment out invalid code. This option will comment out statements such as Load, Unload, and End that are not supported by ActiveX documents.

- Remove original forms after conversion. This option will remove the forms from the current project after the conversion is made. Typically, you will *not* want to check this option because you will want your original project intact.

- Choose whether to convert your project to an ActiveX EXE or ActiveX DLL project. The option defaults to ActiveX EXE. (ActiveX DLL's are used for creating shared components rather than applications.)

FIG. 27.10
Select the options that are appropriate to your needs.

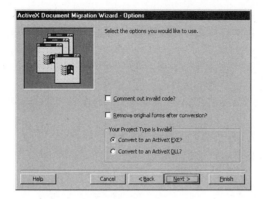

After making your choices, click the Next button to proceed. The final page of the Wizard asks if you would like to see a summary report after the Wizard's part in the conversion has been completed. After making your selection, click the Finish button to begin the conversion. The summary report, shown in Figure 27.11, describes which additional activities you need to perform to complete the conversion process.

FIG. 27.11
The ActiveX Document Migration Wizard uses a summary report to guide you through the rest of the conversion process.

Looking at the Results of the Wizard's Work

When the ActiveX Document Migration Wizard has finished its work, it places the newly cre-ated UserDocument objects in the same project as the original forms. The document source files are stored in the same folder as the original form files and are given similar names, with the appropriate extension. For example, a form stored in the file frmTest1.frm would create a UserDocument stored in the file docTest1.dob. As previously stated, the controls of the form are copied to the UserDocument and their relative positions are preserved. Figure 27.12 shows both the original form and the resulting UserDocument.

Also, as stated previously, most of the code from your original form is copied over to the UserDocument. Invalid code is commented out and identified by the ActiveX Document Migra-tion Wizard. (This assumes that you chose to comment out invalid code on the Options page of the Wizard.) Figure 27.13 shows an example of this process.

Part
V

Ch
27

FIG. 27.12

The UserDocument and the original form have the same user interface.

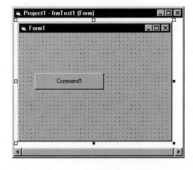 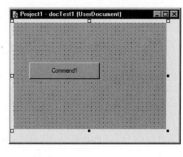

FIG. 27.13

Invalid code is identified by the [AXDW] mark in a comment statement.

Invalid code line

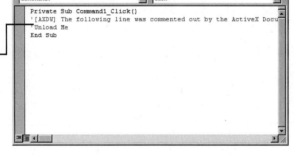

Creating a More Complex Document

Obviously, there is only so much room available on a UserDocument object. Therefore, you are limited in the amount of information that can be displayed in a single document. In this regard, a single document is like an application with a single form. However, you can create additional documents as part of your project and then navigate between the various documents. You can also include standard forms in the applications that you create with ActiveX documents. This section takes a look at what is involved in using multiple documents and forms in your ActiveX document-based application.

Programming Additional Documents

To use additional documents in your ActiveX application, you need to create the additional documents and then provide a mechanism for moving back and forth between the documents. This is a little different than moving between forms in a standard program because the UserDocument object does not support the Load and Unload statements, or the Show and Hide methods that are available to forms.

The first step necessary to add another document to your project is to add another UserDocument object to the project. You do this by choosing the Add User Document item from the Project menu. This places a second (or third, fourth, and so on) document in your project, under the UserDocuments folder. As with the first document you created, you need to specify a name for the document.

The next step required is to draw the interface of the additional document and add the code that enables it to do its tasks. This process is the same as the one you used to create the original document.

Now for the tricky part! Since you cannot use the Show method to display a document (as you can with forms), how do you get back and forth between the various documents in your application? The answer is to use the NavigateTo method of the HyperLink object. The NavigateTo method instructs a container application to go to a particular file or URL and load the page. If the file is an ActiveX document, it gets processed just like your original page.

To move from your first document to your second, you need to run the NavigateTo method as shown in the following line of code:

```
HyperLink.NavigateTo App.Path & "\docnav2.vbd"
```

The App.Path property specifies the path to the current document. By using this as the basis for locating the second document, the document can be loaded without incident, provided that the documents are stored in the same directory. Figures 27.14 and 27.15 show the two pages of a sample document loaded in Internet Explorer. To get from the second document back to the first, you use the NavigateTo method again. For both documents, the method is used in code that responds to an event. The event is typically the Click event of a command button.

FIG. 27.14
The first document of a multiple document application.

Back button is enabled

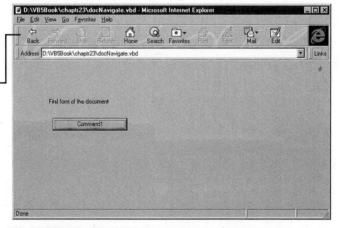

When you moved to the second document of the application, you may have noticed that the Back button of Internet Explorer was enabled. You can use this button to move back to the first document. However, you should provide a direct link using the NavigateTo method because the first document may not always be the previous document in the history list. Also, if the first document has scrolled out of the history list, the NavigateTo method is the only way to get to the document again.

Part
V
Ch
27

FIG. 27.15

The second document of a multiple document application.

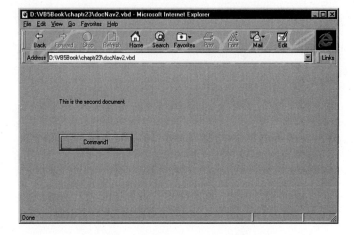

Using and Displaying Forms from the Document

In addition to working with more than one document, you can work with standard forms in your ActiveX document applications. To use a form in a project, you create it the same way you would create a form for a standard project—draw the interface of the form and write the code to perform tasks. To display the form from your document, use the Show method. Then, to remove the form, use the Unload statement.

N O T E For more information about creating forms, see Chapter 4, "Working with Forms and Controls." ■

Although forms can be part of your application, they are not handled the same way as documents. Forms are not contained within the application that contains the ActiveX document. Forms are independent of the container, as shown in Figure 27.16.

FIG. 27.16

Forms are outside the boundaries of the document container.

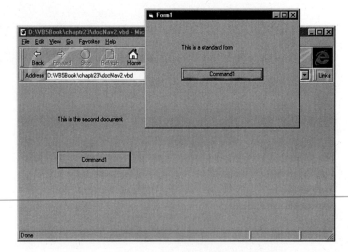

From Here...

This chapter introduced you to the world of ActiveX documents. You have seen how these documents make it easy to create applications that can run inside Internet Explorer or other ActiveX-enabled container applications. You also have seen the similarity between the UserDocument object and the forms of a standard application.

This chapter also touched on some other topics related to the creation of ActiveX documents that are covered in more detail in other chapters. To learn more about these topics, see the following chapters:

- To learn more about designing and creating forms, see Chapter 4, "Working with Forms and Controls."

- To learn more about debugging your programs, see Chapter 8, "Programming Visual Basic."

- To learn more about creating ActiveX controls, see Chapters 24, "Creating ActiveX Controls," and 26, "Creating a User-Drawn Control."

Part
V

Ch
27

Database Programming

CHAPTER 28

Building Database Applications

It's probably fair to say that most business-oriented computer applications work with data in one form or another. This data often is stored in one or more databases. Visual Basic can create powerful data-management programs with a little planning and effort. The most fundamental part of that planning is in how the data is structured. A poorly designed database can doom even the most well-intentioned program from the start. On the other hand, a well-designed database can make a programmer's life much easier.

Creating an organized data structure requires you to learn about two separate tasks. First, you must learn about how to design a database. In the design, you decide what data goes in the database and how it will be organized. Second, you must learn how to translate the design into the actual database. You can do so in a variety of ways. In this chapter, I walk you through the process of designing and creating a sample database that contains information about parents and their children. The database you create here will mirror a portion of the database used in one of my commercial applications that tracks the members of youth groups. ∎

How do you determine the data required for a database?

Learn how to find out which information should be stored in the database.

How do you organize the data in the database?

Data in a database should be stored in a way that makes the information easy to retrieve and maintain.

How can you create a database with a program?

The methods of the Data Access Objects allow you to write programs to create or modify a database.

What can the Visual Data Manager do?

The Visual Data Manager provides an easy way to create and modify databases for your programs.

Can you use Microsoft Access?

If you have Access, you have the best tool for working with database structures.

How are queries used in creating databases?

You can create, delete, and modify tables in a database with SQL queries.

Designing a Database

Like most tasks, building a database starts with a design. After all, you wouldn't try to build a house without a blueprint, and most people wouldn't attempt to prepare a new dish without a recipe. Like these other tasks, having a good design for your database is a major first step to a successful project.

In designing a database application, you must set up not only the program's routines for maximum performance, but you must pay attention also to the physical and logical layout of the data storage. A good database design does the following:

- Provides minimum search times when locating specific records
- Stores data in the most efficient manner possible to keep the database from growing too large
- Makes data updates as easy as possible
- Is flexible enough to allow inclusion of new functions required of the program

Design Objectives

When you're creating the design for your database, you must keep several objectives in mind. Although meeting all these design objectives is desirable, sometimes they are mutually exclusive. The primary design objectives are:

- Eliminate redundant data
- Be able to locate individual records quickly
- Make enhancements to the database easy to implement
- Keep the database easy to maintain

Key Activities in Designing Your Database

Creating a good database design involves the following seven key activities:

- Modeling the application
- Determining the data required for the application
- Organizing the data into tables
- Establishing the relationships between tables
- Setting index and validation requirements for the data
- Creating and storing any necessary queries for the application
- Reviewing the design

Now, look briefly at the initial two activities in the list. First, take a look at modeling the application. When you model an application, you first should determine the tasks that the application is to perform. For example, if you're maintaining a membership list, you know that you want to create phone directories and mailing lists of the members. As you're determining the tasks to be performed by the application, you are creating what is called the *functional specification*. For a project that you are creating, you probably know all the tasks that you want to perform, but writing down these tasks in a specification document is a good idea. This document can help you keep focused on what you want your program to do. If you're creating the program for another person, a functional specification becomes an agreement of what the application will contain. This specification also can show milestones that need to be achieved on a set schedule.

When you're creating the program for other people, the best way to learn what task must be performed is to talk to the people requesting the work. As a first step, you can determine if they already have a system that they are looking to replace, or if they have reports that they want to produce. Then, ask a lot of questions until you understand the users' objectives for the program.

After you determine the functional specifications for the program, you can start determining what data the program needs. In the case of a membership application, knowing that you have to produce directories and mailing lists tells you that the database needs to contain the address and phone number of each of the members. Taking this situation a little further, you know that, by presorting mail by ZIP Code, you can take advantage of reduced rate postage. Therefore, you need an index or query that places the mailing list information in ZIP code order. So, you can see that the model not only tells you the data needed but also defines other components of the database, as well.

Organizing the Data

One of the key aspects of good database design is determining how the data will be organized in the database. To have a good design, you should organize the data in a way that makes the information easy to retrieve and makes maintenance of the database easy. Within a database, data is stored in one or more *tables*. For many database applications, you can accomplish efficient data management by storing data in multiple tables and by establishing relationships between these tables. In the following sections, you learn how to determine what data belongs in each table of your database.

Tables as Topics   A *table* is a collection of information related to a particular topic. By thinking of a key topic for the table, you can determine whether a particular piece of data fits into the table. For example, if a country club wants to track information about members and employees, the club management might be tempted to put both in the same table (because both groups refer to people). However, look at the data required for each group. Although both groups require information about a person's name, address, and phone number, the employee group also requires information about the person's Social Security number, job category, payroll, and tax status. If you were to create just one table, many of the entries would be blank for the members. You also would have to add a field to distinguish between a member and an employee. Clearly, this technique would result in a lot of wasted space. It also could result in slower processing of employee transactions or member transactions because the program would have to skip a number of records in the table. Figure 28.1 shows a database table with the two groups combined. Figure 28.2 shows the reduction in the number of fields in a member-only database table.

FIG. 28.1
Combining the employee and member tables wastes a lot of space.

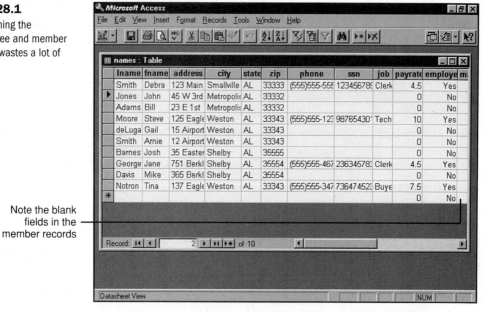

Note the blank fields in the member records

FIG. 28.2
A separate database table for members has only the relevant fields and is more efficient.

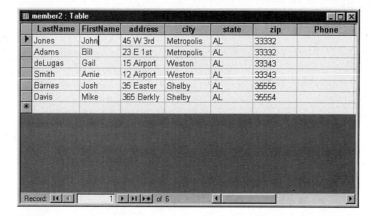

By thinking of the topic to which a table relates, you can determine more easily whether a particular piece of information belongs in the table. If the information results in wasted space for many records, the data belongs in a different table.

Data Normalization   *Data normalization* is the process of eliminating redundant data within a database. Taking data normalization to its fullest extent results in each piece of information in a database appearing only once, although that's not always practical.

Consider the example of order processing. For each item a person orders, you need the item's number, description, price, order number, and order date, as well as the customer's name, address, and phone number. If you place all this information in one table, the result looks like the table shown in Figure 28.3.

FIG. 28.3

Non-normalized data produces a large, inefficient data table.

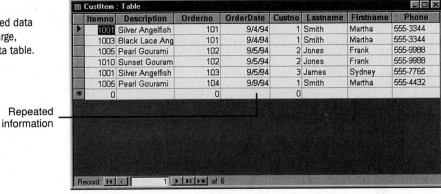

Repeated information

As you can see, much of the data in the table is repeated. This repetition introduces two problems. The first problem is wasted space, because you repeat information. The second problem is one of data accuracy or currency. If, for example, a customer changes his or her phone number, you have to change it for all the records that apply to that customer—with the possibility that you will miss one of the entries. In the table in Figure 28.3, notice that Martha Smith's phone number was changed in the latest entry but not in the two earlier entries. If an employee looks up Martha Smith and uses an earlier entry, that employee would not find Martha's updated phone number.

A better solution for handling the data is to put the customer information in one table and the sales order information in another table. You can assign each customer a unique ID and include that ID in the sales order table to identify the customer. This arrangement yields two tables with the data structure shown in Figure 28.4.

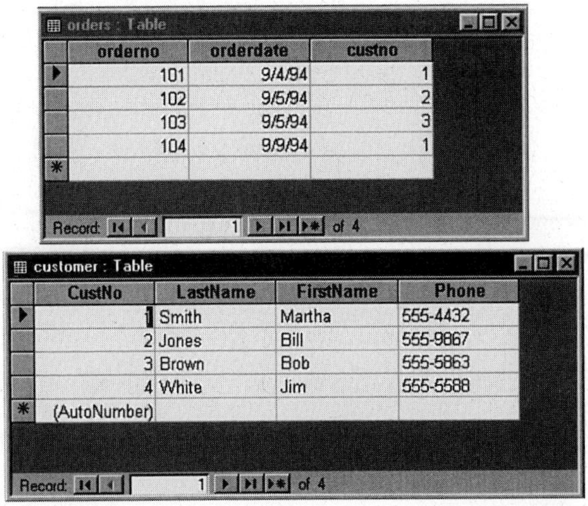

FIG. 28.4

Normalized Customer and Order tables eliminate data redundancy.

With this type of arrangement, the customer information appears in only one place. Now, if a customer changes his or her phone number, you have to change only one record.

You can do the same thing to the items sold and order information. This leads to the development of four tables, but the organization of the tables is much more efficient. You can be sure that when information must be changed, it will change in only one place. This arrangement is shown in Figure 28.5. With the four-table arrangement, the Orders table and the Items Ordered table provide the links between the customers and the retail items they purchased. The Items Ordered table contains one record for each item of a given order. The Orders table relates the items to the date of purchase and the customer making the purchase.

FIG. 28.5

Complete normalization of the tables provides the greatest efficiency.

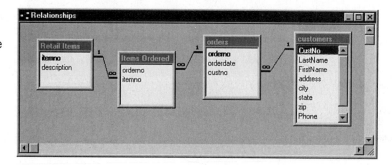

When information is moved out of one table and into another, you must have a way of keeping track of the *relationships* between the tables. You can do so through the use of data keys. For example, your Customers table has a field called CustNo. The Orders table also has a field called CustNo. These tables are said to be linked through that field. If a program needs to obtain information about the customer who made a particular order, that customer's record can be located quickly in the Customers table via the common CustNo field.

Child and Lookup Tables   Another way to handle data normalization is to create what is known as a child table. A *child table* is a table in which all the entries share common information that is stored in another table. A simple example is a membership directory; the family shares a common last name, address, and phone number, but each family member has a different first name. The table containing the common information is called the *parent table,* and the table containing the member's first names is the *child table*. You use this data structure in the Youth system that is created later in the chapter. Figure 28.6 shows a parent table and its related child table.

A *lookup table* is another way to store information to prevent data redundancy and to increase the accuracy of data entry functions. Typically, a lookup table is used to store valid data entries (for example, a state abbreviations table). When a person enters the state code in an application, the program looks in the abbreviations table to make sure that the code exists.

You also can use a lookup table in data normalization. If you have a large mailing list, many of the entries use the same city and state information. In this case, you can use a ZIP Code table as a related table to store the city and state by ZIP Code (remember that each ZIP Code corresponds to a single city and state combination). Using the ZIP Code table requires that the mailing list use only the ZIP Code of the address, and not the city and state. During data entry, you can have the program check an entered ZIP code against the valid entries.

Rules for Organizing Tables   Although no absolute rules exist for defining what data goes into which tables, here are some general guidelines to follow for efficient database design:

- Determine a topic for each table, and make sure that all data in the table relates to the topic.
- If a number of the records in a table have fields intentionally left blank, split the table into two similar tables. (Remember the example of the employee and member tables.)
- If information is repeated in a number of records, move that information to another table and set up a relationship between the tables.
- Repeated fields indicate the need for a child table. For example, if you have Item1, Item2, Item3, and so on in a table, move the items to a child table that relates back to the parent table.
- Use lookup tables to reduce data volume and to increase the accuracy of data entry.
- Do not store information in a table if it can be calculated from data in other tables.

N O T E   As stated previously, the guidelines for defining tables are not hard-and-fast rules. Sometimes it makes sense for you to deviate from the guidelines. ■

Performance Considerations

One of the most frequent reasons for deviating from the guidelines just given is to improve performance. If obtaining a total sales figure for a given salesperson requires summing several thousand records, for example, you might find it worthwhile to include a Total Sales field in the Salesperson table that is updated each time a sale is made. This way, when reports are generated, the application doesn't have to do large numbers of calculations and the report process is dramatically faster.

Another reason to deviate from the guidelines is to avoid opening a large number of tables at the same time. Because each open table uses precious resources and takes up memory, having too many open tables can slow down your application.

Deviating from the guidelines results in two major consequences. The first is increasing the size of the database because of redundant data. The second is the possibility of having incorrect data in some of the records because a piece of data was changed and not all the affected records were updated.

There are tradeoffs between application performance and data storage efficiency. For each design, you must look at the tradeoffs and decide on the optimum design.

Using Indexes

When information is entered into a table, records usually are stored in the order in which they are added. This is the *physical order* of the data. However, you usually want to view or process data in an order different from the order of entry; that is, you want to define a *logical order.* You also frequently need to find a specific record in a table. Doing so by scanning the table in its physical order can be quite time-consuming.

An index provides a method of showing a table in a specific order. An *index* is a special table that contains a key value (usually derived from the values of one or more fields) for each record in the data table; the index itself is stored in a specific logical order. The index also contains pointers that tell the database engine where the actual record is located. This type of index is similar to the index in the back of this book. By using the book's index, you easily can look up key words or topics, because it contains pointers (page numbers) to tell you where to find the information.

Why Use an Index? The structure of an index allows for rapid data search and retrieval. If you have a table of names indexed alphabetically, you rapidly can retrieve the record for a specific name by searching the index. To get an idea of the value of such an index, imagine a phone book that lists the customer names in the order in which they signed up for phone service. If you live in a large city, finding a person's number could take forever, because you have to look at each line until you find the one you want.

A table can have a number of different indexes associated with it to provide different organizations of the data. For example, an Employee table can have indexes on last name, date of birth, date of hire, and pay scale. Each index shows the same data in a different order, for a different purpose.

CAUTION

Although having many different views of the data may be desirable, keeping multiple indexes can take a toll on performance, since all indexes must be updated each time data changes. Once again, you must consider the tradeoffs in the database design.

N O T E You also can create different views of the information in a table by sorting the records or by specifying an order using the ORDER BY clause of a Structured Query Language (SQL) statement. Even though indexes aren't used directly by the SQL engine, their presence speeds up the sorting process when an ORDER BY clause is present. You learn about this topic in detail in "SQL Primer," which is on the companion CD-ROM. ▪

▶ **See** "Setting the Sort Conditions," found in "SQL Primer" on this book's CD-ROM.

Single-Key Expressions The most common type of index is the *single-key index,* which is based on the value of a single field in a table. Examples of this type of index are Social Security number, ZIP Code, employee ID, and last name. If multiple records exist with the same index key, those records are presented in physical order within the sort order imposed by the single-key index. Figure 28.7 shows the physical order of a Names table and how the table appears after being indexed on the last name field.

FIG. 28.7

The physical and logical order of a table can be different. Logical order depends on an index.

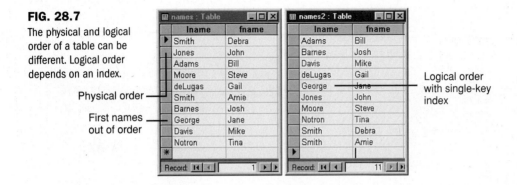

Physical order ——

First names —— out of order

Logical order with single-key index

Multiple-Key Expressions   Although single-key expressions are valuable in presenting data in a specific order, imposing an even more detailed order on the table is often necessary. You can do so by using multiple-key indexes. As you can infer from the name, a *multiple-key index* is based on the values of two or more fields in a table. A prime example is to use last name and first name when indexing a membership list. Figure 28.8 updates the view of the table shown in Figure 28.7 to show how using the first name field to help sort the records changes the order of the table. As with single-key indexes, if the key values of several records are the same, the records are presented in physical order within the index order.

FIG. 28.8

Multiple-key indexes further refine the logical order of a table.

First names now in order

> **CAUTION**
>
> Although this point might be obvious, I must stress that the order of the fields in the index expression has a dramatic impact on the order of the records in the table. Indexing on first name and then last name produces different results than indexing on last name and then first name. Figure 28.9 shows the undesirable results of using a first name/last name index on the table used in Figure 28.7.

FIG. 28.9

An improper index field order yields undesirable results.

Using Queries

When you normalize data, you typically are placing related information in multiple tables. However, when you need to access the data, you want to see the information from all the tables in one place. To do so, you need to create recordsets that consolidate the related information from the multiple tables. You create a recordset from multiple tables by using a SQL statement that specifies the desired fields, the location of the fields, and the relation between the tables. One way of using a SQL statement is to place it in the OpenRecordset method, which you use to create the recordset. However, you also can store the SQL statement as a query in the database.

Using stored queries presents several advantages:

- You can use the SQL statement more easily in multiple locations in your program or in multiple programs.

- Making changes to the SQL statement in a single location is easier.

- Stored queries run faster than those that are handled by parsing the statement from code.

- Moving your application up to a client/server environment is easier.

Implementing Your Design

The first step in implementing the database design is to create the database itself. There are three main methods of creating an Access database for use with Visual Basic. You can use the following:

- Data access objects within a program
- The Visual Data Manager application provided with Visual Basic
- Microsoft Access

Creating the Database

You can use Visual Basic's database commands to write a program that creates a database for use in your design work or to write a program that creates a new database while the program is running. Using the database creation commands is the only way you can make a new database at runtime. Using the program to create the database is particularly useful in creating and distributing commercial applications, because you don't have to worry about including and installing the database files with the application. If the code is included in your program, the database can be created the first time the user runs your application. Also, if future releases of the program require modifications of the database structure, you can use program commands to update the database on-the-fly, without requiring the user to handle conversions from the old format to the new.

Creating files at runtime also is useful if the user is expected to create different database files with the same structure but different user-defined names. Each time the user wants to create a new file, the program asks for the file name and then creates the database accordingly. As an example, a user might create a different database to hold data for each calendar year.

N O T E In order to do any work with databases in your program, you must add a reference to the appropriate DAO object library (typically the Microsoft DAO 3.5 Object Library). This is done in the References dialog box, which is accessible by choosing Project, References. ■

To create a new database, follow these eight steps:

1. Create a new database object variable with the `Dim` statement.
2. Use the `CreateDatabase` method to create the new database.
3. Create `TableDef` objects with the `Dim` statement and `CreateTableDef` method.
4. Set the properties for the new tables.
5. Create `Field` and `Index` objects with the `Dim` statement and `CreateField` and `CreateIndex` methods.
6. Set the properties for the fields and indexes.
7. Use the `Append` method to add fields and indexes to the tables.
8. Use the `Append` method to add the table to the database.

The heart of Visual Basic's data access object structure is the `DBEngine` object, which represents the database engine that Visual Basic programs use to interface with physical databases. All data access objects are contained within the `DBEngine` object. Programs interface with the `DBEngine` object through `Workspace` objects, which represent sessions with the `DBEngine` object and are members of the `DBEngine`'s `Workspaces` collection. Visual Basic creates a default `Workspace` object, `Workspaces(0)`, that is used unless the program explicitly creates another one. When a program references the various data access objects, Visual Basic assumes that the objects are contained in this default `Workspace` object unless another one is named.

You will be using the CreateDatabase method, which is a method of a Workspace object, to create a database. Listing 28.1 shows the statements you will use in this example to define Database and Workspace objects, and then actually create a database using the Workspace object's CreateDatabase method.

Listing 28.1 Defining a Database Object and Creating a Database

```
'***********************************
'Full syntax of CreateDatabase method
'***********************************
Dim NewDb As Database, NewWs As Workspace
Set NewWs = DBEngine.Workspaces(0)
Set NewDb = NewWs.CreateDatabase("C:\YOUTH\YOUTHTRK.MDB",dbLangGeneral)
```

You can define any valid variable name as a database object by using the Dim statement. Although a literal file name ("C:\YOUTH\YOUTHTRK.MDB") is specified explicitly in the argument of the CreateDatabase method, you can use a string variable to hold the name of the database to be created. This arrangement gives the user the flexibility of specifying a database name meaningful to him or her, or it enables you to create multiple databases with the same structure.

TIP If your program allows the user to create a database, you might want to use the CommonDialog control's File Open dialog box to retrieve the file name and path for the new database.

The constant dbLangGeneral represents the required *Locale* argument of the CreateDatabase method. It specifies the database's collating order (how strings are sorted and compared), which may be different depending upon the language and culture in which the program will be utilized. The constant dbLangGeneral that you used specifies that the database engine should use English sorting rules. The Visual Basic help screen "Data Access Objects (DAO) Constants" lists the constants that you can use for different languages in the CollatingOrder section.

Another (optional) argument, the *options* argument, is available for the CreateDatabase method that enables you to specify which version of the Jet database engine to use to create the database, and to specify whether the database should be encrypted. The default Jet engine for both Windows 95 and Windows NT is version 3.5.

To specify the options argument, supply the sum of the Visual Basic constants that define the options you want. The following lines show how you can change the code in Listing 28.1 to create a Jet 2.5 database and encrypt it (if, for instance, your program needed to share data with 16-bit applications):

```
Dim NewDb As Database, NewWs As Workspace
Dim DbOpts As Long, DbName As String
Set NewWs = DBEngine.Workspaces(0)
DbName = "C:\YOUTH\YOUTHTRK.MDB"
DbOpts = dbVersion25 + dbEncrypt
Set NewDb = NewWs.CreateDatabase(DbName, dbLangGeneral, DbOpts)
```

> **CAUTION**
>
> When you use the `CreateDatabase` method, a trappable error occurs if the file name to be created already exists. Include a trap for this error in your error-handling routine or, better yet, check for the existence of the file name before invoking the function, while you're still got a chance to specify a different name.

Creating a Table

Creating a database using the code in Listing 28.1 creates only a file on a disk. You can't do anything with that file until you create the tables and add them to the database (refer to Steps 3 through 8 in "Creating the Database," earlier in this chapter). You can think of the `CreateDatabase` method as simply building the shell of a warehouse. To store items, you still have to lay out the aisles and build the shelves. You do just that when you create the tables.

Defining the *TableDef* Object   The first step in creating a new table is to create a new `TableDef` object. `TableDef` is short for "Table Definition." When you create a `TableDef`, you define what type of information will be stored in a table and some optional properties of that table. Using the `TableDef` object, you can set the properties for the new table. The following lines of code show how to create a `TableDef` object and give the table a name:

```
Dim NewTbl As TableDef
Set NewTbl = NewDb.CreateTableDef("Youth")
```

The `Name` property of the table is only one of several properties for the `TableDef` object, but it is typically the only one required for the creation of a Jet table. You can use some of the other properties (`Attributes`, `Connect`, and `SourceTableName`) when attaching an external table to the database; these can be set in successive arguments of the `CreateTableDef` method. You also can specify other properties by setting them equal to a value after the `TableDef` object has been created, as you do if you want to set the validation rule and validation error message for a table (as shown in the following section). These statements follow the `CreateTableDef` method:

```
NewTbl.ValidationRule = "Age > 0"
NewTbl.ValidationText = _
    "You cannot enter an age of 0 or less."
```

Defining the Fields   After defining the `TableDef` object for the new table, you must define one or more `Field` objects. For each field, you must define its name and type. Depending on the type of field, you might be required to define other properties, or you might want to set some optional properties.

For text fields, you must set the `Size` property to specify how long a string the field can contain. The valid entries for the `Size` property of the text field are 1 to 255. If you want to allow longer strings, you can set the field type to `Memo`, which allows over a gigabyte of text.

Listing 28.2 shows how field objects are created and field properties set for the Youth table of the sample application. You can specify the field name, type, and size as optional arguments of the `CreateField` method, or you could use the `CreateField` method without any arguments and then set all the field properties with assignment statements. Listing 28.2 shows both techniques. You must use an assignment statement to set any other properties. As an example of an assignment statement, the listing sets a validation rule for the age field.

Listing 28.2 Creating Field Objects and Setting Properties

```
Dim F1 As Field, F2 As Field, F3 As Field, F4 As Field
Dim F5 As Field, F6 As Field, F7 As Field
'**********************************************************
'Specify field name, type, and size as CreateField arguments
'**********************************************************
Set F1 = NewTbl.CreateField("LastName", dbText, 20)
Set F2 = NewTbl.CreateField("FirstName", dbText, 20)
Set F3 = NewTbl.CreateField()
'******************************
'Explicitly set field properties
'******************************
F3.Name = "Address"
F3.Type = dbText
F3.Size = 30
Set F4 = NewTbl.CreateField("Age", dbInteger)
'************************************
'Set validation properties for a field
'************************************
F4.ValidationRule = "Age > 0"
F4.ValidationText = "A person's age must be greater than 0."
Set F5 = NewTbl.CreateField("City", dbText, 20)
Set F6 = NewTbl.CreateField("State", dbText, 2)
Set F7 = NewTbl.CreateField()
F7.Name = "Birthdate"
F7.Type = dbDate
```

After you define each of the fields to include in the table, use the Append method of the TableDef object to add the fields to the table definition, as shown in Listing 28.3.

Listing 28.3 Adding Fields to the Table Definition

```
NewTbl.Fields.Append F1
NewTbl.Fields.Append F2
NewTbl.Fields.Append F3
NewTbl.Fields.Append F4
NewTbl.Fields.Append F5
NewTbl.Fields.Append F6
NewTbl.Fields.Append F7
```

N O T E If you have a large number of fields, or if you want to create a generic routine for adding fields to a table, consider using an *array* to define your fields. By using arrays, you can write a simple FOR loop to add all the fields to the table (as shown in the following code statements). Depending on the structure of the table, you might be able to use a loop to set the type properties of several fields, although you must still define each field you intend to add to the table:

```
ReDim Fld(1 To 7) As Field
'*************************************************
'Field definition statements go here for each
'array element.
'*************************************************
FOR I = 1 To 7
  NewTbl.Fields.Append Fld(I)
NEXT I
```

Setting Optional Field Properties   In the preceding section, you learned how to specify the name of a field, the type of data it can store, and, for some fields, the size of the field. These elements are the minimum requirements for defining a field. However, you can set several other properties of a field to further define its behavior.

The first of these properties is the Attributes property. Two key settings of this property are applicable to creating fields in a table. The first is the auto-increment setting, which tells the database to increment the value of a numeric field each time a new record is added. This setting can provide a record counter; you can use it to ensure a unique value in that field for each record. You then can use the auto-increment field as a primary key field. The auto-increment setting is valid only for fields with the Long data type. Another optional setting is the updatable setting, which enables you to specify whether a field can be changed. This setting is not typically used in initial table creation but can be useful in limiting access to information, particularly in a multi-user environment.

You set the Attributes property by assigning it a value in a code statement. For example, the following code segment creates a field and then specifies that it be used as a counter field by setting the Attributes property to auto-increment:

```
Set F1 = NewTbl.CreateField("YouthID", dbLong)
F1.Attributes = dbAutoIncrField
```

Note that dbAutoIncrField is a predefined constant that can be used to specify an auto-increment field. The other constants that you can use in the Attributes property are listed in Table 28.1. You can apply multiple settings to the Attributes property by combining the values of the constants and then setting the property to the sum of the values.

Table 28.1   The Attributes Settings to Control the Behavior of a Field

Constant	Function
dbFixedField	The length of the field is fixed.
dbVariableField	The field size can change. (Text fields only.)
dbAutoIncrField	The value of the field is incremented automatically by the database engine.
dbUpdatableField	The value of the field can be changed.

Part

VI

Ch

28

In addition to the `Attributes` property, you can set several other optional properties for individual fields. As with the `Attributes` property, these optional properties are set using assignment statements; they cannot be set as part of the `CreateField` method. Table 28.2 lists optional field properties, their functions, and their default settings, if applicable.

Table 28.2   Optional Properties that Provide You Further Control over the Behavior of a Field

Property	Function
AllowZeroLength	Specifies whether the value of a `Text` or `Memo` field can be a zero-length (empty) string. The default is False; setting this option to True allows zero-length strings.
DefaultValue	Allows you to specify a default value for the field.
Required	Determines whether a value for the field must be entered. The default value is False.
ValidationRule	Specifies criteria that must be met for the field before the record can be updated. The default value is no rule (an empty string).
ValidationText	Specifies the error message that is displayed when the validation rule is not met. The default value is an empty string.

CAUTION

As mentioned, the default setting for the `AllowZeroLength` property is False. A zero-length string, therefore, cannot be used in the field. You might want to change this value for many of the fields you create, as your program might not need values for these fields. For example, you might have a field for a work phone but need to allow a zero-length string for people who don't work or don't provide the information.

Adding the Table to the Database   The final step in creating a database is adding the table or tables to the database. Use the `Append` method of the `Database` object to accomplish this by appending the `TableDef` object you just created to the database's `TableDefs` collection (see the following code). The `TableDefs` collection contains one `TableDef` object for each table in the database. The code also shows the `Close` method, which closes the database file and releases the system resources associated with the `Database` object:

```
NewDb.TableDefs.Append NewTbl
NewDb.Close
```

Using a Query to Create a Table   In the preceding sections, you learned how to use data access objects to create a table in a database. However, you also could use the SQL CREATE TABLE statement in a query to accomplish the same goal with less effort. In this query, you specify the table name, followed by the names, types, and, optionally, sizes of the fields to include in the table. The list of fields is enclosed in parentheses. The query is run using the Database object's Execute method. The following code shows how to create the Youth table containing the LastName, FirstName, Age, and Birthdate fields using a query:

```
Dim SQLSel As String
SQLSel = "Create Table Youth (LastName TEXT(20),FirstName TEXT(20),"
SQLSel = SQLSel & "Age INTEGER,Birthdate DATETIME);"
NewDb.Execute SQLSel
```

The main drawback of using a CREATE TABLE query is that you cannot use it to set optional properties of the fields. You can set these properties only with the data access objects and the CreateField method.

Creating Indexes

Defining indexes for a table is another key aspect of developing your database. The method for creating an index is closely related to the method for creating the table itself. For each index, you must assign a name, define the fields to include in the index, and determine whether the index is a primary index and whether duplicate values are allowed in the fields that comprise the index key.

To create an index, follow these six steps:

1. Use the CreateIndex method of the TableDef object to create the Index object.
2. Set any optional properties of the index (such as primary or unique).
3. Use the CreateField method of the Index object to create the Field objects.
4. Set any optional properties of the Field objects.
5. Append the Field object(s) to the Fields collection of the Index object.
6. Append the Index object to the Indexes collection of the TableDef object.

Two commonly used optional properties of the Index object are the Primary property and the Unique property. A *primary index* is one that is typically used for finding a specific record in a table. To make an index primary, set the Primary property to True. Making an index primary ensures that the value of the index key for each record is unique and that no null values exist.

> **CAUTION**
>
> If you create a primary index, you must include logic in your program to ensure that any records added have unique, non-null values for the fields in the primary index. If you attempt to add a record with a non-unique or null value, an error is generated.

Use the Unique property on a non-primary index to make sure that the values of fields other than the primary index field are unique (for example, to make sure that you enter a unique Social Security number for each employee in a table).

N O T E   You can specify only one primary index per table. ■

For the `Field` objects that will be part of the `Fields` collection of an `Index` object, the only property of concern for creating indexes is the `Attributes` property. This property determines whether the sort order of the field is ascending (from A to Z) or descending (from Z to A). The default value is ascending. If you want to sort the field in descending order, set the `Attributes` property to the constant `dbDescending`.

You can create a multiple-field index (for example, an index on the first and last names of a customer). To create such an index, simply set up multiple fields using the `CreateField` method, and then append these fields one-by-one to the `Index` object's `Fields` collection. Remember that the order of the fields can have a dramatic impact on the order of your records. The order of the fields in an index is determined by the order in which the fields are appended to the index, not the order in which the field objects are created.

As I described in the preceding section, after you create the fields and set the properties of the fields and index, use the `Append` method to add the fields to the index and the index to the table definition.

N O T E   You can create a maximum of 32 indexes per table. ■

For the sample case, create a primary index on the `YouthID` field and an index on the `LastName` and `FirstName` fields. You also might want to create an index on the `Birthdate` field in descending order. Listing 28.4 shows how you accomplish this task.

Listing 28.4   Creating Index Objects, Assigning Properties, and Adding Indexes to the Table

```
'**********************************
'Dimension the data access objects
'**********************************
Dim Idx1, Idx2, Idx3 As Index
Dim Fld1, Fld2, Fld3 As Field
'**********************************
'Create the primary YouthID index
'**********************************
Set Idx1 = NewTbl.CreateIndex("YouthID")
Idx1.Primary = True
Set Fld1 = Idx1.CreateField("YouthID")
Idx1.Fields.Append Fld1
NewTbl.Indexes.Append Idx1
'*********************
'Create the name index
'*********************
Set Idx2 = NewTbl.CreateIndex("Name")
Idx2.Unique = False
Set Fld1 = Idx2.CreateField("LastName")
Set Fld2 = Idx2.CreateField("FirstName")
```

```
Idx2.Fields.Append Fld1
Idx2.Fields.Append Fld2
NewTbl.Indexes.Append Idx2
'**************************************************
'Create the birthdate index in descending order
'**************************************************
Set Idx3 = NewTbl.CreateIndex("Born")
Set Fld1 = Idx2.CreateField("Birthdate")
Fld1.Attributes = dbDescending
Idx3.Fields.Append Fld1
NewTbl.Indexes.Append Idx3
```

Creating Relations

Earlier in this chapter, I described normalizing data and the need to relate normalized tables. The Jet engine relates tables through the use of a `Relation` object stored in the database. The `Relation` object tells the database which two tables are related, which table is the parent, which is the child, and the key fields used to specify the relationship.

Follow these seven steps to create a relationship between two tables:

1. Use the `Dim` statement to define a `Relation` object variable.
2. Create the `Relation` object by using the `CreateRelation` method of the `Database` object.
3. Set the primary table and the foreign table properties of the relationship.
4. Create the relation field for the primary table by using the `CreateField` method of the `Relation` object.
5. Set the foreign field property of the `Field` object.
6. Append the field to the `Relation` object.
7. Append the `Relation` object to the database.

Listing 28.5 demonstrates the creation of a relationship, showing how to create a relation between the Family (primary) table and the Youth (foreign) table of the sample database.

Listing 28.5 Specifying a Relationship Between Two Tables Using the *Relation* Object

```
Dim NewRel As Relation
Dim Fld1 As Field
'**************************
'Create the Relation object
'**************************
Set NewRel = NewDb.CreateRelation("Parents")
'**********************************
'Set the properties of the relation
'**********************************
NewRel.Table = "Family"
```

Part
VI

Ch
28

continues

Listing 28.5   Continued

```
NewRel.ForeignTable = "Youth"
'*************************************************
'Create the relating field and set the properties
'*************************************************
Set Fld1 = NewRel.CreateField("ParentID")
Fld1.ForeignName = "ParentID"
'*********************************************************************
'Append the field to the relation and the relation to the database
'*********************************************************************
NewRel.Fields.Append Fld1
NewDb.Relations.Append NewRel
```

TROUBLESHOOTING

When I try to create a relation in the database, I get the error message `Parents is not an index in this table`. You get this message if you do not have a primary index on the key field in the primary table. In the preceding case, the primary index must be on the `ParentID` field in the Family table. Although the documentation does make this point, you must have a primary key field in your primary table. This field identifies the records to the relationship.

Creating Queries

Using queries is a powerful way of gathering information from more than one table or of selecting information from a table that matches specific criteria (for example, customer records for people who live in Alabama). As you learn in Chapter 31, "Improving Data Access with Data Access Objects (DAO)," an object called a *recordset* can store this type of information for use in your programs. In fact, using a query is one method of creating a dynaset- or snapshot-type recordset. The advantage of creating a query is that the information about it is saved in the database itself, making it convenient to test and store information needed to create recordsets that are used often. You learn a lot more about SQL in "SQL Primer" found on the CD-ROM.

Setting Up the Query   To create a query, you define a `QueryDef` object, and then use the `CreateQueryDef` method of the database. When calling the function, you must specify the name of the query. You can specify the SQL syntax of the query, or you can define the SQL statement in a separate program line. The following code shows two methods of creating a query:

```
Dim OldDb As Database, NewQry As QueryDef
Set OldDb = OldWs.OpenDatabase("C:\YOUTH\YOUTHTRK.MDB")
Set NewQry = OldDb.CreateQueryDef("Local")
NewQry.SQL = "SELECT * FROM Youth Where State = 'AL';"
'***********************************************
'Alternative form of query creation statement.
'***********************************************
Set NewQry = OldDb.CreateQueryDef("Local", "SELECT * FROM
    Youth Where State = 'AL';")
```

The heart of defining queries is the SQL statement. This statement defines the fields to be included, the source of the fields, record filters, and the sort order of the resulting recordset.

N O T E The Jet engine can store queries only for Access (Jet) databases. It can, however, use queries to retrieve the data in many database types, such as FoxPro, Paradox, dBase, SQL Server, and others. ▪

Deleting a Query As with most other objects in the database, if you create a query, you might, at some time, need to delete it. If you have a query that you no longer need in your database, you can remove it by using the following command:

```
OldDb.DeleteQueryDef "Local"
```

> **CAUTION**
>
> When you use a query, you open the query by creating a data access object. Therefore, before deleting a query that has been used, you should close the associated query object. This way, you can ensure that the query is not in use and that no error occurs during deletion. The syntax for closing a query is NewQry.Close.

Creating a Database with Other Tools

Although the data access objects provide you with a way to create a database by using program code, this approach is not the only way to create a Jet database. Several other methods are available to you:

- *Visual Data Manager* Using this Visual Basic add-in, you can create databases, as well as create, modify, and delete tables, indexes, and relations within a database. VisData, as it's also known, represents a major improvement over its predecessor, Data Manager.

- *Microsoft Access* Using this application, you can create Jet databases. It provides the added advantage of enabling you to create relations by using a visual drag-and-drop interface.

- *Third-party programs* A number of other programs, both commercial and shareware, are available to manage Jet (and other) databases. Some are highly specialized, while others are general-purpose utilities much like Visual Data Manager.

Using Visual Data Manager

The Visual Data Manager application that comes with Visual Basic provides you with an interactive way of creating and modifying databases. You can run this application by selecting the Visual Data Manager item from Visual Basic's Add-Ins menu.

N O T E Visual Data Manager can work with Access (Jet), dBase, FoxPro, Paradox, and ODBC databases, as well as text files. Typically, in Visual Basic applications, you will use it to manipulate Access databases.

continues

Part VI

Ch

28

continued

Visual Data Manager is also one of the sample applications that can be found in the Visual Basic folder when you installed Visual Basic. Examining this project can provide a tremendous education into creating database applications in Visual Basic. ■

The first step in creating a new database is to create the database file itself. This provides a physical location for the rest of your work. To do this in Visual Data Manager, first choose File, New. This brings up a submenu that allows you to specify the type of database to create. For the purpose of this discussion, you will create an Access (Jet) database by choosing the Microsoft Access item. This brings up another submenu from which you can choose the version of Access database to create. If you will be sharing data with users on a Windows 3.1 system, you should choose the 2.0 version; otherwise, choose the 7.0 version. Figure 28.10 shows the different menu levels for creating a database. After you have chosen the type of database, you are presented with the Select Microsoft Access Database to Create dialog box. This dialog box allows you to choose a name and folder for your database. After entering a name, click the Save button on the dialog box. This takes you to the design mode shown in Figure 28.11.

FIG. 28.10

The menus allow you to choose the type and version of database to create.

FIG. 28.11

The Visual Data Manager Database window provides access to the design functions for tables, fields, and indexes.

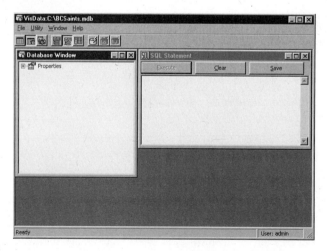

The Visual Data Manager presents the database information in a tree-like view. This type of view allows you quickly to see the tables and queries in the database. It also allows you to open the view further to see the fields and indexes of a table as well as its properties. Finally, you can open the view all the way up to see the properties of the individual fields.

Adding a New Table   After creating the database, the next thing you will want to do is create tables. To create a new table, right-click anywhere in Database Window. Select the New Table item. This brings up the Table Structure dialog box, as shown in Figure 28.12. This dialog box shows you information about the table itself, as well as a list of fields and indexes in the table. There are also buttons in the dialog box to add and remove fields and indexes. To add fields to the table, click the Add Field button to bring up the Add Field dialog box, as shown in Figure 28.13.

FIG. 28.12

In the Table Structure dialog box, you can specify a table name.

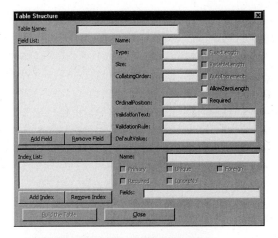

FIG. 28.13

In the Add Field dialog box, you can specify the properties of the fields for a table.

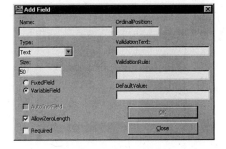

After you are in the Add Field dialog box, you need to follow these steps for each field you want to add:

1. Enter the name of the field.
2. Select the field type from the Type drop-down list.
3. Enter the size of the field (if necessary).
4. Enter any optional parameters, such as validation rules.
5. Click the OK button to add the field to the table.

After you have entered all the fields for your table, click the Close button in the Add Field dialog box. This returns you to the Table Structure dialog box.

Part
VI

Ch
28

If you want to remove a field from the table, select the field name in the dialog box's field list, and then click the Remove Field button. When you are satisfied with the fields in the table, click the Build the Table button to create the table.

Making Changes to the Fields in Your Table After you have created the fields in the table, you can set or change a number of the field properties from the Table Structure dialog box. To modify the properties, select the field name in the Field List. The properties of the field that can be modified appear in the dialog box as enabled text or check boxes. All other properties appear as disabled controls.

 T I P You also can edit the properties of a field from the Database window of the Visual Data Manager. Simply expand the database view to show field properties and right-click the property to be edited. You then can select Edit from the pop-up menu to change the property.

N O T E In Visual Basic, you cannot edit or delete any field that is part of an index expression or a relation. If you need to delete such a field, you must delete the index or relation containing the field and then make the changes to the field. ■

Adding an Index to the Table The Table Structure dialog box also allows you to add, modify, or remove indexes in the table. Any indexes currently in the table appear in the Index List at the bottom of the dialog box, as shown in Figure 28.14.

FIG. 28.14

You can add, edit, or delete indexes for a table from the Table Structure dialog box.

Index List

Editable properties

To add a new index, click the Add Index button; the Add Index dialog box then appears, as shown in Figure 28.15. In this dialog box, first enter an index name. Next, select the fields to be included in the index by clicking the fields in the Available Fields list. As you select each field, it is added to the Indexed Fields list in the order in which it was selected. By default, all fields are indexed in ascending order. To change the order to descending, precede the field name in the Indexed Fields list with a minus sign (-).

FIG. 28.15
The Add Index dialog box provides a visual means of creating the indexes for a table.

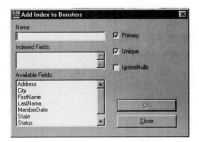

After you define the fields for the index, you can choose to require the index to be unique or to be the primary index (assuming there's not already a primary index) by selecting the appropriate check box in the window. When the index is completed to your liking, save it by clicking OK. The index you have just created is added to the index list on the Table Structure dialog box. To delete an index, simply select it in the list box and click Remove Index.

Returning to the Visual Basic Design Window   Closing the Visual Data Manager window or selecting Exit from the File menu takes you back to Visual Basic's main design window. (You also can switch back and forth between the Data Manager and the Visual Basic design environment.) To manipulate databases without having to start Visual Basic every time, make the Data Manager application a program item in your Visual Basic group.

Using Microsoft Access

Another option for creating a Jet database for use with a Visual Basic application is to use Microsoft Access. Access has a good visual design interface for setting up tables, indexes, queries, and table relationships. Obviously, this option is available only if you own a copy of Access. Note that Visual Basic can work with databases created with any version of Access; however, in order to exploit the power of 32-bit databases, Access 95 or later must be used.

Third-Party Database Designers

In addition to Visual Data Manager and Access, a number of third-party programs enable you to create and maintain Jet databases. Some of them provide you with advanced data modeling capabilities. These modeling capabilities make it easy for you to determine what information goes in which table and to set up the relations easily between the tables. Then, after your data model is complete, the program automatically can generate the database for you.

Modifying the Database Structure

Even if you create the perfect database for an application, sooner or later someone will come along and say, "Well, I really need this program to handle other data, too." At this point, you must modify the structure of your database and tables. Modifications can take the form of new tables, new fields or indexes in tables, or changes in the properties of tables, fields, or indexes. On occasion, you also might have to delete a table, field, or index.

Part
VI

Ch
28

In the following sections, you learn about the modification of a database through the use of Visual Basic code. As with the creation of a database, you also can use Visual Data Manager application or Microsoft Access to perform the modifications.

Adding and Deleting Tables

To add a table, follow the same steps that you took to create tables in a new database:

1. Define the table, field, and index objects by using the Dim statement and appropriate create methods.
2. Define the properties of the table, fields, and indexes.
3. Append the fields and indexes to the table.
4. Append the table to the database.

To delete a table from a database, you need to delete its TableDef object from the database's TableDefs collection, as shown in this statement:

```
OldDb.TableDefs.Delete "Members"
```

> **CAUTION**
>
> Use the Delete method with extreme caution. When you delete a table, all fields, indexes, and—most importantly—data are deleted along with it. And when it's gone, it's gone. The only way to get the data back is to create the table again from scratch and reload all your data.

Adding, Deleting, and Editing Indexes

Adding a new index involves the same steps as creating an index for a new table. You must define an Index object, set its properties, and append it to the Indexes collection of the appropriate TableDef object. An example of these steps was shown earlier in Listing 28.4.

To delete an index, simply use the Delete method as shown in the following line of code. This code deletes the Born index from the Youth table:

```
OldDb.TableDefs("Youth").Indexes.Delete "Born"
```

You cannot modify the properties of an existing Index object. Therefore, if a change to an index is required, you must delete the old index from the table and create a new index with the new properties. You do so by using the methods shown in the section "Creating Indexes," earlier in this chapter.

> **N O T E** You cannot delete an index that is required by a relation. To delete such an index, you first must delete the relation. ■

Adding, Deleting, and Editing Fields

As you learned when creating a new database, you add a field to a table by defining the field object, setting its properties, and appending it to the table. These commands were presented earlier in Listings 28.2 and 28.3.

To delete a field, use the `Delete` method to remove the `Field` object from the appropriate `TableDef` object's `TableDefs` collection, as shown here. This example deletes the `Address` field from the Youth table:

```
NewDb.TableDefs("Youth").Fields.Delete "Address"
```

Unfortunately, you cannot change a field's properties directly. You can, however, accomplish this task in two indirect ways. If the table contains no data, or if you don't care about losing the data in the field, you can delete the field from the table and then re-create it with the new properties. If you have a table that contains data, and you want to preserve the data, you must create a whole new table (making the appropriate changes to the `Field` object), copy the data to the new table, and then delete the old table. The difficulty of this process of making changes to fields dramatically underscores the importance of a good initial design.

To move data from one table to another existing table, follow these steps:

1. Open both tables.
2. Set up a loop to process each record in the table currently containing the data.
3. Then, for each record in the old table, follow these steps:
    a. Retrieve the value of each field to be transferred from the old table.
    b. Add a record to the new table.
    c. Set the values of the field in the new table.
    d. Update the new table.

NOTE If you have Microsoft Access, you can change the properties of a table's fields while preserving the fields' contents. ■

Remember that you cannot delete a field that is part of an index or relation.

Deleting a Relation

If you need to delete a relation, you can use the `Delete` method of the `Database` object to remove the `Relation` object from the database's `Relations` collection. The following statement shows how to delete the relation created earlier in Listing 28.5:

```
NewDb.Relations.Delete "Parents"
```

Using SQL to Modify the Database

Just as you can create a table with SQL statements, you also can modify or even delete a table by using SQL. To modify a table, you can use an ALTER TABLE query. By using this type of query, you can add a new field to the table or delete a field from the table. The following code segment shows how you can use an ALTER TABLE query to add an Address field and delete the Birthdate field from the Youth table created earlier:

```
'********************************
'Add an address field to the table
'********************************
NewDb.Execute "ALTER TABLE Youth ADD COLUMN Address TEXT(30);"
'*********************************************
'Delete the birthdate field from the table
'*********************************************
NewDb.Execute "ALTER TABLE Youth DROP COLUMN Birthdate;"
```

If you want, you also can delete an entire table by using a DROP TABLE query. The following statement deletes the entire Youth table:

```
NewDb.Execute "DROP TABLE Youth;"
```

Why Use a Program Instead of Visual Data Manager?

In this chapter, you have learned that the Visual Data Manager application and Microsoft Access can create, modify, and load data into a database. So the question you might be asking is: "Why do I ever need to bother with the Visual Basic program commands for these functions?" The answer is that, in many cases, you don't. If you have direct control over the database (that is, you are the only user or you can access the database at any time), you may never need to use program commands to create or change a database.

If, however, you have an application with many users—either throughout your company or across the country—using a program for data management offers several benefits. One benefit is in initial installation. If the database creation routines are in the program itself, you don't have to include empty database files on your setup disks. This can reduce the number of disks required, and it certainly reduces the possibility that a key file is left out. Along the same lines, a user accidentally may delete a database file, leading to the necessity to create a new one.

Another benefit occurs when you distribute updates to the program. With changes embedded in a program, your user merely can run the update program to change the file structure. He or she doesn't need to reload data into a new, blank file. Also, by modifying the file in place, you can preserve most structure changes in the database made by the end user.

Another reason for putting database creation and maintenance commands in a program is for performance considerations. Sometimes it is desirable, from a performance standpoint, to create a temporary table to speed up a program or to store intermediate results, and then delete the table at the completion of the program. You also might want to create a temporary index that creates a specific order or speeds up a search.

From Here...

In this chapter, you learned how to design and create a database for use in an application. To use the database, however, you must write a database access application. This topic is covered in other chapters of the book. For further information, refer to the following chapters:

- To learn how to quickly create a database application, see Chapter 29, "Using the Visual Basic Data Control."
- To see how to use bound controls to easily display database information in your programs, see Chapter 30, "Doing More with Bound Controls."
- Creating an application with the data access objects is covered in Chapter 31, "Improving Data Access with the DataAccess Objects (DAO)."
- If you want to create and use SQL statements, see "SQL Primer," on the companion CD-ROM.

Part
VI

Ch
28

CHAPTER 29

Using the Visual Basic Data Control

Visual Basic is designed to enable you, the developer, to create applications for the Windows environment quickly and easily. This ease-of-use extends to the creation of database programs as well. If you have an existing database that you want to access, Visual Basic makes it easy for you to write a complete data management and reporting application with almost no programming. You just drop a few controls on a form and set the properties. In fact, Visual Basic makes the task so easy that it can even create the data entry forms for you.

The components that make all these capabilities possible are the Data control and the data-bound controls for data entry forms and Crystal Reports for report generation. With just these few tools, you can create a wide variety of applications. Of course, as you progress to more complex applications, you need to do more of the programming yourself. But even for more complex applications, these tools provide a good first step in the programming process and enable you to create application prototypes rapidly. ■

Navigating a recordset with the Data control

The Data control provides several buttons that enable you to move from one record to another in a recordset.

Displaying data from a recordset

We examine how the bound controls make it easy to get information from a database to the user's screen.

Adding and deleting records

You will see how to use code to add record management features to your applications.

Using automatic data entry forms

If you want the easiest way to create a data entry form, Visual Basic can create it for you. You'll see how to use a wizard to make this happen.

Running reports from your program

You'll also see how to use Crystal Reports forms from within your program.

Understanding the Data Control

The centerpiece of easy database applications is the Data control. The Data control is one of the controls available in Visual Basic's Toolbox, as shown in Figure 29.1. Setting up the Data control requires only four simple steps:

1. Select the control from the Toolbox.
2. Draw the control on your form.
3. Set the DatabaseName property of the control.
4. Set the RecordSource property of the control.

NOTE Following these four steps is the minimum required to set up the Data control. If you want to access non-Jet databases or use any of the control's other capabilities, you need to set additional properties. These properties are covered in Chapter 30, "Doing More with Bound Controls." ■

▶ **See** "Exploring the Data Control In-Depth," **p. 826**

FIG. 29.1

The Data control is one of the standard components of the Visual Basic Toolbox.

Data control

What Is the Data Control?

Basically, the Data control is a link between information in your database and the bound controls that you use to display the information. As you set the properties of the Data control, you tell it which database and what part of the database to access. By default, the Data control creates a dynaset-type recordset from one or more of the tables in your database.

The Data control also provides the record navigation functions that your application needs. With these buttons, indicated in Figure 29.2, the user can move to the first or last record in the recordset or to a record prior to or following the current record. The design of the buttons makes their use intuitive; they are similar to the buttons you would find on a VCR or a CD player.

The recordset created by the Data control is determined by the settings of the DatabaseName and RecordSource properties. The recordset is created as the form containing the Data control loads and is activated. This recordset is active until the form is unloaded, at which time the recordset is released.

FIG. 29.2
The VCR-like buttons on the Data control indicate their function to the user.

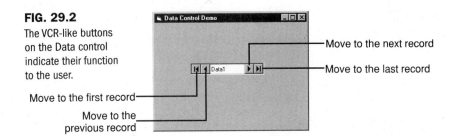

Move to the next record

Move to the last record

Move to the first record

Move to the previous record

N O T E A *recordset* is an object that represents the data in a physical database. Even after a recordset is released or closed, the data in the underlying table(s) is still in the database.

Adding a Data Control to Your Form

The first step in using a Data control is to add the control to your application's form. Select the Data control object from the Visual Basic Toolbox (refer to Figure 29.1). Next, place and size the Data control just as you do any other design object. After you set the desired size and placement of the Data control on your form, you can set its Name and Caption properties.

The Name property sets the control name, which identifies the control and its associated data to the bound controls. The default name for the first Data control added to a form is Data1. Additional Data controls added to a form are sequentially numbered as Data2, Data3, and so on. To change the name of a Data control, select its Name property from the Properties window and type the name you want (see Figure 29.3).

The Caption property specifies the text that appears on the Data control. You usually want the caption to be descriptive of the data the control accesses. The default for the Caption property is the initial setting of the Name property (for example, Data1 for the first Data control). You can change the Caption property the same way you change the Name property (see Figure 29.3).

FIG. 29.3
The Data control's Caption property has been set to a more meaningful value.

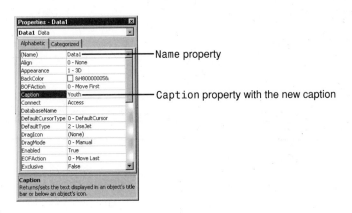

Name property

Caption property with the new caption

For the example you're creating in this chapter, add a Data control with the name datYouth and the caption Youth. Figure 29.4 shows the form with this control added.

TIP   You also can add code to your program to change the Data control's caption to reflect information in the current record, such as a person's name.

FIG. 29.4
Draw the Data control on your form and set its caption appropriately.

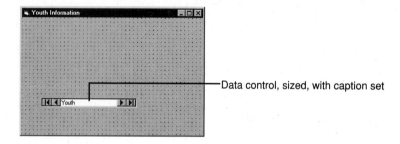

Data control, sized, with caption set

Two Properties Are All You Need to Set

After you place the Data control on your form, you need to make the connection between the Data control and information stored in a database. You do so by setting the Data control's properties. Although several properties can affect the way a Data control interacts with the database, only two properties are required to establish the link to a Jet database: the DatabaseName and RecordSource properties. Specifying these two properties tells the Data control what information to retrieve from the database and causes the Data control to create a recordset that allows nonexclusive, read/write access to the data.

N O T E   The DatabaseName property is not the same as the Name property mentioned earlier. The Name property specifies the name of the Data control object. This name references the object in code. The DatabaseName property specifies the name of the database file that the Data control is accessing.

What's in a Name?   For Jet databases, the DatabaseName property is the name of the database file. To enter the name, select the DatabaseName property from the Properties window and type the database's file name.

If you'd like to locate the database by browsing, click the ellipsis button (...) at the right of the property input line to display the DatabaseName dialog box, as shown in Figure 29.5. Browse to the appropriate database file and click OK. The selected file name and path are automatically entered into the DatabaseName property (see Figure 30.6).

FIG. 29.5
Use the Properties window to set the database name for the control.

FIG. 29.6
You can enter a database name or choose it from the DatabaseName dialog box.

CAUTION

If you browse to the DatabaseName property at design time using the dialog box, the property will include a fully qualified path to the database's file name, for example, C:\MyData\LMS\TMS1112.MDB. This may be dangerous since the database will be expected to be in the same exact location at runtime. It would be better to allow some flexibility in the location of the database: set the DatabaseName property using no path (that is, use TMS1112.MDB), in which case your program would expect to find it in the program's current directory; use a relative path from the current directory (that is, use LMS\TMS1112.MDB); or set the property from code based on user input or some type of program initialization parameters (that is, use Data1.DatabaseName = stDataLocation).

Straight from the Source   After you've set the DatabaseName property, specify the information you want from that database with the RecordSource property. If you are working with a single table as your recordset, you can enter the table name or select it from the list of tables, as shown in Figure 29.7.

FIG. 29.7
You can select the
RecordSource
property from a list of
tables available in the
database.

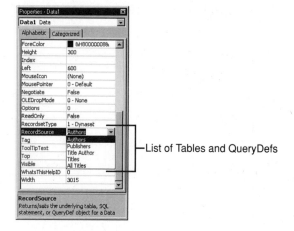

List of Tables and QueryDefs

If you want to use only selected information from a table or use information from multiple
tables, you can use a SQL statement in the RecordSource property. To do this, you can either
set the RecordSource property to the name of a QueryDef in the database that contains a SQL
statement or enter a valid SQL statement as the value of the RecordSource property. You can
use any SQL statement that creates a recordset. (You can also include functions in your SQL
statement.) If you're using a QueryDef, it must be a QueryDef that has already been defined and
stored in the database.

 TIP   To make sure that your SQL statements work correctly, you can test them in Visual Data Manager. Then
copy and paste to place the statements in the RecordSource property.

Getting Acquainted with Bound Control Basics

Bound controls in Visual Basic are controls that are set up to work with a Data control to create
database applications; hence, the controls are "bound" to information in the database. Most of
the bound controls in Visual Basic are simply standard controls that have additional properties
allowing them to perform data access functions. A few custom controls are designed specifically to work with the Data controls. These controls are covered in Chapter 30, "Doing More
with Bound Controls."

▶ **See** "Other Bound Controls," **p. 837**

The controls that you use as bound controls are ones with which you are already familiar:

- TextBox
- Label
- CheckBox
- PictureBox
- Image

These controls are highlighted in the Toolbox shown in Figure 29.8.

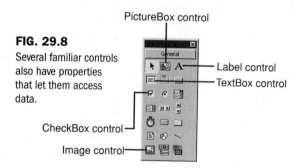

FIG. 29.8
Several familiar controls also have properties that let them access data.

PictureBox control

Label control

TextBox control

CheckBox control

Image control

What Do These Controls Do?

Each bound control is tied to a Data control and, more specifically, to a particular field in the recordset attached to the Data control. The bound control automatically displays the information in the specified field for the current record. As the user moves from one record to another using the navigation buttons of the Data control, the information in bound controls is updated to reflect the current record.

The bound controls are not limited, however, to just displaying the information in the record. Most also can be used to modify the information. To do so, the user just needs to edit the contents of the control. Then, when the current record is changed or the form is closed, the information in the database is automatically updated to reflect the changed values.

> **N O T E** Because the Label control has no editable portion, the data displayed in the Label cannot be changed. Also, if a control is locked or editing is otherwise prevented, the user cannot change the value of the information. ■

You use each of the basic bound controls to edit and display different types of data. With the bound controls, you can handle strings, numbers, dates, logical values, and even pictures and memos. Table 29.1 lists the five basic bound controls and the types of database fields that they can handle. The table also lists the property of the control that contains the data.

Table 29.1   Different Controls Used to Handle Different Types of Data

Control Name	Data Type	Control Property
Label	Text, Numeric, Date	`Caption`
TextBox	Text, Memo, Numeric, Date	`Text`
CheckBox	Logical, True/False	`Value`
PictureBox	Long Binary	`Picture`
Image	Long Binary	`Picture`

Adding Controls to Your Forms

To add a bound control to your form, select the control from the Toolbox and draw it on the form. Figure 29.9 shows a text box added to the form that contains the Data control.

FIG. 29.9

You draw bound controls on your form just as you draw any other control.

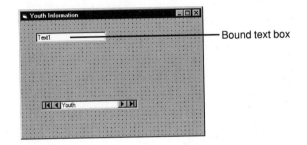

Bound text box

 T I P   Hold down the Ctrl key when you click a control in the Toolbox, and you can add multiple controls of that type to your form. This way, you don't have to click the control's Toolbox button repeatedly. When you're done, click the mouse pointer button in the Toolbox.

Data Display in Two Easy Properties

For a bound control to work with the data from a recordset, you must first tie the bound control to the Data control representing the recordset (recall that we've already discussed how to bind the Data control to physical data). You do this by setting the bound control's `DataSource` property. Depending on the specific control used, you might have to set other properties. By working on the sample Retail Items data entry screen throughout the remainder of this chapter, you will learn several of the bound controls, which properties you must set, and how to set them.

Setting the *DataSource* Property   To set the `DataSource` property, select it from the Properties window for your control. Click the arrow to the right of the input area to see a list of all the Data controls on the current form. To set the `DataSource` property, select one of the controls from the list. Figure 29.10 shows this procedure.

 T I P   Double-click the `DataSource` property to scroll through the available Data controls.

Setting the *DataField* Property   Although the `DataSource` property tells the bound control from which Data control to retrieve data, you still need to tell the bound control what specific data to retrieve. You do so by setting the `DataField` property. This property tells the control which field of the recordset will be handled by this bound control.

To set the `DataField` property of the control, select the `DataField` property from the Properties window, click the arrow to the right of the input area, and select one of the fields from the displayed list. The list includes all available fields from the recordset defined in the specified `DataSource` (see Figure 29.11).

FIG. 29.10

Select the
`DataSource` property
for the bound control
from a list of the form's
Data controls.

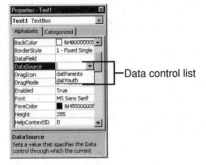

—Data control list

FIG. 29.11

Select the `DataField`
property for the bound
control from the list of
fields in the selected
Data control.

—Field list

 T I P Double-click the `DataField` property to scroll through the available fields.

CAUTION

You cannot select a field for the `DataField` property from a list until the `DataSource` property has
been set.

Creating a Simple Application

To help further illustrate the concepts of creating a data access application, let's walk through
the process of creating a data entry form using the biblio database, which is included with
Visual Basic.

Setting Up the Form

The first step in setting up the data access form is to start a new project. Add a Data control
to the default form. Change the Data control's `Name` property to `dtaMain` and its `Caption` property to `Author Info`. Next, set the `DatabaseName` and `RecordSource` properties of the Data

control. First, set the DatabaseName property to the path to biblio.mdb on your hard drive. After you set the database name, you can set the RecordSource property. From the property's selection list, select the Authors table. The Data control is now ready for use.

The next step in creating the data access form is to add the bound controls. To make the example easy, just use text boxes for each of the fields. Also, for each field, place a label control on the form to identify the information in the text box. For the sample case, you need three text boxes and three corresponding labels. The DataSource property of all the text boxes is dtaMain, which is the name of the Data control you just created. For each text box, you also need to specify a DataField property. Remember that the DataField property ties the control to a specific field in the database. Table 29.2 lists the DataField settings for each text box and the suggested captions for the corresponding label controls. The table uses the default names for the text boxes.

Table 29.2 *DataField* and *Caption* Settings for the Data Access Form

TextBox Name	DataField	Caption for Corresponding Label
Text1	Au_ID	Author ID:
Text2	Author	Name:
Text3	Year Born	Year Born:

After you add the bound controls and set their properties, your form should look like the one shown in Figure 29.12.

FIG. 29.12

You can create a simple data entry form by using just the Data control and bound text boxes.

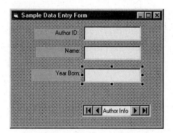

Navigating the Database

Now that you have created the data entry form, try it out by running the program. As the program first starts, you should see the form load, and the information for the first record should appear in the text boxes. Now you can see how the Data control is used to navigate through the records of the database. You can move to the first record, the previous record, the next record, or the last record by clicking the appropriate button on the Data control.

With this simple program you can even update and edit the database. Try typing a year in the Year Born text box and moving to another record. This enters new information into the database.

TROUBLESHOOTING

The records of the database seem to be in random order, not alphabetical order. You have not created an error or done anything wrong in setting up the form. You are seeing the records presented in the physical order of the table, the order in which the records were entered. If you want to see the records in alphabetical order, place the following string in the RecordSource property of the Data control:

```
Select * from Authors Order by Author
```

Then run the program again. You can also set the RecordSource property from code:

```
frmMain.dtaMain.RecordSource = "Select * from Authors Order by Author"
frmMain.dtaMain.Refresh
```

Essential Functions the Data Control Forgot

As you can see, the Data control is quite flexible, but it lacks a few functions that are necessary for most data entry applications—specifically, adding and deleting records. To overcome these shortcomings, you can add the functions to the data entry screen using program commands assigned to a command button.

To add these functions to the sample application, add two command buttons named Add and Delete to the form. To make the buttons functional, add the code segments shown in Listing 29.1 to the Click event of the appropriate button.

> **Listing 29.1   ProgramName.ext—Program Statements Placed in the _Click_ Event of Command Buttons to Add Capabilities to the Data Entry Screen**

```
'Command to add a new record,
'place in click event of Add button
dtaMain.Recordset.AddNew

'Commands to delete a record,
'placed in click event of Delete button
dtaMain.Recordset.Delete
If Not dtaMain.EOF Then
   dtaMain.Recordset.MoveNext
Else
   dtaMain.Recordset.MoveLast
  End If
```

As you can see, this listing does not enter a command to invoke the Update method. (Updates are done automatically by the Data control whenever you move to a new record or close the form.)

> **N O T E**   You add the MoveNext and MoveLast commands to the Delete button to force a move to
> a new record. After a record is deleted, it is no longer accessible but still shows on-screen
> until a move is executed. If you do not force a move and try to access the deleted record, an error
> occurs. ▨

Your data entry form should now look like the one shown in Figure 29.13.

FIG. 29.13

You can add new
capabilities to the data
entry screen by
assigning program
commands to command
buttons.

Creating Forms Automatically

The bound controls make it easy for you to create data entry forms with a minimum of effort.
You just draw the controls on your form, set a few properties, and you're done. What could be
easier?

Well, actually you can create data entry forms in an even easier way—by using the Data Form
Wizard (DFW). The DFW is one of the add-ins that comes with Visual Basic. Using this add-in,
you can select a database and a record source; then it creates your data entry form automatically. Of course, the form might not be exactly like you want it, but you can easily change the
default design and then save the changes. Using the DFW is a great way to create a series of
data entry forms rapidly for a prototype or for a simple application.

Setting Up the Data Form Wizard

As you learned in the preceding section, the DFW is one of the add-ins that comes with Visual
Basic. If, however, you look at the Add-Ins menu in Visual Basic, you don't see this option
initially. You have to first tell Visual Basic that you want access to the form designer. You do so
by choosing Add-Ins, Add-In Manager. The dialog box shown in Figure 29.14 then appears.

To access the DFW, click the box next to the text in the Add-In Manager. A check mark then
appears in the box. Next, click the OK button and you're set. Now, when you select the Add-Ins
menu, you see the DFW as one of the items. Selecting the DFW opens the first dialog box of
the wizard, which you can see in Figure 29.15. This screen tells you a little about the DFW. You
can choose not to have this form presented on subsequent uses of the DFW.

FIG. 29.14

By using the Add-In Manager, you can add capabilities to your Visual Basic design environment.

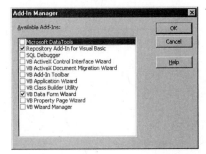

FIG. 29.15

The Data Form Designer automatically creates data entry forms for you.

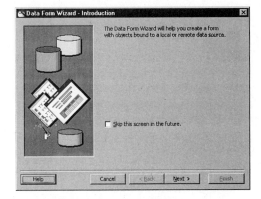

Clicking the Next button on the initial form takes you to the second screen of the DFW. This screen, shown in Figure 29.16, enables you to choose the type of database that your form will be accessing. To choose a database type, simply click the type name in the list and then click the Next button to continue creating your form.

FIG. 29.16

You can choose to create a form from many common desktop databases.

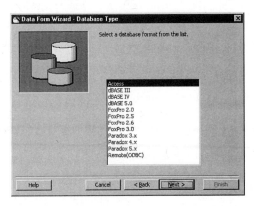

Getting to the Source of Your Data

After you have chosen the type of database to use, you need to choose the actual database and record source with which you will be working. The screen shown in Figure 29.17 enables you either to enter the name of the database or to select the database from a dialog box. Clicking the Browse button on the dialog box presents you with a database dialog box that enables you to choose the database to open. After selecting the database, you are returned to the Database screen of the DFW. You might notice at this point that the file name of the selected database, including the full path, has been entered in the text box on the form.

FIG. 29.17
The Database screen allows you to specify the database and the types of record sources to use.

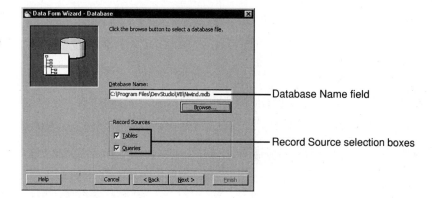

Database Name field

Record Source selection boxes

In addition to specifying the database name, you can also specify the types of record sources that will be displayed for selection in a later screen. You can choose to have tables, queries, or both displayed. You make your selection by clicking the appropriate check boxes. When you have finished, you need to click the Next button to proceed.

The next screen enables you to select the type of data entry form that you want the DFW to create. There are three types of data entry forms that can be created:

- *Single Record*   Allows you to edit the information in the recordset one record at a time. This is the classic data entry type of form.

- *Grid*   Allows you to edit multiple records at a time. This screen is similar to the recordset view in Access or the Browse window in FoxPro.

- *Master/Detail*   Allows you to edit the information of a single parent record along with its associated child records. This type of form might be used to show information about an order along with all the items ordered.

Choosing the type of form to create not only affects the appearance of the form but also determines what recordset(s) must be selected for the form. For a single record or grid form, you only need to select a single record source. For the Master/Detail form, you need to select two record sources. You really don't have to worry too much about this because the wizard guides you through it. That's what wizards are for, right?

CAUTION

If you are creating a Master/Detail form, you need to have established a relation between the tables you select. The relation information is what is used to keep the information synchronized.

Choosing Fields with the Data Form Wizard

After you have selected the database and the type of form, you need to select the table or query to use for the form and the actual fields that you want to have included on the form. This is done on the Record Source screen of the wizard, as shown in Figure 29.18.

FIG. 29.18

You choose the record source and fields using simple combo boxes and lists.

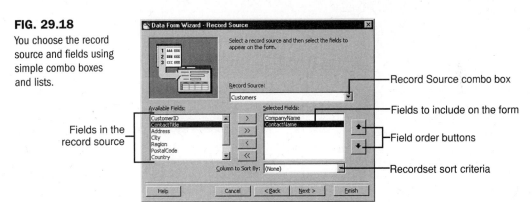

To set up the fields for the form, you need to follow these steps:

1. Select a record source from the combo box.

2. Select the fields to include by clicking the field names in the Available Fields list. You can double-click a field to select it or highlight the field and click the selection button (>).

3. Place the fields in the desired order by moving them in the Selected Fields list. You move a field by highlighting it and then clicking the up or down buttons. (This step is optional.)

4. Select the column on which to sort the recordset by choosing it from the Column to Sort By combo box. (This step is optional.)

5. Click the Next button to move to the next screen.

What Does This Button Do?

After selecting all of the fields that you want on the form, you have one final set of choices to make—the buttons that you want to appear on your form. You make this selection in the Control Selection screen of the DFW, shown in Figure 29.19.

FIG. 29.19

You can choose a number of command buttons to appear on your form.

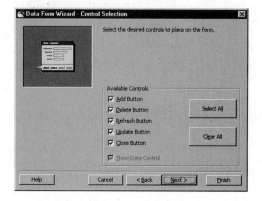

Table 29.3 lists the buttons that you can elect to have appear on your data form.

Table 29.3 Command Button Controls and Their Functions

Available Controls	Function
Add	Adds a new record to the recordset and clears the data entry fields.
Delete	Deletes the current record.
Refresh	Causes the Data control to reexecute the query used to create it. This process is necessary only in a multi-user environment.
Update	Stores any changes made to the data entry fields to the database for the current record.
Close	Closes and unloads the data entry form.

You are now ready for the final step of the DFW—actually creating your form. In the last screen of the DFW, you specify the name of the form (the DFW gives you a default name) and then click the Finish button. This starts the creation process. At this point, you sit back and relax for a minute while the DFW does the work. When it is finished, your program has a new data form, and all you did was answer a few questions and make a few selections. Figures 29.20 through 29.22 show you the various types of data forms that can be created with the DFW.

FIG. 29.20

A Single Record data form created by the Data Form Wizard.

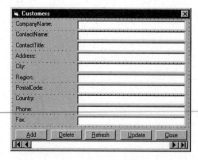

FIG. 29.21

A Grid data form created by the Data Form Wizard.

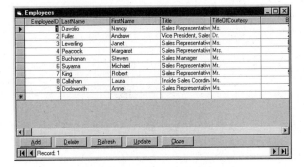

FIG. 29.22

A Master/Detail data form created by the Data Form Wizard.

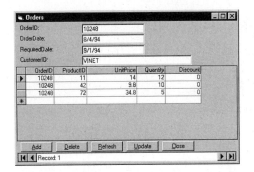

Using Crystal Reports with Visual Basic 5

Although the Data control and bound controls do a great job of enabling you to create forms to enter and display data, they don't have any reporting capabilities. As a result, if you want to display and print reports, you need some additional capabilities. Visual Basic does have a Printer object with which you can send information to the printer. However, trying to set up a custom database report with the Printer object requires a lot of programming and a lot of trial and error.

Fortunately, you can accomplish database reporting in an easier way. Visual Basic comes with a reporting product—Crystal Reports. The Crystal Reports custom control that comes with Visual Basic allows you to access reports from within your Visual Basic program. The Crystal Reports control provides a link between the Crystal Reports engine and the reports you create with the report designer.

Crystal Reports Control

The first step in accessing Crystal Reports is to make the control available to your program. First, you need to add the Crystal Reports control to your Visual Basic Toolbox. To do so, choose Components from the Project menu of Visual Basic. The Components dialog box, shown in Figure 29.23, then appears. In this dialog box, you can specify which custom controls are available in your project.

Selected controls

FIG. 29.23

You must make the
Crystal Reports control
available to your project
by selecting it in the
Components dialog box.

Crystal Reports control

Controls not used

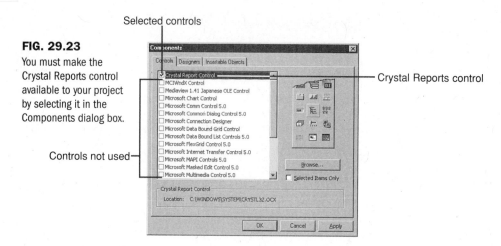

> **T I P**   You also can access the Components dialog box by right-clicking the Toolbox and choosing
> Components from the pop-up menu or by pressing Ctrl+T.

TROUBLESHOOTING

The Crystal Reports control does not show up in the Custom Controls dialog box. If you elected to
perform a custom setup of Visual Basic, you might have left Crystal Reports out of the setup process.
You need to rerun the Visual Basic setup program and add Crystal Reports.

Check Your Version of Crystal Reports!

If you have a version of Crystal Reports on your machine that is greater than version 4.6.1 (the
version that comes standard with VB5), you will need to uninstall it first before you can install the
version that comes with Visual Basic 5. After you have uninstalled your existing version of Crystal
Reports, you can then install the version that comes with Visual Basic 5. If you want to use the
newer version that you previously had, you can reinstall it at this time.

Certain releases of the newest Crystal Reports (version 5.108) DLLs and OCXs may not be completely replaced or overwritten when you install a older version of Crystal Reports. This can produce
reports that work fine on the development machine but produce inconsistent results on the user's
machine.

Setting Up the Control

After the Crystal Reports control is available in your Toolbox, you can use it in your program.
To gain access to the control, simply select it from the Toolbox, and place it on the form from

which you plan to access reports. Because the Crystal Reports control is not visible at runtime, it appears only as an icon on your form. After the control is on the form, you can set the properties that access the reports you create with the report designer.

Specifying the Report to Run   The key property that you need to specify is the `ReportFileName` property. This property specifies the actual report that you will run from your program. You can easily set this property by clicking the ellipsis button that appears to the right of the property in the Properties window. The Crystal Reports Property page, shown in Figure 29.24, then appears. From this page, you can specify the name of the report and whether the report should go to the printer, a preview window, a file, or a message through the MAPI interface.

FIG. 29.24

Select the report name and destination from the Property page of Crystal Reports.

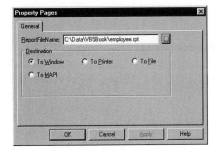

On the Property page, you can either type the name of the report into the field for the `ReportFileName` property or select the report from a file dialog box by clicking the ellipsis button on the Property page.

Selecting the `ReportFileName` is the minimum setup for Crystal Reports. At this point, you can write the line of code necessary to run the report and test it by running your program.

Setting Optional Properties   Although only the `ReportFileName` is required for a report, you might want to use several optional properties with the report. The first of these properties is the `SelectionFormula` property. This property enables you to limit the number of records that are included in the report. The `SelectionFormula` property is similar to the `Where` clause of a SQL statement but uses its own particular format to enter the information. To specify the `SelectionFormula`, you must specify the name of the recordset and the field to be compared. You must express this recordset/field combination in dot notation and enclose it in curly brackets. After specifying the recordset and field, you must specify the comparison operator and the value to be compared. The final result is an expression like the following:

```
{MemberShipList.OrgCode}=1
```

You also can use multiple expressions by including the `And` or `Or` operators.

CAUTION

If you enter a `SelectionFormula` when you're designing your report, any formula you enter in the `SelectionFormula` property of the Crystal Reports control provides an additional filter on the records.

Another optional property is the `CopiesToPrinter` property. This property enables you to print multiple copies of your report easily at one time. You can set this property to any integer value.

Taking Action

After you add the Crystal Reports control to your form and set its properties, you are ready to start printing, right? Well, not quite. You still have to tell Crystal Reports when to print the report. To do so, you write a line of code to initiate the report. The line of code sets the `Action` property of the Crystal Reports control to 1. The report then prints using the report file and other properties that you set. If you have your report set up to preview on the screen, it looks like the one shown in Figure 29.25. The following is the code to run this report (`rptMember` is the name of the Crystal Reports control):

```
rptMember.action = 1
```

FIG. 29.25
Printing the desired report to the screen.

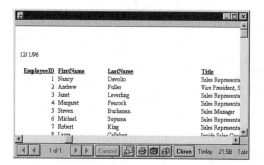

Setting Properties at Run Time

Because you will probably have a number of reports that you need to print, you need to be able to change the Crystal Reports control's properties at run time; otherwise, you would need a separate report control for each of your reports. All the major properties of the Crystal Reports control, such as `ReportFileName` and `SelectionFormula`, are available at run time. You set these properties, like any other properties, to new values using an assignment statement. The following code sets up the Crystal Reports control for a new report and specifies a selection criteria based on user input:

```
rptMember.ReportFileName = "CntyMbr.rpt"
rptMember.SelectionFormula = "{MemberShipList.OrgCode}=" & OrgID
rptMember.action = 1
```

The other property you might need to set at runtime is the `DataFiles` property. This property is not available at design time. The property specifies the name of the database file to be used with the report. Now you might be thinking, "I told the report what file to use when I created it." That is true, but when you created the report, the database file was stored with a path based on your directory structure, and your path might not be the same as the directory structure of your users.

The `DataFiles` property is actually an array with the first element number of 0. If you're using more than one database in your report, you need to set the value of each `DataFiles` array element. For most of your reports, however, you will be using only a single database. The following line of code shows you how to set the value of the `DataFiles` property for the database; this line assumes that the database file is in the same folder as your application:

```
rptMember.DataFiles(0) = App.Path & "\Members.mdb"
```

From Here...

In this chapter, you learned how to set up a database application quickly for an existing database. If you would like to learn more about related topics, check out the following:

- If you want to create your own database, see Chapter 28, "Building Database Applications."

- To learn more about the Data control and bound controls, see Chapter 30, "Doing More with Bound Controls."

- To learn about more advanced ways to work with databases, see Chapter 31, "Improving Data Access with the Data Access Objects (DAO)."

Doing More with Bound Controls

In Chapter 29, "Using the Visual Basic Data Control," you got a first look at the Data control and some of the bound controls that are available in Visual Basic. You saw how the controls can work together to create a good data access application. What you might not have realized is that the Data control and bound controls have a wider range of functionality than that presented in Chapter 29.

In this chapter, we'll learn how to use the Data control in conjunction with the data bound controls to make our data-aware applications extremely powerful and easy to create. ■

Working with other databases using the Data control

While Microsoft Jet (Access) is Visual Basic's database format of choice, the Data control can work with several other types of databases.

Programming the Data control to do more

Some properties of the Data control allow it to perform additional tasks in specific situations.

Changing the recordset of the Data control with code

You are not limited to the recordset that was created when you set the DatabaseName and RecordSource properties at design time.

Bound lists and combo boxes

You can bind list boxes and combo boxes to a Data control. There are also special versions of these controls that automatically can populate themselves from a Data control's recordset.

Windows 95 bound controls

Several of the new Windows 95 controls also can be bound to a Data control.

Working with multiple Data controls on a form

In many situations, you need more than one Data control on your form.

Exploring the Data Control In-Depth

One of the Data control's additional features is the capability to access a number of other database types beside the Jet database. It also can work with all types of recordsets, not just dynaset-type recordsets. In addition to this flexibility, you can use program code to change the properties of the Data control and enhance its capabilities. You get a brief look at this when program code is used to enable you to add and delete records in the data entry application in Chapter 31, "Improving Data Access with the Data Access Objects (DAO)."

What Are Its Advantages and Limitations?

While the Data control does have a lot of capabilities, there are also some things that only can be done with program code. As Chapter 28, "Improving Data Access with the Data Access Objects," shows you, you can create a database application without using the Data control at all. In order to help you determine whether to create your program with the Data control, with just the data access objects, or with a combination of the two, you need to have an understanding of the advantages and limitations of the Data control.

▶ **See** "Creating the Database," **p. 783**

Advantages of the Data Control   The key advantage to using the Data control is that you don't have to do much, if any, programming to develop a data access application. You don't have to provide program code to open a database or recordset, to move through the records, to edit existing records, or to add new records. The Data control makes initial application development quicker and code maintenance easier.

When using the Data control, you also have the advantage of specifying data objects (database and recordset) at design time, and you can select these options from dialog boxes and lists. Selecting options from lists cuts down on typographical errors that you can introduce into the application.

Another advantage of the Data control is that it provides a direct link to the data. You don't have to specifically invoke the Edit and Update methods to modify the data in the database. Consequently, your users' changes show up in the database as soon as they enter them.

In addition to these advantages of using the Data control, there are several bound controls, which provide an easy way to accomplish tasks that are difficult to duplicate with just the data access objects and program commands. These bound controls are the data bound list box, data bound combo box, and data bound grid. (See the sections on these controls in this chapter: "Data Bound Lists and Combos," and "Data Bound Grids.")

Limitations of the Data Control   As useful as the Data control is, it also has a few limitations. These limitations include the following:

- No Add or Delete functions are built in to the Data control.
- Because the Edit and Update functions are automatic, implementing transaction processing in the Data control is more difficult.

■ You can't use the Data control to create a database or a table; it will only work with existing data.

In the section "Programming the Data Control's Events" later in this chapter, you see how to overcome some of these limitations by combining the Data control with program code.

Using Other Databases

The Data control is designed to work best with Jet (Access) databases, but you can work just as easily with other database formats. These formats include some traditional database formats like dBase, FoxPro, and Paradox, as well as data that is not typically thought of as a database—for example, Excel spreadsheets or text files.

For any of the database formats, you still need to set the DatabaseName and RecordSource properties of the Data control. You also need to set the control's Connect property to identify the type of database being used. In addition, the DatabaseName property is treated differently for some database formats than for Jet databases. For example, with dBase files, the DatabaseName property refers to a directory instead of a single file.

Setting the Connect Property   The Connect property tells the Jet engine what kind of database you are using. A listing of Connect property settings for various database types can be found in the *Connect Property (DAO)* topic of Visual Basic's help system.

The Data control makes it easy for you to set the Connect property. To change its value, you select the desired database format from a drop-down list in the Properties window, as shown in Figure 30.1.

FIG. 30.1
The *Connect* property lets you use the Data control with many types of databases.

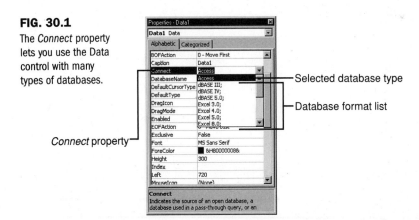

Connect property

Selected database type

Database format list

Considerations for the *DatabaseName* Property   Some database formats, like Jet, store all the tables of the database along with other database information in one database file. Other formats, like FoxPro and dBase, store each table in a separate file, and may even have other files for such things as indexes and Memo field contents. Depending on the database format you select, the information you specify in the DatabaseName property may represent something different. For Jet databases, you just specify the name of the database file. For dBase databases, the DatabaseName property must be set to the name of the folder containing the database files. If you need to use a database type other than Jet, refer to Visual Basic's help system for specific DatabaseName property requirements.

Working Directly with Tables and Snapshots

The Data control, by default, creates a dynaset-type recordset when you specify the RecordSource property. However, you can have the Data control create a snapshot-type recordset or even a table-type recordset to access a table directly. To handle this, you just need to change the setting of the RecordsetType property. You do this by selecting the desired type from a drop-down list in the Properties dialog box (see Figure 30.2).

FIG. 30.2

Use the *RecordsetType* property to determine the type of recordset created by the Data control.

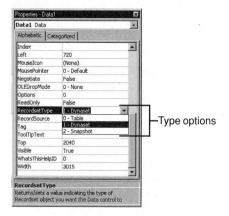

One reason you might want to change the RecordsetType is for performance. For example, if you do not need to be able to edit the contents of the recordset, you might want to use a snapshot-type recordset because it provides faster access than a dynaset-type. In another case, you might want to use a table-type so that you can change the presentation order of the recordset by changing the controlling index of the table, since indexes are supported only by table-type recordsets.

> **CAUTION**
>
> If you specify a RecordsetType that cannot be created in a particular situation, you will get an error when you try to run your program. This is most likely to occur when you set the RecordsetType to Table and use a SQL statement or query in the RecordSource property.

TROUBLESHOOTING

**I tried to set an index for my recordset using the `Index` property of the Data control, but was
unable to do so.** The `Index` property does not refer to a database index, but to the index position in
an array. A Data control, like any other Visual Basic control object, can be part of a control array. If you
have such an array, the `Index` property specifies the position of the current control in that array.
Remember that a Data control, by default, creates a dynaset-type recordset, and you cannot apply an
index to this type of recordset. You can use an index if you specify that the Data control should create
a table-type recordset, but you must set the `Index` property of the `Recordset` object associated with
the Data control, as in this example:

```
datYouth.Recordset.Index = "Name"
```

You can set an index only for the Data control's `Recordset` object if you have set the
`RecordsetType` property to `0 - Table`.

Tracking the Current Record

A recordset has a *record pointer* that keeps track of the current record. There cannot be more
than one current record at any given time.

You may think of the beginning and end of a file as the first and last record, respectively, of
a recordset. However, this is not actually the case. A recordset has a special position called
beginning-of-file (BOF) that is located *before* the first record. Similarly, the special end-of-file
(EOF) position is located *after* the last record. This can create problems in some data access
programs because there is no current record when the record pointer is positioned at the
beginning or the end of the file.

By default, the Data control avoids this problem by setting the record pointer to the first record
when the beginning-of-file is reached and setting the pointer to the last record when the end-of-
file is reached. This assures that there is always a current record for viewing or editing. However, there may be times when you want to know when you have actually reached the BOF or
EOF positions even while using the Data control. You can control what the Data control does at
the beginning or end of the file by setting the `BOFAction` and `EOFAction` properties of the Data
control.

The `BOFAction` property, which tells the Data control what to do when the beginning of file is
reached, has two possible settings:

- Execute the `MoveFirst` method of the Data control's recordset to set the record pointer
  at the first record and the BOF flag to False (property value of `0 - Move First`). This is
  the default setting.
- Set the BOF flag to True (property value of `1 - BOF`).

Part
VI

Ch
30

The EOFAction property, which tells the Data control what to do when the end-of-file is reached, has three possible settings:

- Execute the MoveLast method to set the record pointer at the last record and the EOF flag to False (property value of 0 - Move Last). This is the default setting.
- Set the EOF flag to True (property value of 1 - EOF).
- Execute the AddNew method to set up the recordset for the addition of a new record (property value of 2 - Add New).

You can choose the values of each of these properties from a drop-down list in the Properties dialog box. The 2 - Add New setting of the EOFAction property can be useful if you have an application that needs to add new records. As with most other properties of the Data control, you can reset these properties at runtime.

N O T E   These BOF and EOF actions are triggered only when the user reaches the beginning or end of the file by using the Data control's navigation buttons. They have no effect if the beginning- or end-of-file is reached by using data access methods (such as MoveNext) in code. ■

Other Optional Properties

In addition to the properties already covered, there are three other key properties for the Data control that you can set:

Exclusive   Determines whether others can access the database while your application is using it. You can set the property to True (your application is the only one that can access the database) or False (others can access the database). The default value is False.

ReadOnly   Determines whether your application can modify the data in your defined recordset. You can set the property to True (your application can't modify data) or False (your application can modify data). The default value is False. Setting this property to True is not the same as using a snapshot. Because a snapshot-type recordset is a copy of the data in memory, it is faster than a read-only dynaset-type recordset.

Options   Allows you to specify other properties for the recordset created by the Data control.

Programming the Data Control

There are several ways that you can use program code to work with the Data control and the bound controls. By using program code, you can make your program more flexible than with the Data control alone. The following list gives you a few of the ways that you can have program code work with the Data control:

- Change the properties of the Data control and bound controls in code.
- Place code in the `Validate` event of the Data control to handle user actions.
- Use the methods of the recordset to provide capabilities that the Data control does not have on its own.

Changing Properties On-the-Fly

Like any other control that you have on a form, you can change the properties of the Data control and bound controls at runtime. Most of the properties of the Data control and the bound controls are changeable. Only a few, like the `Name` property, are read-only at runtime.

Properties of the Data Control   You can choose to set (or reset) the `DatabaseName`, `RecordSource`, and `RecordsetType` properties of the Data control at runtime. The following list outlines some of the reasons why you might want to do this:

- To enable the user to select a specific database file from a group of related files. For example, a central office application keeps a separate database for each store of a chain; your application must enable the user to select the store with which he or she wants to work.

- To enable users to set specific conditions on the data they want to see. These conditions can take the form of filters or sort orders (for example, show only salespeople with over $10,000 in sales in order of total sales). Alternatively, your application might have to set the filters as part of an access control scheme, such as allowing a department manager to see data about only the people in his or her department. If the application sets the filters, it incorporates the information into code at runtime instead of at design time. Remember that the initial values of the Data control properties are set at design time.

- You can enable the user to specify the directory in an initialization file (or have your setup program do it for them) and then use the information from the initialization file to set your Data control properties. If you're developing a commercial application, there is no guarantee that the user has the same directory structure as you do. Many users are annoyed if you impose a specific directory structure or drive designation as a requirement for your program.

 TIP   If you distribute your application, you will often need to change the `DatabaseName` property of the Data control to handle differences between your directory structure and that of the user.

If you need to set the parameters at runtime, simply set the properties with code statements like those shown in Listing 30.1. Note that you must specify the name of your Data control, the property name, and the desired property value.

After you set the properties, use the Data control's `Refresh` method to implement the changes, as shown in the last line of Listing 30.1. The changes to the Data control (that is, the creation of the new recordset) take affect *after* the `Refresh` method is invoked.

> **Listing 30.1   Setting or Changing the *DatabaseName* and *RecordSource* Properties of a Data Control at Runtime**
>
> ```
> '*********************************************
> 'Set the value of the DatabaseName property
> '*********************************************
> datMembers.DatabaseName = "C:\YOUTH\YOUTHTRK.MDB"
> '*********************************************
> 'Set the value of the RecordSource property
> '*********************************************
> datMembers.RecordSource = "Family"
> '*****************************************************************
> 'Set the value of the RecordsetType property to table (0)
> '*****************************************************************
> datMembers.RecordsetType = vbRsTypeTable
> '*************************************************
> 'Use the Refresh method to implement the changes
> '*************************************************
> datMembers.Refresh
> ```

Properties of the Bound Control   In a similar manner, you can set the properties of the bound controls at runtime. You can change the `DataSource` of a bound control to access a different Data control on the form. You also can change the setting of the `DataField` property to have the control display the contents of a different field in the recordset.

> **CAUTION**
>
> Be careful when you change the `DataSource` or `DataField` properties in code. If you enter an invalid Data control name or field name, an error will occur.

Recordsets and the Data Control (*Set* Command)

One particularly useful feature of the Data control is the capability to create a recordset with the data access objects and then assign the recordset to the Data control. This gives you increased flexibility in the recordsets that can be used. Because you also can assign the recordset of the Data control to a recordset object, this means you can pass the recordset to other procedures or to class modules for processing. This feature is something that was not available in Visual Basic prior to version 4.

The `Set` statement is the key statement to use when you want to allow recordsets to be moved back and forth between a recordset object and the Data control. Use the `Set` statement any time you want to assign a value to an object. You will also see the `Set` statement used in Chapter 31, "Improving Data Access with Data Access Objects (DAO)," when you open databases and recordsets with the data access objects.

The following code shows you how to use the `OpenRecordset` method to create a recordset:

```
'Create the recordset
SQLSel = "Select LastName, FirstName From Members "
SQLSel = SQLSel & "Where Member Order By LastName, FirstName"
Set datRec = OldDb.OpenRecordset(SQLSel, dbOpenDynaset)
```

After the recordset has been created, this code will assign it to a Data control:

```
'Assign the recordset to the Data control
Set datNames.Recordset = datRec
```

Part

VI

Ch

30

You can use this capability to enable your users to specify sort or filter criteria for a recordset. Then, with the user-defined criteria you can create a recordset using a SQL statement. This recordset then can be assigned to an existing Data control to display the results of the query in a grid or a series of bound controls.

Being able to pass the contents of a Data control to a recordset object enables you to do things like write a generic routine for handling deletions. This way, you can write one procedure or class to query the user for verification of the deletion and then perform the deletion if the user agrees. The code in Listing 30.2 shows you how such a procedure works.

Listing 30.2   Procedures Let You Reuse Code Easily

```
'Define the procedure
Sub DelRecord(Navset As Recordset)
Dim MsgStr As String
'Delete the current record
MsgStr = "Are you sure you want to delete this record"
RetCode = MsgBox(MsgStr, vbYesNo, "Deletion Confirmation")
If RetCode = vbYes Then
      Navset.Delete
End If
End Sub
'**********************************************************
'Call the procedure with the recordset of a Data control
'**********************************************************
DelRecord datNames.Recordset
```

CAUTION

A recordset object and the Data control recordset are identical immediately after the `Set` statement, and at this time, they both point to the same record. However, after a record movement function is performed on either recordset, they are out of synchronization. Therefore, be careful when you are using both a recordset object and a Data control to manipulate the same data.

Programming the Data Control's Events

The Data control has three key events for which you can write program code: the Validate event, the Reposition event, and the Error event. While most of the actions of the Data control are handled automatically, programming for these events can help you add capabilities to your program and help you handle errors.

Using the *Validate* Event   When you create a Jet database, you can specify validation rules to be checked before each record is saved. However, you might have situations where the validation rules for your program are more complex than the Jet engine can handle. In this case, you need to perform the data validation in program code. How can you do this when the Data control saves data automatically?

The Data control has an event, the Validate event, that is triggered whenever the record pointer is *about to be moved*. This event occurs when the user presses one of the navigation buttons on the Data control or when the form containing the Data control is unloaded.

When the Validate event is triggered, the Data control examines all controls that are bound to it to determine if any data in any of the controls has changed. Two parameters then are set for the Validate event: the Save parameter, which tells you whether any data has been changed, and the Action parameter, which tells you what caused the Validate event to fire. The Save parameter can be either True or False. The Action parameter can have one of 12 values, as defined in Table 30.1.

Table 30.1   The Value of the *Action* Parameter Tells You Why the *Validate* Event Fired

Constant	Value	Description
vbDataActionCancel	0	Cancels any Data control actions
vbDataActionMoveFirst	1	MoveFirst
vbDataActionMovePrevious	2	MovePrevious
vbDataActionMoveNext	3	MoveNext
vbDataActionMoveLast	4	MoveLast
vbDataActionAddNew	5	AddNew
vbDataActionUpdate	6	Update
vbDataActionDelete	7	Delete
vbDataActionFind	8	Find
vbDataActionBookmark	9	Sets a bookmark
vbDataActionClose	10	Uses the Close method of the Data control
vbDataActionUnload	11	Unloads the form

Listing 30.3 shows how you can use the Validate event to perform data checking.

Listing 30.3   Data Checking in the *Validate* Event

```
Private Sub datMembers_Validate(Action As Integer, Save As Integer)
    Dim CompStr As String
    If Save = True Then
        CompStr = Trim(txtYouth(0).Text)
        If Len(CompStr) = 0 Then
            MsgBox "First Name cannot be blank"
            Action = vbDataActionCancel
        End If
    End If
End Sub
```

This code checks the Save parameter to see if any of the data in the bound controls has been changed. If it has, the code proceeds to perform the data checking. In this case, the code is checking to make sure a non-null string was entered in one of the text boxes. If the string is zero-length, a message is displayed to the user, and the action that was being processed is canceled by setting the Action parameter to vbDataActionCancel.

N O T E   This particular data verification can be handled by the database engine when you set a validation rule or set the AllowZeroLength property of the field to True. However, many programmers prefer to handle data validation from within the program, rather than relying upon the Jet engine's validation rules. ■

Using the *Reposition* Event   The Reposition event occurs *after* the Data control's current record has changed, as opposed to the Validate event, which occurs *before* the current record changes. This allows you to perform some type of processing once the new record becomes current. For example, you may want to modify the form's caption to reflect the record that is being displayed, or recalculate information such as an invoice total based on data from the new record. This code sample demonstrates how to accomplish both of these tasks:

```
Private Sub Data1_Reposition()
    Dim crTemp As Currency
    Me.Caption = "Invoice Number " & txtInvNumber.Text
    crTemp = Val(txtInvGross) - Val(InvSalesTax)
    lblInvTotal.Caption = Format(crTemp, "currency")
End Sub
```

Handling Errors with the *Error* Event   The other event of note for the Data control is the Error event. The Error event also has two parameters associated with it: the DataErr and the Response parameters. The Error event is triggered when a data access error occurs when no program code is running, such as when the Data control is loaded or the user clicks one of its buttons, but the database specified in the DatabaseName property cannot be found or has been corrupted. When the event is triggered, the error number is reported via the procedure's DataErr parameter. You then can write code in the event procedure to handle the different data access errors.

Part
VI

Ch
30

The Response parameter determines the action to be taken by your program. If the parameter is set to vbDataErrContinue (0), your program attempts to continue with the next line of code. If the parameter is set to vbDataErrDisplay (1), the default value, an error message is displayed. When you write your error handling for the Error event, you can set the Response parameter to vbDataErrContinue for those errors that are corrected by your code and set it to vbDataErrDisplay for all other errors.

Data Control Methods

In addition to being able to respond to events, the Data control also has several methods that you probably will want to use in your programming. We'll discuss these three:

- Refresh
- UpdateControls
- UpdateRecord

The Refresh method causes the Data control to rerun the query that created the recordset and access all data that is currently in the recordset. There are several occasions when you need to use the Refresh method:

- When you change the Data control's RecordSource property.
- When you assign a recordset created with data access objects to the Data control.
- When other users have been accessing simultaneously the same database and tables. Refreshing the Data control shows any additions, modifications, or deletions made by the other users.

The UpdateRecord method forces the Data control to save the information in the bound controls to the recordset. Typically, you will want to place a Save or Update button on any data entry form you create. (This is done automatically if you use the data form designer.) The reason for this is to enable the user to save his work on the current record without having to move to another record. The Data control only saves changes when the record pointer is moved or when the form containing the Data control is unloaded. The following line of code shows how you can force a Data control to update the current record:

```
datYouth.UpdateRecord
```

The companion method to the UpdateRecord method is the UpdateControls method. This method retrieves information from the current record and redisplays it in the bound controls. This has the effect of canceling any changes made by the user. By placing the following line of code in the Click event procedure of a command button, you can implement a cancellation feature:

```
datYouth.UpdateControls
```

Other Bound Controls

In Chapter 29, "Using the Visual Basic Data Control," you were introduced to five bound controls: the TextBox, Label, CheckBox, PictureBox, and Image controls. Visual Basic actually has quite a few bound controls that you can use in your programs:

- TextBox
- Label
- CheckBox
- PictureBox
- Image
- ListBox
- ComboBox
- Data bound ListBox
- Data bound ComboBox
- Data bound Grid
- RichTextBox
- MaskedEdit

▶ **See** "Bound Control Basics," in "SQL Primer," on this book's CD-ROM.

Part

VI

Ch

30

Lists and Combo Boxes

The ListBox and ComboBox controls enable the user to choose one item from a list of items; the ComboBox control also allows the user to enter an item that's not in the list. You can bind either of these controls to a data field to store the user's choices in a field. You do this by setting the `DataSource` and `DataField` properties of the control. To give your user a list of items from which to select, use the control's `AddItem` method. For this sample case, use a combo box to enable users to select the title for the member they are editing (see Figure 30.3). Listing 30.4 shows how to populate the list of choices.

Listing 30.4 Populating the List with the *AddItem* Method

```
Combo1.AddItem "Mr."
Combo1.AddItem "Mrs."
Combo1.AddItem "Ms."
Combo1.AddItem "Miss"
Combo1.AddItem "Dr."
```

 TIP You also can enter the list items at design time by using the `List` property.

FIG. 30.3

Use a list or combo box to present your user with a list of choices.

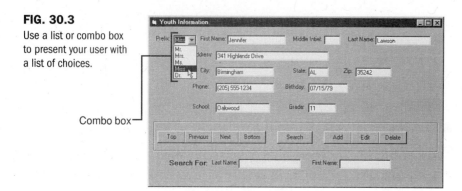

Combo box

Data Bound Lists and Combos

The data bound list box (DBList control) and data bound combo box (DBCombo control) are similar in function to their standard counterparts. They are designed to present the user with a list of choices. The key difference is that the data bound list and combo box controls get their list information from a recordset rather than from a series of AddItem statements.

T I P In order to use the DBList or DBCombo controls, you must add them to the Toolbox. Choose Project, Components. In the Controls tab of the Components dialog box, make sure Microsoft Data Bound List Controls 5.0 is selected.

Consider an example from the sample case. As your users enter data about a member, you want the user to be able to enter easily the county and state names of the member. One of the tables in the database contains county information. You can use the data bound list box to let your users select a county from those contained in the county table. The data bound list takes the county ID selected from the County table and stores it in the appropriate field of the Members table. You might think it would be hard to select the appropriate county if all you can see is the ID. However, the data bound list and combo boxes let you select a second field from the source table to serve as the display in the list. This means that you can display the name of the county in the list box but store only the county ID in the Members table. Figure 30.4 shows this concept graphically.

You set up the data bound list or combo box by specifying five properties. Table 30.2 describes these properties.

Table 30.2 Properties for Data Bound List Box or Combo Box

Property	Sample Case Setting	Description
RowSource	datCounty	The name of the Data control containing the information used to populate the list
BoundColumn	CountyID	The name of the field containing the value to be copied to the other table
ListField	CountyName	The name of the field to be displayed in the list
DataSource	datYouth	The name of the Data control containing the recordset that is the destination of the information
DataField	CountyID	The name of the destination field

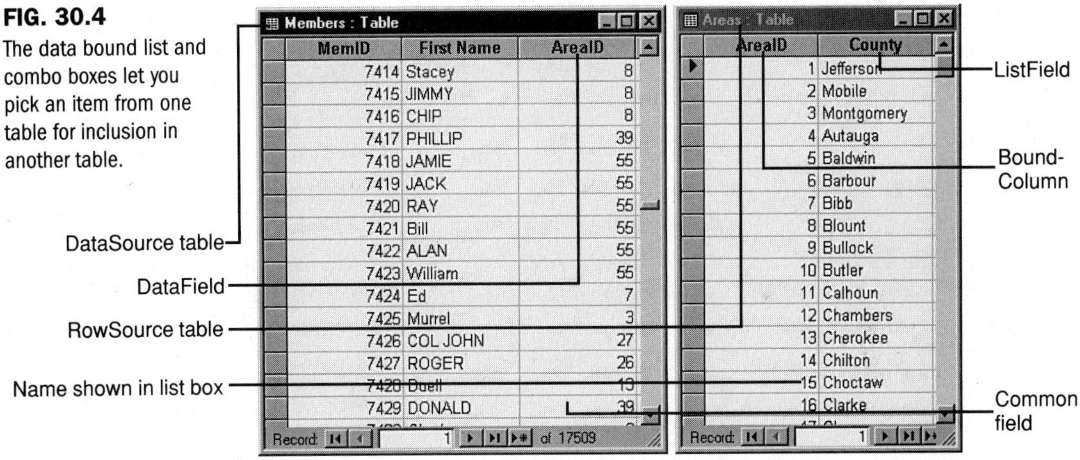

FIG. 30.4
The data bound list and combo boxes let you pick an item from one table for inclusion in another table.

DataSource table
DataField
RowSource table
Name shown in list box

ListField
Bound-Column
Common field

You can set each of these properties by selecting the property from the Properties dialog box and choosing the setting from a drop-down list. When setting the properties of the data bound list and combo boxes, keep in mind the following points:

- The Data controls you specify for the RowSource and DataSource properties can be the same control, or they can be different controls.
- The fields for the BoundColumn and DataField properties must be of the same type.
- You can set the ListField property to the same field as the BoundColumn property.

Figure 30.5 shows the data bound combo box added to a sample data entry form.

FIG. 30.5

A data bound combo box lets the user select from a list of counties.

Data bound combo box

Data control for RowSource

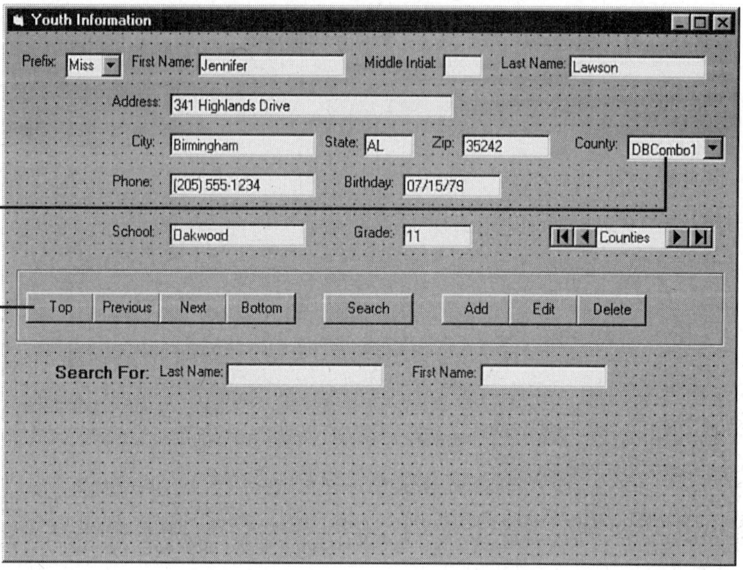

Youth Information

Prefix: Miss   First Name: Jennifer   Middle Initial: Last Name: Lawson

Address: 341 Highlands Drive

City: Birmingham   State: AL   Zip: 35242   County: DBCombo1

Phone: (205) 555-1234   Birthday: 07/15/79

School: Oakwood   Grade: 11   Counties

Top   Previous   Next   Bottom   Search   Add   Edit   Delete

Search For: Last Name: First Name:

Data Bound Grids

The data bound grid (DBGrid control) provides a means to view the fields of multiple records at the same time. The data bound grid is similar to the table view used in Access or the Browse command used in FoxPro. It displays information in a spreadsheet style of rows and columns. You can use it to display any alphanumeric information.

To set up the data bound grid, you need only to specify the DataSource property to identify the Data control containing the data. The grid then displays all fields of all records in the recordset. If the information is larger than the area of the grid you defined, scroll bars are presented to let you view the remaining data.

TIP   To conserve application resources, use a QueryDef or SQL statement in the grid Data control's RecordSource property. This way you can keep the number of records and fields that the grid handles to a minimum.

Your user can select a grid cell to edit by clicking the cell with the mouse. To add a new record, the user positions the pointer in the last row of the grid indicated by an asterisk (*) and enters the desired data. These capabilities are governed by the AllowUpdate and AllowAddNew properties, respectively. The default value of the AllowUpdate property is True; the default value of the AllowAddNew property is False. You can set these properties appropriately either at design time or runtime.

For the sample case, use the data bound grid to display the Members information in a browse mode. Allow the user to switch between the browse mode and single-record mode by using the command button at the lower-right corner of the screen. This saves screen real estate. Figure 30.6 shows the data bound grid for the sample case.

FIG. 30.6
You can use the data bound grid to display information from many records at once.

Data bound grid

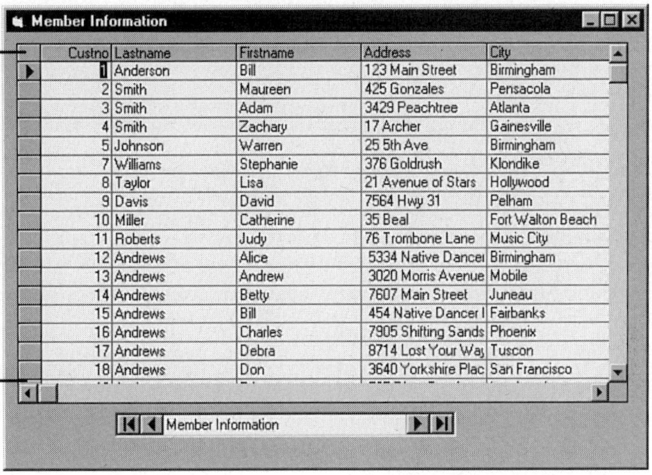

Other Visual Basic Controls

The other bound controls are set up the same way you would set up a text box or check box. Specifically, you set the DataSource property to the name of the Data control containing the data to be displayed and then set the DataField property to the specific field in the recordset.

Third-Party Controls

One of the greatest features about Visual Basic is the capability to extend its functionality through the use of third-party controls. This functionality also extends to bound controls. Many third-party vendors have controls that can be bound to a Data control, and some vendors even market enhanced Data controls. For example, Apex Software Corporation, which developed the DBGrid control included with Visual Basic, sells an enhanced version called True DBGrid Pro, which adds many features to the standard control.

Further Enhancements

In Chapter 29, "Using the Visual Basic Data Control," you saw how you needed to use code to implement some features that were not available with the Data control alone. Specifically, an Add and Delete function were added to the capabilities of the data entry form with some simple coding. There are a few other enhancements that can be implemented with just a little bit of code and some ingenuity.

▶ **See** "Essential Functions the Data Control Forgot," **p. 813**

Find and Seek Operations

Another enhancement to the features provided by the Data control is the capability to search for a specific record. To add this feature, you must use either the Find method or the Seek method of the Data control's Recordset object, depending upon the recordset type. For a table-type recordset, use the Seek method; for the others, use the Find method. To implement the search in our example, add a command button to the form. This command button invokes a dialog box that requests the ID to be found and then uses the appropriate method to perform the search (see Listing 30.5).

Listing 30.5   Use the *Seek* or *Find* Method to Search for a Specific Record

```
'****************************************************************
'The variable SrchCond contains the value of the search criteria
'****************************************************************
If dayYouth.RecordsetType = vbRSTypeTable Then
  datYouth.Recordset.Seek ">=", SrchCond
Else
    datYouth.Recordset.FindFirst "datYouth.Recordset([LastName]) >= " _
        & SrchCond
End If
```

What About Options? (Option Buttons)

Another very useful control is the option button. Unfortunately, it is not a bound control that can be used directly with the Data control. However, this does not have to stop you from using the control. Option buttons come in handy for letting the user select between a number of mutually exclusive choices. A typical use is for selecting gender in a membership application, as shown in Figure 30.7.

FIG. 30.7

Option buttons can be used to present the user with choices.

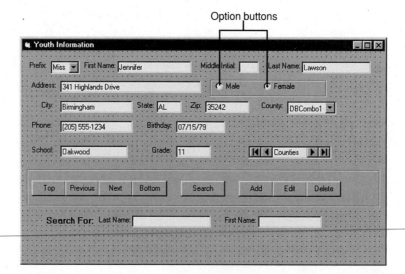

In code, you determine which option button was chosen by checking the Value property of each one. If the value of a button is True, then this was the selected button. Only one option button of a group can be selected. Option buttons can be grouped on a form, in a picture box, or in a frame. It is good practice to set up each group of option buttons in a picture box or frame to avoid conflicts with other groups.

After you have determined which option button was selected, you can assign the desired value for your data field based on the selection. For the membership case, either an M (male) or an F (female) is stored, depending on the option button selected.

 TIP If you have more than two option buttons, you might want to put them in a control array. Then, you can use a loop to look for the selected option, as shown in this code example:

```
isel = 0
'Loop through five option buttons
For I = 0 To 4
    If Option(I).Value Then
        isel = I
        'Exit the loop when the selection is found
        Exit For
    End If
Next I
```

The option buttons are not bound controls, but you can still use them in an application with the Data control. You can place code in the Validate event of the Data control to store the desired value from the option buttons. However, there is a method that I find easier to use. (It's a sneaky way to trick the Data control.) For the field that you are modifying, create a text box and bind it to the field. Then set the Visible property of the text box to False. This keeps the box from being seen by the user. Then, in the Click event of each option button, place a line of code that changes the contents of the text box to the value represented by the option button. Then, when the Data control is invoked to move the record pointer, the field bound to the hidden box is updated along with all other bound fields. For the membership case, the following code would be used:

```
Sub Male_Click()
    txtGender.Text = 'M'
End Sub
Sub Female_Click()
    txtGender.Text = 'F'
End Sub
```

Using this hidden box method has an additional benefit. You can use the Change event of the box to mark the proper option box for each record that is accessed. The code for this follows:

```
If txtGender.Text = 'M' Then
    Male.Value = True
Else
    Female.Value = True
End If
```

While this discussion has focused on how to use the option buttons with the Data control, you also can use them when you program with just the data access objects. In this case, you use an assignment statement to set the value of your field just like you do any other field. For the membership case (assuming the field is named Gender), you would use the following code:

```
OldTbl.Edit
If Male.Value Then
    OldTbl("Gender") = 'M'
Else
    OldTbl("Gender") = 'F'
End If
OldTbl.Update
```

From Here...

This chapter has shown you how to use some additional features of the Data control, what other bound controls are available to you, and how you can add features to enhance your data entry forms. There are other chapters that address other aspects of database applications:

- To see how to create a database, see Chapter 28, "Building Database Applications."
- To learn how to quickly set up a data entry form, see Chapter 29, "Using the Visual Basic Data Control."
- To learn how to create a database application without the Data control, see Chapter 31, "Improving Data Access with Data Access Objects (DAO)."

Improving Data Access with Data Access Objects (DAO)

In Chapters 29, "Using the Visual Basic Data Control," and 30, "Doing More with Bound Controls," you saw how you could write a database application very quickly by using the Data control and bound controls that come with Visual Basic. These chapters showed you that, by setting a few properties, you can create a nearly complete data-entry screen. I say *nearly* complete because, in Chapter 30, you also saw that you needed to write some program code to handle some additional functions of a database application—for example, adding or deleting records or finding a specific record.

These additional functions introduced you to some of the programming that you can do in a database application. However, you can write an entire database application with just program commands and not use the Data control at all. When you use just the program commands, you work with Visual Basic's *data access objects* (DAO).

Use different recordset types

Depending on your application, you might have different data access needs. There are different recordset types to support these needs.

Move from one record to another in a recordset

Recordset navigation is one of the key functions of any database application.

Find a specific record

Most applications also need to be able to find a specific record. The technique you use depends on the type of recordset you open.

Working with multiple records

While data access objects normally work with one record at a time, often you'll want to manipulate records as a group. We'll discuss how this can be accomplished.

Modifying your recordset

You can use filters to narrow down the number of records that you work with, based on specific criteria.

Add, edit, and delete records in a database

What database application would be complete without the capability to add new records and modify old ones.

In this chapter, we'll learn how Visual Basic's data access objects can be used to create complete, robust data-management applications. Data access objects act as a Visual Basic program's internal representation of physical data—data stored in some type of database or data-management engine. Think of the data access objects as special types of variables. These "variables," however, represent data stored *outside* the program rather than information stored in the computer's memory while the program is running. ■

Introduction to DAO

Using the data access objects and their associated program commands is more complex than using the Data control and bound controls, but does offer greater programming flexibility for some applications. The data access objects and programming commands also provide the basis for many of the actions of the Data control and the bound controls. Therefore, they help you understand the concepts behind the controls. As you saw in Chapter 26, even if you use the Data control, you may also need to write some programming code to augment its capabilities.

▶ **See** "Essential Functions the Data Control Forgot," **p. 813**

To demonstrate the similarities and differences between data access objects and the Data control, this chapter instructs you on how to build a data entry screen similar to the ones you created in the previous chapters. This way, you can compare how the programming commands work to how the Data control implements the commands. Figure 31.1 shows the data entry screen that you will build in this chapter.

FIG. 31.1
You can create this data entry screen by following this chapter's instructions.

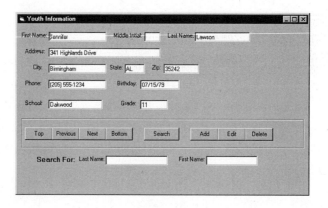

A key reason for using program commands is the flexibility they give you beyond what is available with the Data control. You can perform more detailed input validation than is possible with just data engine rules because program commands do not directly access the database. You also can cancel changes to your edited data without using transactions. The use of program commands also provides an efficient way to handle data input and searches that do not require user interaction. Examples of this are receiving data from lab equipment or across a modem, or looking up the price of an item in a table. Program commands enable you to do transaction processing as well.

Opening an Existing Database

The first step in writing many data access programs is to set up a link to the database with which you want to work. If your application will be working with a database that already exists, you'll need to create a Database object within the program, then use that object to create a link to the existing database. In effect, you are "opening the database" for use in your program. Most of the other data access objects will flow from that Database object.

▶ **See** "Implementing Your Design," **p. 782**

As we discussed in Chapter 24, a database is opened as part of a session with the database engine. The database engine is represented in a program by the DBEngine object; we define sessions by creating Workspace objects within the DBEngine object. You can then open a database with the Workspace object's OpenDatabase method. To use the OpenDatabase method, create a database object and call the method, as shown in this bit of code:

```
Dim OldDb As Database, OldWs As Workspace
Set OldWs = DBEngine.Workspaces(0)
Set OldDb = OldWs.OpenDatabase("C:\YOUTH\YOUTHTRK.MDB")
```

▶ For a detailed discussion of the DBEngine and Workspace objects, **see** "Creating the Database," **p. 783**

TROUBLESHOOTING

When I try to run the preceding commands, I get the error User-defined type not defined. What's happening? In order to use any database capabilities (beyond the Data control and bound controls) in your program, you must have one of the Data Access Object libraries specified in your program references. To set the program references, select the References command from the Project menu and select one of the DAO libraries from the "References – (projectname)" dialog box.

N O T E There are two basic Jet DAO libraries that Visual Basic can include in an application. These external libraries are the "Microsoft DAO 3.5 Object Library" and the "Microsoft DAO 2.5/ 3.5 Compatibility Library." If you will be programming for 32-bit clients only, and using 32-bit Jet (Access 95/97) databases, you should select the 3.5 library. If you have a need to exchange data with 16-bit systems or Access 2.0 applications, you will have to use the 2.5/3.5 compatibility library. ▪

These commands open a Jet database with the default options of read/write data access and shared access. The full syntax of the OpenDatabase method lets you specify that the database should be opened exclusively (no other users or programs can access it at the same time), that it be opened in read-only mode (no updates are allowed), or, if you are connecting to a non-Access database, you can specify the database type. The use of exclusive access and read-only access are usually only required for multiuser applications (as discussed in Chapter 31, "Multi-User Databases").

▶ **See** "Denying Table Access to Others," **p. 929**

Part
VI

Ch
31

However, you might want to use the read-only mode even in a single-user application for a lookup database (for example, a ZIP Code database or a state abbreviations database that you include with your application but do not want the user to be able to modify). To open the database as read-only, change the Set statement to the form shown in the following code. The first parameter after the database name indicates whether the database is opened for exclusive access; the second parameter indicates whether read-only mode is to be used:

```
Set OldDb = OldWs.OpenDatabase("C:\ZIPCODE.MDB",False,True)
```

After you open the database, you have only created a link from your program to the database file itself. You still do not have access to the information in the database. To gain access to the information, you must create and open a Recordset object that links to data stored in one or more of the tables in the database.

Deciding Which Recordset Type to Use

When you create a Recordset object to open a recordset in your program, you can access any entire table, specific fields and records from the table, or a combination of records and fields from multiple tables. There are three types of recordsets available in Visual Basic:

Recordset Type	Definition
Table	Directly represents all records in an entire physical table in a database.
Dynaset	Sets of pointers that provide access to fields and records in one or more tables of a database.
Snapshot	Read-only copies of data from one or more tables. They are stored in memory.

N O T E This chapter refers to tables, dynasets, and snapshots, but it is important to remember that they are all recordsets and can only be accessed using the Recordset object. Specifically, all mentions of tables, dynasets, and snapshots actually refer to table-type recordsets, dynaset-type recordsets, and snapshot-type recordsets, respectively. Previous versions of Visual Basic supported objects that are now outdated: Table objects, Dynaset objects, and Snapshot objects. ▪

The following sections describe each type of recordset, point out some of the advantages and disadvantages of each, and demonstrate the commands used to access the recordset.

Using Tables

A *table* (table-type recordset) is a direct link to one of the physical tables stored in the database. Because all data in a database is stored in tables, using this type of recordset provides the most direct link to the data. Tables are also the only form of recordset that supports indexes; therefore, searching a table for a specific record can be quicker than searching a dynaset or snapshot.

When using tables, data is addressed or modified one table at a time, one record at a time. This arrangement provides very fine control over the manipulation of data. However, it does not give you the convenience of changing records in multiple tables with a single command, such as an action query.

Advantages of Using Tables   Using tables in your programs gives you several advantages:

- You can use or create indexes to change the presentation order of the data in the table during program execution.

- You can perform rapid searches for an individual record by using an appropriate index and the Seek command.

- Changes made to the table by other concurrent users or programs are immediately available. It is not necessary to "refresh" the table to gain access to these records.

Disadvantages of Using Tables   Of course, using tables in your programs also has disadvantages:

- You can't set filters on a table to limit the records being processed to those that meet a certain criteria.

- You can't use the Find commands on a table; the Seek command finds only the first record that meets its criteria. This implies that, to process a series of records in a range, you, the programmer, must provide a means to find the additional records.

You can usually overcome these disadvantages with programming, but the solutions are often less than elegant. This chapter discusses some of the workarounds in its coverage of the various methods for moving through a recordset and for finding specific records. These topics are covered later in this chapter.

▶ **See** "Positioning the Record Pointer," **p. 856**

Opening a Table for Use   To open a table for the program to use, define a Recordset object and then use the OpenRecordset method to access the table. To identify the type of recordset to create, specify the dbOpenTable constant in the parameters of the method, as shown in the following segment of code. This code assumes that you have already opened the database by using the OldDb object and that the database contains a table called "Youth":

```
Dim OldTbl As Recordset
Set OldTbl = OldDb.OpenRecordset("Youth",dbOpenTable)
```

These commands open a table in a Jet database, with the default parameters of shared use and read/write mode. You can include optional parameters in the OpenRecordset method to open the table for exclusive use or to open the table in read-only mode. These options are summarized in Table 31.1.

Table 31.1   Some Options Used to Modify the Access Mode of Tables

Option	Action
dbDenyWrite	Prevents others in a multi-user environment from writing to the table while you have it open.
dbDenyRead	Prevents others in a multi-user environment from reading the table while you have it open.
dbReadOnly	Prevents you from making changes to the table.

Using Dynasets

A *dynaset* is a grouping of information from one or more tables in a database. This information is comprised of selected fields from the tables, often presented in a specific order and filtered by a specific condition. Dynasets address the records present in the base tables at the time the dynaset was created. Dynasets are an updatable recordset, so any changes made by the user are stored in the database. However, dynasets do not automatically reflect additions or deletions of records made by other users or programs after the dynaset was created. This makes dynasets less useful for some types of multi-user applications.

A dynaset is actually a set of record pointers that point to the specified data as it existed when the dynaset was created. Changes made to information in the dynaset are reflected in the base tables from which the information was derived as well as in the dynaset itself. These changes include additions, edits, and deletions of records.

Advantages of Using Dynasets   Some of the advantages provided by dynasets are as follows:

- Dynasets give you the ability to join information from multiple tables.
- You can use Find methods to locate or process every record meeting specified criteria.
- Dynasets enable you to limit the number of fields or records that you retrieve into the recordset.
- Dynasets make use of filters and sort order properties to change the view of data.

Disadvantages of Using Dynasets   Dynasets do have some limitations:

- You can't use indexes with dynasets; therefore, you can't change the presentation order of a dynaset by changing the index or by creating a new one.
- A dynaset does not automatically reflect additions or deletions made to the data by other users or other programs. A dynaset must be explicitly refreshed or recreated to show the changes.

Setting Up a Dynaset   To set up a dynaset for use within a program, you must define the Recordset object with the Dim statement and then generate the dynaset by using the OpenRecordset method with the dbOpenDynaset parameter. For creating a dynaset, the key part of the OpenRecordset method is the SQL statement that defines the records to be included, the filter condition, the sort condition, and any join conditions for linking data from multiple tables.

The code shown in Listing 31.1 shows the simplest form of creating a dynaset, in which all records and fields are selected from a single table with no sort or filter conditions specified. This is the type of dynaset created by default when using a Data control (though you can use a table or snapshot with the Data control). The statements in Listing 31.1 provide you access to the same information as you had by accessing the table directly with the previous code. The only difference is the type of recordset that was created.

Listing 31.1   How to Create a Simple Dynaset

```
Dim OldDb As Database, NewDyn As Recordset,OldWs As Workspace
Set OldWs = DBEngine.Workspaces(0)
Set OldDb = OldWs.OpenDatabase("C:\YOUTH\YOUTHTRK.MDB")
Set NewDyn = OldDb.OpenRecordset("SELECT * FROM Youth", _
    dbOpenDynaset)
```

Part
VI

Ch
31

N O T E   If you want to include all records from one table in a dynaset in no particular order, you can omit the SQL statement and simply use the table name (`Set OldDb = OldWs.OpenDatabase("Youth")`). However, it's a good idea to go ahead and use a SQL statement in case you want to modify it later.

When you create a dynaset, you can use any valid SQL statement that selects records. You can also specify options that affect the dynaset's behavior. Table 31.2 lists these options.

Table 31.2   Some Options Used to Modify the Access Mode of a Dynaset

Option	Action
dbDenyWrite	Prevents others in a multi-user environment from writing to the dynaset while you have it open.
dbReadOnly	Prevents you from making changes to the dynaset.
dbAppendOnly	Enables you to add new records, but prevents you from reading or modifying existing records.
dbSQLPassThrough	Passes the SQL statement used to create the dynaset to an ODBC database server to be processed.

The following code shows how to create a dynaset-type recordset that only allows the user to read the information in the database:

```
Set NewDyn = OldDb.OpenRecordset("Youth", dbOpenDynaset, dbReadOnly)
```

N O T E An *ODBC server* is a database engine, such as Microsoft SQL Server or Oracle, that conforms to the Open Database Connectivity (ODBC) standards. The purpose of a server is to handle query processing at the server level and return to the client machine only the results of the query. ODBC drivers, which are usually written by the vendor of the database engine, handle the connection between Visual Basic and the database server. An advantage of using ODBC is that you can connect to the information on the database servers without having to know the inner workings of the engine. ■

You can also create a dynaset from another dynaset28., as illustrated in Listing 31.2. The reason for creating a second dynaset from an initial dynaset is that you can use the `filter` and `sort` properties of the first dynaset to specify the scope of records and the presentation order of the second dynaset. Creating a second dynaset enables you to create a subset of your initial data. The second dynaset is usually much smaller than the first, which allows faster processing of the desired records. In Listing 31.2, a dynaset was created from the Customer table to result in a national mailing list. A second dynaset was then created, which includes only the customers living in Alabama and sorts them by city name for further processing. Figures 31.2 and 31.3 show the records returned by these two dynasets.

Listing 31.2   How to Set the *filter* and *sort* Properties of a Dynaset and Create a Second Dynaset from the First

```
Dim OldDb As Database, NewDyn As Recordset, ScnDyn As Dynaset
Dim OldWs As Workspace
Set OldWs = DBEngine.Workspaces(0)
Set OldDb = OldWs.OpenDatabase("C:\YOUTH\YOUTHTRK.MDB")
Set NewDyn = OldDb.OpenRecordset("SELECT * FROM Youth", _
    dbOpenDynaset)
NewDyn.Filter = "State = 'AL'"
NewDyn.Sort = "City"
Set ScnDyn = NewDyn.OpenRecordset(dbOpenDynaset)
```

FIG. 31.2

The results of the creation of a dynaset from base tables.

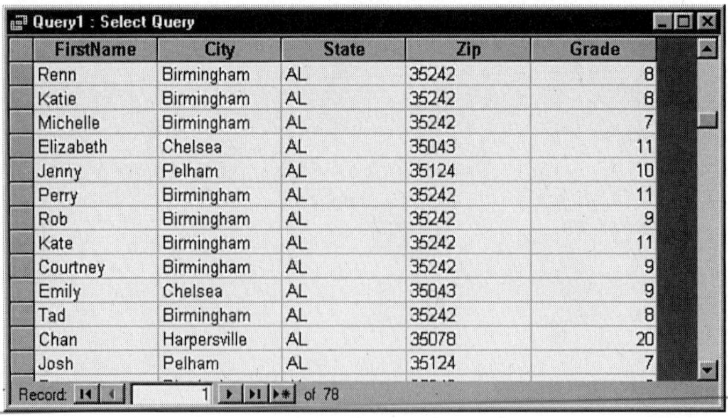

FirstName	City	State	Zip	Grade
Renn	Birmingham	AL	35242	8
Katie	Birmingham	AL	35242	8
Michelle	Birmingham	AL	35242	7
Elizabeth	Chelsea	AL	35043	11
Jenny	Pelham	AL	35124	10
Perry	Birmingham	AL	35242	11
Rob	Birmingham	AL	35242	9
Kate	Birmingham	AL	35242	11
Courtney	Birmingham	AL	35242	9
Emily	Chelsea	AL	35043	9
Tad	Birmingham	AL	35242	8
Chan	Harpersville	AL	35078	20
Josh	Pelham	AL	35124	7

Query1 : Select Query

Record: |◄ ◄| 1 |► ►| ►*| of 78

FIG. 31.3

The results of creating one dynaset from another dynaset after `filter` and `sort` conditions have been set.

FirstName	City	State	Zip	Grade	
Sarah	Birmingham	AL	35124	19	
John	Birmingham	AL	35124	10	
Jay	Birmingham	AL	35242	11	
Brittany	Birmingham	AL	35242	9	
Chris	Birmingham	AL	35242	12	
Misty	Birmingham	AL	35242	9	
Katie	Birmingham	AL	35242	9	
Karen	Birmingham	AL	35242	9	
Brian	Birmingham	AL	35242	12	
Matthew	Birmingham	AL	35242	8	
Mandy	Birmingham	AL	35242	11	
Jeanne	Birmingham	AL	35242	8	
Brett	Birmingham	AL	35242	7	

Record: 1 of 70

Part VI

Ch 31

You might wonder why, if you need the results in the second dynaset, you can't just create it from the base tables in the first place. The answer is that you can do so if your application needs *only* the second table. However, consider a member tracking system in which you want access to all your members (the creation of the first dynaset), and one of the functions of the system is to generate a mailing list for a particular region (the creation of the second dynaset). Because the pointers to all the required information are already present in the first dynaset, the creation of the second dynaset is faster than if it were created from scratch.

Using Snapshots

A *snapshot,* as the name implies, is a "picture," or copy, of the data in a recordset at a particular point in time. A snapshot is very similar to a dynaset in that it is created from base tables, using a SQL statement, or from a QueryDef, dynaset, or another snapshot. A snapshot differs from a dynaset in that it is not updatable. As a general rule, use a snapshot whenever you want a set of data that isn't time-sensitive; that is, it doesn't matter if records in the underlying database are modified after the snapshot is created. The most frequent use of snapshots in a program is to generate reports or informational screens in which the data is static.

Advantages of Using Snapshots   Snapshots provide you with the following advantages:

- You can join information from multiple tables.
- You can use the Find methods to locate records.
- Record navigation and recordset creation can be faster for a snapshot than for a read-only dynaset because a snapshot is a copy of the data, not a set of pointers to the data.

Disadvantages of Using Snapshots   The primary disadvantage of using a snapshot is that it is not an updatable recordset. In addition, you can't use an index with a snapshot to help set the order of the data or locate specific records.

CAUTION

To avoid memory constraints, make sure that a snapshot returns only a small set of records.

Setting Up a Snapshot You can create a snapshot by defining a Recordset object with the Dim statement and then using the OpenRecordset method with the dbOpenSnapshot parameter to assign the records to the object (as shown in Listing 31.3). As with a dynaset, you can specify optional parameters in the OpenRecordset method. Table 31.3 summarizes these parameters.

Listing 31.3 Create a Snapshot in Much the Same Way You Create a Dynaset

```
Dim OldDb As Database, NewSnap As Recordset, OldWs As Workspace
Set OldWs = DBEngine.Workspaces(0)
Set OldDb = OldWs.OpenDatabase("C:\YOUTH\YOUTHTRK.MDB")
Set NewSnap = OldDb.OpenRecordset("Youth",dbOpenSnapshot)
```

Table 31.3 Some Options Used to Modify the Access Mode of a Snapshot

Option	Action
dbDenyWrite	Prevents others in a multi-user environment from writing to the snapshot while you have it open.
dbForwardOnly	Enables only forward scrolling through the snapshot.
dbSQLPassThrough	Passes the SQL statement used to create the snapshot to an ODBC database to be processed.

Using a Forward-Only Recordset

A forward-only recordset is a special type of snapshot that allows only forward scrolling through its records. This means that the MoveFirst, MovePrevious, and Find methods will not work on the recordset. The advantage of using this type of recordset is that it is faster than a snapshot. However, the forward-only recordset should be used only in situations where a single pass through the recordset is needed, such as in report generation routines.

To set up a forward-only recordset, you use the OpenRecordset method and specify the dbOpenForwardOnly constant as shown in the following line of code:

```
Set NewRSet= OldDb.OpenRecordset("Youth",dbOpenForwardOnly)
```

Placing Information On-Screen

Suppose that you have written a data entry screen using the Data control and bound controls. To display information on-screen, you simply draw bound controls and then set the appropriate data fields for the controls. The display of the information is automatic. Using the data access objects, the process is only slightly more involved. You still use control objects (text boxes, labels, check boxes, and so on) to display the information, but you have to assign the data fields to the correct control properties with each record displayed. When used in this manner, the control objects are typically referred to as *unbound controls.* One advantage of using unbound controls is that you can use any control to display data, not just the bound controls specifically designated for use with the Data control.

Information in fields can be accessed through a recordset's `Fields` collection in one of several ways. For example, any of these techniques would suffice for retrieving the contents of a field named `ThisField` in a recordset named `MyRS` and placing it into a text box named `Text1`:

- Use the field's ordinal position in the `Fields` collection: `Text1.Text = MyRS.Fields(0)` (assuming `ThisField` is the first field in the recordset)
- Use the field's name to retrieve it from the `Fields` collection: `Text1.Text = MyRS.Fields("ThisField")`
- Take advantage of the fact that the `Fields` collection is the default collection of a recordset: `Text1.Text = MyRS("ThisField")`
- Use the shorthand method of the previous technique: `Text1.Text = MyRS!ThisField`

N O T E If a field's name contains spaces, you can enclose the entire name in square braces, as in `Text1.Text = MyRS![longer field name].` ■

For an example, we'll detail how to build a member data entry screen based on the Youth table of the sample database we've discussed. You can apply these concepts to any existing database. To begin building this screen, start a new project in Visual Basic. Then, on the default form, add the data labels and text boxes to hold the data from the table. Figure 31.4 shows the form with these controls added.

FIG. 31.4

Use unbound controls to display data from the data access objects.

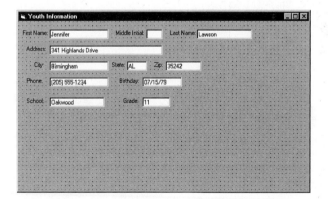

To set up the table for use, you must open the table by using the `OpenRecordset` method. For this case, place the `Dim` statements that define the data access objects (like the ones in Listing 31.3) in the General Declarations section of the form so that the objects are available throughout all the code in the form. You then open the database and table in the `Form_Load` event (see Listing 31.4). At this point, the table is open and you are positioned at the first record in the table.

Listing 31.4 Placing the *OpenDatabase* and *OpenRecordset* in the *Form_Load* Event

```
Set OldWs = DBEngine.Workspaces(0)
'********************************
'Open database and Customer table
'********************************
Set OldDb = OldWs.OpenDatabase("C:\YOUTH\YOUTHTRK.MDB")
Set RcSet = OldDb.OpenRecordset("Youth",dbOpenTable)
'***********************************************
'Move to first record and display information
'***********************************************
RcSet.MoveFirst
Call ShowFields
```

To display the data, assign the value of the desired data fields to the display properties of the controls (captions for labels, text for text boxes, and so on) that contain the data. Listing 31.5 shows this process. Notice that the listing defines the text boxes as a control array; you can use a loop to quickly modify certain properties of the controls such as foreground color or visibility. Also notice that the assignments are placed in a subroutine; you can call the same routine from a number of command button events rather than repeat the code in each event. This arrangement makes the code more efficient and easier to maintain.

Listing 31.5 Assigning Data Fields to the Display Properties of the Form's Controls

```
Private Sub ShowFields()
Text1(0).Text = RcSet("Lastname")
Text1(1).Text = RcSet("Firstname")
Text1(2).Text = RcSet("Address")
Text1(3).Text = RcSet("City")
Text1(4).Text = RcSet("State")
Text1(5).Text = RcSet("Zip")
Text1(6).Text = RcSet("Phone")
End Sub
```

N O T E Because the Text property is the default property of a text box, you do not have to include the property name in the assignment statement. My personal preference is to include the name for readability. ■

Positioning the Record Pointer

Because a database with only one record is fairly useless, a database engine must provide ways to move from one record to another within recordsets. Visual Basic provides six such techniques:

Technique	Description
Move methods	Changes the position of the record pointer from the current record to another record.
Find methods	Locates the next record that meets the find condition. Find methods work on dynasets and snapshots.
Seek method	Finds the first record in a table that meets the requested condition.
Bookmark property	Identifies the location of a specific record.
AbsolutePosition	Moves the record pointer to a specific record position in the recordset.
PercentPosition	Moves the record pointer to the record property nearest the indicated percentage position in the recordset.

Each of these has benefits and limitations, as described in the following sections.

Using the *Move* Methods

You can use the Move methods on any recordsets available in Visual Basic. There are five different Move methods:

Move Method	Action
MoveFirst	Moves the record pointer from the current record to the first record in the opened recordset.
MoveNext	Moves the record pointer from the current record to the next record (the record following the current record) in the opened recordset. If there is no next record (that is, if you are already at the last record), the end-of-file (EOF) flag is set.
MovePrevious	Moves the record pointer from the current record to the preceding record in the opened recordset. If there is no previous record (that is, if you are at the first record), the beginning-of-file (BOF) flag is set.
MoveLast	Moves the record pointer from the current record to the last record in the opened recordset.
Move *n*	Moves the record pointer from the current record *n* records down (if *n* is positive) or up (if *n* is negative) in the opened recordset. If the move would place the record pointer beyond the end of the recordset (either BOF or EOF), an error occurs.

These commands move the record pointer to the record indicated based on the current order of the recordset. The current order of the recordset is the physical order, unless an index was set for a table, or a dynaset or snapshot was created with a specific order specified. To show the use of the MoveFirst, MovePrevious, MoveNext, and MoveLast methods, add command buttons to the data entry screen so that the user can move through the recordset (see Figure 31.5). To activate these buttons, add the code shown in Listing 31.6. The code for each button is preceded by an identifying comment line.

FIG. 31.5

Add command buttons to enable the user to navigate through the recordset.

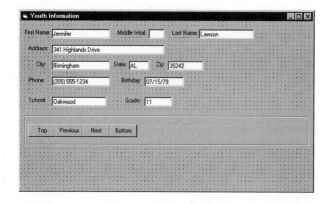

Listing 31.6   Assigning *Move* Methods to Navigation Command Buttons to Make Them Work

```
'***************************************************
'The MoveFirst method activates the "Top" button.
'***************************************************
RcSet.MoveFirst
Call ShowFields
'*******************************************************
'The MovePrevious method activates the "Previous" button.
'*******************************************************
RcSet.MovePrevious
Call ShowFields
'*************************************************
'The MoveNext method activates the "Next" button.
'*************************************************
RcSet.MoveNext
Call ShowFields
'*************************************************
'The MoveLast method activates the "Bottom" button.
'*************************************************
RcSet.MoveLast
Call ShowFields
```

The Move *n* method lets you move more than one record from the current position. The value of *n* is the number of records to move in the recordset. This value can be either positive or negative to indicate movement either forward or backward in the recordset. The following piece of code shows the use of this method to move two records forward from the current record:

```
RcSet.Move 2
```

The Move *n* method also has an optional parameter that enables you to move a specified number of records from a bookmark. You must set the bookmark prior to using this form of the Move method. The following line of code shows how this method is used:

```
RcSet.Move 2, bkmrk
```

Using the *Find* Methods

You can use the Find methods on dynasets and snapshots only. You can't use Find methods on table objects. (Because the data entry screen was created with a table, you can't use the Find methods in the example.) The Find methods are used to locate records that meet specified criteria. You express the criteria in the same way that you specify the Where clause of a SQL command—except without the Where keyword. There are four Find methods:

Find Method	Action
FindFirst	Starting at the top of the database, finds the first record in the recordset with the specified criteria.
FindNext	Starting at the current location in the recordset, finds the next record down with the specified criteria.
FindPrevious	Starting at the current location in the recordset, finds the next record up with the specified criteria.
FindLast	Starting at the bottom of the recordset, finds the last record in the database with the specified criteria.

After the Find method is run, check the status of the NoMatch property of the recordset. If NoMatch is True, the method failed to find a record that matched the requested criteria. If NoMatch is False, the record pointer is positioned at the found record.

Listing 31.7 shows the use of the Find methods to move through a dynaset.

Listing 31.7 How to Move Through Selected Records in a Dynaset Using *Find* Methods

```
'*****************************************
'Set up the database and Dynaset objects
'*****************************************
Dim OldDb As Database, NewDyn As Recordset, FindCrit As String
Dim OldWs As Workspace
Set OldWs = DBEngine.Workspaces(0)
Set OldDb = OldWs.OpenDatabase("C:\YOUTH\YOUTHTRK.MDB")
Set NewDyn = OldDb.OpenRecordset("SELECT * FROM Youth", _
    dbOpenDynaset)
'*********************************************
'Set the search criteria for the find methods
'*********************************************
FindCrit = "State = 'AL'"
'*********************************************
'Find the first record matching the criteria
```

continues

Listing 31.7 Continued

```
'*********************************************
NewDyn.FindFirst FindCrit
Do While Not NewDyn.NoMatch
'*************************************************************
'Loop forward through all records matching the criteria
'*************************************************************
    NewDyn.FindNext FindCrit
Loop
'*********************************************
'Find the last record matching the criteria
'*********************************************
NewDyn.FindLast FindCrit
Do While Not NewDyn.NoMatch
'*************************************************************
'Loop backward through all records matching the criteria
'*************************************************************
    NewDyn.FindPrevious FindCrit
Loop
```

T I P You might want to set a bookmark prior to invoking one of the `Find` methods. Then, if a matching record is not found, you can return to the record that was current before the `Find` was attempted.

The `Find` methods work by scanning each record, starting with the current record, to locate the appropriate record that matches the specified criteria. Depending on the size of the recordset and the criteria specified, this search operation can be somewhat lengthy. The Jet engine can optimize searches if an index is available for the search expression. If you are going to do many searches, consider creating an index for the field or fields in the base table.

T I P In many cases, it is faster to re-create a dynaset by using the search criteria than it is to use the `Find` methods to process all matching records. You can also create a second filtered dynaset from the first dynaset by using the search criteria as the `Filter` condition. The best technique depends upon the amount of data, size of each record, as well as other factors. Try different approaches with your data to see what's best for a given situation. Listing 31.8 shows the comparison of these two approaches.

Listing 31.8 Creating a Dynaset with a *Filter* Condition in the SQL Statement or Creating a Second Dynaset After Setting the *Filter* Property of of the First Dynaset

```
'***********************
'Create Initial Dynaset
'***********************
Dim OldDb As Database, NewDyn As Recordset, ScnDyn As Recordset
Dim OldWs As WorkSpace
Set OldWs = DBEngine.Workspaces(0)
Set OldDb = OpenDatabase("C:\YOUTH\YOUTHTRK.MDB")
```

```
Set NewDyn = OldDb.OpenRecordset("SELECT * FROM Youth", _
    dbOpenDynaset)
'*********************************
'Use Find method to search records
'*********************************
NewDyn.FindFirst "State = 'FL'"
Do Until NewDyn.NoMatch
    NewDyn.FindNext "State = 'FL'"
Loop
'*********************************************************************
'Create second dynaset and use Move methods to process records
'*********************************************************************
NewDyn.Filter = "State = 'FL'"
Set ScnDyn = NewDyn.OpenRecordset()
ScnDyn.MoveFirst
Do Until ScnDyn.EOF
    ScnDyn.MoveNext
Loop
'*********************************************************************
'Create initial dynaset with "Where" clause and use Move
'*********************************************************************
Set NewDyn = OldDb.OpenRecordset _
    ("SELECT * FROM Youth WHERE State = 'FL'", dbOpenDynaset)
NewDyn.MoveFirst
Do Until NewDyn.EOF
    NewDyn.MoveNext
Loop
```

TROUBLESHOOTING

When you use variables as the value to be compared to, you might encounter the error `Cannot bind name *item*` when you run the program. When the field and the variable you are comparing are string (or text) variables, surround the variable name by single quotes (') , as shown in the following sample code:

```
Dim FindCrit As String, FindStr As String
FindStr = "Smith"
FindCrit = "Lastname = '" & FindStr & "'"
NewDyn.FindFirst FindCrit
```

For the sake of readability, you can also assign the single quote to a constant and use that constant in your code.

In the same manner, surround a date variable with the pound symbol (#) to compare it to a date field. You don't need to include any additional symbols when comparing numbers.

When a `Find` method is successful, the record pointer moves to the new record. If a `Find` method is not successful, the recordset's `NoMatch` property is set to True and the record pointer does not move. One way to use the `NoMatch` property is to write an `If` condition that checks the value, as shown in the following code:

```
If NewDyn.NoMatch Then
    'Notify user of event
    MsgBox "Record not found"
Else
    'Process found record.
    command
End If
```

Using the *Seek* Method

The Seek method is the fastest way to locate an individual record in a table; however, it is also the most limiting of the record-positioning methods. The following list outlines the limitations of the Seek method:

- Can be performed only on a table; you can't use it with a dynaset or snapshot.

- Can be used only with an active index; the parameters of the Seek method must match the fields of the index in use.

- Finds only the first record that matches the specified index values; subsequent uses do not find additional matching records.

The Seek method, as shown in Listing 31.9, consists of the method call, the comparison operator, and the values of the key fields. The comparison operator can be <, <=, =, >=, >, or <>. The key values being compared must be of the same data type as the fields in the controlling index. Although you are not required to include the same number of key values as there are fields in the index, you *do* have to include a key value for each field you want to search. These values must appear in the same order as the fields in the index and be separated by commas, as shown in the second part of Listing 31.9.

Listing 31.9   Using the *Seek* Method to Find a Specific Record in a Table

```
Dim OldDb As Database, OldTbl As Recordset
Dim OldWs As WorkSpace
Set OldWs = DBEngine.Workspaces(0)
Set OldDb = OldWs.OpenDatabase("C:\YOUTH\YOUTHTRK.MDB")
Set OldTbl = OldDb.OpenRecordset("Youth",dbOpenTable)
'***********************************
'Set the index property for the table
'***********************************

OldTbl.Index = "Name"
'*********************************************
'Execute the seek for the desired condition
'*********************************************

OldTbl.Seek ">", "Smith"
'*****************************************************************
'Display information or "Not Found" message as appropriate
'*****************************************************************

If OldTbl.NoMatch Then
    MsgBox "Not Found"
Else
    MsgBox OldTbl("Lastname") & ", " & OldTbl("Firstname")
End If
```

```
'*********************************************************
'Seek method with first and last name information supplied
'*********************************************************
OldTbl.Seek ">=", "Smith", "M"
```

You must carefully plan for one behavior of the Seek method. When the Seek method uses the comparison operators =, >=, >, or <>, Seek starts with the first record for the current index and scans forward through the index to find the first matching occurrence. If the comparison operator is < or <=, Seek starts with the last record in the table and scans backward through the table. If the index has unique values for each record, this presents no problem. However, if there are duplicate index values for the key fields being specified, the record found depends on the comparison operator and the sort order of the index. Figure 31.6 shows a table of first and last names indexed on last name and then first name. The table on the top is indexed in ascending order; the table on the bottom is indexed in descending order. Listing 31.10 shows four possible combinations of controlling index and comparison operator for finding a record for the last name of *Smith*. Each of these combinations is labeled in the comments of the code. Note that the comparison operator is a string value that is to be enclosed in quotes, as is the data that is to be compared (if it's in a Text field). Table 31.4 shows the results of each of these Seek operations.

FIG. 31.6

These tables show the difference between using ascending and descending order in an index.

Ascending index order —

Descending index order —

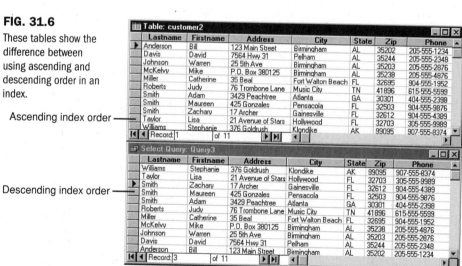

Listing 31.10   Varying Results Are Obtained Using Different *Seek* Operators and *Index* Orders on a Table

```
Dim OldDb As Database, OldTbl As Recordset
Dim OldWs As WorkSpace
Set OldWs = DBEngine.Workspaces(0)
Set OldDb = OldWs.OpenDatabase("C:\YOUTH\YOUTHTRK.MDB")
Set OldTbl = OldDb.OpenTable("Youth", dbOpenTable)
```

continues

Listing 31.10   Continued

```
'*************************
'Set ascending order index
'*************************
OldTbl.Index = "Name"
OldTbl.Seek ">=", "Smith", "A"
printer.Print OldTbl("Lastname") & ", " & OldTbl("Firstname")
OldTbl.Seek "<=", "Smith", "Z"
printer.Print OldTbl("Lastname") & ", " & OldTbl("Firstname")
'*************************
'Set descending order index
'*************************
OldTbl.Index = "Name2"
OldTbl.Seek ">=", "Smith", "A"
printer.Print OldTbl("Lastname") & ", " & OldTbl("Firstname")
OldTbl.Seek "<=", "Smith", "Z"
printer.Print OldTbl("Lastname") & ", " & OldTbl("Firstname")
```

Table 31.4   Different *Seek* Comparison Operators and *Index* Sort Orders Yield Different Results

Seek Comparison Operator	*Index* Order	Resulting Record
">=", "Smith, A"	Ascending	Smith, Adam
"<=", "Smith, Z"	Ascending	Smith, Maureen
">=", "Smith, A"	Descending	Roberts, Judy
"<=", "Smith, Z"	Descending	Smith, Zachary

Notice that you must also be careful when using the > ,< , >=, or <= operator on a descending index. The > (and >=)operator is interpreted as finding the record that occurs later in the index than the specified key value. That is why the ">=", "Smith" search on a descending index returns the record Roberts, Judy. Similar behavior is exhibited by the < and <= operators. As you can see from the preceding example, you must use care when choosing both the index sort order and the comparison operator with the Seek method to ensure that the desired results are achieved.

As with the Find methods, if a Seek is successful, the record pointer moves. Otherwise, the recordset's NoMatch property is set to True and the record pointer does not change. Figure 31.7 shows the Seek Name button and dialog box added to the sample case.

Using the *Bookmark* Property

It is often desirable to be able to return to a specific record after the record pointer moves or new records are added. You can do so by using the Bookmark property of the recordset. The bookmark is a system-assigned variable that is correlated to the record and is unique for each record in a recordset. Listing 31.11 shows how to obtain the value of the bookmark for the current record, move to another record, and then return to the original record by using the bookmark previously obtained.

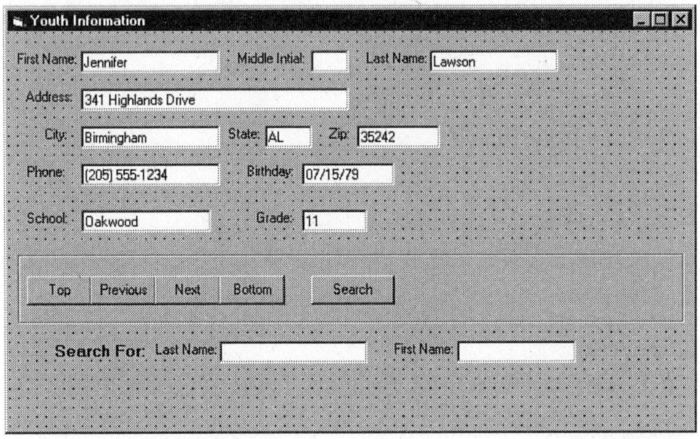

FIG. 31.7
The Seek button presents the user with an opportunity to enter search conditions.

Listing 31.11   Using a Bookmark to Return to a Specific Record in a Recordset

```
Dim OldDb As Database, NewDyn As Recordset
Dim OldWs As WorkSpace
Set OldWs = DBEngine.Workspaces(0)
Set OldDb = OldWs.OpenDatabase("C:\YOUTH\YOUTHTRK.MDB")
Set NewDyn = OldDb.OpenRecordset _
    ("SELECT * FROM Youth", dbOpenDynaset)
'********************************************************
'Set a variable to the bookmark of the current record
'********************************************************
CrntRec = NewDyn.Bookmark
'**********************
'Move to another record
'**********************
NewDyn.MoveNext
'************************************************************
'Return to the desired record by setting the bookmark property
'   to the previously defined value.
'************************************************************
NewDyn.Bookmark = CrntRec
```

CAUTION

If you're working with a database type other than Jet, check the `Bookmarkable` property of the recordset you are using to see whether bookmarks are supported before you execute any methods that depend on the bookmarks.

If you must store multiple bookmark values, consider storing them in an array for faster processing. Listing 31.12 shows code that, while processing a mailing list, uses a bookmark array to identify customers whose birthdays are coming up.

Listing 31.12 Storing Multiple Bookmarks in an Array

```
ReDim BkMrk(1)
nmbkmk = 0
NewDyn.MoveFirst
Do Until NewDyn.EOF
'***************************
'Check for birthday in month
'***************************
    If birthday Then
'********************
'Add bookmark to array
'********************
        nmbkmk = nmbkmk + 1
        If nmbkmk > 1 Then
            ReDim Preserve BkMrk(1 To nmbkmk)
        End If
        BkMrk(nmbkmk) = NewDyn.Bookmark
    End If
    NewDyn.MoveNext
Loop
'****************
'Process bookmarks
'****************
For I = 1 To nmbkmk
    NewDyn.Bookmark = BkMrk(I)
    Debug.Print Lastname, Birthday
Next I
```

Using the *PercentPosition* and *AbsolutePosition* Properties

In addition to the Bookmark property, the Recordset object has two other properties that you can set to establish the position of the record pointer. These properties are AbsolutePosition and PercentPosition.

The PercentPosition property specifies the approximate position in a recordset where a record is located. By setting this property to a value between 0 and 100, you cause the pointer to move to the record closest to that location. Setting the property to a value outside the range causes an error to occur. You can use the PercentPosition property with all three types of recordsets.

The AbsolutePosition property enables you to tell the recordset to move to a specific record. The value of the property can range from 0 for the first record in the recordset to 1 less than the number of records. Setting a value outside of that range causes an error. Therefore, it is a good idea to include error checking in the code used to set the AbsolutePosition property. The AbsolutePosition property can be used only with dynasets and snapshots. Listing 31.13

shows how you can use the `AbsolutePosition` and `PercentPosition` properties. Note the validation of the requested position; this is used to prevent errors.

Listing 31.13 *AbsolutePosition* and Percent*Position* Are Other Ways to Move in a Recordset

```
'Move to the percent position specified
If rcpct > 100 Then rcpct = 100
If rcpct < 0 Then rcpct = 0
NewDyn.PercentPosition = rcpct
  'Move to the absolute position specified
If rcabs > NewDyn.RecordCount Then rcabs = NewDyn.RecordCount
If rcabs < 0 Then rcabs = 0
NewDyn.AbsolutePosition = rcabs
```

Part
VI

Ch
31

Using Filters, Indexes, and Sorts

Filters, sorts, and indexes are properties of the `Recordset` object. You can set these properties by using an assignment statement such as:

```
NewDyn.Filter = "Lastname = 'Smith'"
```

Filters, indexes, and sorts enable you to control the scope of records being processed and the order in which records are processed. *Filters* (which are available only for dynasets and snapshots) limit the scope of records by specifying that they meet certain criteria, such as "last name starts with *M*." *Indexes* (available only for tables) and *sorts* (available only for dynasets and snapshots) specify the order of a recordset based on the value of one or more fields in the recordset. For sorts and indexes, you can also specify ascending or descending sort order.

Setting the *Filter* Property

The `Filter` property is available only for dynasets and snapshots. Although the following discussion refers only to dynasets, the same statements hold true for snapshots. When set, the `Filter` property does not affect the current dynaset, but filters records that are copied to a second dynaset or snapshot created from the first.

You can specify the `Filter` property of a dynaset the same way you specify the `Where` clause of a SQL statement, but without the `Where` keyword. The filter can be a simple statement, such as `State = 'AL'`, or one that uses multiple conditions, such as `State = 'FL' AND Lastname = 'Smith'`. You can also use an expression, such as `Lastname LIKE 'M*'`, to find people whose last names begin with *M*. The following sample code shows how these `Filter` properties are set for a dynaset created from the Youth information table:

```
Dim NewDyn As Recordset, ScnDyn As Recordset
Set NewDyn = OldDb.OpenRecordset("Youth",dbOpenDynaset)
NewDyn.Filter = "State = 'FL' AND Lastname = 'Smith'"
'Second recordset contains only "filtered" records.
Set ScnDyn = OldDb.OpenRecordset(dbOpenDynaset)
```

You can include added flexibility in your `Filter` conditions by using functions in the condition. For example, if you want to filter a dynaset of all states with the second letter of the state code equal to *L,* use the `Mid` function, as shown here:

```
NewDyn.Filter = "Mid(State,2,1) = 'L'"
```

Using functions does work, but it is an inefficient way to filter a dynaset. A better approach is to include the condition in the query used to create the dynaset.

More About Filters

The `Filter` condition of the dynaset has no effect on the current dynaset—only on secondary dynasets created from the current one. The only way to "filter" the existing recordset is to move through the recordset with the `Find` methods. By setting the `Find` condition to your `Filter` condition, you only process the desired records.

If you work with only the filtered dynaset, it is more efficient to create the required dynaset by using the appropriate SQL clause in the `OpenRecordset` method. This method is shown here:

```
Fltr = "State = 'FL' AND Lastname = 'Smith'"
Set NewDyn = OldDb.OpenRecordset("SELECT * FROM Youth WHERE" & Fltr)
```

Setting the *Sort* Property

As with the `Filter` property, the `Sort` property is available only for dynasets and snapshots. Although the following discussion refers only to dynasets, the same statements apply to snapshots. You can specify the `Sort` property by providing the field names and order (ascending or descending) for the fields on which the dynaset is to be sorted. You can specify any field or combination of fields in the current dynaset. The `Sort` condition is similar to the `Order By` clause of a SQL statement. Listing 31.14 shows the syntax for setting the `Sort` property.

Listing 31.14   Two Techniques for Creating a Sorted Dynaset

```
Dim OldDb As Database, NewDyn As Recordset, ScnDyn As Recordset
Dim OldWs As WorkSpace
Set OldWs = DBEngine.Workspaces(0)
Set OldDb = OldWs.OpenDatabase("C:\YOUTH\YOUTHTRK.MDB")
'****************************************************************
'The first method sets the sort property of one dynaset then
'    creates a second dynaset from the first.
'****************************************************************
Set NewDyn = OldDb.OpenRecordset("SELECT * FROM Youth")
NewDyn.Sort = "Lastname,Firstname"
Set ScnDyn = NewDyn.OpenRecordset()
'**********************************************************
'The second method creates the sorted Dynaset directly
'**********************************************************
Set ScnDyn = OldDb.OpenRecordset _
        ("SELECT * FROM Youth ORDER BY Lastname,Firstname")
```

> **CAUTION**
> When specifying a multiple field sort, the order of the fields is important. A sort on first name and then last name yields different results than a sort on last name and then first name.

As was the case for the `Filter` property, the `Sort` property has no effect on the current dynaset; it specifies the order of any dynaset created from the current one. You can also achieve the same results of a sorted dynaset by specifying the `Order By` clause of the SQL statement used to create the dynaset. This alternate technique is shown in Listing 31.14.

Setting the Current Index in a Table

You can use an index with a table to establish a specific order for the records or to work with the `Seek` method to find specific records quickly. For an index to be in effect, the `Index` property of the table must be set to the name of an existing index for the table. An example of how to use a program command to set the current index follows:

```
OldTbl.Index = "NameIndex"
```

The index specified for the table must be one that has already been created and is part of the indexes collection for the given table. If the index does not exist, an error occurs. The index is not created for you!

Creating an Index for a New Situation

If the index you want does not exist, create it and then set the `Index` property of the table to the newly created index. The example shown in Listing 31.15 creates a ZIP Code index for the Youth table by creating a new `Index` object, appending a `Field` object to the `Index` object's `Fields` collection, then appending the `Index` object to the `Recordset` object's `Indexes` collection.

Listing 31.15   Creating a New Index and Setting the *Index* Property

```
Dim Idx1 As Index, Fld1 As Field
Set Idx1 = NewTbl.CreateIndex("Zip_Code")
Set Fld1 = Idx1.CreateField("Zip")
Idx1.Fields.Append Fld1
NewTbl.Indexes.Append Idx1
NewTbl.Index = "Zip_Code"
```

If your program needs an index, why not just create it at design time so you don't have to worry about creating it at runtime? There are several reasons why it may be more beneficial to create an index at runtime:

■ It takes time for the data engine to update indexes after records are added, deleted, or changed. If there are a large number of indexes, this process can be quite time-consuming. It might be better to create the index only when it is needed. Also, indexes take up additional disk resources; therefore, many indexes on a large table can cause your application to exceed available resources.

■ You are limited to 32 indexes for a table. Although this is a fairly large number, if you need more than 32, you must create some indexes as they are needed and then delete them.

■ You cannot anticipate all the ways a user of your application wants to view data. By providing a method for creating indexes, specified by the user at runtime, you add flexibility to your application.

Of these reasons, the performance issue of updating multiple indexes is the one most often considered. To determine whether it is better to add the index at design time or to create it only when you need it, set up the application both ways and test the performance of each.

N O T E   Although it is desirable to limit the number of indexes your table has to keep current, it is advisable to have an index for each field that is commonly used in SQL queries. This is because the Jet engine (starting with version 2.0) employs query optimization that uses any available indexes to speed up queries. ■

Considering Programs that Modify Multiple Records

Some programs, or program functions, are meant to find one specific piece of information in a database. However, the vast majority of programs and functions work with multiple records as a group. There are two basic methods of working with multiple records:

Method	Definition
Program loops	Groups of commands contained inside a DO...WHILE, DO...UNTIL, or FOR...NEXT programming structure. The commands are repeated until the exit condition of the loop is met.
SQL statements	Commands written in Structured Query Language that tell the database engine to process records. SQL is covered in detail in Chapter 29, "Understanding SQL."

Using Loops

Most programmers are familiar with the use of Do...While and For...Next loops. In working with recordsets, all the programming principles for loops still apply. That is, you can perform a loop *while* a specific condition exists or *for* a specific number of records. Loops of this type were shown earlier in this chapter (refer to Listings 31.4 and 31.5).

Another way of working with multiple records forms an *implied loop*. Most data entry or data viewing programs include command buttons on the form to move to the next record or previous record. When a user repeatedly presses these buttons, he or she executes a type of program loop by repeating the move events. A special consideration for this type of loop is what to do when you are at the first record, the last record, or if you have an empty recordset. The problem is that if you move backward from the first record, forward from the last record, or try to move anywhere in an empty recordset, an error occurs. Fortunately, the Jet database engine provides some help in this area. There are properties of the recordset that can tell you when these conditions exist, as described in the following section.

You can use four main recordset properties to control the processing of multiple records in a recordset. Table 31.5 gives the definitions of these properties.

Table 31.5   Properties Used to Control Loop Processing

Property	Indicates
BOF	Beginning of File flag, indicates whether the record pointer is positioned before the first record (BOF = True) or not (BOF = False).
EOF	End of File flag, indicates whether the record pointer is positioned past the last record (EOF = True) or not (EOF = False).
RecordCount	Indicates the number of records in the recordset that have been accessed. This gives a count of the total records in the recordset only after the last record has been accessed (for example, by using MoveLast), unless the recordset in question is a table-type recordset.
NoMatch	Indicates that the last Find method or Seek method was unsuccessful in locating a record that matched the desired criteria.

You can use these properties to terminate loops or prevent errors. Consider the data entry form in Figure 31.5. To prevent an error from occurring when the user presses the Next button, use code that allows the move only if the recordset is not at the end of the file. The following code takes this possibility into account:

```
If NOT OldDyn.EOF Then
    OldDyn.MoveNext
    If OldDyn.EOF Then DolDyn.MoveLast
End If
```

Alternatively, you can disable the Next button when you reach the end of file. You can apply the same principle to the Previous button and the BOF condition. You might also want to check the RecordCount property of a recordset and enable only the Add Record button if the count is zero.

N O T E   After the MoveNext method has been executed, it is possible that the pointer is now at the end of the file (EOF). This would mean that there is no current record. Therefore, if the end of the file is encountered, a MoveLast method is used to make sure the record pointer is positioned at the last record in the recordset. ▪

Using SQL Statements

In addition to processing records with a program loop, you can use SQL statements to handle a number of functions that apply to multiple records. The following sections discuss two main types of functions:

■ Calculation queries provide cumulative information about the requested group of records.

■ Action queries insert, delete, or modify groups of records in a recordset.

Calculation Queries   *Calculation queries* allow you to determine cumulative information about a group of records such as the total; average, minimum, and maximum values; and the number of records. Calculation queries also enable you to specify the filter criteria for the records. For example, you can extract total sales for all salesmen in the Southeast region or the maximum price of a stock on a given day (assuming, of course, that the base data is in your tables). Figure 31.8 shows a table of purchasing data for the fish inventory in an example database. The code in Listing 31.16 shows how to determine the total purchase costs for one type of fish and the minimum, maximum, and average unit cost of all the fish. Figure 31.9 shows the table that results from the SQL query.

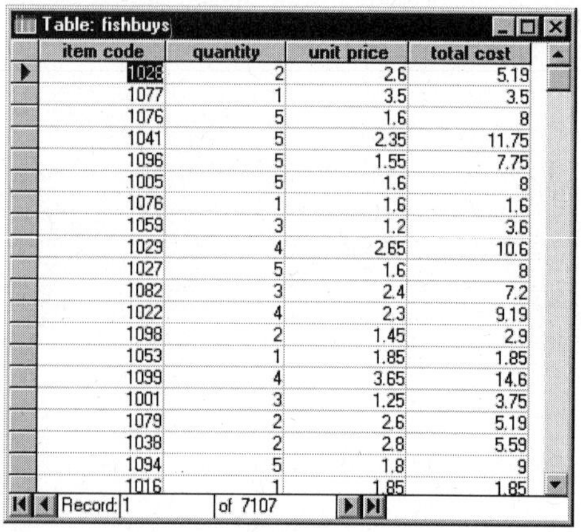

FIG. 31.8

You can process purchasing data shown here with calculation queries or action queries.

Table: fishbuys				
item code	**quantity**	**unit price**	**total cost**	
1028	2	2.6	5.19	
1077	1	3.5	3.5	
1076	5	1.6	8	
1041	5	2.35	11.75	
1096	5	1.55	7.75	
1005	5	1.6	8	
1076	1	1.6	1.6	
1059	3	1.2	3.6	
1029	4	2.65	10.6	
1027	5	1.6	8	
1082	3	2.4	7.2	
1022	4	2.3	9.19	
1098	2	1.45	2.9	
1053	1	1.85	1.85	
1099	4	3.65	14.6	
1001	3	1.25	3.75	
1079	2	2.6	5.19	
1038	2	2.8	5.59	
1094	5	1.8	9	
1016	1	1.85	1.85	

Record: 1   of 7107

Listing 31.16   Using Calculation Queries to Determine Information About Data in the Recordset

```
Dim OldDb As Database, NewDyn As Recordset, _
    NewDyn2 As Recordset, SQL As String
Dim OldWs As WorkSpace
Set OldWs = dbEngine.Workspaces(0)
Set OldDb = OldWs.OpenDatabase("C:\FISH\TRITON.MDB")
'*******************************************
'Use the SUM function to get the total cost.
'*******************************************
SQL = "SELECT SUM([Total Cost]) As Grand FROM Fishbuys _
```

```
             WHERE Fishcode = 1001"
Set NewDyn = OldDb.OpenRecordset(SQL)
Print NewDyn("Grand")
NewDyn.Close
'*******************************************************************
'Use the MIN, AVG, and MAX functions to get unit price statistics.
'*******************************************************************
SQL = "SELECT MIN([Unit Price]) As Mincst, _
         AVG([Unit Price]) As Avgcst, "
SQL = SQL + _
    " MAX([Unit Price]) As Maxcst FROM Fishbuys WHERE Fishcode > 0"
Set NewDyn2 = OldDb.OpenRecordset(SQL)
Print NewDyn2("Mincst"), NewDyn2("Avgcst"), NewDyn2("Maxcst")
NewDyn2.Close
OldDb.Close
```

FIG. 31.9

A calculation query produces a dynaset with a single record containing the results.

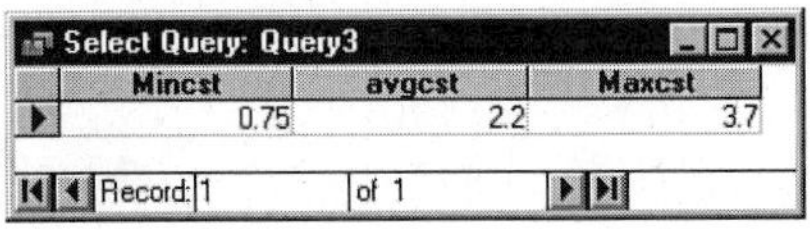

Part

VI

Ch

31

Using a calculation query can replace many lines of program code that would be required to produce the same results. In addition, a query is usually faster than the equivalent program code.

Action Queries   *Action queries* operate directly on a recordset to insert, delete, or modify groups of records based on specific criteria. As with calculation queries, action queries perform the same work that would require many lines of program code. Listing 31.17 shows examples of several action queries.

Listing 31.17   Using Action Queries to Perform Operations on Multiple Records

```
Dim OldDb As Database, NewDyn As Recordset, NewQry As QueryDef
Dim OldWs As WorkSpace
Set OldWs = DBEngine.Workspaces(0)
Set OldDb = OldWs.OpenDatabase("C:\FISH\TRITON.MDB")
'********************************************
'Calculate the total cost of each purchase.
'********************************************
SQL = _
    "Update Fishbuys Set [Total Cost] = [Quantity] * [Unit Price]"
Set NewQry = OldDb.CreateQueryDef("Calc Total", SQL)
NewQry.Execute
NewQry.Close
'************************************
'Delete all records for Fishcode = 1003
'************************************
SQL = "Delete From Fishbuys WHERE Fishcode = 1003"
```

continues

Listing 31.17   Continued

```
Set NewQry = OldDb.CreateQueryDef("Del Fish", SQL)
NewQry.Execute
NewQry.Close
OldDb.DeleteQueryDef ("Calc Total")
OldDb.DeleteQueryDef ("Del Fish")
OldDb.Close
```

CAUTION

When using action queries to modify groups of records, be very careful when specifying the WHERE clause of the query that defines the records to be modified. Improperly setting this clause can produce disastrous results, such as the deletion of all records in a recordset.

Understanding Other Programming Commands

In this chapter, you have learned how to find specific records and how to move through a group of records. However, in most programs, you also must add, modify, and delete records. The commands covered in the following sections apply only to tables and dynasets (remember that snapshots are not updatable).

Adding Records

To add a new record to a recordset, use the AddNew method. AddNew does not actually add the record to the recordset; it clears the copy buffer to allow information for the new record to be input. To physically add the record after you've put data into the record's fields, use the Update method. Listing 31.18 shows how to add a new record to the recordset.

Listing 31.18   Using *AddNew* and *Update* to Add a Record to the Recordset

```
'********************************
'Use AddNew to set up a new record
'********************************
NewDyn.AddNew
'*********************************************************
'Place the necessary information in the recordset fields
'*********************************************************
NewDyn("Lastname") = "McKelvy"
NewDyn("Firstname") = "Mike"
NewDyn("Address") = "6995 Bay Road"
NewDyn("City") = "Pensacola"
NewDyn("State") = "FL"
NewDyn("Zip") = "32561"
'*********************************************************
'Use the update method to add the new record to the recordset
'*********************************************************
NewDyn.Update
```

CAUTION

Because AddNew places information only in the copy buffer, reusing the AddNew method or moving the record pointer with any Move or Find method (before using the Update method) clears the copy buffer. Any information entered in the record is therefore lost.

Editing Records

In a manner similar to adding a record, you use the Edit method to make changes to a record. The Edit method places a copy of the current record's contents into the copy buffer so that information can be changed. As with AddNew, the changes take effect only when the Update method is executed. Listing 31.19 shows the use of the Edit method.

Listing 31.19   Using *Edit* and *Update* to Change the Data in a Record

```
'*********************************************************
'Use the find method to locate the record to be changed.
'*********************************************************
NewDyn.FindFirst "Lastname = 'McKelvy'"
'*************************************************
'Check the NoMatch Property to avoid an error
'*************************************************
If NewDyn.NoMatch Then
    MsgBox "Not Found"
Else
'*******************************************************
'Use the edit method to set up the record for changes
'*******************************************************
    NewDyn.Edit
'*****************************************************
'Change the necessary information in the copy buffer
'*****************************************************
    NewDyn("Address") = "P. O. Box 380125"
    NewDyn("City") = "Birmingham"
    NewDyn("State") = "AL"
    NewDyn("Zip") = "35238"
'***********************************************************
'Use the update method to write the changes to the recordset
'***********************************************************
    NewDyn.Update
End If
```

CAUTION

Because Edit only places information in the copy buffer, reusing the Edit method or moving the record pointer with any Move or Find method (before using the Update method) clears the copy buffer. Any information entered in the record is therefore lost.

Updating Records

The Update method is used in conjunction with the AddNew and Edit methods to make changes to the recordsets. The Update method writes the information from the copy buffer to the recordset. In the case of AddNew, Update also creates a blank record in the recordset to which the information is written. In a multi-user environment, the Update method also clears the record locks associated with the pending Add or Edit method. (Listings 31.17 and 31.18 show the use of the Update method.)

N O T E If you use Data controls to work with recordsets, the use of the Update method is not required. An update is automatically performed when a move is executed by the Data control. ■

Deleting Records

Deleting a record requires the use of the Delete method, as shown in Listing 31.20. This method removes the record from the recordset and sets the record pointer to a null value.

Listing 31.20   Using *Delete* to Remove a Record from the Recordset

```
'***********************************************************
'Use the find method to locate the record to be deleted
'***********************************************************
NewDyn.FindFirst "Lastname = 'McKelvy'"
'***********************************************
'Check the NoMatch property to avoid an error
'***********************************************
If NewDyn.NoMatch Then
    MsgBox "Not Found"
Else
'***********************************************
'Use the delete method to remove the record
'***********************************************
    NewDyn.Delete
End If
```

CAUTION

After you delete a record, it is gone. You can recover the record only if you issued a BeginTrans command before you deleted the record, in which case you can RollBack the transaction. Otherwise, the only way to get the information back into the database is to re-create the record with the AddNew method.

Incorporating *Add*, *Edit*, and *Delete* Functions in the Sample Case

Figure 31.10 shows some command buttons added to the data entry screen for the sample case. These buttons make use of the add, edit, and delete capabilities described in the preceding sections. The Delete Record button deletes the current record. The Add New Record button blanks out the text boxes to prepare them for new input. The Edit Record button prepares the recordset for editing. As a visual indication of editing, the foreground color of the text boxes also changes. Both the Edit Record and Add New Record buttons cause the normal command buttons (the Top, Previous, Next, Bottom, and Seek Name buttons) to be hidden and two new buttons to be displayed. The new buttons are Save and Cancel. The Save button stores the values displayed in the text boxes to the appropriate fields in the recordset and issues the Update method. The Cancel button terminates the Edit or Add process and restores the original information for the current record. After either Save or Cancel is selected, both buttons disappear and the eight main buttons are again shown.

> **N O T E** I stated previously that deletions and changes to the database are made without confirmation by the user. If you want your program to have confirmation built in, you have to provide it in your code. The easiest way to do this is through the MsgBox function. With this function, you can provide a warning to the user and ask for confirmation. ■

FIG. 31.10
Add, Edit, and Delete functions are added to the data entry screen with new command buttons.

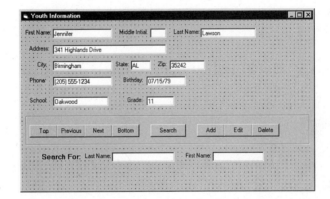

Introducing Transaction Processing

Transaction processing enables you to treat a group of changes, additions, or deletions to a database as a single entity. This is useful when one change to a database depends on another change, and you want to make sure that all changes are made before any of the changes become permanent. For example, you have a point-of-sale application that updates inventory levels as sales are made. As each item is entered for the sales transaction, a change is made to the inventory database. However, you only want to keep the inventory changes if the sale is completed. If the sale is aborted, you want to return the inventory database to its initial state before the sale was started. Transaction processing is a function of the Workspace object and, therefore, affects all databases open in a particular workspace.

Visual Basic provides three methods for transaction processing. These methods perform the following functions:

Transaction Method	Function
BeginTrans	Starts a transaction and sets the initial state of the database.
RollBack	Returns the database to its initial state before the BeginTrans statement was issued. When RollBack is executed, all changes made after the last BeginTrans statement are discarded.
CommitTrans	Permanently saves all changes to the database made since the last BeginTrans statement. After the CommitTrans statement has been issued, the transactions cannot be undone.

Listing 31.21 shows the BeginTrans, RollBack, and CommitTrans methods as they are used in an order entry application. The transactions are used in case the customer cancels the order prior to the completion of the order processing.

Listing 31.21   Using Transaction Processing to Handle Multiple Changes to a Database as One Group

```
OldWs.BeginTrans
'************************************************
'Perform loop until user ends sales transaction
'************************************************
Do While Sales
'************************************************
'Get item number and sales quantity from form
' Input Itemno,SalesQty
' Find item number in inventory
'************************************************
    Inv.FindFirst "ItemNum = " & Itemno
'*************************
'Update inventory quantity
'*************************
    Inv.Edit
    Inv("Quantity") = Inv("Quantity") - SalesQty
    Inv.Update
Loop
'*****************************************
'User either completes or cancels the sale
'*****************************************
If SaleComp Then
    OldWs.CommitTrans
Else
    OldWs.Rollback
End If
```

From Here...

Some of the topics mentioned in this chapter are covered in greater detail in other portions of the book:

■ Chapter 29, "Using the Visual Basic Data Control," explains how to quickly write data access programs by using the Data control.

■ Chapter 30, "Doing More with Bound Controls," shows you how to make applications using the Data control do more.

■ "SQL Primer SQL," found on this book's CD-ROM, explains more about the SQL statements used in creating dynasets, snapshots, and queries.

Part

VI

Ch

31

Using Remote Data Objects (RDO)

So far in the discussions of accessing databases, the focus has been on using PC-based databases. These types of databases include Access, FoxPro, dBASE, and Paradox. However, Visual Basic is also a great tool for creating front ends for client/server applications. These types of applications are used to access data stored in database servers such as SQL Server and Oracle. Most of your front-end work—such as designing forms and writing code to process information—will be the same whether you are writing an application for a PC database or a client/server database. The key difference is in how you make the connection to the data.

In this chapter, we'll discuss how your Visual Basic programs can easily access data stored in a variety of remote locations through the use of Remote Data Objects (RDO). You'll see how the recent addition of RDO to Visual Basic's repertoire makes short work of writing applications that need to work with remote data. ∎

What is client/server computing?

Client/server computing uses a database server to handle many of the data processing tasks. The client works with only a small amount of data returned by the server.

What does ODBC do?

ODBC is a specification that allows your program to communicate with a variety of databases, whether on your local PC or on a mainframe server.

Is there an easy way to work with ODBC databases?

The Remote Data Objects and Remote Data control provide a rich object model that makes working with ODBC databases relatively easy.

How does RDO compare with DAO?

The object model of the Remote Data Objects is very similar to that of the data access objects.

Database Access Philosophies

Before delving further into actually setting up applications that access client/server databases, you'll take a look at the difference in the philosophy of the two types of database access. In the PC-database world, the information is accessed through the database engine, which is part of the application. For Visual Basic, the Jet engine is a part of your database applications. As you issue commands to retrieve information from the database, the commands are interpreted by the Jet engine and the processing of the commands is done locally on your PC. Whether the database file actually resides on your PC or is located on a file server, the database engine remains on your PC. The application itself contains the logic to directly access the database file. In the client/server world, this is not the case. Your application issues a request for information, usually in the form of a SQL statement. This request is passed to the database server which processes the request and returns the results. This is true client/server computing, in which a database server does the actual processing of the request.

Client/server systems have a number of advantages over just sharing a database file. First, database logic is removed to a central, more maintainable location. For example, suppose you have a program that calculates sales tax based on your company's rules. In a client/server environment, the logic for this calculation process would be located on the database server. This means you can make changes to it in one place, without having to rewrite the client application. Other advantages include being able to distribute processing and separating the user interface design from the business logic.

Introducing ODBC

One method used by Visual Basic to communicate with client/server databases is called *Open Database Connectivity*, or ODBC. ODBC is a component of Microsoft's *Windows Open System Architecture* (WOSA). ODBC provides a set of *application program interface* (API) functions, which makes it easier for a developer to connect to a wide range of database formats. Because of the use of ODBC standards, you can use the same set of functions and commands to access information in a SQL Server, Oracle, or Interbase, even though the actual data-storage systems are quite different. You can even access a number of PC databases using ODBC functions.

Understanding ODBC Drivers

ODBC drivers are the DLLs containing the functions that let you connect to various databases. There are separate drivers for each database type. For many standard formats, such as PC databases and SQL Servers, these drivers are provided with Visual Basic. For other databases, the ODBC driver is provided by the server manufacturer.

N O T E   If you use ODBC in your application, make sure the appropriate drivers are distributed with your application. If you selected the Redistributable ODBC option when installing VB, an ODBC subdirectory should have been created in the Visual Basic program directory. Running Setup.exe will install ODBC drivers, although you will still have to set up your data sources. ▪

ODBC drivers can be one of two types: *single-tier* or *multiple-tier.* A single-tier driver is used to connect to PC-based database systems that may reside on either the local machine or a file server. Multiple-tier drivers are used to connect to client/server databases where the SQL statement is processed by the server, not the local machine.

Each ODBC driver you encounter must contain a basic set of functions, known as the *core-level capabilities.* These basic functions are:

- Providing database connections
- Preparing and execute SQL statements
- Processing transactions
- Returning result sets
- Informing the application of errors

Setting Up an ODBC Data Source

Before you can use ODBC to connect to a database, you must make sure of two things:.

- The ODBC drivers are installed on your system.
- You have set up the ODBC data source.

Both of these functions can be accomplished by using the ODBC Manager application. Also, the second function can be accomplished from code, by using the data access objects. Remember, an ODBC driver is used to connect to a *type* of database, for example, SQL Server. An ODBC Data Source is a configuration of an ODBC driver used to connect to a *specific database,* that is, "Accounting Department Database."

Part

VI

Ch

32

> **N O T E** On Microsoft Windows 95 systems, you will find the ODBC manager in the Control Panel, under the Settings item on the Start menu. The icon you are looking for is labeled "32-bit ODBC." You might also have an icon called "ODBC" if you have some older 16-bit programs.

> **N O T E** To ensure that all readers can use the information presented here, the Access ODBC driver is used in all examples. While this is a PC database, the methods used can also be applied to server databases. It is important to remember that connecting to an Access MDB file via ODBC is different than connecting directly through the Jet engine.

Gaining Access to ODBC Drivers   To set up the ODBC Data Sources on your system, you need to use Windows 95's ODBC Data Source Administrator. You will find this in the Control Panel, which is accessible by choosing the Control Panel item from the Settings submenu on the Start menu. The Control Panel is illustrated in Figure 32.1.

FIG. 32.1

The ODBC Data Source Administrator is accessed by selecting the "32-bit ODBC" icon on the Control Panel.

ODBC Data Source Administrator

The ODBC Administrator Dialog Box

If you see different dialog boxes than the ones pictured here when you click the 32-bit ODBC icon, don't panic. As with any product, Microsoft has produced several versions of ODBC. ODBC is included with many of their products, including Office and Visual Basic. Depending on the installation options you chose, you may or may not have the latest version. Older versions of ODBC do not have the "tabbed" dialog style. Fortunately, ODBC is included with VB so you can install it during setup.

When you open the ODBC Manager, you see the ODBC Data Source Administrator dialog box, as shown in Figure 32.2. The Data Source administrator includes several tabs used to add data sources as well as new ODBC drivers.

FIG. 32.2

The Data Source Administrator dialog box allows you to configure ODBC data sources.

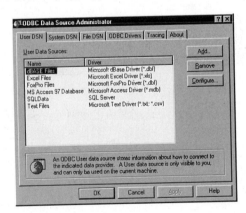

As you'll notice, the titles of the first three tabs in the dialog box end in the letters *DSN*. DSN is an abbreviation for *Data Source Name*. The DSN is the key that your program uses to identify an ODBC Data Source. ODBC takes care of mapping the DSN to the actual driver, server, and database file.

The ODBC Data Sources are divided into three types: user, system, and file. Although the purpose of all DSNs is essentially the same—to provide information about a specific data source—there are differences where and when you can use each type:

■ A System DSN, more applicable in Windows NT than Windows 95, is not associated with a particular user profile. This means that once the DSN has been set up, all programs and services running on the machine can access it. For example, if you are using Internet Information Server to connect to a database, you will probably be setting up a System DSN for the database.

■ A File DSN stores DSN information in a text file. The text file is an INI file containing information about the database driver and location. It is not associated with a particular machine, so it can be on a network drive.

■ A User DSN is the type you will probably use most often. User DSN information is stored in the Registry of the local machine. In Windows NT, each User DSN is associated with a specific user profile and invisible outside of it.

The remaining three tabs in the ODBC Data Source Administrator dialog box are used for informational and debugging purposes. The ODBC Drivers tab, shown in Figure 32.3, displays a list of the ODBC drivers installed on your machine.

FIG. 32.3

The ODBC Drivers tab tells you which drivers are installed on your system.

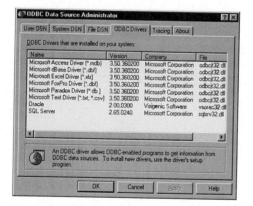

Part
VI
Ch
32

The last tab, the About tab, is very similar to the ODBC Drivers tab. It lists the versions and files used by ODBC itself. You may find these two screens helpful in determining whether or not your users have the correct drivers installed.

Before moving on, note the Tracing tab, pictured in Figure 32.4. This tab allows you to trace each call made by the ODBC Manager to the ODBC Drivers. Remember that ODBC is a means to connect to various databases via some common API functions. The Tracing options allow you to view those API calls. This is something you probably won't do very often, but it is nice to know about.

Creating an ODBC Source with the ODBC Manager   To set up a data source for use in your application, you need to know which driver to use and how to configure it. For example, you will need to know the name of the SQL Server or Access MDB file the data resides in. You also will need to come up with a unique name to identify the data source.

FIG. 32.4
The Tracing tab of the ODBC Administrator is a low-level debugging aid.

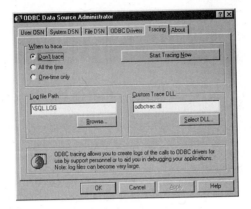

Set up a sample data source now. Go to the User DSN screen and click the A<u>d</u>d button to create a new data source. This presents you with the Create New Data Source dialog box, shown in Figure 32.5. In this first dialog box, you choose the ODBC driver that will be used to access the data.

FIG. 32.5
Selecting the ODBC driver is the first step to setting up a data source.

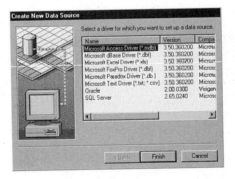

After choosing the driver and clicking the OK button, you are presented with the Setup dialog box for the particular database type associated with the driver. Choose the Microsoft Access Driver and press the Finish button. You will be presented with a dialog box like that in Figure 32.6.

In this dialog box, you provide a name in the Data Source <u>N</u>ame box. This is the name you will use in your applications to refer to the data source. You can also choose to include a <u>D</u>escription of the data source.

After setting the name, you need to choose the actual database file or server you want to use with your program. For the Access driver, this is done by clicking the <u>S</u>elect button of the dialog box. You are then presented with a Select Database dialog box (which is basically an open-file dialog box). Try opening a file by choosing an MDB file on your PC. Figure 32.7 shows a data source called MyDSN linked to the biblio database that comes with Visual Basic.

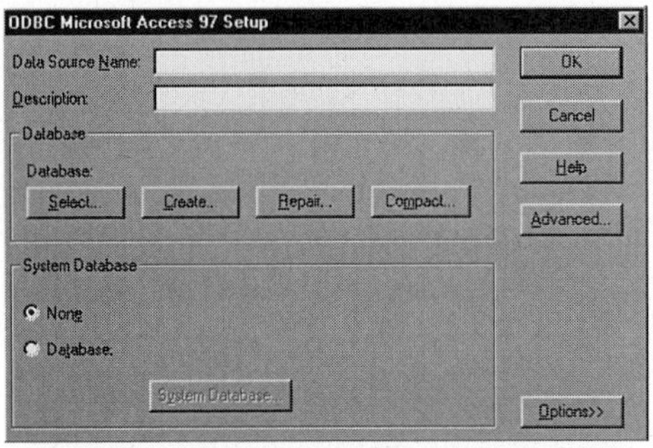

FIG. 32.6
A Setup dialog box lets you specify the information necessary to connect to an ODBC data source.

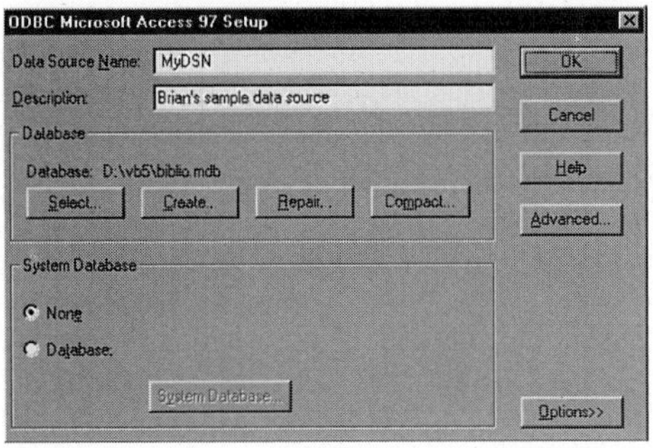

FIG. 32.7
The Access dialog box allows you to select which MDB file you are going to be working with.

Keep in mind that the setup dialog boxes are driver dependent. In each case, however, you specify both a data-source name and the location of the data. Figure 32.8 shows the dialog box for Microsoft SQL Server.

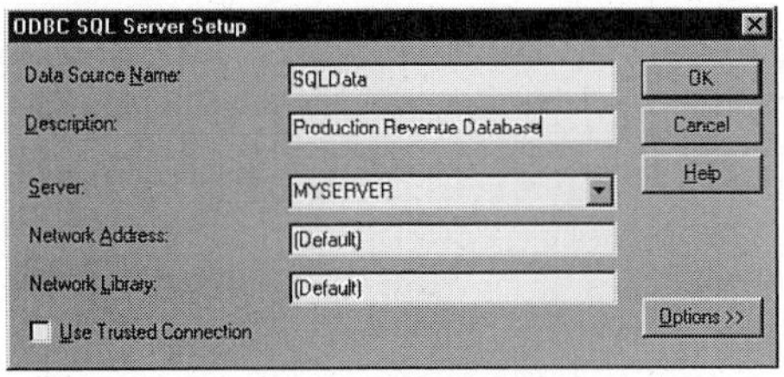

FIG. 32.8
The SQL Server dialog box requires you to specify the server where the information is located.

The DSN screens also give you the capability to Configure or Remove ODBC data sources. To modify a data source, select the data source and then click the Configure button. This presents you with the same dialog box that you used initially to set up the data source. To delete a data source, select it and then click the Remove button.

Part
VI

Ch
32

Using the DAOs to Create an ODBC Source   You are not limited to setting up data sources interactively. There are times, such as application installation, where you might want to add a data source with code. For this purpose, you can use the `RegisterDatabase` method of the `DBEngine` object.

Here is the syntax of the `RegisterDatabase` method:

```
DBEngine.RegisterDatabase dbname, driver, silent, attributes
```

Table 32.1 defines the parameters used in the `RegisterDatabase` method.

Table 32.1   Parameters of the *RegisterDatabase* Method

Parameter	Definition
dbName	A user-definable string expression that specifies the data source name (for example, `"MyDatabase"`).
driver	A string expression that indicates the installed driver's name (for example, `ORACLE`) as listed in the ODBC Drivers tab of the ODBC Administrator. *silent* `True` specifies that the next parameter (*attributes*) indicates all connection information. `False` specifies to display the Driver Setup dialog box and ignore the contents of the *attributes* parameter.
attributes	All connection information for using the ODBC driver. This parameter is ignored if *silent* is set to False.

The following code sample illustrates how the `RegisterDatabase` method is used to create a link to an Access database. Before attempting to use the data access objects, remember to add the appropriate reference.

```
    Dim sAttrib As String
    Dim sDriver As String

    sAttrib = "DBQ=D:\VB5\BIBLIO.mdb"
    sDriver = "Microsoft Access Driver (*.mdb)"
DBEngine.RegisterDatabase "MyDSN", sDriver, True, sAttrib
```

After executing the above code, you can go back to the Data Source Administrator window and verify that a new User DSN has been added.

N O T E   You can also use the `rdoRegisterDataSource` method of the `rdoEngine` to perform the registration task for Remote Data Objects. ▪

Notice that for the Access driver the `"DBQ"` parameter indicates the name of the database file. To determine all the parameters required for a particular ODBC driver, you should create a connection with the ODBC Manager and then examine the settings in the Registry. You will find these under HKEY_USERS\Default\Software\ODBC\ODBC.INI. (To view the Registry, use the REGEDIT application included with Windows 95.) To specify multiple parameters with the `RegisterDatabase` method, separate them with a semicolon.

Using the Remote Data Objects

Data access objects (DAO) are a layer on top of the ODBC API. Before the advent of *Remote Data Objects* in Visual Basic, programmers would sometimes skip this layer by calling the ODBC API directly. The reason, of course, was to make their applications run faster. However, the ODBC API calls are much harder to use than the data access objects. Remote data objects changed this by providing an interface to the ODBC API that uses the familiar operations of setting properties and calling methods. Because properties and methods are used in all Visual Basic programs, this made the access of ODBC databases much easier for developers to understand and accomplish.

Comparison of RDO to DAO

The remote data objects, or RDO, are very similar to the data access objects (DAO), which were covered in Chapter 31, "Improving Data Access with Data Access Objects (DAO)." This similarity not only makes RDO easier to understand, but it also makes the conversion of programs from PC databases to client/server databases much easier. In fact, once the connection to the data source is made, the same code statements can be used to access the data by using RDO as were used for DAO.

To give you a feel for the similarities between the RDO and DAO models, Table 32.2 lists a number of RDO objects and their corresponding DAO objects.

Part VI

Ch 32

Table 32.2   Some RDO Objects and Their DAO Counterparts

RDO Object	DAO Object
rdoEngine	DBEngine
rdoEnvironment	Workspace
rdoConnection	Database
rdoTable	TableDef
rdoResultset	Recordset
rdoColumn	Field
rdoQuery	QueryDef
rdoParameter	Parameter

In addition, the rdoResultset object supports several types of returned sets of records, similar to the recordset types of the Recordset object. Table 32.3 summarizes these similarities.

Table 32.3 *rdoResultset* Types and the Corresponding *Recordset* Types

rdoResultset Types	*Recordset* Types	Definition
Keyset	Dynaset	Updatable set of records in which movement is unrestricted.
Static	Snapshot	Non-updatable set of records that were present when the set was created. Updates by other users are not reflected.
Dynamic	N/A	Similar to a keyset.
Forward-only	Forward-only	Similar to a static resultset or snapshot, but you can move forward only through the set of records. This is the default Resultset type.

Notice that the Remote Data Objects do not support any rdoResultset type that returns a table. This is because the Remote Data Objects are geared to using SQL statements to retrieve subsets of information from one or more tables. You must set the order of the rdoResultset with the Order By clause of the SQL statement used to create the set. Also, because there is no table equivalent, RDO does not support indexes.

As you might expect with the similarity of the objects, there are methods of the RDO that are similar to the methods of the DAO. These methods and their respective objects are summarized in Table 32.4.

Table 32.4 RDO Objects Methods and Related DAO Methods

RDO Method	RDO Object	DAO Method	DAO Object
rdoCreateEnvironment	rdoEngine	CreateWorkspace	DBEngine
BeginTrans	rdoConnection	BeginTrans	Workspace
CommitTrans	rdoConnection	CommitTrans	Workspace
OpenConnection	rdoEnvironment	OpenDatabase	Workspace
RollbackTrans	rdoConnection	Rollback	Workspace
CreateQuery	rdoConnection	CreateQueryDef	Database
Execute	rdoConnection	Execute	Database
OpenResultset	rdoConnection	OpenRecordset	Database

And finally, the rdoResultset object and the Recordset object have the following methods in common:

■ AddNew   Adds a new row (record) to the set

■ Delete   Removes the current row (record) from the set

■ Edit   Prepares the current row for changing the information in the row

■ MoveFirst   Moves to the first row of the set

■ MoveLast   Moves to the last row in the set

■ MoveNext   Moves to the next row in the set

■ MovePrevious   Moves to the previous row in the set

■ Update   Commits the changes made to the copy buffer to the actual record. The copy buffer is a memory location that contains the values of the record with which the user is working

Accessing a Database with RDO

To further illustrate the similarities between the RDO and DAO models, the code in Listings 32.1 and 32.2 perform the same function on the "biblio" database. The difference between the two listings is simply the objects and methods used to create returned records. Once the recordset or resultset is established, the remaining statements simply print each entry in the first field. In the RDO example, the ODBC data source "MyDSN" was created previously with the ODBC Manager.

N O T E   In order to use the Remote Data Objects, you need to add a reference to the "Microsoft Remote Data Object" from the Project, References menu. ■

Listing 32.1   RDOSampl.txt—Access Information in an ODBC Data Source Using the RDO Methods

```
Dim db As rdoConnection
Dim rs As rdoResultset
Dim sSQL As String

Set db = rdoEngine.rdoEnvironments(0).OpenConnection("MyDSN")

sSQL = "Select * From Titles"
Set rs = db.OpenResultset(sSQL, rdOpenKeyset)

rs.MoveFirst
While Not rs.EOF
    Print rs.rdoColumns(0)
    rs.MoveNext
Wend

rs.Close
db.Close
```

Listing 32.2   DAOSampl.txt—Access the Same Information Using the DAO Methods

```
Dim db As Database
Dim rs As Recordset
Dim sSQL As String

Set db = DBEngine.Workspaces(0).OpenDatabase("D:\VB5\BIBLIO.MDB")

sSQL = "Select * From Titles"
Set rs = db.OpenRecordset(sSQL, dbOpenDynaset)

rs.MoveFirst
While Not rs.EOF
    Print rs.Fields(0)
    rs.MoveNext
Wend

rs.Close
db.Close
```

Another thing you will want to explore with RDO is asynchronous execution of database operations. This means control is returned to your program *before* the database operation completes, as in the example below:

```
Set db = rdoEngine.rdoEnvironments(0)._
    OpenConnection("MyDSN", , , , rdAsyncEnable)
While db.StillConnecting = True
    Print "Connecting..."
Wend
```

The constant rdAsyncEnable indicates asynchronous operation. The while loop keeps running until the connection is made and the StillConnecting property becomes False.

Using the Remote Data Control

If you want a faster way to create applications by using ODBC data sources, you can use the *Remote Data control* (RDC). The RDC lets you set a few properties of the control, and then the RDC handles all the tasks of making the connections to the ODBC data source for you. In this way, the RDC automates the methods of the remote data objects in the same way that the data control automates the methods of the data access objects.

After setting up the Remote Data control, you can use the bound controls to display and edit information that is in the resultset created by the data control. The bound controls are set up the same way they would be for use with the Data control that was discussed in Chapter 29, "Using the Visual Basic Data Control," except that now, the DataSource property of the bound controls points to a Remote Data control. Once set up, the bound controls are updated with new information each time a new row is accessed by the Remote Data control.

Comparing the RDC and the Data Control

The Remote Data Objects were compared to the data access objects in the earlier "Using the Remote Data Objects" section; now take a look at the similarities of the Data control and the RDC. As you might expect, many of the properties of the RDC have counterparts in the Data control. These properties and their functions are summarized in Table 32.5.

Table 32.5 Remote Data Control Properties Compared to Data Control Properties

RDC Property	Data Control Property	Purpose
BOFAction	BOFAction	Determines whether the beginning of file flag is set when the user invokes the MovePrevious method while on the first record.
DataSourceName	DatabaseName	Specifies the database containing the desired information.
EOFAction	EOFAction	Determines whether the end of file flag is set or if a new row (record) is added when the user invokes the MoveNext method while on the last record.
ResultsetType	RecordsetType	Determines the type of dataset created by the control.
SQL	RecordSource	The SQL statement that identifies the specific information to be retrieved.

Part
VI

Ch
32

Setting Up the RDC

Setting up the RDC for use in your program is also very similar to setting up the Data control. Before you can use the RDC, you must first add it to your project. You do this by using the Components dialog box, which you access by choosing the Components item from the Project menu. After you close the dialog box, the remote data control is added to your toolbox.

TROUBLESHOOTING

The Remote Data control does not appear as one of the available controls in the Custom Controls dialog box. You may have chosen not to install the remote data control when you first set up Visual Basic. You need to reinstall that portion of Visual Basic. Also, if you do not have the Enterprise Edition of Visual Basic, the remote data control is not available to you at all.

To set up the remote data control, follow these steps:

1. Draw the remote data control on your form.

2. Set the `Name` and `Caption` properties of the RDC to values that have meaning to you.

3. Set the `DataSourceName` property. You may enter a value or choose one from the drop-down list.

4. Set the `SQL` property to a valid SQL statement that specifies the information you need.

As stated in Step 3, you can choose the `DataSourceName` value from a drop-down list. This list contains every registered ODBC data source on your system. An example of this list is shown in Figure 32.8.

FIG. 32.9

You can choose from a list of available ODBC data sources when setting the `DataSourceName`.

After you have set up the remote data control, you then can attach bound controls to it by setting the `DataSource` property. As shown in Figure 32.10, a drop-down list in the `DataSource` property contains the names of any remote data controls or data controls on the current form. After the `DataSource` property has been set, you can select the `DataField` property from a list, just as you did for the controls bound to a data control.

FIG. 32.10

The `DataSource` property list contains all available data controls, remote or not.

From Here...

This chapter has given you a basic understanding of client/server applications. The chapter has also shown you how the Remote Data Objects and Remote Data control make it easier to access the ODBC databases that are part of many client/server programs.

- To learn more about working with the data control, see Chapter 29, "Using the Visual Basic Data Control," and Chapter 30, "Doing More with Bound Controls."

- To learn more about the data access objects, see Chapter 31, "Improving Data Access with the Data Access Objects (DAO)."

- To learn more about creating SQL statements, see "SQL Primer" on the accompanying CD-ROM.

Part
VI

Ch
32

CHAPTER 33

Database Access with ActiveX Data Objects (ADO)

ActiveX Data Objects (ADO) is nearly revolutionary in its concept and scope. It is not a database connector like DAO or ODBC; rather it is an extensible set of data access objects that is a programming model. These objects are based on OLE DB, which operates at the basic API (Application Programming Interface) level. ADO wraps this functionality into an easy to use flexible package that will be the basis of all of Microsoft's future data access development. Even better news is that if you are familiar with DAO or RDO, you will have a very short and shallow learning curve to master ADO.

Microsoft's other new database-connectivity tool, Advanced Data Connector (ADC), is firmly rooted in ADO technology. ADC provides connection to data-aware controls.

Microsoft is making it very clear that DAO and RDO have been developed as far as they will be taken. They will be supported for some time into the future, but will not be enhanced. All future development effort will go toward ADO, so climb aboard and see that the future is here today. ■

OLE DB is the basis of universal data access

OLE DB is the low-level API used to create the data providers for the ADO interface.

ODBC uniformly connects heterogeneous DBs

ODBC provides OLE DBs interface to relational database sources.

SQL unlocks the relational database storage cabinet

Writing syntactically correct SQL statements isn't hard. With some new tools, it's not even necessary.

Much application development today is based on the client/server paradigm

ADO is designed to work well in a client/server application environment. It's very useful in Web development, which is by definition client/server.

The ADO Object Model is easy to understand

The ADO Object Model consists of Connection, Errors, Command, Parameters, Recordset, and Fields objects. All but Errors have a Properties collection.

ADO also works well in a non-Web environment

Building a non-Web example requires small changes from Web-based development.

Understanding ActiveX Data Objects

ADO currently does not come as part of the Visual Basic 5.0 product. It is part of Visual C++ 5.0, Visual InterDev, and Active Server Pages, which is part of Microsoft Internet Information Server 3.0 for Windows NT 4.0 and the Personal Web Server for Windows 95. ADO isn't part of VB 5.0 because ADO wasn't completed when Visual Basic 5.0 was packaged for shipment. ADO definitely will be part of all future releases of Visual Basic. Nevertheless, Visual Basic 5.0 currently works seamlessly with ADO.

In the past, Visual Basic programs were created to provide access to data. The first data was simple ASCII files. This was followed by an interface known as VBSQL that was used to interface with SQL Server databases. The emphasis then shifted to ISAM databases, such as MS Access. Microsoft created the Jet Database Engine and Data Access Objects (DAO) to allow easy access to the Jet. Mixed into all of this was Open Database Connectivity (ODBC), which provided remote access to a heterogeneous group of database engines through ODBC drivers.

The latest and most significant development is OLE DB, which provides access to a heterogeneous group of types of data stores, including relational databases. The ActiveX Data Objects is a programming interface model that gives access to OLE DB.

Understanding Where OLE DB Fits

OLE DB is a low-level OLE API that organizes as either Data Providers or Data Consumers. OLE DB is a set of functionality that is encapsulated in an OLE server. This OLE server uses Data Providers to interface to various types of data stores. The list of data stores will grow over time as more data Providers are written. ADO is a programming model that interfaces to the OLE DB server to provide access to the data.

OLE DB currently uses a Data Provider, code-named Kagera, to interface to ODBC, which then provides an interface to relational and ISAM data stores. There is a plan eventually to create Data Providers for OLE DB that will interface directly to the relational and ISAM data stores, as well as other data stores. OLE DB is being called the universal data access technology.

Understanding ODBC

N O T E ODBC is a subject about which you will need information as you read this chapter. Everything that you need to know about ODBC is explained in the section "Introducing ODBC" in Chapter 32, "Using Remote Data Objects (RDO)." ▪

Reviewing Relational Databases

Relational databases are based on the theoretical work by E. F. Codd. Prior to Codd's concept of relational databases, attempts were made to use a number of database structures. The organizational structures were elegant and performed the task, but the inverted tree and other structures proved inflexible after their creation. Any change to the structure was a major effort and required recompilation of the database. One of the great features of relational databases is the flexibility. Adding another item of data is no problem with the relational model.

A *relational database management system* (*RDBMS*) is a software application that stores data. This data is arranged in such a way as to be available for reading, updating, adding new records, and deleting records. The RDBMS doesn't need a *front end* or user interface. It is sufficient if the database accepts command-line commands (in the form of SQL statements, discussed later in this chapter), executes the command and returns a group of records, updates a record, adds a record, or deletes a record.

The user interface (UI) usually is a separate function that is in a totally separate application program called a *client*. The client/server design concept is explored in a later section of this chapter.

Tables

Data in a relational database is organized in tables. A *table* is a two-dimensional organizational structure that is composed of rows and columns. A *column* contains a specific category of data, such as the names or social security numbers of a group of people, for example. In such an example, the collection of data regarding a particular individual, such as name, social security number, address, and phone number, are contained within a *row*.

Table 33.1 is an example of a table that contains the contact information in a PIM (*Personal Information Manager*).

Table 33.1 A Contacts Table

Last Name	First Name	Area Code	Phone No
Jones	John	520	555-1212
Hansen	Sue	212	555-1212
Adams	Sue	602	444-3434
Adams	Phil	602	444-3434
Smith	Fred	303	222-2323

This looks very much like the information that is kept in many pocket diaries. The rows in the table are not in any particular sequence. The "correct" sequence for the rows in a relational database is in an as-entered chronological sequence.

Primary Keys

One requirement for a table is that each row of the table be unique. This unique identifier can be a specific column that contains an item of information that is unique, such as the social security number of an individual or the serial number of a computer. The primary key can be composed of more than one column.

Notice in Table 33.1 that neither the last name nor the phone number will work as a primary key. Phil and Sue have the same last name and phone number. The first name will not work as the primary key because Sue Hansen and Sue Adams have the same first name. With the data contained in this table, only the combination of the first and last names works as the primary key.

Experience dictates that using the first and last name as the primary key is not a good choice for a table that has many people listed in it. There are certainly many people in the world with the name John Jones. As you design the database table, think of a good choice for the primary key. One strategy is to create a unique number that is attached to each record as the primary key. This works quite well, except for the fact that you can have more than one record for the same individual and not know it.

Normalization

The rules of normalization are of paramount importance in the proper design of a relational database. Application of these rules keeps the database designer from falling into some traps that may cause problems. These rules are called *normalization,* and a database that complies is said to be in the *normal form*. There are three rules or normal forms that are usually applied. These are called the first, second, and third normal forms. What they lack in imaginative naming, they make up for in usefulness.

First Normal Form   A table is in the first normal form if all columns in the table contain *atomic values,* which means a column contains only one item of data such as a phone number or child's name but never two items of the same type of data such as two or more phone numbers or the name of two or more people.

Second Normal Form   A table is in the second normal form if it is in the first normal form and every value is dependent on the primary key value. An example is if you attempt to construct a table composed of first name, last name, and phone number, where the first and last name are used as the primary key. This will work until you attempt to record the second phone number for a person, such as the work and home phone numbers. If you choose to use the phone number rather than the first and last name as the primary key, you would run into the problem of two people having the same phone number. You can begin to see the problems with different database designs and how the normalization rules can help.

> **N O T E**   The language of relational databases can be somewhat arcane and obtuse. The statement that a data item must depend on the primary key is one of these cases. What this means is that without the presence of the primary key, say my social security number, you wouldn't have my name in the record. The two, the SSN and the name, are linked together. ∎

Third Normal Form   A table is said to be in the third normal form if the table is in the first *and* the second normal forms *and* if every value depends on only the primary key. This is the most difficult to understand of the commonly used normal forms. An example is if you are constructing a table that includes pay rates. In your theoretical organization, all people occupying a particular job title are paid the same amount of money, regardless of their time at that job. In this case, the pay rate depends on the job title, not the person occupying the job. If you constructed a database to describe this organization, you would need to create a table of job titles and pay rates and a table of employees. You would place the Key of the job title table in the employee table as a foreign or cross reference key, not the pay rate itself. In other words, the pay rate goes with the job, not the individual. The individual occupies the job and the job title has a pay rate.

> **N O T E**   There are actually five normal forms. The last two are rarely used and delve into mathematical theory that is easy to forget. I have never had occasion to use the fourth and fifth normal forms. ▪

Foreign Keys

Why is this important? Because a well designed relational database does not contain redundant data. An item of information, such as a name, should occur only once in a database so that if the item of data (name) needs to be changed, it needs to be changed only one time.

For example, suppose an employee of your company named Dorothy Rubyslippers marries Cal Combatboots and decides to change her name to Dorothy Combatboots. If her name appears in multiple tables in your company's database, each and every one of the tables containing her name must be located and changed. If the database is properly constructed, however, her name would need to be changed in just one place.

If a table contains multiple instances of an item of information about an individual, such as multiple phone numbers, all the phone numbers should be moved into a separate table. The two tables then need a common item of information that can be used to cross-reference the two tables. As an example, look at Tables 33.2 and 33.3.

Part VI

Ch 33

Table 33.2   Name Table

SSN	Last Name	First Name	Sex
123-45-6789	Jones	John	Male
111-22-3333	Hansen	Sue	Female
012-43-8765	Adams	Sue	Female
888-22-1111	Adams	Phil	Male
666-55-4444	Smith	Fred	Male

Table 33.3 Phone Numbers Table

Key	Foreign Key	Area Code	Phone No
1	123-45-6789	520	555-1212
3	012-43-8765	212	555-1212
9	111-22-3333	602	444-3434
25	888-22-1111	312	444-3434
25	123-45-6789	520	444-3434
72	666-55-4444	215	111-2222
73	012-43-8765	212	222-3333
81	666-55-4444	215	333-4444
88	888-22-1111	312	444-5555
89	111-22-3333	602	555-6666

In Tables 33.2 and 33.3, the social security number (SSN) is used as the common item of information to correlate the two tables because it is the only column of information that has a unique entry for each individual. In the Names table, the SSN is the primary key. In the Phone Number table, a number is assigned as the primary key. The Phone Number table contains the SSN as a foreign key. It is the key from the Names table.

These two tables exist in a parent/child relationship; the Name table is the parent of the child Phone Number table.

The best way to decide whether data should be included in a table or moved to a separate table is to determine if the data item depends on the primary key and there is only one of them. For example, if you create a table that contains data about a group of people, each person will have only one social security number, only one date and place of birth, and will be either male or female. Therefore, all this data can go in one table. However, when you look at other data associated with these individuals, such as the names of their children, the makes of their cars, and their telephone numbers, you realize many of them have more than one of these items. Therefore, each of these items should be in its own separate child table.

Referential Integrity

The *referential integrity* of a database concerns the parent/child relationship between tables. In the preceding example regarding the Names and Phone Numbers tables, there shouldn't be a record in the Phone Number table unless there is a parent record in the Name table. If you delete the record of an individual from the Name table, all of the associated records from the Phone number table should also be deleted. It is a violation of referential integrity if there are records in the Phone Number table that have no associated record in the Name table. In this situation, the records in the Phone Number table that have no parent records are called *orphan records*.

The relationships between tables are classified as one to many, one to one, many to one, and many to many. These relationships are important in the use of the database, which you will find out in the section concerning the Structured Query Language.

NOTE In Microsoft Access, when the relationships between tables are set forth in a database, cascading updates and deletes can be specified. If the database engine does not provide this to be done automatically, then it needs to be done with program code. It is important that you understand the characteristics of the database engine you will be using. ■

Indexes

Because the rows of a table are not organized in any particular order, the RDBMS provides the capability to create one or more indexes. An *index* is a separate table that lists in order, either ascending or descending, the contents of a particular table with pointers to the records in the table. An index provides increased search speed when searching a database table for a specific record or set of records. Instead of reading the entire table, a search of the index is performed and the resulting list of pointers is used to collect the records from the base table.

Views

A *view* is a copy of a table or tables that doesn't exist except as a results set that is created when the view is queried. For example, imagine a table in a company's personnel records database that includes the home phone number of the employee. In this company, as in many, the home phone number is considered confidential information. If the company gives employees access to the personnel table as a company directory, they will have a problem.

The solution is to create a VIEW on the personnel table that doesn't include the column for home phone numbers and then give the employees access to the VIEW. This will protect the security of the data. Because access to a VIEW looks just like access to a table, no one will be able to tell the difference.

Part
VI

Ch
33

Speaking Structured Query Language (SQL)

Structured Query Language, or SQL (pronounced sequel), is a standard that was created, and is maintained, by ANSI (American National Standards Institute). Relational Database Management Systems (RDBMS) are SQL-compliant. This means that the database software system (also called the database engine) is able to accept a SQL statement, parse it, execute it, and return a results set successfully. The current SQL standard is SQL 92. Most RDBMSs are SQL 92-compliant. SQL, in concept, is intended to be English-like and not a cryptic code. An example of a SQL statement is the following:

```
SELECT * FROM TABLENAME
```

This SELECT statement would result in all of the columns and all of the rows of a table being returned as a results set. SQL is divided into two major sections: Data Definition Language (DDL) and Data Manipulation Language (DML).

DDL concerns the creation and alteration of the structure of the database. It includes CREATE and DROP statements. Applications usually don't permit the user to access the structure of the database.

The database application program usually concerns functions that exercise the DML. DML includes statements such as SELECT, UPDATE, INSERT, and DELETE. These are used to manipulate the data in the database, leaving the database structure alone.

SELECT Statements

The simplest SELECT statement will retrieve all the rows of a table in the order in which they occur in the table. As an example, here is a SELECT statement for the Name table.

```
SELECT * FROM Name
```

When the database engine executes this SQL statement, it will create a results set that looks like the following:

```
SSN             Last Name     First Name      Sex
123-45-6789     Jones           John          Male
111-22-3333     Hansen          Sue           Female
012-43-8765     Adams           Sue           Female
888-22-1111     Adams           Phil          Male
666-55-4444     Smith           Fred          Male
(5 row(s) affected)
```

The format of the SELECT statement is to start with the command, which is the SELECT *. This instructs the database engine to select all columns. Followed by FROM Names which tells the database engine which table or view that you want the rows selected from.

You won't always want all the columns from a table or all the rows. In such a case, you can choose the rows that you want to select and set a filter in the form of a WHERE clause to select only certain rows. Using the Name table as an example, a SELECT statement can be typed as follows:

```
SELECT First Name, Last Name FROM Name WHERE First Name = 'Sue'
```

This shows the results set from this SELECT statement.

```
First Name     Last Name
Sue            Hansen
Sue            Adams
 (2 row(s) affected)
```

The WHERE clause filters the records to be selected. One other change you may want to make to your SELECT statement is to have it sorted. To do so, you add an ORDER BY clause, as follows:.

```
SELECT First Name, Last Name FROM Name
    WHERE First Name = 'Sue' ORDER BY Last Name
```

This shows the results set from the SELECT statement.

```
First Name     Last Name
Sue            Adams
Sue            Hansen
 (2 row(s) affected)
```

Notice that in the last two examples the columns are listed in the order they were listed in the SELECT statement, not the order they occur in the table.

There are many other clauses and refinements to clauses that can be added to your SELECT statements. It is not the intention of this chapter to present an exhaustive discussion of the SELECT statement. However, be assured that you can extract from the database the exact data you want in the exact form you want.

> **CAUTION**
>
> A common mistake made when beginning to work with databases is to assume that if the SELECT statement does not return any rows, there must have been an error. An empty results set is a perfectly valid response from a database engine. If you create a WHERE clause and no records meet the criterion, the results set will be empty.

Joins

Joins are the selection of data from more than one table using one SELECT statement. These SELECT statements can require much thought and planning to create them properly. For example, assume that you want to see the first name, SSN, and phone number from all of the people in the database who have the last name "Adams." To get this data, you will need to query two tables.

```
SELECT First Name, SSN, Phone No FROM Name, Phone Number
    WHERE Name.Last Name = 'Adams'
    AND Where Name.SSN = Phone Number.Foreign Key
```

The results set from this SELECT statement is shown in the following code:

```
First Name    SSN             Phone No
Sue           012-43-8765     555-1212
Sue           012-43-8765     222-3333
Phil          888-22-1111     444-3434
Phil          888-22-1111     444-5555
 (4 row(s) affected)
```

Notice in the SELECT statement that fully qualified names are used for the column names in the form of TABLE.COLUMN. This is used to remove any ambiguity about which column forms which table when the SELECT statement refers to more than one table.

INSERT Statements

INSERT statements are used to add new records to the database table. The following is an example of an INSERT statement that is used to add a record to the Name table:

```
INSERT INTO Name (SSN, Last Name, First Name, Sex)
    VALUES ('543-22-1234', 'Jones', 'Tom', 'Male')
```

Notice that the column names are listed in a comma-separated list, enclosed in parentheses. This is followed by the VALUES clause, which has the values for each column in a comma-separated list, again enclosed in parentheses. Likewise, notice that the values are in the same order as the column names. Finally, notice that all of the values are strings and that they are enclosed in single quote (') marks.

The results set from an INSERT is somewhat different than one from a SELECT statement. No row is requested to be returned. Instead, you receive a notification that the INSERT was successful, in the following form:

```
(1 row(s) affected)
```

UPDATE Statements

The UPDATE statement is used to change existing data in a table. The UPDATE statement should always contain a WHERE clause. The WHERE clause selects the rows to be updated. As per an earlier example, assume that the hypothetical employee, Dorothy Rubyslippers, gets married to Cal Combatboots and decides to change her name to Dorothy Combatboots in the company records. Table 33.4 shows the table before the update action is applied.

> **CAUTION**
>
> UPDATE statements are inherently dangerous, as you will see in this section, so make sure that you understand the importance of the WHERE clause.

Table 33.4   Name Table Before a Change

SSN	Last Name	First Name	Sex
123-45-6789	Jones	John	Male
111-22-3333	Hansen	Sue	Female
012-43-8765	Adams	Sue	Female
231-99-2222	Rubyslippers	Dorothy	Female
888-22-1111	Adams	Phil	Male
666-55-4444	Smith	Fred	Male

The UPDATE statement appears as follows:

```
UPDATE Name SET Last Name = 'Combatboots' WHERE SSN = '231-99-2222
```

This produces a results set of:

```
(1 row(s) affected)
```

Now a look at the importance of the WHERE clause in the UPDATE statement. If an UPDATE statement without a WHERE clause is used, such as

```
UPDATE Name SET Last Name = 'Combatboots'
```

the results set informs you:

```
(6 row(s) affected)
```

But the intent is to update only one row. What went wrong? A look at Table 33.5 provides an explanation.

Table 33.5   Name Table With an Improper Update

SSN	Last Name	First Name	Sex
123-45-6789	Combatboots	John	Male
111-22-3333	Combatboots	Sue	Female
012-43-8765	Combatboots	Sue	Female
231-99-2222	Combatboots	Dorothy	Female
888-22-1111	Combatboots	Phil	Male
666-55-4444	Combatboots	Fred	Male

Because the row to be updated is not limited with a WHERE clause, all of the rows of the table were updated. Most actions with a database do not have an undo function. If you imagine a table with 10,000 rows instead of 6, you can appreciate that UPDATE statements not well thought out can produce considerable damage.

DELETE Statements

The DELETE statement is as dangerous as it is simple. A DELETE statement without a WHERE clause deletes the entire contents of a table. As an example, assume that Dorothy Combatboots quits the company and it is now time to delete her record in the Name table. The DELETE statement will be as follows:

```
DELETE FROM NAME WHERE SSN = '231-99-2222'
```

The results set will be:

```
(1 row(s) affected)
```

A look at Table 33.6 shows that the record for Dorothy Combatboots *nee* Rubyslippers is gone, with no evidence that it was ever there.

Table 33.6   Name Table After a Deletion

SSN	Last Name	First Name	Sex
123-45-6789	Jones	John	Male
111-22-3333	Hansen	Sue	Female
012-43-8765	Adams	Sue	Female
888-22-1111	Adams	Phil	Male
666-55-4444	Smith	Fred	Male

Part
VI

Ch
33

Examining the Use of Client/Server Design

Any time two computers are involved in the mutual performance of executing an application, with each performing a different function, you are undoubtedly looking at a *client/server application*. Many definitions of client/server are used. A definition of client/server application is an application that has a client interface and that accesses data on a remote server. The work is distributed between the client system and the remote server system, based on the capabilities of the client and server software applications. Client/server systems usually are efficient because network traffic is minimized and each portion of the application is optimized for a particular function.

Client/server applications function over any type of network, functioning at any speed. These variables are factors that affect the performance of the application, but that do not affect whether the application works.

> **N O T E** Both the client and the server must use a common communications protocol and a common data format. ▪

The essence of a client/server application can be viewed by looking at a database application. Most relational database management systems (RDBMS), such as Microsoft SQL Server, provide a database engine that manages the data but has little or no user interface. (Exceptions are the desktop databases such as MS Access.) The interface to the RDBMS is through command line functions. When working with this type of RDBMS, the developer needs to create the user interface application.

In this instance, the user interface application, the client, formulates a request for data that is transmitted to the system running the database, the server. This request for data will be in the form of a SQL statement, such as a SQL query. The relational database engine will execute the query, create a results set, and transmit the results set back to the client. Figure 33.1 presents this relationship in a diagram.

FIG. 33.1
Client/server actions are always initiated by the client.

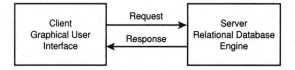

Two-Tiered Client/Server Applications

The client/server diagram shown in Figure 33.1 is called *a two-tiered client/server* because the client communicates directly with the server, with no intermediary. The limitation of this model is that it is not easily scalable. If the server becomes over taxed by client traffic, the usual solution is to upgrade the server hardware to a faster processor with more memory. However, there is an upper limit to how fast the processor can be.

Multi-Tiered Client/Server Applications

It is also possible to have three or more tiers in the client/server design, which is frequently used in Internet applications. This increases the scalability of the application. An example of this multi-tiered approach can be seen with a Web page that accesses a database on the server. Frequently, the database is on a different server than the Web server. This allows the distribution of the load over multiple systems. It also creates scalability. If the database activity becomes a bottleneck for the application, the database activity can be distributed over multiple servers. If the Web server becomes the bottleneck, the Web server can be distributed over multiple servers. Figure 33.2 shows a diagram of multiple Web servers connected to multiple database servers.

FIG. 33.2
The Domain Name Server (DNS) is providing Round Robin service for the client attachments to the Web servers.

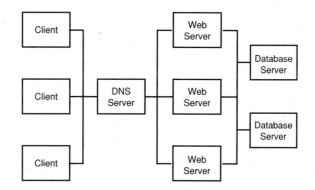

There are other uses of the multi-tier client/server model, including the following two very useful designs. The first design has a middle tier that provides an Online Analysis Processing data warehouse that is extracted from the base layer of operational databases. The second design makes use of a middle tier to enforce business rules. This separate layer for business rules makes the maintenance of the business rules much easier and less disruptive.

Part
VI

Ch
33

Understanding Thin Clients versus Thick Clients

The terms thin client and fat or thick clients are being used with great frequency. The IS world is excited over the prospect of having thin clients. The advent of the thin client is not a new idea. It is a return to the model of the central computer surrounded by "dumb" terminals.

An understanding of the differences between thin and fat clients will provide some insight into the advantages and disadvantages of each.

Client/server implies a division of labor between the client and server systems. The usual division is that the server supplies all of the data and the client displays the data and performs manipulation of the data for the user at the user's system.

A *thin client* is one that provides little to the relationship except the capability to display the data transmitted by the server. The old "dumb" terminal, such as a 3270 or DEC VT 100, are examples of a thin client.

A *fat client* is one that provides extensive logic for the manipulation of the data transmitted by the server. This is the workstation paradigm in which a PC is the client and the data is transmitted for the use of the client and then sent back to the server when the client has finished the task. The server is little more than a data repository.

Viewing this in light of Internet technologies and, in particular, World Wide Web technology, the Web browser is the client and the Web server is the server. In this model, the Web browser is the thin client that requires little or no maintenance for the client/server application to function. Even when client scripting is used, the browser is processing code that is transmitted each time the application is accessed. New versions of the script do not need to be installed on the client.

The primary concern in this scenario is the capability of the Web browser to support various technologies. Not all Web browsers are created equal. The capabilities of Web browsers vary from LYNX, which is a text-only browser, to MS Internet Explorer which supports almost everything. Web browsers vary in their support for different versions and features of HTML. Most browsers support the current 3.2 version of HTML.

In addition to the varying levels of support for HTML, there are varying levels of support for scripting languages. Netscape Navigator supports JavaScript but not VBScript. MS IE 3.0 and later supports JavaScript and VBScript. Add to this mix the complication of ActiveX support, which is present in MS IE 3.0 and later, but not Netscape Navigator without a third-party plug-in.

All of these issues, such as script language and ActiveX support, are moving the thin client of the Web browser toward a fatter client.

The most essential item to consider when analyzing Web browsers as thin clients is whether you are in an environment in which you have control over the Web browser used as a client. If you are not in such an environment, then you need to design to the lowest common denominator and use server logic to provide alternative interfaces for different browsers.

Understanding the ADO Object Model

An understanding of the ADO Object Model will be of great assistance in working with the various components. It will seem complex and overwhelming at first, but it will all fall into place as you gain experience using it. The ADO Object Model is composed of six primary objects, which are shown in Figure 33.3.

Closer examination of each of these objects will provide a greater understanding of them in preparation for building programs using ADO.

FIG. 33.3

The Errors, Parameters, and Fields objects are part of a collection.

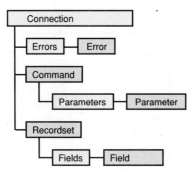

Connection Object

Connection objects can be created independently of any other previously defined object. The Connection object represents a specific unique session with a particular data source. The Connection object contains the following two collections:

- *Errors*   Contains the errors generated on the connection.
- *Properties*   The set of properties for the Connection.

The Connection object contains the following six methods:

- `BeginTrans`   Starts a transaction if the database engine supports transaction processing.
- `Close`   Closes the connection.
- `CommitTrans`   Commits and terminates the transaction.
- `Execute`   Executes the specified SQL statement.
- `Open`   Opens the connection to the data source.
- `RollbackTrans`   Reverses a transaction.

The Connection object also contains nine properties:

- `Attributes`   Reads the `XactAttributeEnum` values for a Connection object. The value can be a sum of any one or more of the `XactAttributeEnum` values.
- `CommandTimeout`   Sets the time to wait for a command to execute before timing out and generating an error.
- `ConnectionString`   Contains the information necessary to establish a connection, such as the DSN and password.
- `ConnectionTimeout`   Determines the time to wait when attempting to establish a connection before timing out and generating an error.
- `DefaultDatabase`   Indicates the default database for the Connection object.
- `IsolationLevel`   Reads or sets the isolation level of a transaction.
- `Mode`   Indicates the permissions that are available in a connection for modifying data.
- `Provider`   Indicates the OLE DB Data Provider for a Connection Object.
- `Version`   Indicates the ADO version number.

Part
VI

Ch

33

http://www.microsoft.com/ado   An excellent source of information on ActiveX Data Objects is available from Microsoft. This site will enable you to keep up to date on this rapidly developing technology. There are also excellent help files available for free download.

Error Object and Errors Collection

An Error object is generated each time an error is encountered in an ADO operation. The Error object is part of an Errors Collection. The Error object contains seven properties:

- `Description`   Explains the Error. This is the description string associated with the error.

- `HelpContext`   Returns a context ID, as a Long integer value, for a topic in a Microsoft Windows Help file.

- `HelpFile`   Returns a String that evaluates to a fully qualified path to a Help file.

- `NativeError`   Indicates the provider-specific error code for a given Error object.

- `Number`   Indicates the number that uniquely identifies an Error object.

- `Source`   Indicates the name of the object that generated the error.

- `SQLState`   Returns a five-character string that follows the ANSI SQL standard.

The Errors collection has one method, the `Clear` method, which removes all of the Error objects in the collection. The Errors collection also has two properties: `Count`, which indicates the total number of Error objects in the collection, and `Item`, which returns a specific Error object.

Command Object

A Command object is the definition of a specific command, such as a SQL statement or stored procedure that you execute on a specific data source. The Command object has two collections:

- *Parameters*   The collection of Parameter objects for the command. A Parameter object represents a parameter or argument associated with a Command object that is based on a parameterized query or stored procedure.

- *Properties*   The set of properties for the Command object.

The Command object also contains two methods:

- `CreateParameter`   Creates a new Parameter object.

- `Execute`   Executes the query, SQL statement, or stored procedure specified in the `CommandText` property.

The Command object has five properties:

- `ActiveConnection`   Indicates the Connection object to which the specified Command object currently belongs.

- `CommandText`   Contains the text of the SQL statement that you want to issue on a specific provider.

- `CommandTimeout`   Determines the time to wait when attempting to establish a connection before timing out and generating an error.
- `CommandType`   Contains the type of the command, for example, a stored procedure.
- `Prepared`   Indicates whether or not to create a prepared or compiled statement from the command before execution.

Parameter Object and Parameters Collection

A Parameter object represents a parameter or argument associated with a Command object that is based on a parameterized query or stored procedure. The Parameter object contains one method, the `AppendChunk` method, which is used to append a large text or binary file to a parameter.

The Parameter object contains eight properties:

- `Attributes`   For the Parameter object, the value is the sum of any one or more of the `ParameterAttributesEnum` values:
  - `Direction`   Shows whether the Parameter represents an input parameter, an output parameter, both, or a return value from a stored procedure.
  - `Name`   The name of a parameter that can be used in references to the parameter rather than its ordinal number in the collection.
  - `NumericScale`   Sets or returns the number of decimal places to which numeric values will be resolved.
  - `Precision`   Sets or returns the maximum total number of digits used to represent values.
  - `Size`   The maximum size, in bytes or characters, of a Parameter object.
  - `Type`   The data type of a Parameter object.
  - `Value`   The value assigned to a Parameter object.

The Parameters collection contains three methods:

- `Append`   Appends a Parameter object to the collection.
- `Delete`   Removes a Parameter object from the collection.
- `Refresh`   Updates the Parameter objects in the collection to show the objects available from, and specific to, the provider.

The Parameters collection also contains the two properties of `Count` and `Item`.

Recordset Object

You do not need to create a `Connection` object to create a `Recordset` object. This is accomplished by passing a connection string with the `Open` method. ADO creates a `Connection` object, but it isn't assigned to an object variable. If you are opening multiple `Recordset` objects over the same connection, you must create and open a `Connection` object. This will assign the `Connection` object to an object variable. If you do not use this object variable when opening your Recordset objects, ADO creates a new Connection object for each new Recordset object, even when you pass the same connection string.

A Recordset object represents the entire set of records from a base table or the results of an executed command. At any time, the Recordset object refers only to a single record within the set as the current record.

The Recordset object contains two collections:

- ■ Fields   Contains all stored Field objects of the Recordset object.
- ■ Properties   Contains all the Property objects for a specific instance of the Recordset object.

The Recordset object contains nineteen methods:

- ■ AddNew   Creates a new record for an updatable Recordset object.
- ■ CancelBatch   Cancels a pending batch update.
- ■ CancelUpdate   Cancels any changes made to the current record or to a new record prior to calling the Update method.
- ■ Clone   Creates a duplicate Recordset object from an existing Recordset object.
- ■ Close   Closes the open Recordset object and any dependent objects.
- ■ Delete   Deletes the current record in an open Recordset object or an object from a collection.
- ■ GetRows   Retrieves multiple records of a Recordset object into an array.
- ■ Move   Moves the position of the current record in a Recordset object.
- ■ MoveFirst   Moves to the first record in the Recordset object and makes that record the current record.
- ■ MoveLast   Moves to the last record in the Recordset object and makes that record the current record.
- ■ MoveNext   Moves to the next record in the Recordset object and makes that record the current record.
- ■ MovePrevious   Moves to the previous record in the Recordset object and makes that record the current record.
- ■ NextRecordset   Advances through a series of commands by clearing the current Recordset object and returns the next recordset.
- ■ Open   Opens a cursor.
- ■ Requery   Updates the data in a Recordset object by re-executing the query that is the basis of the object.
- ■ Resync   Refreshes the data in the current Recordset object from the underlying database.

■ Supports Determines whether a specified Recordset object supports a particular type of functionality.

■ Update Saves any changes you make to the current record of a Recordset object.

■ UpdateBatch Writes all pending batch updates to disk.

The Recordset object contains seventeen properties:

■ AbsolutePage Sets the "page" number on which the current record is located. Uses the PageSize property to logically divide the Recordset object into a series of pages, each of which has the number of records equal to PageSize. The provider must support the appropriate functionality for this property to be available.

■ AbsolutePosition Sets the ordinal position of a Recordset object's current record.

■ ActiveConnection Shows to which Connection object the specified Recordset object currently belongs.

■ BOF Shows that the current record position is before the first record in a Recordset object.

■ Bookmark Returns a bookmark that uniquely identifies the current record in a Recordset object or sets the current record in a Recordset object to the record identified by a valid bookmark.

■ CacheSize Shows the number of records from a Recordset object that are cached locally in memory.

■ CursorType Shows the type of cursor used in a Recordset object; for example, Read Only or Updatable.

■ EditMode Shows the editing status of the current record.

■ EOF Shows that the current record position is after the last record in a Recordset object.

■ Filter Shows a filter for data in a Recordset.

■ LockType Shows the type of locks placed on records during editing.

■ MaxRecords Shows the maximum number of records to return to a Recordset from a query.

■ PageCount Shows how many pages of data the Recordset object contains.

■ PageSize Shows how many records constitute one "page" in the Recordset.

■ RecordCount Shows the current number of records in a Recordset object.

■ Source Shows the source for the data in a Recordset object (Command object, SQL statement, table name, or stored procedure) or the name of the object or application that originally generated an error.

■ Status Shows the status of the current record with respect to batch updates or other bulk operations.

Listing 33.2 Continued

```
        </TR>
        <TR>
            <TD VALIGN=TOP>5</TD>
            <TD VALIGN=TOP>James                    </TD>
            <TD VALIGN=TOP>Monroe                   </TD>
        </TR>
    </TABLE>
    </BODY>
    </HTML>
```

First look at the line of VBScript that creates the Connection object:

```
Set Conn = Server.CreateObject("ADODB.Connection")
```

This creates a connection object on the server. Next, this line opens the connection object:

```
Conn.Open "DSN=PlatVB5;SERVER=SoftCoyote;UID=sa;PWD=password"
```

The Open method is called on the Connection object Conn and the parameters of the DSN, UserID, and password are passed. Next, the Recordset object is created by calling the Execute method on the Connection object. The SQL statement is passed as the parameter for this method.

```
Set RS = Conn.Execute("SELECT * FROM MyTable")
```

You now have a results set as a Recordset object at the Active Server. This Recordset object is complete with the Fields collections, which are used in VBScript that is used to create the table with the values.

The code in Listing 33.3 shows the VBScript that creates the table and manipulates the Recordset object's Fields collection to get the values.

Listing 33.3 Default.ASP Snippet—This VBScript Creates the Table in the Resulting HTML Page Sent to the Web Browser

```
<% Do While Not RS.EOF %>
    <TR>
    <% For i = 0 to RS.Fields.Count - 1 %>
        <TD VALIGN=TOP><% = RS(i) %></TD>
    <% Next %>
    </TR>
    <%
    RS.MoveNext
Loop
```

Finally, the Recordset and Connection objects are closed with the Close method.

```
RS.Close
Conn.Close
```

Adding a Record

To add a record to a table, you first need to collect the data that you want to add. This is done with an HTML form, the contents of which are shown in Listing 33.4.

On the CD

Listing 33.4 InsertRec.HTM—This HTML Form Collects the Data and Transmits It to the .ASP Page

```
<HTML>
<HEAD>
<META NAME="GENERATOR" Content="Microsoft Developer Studio">
<META HTTP-EQUIV="Content-Type" content="text/html; charset=iso-8859-1">
<TITLE>Document Title</TITLE>
</HEAD>
<BODY BGCOLOR="WHITE">
<FORM ACTION="InsertRec.ASP" METHOD=POST>
<TABLE>
    <TR>
        <TD> FIRST NAME </TD>
        <TD> LAST NAME </TD>
    </TR>
    <TR>
        <TD><INPUT TYPE=text SIZE="24" NAME=fname></TD>
        <TD><INPUT TYPE=text SIZE="24" NAME=lname></TD>
    </TR>
    <TR>
        <TD><INPUT TYPE=SUBMIT VALUE="Submit"></TD>
        <TD><INPUT TYPE=RESET VALUE="Reset"></TD>
    </TR>
</TABLE>
</BODY>
</HTML>
```

Part
VI

Ch

33

The INPUT tags create the two text boxes in which the data is entered. Figure 33.5 shows the Web page with the data ready to be submitted to the Active Server for insertion into the database. In Listing 33.10, notice the line of code:

```
<FORM ACTION="InsertRec.ASP" METHOD=POST>
```

This causes the page Insert.ASP to be called.

Figure 33.6 shows the results of the record being submitted. Two pieces of information have been placed on the form: first, a print of the SQL statement used to insert the record, and second, a message that indicates success.

FIG. 33.5
Click the Submit button to send the data to the server.

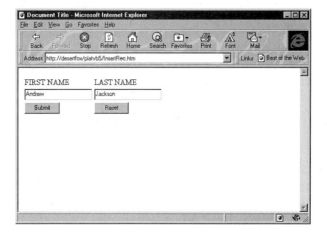

FIG. 33.6
Because there is no results set from an INSERT statement, a message will tell the user that the operation was successful.

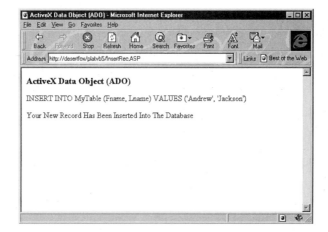

In Figure 33.7, you can see that the record was added to the database.

The contents of the .ASP page that performed the update appear in Listing 33.5.

FIG. 33.7

The table in the ASP page is dynamic and will list all records.

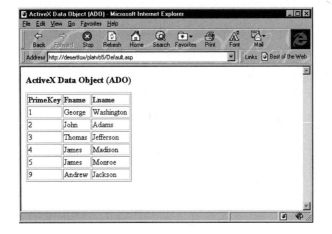

On the CD

Listing 33.5 InsertRec.ASP—The HTML and VBScript that Perform the Insert Operation

```
<%@ LANGUAGE="VBSCRIPT" %>

<HTML>
<HEAD>
<TITLE>ActiveX Data Object (ADO)</TITLE>
</HEAD>
<BODY BGCOLOR=#FFFFFF>
<H3>ActiveX Data Object (ADO)</H3>
<%
Set Conn = Server.CreateObject("ADODB.Connection")
Conn.Open "DSN=PlatVB5;SERVER=SoftCoyote;UID=sa;PWD=password"
%>
<%
Dim SQLState
%>
<%
SQLState = "INSERT INTO MyTable (Fname, Lname) VALUES ('"
%>
<%
SQLState = SQLState & Request.Form("fname")
%>
<%
SQLState = SQLstate & "', '"
%>
<%
SQLState = SQLState & Request.Form("lname")
%>
<%
SQLState = SQLstate & "')"
%>
<%
```

Part

VI

Ch

33

continues

Listing 33.5 Continued

```
Response.Write SQLState
%>
<%
Set RS = Conn.Execute(SQLState)
%>
<P>
Your New Record Has Been Inserted Into The Database
<%
Conn.Close
%>
</TABLE>
</BODY>
</HTML>
```

First the connection is opened, and then the SQL statement is built and executed. As you can see, ADO is very easy to use.

Creating a Non-Web ADO Example

When creating an example that will work in Visual Basic, you will find the syntax very much the same. Listing 33.6 is a simple VB program that opens a connection and creates a Recordset that can then be walked with the MoveNext and MoveFirst methods.

Listing 33.6 PlatVB_5_28_1.FRM—The Visual Basic Code Required for a Simple ADO Connection

```
Option Explicit
Dim RS As Recordset

Public Sub Command1_Click()
    RS.MoveFirst
    Text1.Text = RS.Fields(1)
    Text2.Text = RS.Fields(2)
End Sub

Private Sub Command3_Click()
    RS.MoveNext
    Text1.Text = RS.Fields(1)
    Text2.Text = RS.Fields(2)
End Sub

Public Sub Form_Load()
    Dim conn As ADODB.Connection
    Set conn = CreateObject("ADODB.Connection")
    conn.Open "DSN=PlatVB5;SERVER=SoftCoyote;UID=sa;PWD=password"
    Set RS = conn.Execute("SELECT * FROM MyTable")
    Text1.Text = RS.Fields(1)
    Text2.Text = RS.Fields(2)
End Sub
```

Notice that the following three lines of code are virtually identical with the Web example:

```
Set conn = CreateObject("ADODB.Connection")
conn.Open "DSN=PlatVB5;SERVER=SoftCoyote;UID=sa;PWD=password"
Set RS = conn.Execute("SELECT * FROM MyTable")
```

The only difference is the Server object in the first line before the `CreateObject` method is called. Figure 33.8 shows the VB program with the command buttons used for walking the results set.

FIG. 33.8

This example uses the same database and DSN as the Web example.

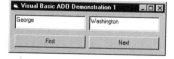

From Here...

In this chapter, you have explored the ActiveX Data Objects. The ADO provide a simple, powerful, and flexible interface to relational databases through the use of an ODBC DSN. Exploring the following chapters will provide further insight into some of the issues involved with database and client/server development. Mastery of database access is one of the most important skills that a programmer can possess:

- Chapter 28, "Building Database Applications," explores the considerations that relate to applications when a database is employed.
- Chapter 31, "Improving Data Access with Data Access Objects (DAO)," examines the use of the Data Access Objects and the Jet.
- Chapter 32, "Using Remote Data Objects (RDO)," reviews the Remote Data Objects, which are a direct ancestor of ADO and share a very similar syntax.
- Chapter 35, "Internet Programming with VBScript," delves into the scripting version of Visual Basic and shows what a powerhouse it is for use on the Web.
- Chapter 36, "Programming Web Pages," explores the techniques of integrating scripting with HTML and ActiveX Controls and components.
- Chapter 37, "Creating Active Server Pages," examines the powerful, browser-independent world of Active Server Pages.
- Chapter 38, "Working with Active Server Page Objects," reviews the Active Server Page Object Model.
- Chapter 39, "Using the Web, Databases, and Visual Basic," puts all of the information together for use in creating powerful Web pages.

Part
VI

Ch
33

- Chapter 40, "Programming Web Functionality into Your Applications," reviews the use of three Microsoft ActiveX controls for use with the Web: the Winsock Control, the Internet Transfer Control, and the WebBrowser Control.

- Chapter 41, "Using Visual Basic in a Client/Server Environment," explores the Client/Server paradigm and techniques in depth.

CHAPTER 34

Multiuser Databases

In preceding chapters, you learned several aspects of database programming, particularly how to develop an application that would be used by a single user on a stand-alone PC. However, many of today's database applications must be written for a network environment, where multiple users will be reading, modifying, deleting, and adding to the data in the database. This type of application presents an additional set of challenges for you as a database developer.

Controlling users' access to the database

For many programs, you want users to be able to access only certain parts of the database.

Using Jet engine security features

Jet has built-in security that you can use to prevent users from accessing sensitive information.

Using locking to keep one user from changing a record while another user is using it

Record-locking schemes keep multiple users from changing the same record at the same time.

Maintaining application performance with multiple users

Many applications slow down when they are distributed across a network, but there are ways you can enhance performance.

Dealing with some common database errors

Because database errors can occur, you need to know what they are so you can deal with them.

Replicating the database and synchronizing multiple database copies

Using replication places the burden of keeping multiple copies of the data on the database engine.

N O T E The examples in this chapter are tailored to a PC-level database, specifically the Jet
database engine. A client/server environment, such as SQL Server, would handle all of
these issues in a different (and usually better) manner. ▪

In addition to multiple users accessing a single database, we will also look at how the multi-user concept works if each user has a separate copy of the database. The Jet engine has special database replication features designed to handle this.

The main considerations involved in multi-user program development are the following:

- Database access
- Database security
- Data currency
- Record-locking to prevent simultaneous update attempts
- Application performance

Even if you don't develop applications for a network environment, you still need to be aware of some multiuser considerations. In Windows or any other multitasking environment, two programs on the same machine can try to access the same data. As an example, consider a PC monitoring a manufacturing process. One program can receive the process data from instruments and store the data in a database. Another program can then generate reports on the data or modify erroneous or abnormal data points. Although the same user can run both programs on the same machine, the two programs appear to the database to be multiple users of the data.

Determining the multiuser needs of the application is part of the design process. And, as with other aspects of programming, a good design helps tremendously in producing a good and efficient application. ▪

Controlling Data Access

Controlling data access involves placing restrictions on part or all of a database. Data access restrictions can be put in place as either user restrictions or function restrictions.

You need user restrictions when you want to prevent certain people (or, as a corollary, to allow only certain people) from looking at sensitive information. An example is a payroll system, in which most people can view the names of employees, but only a select few can see or modify the actual pay information. These restrictions are usually handled through user IDs and passwords and are the basis of data security.

Function restrictions, on the other hand, place limits on specific parts of a program, regardless of who the user is. An example is opening a price table in read-only mode in an order-entry system. You add function restrictions so that a user cannot inadvertently change the price of an item while processing an order.

You can handle the restrictions in an application in two ways: using *programmatic controls* or using *database engine controls*. A programmatic control is one that you put into the application itself. Engine-level controls restrict any program trying to access the information in the database.

Using a Database Exclusively

The most restrictive limit that you can place on a database is to open it exclusively. This limit prevents any other user or program from gaining access to any information in the database while it is in use. Because this method is so restrictive, you should use it only for operations that affect the entire database. These operations include the following:

- Compacting a database
- Updating entire tables (for example, using the UPDATE query)
- Changing the structure of the database by adding or deleting tables, fields, or indexes
- Handling special user needs, such as posting accounting information

Within a program, you can open a database exclusively using the options portion of the Data Access Object OpenDatabase method, as shown in the following code:

```
Dim db  As Database
Set db = DBEngine.Workspaces(0).OpenDatabase("D:\VB5\BIBLIO.MDB", True, False)
```

If the database is not in use, it opens and no one else can access it until it is closed again. If the database is in use, an error is returned. (Handling errors is discussed later in this chapter in the section "Handling Errors and Conflicts.")

Denying Table Access to Others

In addition to opening the database exclusively, you can also open recordsets exclusively. This is a less restrictive way to lock part of a database. When you create a recordset, you can deny other users or programs access to the table being used by your program function. You can do so by using the options of the OpenRecordset method to deny read or write access to the information with which you will be working. Similarly, you can deny write access to the information in a dynaset-type recordset by using the options of the OpenRecordset method.

> **CAUTION**
>
> When you use the Deny options on a recordset created from multiple tables, other users are restricted from the base tables used to create the recordset.

You should use these options, as with exclusive access, only for administrative functions, when you don't want others viewing or updating any of the table's information during the process.

Using the Deny Read Option (*dbDenyRead*)   The dbDenyRead option for the OpenRecordset method prevents other users from looking at the data in the affected table until you close the table. You use this option if you need to update information in the entire table, such as a global price increase. The following code shows the use of this option:

```
Dim tblMain As Recordset
Set tblMain = db.OpenRecordset("Titles", dbOpenTable, dbDenyRead)
```

Part

VI

Ch

34

N O T E   The dbDenyRead option is available only for table type recordsets. You cannot use it with dynasets or snapshots. ■

Using the Deny Write Option (*dbDenyWrite*)   The dbDenyWrite option used in the OpenRecordset method also restricts other users' access to information. In this case, however, the users can view but not update information in the affected table or tables. Again, other users' access is restricted only until you close the recordset. You might use the dbDenyWrite option if you're inserting new records into a table but not making changes to existing records. The dbDenyWrite option is available for both table- and dynaset-type recordsets. Listing 34.1 shows the use of the dbDenyWrite option for the two functions.

Listing 34.1   Use *dbDenyWrite* to Prevent Others from Updating Tables While You Are Working with Them

```
Dim tblTitles As Recordset
Dim rsAuthors As Recordset
Dim sSQL As String

' Open a table with the dbDenyWrite option.
Set tblTitles = db.OpenRecordset("Titles", dbOpenTable, dbDenyWrite)

' Create a Recordset with the dbDenyWrite option.
sSQL = "Select * From Authors"
Set rsAuthors = db.OpenRecordset(sSQL, dbOpenDynaset, dbDenyWrite)
```

Using the deny options does not restrict other users' access to information in the database all the time. They are denied access only if they attempt to open a table while you are using it with one of the options in effect. In other words, this is not really a security feature but a way to manage multiple updates to the database.

Using Read-Only Tables

Often you might have functions in your applications that have data you don't want the users to be able to modify at any time. You might also have some tables that you want only certain people to modify. In these cases, you can open a table or recordset in read-only mode, or you can use a snapshot-type recordset.

Using Lookup Tables   One example of a read-only table is a lookup table. A *lookup table* contains reference information that is necessary for the users to see but that the users do not need to change. For instance, your application might use a ZIP Code table for a mailing list application or a price table for an order-entry system. In either of these cases, you open the table in read-only mode using the options shown in Listing 34.2. Unlike the deny options, the read-only option does not restrict other users' access to the information.

> **Listing 34.2 Use the Read-Only Option to Prevent Users from Modifying Data**
>
> ```
> Dim rsPubs As Recordset
> Set rsPubs = db.OpenRecordset("Publishers", dbOpenTable, dbReadOnly)
> ```

N O T E You can open an entire database in read-only mode by setting the `ReadOnly` parameter of the `OpenDatabase` method to `True`. ▦

Using Snapshots   Another way to restrict a program function to read-only is to use a snapshot-type recordset. Jet engine snapshots are always read-only. You can use a snapshot when data in the base tables is not being changed frequently by others or when a point-in-time look at the data is sufficient. Snapshots are usually used for reporting functions. An advantage to using snapshots is that they are stored in memory. Therefore, some operations using snapshots are faster than the same operations using tables or dynasets. However, because of the memory requirements for a snapshot and the time that it takes to load the data into memory, snapshots are best used for queries that return fewer than 200 records.

Restricting Specific Users   Finally, you might have occasion to want to restrict certain users to read-only access, no matter what program functions they are performing. You can do so only through the Jet security system. These security features are described later in this chapter in the section "Exploring Jet Security Features."

Understanding Record-Locking Schemes

The features described in the preceding section place restrictions on an entire table or even the entire database. In this section, we discuss locking the database at the record level. One of the main considerations in multiuser programming is assuring that a record is not in use by another user at the same time that you are trying to update it. You do so through the use of record locks. A *record lock* temporarily limits the access of other users to a specific record or group of records.

In a typical application, a record lock is set while a user updates the data in the record and then is released after the update is completed. As the developer, you must take into account the following considerations in the use of record locks:

- What to do if the record cannot be locked (for example, if another user is already accessing the record)
- How to prevent a user from keeping a record locked for too long
- Whether to lock the record when the user first accesses it or only when the changes are being written to the database

How you handle these considerations has an impact on many aspects of the application development. Therefore, you should address these issues as much as possible in the design phase of the application.

Part
VI

Ch
34

Page-Locking versus Record-Locking

The Jet engine does not support true record-locking. In record-locking, only the individual record currently being accessed by the user is locked. Instead, Jet uses a page-locking scheme. Jet reads data in pages of 2K (2,048 bytes). When it places a lock on a record, it locks the entire page containing the record.

In this locking scheme, multiple records are locked each time a lock is issued. The number of records locked depends on the size of each record. For example, suppose each record in a sample table is 230 bytes long. Nine records therefore are locked each time. On the other hand, if the table has records that are only 30 bytes long, each record lock affects 68 records.

When a page is locked by one user, another user cannot modify any records on that page (although the second user can read the records). This is true even if the first user is working with only one of the records. This aspect of page-locking requires you to be even more careful in the application of record locks, because it increases the chances of a conflict between users.

Visual Basic has no commands to specifically request a record lock. Instead, the record locks are automatically created and released when the Add, Edit, and Update methods are used. Visual Basic supports two locking schemes: pessimistic and optimistic.

Pessimistic Locking

Pessimistic locking locks the page containing a record as soon as the Edit method is used on that record. The lock on the page is released when the Update method is used and the data is written to the file. The advantage of this approach is that it prevents other users from changing the data in a record while one user is editing it. The disadvantage is that it keeps the record locked for a longer period of time. In the worst case, a user could open a record for editing, place a lock on it, and then head out to lunch. This lock would keep other users from editing that record, or any others on the same page, for a long time.

N O T E   To prevent locks from being held too long, you can put a timer in your code that releases the record after a specified period of inactivity. You would do this by placing code in the Timer event of the Timer control. This code would use the Idle method of the database engine as shown in the following line of code:

```
DBEngine.Idle dbFreeLocks
```

Optimistic Locking

Optimistic locking locks the page containing a record only when the Update method is invoked. The lock on the page is immediately released when the update operation is completed. The advantage of optimistic locking is that the lock is on the page for only a short period of time, reducing the chance that another user might try to access the same data page while the lock is in place. The disadvantage is that another user can change the data in the record between the time the Edit and Update methods are used. If the data has changed in that time period, VB issues an error message.

Which Locking Method to Use and When

For most database applications, optimistic locking is the better choice of the two methods. The probability that someone else will change or delete the record you are working on is less than the probability that someone will try to access a record on the page that you have locked. If, however, you have an application in which many users are accessing and editing records simultaneously, you might want to use pessimistic locking to ensure that the record is not changed while you are performing your edits. In this case, you should put some method in place to limit the time that the record is locked.

Pessimistic locking is the default record-locking scheme used by Visual Basic. To set the method of record-locking, you must set the LockEdits property of the table or dynaset with which you are working. Setting the property to True gives you pessimistic locking. Setting the property to False yields optimistic locking. Listing 34.3 shows how to set the LockEdits property for pessimistic and optimistic locking, respectively.

Listing 34.3   Set the Recordset's *LockEdits* Property to Choose How Record-Locking Works

```
Dim rsTemp As Recordset

'Set the locking method to pessimistic
rsTemp.LockEdits = True

'Set the locking method to optimistic
rsTemp.LockEdits = False
```

Releasing Locks

As stated previously, the record locks are released automatically when the Update method has completed. However, releasing record locks is a background process, and sometimes other activities are occurring so rapidly that the database does not have time to catch up. If you are developing a data-entry-intensive program, you might need to pause the processing in the application momentarily. You can do so by using the Idle method of the database engine.

The Idle method pauses the application and allows the database engine to catch up on its housekeeping work. The following line shows the syntax of the Idle method:

```
DBEngine.Idle dbFreeLocks
```

Using the Data Control

Because the data control uses tables or dynasets (the default) as its record source, the same locking schemes mentioned previously are used with the data control. Pessimistic locking is the default; therefore, as each record is accessed, the data control automatically performs the Edit method, which in turn automatically locks the record's page. When you move from one record to another, the lock on the current record is released by the Update method, and a lock is placed on the next record by the `Edit` method. In a multiuser system in which you want to use optimistic locking, you need to change the locking scheme of the data control. You do so by adding a `LockEdits` statement, as shown in Listing 34.3, to the `Activate` event of the form containing the data control.

> **CAUTION**
>
> You must be careful when using transactions in a multiuser environment. Any record locks that are set by the `Edit` or `Update` method are not released until the transaction is committed or rolled back. Therefore, keeping transactions as short as possible is best so that you can avoid having a large number of records locked for a long period of time. In addition, you should be careful when using cascaded updates or deletes because they create more transactions and, therefore, more locks.

Exploring Jet Security Features

Another consideration of multiuser database programming is database security. Because a network environment can allow other people access to your database file, you might want to use methods to prevent them from viewing specific information in your database or possibly prevent them from viewing any of the information.

The Jet engine provides a database security model based on user IDs and passwords. In this model, you can assign to individual users or groups of users permissions to the entire database or any parts of the database. As each user is added to the security file, you must assign him or her to one or more user groups. That user then inherits the permissions of that group. In addition, you can assign other permissions to the user.

If you're working with a secured database, you must perform the following three steps to gain access to the database from your VB program:

- Determine the location of the system database. (The system database is a separate file that stores your security settings.) The default install sets it up as SYSTEM.MDW in the \Windows\System directory.

- Set the `IniPath` or `SystemDB` property of the database engine to tell the program where the system database is located. (Note that for 32-bit operating systems, the location of the system database is in the Registry, not an INI file.)

- Use the `CreateWorkspace` method with the workspace name, user ID, and user password specified to create a workspace to contain the database.

The syntax for each of these statements is shown in Listing 34.4.

Listing 34.4 · Gaining Access to a Secured Database

```
Dim wsTemp As Workspace

    DBEngine.SystemDB = "C:\Windows\System\System.mdw"
```

```
Set wsTemp = DBEngine.CreateWorkspace("MYWSPACE", "MyName", "MyPassword", _
    dbUseJet)
```

For the preceding code to work, the user name and password must be set in the system database first. To do this, read the section "Setting Up the Security System" later in this chapter. By default, the SYSTEM.MDW contains an administrator account whose username is admin with no password.

Database Permissions

Within the Jet security system, you can set two database-level permissions: Run/Open and Open Exclusive. The Run/Open permission is required for anyone who needs access to the database. Without this permission, a user cannot open a database for any function. The Open Exclusive permission allows users to open a database exclusively, as described previously. You should give this permission only to administrative users. Otherwise, another user of an application might inadvertently lock everyone else out of the database until he closes it.

Table Permissions

Although database permissions affect the entire database (and every table in it), you often need finer control over access to individual tables. Using the Jet engine, you can set table-level permissions for any table in a database. As with the database permissions, the table permissions can be assigned to individual users or groups of users. The following seven table-level permissions are available with the Jet engine:

- *Read Design*   Enables the user to view the structure of the table
- *Modify Design*   Enables the user to change the structure of the table
- *Administer*   Gives the user full control over the table
- *Read Data*   Enables the user to read information from the table but not to make any changes
- *Modify Data*   Enables the user to modify existing data but not to add or delete data
- *Insert Data*   Enables the user to add new data to the table
- *Delete Data*   Enables the user to remove data from the table

With the Read and Modify Design permissions, the user can work with the structure of the table. The Administer permission gives a user full access to a table, including table-deletion capabilities. The four Data permissions control the type of access a user has to the actual data in the table. You can assign these permissions by table, and you can grant different users different access rights to each table. For the constants used to set permissions, see "Permissions Property" in the help file.

Setting Up the Security System

Visual Basic has no means of creating the system database file needed for the security system. You can create this file using only Microsoft Access. Access also provides the easiest means of establishing and modifying user IDs and setting database and table permissions. However, after the file exists, you can use VB code to create new user IDs, assign users to existing groups, and delete users as described in the following list:

- To add a new user, you create the user object by specifying the user name, user ID, and password. You then append the new user to the workspace. This procedure adds the new user to the system database that was in use when the workspace was created.

- To add a user to an existing user group, you create the user object and then add the user to the Groups collection.

- To delete a user, you use the delete method for the Users collection of the workspace.

Each of these activities is shown in Listing 34.5.

Listing 34.5   Performing Security System Maintenance from Visual Basic

```
Dim wsTemp As Workspace
Dim NewUser As User
Dim NewGrp As Group

'Add a new user to the system database
DBEngine.SystemDB = "C:\Windows\System\System.mdw"
Set wsTemp = DBEngine.Workspaces(0)
Set NewUser = wsTemp.CreateUser("BSILER", "12345", "PASSWORD")

'Add the user to the "Users" group
wsTemp.Groups("Users").Users.Append NewUser

'Delete the user from the system database
wsTemp.Users.Delete "BSILER"
```

Encryption

In addition to the security system, the Jet engine provides a means of encrypting a database that you create. *Encryption* is a method of disguising the data in a database so that someone using a disk-editing program cannot view the contents of the database. You can specify encryption when first creating the database by using the options portion of the CreateDatabase function. After a database has been created, you can add or remove encryption by using the CompactDatabase function. The use of these functions for encrypting data is shown in Listing 34.6.

Listing 34.6   Adding Encryption to Your Database

```
'Create an encrypted database
   Dim dbNew As Database
   Set dbNew = DBEngine.Workspaces(0).CreateDatabase("D:\TEST.MDB",_
        dbLangGeneral, dbEncrypt)
```

```
'Encrypt an existing database
DBEngine.CompactDatabase "D:\TEST.MDB", "D:\TEST2.MDB", , dbEncrypt

'Remove encryption from a database
DBEngine.CompactDatabase "D:\TEST2.MDB", "D:\TEST3.MDB", , dbDecrypt
```

The encryption method used by the Jet engine encrypts the entire database, including table definitions and queries. Also, the encryption results in a performance degradation of about 10 to 15 percent.

For some applications, you might want to encrypt only a portion of the data. For instance, in a payroll system, you might need to encrypt only the actual pay rates, not the entire database. Although no built-in method is available for this type of encryption, you can create your own encryption schemes for these situations.

As an example, a simple encryption scheme for numeric data is to convert each digit (including leading and trailing zeroes) to a character, invert the character string, and then store the data as text. In this way, the number 2534.75 can be stored as EGDCEB. Although this type of encryption is by no means foolproof, it does provide some data security from casual lookers.

Application Passwords

In addition to, or in place of, the security built into the database, you also can choose to put a user ID and password system into your application. With an application-level system, you control the type of access people have to the functions of your application. The drawback to this approach is that someone could access your database by using another program. However, this type of security is fairly easy to implement. Visual Basic even includes a form template for a login box.

Using Network Security

Finally, most network operating systems have their own security system built in. Many of these systems are quite good and can prevent unauthorized users from even knowing that the database exists. For example, the path on the file server containing the database could simply be restricted from unauthorized users. This might be the easiest way to secure your database, because it would involve no programming. To determine the capabilities of your network's security system, refer to your network program manuals or contact your network administrator.

Part
VI

Ch

34

Maintaining Data Currency

Currency of the data is a big issue in multiuser applications, especially those that handle a high volume of data entry and modification. Maintaining currency refers to making sure that the data at which you are looking is the most up-to-date information available. The data you're working with becomes noncurrent if another user changes or deletes the records since you retrieved them. Additionally, your recordset might be noncurrent if other users have added records since you retrieved data.

Using Only Tables

The only way to be sure that your data is always the most current is to work exclusively with tables. Only a table immediately reflects changes, additions, or deletions made by other users. If your application or function works with only one table, using the table instead of a dynaset is probably the best way to go. If your application must work with multiple tables, the drawback to using just the tables is that you have to maintain the table relationships instead of using a dynaset to do it. To decide whether to use tables or dynasets, you must determine the probability that your data will not be current, the consequences of having noncurrent data, and the effort involved in maintaining the table relationships. Weighing these three factors will help you decide which access method is best.

Requerying a Dynaset

If you need to work with a dynaset-type recordset in a multiuser application, you can use the `Requery` method to make it current with the database. The `Requery` method, shown here, basically re-executes the SQL query:

```
rsTemp.Requery
```

You can requery a dynaset only a limited number of times. Therefore, after several requeries, you should close the dynaset and re-create it completely.

> **NOTE** Depending on how the recordset was created, the `Requery` method might or might not be available. You should check the `Restartable` property of the recordset to verify that it supports the `Requery` operation. ▪

Probing Performance Considerations

The performance of your multiuser application is dependent on, among other things, the type of network, the number of users, and the size of the databases with which you're working. At best, with you as the only user attached to a server, the data-transfer rates across a network are a lot slower than from your local hard drive. This means that you have to work harder in a network environment to keep the performance of your application crisp. In the following sections, I list some ideas for helping the performance of your application.

Keep Recordsets Small

The trick to keeping your recordsets small is to make your queries as specific as possible. This way, you can avoid repeatedly reading data across the network as you move through the records. For example, consider the "Titles" table in the BIBLIO.MDB sample database. Suppose you wanted to print a list of all the titles in the table. One way to do this would be to open a recordset as follows:

```
sSQL = "Select * From Titles"
Set rs = db.OpenRecordset(sSQL, dbOpenDynaset)
rs.MoveFirst
```

```
    While Not rs.EOF
        Print rs.Fields("Title")
        rs.MoveNext
Wend
```

However, note that the SQL statement brings back all the fields for each record. Because you only care about the Title field, a better SQL statement would be

```
sSQL = "Select Title From Titles"
```

Copy a Database or Table to a Local Drive

If you have a database that is used for lookup purposes, such as a ZIP Code database, you can make a copy of the database on your local drive. This approach improves the speed of access during searches and queries. For example, the following code copies a database to your drive if the network copy is newer:

```
    Dim sLocalMDB As String
    Dim sNetMDB As String

    sLocalMDB = "C:\ZIPCODES.MDB"
    sNetMDB = "\\MYSERVER\MYPATH\ZIPCODES.MDB"

    'Make sure your copy of the database
    'is closed before attempting this.
    If FileDateTime(sNetMDB) > FileDateTime(sLocalMDB) Then
        FileCopy sNetMDB, sLocalMDB
End If
```

For other databases that might change only occasionally (such as a price database), you might consider making the changes at a time when no one else is using the database. That way, the data is always static to the users of the system. In other words, do your data maintenance at night.

Use Snapshot-Type Recordsets Where Possible

Because snapshots are read-only copies of the data stored in memory, they access the network only when the snapshots are created. Therefore, if you don't need to make changes to the data, use a snapshot—but only if the recordset is small. A large snapshot can choke your memory and resources in a hurry.

Use Transactions for Processing Updates

Each time an update is issued, data is written to the database, requiring a disk write—that is, unless transaction processing is used. All the updates between a `BeginTrans` and a `CommitTrans` are stored in memory until the transaction is committed. At that time, all the updates are processed at once. This approach cuts down on the amount of writes being performed across the network. However, you should be careful not to allow too many updates to stack up at one time because of the record-locking concerns described earlier.

Using Database Replication to Handle Multiple Users

Although database replication might not be multiuser in the strictest sense of the concept (multiple users accessing the same database at the same time), you can use this process to handle a number of situations in which multiple users need to work with a database. The most easily visualized of these situations is one in which a sales force in different locations works with a common database and then sends information back to a central site where summary reports are developed.

With database replication, each person can work with a copy of the data in a database. Then, at certain times, the individual databases are recombined with the master database. At the same time that the data from the replica databases is passed back to the master database, any structure changes made to the master can be passed to the replicas.

You also can use database replication to create a read-only copy of a database for a user. You do so to make a complete copy of a network database on a user's local machine. You can use this approach to speed up the processing of large reports or queries when the user has no need to modify the base information.

Managing database replication involves four basic steps:

1. Making a database replicable (that is, capable of being replicated)
2. Making copies (replicas) of the database
3. Periodically synchronizing the copies of the database
4. Handling synchronization conflicts

N O T E   Database replication features are available only for Jet version 3.0 or later databases. ▪

Making a Replicable Database

To create a database that can be replicated, you must use a user-special, user-defined property of the database—the `Replicable` property.

N O T E   User-defined properties were first introduced in Visual Basic 4. Using these properties, you can add properties to a database, `Querydef`, table, index, or field object of your database. User-defined data objects are described in detail in Chapter 31, "Improving Data Access with Data Access Objects(DAO)." ▪

Making a database replicable requires only a few lines of code and a single user-defined property, as shown in the following code example. This property is a text property with the name `Replicable` and a value of `T`:

```
Dim RepProp As Property
Set OldDb = OldWs.OpenDatabase(DataName, True)
```

```
Set RepProp = OldDb.CreateProperty()
RepProp.Name = "Replicable"
RepProp.Type = dbText
RepProp.Value = "T"
OldDb.Properties.Append RepProp
OldDb.Close
```

> **N O T E** A database must be opened exclusively in order to make it replicable. ▪

Making Copies of the Database

After you change your database so that it can be replicated, you should make copies of the database to give to the various users. You do so by using the MakeReplica method of the database object, which is shown in the following code:

```
'(dbMaster is a database that has been opened previously)
dbMaster.MakeReplica "E:\REPLTEST\REPLICA2.MDB", "Copy Number 2"
```

With the MakeReplica method, you supply a name and description for the database copy. There also is a third optional parameter that indicates whether the copy should be read-only. If you want the copy to be read-only, use the constant dbRepMakeReadOnly as the third argument. Another constant, dbRepMakePartial, is used to copy only some of the data to the replica. In the sales force example, this would be useful to provide each mobile person with the information for their region only, which would then be synchronized back into the "master" database. The help file has details on how to determine which information goes into a partial replica.

Putting the Database Back Together

Finally, after making changes to the master database or one or more of the replicas, you should make the data and structure consistent between all the databases by using the Synchronize method. This method synchronizes the data between two databases. You define one of the databases as the database object, which is running the Synchronize method. You specify the other database (defined by its path and file name) as an argument of the method. The data exchange between the files can be one of the following three types as defined by the constants shown in parentheses:

- ▪ *Export*   Changes are passed from the current database object to the target file (dbRepExportChanges).
- ▪ *Import*   Changes are received by the current database object from the target database (dbRepImportChanges).
- ▪ *Bidirectional*   Changes are made in both directions (dbRepImExpChanges).

> **N O T E** A fourth option, dbRepSyncInternet, is available in the Office 97 developer edition. ▪

Part
VI

Ch

34

The `Synchronize` method is shown in the following code:

```
Set OldDb = OldWs.OpenDatabase(DataName)
OldDb.Synchronize "E:\REPLTEST\REPLICA2.MDB", dbRepImportChanges
OldDb.Close
```

Handling Errors and Conflicts

In a multiuser application, errors are triggered when you attempt to open a table or update a record that is locked by another user. These errors can be trapped by your code, and appropriate steps can be taken to either retry the operation or exit the application gracefully. In the following sections, you look at these errors in three major groups:

- Database- and table-locking errors
- Record-locking errors
- Permission errors
- Synchronization conflicts

The way to handle most errors that occur when trying to lock a table, database, or record is to wait for a few seconds and then try the operation again. Unless the other user who has the record locked maintains the lock for a long time, this method will work. In an interactive environment, I usually give the user the choice of retrying or aborting the operation.

Database- and Table-Locking Errors Database- or table-locking errors occur when you try to access information that is currently locked or in use by another user. These errors occur either when you try to open the database or table, or when you try to lock them. When the errors occur, you need to wait until the other user has released the lock or quit using the recordset. Table 34.1 lists the error numbers and when they occur.

Table 34.1 Locking Errors that Apply to Tables and Databases

Error Number	Error Occurs When
3008	You attempt to open a table that is exclusively opened by another user.
3009	You attempt to lock a table that is in use by another user.
3211	Same as 3009
3212	Same as 3009, except that this error provides information about the user and machine using the table.

Each of these errors can be handled as described previously, with a choice by the user to abort or retry the operation.

Record-Locking Errors Record-locking errors occur when you try to add, update, or delete records on a page locked by another user. Depending on the type of locking you use, the error can occur either when you use the `Edit` method (pessimistic locking) or when you use the `Update` method (optimistic locking). To determine which locking method is in effect when the error occurs, you can check the `LockEdits` property of the recordset you are attempting to lock by using the routine shown in Listing 34.7. Then, if you choose to retry the operation, you can re-execute the correct method.

Listing 34.7   Determine Which Locking Method Is in Effect When an Error Occurs

```
'****************************************
'Determine the type of locking being used
'****************************************
If NewDyn.LockEdits Then
'********************************
'If pessimistic locking, retry Edit
'********************************
   NewDyn.Edit
Else
'********************************
'If optimistic locking, retry Update
'********************************
   NewDyn.Update
End If
```

Most of the record errors pertain to problems encountered while locking the record. However, one error requires special handling. This error (3197) occurs when a user attempts to update a record that has already been changed by another user. This error occurs only when optimistic locking is in effect. When it occurs, you need to present your user with the choices of "Make the new changes anyway" or "Keep the changes made by the other user." Showing the other user's changes also is beneficial. If the user decides to make the changes anyway, he or she can execute the `Update` method a second time to make the changes.

Several other errors might occur when you attempt to lock a record. Table 34.2 lists the error numbers for these errors and when they occur.

Table 34.2   Other Record-Locking Errors

Error Number	Cause
3046	You attempt to save a record locked by another user.
3158	You attempt to save a record locked by another user.
3186	You attempt to save a record locked by another user. The message gives the name of the user who placed the lock.
3187	You attempt to read a record locked by another user.
3188	You attempt to update a record that another program on your machine already has locked.
3189	You attempt to access a table that another user has exclusively locked.

continues

Table 34.2   Continued

Error Number	Cause
3218	You attempt to update a locked record.
3260	You attempt to save a record locked by another user. The message gives the name of the user who placed the lock.

Permission Errors   The other major group of errors is permission errors. These errors occur when the Jet security is in operation and the current user does not have the appropriate permission to perform the operation. The only way to handle these errors is to inform the user of the error and abort the operation. Table 34.3 summarizes the permission errors.

Table 34.3   Permission Errors that Occur When a User Does Not Have the Appropriate Rights for an Operation

Error Number	Permission Required
3107	Insert
3108	Update
3109	Delete
3110	Read Definitions
3111	Create
3112	Read

Handling Synchronization Conflicts   One type of error occurs when you attempt to synchronize incompatible databases. When you use Jet's replication and synchronization features, you are essentially working with a set of databases—a master database and a bunch of replicas. When a replica is created with the MakeReplica method, it is given a unique ID. This ID is stored in the ReplicaID property of the database. Similarly, there is a property called DesignMasterID which identifies one of the databases as having the database design upon which all replicas are based. Together these IDs identify a *replica set*. If you attempt to synchronize across different sets, an error will occur.

Other types of errors that occur are due more to data conflicts than errors in the synchronization process. In the sales force example, suppose there are only two salespeople, each with his own database replica. Let's say the database includes a table that lists customers along with a field called LastVisitDate, which represents the last time any salesperson visited the customer. If synchronization is performed after each visit, conflicts won't occur and the LastVisitDate field will be the same in both replicas. However, suppose our entire sales force visits the same customer and then attempts to synchronize their databases. Which salesman's LastVisitDate field will be propagated to both databases?

The answer is neither. Resolving conflicts like this must be handled by your program code. This makes sense, because Visual Basic cannot be expected to know that the later of the two dates is the logical choice for this database. What Jet does do, however, is give you all the information necessary to resolve a conflict. It does this by creating a new table, the *conflict table*, and placing the conflicting record(s) in it. Your program can then look at the records and make a decision to overwrite the existing one. In our fictional situation, we would simply take the later of the two dates.

Both types of synchronization errors discussed in the preceding can be avoided with better database design. For example, if our sales force of two had a third database located at the sales company, each salesperson could synchronize with that database rather than with each other.

From Here...

As you can see, many more design considerations are involved in creating a multiuser application than in a single-user application. This process is made even more difficult by the fact that each multiuser situation is different, in terms of hardware and network software used, the number of users of the system, and the functional requirements of the individual application. The intent of this chapter was not to provide specific solutions but to make you aware of the challenges involved in multiuser programming and some of the tools available in Visual Basic to help you meet the challenges. Refer to the following chapter for more information:

- See Chapter 28, "Building Database Applications," to learn about general database design considerations.

On the CD

- See "Building Security into Your Applications," on the CD-ROM, for more information on how you can build secure databases and tables within your applications.

Part
VI

Ch
34

Web Programming

CHAPTER 35

Internet Programming with VBScript

HTML elements provide a rich and compelling way for users to interact with Web sites. Sites that can accept user input and provide visual and aural experiences are fast becoming the most popular stops on the Information SuperHighway. HTML elements combined with VBScript allow users to extend the scope and functionality of Web Pages to include a higher degree of interactivity and control than was previously possible without incurring a lot of client/server transactional overhead. And, when you use VBScript to bring life into your site, you build upon skills you have already developed from previous experience programming with Visual Basic. In this chapter, you learn how VBScript can be used to bring a new dimension to a two-dimensional Web site. ■

Interactive Web pages

Change a static Web page into an interactive, dynamic page by using VBScript and the Internet Explorer Object Model.

HTML Form Elements

Leverage your knowledge of the Visual Basic standard controls to use the HTML 3.0 Form Elements.

Microsoft Forms Intrinsic Controls

Go beyond the HTML form elements with the Internet Explorer Intrinsic Controls.

Writing procedures in VBScript

Enhance and extend your VBScript with event handlers and user-defined Subs and Functions.

Understanding the HTML *<FORM>* Elements

The original purpose of an HTML form was to collect and organize data to be used by the Internet Server. Over time HTML forms have evolved far beyond that original purpose. Although you can still use HTML forms to do standard CGI-based, client/server, and Web-based interactions over the Internet, with the help of a scripting language such as JavaScript or VBScript, you can also use them to analyze and process data on the client side. Thus, you reduce the transactional burdens you place on your server-side programming, making your code more concise and robust.

N O T E *CGI* The *Common Gateway Interface* is a specification that defines a set of standards by which data enters and leaves an Internet server consistently and predictably. Originally developed for the UNIX environment, CGI is used for Internet-based data processing and decision-making routines such as queries and lookups. Programs that do this sort of server-side processing are called *CGI scripts*. Usually, they are written in a language such as Perl or C. ■

A Word on HTML Coding Style

HTML keywords are not case sensitive, nor do non-white space value strings require quotation marks. Thus,

```
<INPUT TYPE=RADIO NAME=opFoo VALUE=fooFighter1>
```

is operationally the same as:

```
<input type=radio Name=opFoo Value=fooFighter1>
```

or

```
<INPUT TYPE=RADIO name=opFoo value=fooFighter1>
```

Quotation marks are optional for non-white space value assignments but *are* required if you use value assignments with more than one word. Thus,

```
<INPUT TYPE=SUBMIT NAME=submit VALUE=Clear>
```

will work. However,

```
<INPUT TYPE=SUBMIT NAME=submit VALUE=Clear Form>
```

will *not* work. Rather the correct syntax is:

```
<INPUT TYPE=SUBMIT NAME=submit VALUE="Clear Form">
```

There is lot of variety to HTML coding style in the HTML development community. The important thing to consider when you create your pages is that your code should be consistent, well organized, and easy to read.

The *<FORM>* Element

HTML forms begin with the tag `<FORM>` and ends with the tag `</FORM>`. The `<FORM>` element takes the format:

```
<FORM ACTION = URL METHOD= post (or get) NAME=aname>
.
.
</FORM>
```

Where:

ACTION is the server-side Uniform Resource Locator to which the form's data will be passed. Typically, this is a CGI script. However, with the emergence of Microsoft's Active Server Pages initiative, many more URLs are referencing an Active Server Page.

METHOD is the way the data is passed. You can choose from either the POST method or the GET method.

A Word About *POST* and *GET*

The GET and POST are the most used methods for sending user information to scripts. The GET method is typically the default method if no method is specified.

The GET method sends the user-entered information to the script in the environment variable, QUERY_STRING, which is limited to 255 characters. Usage of the GET method is shown in the following example.

```
<FORM ACTION="SendData" METHOD="GET">
```

The POST method sends the user-entered information to the script via the server's STDOUT and the script's STDIN. The POST method has no limitations on the amount of character data it can process. Usage of the POST method is shown in the following example.

```
<FORM ACTION="SendData" METHOD="POST">
```

NAME is a user-defined ID that identifies the form. This feature is particularly useful when you have Web pages that contain more than one form.

Thus:

```
<FORM ACTION=http://www.mysite.com/cgi-bin/myscript.exe
➥METHOD=post NAME=myform>
.
.
.
</FORM>
```

denotes a form that will pass its data to a CGI script, myscript.exe on the server www.mysite.com. The form will use the POST method. The name of the form is myform.

Forms are parent elements. This means that the information they gather is generated by other HTML elements that live between the <FORM> and </FORM> tags. An element that lives within a <FORM> is called a *child element*. This notion of parent and child elements becomes very important when you work with VBScript or JavaScript and the IE Object Model.

You can have more than one form on a page. The NAME attribute of the form delineates one form from another. Figure 35.1 shows the HTML for a Web page with two forms, frmAnimal and frmStooge. Figure 35.2 shows what the HTML looks like when viewed in Internet Explorer.

FIG. 35.1
The <FORM> element is
the basic building block
for using HTML
elements.

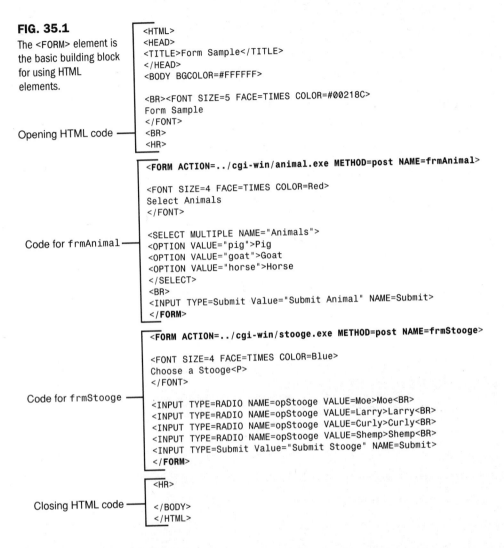

Opening HTML code ———

Code for frmAnimal ———

Code for frmStooge ———

Closing HTML code ———

```
<HTML>
<HEAD>
<TITLE>Form Sample</TITLE>
</HEAD>
<BODY BGCOLOR=#FFFFFF>

<BR><FONT SIZE=5 FACE=TIMES COLOR=#00218C>
Form Sample
</FONT>
<BR>
<HR>

<FORM ACTION=../cgi-win/animal.exe METHOD=post NAME=frmAnimal>

<FONT SIZE=4 FACE=TIMES COLOR=Red>
Select Animals
</FONT>

<SELECT MULTIPLE NAME="Animals">
<OPTION VALUE="pig">Pig
<OPTION VALUE="goat">Goat
<OPTION VALUE="horse">Horse
</SELECT>
<BR>
<INPUT TYPE=Submit Value="Submit Animal" NAME=Submit>
</FORM>

<FORM ACTION=../cgi-win/stooge.exe METHOD=post NAME=frmStooge>

<FONT SIZE=4 FACE=TIMES COLOR=Blue>
Choose a Stooge<P>
</FONT>

<INPUT TYPE=RADIO NAME=opStooge VALUE=Moe>Moe<BR>
<INPUT TYPE=RADIO NAME=opStooge VALUE=Larry>Larry<BR>
<INPUT TYPE=RADIO NAME=opStooge VALUE=Curly>Curly<BR>
<INPUT TYPE=RADIO NAME=opStooge VALUE=Shemp>Shemp<BR>
<INPUT TYPE=Submit Value="Submit Stooge" NAME=Submit>
</FORM>

<HR>

</BODY>
</HTML>
```

The *<INPUT>* Element

The <INPUT> elements are what you provide the user into which they enter form data and trigger a submission of the form's data to a server on the Internet.

HTML has a standard set of <INPUT> *types* just as VB has a standard set of controls that you adapt to a particular purpose. And, as with VB control properties, each <INPUT> element has attributes that you configure to accommodate a particular layout need. These <INPUT> element attributes are shown in Table 35.1

FIG. 35.2

HTML elements look
and behave very much
like the standard Visual
Basic controls.

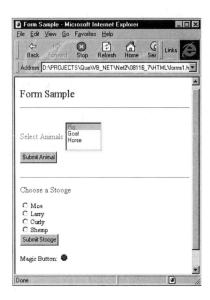

Table 35.1   The *<INPUT>* Element's Attributes

Attribute	Description
NAME	Defines name of <INPUT>'s data, similar to a variable name.
VALUE	<INPUT>'s data, similar to the value of a variable.
TYPE	Defines the type of <INPUT> element—for example, Text, Radio, CheckBox, and so on.
MAXLENGTH	Specifies the maximum number of characters permitted to be entered in an <INPUT>'s field.
SIZE	Defines the size (width) of the <INPUT>'s field. Used for Text or Password.
CHECKED	Sets a check in a CheckBox or sets a Radio to true.

The <INPUT> element types are described in the following sections.

Text   You use the Text type to allow the user to enter textual data. The following code produces the text input box in Figure 35.3:

```
Name: <INPUT TYPE=Text NAME=txtMain VALUE="Enter your name here"
       SIZE=40 MAXLENGTH=36>
```

FIG. 35.3

You can set a default value for <INPUT TYPE=Text> by setting the VALUE to the data you want to show as default.

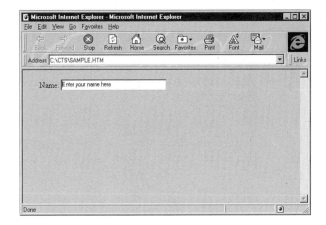

Password   A Password type is similar to a Text <INPUT> element type, but the characters that the user enters are masked with asterisks (see Figure 35.4). Though the type does offer some measure of security, the type's security can be breached with little difficulty if you do *not* have a secure transaction. The following example shows how to produce a password box:

```
Password: <INPUT TYPE=Password NAME=pswMain>
```

FIG. 35.4

Using a Password <INPUT> type does NOT necessarily mean total password security.

Submit   The Submit button is the <INPUT> type you use to create a button that, when clicked, triggers the submission of a form's data to an Internet server. The browser will show the caption of the Submit type to be the string "Submit," unless the VALUE is assigned another string. The following example assigns the caption Submit Profile, which is shown in Figure 35.5:

```
<INPUT TYPE=Submit Value="Submit Profile" NAME=Submit>
```

FIG. 35.5

You can customize the caption of the Submit <INPUT> type by changing the VALUE= data.

Reset   The Reset type creates a button that, when clicked, clears the data from all fields on an HTML form and returns the fields to their default settings (see Figure 35.6).

```
<INPUT TYPE=Reset Value="Clear Profile" NAME=Reset>
```

FIG. 35.6
You can custom
configure the Reset
caption by adjusting
the VALUE= attribute.

Button This feature creates a button that can be referenced with VBScript or JavaScript. You can't really use this <INPUT> type in standard, non-scripted HTML (see Figure 35.7).

```
<INPUT TYPE=Button Value="Go Back" NAME=cmdBack
 LANGUAGE=VBScript OnClick=History.Back>
```

FIG. 35.7
Button <INPUT> types
can be used pretty
easily with VBScript or
JavaScript.

Radio Radio buttons are used to make exclusive choices. They are used in much the same way that you use an Option control in VB (see Figure 35.8). The tricky thing about Radio <INPUT> types is to understand that, in order to group a set of Radio types to be exclusive of one another, all Radio types to be grouped *must* have the same value attached to their NAME attribute. When you submit the form, only the VALUE of the chosen Radio type will be sent to the server.

```
<B>Your gender:</B><BR>
<INPUT TYPE=RADIO NAME=opMain VALUE=Male CHECKED>Male<BR>
<INPUT TYPE=RADIO NAME=opMain VALUE=Female>Female<BR>
```

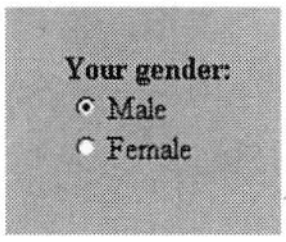

FIG. 35.8
If you want to set a
default Radio, include
the CHECKED attribute
when you define the
<INPUT> tag.

CheckBox CheckBoxes are used to make inclusive choices. The value of the NAME attribute for each CheckBox must be different (see Figure 35.9). When you submit the form, if a CheckBox is checked, its name-value pair will be sent to the server.

```
<B>Have you had:</B><BR>
<INPUT TYPE=CHECKBOX NAME=ckMumps>Mumps<BR>
<INPUT TYPE=CHECKBOX  NAME=ckMeasles>Measles<BR>
<INPUT TYPE=CHECKBOX  NAME=ckChickePox >ChickPox<BR>
<INPUT TYPE=CHECKBOX  NAME=ckNone CHECKED>No Disease<BR>
```

Part
VII

Ch
35

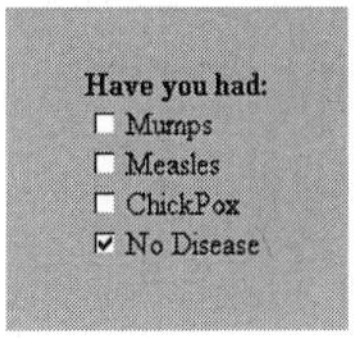

FIG. 35.9

If you want to default set a check on a CHECKBOX, include the CHECKED attribute in the tag definition.

N O T E *NAME-VALUE pair* When you make an <INPUT> element, you define a TYPE and you assign values to the NAME and VALUE attributes of the element. When the form's data is submitted to the server on the Internet, the NAME and VALUE data for the <INPUT> element is sent as a pair associated with the "=" sign. This association is called a NAME-VALUE pair. NAME-VALUE pairs are usually passed to a server side CGI Script or an Active Server Page. The server-side script or ASP (Active Server Page) then parses the VALUE data from the NAME data and acts upon the data as defined in the script or ASP.

For example:

You create a TEXT <INPUT> element in which the user is to enter a favorite baseball team. The HTML syntax is:

`Favorite Team<INPUT TYPE=TEXT NAME=txtTeam SIZE=40><BR>`

The user enters the string "Yankees" in the <INPUT TYPE=TEXT> element. When the form is eventually submitted to the server the NAME-VALUE pair that will be sent is txtTeam=Yankees, where,

> txtTeam is the value of the NAME attribute

and

> Yankees is the value of the VALUE attribute. ■

Hidden Hidden <INPUT> types are, well, hidden. They're never shown on the form. They are a good way to send in some data from the form to the server without the user's knowledge. It's as if you have a piece of data embedded in the form that you can send back to the server on a free-ride basis. In the following code example, the author of the HTML attached the name of "VIP Customer" to a HIDDEN input type. When the data is sent back to the server, the value of the HIDDEN input type will also be sent to the server without the user knowing about it.

`<INPUT TYPE=Hidden NAME=hidStatus VALUE="VIP Customer">`

Image An IMAGE <INPUT> type displays a .GIF image that has the behavior of a SUBMIT <INPUT> type (see Figure 35.10).

`<B>Magic Button:</B><INPUT TYPE=image NAME=imgMain SRC=gifs/gifbut.gif>`

FIG. 35.10

You can give some artistic variety to your form with an IMAGE <INPUT> type.

Magic Button: ●

The *<SELECT>* Element

A <SELECT> element is similar to an <INPUT> element in that it allows users to input data to be submitted to an Internet server. However, the <SELECT> element is a little more powerful in that it has the behavior of a Visual Basic listbox or combobox.

The tag begins with <SELECT> and ends with </SELECT>. Within the <SELECT> element you place <OPTION> elements. If you use the attribute, MUTLIPLE, in the tag definition, the element will appear as a list, similar to the Visual Basic listbox. When the element appears as a list, you can submit multiple <OPTION>s to the server. If you omit the MULTIPLE attribute, the element will appear as a drop-down box, similar to a VB combobox, from which you can chose only one <OPTION> (see Listing 35.1 and Figure 35.11).

Listing 35.1   FORM2.HTM—HTML for Single and Multiple Selection *<SELECT>* Elements

```
<FORM METHOD=post ACTION=../cgi-win/ark.exe NAME=frmArk>

<FONT SIZE=4 FACE=TIMES COLOR=Red>
Select Animals
</FONT>

<!--Allow multiple selections-->
<SELECT MULTIPLE NAME="Animals">
<OPTION VALUE="pig">Pig
<OPTION VALUE="goat">Goat
<OPTION VALUE="horse">Horse
</SELECT>
<P>

<FONT SIZE=4 FACE=TIMES COLOR=Red>
Select a Flower
</FONT>
<!--Allow only one selection-->
<SELECT NAME="Flowers">
<OPTION VALUE="rose">Rose
<OPTION VALUE="lily">Lily
<OPTION VALUE="daisy">Daisy
</SELECT>

<P>
<INPUT TYPE=Submit Value="Submit" NAME=Submit>
</FORM>
```

Part

VII

Ch

35

FIG. 35.11
<SELECT> elements
are similar to a Visual
Basic listbox or combo
control.

The <TEXTAREA> Element

The <TEXTAREA> element is similar to a TEXT <INPUT> type, the difference being that a <TEXTAREA> element can accept multiple lines of text.

The tag definition begins with <TEXTAREA> and ends with </TEXTAREA>. Any text that appears between the begin and end tags will show up in the field of the <TEXTAREA> (see Listing 35.2 and Figure 35.12).

The <TEXTAREA> element has three attributes, listed in Table 35.2.

Table 35.2   <TEXTAREA> Attributes

Attribute	Description
NAME	The name of the element (required)
ROWS	The number of rows in the <TEXTAREA> field
COLS	The width of the field in characters

Listing 35.2   FORM2.HTM—HTML Syntax for a <TEXTAREA> Element

```
<FORM METHOD=post ACTION=../cgi-win/poll.exe NAME=frmComment>

<FONT SIZE=4 FACE=TIMES COLOR=Blue>
Do you have a comment?<P>
</FONT>

<TEXTAREA ROWS=5 COLS=30 NAME=taComment>Enter your comment here.
Don't forget to erase
this message or it will show up in you comments
and that's not something that you would like to
happen.
</TEXTAREA>
<P>
<INPUT TYPE=Submit Value="Submit Comment" NAME=Submit>
</FORM>
```

FIG. 35.12

You can use a
<TEXTAREA> element
as a memo field.

The *<SCRIPT>* Element

The <SCRIPT> element denotes a section of script code within a Web page's HTML. The tag definition begins with <SCRIPT> and ends with </SCRIPT>. The element has an attribute LANGUAGE that indicates the scripting language used. Listing 35.3 is a snippet of HTML that shows a <SCRIPT> element that is defining an OnClick event handler in VBScript.

Listing 35.3   VALNAME3.HTM—HTML Syntax for the *<SCRIPT>* Element

```
<SCRIPT LANGUAGE="VBScript">
<!--
Sub cmdSubmit_OnClick
  Dim TheForm
  Dim i
  Dim MyMsg

  MyMsg = "All fields must be filled in. If a field is empty, please type: NONE."

  Set TheForm = Document.frmPurchase

  For i = 0 to CInt(TheForm.Elements.Length) - 1
    If TheForm.Elements(i).Value = "" Then
      Alert (MyMsg)
      Exit Sub
    End If
  Next

End Sub
-->
</SCRIPT>
```

Using the HTML *<FORM>* Elements

As discussed in the preceding section, you use an HTML <FORM> element to group, collect, and submit data to a server on the Internet. The type of circumstances that you would typically apply a <FORM> to are situations in which you want to collect personnel data, input sales order information, or get lookup information for an Internet search.

Part
VII

Ch
35

Submitting Data to a Server

Figure 35.13 shows an illustration of a Web site that uses the HTML <FORM> elements, <INPUT TYPE=RADIO>, <TEXTAREA>, <INPUT TYPE=IMAGE>, and <INPUT TYPE=HIDDEN> to create a form that allows a user to submit a term or keyword to a server to do a lookup query. Listing 35.4 shows the HTML that's used to create the page.

FIG. 35.13

Lookup and retrieval
Web pages use HTML
forms.

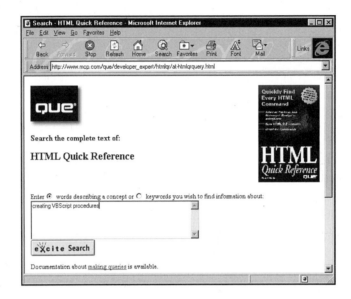

Notice that instead of using a <TYPE INPUT=SUBMIT> element type to create a Submit button, the creator of this page cleverly uses an <INPUT TYPE=IMAGE> that uses a custom illustration to create a unique Submit button. If the user enters the lookup terms "creating VBScript procedures" in the TEXTAREA, when the user submits the form's data, the following query string will be sent on to the server:

mode=concept&search=creating+VBScript+prodcures&sp=sp

Where

> mode=concept is the NAME-VALUE pair for the selected Radio.
>
> & is the character used in HTML to separate NAME-VALUE pairs.
>
> search=creating+VBScript+prodcures is the NAME-VALUE pair that describes that data entered in the <INPUT TYPE=TEXTAREA>.
>
> The "+" character is used in HTML to indicate a space between words.
>
> sp=sp is the NAME-VALUE pair corresponding to the <INPUT TYPE=HIDDEN> element.

N O T E *query string*   A query string is the string passed to an Internet server when a user clicks a Submit button in an HTML form.

The string is constructed from the NAME=VALUE pairs of the elements in the form which is being submitted. ■

Listing 35.4   QUE_SRCH.HTM—A Web Page that Uses an HTML Form to Do a Lookup

```
<HTML>
<HEAD>
<TITLE>Search - HTML Quick Reference</TITLE>
</HEAD>

<BODY BGCOLOR="#FFFFFF">

<!-- -->
<!-- HEADER -->
<TABLE WIDTH=600>
<TR><TD WIDTH=600>
<IMG SRC="q08671.gif" ALT="book cover" ALIGN=RIGHT>
<A HREF="/que/"><IMG SRC="../sevb4/que_sq.gif" ALT="QUE" Border=0></A>
<H3>Search the complete text of:</H3>
<H2>HTML Quick Reference</H2>
</TD>
</TR>
</TABLE>

<!-- -->
<!-- INPUT FORM (DO NOT CHANGE)-->
<TABLE WIDTH=600>
<TR><TD WIDTH=600>
<FORM ACTION="/cgi-bin/AT-htmlqrsearch.cgi" METHOD="POST">
Enter<INPUT TYPE="radio" NAME="mode" VALUE="concept"
➥CHECKED> words describing a concept or<INPUT TYPE="radio"
➥NAME="mode" VALUE="simple"> keywords you wish to find
➥information about:<BR>
<TEXTAREA NAME="search" COLS=70 ROWS=4></TEXTAREA><BR>
<INPUT TYPE="image" NAME="SearchButton" BORDER=0
➥SRC="/Architext/pictures/AT-search_button.gif">
<INPUT TYPE="hidden" NAME="sp" VALUE="sp">
</FORM>
<P>
Documentation about <a href="/Architext/AT-queryhelp.html"
➥>making queries</a> is available.
<P><P>
<B>TIP:</B> If you plan on making multiple queries,
➥you might wish to make a bookmark for this page.
<P>
</TD>
</TR>
```

continues

Listing 35.4   Continued

```
</TABLE>


<HR SIZE=1 NOSHADE ALIGN=LEFT WIDTH=600>
<!-- -->
<!-- NAVIGATIONAL TOOLBAR -->
<TABLE WIDTH=600>
<TR><TD ALIGN=CENTER>
¦ <A HREF="/que/developer_expert/htmlqr/">Book Home Page</A> ¦
<A HREF="/que/developer_expert/htmlqr/toc.htm"
➥>Table of Contents</A> ¦ <A HREF="/cgi-
bin/placeorder?express=0-7897-0867-1">Buy This Book</A> ¦
<P>
¦ <A HREF="/que/">Que Home Page</A> ¦
➥<A HREF="/que/bookshelf/">Digital Bookshelf</A> ¦ <A
HREF="/que/bookshelf/disclaim.html">Disclaimer</A> ¦
<P>
</TD></TR>
</TABLE>



<!-- -->
<!-- FOOTER -->
<HR SIZE=8 ALIGN=LEFT WIDTH=600>
<TABLE WIDTH=600>
<TR><TD ALIGN=CENTER><FONT SIZE=1>
To order books from QUE, call us at 800-716-0044 or 317-361-5400.
<P>
For comments or technical support for our books and software, select
<A href = "/general/support/index.html" >Talk to Us</a>.
<P>
&#169; 1997, QUE Corporation, an imprint of Macmillan
➥Publishing USA, a Simon and Schuster Company.
<P>
</FONT></TD></TR>
</TABLE>

</BODY>
</HTML>
```

Limitations of HTML

Though HTML forms and <FORM> elements are powerful tools to have in your development toolbox, they are limited. The most fundamental limitation is that the only dynamic interactions you can do with them on the client side are to submit data to an Internet server or clear the form. Conceptually, you have only one event—Click—and two operational client-side methods—submit the data and clear the form's data. That's it! Any other validation or modifications that you may want to make have to be done through a plethora of client/server interactions. This is time-consuming and incurs a heavy burden of server-side transactions and programming to accommodate those transactions.

However, there is a solution to this problem and that is to extend the functionality of standard HTML forms with a scripting language such as VBScript or JavaScript. You'll take a look at this solution in the section "Using VBScript with the HTML <FORM> Elements and Intrinsic Controls," which comes later in this chapter.

VBScript and the Internet Explorer Intrinsic Controls

When you install Internet Explorer on you computer, you get more than full multimedia access to the Internet and an OLE container in which you can view documents with full OLE functionality (provided the "maker" applications are installed on your system). You also get a full-blown programming environment, VBScript, and the Intrinsic Controls. Just about all the stuff you get with Standard VB you get with Internet Explorer. You can make programs using VBScript that can use CommandButton, OptionButton, CheckBox, and ComboBox controls, and much more. These controls that are built right into the browser are called *Intrinsic Controls*.

On the Web

http://www.microsoft.com/vbscript The latest version of VBScript (v. 2.0) allows you to create code that more closely resembles that of Visual Basic. For more information on VBScript, visit the VBScript Web page. This site includes the complete online documentation and numerous other VBScript specific resources.

> **N O T E** VBScript now has a debugger! The only provision is that you are using IE 3.02 or greater.
>
> At the VBSript Web page you can download a debugger that allows you to debug your VBScript code. The debugger embeds itself as part of Internet Explorer, making the executing and debuging process a little simpler than using a separate executable. ■

The Internet Explorer Intrinsic Controls

The Internet Explorer Intrinsic Controls enable you to create Web pages that look like a typical Visual Basic application. The underlying code for these controls you create through the VBScript scripting engine. A complete listing of the Intrinsic Controls with their VB and HTML <FORM> counterparts can be found in Table 35.3.

Table 35.3 The Microsoft Forms 2.0 Controls		
Microsoft Forms Control	VB Standard Equivalent	HTML Element Equivalent
CheckBox	CheckBox	`<INPUT TYPE=CHECKBOX>`
ComboBox	ComboBox	`<SELECT>`

continues

Table 35.3   Continued

Microsoft Forms Control	VB Standard Equivalent	HTML Element Equivalent
CommandButton	CommandButtons	`<INPUT TYPE=BUTTON>`
Frame	None	`<FRAME>`
Image	Image	`<INPUT TYPE=IMAGE>`
Label	Label	none
ListBox	ListBox	`<SELECT MULTIPLE>`
OptionButton	OptionButton	`<INPUT TYPE=RADIO>`
ScrollBar	ScrollBar	none
SpinButton	SpinButton	none
TabStrip	TabStrip	none
TextBox	TextBox	`<INPUT=TEXT>`
ToggleButton	none	none

Using the *<OBJECT>* Tag to Insert Intrinsic Controls

You manipulate the Intrinsic Controls at runtime by using VBScript. You insert and define these controls at design time by using the `<OBJECT>` tag. The tag definition begins with `<OBJECT>` and ends with `</OBJECT>`. The attributes for the `<OBJECT>` tag, as they pertain to the Intrinsic Controls, are shown in Table 35.4.

Table 35.4   The Attributes of the *<OBJECT>* Tag for Intrinsic Controls

Attribute	Description
`ID`	Specifies the object. For Intrinsic Controls and ActiveX controls, this is similar to the Visual Basic `Name` property.
`CLASSID`	The ActiveX Control Identifier. All ActiveX controls have a unique number by which they can be identified by your system.
`HEIGHT`	The height of the control, similar to the Visual Basic `Height` property.
`WIDTH`	The width of the control, similar to the Visual Basic `Width` property.
`CODEBASE`	The server location of the control to be downloaded if the control is not on the client computer. This is not relevant for the Intrinsic Controls because they are built right into Internet Explorer.

With regard to the Intrinsic Controls, the `<OBJECT>` tag also has a child tag, `<PARAM>`. The `<PARAM>` tag is used to set properties of an Intrinsic Control.

The `<PARAM>` tag takes the form

```
<PARAM NAME=PropertyName VALUE=PropertyValue>
```

For example, if you want to set the caption of an intrinsic CommandButton with the ID `cmdEnter` to "Enter", the `<PARAM>` tag would be:

```
<PARAM NAME="Caption" VALUE="Enter">
```

This is the Visual Basic syntactical equivalent of

```
cmdEnter.Caption = "Enter".
```

Figure 35.14 shows a Web page that uses two Intrinsic Controls: a CommandButton, `cmdClickMe`, and a TextBox, `txtMain`. The HTML for the page is shown in Listing 35.5.

FIG. 35.14

Intrinsic Controls can interact with one another without the need to incur a lot of client/server transactions.

Listing 35.5 SMPLVB.HTM—Using Intrinsic Controls with HTML

```
<HTML>
<HEAD>
<TITLE>Simple VBScript</TITLE>
</HEAD>
<SCRIPT LANGUAGE="VBScript">
<!--
Sub cmdClickMe_Click()
   txtMain.Text = "Clicked!"
End Sub
-->
</SCRIPT>
<BODY>
    <OBJECT ID="txtMain" WIDTH=127 HEIGHT=24
      CLASSID="CLSID:8BD21D10-EC42-11CE-9E0D-00AA006002F3">
        <PARAM NAME="VariousPropertyBits" VALUE="746604571">
```

continues

Part

VII

Ch

35

Listing 35.5 Continued

```
        <PARAM NAME="Size" VALUE="3329;635">
        <PARAM NAME="FontCharSet" VALUE="0">
        <PARAM NAME="FontPitchAndFamily" VALUE="2">
        <PARAM NAME="FontWeight" VALUE="0">
    </OBJECT>

<P>

    <OBJECT ID="cmdClickMe" WIDTH=96 HEIGHT=32
     CLASSID="CLSID:D7053240-CE69-11CD-A777-00DD01143C57">
        <PARAM NAME="Caption" VALUE="ClickMe">
        <PARAM NAME="Size" VALUE="2540;847">
        <PARAM NAME="FontCharSet" VALUE="0">
        <PARAM NAME="FontPitchAndFamily" VALUE="2">
        <PARAM NAME="ParagraphAlign" VALUE="3">
        <PARAM NAME="FontWeight" VALUE="0">
    </OBJECT>
</BODY>
</HTML>
```

Handling Events

Having more controls available to readily add to your Web pages wouldn't have much of a payoff unless you had a way to interact with them. Using a CommandButton without having access to the Click event or a SpinButton without access the SpinDown event would be a waste of time. Fortunately, this limitation does not exist.

Take a look at the code in Listing 35.5. Notice that in addition to some <OBJECT> tags to accommodate the inclusion of the CommandButton and Textbox controls, at the top of the page you have a <SCRIPT> tag that references a Sub, cmdClickMe_OnClick. This is called an *event handler*. This piece of VBScript is what will be executed when the user clicks the cmdClickMe button.

An event handler is a Sub. In Visual Basic, event handler code blocks are automatically generated by the Visual Basic IDE (Integrated Development Environment). When using VBScript within HTML, you must create the event handlers yourself.

The syntax for an event handler is:

```
<SCRIPT LANGUAGE="VBScript">
<!--
Sub ControlID_Event
    'handler code
  .
  .
  .
End Sub
-->
</SCRIPT>
```

Where,

> `ControlID` is the ID of the control whose event you are handling.
>
> `Event` is the event to be handled.

Thus, as coded in the event handler `cmdClickMe_OnClick`, in Listing 35.5, when the user clicks the `CommandButton`, `cmdClickMe`, the `Text` property to the TextBox, `txtMain`, is set to "Clicked!".

Trying to remember all the events and all the event handler syntax that goes with any given Intrinsic Control can be a chore. To make programming Intrinsic Controls with VBScript easier, Microsoft created a tool to handle most of the drudgery of these sorts of tasks. It's called ActiveX Control Pad. You can get it by downloading it from the Microsoft SiteBuilder site on the Internet. After you get the hang of it, it will save you a lot of time in your programming endeavors.

Figure 35.15 shows the ActiveX Control Pad Script Wizard. Script Wizard is one the many features of ActiveX Control Pad. Script Wizard allows you to write a lot of VBScript with nothing more than a point and a click.

FIG. 35.15

You can use the ActiveX Control Pad's Script Wizard to code a control's event handler.

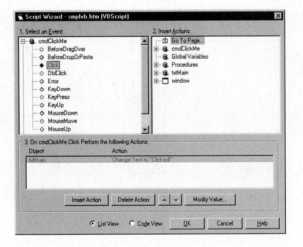

www.microsoft.com/sitebuilder/   Download the ActiveX Control Pad from the Microsoft SiteBuilder site.

On the Web

Part
VII

Ch
35

Subs and Functions

In addition to using VBScript to write event handlers for Intrinsic Controls, you can also use it to write user-defined subs and functions, just as you would in standard Visual Basic. The benefit of this is that you can write some fairly complex event handlers, the tasks of which are encapsulated in other subs and functions. Using subs and functions helps you avoid writing code that has minimal reuse and is hard to read.

A Word About Commenting

The HTML comment tag begins with <!-- and ends with -->. Anything that appears between these tags is considered to be a comment and not read by the browser.

For example:

```
<!--I am a comment.

    I am a another comment on another line-->
```

For commenting within a VBScript block, you use the "'" character, just as you would in standard Visual Basic.

For example:

```
<SCRIPT LANGUAGE=VBScript>
<!--
  'Send out an error message
  Alert "Error Message"
-->
 </SCRIPT>
```

You write user-defined Subs and Functions in VBScript just as you would in standard Visual Basic, only you place them within the <SCRIPT> tag. You can place more than one Sub or Function within a set of <SCRIPT></SCRIPT> tags.

Figure 35.16 is an illustration of the Web page, FORM3.HTM. The HTML for this page is shown in Listing 35.6. This page is an example of using a user-defined Sub to extend an event handler, in this case the OnSubmit event for the HTML form, frmLookup. (The OnSubmit is the method of the Form object. VBScript considers the <FORM> element to be a Form object.)

FIG. 35.16

Data validation is a typical use for VBScript.

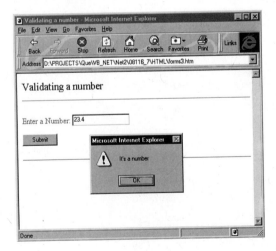

Listing 35.6 FORMS3.HTM—The HTML for a User-Defined *Sub*

```
<HTML>
<HEAD>
<TITLE>Validating a number</TITLE>
</HEAD>
<SCRIPT LANGUAGE=VBScript>
<!--
'''''''''''''''''''''''''''''''''''''''
'Checks a value to see if it looks
'''''''''''''''''''''''''''''''''''''''
like a number
Sub CheckNum(NumToCheck)
  If IsNumeric(CStr(NumToCheck)) Then
    Alert ("It's a number")
  Else
    Alert ("It's not a number")
  End If
End Sub

Sub frmLookUp_OnSubmit
  CheckNum(frmLookup.txtNumber.Value)
End  Sub

-->
</SCRIPT>

<BODY BGCOLOR=#FFFFFF>
<FONT SIZE=5 FACE=TIMES COLOR=#00218C>
Validating a number
</FONT>
<HR>

<FORM METHOD=post ACTION=../cgi-win/lookup.exe NAME=frmLookup>

<FONT SIZE=4 FACE=TIMES COLOR=Red>
Enter a Number:
<INPUT TYPE=TEXT NAME=txtNumber>
</FONT>

<P>
<INPUT TYPE=Submit Value="Submit" NAME=Submit>
</FORM>
<HR>
</BODY>
</HTML>
```

You'll notice that the event handler, frmLookUp_OnSubmit calls the user-defined Sub, CheckNum(NumToCheck). CheckNum is pretty straightforward. It takes the value to check as an argument and passes that value on to the intrinsic VB function, IsNumeric(). (You're probably pretty familiar with IsNumeric. It's been around in VB for years!) If the return is true, the Sub displays an Alert Box containing the string, "It's a number". If it's false, the Alert displays, It's not a number. (The Alert method is the VBScript equivalent of the VB MsgBox statement.)

http://www.microsoft.com/vbscript/us/vbslang/vbstoc.htm A complete illustration and discussion of the VBScript Intrinsic Functions are outside of the scope of this chapter. For the most part, all of the VB functions that are not operating system dependent exist in VBScript. In a few cases, the syntax may be modified a bit. For a detailed reference of the VBScript Language go to the Microsoft site.

The significance of the illustration in Listing 35.6 is that it shows you how to use a user-defined Sub to extend a control's event handler. However, as you read this you might be a bit disconcerted. How can you reference an HTML <FORM> element as you would an Internet Explorer Intrinsic Control? Well, while it is true that a <FORM> is not an Intrinsic Control, it is an object in the Internet Explorer Object Model and can be accessed as such. The trick is understanding the Internet Explorer Object Model for Scripting.

The Internet Explorer Object Model

Many HTML elements can also be treated as Internet Explorer Scripting Objects. In order to work effectively with VBScript and HTML elements and to see how they can intermingle, you need to understand the Internet Explorer Scripting Object Model.

The Object Model is pretty straightforward, if you understand the "object-ness" of Visual Basic. At the top of the IE Object Model hierarchy is the Window object, which is the parent to all other objects. This arrangement is similar to the Form-Custom Control architecture in Visual Basic (see Figure 35.17). Object referencing works the same in VBScript as in VB:

```
parent_object.child_object.property = somevalue
```

Be advised that variable scope and types are a bit tricky. The scope of VBScript variables is described as procedure scope and script scope. What procedure and script scope means is that the variable can be seen only in the Sub or Function if it is declared inside the procedure. If it is declared outside a procedure, it has script-wide scope. A script in this case means an HTML page. All variables in VBScript are of the data type Variant but you must watch the subtype.

The following sections are a brief description of the objects in the IE Object Model. The files used in Listings 35.7 through 35.15 can be found in the /HTML directory on the CD-ROM that comes with this book.

Window   The Window is the object at the top of the IE Scripting Object Model. Operationally, it is the Internet Explorer. In Listing 35.7, you see an example of how to use the Alert method to send a message to a user.

Methods: alert, confirm, prompt, open, close, setTimeout, clearTimeout, navigate

Events: onLoad, onUnload

Properties: name, parent, opener, self, top, location, defaultStatus, status, frames, history, navigator, document

FIG. 35.17
The Internet Explorer
Scripting Object Model
Hierarchy.

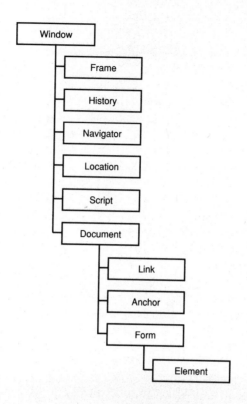

On the CD

**Listing 35.7   HELLO.HTM—Use the *Alert* Method to Send a Message
to a User**

```
<HTML><HEAD>
<TITLE>Hello</TITLE>
<SCRIPT LANGUAGE=VBScript>
<!--
Sub window_onLoad
    window.Alert "Hello World"
End Sub
-->
</SCRIPT>
</HEAD>
```

Frame   The Frame object is similar to and descends from the Window object. Although you can
have a collection of frames, each frame has its own property values and its own document.

Methods: See Window object

Events: See Window object

Properties: See Window object

Part
VII

Ch

35

History   The History object holds information about what has been in the window before. It gets this information for the browser's History list (see Figure 35.18). In Listing 35.8, you see an example of how to return to a previously viewed Web page.

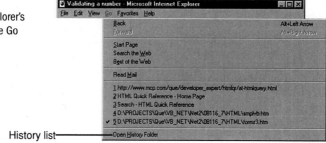

History list

Methods: back, forward, go

Events: none

Properties: length

Listing 35.8   BACK.HTM—Use the *History* Object's *Back* Method to View Previous Pages

```
<HTML><HEAD>
<TITLE>Back</TITLE>
<SCRIPT LANGUAGE=VBScript>
<!--
Sub window_onLoad
     History.back 1
End Sub
-->
</SCRIPT>
</HEAD>
```

Navigator   The Navigator object gives you information about the browser in use. You can find out what browser your client is using by using the appName property of the Navigator object as shown in Listing 35.9.

Methods: none

Events: none

Properties: appCodeName, appName, appVersion, userAgent

Listing 35.9 N_GATOR.HTM—An Easy Way to Determine What Browser to Code Your Web Pages for

```
<HTML><HEAD>
<TITLE>Navigator</TITLE>
<SCRIPT LANGUAGE=VBScript>
<!--
Sub window_onLoad
     Alert Navigator.appName
End Sub
-->
</SCRIPT>
</HEAD>
```

Location   The Location object encapsulates an URL. You can use the protocol property of the location object to determine the protocol that is currently in use. (see Listing 35.10)

Methods: none

Events: none

Properties: href, protocol, host, hostname, port, pathname, search, hash

Listing 35.10   LOCATION.HTM—To Find Out the Protocol that Your Document Is Presently Using, Use the *Protocol* Property

```
<HTML><HEAD>
<TITLE>Location</TITLE>
<SCRIPT LANGUAGE=VBScript>
<!--
Sub window_onLoad
     Alert Location.protocol
End Sub
-->
</SCRIPT>
</HEAD>
</HTML>
```

Script   The Script object defines the script used in the Window. Granted, this description is rather vague. At some point, Microsoft will probably extend and enhance the utility of this object.

Document   The Document object encapsulates the document in the current window as well as the elements in the document, that is, links, forms, buttons, and ActiveX objects. The objects Link, Anchor, and Form descend from the Document object. An interesting use of the Document object is to write a line of text to the browser, as shown in Listing 35.11

Part
VII

Ch
35

Methods: write, writeLn, open, close, clear

Events: none

Properties: linkColor, aLinkColor, vLinkColor, bgColor, fgColor, anchors, links, forms, location, lastModified, title, cookie, referrer

Listing 35.11 DOCUMENT.HTM—The *Write* Method of the *Document* Object Allows for Writing Text to the Browser

```
<HTML><HEAD>
<TITLE>Document</TITLE>
<SCRIPT LANGUAGE=VBScript>
<!--
    document.write ("I am writing a line.")
-->
</SCRIPT>
</HEAD>
</HTML>
```

Link The Link object is an encapsulation of an HTML <A HREF...> tag on a given page. It is read-only. Because a link is a member of the links collection (an array of <A HREF...> tags), you need to access an a particular link through the Document object's Links property. To find out how many <A HREF...> tags are on a page, use the Document object Property links. To determine the text of an <HREF>, use the href property of the Link object, as shown in Listing 35.12

Methods: none

Events: onMouseMove, onMouseOver, onClick

Properties: href, protocol, host, hostname, port, pathname, search, hash, target

Listing 35.12 LINK.HTM—The *<HREF>* Property Can Be Used to Count the Number of Links on a Page

```
<HTML><HEAD>
<TITLE>Document</TITLE>
<SCRIPT LANGUAGE=VBScript>
<!--

Sub window_onUnLoad
  Dim NumOfLinks
  Dim MyAlertMsg
  NumOfLinks = Cstr(document.links.length)
  MyAlertMsg = "There are " & NumOfLinks & " links on this page."
  MyAlertMsg = MyAlertMsg & Chr(10) & Chr(13)
  MyAlertMsg = MyAlertMsg & "The first link is " & document.links(0).href
```

```
   Alert MyAlertMsg
End Sub
-->
</SCRIPT>
</HEAD>

<BODY>

<P>
<A HREF="http://www.whitehouse.gov"> Go to the White House.</A>
<P>
<A HREF="http://www.senate.gov"> Go to the Senate. </A>
</BODY>
</HTML>
```

Anchor   The Anchor object is similar to a Link object. The difference is that the Anchor object references all <A> tags in a given document as opposed to <A HREF...> objects.

Methods: none

Events: none

Properties: name

Form   The Form object represents an HTML <FORM> element in a Document object. You can reference a Form object by either a name or an array index (see Listing 35.13). The Element object is a child of the Form object.

Methods: submit

Events: onSubmit

Properties: action, encoding, method, target, elements

On the CD

Listing 35.13   OM_FORM.HTM—A Simple Form Element

```
<HTML>
<HEAD>
<TITLE>The Virtual Music Store</TITLE></HEAD>
<FORM method=post action=/cgi-win/mycgi.cgi>
Enter your name: <INPUT TYPE=TEXT NAME=yourname>
<BR>
<INTPUT TYPE=Submit NAME=submit VALUE="Enter Name">
</FORM>
</BODY></HTML>
```

Part
VII

Ch
35

Element   The Element object is a control placed in your HTML document by using the <INPUT> tag or the <OBJECT> tag. The <INPUT> tags refer to HTML elements. The <OBJECT> tags refer to Intrinsic Controls and ActiveX Controls. To handle a Click event of an Element object of type Button, code the onClick event of the Element object, as shown in Listing 35.14.

Methods: click, focus, blur, select

Events: onClick, onFocus, onBlur, onChange, onSelect

Properties: form, name, value, defaultValue, checked, defaultChecked, length, options, selectedIndex

---

**Listing 35.14   ELEMENT.HTM—The *onClick* Event Will Trap for a *Click*
Event of Object**

```
<HTML><HEAD>
<TITLE>Element</TITLE>
<SCRIPT LANGUAGE=VBScript>
<!--

Sub btnOK_onClick
     frmMain.btnOK.Value ="Thank you!"
End Sub
-->
</SCRIPT>
</HEAD>

<BODY>
<FORM NAME=frmMain>
<INPUT TYPE=button NAME=btnOK VALUE="Click me">
</FORM>
</BODY>
</HTML>
```

Using VBScript with the HTML *<FORM>* Elements and Intrinsic Controls

Now that you have gotten a pretty extensive overview of HTML elements, the IE Intrinsic Controls, and the IE Object Model, tie it all together. Listing 35.15 shows the HTML for a customer information registration Web page. This code implements many of the features and techniques you read about in this chapter.

**Listing 35.15   CUSTREG.HTM—The HTML for a Customer Registration
Web Page**

```
<!--04-20-97-->
<HTML>
<HEAD>
<TITLE>The Square Company</TITLE>
<SCRIPT LANGUAGE="VBScript">
<!--
```

```
Sub submit_OnClick
'********************************
'Sub: submit_OnClick
'
'Remarks: This sub checks to make sure that:
'  1. All fields are filled in
'  2. The password matches the password confirmation
'  3. The CC expiration date string is a valid date format
'  It then submits to the form data to the CGI script, TRANSACT.EXE
'  to the "register" CASE.


'Copyright:  1997 Macmillan Publishing
'********************************

    Dim TheForm      'declare a variable for the form object
    Dim i            'declare a counter variable
    Dim MyErrMsg     'declare a variable to hold the error message
    Dim PassWord     'declare a variable to hold the password
    Dim ConfirmWord  'declare a variable to hold the confirmation
    Dim s            'declare a general string variable
    'Assign the blank error message to the message variable
    MyErrMsg = "All field must be filled in. "
    MyErrMsg = MyErrMsg + "If a field is empty, please type: NONE."

    'Assign the purchase form to the object variable
    Set TheForm = Document.frmRegInfo
    'Transverse all the elements in the form to
    'make sure that all the fields are filled in.
    For i = 0 to CInt(TheForm.Elements.Length) - 1
      If TheForm.Elements(i).Value = "" Then
        'If you get a blank, show the error message and
        'set the cursor to the offender and leave the Sub.
        Alert (MyErrMsg)
        TheForm.Elements(i).focus
        Exit Sub
      End If
    Next

    'Assign the password and the confirmation to the
    'corresponding variables
    PassWord = frmRegInfo.txtPassword.value
    ConfirmWord = frmRegInfo.txtPassConfirm.value

    'Create the password mismatch error message
    MyErrMsg = "The password and the confirmation do not match"




    'Check to make sure the values match
    If PassWord <> ConfirmWord then
      'If you have  mismatch, show an Error message
      Alert (MyErrMsg)
```

Part

VII

Ch

35

continues

Listing 35.15   Continued

```
      'Set the focus back to the confirmation textbox
      frmRegInfo.txtPassConfirm.focus
      'HiLite the confirmation textbox
      frmRegInfo.txtPassConfirm.select
      Exit Sub
   end if

  'Check to make sure that the CC expiration date string is a date
  MyErrMsg = "The Expiration Date entry must be in a valid date format."

   'Go to the <INPUT TYPE=text NAME=
   s = frmRegInfo.txtExpDate.value
   If IsDate(s) = 0 then
     Alert (MyErrMsg)
     frmRegInfo.txtExpDate.focus
     frmRegInfo.txtExpDate.select
     Exit Sub
   End if

   'If you've gotten to here, everything is OK
   'Submit the data
   TheForm.Submit

End Sub

Sub cmdReturn_OnClick
'********************************
'Sub: return_OnClick
'
'Remarks: This sub returns the user to their previous URL
'
'
'Copyright:  1997 Macmillan Publishing
'********************************
   history.back 1
End Sub
-->
</SCRIPT>
</HEAD>
<BODY BGCOLOR=#FFFFFF>
<CENTER>
<IMG SRC=gifs/logo.gif>
<BR><FONT SIZE=6 FACE=TIMES COLOR=#00218C>
Customer Registration</FONT>
<BR>

<TABLE BORDER=1 WIDTH=80%>
<FORM NAME=frmRegInfo METHOD=post ACTION=../cgi-win/transact.exe>
<INPUT TYPE=hidden NAME=transaction VALUE= hidRegister>

<!--Name Data-->
<TR>
<TD COLSPAN=2><FONT SIZE=2 COLOR=#840084 FACE=arial>
```

```
First Name:<BR><INPUT TYPE=text SIZE=40 NAME=txtFirstName></TD>
</TR>

<TR>
<TD COLSPAN=2><FONT SIZE=2 COLOR=#840084 FACE=arial>
Last Name:<BR><INPUT TYPE=text SIZE=50 NAME=txtLastName></TD>
</TR>

<!--Address Data-->
</TR>
<TD COLSPAN=4><FONT SIZE=2 COLOR=#840084 FACE=arial>
Address 1:<BR><INPUT TYPE=text SIZE=60 NAME=txtAddress1></TD>
</TR>

<TR>
<TD COLSPAN=4><FONT SIZE=2 COLOR=#840084 FACE=arial>
Address 2:<BR><INPUT TYPE=text   SIZE=60 NAME=txtAddress2></TD>
</TR>

<!--City  State Zip Country-->
<TR>
<TD COLSPAN=2><FONT SIZE=2 COLOR=#840084 FACE=arial>
City: <BR><INPUT TYPE=text SIZE=50 NAME=txtCity></TD>

<TD><FONT SIZE=2 COLOR=#840084 FACE=arial>
State: <BR><INPUT TYPE=text NAME=txtState></TD>
</TR>

<TR>
<TD><FONT SIZE=2 COLOR=#840084 FACE=arial>
Zip: <BR><INPUT TYPE=text NAME=txtZip></TD>

<TD><FONT SIZE=2 COLOR=#840084 FACE=arial>
Country: <BR><INPUT TYPE=text NAME=txtCountry></TD>
</TR>

<!--E-mail, Phone, URL-->
<TR>
<TD><FONT SIZE=2 COLOR=#840084 FACE=arial>
E-Mail <BR><INPUT TYPE=text NAME=txtEmail></TD>

<TD><FONT SIZE=2 COLOR=#840084 FACE=arial>Phone: <BR>
<INPUT TYPE=text NAME=txtPhone></TD>

<TD COLSPAN=2><FONT SIZE=2 COLOR=#840084 FACE=arial>
URL: <BR><INPUT TYPE=text SIZE=30 NAME=txtURL></TD>
</TR>
</FONT>

<!--Put in a line across the TABLE-->
<TR>
<TD COLSPAN=4>
<HR>
</TD>
</TR>
```

Part

VII

Ch

35

continues

Listing 35.15 Continued

```
<!--Customer ID and Password-->
<TR>
<TD><FONT SIZE=2 COLOR=#FF0639 FACE=arial>
Customer ID: <BR><INPUT TYPE=text NAME=custID></TD>

<TD><FONT SIZE=2 COLOR=#FF0639 FACE=arial>
Password: <BR><INPUT TYPE=password NAME=txtPassword></TD>

<TD><FONT SIZE=2 COLOR=#FF0639 FACE=arial>
Password Confirmation: <BR><INPUT TYPE=password NAME=txtPassConfirm></TD>
</TR>
</FONT>


<!--Credit Card-->
<TR>
<TD COLSPAN=4>
<HR>
</TR>
<TR>


<!--Credit Card Type-->
<TD><FONT SIZE=2 FACE=ARIAL COLOR=#00218C>Credit Card Type:<BR></TD>
<TD  COLSPAN=3 ALIGN=CENTER><FONT SIZE=2 FACE=ARIAL COLOR=#00218C>
<INPUT TYPE=radio NAME=radCcType VALUE=visa>Visa
<INPUT TYPE=radio NAME=radCcType VALUE=mc>MasterCard
<INPUT TYPE=radio NAME=radCcType VALUE=amex>American Express
<INPUT TYPE=radio NAME=radCcType VALUE=disc>Discover
</TD>


<!--Credit Card Number-->
<TR>
<TD  COLSPAN=2><FONT SIZE=2 FACE=ARIAL COLOR=#00218C>
Credit Card Number:<BR><INPUT TYPE=text SIZE=50 NAME=txtCcNumber></TD>
</TR>


<!--Credit Card Expiration-->
<TR>
<TD  COLSPAN=2><FONT SIZE=2 FACE=ARIAL COLOR=#00218C>
Expiration Date:<BR><INPUT TYPE=text NAME=txtExpDate></TD>
</TR>


<TR>
<TD></TD>
<!--Submit Button-->
<TD><INPUT TYPE=button NAME=submit  VALUE="Submit Customer Info"></TD>
<!--Clear Button-->
<TD><INPUT TYPE=reset VALUE="Clear Customer Info"></TD>
<TD></TD>
</TR>
</FONT>


<TR>
```

```
<TD  COLSPAN=2>
<!--Return Button-->
<INPUT TYPE=button NAME=cmdReturn VALUE="< Return"></TD>
</TR>

</FORM>
</TABLE></CENTER>
</BODY>
</HTML>
```

Notice that the page contains a frmRegInfo and that the form is populated with TEXT, PASSWORD, RADIO, SUBMIT, RESET, and BUTTON <INPUT> types (see Figure 35.19). However, all the data is analyzed and manipulated by using VBScript. These <INPUT> elements are referenced as children objects of the IE Object Model, Form object. Notice too, that the SUBMIT element's default submission behavior (which happens when you press an HTML <INPUT TYPE=SUBMIT> element) is modified by using the OnClick method of the IE Submit object. Thus, you are able to overcome one of the pivotal shortcomings of HTML elements—the ability to analyze and respond to user input before such input is sent on to a server on the Internet.

FIG. 35.19

You can use the <TABLE> element to better organize your forms.

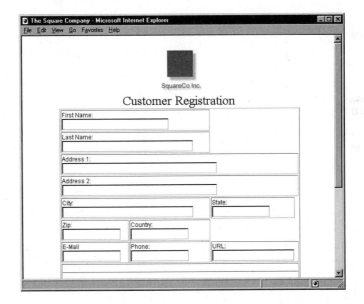

To validate that all <INPUT TYPE=TEXT> element's VALUEs are not empty, the code takes advantage of VBScript's ability to reference elements as members of a collection, thus averting the need to explicitly query the VALUE of every element by name. This is done by querying each item in the Form object's ELEMENTS collection by using a For...Next loop and then using a Window object's Alert method and the Element object's Setfocus and Select methods if errors are encountered.

Part
VII

Ch

35

The `History` object's `Back` method is used within the `OnClick` event of the custom-created Return button. This button was created *not* as an IE Intrinsic Control, but rather as an HTML element upon which an event handler has been imposed by using VBScript (see Figure 35.20).

FIG. 35.20

You can make a Return button by using HTML elements and VBScript.

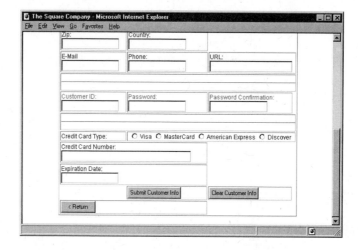

Using a scripting language such as VBScript in conjunction with HTML elements is a very flexible, powerful programming technique. You can use this methodology not only with Internet Explorer by using VBScript, but also with Netscape Navigator. All you need to do to have HTML elements be interactive within Netscape Navigator is to use JavaScript instead of VBScript. If you are reticent about taking the time to learn another scripting language, while it is true that JavaScript is syntactically different than VBScript, they are conceptually similar and *Internet Explorer supports JavaScript*! It might not be the superfluous use of time that you might think it is. In the next chapter, you take a look at how Java and VBScript can be used to create Web pages.

From Here...

In this chapter, you looked at HTML elements and how you can use them in your Web pages. You also looked at the Internet Explorer Intrinsic Controls and the Internet Explorer Object Model. You've looked at how VBScript can be used to tie all of these different tools and techniques together to form a working Web site, as well.

The following chapters will provide you with additional coverage on creating Web pages:

- Chapter 36, "Programming Web Pages," continues to look at VBScript by creating additional Web pages and introducing a few new tools and techniques.
- Chapter 37, "Creating Active Server Pages," discusses how you can use Active Server Pages to provide a Web site that responds to your users' requests.

■ Chapter 39, "Using the Web, Databases, and Visual Basic," shows you how you can connect your Web site to a database.

You might want to check out the following Que books for additional information on VBScript and Web page development:

■ For more information about HTML Elements, see Que's *Special Edition Using HTML* (ISBN 0-7897-0758-6), Chapter 21, "Forms and How They Work," on pp. 489-502.

■ For more information about The Internet Explorer 3.0 Object Model for Scripting, see Que's *Special Edition Using VBScript* (ISBN 0-7897-0809-4), Chapter 11, "Using the Internet Explorer 3.0 Object Model," on pp. 197-199.

■ For more information about using ActiveX Control Pad, see the Que book, *Special Edition Using VBScript* (ISBN 0-7897-0809-4), Chapter 4, "Creating a Standard HTML page," on pp. 84-98.

You might want to check out the following Web sites for additional information on the topics covered in this chapter:

■ For detailed documentation online about The Internet Explorer 3.0 Object Model for Scripting, go to **http://www.microsoft.com/workshop/prog/sdk/docs/scriptom/** on the Internet.

■ For a copy of the ActiveX Control Pad and numerous other ActiveX resouces, go to **http://www.microsoft.com/sitebuilder/** on the Internet.

■ For more information about VBScript and numerous resources including a VBScript debugger, go to **http://www.microsoft.com/vbscript/** on the Internet.

Part
VII

Ch
35

CHAPTER 36

Programming Web Pages

HTML pages should be interesting as well as functional. The average Web user is familiar with a computer environment in which functionality is provided by visually pleasing controls, such as a toolbar or a menu list. While the HTML controls add basic visual support, such as the button, they lack the range of visual functionality familiar to the user. ActiveX controls are a great way to make Web pages interesting while still providing a great deal of additional functionality. A Web page that contains a few common ActiveX controls gives users the visual benefits of a regular computer application along with the capability to interact with the Web page.

At the time of this writing, the only Web browser that fully supports ActiveX controls is the Microsoft Internet Explorer 3.01 (or higher). The HTML standard that describes the inclusion of ActiveX controls can be found at **http://www.w3.org/pub/WWW/TR/WD-object.html**. The HTML tag that supports ActiveX controls is the <OBJECT> tag. I will assume that you are currently using Internet Explorer as your main browser from this point on. ■

ActiveX controls and HTML

Include ActiveX controls in your Web pages with the help of the HTML tag <OBJECT>.

Setting ActiveX control properties with VBScript

Learn how to set the properties of an ActiveX control with VBScript.

Triggering VBScript subroutines with ActiveX control events

Learn how ActiveX controls and VBScript can act together to accomplish tasks.

Using Visual Interdev to create Web pages

Discover how easy it is to create rich Web pages with Microsoft's Visual Interdev.

JavaScript and Java applets

Discover how JavaScript and Java applets can be used with VBScript to create browser-independent Web pages.

Understanding the HTML *<Object>* Tag's Purpose

The Object tag's original purpose was to replace the current tags of IMG, EMBED, and APPLET. These tags all load specific objects. The object tag makes the HTML code nonspecific but includes an attribute to specify which type of object it is. But the Object tag does more than just support ActiveX controls.

The Object tag allows the browser to determine if it can support the object type (MIME type) before it downloads the object from the server. If the browser doesn't support the mime type, the HTML code between <OBJECT> and </OBJECT> can point to an alternative object type to download. For example, there are many sound file types. Some provide for richer sound quality but also require special applications to play their types of sound.

In this example, the Object tag can specify the special application but can still provide a different, lower-quality sound file as an alternate type. The alternative should be a generic type that is widely supported on the Internet. If no suitable alternative object exists, HTML text can be added to tell the user that something is not being loaded and can perhaps point to a download location for the appropriate application, such as the advanced sound file. Microsoft Internet Explorer has limited support for non-ActiveX actions of the Object tag; the example of the advanced sound files' use of the Object tag is not fully supported in the Microsoft 3.0 browser.

http://www.blooberry.com/html/intro.htm   This is a great resource for information on which browser supports which tag and which attributes.

Listing 36.1 illustrates the general use of an Object tag. (Don't worry about the syntax, which will be explained later.) The object type and mime type in the listing are meant to be placeholders only. They have no corresponding object. Therefore, the text and image should be displayed instead of the fake object. This listing shows you how to compensate for the browser's inability to load the object. Every Object tag should have an alternate display, such as a link or text, so that browsers that don't support objects can still go through your site. Do not expect this page to work in your browser; the following code is meant to be an example.

T I P

You will be using the code in Listing 36.1 as a template to create the next couple of projects in this book. You can also use this for your own development efforts by placing any additional code after the <BODY> tag.

Listing 36.1   template.htm—Alternative Text Can Be Displayed Instead of the Object

```
<HTML>
<HEAD>
<TITLE>Object with Alternative Text</TITLE>
</HEAD>
<BODY>
```

```
<OBJECT
DATA = mydata.abc
```

```
TYPE = "Application/myapp">
<A HREF="http://www.download.com">Download
➥</A> the necessary application
from here.
</OBJECT>
</BODY>
</HTML>
```

The Object tag has a beginning and an ending tag. The attributes placed in the opening tag give object information, such as the object's name and where to download it. The object can have parameters, so the <PARAM> tag is provided to support passing parameters to the object when it is loaded. For an ActiveX object, these parameters are the ActiveX control's properties. The browser displays any HTML text or tags that are between the Object tags if it cannot load the object. If the Object cannot be loaded, then the Param tags are ignored. Any supported HTML tags can be placed in between the Object tags.

> **CAUTION**
>
> You can't guarantee that you will always have access to the <PARAM> tag to set properties in an ActiveX control unless it was created using Visual Basic 5.0.
>
> If the control is created with Visual C++ or another high-level language, the capability to set properties through the <PARAM> tag *must* be programmed by the developer via the PropertyBag, or the developer must use the Data tag. The Data tag is described in the following section.

The HTML *<Object>* Tag's Attributes

The Object tag's attributes let the browser know how to display the object. Before the object is fully displayed, the ActiveX layer in Microsoft Internet Explorer attempts to load the control based on those attributes. Table 36.1 lists all of the attributes that apply to ActiveX controls. (There are more attributes in the specification, but they are not related to ActiveX controls.) One good place for getting the complete ActiveX specification is at **http://www.microsoft.com/activex/**. Another possibility is the ActiveX SDK, although the SDK is currently undergoing revisions on a continual basis.

Table 36.1   Object Tag Attributes

Attribute Name	Function
Align	Position of the object
Border	Border of the object
Classid	Class identifier of the object
Codebase	URL location of the object

continues

Table 36.1   Continued

Attribute Name	Function
Data	Encoded initialization information (See the caution in the following section, "Attributes that Load the ActiveX Control.")
Declare	Object is declared but not loaded until it is referenced
Height	Height of the object
Hspace	Horizontal gutter of the object
Id	Reference name of the object
Name	Name of object when passed in a Form tag
Type	Mime type
Vspace	Vertical gutter of the object
Width	Width of the object

Some of the Object tag attributes are used to load the control correctly, while others are used to reference the object (such as in a VBScript). Still others are used to visually display the control. The first set of attributes focuses on the loading attributes, the second set focuses on referencing the attribute with code, and the third set of attributes focuses on the display of the control.

Attributes that Load the ActiveX Control

While some of the attributes are not critical to the object loading, a couple of attributes have to be set in order correctly for the object to be loaded. The main attributes of an ActiveX object are the CLASSID (this should be familiar to you by now) and the CODEBASE. The classid, the unique identifier for this control, allows the browser to find the control. The codebase is where you download the control. As with all attributes, the correct syntax is `Attribute="value"` when the attribute name is not case-sensitive. The following examples show how the CODEBASE attribute could be used.

```
CODEBASE="http://www.mydomain.com/myindex.html"
```

or

```
codebase="http://www.mydomain.com/myindex.html"
```

In the preceding examples CODEBASE will be treated the same as codebase because the attribute portion is case-insensitive.

The *CLASSID* Attribute   The CLASSID attribute value should include the classid of the object, prefaced with the characters `classid:`. The classid value can be found in The Registry at HKEY_CLASSES_ROOT*XYZ*\\CLSID; XYZ is the name of the control. Figure 36.1 shows a picture of The Registry on a Windows 95 machine for the control names MSGrid.Grid. Notice that the classid on the right side of the figure is a huge number. This is the number you want to place in the classid attribute. The following example shows how the classid for the MSGrid control would be placed in the CLASSID attribute.

```
classid="classid:A8C3B720-0B5A-101B-B22E-0AA0037B2FC".
```

FIG. 36.1

The Registry on Windows 95 and NT 4.0 holds the classid for each control registered on your system.

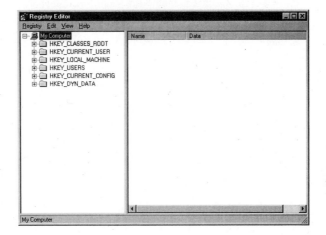

The Registry in Windows NT 4.0 can be accessed via the REGEDIT.EXE application (just as in Windows 95). This application is used to navigate through The Registry just as the Windows file system can be navigated with the Explorer.

When you get to the point where the regedit application looks like Figure 36.1, you can double-click the entry on the right side. This action brings up a dialog box. You can select that text (the classid) and copy it (Ctrl+C). You can then paste the number into your HTML page. Do *not* alter the number in any way. If you do, your browser cannot find the control.

The preceding example, ComCtl2.Animation.1, contains the version number. By looking at this name, you can see that the version number is 1.

Listing 36.2 illustrates how a Web page can use just the classid attribute. The Web page is entirely correct only if the control does not need any initialization data (such as properties), is not referenced via VBScript, and is already on the machine. Few controls meet that criteria. Do not expect this page to load a control in your browser; this code is meant to be an example.

Listing 36.2   classid.htm—A Web Page that Uses the Object Tag with the Classid Attribute

```
<HTML>
<HEAD>
<TITLE>Basic ActiveX Control Page</TITLE>
</HEAD>
```

continues

Listing 36.2   Continued

```
<BODY>

My interesting Web page.
<!-- added Classid reference ‡
<OBJECT CLASSID="CLSID:978C9E23-D4B0-11CE-BF2D-00AA003F40D0">
</OBJECT>

</BODY>
</HTML>
```

The *CODEBASE* Attribute   The CODEBASE attribute should be the URL location where you download the control. The URL should look like any Web address: http://www.mysite.org/controls/mycontrol.ocx, for example. As long as the control's extension is .OCX, you don't need to supply any more information. OCX should be the default extension if the control is built with Visual Basic 5. If you know that the control is already on the client's machine (such as a company intranet of only Windows machines), you don't need to use the CODEBASE attribute.

Before the browser downloads the control, it checks to see if the control currently exists on the system. If the control does exist, the browser checks to see if the control is the correct version (if one is specified). The browser is finished with the CODEBASE attribute if the control is the correct version. If the version is not correct (but the control is on the machine), the browser downloads the control and registers it. If the control does not exist on the client machine, the browser downloads the control and registers it.

The control's version is denoted in the CODEBASE attribute by adding a #Version= and then the version number. The version number's syntax is a four-part number, each part of which is comma-delimited. If you right-click an executable file (EXE) in your Windows operating system, the version property page will have the version number, such as 4.00.31.85. The periods are replaced with commas for the HTML page. The program automatically adds the version to the control when the programmer builds it. The programmer must ensure that different "versions" of the same control have different version numbers. The higher the version number, the more recent it is. 4.00.31.85 is a newer version than 4.00.31.70.

Developers can easily choose any extension for the control they want. If the extension is not OCX, then the download has to be a *.cab (short for cabinet) file. The cab file is a compression technique that makes the control smaller as it is shipped across the Internet. One file that can go in the cab file is the information file (*.inf), which tells the browser what to do with the control and any files that are in the cab file. Because this book assumes that controls are built with Visual Basic 5, you can assume that controls used in this book have the extension of OCX. Visual Basic 5's Books Online has a section about cab files.

http://www.microsoft.com/workshop/prog/cab/   There is a complete Cabinet Developer's SDK at the Microsoft site. The SDK can be used to create Cabinet and Diamond files for your ActiveX controls and Java applets.

> **CAUTION**
>
> Building a cab file can be a simple task or a complex task, depending on what you want to happen to the files in the cab file. For example, if the control has an extension of *.XYZ* and isn't dependent on any other files, the only action the browser needs to perform is to register the control. The browser automatically registers the control if the extension is OCX. However, if the control is dependent on several other files (such as initialization files or other dynamic link libraries), the browser needs to be told where to put those files and any information that must be added to the system Registry.

Listing 36.3 defines a Web page that uses the classid and the codebase. The codebase can be an absolute reference to a Web page (the first object on the page), or it can be a relative reference from the location of the calling Web page (the second object on the page). Do not expect this page to load a control in your browser. This code is meant to be an example only.

Listing 36.3   codebase.htm—A Web Page that Uses the Object Tag with the Classid Attribute and the Codebase Attribute

```
<HTML>
<HEAD>
<TITLE>Basic ActiveX Control Page</TITLE>
</HEAD>
<BODY>

My interesting Web page.

<OBJECT
CLASSID="CLSID:978C9E23-D4B0-11CE-BF2D-00AA003F40D0"
<!-- Added codebase to point to mycontrol.ocx ‡
CODEBASE="www.mysite.com/scripts/mycontrol.ocx">
</OBJECT>
<OBJECT
CLASSID="CLSID:978C9E23-D4B0-11CE-BF2D-00AA003F40D0"
<!-- added codebase reference ‡
CODEBASE="/../../scripts/mycontrol.ocx">
</OBJECT>

</BODY>
</HTML>
```

You use the DATA attribute to initialize the ActiveX control properties through 64-bit encoding. You cannot read the properties' values after they have been initialized because the initialization is encoded. The encoding is meant for small, but complex initialization. If an ActiveX control is poorly developed in a high-level language, 64-bit encoding is used for the initialization of all of the properties. There are two drawbacks to using the data attribute. You have to know how to generate the 64-bit encoding, and debugging is difficult because the coding is so hard to read. (If you don't have to use the DATA attribute, use a much easier equivalent, PARAM tags, discussed in "Working with the *<PARAM>* Tag" later in this chapter.)

Listing 36.4 illustrates a sample Web page that uses the data attribute. Notice that the value of the attribute is prepended with information about the encoding and the MIME type. The control in this listing is the Calendar Control 40.0.

Listing 36.4   activex1.htm—Initializing an ActiveX Control's Properties Using the *DATA* Attribute in a Web Page

```
<HTML>
<HEAD>
<TITLE>Basic ActiveX Control Page</TITLE>
</HEAD>
<BODY>

My interesting Web page.

<OBJECT ID="Calendar1" WIDTH=288 HEIGHT=192
  CLASSID="CLSID:8E27C92B-1264-101C-8A2F-040224009C02"
  DATA="DATA:application/x-oleobject;BASE64,K8knjmQSHBCKLwQCJ
ACcAgAACADEHQAA2BMAAM0HBAAXAA8AAIAAAAAAACg
ABAAAIAAAKAAAQABAAIAAAABAAAAAQAAAAEAAAABAAAAAQAAAAEAAAAAAAAA
AAAAAAAAAAAAAAAAAAAAAAAAAAAAAAAAAAAAAAAAAAAAAAAAAAAAAAAAAAAAAA
AAAAAAAAAAAAAAAAAAAAAAAAAAAAAAAAAAAAAAAAAAAAAAAAAAAAAAAAAAAAAA
AAAAAAAAAAAAAAAAAAAAAAAAAAAAAAAAAAAAAAAAAAAAAAAAAAAAAAAAAAAAAA
AAAAAAAAAAAAAAAAAAAAAAAAAAAAAAAAAAAAAAAAAAAAAAAAAAAAAAAAAAAAAA
AAAAAAAAAAAAAAAAAAAAAAAAAAAAAAAAAAAAAAAAAAAAAAAAAAAAAAAAAAAAAA
AAAAAAAAAAAAAAAAAAAAAAAAAAAAAAAAAAAAAAEAAAC8AkRCAQAFQXJp
YWwwBAAAAkAFEQgEABUFyaWFsAQAAALwCwNQBAAVBcmlhbhA==">
</OBJECT>
</BODY>
</HTML>
```

TIP   If you have a hard time deciphering the encoding of the preceding listing, two Microsoft programs are designed to make this type of work easy. Microsoft's ActiveX Control Pad (free on the Microsoft Web site) is an elementary application that adds ActiveX controls to a Web page. Because it is free, the functionality is bare and the support from Microsoft is nonexistent.

Microsoft's Visual InterDev (part of the Developer Suite) has an advanced version of the ActiveX Control Pad. Once you select the object you want to add to the page, a property sheet appears (just as it does in Visual Basic). You fill in the property sheet and design the visual properties of the object. When you insert the control into the page, the properties are set for you, either through the Data attribute or the Param tag (discussed in "Working with the <PARAM> Tag" later in this chapter).

The *DATA* and *TYPE* Attributes   If you use the DATA attribute and the data is just an URL (instead of encoding), you need to use the TYPE attribute to let the browser know what type of data is being retrieved. If the browser doesn't support that MIME type, the data is not downloaded and the object is not initialized. Remember that using the data attribute as an URL is the hard way to work with the popular controls on your Windows 95 or Windows NT machine (depending on the control, doing so may be impossible). The popular controls generally need for the properties to be set through the data attribute that is encoded or set through the PARAM tag (discussed in "Working with the *<PARAM>* Tag" later in this chapter). If you have created your own control, using the DATA attribute as an URL and using the TYPE attribute to specify the MIME type may work for you.

Listing 36.5 illustrates how to use the DATA and TYPE attributes together. Do not expect this page to load a control in your browser; this code is meant to be an example. If you compare Listings 36.5 and 36.4, you can see that when the data is encoded, the data type is already included. When the data is not encoded, the MIME type has to be specified via the TYPE attribute.

Listing 36.5 activex2.htm—Initializing an ActiveX Control by Using the *DATA* and *TYPE* Attributes Together

```
<HTML>
<HEAD>
<TITLE>Declare Attribute</TITLE>
</HEAD>
<BODY>
    <OBJECT ID="MyControl"
      CLASSID="CLSID:0713E8A2-850A-131b-AXC0-4210302A8DA7"
      DATA="http://mysite/mydirectory/mydata.xyz"
TYPE="application/x-oleobject">
    </OBJECT>
</BODY>
</HTML>
```

The *DECLARE* Attribute   The DECLARE attribute lets the browser know which object to load and when to load it (after it is referenced). This is a cool feature in two situations—when you have a link point to an object that could not be referenced from a single URL and when one object is a parameter to another object.

An example of the latter situation is the ever-popular tree control. The tree control is generally used with a control of images. A tree element of type X has an image that illustrates X and a tree element of type Y has an image that illustrates Y. In order for the image control to be a parameter of the tree control, the tree control lists the image control as a parameter with the PARAM tag (discussed later). The image control then uses the DECLARE attribute so that it is loaded only when the tree control needs it. Loading the control only when it is referenced is called *late binding*.

Listing 36.6 illustrates how to use the DECLARE attribute. The first control is the tree control, which has a property called ImageList. The # sign in front of the reference to ImageList1 in the tree control indicates that the referenced control is on the same page as the ActiveX control. The ImageList control is the second control that needs to be referenced. The ImageList control must also include the declare statement so that it is loaded only when the tree control is initialized.

If you run this page as it is written in Listing 36.6, it does not run. This code is for discussion purposes only. Using the tree control and the ImageList control actually requires much more code to function than other controls, but these controls are perfect examples of how to use the DECLARE attribute. The tree control and the ImageList use the DATA attribute to initialize the control. I've reduced the value of the DATA attribute so that the code listing is easier to read than it usually is.

Listing 36.6   activeX3.htm—Declaring an ActiveX Control that Is Initialized by Another Control on the Same Web Page

```
<HTML>
<HEAD>
<TITLE>Declare Attribute</TITLE>
</HEAD>
<BODY>

    <OBJECT ID="TreeView1"
    CLASSID="CLSID:0713E8A2-850A-101b-AFC0-4210102A8DA7"
    DATA="DATA:application/x-oleobject;BASE64...">
<!-- referencing the control ‡
    <PARAM NAME="ImageList" VALUE="#ImageList1"
VALUETYPE="OBJECT">
    </OBJECT>
<!-- declaring imagelist ‡
    <OBJECT ID="ImageList1" DECLARE
    CLASSID="CLSID:58DA8D8F-9D6A-101b-AFC0-4210102A8DA7"
    DATA="DATA:application/x-oleobject;BASE64...">
    </OBJECT>
</BODY>
</HTML>
```

Attributes that Reference the ActiveX Control

Only two attributes are used to reference the ActiveX ImageList control—NAME and ID. The NAME attribute should be familiar to you. Any information passed in a Form uses the NAME attribute. The NAME attribute is used on the Web server when the page is returned to reference the data sent back. The ActiveX control is used in the same way. If you use the control inside a FORM from which some information is being sent back to the server, the object tag must use the NAME attribute. The name can be any string value you want, such as MyControl or TreeControl, or just CNTR. Listing 36.7 illustrates how to include the NAME attribute on the Web page. The NAME attribute has no effect on any of the other attributes. The browser only uses it to pass values back to the Web server.

Listing 36.7   activeX4.htm—By Using the *NAME* Attribute, ActiveX's Properties Can Be Passed in a *FORM*

```
<HTML>
<HEAD>
```

```
<TITLE>The Name Attribute</TITLE>
</HEAD>
<BODY>

<FORM METHOD="GET" ACTION="nextpage.htm">
    <OBJECT
    CLASSID="CLSID:978C9E23-D4B0-11CE-BF2D-00AA003F40D0"
    NAME="MyControl">
    </OBJECT>
</FORM>
</BODY>
</HTML>
```

Remember that forms use the name/value pair to pass information back to the server. The NAME attribute and the VALUE attribute have to be set. The preceding example is valid according to the HTML specification but will probably not be used in this manner for Internet Explorer 3.x. The problem is that the VALUE attribute is not listed in the object tag, and the browser can't assume that it is any particular attribute. In order to pass back a value to the server in a Form from an ActiveX object, you probably want to set the name and value in VBScript and then include that information in an input tag of the Form tag. The value could be any number of things—a property, a result of a method call, or a value generated as a result of a user event. This functionality may change in the 4.0 version of Microsoft's Internet Explorer.

The other reference attribute is the ID attribute. If you plan to manage the control in script, the ID is mandatory. The only way you can reference the control in script is from the ID. The ID is a string that you choose. Although this string can be just about anything, it is wise to name the ID something that reflects what the control does. Any reference to the control's methods, properties, and events in script has to be prefixed with the ID. (The requirements are the same for the name of the control in a true Visual Basic application.) Listing 36.8 illustrates how you would reference a control from VBScript. Don't concentrate on the syntax of the script; this script is only meant to be an example. A more detailed discussion of VBScript and ActiveX follows later in this chapter in the section "The VBScript Web Page." Notice that Procedure1 changes the background color of the label to green. The object name is Label1 and the property is BackColor.

> **Listing 36.8   label.htm—By Using the ID Attribute, the ActiveX Control Can Be Manipulated in VBScript or JavaScript**

```
<HTML>
<HEAD>
<TITLE>The ID Attribute</TITLE>

<SCRIPT LANGUAGE="VBScript">
<!--
Sub Procedure1()
    Label1.BackColor = "GREEN"
end sub
```

continues

Listing 36.8   Continued

```
-->
</SCRIPT>

</HEAD>
<BODY>
    <OBJECT ID="Label1" WIDTH=132 HEIGHT=28
      CLASSID="CLSID:978C9E23-D4B0-11CE-BF2D-00AA003F40D0">
        <PARAM NAME="Caption" VALUE="My Cool Label Control">
        <PARAM NAME="Size" VALUE="3493;741">
        <PARAM NAME="BorderStyle" VALUE="1">
        <PARAM NAME="FontCharSet" VALUE="0">
        <PARAM NAME="FontPitchAndFamily" VALUE="2">
    </OBJECT>
</BODY>
</HTML>
```

Attributes that Control the Visual Display of the ActiveX Control

Several attributes affect how the control appears on the page, including ALIGN, BORDER, HEIGHT, HSPACE, VSPACE, and WIDTH. This section focuses on how these familiar attributes relate to ActiveX controls.

Attribute	Function
ALIGN	Focuses on the position of the control in relation to the objects around it. The values for align are left, text, middle, textmiddle, baseline, textbottom, center, and right.
BORDER	Specifies how large the border around the object should be.
HEIGHT and WIDTH	Specify how large the object should be.
HSPACE and VSPACE	Specify how much space should be between the control and neighboring objects.

Working with the *<PARAM>* Tag

You have two choices of how to set the parameters of the ActiveX control. The first is through the DATA attribute of the OBJECT tag. The second is through the PARAM tag. The PARAM tag is much easier to use because it follows the HTML standard name/value pair model. The data is not encoded so it is easy to see what has been passed to the control. The PARAM tag is enclosed within the OBJECT's beginning and ending tags.

The PARAM tag has two obvious attributes, NAME and VALUE. NAME is the property of the ActiveX control, which is initialized to the VALUE. The PARAM tag has two more attributes, VALUETYPE and TYPE. The VALUETYPE attribute was used in Listing 36.6 to describe what type of information was contained in the VALUE attribute. The value can be DATA (not encoded),

OBJECT (meaning an object's name, as in Listing 36.6), or REF (meaning a Web address reference). The TYPE attribute, which indicates the MIME type of the data, is used in conjunction with the VALUETYPE attribute (when the VALUETYPE attribute is equal to REF). Because the parameter VALUEDATA is a Web site, the browser must know what type of data is being retrieved at that Web site. Listing 36.9 illustrates a couple of different controls that use the PARAM tag. This listing is meant to be an example and may not load in your browser.

Listing 36.9   label2.htm—Using the PARAM Tag

```
<HTML>
<HEAD>
<TITLE>The ID Attribute</TITLE>


</HEAD>
<BODY>
    <OBJECT ID="Label1" WIDTH=132 HEIGHT=28
     CLASSID="CLSID:978C9E23-D4B0-11CE-BF2D-00AA003F40D0">
        <PARAM NAME="Caption" VALUE="My Cool Label Control">
        <PARAM NAME="Size" VALUE="3493;741">
        <PARAM NAME="BorderStyle" VALUE="1">
        <PARAM NAME="FontCharSet" VALUE="0">
        <PARAM NAME="FontPitchAndFamily" VALUE="2">
    </OBJECT>


    <OBJECT ID="Marquee1" WIDTH=148 HEIGHT=40
     CLASSID="CLSID:1A4DA620-6217-11CF-BE62-0080C72EDD2D"
     CODEBASE="text.htm">
        <PARAM NAME="_ExtentX" VALUE="3916">
        <PARAM NAME="_ExtentY" VALUE="1058">
    </OBJECT>
</BODY>
</HTML>
```

The DATA attribute (encoded data) and the PARAM tag can be used together. However, they rarely are. Most controls use either the DATA attribute or the PARAM tag.

Writing Web Pages with Microsoft Visual Interdev

Writing Web pages that have ActiveX controls can be simple if the control is simple. The controls that have great functionality are usually more complex, however. Microsoft has developed an environment that makes writing these pages easier. This tool is called Visual Interdev. It is sold separately or as part of the Visual Developer suite. To illustrate how easy it is to write a Web page with Visual Interdev, I will write a Web page that uses a tab page control.

N O T E The first control used in this section is Calendar Control 40.0. The OCX file for this control is mscal.ocx . The second control used is Microsoft Forms 2.0 Textbox. The file name is fm20.dll. ■

Using ActiveX Controls with Visual Interdev

First, start up Visual Interdev and insert the control. Figure 36.2 shows the dialog box used to add a new HTML page. To open this dialog box, choose File, New and then select the Files tab. Choose HTML page. After you select these options, Visual Interdev creates a basic HTML file for you and indicates at which point you should start including your own HTML or ActiveX.

FIG. 36.2

Creating a new HTML page is the first thing you do after starting Visual Interdev.

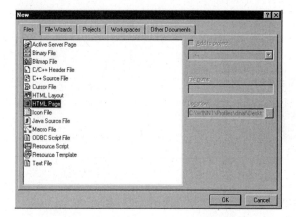

When you want to add an ActiveX control, choose Insert, Into HTML, ActiveX Control. A window of all of the ActiveX controls registered on the system will be displayed. If you have developed a control but it is not displayed in this dialog box, make sure it is registered. Figure 36.3 illustrates the dialog box of all of the controls on this system. The calendar control is highlighted. Notice that behind this dialog box is the HTML file that Visual InterDev has written for you.

T I P If your control is not registered, you can register it in Visual InterDev from the Tools, Register Control menu item. Or you can go to a command prompt and type **regsvr32 x** (**x** is the path and file name of the control). If you just type **regsvr32**, a dialog box displays all of the options for using the regsvr32 application.

Figure 36.4 illustrates what happens once you choose the control and click OK. The HTML page is still open but is displayed behind the dialog box shown in this figure. The HTML page is where you design the control. You can set the properties displayed in the Properties dialog box or you can resize the object.

FIG. 36.3

The next step is to select the ActiveX control.

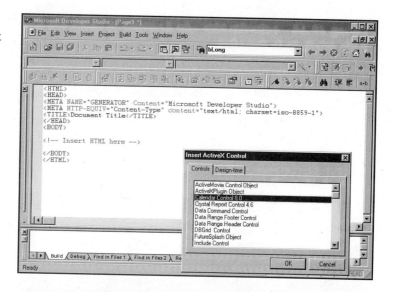

FIG. 36.4

You need to design the physical properties and programmable properties of the ActiveX control next.

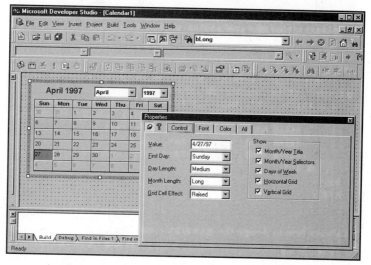

The HTML page created when you accept the default properties and don't resize the object is illustrated in Listing 36.10. Notice that Visual InterDev adds Meta tag information. Visual InterDev has completely filled in the calendar control object tag. The default property of the calendar control has no codebase value. In order for this control to download, that attribute needs to be added. The codebase value is not added to any control you choose. You can either add the text to the HTML page yourself or have Visual InterDev do it.

Listing 36.10 calendar.htm—An Example of Using the Calendar Control; the *DATA* Attribute Is Encoded

```
<HTML>
<HEAD>
<META NAME="GENERATOR" Content="Microsoft Developer Studio">
<META HTTP-EQUIV="Content-Type" content="text/html; charset=iso-8859-1">
<TITLE>Document Title</TITLE>
</HEAD>
<BODY>

<OBJECT ID="Calendar1" WIDTH=288 HEIGHT=192 HSPACE=20
➥VSPACE=20 ALIGN="CENTER"
    CLASSID="CLSID:8E27C92B-1264-101C-8A2F-040224009C02"
    DATA="DATA:application/x-oleobject;BASE64,
➥K8knjmQSHBCKLwQCJACcAgAACADEHQAA2BMAAM0HBAASAA8AAIAAAAAAAACg
ABAAAIAAAKAAAQABAAIAAAABAAAAAQAAAAEAAAABAAAAAQAAAAEAAAAAAAAA
AAAAAAAAAAAAAAAAAAAAAAAAAAAAAAAAAAAAAAAAAAAAAAAAAAAAAAAAAAAA
AAAAAAAAAAAAAAAAAAAAAAAAAAAAAAAAAAAAAAAAAAAAAAAAAAAAAAAAAAAA
AAAAAAAAAAAAAAAAAAAAAAAAAAAAAAAAAAAAAAAAAAAAAAAAAAAAAAAAAAAA
AAAAAAAAAAAAAAAAAAAAAAAAAAAAAAAAAAAAAAAAAAAAAAAAAAAAAAAAAAAA
AAAAAAAAAAAAAAAAAAAAAAAAAAAAAAAAAAAAAAAAEAAAC8AkRCAQAFQXJp
YWwBAAAAkAFEQgEABUFyaWFFsAQAAALwCwNQBAAVBcmlhA==
">
 </OBJECT>
<BR>
    <OBJECT ID="TextBox1" WIDTH=196 HEIGHT=112
➥ALIGN="CENTER" HSPACE=20 VSPACE=20
    CLASSID="CLSID:8BD21D10-EC42-11CE-9E0D-00AA006002F3">
        <PARAM NAME="VariousPropertyBits" VALUE="2894088219">
        <PARAM NAME="Size" VALUE="5186;2963">
        <PARAM NAME="FontCharSet" VALUE="0">
        <PARAM NAME="FontPitchAndFamily" VALUE="2">
    </OBJECT>
</BODY>
</HTML>
```

It's always best to design the appearance and functions of the Web page before creating it. The Web page being created will display both a text box (ActiveX control) and a calendar (ActiveX control). As a user maneuvers through the calendar, any special information about that day will be displayed in the text box. At this point, I have added the TextBox control. Script needs to be written to handle and trap for the events needed to make the TextBox control contain useful information.

Figure 36.5 illustrates what the page looks like in a browser. No additional text has been added to the page, so you can see what the two controls (the text box and the calendar) look like without having to figure out what goes with the control. The system day and month are chosen. Any month and year can be selected from a drop-down box list. The text box is empty because nothing has been added to it.

FIG. 36.5

The calendar control and the text box could be the foundation for several Internet applications.

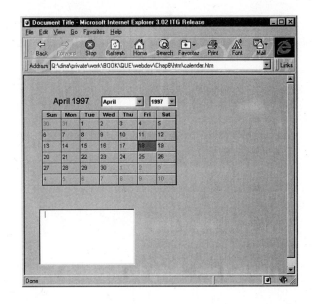

N O T E Remember that an ActiveX control has properties, events, and methods. A *property* is a value of the object, such as color or text. An *event* is a procedure that is triggered when a certain user interaction happens, such as clicking an object. A *method* can set or get a property value. It can perform a function (such as arithmetic) or fire off an event. ■

Scripting with Visual Interdev

The text box information changes based on user input, so the script must be associated with the events of the control. To add these events, the Visual InterDev Script Wizard (choose View, Script Wizard) should be used. Figure 36.6 is the Script Wizard dialog box. The upper half of the dialog box is divided into two sections. The events are on the left side. The properties and methods are on the right side. The icon for methods is a square with an exclamation point in it. The icon for properties is a square with lines (denoting the property sheet).

The NewMonth event is used to place the text in the text box. The NewMonth event of the TextBox control can be fired off in one of two ways any time the current month is changed. The first way is to change the month in the drop-down list box. The second way is to click a grayed-out day number (the grayed-out number indicates that the day is not in the current month). In order to set the text box, the text box control name has to be referenced. The code in this figure (the entire HTML page) appears in Listing 36.11. Only the DATA attribute has been shortened, although it has not changed from Listing 36.10.

Notice that the Script Wizard has added the required <SCRIPT> tag as well as the code about the NewMonth event that was typed into the event window. You do not need Visual InterDev to write this Web page, but it does make programming ActiveX Web pages easier. The type of script language has to be set in the SCRIPT tag. The two choices are VBScript and Java.

FIG. 36.6

The Script Wizard enables you to write code in either VBScript or JavaScript.

Listing 36.11 calendar2.htm—Using the *NewMonth* Event of the Calendar Control

```
<HTML>
<HEAD>
<META NAME="GENERATOR" Content="Microsoft Developer Studio">
<META HTTP-EQUIV="Content-Type" content="text/html; charset=iso-8859-1">
<TITLE>Document Title</TITLE>
</HEAD>
<BODY>
    <SCRIPT LANGUAGE="VBScript">
<!--
Sub Calendar1_NewMonth()
Dim sMonth
sMonth = Calendar1.Month
TextBox1.Text = "New Month = " & sMonth
end sub
-->
    </SCRIPT>
    <OBJECT ID="Calendar1" WIDTH=288 HEIGHT=192
➥HSPACE=20 VSPACE=20 ALIGN="CENTER"
    CLASSID="CLSID:8E27C92B-1264-101C-8A2F-040224009C02"
    DATA="DATA:application/x-oleobject;BASE64,...">
    </OBJECT>
<BR>
    <OBJECT ID="TextBox1" WIDTH=196 HEIGHT=112
➥ALIGN="CENTER" HSPACE=20 VSPACE=20
    CLASSID="CLSID:8BD21D10-EC42-11CE-9E0D-00AA006002F3">
        <PARAM NAME="VariousPropertyBits" VALUE="2894088219">
        <PARAM NAME="Size" VALUE="5186;2963">
        <PARAM NAME="FontCharSet" VALUE="0">
        <PARAM NAME="FontPitchAndFamily" VALUE="2">
    </OBJECT>
</BODY>
</HTML>
```

T I P If you are not using Visual InterDev or Microsoft ActiveX Control Pad, your ActiveX layout software must have some way of discovering methods, properties, and events. Some controls have documentation, and some don't.

CAUTION

In Listing 36.11, the script code (but not the script tags) are enclosed in the HTML comments `<!--"` and `"-->`. If you are writing this code in a different editor than Visual InterDev, you still must include these comments. Several older browsers do not support scripting. The older browser ignores the `<SCRIPT>` tag and displays the script code as text (because the browser thinks that the script code is text). Microsoft's IE browser treats any VBScript inside the `<SCRIPT>` tag as script and ignores the fact that this script is HTML commented. This feature lets the page work on different browsers.

When you write a procedure for events, the procedure name must begin with the control ID (ID attribute), followed by an underscore and the event name. In Listing 36.11, the script for the new procedure is `Calendar1_NewMonth()`. `Calendar1` refers to the ID attribute of the control, and `NewMonth` is the event name. Notice that no parameters are passed to this procedure. (They are not passed because the event is triggered by the system.) With this code, the text box displays `New Month = 5` for May. Because the control stores months as numbers, the programmer must switch from the numeric representation to the character representation.

Enhancing the Control

Now it's time to add a bit more work to the control. The Web page should be designed so that if a new month or a particular day is chosen, any corresponding information is added. To ensure that the text box information includes the month and the day information, a couple of global variables are added. `DayInfo` stores the current day's information. `MonthInfo` stores the current month's information. `TextInfo` stores the combination of `DayInfo`, `MonthInfo`, and anything else added to the text box.

Choose Global Variables from the right side of the Script Wizard dialog box and right-click it. New Global Variable and New Procedure are your options. Choose New Global Variable, type in the name of the month or day, and click OK. Additions to the Web page have only been made in the script section. Listing 36.12 is the new script section. The only added text is the `Dim` *variablename*. Dim (short for dimension) is the VB way of defining variables.

Listing 36.12   calendar3.htm—Adding Global Variables to a Web Page in the VBScript Section

```
<SCRIPT LANGUAGE="VBScript">
<!--
dim MonthInfo
dim DayInfo
```

continues

Listing 36.12 Continued

```
Sub Calendar1_NewMonth()
Dim sMonth
sMonth = Calendar1.Month
TextBox1.Text = "New Month = " & sMonth
end sub
-->
</SCRIPT>
```

N O T E Listing 36.12 includes dim and DIM. The global variable dims were written by Visual InterDev's Script Wizard. The DIM in Calendar1_NewMonth() was written outside of the Script Wizard. VBScript doesn't care about the case of the keywords; it is case-insensitive just as Visual Basic is. ■

T I P When I first wrote the script for this control, some of the events were not fired when I expected them to fire. To debug this problem, I used the ActiveX control test container to watch the events as they were fired. Figure 36.7 illustrates what the messages look like when the calendar control events are fired.

FIG. 36.7
Use the ActiveX control test container to see events as they are fired off.

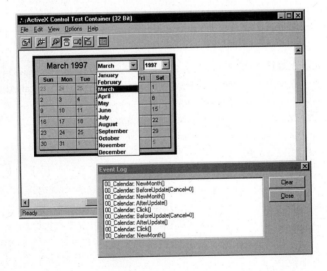

Listing 36.13 is the Web page with the code needed to update the text box. It doesn't matter which procedure is first. Figure 36.8 illustrates what the Web page will look like. There is very little code here. But the user can interact with the calendar control, and the test control can be updated.

Listing 36.13   newmonth.htm—Updating the Text Box Based on Events of the ActiveX Calendar Control

```vbscript
<SCRIPT LANGUAGE="VBScript">
<!--
dim YearInfo
dim MonthInfo

Sub Calendar1_NewYear()
iYear = Calendar1.Year
YearInfo = iYear
MonthInfo = Calendar1.Month
TextBox1.Text = YearInfo  & MonthInfo
end sub

Sub Calendar1_NewMonth()
iMonth = Calendar1.Month
select case (iMonth)
case 1
    MonthInfo = " January is a cold month."
case 2
    MonthInfo = " February is a snowy month"
case 3
    MonthInfo = " March is a green month"
end select
YearInfo = Calendar1.Year
TextBox1.Text = YearInfo  & MonthInfo
end sub
-->
    </SCRIPT>
```

FIG. 36.8

The calendar control updates the text box based upon the date and month displayed.

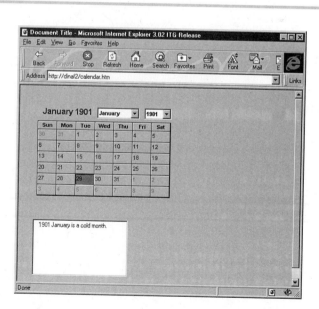

Examining Different Types of ActiveX Controls

There are several types of controls. The last example in Listing 36.13 used a control that "sat" on the page (contained inside the browser window). Some controls can "hover" over the browser, such as the common control dialog (choose File, Open). Some controls are not visible to the user at all. You should look for controls that either add to the functionality of the page or save the user from having to do "extra" work. Adding functionality and helping the user avoid extra work affects the number of visitors that return to your page.

Accessing the System Information File

In this example, the Web page has an invisible ActiveX control that reads the system information of the user's machine and fills in a form. The user can then submit the form back to the Web server. If you want to inventory a company's machines but don't want to walk to each machine, add this invisible control to your Web page.

Use the *Microsoft SysInfo Control, Version 5.0*, with a file name of SYSINFO.OCX. The control needs to be able to read the system information of the user's machine as soon as the Web page is loaded. To do that, use the window_onLoad event. The SysInfo control doesn't have any events or methods—it just has system information properties. As soon as the system information is loaded, you need it to fill in the three text boxes in a form so that the user only has to press the SUBMIT button. This particular form shows the user what is being passed back to the Web server. If the INPUT tags were of type HIDDEN, the user would never have known that the information was being passed back.

Listing 36.14 includes the entire contents of the Web page. Figure 36.9 shows how the page loads in the browser. To load the text boxes of the form when the page is first loaded, the window_onLoad procedure needs to have the name of the text box. Because the text box is in an INPUT tag, and the INPUT tag is in a form, the name of the text box is FORM.ELEMENT.VALUE. The INPUT tag is set directly by the SysInfo control's properties. And that is all there is to this simple procedure.

Listing 36.14   sysinfo.htm—Use the System Info ActiveX Control on a Web Page

```
<HTML>
<HEAD>
<META NAME="GENERATOR" Content="Microsoft Developer Studio">
<META HTTP-EQUIV="Content-Type" content="text/html; charset=iso-8859-1">
<TITLE>Document Title</TITLE>
    <SCRIPT LANGUAGE="VBScript">
<!--
Sub window_onLoad()
    MySysInfoForm.InputSysBuild.value = SysInfo1.OSBuild
    MySysInfoForm.InputSysPlatform.value = SysInfo1.OSPlatform
    MySysInfoForm.InputSysVersion.value = SysInfo1.OSVersion
end sub
-->
```

```
        </SCRIPT>
</HEAD>
<BODY>
Thank you for visiting my page. Here is your system information.
    <OBJECT ID="SysInfo1" WIDTH=39 HEIGHT=39
      CLASSID="CLSID:6FBA474B-43AC-11CE-9A0E-00AA0062BB4C">
        <PARAM NAME="_ExtentX" VALUE="1005">
        <PARAM NAME="_ExtentY" VALUE="1005">
        <PARAM NAME="_Version" VALUE="327680">
    </OBJECT>
    <FORM ACTION="sysinfo.asp" METHOD="GET" NAME="MySysInfoForm">
        <INPUT TYPE=TEXT NAME="InputSysBuild">
Build Number<BR>
        <INPUT TYPE=TEXT NAME="InputSysPlatform">
Platform<BR>
        <INPUT TYPE=TEXT NAME="InputSysVersion">
         System Version<BR>
        <INPUT TYPE=SUBMIT NAME="SUBMIT">
    </FORM>
</BODY>
</HTML>
```

FIG. 36.9

System information of
the visitor is displayed
in a Web page.

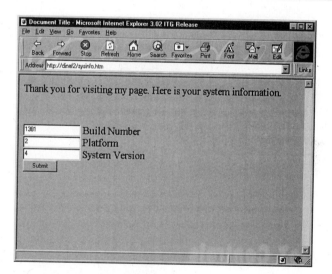

Using the Common Dialog Control

The last example uses the CommonDialog control, which "hovers" over the browser window.
In this example, the event is fired from inside a button, which is inside a form. No separate
VBScript section is needed. The `onClick` event of the button contains the code. The code must
display the dialog box and then set the text box with the file name. Both of these actions happen within the `onClick` event.

Listing 36.15 illustrates how easy it is to make these activities happen. The first thing the onClick event does is to pop up the dialog box in order to find the file, CommonDialog1.ShowOpen(). Next, the onClick event assigns the file chosen to the text box in the form, FINDFILE.strFile.value. The objects in the form should have names. Figure 36.10 illustrates this Web page when the file is being chosen.

Listing 36.15   findfile.htm—Use the Common Dialog Control to Find a File from a Web Page

```
<HTML>
<HEAD>
<META NAME="GENERATOR" Content="Microsoft Developer Studio">
<META HTTP-EQUIV="Content-Type" content="text/html; charset=iso-8859-1">
<TITLE>Document Title</TITLE>
</HEAD>
<BODY>
Step 1) Please find the file you want to send to the server.
    <FORM NAME="FINDFILE">
        <INPUT LANGUAGE="VBScript" TYPE=BUTTON
          ONCLICK="call CommonDialog1.ShowOpen()
          FINDFILE.strFile.value = CommonDialog1.FileName"
         NAME="bFINDFILE" VALUE="Find File"><P><P>
        Step 2) You choose <INPUT TYPE=TEXT NAME="strFile">
    </FORM>
    <OBJECT ID="CommonDialog1" WIDTH=32 HEIGHT=32
      CLASSID="CLSID:F9043C85-F6F2-101A-A3C9-08002B2F49FB">
        <PARAM NAME="_ExtentX" VALUE="847">
        <PARAM NAME="_ExtentY" VALUE="847">
        <PARAM NAME="_Version" VALUE="327680">
        <PARAM NAME="DefaultExt" VALUE="*.*">
        <PARAM NAME="DialogTitle" VALUE="My Common Dialog Control">
        <PARAM NAME="InitDir" VALUE="c:\">
    </OBJECT>
</BODY>
</HTML>
```

Using ActiveX Controls

Please don't try to use any controls that have been downloaded to your machine from the Web except on the Web page they were downloaded with. They may be from reputable software manufacturers, such as Microsoft, or they may be written by an individual. In either case, you cannot guarantee what the control will do, and the only "documentation" you have for that control is your discovery of it for properties, methods, and events.

Any control downloaded from the Web should be treated with the same respect as a shareware product unless it is Verisigned. Verisign authentication means the code and company have been registered and can be held responsible for the behavior of their ActiveX component. If the control does not have a Verisign authentication, you have no way of knowing who wrote it or to what extent it functions.

FIG. 36.10

Find the file by using the CommonDialog control.

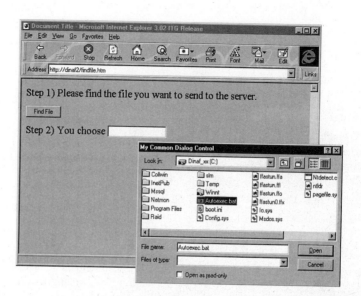

http://www.microsoft.com/gallery.asp   If you want to ensure a quality Web site and experience for your users, either purchase a control (there are several well-respected manufacturers) or make your own. A list of ActiveX control manufacturers can be found at a site known as the ActiveX Gallery.

Do not assume that a control that comes from Microsoft is of Microsoft quality. Microsoft has delegated the development of controls to third-party companies, such as those listed in the ActiveX Gallery. The controls in the Gallery that come from Microsoft are meant to have low functionality, and they generally have no support.

You may be under the impression that the controls are free because you are not charged for them when they are downloaded to your machine. That is incorrect. Just because a control comes from the Web does not mean it is free. ActiveX components are purchased and used the same way as any other software.

JavaScript and Java Applets

JavaScript is a scripting language that you write along with the HTML in your Web pages to do the same kinds of tasks you do with VBScript. These two scripting languages have essentially the same capabilities and can be used to accomplish the same tasks. The only difference between them is in the languages themselves. You know that VBScript is a subset of Visual Basic. It is very familiar to those who are used to programming in Visual Basic. JavaScript, on the other hand, is loosely based on Java, which, in turn, is loosely based on C++. So if you come from a C++ or Java background, you will probably prefer JavaScript.

You may have heard that JavaScript is a "simplified Java." It is not. It is a completely different language, which is designed specifically for scripting tasks and is only loosely based on the Java language.

Can you do everything you want to do with Visual Basic? Maybe, but think about these questions: Do you want to be able to use controls and applications written by others? Is the ability to run your applications on more than one platform important? If you answered yes to either of these questions, you definitely need to give Java a second look.

Creating Java Applets

Java can be compiled and used to create stand-alone applications just as Visual Basic and C++ can create stand-alone applications. But Java can also be used to create Java applets. An applet, as the name implies, is a small application that can be downloaded when a browser pulls up your Web page. Once the applet is downloaded, the applet is executed and the results appear on your page. These results might show up in the form of an animation, a mortgage calculator, or a game.

Comparing Java Applets and ActiveX Controls

So what's the difference between a Java applet and an ActiveX control? Functionally, there isn't much of a difference. You can use both to enhance and activate your Web pages in a variety of ways. But there is a big difference in the way they are implemented.

First, Java applets are always written in Java. ActiveX controls can be written in any language. Second, ActiveX controls are generally platform-specific to Windows (generally because you can write ActiveX controls in Java). But even when ActiveX controls are written in Java, you cannot automatically use them wherever you use Java applets. ActiveX controls are built on top of Microsoft's COM Architecture, which is built into Windows. This architecture needs to be in place before the ActiveX control can work. Fortunately, the COM Architecture has been ported to the Macintosh and to some flavors of Unix. Therefore, everywhere you have the COM Architecture, you can port Java-written ActiveX controls.

Java applets don't have any inherent dependence on architecture as do ActiveX controls, but they do sometimes make use of platform-specific libraries. If you use a user-interface library for your Java applet that was written exclusively for Windows, then you've negated the multiplatform benefit of Java. Although many libraries strive to be multiplatform, you still have to be careful what libraries you use.

So which language is better? That depends on who you ask. Java proponents could emphasize the multiplatform benefits of the applet, while ActiveX proponents could point both to the higher level of integration that an ActiveX control provides and to the proven success of the ActiveX (formerly OLE) architecture in Windows applications.

In the final analysis, you probably want to be able to work freely with both ActiveX controls and Java applets when you create your own Web pages. Fortunately, it isn't difficult to do so.

Using a Java Applet in a Web Page

Up until now you have focused your attention on creating Web pages that use ActiveX controls. This is not the only way that feature-rich Web pages can be created. Java applets can provide your Web page with a broad range of creative expression. In the following sections you see just how easy it is to use Java applets on a Web page.

Anatomy of an Applet

You are familiar with the `<OBJECT>` tag that is used to insert ActiveX controls into your HTML document. There is a different tag for Java applets: `<APPLET>`.

Listing 36.16   sample.htm—Sample of How to Use an Applet in a Web Page

```
<APPLET CODEBASE="applets/java"
  CODE=CardGame.class
  WIDTH=150
  HEIGHT=220
  ALIGN=LEFT
  ALT="The Card Game"
  ID=game>
</APPLET>
```

The following list describes the different components of the preceding example:

- `CODEBASE` identifies what subdirectory contains the Java applets.

- `CODE` provides the actual file name of the Java applet. `CODE` always ends in .class. `CODE` is required.

- `WIDTH` and `HEIGHT` specify, in pixels, the area that the Java applet takes up on the Web page. Remember, though, that a Java applet *can* resize itself. `WIDTH` and `HEIGHT` are also required.

- `ALIGN` determines how text flows around the Java applet on the HTML page. `LEFT`, for example, means that the applet appears to the left of the text. Other options are `RIGHT`, `CENTER`, `TOP`, `MIDDLE`, and `BOTTOM`. These options correspond exactly to the values for the `ALIGN` property of the `<IMG>` HTML tag.

- `ALT`, as it does or other tags, provides alternative text that is displayed in text-only Web browsers.

- `ID` isn't required, but is important if you intend to access this applet from VBScript. ID is the name you use to access it.

Other interesting properties are also available:

- `VSPACE` and `HSPACE` identify how much empty space should frame the applet vertically and horizontally. These properties work just like the corresponding `<IMG>` tag properties.

- `DOWNLOAD` provides a number, which is compared to the `DOWNLOAD` property on other objects and images on this page so that the order in which they should be downloaded can be determined.

- `NAME` provides another way of naming the applet. This name may be used by other applets on the page.

There is often nothing between the <APPLET> tag and its ending tag. You can create Java applets that accept parameters from the Web page. These parameters are specified between the beginning and ending tags in this form:

```
<PARAM NAME="parametername" VALUE="value">
```

There can be any number of <PARAM> tags between the begin and end <APPLET> tags. The name of the parameter is specified using the NAME property, and the value you give the parameter is assigned to the VALUE property. Again, the Java applet must be designed to accept parameters before you can pass them.

The </APPLET> ending tag is required.

Accessing the Java Applet

You can access and manipulate Java applets right from your VBScript code in almost exactly the same way that you access ActiveX controls:

```
<SCRIPT language = "VBScript">
<!--
Sub Document_OnLoad
document.game.DealCards
End Sub
-->
</SCRIPT>
```

The preceding code calls the function named DealCards in the Java applet that is inserted into the Web page in the last section. You must always prefix the name of the applet with the word document. You can refer to any public property or call any public function in the class.

Creating Applets to Use from VBScript

You cannot simply insert an applet into your page and begin manipulating it from VBScript. The applet must be designed to allow you to take advantage of its capabilities.

There are several requirements for designing the applet. First, if you create the class in Java, you must inherit that class from the applet class. If you want to make properties and methods from other classes available, you must create wrapper properties and methods in the applet-derived class and then delegate to the properties and methods of the other classes.

Second, you must make all of the properties and methods you want access to in VBScript public. All public properties and methods of your applet-derived class can be manipulated in VBScript.

Finally, the parameters that can be specified in the <APPLET> tag are not the same as the public variables that can be manipulated by VBScript. In order to make use of parameters, you must use the getParameter() function.

Creating a Sample Java Applet Scoreboard

The Java applet's name is scoreboard.java. The applet displays a number in big, bold text. The idea is that you can create a game using VBScript and other Java or ActiveX controls and then use this applet to display the current score.

Listing 36.17 is the source code for the scoreboard applet.

Listing 36.17 scoreboard.txt—The Scoreboard.Java Applet

```
import java.applet.*;
import java.awt.*;

public class scoreboard extends Applet {

public int score=0;

public void updatescore() {
  repaint();
}

public void paint(Graphics g) {
  Font fnt = new Font("Helvetica", Font.BOLD, 24);
  g.setFont(fnt);
  g.drawString(String.valueOf(score), 20, 20);
  }
}
```

If you know Java, you can easily understand how this applet works. If you don't, teaching you Java is well beyond the scope of this chapter. Even if you've never seen Java code before, you should be able to follow along how this applet works.

The first two lines, which are needed by the applet, include some standard Java libraries. The libraries enable you to create an applet and to use input/output commands.

The next line creates a new class called scoreboard, which is inherited from the class named applet. All applets are descendants of the applet class or one of applet's descendants. The rest of the listing fills in the details about this new scoreboard class. You know this is the case because all of the rest of the code is wrapped between the curly brackets ({ and }).

The next line creates a public integer variable named *score* that is initialized to 0. This is the variable that always holds the current score. Again, notice that the variable is public; therefore, it is available to you when you write your VBScript code.

Next, a public function is created called updatescore. The *void* indicates that the updatescore() doesn't return a value, and the empty parentheses after the void indicates that this function doesn't expect any arguments. All the updatescore() does is to call the repaint() function. This action causes the applet to repaint itself and to execute any code in the paint function.

The last function is the `paint` function. This function is automatically called by the system whenever the applet is repainted, which happens when the applet is first loaded into the page and any time the `repaint()` function is called. This function accepts a argument that identifies the graphic workspace on the applet. This workspace is where you print the score.

The code in the `paint` function first creates a font object with a bold, Helvetica, 24-point font. That object is then passed to the `setFont()` function to make it the current font. Finally, the `drawString()` function is called. The number contained in the `score` variable is converted to a string and passed to the function to be printed. The `20, 20` indicates the part of the applet on which the text appears.

Note three key things about this simple applet. First, it defines a class that is descended from the applet class. VBScript can only access variables and functions from descendants of the applet class.

The other two things you should notice are the public variable `score` and the public function `updatescore`. Because these are public, you should be able to call them from VBScript.

The VBScript Web Page

In order to put this applet to work, you need a Web page. Listing 36.18 shows a sample page.

Listing 36.18   score.htm—The Web Page Demonstrating the Scoreboard Applet

```
<HTML>
<HEAD>
<TITLE>Game</TITLE>
</HEAD>
<BODY>
<h1>Game</h1>
The Score Is:<p>
<APPLET CODE="scoreboard.class"
CODEBASE="d:\javaproj\game"
ID=sign
WIDTH = 70
HEIGHT = 30>
</APPLET>
<p>
<INPUT TYPE=button VALUE="Score + 10" NAME="BtnScoreTen">
<SCRIPT LANGUAGE="VBScript">
<!--
Sub BtnScoreTen_OnClick
  document.sign.score = document.sign.score + 10
  document.sign.updatescore
End Sub
-->
</SCRIPT>

</BODY>
</HTML>
```

This sample page is very basic. It just shows you how to drop the applet into a Web page and how to work with it. You could easily expand on this page to form the heart of an interesting Web application.

Notice the <APPLET> tag. It identifies the name of the class that uses the CODE attribute and where on your system that code might be found. An appropriate WIDTH and HEIGHT are specified. Even more importantly, the applet is given an ID for VBScript to use when it references the applet.

A simple form-style button is then used to kick off the BtnScoreTen_OnClick VBScript subroutine. The number in the applet's score variable is increased by 10. And the updatescore function is called so that the user can see the change. Notice that the document and then the applet name are specified in order to qualify the applet variable and the updatescore function.

When you bring up the page, you see a box holding the number 0. Every time you click the button, the score is increased by 10. Nothing to it!

A Final Thought on Java Applets and VBScript

Java applets provide you with an alternative to using ActiveX controls to activate your Web pages. Each of these methods has advantages and disadvantages when weighed against the alternative method. Fortunately, you don't have to choose one or the other. You can use both very easily and from VBScript's perspective, almost seamlessly. This seamless interaction gives you the flexibility to design your Web page so that it is both dynamic and content-rich, no matter what browser you use to view it.

From Here...

Before you design a Web page to include an ActiveX control, you should check out a few things. Make sure the page is gaining information from the client. If you are performing a function that can be done just as easily on the Web server, then it should be done there. But if you want to jump into writing ActiveX Web pages, first get the documentation for the controls and a good editor (such as Visual InterDev).

For related material on ActiveX, see the following chapters:

- Chapter 33, "Database Access with ActiveX Data Objects (ADO)," shows you how to create ActiveX applications that connect to databases using ADO.
- Chapter 38, "Working with Active Server Page Objects," shows you how easy it is to create feature-rich, dynamic Web pages.
- Chapter 40, "Programming Web Functionality into Your Applications," guides you through the process of Web enabling your applications.
- Chapter 42, "Using Visual Basic with Microsoft Transaction Server," shows you how to create transaction-based Web applications without using CGI.

CHAPTER 37

Creating Active Server Pages

Static Web pages are a thing of the past and dynamic content is here to stay. As the Internet becomes increasingly congested with information, sites must be up-to-date to be successful. People won't keep coming back to a Web site if the "Headlines of the day" start becoming the headlines of the month. Only by modifying and adding information on a daily basis can a site stay successful and keep attracting visitors. The time and expense involved to do this can be overwhelming and is not feasible for many individuals and companies.

The solution is not to hire more Web page editors, it is to design and build sites that keep themselves current. This doesn't mean artificial intelligence, just the application of client/server knowledge to the Internet. Web sites that automatically update themselves are not new, but how you create one is changing all the time. One of the newest, and most popular, technologies is Active Server Pages (ASP). By using ASP, you can create Web sites that do almost anything and do it quickly. ■

Determining the difference between static and dynamic Web sites

When should a site be static? When can dynamic content help? And when is dynamic content essential? Learn the general reasons for each approach and how to decide what is best for your Web projects.

Exploring Active Server Pages (ASP)

Server-Side Scripting provides the power to create dynamic content available to any browser. Bring the business advantages of client/server technology to the Internet.

Running Active Server Pages

Receive an overview on how to get Active Server Pages running.

Getting started programming Active Server Pages

An introduction into Server-Side Scripting. Transfer your knowledge of Visual Basic to Web development.

Troubleshooting your Active Server Pages

A discussion of the common problems and the solution or work-around required to correct them.

Static versus Dynamic Content

Whether you know it or not, you probably have already seen examples of both static and dynamic Web sites. *Static content*, or a static Web site, is made up of pages whose content does not change on its own. Any Web page can be changed by its owner through an editor, but that doesn't make it dynamic. Consider the example of billboards. Like Web pages, billboards can be either dynamic or static. Most billboards advertise such things as the distance to the advertiser's next fast food restaurant or gas station. These billboards have static content; it doesn't change unless someone manually changes it.

On the other hand, some billboards display such things as the current time and temperature. This is *dynamic content*; it changes as the information displayed changes. Obviously, some types of billboards are more suited for static content than dynamic content. The distance to the fast food restaurant isn't likely to change, so a dynamic electronic sign wouldn't be very useful. The reverse is also true—a painted sign displaying the time and temperature would always be wrong. It is usually clear from the content whether a dynamic or static billboard is called for.

Dynamic HTML

In this chapter, you spend a lot of time reading about Dynamic Web pages. It is important not to get this confused with Dynamic HTML, which is another important technology from Microsoft that is being released as part of its latest Internet browser (Internet Explorer 4.0).

Whereas *Dynamic Web pages* are called dynamic because their content may change every time you visit the site (reload the page), *Dynamic HTML* is a technology that enables Web pages to change appearance on the client side (without reloading). For example, text that changes as you move your mouse over different sections, or displaying database records that you can browse through without the page having to reload. Look for more information on this hot new technology in upcoming Que books, particularly *Special Edition Using Visual Studio*.

The same rules that apply to billboards apply to Web pages. The nature of the content determines whether the site should be dynamic or static. Dynamic content is relatively new to the Web and, until recently, it was difficult to achieve. Difficulty often translates into expense and, consequently, simplistic Web sites are popping up all the time.

If a plain wooden sign were put up to display the time and temperature and a painter were hired to repaint the sign every few minutes to update it, people would think the advertiser was crazy. But many of the sites on the Web today are tantamount to a painted time and temperature billboard. Sites are created as static pages, displaying information (such as news headlines, tips of the day, and so on) that changes on a regular basis, but the person (the "painter") hired to update the page works only once a week or month. Fortunately, this is changing.

When to Build Dynamic Sites

Two key questions determine the need for dynamic content:

■ Does the information that the site displays change often?

■ Is that information available (through a database, live feed, and so forth) to the Web server?

For example, a site that displays stock price information must be dynamic. The information changes every second and those changes need to be fed electronically to the Web server. Conversely, a site that displays the names of the 50 states of the U.S. probably doesn't need to be dynamic. While the states' names are available in electronic form, they don't change and therefore such a site doesn't require dynamic features. It is important to justify the extra time or money required to build a dynamic site. As an example, take a look at the following case scenario for a proposed Web site project and compare the choice of a static site versus a dynamic site.

Part

VII

Ch

37

Suppose a company that offers courses on a variety of computer-related topics decides it wants to create a Web site. The function of this Web site is to serve as an Online Course Catalog. Visitors to the site can browse a list of available courses, view schedule information to determine course schedules, and register for courses if interested—all through the Internet.

The reason for creating this site is clear to the training company: the paper catalog it currently produces is too expensive and becomes outdated too quickly. In many industries, such as technical education, things change so rapidly that information becomes outdated in the time it takes to develop and print a brochure or catalog. Even if the catalog is correct when it is first sent out, there is no way to deal with changes that occur the very next day. If a course is cancelled, it isn't removed from the catalog, and if a course is added, it won't suddenly appear in the catalog.

The cost of the catalog includes much more than the time and money required to create it. Keeping the catalog current means reprinting it frequently, which can quickly begin to cost a great deal more than the original printing. A Web-based catalog doesn't require reprints; changes occur instantly. The Web version of this course catalog would provide online registration capabilities that would enable the school to cut personnel costs of staffing employees to answer phone calls from students who want to register. If the site were expanded to allow direct payment with a credit card through a secure connection, the entire process could be completely automated, reducing the personnel costs even further.

So, what the company needs is a Web site that

■ Displays a list of all its currently available courses

■ Displays a schedule of when each course is offered

■ Allows users to register simply by clicking scheduled courses

■ Accepts payment online through a secure connection

Given these specifications, a decision must be made regarding which type of site to build— dynamic or static.

A static Web site could be developed quickly. It would be relatively easy to convert the pages of the print catalog into corresponding Web pages. A listing of the courses available could be created in any HTML editor, as could a schedule of dates and places the courses are offered.

Some small, pre-built CGI component (such as the WebBot features built into Microsoft FrontPage) could be used to save registration information to a file, but in general, the entire site could be built as standard, static Web pages.

Assume that a static site can be created quicker than a dynamic version of the same site. The dynamic pages would get the course list and schedule from a database, but otherwise, the site would look identical to its static counterpart. (Of course, programmers know better, but they usually aren't the ones making these decisions.) To some people, the choice is obvious: if the static site costs less to develop and the two versions look the same, why would any company choose a dynamic solution?

The advantages of a dynamic site are not immediately obvious—until a change needs to be made. For example, suppose a course currently labeled as NT 3.51 Administration needs to be called NT 4.0 Administration. Making this change in the static site involves the Web designer (or someone else with Web page skills) coming in and changing the listings page, the schedule page, and perhaps a few other pages where the course names are being used in such things as drop-down lists. This change could take an hour or more, plus the time for the Web designer to arrive. Even if the Web builder is available the next day, that is one entire day with incorrect information being shown to potential clients of the company.

In contrast, to make this change in the dynamic site, the training administrator (or another company employee) opens a standard database-editing program (custom made through MS Access or similar program) and changes the few characters that need editing. Instantly, the information displayed on every part of the Web site is correct. With that one change, the company has started to recoup the increased cost of building a dynamic Web site. Likewise, if such changes are required often (as is typical), the cost benefit of the dynamic site grows quickly. The entire investment eventually will be recouped and the Web site will begin to save the company money almost immediately.

How to Build Dynamic Sites

Determining that you need a dynamic site isn't the end of the process; now you have to build it, and this isn't necessarily easy. To create a dynamic site, you need to pick a technology to use. The technology most commonly used for this purpose is CGI (Common Gateway Interface). This generic term describes programs that interface with Web servers and respond to requests by sending back Web pages, using a combination of parameters and back-end data to determine its content. These applications can do almost anything you want with a Web site, and can be written in several languages, including C and Perl—so why would you use anything else?

CGI is difficult; it involves the creation of low-level programs in languages that lack most of the features of new development tools (like Visual Basic). Many of the functions required to generate the Web page, such as database access, are not provided to the programmer; you would have to build those functions your self. Most CGI applications do not support ODBC (Open Data Base Connectivity), DAO (Data Access Objects), or many other features programmers have become used to.

▶ **See** "Improving Data Access with Data Access Objects (DAO)," **p. 845**

▶ **See** "Introducing ODBC," **p. 882**

A major problem, and one that is of major importance to Visual Basic programmers, is that most CGI applications do not support the Component Object Model (COM), making it virtually impossible to reuse business logic contained in Visual Basic applications. Chapter 23, "Using Microsoft's Object Technologies," covers this topic in more detail. In today's environment, with more and more systems being designed with a 3-tier architecture, the business rules are contained within (middle-tier) objects accessed by many client applications. If the Web interface to that same business data cannot use those same objects, then a duplication of code and a deviation from the rest of the system is required.

In addition to those problems, CGI applications are inefficient. Each concurrent request against a CGI application creates another process on the server, resulting in poor performance and higher memory usage. In general, CGI is out of date; the concept is good, but it is not up to the task. The need for dynamic Web sites still exists and it is steadily increasing—so what should be used to create them?

Active Server Pages

Programmers want all the functionality of existing CGI applications, combined with the ease of use and support for language standards such as Visual Basic. Programmers want Active Server Pages (ASP). ASP is the perfect replacement for CGI, and it is still a handy TLA (three-letter acronym). It is built on the same standards programmers have become used to, allowing the use of COM objects directly. You can connect to the same middle- or back-end objects as your client VB applications do, and do it almost exactly the same way. It uses VBScript (or any other ActiveX Scripting Language, such as JavaScript), thus allowing programmers to transfer their knowledge of Visual Basic directly into this new environment.

How ASP Works

Well, now that you know that ASP is wonderful, let's discuss why. To understand what ASP is, it is important to discuss first what happens when a Web page is viewed.

The first step in the viewing process is the browser request. When the user types an URL (uniform resource locator) into their Web browser, or clicks an existing hyperlink that points to that URL, the browser initiates a request. For the purposes of this example, let's assume the user typed in the following URL: **http://www.microsoft.com/ie/default.htm**. The browser first looks at the address to determine which server to send the request to (in this example, this would be **www.microsoft.com**) and what to ask for (the document **/ie/default.htm**). This request is sent to the server by using HTTP (Hypertext Transfer Protocol), a common language that both the browser and the server understand.

The second step starts when the server gets involved. When the server receives the request, it begins to process it. In the case of a simple Web page, this processing isn't very involved; the content of the appropriate file on the server is read from the server's hard disk and sent back to the browser, unchanged.

The final part of the cycle occurs when the requesting browser receives the Web server's response. In this case, the response consists of the text contained in the requested file. The browser uses the HTML tags contained in the response to determine how to display the page to the user.

N O T E The server's response, before being parsed by the browser, is available for any page you are viewing through the View Source menu option. ■

In the case of Active Server Pages, the server side of the request-response process becomes a little different. Once again, the browser is directed to an URL, and it creates a request (as above, but the URL would end in a .asp instead of .htm). The Web server is contacted and the request is sent. Up until this point, nothing occurs any differently then for a regular HTML page; the difference occurs when the server becomes involved.

When the server receives a request for a page, it looks at the extension to determine how to handle it. If the extension is .htm or .html, it treats the page like a standard HTML document, but if the extension is .asp, further processing is required. A special program on the server reads in the scripting code contained in the Active Server Page, and then executes it. The results of that code execution are then sent back to the browser. This response is standard HTML, no different than the results sent back from a regular page.

N O T E ASP is actually implemented as an ISAPI (Internet Server API) extension to IIS 3.0. ISAPI enables programmers to create programs that run along with the Web server that is performing content-filtering and some page-generation services. You can build your own ISAPI extensions by using Visual C++ if you need to integrate yourself closely with the Web server itself. ■

Browser Independence

Although there are common elements between ASP and other Internet technologies such as client-side scripting (VBScript) and ActiveX controls, there is also one important difference— ASP occurs completely on the server. What does this mean? If you write an ActiveX control and put it on your Web page, it is up to the browser to download, install, and use that control. If you view that page with a browser that doesn't support ActiveX controls, such as Mosaic, it wouldn't work. Similarly, if you include VBScript in your page, attached to a button click for instance, it won't work on a browser that doesn't support VBScript. These are examples of client-side technologies, and they are browser dependent.

ASP does not involve the browser. All of the code is executed on the server; the browser just receives standard HTML from the server and displays it. The fact that the HTML was generated is hidden from the client-side of the process. This makes ASP browser independent, an important feature that makes ASP perfect for the Internet, where you have no control over what type of browser people are using. Of course, it is still possible to use client-side scripting and ActiveX controls in the pages generated by ASP, if browser independence is not required.

Support for Standards

A big selling point of Active Server Pages is that they support the same existing standards that Visual Basic does. Because the server components that interpret and execute the Active Server Page code are designed using COM, it isn't surprising that the scripting languages used to write the actual pages also support COM. Intrinsic objects in ASP allow the script to create COM objects and use their properties and methods directly. This gives ASP its greatest power—the capability to use existing objects, which could be written in Visual Basic, directly in the Web application.

Active Server Pages use the ActiveX Scripting Engine to provide the interpreting and execution functionality of their pages. The obvious benefit of this is that it supports the use of any scripting language written to that standard. This currently includes two languages from Microsoft, VBScript (discussed in Chapter 35, "Internet Programming with VBScript") and JavaScript, as well as several languages from other third-party vendors, including an implementation of Perl. The side effects of choosing to implement ASP in this way are that any additional languages, or language features, that are added to the Scripting Engine will immediately be available to developers of ASP applications.

The two main features of ASP—support for COM and support for VBScript—have the general effect of enabling programmers to use their existing knowledge in this new environment. VBScript uses the same syntax and supports many of the same functions as full-blown Visual Basic, smoothing the ASP learning curve considerably. COM support provides for more direct code transfer through the reuse of objects that were written in VB, or for use in VB. The mortgage approval object currently in use by your client/server Visual Basic system now also can be used by your ASP version of the same interface. If a change in the workings of the object is made, both the traditional system and the new Web application will be automatically affected. Redundant code is avoided, and the existing investment that you or your company have made in a system doesn't have to be lost.

Visual Basic is one of the most popular programming environments in the world. By maintaining such a high level of compatibility between it and ASP, Microsoft has made this technology a success from the moment it was released.

Programming Active Server Pages

We know that the server looks at the contents of an ASP file on the server and generates an HTML file to send back to the browser, but how does it determine what to send back? The ASP file on the server contains scripting code, which code is executed by the server, resulting in HTML. The scripting code itself is what you, as the Web site developer, create. This code may be written in various ways and by using different languages but, regardless of these details, it is still programming. If you know how to program a non-Web application, then you already understand the fundamentals of programming in ASP. To get started, the general structure and flow of ASP pages will be covered next through the use of some simple examples.

The Basics

As previously discussed, the code required to program ASP can be written in any supported scripting language that is available for client-side scripting. At the moment, the two most commonly used languages for this purpose are VBScript and JavaScript. This section will discuss VBScript only. JavaScript is a dialect of Java. VBScript is a language that is related to Visual Basic. There are differences between the two, but general coding syntax and methods are the same. Because of the similarity between ASP and VB, which you already have at least some familiarity with, the best way to learn is to get right into it, so take a look at the example file in Listing 37.1.

> **N O T E**   All the commands and functions of VBScript and JavaScript are available in ASP, but the object model is different. Many of the objects you have seen in client-side scripting, such as `Document`, `Frame`, and `Window`, have no place in server-side scripting, and thus are not available. Don't worry, though. ASP has its own powerful set of objects that will be addressed in the next chapter, "Working with Active Server Page Objects." ▪

On the CD

Listing 37.1   sample.asp—Programming a Simple Loop in ASP

```
Response.Write "<HTML>"
Response.Write "<HEAD><TITLE>Example Page</TITLE></HEAD>"
Response.Write "<BODY>"
<%
For j = 1 to 10
        Response.Write  "<P>Line: " & j & "</P>"

Next j
Response.Write "</BODY>"
Response.Write "</HTML>"
%>
```

The first thing that will help you understand this code is the `Response.Write` statement. It is a type of print function that outputs information to the browser. Anything sent out by one of these statements is sent directly—unmodified—as part of the server's response. The `For` loop is the other piece of code in this example, but it doesn't look any different than the Visual Basic equivalent, and it behaves exactly the same. The code in Listing 37.1 produces the HTML code shown in Listing 37.2, which is then sent back to the browser that requested the page.

Listing 37.2   Output from *sample.asp*

```
<HTML>
<HEAD><TITLE>Example Page</TITLE></HEAD>
<BODY>
<P>Line: 1</P>
<P>Line: 2</P>
<P>Line: 3</P>
```

```
<P>Line: 4</P>
<P>Line: 5</P>
<P>Line: 6</P>
<P>Line: 7</P>
<P>Line: 8</P>
<P>Line: 9</P>
<P>Line: 10</P>
</BODY>
</HTML>
```

The `Response.Write` statement is just one way to send output back to the browser. Plain HTML may also be written directly into the .asp file. Scripting code can be placed around the HTML to insert variables into the HTML statements. The `<%` and `%>` symbols around the scripting code in Listing 37.1 are delimiters used to mark where scripting code begins and ends. If the sample.asp file is redone using this other method, it looks like Listing 37.3.

On the CD

Listing 37.3 NEWSAMP.ASP—Another Method of Creating the Same Output as *sample.asp*

```
<HTML>
<HEAD><TITLE>Example Page</TITLE></HEAD>
<BODY>
<%
For j = 1 to 10
%>
<P>Line:<%=j%></P>
<%
Next j
%>
</BODY>
</HTML>
```

The preceding code will produce the exact same output as the previous method (see Figure 37.1), but it is much easier to use and understand. The line `<P>Line:<%=j%></P>` is an example of using ASP to insert a variable into HTML. When that line is processed by the server, it will just replace `<%=j%>` with the current value of j. This combination of using standard HTML, scripting code, and variable substitution is how most Active Server Pages are written, and it's how the examples will be done from here forward.

N O T E If you haven't worked in VBScript before, you may wonder why the variable j wasn't declared before it was used. Unlike Visual Basic, all variables are considered to be of type Variant and, therefore, there is little advantage to declaring them. Variable declaration is only required for arrays, as in `Dim month_array(12)`, but these arrays are still composed only of variants. ■

FIG. 37.1

A simple list of numbers, created from an Active Server Page script.

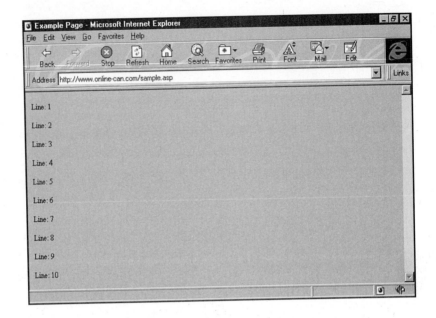

It is helpful to try out these examples as you progress (you can modify them and see what happens) to get a better understanding of what the end result will look like.

Generating HTML from Active Server Pages

When designing Active Server Pages, you really are creating programs that will create Web pages completely from scratch; no portions of the page are being generated for you. If you miss important parts of the page or create them improperly, the results of your page will not be what you expect. It is important that you understand what you are trying to create. If you were writing a VB program to generate MS Word documents, you certainly would want to find and study a reference on that file format. The same applies to HTML. Que's *Special Edition Using HTML 4*, Third Edition, provides a full reference and discussion of the HTML language.

Everything in HTML is based on tags, matching delimiters in the form <TAG>TEXT</TAG>, that indicate the formatting or meaning of text contained between them. The key tags you need to know when learning ASP are those at the top of every HTML page.

The first tag that you should see in the output from any ASP you create is <HTML>. This marks the page as HTML and delimits the beginning and ending of the page's content. No other HTML tags or any other content that you want the Web browser to see should come before <HTML> or after its corresponding end tag, </HTML>. Following immediately after the HTML tag is <HEAD> (for header), nested inside of which should be the tag <TITLE>. Text placed between the <TITLE></TITLE> tags specifies the page's name for display in the title bar of the browser window.

In almost all HTML pages (except frame sets, which are not be covered in this discussion), after the closing tags of both </TITLE> and </HEAD> comes the <BODY> tag. This tag is a little more complicated and has a few options, including the capability to set the background image and color for the page. In its most basic form, it is just <BODY>, but it can also contain any combination of the following parameters: BGCOLOR, TEXT, LINK, VLINK, ALINK, or BACKGROUND. The most commonly used tags inside <BODY> are BGCOLOR (to set the background color) and BACKGROUND (to set a background image). The following are a few examples to illustrate the use of this tag.

Part
VII

Ch
37

For a page that has a black background and no background image, you would use:

```
<BODY BGCOLOR="#000000">
```

For a page with a background image of "swirls.jpg" and a specified background color of white, you would use:

```
<BODY BACKGROUND="swirls.jpg" BGCOLOR="#FFFFFF">
```

> **CAUTION**
>
> It may seem pointless to specify a background color when you have already set an image, but the color you set will be used as a background if the image is unavailable or images have been turned off in the browser. This can be very important if you choose a particular text color because it will display well on the specified background image. If you don't specify a background color, the text may be unreadable against the browser's default background.

This <BODY> tag, like most others, requires a closing tag, but it doesn't appear until after the content of the page is finished. The last couple lines in a Web page are usually

```
</BODY>
</HTML>
```

to mark the end of the body of the page, and then the end of the page itself.

Once past the header portion of the page, there is a very large number of tags and options available, but only a few others are required to build and test some simple Active Server Pages.

The Paragraph Tag

```
<P></P>
```

These tags mark the beginning and ending of a paragraph.

The Break Tag

```
<BR>  (this tag has no matching end tag)
```

This tag is the equivalent of a soft return and can be used within a body of text to define the line-break point without forcing any space between the two lines. You can use <BR> between the <P></P> tags.

The Heading Tags

`<H#></H#>` (where # is a number from 1 to 6)

These tags denote that the text contained within the tags is a heading. The lower the number is from 1 to 6, the more important the heading contained within the tags. Browsers usually display lower heading numbers as progressively larger, bold font. For example, if you were to have the following lines in your Web page:

```
<H1>My Web Page</H1>
<H2>by Jane Doe</H2>
```

the first line, your main heading, would be displayed larger and with a heavier boldface than the second, your subtitle.

Hyperlinks

`<A HREF = URL></A>`

This is a very useful tag that is used to mark a piece of text as a hyperlink to an URL. This URL might represent another Web page, a file, or even someone's e-mail address. A link pointing to the Microsoft Site might look like this:

```
<A HREF="http://www.microsoft.com/">Click here to go
to the Microsoft Web Site </A>
```

The text `Click here...` will appear as a link in the Web browser, which means that it will be underlined, colored differently, or otherwise distinguished. When this text is clicked in the browser, it causes the browser to initiate a request for the page this link points to.

Other Tags　It is likely that the tags just discussed will not be enough to build a proper Web site, but there are many more available. To find out more about these other tags, look at an HTML reference, look at the source for other people's pages, or use a Web page editor, such as Microsoft FrontPage. The advantage of using an editor is that it enables you to quickly create the look of your pages, using all of the tags needed, through an interface that provides the capability to tweak details of the page's appearance. Once you have the prototype page completed, replace portions of the HTML (created by the editor) with your scripting variables, or copy some of that HTML into your .asp files. The FrontPage Editor is, of course, available as part of the FrontPage 97 product, but it is also included in Microsoft Visual InterDev.

Microsoft Visual InterDev

Visual InterDev is Microsoft's development tool for building Active Server Pages, and it has many features that can help you build ASP applications. As part of Visual Studio 97, it uses the common development environment found in Visual C++ and Visual J++, and it is similar to the environment of Visual Basic (see Figure 37.2). This environment provides all of the editing bells and whistles you are used to, including code highlighting, direct access to comprehensive help information (that reference material alone makes the product worthwhile, in my opinion), and other time-saving features specific to the creation of dynamic Web sites.

FIG. 37.2

Visual Interdev gives you an integrated development environment in which to create and modify ASP files, while providing instant access to a large library of reference material.

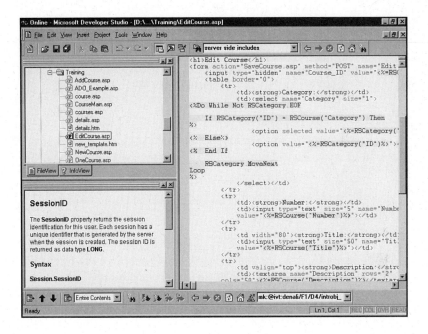

Visual InterDev has the capability to connect to a Web site, whether created with InterDev or not, and display it using a link view (showing all of the pages, by the hyperlinks joining them) or an explorer tree view (basically showing the files and directories that exist on the Web server). This is similar to the functionality of the FrontPage Explorer, but page editing can take place right next to the tree view (in a dockable, resizable window), making coding a quicker process. For straight HTML editing or for creating HTML sections to include in your .asp files, the FrontPage 97 Editor is included. Several wizards and Design Time Controls (DTC) are also included, enabling you to generate quickly large amounts of ASP script customized to your purpose.

The shared development environment (Dev Studio) means that Visual InterDev is fully scriptable (using VBA) and can support the addition of new tools (through Add-Ins, such as Visual Basic). Built-in support for Visual Source Safe enables multiple programmers to work on the site together without fear of overwriting pages.

In conclusion, Visual Interdev is a great alternative to creating ASP files directly in Notepad or other text editors, especially if you are used to working in Dev Studio because of Visual C++ or J++. Visual Interdev is very affordable if purchased as part of the entire Visual Studio 97 package (including Visual Basic 5, Visual Fox Pro 5, Visual C++ 5, Visual J++ 1.1, Visual Source Safe 5, and other development tools). It isn't required (you can build any size ASP application without it), but for a large project, it quickly justifies its cost.

The ASP examples in this book can be created, edited, and run without Visual InterDev as well, so don't worry if you don't have it available at the moment.

Running Active Server Pages

As you work through the remainder of this chapter and the next two chapters dealing with ASP, you will want to try it out for yourself. Due to the nature of ASP as a server-side component, setting up a machine to test the pages can be somewhat involved.

Software Requirements

To run the examples shown in this book, or any other programs you find or create, you will need:

- A Web server that supports ASP
- For examples involving databases, a 32-bit ODBC on the server and an ODBC connection to your database
- A Web browser

You need a Web server due to the way in which ASP works; if you look at an asp file directly (without a server) using an URL such as **file://c:\sample.asp**, it simply asks if you want to save the file to disk. When the same file is requested through the server (**http://www.online-can.com/sample.asp**), it intercepts requests for .asp files and processes them, returning the results to the browser, not the page. If the request doesn't go through the server, no processing will take place.

At the moment, there are two Web servers available that support Active Server Pages. For Windows NT (version 4.0), there is Internet Information Server 3.0 (IIS), a true production-level Web server, which is recommended for development and deployment of your application. Not everyone will have access to a computer running NT Server, so the Personal Web Server (PWS) for Windows 95 is also available. This Web server, which is not really suited to running a production site, enables you to do much of your development and experimenting without having to purchase the hardware and software required for Windows NT.

Internet Information Server is tightly integrated with Windows NT; to properly use it as your Web server, you need to understand its functionality as much as possible. This book can't teach you everything about Windows NT and IIS, but the key areas that impact ASP are discussed in the section "Troubleshooting ASP Files."

ASP is included with IIS 3.0, but you will need to install it separately if you are using PWS for Windows 95. Fortunately, ASP is available as part of several different products from Microsoft, including Visual InterDev, and it shouldn't be too difficult to find.

Any database access that takes place occurs on the server, so it is there that ODBC is required (software allowing use of the Open Database Connectivity standard to connect to databases). ODBC is the method used by most Active Server Pages (including all of the database-orientated examples in this chapter) to access databases. 32-bit ODBC must be installed on the server, and a System DSN must be set up for the desired data source. To determine if ODBC is installed, check for an ODBC 32 icon in the Control Panel of your server (as shown in Figure 37.3). If present, this control panel provides access to create and configure ODBC entries. For more information on ODBC and setting up DSNs, see Chapter 32, "Using Remote Data Objects (RDO)." Although not installed by default in Windows NT, ODBC is included with many other products, including Microsoft Visual Basic 5.0, Microsoft SQL Server, Microsoft Access, and Microsoft Visual InterDev, and is also available free of charge from Microsoft (**www.microsoft.com**).

▶ **See** "Setting Up an ODBC Data Source," **p. 883**

FIG. 37.3
Looking for the ODBC 32 icon.

Part **VII**
Ch
37

ODBC icon

CAUTION
Database connections from Active Server Pages require the 32-bit version of ODBC.

You need a Web browser to test the pages. The type or brand of browser required is dependent on what you choose to do in your pages. If you are producing standard HTML only, then you should be able to use any browser, but if you are also working with ActiveX controls or VBScript on the client side, you will need Internet Explorer (free from Microsoft at **http://www.microsoft.com/ie**). If you want your pages to be browser independent, you should use multiple browsers to test your pages to ensure that you get the desired results on each browser.

Troubleshooting ASP Files

After everything is set up, you should be able to run .asp files without any trouble. If you do run into problems, the following sections provide descriptions of some common errors that occur while using ASP, possible causes of these errors, and suggestions for solving these problems.

Browser Doesn't Open the Page   If the browser doesn't show your page, but instead puts up a dialog box asking if you want to open the .asp page or save it to a disk (see Figure 37.4), the URL you are attempting to go to is not a format you can view from your browser. The same message appears when you click a link or type in an URL that points at an .exe file.

FIG. 37.4

The Browser dialog box that is shown when a Web browser doesn't understand how to display your page.

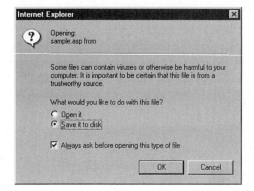

This problem occurs because the ASP files are not directly supported by your browser, although the results of them are. This error means that the .asp file is not being executed for one of the following reasons:

- You do not have ASP installed (properly), on your Web server; try (re)installing it again.

- You are not going through the Web server; check your URL to make sure it really is going through your server.

- You do not have execute permissions on the .asp file; this can be a complicated problem—see the section "Security Settings in Windows NT, IIS, and ASP," later in this chapter.

Browser Requests Username and Password   If your browser displays a dialog box that asks you to provide a username and password (see Figure 37.5), or the result of the page states that access is denied, then you don't have sufficient access rights on the Web server to execute the ASP file. The anonymous Web user, commonly named "IUSR_<Server Name>", must have at least "Read & Execute (RX)" rights to the file. See the section "Security Settings in Windows NT, IIS, and ASP," later in this chapter.

FIG. 37.5

The Browser dialog box requests authentication information to access an Active Server Page on the server.

An Error Message Appears on Your Page   An error message is displayed directly on the page; see Figure 37.6 for an example. This usually means there is an error in your script (as opposed to a system setting, file access, or other form of problem).

FIG. 37.6

These are the results of an Active Server Page that contains an error in its scripting code.

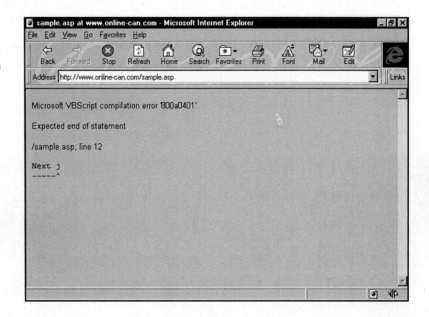

This type of error is equivalent to a compile-time or run-time error in Visual Basic. There is an error in your scripting code, and the text displayed should contain the error number and description.

This is the best error to get: All it means is that something is wrong with your code—and the error message is the best place to determine what that something is. Debugging code is simply part of the process, and this message, in fact, suggests that ASP is working correctly. The extremely straightforward, simple error messages that are returned make it easy to fix the problem (refer to Figure 37.6). (Where are those <SARCASM></SARCASM> tags when you need them?)

Page Takes Too Long to Load   This problem presents itself as a page that seems to be loading but never stops; part of the page may display, but the entire page never completely loads. A dialog box may appear on the browser stating that a script is taking a long time to execute, and it usually gives the user the option to cancel (see Figure 37.7).

ASP sends back results from the .asp file as it generates them; there is no real limit to how long that processing will take, so the first few lines of the page can arrive well before the rest of the page. The browser will continue to indicate that it is loading until the .asp file stops executing on the server. There is a server setting (see SCRIPT.TIMEOUT in the next chapter) that will stop the execution of the .asp script if it takes too long, but this is usually set high enough that you will notice that the page isn't loading completely long before an actual timeout occurs.

Part
VII

Ch
37

FIG. 37.7

An error message displays when an ASP script has taken too long to execute.

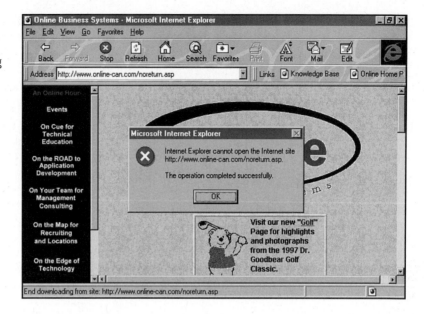

There really is only one possible cause—the .asp file's script is taking a long time to finish execution—but there are many reasons why that can happen:

- The obvious cause is that the script really is taking that long. In most cases, this is not likely to happen; the server should be able to execute most scripts in a period of seconds or less.

- The script may contain an infinite loop, which means that it will never complete its execution.

- A function call or object reference inside the script may not be returning control to the script. If this is the cause of the error, the script eventually will time out and an error will be returned to the browser.

- A problem related to the previous bullet is that some object external to ASP has put up a dialog box and is waiting for a response. Because ASP executes on the server, that dialog box would appear on the server, which may be unattended, making a response unlikely. This would hold up execution of the .asp file indefinitely.

Security Settings in Windows NT, IIS, and ASP

This section is a continuation of the "Troubleshooting" section, as many errors in ASP are really caused by incorrect security settings on the Web server. In general, these types of problems are found only on Web servers running under Windows NT. Therefore, this section begins with a general discussion of security in ASP and NT. If you already are an advanced NT user, you may find this discussion unnecessary, but for anyone else, it should provide a quick overview of a very complex topic.

File Systems   Windows NT supports the use of several different file systems, two of which, FAT and NTFS, are most often used and thus will be the focus of this section. The FAT (File Allocation Table) file system is the standard used in most DOS systems and in Windows 95. NTFS (NT File System) is designed and used exclusively by Windows NT. The primary difference, and of most relevance to a discussion of Active Server Pages, is that FAT does not provide grant or denial of access to users and groups on a file or directory basis—NTFS does.

Although you can run NT and Internet Information Server on a FAT volume, it is recommended that you use NTFS. The ability to control access down to the file and directory level is very important in running a secure Web server. Each user or group that is set up in NT (using the User Manager program, as shown in Figure 37.8) can be given a set of security rights to distinct files or directories. This is a huge difference from FAT, where the entire file system is open for access to any user.

Part

VII

Ch

37

FIG. 37.8
Here is the Windows NT
User Manager, where
you can add, edit, or
remove users and
groups.

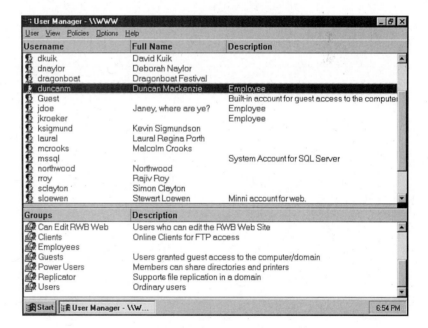

File and Directory Access Rights   NT Security, using NTFS as previously described, provides the administrator with the capability to control exactly which users (or groups of users) can access each particular file and directory on the server (see Figure 37.9). For each file, a user (or group) can be assigned any of the access types shown in Table 37.1.

FIG. 37.9

Through a series of dialogs, the exact security rights can be set for a file or directory.

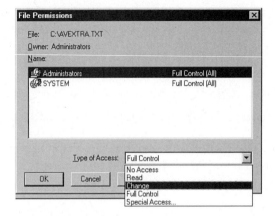

Table 37.1   File Permissions (Windows NT)

Setting	Meaning
Read	The user can only read the file. Sufficient for static HTML pages.
Execute	The file can be run. Necessary for script files, Dlls, or other programs.
Change	The user can read and modify the file. Usually not required for Web pages.
Full Control	The user can read, write, or delete the file. Should not be given to any user unless necessary.

For a directory, the permissions are a little different. There are two additional settings: List, which means that the user has the right to see the list of files contained within a directory, and Add, which gives the user the right to create new files in a directory. When changing the permissions for a directory, you have the option of setting all subdirectories of the current directory to have the same permissions, or to have the settings changed for all files under the directory.

When someone attempts to connect to an NT Server, authentication is required from him/her through the use of a userid/password combination, enabling the server to determine exactly who he/she is. After the server knows the individual's userid, it can determine that individual's security rights to files on the server. Each file-system access involves a check of the user's permissions for that portion of the file system. In the case of a Web server, there are unique problems. If the pages are designed for public browsing, then visitors to the page will not have to log in, so the server needs to have a default user setup to handle the special case of anonymous Web users.

Anonymous Access to Your Web Site   The userid that is used for anonymous users is set up in the WWW service properties dialog box, which is accessible from the Internet Service Manager of IIS. Your screen may look different, depending on the services you have installed. For each service listed, you can stop, start, pause, or edit its properties from this screen. Right-clicking the WWW Service gives you a menu of these options (see Figure 37.10). Choose Service Properties to bring up the Service Properties dialog box (see Figure 37.11).

FIG. 37.10

The Service Manager program, installed with Internet Information Server, gives you access to many of your Web server's most important settings.

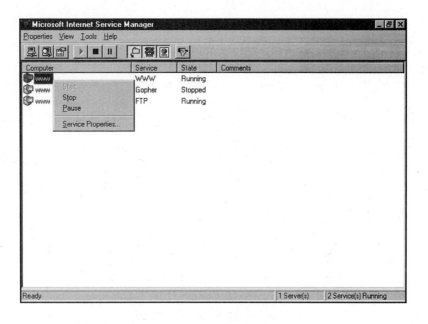

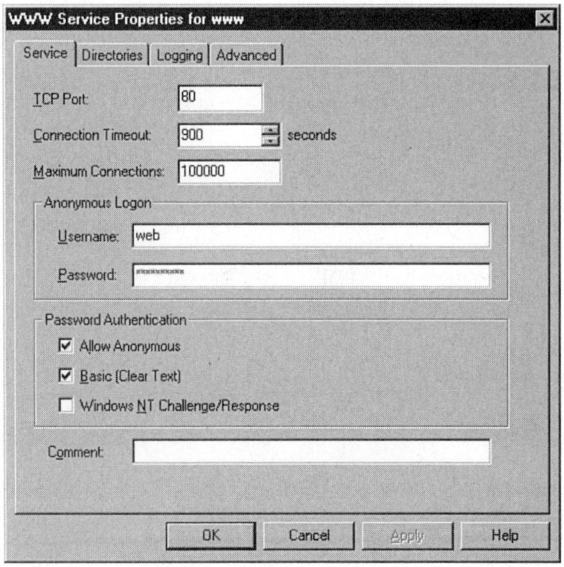

FIG 37.11

Here is the WWW Service Properties properties sheet, Service Tab.

This properties dialog box includes four tabs:

- *Service*   Allows you to set general options, including authentication and port information.

- *Directories*   Allows you to create, edit, and delete virtual directories. Functioning in the same way as mapped network drives, virtual directories map URL paths to physical paths on your server.

- *Logging* Allows you to start, stop, and change the settings for the Web server's log files.
- *Advanced* Allows you to set the less commonly used options of your Web server, including server usage and TCP/IP address restrictions.

The Service Tab The settings on the first tab deal primarily with security settings, but the tab also contains the TCP/IP port for the service. You shouldn't change this field (the default is 80) unless you know what you are doing. Web browsers look for servers on the default port and won't be able to connect to your site if you aren't using that port. The remainder of the settings on this tab deal with security issues, enabling the administrator to control which authentication methods are allowed. The Web server can be set up to use any combination of the three types listed, as long as at least one method is selected. A description of each of the three types of authentication and of their positive and negative features is discussed next.

Windows NT Authentication allows the server to use pass-through authentication with the Microsoft Networking client software on the browser end of the connection. Two main advantages of this method are:

- It is secure—the user ID and password are never exposed during authentication.
- It usually functions transparently to the users—they do not have to enter their passwords or user IDs to enter the site.

There are also disadvantages, a key one being that (at the moment) only Microsoft's browsers support this authentication method. Another problem with Windows NT Authentication is that it doesn't function through all types of firewalls. This authentication method is best used for secure intranet sites, where the browser can be a controlled choice, and a firewall isn't an issue. It isn't very well-suited for a public site.

Basic Authentication is the general method of requesting identification for Web page access. The browser is told that a user ID and password are required for access to the page it has requested, and it takes care of putting up a dialog box asking for that information (see Figure 37.5, in the troubleshooting section). Whatever the user enters is unencoded and is included in the HTTP request for the page. This method has the advantage of being supported by most browsers (including Netscape and Microsoft), but is relatively unsecured. The HTTP request (containing the authentication information) can be intercepted during transmission and decoded to obtain the user's ID and password. Chapter 39, "Using the Web, Databases, and Visual Basic," discusses a possible solution to the security problems of Basic Authentication.

The remaining option is *Anonymous Access*, which is not really a method of authentication but instead a choice to allow access without authentication. If it is checked, then HTTP requests are treated as being from the user specified as the Anonymous User.

N O T E During installation of IIS, an anonymous user account is created for you. It is named `IUSR_<Machine Name>`, where machine name is the name of the server. You do not have to use this account and may instead specify one of your own choosing. ■

The specified user ID is then used to determine access rights to files on the server. If a file is requested that requires more access than the anonymous user has, then further authentication is requested, using one of the other methods that are checked off. If no other method is checked, then anonymous access only is allowed, meaning that any request will fail if it requires more rights than the anonymous user has.

> **CAUTION**
>
> No check is performed on the password entered for the anonymous user—you must make sure it is correct. If you change the password for the user specified through the User Manager or other means, then this screen must be updated as well. If the true password and the entry on this screen are not the same, no anonymous access will work, which may prevent any access to your Web site.

When attempting to view .asp files on your Web server, it is important to realize which set of permissions you are using. Your page and any components it calls execute in the context of the user account you are logged in as. In general, you will be logged into the server as the anonymous user if you aren't using Windows NT Authentication and you haven't been prompted by the browser to enter a user ID and password. If you receive errors at this point or the page doesn't seem to work properly and you suspect permissions are the problem, there is a quick way to check. Go into the User Manager of your Web server and add the anonymous user to the administrators group. This should give the anonymous user them full control rights on every file. Test your page. If it now works, then permissions are the problem. The error `Access Denied` usually implies you do not have permissions to the page you are requesting, but other errors (such as `ASP:0115`) can be caused by insufficient permissions on other files that ASP, or some component of ASP, needs.

> **CAUTION**
>
> If you add the anonymous user to the Administrators group for the purposes of testing, make sure you remove the user afterwards!! Leaving the anonymous user set as a member of the Administrators group would give that userid full access to every single file on your server. Using Front Page or even just FTP, any person on the Internet could potentially destroy, copy, or modify your information.

The following are common areas where the browsing user needs access:

- The Common Files directory (C:\Program Files\Common Files) contains many ODBC DLLs (Dynamically Linked Libraries), as well as other components your pages may be using. READ and EXECUTE permissions should be sufficient.

- C:\Winnt\System32 is home to many DLLs that need to have READ and EXECUTE permissions turned on. It isn't recommended that you give blanket rights to this directory; try to determine exactly which files are giving you problems. Likely candidates are the ODBC set of files and any ActiveX components you are using.

- C:\Winnt\System32\LogFiles contains the system logs, as well as the IIS logs. The Web users require CHANGE permissions in this directory to allow the system to add entries to the log during their sessions.

- If you are using Microsoft Jet (Access Databases) as your server-side database, you need to give users READ and EXECUTE permissions to the MDB file (and CHANGE, if they can add or edit records in the database). In addition, they need ADD, READ, and EXECUTE permissions on the directory containing your MDB file to create the LDB (locking file for Jet).

To track down the exact file to which you do not have access, use NT's auditing features, which will log all failed access attempts to the NT Security Log. Tracking down permission problems can be frustrating and time-consuming, and it is often tempting just to give the anonymous user account Full Control rights over the whole drive, but doing so completely removes security on your system and is not a good solution. Further details on NT Security are beyond the scope of this book, but if you need more information on this issue, Que publishes several good references on NT 4.0, such as *Platinum Edition Using Windows NT 4.0* and *Windows NT Server 4.0 Administrator's Desk Reference,* which will be of assistance.

The Directories tab, shown in Figure 37.12, contains the directory setup for use by the Internet Information Server. The first directory listed is the root of your Web server, the directory pointed to when someone goes to `http://<your server>` with a Web browser. If your root directory is C:\INetPub\wwwroot, then when someone browses to `http://<your server>/ default.asp`, the Web server translates that request (using this list of directories) into `C:\INetPub\wwwroot\default.asp`.

FIG. 37.12

This is the Directories tab of the WWW Properties dialog box.

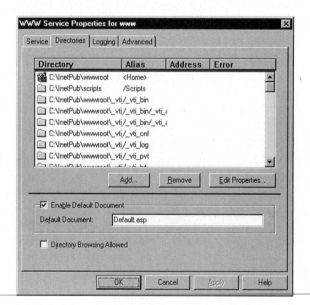

The remaining entries in this list are *Virtual Roots*. Virtual Roots enable you to specify physical locations on your server for subdirectories of your Web server. If you want to have the URL `http://<your server>/Training` point to a directory other than one physically located under your Web server's root (`C:\INetPub\wwwroot\Training`), then you must create a *Virtual Root*. When creating or editing a *Virtual Root*, as shown in Figure 37.13, you must specify the URL path you want to create a mapping for (such as `/Training`); the physical path it maps to; and several additional settings that involve access rights. The two check boxes, READ and EXECUTE, control what type of requests are allowed to come through the Web server against files under this Virtual Root. If .asp files are going to exist under a root, then you must check the EXECUTE option, but READ is sufficient for regular HTML files.

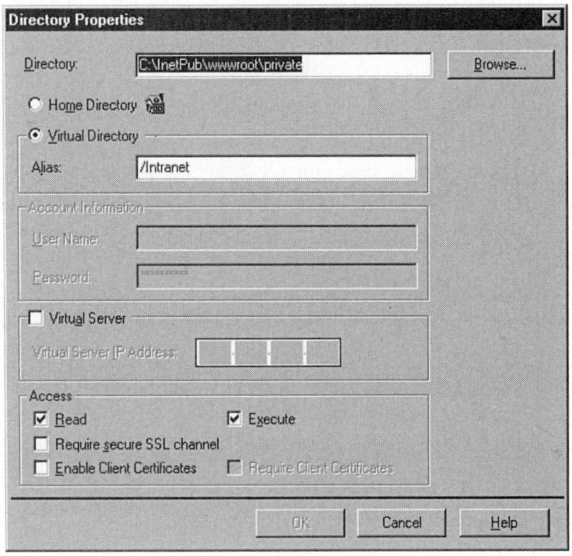

Part VII

Ch 37

FIG. 37.13

Editing a Virtual Root. When the EXECUTE option is selected, Active Server Pages are allowed to exist under this root.

This discussion of URLs and paths brings up a related point: what file is shown to the Internet user when that user requests an URL that doesn't specify a file (such as **http://www.online-can.com**)? How this common situation is handled is dependent on the two options at the bottom of this page: Enable Default Document and Directory Browsing Allowed.

The first option allows you to specify what page is shown as the default in each directory. This is set to `default.htm` initially, but you may want to change it to `main.htm`, or something similar. The second option controls whether Internet users can look at the contents of directories on your Web site. If this option is enabled and the default page is either disabled or doesn't exist for a specific directory, then Web users will see a list of files on your Web site if they browse to that directory.

CAUTION

Be extremely careful with the Directory Browsing option. Leaving this on can make hacking your site easier, allowing people to view files and directories other than those you link to on your Web pages.

The Logging Tab of the WWW Service Properties dialog box contains options allowing you to control your server's logging of HTTP requests. You can set how often new files are created, whether or not a database should be used instead of just logging to text files, and even turn off logging altogether. Many shareware and third-party utilities exist to help analyze the contents of Internet Information Server's log files.

The final tab, containing Advanced options, is shown in Fig 37.14. On this dialog box you can change the settings for two types of restrictions—access by TCP/IP addresses, and how much Internet traffic should be allowed for WWW services. The TCP/IP restriction settings allow you to prevent or grant only certain addresses (or ranges of addresses) to access your Web server. This could be used to limit your visitors to those using the same ISP as your server, while still having your server on the Internet. Denying access by IP address is a little less common but could be used to block certain users or all users connecting from a certain ISP.

The Network Usage options are designed to prevent a busy Web server from creating too much traffic on your network connection. If this option is not set, then surges in HTTP requests could bring down your entire network, but setting it to a low value will reduce the server's ability to respond to multiple requests. It is better to not use this option unless you are encountering network problems during busy periods on the server.

FIG. 37.14

This is the Advanced tab of the WWW Service Properties dialog box.

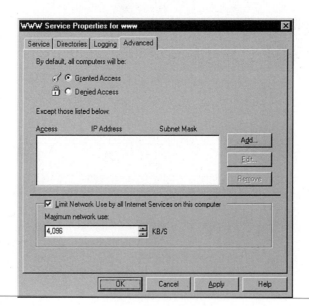

> **CAUTION**
>
> It is important to note that improper settings in this section of the Properties dialog box could easily prevent all or most of your intended audience from seeing your site.

From Here...

The need for dynamic Web sites is steadily increasing. Current technologies (CGI) are out-of-date and difficult to use. Active Server Pages are the successor to those technologies, and they improve upon them in every way. The open, COM-based architecture of ASP allows the use of existing objects, code, and standards from many other development tools. Programmers, especially Visual Basic programmers, who want to start making dynamic sites need to learn this new technology now.

The programming basics discussed in this chapter only scratch the surface of ASP programming. The following related chapters in this book will be useful as you continue deeper into ASP:

- Chapter 38, "Working with Active Server Page Objects," provides details on the intrinsic objects available in ASP, including Server, Session, Application, Response, and Request.

- Chapter 39, "Using the Web, Databases, and Visual Basic," goes into details on integrating databases with ASP and steps through the creation of an entire Web site.

Working with Active Server Page Objects

A ctive Server Pages (ASP) are used to create dynamic Web applications. The previous chapter introduced the basics of programming these pages, but those basics are not enough to create a truly dynamic site. Listing 38.1 in Chapter 37, "Creating Active Server Pages," created a Web page with ten lines—always ten, always the same lines. Not very dynamic.

To go beyond that level of dynamic content, you must have access to external input—more than just simple things, such as the current time. The input can be from a database, from users' actions on their browsers, or from some form of live data feed. It doesn't matter what. Using VBScript (or JavaScript) alone, you can't get that input. That is where objects come in to play; they are the window to everything that lies outside the page. ∎

Using objects in ASP

Learn what objects are available in ASP and how and when to use them.

Making interactive pages by using the Request and Response objects

Basic input and output in Active Server Pages, the basis for any of your scripts.

Maintaining state between pages and users by using the application and session objects

Share information between pages for one or all of the visitors to your site.

Using the ActiveX (COM) Components that come with ASP and those you obtain from other sources

Components provide prepackaged functionality you can use from your scripts.

Writing your own components for use with Active Server Pages

Bring the power of Visual Basic to your ASP applications by creating reusable components. Allow your Web pages to access the same business objects as your desktop applications.

Introducing Objects

Objects in ASP are very similar to objects in VB. You probably have already seen and used objects a fair bit, so this introduction is brief. You work with objects through their properties and methods and respond to their events. What the various parts do depends on the object, but in general, properties enable you to retrieve and set values, methods perform actions, and events occur when something happens (or at least they should—see the following Note).

> **N O T E** If you have created your own objects by using classes in Visual Basic, you know that you can have properties or methods that behave any way you want. You can make your object perform an action when the user sets a property or provide a method that takes a parameter and just sets an internal variable. Please don't. The key to creating reusable objects is following standards; use properties and methods as they are intended and other programmers won't get annoying surprises. If you are unsure of how a certain feature should be implemented, look at the objects provided by Microsoft for good examples. ■

The objects can be ActiveX (COM) objects, but they don't have to be. Both VB and ASP provide a built-in set of objects (sometimes referred to as their *Object Model* or as *intrinsic objects*) that give the environment a wide range of functionality. Each of these objects can be accessed directly; they don't need to be created, declared, or initialized. *External objects* (discussed later) expand the functionality of the language. Later in this chapter, you will be introduced to several ASP Components that you can use as external objects in your site. The intrinsic objects are available all of the time and generally are used more often (at least when just starting out) than external objects, so you will be spending more time on intrinsic objects than on other components.

COM, OLE, ActiveX, ASP Components, Enough Already!

Throughout Visual Basic magazines and books (including this one), you can find references to ActiveX objects, COM objects, OLE Automation, and now ASP Components. If you were wondering "what are all these things?" you wouldn't be alone.

Don't worry. You're not going crazy. They're all the same thing: COM. The *Component Object Model* has been around for quite a while. It started out as OLE, *Object Linking and Embedding*, gained new power with OLE2, which included, among other new features, OLE Automation (which didn't include a lot of linking or embedding, but that darn OLE stuck around anyway). Now, due to some good marketing, COM has become known to many programmers as ActiveX. They are all parts of the whole technology that is COM, each one being some subset of the full functionality. It would be nice to use one term only through the entire book, but that can't be helped. The buzzwords are stuck in our minds.

ASP Intrinsic Objects

There are five objects built into ASP:

- The Request and Response objects   These objects deal, respectively, with getting information from the browser and sending information back to the browser.
- The Application and Session objects   These objects are used to maintain information beyond the scope of the current page.
- The Server object   This object gives your Active Server Page (ASP) access to some general functions, including the powerful CreateObject method.

The following sections cover the properties, methods, and events (for those that have events) of each of the objects. You will learn what each object does and how to use it, and you will be given examples of where it is most useful. As each object is covered, some related aspects of programming Active Server Pages will also be touched on, such as the global.asa file.

The *Request* Object

The Request object contains information about the browser request for the current page. Each request can contain a large number of parameters in several different categories. To handle all of this information, the Request object uses collections. *Collections*, which are common to VB, VBA, and VBScript, generally function like linked lists or dynamic arrays, holding a list of information. You can access the information through a loop (using the For Each...Next construct), directly (using a string key), or as an ordered list (using an integer index). Chapter 10, "Using the Windows Common Controls," and Chapter 18, "Introduction to Classes," contain coverage of collections, including several examples.

▶ **See** "Creating a Toolbar with Code," **p. 247**

▶ **See** "Creating Classes that Contain Collections," **p. 505**

The following collections can be accessed through the Request object:

- QueryString
- Form
- ServerVariables
- ClientCertificates
- Cookies

Each collection contains a set of values that are all accessed in the same manner: *<Collection>*("*<Variable Name>*"). In this section, you go through the collections (except Cookies, which are covered in a separate section) and the values they contain, but you can also quickly write ASP code that will provide a list of the available variables using For Each...Next. The code in Listing 38.1 loops through each collection and outputs all the variable names and values. You can use similar code to display the contents of any collections.

On the CD

Listing 38.1   COLLECTIONS.ASP—Displaying the Content of Collections

```
<%@ LANGUAGE="VBSCRIPT" %>
<HTML>
<HEAD><TITLE>Collections</TITLE></HEAD>
<BODY>
<H1 align="center">Request Collections</H1>
<HR>
<H1 align="center">Query String</H1>
<% For Each item in Request.QueryString %>
<STRONG><%=item%></STRONG>=<%=Request.QueryString(item)%><BR>
<% Next %>
<HR>
<H1 align="center">Form</H1>
<% For Each item in Request.Form %>
<STRONG><%=item%></STRONG>=<%=Request.Form(item)%><BR>
<% Next %>
<HR>
<H1 align="center">ClientCertificate</H1>
<% For Each item in Request.ClientCertificate %>
<STRONG><%=item%></STRONG>=<%=Request.ClientCertificate(item)%><BR>
<% Next %>
<HR>
<H1 align="center">Server Variables</H1>
<% For Each item in Request.ServerVariables %>
<STRONG><%=item%></STRONG>=<%=Request.ServerVariables(item)%><BR>
<% Next %>
<HR>
<H1 align="center">Cookies</H1>
<% For Each item in Request.Cookies %>
<STRONG><%=item%></STRONG>=<%=Request.Cookies(item)%><BR>
<% Next %>
</BODY>
</HTML>
```

This is an important sample that you should try out on your own, as it will be referred to from time to time in the rest of this section. When you do run this script, you may be surprised to see that some of the collections appear to contain no items. That isn't a mistake in the code. Other than the SERVERVARIABLES collection, there shouldn't be any visible items at this point. As you go through each collection, you'll understand why this is the case.

> **N O T E**   In Listing 38.1, there is a line that hasn't been used in any examples thus far, <%@ LANGUAGE="VBSCRIPT" %>. This line (placed at the very beginning of the .asp file) tells ASP what scripting language is being used in this file. By default, the server assumes you are using VBScript, so this is not really necessary. It is a good idea to include it anyway, both to make it clear what language you're using, and to take due precaution in case the default language of the server has been changed. ▪

QUERYSTRING   The QUERYSTRING collection is used to get the values of any parameters that were sent to the ASP file. Like parameters in procedures in Visual Basic, ASP files use the parameters to pass information from one page to another. The syntax for passing parameter values is to append them in name/value pairs to the end of the page's URL. For example, if the ASP file you are calling is http://www.online-can.com/qsexample.asp and you want to send it a parameter called ID with a value of 5, you append ?id=5 onto the end of the original URL, making it http://www.online-can.com/qsexample.asp?id=5. Multiple parameters can be sent at once, separated by an ampersand (&), as follows: http://www.online-can.com/qsexample.asp?id=5&code=UT. The receiving page can retrieve these values from the QUERYSTRING collection using the parameter names as keys, as shown in Listing 38.2.

On the CD

Listing 38.2   QSEXAMPLE.ASP—Retrieving Variables from the *QueryString* Collection

```
<%@ LANGUAGE="VBSCRIPT"%>
<HTML>
<HEAD><TITLE>Query String Example</TITLE></HEAD>
<BODY>
<H2>The ID is <%=Request.QueryString("ID")%></H2>
<H2>The Code is <%=Request.QueryString("CODE")%></H2>
</BODY>
</HTML>
```

Part
VII

Ch

38

A big difference between these parameters and parameters in VB is that in ASP the parameters are not predefined. In VB your procedure expects a certain number of parameters of certain data types in a certain order. In the preceding example, two parameters were sent to qsexample.asp, but three could have been sent, or one, without generating any sort of error.

The URLs http://www.online-can.com/qsexample.asp?ID=5&CODE=UT and http://www.online-can.com/qsexample.asp?CODE=UT&ID=5&OTHERCODE=TU would both produce the exact same output (see Figure 38.1). The example page looks in the QUERYSTRING collection for two values—it doesn't matter which order they were sent or if there were other values sent that it isn't using. If the parameter you expect hasn't been sent, http://www.online-can.com/qsexample.asp?id=5 for instance, then you'll receive an empty string when you try to retrieve it with Request.QueryString("CODE").

All parameters are treated as *Variants* (general purpose data type that can hold almost any type of information), but your page may still be expecting a certain type of data for each parameter. In the previous example, ID is a numeric value, but nothing prevents someone from sending a string instead. If you planned on using that ID value as a number (in a SQL statement or a calculation), you would have a problem.

FIG. 38.1

Displaying the contents of the *QUERYSTRING* collection.

None of these things (parameter not sent, wrong data type, and so forth) cause errors on their own, but they can cause your ASP file to produce unexpected results or (its own) errors. It is a good idea to check for the existence of a parameter before you start using the ASP file. Data type errors are difficult to check for, but the VBScript functions IsDate and IsNumeric can help. An example of this is provided in Listing 38.3, which uses the same ID parameter. Try this page out by sending it different types of values, such as http://www.online-can.com/qs_datatype.asp?id=fred or http://www.online-can.com/qs_datatype.asp?id=12.

Listing 38.3   QS_DATATYPE.ASP—Checking the Data Type of Parameters

```
<%@ LANGUAGE="VBSCRIPT"%>
<HTML>
<HEAD><TITLE>Data Type Example</TITLE></HEAD>
<BODY>
<%If IsEmpty(Request.QueryString("ID")) Then %>
    <H2>No ID Value Passed</H2>
<%Else%>
    <%If IsNumeric(Request.QueryString("ID")) Then %>
        <H2>Numeric ID Passed: <%=Request.QueryString("ID")%></H2>
    <%Else%>
        <H2>Non-Numeric ID Passed: <%=Request.QueryString("ID")%></H2>
    <%End If%>
<%End If%>
</BODY>
</HTML>
```

> **N O T E**   ASP doesn't format your code in any way; you don't have to indent code within If blocks or anything else. Listing 38.3 does indent, and it is recommended that you do so to keep your pages easy to read and understand. ■

In addition to flexibility in parameter type and order, ASP allows you to send multiple parameters of the same name, such as **http://www.online-can.com/qsexample.asp?ID=5&ID=6&CODE=UT&CODE=TU**. If multiple values have been set for one parameter, then the value for that parameter, Request.QueryString("ID"), becomes a collection itself. This means you can iterate through its values or determine how many values it contains, just like a regular collection (see Listing 38.4).

Listing 38.4   QS_COLLECTIONS.ASP—Working with Collections of Parameter Values

```
<%@ LANGUAGE="VBSCRIPT"%>
<HTML>
<HEAD><TITLE>Query String Collections Example</TITLE></HEAD>
<BODY>
<%For i = 1 to Request.QueryString("ID").Count %>
    <H2><%=i%>:<%=Request.QueryString("ID")(i)%></H2>
```

```
<%Next%>
</BODY>
</HTML>
```

When creating ASP-based Web sites, you use the parameters feature almost continually. Although you can type the parameters directly as part of the URL, it is more common to use them in hyperlinks from other pages. The following two listings (see Listings 38.5 and 38.6) represent two pages. The first is a standard HTML page with several links to the other file, which contains scripting code. If you want to run these pages, you should place them into the same directory (so that the hyperlinks work properly).

Listing 38.5 CALLER.HTM—Calling Page for Hyperlink Example

```
<HTML>
<HEAD><TITLE>Calling Page Example</TITLE></HEAD>
<BODY>
<H1>Select the Biography you wish to see:</H1>
<a href="bio_page.asp?id=1">John</a><BR>
<a href="bio_page.asp?id=2">Frank</a><BR>
<a href="bio_page.asp?id=3">Susan</a><BR>
</BODY>
</HTML>
```

Part
VII

Ch
38

Listing 38.6 BIO_PAGE.ASP—Page Called in Hyperlink Example

```
<%@ LANGUAGE="VBSCRIPT"%>
<HTML>
<%
Select Case Request.QueryString("ID")
    Case 1 'John
%>
     <HEAD><TITLE>John</TITLE></HEAD>
     <BODY bgcolor="#FFFFFF">
     <H1>John</H1>
     <P><STRONG>John is a wonderful guy who has
 been working in our production department for
 years now. He stacks the boxes during the morning,
 then unstacks them in the afternoon. He never lets
 the fact that his job is pointless make him
 depressed.</STRONG></P>
<%
    Case 2 'Frank
%>
     <HEAD><TITLE>Frank</TITLE></HEAD>
     <BODY  bgcolor="#FFFFFF" >
     <H1>Frank</H1>
     <P><STRONG>Frank has always been working here.
 Filling various positions, from the mail room
 to the board room, he is an asset to the company
 and we are sad to hear that he is retiring next
```

continues

Listing 38.6 Continued

```
week at the age of 105.</STRONG></P>
<%
    Case 3 'Susan
%>
    <HEAD><TITLE>Susan</TITLE></HEAD>
    <BODY bgcolor="#FFFFFF" >
    <H1>Susan</H1>
    <P><STRONG>Susan, our illustrious President, was one
of the founding members of our company, and as such
is responsible for much of our success. Of course,
since this is a fictional company, our success has
been limited.</STRONG></P>
<%
    Case Else
%>
    <HEAD><TITLE>Error</TITLE></HEAD>
    <BODY bgcolor="#FFFFFF">
    <H1>This employee doesn't exist.</H1>
<%
End Select
%>
</BODY>
</HTML>
```

In the first page, Caller.htm, three links are available. They all point at the same .asp file, but with different parameter values. From the user's point of view, they can go to three separate pages (see Figures 38.2, 38.3, and 38.4), and each displays different information. However, you know that there is just one.

FIG. 38.2

This is the result of clicking the first link.

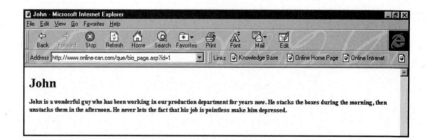

FIG. 38.3

This is the same page, requested with different parameter values.

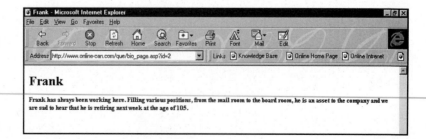

FIG. 38.4
Here is the same page again, with a different ID value specified.

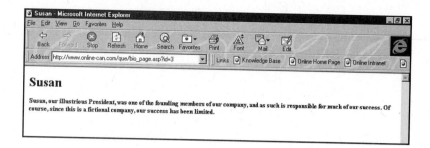

This method of having many hyperlinks to the same ASP file, each with different parameters, is very useful. It enables you to maintain one file instead of many separate pages, and it lends itself well to database-driven Web sites. This technique is used throughout the next chapter, in which an example Web site is built.

FORM The FORM collection is for use with HTML forms. An HTML form is a collection of text fields, buttons, check boxes, and other controls that are set up to allow the user to fill in and submit information. What happens when a user submits information? That is controlled by setting the action option of the <FORM> tag. The action option is set to an URL, which can point to a program or script designed to handle the results of the HTML form. This used to be limited to a CGI application or Perl script, but because the action option is just an URL, it can be the address of an Active Server Page. When the user submits the form (usually by pressing a certain button), all the information entered into the form is sent to the URL specified in the action clause.

How the information is sent depends on the method option of the <FORM> tag. If it is set to GET, then the field names and values are sent in the same manner as parameters (discussed earlier) and can be retrieved from the QueryString collection. If, on the other hand, it is set to POST, then the information is embedded into the HTTP Request sent to the page and is available through the Form collection. Listing 38.7 contains an HTML form with various types of controls on it (see Figure 38.5) and the action option set to point to Collections.asp (refer to Listing 38.1, which must be located in the same directory as this page).

On the CD

Listing 38.7 FORMSAMP.HTM—Sample Form for *Request.Form* Example

```
<HTML>
<HEAD>
<TITLE>Form Sample</TITLE>
</HEAD>
<BODY BGCOLOR="#FFFFFF">
<H1>Please Fill Out The Form Below:</H1>
<P> </P>
<form action="collections.asp" method="POST" name="Sample">
    <TABLE BORDER="0">
        <TR>
            <TD>Name:</TD>
            <TD><INPUT TYPE="text" size="50" name="txtName"></TD>
        </TR>
```

continues

Part
VII

Ch
38

Listing 38.7 Continued

```
        <TR>
            <TD>Organization:</TD>
            <TD><INPUT TYPE="text" size="50" name="txtOrganization"></TD>
        </TR>
        <TR>
            <TD>Phone Number:</TD>
            <TD><INPUT TYPE="text" size="15" name="txtPhoneNumber"></TD>
        </TR>
        <TR>
            <TD>Country:</TD>
            <TD>
              <SELECT NAME="cboCountry" size="1">
                    <OPTION SELECTED>Canada</OPTION>
                    <OPTION>United States</OPTION>
                    <OPTION>Mexico</OPTION>
                    <OPTION>France</OPTION>
              </SELECT>
            </td>
        </tr>
    </table>
    <P ALIGN="center">
     <INPUT TYPE="submit" name="cmdSubmit" value="Submit">
    </P>
</form>
<P> </P>
<H1 ALIGN="center">Thank You</H1>
</BODY>
</HTML>
```

N O T E   In Listing 38.7, the method (line 8) is set to POST; if you want to see the results of the other method, you can change this to GET. ▪

SERVERVARIABLES   When a Web page is requested from a browser, the Web server is sent various pieces of information about the requester. Those pieces of information, combined with various server-side environment variables, are all contained in the Server Variables collection. Following are the more useful members of this collection, but you can always look at the others on your own (refer to Listing 38.1).

- ■ `LOGON_USER`   This variable holds the NT user ID that the requester is currently logged in as. If he/she is logged in as the anonymous user, this value is blank.

- ■ `PATH_INFO`   When a browser makes a request, it places the non-root portion of the request's path into this variable.

    For example, if the request were for "http://www.online-can.com/webtest.asp", then this variable would hold "/webtest.asp". This is useful for ASP files that want to call themselves without hard coding their own path into the file.

- ■ `PATH_TRANSLATED`   The translated path is the actual physical path to the Web page on the Web server.

FIG. 38.5

A Simple Example HTML Form, viewed when it is submitted.

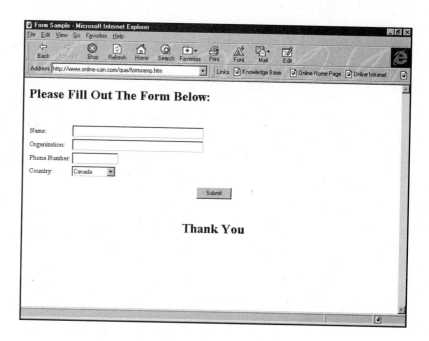

Using the same request example as was mentioned previously (http://www.online-can.com/webtest.asp), this variable will be set to "C:\INetPub\wwwroot\webtest.asp" because "C:\INetPub\wwwroot" is the root path of the Web server.

This value is extremely helpful and difficult to duplicate manually. If you are using an external COM object (to create a table of contents listing, for example) that works with directories or files, it will probably require the true path to your page. Translating the virtual Web server path into this form requires a large amount of work, which this variable allows you to avoid.

■ QUERY_STRING   Contains the parameters passed as part of this HTTP Request. Everything after the "?" in the URL is placed into this variable.

Given the request "http://www.online-can.com/webtest.asp?id=5&name=fred&j=3", this variable would contain the value "id=5&name=fred&j=3". The values contained within this variable are very useful, but it is easier to retrieve them from the QueryString collection directly, letting the system parse this string for you.

■ REMOTE_ADDR/REMOTE_HOST   Filled in with the IP address and host name (if available), respectively, of the computer making the HTTP Request. This information is generally used for logging purposes, but you can select content based on this value as well.

■ SERVER_NAME   Gives you the server name portion of the current page's URL. In the prior example ("http://www.online-can.com/webtest.asp"), this would be "www.online-can.com". It is primarily used for scripts that want to reference themselves but do not want to have any hardcoded values (see PATH_INFO).

Part
VII

Ch
38

- ▓ HTTP_UA_PIXELS   Contains the screen resolution of the browser making the request, in the form "800 × 600", "640 × 480", and so on. This is one of several User Agent values used to customize your page layout or content based on the specifications of the browser making the request.

- ▓ HTTP_UA_COLOR   Gives the number of colors available on the client machine—"color16" for 16-bit color, "color8" for 8-bit, and so on.

- ▓ HTTP_UA_OS   Set to a string representing the Operating System used by the client machine, of the form "Windows 95". Could be used for logging purposes, customization of content (use of 32-bit ActiveX controls, for instance) or to preselect form options during software download or a related process.

- ▓ HTTP_USER_AGENT   Contains a string representing all available information about the type of browser in use. The various values available for this variable map directly to certain brands and versions of browsers, such as "Mozilla/2.02 (Win95; U)" for Netscape 2.0, or "Mozilla/2.0 (compatible; MSIE 3.01; Windows 95)" for Internet Explorer 3.01 on Windows 95.

  Your page could base its content (use of frames, tables, ActiveX controls, VBScript, and so on) on the value of this variable, but there are a large number of possible values for which you would have to check, making this a complicated process. It is easier to use the Browser Capabilities COM object that is included with ASP (discussed later in this chapter) to determine what HTML features are supported by the client browser.

Client Certificates   *Certificates* are digital documents that uniquely identify an object, whether that is an individual, a company, or a specific Web server. Each certificate is issued by some signing authority (Verisign is a common authority; see **http://www.verisign.com**) and contains a series of fields used to identify the object attached to the certificate. The fields in a particular certificate can vary, but usually include standard information such as Name, Country, Organization, and so forth.

Client Certificates refer to the use of these certificates by visitors to a secure Web site as a means of identification. If certain options are selected for the virtual directory being browsed (see Figure 38.13, in the previous chapter), the server will request a certificate from the client for identification. If a certificate is provided, your pages may use the Client Certificate collection to query the values contained within the document. This provides your pages with a way to determine the client's name or other identifying information, in order to control access to secure information. More information on certificates and Secure Web Sites is available in the next chapter.

The *Response* Object

The Response object is used to send information to the client. Unlike Request, this object contains only one collection, Cookies. The Cookies collection is not discussed here, but is covered in-depth later in the chapter in a section on working with Cookies, which covers both the Request and Response objects. Most of the functionality of the Response object is accessed through its series of properties and methods. Each item will be covered as well, with some related examples.

Properties   The Response object has several properties, each of which is used to affect the information returned to the browser in some way. Setting any of these values after information has been returned to the browser (which occurs as soon as the <HTML> tag is reached) will cause an error.

■ Expires   Expires is the property you'll probably use the most in your ASP applications. This value represents the number of minutes before the page's content expires from the browser's cache. This means that if a particular client returns to this page within the time set by Expires, then the cached content is used. If it has been longer than the time specified, the page is requested from the server again. To ensure that users are always seeing the most up-to-date information on pages, usually you'll set this property to zero, telling the browser not to cache the page at all—to always go back to the server for a fresh copy.

Listings 38.8 and 38.9 show how this property can affect page updating. To view the examples, place each one onto your Web server and then go to them through your browser. Once the pages have been displayed, browse to a different page and return to each example page quickly (within 5 minutes). The page with Expires set to 5 minutes will still show the time of your first visit, while the other page will show the time of your current visit. For your applications, you can adjust this property as necessary to balance between too frequent of a return query to your page and making sure you have the most current information.

Part VII

Ch

38

Listing 38.8   NEVERCACHE.ASP—Setting *Response.Expires* to Zero

```
<%@ LANGUAGE="VBSCRIPT"%>
<%Response.Expires=0%>
<HTML>
<HEAD><TITLE>Never Cache This Page</TITLE></HEAD>
<BODY>
<H1>The Current Date and Time is:</H1>
<P align="center"><%=Now%></P>
</BODY>
</HTML>
```

Listing 38.9   CACHE_5MIN.ASP—Setting *Response.Expires* to Five Minutes

```
<%@ LANGUAGE="VBSCRIPT"%>
<%Response.Expires=5%>
<HTML>
<HEAD><TITLE>Cache This Page for 5 minutes</TITLE></HEAD>
<BODY>
<H1>The Current Date and Time is:</H1>
<P align="center"><%=Now%></P>
</BODY>
</HTML>
```

- **ExpiresAbsolute** This is a similar property to Expires, but instead of specifying the number of minutes before the cached copy of the page expires, you specify a date and time. This version of the Expires property is useful for information that is current up to a certain time each day or every week. An example is a page displaying currency exchange rates, or other information that is updated only at certain specific times. Expiration dates and times (for this property and the previous one) are client-based, meaning that if you moved your clock forward on the client machine, the cached pages would expire early.

- **ContentType** The ContentType property changes the HTTP header of the page to indicate what type of data the page contains. Pages are sent back as "text/HTML" by default, indicating that they are text files containing HTML tags and should be interpreted as such by the browser. If you set this to "text/plain", as in Listing 38.10, the browser displays the entire page, including all of the HTML source. This property can be used to generate text files from ASP for use in other objects or to send out to the client browser. For instance, you can use ASP to generate a comma-delimited text file from a database so that the user can import that information into Microsoft Excel or similar applications. A more advanced use of the content type property is to use ASP to return a picture (which can be stored as binary information in a database or created at run time by a COM object) to the browser. (A quick sample of this is shown in Listing 38.15 under "RESPONSE.BINARYWRITE Method.")

On the CD

Listing 38.10   TEXT.ASP—Outputting Text from an Active Server Page

```
<%@ LANGUAGE="VBSCRIPT"%>
<%Response.ContentType="text/plain"
For j = 1 to 100
    Response.Write j & "," & (j * 2) & "," & (j * 3) & chr(13) & chr(10)
Next
%>
```

- **Status** This property allows you to set the HTTP Status line that is returned to the browser. This line consists of a three-digit status code and a message, such as 404 Page Not Found. You can set this property to whatever message you want, but it is better if you attempt to follow standard formats for Web servers. The current list of status codes and messages is part of the HTTP specification, which can be found at **http://www.w3.org/ pub/WWW/Protocols/Overview.html**.

- **Buffer** This property controls whether page content generated from your ASP script is returned to the browser as it is generated or all at once when your page has finished executing.

    This becomes important when your script modifies the HTTP headers. Any property or method that changes some part of those headers (Response.Redirect, Response.Expires, Response.AddHeader, Response.Status, and so on) must occur before any content is returned to the browser. If Response.Buffer is set to false (buffering is off), then those commands must all occur before the opening <HTML> tag. If buffering is on, then those commands can be used anywhere in the page because the entire page will be executed before any content is returned.

Normally, it is not a problem to place these commands before the <HTML> tag, it is just a matter of moving your script around, but in certain cases (such as error handling code, as in Listing 38.11), you can't control when it is executed. In those cases, you must use buffering.

On the CD

Listing 38.11 BUFFERING.ASP—Buffering Output to Allow Error Handling

```
<%@ LANGUAGE="VBSCRIPT"%>
<%

Response.Buffer=TRUE

On Error Resume Next

%>
<HTML>
<HEAD><TITLE>Buffering Example</TITLE></HEAD>
<BODY>
<%

Set Obj = Server.CreateObject("SyncDateTime.clsSyncDateTime")
If Err.Number > 0 Then

    ErrorURL = "ErrorHandler.asp"
    ErrorURL = ErrorURL & "?Source=" & Server.URLEncode(Err.Source)
    ErrorURL = ErrorURL & "Number=Err.Number"

    Err.Clear

    Response.Redirect ErrorURL
        ' Buffering allows us to do a redirect at any point in the page.

Else

    Obj.DateTime = Now
    Response.Write Obj.DateString
End If
%>
</BODY>
</HTML>
```

Part

VII

Ch

38

CAUTION

Regardless of how you plan to use buffering, setting the Response.Buffer property must occur at the very beginning of your page, before any other commands or any content.

The other reasons for choosing to turn buffering on or off are mostly aesthetic; buffering affects the apparent speed of your page. Buffering can hide the fact that the generation of one particular section of the page is taking longer than the rest but can also make the entire page seem to take too long. If the page takes a long time to execute, this can result in a long wait before any part of the page is displayed at the client end.

Methods   The Response object's methods allow you to directly affect the return of information to the browser. Several of these methods involve the concept of buffering, see the Buffer property previously discussed for more information.

- ■ Write Response.Write is the ASP equivalent of a print command. It enables you to place text directly into the page's output. In many cases, this method is unnecessary because you can use inline sections of text and variable substitution. (See Listings 38.1 and 38.2 in Chapter 37, "Creating Active Server Pages," for an example and a comparison of the two methods.)

▶ **See** "The Basics," **p. 1024**

- ■ Redirect This method enables you to move to a different URL, which allows you to control a user's navigation through your site based on whatever criteria you want. Listing 38.12 redirects the user to a page based on the operating system he/she is using. Two users could go to the same page, click the same link, and yet be shown different information from different pages, each page containing information targeted at their specific operating system. This type of processing is one of the keys to dynamic Web sites: showing users content tailored to their needs.

Listing 38.12   REDIRECT.ASP—Redirection Based on Client OS

```
<%@ LANGUAGE="VBSCRIPT"%>
<% Select Case Request.ServerVariables("HTTP_UA_OS")

    Case "Windows95"

        Response.Redirect "Win95.htm"

    Case "WindowsNT"

        Response.Redirect "WinNT.htm"

    Case "MacOS"

        Response.Redirect "MacOS.htm"

    Case Else

        Response.Redirect "Other.htm"

End Select

%>
<HTML>
<HEAD><TITLE>Redirection</TITLE></HEAD>
<BODY>
</BODY>
</HTML>
```

CAUTION

`Response.Redirect` modifies the HTTP headers, so it must occur before any content is returned to the browser (see `Response.Buffer` in Listing 38.11 for more information).

- Buffering Related Methods, `Clear/Flush`   When buffering is on (see `Response.Buffer`, Listing 38.11), nothing is returned to the browser until the script is finished executing. These two methods give you some control over that buffered information. `Clear` removes any page content from the buffer, and `Flush` sends the current contents of the buffer immediately (even if the page has not finished executing) to the browser. Calling either of these methods when buffering is off causes an error.

- `End`   The `End` method stops execution of your program immediately when it is called (see Listing 38.13). It doesn't do anything about content already sent to the browser or content that is in the buffer (which would be sent to the browser at this point). You shouldn't use this method unless you have to, and you don't ever have to. If you are responding to an error condition, then redirect the user to an error screen or some form of "Oops!!" page. If you are not buffering and therefore can't use the redirect option, at least write out some sort of error message to the browser before aborting. Sending `Response.End` on its own just leaves users staring at a partially completed or empty browser and wondering what happened.

On the CD

Listing 38.13   END.ASP—Stopping Execution of an Active Server Page

```
<HTML>
<HEAD><TITLE>Stopping an ASP</TITLE></HEAD>
<BODY>
<% For j = 1 to 200 %>
<P><%=j%></P>
<%
    If j > 40 Then
        Response.End
    End If
Next
%>
</BODY>
</HTML>
```

- `AddHeader`   The `AddHeader` method is used to create a new HTTP header and return it, along with your page, to the browser. It takes a name/value pair as parameters (for example, `Response.AddHeader "NOTE","I made this page!"`) to create the new header, one called NOTE with a value of "I made this page!". This is a relatively low-level function and shouldn't be used until you have become comfortable with the more common properties and methods.

- `AppendToLog`   This method allows you to append text to the Web server's log entry for this HTTP request. Whatever string you send as a parameter to this method is added to the end of the log entry that is normally created. The example given in Listing 38.14 produces the following log entry (all as one line):

```
207.161.119.76, -, 7/3/97, 21:23:17, W3SVC, WWW,
205.200.204.200, 30, 413, 259, 200, 0, GET,
/append.asp, This is a test of the AppendToLog method,
```

Of course, some fields (such as the IP address) will contain different values if you try out this example yourself.

On the CD

Listing 38.14 APPEND.ASP—Appending Text to the Web Server's Log

```
<%Response.AppendToLog "This is a test of the AppendToLog method" %>
<HTML>
<HEAD><TITLE>Example Page</TITLE></HEAD>
<BODY>
</BODY>
</HTML>
```

CAUTION

Web Server log entries are comma-delimited, so the string you append cannot contain any commas.

- `BinaryWrite` This method is similar to the `Response.Write` Statement, but not for textual data. You pass it binary data (with the same syntax as passing a string to `Response.Write`), and it sends that data out to the browser.

   Where is this useful? Many types of files commonly viewed in Web browsers are binary in nature, including images, sounds, and even documents, such as Excel spreadsheets. To use this method to send back files of those, or other, types, you will also need to use the `RESPONSE.CONTENTTYPE` property. An example of this type of application is shown in Listing 38.10.

Suppose you create an employee directory for a large company. For each employee, you would go to an Active Server Page to display his/her information, sending a parameter of the employee's ID. Your database would also include pictures for each employee, stored as binary data in a field of the employee table. In this case, you would need to create another .asp file, called picture.asp, for example, and in your details page, use it as the source for your picture, such as `<img src="picture.asp?id=<%=EmpID%>">`. The picture page (see Listing 38.15) would use `RESPONSE.CONTENTTYPE="image/jpeg"` to tell the browser that it should be treated like a picture and would then call RESPONSE.BINARYWRITE to output the contents of the picture field from the database.

On the CD

Listing 38.15 PICTURE.ASP—Outputting Binary Data

```
<%
'Create ADODB Object, Connect to Database and execute query
Set conn = Server.CreateObject("ADODB.Connection")
Conn.Open "DSN=EmployeeDB"
SQL = "SELECT Employee.Picture FROM Employee "
SQL = SQL & "Where Employee.ID=" & Request.QueryString("ID")
```

```
Set RSPicture = Conn.Execute(SQL)
Response.ContentType="image/JPEG"
Response.BinaryWrite RSPicture("Picture")
%>
```

N O T E The example shown in Listing 38.15 isn't complete: the database access involved has been skipped. This is to allow you to focus on the particular feature without bringing in a lot of unrelated code. If you want to try out this specific type of example in full, you will need an ODBC connection to a database that supports BLObs (Binary Large Objects) and has a table set up that contains JPEG format binary data. ■

Controlling State, the *Application* and *Session* Objects, and the Global.asa File

Variables used in ASP or in any programming environment have a certain *scope*, meaning that variables created inside a procedure exist for that procedure only. These types of variables are fine for most things you do, in any language, but occasionally you need to keep some piece of information available in all of your procedures. A good example is the user IDs of the logged-on users. They may have logged on at the very beginning of the program, but you need to know that information throughout your application.

This situation is usually handled by creating a global variable (for example, Public Userid as string), which can then be used anywhere you want without having to pass it to any procedure. To do this in ASP, you first have to determine what *global* means in the context of Active Server Pages. In Visual Basic, it means that the variable has *Application-level scope* or, more clearly, that the variable is available to every part of that VB Application. In ASP, because there is no project file to define your application, you have to use a different method to determine what global means.

An ASP application is defined as all of the ASP files within one *Virtual Root* (refer to Chapter 37, "Creating Active Server Pages"). Two different levels of variables are supported for ASP: *Session* variables, which are closest to VB global variables, and *Application* variables. Session variables exist on a user-by-user basis, while Application variables are available to all users of that application. The Session and Application objects, which enable you to create and access the different types of global variables, are discussed later in the chapter. Unlike the objects previously discussed (such as the Request object), these objects have more than just properties and methods; they also have *events*.

▶ **See** "Security Settings in Windows NT, IIS, and ASP," **p. 1034**

In Visual Basic, code is written to be executed on an event by placing that code into special procedures that are defined at the same level as the object. ASP handles the Application and Session events in the same fashion, and the code is placed into a special file named "global.asa," which must be located at the root of the ASP application. These events, and the "global.asa" file, will be described later.

The *Application* Object

Variables are placed into and accessed in the Application object in the same manner as other collections. Any type of variable, even instances of objects, may be placed into the Application and Session objects (with the single exception of ASP *Intrinsic* objects) so that the line Application("Test")=Response would cause an error.

This code, APPLICATION("STARTDATE")=Now would store the date and time into an application variable named *StartDate*. To access this information again is equally straightforward. The code RESPONSE.WRITE APPLICATION("STARTDATE") would output that date to the browser. Because of the multiuser nature of the Application object, two methods are provided: Lock and Unlock. These methods are similar to the idea of locking a database record before updating it because they allow you to prevent anyone else from modifying the Application object at the same time as you. You should try to minimize the amount of code that occurs while you've locked the Application object, as no other users can modify any Application level variable during that time. Listing 38.16 and Listing 38.17 show two possible ways to assign the results of a complex function to the Application object. The second method is preferred, as it performs the calculation outside of the Lock/Unlock, reducing the amount of time the lock is in effect.

Listing 38.16 LOCKSAMP1.ASP—Locking the Application Object for a Long Time

```
<%
Application.Lock
Application("MyResult")=ComplexFunction(3,223,29)
Application.Unlock
%>
```

Listing 38.17 LOCKSAMP2.ASP—Locking the Application Object for the Shortest Time Possible

```
<%
TempValue = ComplexFunction(3,223,29)
Application.Lock
Application("MyResult")=TempValue
Application.Unlock
%>
```

A single instance of the Application object is created when the first person accesses any Active Server Page in that ASP application and is released when the Web service is shut down or restarted. At each of these times, an OnStart or OnEnd event is triggered, as appropriate. Code that you want to run at either of these times can be placed into the global.asa, as shown in Listing 38.18.

Listing 38.18   GLOBAL.ASA—Working with Application Events

```
<SCRIPT LANGUAGE=VBScript RUNAT=Server>

Sub Application_OnStart

        Application("StartDate") = Now
        Application("Counter") = 0

End Sub

</SCRIPT>
```

N O T E   In Listing 38.18, the <SCRIPT> tag is used, which you may have seen when dealing with client-side scripting (refer to Chapter 35, "Internet Programming with VBScript"). This is required in the global.asa file because that file is not really a true ASP file and doesn't support the use of the script delimiters (<% and %>). ■

▶ **See** "Using the HTML <*FORM*> Elements," **p. 950**

▶ **See** "The <*SCRIPT*> Element," **p. 959**

The *Session* Object

Like the Application object, the Session object uses the same syntax to store and retrieve values, and its two event routines, Session_OnStart and Session_OnEnd, are handled in the global.asa file (refer to Listing 38.18). There are two differences between the two objects—when the instances of them are created or destroyed, and who can access those instances.

A Session starts when a user requests any page within an ASP application. It ends when the session times out, or when a script Abandons the session (see the following sections, Abandon and Timeout). All values/objects stored in Session variables are lost when the session ends.

Variables stored in the SESSION object are available only to the user who owns the session, whereas the APPLICATION object is available to all users. This difference allows the Session object to function safely without any form of the Lock/Unlock methods present in the Application object.

Abandon   The SESSION.ABANDON method ends the current session immediately. This causes any script in the SESSION_ONEND procedure to be called and the destruction of any session-level variables or objects.

Timeout   Each Session instance is maintained on the server until it is explicitly closed (as with the preceding Abandon method) or until a certain amount of time has passed since the application received the last request for that session (any page access within that ASP application). The second condition is known as a timeout.

This property returns or sets the number of minutes before the current session times out. The default is 20 minutes, and modifying the value for this property changes only the timeout for the current session. Changing this, or any other default ASP setting, involves modifying the Web server's Registry entries.

SessionID   This property is read-only and holds the ID used to uniquely identify a session (see the "Oh, It's Just You Again" sidebar). This value is unique only across the current `Application` instance, and it may repeat after the Web service has been restarted.

Oh, It's Just You Again

When a user first requests a page inside an ASP application, he/she has started a Session. Values stored into Session variables are kept at the server and are made available to that user for the duration of his/her session. To accomplish this task, the server has to keep track of who owns which session. Communication between the server and the browser consists of requests and responses; there is no permanent connection. Every time the user requests the page, the server has to determine if the user already has a session or if a new session should be created.

It manages this little trick by using a cookie. This cookie stores (at the client side) a unique ID that it sends to the server every time it requests a page. The server then uses this ID to find the user's current session. If the ID isn't present on the client, or the session has been removed on the server, a new session is started, and a new ID is stored into the cookie.

If the client's browser doesn't support cookies, or the user chooses not to accept the cookie containing the `SessionID`, then no Session can be set up for that client, and session-based variables and objects will not work.

Cookies

Cookies are a unique feature in the world of HTML and HTTP. They allow pages and sites to store information on the client. This capability became a need as Web sites attempted to become more customized. Sites, such as **http://home.microsoft.com**, that show you personalized content immediately upon your arrival to the page (without any form of login) are using cookies to determine who you are. When you first go to the page, they create a server-side record of you (in a database or something similar) and store a unique identifier into a cookie on your machine. When you return to that page, it looks at the cookie to get your unique ID, uses it to retrieve the server-side information, and then creates a page that is customized for you. If cookies didn't exist, you would have to identify yourself (most likely through a logon screen) every time a site wanted to show you a personalized appearance.

Most browsers support cookies, so that isn't usually an issue, but many (including Microsoft's and Netscape's browsers) give users the option not to accept cookies (see Figure 38.6). If users take this option, then when they go to sites that attempt to send out a cookie, they have the option to not accept it (see Figure 38.7). Without that cookie, the sites (which could potentially include yours) will be unable to work as expected. With ASP, this means more than just requiring a logon screen—it means that Session variables are not available. Many sites rely heavily on storing information in the `Session` object and, therefore, depend on cookies to function. Even if you are not using the Session features of ASP, it still creates a session for you and thus still sends out cookies.

FIG. 38.6

Disabling Cookies in
Internet Explorer 3.01.

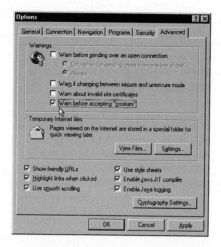

FIG. 38.7

Cookie Security
Warning when
accessing an ASP site.

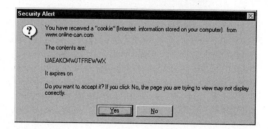

Now that you have an idea what cookies are and what problems can exist with them, you may want to use them in your own ASP applications. If so, you are in luck because it is very easy to use them. The `Response.Cookies` collection enables you to create cookies and place values into them, and the `Request.Cookies` collection enables you to retrieve values from the cookies. The following example shows how to place a value into a cookie and then retrieve it. Each time you refresh or return to this page, the value increases. Try disabling cookies or turning on the "warn before sending" option of Internet Explorer when viewing this page to see what effect it has on the script (refer to Figure 38.6).

Listing 38.19 demonstrates setting individual values in a cookie (`Response.Cookies("Counter")`), but you can also set and access individual subkeys of a Cookie by using a second index. This example—`Response.Cookies("Counter")("main")=6`—would set the `"main"` subkey of this Cookie to `6`. A cookie cannot have both types of values—if you used the storage method, setting the value using one index would overwrite any subkeys that were in use, and vice versa. The read-only property `HasKeys` (as in `Response.Cookies("Counter").HasKeys`) can be used to determine if subkeys are in use for a particular Cookie. When setting the Cookie's value by using the `Response` objects, several other properties of the cookie are available, such as `Expires`, `Domain`, `Path`, and `Secure`.

Listing 38.19   COOKIES.ASP—Demonstration of Setting and Retrieving Cookie Values

```
<%
Counter = Request.Cookies("Counter")
If len(Counter) = 0 Then
     Counter = 0
Else
     Counter = Counter + 1
End If
Response.Cookies("Counter") = Counter
%>
<HTML>
<HEAD><TITLE>Cookie Demonstration</TITLE></HEAD>
<BODY>
<H1>Cookie Value: <%=Counter%></H1>
</BODY>
</HTML>
```

The *Server* Object

This object's name suggests that it gives access to the Web server itself, which is not quite true. The properties and methods are more related to the Web server than the other intrinsic objects but are really just general utility functions.

ScriptTimeout   This property controls how long an ASP script can execute on the server before it is considered to have timed out and an error message is returned to the browser. The default value for this property, which is contained in the Registry, is usually 90 seconds. This property can be used only to increase that value, and if you set the timeout to a value less than the default, the default will still be used.

CreateObject   This method of the Server object is the most powerful aspect of ASP, providing the capability to create instances of COM objects. Using the VBScript Set command, you can create an instance of a component and assign it to a variable for use in your pages. You can also take these instances and store them into the Application or Session objects to allow those objects to be used across your ASP application. The example script in Listing 38.20 shows the creation of a component that is used to output lines back to the browser. Later, in the sections dealing with external objects, you will see this method in every Active Server Page used. The syntax of the method is straightforward, and is identical to the CreateObject statement in VB because it takes just one parameter (the ProgID.ClassId string of the object you are trying to create).

Listing 38.20   TOC.ASP—Example Using the *CreateObject* Method

```
<%
Response.ContentType = "text/plain"

Set NAV = Server.CreateObject("Navigation.clsWebDirUtils")
```

```
TOCLine = "1 -t main.htm " & """" & "Employee Policy Manual" & """"

Response.Write TOCLine
Response.Write vbNewLine

NAV.FilePath = Server.MapPath(".")

NAV.OutputFormat = NAV.obsTOC

NAV.ListFiles 2

i = 0

if NAV.LineCount > 1 Then

    for i = 2 to NAV.LineCount

        OutputString = NAV.lines(i + 1 - 1) & " "

        Response.write OutputString & vbNewLine

    next

end if

%>
```

HTMLEncode   Certain characters can't be written out directly to the browser. These characters, including < and >, as well as both double and single quotes, have special meaning to the browser and will not be displayed as you would expect. If you are entering text into a Web page editor, such as FrontPage, then these characters are automatically converted into special character combinations (such as &lt for <) for you. If, as is more often the case in ASP, you are pulling text out of a database or other external source, then you need to perform this conversion yourself (at run time). It is possible to write a VBScript routine to do this or to create an external object in VB or VC++ for this purpose, but you don't have to do so. Server.HTMLEncode will take any string as a parameter and output the converted value for use in your page. The example Active Server Page in Listing 38.21 produces the HTML output shown in Listing 38.22.

Listing 38.21   HTMLENCODE.ASP—Converting Text with *Server.HTMLEncode*

```
<HTML>
<HEAD>
<TITLE><%=Server.HTMLEncode("John & Debbie's Web Page")%></TITLE>
</HEAD>
<BODY BGCOLOR="#FFFFFF">
<H1 align="center">
<%=Server.HTMLEncode("Welcome to John & Debbie's Place")%>
</H1>
<H2 align="center">
<%=Server.HTMLEncode("Where it's <COOL> to use tags!")%>
</H2>
```

continues

Listing 38.21   Continued

```
<P><%=Server.HTMLEncode("John specializes in " & _
"creating Web pages. Using only the <BODY>")%><BR>
<%=Server.HTMLEncode("and </BODY> tags he is able to " & _
"generate a complete site in minutes.")%></P>
<HR>
<P><%=Server.HTMLEncode("Debbie prefers to create" & _
" graphics.  Wherever you have an <IMG> tag,")%><BR>
<%=Server.HTMLEncode("you could use Debbie's " & _
"""" & "Special Touch" & """")%></P>
</BODY>
</HTML>
```

On the CD

Listing 38.22   HTMLRESULTS.HTM—Results of HTML Encode

```
<HTML>
<HEAD>
<TITLE>John &amp; Debbie's Web Page</TITLE>
</HEAD>

<BODY BGCOLOR="#FFFFFF">

<H1 align="center">Welcome to John &amp; Debbie's Place</H1>
<H2 align="center">Where it's &lt;COOL&gt; to use tags!</H2>
<P>John specializes in creating Web pages.
 Using only the &lt;BODY&gt;<BR>
and &lt;/BODY&gt; tags he is able to generate
a complete site in minutes.</P>
<HR>
<P>Debbie prefers to create graphics.
Wherever you have an &lt;IMG&gt; tag,<BR>
you could use Debbie's &quot;Special Touch&quot;</P>
</BODY>
</HTML>
```

The HTML output, now properly encoded, is returned to the browser and produces the desired output, as you can see in Figure 38.8.

URLEncode   Similar to the encoding just described for text inside an HTML page, text attached to an URL (as a parameter, for instance) also cannot use certain characters. In an URL, characters such as a space or a backslash take on other meanings. URLEncode takes any string and, using special escape characters, converts it into a string suitable for use in an URL. For example, see the following line of scripting code:

```
<A HREF="collections.asp?text="
<%=Server.URLEncode("Why do we need to encode things?")%>
">Test</A>
```

```
        </TD>
</TR>
<TR>
        <TD>
        <STRONG>Position:</STRONG>
  </TD>
        <TD>
        <INPUT TYPE="text" SIZE="60" NAME="Position">
  </TD>
</TR>
<TR>
        <TD>
        <STRONG>Address:</STRONG>
  </TD>
        <TD>
        <INPUT TYPE="text" SIZE="60" NAME="Address">
  </TD>
</TR>
<TR>
        <TD>
        <STRONG>City/Town:</STRONG>
  </TD>
        <TD>
        <INPUT TYPE="text" SIZE="60" NAME="City">
  </TD>
</TR>
<TR>
        <TD>
        <STRONG>Postal Code:</STRONG>
  </TD>
        <TD>
        <INPUT TYPE="text" SIZE="20" NAME="PostalCode">
        </TD>
</TR>
<TR>
    <TD WIDTH="80">
        <STRONG>Email:</STRONG>
    </TD>
    <TD>
        <INPUT TYPE="text" SIZE="60" NAME="EMail">
    </TD>
</TR>
<TR>
    <TD WIDTH="80">
        <STRONG>Phone:</STRONG>
  </TD>
    <TD>
        <INPUT TYPE="text" SIZE="20" NAME="Phone">
    </TD>
</TR>
<TR>
    <TD WIDTH="80">
        <STRONG>Fax:</STRONG>
  </TD>
    <TD>
```

continues

Listing 39.18   Continued

```
                 <INPUT TYPE="text" SIZE="20" NAME="Fax">
           </TD>
        </TR>
        <TR>
           <TD WIDTH="80"> </TD>
           <TD ALIGN="right" VALIGN="bottom">
              <P ALIGN="right">
                    <INPUT TYPE="submit"
                    NAME="Submit Form"
                    VALUE="Submit Registration Form">
              </P>
           </TD>
        </TR>
     </TABLE>
  </FORM>
  </BODY>
  </HTML>
```

All of the fields in a form, whether visible or not, are available to the target page as part of the `Request.Form` collection. A registration system may take a variety of information, depending on the needs of the system; but in your case, all you want is standard name and address style information. If you want to collect different information, you have to modify the Form, the receiving Active Server Page, and the database, for everything to work properly. The receiving page is where the actual information saving occurs, using the `AddNew` method of a `Recordset` (see Listing 39.19). After you have added a new record, you can put values into each field through straight assignment, `RSSave("Name")=Request.Form("Name")`, making for pretty easy, though somewhat repetitive code. It is standard practice to put up some sort of confirmation message, as shown in Listing 39.19, or to display any field validation errors encountered. Regardless of what you choose to display, it is better than a blank page—users require some feedback; otherwise, they will register over and over again.

On the CD

Listing 39.19   SAVEREG.ASP—Script to Save Results of an HTML Form

```
<%@ LANGUAGE="VBSCRIPT" %>
<HTML>
<head>
<TITLE>Save Registration Form</TITLE>
</HEAD>
<%
Set conn = Server.CreateObject("ADODB.Connection")
Conn.Open "DSN=Training"
Set RSSave = Server.CreateObject("ADODB.Recordset")
SQL = "SELECT registration.* FROM registration"
RSSave.Open SQL,Conn , 1, 2
%>
<BODY BGCOLOR="#FFFFFF">
<%
     RSSave.AddNew
     RSSave("Course_Name") = Request.Form("Course_Name")
```

```
      RSSave("Course_Date") = Request.Form("Course_Date")
      RSSave("Name") = Request.Form("Name")
      RSSave("Organization") = Request.Form("Organization")
      RSSave("Position") = Request.Form("Position")
      RSSave("Address") = Request.Form("Address")
      RSSave("City") = Request.Form("City")
      RSSave("Postal Code") = Request.Form("Postal Code")
      RSSave("Email") = Request.Form("Email")
      RSSave("Phone") = Request.Form("Phone")
      RSSave("Fax") = Request.Form("Fax")
      RSSave("TimeRegistered")=Now()
      RSSave.Update
%>
<H1>Registration Saved Successfully...</H1>
<H3>Click here to return to the
<A HREF="default.asp">Training Page</A></H3>
</BODY>
</HTML>
```

NOTE In Listing 39.19 the Open method of a Recordset object is used instead of just using the Execute method of the Connection object. This is different than what has been done in the previous examples because you are adding a new record in this example. The Open method of a Recordset enables you to specify more options. The parameters of the Open method are as follows:

- The command to execute (your SQL query)
- The connection to use
- The type of cursor you want to open (1 for a Keyset Cursor)
- The type of locking you want to have on your recordset (2 for Pessimistic Locking)

You will be using this syntax whenever you need to add or modify a record from here on. ■

Part
VII

Ch
39

You now have everything your client asked for: the site displays the right information, in several different ways, and users can easily register for any scheduled course. Are you done? Although the site does everything that was requested, there is still one thing unaccounted for. How will your client update this information? Your goal was to make it easy to change this information on a regular basis, easier than a paper catalog. You have stored all their courses, schedules, locations, and instructors into a fancy database, but you haven't given them any method for modifying it.

There are really two alternatives (three if you count going directly to the database, but that isn't really a solution):

■ Create an ASP interface to add, edit, and remove records from each of the tables

■ Create some other type of application to work with the data

The second option is easy. You can create this application right in Access, or you can create in Visual Basic. The choice of creating an ASP interface is more difficult. For most programmers, creating a full database interface using Active Server Pages is relatively unknown. Fortunately for you, you have this book to help you get started. In the end, the extra work required to create an ASP interface will be justified by its advantages over a traditional application:

- No installation issues

    All that is required on the client's machines is an Internet browser.

- No upgrade issues

    When you fix bugs in your program or add new features, you do not need to worry about distributing patches or new installations. Every time the client connects to administer their database they will automatically be working with the latest version of your pages.

- Access from anywhere

    Being on a Web server means that, with the proper passwords, the client can edit the database from anywhere on the Internet. If they notice a problem from home, they can fix it right from there.

- Instant cross-platform support

    An ASP application can be accessed from a PC, a Macintosh, or even a UNIX workstation, without any recoding on your part.

Editing Database Records

Creating the full application to administer this training catalog goes beyond the scope of this chapter, but one example will be provided that you can use as a reference for any others you decide to create. You'll be constructing a page (really a set of pages) to edit, add, and delete courses.

The first page you'll need to create is another list view, almost identical to the one shown in Listing 39.14, but with different hyperlinks for each course. Make a copy of the original code from Listing 39.8 and change the links pointing at "details.asp" to point to "EditCourse.asp", still supplying the Course ID as a parameter. From this list, which should be restricted to administrators of the site, you will be able to pick the course you want to edit simply by clicking its name. The editing form, "EditCourse.asp", is the first example page we are going to cover. Once again, you'll start on making this page by creating a template in HTML. The finished page will basically be a Form, as shown in Figure 39.16, with some simple scripting code added in.

Unlike this chapter's registration example, the data you retrieve needs to appear directly in the fields of your Form. You can achieve this effect by substituting the database field references into the value parameters of the appropriate input fields. This is done a little differently in the case of the <TEXTAREA> fields, which you need for editing Memo fields. For the <TEXTAREA> fields, you just place your data between the tags, and it will be placed into the field at runtime.

Another difference from the previous form example is that you will require more than one submit button, each of which will be labeled (and named) differently. When clicked, they will all submit the form using the same target page, but one of the button fields will have a different value. Later on in this section, you will see how to determine which button was clicked. This enables you to have both a delete button and a save button handled through the same form.

The functionality of adding a course will be handled by placing a special link onto your list view, which will be covered a little later in this chapter. The source for this form page is shown in Listing 39.20, with the form's Action URL set to "SaveCourse.asp." Notice the category combo box, and the code required to fill it. A page with several such combo boxes would quickly grow complicated.

FIG. 39.16

Editing a course.

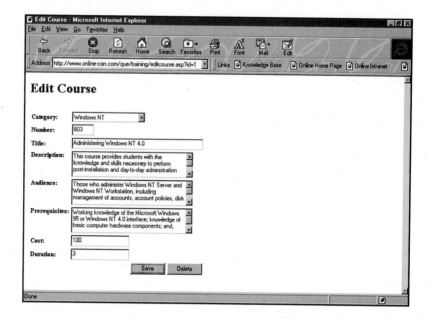

On the CD

Listing 39.20   EDITCOURSE.ASP—Source for Your Editing Page

```
<HTML>
<%
Set Conn=Server.CreateObject("ADODB.Connection")
Conn.Open "DSN=Training"
SQL = "Select Course.* From Course Where Course.ID = "
SQL = SQL & Request.QueryString("ID")
Set RSCourse = Conn.Execute(SQL)
SQL = "Select Category.* From Category"
Set RSCategory = Conn.Execute(SQL)
%>
<HEAD>
<TITLE>Edit Course</TITLE>
</HEAD>
<BODY BGCOLOR="#FFFFFF">
<H1>Edit Course</H1>
<form action="SaveCourse.asp"
method="POST"
name="Edit Course">
    <INPUT TYPE="hidden" name="Course_ID"
     value="<%=RSCourse("ID")%>">
    <TABLE BORDER="0">
```

Part
VII

Ch
39

continues

Listing 39.20 Continued

```
        <TR>
            <TD><STRONG>Category:</STRONG></TD>
            <TD><SELECT NAME="Category" size="1">
<%Do While Not RSCategory.EOF
    If RSCategory("ID") = RSCourse("Category") Then
%>
        <OPTION SELECTED VALUE="<%=RSCategory("ID")%>">
        <%=RSCategory("name")%></OPTION>
<%      Else%>
        <OPTION VALUE="<%=RSCategory("ID")%>">
        <%=RSCategory("name")%></OPTION>
<%      End If
    RSCategory.MoveNext
Loop
%>
            </SELECT></TD>
        </TR>
        <TR>
            <TD><STRONG>Number:</STRONG></TD>
            <TD><INPUT TYPE="text" size="5" name="Number"
            value="<%=RSCourse("Number")%>"></TD>
        </TR>
        <TR>
            <TD WIDTH="80"><STRONG>Title:</STRONG></TD>
            <TD><INPUT TYPE="text" size="50" name="Title"
            value="<%=RSCourse("Title")%>"></TD>
        </TR>
        <TR>
            <TD VALIGN="top">
                <STRONG>Description:</STRONG></TD>
            <TD><textarea name="Description" rows="2"
        cols="50"><%=RSCourse("Description")%>
            </TEXTAREA></TD>
        </TR>
        <TR>
            <TD VALIGN="top">
                <STRONG>Audience:</STRONG></TD>
            <TD><TEXTAREA NAME="Audience" rows="2"
        cols="50"><%=RSCourse("Audience")%>
            </TEXTAREA></TD>
        </TR>
        <TR>
            <TD VALIGN="top">
                <STRONG>Prerequisites:</STRONG></TD>
            <TD><TEXTAREA NAME="Prerequisites" rows="2"
        cols="50"><%=RSCourse("Prerequisites")%>
            </TEXTAREA></TD>
        </TR>
        <TR>
            <TD><STRONG>Cost:</strong></TD>
            <TD><INPUT TYPE="text" size="20" name="Cost"
            value="<%=RSCourse("Cost")%>"></TD>
```

```
        </TR>
        <TR>
            <TD><STRONG>Duration:</STRONG></TD>
            <TD><INPUT TYPE="text" size="20" name="Duration"
            value="<%=RSCourse("Duration")%>"></TD>
        </TR>
        <TR>
            <TD> </TD>
            <TD><P ALIGN="right"><input type="submit"
            name="Submit" value="Save"><INPUT TYPE="submit"
            name="Submit" value="Delete"></P>
            </TD>
        </TR>
    </TABLE>
</FORM>
</BODY>
</HTML>
```

N O T E To test this page without building the list view or "SaveCourse.asp", you can go directly to the page by specifying its URL in your browser. Attach a parameter to the URL for the Course ID ("EditCourse.asp?ID=1"). This type of testing will work for any of your Active Server Pages. ∎

As you might have guessed, the page containing our form (refer to Listing 39.20) isn't really that difficult; all the code that actually modifies the database is contained in the Action page, "SaveCourse.asp". This page can be called to perform two separate tasks: delete the record or save changes to it. The value of your Form fields will be checked right at the beginning of the page to determine which of the two possible tasks (deleting or editing) is intended to be (see Listing 39.21).

On the CD

Listing 39.21 SAVECOURSE.ASP—Determining If We Are Saving or Deleting a Course

```
<%
    If Request.Form("Submit") = "Delete" Then

        'We are deleting the record
    Else
        'We are saving it

    End If
%>
```

If you are deleting the record, then you don't need to worry about any of the form fields except for the Course ID. The code to perform the delete by using a SQL Delete statement is shown in Listing 39.22. After the delete has been performed, display a completion statement, and provide a link back to the list view page ("EditList.asp").

On the CD

Listing 39.22 SAVECOURSE.ASP—Deleting the Record

```
<%
'Delete Record
Set Conn = Server.CreateObject("ADODB.Connection")
SQL = "Delete * FROM Course Where Course.ID = " & Request.Form("Course_ID")
Conn.Execute SQL
%>
```

N O T E In this example, you haven't given the user any chance to confirm the deletion—no "Are you sure?" If you want to, you can set up something like that by displaying a simple form on this page with two buttons (Yes and No). Clicking either button would take the user to another page, "delete.asp", that would either delete the record or redirect the user back to the editing page, based on which button is chosen. ■

If you do not delete the record, then you are saving the changes. You can use a SQL Insert statement to modify the fields, but when you have Memo fields involved (text fields of indeterminate length), it is a better idea to work with the record directly. Using the Course ID, create a recordset containing only that one record. Now, just go through all the fields, set the database field equal to the value of its equivalent Form field, display a completion message, and then you are done. The complete listing for the "SaveCourse.asp" page is provided in Listing 39.23, including both the deletion and editing code.

On the CD

Listing 39.23 SAVECOURSE.ASP—Scripting Code to Save or Delete a Course

```
<%@ LANGUAGE="VBSCRIPT" %>
<HTML>
<HEAD>
<TITLE>Save Registration Form</TITLE>
</HEAD>
<BODY BGCOLOR="#FFFFFF">
<%
Set Conn = Server.CreateObject("ADODB.Connection")
If Request.Form("Submit") = "Delete" Then
     'Delete the Record
     SQL = "Delete * From Course Where Course.ID = "
& Request.Form("Course_ID")
     Conn.Execute SQL

     Response.Write "<H1>Record Deleted</H1>"
Else
     SQL = "Select * From Course Where Course.ID = "
& Request.Form("Course_ID")
     Set RSCourse = Server.CreateObject("ADODB.Recordset")
     Conn.Open "DSN=Training"
     RSCourse.Open SQL,Conn,1,2

     RSCourse("Category") = Request.Form("Category")
```

```
        RSCourse("Title") = Request.Form("Title")
        RSCourse("Number") = Request.Form("Number")
        RSCourse("Description") = Request.Form("Description")
        RSCourse("Audience") = Request.Form("Audience")
        RSCourse("Prerequisites") = Request.Form("Prerequisites")
        RSCourse("Cost") = Request.Form("Cost")
        RSCourse("Duration") = Request.Form("Duration")
        RSCourse.Update

        RSCourse.Close
        Response.Write "<H1>Record Saved</H1>"
    %>
    </BODY>
    </HTML>
```

N O T E Using DAO or RDO, you have to use the `Edit` method before changing those values. In
ADO, the Edit command is assumed. ■

Adding a New Record

With those last two pages completed, you have the capability to edit or delete any course from
your database. The last thing you have to build is the page to add a new course, which you will
provide as a link from your administrative list view, "EditList.asp". A simple hyperlink to a page,
"NewCourse.asp" in your example, is all you need. Because you are adding a new record, no
parameters are necessary.

You don't need to look at the Course table to display this page—the form starts out blank—but
you do have to open a recordset of the Category table to fill in your combo box. The source for
"NewCourse.asp" is displayed in Listing 39.24. As in the edit/delete form, most of the code is
contained in the Action URL, which, in this case, points at the file "AddCourse.asp".

On the CD

Listing 39.24   NEWCOURSE.ASP—Form to Add a New Course

```
<HTML>
<%
Set Conn = Server.CreateObject("ADODB.Connection")
SQL = "Select * From Category"
Set RSCategory = Conn.Execute(SQL)
%>
<HEAD>
<TITLE>New Course</TITLE>
</HEAD>
<BODY BGCOLOR="#FFFFFF">
<H1>Add Course</H1>
<FORM ACTION="AddCourse.asp" method="POST" name="New Course">
    <TABLE BORDER="0">
        <TR>
            <TD><STRONG>Category:</STRONG></TD>
            <TD><SELECT NAME="Category" size="1">
<%Do While Not RSCategory.EOF
```

continues

Listing 39.24   Continued

```
                <OPTION VALUE="<%=RSCategory("ID")%>">
                <%=RSCategory("name")%></OPTION>
<%
      RSCategory.MoveNext
Loop
RSCategory.Close
%>
            </SELECT></TD>
        </TR>
        <TR>
            <TD><STRONG>Number:</STRONG></TD>
            <TD><INPUT TYPE="text" size="5" name="Number"></TD>
        </TR>
        <TR>
            <TD WIDTH="80"><STRONG>Title:</STRONG></TD>
            <TD><INPUT TYPE="text" SIZE="50" NAME="Title"></TD>
        </TR>
        <TR>
            <TD VALIGN="top"><STRONG>Description:</STRONG></TD>
            <TD><TEXTAREA NAME="Description" rows="2"
        COLS="50"></TEXTAREA></TD>
        </TR>
        <TR>
            <TD VALIGN="top"><STRONG>Audience:</STRONG></TD>
            <TD><TEXTAREA NAME="Audience" rows="2"
        COLS="50"><%=RSCourse("Audience")%></TEXTAREA></TD>
        </TR>
        <TR>
            <TD VALIGN="top">
              <STRONG>Prerequisites:</STRONG>
            </TD>
            <TD><TEXTAREA NAME="Prerequisites" rows="2"
        COLS="50"></TEXTAREA></TD>
        </TR>
        <TR>
            <TD><STRONG>Cost:</STRONG></TD>
            <TD><INPUT TYPE="text" SIZE="20" NAME="Cost"></TD>
        </TR>
        <TR>
            <TD><STRONG>Duration:</STRONG></TD>
            <TD>
              <INPUT TYPE="text" SIZE="20" NAME="Duration">
            </TD>
        </TR>
        <TR>
            <TD> </TD>
            <TD><P ALIGN="right"><INPUT TYPE="submit"
            NAME="Submit" VALUE="Add"></P>
            </TD>
        </TR>
    </TABLE>
</FORM>
</BODY>
</HTML>
```

Within your code for "AddCourse.asp" you go through a series of validation checks to ensure the values are correct before adding the record to the database. If everything is okay, you can open a Recordset from the Course table and proceed to add your record. From this point on, there isn't a great deal of difference between saving this record and saving a registration. You call the AddNew method of your Recordset, set the values of the database fields to the values from your Form, and display a completion message. That's it, you're done. The source for the finished page is in Listing 39.25.

On the CD

Listing 39.25 ADDCOURSE.ASP—Adding a New Course

```
<%@ LANGUAGE="VBSCRIPT" %>
<HTML>
<HEAD>
<TITLE>Save Registration Form</TITLE>
</HEAD>
<BODY BGCOLOR="#FFFFFF">
<%
Error = False
If Not IsNumeric(Request.Form("Number")) Then
    Response.Write "<H2>Course Number has to be a Number</H2>"
    Error = True
End If
If Not IsNumeric(Request.Form("Cost")) Then
    Response.Write "<h2>Cost has to be a Number</h2>"
    Error = True
End If
If Not IsNumeric(Request.Form("Duration")) Then
    Response.Write "<H2>Duration has to be a Number</H2>"
    Error = True
End If
If Not Error Then
    Set Conn = Server.CreateObject("ADODB.Connection")
    Set RSCourse = Server.CreateObject("ADODB.Recordset")
    Conn.Open "DSN=Training"
    SQL = "Select * From Course"
    RSCourse.Open SQL,Conn , 1, 2
    RSCourse.AddNew

    RSCourse("Category") = Request.Form("Category")
    RSCourse("Title") = Request.Form("Title")
    RSCourse("Number") = Request.Form("Title")
    RSCourse("Description") = Request.Form("Description")
    RSCourse("Audience") = Request.Form("Audience")
    RSCourse("Prerequisites") = Request.Form("Prerequisites")
    RSCourse("Cost") = Request.Form("Cost")
    RSCourse("Duration") = Request.Form("Duration")
    RSCourse.Update

    RSCourse.Close
    Response.Write "<H1>Record Added</H1>"
End If
%>
</BODY>
</HTML>
```

Part
VII

Ch
39

Through the examples in the last few sections, you have the information you need to build a complete ASP application to maintain most database-driven sites. Don't just assume a Web-based administration system is necessary though; an Access application will fit the needs of many sites and could take a lot less work. If your client, or company, needs the capability to edit the database from anywhere, or if so many people require editing capability that it makes distribution a problem, then an Internet-based solution is probably best. If, on the other hand, one person will be doing the editing, always from the same place, then a more traditional system is probably the correct choice.

Finishing Touches

If you only create the pages in this chapter, you wouldn't be done. There are many other static pages to build, images to include in the pages, and general tweaking of the entire site. You are not ever really finished until the site is completely ready to be opened to the public, and even then additions will be asked for. Some potential additions to the example Training site are almost guaranteed to be requested, such as a visitor counter, or other bells and whistles (such as "tips of the day" or extensive search capabilities).

Personalization

Personalization is customizing the behavior or appearance of your pages based on whom the visitor is. The "Internet Start" site from Microsoft, **http://home.microsoft.com** is an excellent example. By providing information and selecting options, such as what sports you are interested in, or where you live, this site generates custom content that can be different for everyone who views it. Just using a person's name on your site, such as "Good Morning, Dave!" is a form of personalization.

There are two parts to creating a personalized Web site. The obvious one is the actual customization, as just described. The other part is the tricky one: getting the information. Asking a user to enter information into a survey form just so you can say "Welcome, Dave!" isn't very worthwhile. A preferred way is to work backwards—figure out what information you are already collecting, or should be collecting, about the user, and then see what you can do with that information.

In the Training Catalog example, a user provides information only through the registration process, so that is where you would attempt to customize the site. If a user registers for a course on your client's site, then, at some time in the future, the same user registers for another course, they will have to re-enter all their information. If you design the site so that it automatically brings up the user's previous entries, while still enabling the user to change the information if needed, then registration becomes personalized, easier, and quicker.

Registration entries are already being time-stamped, so it is easy to pull up the last entry made by a particular person. Before doing that, you must first identify the current user, which in this case, you can do through their e-mail address. By showing a small form to users that asks them to provide their e-mail address and a password before entering the actual registration page, you can find and load up the last information they entered. The lookup of information would be accomplished using a SQL query such as this one; `SELECT * FROM USERS WHERE USERS.EMAIL="<ENTERED EMAIL ADDRESS>"`.

If this is the user's first time in your client's system, a new record has to be created for them (in the database) containing their e-mail address and password. You could design the system to e-mail them their password to ensure security.

Putting a Counter on a Site

A common addition requested for Web sites is a counter, some method of tracking how many times the site, or particular pages, have been accessed. When using IIS 3.0, all this information is already being saved to log files. Although you can pull information out of those files to create statistical reports about your site, it doesn't provide the same thing that a counter does: instant visual update of hits to your page. Many companies can provide a site with a Web-counter service, but you can accomplish the same thing yourself.

To create a counter, you need to maintain a numeric value in a database, one for each page on which you are tracking hits, and then increment that value every time that page is loaded. At the same time as you are accessing the database to update it, you can return the value for display on your site. A database table that contains two fields: one to hold the path of your page, and one to hold the number of hits. The example shown in Listing 39.26 updates the value and displays it (the ODBC DSN, table name, and field names will change depending on how you set up your database).

Part
VII

Ch
39

On the CD

Listing 39.26   HOMEPAGE.ASP—Example of Using ASP to Track Visitors to a Site

```
<HTML>
<HEAD><TITLE>Our Home Page</TITLE></HEAD>
<BODY>
<Our Page's Content>
<%
Set Conn=Server.CreateObject("ADODB.Connection")
Set RSCounter = Server.CreateObject("ADODB.Recordset")
Conn.Open "DSN=Counter"
SQL = "Select * from Pages "
SQL = SQL & "Where Pages.Page='"
SQL = SQL & Request.ServerVariables("PATH_TRANSLATED") & "'"
RSCounter.Open SQL, Conn, 1, 2
If RSCounter.EOF Then 'There is no record for this page
     RSCounter.AddNew
     RSCounter("Page") = Request.ServerVariables("PATH_TRANSLATED")
     RSCounter("Hits") = 1
     Response.Write "<P><STRONG>This page has been visited
     one time</STRONG></P>"
Else
     RSCounter("Hits") = RSCounter("Hits") + 1
     Response.Write "<P><STRONG>This page has been visited "
& RSCounter("Hits") & " times</STRONG></P>"
End if
```

continues

Listing 39.26   Continued

```
RSCounter.Update
RSCounter.Close
%>
</BODY>
</HTML>
```

N O T E   In Listing 39.26, the PATH_TRANSLATED Server Variable is used, which contains the physical path to the file to uniquely identify your pages. This is done because, while there can be more than one virtual path to a Web page, there can only be one physical path, making it perfect to use as a unique identifier. ■

Using VB Across the Internet

As this is a Visual Basic book, many of you are probably interested in knowing how you can use VB with the Internet. Creating components for ASP is one way to do this, but it isn't really anything new. Your component runs on the server, accesses data on the server, and works with a client (the ASP page) that is also on the server. Nothing different than a standard VB application on one machine, or on an office LAN. ActiveX controls are very different, but still are not really considered using the Internet—the control is installed on the client, runs on the client, and is working together with a program on the client side (the browser). The fact that the control is downloaded across the Internet doesn't really make it an Internet application.

A true VB Internet application has to run on one machine and work with or access data from another machine, across the Internet. Several technologies (from Microsoft) exist to enable you to create applications (and components) such as the Advanced Data Connector (ADC), the Advanced Data Space (ADS), and the Advanced Data Factory (ADF).

Advanced Data Connector

ADC is the name for a set of objects from Microsoft that are designed to give your client-side program the capability to access Databases across the Internet. By specifying the URL of a Web server (such as **http://www.online-can.com**) and an ODBC Connection String, including the server-side DSN, you can execute queries against that remote database. ADC returns the results of these queries to your client program in an ADO-style Recordset. You can add, delete, or modify records; changes made to the recordset are made to the server database, just like in regular ADO. Setting up ADC for use is relatively easy. After it has been installed on your client machine, Visual Basic applications can create instances of its objects by using the CreateObject command. Examples of using this object are given in "A Sample Application."

N O T E   If you have ever programmed in Powerbuilder (a development tool from Powersoft), you may have noticed a very interesting feature of that program. After you receive a "recordset" back from your DBMS, you can change the filtering or ordering of the records, without having to talk to the database again. ADO allows this same thing, avoiding unnecessary network traffic. ■

A Sample Application

The sample application created in this section shows the use of two main components: the *Advanced Data Space* object, which allows you to create objects on the server and access them remotely, and the *Advanced Data Factory*, which is created on the server, and handles the database access and returns the query results.

In the Training catalog example, you are going to quickly fill a list box with course names from the server. This uses the existing database for the Training catalog example and assumes that an appropriate DSN is still set up on the server.

To create and run the example, perform the following steps:

1. Ensure that ADC is installed on the server and the client.

   Visit the Microsoft ADC site for more information at **http://www.microsoft.com/adc**.

2. Create a new project (Standard EXE) in Visual Basic 5.0.

   A new form (Form1) will be created by default.

3. Put a ListBox control onto the form, which will be named "list1".

4. Put a CommandButton control onto the form (Command1).

5. Double-click the button to view the code for its Click event.

6. Enter in the following code from Listing 39.27.

7. Make sure you are connected to the Internet.

8. Run the project (F5 or the Start button).

9. When Form1 comes up, click the Command1 button.

   The list box should fill with the results of your query (see Figure 39.17).

Listing 39.27 FORM1.FRM—Command1_Click Code

```
Dim objADF as object
Dim objADS as object
Dim RSCourses as object
Dim sConnection as Variant
Dim sSQL as Variant
Set objADS = CreateObject("AdvancedDataSpace")
Set objADF = objADS.CreateObject("AdvancedDataFactory", _
             "http://www.online-can.com")
             'Replace this server name with yours
sConnection = "DSN=Training"
sSQL = "Select Course.Title From Course"
Set RSCourses = objADF.Query(sConnection, sSQL)
Do While Not RSCourses.EOF
    List1.AddItem RSCourses("Title")
    RSCourses.MoveNext
Loop
```

FIG. 39.17
Our sample application.

FIG. 39.17
Our sample application.

From Here...

You've seen how to create a simple database-driven Web site using ASP, but that is not the limit of what you can do. With the ability to access any COM object, including those written in VB, you can create Web sites that do almost anything. The Advanced Data Connector and its related components opens up a whole new group of possible applications. Your Visual Basic programs can now work across the Internet, making distributed computing easier than ever. Overall, developing Internet applications has become easier than ever and Visual Basic programmers now have the edge.

For more information on the topics discussed in this chapter, see the following chapters:

- Chapter 33, "Database Access with ActiveX Data Objects (ADO)," which provides a more detailed look at using this new form of data access.
- Chapter 40, "Programming Web Functionality into Your Applications," discusses more ways that you can include the Internet into your VB applications.
- Chapter 42, "Using Visual Basic with Microsoft Transaction Server," provides information on designing and implementing components that are to be used as server-side objects.

There are also many Web sites that offer useful information on ASP, building ASP components, ADO, and ADC. Here are a few examples:

- The ASP Developer's Site—**http://www.genusa.com/asp/**
- The Active-Server BBS—**http://www.activexserver.com/**
- The Microsoft ADO site—**http://www.microsoft.com/ado**
- The Microsoft ADC site—**http://www.microsoft.com/adc**
- The Active Server Pages newsgroup—**news://msnews.microsoft.com/ microsoft.public.inetserver.iis.activeserverpages**

CHAPTER 40

Programming Web Functionality into Your Applications

Including Web functionality in an application in the past involved Winsock programming. Winsock programming has been perceived as a barrier by many programmers. Development involving TCP/IP networking appeared to be an arcane craft known only to initiates of the black arts. For Microsoft to reach its goal of making the Internet— and the use of Internet technology for intranets— accessible to all, this barrier needed to be removed. To this end, Microsoft developed a superb suite of tools.

Three of the tools that Microsoft created for use in Visual Basic 5.0 are ActiveX controls that ease the road to Internet functionality. One of these ActiveX controls is the Microsoft Winsock Control Version 5.0. This control parks invisibly on a Visual Basic form, which acts as a client, and provides TCP/IP communication with a server program that also has a Winsock control. Another of the three controls is the Microsoft Internet Transfer Control Version 5.0. This control is used to transfer files between clients and servers on a TCP/IP network by using protocols such as HTTP and FTP. The third of the ActiveX

TCP/IP communications fundamentals

Ports and friendly names, among other issues, are examined to provide understanding of the requirements of the protocol.

Properties, methods, and events

The Winsock API has been encapsulated in the methods, properties, and events of the Microsoft Winsock Control, the Microsoft Internet Transfer Control, and the WebBrowser Control. Understanding these is essential to effective use of these controls.

Building a client application

Moving step by step through the development of a client application provides you with an understanding of the potential power of the Winsock, Internet Transfer, and WebBrowser Controls.

Building a server application

A client without a server is only half the story. You examine how the server handles the request for service from the client.

Testing the client/server application and building fault tolerance

Most server applications run unattended. Errors need to be reported to the client for action to occur.

controls is the WebBrowser Control, which is used to display HTML pages. The Winsock API is wrapped in these controls and exposed through their properties, methods, and events. If you can write a Visual Basic "Hello World" application, you can create powerful client/server applications that will communicate over a TCP/IP network link.

Use of the Winsock Control is not limited to the Web browser paradigm or to the use of the HTTP or FTP protocols. It lives at a lower level, using the TCP and UDP protocols. The other Microsoft controls encapsulate the specifics of the HTTP and FTP protocols.

In this chapter, you will explore TCP/IP fundamentals; examine in some detail the Microsoft Winsock Control, Internet Transfer Control, and the WebBrowser Control; and build a working client/server application. ■

TCP/IP Communications Fundamentals

Winsock is a short name for *Windows Sockets*. Sockets provide a standard programming interface for communications programming with the TCP/IP protocol. The Win32 API includes the Winsock API, which is a fairly straight port of the Berkeley Sockets API for Windows. It encompasses the event-driven nature of Windows programming. Microsoft has added extensions to the Winsock API, which constitute the INetAPI. These extensions are aimed at extending the functionality of HTTP, FTP, and Gopher.

> **N O T E** There are several excellent books on TCP/IP and Microsoft TCP/IP, which is Microsoft's implementation of TCP/IP. In the Microsoft world of TCP/IP, you might also want to explore DHCP (Dynamic Host Configuration Protocol) and WINS (Windows Internet Name Service). The information in this chapter will enable you to use the Winsock Control with little or no trouble. ■
>
> ▶ **See** Sams' *TCP/IP Unleashed*, Second Edition, for in-depth coverage of TCP/IP.

Clients and Servers

Networked applications often use the paradigm of client/server. The client contacts the server and requests information or service from the server application. The server responds by providing the data or service.

In the world of Winsock communications, the important aspect of the client/server relationship is who establishes the connection. Chapter 41, "Using Visual Basic in a Client/Server Environment," covers the client/server world in more depth. The client is always the initiating application. The client sends a request for connection to the server. After the connection has been established, the server can request information from the client and vice versa. Once the connection has been established, a peer relationship exists, with either application being able to initiate communication.

IP Addresses and Host Names

When a system is part of a TCP/IP network, it needs to have an identification address. This address, called the IP or Internet Protocol address, is a 32-bit number that is usually represented by four numbers separated by periods. An example is 190.137.48.1. This is the decimal representation of four bytes. When assigned to your computer, this number is its node address, whether your system is attached to the Internet, to your company LAN, or to a system of two computers at home that you have attached in a small local LAN.

Domain Name Services (DNS)

Because numbers can be hard to remember, a system of "friendly" names has been created wherein each computer has a name—the *domain name*. An example is the Microsoft domain name of www.microsoft.com. In the friendly name system, this represents a node on the network.

> **N O T E**   The domain name www.microsoft.com is actually composed of multiple computers that are all reached by the domain name of www.microsoft.com. A system called *round robining* is used to have multiple computers available to respond when one friendly domain name is used. As Microsoft is one of the busiest Web sites in the world, it is understandable that one system can't handle the load. ▪

Friendly names are difficult for computers to work with as addresses, so a system called the *Domain Name Service* (DNS) was devised. Domain Name Service translates the friendly names into IP addresses. This is accomplished by computers on the network that are *Domain Name Servers*. When you enter a request for service on the World Wide Web, the address is specified as an URL, or *Universal Resource Locator*. **http://www.microsoft.com** is an example. http is the protocol used and www.microsoft.com is the name of a system somewhere on the Internet. The essence of the process is that the www.microsoft.com address is translated by a DNS into an IP address, such as 190.137.12.4. Now the network can work with the address and locate the system to which you want to attach.

The key factor to remember is that a system on a network can be referred to by either the IP address or the friendly name. If there is a system on the network providing Domain Name Services, the name will be resolved into an IP address. The IP address is the "real" address. The friendly name is an "alias" that is easier to remember.

Part **VII**

Ch **40**

UDP and TCP

When data is moved across the network with the TCP/IP protocol, there are two methods used: *User Datagram Protocol* (UDP) and *Transmission Control Protocol* (TCP). UDP and TCP are quite different and each has its uses. One is not better than the other. Both are available to you when using the Winsock Control, for example. In the use of HTTP or FTP, the protocol decides which will be used. In general, if you are not sure which one to use, TCP will always work, but it imposes a higher overhead cost.

UDP   UDP is somewhat like mailing a letter. When a message is sent over the network with UDP, the message is packaged up with a *destination address* (the IP address of the system to which it is being sent) and the address of the system sending the message (again, an IP address). The theoretical maximum size for a UDP message is 65K bytes. Many implementations are less than this size. A size of 8192 bytes is the usual smallest maximum size that all implementations will accommodate. If the Datagram exceeds the maximum permissible size for the implementation, the message is simply truncated. After the message is packaged with the destination and origin addresses, it is sent on a best-efforts basis, with no guarantee that it will arrive and no checking performed by the protocol to see if it did arrive. Any checking must be performed in the application.

This is a connectionless communication. There is no checking to see if the destination system is capable of receiving a message.

The UDP message also contains the source port and the destination port numbers. Ports are discussed later in this chapter in the section "Ports."

An example of a service that uses UDP is the Simple Mail Transport Protocol (SMTP) for e-mail messages. This is very much like mailing a letter. There is no assurance that it will arrive. This is an unreliable communication protocol.

TCP   With TCP, there is no maximum message length. When a message passed to the TCP protocol is too large to be sent in one piece, the message is broken up into chunks or packets and then sent one chunk or packet at a time to the destination address. The TCP packet contains the addressee information, as does the UDP message, with one addition: The TCP message also contains a packet number and the total number of packets. Because of the nature of the TCP/IP protocol, the packets might travel different paths and might arrive in a different order than when sent. TCP reassembles the packets in the proper order and requests the retransmission of any missing or corrupted packets.

Unlike UDP, TCP is a connection-oriented, reliable communication protocol. Using it is somewhat like dialing a telephone and waiting for someone to answer before beginning to talk or send data.

With TCP, the client system sends a request for connection, as previously discussed. As with the UDP protocol, the TCP messages contain destination and origin port numbers.

Ports

The TCP/IP protocol is used for communication between computer systems. Port numbers are used for communicating between applications on the two systems. Ports are also called *sockets*. This is the origin of the Winsock terminology.

When two applications are communicating by using the TCP/IP protocol, the applications use port numbers to identify themselves to the other application. When a server receives a request for a connection, the request is directed to a particular TCP/IP port. The server then knows which application is being contacted because it has the port number associated with the application.

This is analogous to having two phones in your house, one for business and one for personal use. If the business phone rings, you know that when you answer, the caller will request the attention of your business persona, not your private persona.

Servers listen on a particular port, and clients send requests to that port. In the everyday world of Internet usage, there are *Well Known Ports*. Some of these ports have become standard. The World Wide Web uses Port 80, and FTP uses Port 21. WWW would function just as well on Port 37, but "everyone" has agreed that Port 80 will be used.

This is similar to the use of 911 for an emergency phone number. 919 would have worked just as well, but the use of 911 has been accepted almost nationwide.

A particular server application listens on a specific port number for requests to connect to that server. If you have a system that is used for both WWW and FTP, it will listen on both Ports 21 and 80. If the request for connection comes in on Port 80, the Web server application handles the communication.

Having a system work as a server for one application does not prevent it from being a client for another application. A system can be a Web server listening on Port 80 and communicate contemporaneously with another system on another Port for a different application.

An important point to remember is that the client system does not have to send the request for service from the same port on which the server is listening. For example, if the server ABC application is listening on Port 239, the client may send its request for service from its Port 1593 to the server's Port 239. This works because the client tells the server the port number that its request came from, so the server responds to the client by sending the response to Port 1593.

The essential parts of the message sent from one computer system to another are the following:

- ■ *Destination IP Address*   This is a dotted quartet—for example, 191.187.39.55. This is how the network identifies the node of the network for which the message is bound.
- ■ *Origin IP Address*   This is also a dotted quartet; it is used if any replies or requests for retransmission are required.
- ■ *Destination Port Number*   This identifies the socket for which the message is bound. Because sockets or ports are linked or bound to one application, this is the "address" of the application on the system.
- ■ *Origination Port Number*   This is used for any replies that are sent to the originating system to identify to the TCP/IP protocol. This application is the intended recipient of the message.
- ■ *Data*   This is the information that the applications are sending to each other.

There are other components of the message, but they are not important for this discussion.

Hypertext Transfer Protocol (HTTP)

HTTP is one of the protocols that uses the basis of TCP/IP in a specific implementation. This is the protocol of the World Wide Web. You may hear reference to an HTTPD server, which refers to the Hypertext Transfer Protocol Daemon.

Part
VII

Ch
40

> **N O T E** *Daemon* is UNIX-speak for a program or process that runs continuously in the background. In Windows NT-speak, this is usually a service or server, such as a Web server or an FTP server that listens on a port for incoming requests for service. If a daemon is not running, no connection can be made. This is why failed e-mail is often returned by a daemon. ■

HTTP currently is in version 1.0 and moving toward version 1.1. Most Web servers will be updated in the near future to support 1.1, as will Web browsers. There will be backward compatibility for both servers and browsers.

HTTP is a very simple protocol. The client, usually called a *browser*, issues a request to the server. The server responds with the requested file and closes the connection.

There are two HTTP message types: requests and responses. There are three types of requests: GET, HEAD, and POST. In a GET request, a file is requested. In a HEAD request, only the server header information is returned. In a POST request, the BODY is transmitted to the server, and it contains data such as an HTTP form or a MAIL message.

HTTP Request The format of an HTTP request is the following:

```
request-line
headers (0 or more)
<blank line>
body (only for POST requests)
```

The format of the request-line is:

```
request request-URL HTTP/Version
```

An example of a request-line is:

```
GET /afile.htm HTTP/1.0
```

HTTP Response The format of the HTTP response is:

```
status-line
headers (0 or more)
<blank line>
body
```

The body usually will be an html file that contains formatting tags and links that are used in other requests. The format of the status-line is:

```
HTTP/version response-code response-phrase
```

An example of a status-line is:

```
HTTP/1.0 200 OK
```

There are a number of other status codes. If you have spent any time on the Web, you have seen the 404 Not Found response.

File Transfer Protocol (FTP)

FTP is the TCP protocol that is widely used to transfer files. A brief description of the details of the FTP protocol will help you understand the details of an FTP session.

There are two types of connections established in an FTP session: a control connection and a data connection.

Control Connection   The *control connection*, which is maintained throughout the FTP session, is used to transmit commands between the client and the server.

The first step in the FTP session process consists of the server listening on FTP's well-known port, Port 21. The FTP server listens by performing a passive open of a control connection, which waits for an active open control connection request.

The second step in the FTP session process consists of the client sending an active open control connection request to the FTP server, which request is addressed to Port 21. If all of the logon requirements are met, an active control connection is created between the client and the server. This connection stays open throughout the FTP session. Commands and replies are communicated over this connection.

Data Connection   A *data connection* is established each time a file is transferred and is maintained only so long as the file transfer is in process.

The client establishes a data connection to either upload or download a file. When the file has been transferred, the data connection is terminated.

When the client is finished with the FTP session, a command terminating the control connection is sent to the server and the FTP session is terminated.

> **N O T E**   *Gopher* essentially is a menu-driven front end to an anonymous FTP. It is quite similar to HTTP in its usage. However, Gopher is declining in usage and might fall into complete disuse in the near future. Gopher uses Port 70. It is considered a legacy protocol by many Web users. Most Web browsers support the Gopher protocol, and it is one of the protocols supported by the Microsoft Internet Transfer Control. ▨

Part VII

Ch 40

Microsoft Winsock Control Version 5.0

The Winsock Control operates at a very basic level of TCP/IP. It does not use the HTTP or FTP protocols. For example, it could be used if you wanted to create your own two-person chat room application to create and maintain the connection and manage the details of the data transfer.

As stated earlier, the Winsock API is wrapped in the Winsock Control. The API functions are accessed through the properties, methods, and events of the Winsock Control, which are discussed in detail in the following sections.

Properties

Properties have several attributes, such as:

- Some can be set at design time
- Some are read-only at run time and unavailable at design time

■ Some can be set only at design time and are read-only at run time

■ Some can be set at both run time and design time

Another aspect of a property is the data type of the value. This can be a string, an integer, a long integer, or any other data type.

The third important aspect of a property is the syntax or usage of the property in code.

BytesReceived Property   The `BytesReceived` property tells you the number of bytes that are currently in the receive buffer. It is read-only and is unavailable at design time. The value returned is a long integer. An example of the syntax is:

```
myvar = MyWinsockControl.BytesReceived
```

You might use the `BytesReceived` property to determine the size of a display area for the data or to see if there is any data in the buffer.

LocalHostName Property   The `LocalHostName` property returns the name of the local host system. `LocalHostName` is read-only and is unavailable at design time. The value returned is a string. An example of the syntax is:

```
myvar = MyWinsockControl.LocalHostName
```

LocalIP Property   The `LocalIP` property returns the local host system IP address in the form of a string, such as *XXX.XXX.XXX.XXX*, where the *X*'s represent the numbers in an IP address. This property is read-only and is unavailable at design time. The value returned is a string. An example of the syntax is:

```
myvar = MyWinsockControl.LocalIP
```

LocalPort Property   The `LocalPort` property returns or sets the local port number. `LocalPort` is both read and write and is available both at design time and at run time. The value returned is a long integer. An example of the syntax to read the property is:

```
myvar = MyWinsockControl.LocalPort
```

To set the property, you use:

```
MyWinsockControl.LocalPort = 1001
```

An example of using this property is setting the port prior to using the `Listen` method to set the port number for the application. This allows selection of the port at run time.

Protocol Property   The `Protocol` property returns or sets the protocol of either UDP or TCP. This property is both read and write and is available both at design time and at run time. (Note that at run time the control must be closed—see the upcoming `State` property.) The value returned is 0, or the constant `sckTCPProtocol`, or 1, or `sckUDPProtocol`. An example of the syntax to read the property is:

```
myvar = MyWinsockControl.Protocol
```

To set the property, you use:

```
MyWinsockControl.LocalPort = sckTCPProtocol
```

RemoteHost Property   The RemoteHost property returns or sets the remote host. RemoteHost is both read and write and is available both at design time and at run time. The value returned is a string and can be specified either as an IP address (*XXX.XXX.XXX.XXX*) or as a friendly name, such as www.microsoft.com. An example of the syntax to read the property is:

```
myvar = MyWinsockControl.RemoteHost
```

To set the property, you use:

```
MyWinsockControl.RemoteHost = "192.143.29.47"
```

Setting this property at run time allows the remote host to be selected when the application starts or to be selected based upon some criteria.

RemotePort Property   The RemotePort property returns or sets the remote port number. This property is both read and write and is available both at design time and at run time. The value returned is a long integer. An example of the syntax to read the property is:

```
myvar = MyWinsockControl.RemotePort
```

To set the property, you use:

```
MyWinsockControl.RemotePort = 1001
```

This property can be used to select the application that is to be contacted at the remote host.

State Property   The State property returns the state of the control as expressed by an enumerated list. This property is read-only and is unavailable at design time. The State property is set by using various methods and events. The syntax to read the property is:

```
myvar = MyWinsockControl.State
```

The settings for the State property are set forth in Table 40.1.

Table 40.1   Settings for the State Property

Constant	Value	Description
sckClosed	0	Default Closed
sckOpen	1	Open
sckListening	2	Listening
sckConnectionPending	3	Connection pending
sckResolvingHost	4	Resolving host
sckHostResolved	5	Host resolved
sckConnecting	6	Connecting
sckConnected	7	Connected
sckClosing	8	Peer is closing the connection
sckError	9	Error

Part
VII

Ch
40

The State property needs to be checked before state-changing methods are used. For example, attempting to open a closed Winsock Control will result in an error.

Methods

Methods are predefined functions that are used to perform various tasks on the control. There are methods that open and close a connection and methods that accept a request for the connection. Some of the important methods used with the Winsock Control are discussed in the following sections.

Accept Method The Accept method is used for the TCP server applications only. It accepts the request for connection from a client system. For the Accept method to be used, the control must be in a *listening state*. This method is used in conjunction with the ConnectionRequest event, which is discussed below.

The syntax for the Accept method appears as follows:

```
Private Sub MyWinsockControl ConnectionREquest (ByVal requestID as Long)
    MyWinsockControl.Accept
End Sub
```

Close Method The Close method is used to terminate a TCP connection from either the client or server applications. The syntax is:

```
MyWinsockControl.Close
```

GetData Method GetData is the method used to retrieve the current block of data from the buffer and then store it in a variable of the variant type. The syntax is:

```
MyWinsockControl.GetData myvar
```

Listen Method The Listen method is invoked on the server application to have the server application wait for a TCP request for connection from a client system. The syntax is:

```
MyWinsockControl.Listen
```

SendData Method The SendData method is used to dispatch data to the remote computer. It is used for both the client and server systems. The syntax is:

```
MyWinsockControl.SendData myvar
```

Events

Events are the triggers that invoke the methods. An example of an event is a mouse click. The events from other objects, such as a command button, are used to trigger some of the methods in the preceding section. The Winsock Control generates events that also can be used. Some of these events, such as the ConnectionRequest event, happen at the server system as a result of an action taken at the client system. The events generated by the Winsock Control make it possible for an unattended system to participate in a network communications session.

Close Event The Close event occurs when the remote computer closes the connection. The event can be used to do cleanup work at the end of a session. The syntax is:

```
Private Sub MyWinsockControl_Close()
```

Connect Event   The Connect event occurs after the connection with the remote computer has been made. The syntax is:

```
Private Sub MyWinsockControl_Connect()
```

ConnectionRequest Event   The ConnectionRequest event occurs when the server receives a request for connection from a client system. The syntax is:

```
Private Sub MyWinsockControl_ConnectionRequest(requestID As Long)
```

DataArrival Event   The DataArrival event occurs when new data arrives. The syntax is:

```
Private Sub MyWinsockControl_DataArrival (ByVal bytesTotal As Long)
```

Winsock Control Example—Building a Client/Server Application

The client always initiates the conversation, and the server must provide appropriate answers. At any point, if either party does not keep the exchange going, the connection is broken and the conversation ends. If the conversation ends without the proper cleanup, the conversation cannot be reinitiated until the applications have been reset.

The sample application that is contained in this chapter is a form of chat, in which both the client and server are capable of sending text to one another.

This is a very simple application. There is no error trapping, so the application is not robust. When an error occurs, both the client and the server must be closed and reopened. This way, you have all the fun of adding the error trapping. The complete code for this application is on the companion CD and is yours to use.

The project is contained in the Chapter 41 directory. Both the Visual Basic projects and a compiled version of the programs are there.

When the project is started, two controls must be added to the default Visual Basic Toolbox. These controls are the RichTextBox control and the Microsoft Winsock 5.0 Control. These are added by choosing Project, Components and then selecting the two components in the list presented.

Designing the Client Application

When designing this sample client application, the designers determined that the user would want to see messages and replies in two separate text boxes. RichTextBoxes were selected because of their capability to use text formatting, and these text boxes were designated InBound and OutBound.

A command button was added to initiate the connection.

Two more text boxes were added to enter the remote host name or IP address and the remote port, which enables the host and port to be selected and set at run time.

A final text box was added to display the local port number. This local port number can be read before the connection is created and after the connection is made.

 And last, but certainly not least, a Microsoft Winsock Control 5.0 is added. This Winsock Control manages the communications between the client and server systems.

Laying Out the Form   The Visual Basic form for the client application at design time is shown in Figure 40.1. When the application runs, you need to enter the remote host name or IP address and the remote port number before clicking the Connect button. After the connection is established, you can enter text in the Outbound Text box. When entered, text is automatically dispatched to the Server application. When you enter a character in the Outbound text box, a change event is triggered, and its attached event handler sends the contents of the text box to the remote host.

FIG. 40.1

Notice that the Winsock Control is visible at design time.

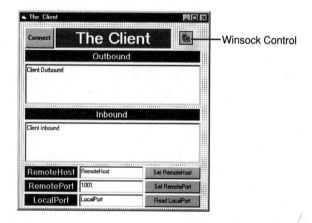

Winsock Control

In Figure 40.2, the appearance of the form at run time is the same as the design-time appearance, with the exception that the Winsock Control is not visible.

FIG. 40.2

The Remote Host and Remote Port setting must be entered before the connection is attempted in this example program.

Adding the Code   This section examines the code from the client application, just as it appears in the program. Take notice of the small amount of code that is required to create the functionality of the application. The addition of error handling would more than double the code. Here, you can see the power of the Winsock Control. In a very few lines of code, full TCP/IP communication is accomplished.

In Listing 40.1, a command button is used to initiate the connection. The Connect method is used. This method gathers the current values in two properties, the RemoteHost property and the RemotePort property, and creates the TCP message that contacts the remote host and requests the connection. By setting two properties and calling one method, you have accomplished what could have required hours or even days of programming to accomplish if you were not using the Winsock API.

Listing 40.1   Sub cmdConnect_Click()—The *Click* Event that Creates the Connection

```
Option Explicit

Private Sub cmdConnect_Click()

    'The command button click event is used to create the
    'connection.
    '    The connection request string is sent to the RemoteHost
    '    on the RemotePort.
    '    The Connect method takes two arguments, in the form of
    '        object.Connect remoteHost, remotePort
    '    If the two properties are blank and the arguments are
    '    not supplied an error occurs.
    '    The two properties were set in the Form_Load
    '    event which occurs prior to the Command_Click event.

    wskClient.Connect

End Sub
```

Listing 40.2 shows the sub that is provided to enable you to see that the local port is set to 0 before the connection is made, and will be set to a value selected by the system in the process of making the connection.

Listing 40.2   Sub cmdReadLocalPort_Click()—The *Click* Event that Displays the Local Port Number

```
Private Sub cmdReadLocalPort_Click()

    'This will read and display the value of the LocalPort
    'property in txtLocalPort.Text

    txtLocalPort.Text = wskClient.LocalPort

End Sub
```

Listing 40.3 shows the sub that enables the RemoteHost property to be set at run time. If the client is always going to communicate with the same server, the RemoteHost property can be set at design time.

Listing 40.3   Sub cmdSetRemoteHost_Click()—The *Click* Event that Sets the RemoteHost Property

```
Private Sub cmdSetRemoteHost_Click()

    'This will set the value of the RemoteHost property to the
    'value in txtRemoteHost.Text

    wskClient.RemoteHost = txtRemoteHost.Text

End Sub
```

Listing 40.4 shows the sub that enables the RemotePort property to be set at run time. If the client is always going to communicate with the same port number, the RemotePort property can be set at design time.

Listing 40.4   Sub cmdSetRemotePort_Click()—The *Click* Event that Sets the *RemotePort* Property

```
Private Sub cmdSetRemotePort_Click()

    'This will set the value of the RemotePort property to
    ' the value in txtRemotePort.Text

    wskClient.RemotePort = txtRemotePort.Text

End Sub
```

Listing 40.5 shows another method for setting the RemoteHost and RemotePort properties in code.

Listing 40.5   Sub Form_Load()—The Form_Load Event Can Be Used to Perform Initiation Tasks

```
Private Sub Form_Load()

    'The name of the Winsock control for the client is wskClient
    '    This name is the object when setting a property such as
    '    object.property or wskClient.Property

    'The name of the remote host can be set at design time in the
    '    properties dialog or it can be set at runtime in code.
    '    Either the IP address "XXX.XXX.XXX.XXX" or a
```

```
'    friendly host
'    name may be used such as "http://www.microsoft.com"
'    The RemoteHost property has a data type of string.

wskClient.RemoteHost = "SomeJunk"

'The RemotePort property can be set at design time
'or in code at run time.
'    The RemotePort property has a data type of Long Integer.
'    This is port number on which the Server will be
'    listening.

wskClient.RemotePort = 1002

End Sub
```

Using the Change event to send the entire contents of a RichTextBox, as shown in Listing 40.6, is an inefficient technique because the entire message is retransmitted with each change in the contents. However, it does illustrate the simplicity of sending data with the SendData method.

Listing 40.6   Sub rtbClntOutBound_Change()—The *Change* Event Is Used to Send Data

```
Private Sub rtbClntOutBound_Change()

    'The RichTextBox_Change event is being used to send data.
    'The contents of the
    '    RichTextBox rtbClntOutBound will be transmitted each
    '    time the contents of the
    '    Text property is changed.  The SendData method is used
    '    with the argument of
    '    RichTextBox.Text

    wskClient.SendData rtbClntOutBound.Text

End Sub
```

Listing 40.7 shows a two-step process of moving the data from the buffer into a variable and then placing the variable contents into the Text property of the RichTextBox control. It can be placed directly into the Text property of the RichTextBox control.

Listing 40.7   Sub wskClient_DataArrival(ByVal bytesTotal As Long)—The *Data Arrival* Event Is Used to Display the Data in a Text Box

```
Private Sub wskClient_DataArrival(ByVal bytesTotal As Long)

    'The variable strData is declared to hold the incoming data.
    'It is stored as a variant.
```

continues

Listing 40.7 Continued

```
Dim strData As String

'The GetData method takes the data from the incoming buffer
'and places it in the strData variable.

wskClient.GetData strData

'The strData variable contents are placed in the
'RichTextBox rtbClntInBound.Text property

rtbClntInBound.Text = strData

End Sub
```

The salient feature of the client application program code is its simplicity. The assertion made at the beginning of the chapter was not an exaggeration—if you can write a "Hello World" application, you can use the Winsock Control.

Designing the Server Application

When the sample server application was designed, the primary requirement was that the application be capable of servicing the needs of the client application. The server application looks like a mirror image of the client application, with the exception that it cannot initiate a connection.

The users see their messages and the replies in two separate text boxes. RichTextBoxes were selected to correspond to the client application. The RichTextBoxes were, again, designated InBound and OutBound.

A text box is added to display the Remote Port number. This enables you to see that the Local Port on the Client Application and the Remote Port on the Server Application are the same.

Another text box is added to display the State property of the server. This changes from 2 (listening) to 7 (connected) as the application runs.

A final text box is added to display automatically the requestID that is sent by the client application or, optionally, to display the Local Port number for the server.

Of course, a Microsoft Winsock Control 5.0 is added to manage the communications between the client and server systems.

Laying Out the Form The Visual Basic form for the server application at run time is shown in Figure 40.3. When the application runs, the server application is in a listening state. It waits for a client system to initiate a connection.

Adding the Code This section examines the code from the server application. Notice the small amount of code that is required to create the functionality of the application. The addition of error handling would, at the very least, double the total amount of code. Just as with the client application, very little code is required to utilize the power of the Winsock Control.

FIG. 40.3

There is no command button to initiate the connection on the server application form.

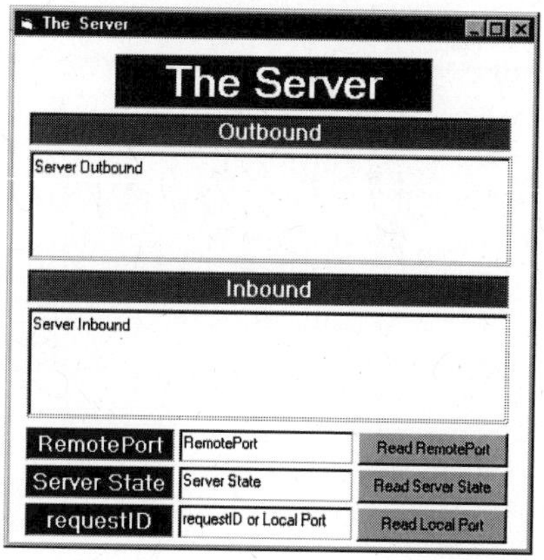

In Listing 40.8, a command button `Click` event is used to display the local port number. Because this is set by the `From Load` event, it will read `1001`, as set in the `Sub Form_Load()` section.

Listing 40.8   Sub cmdReadLocalPort_Click()—The *Click* Event that Displays the Local Port Number

```
Option Explicit

Private Sub cmdReadLocalPort_Click()

    'This reads and displays the LocalPort property.

    txtrequestID.Text = wskServer.LocalPort

End Sub
```

The code in Listing 40.9 displays the remote port number. Display this number before and after the connection is made and you will see that the remote port number is set at the time the connection is made.

Listing 40.9   Sub cmdReadRemotePort_Click()—The *Click* Event that Displays the Remote Port Number

```
Private Sub cmdReadRemotePort_Click()

    'Read the RemotePort property and display
    'in the txtRemotePort.

    txtRemotePort.Text = wskServer.RemotePort

End Sub
```

Part
VII

Ch
40

Server state is an enumerated list. A ServerState of 2 is currently listening, and a ServerState of 7 is connected. The code in Listing 40.10 displays the current server state.

Listing 40.10   Sub cmdReadServerState_Click()—The *Click* Event that Displays the Server State

```
Private Sub cmdReadServerState_Click()

    'Read and Display the current Server State

    txtServerState.Text = wskServer.State

End Sub
```

In Listing 40.11, the Form_Load event is setting the local port number for the Server Winsock Control and is using the Listen method to place the server application in a listening state.

Listing 40.11   Sub Form_Load()—The *Form_Load* Event Is Used to Set Various Properties

```
Private Sub Form_Load()

    'The name of the Winsock control for the server is wskServer
    '    This name is the object when setting a property such as
    '    object.property or wskServer.Property

    'The LocalPort property can be set at design time or in
    'code at runtime.
    '    The LocalPort property has a data type of Long Integer.
    '    This is port number on which the Server will be listening
    '    and must match the RemotePort property of the Client.

    wskServer.LocalPort = 1001

    'The Listen method is used to start the server monitoring
    'incoming requests for a connection.

    wskServer.Listen

End Sub
```

Listing 40.12 shows the RichTextBox_Change event being used to send data to the client application.

Listing 40.12   Sub rtbServOutBound_Change()—The *RichTextBox_Change* Event Is Used to Send Data

```
Private Sub rtbServOutBound_Change()

    'The RichTextBox_Change event is being used to send data.
    'The contents of the RichTextBox rtbServOutBound will be
    '   transmitted each time the contents of the
    '   Text property is changed.  The SendData method is used
    '   with the argument of RichTextBox.Text

    wskServer.SendData rtbServOutBound.Text

End Sub
```

Listing 40.13 shows the ConnectionRequest event being used to open the connection. The Accept method establishes the connection. The request ID is also displayed in a text box.

Listing 40.13   Sub wskServer_ConnectionRequest(ByVal *requestID* As Long)—The *ConnectionRequest* Event Is Used to Open the Connection

```
Private Sub wskServer_ConnectionRequest(ByVal requestID As Long)

    'Check to determine whether the WinSock Control's state is
    'closed.
    '   If it is not, then close the control before using the
    '   Accept method.

    If wskServer.State <> sckClosed Then wskServer.Close

    'The control is now prepared to use the Accept method
    '   which will receive the
    '   ConnectionRequest from the Client.
    '   The argument for the Accept method is requestID

    wskServer.Accept requestID

    'The requestID is displayed

    txtrequestID.Text = requestID

End Sub
```

Listing 40.14 uses the DataArrival event to display the data in a RichTextBox.

Part

VII

Ch

40

**Listing 40.14 Sub wskServer_DataArrival(ByVal bytesTotal As Long)—
The *DataArrival* Event Is Used to Display the Data**

```
Private Sub wskServer_DataArrival(ByVal bytesTotal As Long)

    'The variable strData is declared to hold the incoming data.
    '  It is stored as a variant.

    Dim strData As String

    'The GetData method takes the data from the incoming
    '   buffer and places it in the strData variable.

    wskServer.GetData strData

    'The strData variable contents are placed in the
    '   RichTextBox rtbClntInBound.Text property

    rtbServInBound.Text = strData

End Sub
```

As with the code for the client application, the code required for the server Winsock Control is only a few lines. This is a truly powerful control.

Running the Winsock Control Client/Server Application

The client/server application can be run on the same system or on two different systems that are on the same network. The application will run on a Windows NT 4.0 or Windows 95 system. The primary requirement is that TCP/IP be installed on the system and that the TCP/IP stack is running. This usually is not a problem on a Windows NT system. Occasionally, you may need to start the TCP/IP stack on a Windows 95 machine. One of the easiest ways to do this is to open a connection to your ISP (Internet Service Provider). This starts the TCP/IP stack on a Windows 95 machine and allows the Winsock Control to be used.

To run the application, use the Windows Explorer to go to the Chapter 41 directory on the CD and then double-click both WebDev05Client.exe and WebDev05Server.exe. This starts both programs, as shown in Figure 40.4.

When both programs are running, you need to set the remote host name in the client application. You accomplish this by entering the name of the system or the IP address of the system that is running the server application in the text box labeled Remote Host and then clicking the Set RemoteHost button. You also need to click the Set RemotePort button. Leave the default value of 1001. Now click the Connect button on the client application. A requestID number should appear in the requestID text box on the server system, as shown in Figure 40.5.

FIG. 40.4

These programs can be run on two systems that are connected on a local network by using the TCP/IP protocol.

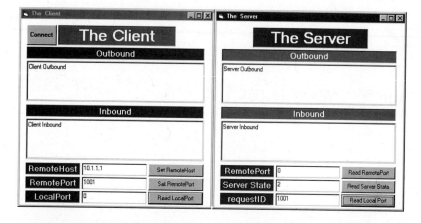

FIG. 40.5

The Read buttons at the bottom of the application windows can be used to show various properties.

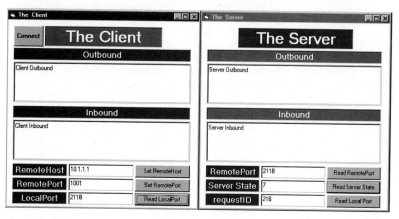

You are now ready to use the application for its designed purpose—a simple chat application. By typing inside the Outbound text boxes, you will see the information that you enter displayed in the Inbound box of the other application window, as shown in Figure 40.6.

FIG. 40.6

The information entered is displayed on a character-by-character basis.

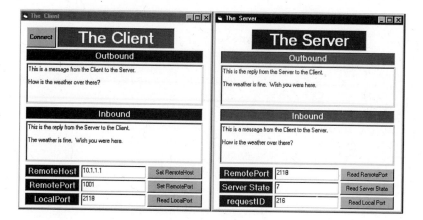

Part
VII

Ch
40

The code and project for this demonstration program is also on this book's companion CD-ROM. As you experiment with the programs, you will find that the principles of the program are very simple. The Winsock Control is very easy to use.

Microsoft Internet Transfer Control

The Microsoft Internet Transfer Control enables the implementation of two of the most significant and widely used Internet protocols: Hypertext Transfer Protocol (HTTP) and File Transfer Protocol (FTP) are the workhorses of the Internet. With HTTP, you can connect to World Wide Web servers and retrieve HTML and other documents. By using FTP, you can download and upload files between systems on the Internet or an intranet.

The Internet Transfer Control has properties, methods, and events, just as all ActiveX controls have. Understanding these properties, methods, and events is the key to understanding the control and what can be done with it.

Properties

Some properties are available to be set at design time, while others are read-only at run time and unavailable at design time. Still others can only be set at design time and are read-only at run time. Some properties, though, can be set at both run time and at design time.

The data type of the property is important to know and understand. A data type can be a string, an integer, a long integer, or any other data type.

You also must understand the syntax for using the property in code.

***AccessType* Property**   The AccessType property determines whether the control will directly access the network (Internet or intranet) or access the network through a proxy.

> **N O T E**   Proxies can be used to link LANs to the Internet. In addition to providing access to the Internet, these proxies act as a firewalls, preventing unwanted intrusion into the LAN from the Internet. ▓

The syntax for AccessType is:

```
MyInetControl.AccessType = type
```

Following is an enumerated list of integers and constants for the AccessType:

Integer	Value	Description
icUseDefault	0	The control uses the default setting found in The Registry.
icDirect	1	The connection is direct to the Internet.
icNamedProxy	2	The control uses the proxy server named in the Proxy property.

***Document* Property**   The Document property sets the file or document that will be used in the Execute method. If this property is blank, the server returns the default document. The syntax is:

```
MyInetControl.Document = "MyFile.Htm"
```

***Name* Property**   The Name property is the name that the control is called in code (MyInetXfer, for example). VB assigns a default name at the time a control is created, such as Inet1. The name assigned should follow your chosen coding convention. The rules for names require that the name start with a letter and be no longer than 40 characters. It can contain underscore (_) characters, but it cannot contain punctuation, such as commas and periods.

***Password* Property**   How a password is used in the Microsoft Internet Transfer Control depends upon the protocol being used. If the protocol is HTTP, the password is not sent with the request because HTTP mostly uses anonymous connections. If the protocol is FTP and these criteria are met—the UserName property is blank, and the Password property is blank—then the control sends the e-mail address of the user. However, if the UserName property has an entry, the control sends the contents of the Password property. The syntax is:

```
MyInetControl.Password = "aPassWord"
```

The password is a string; its content and form depend on the system to which it is being attached. Most passwords are case-sensitive, meaning that you must use uppercase and lowercase letters exactly as they appear in the original password that is assigned.

***Protocol* Property**   The Protocol property returns or sets the protocol that will be used with the Execute method for the control. The syntax for the Protocol property is:

```
MyInetControl.Protocol = type
```

These protocol types are shown in the following enumerated list of integers:

Integer	Value	Description
icUnknown	0	The protocol is unknown
icDefault	1	The default protocol in The Registry is used
icFTP	2	File Transfer Protocol
icReserved	3	Reserved for future use
icHTTP	4	Hypertext Transfer Protocol
icHTTPS	5	Secure Hypertext Transfer Protocol

***Proxy* Property**   If the Access property is set to use a named proxy, the Proxy property is where that name is set. The syntax is:

```
MyInetControl.Proxy = Myproxy
```

This also can be the IP address of the proxy server.

***RemoteHost* Property**   The RemoteHost property returns or sets the host to which the Internet Transfer Control sends the request. This can be either the remote host domain name—such as **ftp.microsoft.com**—or the dotted quartet IP address, as in 190.190.28.1. The syntax is:

```
MyInetControl.RemoteHost = "ftp.microsoft.com"
```

RemotePort Property   The `RemotePort` property sets or returns the port number to which requests are sent. The `Protocol` property automatically sets the `RemotePort` property to a well-known port—if one exists— such as Port 80 for HTTP or Port 21 for FTP. The syntax is:

```
MyInetControl.RemotePort = 80
```

RequestTimeout Property   The `RequestTimeout` property is the time (in seconds) that the control waits for a response before an error is generated. If the request is made with the `OpenURL` method, an error is generated. If the `Execute` method is used, a `StateChanged` event is generated, with the state being an error. Setting the property to `0` indicates infinity. The syntax is:

```
MyInetControl.RequestTimeout = 20
```

ResponseCode and ResponseInfo Properties   When a request is made of a server, the server might generate an error that is transmitted to the client system. An example is the `404 Not Found` error with which you are probably familiar. This is transmitted in two parts: the response code and the response information. These two properties are used by the client system to return this information for display. The syntax is:

```
MyCode = MyInetControl.ResponseCode
```

```
MyInfo = MyInetControl.ResponseInfo
```

StillExecuting Property   The `StillExecuting` property is used to test whether the control is busy. The value is Boolean, with `-1` indicating `True` and `0` equaling `False`. The syntax is:

```
If MyInetControl.StillExecuting = -1 Then...
```

URL Property   The `URL` property sets or returns the URL that is used by the `OpenURL` or `Execute` method. The syntax is:

```
MyInetControl.URL = "http://www.microsoft.com"
```

UserName Property   Whether the `UserName` property is transmitted to the remote host system depends on the protocol being used. If the protocol is HTTP, no name is transmitted. If the protocol is FTP, a user name is transmitted. If the `UserName` property is blank, the user name anonymous is sent. The syntax is:

```
MyInetControl.UserName = "MyName"
```

Methods

Methods are predefined functions that are used to perform various tasks on the control. There are methods that open a connection and methods that retrieve data from a buffer. The methods used with the Microsoft Internet Transfer Control are discussed in the following sections.

***Cancel* Method**   The `Cancel` method cancels the current request and closes all currently open connections. The syntax is:

`MyInetControl.Cancel`

***Execute* Method**   The `Execute` method sends a request to a remote server. The request must be valid for the specified protocol. The syntax is:

`Object.Execute url, operation, data, requestHeaders`

Table 40.2 examines the elements of the syntax.

Table 40.2   The Execute Syntax Elements

Element	Example	Description
object	`MyInetControl`	An object expression that evaluates to the control `Name` property.
url	`http://www.micro`	The Universal Resource Locator to which the control should connect.
operation	`POST`	Specifies the operation to be executed.
data	`MyVar: vardata`	Contains the data that may be required by the operation.
requestHeader	`Header name: value`	Specifies additional headers to be sent by the server.

***GetChunk* Method**   The `GetChunk` method is used to retrieve data from the buffer that is created by the Internet Transfer Control. The syntax is:

`MyInetControl.GetChunk(size,datatype)`

`size` is a long integer and `datatype` is optional, with the default being text. The other type is a byte array. These types are an enumerated list, as shown in the following table:

Integer	Value	Description
icString	0	Retrieves data as a string
icByteArray	1	Retrieves data as a byte array

An example of using the `GetChunk` method is shown in Listing 40.15. The `StateChanged` event is being used to initiate the use of the `GetChunk` method.

Listing 40.15   Code Snippet—The *GetChunk* Method in Context

```
Private Sub Inet1_StateChanged(ByVal State As Integer)
    ' Retrieve server response using the GetChunk
    ' method when State = 12. The example data is text.
```

continues

Listing 40.15 Continued

```
    Select Case State
    ' ... Other cases not shown.

    Case icResponseReceived ' 12
        Dim MyData As Variant ' Data variable.
        Dim MystrData As String: MystrData = ""
        Dim bFinished As Boolean: bFinished = False

        MyData = Inet1.GetChunk(1024, icString)

        Do While Not bFinished

strData = Data & MyData
            ' Get next chunk.
            MyData = Inet1.GetChunk(1024, icString)
            If Len(vtData) = 0 Then
                bFinished = True
            End If
        Loop

        txtData.Text = strData
    End Select

End Sub
```

This Sub would place the data in a text box named txtData.

***GetHeader* Method**   The GetHeader method retrieves additional headers from the server. If no header name is specified, then all headers are retrieved. The headers contain such information as the date last modified and the content length. The syntax is:

MyInetControl.GetHeader(headername)

Some of the headers usually available are:

Header	Description
Date	Contains the time and date of the document's transmission
MIME-Version	Contains the MIME protocol version
Server	Contains the server name
Content-length	The length of the content file (in bytes)
Content-type	Reveals the MIME content-type
Last-modified	The time and date the file was last modified

***OpenURL* Method**   The OpenURL method is used to retrieve the document specified in the URL. The syntax is:

object.OpenURL url, datatype

An example of the use of the syntax is:

```
MyInetControl.OpenURL "http://www.microsoft.com", icString
```

The following are the data types for the OpenURL method:

Integer	Value	Description
icString	0	Retrieves data as a string
icByteArray	1	Retrieves data as a byte array

Events—*StateChanged* Event

Events are the triggers that invoke the methods. The Microsoft Internet Transfer Control generates only one event, the StateChanged event. The values for the State property usually are used in a Case statement that executes the proper functions based on the State value. The State values are shown in Table 40.3.

Table 40.3   The Execute Syntax Elements

Constant	Value	Description
icNone	0	No state to report
icHostResolvingHost	1	The IP address is being resolved by a DNS
icHostResolved	2	The IP address has been resolved
icConnecting	3	The connection to the server is being established
icConnected	4	The connection has been successfully completed
icRequesting	5	The request is being transmitted to the server
icRequestSent	6	The transmission of the request is complete
icReceivingResponse	7	The response from the server is being received
icResponseReceived	8	The response from the server has been successfully received
icDisconnecting	9	The client is disconnecting from the server
icDisconnected	10	The disconnect process is complete
icError	11	An error has occurred in the communication with the server
icResponseCompleted	12	The data requested has been successfully received

Part

VII

Ch

40

Microsoft Internet Transfer Control Example

A simple example using the Internet Transfer Control demonstrates how powerful the control is and how easy it is to use. In this example, a new project has been created in Visual Basic. The Microsoft Internet Transfer Control Version 5.0 and the Microsoft RichTextBox Control Version 5.0 have been added to the project.

The following controls have been added on the project form:

Button	Name	Caption
	RichTextBox	RichTextBox1
	Internet Transfer	Inet1
	Command1	OpenURL
	Command2	GetHeader
	Command3	FTP
	Command4	Cancel

The arrangement of the controls at design time is shown in Figure 40.7.

FIG. 40.7
Notice that the Microsoft Internet Transfer Control is visible at design time.

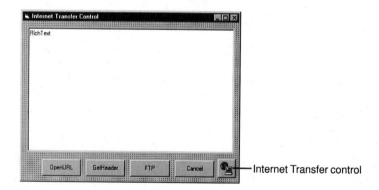

Internet Transfer control

The amount of code required to use the control is surprisingly small. Opening a connection to a server and retrieving a file requires only three lines of code, as shown in Listing 40.16. Here, the OpenURL command button was clicked.

Listing 40.16   OpenURL Method—The *OpenURL* Method Creates a Connection to a Web Server

```
Private Sub Command1_Click()
    RichTextBox1.Text = Inet1.OpenURL("http://www.microsoft.com")
End Sub
```

The results of this connection are shown in Figure 40.8. Notice that the HTML has not been formatted. This is because the file is displayed as transferred.

FIG. 40.8

The display in a rich text box preserves the original file formatting.

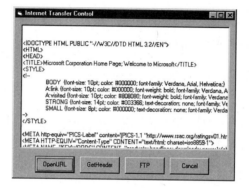

The Click event for the GetHeader command button is equally simple and straightforward, as shown in Listing 40.17.

Listing 40.17   GetHeader Method—The *GetHeader* Method Requests Headers from the Server

```
Private Sub Command2_Click()
    RichTextBox1.Text = Inet1.OpenURL("http://www.microsoft.com")
    RichTextBox1.Text = Inet1.GetHeader
End Sub
```

The result of Listing 40.17 is displayed in Figure 40.9. The headers are in a header-name: header-data format. In the code, no header name was specified, so all headers were transferred.

The FTP command button specifies a file to be transferred. The file is transferred and displayed, as shown in Figure 40.10; the accompanying code appears in Listing 40.18.

Part

VII

Ch

40

> ### Listing 40.18 OpenUrl Method—The *OpenURL* Method Specifies a File to Transfer

```
Private Sub Command3_Click()
    RichTextBox1.Text =
➥Inet1.OpenURL("ftp://ftp.microsoft.com/disclaimer.txt")
End Sub
```

FIG. 40.9

The headers available will vary from server to server.

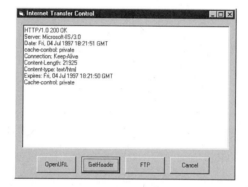

FIG. 40.10

The text file is displayed as it is formatted.

The final command button, the `Cancel` button, simply breaks the connection to any server. The code is shown in Listing 40.19.

> ### Listing 40.19 Cancel Method—The *Cancel* Method Closes Any Connections

```
Private Sub Command3_Click()
    Inet1.Cancel
End Sub
```

As you can see, the Microsoft Internet Transfer Control is both very easy to use and very powerful. The broad set of properties and methods provides a very detailed level of control when required, but it can also be very simple to use.

WebBrowser Control

The WebBrowser control is the ActiveX control DLL Shdocvw.dll, which is part of Microsoft Internet Explorer. The WebBrowser control can add browsing of documents on the local system or on the Web. It also parses HTML documents and keeps a history log so that you can return to previously displayed documents. Because this control can view richly formatted documents, it can host Excel spreadsheets and Microsoft Word documents. This control needs to be added to the toolbox. It is the Microsoft Internet Controls.

A review of some of the properties, methods, and events of the WebBrowser control will provide insight into some of its possible uses.

Properties

A few of the properties are available to be set at design time. Some are read-only at run time and unavailable at design time. Others can be set only at design time and are read-only at run time. But some properties can be set both at run time and at design time.

Important information is contained in the data type of the property. The data type can be a string, an integer, a long integer, or any other data type.

***LocationName* Property**   The LocationName property returns the name of the resource that is currently being displayed as a string. The syntax is:

```
MyVar = MyBrowser.LocationName
```

***LocationURL* Property**   The LocationURL property returns the URL of the resource that is currently displayed as a string. The syntax is:

```
MyVar = MyBrowser.LocationURL
```

***Type* Property**   The Type property returns the type name of the resource that is currently displayed as a string. The syntax is:

```
MyVar = MyBrowser.Type
```

Methods

Methods are predefined functions that are used to perform various tasks on the control. For example, there are methods that move forward and backward in the history list. The methods used with the WebBrowser control are discussed in the following sections.

***GoBack* Method**   The GoBack method navigates back one item in the history list maintained by the control. The syntax is:

```
MyBrowser.GoBack
```

***GoForward* Method**   The GoForward method navigates forward one item in the history list maintained by the control. The syntax is:

```
MyBrowser.GoForward
```

Part
VII

Ch
40

***GoHome* Method**   The GoHome method navigates to the home or start page, as defined in the Internet Explorer Options Dialog box. The syntax is:

```
MyBrowser.GoHome
```

***GoSearch* Method**   The GoSearch method navigates to the search page, as defined in the Internet Explorer Options Dialog box. The syntax is:

```
MyBrowser.GoSearch
```

***Navigate* Method**   The Navigate method navigates to the resource identified in the URL parameter of the method. The syntax is:

```
MyBrowser.Navigate URLVar
```

***Refresh* Method**   The Refresh method reloads the page that is currently displayed by the WebBrowser control. The syntax is:

```
MyBrowser.Refresh
```

***Stop* Method**   The Stop method cancels any pending navigation, any download operation, and any dynamic page elements, such as animation or background music. The syntax is:

```
MyBrowser.Stop
```

Events

Events fire when certain actions take place. The WebBrowser control fires a number of events; these events can be handled to provide functionality for code that is attached to the control. An example is the DownloadComplete event, which can be used to clean up after a file download.

Some events that are generated by the WebBrowser control include the following:

- BeforeNavigate
- CommandStateChange
- DownloadBegin
- DownloadComplete
- NavigateComplete
- NewWindow
- ProgressChange
- StatusTextChange
- TitleChange

WebBrowser Control Example

A very simple sample Web browser has been created to show how easy it is to use the WebBrowser control (see Figure 40.11 for the browser as it appears at design time).

FIG. 40.11

The URL is entered in the text box and then the Navigate button is clicked.

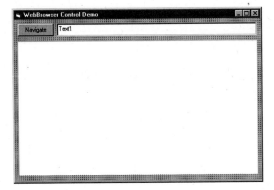

The Web Browser consists of a command button with the caption "Navigate," a text box in which you enter the URL, and the WebBrowser control. Figure 40.12 shows the Web Browser when it is first opened. The code activated by the Navigate button is shown in Listing 40.20.

FIG. 40.12

The simplest of all Web browsers is functionally useable.

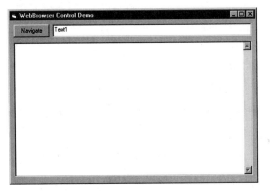

Listing 40.20   Navigate Method—The *Navigate* Method Only Requires an URL

```
Private Sub Command1_Click()
    WebBrowser1.Navigate Text1.Text
End Sub
```

Figure 40.13 shows the WebBrowser displaying the Microsoft Home Page. The WebBrowser control is extremely easy to use and can be controlled at a very detailed level.

FIG. 40.13

Construction of a Web browser is quite simple with the WebBrowser control.

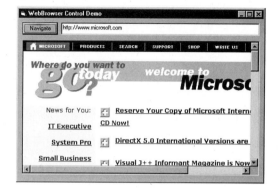

From Here...

In this chapter, you have examined three controls that can be used in Visual Basic to enable your applications on the Web: the WebBrowser Control, the Internet Transfer Control, and the Winsock Control. These controls are easy to use. The only limit to the applications that you can create for the Web with these controls is your imagination. The following chapters provide additional insight into Web applications:

- Chapter 33, "Database Access with ActiveX Data Objects (ADO)," looks at databases as part of a Web application.

- Chapter 35, "Internet Programming with VBScript," explains how to use VBScript in Web pages.

- Chapter 36, "Programming Web Pages," goes deeper into the realm of VBScript to explore this powerful tool.

- Chapter 37, "Creating Active Server Pages," looks at the flexibility and browser-independence provided by Active Server Pages.

- Chapter 38, "Working with Active Server Page Objects," explores the Active Server Page Object Model.

- Chapter 39, "Using the Web, Databases, and Visual Basic," brings together the use of databases for dynamic Web applications.

P A R T VIII

Distributed Client/Server Environment Programming

Using Visual Basic in a Client/Server Environment

The most common use of client/server technology is in the database field. Client/server databases are very popular because they provide most of the advantages of mainframe databases, such as security and transaction processing, while maintaining the ease of use and lower life-cycle cost of distributed hardware and software.

This chapter uses Microsoft SQL Server 6.5, which runs under Windows NT Server 4.0, for its examples. SQL Server is, as its name implies, a database server. It was designed to be a powerful and reliable back-end server for use with front-end tools, such as Visual Basic. Those front-end tools provide the user interface.

This chapter explores how to build applications using Visual Basic and SQL Server. ■

Understanding the client/server architecture

Client/server computing is a modern trend in PC-based applications. Learn what the key components are and how they interact.

The role of Microsoft SQL Server

SQL Server provides a powerful database engine which can be used with Visual Basic in a client/server environment.

Installing SQL Server

You walk through a typical SQL Server installation and understand the important decisions that must be made.

Creating and maintaining data

You learn how to create databases, tables, and other objects, as well as how to add data to a table, and query the data in that table.

Using SQL server from Visual Basic

You see how to access the data stored in a SQL server environment from within your Visual Basic programs.

Client/Server Databases

The client/server architecture is fairly easy to understand. A client program sends a request across a network to a centralized database engine (or server), which processes the request and returns the results over the network to the client. Just as the Internet is today's hot topic, client/server has been a key concept in modern computing for some time. Data exists everywhere in the enterprise—in ancient mainframe databases, in file cabinets, on purchase orders, in spreadsheets, and so on. Frequently, the goal of a client/server system is to bring together this information in a SQL database and provide a front end for reporting and analysis. In years past, a small subset of this data was transferred into mainframe databases where it could be widely viewed. However, a PC-based client/server system has several advantages, including usability and lower cost.

During recent years, as desktop computers have proliferated throughout corporations, single-user databases have been created using dBASE, Lotus 1-2-3, Access, and other desktop database programs. These databases have produced a cost savings over paper systems and have made some data available electronically for the first time.

Once data is stored electronically, it begins to attract attention. Other departments perceive that an integration of this data with their own internal data could yield some very interesting information. Those departments begin asking first for reports, then for disks, and finally for online access to this data.

This process is wonderful for the enterprise because it improves the organization's ability to make sound decisions. However, the person on whose desktop the database resides faces new difficulties, including such issues as data integrity, concurrent access, security, and performance. Those issues are the province of computer scientists, not of individual users.

The client/server architecture moves the desktop database to a departmental server where a database administrator can maintain it. Because server databases such as SQL Server are fully functional in the areas of transaction processing, crash recovery, and performance, they have many of the same advantages as mainframe databases. Server databases usually reside on a departmental server and are usually maintained by an employee of the department, so they fit the political reality of companies and governmental organizations.

Performing this conversion of a desktop database to a server database is a booming business. The computer specialists who can master the art of performing this task are in demand both inside traditional companies and in consulting firms that specialize in that type of work.

Microsoft SQL Server

One of the most popular client/server database platforms is Microsoft SQL Server. SQL Server is a back-end processor that is designed to perform back-end tasks, such as fast updates and retrieval. It stores and retrieves data as quickly as possible while protecting that data from disaster. This separation of the front end from the back end of this server enables the customer to benefit from the advantages of both the mainframe and the PC world. The multiuser support, centralized administration, and security features of a mainframe are combined with the low cost-per-user and rich graphical interactive tools available on a PC platform.

Optional components provide gateways to mainframe and minicomputer database management systems, including IBM DB2, AS/400, and ORACLE.

ODBC drivers are widely available. They connect the SQL server to any front-end development tool that supports ODBC. For more information on ODBC, see Chapter 32, "Using Remote Data Objects (RDO)," and Chapter 33, "Database Access with ActiveX Data Objects (ADO)."

▶ **See** "Introducing ODBC," **p. 882**

▶ **See** "Understanding ODBC," **p. 898**

Installing SQL Server

Microsoft SQL Server runs under the Microsoft Windows NT Server network operating system. (There is also a developer's version named "Microsoft SQL Workstation" that runs under NT workstation.) Installation is not difficult, and it usually proceeds without any problems. However, some important choices must be made during installation, so the installation process is briefly reviewed here. To install SQL Server, you need to be at the server console. When setup starts, you are prompted for your name, organization, and product ID. Then the setup Options dialog box appears, as shown in Figure 41.1.

FIG. 41.1

The number of setup options available during installation varies, depending on whether the SQL server has ever been installed before.

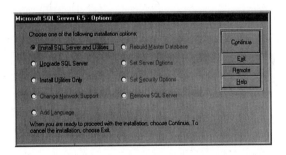

The grayed-out options become available when you run setup again after SQL Server has already been installed. In Figure 41.1, the default option is to install both the database server and the utilities. The utilities are tools that let you administer the server and run queries against it, among other things. After performing the main installation on the server, you need to use the third option, Install Utilities Only, on the machines of the developers and the database administrator.

The next screen that appears, shown in Figure 41.2, enables you to choose the licensing mode. Remember, multiple clients will connect to this server, so make sure that all of them are legally allowed to do so.

FIG. 41.2

Stay legal by setting the licensing options appropriately.

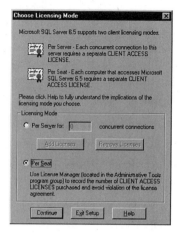

The first option, Per Server, enables you to specify the number of licenses you have purchased for this server. For example, suppose you set your server up for 20 connections. This means you could have any number of installations of your application, but would be allowed only 20 connections at a time. The second option, Per Seat, requires you to purchase licenses for the clients rather than for the server. In this case, everyone who connects to the server is supposed to have a license.

After selecting the licensing method, choose the installation path. The default path is C:\MSSQL. Depending on how your server's disk drives are arranged, you may want to change your installation to another drive to separate SQL Server from the NT operating system.

Next, you are prompted to create the master database device. This dialog is shown in Figure 41.3. SQL Server stores data in its own file system. Devices can be thought of as named logical disk drives within that file system. From NT's point of view, the device is just a file. In Figure 41.3, the NT file name is MASTER.DAT.

FIG. 41.3

The device size does not have to be very large because the master database stores information about other databases rather than actual data.

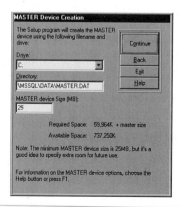

As you probably already know, one SQL server can have multiple databases. For example, you might have a payroll database, a human resources database, and a budgeting database on the same SQL server. Each of these databases can be stored on one or more devices. The master database is a special database that is created during the installation of SQL Server. It stores information about the other databases on your SQL server.

When you continue the installation, you are eventually presented with the Installation Options dialog box, shown in Figure 41.4.

FIG. 41.4

Pay special attention to the Installation Options dialog box; some of these options can only be changed by re-installing SQL Server.

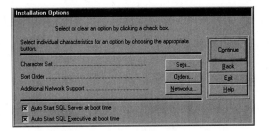

The first two options, Sets and Orders, are important because if you need to change them at a later time, you must rebuild your databases. In addition, database backups made from another SQL server can only be restored to a server with the same sort order and character set.

The character set is exactly what it sounds like—the set of allowable characters that can be stored in the database. I usually choose the recommended default, the ISO Character Set. You must decide whether to make your sort order; the big decision to make is whether or not to be sensitive. Although case-sensitive sorting is supposedly faster, I recommend a case-insensitive sort because it is less complicated for the programmer and for the users.

The third option on the dialog, Network Support, determines the network protocols that clients must use to connect to the SQL Server.

Finally, the two boxes at the bottom of the screen determine whether the SQL services are started automatically. The SQL Server is like any other Windows NT service: It must be "started" before anyone can use it.

These installation options can be changed at any time from the Services icon in the Control Panel. The first option, Start SQL Server at boot time, should always be checked because it represents the database server itself. The second box determines whether the SQL Executive service is started. The SQL Executive is a utility that can be used to automate some administrative functions. During installation, you are asked which NT user account the SQL Executive service should use. This choice is not critical now because whatever you select can be easily changed from the Control Panel.

Upon completion of the installation, a new program group—which is shown in Figure 41.5—is added to the server's Start menu.

Part
VIII

Ch
41

FIG. 41.5

The program group on the server's desktop contains all of the utilities you need to manage a SQL server.

The SQL Server Program Group

The most important program in this group is *SQL Enterprise Manager*. With SQL Enterprise Manager, you can run queries and configure, administer, and control most aspects of the multiple SQL servers on your network. The remaining icons, which serve various other purposes, are described briefly here:

- *SQL Service Manager*   This allows you to start and stop the database server. (This function can also be performed remotely from SQL Enterprise Manager.)

- *SQL Client Configuration Utility*   This determines which network protocol and which library (DLL) a client will use to connect to the SQL server.

- *SQL Security Manager*   When using SQL Server's integrated security, you can use this program to give NT accounts user and system administrator privileges on your SQL server. You can use this program when using SQL Server's integrated security.

- *SQL Server Web Assistant*   A wizard that instructs SQL Server to build an HTML file (Web page) from the data in your database. This process can be scheduled to update the Web page whenever the data changes.

- *ISQL_w* This enables you to execute SQL commands interactively against the database. (You can also run SQL commands from SQL Enterprise Manager's Query window.)

- *MS Query*   This creates queries graphically. This query tool is also included with Microsoft Office.

- *SQL Performance Monitor*   This uses a graph to monitor the performance of the SQL server.

- *SQL Trace*   This allows you to view the SQL commands being executed on the server by one or more clients.

- *SQL Setup*   This allows you to run setup and install additional components or to remove SQL Server from your system.

- *Help Files and Books Online*   This provides additional documentation for various parts of SQL Server. For help with the SQL language itself, choose Help, Transact-SQL Help from SQL Enterprise Manager.

By using these programs, the database administrator can perform all of the tasks required to support production systems. The additional support services just discussed make the SQL Server a robust departmental server capable of handling a large number of users.

Testing the SQL Server Installation

Before continuing, make sure the SQL Server is running. Start the SQL Service Manager. You should see the screen shown in Figure 41.6.

FIG. 41.6

If you have the "green light," SQL Server is running.

If the traffic light is red, double-click Start/Continue to start the SQL service.

The server is now ready to receive commands from the database administrator and from user applications (once they are written).

Configuring Enterprise Manager

Now that the server is running, you need to configure SQL Enterprise Manager so that it can connect to that server. SQL Enterprise Manager is designed to control multiple SQL servers. Each server you want to access has to be registered with SQL Enterprise Manager. If you have not run SQL Enterprise Manager before, the Register Server dialog appears automatically. Otherwise, you can choose Server, Register Server. The dialog box is pictured in Figure 41.7.

FIG. 41.7

To use a SQL server with Enterprise Manager, the server must be registered.

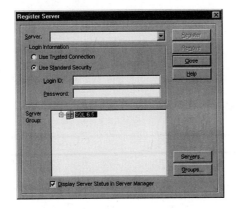

Now you should go through the steps to register a new server. First, type the name of your server in the box labeled Server.

N O T E   The name of the SQL server is the name of the Windows NT server you installed it on. This
is by design, because often an entire NT server is dedicated to running the SQL service.
Companies have used a wide range of server-naming conventions, from movie star names to planets in
the solar system. The examples in this chapter use the name EINTSVR, which stands for Enterprise
INTranet SerVeR. ■

Next, you need to specify how Enterprise Manager should log in to SQL Server. You have two
options, using a "trusted connection" or specifying a "standard security" login. A trusted connection means that login information is integrated with NT security. For the purposes of this
chapter, however, standard security will be used. (Integrated NT security is more complicated
and not available over all of the network protocols.)

SQL Server has its own user logins, which are used by client programs to gain access to the
server. One of these logins, the sa login, is meant to be used by the SQL system administrator.
By default, the sa account has no password. To register the server, select "standard security"
and type sa in the Login ID box. Press Register and then Close to close the dialog box.

T I P   You will want to change the sa account's password. Choose <u>M</u>anage, <u>L</u>ogins. After you have changed
the password, you must register the server again.

After the server has been registered, it shows up in the Server Manager window of SQL Enterprise Manager. This window shows all of the registered SQL servers, as illustrated in Figure
41.8.

FIG. 41.8

The previous example
shows SQL Enterprise
Manager with six
registered servers. Note
that with the proper
scripts installed, SQL
Enterprise Manager will
work with older versions
of SQL Server.

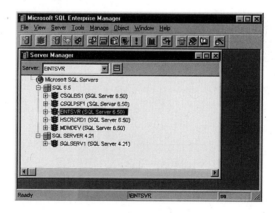

To work with a particular server, select it in the list. Click the plus symbol next to the server
name to expand the tree. When you do so, the SQL Enterprise Manager will connect to the
selected server and retrieve additional information about it.

Creating a Database

With the server running, you are now ready to create a database. In this section we will create a sample "employee" database, which could be used to store an employee phone directory. Creating this database will be a two-step process. You will need to create both a *database device* and the actual database.

Creating a Database Device

Prior to creating a database, you must create a *device* for the database to reside in. Devices are files that can hold one or more databases and transaction logs. Devices can be thought of as named logical disk drives. When SQL Server is first installed, several devices that hold system information and sample databases are created. To see the devices, expand the Database Devices tree in the Server Manager window. No devices have been added to the server EINTSVR in Figure 41.9 except the defaults.

FIG. 41.9
In addition to the master device, the SQL installation creates two other devices, MSDBData and MSDBLog.

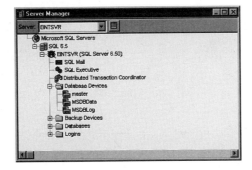

To add a new device, first choose <u>M</u>anage, Database De<u>v</u>ices. This brings up the Manage Database Devices window, shown in Figure 41.10.

FIG. 41.10
The Manage Database Devices window shows a color-coded graph of the free and used disk space for each device.

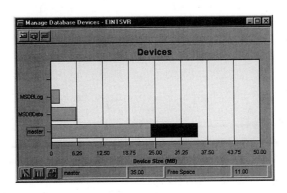

Part
VIII

Ch
41

To add a database device, click the New Device icon (upper-left corner) to display the New Database Device dialog box in Figure 41.11. Name the new device "MyDevice." Set the size to 10M, which will be more than enough for your sample database.

N O T E As you type the device name, the physical location of the device is filled in automatically. The physical location is a file on the NT server. Remember that even if you are creating a device remotely, the location is on the hard drive of the server, not on your PC. ■

FIG. 41.11
Creating a new device requires you to specify a file name and size.

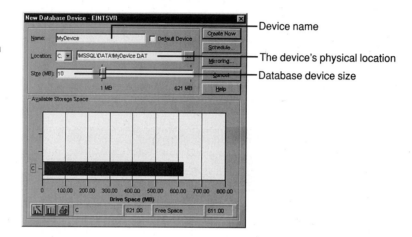

Device name
The device's physical location
Database device size

Press Create Now. After the device has been created, it shows up in both the Server Manager window and the Manage Database Devices window.

Creating the Actual Database

Now that you have a device to store the database in, you can create the employee database (which is created in much the same way as a device). First, choose Manage, Databases to bring up the Manage Databases window (see Figure 41.12).

New Database button

FIG. 41.12
The Manage Databases window is used to create, edit, and remove databases.

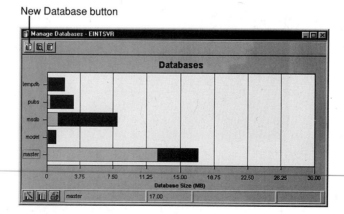

Next, click the New Database button (in the upper-left corner) to display the New Database dialog box, pictured in Figure 41.13. Enter the name "employee" in the Name box so that your sample database will store information about employees.

FIG. 41.13
In the New Database dialog box, specify the name and size of your database.

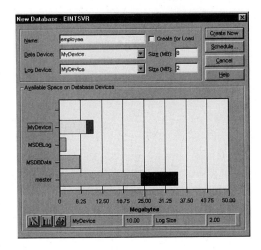

Databases in SQL Server generally have space for both the actual data and the transaction log. The log space is used for recovery purposes, as well as for rolling back server transactions. Multiple databases can share a device, and devices can be expanded if the need arises. You should read the included documentation carefully regarding transaction log space and database devices.

For the purposes of your sample database, store both the data and log on the "MyDevice" device. Select "MyDevice" from the Data Device box and enter **8** for the size. Make the log size **2M.** Press Create Now. The new database appears in both the Manage Databases and Server Manager windows (see Figure 41.14).

FIG. 41.14
The newly created employee database is added to the list of databases.

Part
VIII

Ch
41

Armed with a real database, you are now ready to begin adding objects to it.

Creating a Table

Once the database is created, the next task is to create a table. The Transact SQL language contains commands to create tables using the SQL syntax. SQL Enterprise Manager includes a way to create tables graphically using the SQL syntax. In this section you see a quick rundown of each method. You learn to create a table named "phonenumbers" that can store employees' names and office phone numbers. The four fields in the table will be employeeid, fname, lname, and phone.

Creating a Table with SQL

To create this sample table, use the CREATE TABLE command. The syntax is easy to pick up if you look at an example:

```
CREATE TABLE phonenumbers
(
 employeeid int NULL,
 fname char(35) NULL,
 lname char(35) NULL,
 phone char(12) NULL
)
```

As you can see, the field names are listed, followed by the data type. The word NULL indicates that that field is allowed to contain a null value. The CREATE TABLE command has many additional options. See the help file for a complete list.

You can run the CREATE TABLE command or any other SQL command from the SQL Query Tool. To start the SQL Query Tool, select Tools, SQL Query Tool. The SQL Query Tool window is divided into three tabbed sections, as illustrated in Figure 41.15.

FIG. 41.15

To execute a SQL statement, first enter it in the Query tab's edit window. There are several ways to execute a query: press the Play button, Alt+X, or Ctrl+E.

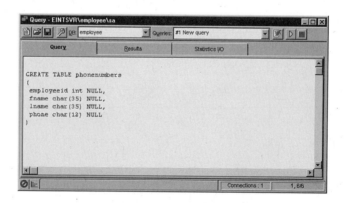

The Query tab is where you type the SQL statements (or queries). After typing a query, press Alt+X to execute it. The SQL Query Tool automatically switches to the Results tab to display any returned information or results. The third tab, Statistics I/O, (which is not covered in this section) is used to track the execution of your queries. Try to execute the CREATE TABLE command listed previously. (If you need to delete a table, a corresponding DROP TABLE command takes the table name as a parameter.)

N O T E   When working with the SQL Query Tool, it is useful to know that you can enter multiple SQL statements in the Query tab. If you select text with the mouse before executing the query, the server only processes the selected text. If no text is selected, the entire contents of the Query tab are sent to the server, which may cause multiple messages and/or table listings to appear in the Results tab. ■

Creating a Table Graphically

SQL Enterprise Manager also has a graphical interface for creating tables. To begin, choose Manage, Tables to display the Manage Tables window. From this window you can view the structure of tables in the current database, as well as create a new table. If you enter the field information for the phonenumbers table, your screen should look like Figure 41.16.

FIG. 41.16

If you do not want to create tables with SQL code, the Manage Tables Window provides an easy alternative.

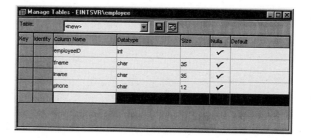

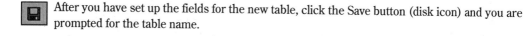

After you have set up the fields for the new table, click the Save button (disk icon) and you are prompted for the table name.

A Word About Tables

There are a few things about tables that every SQL newbie needs to know to survive. On the road to understanding SQL Server, you will find several little conceptual "speed bumps" to get over. Another is the fact that most system objects in SQL Server are defined in the same way as the objects in all of your databases. For example, every user database contains a table called sysobjects that describes the objects in the database. When you created the phonenumbers table, SQL Server updated the sysobjects table with information about the phonenumbers table. The "sys-" prefix indicates that sysobjects is a "system" table. However, it behaves just like a user table. For example, you could run the following query against it in order to list all of the objects in your database:

```
select * from sysobjects
```

TIP If you want to list all of the user tables in a database, use the following SQL statement:

```
select name from sysobjects where type = 'U' order by name
```

Of course, you could also just look at the table list in Enterprise Manager, but using this statement is sometimes quicker for fast typists.

Another good example of a system table is the sysprocesses table, located in the master database. It contains information about the currently connected users and which databases they are using.

Yet another useful item is the sp_help stored procedure. (Stored procedures are discussed later; for now, just think of them as SQL commands that are similar to SELECT.) The sp_help command, when executed without a parameter, lists all of the user tables in the current database. If you pass the sp help command a specific table name, it presents the table definition. It is used in the following manner:

```
sp_help phonenumbers
```

Adding Data to the Table

Now that you have created a table, you can add data to it. In the first part of this section, you see how to insert a record that includes a SQL statement. However, this method alone is not sufficient because SQL databases are frequently the gathering place for data from a variety of sources. You can use BCP, the SQL utility described in the second part of this section, to import data from an external file.

Adding Data with SQL

It is very easy to add records to a table with the SQL INSERT statement. Demonstrate this by adding an entry to the phonenumbers table created earlier.

First, start the SQL Query Tool by choosing Tools, SQL Query Tool. Next, enter the following SQL code:

```
INSERT INTO phonenumbers
    VALUES ( 1234, "Stan ", "McFarley",   "901-555-1212")
```

The syntax is fairly obvious, even if you are new to SQL. INSERT INTO specifies which table to affect. VALUES specifies the data values that you want entered.

After executing the INSERT statement, return to the Query tab and enter the following SELECT statement:

```
SELECT * FROM phonenumbers
```

The SELECT * statement means that you want to see all of the fields in the phonenumbers table. The results of this query are shown in Figure 41.17.

FIG. 41.17
The output of the
SELECT query appears
in the Results tab.

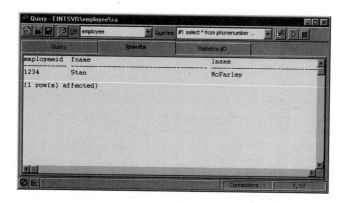

A Note About Referencing Tables

You may have noticed that a drop-down box in the Query Tab lists the current database. This box indicates your queries are executed in the context of the current database and that you can reference a table (like phonenumbers) by using only its name:

```
select * from phonenumbers
```

However, suppose you are not in the employee database but want to look at the phonenumbers table without changing the current database. If that is the case, the following statement would work:

```
select * from employee..phonenumbers
```

The official syntax is the database name, followed by the table owner, and finally the name of the table itself. A period separates each item from the other items. By omitting the table owner name in the previous line, you are assuming that the person currently logged in (sa) is the owner of the table.

The SQL Query Tool displays the data and the field names in the Results tab. If you were developing in VB, you might use the Query tool to test your SQL queries here first. It is important to verify that the data is in the table before attempting to do a remote query. Often, network problems or ODBC setup problems prevent the query from working properly from the client side. Ensuring that this data is in the server's database can speed up the debugging process because one source of the failure has been eliminated.

Part
VIII
Ch
41

Adding Data with BCP

When you develop a SQL Server application, especially one that relies on data from other systems, you need a way to import large quantities of data in an automated fashion. The Bulk Copy Procedure, or BCP, is a simple way to do this. It can take information from a text file and load it into a database table. It can also copy the data from a table out to a text file. BCP itself is a command line utility, but there are some APIs which can be used to call BCP functions from VB. This feature is especially useful if your SQL database application needs to interact with a mainframe via text files. You can demonstrate the capabilities of the BCP utility by importing several rows from a text file into the phonenumbers table.

First, you can create a sample text file to import. BCP is not very smart, so you must use a consistent format throughout the text file. Your `phonenumbers` table has four fields. To create an import file, just type values for each field into Notepad, separating those values with commas. Each record should begin on a new line. The completed data file, named IMPORT.TXT, is pictured in Figure 41.18.

FIG. 41.18

Many different types of text files can be imported into SQL Server, including tab delimited, comma separated, and fixed width.

```
1111,Brian,Siler,202-456-1414
7557,Pam,Anderson,750-123-4567
1335,Shemp,Howard,888-272-1234
1576,Wesson,Smith,901-555-1736
8765,Leena,Wayback,901-555-6789
2213,Willie,Makeit,678-376-3456
3289,Cathy,Perna,821-012-3230
9873,Jenny,Doherty,723-743-7399
7863,James,Morrison,823-976-7388
```

For SQL Server to understand the structure of IMPORT.TXT, you must also provide a *format file*. The format file is another text file that describes the input file to SQL Server. The sample format file, IMPORT.FMT, is shown in Figure 41.19.

FIG. 41.19

Format files can be typed in by hand or created by the BCP utility.

```
6.0
4
1       SQLCHAR     0     4      ","      1     employeeid
2       SQLCHAR     0     35     ","      2     fname
3       SQLCHAR     0     35     ","      3     lname
4       SQLCHAR     0     12     "\r\n"   4     phone
```

The first line of the format file, 6.0, is the BCP version number. The number 4 represents the number of fields in the destination table. Next, there is a line for each individual field. Note that the fifth column indicates the field delimiter. The fourth field's delimiter is a newline character (carriage return + line feed, represented by "\r\n"), while the rest are commas.

After you create the sample format file and data file, you can run the BCP utility. However, one more step is usually performed on the server. That step is to set an option to allow non-logged BCP. Remember, when you created the database you allocated 2M for log space. If you are importing thousands of rows, and SQL Server tries to log each BCP operation, that log space will fill up quickly. For your sample database, this problem is unimportant. But as a general rule, you should open the Edit Database dialog box and choose Select Into/Bulk Copy from the Options tab. This option is pictured in Figure 41.20.

The final step is to run the BCP utility. BCP.EXE is located in your SQL Enterprise Manager directory, usually in C:\MSSQL. BCP commands can be executed from an MS-DOS prompt window or batch file. The BCP command line is pretty long because you have to specify login and table information as well as specify all of the files involved:

```
BCP employee..phonenumbers in import.txt
➥/Usa /P /SEINTSVR -fimport.fmt
```

FIG. 41.20

If you plan to use the BCP utility, check the option for non-logged bulk copy.

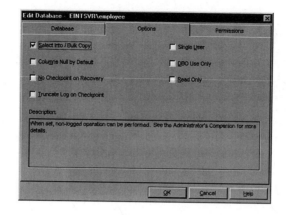

N O T E   The password ("/P" parameter) is blank in the previous example because you have not yet changed the default (sa user's) password. You can see the exact BCP syntax by typing "BCP" at the DOS prompt (with no additional parameters). ▪

After the BCP command has finished executing, it reports how many rows were copied and the time that elapsed. You can then run a SQL query to verify that the data has indeed been inserted into the phonenumbers table (see Figure 41.21).

FIG. 41.21

The results of a successful BCP operation are confirmed when you run a SELECT query on the destination table.

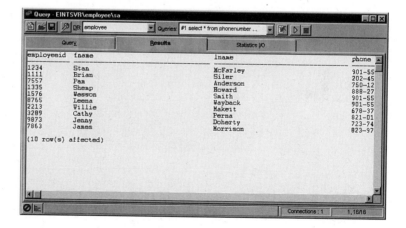

Making the ODBC Connection

Now that your database contains valid data, you can set up the ODBC connection on the client side. This connection is necessary to use the SQL server from VB. To add an ODBC data source name, open the Control Panel. Double-click the 32-bit ODBC icon to display the ODBC Data Source Administrator, as seen in Figure 41.22.

Part
VII

Ch
41

FIG. 41.22
You can install ODBC on client machines by running SETUP.EXE in Visual Basic's ODBC subdirectory.

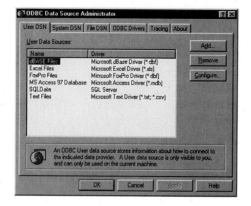

As you'll notice, the titles of the first three tabs in the dialog box end in the letters "DSN." DSN is an abbreviation for Data Source Name. Your program uses the DSN to identify an ODBC Data Source. ODBC maps the DSN to the actual driver and to the database server.

To define a data source for a SQL server, click the Add button on the User DSN tab. You are presented with the Create New Data Source dialog box, shown in Figure 41.23. In this first dialog box, choose the ODBC driver you will use to access the data.

FIG. 41.23
To configure a new data source, you must have the appropriate driver available on your system.

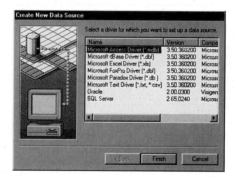

After choosing the driver and clicking the OK button, you are presented with the Setup dialog box for the particular database type associated with the driver. Choose the SQL Server Driver and press the Finish button.

The SQL Server Setup dialog box, pictured in Figure 41.24, contains the following important text input boxes that contain information about the new data source:

- *Data Source Name* This identifies the data source.
- *Description* This is a free-format description of the source.
- *Server* This server is where the database is located.

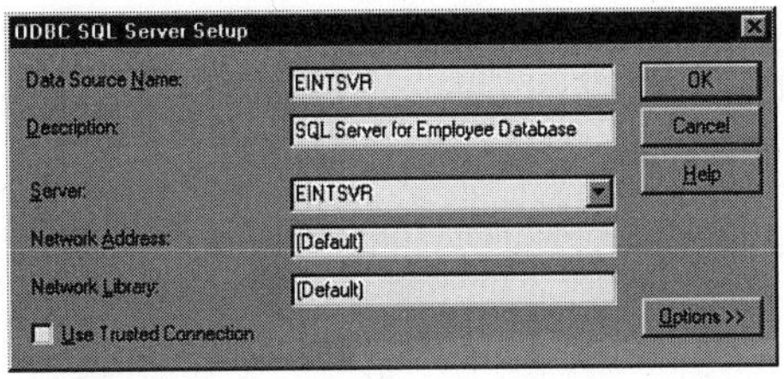

FIG. 41.24
To actually set up the data source, you must provide the server name and a unique data source name.

Having completed the definition, the data source can now be seen in the User Data Sources tab.

Accessing SQL Server Data

Accessing data stored in a SQL Server database from within Visual Basic can be done in a number of ways:

- Directly, using data access objects (DAO)

- Using a Data control (and associated bound controls) bound directly to a SQL Server data source

- Using DAO or bound controls with a temporary Microsoft Access database that has one or more tables linked to SQL Server data (This method may sound convoluted, but it usually achieves the best performance.)

Using any one of these basic data access techniques is basically the same as working with data stored in a local Access (Jet) database. The main difference is that the object(s) that work with the data are not set up and initialized in the same way.

In the remainder of this chapter, you'll learn how to set up the objects in your program so that they can connect to SQL Server data in each of the three ways just discussed. Once the objects are properly set up so that they can "see" the SQL Server data, you can use familiar methods for the rest of your program development, as you would if the data were stored in a local database.

Security Issues

Before you learn how to open the data, you should be aware of a common problem encountered in dealing with client/server database management systems: the security and permissions issue. PC DBMS programmers assume that only one user at a time will access data from their systems. In contrast, client/server programmers assume that the whole enterprise might try to access the data from their systems at the same time. They also assume that some attempted accesses will be unauthorized. Therefore, client/server systems are set up to guard against unauthorized attempts.

Part
VIII

Ch
41

The SQL Server (like other client/server systems) requires a login and a password before you can gain access to the data in its databases The SQL Server Login dialog box (see Figure 41.25) appears when the server is attaching tables to the database. If you enter a valid Microsoft SQL Server Login ID and Password, part of the security requirement will be satisfied.

FIG. 41.25

You must supply a valid SQL Server Login ID and Password to access a SQL Server table.

SQL Server also controls user access at the individual permission level. Even if a user attempting to connect with the SQL Server database uses a valid Login ID and Password, access might still be denied if the Database Administrator (DBA) has not given the user the appropriate permission on the requested table. Recall that in earlier examples you created the phonenumbers table with the sa (system administrator) account. Security was not a problem because you executed all of your queries while using the sa account. However, in the real world, users and client programs should not connect with the sa account. In addition, you might want to restrict permissions so that certain users can read from but not update certain tables.

Create a new login, QueUser. The QueUser account will grant permission to read from, but not modify, the phonenumbers table.

To create a new login, first run SQL Enterprise Manager. Choose Manage, Logins, which opens the Manage Logins dialog box. In the Login Name box, enter QueUser and type **elvis** for the password.

In order to restrict the QueUser login to only the employee database, unselect the Permit boxes for all other databases. In addition, make sure the Default box for the employee database is selected. Any ODBC connections made under this login should now have employee as their current database. Your screen should look like Figure 41.26 when you are finished.

FIG. 41.26

The Manage Logins dialog box enables you to assign and revoke the users' access to tables.

Now that the new login has been created, you should ensure that it will give your user the appropriate access to the phonenumbers table. Open the tree in the Server Manager window to the phonenumbers table and select it (single-click) with the mouse. Choose Object, Permissions. You should see the Object Permissions dialog box (see Figure 41.27).

FIG. 41.27
You can grant or revoke specific levels of access for a particular table from the Object Permissions dialog box.

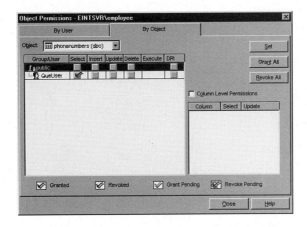

The Object Permissions dialog box shows group and user permissions related to the phonenumbers table. Notice that QueUser is a member of the Public group. All users in a group will have all of the permissions of their parent group. Therefore, unselect all of the boxes next to public so that full access is not granted by default to all Public members. In the QueUser row, leave only the Select permission selected, which means that the user can view but not modify the data. After you've set the permissions as desired, click the Set button to save them.

Now that you have granted the appropriate permissions, you can test your new login from a VB program, as described in the next section, or you can run the ISQL_w utility and log in as QueUser. If you try to run a delete statement while logged in as QueUser, you will receive an error message.

You can also control permissions with SQL statements. Suppose you want to grant update permission to QueUser. First, open a SQL Query Tool Window in the employee database while logged in as sa. Next, execute the following SQL query:

```
GRANT UPDATE ON phonenumbers TO QueUser
```

The SQL GRANT statement enables you to grant permissions for objects to specific users. Its companion statement, REVOKE , enables you to take specific permissions away from users.

Accessing SQL Server Data Through DAO

If you are already familiar with using data access objects to work with data stored in a local Jet (or other) database, it's pretty simple to use them to work with SQL Server data as well. The only thing that's different is the way the data access objects, specifically Database objects, are created.

Part
VIII

Ch
41

Accessing Data Stored in a Local Database   When you access data in a local database, you have probably used the OpenDatabase and OpenRecordset methods in a manner similar to this example:

```
sDBLocation = "C:\Data\employee.mdb"
Set MyDB = DBEngine.Workspaces(0).OpenDatabase(sDBLocation,
➥    False, False)
Set MyRS = MyDB.OpenRecordset("select * from phonenumbers")
```

In this example, MyRS becomes a Dynaset-type Recordset object that lets you work with the data stored in the underlying phonenumbers table. You could locate specific records by using the FindFirst, FindNext, FindPrevious, and FindLast methods. The following code searches for the first match for a specific last name and first name combination and displays the employee's phone number if found:

```
sCriteria = "lname = 'Doherty' and fname = 'Jenny'"
MyRS.FindFirst sCriteria
If MyRS.NoMatch Then
    MsgBox "No match.", vbExclamation, "Phone Book"
Else
    MsgBox "That employee's phone number is " & MyRS!phone & "."
End If
```

Additionally, you could edit an existing record with the Edit and Update methods, or you could add a new record with the AddNew and Update methods. All of these techniques are discussed in Chapter 32, "Improving Data Access with Data Access Objects (DAO)."

Accessing Data Stored in SQL Server   Accessing data stored in SQL server is just as easy as working with a local database. As was already mentioned, the main difference is in the way the Database object is created. To connect a Database object to SQL Server, utilize the *connect* argument of the OpenDatabase method. The *connect* argument, which in essence sets the Database object's Connect property, provides information about the source of the data being opened. To connect to a SQL Server database, use the ODBC version of the connect string. For example, if the data mentioned in the previous example were moved to the SQL Server database you created earlier in this chapter, you could replace the OpenDatabase portion of the previous code as follows:

```
sConnect = "ODBC;DSN=eintsvr;UID=QueUser;PWD=elvis;DATABASE=employee"
Set MyDB = DBEngine.Workspaces(0).OpenDatabase("", False, True, sConnect)
```

In this example, note the syntax of the connect string (stored in the variable sConnect) that is used to connect to the SQL Server. The components of the connect string are separated by semicolons. The connect string begins with the ODBC string so that the type of connection being sought is immediately identified. DSN=eintsvr identifies the ODBC source; in this case, the SQL Server named eintsvr. (Note that the ODBC source must have been configured in the Windows Control Panel's ODBC applet.). UID=QueUser and PWD=elvis are the Login ID and Password, respectively. The data source will use the Login ID and Password to log in the user. DATABASE=employee identifies the database that contains the data your program needs.

Once the Database object is created properly, the remainder of the code is the same as the code in the phonenumbers table you created earlier. It is still appropriate to use the instruction

```
Set MyRS = MyDB.OpenRecordset("select * from phonenumbers")
```

to open the Recordset object because the phonenumbers SQL Server table has the same name as the phonenumbers table in the previous example. In addition, the remaining example code—which searches for a particular record—can be used with no modifications.

Creating a Generic Data Access Procedure   Because using DAO with SQL Server is almost the same as using DAO with local databases, it would be wise to set up a procedure in your programs that would create the data access objects and open them appropriately. Use initialization strings of some type—which could be stored in the Registry or in .INI files—to provide an easily modified, generic data-opening routine, as shown in Listing 41.1.

Listing 41.1   Use this Generic Data-Opening Function for Both Local and Client/Server Databases by Modifying the Values of *sDBLocation* and *sConnect*

```
Function OpenData() As Boolean
    On Error GoTo OpenDataError
    OpenData = False

    'Assume that sDBLocation and sConnect are Public variables
    '  that contain the appropriate data connect information
    Set MyDB = DBEngine.Workspaces(0).OpenDatabase(sDBLocation,
    ➥False, True, sConnect)
    Set MyRS = MyDB.OpenRecordset("select * from phonenumbers")

    'If we made it this far, we've succeeded.
    OpenData = True
    GoTo OpenDataExit

OpenDataError:
    Dim sErrorInfo As String
    sErrorInfo = "Error number " & Err.Number & ": "
    sErrorInfo = sErrorInfo & Err.Description
    If MsgBox(sErrorInfo, vbCritical + vbRetryCancel) = vbRetry Then
        Resume 0
    Else
        OpenData = False
    End If
OpenDataExit:
    On Error GoTo 0

End Function
```

Part

VIII

Ch

41

Accessing SQL Server Data Through Bound Controls

Just like using DAO, connecting bound controls to SQL Server data is merely a matter of getting your program's objects set up correctly. Once bound controls are properly initialized, they work the same connected to SQL Server data as they would if they were attached to a local database.

If you've worked with the Data control and bound controls before, you know the steps needed to connect them to data properly:

- Set the Data control's DatabaseName property to the name of the local database the control should attach to. You can do this at design time or at run time.
- Set the Data control's RecordSource property to the name of the local database table (or query) that the control will retrieve its data from. You can do this at design time or at run time, but not until you have set the DatabaseName property.
- Set each bound control's DataSource property to the name of the Data control that will provide its data. You must do this at design time.
- Set each bound control's DataField property to the name of a field (in the table or in the query) that the Data control is bound to. You can do this at design time or at run time, but not until you set all of the three properties previously mentioned.

Using bound controls with client/server database systems, such as SQL Server, is very similar to using them with local databases. The main difference is that you must set the Data control's Connect property instead of its DatabaseName property. (The connect string used to set the Connect property is the same one described in the previous section.) After you've set the Connect property, you can set the Data control's RecordSource property. Then you can set the DataField property of any bound control.

Use the data model described in the previous section to set up bound controls that can access data from client/server database systems. First, add a Data control to a form. Next, add a text box (or some other control) that will be bound to the Data control. At design time, you must set the DataSource property of the bound control(s) to the name of the appropriate Data control. The rest of this task can be accomplished with code. The following example sets up a TextBox control that is bound to the phone field of the phonenumbers table in your SQL Server's employee database:

```
sConnect = "ODBC;DSN=EINTSVR;UID=QueUser;PWD=elvis;DATABASE=employee"
Data1.Connect = sConnect
Data1.RecordSource = "phonenumbers"
Text1.DataField = "phone"
Data1.Refresh
```

After is is configured, the Data control and its bound controls work just as they would if they were bound to a local database.

▶ **See** "Understanding the Data Control," **p. 804**

▶ **See** "Getting Acquainted with Bound Control Basics," **p. 808**

Attaching a Table to a Jet Engine Database

Attaching an ODBC table to a Jet (Access) table appears to be the fastest way to connect Visual Basic to a non-Access database. Doing so speeds up processing. The Jet Database Engine maintains all of the data needed to process transactions in its internal control blocks, which removes the need for Visual Basic to retrieve that information for every transaction.

The simplest way to attach an ODBC table to a Jet (Access) table is to create a "dummy" database. This database should contain a linked, or attached, table for each ODBC table you need to use. The database can be created using Microsoft Access. However, the following section will demonstrate how they can be created with the Visual Data Manager (VisData) application included with VB.

Creating a Dummy Database   First, start the VisData by choosing Add-Ins, Visual Data Manager. Then create a new 32-bit Jet database by choosing File, New, Microsoft Access, Version 7.0 MDB, as shown in Figure 41.28. You are then prompted for the name and location of your database. An empty database is created, such as the one shown in Figure 41.29.

FIG. 41.28
Visual Data Manager provides a convenient way to create a new database.

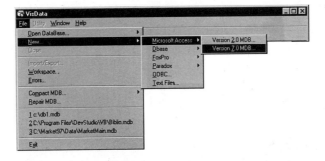

FIG. 41.29
An empty database is ready for tables to be added to it.

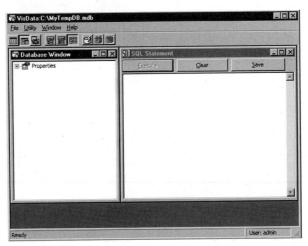

Part

VIII

Ch

41

Once the database has been created, you need to attach the desired ODBC/SQL Server table(s) to it. From VisData's Attachments window, which is shown in Figure 41.30, select Utility, Attachments.

FIG. 41.30

VisData's Attachments window helps you manage attached tables.

Click the New button to bring up the New Attached Table window. Supply the appropriate information to attach to the desired table, as shown in Figure 41.31.

FIG. 41.31

You can enter ODBC connection information in the New Attached Table window.

Be sure to select the `AttachSavePWD` check box so that the user isn't asked for the ODBC password every time the table is used. Once you've entered the connection information, you need to navigate to the appropriate ODBC (or other) data source where the data is located. Once you have reached this data source, the Attachments window is updated to reflect your new attached table (see Figure 41.32).

FIG. 41.32

The Attachments window lists the database's linked tables.

Finally, select Close from the Attachments window to return to VisData's main database window, which is shown in Figure 41.33.

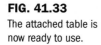

FIG. 41.33
The attached table is
now ready to use.

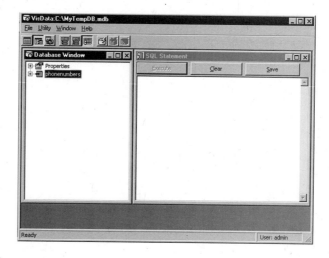

Now the hard part is over. Your database is ready to use. You can use the attached table as a source for DAO and/or bound control processing just as if the table were a local database. In fact, it *is* a local database. The Jet engine manages the attachment so that your program can work with it locally.

Why Work So Hard?

The motivation for going to this much trouble must now be clear. A considerable database engine is required to run a full-blown, 100+ user system over a network. Issues of performance, concurrent access, and security become incredibly significant when large numbers of users are accessing a database. In the past, the solution was to buy a huge mainframe and connect everyone to a terminal. Although this solution did eliminate some problems, such architecture, which requires that all data be stored in a central location, does not work well with the "data everywhere" enterprises of the late 1990s.

When Visual Basic and SQL Server work together, users can manipulate remote data as if it were local to their machines and still maintain the data integrity and security of a mainframe.

Stored Procedures

In addition to running queries and simple select statements executed from client programs, SQL server is capable of running *stored procedures*. Stored procedures are lines of SQL code stored as part of the database on the SQL server. Like Visual Basic functions, stored procedures can include parameters, local variables, return values, and calls to other stored procedures. They can be executed directly from a Query Window or client program. SQL server has many built-in stored procedures, such as the sp_help procedure described earlier.

Part
VIII

Ch
41

N O T E The "sp_" prefix is a naming convention for stored procedures. Since SQL Server's built-in
system procedures use the "sp_" prefix (and "xp_" for "extended stored procedure"), you
might want to come up with your own prefix for user procedures. In this chapter, "gp_" will be used to
indicate a general-purpose procedure. ▪

The main uses for stored procedures are the following:

- *Triggers* These are procedures that are executed by SQL Server whenever you modify
  the data in a specific table. For example, information being loaded into a SQL table from
  the mainframe could "trigger" the processing of that new information.

- *Rules* These regulate what you can or cannot enter in a column of a table. Rules enable
  the database administrator to restrict the data allowed in the database. For example, a
  rule could be written that would reject Social Security numbers that contained alphabetic
  characters.

- *Stored Procedures* Like full-blown programs, stored procedures manipulate data on the
  server. These procedures are discussed further in the following section.

Creating a Simple Stored Procedure

You can create stored procedures from the Query window in Enterprise Manager or from the
Stored Procedures command in the Manage menu. Open a Query window in your sample
employee database by choosing Tools, SQL Query Tool. Use the CREATE PROCEDURE statement
to create a simple stored procedure.

First, you need to come up with something for your stored procedure to do. For example,
suppose you want to retrieve a phone list for a specific area code. From a standard SQL statement, this is pretty easy to do:

```
SELECT lname, fname, phone FROM phonenumbers
    WHERE substring(phone,1,3) = "901"
```

However, suppose you want to make the previous statement more generic, like a function. An
input parameter for the area code is required to do so. The user should not have to put quotes
around the area code parameter because it is an integer. However, your SQL statement should
still require a string in its WHERE clause.

Like most programming concepts, the best way to learn is by doing. Execute the following
code in a Query Tool window. A new stored procedure, gp_listarea, is created.

```
CREATE PROCEDURE gp_listarea
@areacode SMALLINT
AS
DECLARE @strarea char(3)
SELECT @strarea=convert(char(3),@areacode)
SELECT lname, fname, phone FROM phonenumbers
    WHERE substring(phone,1,3) = @strarea
```

The first line in the previous code is the beginning of the CREATE PROCEDURE statement, which
is followed by the new procedure name. Next, any input parameters are listed—in this case, the
"@areacode" parameter.

The keyword AS separates the procedure declaration from the local variables and the SQL code. Note the way the first SELECT statement is used to assign a value to the @strarea value. The next SELECT statement, unlike the first SELECT statement, returns a result set to the user.

Once the stored procedure has been created, it can be executed from the Query window. First use its name and then use the input parameters in order:

```
gp_listarea 901
```

Stored procedures can also be executed from Visual Basic, as discussed in the next section.

Calling Procedures from Visual Basic

It is important to remember that stored procedures and the methods of calling them are DBMS-specific and as such are outside the scope of the ODBC standard. For this reason, stored procedures called from Visual Basic programs must be called as *SQL pass-through* queries. When you use this option, Visual Basic does not interpret the query; it simply passes the entire query directly through to SQL Server (or another ODBC database source), which will interpret and execute the query.

Visual Basic provides two methods of executing a SQL pass-through query:

- A Database object's Execute method can be used to execute queries that do not return a value or record set. The Execute method's dbSQLPassThrough option causes the query to be passed through to the back-end database engine.

- The OpenRecordset method's dbSQLPassThrough option can be used when the procedure returns a value or record set.

In the past, applications consisted of programs and data files. Because the data files were application-specific, you could incorporate all data validation checks in the applications and thus ensure the integrity of the data. However, when using DBMS, such as SQL Server, incorporating the data validation checks is not enough. You can still build applications that can carry out all of the data validation and store the data on the server. But your users are free to connect to the server with MS Access or MS Excel and carry out modifications to the data, thus bypassing your data validation routines.

To overcome this problem, create data validation and triggers in the database. However, this solution falls short when you try to implement business rules. For example, assume that Northwind Traders decides that important customers should receive an extra discount. An important customer is defined as a person to whom you have sold more than $5,000. How would you implement the rule that defines what an important customer is?

You could always code it up in your application, but this would cause a problem. People using Access or Excel to modify data would also have to code it up. In addition, when the rule changed you would have to ensure that all applications that used the rule were changed. To avoid these problems, you can implement this rule as a stored procedure on the server and have each application call it.

Part
VIII

Ch
41

To implement the rule for Northwind Traders, you need to total all of the orders for a given customer. and somehow indicate that the customer is an important customer if the total is greater than $5,000. The first element of your procedure is to write the SQL statement to summarize the orders as follows:

```
SELECT SUM(order_amount) FROM orders
    WHERE customer_id = @CUST_ID
```

This statement summarizes the orders for a customer. The `customer_id` is equal to the variable `CUST_ID`. (`@CUST_ID` is the format used to indicate a variable in Transact SQL.)

Next, you need to add the code to see if the total is over $5,000. As you might have suspected, the `IF` statement is used in the following way:

```
IF (SELECT SUM(order_amount) FROM orders
        WHERE customer_id = @CUST_ID) > 5000
    /* An important customer */
ELSE
    /* A normal customer */
```

The final element of your procedure is to return the value to Visual Basic. Transact SQL provides the following three methods of doing this:

- A `SELECT` statement
- A `RETURN` statement
- A `PRINT` statement

Visual Basic cannot retrieve values that are returned via the `RETURN` statement, so you can rule that method out. If you use the `SELECT` statement, your procedure will be the following:

```
IF (SELECT SUM(order_amount) FROM orders
        WHERE customer_id = @CUST_ID) > 5000
    /* Important Customer */
    SELECT 1
ELSE
    /* Normal Customer */
    SELECT 0
```

If you use the `PRINT` statement, the procedure will be the following:

```
IF (SELECT SUM(order_amount) FROM orders
        WHERE customer_id = @CUST_ID) > 5000
    /* Important Customer */
    PRINT "Important Customer"
ELSE
    /* Normal Customer */
    PRINT "Normal Customer"
```

The only other task to be carried out that involves the stored procedure is to implement the stored procedure on MS SQL Server. The code required to create the procedure using the `PRINT` statement is as follows (the code to create the procedure is similar and is not reproduced here):

```
CREATE PROCEDURE IMPORTANT_CUSTOMER @CUST_ID VARCHAR(5),
AS
IF (SELECT SUM(order_amount) FROM orders
        WHERE customer_id = @CUST_ID) > 5000
    /* Important Customer */
    PRINT "Important Customer"
ELSE
    /* Normal Customer */
    PRINT "Normal Customer"
```

This code tells MS SQL Server to create your stored procedure IMPORTANT_CUSTOMER and also tells the server that the procedure accepts a certain parameter, CUST_ID.

Having implemented the procedure on the server, you should now learn how to call it from Visual Basic. The method you should choose depends on whether or not the procedure returns a value. In this case, both procedures return a value, so call it via an SQL Pass-Through query.

Because the query using the SELECT statement is simpler to call, start with it. The code required to create and execute the query is as follows:

```
Private Sub cmdProc_Click
    ' Demo calling stored procedure that returns
    ' a value via a select statement
    Dim db As Database
    Dim qry As QueryDef
    Dim rsStoredProc As Recordset
    Set db = DBEngine(0).OpenDatabase(App.Path & "\PROCS.MDB",
➥False, False)
        Set qry = db.CreateQueryDef("ImportantCustomer")
        qry.SQL = "EXEC IMPORTANT_CUSTOMER 'ALWAO'"
        qry.Connect = "ODBC;DATABASE=Northwind;DSN=NWIND;UID=Sa;
        ➥PWD="
        qry.ReturnsRecords = True
        Set rsStoredProc = qryTemp.OpenRecordSet()
        MsgBox "Returned value was :" & Str$(rsStoredProc(0))
        qry.Close
        rsStoredProc.Close
    db.Close
end Sub
```

In this segment of code, you create a QueryDef named ImportantCustomer. Set its SQL property to the MS SQL Server-specific command required to call the stored procedure. Set its Connect property to the values required to connect to the server. Indicate that it will return records by setting its ReturnsRecords property. Once you have created the query, create a record set based on it to obtain the return value.

In the case of your stored procedure that uses the PRINT statement, things are little different. Rather than returning a result set, the query returns a message. These messages are trapped by the Jet engine and stored in a table, based on the user's name. First look at the code required to call the procedure and then examine the database to find out how the message is stored.

```
Private Sub cmdProc_Click
    ' Demo calling stored procedure that returns
    ' a value via a select statement
    Dim db As Database
    Dim qry As QueryDef
    Set db = DBEngine(0).OpenDatabase(App.Path & "\PROCS.MDB",
    ➥False, False)
        Set qry = db.CreateQueryDef("ImportantCustomer")
        qry.CreateProperty("LogMessages", dbBoolean, True)
        qry.SQL = "EXEC IMPORTANT_CUSTOMER 'ALWAO'"
        qry.Connect = "ODBC;DATABASE=Northwind;DSN=NWIND;UID _
        =Sa;PWD="
        qry.ReturnsRecords = False
        qry.Execute
        qry.Close
    db.Close
end Sub
```

In dealing with the PRINT statement, start out the same way as you did for the SELECT statement. Create a QueryDef and set its properties. In addition to setting the Default properties, create one user-defined property, LogMessages. This property tells Jet to log the messages returned by the PRINT statement to a table in the local database, PROCS.MDB.

From Here...

You have now learned how to use a commercial database product, Microsoft SQL Server, to implement Visual Basic programs that access data stored on a server. This approach frees Visual Basic programs from the limitations of ordinary PC-based database management products. It enables you to implement systems that scale to hundreds of users, while maintaining Visual Basic's application development advantages.

To increase your understanding of databases and client/server, you should examine the following chapters:

- See Chapter 28, "Building Database Applications," for information on creating Visual Basic databases.

- Go to Chapters 29, "Using the Visual Basic Data Control," and 30, "Doing More with Bound Controls," for information about the Data control and bound controls.

- See Chapter 31, "Improving Data Access with Data Access Objects (DAO)," for coverage of data access objects.

- Go to Chapters 32, "Using Remote Data Objects (RDO)," and Chapter 34, "Database Access with ActiveX Data Objects (ADO)"for information about connecting to remote databases.

- See Chapter 39, "Using the Web, Databases, and Visual Basic," for a discussion of databases and the World Wide Web.

CHAPTER 42

Using Visual Basic with Microsoft Transaction Server

There has been a lot of discussion in the client/server industry over the past few years about second-generation and three-tier architectures. These are applications infrastructures where the applications processing is not divided into the traditional two parts—the front-end user interface and the back-end database—but into at least three separate and distinct parts. There are several reasons that this application architecture is superior to the original client/server model:

Distributed transaction processing

Distributed transaction processing involves spreading the logical and business rule processing over multiple computers. You learn how this works, and how it requires you to design your applications differently from traditional client/server applications.

Microsoft's Transaction Server

Microsoft recently released its own Transaction Server for use in building distributed transaction architectures. You see how Transaction Server works, and how it uses Microsoft's Distributed Common Object Model (DCOM) technology to provide a transparent platform for building distributed applications.

Visual Basic and Transaction Server

One key advantage offered by Microsoft's Transaction Server is the ability to build modules by using Visual Basic (along with Microsoft's other development languages). You learn what is involved in building modules with Visual Basic that integrate with Transaction Server.

- *Scalability*   The capability of an application architecture to scale up to hundreds of simultaneous users

- *Manageability*   The ease with which problems can be isolated, updates distributed, and configurations managed

- *Transparency*   The capability to switch server processing from one particular computer to another, as dictated by scheduled or unexpected system outages

One key difference between traditional, or two-tier, client/server models and second generation, or three-tier (also known as *n*-tier, where *n* is any number greater than two), client/server architecture is in the use of what is known as *middleware*. Some of the most popular kinds of middleware are *Transaction Monitors* and *Object Request Brokers (ORB)*. Microsoft's Transaction Server is a combination of these two technologies, providing you with a flexible and powerful middleware component that can be used to build very large-scale distributed processing applications with minimal coding and configuration effort on your part.

N O T E   The typical three-tier architecture is composed of the following three tiers:

- The presentation tier, which consists primarily of the user-interface, running on the desktop computer.

- The business-logic tier, which consists of shared application processing logic modules, running on one or more application servers. Each application server is connected to multiple desktop computers.

- The data server tier, also known as the database server. Usually, one database server serves multiple application servers. If there are multiple database servers, they are normally spread out over a large geographical area with the common data replicated between them. ■

In this chapter, you take an in-depth look at Transaction Server, how it works, and how you can use it in building applications. You also look at what's involved to use Transaction Server with Visual Basic, and how you can design and code Visual Basic objects that can be integrated into Transaction Server to provide a large, distributed application. In the chapters immediately following this one, you look at how Transaction Server can be integrated into a Web site to provide the ability to build an integrated enterprise-wide application system that stretches far beyond what most Web sites currently are capable of. ■

Understanding Distributed Transaction Processing

Imagine that your company has several independent database systems: one for maintaining the current inventory in the company warehouse, one for maintaining all items that have been requisitioned and should be arriving on the receiving dock, and a third database for maintaining customer orders and shipping information, as shown in Figure 42.1.

In this company, when an order comes in, the order is entered into the order entry system, which produces a shipping order. This order is then taken to the warehouse, where each item in the order is removed and taken to the shipping dock to be packaged and sent to the customer. While at the warehouse, the employee filling the order finds that one or two items are out of stock. The employee then takes the order to the requisition department and has the missing items back ordered for later shipping.

At each of these points, the individual systems have to be updated so that they are up-to-date. Even the Shipping Dock system has to be updated to produce an accurate shipping bill-of-lading, which correctly reflects the back-ordered items.

FIG. 42.1

A typical catalog company has systems to track current inventory, requisitioned or back-ordered items, and shipping orders.

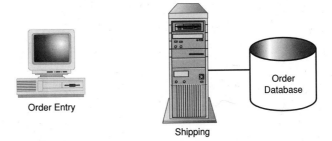

Order Entry

Order Database

Shipping

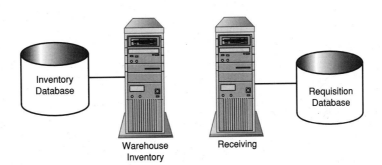

Inventory Database

Warehouse Inventory

Receiving

Requisition Database

This seems like a lot of wasted and duplicated effort. Wouldn't it make a lot more sense to connect all these systems so that they could all exchange the necessary information to perform most of these tasks themselves? If you put a network in place and connect all these systems to the network, as in Figure 42.2, the potential for these systems to exchange the appropriate information can be realized.

Unfortunately, anyone who has attempted to connect separate systems in this way knows that after you have all the systems on a network, the work is just beginning. Enabling all these systems to work together is what middleware is all about.

Part
VIII

Ch
42

FIG. 42.2

A network can be used to connect all the company systems so that they can exchange information with each other.

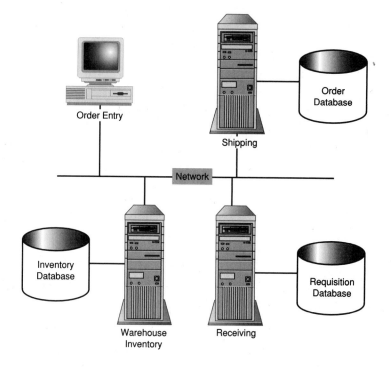

Order Entry

Shipping

Order Database

Network

Inventory Database

Warehouse Inventory

Receiving

Requisition Database

Transaction Monitors

The original idea behind the client/server computing model was to split the application processing between two computers. This split was normally made where the database processing was all performed on the server, while all application processing was performed on the client, as in Figure 42.3. This model works reasonably well, except that it is fairly easy to overload the client system with data, if the application allows the database to return more data than the client computer can handle. (Remember, this model was used when the standard desktop computer was a 386 with 4M of RAM, and a 486 was a high-end workstation.)

As the number of active users of these early client/server systems increases, the workload on the database increases. A normal application maintains an open connection to the database server for the entire time the application is running, as in Figure 42.4. This requires the database server to have additional processing power to service all those open connections, even if they are sitting idle. This also increases the cost associated with the database itself, as most traditional database license prices are based on the number of users that can be connected to the database simultaneously.

As the number of databases that an application needs to interact with increases, the number of open connections that the application must maintain also increases. This adds to the processing load on the client computer, as well as the network management and configuration. The total number of connections that must be maintained can be calculated as the number of clients times the number of database servers to which the client connects (see Figure 42.5).

FIG. 42.3

The original idea behind client/server computing was to split application processing between the client and the database server.

FIG. 42.4

As the number of users increases, the number of active connections that must be serviced by the database increases.

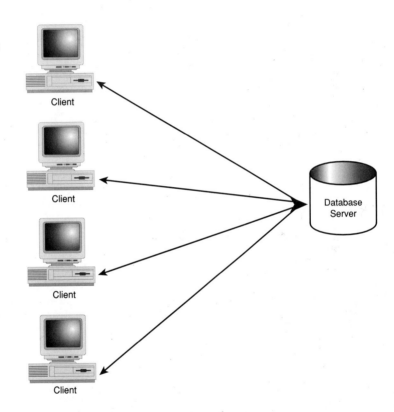

This is a lot of configuration information that has to be maintained for each client computer. If one of the databases that an application uses has to be taken offline and the backup database brought online, the configuration of each and every client that connects to the database has to be updated to reflect the new database server (with care taken not to update the wrong database server information).

FIG. 42.5
The total number of open connections that must be maintained can be calculated as the number of clients times the number of servers.

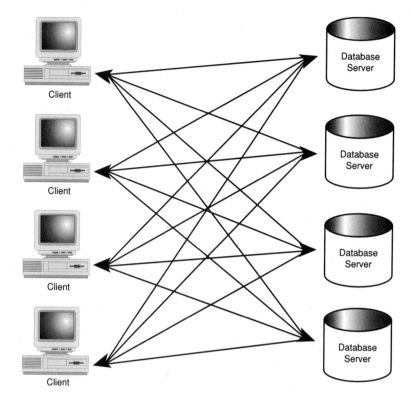

This is one of the primary problems that Transaction Monitors were designed to solve. A Transaction Monitor goes between the client systems and the database servers, as in Figure 42.6. Each client maintains a single connection to the Transaction Monitor instead of the database servers. Likewise, the Transaction Monitor maintains connections to each database server. This allows the Transaction Monitor to act as a traffic cop, passing each database query or update to the appropriate database, and to maintain only as many open database connections as are currently required, which allows the database servers to run more efficiently.

Object Request Brokers

Object Request Brokers (ORBs) fall into a different category of middleware from Transaction Monitors. ORBs provide location transparency to application modules and services. What *location transparency* means is that when an application needs to interact with a server process, the application does not need to know where that specific server process is located on the network. The only process that the application knows the location of is the ORB client stub located on the same machine as the application.

FIG. 42.6
A Transaction Monitor reduces the number of open connections to the number of clients plus the number of database servers.

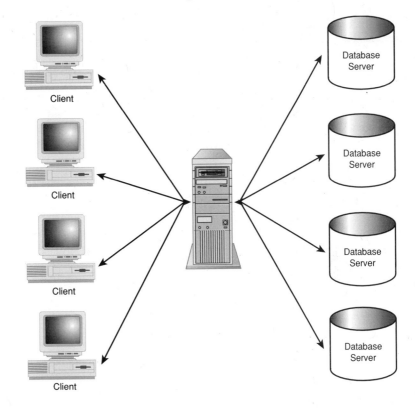

The ORB knows where all server processes are running, or on which machines the server processes can be run. If a particular server process is not running when an application requests access to it, the ORB starts the server process on one of the machines for which the process is configured to run. The client application does not know on which server the requested process is running, or if it's even running. The ORB keeps track of all server processes for the client applications. The ORB can even perform load balancing between two or more servers running the same process so that each server is servicing around the same number of requests.

Returning to your catalog sales company, it is reasonable to expect that the order entry system would use various services that could be located on a series of servers on the company network. One of these services could be a sales tax engine, which calculates the tax for each of the customer orders. It makes sense to keep this set of calculations on a server, as tax laws have a tendency to change. By keeping this processing module on the server, it would be a lot easier to update in this one location every time the tax laws changed, as opposed to having to update every order entry workstation in the company.

Part

VIII

Ch

42

Another service the order entry systems might take advantage of is a credit check application. By having all the credit authorization requests go through a single server, it would be easy for that one server to maintain an open connection to the credit clearinghouse, as compared to outfitting each workstation with a modem and the software to call up the credit authority (not to mention all the additional phone lines this would require).

A third service the order entry systems might use is the business rules engine. This system would calculate shipping costs based on the quantity or weight of the ordered items or enforce minimum purchase rules. By keeping this module on one or two servers, you could easily update the module as the powers-that-be within the company change the business rules that this module has to enforce.

Considering that the functions provided by these server modules are critical to the core business of your catalog sales company, it's important to make sure that these modules are always available for the order entry systems. To make sure that these systems have high availability, they are probably loaded onto more than one system. If the order entry application made direct accesses to these services, each copy of the application would have to know which machines each service is running on at all times. By using an ORB, the individual copies of the order entry application don't know and don't care what servers any of these services are running on. The ORB takes care of making the connections and passing the results back to the order entry application, as seen in Figure 42.7.

FIG. 42.7

The ORB relieves the client application from having to know which server computer each service is running on.

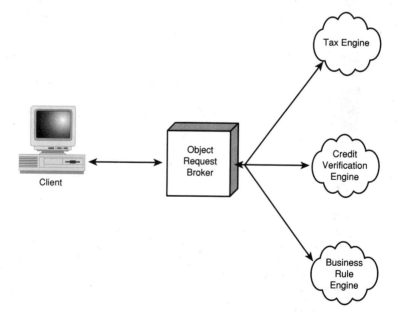

Introducing Microsoft Transaction Server

Microsoft's Transaction Server is somewhat of a cross between a Transaction Monitor and an ORB, although it tends to lean more toward the ORB set of functionality. If you are running an application on a Windows NT system that has Transaction Server installed and you are using ODBC to access a database, Transaction Server transparently inserts itself between your application and the database to manage that connection (as well as all the other open connections to the same database). Transaction Server also allows application functionality to be built as a series of ActiveX DLLs and distributed across a network. You take a quick look at how Transaction Server provides this functionality.

Managing Database Connections

When an application is using the ODBC interface to access a database, Transaction Server takes control of the database connection to provide a more consistent access, quicker connection, and transaction control. By placing itself between the application and the database, Transaction Server can open its own connection to the database and provide the application with a connection to Transaction Server instead of the database. This allows Transaction Server to limit the actual number of database connections to only as many as are necessary to service all the application requests, as seen in Figure 42.8. This relieves the work of maintaining all those connections from the database, allowing the database to perform better and be more responsive.

FIG. 42.8
By inserting itself between the applications and the database, Transaction Server can limit the number of active connections that the database has to service.

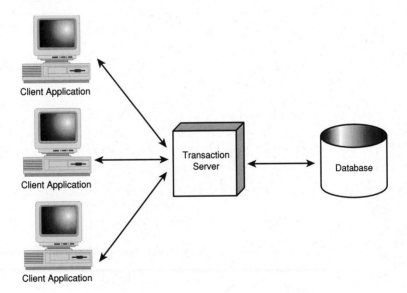

Client Application

Client Application

Client Application

Transaction Server

Database

Part
VIII

Ch
42

When an application closes its connection to the database, Transaction Server maintains the open database connection so that the connection can be reused either by the application that closed the connection, or by another application (or client) that needs the same connection to the database. This allows application modules to be written in such as way that they maintain only open connections to a database for those periods of time that the application really needs to have the connection open. The performance penalty for closing and reopening a database connection is removed, making it more attractive to write applications that release the associated resources when they are not needed.

N O T E By combining Transaction Server with OLEISAPI2 applications, the remaining bit of overhead that you want to eliminate by using a SAPI interface is removed by allowing the OLEISAPI2 application to disconnect each time it finishes servicing a client call, and to reopen the database connection with each new call. ▓

Managing Distributed Objects

Transaction Server provides a facility for building distributed applications by allowing you to build functionality into a series of ActiveX server DLLs and then distribute them across your network. Transaction Server keeps track of where each DLL is located and performs all the communications between them and your application. This allows you to move your functionality modules to the most suited computer on your network, based on the processing load that each module requires to service all the requests from applications needing the services of the module. You can even double up and place the same module on multiple computers and allow Transaction Server to load balance between the copies.

Transaction Server also provides you with the ability to easily mix and match modules of functionality that are built in a number of different programming languages. Any language that can be used to build ActiveX Server DLLs can be used to build modules to be used with Transaction Server. This includes not just Microsoft's Visual Basic, Visual C++, and Visual J++, but also Borland's Delphi, Symantec's Café, and Micro Focus's Visual Object COBOL. This enables you to pull functional modules together into a large distributed application, regardless of what language was used to build the individual modules, as seen in Figure 42.9. This capability of Transaction Server allows you to build an extensive application using best-of-breed modules and components.

Transaction Coordination

One of the many beneficial features of Transaction Server is its capability to provide coordinated transaction control through many objects and over multiple databases. Transaction Server accomplishes this by using the Microsoft *Distributed Transaction Coordinator (DTC)*. The DTC was first released as part of SQL Server 6.5 and is included with Transaction Server. It provides a low-level infrastructure for distributed transactions, controlling and guaranteeing the outcome (either commit or rollback) across multiple databases and database connections. The DTC uses a two-phase commit protocol to ensure the outcome of these transactions.

FIG. 42.9
By using Transaction Server, you can use functional modules that were built by using many different languages together in a single application.

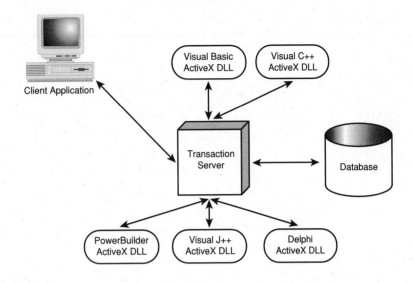

Two-Phase Commit

A *two-phase commit* is where a data change (insert, update, or delete) to two or more databases absolutely has to be successful in all, or unsuccessful in all. If the situation dictates that the changes to the data cannot be committed in one of the databases without being committed in the others, then two-phase commit is necessary.

Integrating Visual Basic Classes with Transaction Server

When building server objects for use with Transaction Server, a couple of basic details have to be taken into consideration. These details affect the design of your objects and add a small amount of Transaction Server-specific code. You look at each of these aspects as you build a simple Server object. You'll add on to this object with additional objects a little later.

Initializing the Visual Basic Project

All server objects for use with Transaction Server have to be built as ActiveX DLLs, regardless of which programming language is used. After you have started a new Visual Basic project with the target being an ActiveX DLL, you need to include a reference to the Microsoft Transaction Server Type library by choosing Project, References, as seen in Figure 42.10.

On the CD

The object that you are building is the warehouse inventory adjuster object for your catalog order company. For now, you'll be using just two database tables in a SQL Server database. These tables are the Products table, shown in Table 42.1, and the Inventory table, shown in

Table 42.2. You'll be adding additional tables as you expand the scope of this system later in this chapter. The SQL to create these tables and populate them with some initial data can be found on the CD.

FIG. 42.10
You need to include a reference to the Transaction Server Type library when building a server object for use with Transaction Server.

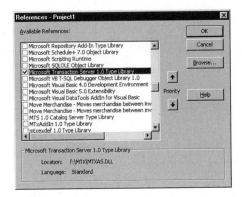

Table 42.1 The Products Table

Column Name	Data Type	Size
Prd_ID	int	
Prd_Name	char	8
Prd_Desc	varchar	40
Prd_StandardStock	smallint	

N O T E The int and smallint data types in SQL Server are a fixed size and thus do not require a column size to be specified. An int data type is defined as 4 bytes, and a smallint is defined as 2 bytes. The available number range that can be stored in each of these data types depends completely on what range of numbers can be represented by each of these storage allocations. ▪

Table 42.2 The Inventory Table

Column Name	Data Type
Prd_ID	int
Inv_Count	smallint

To wrap up your project initialization, name your project InvMaint and give the project a description to remind yourself what this module does at a later time. You'll also mark this module for unattended execution so that it can run in a multithreaded environment. You have a single class in this project, and you name it InvMnt.

TIP It a good idea to provide a project description for the modules that you are building in this and the following chapters. You will be building several DLLs and including references to DLLs that you have already built. By including a description, the project description will show up in the Project References dialog box. If you don't provide project descriptions, only the project name will show up in the References dialog box.

Stateless Objects

One key to designing and building well-performing components for use with Transaction Server is to design the objects and methods to be *stateless*. This means that there are no variables and conditions that are held within the object, all variables are received as parameters to the methods that are exposed, and all results are returned either as the result of the method or through method parameters that were passed by reference.

The primary reason for building stateless objects is because the same method can be called as part of several different applications. These calls can happen simultaneously or sequentially; regardless, it is a high likelihood. Keep in mind that this is the same approach that you need to take when building thread-safe objects. It is possible to build stateful objects for use with Transaction Server, but these objects entail a lot more overhead and will not perform as well when the system is under load.

There are a few exceptions to the rule of building stateless objects. These exceptions consist primarily of information that the object will be using across all processes, such as the database connection information. To build your server object in a stateless manner, your declarations are limited to the database connect string and the error number that you will be raising in the event of an error. This gives us the class declaration section found in Listing 42.1.

Listing 42.1 INVMNT.CLS—Error Number and Database Connection Information

```
Option Explicit
'We always return the same error number
Private Const ERROR_NUMBER = vbObjectError + 0
'The database connect string
Private Const strConnect = "DSN=InvMntDB;UID=TxsVB;PWD=vbtxs;"
```

Transaction Context

When an object is running with Transaction Server, it is running in the context of a transaction. A transaction attribute controls how the objects interact with the current transaction within their context. This transaction attribute can have any one of four values, as seen in Table 42.3.

Table 42.3   The Transaction Attribute Values

Value	Description
Requires a transaction	Objects with this transaction attribute must execute within the scope of a transaction. If the object that called this object was executing within a transaction, this object executes within the scope of the same transaction as the calling object. If the calling object is not executing within a transaction, this object starts (and completes) a new transaction.
Requires a new transaction	Objects with this transaction attribute always begin (and complete) a new transaction, whether or not the calling object was running within a transaction.
Supports transactions	Objects with this transaction attribute execute within the scope of the transaction of the calling object, if that object was executing within a transaction. If the calling object was not executing within a transaction, this object executes without a transaction.
Does not support transactions	Objects with this transaction attribute always execute outside the scope of any transactions, regardless of the transaction state of the calling object.

By using the transaction attribute on all objects running within Transaction Server, you can configure an extensive transaction model, separating objects into distinct transactions that are executed within the midst of other transactions.

For example, take the collection of objects in Figure 42.11. In this model, Object A calls Object B, which calls Object C. All three objects have their transaction attributes set to Requires a transaction. The transaction in which all three objects are executing will commit the changes made by these objects only if all three objects execute successfully. If any one of the three has an error, the entire transaction is rolled back.

Notice that Object D is also called by Object B; only Object D has its transaction attribute set to Does not support transactions. This means that Object D does not affect the transaction within which Objects A, B, and C are executing. Object E, which is called by Object D, might have its transaction attribute set to either Requires a transaction or Requires a new transaction. Because Object D does not support transactions, Object E always starts a new transaction, which is completely independent of the transaction of Objects A, B, and C. If Object E is set to Requires a transaction and Object D is set to Requires a new transaction the transaction of A, B, and C would continue to be independent of the transaction of D and E.

FIG. 42.11

The transaction attribute enables you to define separate transactions within other transactions.

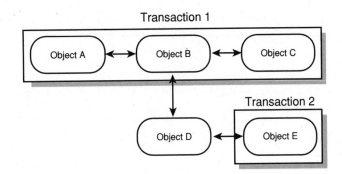

Being able to tell Transaction Server whether an object was successful—or that it ran into problems—requires a few lines of code. The first task is to get a reference to the transaction context object, which is the transaction context within which the object is executing. This is done with the GetObjectContext() function, as in the following code:

```
Dim ctxObject As ObjectContext
Set ctxObject = GetObjectContext()
```

After you have the transaction context, you can use the context object's two methods, SetComplete and SetAbort, to tell Transaction Server whether the object was successful or not. If your object executed without any problems, you use the following call to tell Transaction Server that you are finished and that the transaction can be committed:

```
ctxObject.SetComplete
```

If your object ran into problems, you can use the SetAbort method to tell Transaction Server that the transaction should be rolled back, as follows:

```
ctxObject.SetAbort
```

N O T E The context object (ctxObject) does more than just control the transaction. It also controls the objects and the resources that those objects are consuming. When an object calls SetComplete or SetAbort, the object is informing Transaction Server that the object is finished processing and can be deactivated, and all the system resources being used by the object can be reallocated to other objects. If SetComplete or SetAbort are not called, Transaction Server does not know when it can release those resources for use by other objects. This eventually bogs down system performance. ■

You can take this understanding of how to use the context object to build your first object, which will maintain the current inventory of a particular product in the warehouse. Name your method ChangeInv, and pass it a product identification number and the number of the product that you want to move. A positive number adds inventory to the warehouse, and a negative number removes inventory from the warehouse. You also have this object tell how much of the product remain in stock after your request, and (in the case of a negative number) how much needs to be back-ordered to fulfill your request. You can do this with the code in Listing 42.2.

Listing 42.2 INVMNT.CLS—Adding and Removing Inventory from the Warehouse with the *ChangeInv* Method

```
Public Function ChangeInv(aiPrdID As Long,aiChange As Integer, _
                           ByRef aiBackOrder As Integer, _
                ByRef aiStockRemain As Integer ) As Integer
    Dim ctxObject As ObjectContext
    Dim rdoConn As rdoConnection
    Dim strSQL As String
    Dim rdoRS As rdoResultset

    'Get our object context
    Set ctxObject = GetObjectContext()

    'Set up error handling
    On Error GoTo ErrorHandler

    'Obtain the RDO environment and connection
    Set rdoConn = rdoEngine.rdoEnvironments(0).OpenConnection("", _
                            rdDriverNoPrompt, False, strConnect)

    'Update the Inventory
    strSQL = "UPDATE Inventory SET Inv_Count = Inv_Count + " _
            + Str$(aiChange) + " WHERE Prd_ID = " + Str$(aiPrdID)
    rdoConn.Execute strSQL, rdExecDirect
    'Get resulting inventory which may have been further
    'updated via triggers
    strSQL = "SELECT Inv_Count FROM Inventory WHERE Prd_ID = " _
                                        + Str$(aiPrdID)
    Set rdoRS = rdoConn.OpenResultset(strSQL, rdOpenForwardOnly, _
                            rdConcurReadOnly, rdExecDirect)
    'Did we retrieve anything?
    If rdoRS.EOF <> True Then
        'Yes, get the current inventory count
        aiStockRemain = rdoRS.rdoColumns("Inv_Count")
        'Check if the inventory is overdrawn
        If aiChange < 0 And aiStockRemain < 0 Then
            'Set the number of items that are backordered
            aiBackOrder = 0 - aiStockRemain
            'Update the inventory count
            strSQL = "UPDATE Inventory SET Inv_Count = 0 WHERE Prd_ID = " _
                                        + Str$(aiPrdID)
            rdoConn.Execute strSQL, rdExecDirect
            aiStockRemain = 0
```

```
        Else
            'We are not overdrawn, so we don't need to back order anything
            aiBackOrder = 0
        End If
    Else
        'No, there is a problem as no product inventory record was found
        Err.Raise ERROR_NUMBER, "Could not find product inventory record."
    End If

    'Close the database connection
    rdoConn.Close

    'Tell Transaction Server that we have successfully completed our task
    ctxObject.SetComplete

    'Return a 0 to signal that we were successful
    ChangeInv = 0

  Exit Function
ErrorHandler:
    'Have we connected to the database yet?
    If Not rdoConn Is Nothing Then
        'If so, then close the connection
        rdoConn.Close
    End If

    'Tell Transaction Server that we had problems
    ctxObject.SetAbort
    'Indicate that an error occured
    ChangeInv = -1
End Function
```

Registering Visual Basic DLLs with Transaction Server

After you have built your Visual Basic project into an ActiveX DLL, you need to register it with Transaction Server before it can be used. You do this through the Transaction Server Explorer. After you have started up the Transaction Server Explorer, you need to make sure that the DTC is running. You can tell if the DTC is running by looking at the color of the screen in the computer icon for your computer. When the DTC is running, the screen on the computer icon is green, and when the DTC is not running, the computer screen is black. If the DTC is not running, click the Computer icon for your computer, and then choose Tools, MS DTC, Start.

Creating Packages Before you can start registering components in Transaction Server, you must have a package into which you are going to install the components. *Packages* are logical groupings of objects that are generally used as a unit. As a general rule, you will want to create one package for every set of applications that uses Transaction Server. You can create a package by following these steps:

1. Select the Packages Installed folder.

2. Choose <u>F</u>ile, <u>N</u>ew from the main menu.

3. On the first screen of the Package Wizard, choose Create an Empty Package, as seen in Figure 42.12.

FIG. 42.12

For registering components that you have built, you need to create an empty package into which the components will be installed.

4. Type a name for the package, as shown in Figure 42.13. For your catalog sales company package, call it **Inventory**. Then click the <u>N</u>ext button.

5. If the objects in the package need to run under a specific login account, select the <u>T</u>his User radio button and provide the user name and password. Otherwise, leave the default radio button selected, as in Figure 42.14, which runs all the objects in the package under the account of the users using the applications that use the objects in this package. (This can affect the availability of resources for the process components, depending on how the access privileges are configured in the system security.)

6. Click the Finish button to complete the process.

Installing Components   After you have a package, you can begin installing components into it. This is where you register the ActiveX DLLs that you have and will be creating with Visual Basic. You can register your components by following these steps:

N O T E   In the following section, the terms *install* and *register* are used interchangeably. Installing components into Transaction Server and registering components with Transaction Server are two ways of referring to the same process. ■

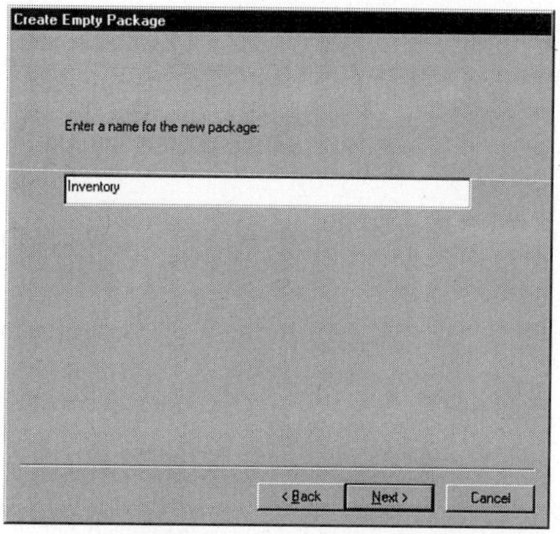

FIG. 42.13

Provide the package with a name that reflects the functionality, or family of applications, that the components in the package will be providing.

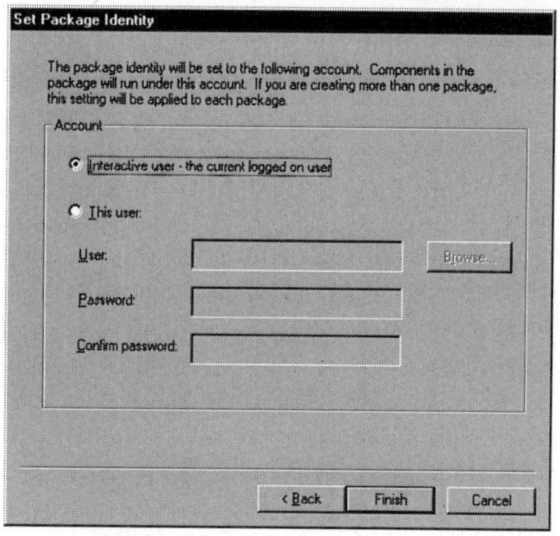

FIG. 42.14

If you need the components in the package to execute as a specific user login, for resource access purposes you need to specify the user login and password.

1. Select the Components folder in the package into which you want to install the components, as seen in Figure 42.15.

2. Click the Install New Component(s) button, as seen in Figure 42.16.

3. Click the Add Files button and select the ActiveX DLL that you are wanting to register, as seen in Figure 42.17.

4. When you return to the Install Components dialog box, the upper list box should show the DLL that you are installing, and the lower list box should show all the visible classes within the DLL, as in Figure 42.18.

FIG. 42.15
Select the Components folder in the package that you have created to install the newly created Inventory package.

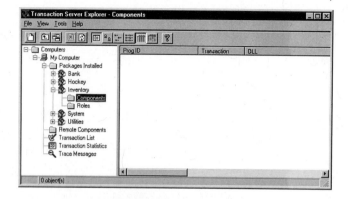

FIG. 42.16
If you are installing components that you have built, you need to select the Install New Components option.

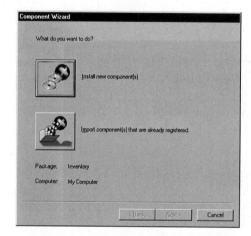

FIG. 42.17
You need to select the DLL containing the components that you are installing.

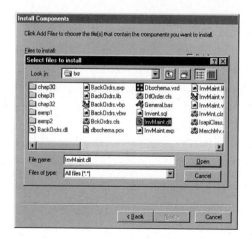

FIG. 42.18

The Install Components dialog box displays all the components found in the specified DLL.

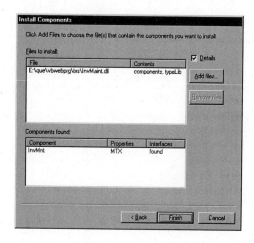

5. Click the Finish button, and the components are installed in Transaction Server, as seen in Figure 42.19.

FIG. 42.19

After you install the components, they show up in the Transaction Server Explorer.

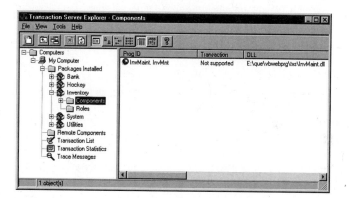

6. Select the components you just installed, one at a time, and right-click the mouse. Select Properties from the pop-up menu. On the component Properties Editor, select the Transaction tab, and select the transaction attribute desired for the currently selected component, as in Figure 42.20.

Whenever you recompile any ActiveX DLL built in Visual Basic, you need to refresh the component information in Transaction Server. This can be easily done by deleting the component from the Transaction Server Explorer and reinstalling the component by following the same steps as were followed to install the component originally. Another way of refreshing the component information in Transaction Server is by choosing Tools, Refresh All Components.

Part
VIII

Ch
42

FIG. 42.20
You need to open the
properties dialog box for
the installed component
to specify the transac-
tion attribute setting.

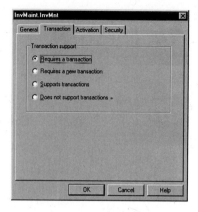

A Note from the Authors

In working with Transaction Server 1.0, the Refresh All Components menu option often scrambles the
component names in the package that we were working with. We end up with what looks like two or
three copies of the same component in the package, and some components appear to be missing.
We do not notice any problems when attempting to run the applications that used these components, but most often end up deleting all the components from the package and reinstalling them.
Hopefully, this behavior will be corrected in an upcoming service pack.

Calling Transaction Server Objects from Visual Basic

Now that you have a component built and registered with Transaction Server, how do you call
the method in this object from a Visual Basic application? First, the Visual Basic application has
to get a reference to the Transaction Server object. After the reference has been acquired, the
object's methods can be called. A reference to a Transaction Server object can be acquired in
three ways:

- Using the CreateObject function
- Using the GetObject function
- Using the New keyword

N O T E   A fourth method for acquiring a reference to a Transaction Server object by another
Transaction Server object is through the use of the Context Object's CreateInstance
method, which creates the object reference in the same transaction context of the current object
(depending on the new object's transaction attribute). You see this method in use in the following
chapters. ■

From a Visual Basic application, you can create your reference to your Inventory Maintenance
object with the following code:

```
Dim obj As Object
Set obj = CreateObject("InvMaint.InvMnt")
```

N O T E The same Transaction Server object could have been created with the New keyword by using the following code:

```
Dim obj As New InvMaint.InvMnt
```

As a general rule, all Transaction Server components can be referenced in the same way as all other ActiveX server objects. Transaction Server works with the operating system to make sure that when Transaction Server components are requested, they are created and called within Transaction Server. ■

From here, you can call the object methods by referencing them via the object you have just created, as so:

```
obj.ChangeInv(iiProductID, CLng(txtCount.Text), iBackOrder, iCurInventory)
```

If you build a simple little applet by using the Remote Data Control and the Data Bound Combo Box, you can call your object and see how Transaction Server works. The first thing you need to do is to add the Remote Data Control and the Data Bound List Controls to your Toolbox. You do this by choosing Project, Components, as seen in Figure 42.21.

FIG. 42.21

You have to include the Data Bound List Controls and the Remote Data Control into your Visual Basic project before you can use them.

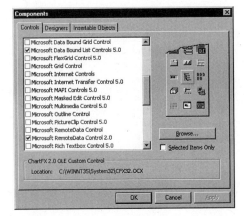

With these two controls, you can build a simple form that provides a drop-down list box, containing the product descriptions from the Products table in the database. You accomplish this by binding the Remote Data Control to the ODBC configuration you have set up for your database, providing the user name and password that you have configured, and using the following SQL to populate the Remote Data Control:

```
SELECT * FROM Products
```

Next, specify the Remote Data Control as the row source for the Data Bound Combo Box and specify the Prd_Desc column as the ListField, DataField, and BoundColumn. You add a text box for the user to enter the number to add or remove from the inventory, and you have the form seen in Figure 42.22. The complete source code for this form can be found on the CD.

Part

VIII

Ch

42

FIG. 42.22

Use a very simple form to call the method in the object you registered with Transaction Server.

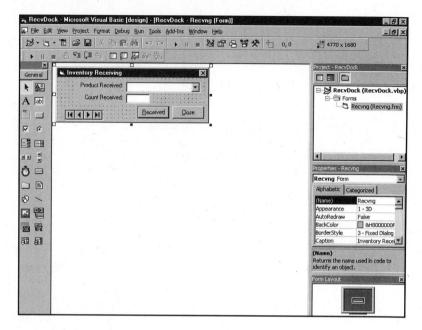

Setting the Product ID

When the user selects a product, you need to have a variable into which to place the selected product ID, so you declare a variable in the form declarations by using the code in Listing 42.3.

Listing 42.3 RECVNG.FRM—Declaring a Variable for Holding the Selected Product ID

```
Option Explicit
'We always return the same error number
Private Const ERROR_NUMBER = vbObjectError + 0
'The currently selected product ID
Dim iiProductID As Long
```

You set the product ID into this variable whenever the user selects a product from the list by navigating in the Remote Data Control to the currently selected row, and then getting the Prd_ID column from that row, as in Listing 42.4.

Listing 42.4 RECVNG.FRM—Grabbing the Product ID from the Remote Data Control When the User Selects a Product

```
Private Sub dbcProduct_Click(Area As Integer)
    Dim varCurRecord As Variant

    'What is the currently selected item?
    varCurRecord = dbcProduct.SelectedItem
```

```
'Move to the selected record in the result set
MSRDC1.Resultset.Move 0, varCurRecord
'Grab the product ID
iiProductID = MSRDC1.Resultset!Prd_ID.Value
End Sub
```

CAUTION

The code that you are using to grab the selected product ID is dependent on the Remote Data Control being used for the `ListField`, `DataField`, and the `BoundColumn`. If you use the Remote Data Control for just the `ListField`, the `dbcProduct_Click` method will error out with an invalid bookmark error when you first click it to select a product. This is due to the fact that the control starts out with the selected item of 0, which the Remote Data Control interprets as an invalid row. It is after you have selected a row that the control has a valid row number, but you cannot get to that point.

N O T E You could easily have waited until the user clicked the Received button when calling the Transaction Server object to determine the selected item. Calling the object in this way requires additional code in the specific method isolated by using the method that you have. This is not really better, but it does isolate the functionality, allowing you to focus on the core functionality that you are implementing in each method. ■

Calling the Transaction Server Object

When the user clicks the Received button, you can create a reference to the Transaction Server object that you created by using the earlier code snippets, and you can display for the user the resulting stock and back-order amounts with the code in Listing 42.5.

Listing 42.5   RECVNG.FRM—Creating a Reference to Your Transaction Server Object and Calling the Method That You Created in the Object

```
Private Sub cmdReceived_Click()
    Dim iBackOrder As Integer
    Dim iCurInventory As Integer
    Dim ProgID As String
    Dim obj As Object

    'Set up the error handling
    On Error GoTo ErrorHandler

    'Decide which component to use
    ProgID = "InvMaint.InvMnt"

    'Create the appropriate object
    Set obj = CreateObject(ProgID)
    'Were we able to create the object?
    If obj Is Nothing Then
```

Part

VIII

Ch

42

continues

Listing 42.5 Continued

```
        MsgBox "Create object " + ProgID + "failed."
        Exit Sub
    End If
    'Call the object method
    If obj.ChangeInv(iiProductID, CLng(txtCount.Text), iBackOrder, _
                                iCurInventory) = -1 Then
        Err.Raise ERROR_NUMBER
    End If

    'Release the object
    Set obj = Nothing

    'Display for the user what the current inventory is
    MsgBox "New Inventory received, current backorder count = " _
            + Str$(iBackOrder) + " and current inventory = " _
            + Str$(iCurInventory)
    Exit Sub

ErrorHandler:
    'Show the user the error message
    MsgBox "Error " + Str$(Err.Number) + " : " + Err.Description
    Exit Sub
End Sub
```

Before you run your form, let's change the view in the Transaction Server Explorer to show the status of your object. You do this by selecting the Components folder in the package you have created. Next, choose View, Status. The right side of the Explorer now shows the activity status of your object. If you run the form with the Transaction Server Explorer where it can be seen, you can watch as the object that you created earlier is instantiated and executed, as seen in Figure 42.23.

FIG. 42.23

When the form that you have created calls the object that you registered in Transaction Server, you can watch as the object is created and run.

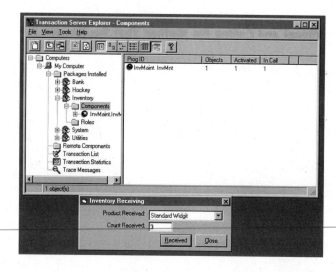

From Here...

In this chapter, you learned about the different types of middleware, and how they enable client/server applications to be scaled for use by many more users than traditional client/server applications. You saw how Microsoft's Transaction Server is somewhat of a cross between a Transaction Monitor and an Object Request Broker, providing all the functionality of the first with a substantial amount of the functionality of the latter. Later, you saw how you can build objects with Visual Basic that can be registered with Transaction Server for use by applications running on client systems. Finally, you saw how you can build a front-end application that uses the object that you built and loaded into Transaction Server.

From here, you might want to check out the following chapters:

- For information about connecting to remote databases, see Chapters 32, "Using Remote Data Objects (RDO)," and 33, "Database Access with ActiveX Data Objects (ADO)."

- For discussion of databases and the World Wide Web, see Chapter 39, "Using the Web, Databases, and Visual Basic."

- For a look at using Visual Basic in a client/server context (with SQL Server as the example), see Chapter 41, "Using Visual Basic in a Client/Server Environment."

- To learn about some of the security systems that you might want to put in place before opening up your systems, check out, "Building Security into Your Applications" on the accompanying CD-ROM.

Part

VIII

Ch

42

Advanced Topics

CHAPTER 43

Creating a Visual Basic Add-In

However sophisticated the VB5 Integrated Development Environment (IDE) may be, there is always something that is missing. Sometimes you want advanced word processor-like capabilities in your code editor (a spell checker, for instance); other times you need a more flexible way to align, center, and resize the controls on your forms.

It is understandable that Microsoft couldn't anticipate all of the wishes of every Visual Basic programmer on earth, so they made a smarter move: if you need a special capability in the VB environment, you only have to write an add-in and install it within the VB5 IDE. ■

Introducing add-ins

VB5's Integrated Development Environment (IDE) is highly customizable, using software components written in Visual Basic itself.

Discovering the add-ins included with Visual Basic

You find many good examples of add-ins in the VB package, including the little known Template Manager that lets you reuse the controls, the menu, and the routines that you use on a regular basis.

Exploring the inner life of an add-in

Understanding what happens when the VB environment is launched and when it activates your add-ins is invaluable knowledge when trying to write bulletproof add-ins.

Analyzing the VB IDE object model

Your add-ins can do almost anything that a programmer does manually while working with the VB environment, provided that you spend some time learning the intricacies and subtleties of the VB IDE object model.

Introducing Add-Ins

The concept of *add-ins* dates back to Visual Basic 3.0, when a few third-party software companies created and marketed a number of utility programs that looked as if they were part of the VB environment, while adding many features that the environment itself did not offer. The most successful product of this category is Sheridan's VB Assist, which is still one of the most popular accessories for VB programmers.

These add-ins usually offer a wide range of functions—VB Assist currently has more than fifty—ranging from simple code generators for message boxes and common dialogs, to complex stuff, such as a customized Property Window and a palette to resize and align controls on the active form at design time. Many add-ins include other useful utilities, such as screen-capture programs, icon extractors (a tool that extracts icons from DLLs, EXEs and other files), or clipboard enhancers (to keep multiple code fragments in the clipboard).

Writing a VB3 add-in was not simple at all. The big problem wasn't writing the code to implement the utility function itself; rather, it was integrating the add-in with the VB editor. In fact, Microsoft never made public the internal details of the VB3 environment, and add-in developers had to find out everything by themselves, using several unorthodox techniques and tools, including reverse engineering, debuggers, and spy programs. This approach worked 99 percent of the time, but certainly did not contribute to the overall robustness of the majority of add-ins on the market.

The situation dramatically changed when VB4 was released. In fact, this version of the Integrated Development Environment (IDE) exposes several internal structures to the outside in the form of objects that can be controlled by an external program, written in VB or most other programming languages. This innovation enabled developers to build more reliable add-ins and, in fact, the number of such tools increased significantly, especially in the shareware market. Generally speaking, add-ins were more robust and reliable and it seemed it was no longer necessary to resort to all sorts of unorthodox tricks to make them work.

Unfortunately, Visual Basic 4.0 exposed only a small number of objects to the outside; they only permitted to add a menu item to the Add-Ins menu, to handle the controls on the current form and to intercept a few user actions, such as saving or loading a new project. These features enabled Microsoft to enhance the VB IDE with Visual SourceSafe—a well-known and powerful control version program that was, and still is, included in the Enterprise Edition—but were not enough for the demanding add-in developers who were forced to continue to use non-standard techniques for their programs to work flawlessly in the VB IDE.

Visual Basic 5.0 has completely changed the picture. The VB5 IDE exposes nearly every internal structure to the outside, from the active project down to the individual forms, controls, and procedures; it also exposes all its windows, menus, and toolbars. You now may add new items to any menu—not just the Add-Ins menu—and to any toolbar. Finally, you can intercept most of the actions performed in the environment by the developer: when a new component is loaded, saved, or becomes the current one, when a control is selected, when a menu or toolbar command is invoked, and so on. In other words, you now have the capability to control almost every aspect of the environment and, therefore, you can write powerful add-ins that automate many complex or boring routine tasks.

Most VB programmers are interested only marginally in building add-ins, which they perceive as tools that should be purchased from specialized vendors. However, I strongly believe that add-ins are a great opportunity for the smart developer. In fact, even if third-party add-ins are very useful and likely to significantly reduce your development time, they cannot cover every possible need.

Add-ins are especially helpful to corporate programmers, who often have to adhere to a set of rules for writing source code—from consistent names for variables and controls, to coherent indentation of loops, If, and Select blocks. Thus, a wise team manager might decide to write down these standards and build an add-in that enforces them. Imagine an add-in that pops up whenever a developer creates a new control, asking for its name and rejecting default, meaningless strings such as Text1 or Command1.

However, add-ins are not for corporate programmers only. The time you spend writing and testing your personal add-in will save you time whenever you use it. Not convinced yet? Just think of this: Suppose you write a trivial code generator that saves you about five minutes a day. This means that you save about 20 hours in a year, not counting all the time you save by not having to debug the code generated by the add-in. Once you are familiar with add-ins, you might be able to write such simple utilities in just two or three hours; thus, you can save at least sixteen or seventeen hours!

Installing, Activating, and Using VB5 Add-Ins

You should be familiar with the concept of add-ins already as a number of such utilities were shown in action in previous chapters. This section summarizes what you've learned so far and illustrates a few details of their inner workings, which are not immediately apparent.

The Add-Ins in the VB5 Package

The following list is a quick review of all the add-ins that come with Visual Basic 5.0:

- *Application Wizard* Produces the complete skeleton of an SDI or MDI application, including menus, toolbars, and data-access forms. This is likely to be the first add-in that you learn to use, as well as the most useful one.

- *Data Form Wizard* Creates forms that read and save data to database tables, including forms that access data in a master-detail relationship (see Figure 43.1).

- *Class Builder* Lets you both create new classes and hierarchies and add new properties, methods, and events to existing ones.

- *ActiveX Control Interface Wizard* Enables you to save hours of hard, error-prone manual work when building ActiveX controls that are based on existing, simpler constituent controls.

- ■ *Property Page Wizard* Simplifies greatly the creation of property pages to associate with existing ActiveX controls.

- ■ *ActiveX Document Migration Wizard* Converts a regular application and its forms into an ActiveX Document that can be sent over the Internet and viewed from within a compatible browser, such as Internet Explorer.

▶ **See** Chapters 24, "Creating ActiveX Controls," 25, "Extending ActiveX Controls," and 27, "Creating ActiveX Documents," for more information about ActiveX Controls, Property pages, and ActiveX Documents.

- ■ *Wizard Manager* Makes the creation of wizard-like applets a visual job.

- ■ *API Viewer* Offers a quick way to add declarations of external Windows API functions to your program by using a simple and intuitive interface. It is an executable program that also can be installed in the Add-Ins menu (see Figure 43.1).

▶ **See** Chapter 46, "Accessing the External Functions: The Windows API," for more information about Windows API.

FIG. 43.1

Two of the many add-ins that come with Visual Basic 5.0.

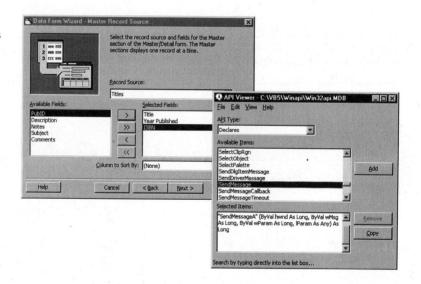

- ■ *Add-In Toolbar* Appears as a toolbar that enables you to quickly launch other add-ins (an example is provided later in this chapter).

Users of the Visual Basic 5.0 Enterprise Edition have the following two additional add-ins to use:

- ■ *Microsoft Data Tools* Visually organizes remote SQL Server databases and related queries.

- ■ *T-SQL Debugger* A precious tool for those programmers who need to run Transact SQL stored procedures on a SQL Server database and want to trace their execution and debug them from a remote workstation.

The Template Manager Add-In

There is one more add-in of which you might not be aware—the Template Manager add-in. This add-in comes in the Tools\Unsupprt\Templmgr directory and is not automatically installed by the Visual Basic Setup procedure. It adds three new items to the Tools menu that enables you to easily reuse code snippets and individual routines, controls and their related code, and entire menus (see Figure 43.2).

FIG. 43.2

The Tools menu after you have correctly installed the Template Manager.

The installation procedure of the Template Manager is completely manual and requires that you carefully follow these steps (the instructions assume that your CD-ROM drive is D: and that Visual Basic has been installed in the directory c:\vb5):

1. Copy the Template Manager DLL into the VB5 directory; from the MS-DOS prompt, execute the following command:

   ```
   copy d:\Tools\Unsupprt\TmplMgr\Tempmgr.dll c:\vb5
   ```

2. Register the DLL by using the RegSvr32 utility in the \Tools\RegUtils directory:

   ```
   d:\Tools\RegUtils\RegSvr32 c:\vb5\Tempmgr.dll
   ```

3. Create the directories for menu, control, and code templates and then copy the templates that come on the CD-ROM:

   ```
   xcopy d:\Tools\Unsupprt\TmplMgr\Template\*.* c:\vb5 /s
   ```

4. Using Notepad or another text editor, open the VBADDIN.INI file in the \WINDOWS directory and add this line at the end of the [Add-Ins32] section:

   ```
   TempMgr.Connect=1
   ```

5. Run Visual Basic: If everything is okay, you should find three more items in the Tools menu (refer to Figure 43.1).

Now you can easily add standard menus to your forms (see Figure 43.3), as well as controls and routines, and you can even create your own customized templates with the following directions:

- For customized menu templates, create a blank form, add the menus that you want to include in the template, and then save the form with a descriptive name in the c:\vb5\Template\Menus directory.

- For customized control templates, create a blank form, add one or more controls to it, and then save the form in the c:\vb5\Template\Controls directory.

■ For customized code snippet templates, create a blank BAS form, add the routine(s) you want to include in the template, and then save the file with a descriptive name in the c:\vb5\Template\Code directory.

FIG. 43.3

Three standard menus have been added to the underlying form by double-clicking the corresponding menu icon.

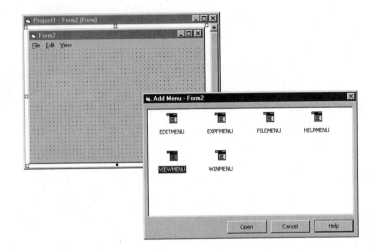

Activating an Add-In

As a developer, you probably already know how to activate an add-in, especially if you already used the add-ins that were provided with Visual Basic 4.0. However, a few minor details have changed, so it's better to tell the whole story from the beginning.

Note that this section discusses *activating* an add-in, not *installing* it. The installation process consists of copying the relevant files to the hard disk; an add-in should have been properly installed by using its own setup procedure—before being activated.

Using the Add-In Manager

The most common way to activate one all of the add-ins that comes in the VB5 package, or that you buy from third-party vendors, is through the Add-In Manager, a command found in the Add-Ins menu.

The Add-In Manager dialog box shows all of the VB5 add-ins currently installed in the system (see Figure 43.4). You activate and deactivate individual items simply by marking and unmarking the corresponding check box.

In most cases, as soon as you activate an add-in, a new item is added to the Add-Ins menu; in other cases, you'll see a brand new submenu. However, there are add-ins that affect menus other than the Add-Ins menu (for instance, the Template Manager, discussed previously), or that add a custom toolbar. Finally, there also may be add-ins that do not have any user interface, which quietly work in the background until the developer does something that wakes them up.

FIG. 43.4

The Add-In Manager dialog box, which lists all the add-ins that have been installed on the system.

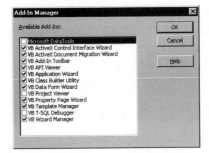

Customizing a Toolbar for Easy Add-In Access

If you work intensively with add-ins, you may find it convenient to prepare a customized toolbar—or add a custom icon to an existing toolbar—that gives you quick access to the Add-In Manager dialog box (see Figure 43.5).

FIG. 43.5

Take advantage of VB5 customizability to build a personal toolbar with all your favorite commands, including a shortcut to the Add-In Manager dialog box.

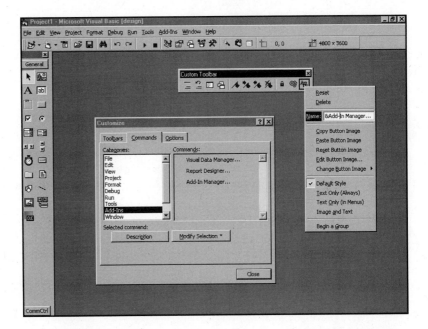

To create a custom toolbar, follow this procedure:

1. Right-click any existing toolbar; then select the Customize command.

2. In the Toolbar tab of the Customize dialog box, click the New button and then create a new toolbar.

3. In the Command tab, select a menu in the leftmost list box, then drag-and-drop selected items onto the toolbar just created.

4. Right-click the new toolbar, then use the commands on the pop-up menu to customize each toolbar button with a caption, an icon, group separators, and so on.

Editing the VBADDIN.INI File

Behind the scenes, the Add-In Manager modifies the VBADDIN.INI file found in the \WINDOWS directory. This is a text file that includes a list of all the add-ins currently installed in the system. The format of the list is rather intuitive; here are the contents of a typical VBADDIN.INI file:

```
[Add-Ins32]
VBSDIAddIn.Connect=0
AppWizard.Wizard=1
WizMan.Connect=1
ClassBuilder.Wizard=1
AddInToolbar.Connect=1
ControlWiz.Wizard=1
DataFormWizard.Wizard=1
ActiveXDocumentWizard.Wizard=1
PropertyPageWizard.Wizard=1
APIDeclarationLoader.Connect=1
PrjViewer.Connect=0
TempMgr.Connect=1
```

As you can see, the format of all the lines, apart from the [Add-Ins32] header, is the same:

```
server-name.class-name = 0¦1
```

The server name is unique to the add-in, and usually resembles the add-in's descriptive name. The class name is the name of the class that the add-in exposes to the VB5 IDE (more on this later in the chapter). Often, this class is called Connect or Wizard, but this is just a convention, not a strict rule. For instance, all the add-ins that you create using VB5's Add-In template expose a Connect class, unless you manually change this name before compiling.

The digit that follows the equals (=) symbol is 1 if the add-in is to be activated as soon as the VB5 IDE is loaded into memory, and 0 if the add-in is installed but is not automatically activated at VB5's startup. In practice, all add-ins that are marked with 1 appear in the Add-ins menu, while the others do not.

Each time you modify the settings inside the Add-In Manager dialog box, the VB5 IDE modifies this file, so that the next time you run the Visual Basic environment, you'll find exactly the same set of add-ins that you left in the previous session.

Of course, now that you know what happens behind the scenes, you can also edit the VBADDIN.INI file yourself by using any text editor, such as Notepad. In fact, you probably will be obliged to do so when you have to install an add-in that comes without a professional setup procedure, exactly as you did for the Template Manager add-in.

Note that you cannot add a line to the VBADDIN.INI file unless you know the exact add-in name and class name used by the add-in. This information usually is found in the documentation or a Readme.txt file that comes with the add-in. This is not a problem with the add-ins that you create on your own.

The Add-In Toolbar

The Add-In Toolbar is an add-in provided with Visual Basic 5.0; its function is to provide a way to activate any add-in quickly. You can activate the Add-In Toolbar exactly as you do with any other add-in: by using the Add-In Manager dialog box.

There are two methods to make the Add-in Toolbar show the icon of a given add-in:

■ You can manually add (or remove) an add-in to the Add-In Toolbar: just click the +/- button (the leftmost button on the toolbar), then choose the Browse command and select the DLL or EXE file corresponding to your add-in (see Figure 43.6).

■ The add-in automatically adds itself to the Add-In Toolbar during its setup routine; the majority of the add-ins that come with VB5 follow this approach. It is also said that the add-in *registers* itself with the Add-In Toolbar. For more information about this registration procedure, see the language manuals.

FIG. 43.6

You can manually add any add-in to the Add-In Toolbar by clicking its +/- button, and then selecting the right DLL or EXE file.

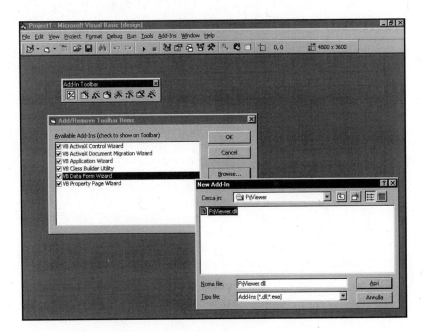

It is interesting that the list of the add-ins recognized by the Add-In Toolbar is distinct from the list that you see in the Add-In Manager dialog box. In fact, the Add-In Toolbar is capable of dealing with add-ins that are not registered in the VBADDIN.INI file, even if this opportunity is rarely exploited by commercial add-ins.

The Add-In Toolbar offers two important advantages to the add-in user. First, the add-in is always available and highly visible on a toolbar, without having to be activated through the Add-In Manager dialog box or invoked from the Add-Ins menus. Second, the add-in is launched only when the user actually needs its functions.

The latter point is very important because when Visual Basic starts, it activates all the add-ins that are marked with a 1 in the VBADDIN.INI file; this initialization step must be performed for every add-in in the list, and therefore may take several seconds.

Conversely, when an add-in is registered only in the Add-In Toolbar (and not in the Add-In Manager), Visual Basic won't initialize it during its startup, thus saving some precious time. Of course, you have to activate the Add-In Toolbar itself, which is one add-in, but this takes only a fraction of the time it would take to load all the add-ins you might have installed.

The first time you run a given add-in from the Add-In Toolbar, it goes through its initialization procedure; therefore, you are not really saving any time—you are simply procrastinating the initialization step until you really need the add-in's services. In other words, you are able to quickly start Visual Basic without having to initialize a bunch of add-ins that you'll probably never use in the current session.

The Nature of Add-Ins

At this point, you should have a clear picture of what an add-in is and how it is activated, at least from the users' standpoint. Since this chapter discusses *developing* an add-in, you must understand the real nature of this kind of application. The following concepts may sound a bit too theoretical at first, but it is strongly suggested that you *do not* jump over this section: if you have the patience to follow me in this digression, you'll find no difficulty in learning all the practical, nitty-gritty details of add-in programming.

The Add-In as an OLE Client

As mentioned at the beginning of this chapter, the VB5 IDE exposes an extensive object hierarchy through which an external program can access all its inner structures and components. It is evident that any add-in that needs to manipulate such real entities (windows, controls, code procedures, and so forth) actually has to work with these objects. There is an OLE client-server relationship between the VB IDE and the add-in, where the IDE is the server that exposes the objects, and the add-in is the client that handles them.

The most important item of Visual Basic's IDE object model is the VBE object, which represents the environment that has activated the add-in. The complete VB/IDE object model is a complex tree—and I won't discuss it until later—but it is important to note that all the other entities in the hierarchy are dependent objects that are children (or grandchildren, or great-grandchildren) of the VBE object.

This hierarchical relationship means that the add-in must have a reference to the root VBE object to completely explore the object tree. As will be seen in a moment, this reference is passed to the add-in during its initialization process, when Visual Basic starts and launches all of the add-ins whose entry in VBADDIN.INI is set to 1, or when the add-in is selected later in the Add-In Manager dialog box. The add-in must save this reference somewhere for future use.

Adding the Necessary References   Because the add-in has to know how to deal with the VBE objects, and all the other objects exposed by the Visual Basic environment, when you start coding it, you must add the correct type libraries in the References dialog box. Add-ins require that the following two distinct type libraries be available; the third one is optional (see Figure 43.7):

- *The Microsoft Visual Basic 5.0 Extensibility type library, embedded in the VB5EXT.OLB file*   This library includes all the VB IDE objects (windows, components, and so forth) except those exposed by the library that is explained next.

- *The Microsoft Office 8.0 Object library, contained in the MSO97.DLL file*   This library includes a small number of user interface elements, namely menus and toolbar buttons.

- *The VB Add-In Toolbar type library, included in the AITOOL.DLL file*   This reference is necessary only if you want to register your add-in programmatically with the Add-In Toolbar

FIG. 43.7
You need to add
two types of library
references when writing
your add-ins, or three
if you also want to
register your program
with the Add-In Toolbar.

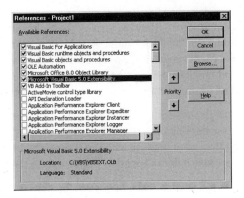

The Add-In as an OLE Server

While it is easy to understand that the add-in works as an OLE client, it is less obvious that—at the same time—the add-in also works as an OLE server, and the VB IDE works as an OLE client.

To understand why this is necessary, think of what happens when the Visual Basic IDE activates an add-in: it looks in the VBADDIN.INI file for the corresponding pair *server-name.class-name* and then asks the OLE subsystem to create an object of that class. This action brings up the add-in, which is now ready to respond to Visual Basic's requests.

The add-in therefore must expose a Public class to the VB IDE. In other words, at this stage of the process, the add-in is the OLE server, and the Visual Basic environment is the client. During the regular use roles are reversed, as seen in the previous section: the add-in handles the objects exposed by the IDE and, therefore, is the client. However, when the user requests to deactivate the add-in from the Add-In Manager dialog box, or the IDE is shutting down, the environment calls the add-in to inform it that it should remove all the menu or toolbar items it has created. Once again, the VB IDE acts as the client and the add-in acts as the server.

To summarize, it makes little sense to specify whether an add-in is an OLE client or server; the truth is that the VB IDE and the add-in communicate through OLE in a bidirectional fashion. This means that both of them have to expose a Public object that the other can see and use.

In-Process versus Out-Process Add-Ins   Visual Basic is capable of creating both in-process and out-process OLE servers. The following bullets briefly summarize the differences between the two:

- *In-process servers*   DLLs that are loaded in the same address space as the program that is using them (the client program).
- *Out-process servers*   Regular EXE programs that also expose a number of objects and, therefore, are programmable from the outside. Out-process servers are distinct processes and don't share the address space with their client applications.

It turns out that in-process DLLs generally are faster because the communication with their clients occurs in the same address space. Conversely, while EXEs are slowed down by the relatively slow cross-process communication, they offer a few advantages. First, they can be used as stand-alone applications; second, they can exploit the multitasking nature of Windows 95 and NT and can execute tasks in the background. Besides, a stand-alone OLE server can expose its objects to multiple client applications, while a DLL can serve only one client (however, multiple clients can load multiple instances of the DLL, even though these instances might take more memory and cannot communicate easily among each other).

The Visual Basic environment deals with both kinds of add-ins. However, the only out-process add-in included in the Professional Edition is the API Viewer. All the other add-ins in the box are DLLs, probably because they communicate with the IDE at a higher speed (this is not an issue with the API Viewer because it doesn't send too much data to the VB environment).

If you expect that your add-in will need to make heavy use the objects in the IDE, you should compile it as an in-process OLE server. However, you can decide which kind of server to create just before compiling the program. In other words, you initially can work with out-process components (that are easier to debug), and then switch to in-process servers if you discover later that the out-process components are too slow, often without changing one single line of code.

The *IDTExtensibility* Interface

There is one more detail to discuss. While the VB IDE can easily create an instance of the class exposed by the add-in (whose name is found in the VBADDIN.INI file), this action is not sufficient to establish a robust communication between the two programs. This communication is possible only if the VB IDE calls a specific method in the class exposed by the add-in. But, which method should the IDE call? And, above all, how can the IDE be sure that the add-in class actually exposes that method?

This is where the IDTExtensibility interface comes into action. IDTExtensibily is not a class used to create an object; rather, it is an abstract class used to define an *interface*, the set of properties and methods exposed by a class. If class A exposes a given set of properties and methods, and class B exposes the same set of members, class B is said to *implement* the A interface. This simple concept is very important both when writing robust object-oriented applications, and when working with advanced OLE concepts. Find out next what this has to do with add-ins.

Add-ins are not required to include a class with a given name—in fact, the name of the class exposed to the VB IDE is completely arbitrary—as long as that class implements the IDTExtensibility interface. This particular interface consists of the following four methods: OnConnection, OnDisconnection, OnStartupComplete, and OnAddinsUpdate.

Because the VB IDE can assume that the Public class exposed by the add-in implements this particular interface, it can invoke one of those methods without the risk of raising a runtime error. The environment invokes one of the methods when it has something to inform the add-in about its current status, as follows:

- The OnConnection method is called by the VB IDE when the add-in is being connected to the environment; this can occur when VB is starting, when the user selects the add-in in the Add-In Manager dialog box, or when the user clicks the corresponding icon in the Add-In Toolbar.

- The OnDisconnection method is invoked when the environment is about to disconnect the add-in; this occurs when the user deselects the add-in from the Add-In Manager dialog box, or when VB shuts down.

- The Visual Basic IDE calls the OnStartupComplete method when it has completed its initialization. This method is called after OnConnection only for those add-ins that are loaded at VB startup, and is never called for add-ins that are activated at a later time through the Add-In Manager or the Add-In Toolbar.

- The Visual Basic IDE calls the OnAddinsUpdate method whenever the VBADDIN.INI file has been modified.

The OnConnection and OnStartupComplete methods are similar in that they both offer the add-in an opportunity to perform all the initialization chores, such as adding one or more menu items or toolbar buttons to the VB environment user interface. The difference between the two is subtle: when the OnStartupComplete method is invoked, the add-in has an opportunity to learn which add-ins have been loaded at startup, which is not possible within the OnConnection method.

N O T E When the OnConnection method is fired, the VB IDE is still loading and might be in an unstable state: that's why it's suggested that you not act on VB IDE objects before the OnStartupComplete method is executed. ■

The OnDisconnection method is where the add-in destroys the menu items and toolbar buttons it created and, in general, restores the previous state of the environment.

The fourth method, OnAddinsUpdate, is of limited use. It fires when an item is added or removed from the list of active add-ins. You probably will need to write code for this method only if you are writing an add-in that manages other add-ins (as in the case of the Add-In Toolbar add-in).

The Life Cycle of an Add-In

It's time to see some code in action. Even if all add-ins differ from each other in their functionality and user interface, there clearly are some recurring patterns. This section introduces the routines that you're likely to find in a typical add-in.

Registration

To be recognized by the Visual Basic environment as an add-in, an application must meet the following two conditions:

- The add-in must be an OLE server and correctly registered as such in the system Registry.
- The complete name of its main Public class—the class that works as the connection with the VB IDE—must be listed in the VBADDIN.INI file.

Registering an Out-Process Add-In   If the add-in is an out-process OLE server—in other words, it is an executable stand-alone program—it can be run from the Start menu or from the Windows Explorer without being registered in the Registry or the VBADDIN.INI file. This enables the add-in to perform the registration by itself, without the need of any other support utility.

All OLE servers created in Visual Basic self-register themselves in the system Registry the first time they execute; thus, if you are building an executable add-in, you don't need to worry about the registration in the Registry, which will be handled by the VB runtime. However, it is up to you to register the add-in in the VBADDIN.INI file. This can be done using the code in Listing 43.1.

Listing 43.1   The Code that Registers the Add-In into VBADDIN.INI

```
Declare Function GetPrivateProfileString Lib "kernel32" _
    Alias "GetPrivateProfileStringA" _
    (ByVal AppName As String, ByVal KeyName As String, _
    ByVal keydefault As String, _
    ByVal result As String, ByVal resultSize As Long, _
    ByVal filename As String) As Long
Declare Function WritePrivateProfileString& Lib "Kernel32" _
    Alias "WritePrivateProfileStringA" _
    (ByVal AppName$, ByVal KeyName$, ByVal keydefault$, _
    ByVal FileName$)
' the name of the addin (modify as required)
Public Const AddInName = "PrjViewer"
Sub Main()
    Call RegisterAddIn
End Sub
Sub RegisterAddIn()
'------------------------------------------------------------
' Add a reference in the VBADDIN.INI file
'------------------------------------------------------------
Dim result As String
```

```
' skip the block if the add-in has been invoked by the OLE
' sub-system (in this case we are sure it is already
' installed as an add-in)
If App.StartMode = vbSModeStandalone Then
      ' try to read the entry in VBADDIN.INI
      result = Space$(256)
      GetPrivateProfileString "Add-Ins32", AddInName & ".Connect", _
          "***", result, _
          Len(result), "vbaddin.ini"
      If Left$(result, 3) = "***" Then
          ' the entry is not there, so we must record it
          WritePrivateProfileString("Add-Ins32", _
              AddInName & ".Connect", _
              "0", "vbaddin.ini")
      End If
End If
End Sub
```

The logic behind this routine is simple: when the program is launched, its `Main` procedure is executed, which in turn calls the `RegisterAddIn` routine. This routine uses the `App.StartMode` property to discern if the program is being activated by the user (`vbSModeStandalone`) or by the OLE subsystem (`vbSModeAutomation`); in the latter case, it obviously means that the program is already running as an add-in; therefore, the registration procedure can be conveniently skipped.

The rest of the procedure searches the VBADDIN.INI file for the *server-name.class-name* string, where *server-name* is the name of the add-in project, as appears in the Project Properties dialog box, and *class-name* is the name of the class that is instantiated by Visual Basic (the name of this class is often "Connect," "Wizard," or something similar). You can change the name of the project in the Project Properties dialog box (see Figure 43.8). If the search fails, the following line is appended to the file:

```
PrjViewer.Connect=0
```

On the other hand, if the file already contains a reference to the add-in, it is left undisturbed. This approach does not modify the current activation status of the add-in (for example, 1 if the add-in has to be loaded at Visual Basic's startup, otherwise 0).

FIG. 43.8

The name of the add-in listed in the VBADDIN.INI file is in the form *server-name.class-name*; you can modify the server name from the Project Properties dialog box.

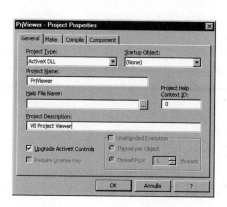

While it might be possible to manually open the VBADDIN.INI file and perform the search and creation of the line of text, the RegisterAddIn procedure follows a different, simpler approach. It uses a couple of Windows API functions that are very useful when dealing with INI files.

The GetPrivateProfileString reads an INI file for a given key and returns that associated value, or the provided default value if the key is not found. In this case, the routine searches for the PrjViewer.Connect key and returns *** if it is not found; if this happens, it manually appends the key by using another API function, WritePrivateProfileString.

▶ **See** "Calling Basic API and DLLs," **p. 1344**

If your add-in often works as a standalone program, you may decide to save a call to the RegisterAddIn—which is a relatively slow process because it involves reading, and possibly writing, a file—and execute it only when the user specifies a particular switch on the command line:

```
Sub Main
    If Command$ = "/REGISTER" Then
        Call RegisterAddIn
    End If
End Sub
```

Registering an In-Process Add-In   Unfortunately, in-process add-ins do not have a chance to run as stand-alone programs and therefore cannot register themselves either in the system Registry or in the VBADDIN.INI file. If an in-process add-in is running, it means that Visual Basic has already found a way to invoke it; therefore, registration is no longer needed.

Hence, it is evident that an in-process add-in can't register itself and, instead, has to rely on some external setup procedure to do it. The following instructions provide a "manual" procedure that you should follow to get your add-in up and running.

First, you need to register the add-in in the system Registry. The simplest way to accomplish this task is to use the RegSvr32.exe utility that comes on the Visual Basic CD-ROM, in the \Tools\RegUtils directory; just run these commands from the command prompt:

```
copy myaddin.dll c:\vb5
c:\vb5\Tools\RegUtils\RegSvr32.exe c:\vb5\myaddin.dll
```

Of course, you need to modify the paths to match the directory names on your system.

At this point, you have to edit only the VBADDIN.INI file to inform Visual Basic that a new add-in is available. You can do this in a number of ways—using Notepad, for example—but the simplest one is, by far, executing the RegisterAddIn procedure from the Immediate window of the VB environment.

Connection

When Visual Basic needs to activate an add-in, it looks in the VBADDIN.INI file and creates an instance of a class with that name; then it invokes the OnConnection method of the IDTExensibility interface of that instance to let the add-in know that it is now active. Here is the syntax for this method:

```
'--- class Connect
Implements IDTExtensibility
Private Sub IDTExtensibility_OnConnection(ByVal VBInst As Object, _
    ByVal ConnectMode As vbext_ConnectMode, _
    ByVal AddInInst As VBIDE.AddIn, custom() As Variant)
End Sub
```

Note that you really don't have to type the method definition yourself. As soon as you specify that the Connect class exposes the IDTExtensibility secondary interface, you'll find the four methods that belong to this interface right in the Visual Basic Code window (see Figure 45.9).

FIG. 43.9

If the Connect class exposes the IDTExtensibility interface, you have its four methods ready in the upper-right combo box.

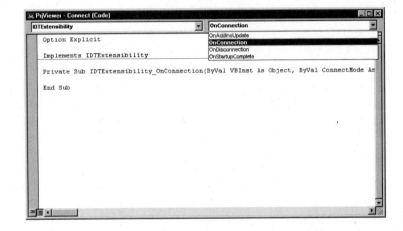

Let's see the meaning of each argument passed to the OnConnection method. The VBInst object is a reference to the VBE object that represents the root of the VB IDE that is invoking the add-in. Please note that there could be more than just one instance of VB running on the machine, and the add-in has to know which one has called it. For this reason, it has to save this reference in a Public property of the class itself, as follows:

```
'--- class Connect
Implements IDTExtensibility
' the instance of the VB IDE
Public VBInstance As VBIDE.VBE
Private Sub IDTExtensibility_OnConnection(ByVal VBInst As Object, _
    ByVal ConnectMode As vbext_ConnectMode, _
    ByVal AddInInst As VBIDE.AddIn, custom() As Variant)
    'save the vb instance
    Set VBInstance = VBInst
End Sub
```

Why can't you use a global variable in a BAS module? Again, never forget that the add-in is an OLE server and therefore can be invoked by more than one VB environment (however, this is true only for out-process servers: in-process servers always belong to only one instance of the VB environment). Hence, if the VBInst value is saved in a global, shared variable, then when the second instance of VB activates the add-in, it overwrites the value stored there by the first instance. This is not a problem if you store the reference to the VBE object in a public property of the Connect class—in this case, each instance of the class will refer to its local value.

The `ConnectMode` argument informs the add-in when and how it is being activated. It can be one of the following symbolic constants:

- `vbext_cm_Startup`   The add-in is being activated as part of the Visual Basic's startup process (this means that the corresponding entry in VBADDIN.INI was 1).

- `vbext_cm_AfterStartup`   The user has activated the add-in from the Add-In Manager dialog box (this means that the corresponding entry in VBADDIN.INI was 0).

- `vbext_cm_External`   The add-in is being activated by another program, most likely the Add-In Toolbar (this means that the corresponding entry in VBADDIN.INI was 0 or missing completely).

`AddInInst` is a reference to the `Addin` object held in the VBE hierarchy and corresponds to the add-in being activated. The meaning of this argument becomes apparent when exploring the VB IDE object tree; however, for now, suffice it to say that this argument is rarely used. Likewise, the `custom()` array is of no use in most add-ins.

If the add-in has been connected at VB5 startup, the `OnStartupComplete` method is fired some time after the `OnConnection` method, when the IDE has completed its loading and all add-ins are ready to be used. Basically, there are two reasons for writing code within this method. One reason is that you want to find out which other add-ins are currently activated in the environment. The second reason is that you need to show a form or some other message to the VB programmer, as in the following code:

```
Private Sub IDTExtensibility_OnStartupComplete(custom() As Variant)
    ' this add-in interacts with the user through a form
    frmAddin.Show
End Sub
```

It is important to understand that you cannot show a form from within the `OnConnection` method because the IDE is still loading and is not stable. On the other hand, as stated previously, the `OnStartupComplete` method is never called for those add-ins that are loaded manually through the Add-In Manager or the Add-In Toolbar. This is an interesting problem because you must differentiate between two cases: if the add-in is loaded when the IDE is launched, you must show its form from within the `OnStartupComplete` method, whereas, if the add-in is loaded manually, the form must be shown from within the `OnConnection` method because the `OnStartupComplete` method will never be called. Listing 43.2 shows a complete implementation of this concept.

Listing 43.2   A Typical *OnConnection* Method

```
'--- class Connect
Implements IDTExtensibility
' the instance of the VB IDE
Public VBInstance As VBIDE.VBE
Private Sub IDTExtensibility_OnConnection(ByVal VBInst As Object, _
    ByVal ConnectMode As vbext_ConnectMode, _
    ByVal AddInInst As VBIDE.AddIn, custom() As Variant)
    'save the vb instance
```

```
        Set VBInstance = VBInst

        ' show the form if the add-in is being loaded manually
        If ConnectMode <> vbext_cm_Startup Then
                ShowForm
        End If
End Sub
Private Sub IDTExtensibility_OnStartupComplete(custom() As Variant)
        ShowForm
End Sub
Private Sub ShowForm()
        frmAddin.Show
        ' add here all the other initialization code ...
End Sub
```

Note that a separate ShowForm routine was created so that more code can easily be added to be executed when the add-in finally becomes visible. The same approach should be followed if your add-in has to interact with other add-ins, which names are not available during the OnConnection method if the ConnectMode argument is equal to vbext_cm_Startup.

Adding User Interface Elements

If the add-in immediately shows a form and such form represents the only way for the VB programmer to interact with the add-in, you may skip this section. However, most add-ins do not use this approach; instead, they add some user interface element to the VB IDE—such as a menu item or a toolbar button—so that programmers can invoke them anytime they actually need its services.

Adding an interface element to the VB IDE is rather simple, but complete comprehension of this process requires an in-depth knowledge of the IDE object hierarchy, which is discussed later in this chapter. For now, suffice it to say that the VB environment exposes the CommandBars collection, where each CommandBar object is either a menu or a toolbar. The first element in this collection—the VBInstance.CommandBars(1) object—is the main IDE menu, and each member of the collection can be referenced by using a name, as in VBInstance.CommandBars("Tools").

Each CommandBar object contains a Controls collection, which is a collection of CommandBarControls objects that lets you reference all the items in a menu, or the buttons of a toolbar. Thus, VBInstance.CommandBars("Tools").Controls(1) is the first item in the Tools menu, which can also be referred to as VBInstance.CommandBars("Tools").Controls ("Add Procedure...").

CAUTION

When referencing a menu or toolbar item, it is preferable that you use its caption, rather than its numerical index in the menu or the toolbar, because users can customize the VB environment and move all interface items according to their tastes.

continues

continued

Also, the string used as a key in the `CommandBars` or `Controls` collection must match *exactly* what appears on the menu, including the trailing ellipsis, if any. However, if the caption includes a hot key, you optionally may omit the ampersand (`&`) character. For instance, the following two references are equivalent:

```
VBInstance.CommandBars("Tools")
```

```
VBInstance.CommandBars("&Tools")
```

Because it is a collection, you also can add new items to the `Controls` collection by using the `Add` method. In other words, you effectively can add new menu items, as well as set their captions and other properties, as in the following example:

```
Dim newMenuItem As Office.CommandBarControl
Set newMenuItem = VBInstance.CommandBars("Add-Ins").Controls.Add(1)
newMenuItem.Caption = "My Great Add-in"
```

You have added a new menu item, but you don't know how to receive notification when the user selects it. In other words, your add-in has made itself available in the Add-Ins menu, but has no means to activate itself when the user needs to use it.

To receive notification when the user selects the new menu item, you must declare an object of yet another type, `CommandBarEvents`, and use it to receive an event when the menu item is selected. The source code in Listing 43.3 shows how to perform those tasks.

Listing 43.3   How to Receive an Event when the User Clicks a Menu Item

```
' this is a form-level variable
Dim WithEvents MenuHandler As CommandBarEvents
Private Sub Form_Load()
    Set MenuHandler = VBInstance.Events.CommandBarEvents(newMenuItem)
End Sub
Private Sub MenuHandler_Click(ByVal CommandBarControl As Object, _
    handled As Boolean, CancelDefault As Boolean)
        ShowForm
End Sub
```

The `CommandBarEvents` object exposes only one event, `Click`, which obviously fires when the user selects the corresponding menu item or the toolbar button (depending on the type of the `CommandBar` object). Within the `Click` event, you can do whatever you want with the VBIDE by using the many objects that will be introduced later in this chapter.

Disconnection

An add-in can be shut down in several ways (through the Add-Ins Manager or automatically when VB closes, for instance), but this usually is of no concern to the add-in programmer, in the sense that the sequence of the operations to be performed most often is identical in all cases.

Generally speaking, in the `OnDiconnection` method, the add-in should release all the resources it took previously, destroy all the user interface elements it created, and so on. Here is a typical `OnDisconnection` method, which completes the previous example:

```
Private Sub IDTExtensibility_OnDisconnection(ByVal RemoveMode _
    As vbext_DisconnectMode, custom() As Variant)
        'delete the menu item
        newMenuItem.Delete
        ' unload the form
        Unload frmAddIn
        Set frmAddIn = Nothing
End Sub
```

When the `OnDisconnection` method is fired, you should assume that your add-in is not executing anymore and, in fact, you shouldn't try to keep it alive (by keeping a form visible, for example). You should be aware that, after this method is executed, the `VBInstance` reference is not valid anymore and you absolutely should not reference it or any of its dependent objects.

A Simple Example

You can finally put everything together and prepare your first complete example of a working add-in. Because the complete VB IDE object model hasn't been introduced yet, you are still unable to write complex (and very useful) add-ins at this point; nevertheless, you can put to good use what you have read thus far.

A Simple Property Code Generator

Even the simplest example should be somewhat useful; therefore, this example prepares an add-in that many of you will appreciate: a simple code generator that improves upon the "Add Procedure" standard menu command. As you may recall, this command lets you quickly create subs, functions, and Get/Let property procedure pairs, but has a number of shortcomings: It creates code for Variant properties only, and it knows nothing about Property Set procedures or Friend keywords. Above all, it isn't any help when you have to create properties that wrap around member variables.

▶ **See** "Working with Procedures," **p. 464**

A *member variable* is a variable that is private to a class and whose value is exposed to the outside world using a couple of wrapper property procedures. Suppose you have a `LastName` public property—you can implement it in two different ways. The simplest way to implement it is to use a Public variable, as in:

```
Public LastName As String
```

In the second method, which is preferred by most VB developers, you wrap the real value of the property between a couple of Property procedures, as follows:

```
Private m_LastName As String
Public Property Get LastName() As String
    LastName = m_LastName
End Property
```

```
Public Property Let LastName (newValue As String)
    m_LastName = newValue
End Property
```

Why are property procedures to be preferred to member variables? For one thing, these property procedures let you have greater control over which value is assigned to the property, which helps to create more robust and bug-free applications. Here is a simple example:

```
Public Property Let LastName (newValue As String)
    ' refuse to assign null strings
    If newValue <> "" Then
        m_LastName = newValue
    End If
End Property
```

On the other hand, writing all this code just for a property is a lot of work, and in this respect, the Add Procedure command is almost completely useless. However, you can build an add-in that does exactly what you need it to do. This add-in will, in fact, let you set all your desired options and will copy the generated VB code to the system clipboard, ready to be pasted in the appropriate position in the project that is under development.

The PropertyBuilder Project

You can create an add-in in several ways, one of which is loading the Add-In template project from the dialog box that appears when you invoke the File-New Project command. If this command doesn't lead you to the New Project dialog box shown in Figure 43.10, you should set the appropriate option button in the Environment tab of the Tools-Option dialog box.

FIG. 43.10

The quick way to create an add-in: simply invoke the File-New Project menu command and select the correct template.

However, your current PropertyBuilder project does not use the provided add-in template, which is too sophisticated for this simple example. Besides, it is more interesting to see what occurs "behind the scenes" than simply letting a template do all the work. To create your add-in from scratch, just follow these simple steps:

1. Execute the File-New Project command and create an ActiveX EXE project.
2. Change the name of the class module to **Connect**.
3. Add a regular form and name it **frmAddin**.

4. Add a regular BAS module and name it **AddIn.bas**.

5. Invoke the Project-Properties command and modify the project's attributes as shown in Figure 43.11.

6. Go to the Component tab of the same dialog box and set the StartMode option to ActiveX Component.

7. Press F2 to show the Object Browser, right-click the Connect class in the leftmost pane, and select the Properties menu command. In the Member Options dialog box, set the description of the Connect class equal to the text that you want to appear in the Add-In Manager (see Figure 43.12).

FIG. 43.11

All the project attributes you need to create an add-in.

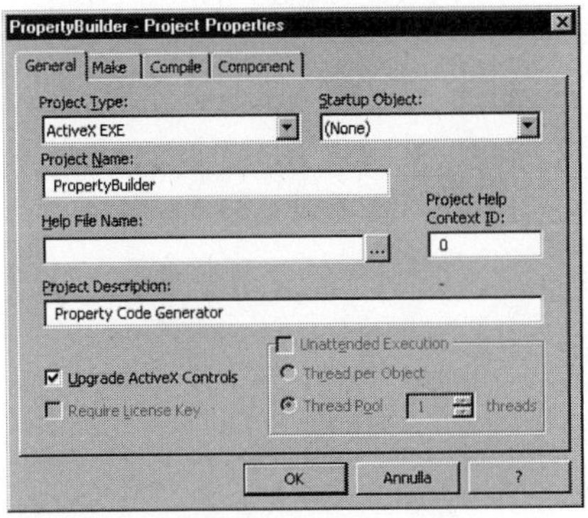

FIG. 43.12

The description associated to the Connect class is the string that users will see in the Add-In Manager.

The project name, as set in Step 5, is very important because it will be added to the class of the Connect class to form the complete name of the class, as it will appear in the VBADDIN.INI file. In this case, the resulting name is PropertyBuilder.Connect.

This last step is somewhat undocumented in the language manuals. In fact, many programmers mistakenly believe the description that appears in the Add-In Manager comes from the Description attribute of the add-in project, while it actually comes from the Description attribute of the Connect class. This might sound counterintuitive, but it makes perfect sense: after all, the same add-in project could theoretically install several add-ins (even though I never saw such a program), thus the add-in's description should be an attribute of the individual Connect class, not of the project.

The Connect Class

See Listing 43.4 for the code in the Connect class that reacts to VB IDE notifications.

Listing 43.4   CONNECT.CLS—The Source Code of the Connect Class

```
Option Explicit
Implements IDTExtensibility
' the VBIDE instance connected to this addin
Private VBInstance As VBIDE.VBE
' the new menu item added to the Add-Ins menu
Private newMenuItem As Office.CommandBarControl
' the Event object used to get a notification when
' the user clicks on newMenuItem
Private WithEvents MenuHandler As CommandBarEvents
' this is the form corresponding to this instance of the class
Dim frmAddin As New frmAddin
Private Sub IDTExtensibility_OnConnection(ByVal VBInst As Object, _
    ByVal ConnectMode As vbext_ConnectMode, ByVal AddInInst As VBIDE.AddIn, _
    custom() As Variant)
    On Error GoTo OnConnection_Error

    'save the VB instance
    Set VBInstance = VBInst

    If ConnectMode <> vbext_cm_Startup Then
        ' if no AfterStartup method will be called, this is the right
        ' place to add a menu item to the Add-Ins menu
        CreateMenuItem
    End If
    Exit Sub

OnConnection_Error:
    MsgBox "Unable to correctly connect the add-in", vbCritical
End Sub
Private Sub IDTExtensibility_OnStartupComplete(custom() As Variant)
    ' if the add-in is being loaded at VB startup, this is
    ' the right place to add a menu item to the Add-Ins menu
    CreateMenuItem
End Sub
Sub CreateMenuItem()
    Dim addInMenu As Object
    On Error Resume Next

    ' search the Add-Ins menu, exit if not found
    ' (very unlikely)
    Set addInMenu = VBInstance.CommandBars("Add-Ins")
    If (Err <> 0) Or (addInMenu Is Nothing) Then Exit Sub

    ' add a new item to the Add-In menu, after existing ones
    Set newMenuItem = addInMenu.Controls.Add(1)
    ' set its caption to a suitable string, with a hotkey
    newMenuItem.Caption = "&Property Builder..."
```

```
      ' create a menu handler object that will receive
      ' a click event when the user selects the menu command
      Set MenuHandler = VBInstance.Events.CommandBarEvents(newMenuItem)
End Sub
Private Sub MenuHandler_Click(ByVal CommandBarControl As Object, _
      handled As Boolean, CancelDefault As Boolean)
          frmAddin.Show
End Sub
Private Sub IDTExtensibility_OnDisconnection(ByVal RemoveMode _
      As vbext_DisconnectMode, _
      custom() As Variant)
          On Error Resume Next

          'delete the menu item
          newMenuItem.Delete
          ' clear the menu handler object
          Set MenuHandler = Nothing
          ' unload the form, if necessary
          Unload frmAddin
          Set frmAddin = Nothing
End Sub
Private Sub IDTExtensibility_OnAddInsUpdate(custom() As Variant)
        ' a placeholder remark
End Sub
```

The OnConnection method of the IDTExtensibility interface must save the reference to the calling VBIDE object in the VBInstance variable and decide whether it is the right time to add a menu item to the Add-Ins menu.

The OnStartupComplete method is much simpler. It will be invoked by VB only for those add-ins that are loaded when the environment is launched, and in this context its only purpose is to create the menu item, which was not possible within the OnConnection method:

See what happens in the CreateMenu procedure. Basically, it does three things. First, it checks that the Add-Ins menu actually is there (in the unlikely case that the add-in is being installed by something different from the VB environment), then it adds a new element to the Controls collection of the Add-In menu. Finally, it creates a menu-handler object that then will be used to receive an event when the user clicks the brand new "Property Builder" menu item:

Now that you have a menu handler object, you can write code for its Click event, but there is a subtle detail to which you must pay attention. While the project does include a frmAddIn form, here you actually are accessing a local variable with the same name, and declared as:

```
Dim frmAddin As New frmAddin
```

In other words, each instance of the Connect class will create a new frmAddIn form and will show a different form. Again, this permits you to create a single add-in that is capable of serving several instances of the VB environment.

The OnDisconnect method's purpose is to undo whatever was done during the connection stage.

Lastly, you have to create an empty `OnAddInsUpdate` method. This is necessary because you used the `Implements` keyword to create the IDTExtensibility secondary interface, and this program won't even compile until this method is implemented in the class. The simplest way to complete the implementation of the `IDTExtensibility` secondary interface is creating an OnAddInsUpdate method with a remark in it.

The *frmAddIn* Form

When the user invokes the new "Property Builder" command in the Add-Ins menu, a `MenuHandler_Click` event will be raised, which in turn will pop up a form that lets the user enter the details of the Property procedure that he or she is about to create (see Figure 43.13).

FIG. 43.13

The `frmAddIn` form at design time. The `cboDataType` combo box already contains the names of all native VB's data types.

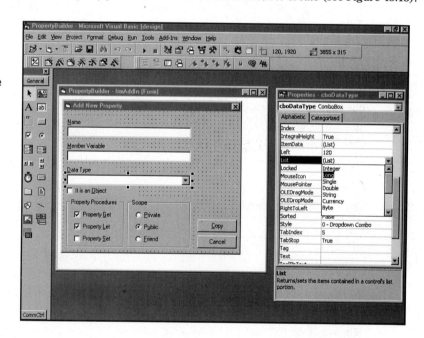

Most of the code in this form serves to implement a sensible interaction with the user (see Listing 43.5):

Listing 43.5   The Code in frmAddin.frm that Reacts to User's Action

```
' this is the standard prefix used to build Member variable names
Const DEFAULT_PREFIX As String = "m_"

Private Sub Form_Load()
    ' restore defaults
    txtVariable = DEFAULT_PREFIX
    cboDataType.Text = "String"
End Sub
```

```
Private Sub txtName_Change()
    ' build the name of the member variable
    txtVariable.Text = DEFAULT_PREFIX & txtName.Text
End Sub

Private Sub cboDataType_Click()
    ' delegate to the Change event
    Call cboDataType_Change
End Sub
Private Sub cboDataType_Change()
    ' enable or disable the "Property Set" checkbox according
    ' to which data type has been selected
    Select Case LCase$(cboDataType.Text)
        Case "integer", "long", "single", "double", _
             "currency", "string", _
             "date", "byte", "boolean"
                chkObject.Enabled = False
        Case "object"
                chkObject.Enabled = True
                chkObject.Value = vbChecked
        Case Else
                chkObject.Enabled = True
    End Select
End Sub

Private Sub chkObject_Click()
    chkSet.Enabled = chkObject.Value
End Sub

Private Sub cmdCopy_Click()
    Clipboard.setText GeneratedCode
    Unload Me
End Sub
Private Sub cmdCancel_Click()
    Unload Me
End Sub
```

Both the Copy and the Cancel command buttons cause the form to be closed, but the former also places the generated code into the system clipboard.

Next comes the smart part of the program that generates the code, based on the contents of the fields on the form. The code in Listing 43.6 should be rather simple to follow, without any further comments.

Listing 43.6   The Routine that Actually Builds the Code of Property Procedures

```
Private Function GeneratedCode() As String
    Dim codeText As String
    Dim scopeText As String
    Dim setText As String
```

continues

Listing 43.6 Continued

```
    ' retrieve the scope
    If optScope(0).Value Then
        scopeText = "Private "
    ElseIf optScope(1).Value Then
        scopeText = "Public "
    Else
        scopeText = "Friend "
    End If

    ' should we use "set" when assigning?
    If chkObject.Enabled And chkObject.Value = vbChecked Then
        setText = "Set "
    End If

    ' create the declaration of the member variable
    codeText = "Private " & txtVariable & " As _
    " & cboDataType & vbCrLf & vbCrLf

    ' add the Property Get code, if requested
    If chkGet.Value Then
        codeText = codeText & scopeText & "Property Get " _
        & txtName & "() As " _
            & cboDataType.Text & vbCrLf _
            & vbTab & setText & txtName & " = " _
            & txtVariable & vbCrLf _
            & "End Property" & vbCrLf & vbCrLf
    End If

    ' add the Property Let code, if requested
    If chkLet.Value Then
        codeText = codeText & scopeText & "Property Let " _
            & txtName _
            & "(newValue As " & cboDataType.Text & ")" _
            & vbCrLf _
            & vbTab & txtVariable & " = newValue" _
            & vbCrLf _
            & "End Property" & vbCrLf & vbCrLf
    End If

    ' add the Property Let code, if requested
    If setText <> "" And chkSet.Value Then
        codeText = codeText & scopeText & "Property Set " _
            & txtName _
            & "(newValue As " & cboDataType.Text & ")" _
            & vbCrLf _
            & vbTab & setText & txtVariable & " = newValue" _
            & vbCrLf _
            & "End Property" & vbCrLf & vbCrLf
    End If

    GeneratedCode = codeText

End Function
```

The *Addin.Bas* Module

The only module left to illustrate is `Addin.Bas`, that contains the Sub Main procedure that is fired when the add-in starts its execution.

Apart from the Main procedure, it only includes a routine that adds the proper string to the VBADDIN.INI file:

```
Declare Function WritePrivateProfileString& Lib "Kernel32" Alias _
    "WritePrivateProfileStringA" (ByVal AppName$, ByVal KeyName$, _
    ByVal keydefault$, ByVal FileName$)

Sub Main
    frmAddin.Show
End Sub

Sub RegisterAddin()
    WritePrivateProfileString "Add-Ins32", "PropertyBuilder.Connect", "0",
"vbaddin.ini"
End Sub
```

You may also use the more sophisticated `RegisterAddIn` routine, illustrated in Listing 43.1, if you want to.

Testing the Add-In

Your add-in is finally completed, and you only have to install it and check that it behaves as expected. This is the simplest part of the whole job; just follow these steps:

1. Run the `RegisterAddIn` procedure from within the Immediate window.

2. Press Ctrl+F5 to run the program with the Full Compile option.

3. Start another instance of VB5, open the Add-In Manager dialog box, and check that your add-in is there and ready to be activated (see Figure 43.14). Select the corresponding check box and close the dialog box.

4. Open the Add-Ins menu: a new "Property Builder" command should have been added to the bottom of the menu.

FIG. 43.14

The Property Code Builder add-in is finally available in the VB environment.

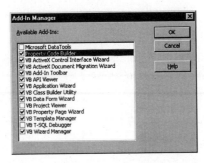

To test the add-in, run it from the Add-Ins menu and try to create several kinds of properties, including read-only properties and object properties (see Figure 43.15).

FIG. 43.15
It takes less than ten
seconds to create a
property; the generated
code is visible in the
Code window behind
the add-in dialog box.

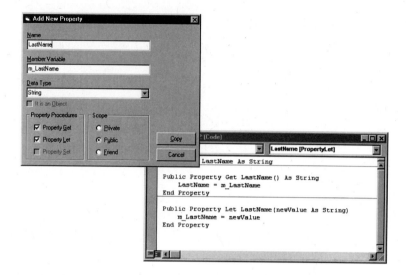

Of course, you are by no means limited to this first, simple version of the add-in, and you are encouraged to improve it with many other features. For instance, you could add the support for one or more arguments, or for automatic insertion of a remark banner reporting who wrote this property, and when it was written. Another interesting addition might be the capability to define multiple properties and then paste them all into the VB project in just one operation.

To produce a stand-alone add-in, you must compile it into an EXE file. Note that this particular add-in may also work as a stand-alone program because it really doesn't interact with the VB IDE object model. In that case, you must run it from the Start menu or a desktop icon instead of as an item in the Add-Ins menu.

The VB IDE Object Model

Now that you know how to create add-ins, you probably are wondering what you can do with them. The answer is: Everything that you can do with your mouse and keyboard from within the VB environment, including opening and closing windows, creating new projects and files, finding routines and adding new ones, manipulating controls on a form, and so on. Well, in truth, there are a few things that are still beyond the reach of add-ins, but they are mostly minor issues (adding and removing breakpoints and bookmarks or trapping user actions within a code window, for example).

To leverage the power of VB5 add-ins, you have to spend some time on the VB IDE Object Model, which is rather complex. This section introduces you to the intricacies of the VB IDE Object Model, but there simply is not enough space available to explain every single detail. In many cases, you'll have to gather more information from the Object Browser and online help, and write some test programs to see if things work as expected. However, all the main objects of the hierarchy and their most useful properties and methods will be explained, and you can use the many code samples in this section as guidelines for your own complete add-ins.

One of the difficulties you'll find while exploring this object model is that the model itself often is recursive, so you have to know where to stop when you dive into its many branches. One example is the CommandBarsControl objects—they expose a Controls collection (menu items or toolbar buttons) that, in turn, can be other CommandBarControls (sub-menus, in this case).

The *VBE* Object

The VBE is the object at the top of the object model, and represents the VB environment itself. This object is passed to the add-in as an argument of the OnConnection method, and the add-in is supposed to store it somewhere for further reference (see Figure 43.16).

FIG. 43.16
The VB IDE object hierarchy; subsequent figures show the various object levels in more detail.

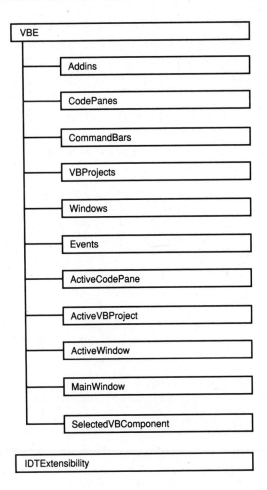

The following list describes the main level objects, collections, and properties:

- ■ Addins collection   Includes all the add-ins active in the environment.
- ■ CodePanes collection   All the code windows that are currently open.

- **CommandBars** collection   All the top level menus and toolbars in the environment, including toolbars that are not currently visible.
- **VBProjects** collection   All the projects that are loaded in the environment.
- **Windows** collection   All of the windows that belong to the environment, excluding the main window, but including all the windows that are currently hidden.
- **Events** object   This doesn't represent a real, visible object, and is only used to return objects that handle events generated by the user within the environment (for example, when the user loads a new project or adds a new control).
- **ActiveCodePane** property   The code window that is currently active.
- **ActiveVBProject** property   The project that is currently active.
- **ActiveWindow** property   The window that is currently active.
- **MainWindow** property   The main window of the VB IDE, in other words, the window that hosts the main menu and acts as a container for all the others (if the IDE is in MDI mode).
- **SelectedVBComponent** property   The VBE object's SelectedVBComponent property, used to reference the active component.
- **IDTExtensibility** interface   An abstract class used to define an *interface*, the set of properties and methods exposed by a class.)

The VBE object also exposes a number of properties that you can use to retrieve additional information regarding the current state of the environment. For instance, the DisplayModel property lets you set or retrieve the current display model, MDI or SDI; the FullName property returns the full path name of the Visual Basic application. Finally, the Quit method lets you programmatically exit the environment.

The *VBProjects* Collection and the *VBProject* Object

The VBProjects collection holds all the VB projects that are currently loaded in the environment, so you can enumerate them by using a simple For Each loop. Alternatively, you can exploit the VBE.ActiveVBProject object that points to the active project. In all cases, you end up with a reference to a VBProject object (see Figure 43.17).

Here is a short code snippet that shows how to load into a list box the name and the path of all loaded projects, and how to highlight the project that is currently active:

```
Sub LoadProjects(Target As Listbox)
    Dim vbp As VBIDE.VBProject
    Target.Clear
    For Each vbp In VBInstance.VBProjects
        Target.AddItem vbp.Name & " - " & vbp.FileName
        If vbp Is VBInstance.ActiveVBProject Then
            Target.ListIndex = Target.ListCount - 1
        End If
    Next
End Sub
```

FIG. 43.17

The `VBProjects` collection and its dependent objects.

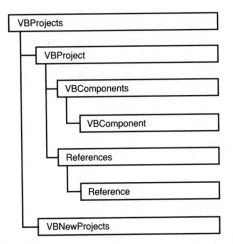

The `VBProjects` collection also includes a number of interesting properties and methods. The `StartupProject` property lets you set or get a reference to the project that runs when you press F5; the `FileName` property returns the fully qualified path of the VBG file that gathers all the projects in a group. The `Add` method lets you add a blank project of the desired type (standard EXE, ActiveX DLL or EXE, ActiveX Control or Document, and so forth), and you can load an existing project with `AddFromFile`, or by using a template with `AddFromTemplate`. Because you can use the latter two methods to add a VBG file, they return a `VBNewProjects` collection of `VBProject` objects that you can enumerate to learn which projects have been added, as follows:

```
' load a project or project group and list which projects have been added
Dim vbg As VBIDE.VBNewProjects
Dim vbp As VBIDE.VBProject
Set vbg = VBInstance.VBProjects.AddFromFile "c:\vb5\prova.vbg"
For Each vbp In vbg
    Debug.Print vbp.Name & " - " & vbp.FileName
End Sub
```

The `VBProject` object is rather powerful and complex. It exposes a large number of properties that let you query or modify what the programmer has typed into the Options dialog box. A number of properties are rather self-explanatory, such as `FileName`, `Description`, `HelpFile`, `HelpContextID`, `Type` (Standard EXE, ActiveX Control or Document, ActiveX DLL or EXE), `StartMode` (stand-alone or ActiveX Component), and `BuildFileName` (the name of the EXE or DLL file that will be produced by the compilation process).

There are also a few useful methods, such as `MakeCompiledFile` and `SaveAs`. The `AddToolboxProgID` command lets you add an OCX to the Toolbox, and the `ReadProperty`/`WriteProperty` pair enables you to read and modify selected portions of the VBP file, including the version of the project and all the compiler optimization settings.

The `VBProject` object also exposes the `References` and the `VBComponents collections`; the latter is undoubtedly one of the more interesting elements in the hierarchy, and is explained in more detail in the next section.

The *VBComponents* Collection and the *VBComponent* Object

The VBComponents collection gives you access to all the individual components of the projects (see Figure 43.18), including forms, code and class modules, ActiveX Control and Document designers, and so on. You can use its StartupObject to learn which VBComponent object is executed when F5 is pressed (usually, the code module that contains Sub Main, or the startup form, but it could also be "(none)" for ActiveX components).

FIG. 43.18
The VBComponents collection and its dependent objects.

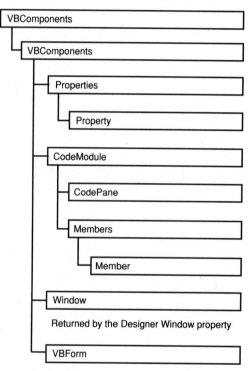

This collection also exposes three methods for adding new items: Add creates a blank component of a given type (code or class module, form, and so forth); AddFromTemplate and AddFromFile let you create a component from a template or load an existing component, respectively. Regardless of how you load a component, you can unload it by using the Remove method.

The VB environment does not offer a quick way to add multiple components in one single operation and it requires that you issue several Project-Add File commands. Listing 43.7 shows a useful routine that you can encapsulate in your add-ins to automatically add all the files in a given directory:

Listing 43.7   Adding Multiple Components

```
Sub AddMultipleComponents(ByVal path As String, _
    Optional extension As String)
    Dim filename As String
    Dim vbc As VBIDE.VBComponent
    ' add a trailing backslash, if needed
    If Right$(path, 1) <> "\" Then path = path & "\"

    If extension <> "" Then
        ' if an extension was given, add all components
        ' with that extension
        filename = Dir$(path & "*." & extension)
        Do While filename <> ""
            Set vbc = VBInstance.ActiveVBProject._
                VBComponents.AddFile(path & filename)
            ' this is necessary to work around a VBIDE bug
            vbc.IsDirty = True
            vbc.IsDirty = False
            ' read the next file in the directory
            filename = Dir$
        Loop
    Else
        ' otherwise, recursively call this routine with
        ' all standard extensions
        AddMultipleComponents path, "frm"
        AddMultipleComponents path, "bas"
        AddMultipleComponents path, "cls"
        AddMultipleComponents path, "ctl"
        AddMultipleComponents path, "dob"
        AddMultipleComponents path, "pag"
    End If
End Sub
```

The AddMultipleComponents routine shows a couple of interesting points. First, it is a simple but effective example of how to use recursion: if the routine is called with just one argument, it recalls itself once for each of the existing extensions. Second, it works around a bug in the environment: under some circumstances, the VB IDE ignores the components added through the AddFile method of the VBComponents. To prove it, comment out the two lines containing a reference to the IsDirty property and run the procedure. If you issue a File-New Project command, VB will ask if you want to save modified files, but won't show all the components that have been added in this way.

The VBComponent object is also rich of properties and methods. The meaning of a few of them is rather evident: Name, Type, Description, HelpFile, HelpContextID, and IsDirty. The FileNames and FileCount properties, however, require a more detailed explanation: some components—namely, Forms, UserControls, and UserDocuments—are associated to *designer* modules and are stored into two different files, one for the code and regular properties, the other to hold binary properties. For instance, forms are stored in FRM and FRX files and, similarly, UserControl modules require CTL and CTX files. In this case, the FileCount property returns 2 and you can query the names of the files with `FileNames(1)` and `FileNames(2)`. When the component is associated to a designer, you also can query the `HasOpenDesigner` Boolean property, which returns `False` if the form is currently closed.

The `Properties` collection stores all the properties related to a component. Such properties correspond to what you see when you press the F4 key when the component has the focus. Code modules have only one item in this collection (`Name`), class modules have two (`Name` and `Instancing`), and all components that correspond to a designer may have dozens. Here is a simple routine that shows all the properties for the component that is currently selected:

```
Dim prop As VBIDE.Property
On Error Resume Next
For Each prop In VBInstance.SelectedVBComponent.Properties
    Print prop.Name & " = " & prop.Value
Next
```

This code references the active component by using the `SelectedVBComponent` property of the `VBE` object. Note that you must add error trapping because there might be one or more properties that return an object or that have several values, and in both cases, the `Print` method will fail. You can use this collection to modify an existing property, as in:

```
VBInstance.SelectedVBComponent.Properties("Width").Value = 1000
```

There are two more items that are worth examining: the `CodeModule` property returns a reference to the code module associated to the component; the `Designer` property returns a reference to the `VBForm` object that represents the designer on which you place controls. Both types of objects will be explained in a moment.

`VBComponent` objects also expose a few methods. `InsertFile` has the same effect as the Edit, Insert File menu command (it merges the contents of a file at the current position of the cursor), `Activate` makes the component active, `Reload` discards all changes from the last Save operation, and `SaveAs` writes the component to disk using a different file name.

The *VBForm* and *VBControl* Objects

Don't confuse the `VBForm` object with the usual form object: in the add-in jargon, the visible form object corresponds to the `VBComponent` object, while the `VBForm` is the designer on which you place controls, and has no correspondence to any visible entity in the environment. In fact, you can enumerate a form's properties by using the `Properties` collection of the corresponding `VBComponent` object, as seen above, not of the `VBForm` object (which doesn't expose any `Properties` collection). To retrieve the `VBForm` object related to a given `VBComponent`, you just query its `Designer` property.

The `VBForm` object indeed has a very limited use in that it only exposes the `Paste` and `SelectAll` methods and the `CanPaste` boolean property. Its main function is as the container for three important collections: `VBControls`, `SelectedVBControls`, and `ContainedVBControls` (see Figure 43.19).

FIG. 43.19

The VBForm and
VBControl objects.

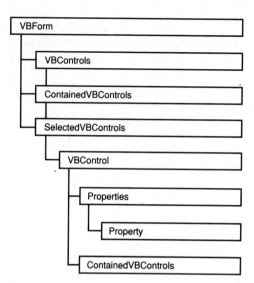

All of them contain VBControl objects, which correspond to the controls that a VB programmer picks from the toolbox and drops onto the form. The only difference among these three collections is in the controls they contain: the VBControls collection gathers all the controls on the form; the SelectedVBControls collection returns only the controls that are currently selected; the ContainedVBControls collection returns only the controls that are on the form's surface (as opposed to controls contained in other controls, such as a frame or a picture box).

You can create new controls on the form by simply adding a new VBControl object to the VBControls or ContainedVBControls collection, using their Add method. Here's how you can add a textbox to the currently selected form (or UserControl or UserDocument):

```
Dim frm As VBIDE.VBForm
Dim ctr As VBIDE.VBControl
On Error Resume Next
Set frm = VBInstance.SelectedVBComponent.Designer
Set ctr = frm.VBControls.Add("VB.TextBox")
```

After you have a reference to a VBControl object—retrieved from one of the collections or just created by yourself, as in the previous code example—you can modify its properties by using its Properties collection:

```
' set its name
ctr.Properties("Name") = "txtLastName"
' move to the upper-left corner
ctr.Properties("Left") = 0
ctr.Properties("Top") = 0
```

You can do a lot of other interesting things by using these objects and collections. For instance, whenever you add a textbox to a form, VB initializes its Text property to something meaningless, such as "Text1", whereas in most cases, you will prefer to have it blank. What's worse is that, while you can usually select more controls on the form and use the Properties window to change all the properties they have in common, this is not possible with the Text property, and you have to blank this property for each individual control. Here is a better solution:

```
Dim ctr As VBIDE.VBControl
For Each ctr in VBInstance.SelectedVBComponent.Designer.VBControls
    If ctr.ProgId = "VB.TextBox" Then
        ctr.Properties("Text") = ""
    End If
Next
```

This code clears the Text property for all the textbox controls on the active form. Since you probably want to do the same as well with other similar controls, such as combo boxes or MaskedEdit controls, there is an alternative solution that you might like more:

```
Dim ctr As VBIDE.VBControl
On Error Resume Next
For Each ctr in VBInstance.SelectedVBComponent.Designer.VBControls
    ctr.Properties("Text") = ""
Next
```

This code attempts to clear the Text property of each control on the active form, and relies on the On Error statement to avoid fatal errors if a given control does not support that property.

Finally, note that each VBControl object exposes a ContainedVBControls collection, which returns all the child VBControl objects, or Nothing if the control is not a container or doesn't contain any child control. Because it is perfectly legal for a container control to host other controls that work as containers—for example, a picture box that contains a frame control that contains an array of option buttons—this is another case of recursion in the object model. If you plan to write an add-in that explores all the controls on a form, you should take this issue into account.

The *CodeModule* Object

This probably is one of the most interesting objects in the VBE hierarchy, wherein it appears as a child of the VBComponent object. Each VBComponent object exposes a CodeModule property that returns a reference to the object that represents the source code behind a component.

Thanks to the many properties of the CodeModule object, it is possible to read and modify individual lines of code, single routines, or blocks of code of any size. The CountOfLines property returns the total number of lines in the module, while CountOfDeclarationLines returns the number of lines in the declaration section. If you know the name of a procedure, you can retrieve its position and length by using the ProcStartLine and ProcCountLines properties respectively. Note, however, that the value returned by the ProcStartLine property keeps remarks and blank lines into account: if you want to learn the position of the first actual line of code, you must use the ProcBodyLine property (this detail is not documented in the language manuals).

After you know in which lines you are interested, you may read them by using the Lines property, delete them by using the DeleteLines method, use the ReplaceLine method to replace the code, or insert new statements by using the `InsertLines` method. Finally, you can use the `AddFromFile` and `AddFromString` methods to merge the contents of a file or a string into the module.

To fully exploit the potential of the `CodeModule` object, you have to introduce one more element, the `Members` collection. This collection holds `Member` objects, which correspond to the individual items in the code. You can iterate on the `Members` collection to retrieve the name of each variable, event, and procedure in the module. The routine shown in Listing 43.8 fills a listbox with information on all the members of a given component:

Listing 43.8   Adding the List of Component Members to a Listbox

```
Sub MemberListToListbox(ctrl As ListBox, projectName _
    As String, componentName As String)
    '-------------------------------------------------
    ' Add the list of component members to a listbox
    '-------------------------------------------------
    Dim cmp As VBIDE.VBComponent
    Dim mbr As VBIDE.Member
    Dim text As String

    On Error Resume Next

    ' get component reference - exit if error
    Set cmp = VBInstance.VBProjects(projectName).VBComponents_
        (componentName)
    If Err Then Exit Sub

        ' iterate on all members
    For Each mbr In cmp.CodeModule.Members
        text = mbr.Name
        ' add member scope
        Select Case mbr.Scope
            Case vbext_Friend
                text = text & vbTab & "Friend"
            Case vbext_Private
                text = text & vbTab & "Private"
            Case vbext_Public
                text = text & vbTab & "Public"
        End Select
        ' add member type
        Select Case mbr.Type
            Case vbext_mt_Const
                text = text & vbTab & "Const"
            Case vbext_mt_Event
                text = text & vbTab & "Event"
            Case vbext_mt_Method
                ' this could be a real method or an ingoing event
                ' the following code is not bullet-proof
                If InStr(mbr.Name, "_") _
                    And mbr.Scope = vbext_Private Then
```

continues

Listing 43.8   Continued

```
                                text = text & vbTab & "Event proc"
                        Else
                                text = text & vbTab & "Method"
                        End If
                Case vbext_mt_Property
                        text = text & vbTab & "Property"
                Case vbext_mt_Variable
                        text = text & vbTab & "Variable"
        End Select
                If mbr.Static Then text = text & " Static"
            ' add to the listbox
            ctrl.AddItem text
    Next
End Sub
```

This procedure makes good use of the Name, Type, Scope, and Static properties of the Member object, but there are other properties that you might find interesting, such as Description, Hidden, and HelpContextID. In general, all those values that appear in the Procedure Attributes dialog box can be read or modified by using these properties. For instance, you may write an add-in that warns you if any Public property or method in a UserControl component is not associated to a description or a HelpContextID value (see Listing 43.9). Because Public properties and methods are those that are visible to the developer who uses your ActiveX control, you have to complete the documentation for the control:

Listing 43.9   An Add-In that Warns You if Public Properties Are Not Associated

```
Sub CheckAttributes(list As ListBox, projectName As String, _
    componentName As String)
    '----------------------------------------------------------
    ' Check the attributes of all the members in a component
    ' Fill a listbox with the names of all members whose
    ' description or HelpContextID is missing
    '----------------------------------------------------------
    Dim cmp As VBIDE.VBComponent
    Dim mbr As VBIDE.Member
    On Error Resume Next

    ' get component reference - exit if error
    Set cmp = VBInstance.VBProjects(projectName).VBComponents(componentName)
    If Err Then Exit Sub

        ' iterate on all members
    list.Clear
    For Each mbr In cmp.CodeModule.Members
        If mbr.Scope = vbext_Public Then
```

```
          If mbr.Description = "" Or mbr.HelpContextID = 0 Then
              List.AddItem mbr.Name
          End If
      End If
  Next
End Sub
```

The *CodePanes* Collection and the *CodePane* Object

The CodePanes collection, as shown in Figure 43.20, is directly exposed by the root VBE object and represents all of the code windows that are open at a given time. Each CodePane object exposes several properties, such as TopLine (the first visible line in the window), CountOfVisibleLines (the number of lines showed in the window), and CodePaneView (which lets you alternate between procedure or full-module view). You can learn which lines are currently highlighted by using GetSelection, or move the selection with SetSelection. Here is a simple usage of the CodePanes collection:

```
' reset full module view for each code module
' and scroll it to the first line of the module
Dim cpa As VBIDE.CodePane
For Each cpa In VBInstance.CodePanes
    cpa.CodePaneView = vbext_cv_FullModuleView
    cpa.TopLine = 1
Next
```

It is important to remember that CodePane objects do not give you access to the actual code, not immediately at least. However, each CodePane object exposes the underlying CodeModule object, which you use to read and modify the code shown in the window.

FIG. 43.20

The CodePanes collection and its dependent objects.

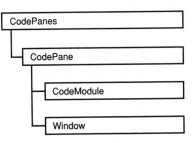

For instance, if you want to retrieve the code that is currently selected, you first must get a reference to the active code pane by using the ActiveCodePane property of the VBE object, then apply its GetSelection method, and finally, use the Lines method of the related CodeModule object to return the actual code. Listing 43.10 shows the complete routine.

Listing 43.10   A Procedure that Retrieves the Code Currently Highlighted

```
Function GetSelectedText() As String
    Dim startLine As Long, startCol As Long
    Dim endLine As Long, endCol As Long
    Dim codeText As String
    Dim cpa As VBIDE.CodePane
    Dim cmo As VBIDE.CodeModule

    On Error Resume Next

    ' get a reference to the active code window and the
    ' underlying module
    ' exit if no one is available
    Set cpa = VBInstance.ActiveCodePane
    Set cmo = cpa.CodeModule
    If Err Then Exit Sub

    ' get the current selection coordinates
    cpa.GetSelection startLine, startCol, endLine, endCol
    ' exit if no text is highlighted
    If startLine = endLine And startCol = endCol Then Exit Sub

    ' get the code text
    If startLine = endLine Then
        ' only one line is partially or fully highlighted
        codeText = Mid$(cmo.Lines(startLine, 1), startCol, _
        endCol - startCol)
    Else
        ' the selection spans multiple lines of code
        ' first, get the selection of the first line
        codeText = Mid$(cmo.Lines(startLine, 1), startCol) & vbCrLf
        ' then get the lines in the middle, that are fully highlighted
        If startLine + 1 < endLine Then
            codeText = codeText & cmo.Lines(startLine + 1, _
            endLine - startLine - 1)
        End If
        ' finally, get the highlighted portion of the last line
        codeText = codeText & Left$(cmo.Lines(endLine, 1), endCol - 1)
    End If

    GetSelectedText = codeText
End Sub
```

As you can see, getting the selected text is not immediate: the Lines property of the underlying CodeModule can retrieve entire lines only, while a selection can start or end at any column. For this reason, you must deal with different cases, depending on whether the selection spans multiple lines.

Modifying the text that appears in a code pane is a bit more difficult because you must resort to the Replace method of the related CodeModule object, and this method only works on single lines. The routine shown in Listing 43.11 converts the highlighted code to uppercase.

Listing 43.11   A Routine that Converts the Highlighted Text to Upper- or Lowercase

```
Sub ConvertSelectedText(Optional conversion As Long = vbUpperCase)
    Dim startLine As Long, startCol As Long
    Dim endLine As Long, endCol As Long
    Dim codeText As String
    Dim cpa As VBIDE.CodePane
    Dim cmo As VBIDE.CodeModule
    Dim i As Long

    On Error Resume Next

    ' get a reference to the active code window and the
    ' underlying module
    ' exit if no one is available
    Set cpa = VBInstance.ActiveCodePane
    Set cmo = cpa.CodeModule
    If Err Then Exit Sub

    ' get the current selection coordinates
    cpa.GetSelection startLine, startCol, endLine, endCol
    ' exit if no text is highlighted
    If startLine = endLine And startCol = endCol Then Exit Sub

    ' get the code text
    If startLine = endLine Then
        ' only one line is partially or fully highlighted
        codeText = cmo.Lines(startLine, 1)
        Mid$(codeText, startCol, endCol - startCol) = _
            StrConv(Mid$(codeText, startCol, _
            endCol - startCol), conversion)
        cmo.ReplaceLine startLine, codeText
    Else
        ' the selection spans multiple lines of code
        ' first, convert the highlighted text on the first line
        codeText = cmo.Lines(startLine, 1)
        Mid$(codeText, startCol, Len(codeText) + 1 - startCol) = _
            StrConv(Mid$(codeText, startCol, Len(codeText) _
            + 1 - startCol), conversion)
        cmo.ReplaceLine startLine, codeText

        ' then convert the lines in the middle, that are
        ' fully highlighted
        For i = startLine + 1 To endLine - 1
            codeText = cmo.Lines(i, 1)
            codeText = StrConv(codeText, conversion)
            cmo.ReplaceLine i, codeText
        Next

        ' finally, convert the highlighted portion of the last line
        codeText = cmo.Lines(endLine, 1)
```

continues

Listing 43.11 Continued

```
        Mid$(codeText, 1, endCol - 1) = StrConv(Mid$(codeText, 1, _
        endCol - 1), conversion)
        cmo.ReplaceLine endLine, codeText
    End If

    ' after replacing code we must restore the old selection
    ' this seems to be a side-effect of the ReplaceLine method
    cpa.SetSelection startLine, startCol, endLine, endCol
End Sub
```

Note that you also can use the `ConvertSelectedText` routine for converting the highlighted code to lowercase or proper case (for example, "This Is A Sentence In Proper Case"), by simply passing a suitable value for the optional parameter, as in

```
ConvertSelectedText vbLowerCase
```

or

```
ConvertSelectedText vbProperCase
```

As an exercise, it is left to you to create an add-in that adds three menu commands to the Edit menu to make these conversion routines available to the VB environment.

The *Windows* Collection and the *Window* Object

The `VBE` object exposes the `Windows` collection (see Figure 43.21), which includes all the windows of the environment, except the main window. All the child windows used in the IDE appear in this collection, even if they currently are not visible. After you have the reference to a `Window` object, you can query its `Type` property (toolbox, color palette, immediate, and so forth—each window has a distinctive type); move or resize it by using the standard `Left`, `Top`, `Width` and `Height` properties; hide or show it by means of the `Visible` attribute; and maximize or minimize it by using the `WindowState` property.

FIG. 43.21

The `Windows` collection.

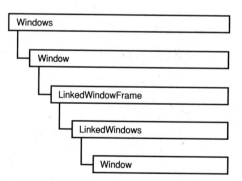

The Windows collection is not the only set of objects that gives you access to the windows used in the environment. Each CodePane object exposes a Window property, which returns a reference to the corresponding Window object, and the VBE object also exposes the ActiveWindow property, which returns a reference to the window that currently has the input focus.

What can you do with the Windows collection? Just try out this handy routine, which closes all the forms and code windows in the environment, except the one with which you are currently working. Call this routine from within an add-in, and you'll have a quick way to reduce the clutter on your screen:

```
Sub CloseUnusedWindows()
    Dim win As VBIDE.Window
    For Each win In VBInstance.Windows
        If win Is VBInstance.ActiveWindow Then
            ' it's the active window, do nothing
        ElseIf win.Type = vbext_wt_CodeWindow Or win.Type _
            = vbext_wt_Designer Then
            ' close it if it is a code pane or a designer window
            win.Close
        End If
    Next
End Sub
```

The *Events* Object

Don't let the "s" fool you—this is an object, not a collection. By itself, this object is useless and serves only to expose six properties that return a reference to other objects: CommandBarEvents, FileControlEvents, ReferencesEvents, SelectedVBControlsEvents, VBComponentsEvents, and VBControlsEvents (see Figure 43.22). All these objects let your add-in receive an event from the VB environment when something interesting happens.

FIG. 43.22
The Events objects and its dependent objects in the VB IDE hierarchy.

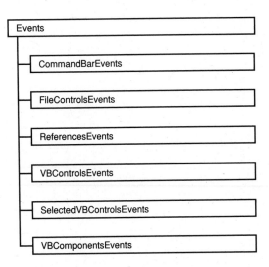

Events

CommandBarEvents

FileControlsEvents

ReferencesEvents

VBControlsEvents

SelectedVBControlsEvents

VBComponentsEvents

The `CommandBarEvents` object was shown in action in the earlier section of this chapter, "Adding User Interface Elements." All add-ins that add a menu item to the Add-Ins menu have to create an object of this type to get a notification when the user clicks it. However, you can intercept actions related to any other menu or toolbar item, not just those that you added to the environment. Listing 43.12 shows how easy intercepting the File, Print command is.

Listing 43.12   How to Intercept the File, Print Menu Command

```
' form level variable
Private WithEvents PrintMenuHandler As CommandBarEvents

Private Sub Form_Load()
    Dim cbc As Office.CommandBarControl
    Set cbc = VBInstance.CommandBars("File").Controls("Print...")
    Set PrintMenuHandler = VBInstance.Events.CommandBarEvents(cbc)
End Sub

Private Sub PrintMenuHandler_Click(ByVal CommandBarControl As Object, _
    Handled As Boolean, CancelDefault As Boolean)
        ' user is trying to print something
        ' remind to connect the printer
        If MsgBox("Have you connected the printer?", vbYesNo) = vbNo Then
            ' if the user replies "No", don't proceed with command
            CancelDefault = True
        End If
End Sub
```

Admittedly, this example really is not useful, but it shows a number of interesting points. After you get a reference to an existing menu item, using the `CommandBars` property (`cbc` in this example), you pass it to the `CommandBarEvents` property to get a reference to a `CommandBarEvent` object (`PrintMenuHandler` in the example). Since you want to use this object to trap events, it must be declared as a form-level variable by using the `WithEvents` clause. You can then write an event procedure that fires when the user selects the corresponding menu command (File-Print, in this case), and you can even cancel the command by setting the `CancelDefault` parameter to `True`.

After you are familiar with this pattern, you'll find no difficulty in understanding how all the other properties of the `Events` object work.

The `VBControlsEvents` property enables you to receive notification when a new control is added on a given form (or any form in the environment), or an existing control is deleted or renamed. Once again, you have to declare an object that will act as a receiver for the IDE events and initialize it properly in the `Form_Load` event (or where you find it more appropriate). See Listing 43.13 to learn you can trap the `ItemAdded`, `ItemRemoved` and `ItemRenamed` events.

Listing 43.13 Intercepting the Events Associated to Controls

```
' form level variable
Private WithEvents CtrlHandler As VBControlsEvents

Private Sub Form_Load()
    ' the syntax (Nothing, Nothing) means that we are asking to
    ' receive events from any project and any component
    Set CtrlHandler = VBInstance.Events.VBControlsEvent(Nothing, Nothing)
End Sub

Private Sub CtrlHandler_ItemAdded(ctrl As VBControl)
    ' a new control has been added
End Sub

Private Sub CtrlHandler_ItemRemoved(ctrl As VBControl)
    ' a control has been deleted
End Sub

Private Sub CtrlHandler_ItemRenamed(ctrl As VBControl, oldName _
    As String, oldIndex As Long)
    ' a control has been renamed or its index has been modified
End Sub
```

You might use the ItemAdded and ItemRenamed events to ensure that the programmers assign a no-nonsense name to the control, instead of sticking to those dumb "Text1" and "List1" default strings. The ItemRemoved event might be useful to delete all the code related to the control, which often is left forgotten in the source code, even though it will never be executed.

You can take advantage of the SelectedVBControlsEvents property to learn when a control is selected (or deselected) on the current form. For instance, if your add-in offers a toolbar that aligns controls, you might enable it when there are at least two selected controls, and disable (or hide) it when there are zero or one selected controls.

The remaining event properties are less likely to be useful, unless you are writing a source code-maintenance utility. The VBComponentsEvents property lets you trap events related to components (for example, when a new module is added or an existing form is removed from the project). The ReferencesEvents property is useful only to get a notification when a reference is added or removed from the current project. Finally, the FileControlEvents property exposes a huge number of events that are related to files. You can be notified when a file is added to the project, when it is renamed or written back to disk, and so forth.

The *References* Collection and the *Reference* Object

Each VBProject object exposes a References collection, which holds one Reference object for each selected item in the Reference dialog box. Each individual Reference object exposes useful properties, such as Name, Guid, Type, Description, FullPath, BuiltIn (which returns True for those references that cannot be removed, for example, VB and VBA object libraries), and Major and Minor (which return version information). Another interesting property is

IsBroken, which is True if the reference does not correspond to a valid entry in the system registry and, therefore, can be used for diagnostic purposes, as in the routine shown in Listing 43.14.

Listing 43.14   You Can Programmatically Check that All References Are Okay

```
Dim ref As VBIDE.Reference

For Each ref In VBInstance.ActiveVBProject.References
    Print "Name: " & ref.Name
    Print "Type: " & IIf(ref.Type = vbext_rk_Project, _
        "Project", "Type Library") _
        & IIf(ref.BuiltIn, " (Built-in)", "")
    Print "Path: " & ref.FullPath
    Print "Version: " & ref.Major & "." & ref.Minor
    Print "Guid: " & ref.Guid
    Print "Description: " & ref.Description
    If ref.IsBroken Then Print "WARNING: the reference appears to be invalid"
    Print
Next
```

You can also programmatically add new references to the project, using the AddFromFile and AddFromGuid methods of the References collection, and discard them by using the Remove method.

The *Addins* Collection and the *Addin* Object

As implied by its name, the Addins collection holds one reference for each add-in installed in the environment, either active or not. Each Addin object represents one entry in VBADDIN.INI and exposes properties such as Guid, ProgID, and Description. The most important property is Connect, which is True if the add-in is active and is otherwise False. To activate and deactivate other add-ins, you simply modify this setting and execute the Update method of the Addins collection. However, unless you are writing an alternative add-in manager, you are not going to use the Addin objects very often.

Hints and Suggestions

At this point, you should be aware of the many things that you can accomplish by using add-ins. The VB IDE object model is very complex and powerful at the same time, and it is impossible to cover all of its intricacies in a single chapter. However, the information contained in this chapter should be sufficient for you to start exploring it on your own. When in doubt, you may resort to official documentation and online help.

The next section provides you with some ideas to be implemented in your own add-ins:

- *Code formatter*   Modifies your source code by providing the correct indentation for `If` and `Select Case` blocks and loops, by inserting blank lines where desired, by breaking longer lines, and so on.

- *Print routine*   Prints selected portions of the source code (for instance, only the procedures modified after a specified date); uses different styles for such things as keywords, variables, and statements; adds informative headers and footers; and other related printing styles.

- *Cross-reference utility*   Shows where a variable is initialized, modified, and referenced; where a procedure or method is invoked; and so forth.

- *Code optimizer*   Spots which variables are declared but not used, and which routines are never executed (the so-called *dead code*). A decent optimizer would also point to inefficient Variant variables and arguments, or to invariant expressions within loops, which could be optimized simply by evaluating the expression outside the loop and assigning it to a temporary variable.

- *Palette for control alignment*   While VB5 offers many commands to align and resize the controls on a form, you might find that something is still missing. For example, while it is possible to center a control on its parent form, you cannot center a control within its container control.

- *Repository for code routines*   A database where you store your routines, and retrieve them by using intelligent queries (for example, "show me all the routines that deal with graphics").

- *Naming Style enforcer*   A utility that helps to enforce a set of rules for control and variable naming (for instance, all command buttons should be prefixed by "cmd", all text box controls should be prefixed by "txt", and so forth).

- *Interface guidelines enforcer*   An add-in that checks that a number of rules are met while building the user interface of your application. For instance, it can check that there are no duplicate hot keys in menus and controls, that all controls are properly aligned, that no form is greater than 640 × 480 pixels (if you want your apps to run in VGA mode), and so on.

- *Wizards*   Automate several phases in the process of software development, such as the many wizards included in the VB package.

- *Common dialog code generators*   A common task for add-ins is the generation of code for building message boxes, Open and Save dialogs boxes, and all the other types of Windows common dialogs boxes.

- *Common styles for controls*   Build *control styles*, a well defined set of properties and related values that you can then apply to any control or group of controls that you place on a form.

- *Code spell-checkers*   It is rather easy to build an add-in that extracts all the quoted strings in an application and passes them to an external spell checker (such as the one included in Microsoft Word).

- *Tools for code localization*   Similar to the spell-checker, but instead helps translate a program to a different language, while checking that hot keys are consistent and that the new translated strings are short enough to appear on-screen (this is especially useful for messages that appear in label controls).

- *Homemade source control utilities*   While it is strongly suggested that you use full-fledged tools, such as Microsoft Visual SourceSafe, for any nontrivial requirement in this area, you can do many interesting things with your own add-ins, such as automatic compression and backup of all the source files as soon as they are written to disk, or immediate notification to the team administrator—through e-mail, for instance—that a programmer has opened or saved a shared file.

From Here...

This chapter explained what add-ins are and how you can implement them. It also showed a number of advanced routines that you may reuse in your own add-ins, and gave you many hints that you may want to develop on your own.

Much of the code illustrated in this chapter based on many advanced concepts that may be discussed in more depth elsewhere in this book:

- Chapter 17, "Managing Your Projects," covers functions and procedures, and explains argument passing.

- Chapter 18, "Introduction to Classes," contains details on the implementation of properties and methods, that are essential to understand all the issues related to add-ins.

- Chapter 44, "Building a Wizard," is a good companion to this chapter because many add-ins are written in the form of wizards—find out how to couple the two concepts.

Building a Wizard

This chapter introduces the concept of using wizards and provides guidance on why and when to use wizards. You'll be guided through planning an example application by using the wizard paradigm. Then you'll be taken step-by-step through building the application and, along the way, you'll learn how to build an intuitive process flow and how to avoid design pitfalls in your own wizard applications. ■

Presenting a wizard overview

Discover how to use the wizard paradigm to design effective user interfaces.

Designing and building wizards

Learn the concepts of designing and building intuitive wizards.

Presenting the Wizard Manager

Find out how to use the Wizard Manager to accelerate and simplify the process of building and managing wizard forms.

Mastering the wizard

Learn methods of error handling and checking for omissions to insure fail-safe functioning of your wizard applications.

Defining a Wizard

When you examine the workflow of many user interfaces, you'll often find that the user is processing the same series of tasks over and over again. There are instances where the application asks the user a series of questions and builds a response set or a finished product. This may be an appropriate place to design a wizard interface for your application. Later in this chapter, you'll learn how to design and build a wizard, but first, some application tasks that are suitable for a wizard will be discussed.

If you've ever used Microsoft Access, then you probably are already familiar with using wizards. The Access Report Wizard is one of the best examples of a successful implementation of the wizard paradigm. The Report Wizard prompts the user for information about which tables or queries to use, which fields to use in the report, and in which order to use them. The Report Wizard then asks if the user wants totals and subtotals, and how to group and sort the report. When the Report Wizard has collected all the essential information from the user, it asks the user to select a presentation format for the report. Then the Report Wizard assembles all this information and presents the user with a complete, finished product: a professional-looking report.

When to Use a Wizard

Now examine what happens in the process of using the Report Wizard. The program asks a series of questions. The Report Wizard gathers essential information from the user in the form of answers to questions and then presents a finished product to the user. Keep in mind that, to a user, a wizard appears only to ask a series of questions. Each question usually has a finite number of answer choices. After the wizard has gathered all the necessary information, it processes the information *behind the scenes*—that is, the processing is transparent to the user— before presenting the finished product.

Many applications lend themselves to this sort of querying process interface, such as the following:

- Order-entry systems
- Aptitude tests
- Diagnostic systems
- Loan applications
- Computer-based training

Effective Wizard Design

When designing a wizard, it is necessary to break the essential pieces of information into logical units first. Then these logical units must be placed in an appropriate order. For example, a report-building wizard would not ask about sorting fields before asking the user to select fields. First the user would be asked what information to include and then would be asked how to present that information. Similarly, a loan calculator wizard would not ask a user to select interest rates—this information would come from a database. Instead, the program would ask about the principal of the loan, frequency of payments, duration of the loan, and so forth. Lastly, the user can be presented with a choice about the presentation or routing of the finished information.

Introducing the Wizard Manager

The Wizard Manager simplifies the daunting task of building a wizard with Visual Basic 5.0. If you wanted to create a wizard in earlier versions of Visual Basic, you had to build your own wizard from scratch. The process was not complex, but it was certainly cumbersome. At the time, the accepted method was to create a single form with individual frames, which contained the controls for each step of the wizard. Then the frames were either shown or hidden to present individual screens to the user. A few enterprising developers built reusable classes from these models, but it was still slow and cumbersome work. With Visual Basic 5.0, this approach has been incorporated as the Wizard Manager, which is now included as an Add-In tool.

Part

IX

Ch

44

A Note from the Author

There is very little documentation about the Wizard Manager on the Visual Basic disks. In fact, you cannot find "Wizard Manager" when searching the help index, but you will find a very brief overview under "Wizard Wizard."

What the Wizard Manager Will Do for You

The Wizard Manager automates much of the tedious work involved in building a wizard application. The Wizard Manager builds the necessary frames and essential controls, and creates the code to control the behavior of the interface elements (for example, navigation buttons). When you use the Wizard Manager to create a skeleton wizard, you can be assured that the design of your wizards will be consistent.

What the Wizard Manager Won't Do for You

While the Wizard Manager greatly speeds up your wizard development, it doesn't do all the work for you. Remember that the Wizard Manager only builds a template, a skeleton wizard. You still have to add the controls and the code specific to your interface needs, and you have to write the code to process the information that your wizard gathers from the user. Although the Wizard Manager provides some rudimentary error handling, if you want more sophisticated error handling or conditional branching, you have to provide that code yourself.

Installing and Running the Wizard Manager

First, you need to install the Wizard Manager Add-In. From the Visual Basic toolbar, select Add-Ins; then click the Add-In Manager. You will see the available add-ins. Check the box next to VB Wizard Manager, as illustrated in Figure 44.1.

FIG. 44.1
Here is the Visual Basic Add-In Manager, which shows the screen when the new VB Wizard Manager is selected.

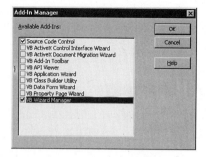

Next, return to the Visual Basic menu bar and select the Add-Ins option. Note that the Wizard Manager has been added to the submenu. Select this option and you will see the Wizard Manager form, as shown in Figure 44.2.

FIG. 44.2
You can create a template wizard by following the prompts from the Wizard Manager Add-In.

Wizard Manager menu ─

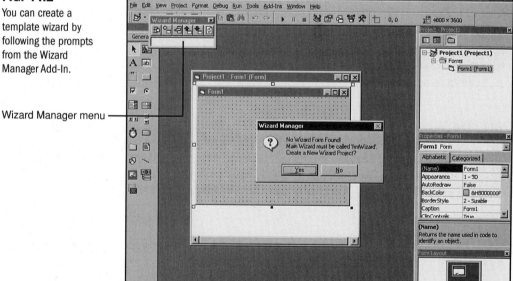

You are almost ready to begin building your wizard, but first you must complete the most important step: planning.

Planning the Pizza Wizard

Obviously, it is important to plan every application, but all too often, developers simply sit down at the keyboard with a rough idea of what they want and begin to code. While this is undeniably bad practice, the result can be even worse with a highly specialized interface, such as a wizard. So, before you begin to design or code anything, *stop and think* about the design. How will the design be most intuitive to the user? Careful design *now* will not only make your program more usable, but it will also make it easier to develop—and you certainly will reduce the chances that you will have to go back and redesign the application.

Most wizards today are extensions of existing larger applications. But a wizard can be the *entire* application, as is the case in the example you'll be building in this chapter.

The application you will design is a user interface for ordering a pizza, in which the user is asked a series of questions, and the wizard then builds the order and asks the user if the order is correct. If the user answers affirmatively, the order is built and e-mailed to the appropriate pizza kitchen. You'll see from this relatively simple demonstration application that you can easily build powerful intranet applications.

To start, you need to determine what information your application must obtain from the user. First, you need to identify the user. Presuming that there is a database with previous orders on file, you will ask the user to enter a telephone number.

N O T E If you want to build a truly powerful intranet application from this example, add an interface to a telephone database and match the users' telephone numbers with their addresses. ∎

Now you need to ask the users what kind of pizza they would like. You should build the pizza logically, from size, to crust, to sauce, to toppings. Finally, ask the users whether they want to order add-on items, such as garlic bread and soft drinks.

Now pause a minute and re-read the preceding paragraph. These descriptions are very logical, discrete units. In essence, then, you are defining the steps of the pizza-order process. From looking at these units, you should begin to understand how to build the wizard screens.

The wizard needs a splash or welcome screen and a summary screen at the end. You can design the entity diagrams, or logical units, for these screens. As you go through them, there may be quite a few toppings you want to include. Thus, you should subdivide toppings into two types—meat and cheese, and vegetables. Perhaps you can combine the crust and sauce type screens. If you block these screens out into an entity diagram, you'll have the high levels of your wizard screens defined, as in Figure 44.3.

Now that the entities, or logical units, have been clearly delineated, you are ready to begin designing the screen frames for the application.

Constructing the Pizza Wizard Application

A wizard should always start with an introductory, or *splash*, screen. The splash screen should identify the application wizard and tell the user some basic information about what to expect—for example, that the wizard will ask questions and present a series of options to make the process as simple as possible. The Wizard Manager will create a basic introductory screen—you'll add appropriate text and graphics to it later on.

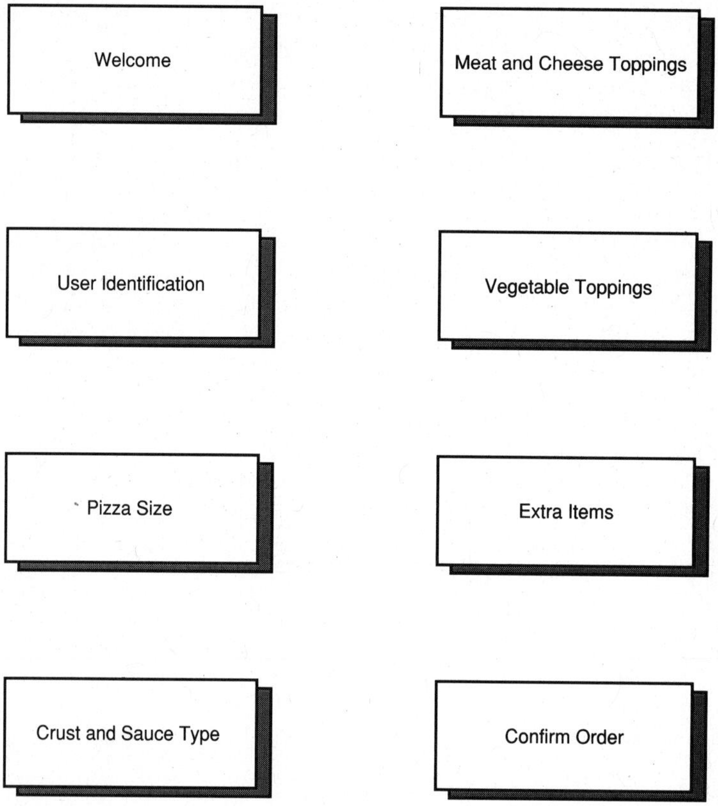

FIG. 44.3
After the order process
is broken into eight
logical units, eight
screens are defined for
the Pizza Wizard.

Welcome	Meat and Cheese Toppings
User Identification	Vegetable Toppings
Pizza Size	Extra Items
Crust and Sauce Type	Confirm Order

Generating the Wizard Template

To begin, start a new project and name it "Pizza Wizard." Now select Add-Ins from the menu bar and select the Wizard Manager. Immediately, you see the template forms for a generic wizard in the Wizard menu frame. If you don't see the pre-built steps—Introduction, Steps 1, 2, 3, 4, and Finished!—right-click the Wizard Manager and select New Wizard. The Wizard Manager creates two forms automatically (Wizard.frm and Confirm.frm) and opens the Wizard template screens, as shown in Figure 44.4.

N O T E You must name the main form in your wizard application frmWizard! ■

You're now ready to get into the meat, as it were, of building your Wizard application.

Using the Template to Build the Pizza Wizard

 Now you are ready to begin modifying the template Wizard to build your own Wizard. By default, the Wizard Manager creates four Step *x* template screens. Because you will need six screens, click the Add A Step button and add two more. You'll be asked for names, but for now, just name them Step 5 and Step 6.

FIG. 44.4
The Wizard Manager
pre-builds the wizard
template forms, which
you can modify for your
own wizard application.

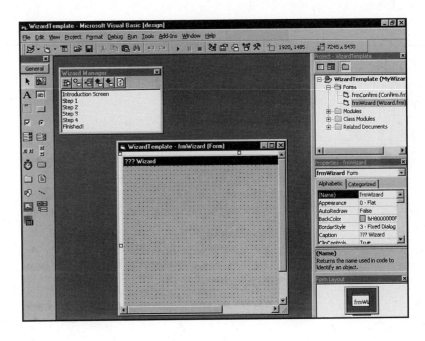

Next, double-click each of the Step *x* captions and change them, as set forth in Table 44.1 and shown in Figure 44.5.

Table 44.1 The Pizza Wizard Steps

Original Caption	New Caption
Introduction	(no change)
Step 1	Step 1: Your Telephone Number?
Step 2	Step 2: What Size Pizza?
Step 3	Step 3: Crust & Sauce
Step 4	Step 4: Meat and Cheese Toppings
Step 5	Step 5: Vegetable Toppings
Step 6	Step 6: Accompaniments
Finished!	(no change)

 If you mix up the screen order, you can always rearrange the order by clicking the Move Up and Move Down buttons on the Wizard Manager.

FIG. 44.5

After you have set all the captions, you will have eight screens in the Pizza Wizard.

TIP You don't have to rename the items in the Wizard Manager, but you'll find it easier to maintain your wizards if you give the frames meaningful names instead of something overly generic, such as Step 3.

Now change the project startup form to `frmWizard` and run the application. You'll see that the Wizard Manager has inserted the appropriate navigation buttons into the form for you. Now just add graphics and appropriate text to create the visual portion of the interface.

Now close the application and return to Visual Basic. Examine the Wizard form and note how you can navigate among the various frames by clicking the appropriate screen title in the Wizard Manager, as explained earlier.

The various Wizard screens are saved on frame controls. Start by selecting the first frame in the array. This form has only three controls on it: a picture box, a label, and a check box. Usually, the check box should be left as it is, which enables users to select the `Skip this screen in the future` option. The Wizard Manager creates the code to activate this check box option, too. The Step frames, however, have only two controls each: the picture box and a single label. These controls are all control arrays; thus, it is simple to correlate them with the frame names as you work.

Create your own version of the Pizza Wizard by using the following figures and control name tables as a guide. Figures 44.6 through 44.12 illustrate the remaining screen modifications. Begin by modifying `Frame(0)`, the Introduction screen, as in Figure 44.6.

FIG. 44.6

Add an appropriate graphic to the PictureBox control.

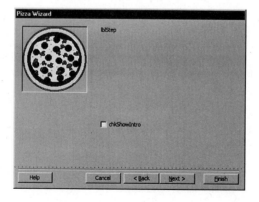

Add the controls listed in Table 44.2 to the frame Step 2: "What Size Pizza?"

FIG. 44.7
Add a graphic, as you did for Figure 44.6, to the second screen, and add a text box for a telephone number.

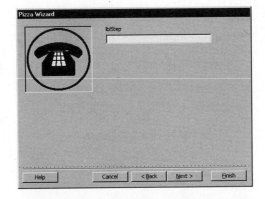

FIG. 44.8
Add option buttons for the "Step 2: What Size Pizza?" choice.

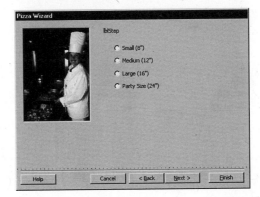

Table 44.2 Controls for the Pizza Size Frame (Step 2)

Control Type	Name	Caption or Text
OptionButton	optSizeSmall	Small (8")
OptionButton	optSizeMedium	Medium (12")
OptionButton	optSizeLarge	Large (16")
OptionButton	optSizeParty	Party Size (24")

Table 44.3 Controls for the Crust and Sauce Frame (Step 3)

Control Type	Name	Caption
Frame	fraCrust	Crust Type
OptionButton	optCrustRegular	Regular

continues

Table 44.3   Continued

Control Type	Name	Caption
OptionButton	optCrustWholeWheat	Whole Wheat
OptionButton	optCrustGarlic	Garlic Sourdough
Frame	fraSauce	Sauce
OptionButton	optSauceRegular	Regular Tomato
OptionButton	optSauceSpicy	Spicy Tomato
OptionButton	optSaucePesto	Pesto

FIG. 44.9

On the third screen, as depicted in this figure, you have two frames, one for crust type and one for sauce (see Table 44.3).

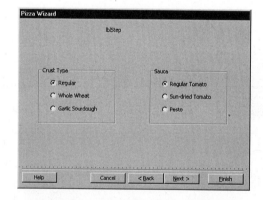

FIG. 44.10

The Step 4 frame has multiple check boxes so that the user can select multiple toppings (see Table 44.4).

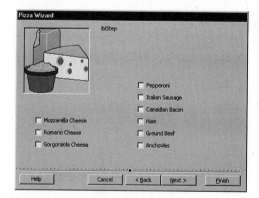

Table 44.4   Meat and Cheese Toppings (Step 4)

Control Type	Control Name	Caption or Text
CheckBox	chkMozzarella	Mozzarella Cheese
CheckBox	chkRomano	Pecarino Romano Cheese

Control Type	Control Name	Caption or Text
CheckBox	chkGorgonzola	Gorgonzola Cheese
CheckBox	chkPepperoni	Pepperoni
CheckBox	chkSausage	Italian Sausage
CheckBox	chkCanadianBacon	Canadian Bacon
CheckBox	chkAnchovies	Anchovies

FIG. 44.11
As with the meat and cheese topping screen, the Step 5, "Vegetable Toppings," frame has a number of check boxes so that the user can select multiple toppings (see Table 44.5).

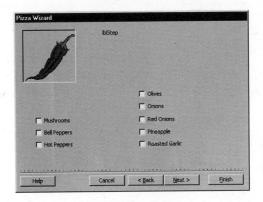

Table 44.5 Vegetable Toppings (Step 5)

Control Type	Control Name	Caption or Text
CheckBox	chkOnion	Onion
CheckBox	chkRedOnion	Red Onion
CheckBox	chkGarlic	Roasted Garlic
CheckBox	chkOlive	Olives
CheckBox	chkPineapple	Pineapples
CheckBox	chkMushroom	Mushrooms
CheckBox	chkHotPepper	Hot Peppers
CheckBox	chkBellPepper	Bell Peppers

Table 44.6 Accompaniments

Control Type	Control Name	Caption
CheckBox	chkGarlicBread	Garlic Bread (Serves 6)
CheckBox	chkBuffaloWingsSpicy	Spicy Buffalo Wings (1 dozen)

continues

Table 44.6   Continued

Control Type	Control Name	Caption
CheckBox	chkBuffaloWingsMild	Mild Buffalo Wings (1 dozen)
CheckBox	chkColaRegular	Regular Cola (6-pack)
CheckBox	chkColaDiet	Diet Cola (6-pack)

FIG. 44.12

The final step in collecting information from the user is the Accompaniments frame, where you have two option groups. Because they contain check boxes, the frames are optional (see Table 44.6).

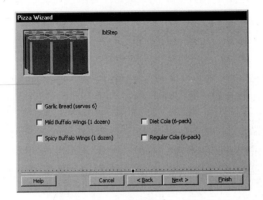

The wizard now should be able to gather all the information necessary to process the customer's order. But good wizard design dictates that the program process the information and present it to the user so that the user can go back and change it if necessary. For a typical wizard application, the Finish button is active only on the final frame. The Wizard Manager creates the "Finished!" frame for you; in most cases, there is no need to change this frame. For this particular application, the text on the command button could be changed to "Place Order." The chkSaveSettings control can be used to enable the customer to make the same order next time.

The Confirm dialog box, illustrated in Figure 44.13, appears last. It is a separate form that serves to confirm that the order has been sent. In the background, the program assembles the information and e-mails it to the proper pizzeria.

FIG. 44.13

The Confirm dialog box is a separate form that appears after the user has clicked the Finish button on the last frame of the wizard.

You have created an interface with the help of the Wizard Manager, but as noted earlier in this chapter, the Wizard Manager doesn't make your wizard do anything. You still have to write most of the functional code.

The Example in Action

In this section, you learn how to modify the code the Wizard Manager created. You also look at some error-handling techniques for the wizard paradigm. Finally, you learn how to use resource files to create wizard libraries that you can quickly modify for easy maintenance.

Modifying the Template Code

Now that you have built the interface, you can run the wizard, and even compile it, but it is still just a series of screens. In fact, notice that the form caption doesn't change properly, and the Finish button appears prematurely. It's time to look at the code built by the Wizard Manager and make the essential changes. The declarations section code generated by the Wizard Manager is provided in Listing 44.1.

Par
IX

Ch

44

On the CD

Listing 44.1   WIZARD.FRM—Declarations Created by the Wizard Manager

```
Option Explicit

Const NUM_STEPS = 8

Const RES_ERROR_MSG = 30000

'BASE VALUE FOR HELP FILE FOR THIS WIZARD:
Const HELP_BASE = 1000
Const HELP_FILE = "MYWIZARD.HLP"

Const BTN_HELP = 0
Const BTN_CANCEL = 1
Const BTN_BACK = 2
Const BTN_NEXT = 3
Const BTN_FINISH = 4

Const STEP_INTRO = 0
Const STEP_1 = 1
Const STEP_2 = 2
Const STEP_3 = 3
Const STEP_4 = 4
Const STEP_FINISH = 5

Const DIR_NONE = 0
Const DIR_BACK = 1
Const DIR_NEXT = 2

Const FRM_TITLE = "Blank Wizard"
Const INTRO_KEY = "IntroductionScreen"
Const SHOW_INTRO = "ShowIntro"
Const TOPIC_TEXT = "<TOPIC_TEXT>"

'module level vars
Dim mnCurStep       As Integer
Dim mbHelpStarted   As Boolean

Public VBInst       As VBIDE.VBE
Dim mbFinishOK      As Boolean
```

Several values in the Declarations section need to be changed; the necessary changes for the sample are noted in Listing 44.2.

Listing 44.2 WIZARD.FRM—The Modified Declarations for *frmWizard*

```
Option Explicit

Const NUM_STEPS = 8

Const RES_ERROR_MSG = 30000

'BASE VALUE FOR HELP FILE FOR THIS WIZARD:
Const HELP_BASE = 1000
Const HELP_FILE = "PIZZAWZD.HLP"     ' Help file name

Const BTN_HELP = 0
Const BTN_CANCEL = 1
Const BTN_BACK = 2
Const BTN_NEXT = 3
Const BTN_FINISH = 4

Const STEP_INTRO = 0
Const STEP_1 = 1
Const STEP_2 = 2
Const STEP_3 = 3
Const STEP_4 = 4
Const STEP_5 = 5             ' Constant added
Const STEP_6 = 6             ' Constant added
Const STEP_FINISH = 7        ' Constant changed

Const DIR_NONE = 0
Const DIR_BACK = 1
Const DIR_NEXT = 2

Const FRM_TITLE = "Pizza Wizard"    ' Form caption changed
Const INTRO_KEY = "IntroductionScreen"
Const SHOW_INTRO = "ShowIntro"
Const TOPIC_TEXT = "<TOPIC_TEXT>"

'module level vars
Dim mnCurStep        As Integer
Dim mbHelpStarted    As Boolean

Public VBInst        As VBIDE.VBE
Dim mbFinishOK       As Boolean
```

Now that changes have been made in the Declarations, it is necessary to change the SetStep() subroutine accordingly, as noted in Listing 44.3.

Listing 44.3   WIZARD.FRM—Corresponding Changes in the *SetStep* Subroutine

Part

IX

Ch

44

```
Select Case nStep
        Case STEP_INTRO

        Case STEP_1

        Case STEP_2

        Case STEP_3

        Case STEP_4

        Case STEP_5

        Case STEP_6
            mbFinishOK = False

        Case STEP_FINISH
            mbFinishOK = True

    End Select
```

The purpose of the code in Listing 44.3 is to change the mbFinishOK variable to be called on the sixth, or last step, rather than the fourth, or default frame. Otherwise, the user sees the finish button enabled prematurely in the fourth screen frame.

If you want to use conditional branching, that is, present different options on subsequent wizard screens, you can insert it into the code in Listing 44.3.

Error Handling

An essential feature of any wizard is error handling. The wizard must check, for instance, that the user has entered the necessary data in the required fields.

For the purposes of this example, you have enabled the essential error handling on only one screen. But, from the techniques in the example, you will be able to see how to insert more sophisticated error handling, and even conditional branching routines, into your own wizard interfaces.

The Wizard Manager creates a subroutine called IncompleteData, which displays error messages. First, however, the Wizard needs criteria to detect errors or omissions. You must pass this information to the IncompleteData subroutine. This error checking is the purpose of the CheckForIncompleteData subroutine. The subroutine in Listing 44.4 is not created by the Wizard Manager; you must add it.

On the CD

Listing 44.4 WIZARD.FRM—Using the *CheckForIncompleteData* Subroutine

```
Sub CheckForIncompleteData(nStep As Integer)

    Select Case nStep
        Case STEP_INTRO

        Case STEP_1
            If txtTelephoneNumber.Text = "" Then
                IncompleteData (mnCurStep)
            End If

        Case STEP_2

        Case STEP_3

        Case STEP_4

        Case STEP_5

        Case STEP_6

        Case STEP_FINISH

    End Select


End Sub
```

To call the subroutine from the next button, simply call the function with a simple `If...Then`
statement, as in Listing 44.5.

**Listing 44.5 WIZARD.FRM—Calling the *CheckForIncompleteData* Subroutine
from the *cmdNav_Click* Procedure**

```
Private Sub cmdNav_Click(Index As Integer)
    Dim nAltStep As Integer
    Dim lHelpTopic As Long
    Dim rc As Long
    CheckForIncompleteData (mnCurStep)

    Select Case Index
        Case BTN_HELP
            mbHelpStarted = True
            lHelpTopic = HELP_BASE + 10 * (1 + mnCurStep)
            rc = WinHelp(Me.hwnd, HELP_FILE,
            ➥HELP_CONTEXT, lHelpTopic)

        Case BTN_CANCEL
            Unload Me

        Case BTN_BACK
```

```
                    'place special cases here to jump
                    'to alternate steps
                    nAltStep = mnCurStep - 1
                    SetStep nAltStep, DIR_BACK

            Case BTN_NEXT
                    'place special cases here to jump
                    'to alternate steps
                    nAltStep = mnCurStep + 1
                    SetStep nAltStep, DIR_NEXT

            Case BTN_FINISH
                    'wizard creation code goes here

                    Unload Me

                    If GetSetting(APP_CATEGORY, WIZARD_NAME,
                    ➥CONFIRM_KEY, vbNullString)
                    ➥= vbNullString Then
                        frmConfirm.Show vbModal
                    End If

        End Select
End Sub
```

If you want to include more sophisticated branching or error handling, the cmdNav_Click procedure is the appropriate place to insert this code.

Working with the Wizard Resource File

The Wizard Manager creates an easily maintainable program skeleton, which requires the minimal code manipulation listed in the previous sections. Much of what the user sees in the interface, however, is customized and controlled from a resource file.

A resource file can be added and removed from the Visual Basic project just as any other object can, except that you can't work with the file directly from Visual Basic. First, you need to create the source file, then compile it into a resource .res file.

The Wizard Manager creates a template resource file that holds strings for the captions of the various buttons and labels in the wizard application. The source code created by the Wizard Manager for the template resource file is contained in Listing 44.6.

On the CD

> **Listing 44.6   WIZARD.RC—The Resource File Source Code as Generated by the Wizard Manager**

```
STRINGTABLE DISCARDABLE
BEGIN
        //Wizard Caption
        10        "Wizard Template"
        15        "Wizard Template..."
```

continues

Listing 44.6   Continued

```
//Button Captions for Navigation Control:
100        "Help"
101        "Cancel"
102        "< &Back"
103        "&Next >"
104        "&Finish"

//Intro Info:
1000       "Introduction"
1001       "The ??? Wizard will help you ..."
1002       "&Skip this screen in the future."

//Other Step Control Captions:
2000       "Step 1"
2001       "Instructions for this step."
2002       "Step 2"
2003       "Instructions for this step."
2004       "Step 3"
2005       "Instructions for this step."
2006       "Step 4"
2007       "Instructions for this step."


//Finish Step:
3000       "Finished!"
3001       "The ??? Wizard is finished
           ➥collecting information.\r\n\r\n_"
3002       "To build your ???, press Finish!"
3003       "Save current settings as default"

//Confirmation dialog
10000      "??? Created"
10001      "The ??? has been created."
10002      "Don't show this dialog in
           ➥ the future."
10003      "OK"

//Misc strings:
20000      "(None)"

//Error messages:
30000      "Incomplete Data."
30001      "You must ...
           ➥before you can continue."

END


5000    BITMAP    wizmenu.bmp
```

You can modify each of the strings in the preceding source code to match what you want your wizard to say to the user. The numbers to the left of each string refer to the Tag property of the controls on the wizard. Note that the /r/n characters in the resource file signal the compiler to insert a carriage return and new line into your text.

N O T E If you are interested in seeing how the code refers to the Tag property, examine the code in the Wizard.bas module on the companion CD. ▪

To modify your own resource file, use a text editor and open the file wizard.rc in your working directory. Make the changes listed in Listing 44.7 to the source code.

Listing 44.7 WIZARD.RC—Modify the Source Code for the Resource File to Your Wizard's Requirements

```
STRINGTABLE DISCARDABLE
BEGIN
        //Wizard Caption
        10          "Pizza Wizard"
        15          "Pizza Wizard..."

        //Button Captions for Navigation Control:
        100         "Help"
        101         "Cancel"
        102         "< &Back"
        103         "&Next >"
        104         "&Finish"

        //Intro Info:
        1000        "Introduction"
        1001        "The Pizza Wizard will take you step-by-step
                    ➥ through the order process.\r\n\r\nThe Wizard will ask a
                    series of questions about how you like your pizza, and then
                    ➥ your order will be prepared!"
        1002        "&Skip this screen in the future."

        //Other Step Control Captions:
        2000        "Step 1"
        2001        "Enter your telephone number below:"
        2002        "Step 2"
        2003        "What size pizza would you like?"
        2004        "Step 3"
        2005        "Select a sauce and crust type."
        2006        "Step 4"
        2007        "Select your favorite meat and cheese toppings."
        2008        "Step 5"
        2009        "Select your favorite vegetable toppings."
        2010        "Step 6"
        2011        "Don't forget beverages and side orders to
                    ➥ go with your pizza!"
```

continues

Listing 44.7   Continued

```
//Finish Step:
3000       "Finished!"
3001       "The Pizza Wizard is finished collecting
          ➥ information.\r\n\r\nTo send your pizza order,
          ➥ press Finish!"
3003       "Save current settings as default"

//Confirmation dialog
10000       "Order Created"
10001       "Your pizza order has been created."
10002       "Don't show this dialog in the future."
10003       "OK"

//Misc strings:
20000       "(None)"

//Error messages:
30000       "Incomplete Data."
30001       "You must enter required information before
          ➥ you can continue."

END
```

Note that most of the modifications in the code in Listing 44.7 are simply changes to the text strings. But as you have added screens, you need to go back to the interface and check the `Tag` properties on the controls for the screens that you added. If you neglect this step, your controls will not display the label text you entered in Listing 44.7.

TIP If you want to customize your wizard further, you can change the &Finish string to &Send Order.

Now you're ready to compile your resource file. But first you need to make sure that the Resource Compiler is installed on your system.

NOTE The modified code does not include any bitmaps. In the example on the CD-ROM, the bitmaps are imbedded directly into the controls. However, you may want to refer to your own wizards in the resource file. If you do, make sure that they are in the application directory, where the wizard is installed. ■

Installing and Using the Resource Compiler

If the Resource Compiler is not already installed on your system, you need to copy it from the Visual Basic CD. You'll find it in the Tools\Resource\ directory. There is no install process; simply copy the rc.exe and rcdll.dll files to your hard drive. You will find it helpful to copy the Resource Compiler directly into the directory where you are working with your wizard.

The Resource Compiler is discussed extensively in the VB Books Online on your Visual Basic CD and in the readme file in the Resource Compiler tool directory, but you only need to know the basics to compile your resource file. To compile the file, run the following in the working directory:

```
RC /v /r wizard.rc
```

The `RC` runs the Resource Compiler, the `/v` parameter turns on messages (so that you can see what the compiler is doing), the `/r` parameter tells the compiler to create the `.res` file, and the `wizard.rc` specifies the file name.

If you run the Resource Compiler and receive an error message, the `/v` parameter tells you which line(s) you need to correct. When you have successfully compiled the resource `.res` file, return to Visual Basic, open the Pizza Wizard project, and run it. You will now see your changes in the resource file reflected in the program, as illustrated in Figure 44.14.

FIG. 44.14
The control tags are associated with the appropriate strings in the compiled resource file.

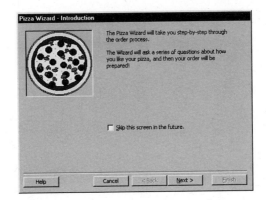

Assembling the Order

Now that you have received the essential order information from the user and have verified it, the Pizza Wizard is ready to assemble the pizza order. Depending on the nature of the environment, the order can be e-mailed to the appropriate pizza deli, or simply printed in the kitchen.

From Here...

In this chapter, you learned how to build a simple wizard, collect the necessary information from the user, and check for errors or omissions. When you are ready to build more complex wizards or explore the possibilities of Internet-enabled Wizard interfaces, explore these sources:

- Find further information about working control arrays in Chapter 12, "Using Control Arrays."

- Discover more about creating Internet Web-enabled applications in Chapter 27, "Creating ActiveX Documents," Part VII, "Web Programming," or Que's *Web Development with Visual Basic 5.*

CHAPTER 45

Accessing the Windows Registry and INI Files

The Windows 95 Registry and INI files are just two of the key elements within the Windows 95 operating system. Windows 95 as well as many other Windows based application make extensive use of INI files and the Registry. Since these two elements play such an important role in the system, your Visual Basic application will, from time to time need to either read the information stored in one of these sources of information or, need to update information stored in either of these locations.

There are various methods that can be used in order to access information stored in INI files, and the Windows 95 Registry. These access methods consist of native Visual Basic 5.0 funcation, as well as functions that are provided as part of the Windows 95 API.

In this chapter you look at both the structure of INI files, and the Registry, as well as the various methods that can be used in order to both read and update the information storedin these two within Windows 95. ■

The structure of INI files and the Windows 95 Registry

Learn about the contents of INI files and the Windows 95 Registry.

Access the information stored in the INI files

Use the Windows 95 API to access data that is stored in INI files.

Access the Registry by using Visual Basic 5.0 functions

Use native Visual Basic 5.0 commands to access the data stored in the Windows 95 Registry.

Access the Registry using Windows 95 API functions

Use the Windows 95 API to access the data stored in the Windows 95 Registry.

Introducing INI Files and the Windows Registry

This section covers the following topics:

- What is the purpose of INI files, and how were they initally used within the Windows environment.
- How the data contained in an INI file is stored.
- The structure of INI files, and how an INI file could be used by an application.
- The purpose of the Windows 95 Registry, and how the Registry is used within the Windows Environment.
- The structure of the Windows 95 Registry. The different types of data that can be stored in the Registry. How the data contained within the Windows 95 Registry is stored.

What INI Files Are

INI files, or Windows Initialization files, are holdovers from the days of 16-bit Windows. There are two types of INI files, system INI files, such as the WIN.INI file—primarily used by Windows 95—and private INI files, which are used by applications other than Windows 95.

An initialization file is a text-format file that is used to store an application's parameters or any additional information the application might need at run time. An example of this is the local date format.

N O T E   The discussion of INI files might seem inappropriate because this book covers Visual Basic 5.0, which is strictly a 32-bit application, and 32-bit applications primarily use the Registry. ▪

You might find that it is easy to store application-based parameters in an INI file format while you are developing an application because they can quickly be changed using any text editor. Some applications make use of a mix of INI settings, as well as Registry settings. A good example of this is Windows 95 itself. Windows 95 stores the majority of its application-specific information in the Registry, but it still makes use of the SYSTEM.INI file, as well as assorted other INI files, to store additional information.

Under Windows NT, most of the contents of the WIN.INI file are mapped directly to the Registry. Therefore, if you update or query any of the sections of the WIN.INI file, you will be reading and writing directly to the Registry. You can modify the contents of INI files using any text editor or the Windows 95 API. Later in this chapter, in the section "INI Files and the Windows API," you learn how to access INI files with the Windows 95 API.

The Structure of INI Files

All INI files have the same standard structure, which is made up of the following elements:

- *Section name*   Defined by a statement enclosed in square brackets ([ ]). The section name is used to group related items. An example of a section name is the [BOOT] section name contained in the SYSTEM.INI file.

■ *Keynames* Contained in each section are keynames. The keyname is used to identify a setting and its value. Keynames are made up of two parts, a key followed by an equal sign (=), and then the key value. An example of a key is the shell setting `shell=Explorer.exe`, which is contained in the SYSTEM.INI file.

Listing 45.1 illustrates the contents of a VB5.ini file.

N O T E The contents of your VB5.ini file might be different from that in the listing, depending on the options that you have installed. ■

Listing 45.1 VB5.INI—The Contents of the VB5.ini File

```
[VBX Conversions32]
threed.vbx={0BA686C6-F7D3-101A-993E-0000C0EF6F5E}#2.0#0;
➥C:\Sheridan\ActiveThreed\Threed20.ocx
[Add-Ins32]
RoseAddInMenues.Connector=1
```

Part IX

Ch

45

As you can see from Listing 45.1, the VB5.ini contains two sections. The first section contains VBX conversion items (in this example, there is only one item that will be converted automatically). The second section contains information about 32-bit add-ins. There is additional add-in information stored in the VBADDIN.ini file.

▶ **See** "Editing the VBADDIN.INI File," **p. 1232**

What the Registry Is

The Registry has been a part of Windows since Windows version 3.1. Originally, the Registry was used to store information on how an application would open and print a file. With the advent of Windows 95 (with its multiple hardware and user profiles), a method of storing information was required. Due to limitation in the INI file architecture, Microsoft elected to use the Registry. The Registry is used to store hardware, user profile, and software configuration information.

The contents of the Registry are physically stored in two files: System.dat and User.dat. The System.dat file, which is located in the WINDOWS directory, contains the hardware and software configuration of the system. The User.dat file is located in the WINDOWS directory. There is one User.dat file for each user that has access to the system. The User.dat file contains user-specific information, pertaining to the user's preferences, as well as any user-specific security and application setup.

To accommodate the variety of information that needs to be stored in the Registry, provisions have been made to store various formats of data. Table 45.1 illustrates the various data formats stored in the Registry.

Table 45.1   Formats of Data Stored in the Registry

Data Type	Description
REG_BINARY	Binary Data
REG_DWORD	Long Data Type
REG_DWORD_BIGENDIAN	Long Data Type
REG_DWORD_LITTLE_ENDIAN	Long Data Type
REG_EXPAND_SZ	Compressed Environment String
REG_LINK	Symbolic Link
REG_MULTI_SZ	List of Strings separated by Null characters
REG_NONE	Undefined Data type
REG_RESOURCE_LIST	Device driver Resource list
REG_SC	String bate type terminated by a null character

Detailed Description of Windows 95 API Registry Manipulation Functions

To access information that is stored in the Registry, you can use the Microsoft-supplied application Regedit. To access Regedit, choose Start, Run. Type **regedit** in the Open box and then press Enter.

N O T E   All of the items in the Data Type column are also available as Constants. See the sample in the section "Detailed Description of Windows 95 API Registry Manipulation Functions" for their definitions. ■

Figure 45.1 shows the top level view of the Registry as it is seen in the Regedit application.

Structure of the Registry

The Registry, much like INI files, is divided into many sections. In the Registry, these sections are referred to as *keys*. Each key contains related subkeys and values. The Registry contains two major keys and four minor keys containing data that is derived from the two major keys.

Major Registry Keys:

HKEY_LOCAL_MACHINE

HKEY_USERS

Minor Registry Keys:

HKEY_CLASSES_ROOT

HKEY_CURRENT_USER

```
HKEY_CURRENT_CONFIG

HKEY_DYN_DATA
```

FIG. 45.1

This top level view of the Registry shows all of the major Registry keys seen through the Regedit application.

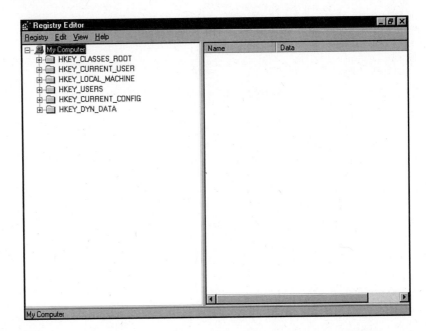

The following portions of this chapter describe these Registry sections. You might also want to consult Que's *Windows 95 Registry and Configuration Handbook*, Second Edition, for even more coverage of the Windows 95 Registry.

Major Registry Keys

HKEY_LOCAL_MACHINE

The HKEY_LOCAL_MACHINE section of the Registry contains all of the Registry values that relate to the hardware and software configuration of the computer.

HKEY_USERS

The HKEY_USERS section of the Registry contains the default windows settings for all new users of the current systems. When a new user is initially created, the registry settings contained in the HKEY_USERS section will be used in order to determine the initial Windows 95 settings.

Minor Registry Keys

HKEY_CLASSES_ROOT

The HKEY_CLASSES_ROOT section of the Registry contains a duplicate of the information that is stored in the Software\Classes section of the HKEY_LOCAL_MACHINE section of the Registry.

Figure 45.2 illustrates the setting for the VBP type of files.

Part

IX

Ch

45

FIG. 45.2

This is the Visual Basic Association section of the Registry, as viewed through Regedit. The currently opened key displays the Open Visual Basic Project Registry Entry.

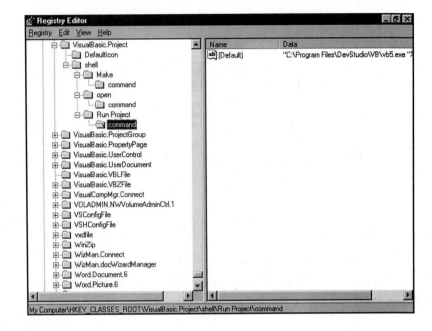

HKEY_CURRENT_USER

The HKEY_CURRENT_USER section of the Registry contains all of the Windows and software settings for the user currently signed onto the system. Figure 45.3 illustrates various keys stored in the HKEY_CURRENT_USER section.

FIG. 45.3

These are the keys contained in the HKEY_CURRENT_USER section of the Registry.

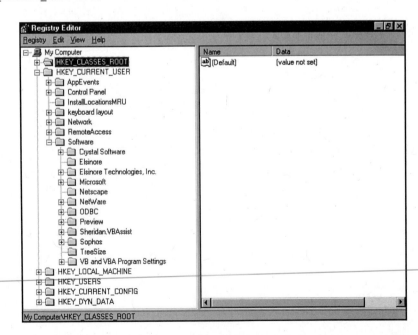

HKEY_CURRENT_CONFIG

The HKEY_CURRENT_CONFIG section of the Registry contains all of the Registry information relating to the current configuration of Windows 95. The section is rebuilt every time Windows 95 is restarted.

HKEY_DYN_DATA

The HKEY_DYN_DATA section of the Registry contains information relating to currently running device drivers. This section is rebuilt every time Windows 95 is restarted.

INI Files and the Windows API

You can most easily and quickly access the data stored in INI files by using the Windows 95 API. The Windows 95 API provides functions with which you can read and update data from INI files. In this section, you learn about the various Windows 95 API functions that you can use to access INI files. You also learn to create a sample application to edit the contents of INI files.

Introduction to Windows 95 INI Manipulation Functions

In this section you learn how to use the various API functions contained in the Windows 95 API to edit and update INI files.

As mentioned previously, there are two different types of INI files—system INI (WIN.INI) files and private or application INI files. Therefore, there are two sets of similar Windows 95 API functions—one set for system files and another for private files.

N O T E You can use the private INI functions to open system INI files. ■

Table 45.2 lists the various Windows 95 API functions that are available and gives a brief description of each function.

Table 45.2 Available Windows API Functions

API Function	Description
GetProfileString	Retrieves a string value from a named key in the WIN.INI file
GetProfileSection	Retrieves all of the values stored in a named section of the WIN.INI file
GetProfileInt	Retrieves an Integer value from a named key in the WIN.INI file
GetPrivateProfileString	Retrieves a string value from a named key contained in a private INI file

continues

Table 45.2 Continued

API Function	Description
GetPrivateProfileSection	Retrieves all of the values stored in a named section of a private INI file
GetPrivateProfileInt	Retrieves an Integer value of a named key contained in a private INI file
WriteProfileString	Updates the value of a named key contained in the WIN.INI file (If the key did not previously exist, it is created.)
WriteProfileSection	Updates a complete section contained in the WIN.INI file (If the section or any of the values did not previously exist, they are created.)
WritePrivateProfileString	Updates the value of a named key contained in a private INI file (If the key did not previously exist, it is created.)
WritePrivateProfileSection	Updates a complete section contained in a private INI file (If the section or any of the values did not previously exist, they are created.)

The description of both the Windows 95 API calls and the parameters needed for each function is discussed in the following section.

Detailed Description of Windows 95 API INI Manipulation Functions

In this section, you learn about the various Windows 95 API functions that you can use to manipulate INI files. In the final part of this section, you learn how to create a small application that can be used as a generic INI file editor.

The *GetProfileString* Function   The declaration that must be included in your Visual Basic application for the GetProfileString function is:

```
Declare Function GetProfileString Lib "kernel32" Alias _
"GetProfileStringA" (ByVal lpAppName As_ String, _
ByVal lpKeyName As String, ByVal lpDefault As String, _
 ByVal lpReturnedString As String, _ bevel nSize As Long) _
As Long
```

The GetProfileString function requires the use of the following parameters:

Parameter	Description
lpAppName	The section in the INI file that contains the key that you want to obtain the value for
lpKeyName	The name of the key whose value you want to retrieve
lpDefault	The default value to be returned to your program if neither the section of the INI file nor the key is found

Parameter	Description
lpReturnedString	The variable that is used to store the value retrieved by the API call (If this value is Null, the value defined in lpDefault is used.)
nSize	The maximum number of characters to retrieve from the INI file

The GetProfileString function returns a Long value indicating the number of bytes that have been read.

The *GetProfileSection* Function   The declaration that must be included in your Visual Basic application for the GetProfileSection function is:

```
Declare Function GetProfileSection Lib "kernel32" Alias _
"GetProfileSectionA" _(ByVal lpAppName As String, _
ByVal lpReturnedString As String, ByVal nSize As Long) _
 As Long
```

The GetProfileSection function requires the use of the following parameters:

Parameter	Description
lpAppName	The section in the INI file of which you want to obtain the contents.
lpReturnedString	The variable that is used to store the value retrieved by the API call. Each key contained in this string is separated by a Null value, and the end of the string is marked by two Null values.
nSize	The maximum number of characters to retrieve from the INI file.

The GetProfileSection function returns a Long value indicating the number of bytes that have been read.

***GetProfileInt* Function**   The declaration that must be included in your Visual Basic application for the GetProfileInt function is:

```
Declare Function GetProfileInt Lib "kernel32" Alias _
"GetProfileIntA" (ByVal lpAppName As String, _
ByVal lpKeyName As String, _
ByVal nDefault As Long) As Long
```

The GetProfileInt function requires the use of the following parameters:

Parameter	Description
lpAppName	The section in the INI file that contains the key you want to obtain the value for
lpKeyName	The name of the key whose value you want to retrieve
nDefault	The default value to be returned to your program if neither the section of the INI file nor the key is found

The GetProfileInt function returns a Long value containing the value that was retrieved by the API function.

The *GetPrivateProfileString* Function   The declaration that must be included in your Visual Basic application for the GetPrivateProfileString function is:

```
Declare Function GetPrivateProfileString Lib "kernel32" Alias _
"GetPrivateProfileStringA" (ByVal lpApplicationName _
 As String, _ByVal lpKeyName As String, ByVal lpDefault As String, _
 ByVal lpReturnedString _As String, ByVal nSize As Long, _
 ByVal lpFileName As String) As Long
```

The GetPrivateProfileString function requires the use of the following parameters:

Parameter	Description
lpApplicationName	The section in the INI file that contains the key for which you want to obtain the value
lpKeyName	The name of the key whose value you want to retrieve
lpDefault	The default value to be returned to your program if neither the section of the INI file nor key is found
lpReturnedString	The variable that is used to store the value retrieved by the API call (If this value is Null, the value defined in lpDefault is used.)
nSize	The maximum number of characters to retrieve from the INI file
lpFilename	The name and location of the INI file from which you want to retrieve information

The GetPrivateProfileString function returns a Long value that indicates the number of bytes that have been read.

The *GetPrivateProfileSection* Function   The declaration that must be included in your Visual Basic application for the GetPrivateProfileSection function is:

```
Declare Function GetPrivateProfileSection Lib "kernel32" Alias _
"GetPrivateProfileSectionA" _(ByVal lpAppName As String, _
 ByVal lpReturnedString As String, ByVal nSize As Long, _
 ByVal lpFileName As String) As Long
```

The GetPrivateProfileSection function requires the use of the following parameters:

Parameter	Description
lpAppName	The section in the INI file that contains the key for which you want to obtain the value.
lpReturnedString	The variable that is used to store the value retrieved by the API call. Each key contained in this string is separated by a Null value, and the end of the string is marked by two Null values.

Parameter	Description
nSize	The maximum number of characters to retrieve from the INI file.
lpFilename	The name and location of the INI file from which you want to retrieve information.

The GetPrivateProfileSection function returns a Long value that indicates the number of bytes that have been read.

The *GetPrivateProfileInt* Function The declaration that must be included in your Visual Basic application for the GetPrivateProfileInt function is:

```
Declare Function GetPrivateProfileInt Lib "kernel32" Alias _
"GetPrivateProfileIntA" (ByVal lpApplicationName As String, _
 ByVal lpKeyName As String, ByVal nDefault As Long, _
 ByVal lpFileName As String) As Long
```

The GetPrivateProfileInt function requires the use of the following parameters:

Parameter	Description
lpApplicationName	The section in the INI file that contains the key for which you want to obtain the value
lpKeyName	The name of the key whose value you want to retrieve
nDefault	The default value to be returned to your program if neither the section of the INI file nor the key is found
lpFilename	The name and location of the INI file from which you want to retrieve information

The GetPrivateProfileInt function returns a Long value containing the value that was retrieved by the API function.

N O T E In each INI API function, the size of the lpReturnedString variable must be predefined. ▨

Accessing and Updating INI Files Using the Windows 95 API

In this section, you create a small application with which you can read, change, and update the contents of an INI file. After you complete this application, you will have an easy-to-use general purpose INI file editor.

To create the application, perform the following steps:

1. Start Visual Basic and select the option to Open a New Standard EXE project.
2. Choose Project, Components. Add the Microsoft Common Dialog Control to your project by selecting the box next to the name and clicking OK.
3. Choose Project, Add Module to add a standard module to the project.

Part
IX

Ch
45

4. Enter the code contained in Listing 45.2 into the Declarations section of the newly added standard module. This code contains all of the Windows 95 API calls that you will use in the example. Alternatively, you might want to copy the listing from file exam1.bas, which is included on the CD accompanying this book.

Listing 45.2   EXAM1A.BAS—INI File API Declarations that Need to be Placed in *Module1*

```
Declare Function GetProfileInt Lib "kernel32" Alias _
 "GetProfileIntA" (ByVal lpAppName As String, _
 ByVal lpKeyName As String, ByVal nDefault As Long) _
 As Long
Declare Function GetProfileSection Lib "kernel32" Alias _
 "GetProfileSectionA" (ByVal lpAppName As_ String, _
 ByVal lpReturnedString As String, ByVal nSize As Long) _
 As Long
Declare Function GetProfileString Lib "kernel32" Alias _
 "GetProfileStringA" (ByVal lpAppName As_ String, _
 ByVal lpKeyName As String, ByVal lpDefault As String, _
 ByVal lpReturnedString As String, _ ByVal nSize As Long) _
 As Long
Declare Function GetPrivateProfileInt Lib "kernel32" Alias _
 "GetPrivateProfileIntA" (ByVal_ lpApplicationName As String, _
 ByVal lpKeyName As String, ByVal nDefault As Long, _
 ByVal lpFileName_ As String) As Long
Declare Function GetPrivateProfileSection Lib "kernel32" _
 Alias _
 "GetPrivateProfileSectionA" (ByVal_ lpAppName As String, _
 ByVal lpReturnedString As String, ByVal nSize As Long, _
 ByVal lpFileName As_ String) As Long
Declare Function GetPrivateProfileString Lib "kernel32" _
 Alias "GetPrivateProfileStringA" (ByVal_
 lpApplicationName_As String, _
 ByVal lpKeyName As String, ByVal lpDefault As String, _
 ByVal_ lpReturnedString As String, ByVal nSize As Long, _
 ByVal lpFileName As String) As Long
Declare Function WritePrivateProfileSection Lib "kernel32" _
 Alias _"WritePrivateProfileSectionA" _ (ByVal lpAppName As String, _
 ByVal lpString As String, ByVal lpFileName As String) As Long
Declare Function WritePrivateProfileString Lib "kernel32" _
 Alias "WritePrivateProfileStringA" _
 (ByVal lpApplicationName As String, ByVal lpKeyName As String, _
 ByVal lpString As String, ByVal lpFileName_ As String) As Long
Declare Function WriteProfileSection Lib "kernel32" Alias _
 "WriteProfileSectionA" (ByVal lpAppName_ As String, _
 ByVal lpString As String) As Long
Declare Function WriteProfileString Lib "kernel32" Alias _
 "WriteProfileStringA" (ByVal lpszSection As String, _
 ByVal lpszKeyName As String, ByVal lpszString As String) As Long
```

5. If no form is contained in the current project, choose Project, Add Form to add a form to the project.

6. Add the following controls to the form (don't worry about their properties because you set them in the next step):

Control	Description
A	Four Label controls
[ab]	Two TextBox controls
	Two ComboBox controls
	Three CommandButton controls
	One CommonDialog control

7. Set the following properties for the four Label controls:

```
Name = lblValue
Caption  =   Value
Height  =    270
Left  =     270
Top  =  1440
Width  =   1245

Name = lblEntryName
Caption =  Entry Name
Height  =    270
Left  =    240
Top  =    1050
Width  =   1245

Name = lblSection
Caption  =   Section
Height  =    270
Left  =    240
Top  =   660
Width  =   1245

Name = lblIniFile
Caption  =   INI File
Height  =    270
Left  =    240
Top  =     240
Width  =   1245
```

8. Set the following properties for the two TextBox controls:

```
Name = txtFileName
Height  =    300
Left =    1560
TabIndex =    0
ToolTipText  =    Enter the Path/Name of the INI file or
```

```
Depress the ""?"" button to Select an INI file
Top  =   240
Width =   2505


Name = txtValue
Height  =   300
Left  =   1560
TabIndex  =   3
Top  =  1440
Width  =   2505
```

9. Set the following properties of the two ComboBox controls:

```
Name = comEntry
Height =   315
Left  =   1590
Style =   2  'Dropdown List
TabIndex  =   2
ToolTipText =   Selection The Section You Wish to View
Top  =  1020
Width  =   2505


Name = comSection
Height =   315
Left  =   1560
Style =   2  'Dropdown List
TabIndex  =   1
ToolTipText =   Selection The Section You Wish to View
Top  =   630
Width =   2505
```

10. Set the following properties for the three CommandButton controls:

```
Name = cmdSave
Caption =   &Save
Height =   300
Left  =   3450
TabIndex =   4
ToolTipText =   Save The Changes
Top =   2910
Width =   700


Name =  cmdSelect
Caption  =   &?
Height  =   315
Left  =   4170
TabIndex =   7
ToolTipText =   Select INI File
Top  =   240
Width  =   345


Name = cmdExit
Caption  =   E&xit
Height =   300
Left  =   4260
TabIndex  =   5
ToolTipText =   Exit the Application
```

```
Top  =   2910
Width  =   700
```

11. Set the following properties for the CommonDialog control:

```
Name = diaexam1
Left =   660
Top  =   2760
CancelError    =    -1  'True
DialogTitle =   Select File to Open
FileName   =   *.ini
Filter  =   Initialization file (*.ini)¦*.ini
```

12. Set the following properties for the form that contains the newly added controls:

```
Name = exam1a
Caption  =   INI Files Sample 1
Height  =   3345
Width   =   5400
```

13. Enter the following code in the `From_Unload` event:

```
Set frmChp531a = Nothing
```

14. Enter the following code in the `cmdExit_Click` event:

```
Unload Me
```

15. Enter the following code in the `cmdSave_Click` event:

```
Dim nbytes As Long
nbytes = WritePrivateProfileString(comSection.Text, _
 comEntry.Text, txtValue.Text, txtFileName.Text)
```

On the CD

16. Enter the following code in the `cmdSelect_Click` event. This code will be used to retrieve all of the section names contained in the selected INI file. Alternatively, you might want to copy the listing from file exam1a.frm, which is included on the CD accompanying this book.

```
Dim nBytes As Long
Dim csection As String
Dim cbuffer As String
Dim cstring As String
Dim nfirst As Integer
On Error Resume Next
If Len(txtFileName.Text) = 0 Then
    diaexam1.filename = ""
    diaexam1.ShowOpen

    If Err = cdlCancel Then
        ' the user depressed cancel
        Exit Sub
    End If

    txtFileName.Text = diachp531.filename
End If
comSection.Clear
If Len(txtFileName.Text) = 0 Then
' There has not been a file selected exit
```

```
        Exit Sub
    End If
    If Len(Dir$(txtFileName.Text)) = 0 Then
    ' invalid file name
        Exit Sub
    End If
    Open txtFileName.Text For Input As #1
    Do While EOF(1) = False
        cstring = Input$(1, #1)

        If cstring = "[" Then
            nfirst = True
            ' Drop the Bracket
            cstring = ""

        End If

        If cstring = "]" Then
            If nfirst = True Then

                If Len(csection) > 0 Then

                    'Add it to the selction list
                    comSection.AddItem csection
                    ' Drop The trailing Bracket
                    csection = ""

                End If

                nfirst = False

            End If

            nfirst = False

        End If

        If nfirst = True Then

            csection = csection & cstring

        End If



    Loop
    comSection.ListIndex = 0
    Close #1
    On Error GoTo 0
```

17. Enter the following code in the comEntry_Click event. This code will be used to retrieve the value of the selected INI Key:

```
Dim nBytes As String
Dim cvalue  As String
' Initialize returned string
```

```
'---------------------------
cvalue = Space$(4096)
nBytes = GetPrivateProfileString((comSection.Text), _
 (comEntry.Text), "", cvalue, 4096, txtFileName.Text)
txtValue.Text = cvalue
```

18. Enter the following code in the comSection_Click event. This code will be used to retrieve all of the entries contained in the selected section on the INI file:

```
Dim nBytes As Long
Dim cvalues As String * 32767
Dim cbuffer As String
Dim x As Integer
Dim y As Integer
Dim ctext As String
Dim nend As Integer
comEntry.Clear
nBytes = GetPrivateProfileSection((comSection.Text), _
 cvalues, 32767, txtFileName.Text)
' get all of the values
x = 1
y = 0
Do While Not nend = True
    x = InStr(y + 1, cvalues, Chr(0))

    ctext = Mid$(cvalues, y + 1, x - y - 1)
    If Len(ctext) = 0 Then
        Exit Do
    End If
    '
    'Strip off the "=" and value

    comEntry.AddItem Mid$(ctext, 1, InStr(ctext, "=") - 1)
    y = x
Loop
```

19. Enter the following Code into the txtSelection_LostFocus event. This code will be used to instigate a click of the Select button:

```
If Len(txtFileName.Text) > 0 Then
    cmdSelect_Click
End If
```

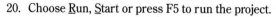

20. Choose <u>R</u>un, <u>S</u>tart or press F5 to run the project.

21. After the project has started, enter the following in the INI File text box: **c:\windows\system.ini**. When you press Tab, the value in the combo box defaults to Boot. If you select Shell from the Entry Name combo box (providing you are using Explorer as the Shell for Windows 95), Explorer.exe appears in the Value box. If you want to change this (which I do not recommend), enter the new value in the text box and click Save to save the change.

Figure 45.4 illustrates the sample application.

FIG. 45.4

Access INI Files through the Windows API.

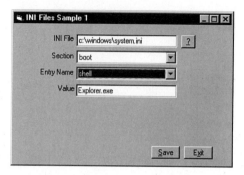

You have now seen various aspects of accessing INI files through the use of the Windows 95 API. In the next sections, you learn to access and alter the Windows Registry by using built-in Visual Basic functions.

Using Visual Basic to Access the Windows 95 Registry

In this section, you learn various ways to access and manipulate information that is stored in the Windows 95 Registry. First, you learn how to access the information using built-in Visual Basic commands. Second, you learn how to access information contained in the Windows 95 Registry by using Windows 95 API functions.

Accessing the Registry Through Visual Basic Commands

Visual Basic version 5.0 provides four commands that allow your application to access the Registry. The provided commands do not give you access to all of the data that is stored in the Registry. Instead, you are restricted to items that can be found under the following key:

HKEY_CURRENT_USER\Software\VB and VBA Program Settings

Figure 45.5 displays the contents of this key. While this protects the programmer from working havoc on the Registry, it is also very restrictive. If your application needs to access other information that is stored in the Registry, then you will have to use Windows 95 API calls as discussed later in the section "The Registry and the Windows 95 API."

Table 45.3 lists all of the Registry-related functions that are available in Visual Basic 5.0, as well as a brief description of each function.

Table 45.3   Registry Functions Available in Visual Basic 5.0

Visual Basic Function	Description
DeleteSetting	Allows you to delete a Registry setting as well as the Registry key

Visual Basic Function	Description
GetSetting	Allows you to retrieve the value of a specified Registry key
GetAllSettings	Allows you to retrieve all of the Registry keys and their settings for a specified application
SaveSetting	Allows you to save a key and its value to the Registry (If the key did not previously exist, it is created.)

FIG. 45.5

This Registry section is available to Visual Basic functions.

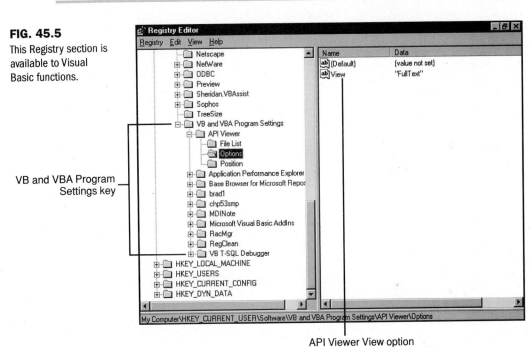

VB and VBA Program Settings key

API Viewer View option

A further description of the Visual Basic functions, as well as examples of their use, is discussed in the following section.

Detailed Description of Visual Basic Registry Manipulation Functions

In this section, you see the various parameters for the functions discussed in the preceding section, as well as their use in the Visual Basic Registry manipulation functions.

The *DeleteSetting* Function   The DeleteSetting function uses the following syntax:

```
DeleteSetting capplication, csection,Key
```

The DeleteSetting function requires the use of the following parameters:

Parameter	Description
capplication	This string setting, which is contained in the upper key of the applications setting, is one that you would like to delete. (This value must be supplied.)
csection	This string setting contains the section of the Registry that contains the key that you want to delete. (This value must be supplied.)
Key	This optional parameter contains the name of the key that you want to delete. If this parameter is left empty, all of the keys in the named section are deleted.

If the named section or key does not exist, the DeleteSetting function takes no action, nor does it return an error.

The following example deletes the View option settings of the API Viewer application from the Windows 95 Registry (refer to Figure 45.5):

```
DeleteSetting "API Viewer, "Options","View"
```

GetSetting Function   The GetSetting function uses the following syntax:

```
GetSetting capplication, csection, key, cDefault
```

The GetSetting function requires the use of the following parameters:

Parameter	Description
capplication	This string setting contains the upper key of the applications setting that you would like to retrieve. (This value must be supplied.)
csection	This string setting contains the section of the Registry that contains the key you want to retrieve. (This value must be supplied.)
key	This string setting contains the name of the key whose value you want to retrieve. (This value must be supplied.)
cDefault	This parameter is used to supply your application with a default value if the key in the specified section does not exist. (This value is optional.)

The GetSetting function returns a Variant value containing the value of the key; if the key is not found, the cDefault value is returned.

The following example retrieves the values of the View Registry entry used by the API Viewer (refer to Figure 45.5). If the Value had been deleted, as illustrated in the previous example, the function would return a Null String.

```
vValue= GetSetting("API Viewer, "Options","View","")
```

The *GetAllSettings* Function   The `GetAllSettings` function uses the following syntax:

`GetAllSettings capplication, csection`

The `GetAllSettings` function requires the use of the following parameters:

Parameter	Description
`capplication`	This string value contains the upper key of the applications setting that you would like to retrieve. This value must be supplied.
`csection`	This string setting contains the name of the section of the Registry whose values you want to retrieve. This value must be supplied.

The `GetAllSettings` function returns a two-dimensional array of Variant values. This array contains the keys as well as the values from the named section of the Registry.

The following example retrieves all of the View options of the API Viewer Registry setting (refer to Figure 45.5). If the value is not found, the function returns a `Null Variant` value.

`vValue= GetAllSettings("API Viewer, "Options")`

Accessing and Updating the Registry Using Visual Basic Functions

In this section, you learn how to create a small application that reads, changes, and updates the contents of the Windows 95 Registry. This example accesses the information that pertains to add-ins available on your system. In addition, the application will save and restore its own setting regarding the size and position of the main form.

> **N O T E**   The add-ins are hard-coded in the `Form_Load` event. The three most common entries have been selected , but your system might have different values. If you want to double check what your system's values are, use the Windows-supplied Regedit program to manually check the Registry entries on your system and update the `Form_Load` procedure appropriately. ■

> **N O T E**   Prior to altering any of the data stored in the Windows 95 Registry, perform a backup of the information contained in the Registry. You can back up the Registry by choosing Registry, Export Registry when using the Regedit application. ■

To create the application, perform the following steps:

1. Start Visual Basic and select the option to Open a New Standard EXE project.

2. If no form is contained in the current project, choose Project, Add Form to add a form to the project.

3. Add the following controls to the form; don't change any of their properties as you will set them in the next step:

Control	Description
A	Three Label controls
ab	One TextBox control
	One ComboBox control
	Three CommandButton controls
	One ListBox control

4. Set the following properties for the three Label controls:

```
Name = lblKeyValue
Alignment =   1  'Right Justify
Caption =   Key Value
Height  =   195
Left  =   510
Top =   2130
Width =   1275


Name = lblKeys
Alignment =   1  'Right Justify
Caption =   Keys
Height  =   195
Left =   510
Top  =   810
Width =   1275


Name = lblAddin
Alignment =   1   'Right Justify
Caption  =   Add in
Height  = .195
Left =   510
TabIndex =   5
Top =   360
Width  =   1275
```

5. Set the following properties for the TextBox control:

```
Name = txtValue
Alignment =   1   'Right Justify
Height =   300
Left =   1920
TabIndex  =   2
ToolTipText  =   Alter the Value of the Key if it is Incorrect
Top  =   2100
Width =   2475
```

6. Set the following properties for the ComboBox control:

```
Name = comAddin
Height =   315
```

```
Left   =   1950
Style =    2   'Dropdown List
TabIndex =   0
ToolTipText =    Select The Addin You Would like
Additional Information About
Top =   360
Width =   2445
```

7. Set the following properties for the three CommandButton controls:

```
Caption =   &Delete
Height =   345
Left =   1800
TabIndex   =   5
ToolTipText =    Delete the Key
Top =   2610
Width =   855


Name = cmdSave
Caption =   &Save
Height =   345
Left =   2700
TabIndex   =   4
ToolTipText =    Save The Changes
Top =   2610
Width =   855


Name = cmdExit
Caption =   E&xit
Height Name =   cmdDelete
=   345
Left =   3600
TabIndex   =   3
ToolTipText =    Exit the Application
Top =   2610
Width =   855
```

8. Set the following properties for the ListBox control:

```
Name =   lstKeys
Height =   1230
Left =   1920
TabIndex =   1
ToolTipText =    Select the Key to Retrieve the Setting for
Top =   780
Width   =   2505
```

9. Set the following properties for the form containing the newly added controls:

```
Name = frmChp532
Caption   =   Chapter 53 Sample 2
Height   =   3465
Width   =   4500
```

10. Enter the following code in the Form_Load event. This code adds three items in the ComboBox and accesses the Registry to retrieve the application's form placement settings. (If the settings are not found, the design time values will be used):

```
' Set up the ComboBox with Known Data
comAddin.AddItem "VBAddinToolbar"
comAddin.AddItem "VisData"
comAddin.AddItem "VisualComponentManager"
comAddin.ListIndex = 0
If Len(GetSetting("exam2", "Position", "top")) <> 0 Then
    Me.Top = GetSetting("exam2", "Position", "top")
End If
If Len(GetSetting("exam2", "Position", "left")) <> 0 Then
    Me.Left = GetSetting("exam2", "Position", "left")
End If
If Len(GetSetting("exam2", "Position", "width")) <> 0 Then
    Me.Width = GetSetting("exam2", "Position", "width")
 End If
If Len(GetSetting("exam2", "Position", "Height")) <> 0 Then
    Me.Height = GetSetting("exam2", "Position", "Height")
End If
```

11. Enter the following code in the `Form_Unload` event:

    ```
    Set exam2 = Nothing
    ```

12. Enter the following code in the `cmdDelete_Click` event. This code will delete the application's Registry values for the Key specified in the ComboBox:

    ```
    DeleteSetting "Microsoft Visual Basic Addins", comAddin.Text, _
      lstkeys.Text
    ```

13. Enter the following code in the `cmdExit_Click` event. This code saves the form's current position and size in the Windows 95 Registry:

    ```
    SaveSetting "exam2", "Position", "top", Me.Top
    SaveSetting "exam2", "Position", "left", Me.Left
    SaveSetting "exam2", "Position", "height", Me.Height
    SaveSetting "exam2", "Position", "width", Me.Width
    Unload Me
    ```

14. Enter the following code in the `cmdSave_Click` event. This code updates the value of the data stored for the Key (which has been selected in the Key ListBox) to the value the has been entered in the Key Value TextBox:

    ```
    SaveSetting "Microsoft Visual Basic Addins", _
      comAddin.Text, _lstkeys.Text, txtValue.Text
    ```

15. Enter the following code in the `comAddin_Click` event. This code retrieves all of the Keys that are stored under the Add-in, which was selected in the ComboBox:

    ```
    Dim vValues As Variant
    Dim nCount As Integer
    vValues = GetAllSettings("Microsoft_
     Visual Basic Addins", comAddin.Text)
    For nCount = LBound(vValues, 1) To UBound(vValues, 1)
        lstkeys.AddItem vValues(nCount, 0)
    Next nCount
    ```

16. Enter the following code in the `lstKeys_Click` event. This code will retrieve the value of the Key that has been selected in the Keys ListBox:

```
txtValue.Text = GetSetting("Microsoft Visual_
    Basic Addins", comAddin.Text, lstkeys.Text)
```

 17. Choose <u>R</u>un, <u>S</u>tart or press F5 to run the project.

After the Project is started, you should have a form on your display similar to that illustrated in Figure 45.6.

FIG. 45.6

Here is the Sample Registry Viewer Application.

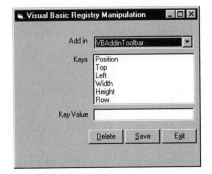

If you select any of the items in the Keys list box, its Registry value is displayed in the Key Value text box. If you want to change the value in the text box, type in a new value and then click <u>S</u>ave to update the value in the Registry. If you click the <u>D</u>elete button, the information is removed from the Registry.

After you have clicked the E<u>x</u>it button, start the Regedit program and open the following keys:

```
HKEY_CURRENT_USERS\Software\VB AND VBA Program Setting\exam2\Position
```

You should then see Registry settings similar to those illustrated in Figure 45.7. These settings represent the position and size of the form in the project when the Exit button is pressed. If you resize the form or move it prior to pressing Exit, the new settings are saved. The form will be restored to these settings the next time the project is run.

In this section, you have learned various aspects of accessing the Windows 95 Registry through the use of Visual Basic's built-in function. Although you only have limited access to the Registry, this is probably enough for most uses. The next section discusses accessing the Registry through the Windows 95 API, where there are very few, if any, limitations.

Windows 95 API Registry Functions

In this section, you create a small application that can be used to read, change, and update the contents of the Windows 95 Registry. This application will use the Windows 95 API function calls to access and update the information stored in the Windows 95 Registry. Once this application is complete, you can use it as a substitute for the Microsoft-supplied Regedit program.

FIG. 45.7

The Registry settings containing the sample forms position information.

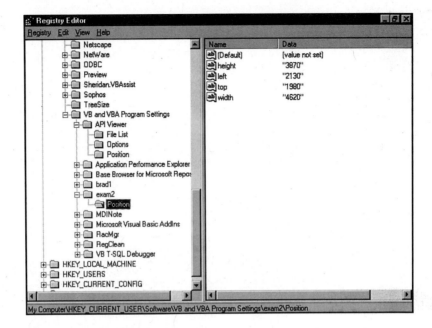

Accessing the Registry Using the Windows 95 API

While Visual Basic provides four commands that allow your application to access the Registry, the Windows 95 API provides more than 20 functions. The Windows 95 API gives you full access to all of the keys and to the values of the data stored in the Registry. The commands that are provided allow you access to all of the data that is stored in the Registry.

N O T E Unlike most Windows API functions, the Registry-related functions are not stored in one of the major Windows libraries (such as Kernel32). Instead, the Registry functions are contained in the advapi32.dll. This library, which is known as the Advanced API services library, contains all of the Registry as well as security Windows 95 API functions. ◼

Table 45.4 lists all of the Windows API Registry-related functions, as well as brief descriptions of each.

Table 45.4   Windows API Registry-Related Functions

Function	Description
RegCloseKey	Closes a Registry key that has previously been opened by another API function. You must always close the Registry key when you are finished with it.
RegConnectRegistry	Allows you to access a certain part of the Registry that is stored on a connected computer.

Function	Description
`RegCreateKey/RegCreateKeyEx`	Allow you to create a new key in the Registry. If a key with the same attributes already exists, that key is opened. The `RegCreateKeyEx` function allows you to provide additional security information that can be placed on the Registry entry.
`RegDeleteKey`	Deletes a specified Registry key and its associated value.
`RegDeleteValue`	Deletes the value of the specified Registry key entry.
`RegEnumKey/RegEnumKeyEx`	Allow you to step through the name of each subkey located under a specified key.
`RegEnumValue`	Allows you to step through the values of each subkey located under a specified key.
`RegFlushKey`	Forces an immediate write of information to the Registry.
`RegLoadKey`	Loads the Registry information from a file that was previously created using the `RegSaveKey`.
`RegNotifyChangeKeyValue`	Allows your application to monitor a Registry key and receive notification when that key has been changed.
`RegOpenKey/RegOpenKeyEx`	Open a specified key. `RegOpenKeyEx` also opens a key but has additional security parameters.
`RegQueryInfoKey`	Allows your application to obtain information about the key.
`RegQueryValue/RegQueryValueEx`	Retrieve the default value for the key. The `RegQueryValueEx` also retrieves the security information of the key.
`RegReplaceKey`	Replaces Registry information from a disk file. In addition, the `RegReplaceKey` creates a backup file of the information that has been replaced.
`RegRestoreKey`	Restores Registry information from a file, which was created by the `RegReplaceKey` function.
`RegSaveKey`	Saves a Registry key as well as all of its subkeys to a disk file. This file can later be used by the `RegLoadKey` function.
`RegSetValue/RegSetValueEx`	Change the value of a specific key.
`RegUnLoadKey`	Closes and removes from memory a key previously opened with the `RegLoadKey` function.

Part

IX

Ch

45

A detailed description of the Windows 95 API Registry functions will be provided later in this section. The next section details the various Constants that are used by the Windows 95 API Registry function.

Detailed Description of Windows 95 API Registry Manipulation Functions

This section discusses the usage of the various parameters of the Windows 95 API Registry manipulation functions.

When accessing the Registry through the Windows API, you must use certain predefined constants to represent the different branches of the Registry.

Table 45.5 lists the constants and their values.

Table 45.5 Registry Key Constants

Constant	Value
HKEY_CLASSES_ROOT	&H80000000
HKEY_CURRENT_CONFIG	&H80000005
HKEY_CURRENT_USER	&H80000001
HKEY_DYN_DATA	&H80000006
HKEY_LOCAL_MACHINE	&H80000002
HKEY_PERFORMANCE_DATA	&H80000004
HKEY_USERS	&H80000003

When creating keys in the Registry, specify the type of operations that will be allowed on the key. Table 45.6 lists all of the operations constants and their values.

Table 45.6 Key Creation Constants

Constant	Value
KEY_CREATE_LINK	&H20
KEY_CREATE_SUB_KEY	&H4
KEY_EVENT	&H1
KEY_NOTIFY	&H10
KEY_QUERY_VALUE	&H1
KEY_ALL_ACCESS	&H3F
KEY_SET_VALUE	&H2

The next section will take a closer look at the Windows 95 API Registry functions.

The *RegCloseKey* Function   The declaration that must be included in your Visual Basic application for the RegCloseKey function is:

```
Declare Function RegCloseKey Lib "advapi32.dll" _
(ByVal hKey As Long) As Long
```

The RegCloseKey function requires the use of the following parameter:

hkey   The Long integer that was returned by the RegOpenKey/RegOpenKeyEx function

The RegCloseKey function returns a Long value of 0 if the function was successful; any other values should be treated as error code.

The *RegConnectRegistry* Function   The declaration that must be included in your Visual Basic application for the RegConnectRegistry function is:

```
Declare Function RegConnectRegistry Lib "advapi32.dll" _
 Alias "RegConnectRegistryA" (ByVal lpMachineName As String, _
 ByVal hKey As Long, phkResult As Long) As Long
```

The RegConnectRegistry function requires the use of the following parameters:

Parameter	Description
lpMachineName	The name of the computer whose Registry you want to access.
hkey	The name of the key to open (can only be HKEY_LOCAL_MACHINE or HKEY_USERS).
phkResult	If the function completes successfully, phkResult contains the handle to the specified key.

The RegConnectRegistry returns a Long value of 0 if the function was successful; any other values should be treated as error codes.

The *RegCreateKey* Function   The declaration that must be included in your Visual Basic application for the RegCreateKey function is:

```
Declare Function RegCreateKey Lib "advapi32.dll" Alias _
 "RegCreateKeyA" (ByVal hKey As Long, ByVal lpSubKey As String, _
 phkResult As Long) As Long
```

The RegCreateKey function requires the use of the following parameters:

Parameter	Description
hkey	The root key under which to create the new key (refer to Table 45.5 for the valid constants).
lpSubKey	The name of the new subkey to create.
phkResult	If the function completes successfully, phkResult will contain the handle to the new key.

Part

IX

Ch

45

The RegCreateKey returns a Long value of 0 if the function was successful; any other values should be treated as error codes.

The *RegCreateKeyEx* Function   The declaration that must be included in your Visual Basic application for the RegCreateKeyEx function is:

```
Declare Function RegCreateKeyEx Lib "advapi32.dll" _
Alias "RegCreateKeyExA" (ByVal hKey As Long, _
 ByVal lpSubKey As String, ByVal Reserved As Long, _
 ByVal lpClass As String, ByVal dwOptions As Long, _
 ByVal samDesired As Long, _
 lpSecurityAttributes As SECURITY_ATTRIBUTES, _
 phkResult As Long, lpdwDisposition As Long) As Long
```

The RegCreateKeyEx function requires the use of the following parameters:

Parameter	Description
hKey	The root key under which to create the new key (refer to Table 45.5 for the valid constants).
lpSubKey	The name of the new subkey to create.
Reserved	Not used. Set to 0.
lpClass	The class of the new key (generally set to Null).
dwOptions	The value of this parameter must be 0; any other value causes the key to be unavailable after the computer system is restarted.
samDesired	A key access constant (refer to Table 45.6 for valid constants).
lpSecurityAttributes	A structure defining the key security. Not applicable under Windows 95.
phkResult	If the function completes successfully, phkResult will contain the handle to the new key.
lpdwDisposition	The value of this parameter indicates whether a new key should be created or an existing key should be opened. Use one of the following two constants: REG_CREATED_NEW_KEY = &H1 REG_OPENED_EXISTING_KEY = &H2

The RegCreateKeyEx returns a Long value of 0 if the function was successful; any other values should be treated as error codes.

The *RegDeleteKey* Function   The declaration that must be included in your Visual Basic application for the RegDeleteKey function is:

```
Declare Function RegDeleteKey Lib "advapi32.dll" Alias _
 "RegDeleteKeyA" (ByVal hKey As Long, ByVal lpSubKey As String) _
 As Long
```

The `RegDeleteKey` function requires the use of the following parameters:

hKey   The handle of the open key or a key access constant (refer to Table 45.5 for the valid constants).

lpSubKey   The name of the subkey to delete. All keys and their values located under this subkey are deleted.

The `RegDeleteKey` returns a `Long` value of `0` if the function was successful; any other values should be treated as error codes.

The *RegDeleteValue* Function   The declaration that must be included in your Visual Basic application for the `RegDeleteKey` function is:

```
Declare Function RegDeleteValue Lib "advapi32.dll" Alias _
 "RegDeleteValueA" (ByVal hKey As Long, _
 ByVal lpValueName As String) As Long
```

The `RegDeleteValue` function requires the use of the following parameters:

Parameter	Description
hKey	The handle of the open key or a key access constant (refer to Table 45.5 for the valid constants).
lpValueName	The section of the key to delete (setting parameter to Null causes all values to be deleted).

The `RegDeleteValue` returns a `Long` value of `0` if the function was successful; any other values should be treated as error codes.

The *RegEnumKey* Function   The declaration that must be included in your Visual Basic application for the `RegEnum` function is:

```
Declare Function RegEnumKey Lib "advapi32.dll" Alias _
 "RegEnumKeyA" (ByVal hKey As Long, ByVal dwIndex As Long, _
 ByVal lpName As String, ByVal cbName As Long) As Long
```

The `RegEnumKey` function requires the use of the following parameters:

Parameter	Description
hKey	The handle of the open key or a key access constant (refer to Table 45.5 for the valid constants)
dwIndex	The index of the subkey that you want to retrieve
lpName	The function retrieves the name of the key to this variable
cbName	The size of the `lpName` variable

The `RegEnumKey` returns a `Long` value of `0` if the function was successful; any other values should be treated as error codes.

The *RegEnumKeyEx* Function   The declaration that must be included in your Visual Basic application for the `RegEnumKeyEx` function is:

```
Declare Function RegEnumKeyEx Lib "advapi32.dll" Alias _
"RegEnumKeyExA" (ByVal hKey As Long, ByVal dwIndex As Long, _
 ByVal lpName As String, lpcbName As Long, lpReserved As Long, _
 ByVal lpClass As String, lpcbClass As Long, _
 lpftLastWriteTime As FILETIME) As Long
```

The RegEnumKeyEx function requires the use of the following parameters:

Parameter	Description
hKey	The handle of the open key or a key access constant (refer to Table 45.5 for the valid constants).
dwindex	The index of the subkey that you want to retrieve.
lpName	The function retrieves the name of the key to this variable.
lpcbName	The size of the lpName variable.
lpReserved	Not used. Set to 0.
lpClass	A string used to identify the class of the key (can be set to Null).
lpcbClass	The size of the lpClass variable.
lpftLastWriteTime	The time and date the Registry entry was last modified.

The RegEnumKeyEx returns a Long value of 0 if the function was successful; any other values should be treated as error codes.

The *RegEnumValue* Function   The declaration that must be included in your Visual Basic application for the RegEnumValue function is:

```
Declare Function RegEnumValue Lib "advapi32.dll" Alias _
"RegEnumValueA" (ByVal hKey As Long, ByVal dwIndex As Long, _
 ByVal lpValueName As String, lpcbValueName As Long,
lpReserved As Long, lpType As Long, lpData As Byte, _
 lpcbData As Long) As Long
```

The RegEnumValue function requires the use of the following parameters:

hKey	The handle of the open key or a key access constant (refer to Table 45.5 for the valid constants).
dwindex	The index of the subkey that you want to retrieve.
lpValueName	The name of the Value located at the specified index.
lpcbValueName	The size of the lpValueName variable.
lpReserved	Not used. Set to 0.
lpType	The type of data to retrieve. (see the RegQueryValueEx definition for a list of valid constants).
lpData	The data to retrieve.
lpcbData	The size of the lpData variable.

The RegEnumValue returns a Long value of 0 if the function was successful; any other values should be treated as error codes.

The *RegFlushKey* Function   The declaration that must be included in your Visual Basic application for the RegFlushKey function is:

```
Declare Function RegFlushKey Lib "advapi32.dll" _
 (ByVal hKey As Long) As Long
```

The RegFlushKey function requires the use of the following parameter:

hKey   The handle of the open key or a key access constant (refer to Table 45.5 for the valid constants).

The RegFlushKey returns a Long value of 0 if the function was successful; any other values should be treated as error codes.

The *RegLoadKey* Function   The declaration that must be included in your Visual Basic application for the RegLoadKey function is:

```
Declare Function RegLoadKey Lib "advapi32.dll" Alias _
 "RegLoadKeyA" (ByVal hKey As Long, ByVal lpSubKey _
 As String, ByVal lpFile As String) As Long
```

The RegLoadKey function requires the use of the following parameters:

Parameters	Description
hKey	The handle of the open key or a key access constant (refer to Table 45.5 for the valid constants)
lpSubKey	The name of the new key to create
lpFile	The name of the file counting the Registry information that you want to load

The RegLoadKey returns a Long value of 0 if the function was successful; any other values should be treated as error codes.

The *RegNotifyChangeKey* Function   The declaration that must be included in your Visual Basic application for the RegNotifyChangeKey function is:

```
Declare Function RegNotifyChangeKeyValue Lib "advapi32.dll" _
 (ByVal hKey As Long, ByVal bWatchSubtree As Long, _
 ByVal dwNotifyFilter As Long, ByVal hEvent As Long, _
 ByVal fAsynchronus As Long) As Long
```

The RegNotifyChangeKey function requires the use of the following parameters:

Parameter	Description
hKey	The handle of the open key or a key access constant (refer to Table 45.5 for valid constants).

Part

IX

Ch

45

continues

continued

Parameter	Description
bWatchSubtree	Set this value to True if you want to be informed about changes to the subkeys of the key handle contained in the hKey parameter.
dwNotifyFilter	The type of key change that you want to detect. Must be one of the following constants: REG_NOTIFY_CHANGE_ATTRIBUTES = &H2 REG_NOTIFY_CHANGE_LAST_SET = &H4 REG_NOTIFY_CHANGE_NAME = &H1 REG_NOTIFY_CHANGE_SECURITY = &H8
hEvent	A handle to an event that caused the change.
fAysynchrous	If this parameter is set to False, the function will not return a value until a change has been detected in the Registry. Otherwise, the function will return a value when the event specified in the hEvent parameter occurs.

The RegNotifyChangeKey returns a Long value of 0 if the function was successful; any other values should be treated as error codes.

The *RegOpenKey* Function   The declaration that must be included in your Visual Basic application for the RegOpenKey function is:

```
Declare Function RegOpenKey Lib "advapi32.dll" Alias _
 "RegOpenKeyA" (ByVal hKey As Long, ByVal lpSubKey As String, _
 phkResult As Long) As Long
```

The RegOpenKey function requires the use of the following parameters:

Parameter	Description
hKey	The handle of the open key or a key access constant (refer to Table 45.5 for the valid constants).
lpSubkey	Name of the subkey to open.
phkResult	If the function successfully completes, phkResult contains the handle to the key.

The RegOpenKey returns a Long value of 0 if the function was successful; any other values should be treated as error codes.

The *RegOpenKeyEx* Function   The declaration that must be included in your Visual Basic application for the RegOpenKeyEx function is:

```
Declare Function RegOpenKeyEx Lib "advapi32.dll" Alias _
 "RegOpenKeyExA" (ByVal hKey As Long, ByVal lpSubKey As String, _
 ByVal ulOptions As Long, ByVal samDesired As Long, _
 phkResult As Long) As Long
```

The RegOpenKeyEx function requires the use of the following parameters:

Parameter	Description
hKey	The handle of the open key or a key access constant (refer to Table 45.5 for the valid constants).
lpSubkey	Name of the subkey to open.
ulOptions	Not used. Set to 0.
samDesired	A key access constant (refer to Table 45.6 for valid constants).
phkResult	If the function completes successfully, phkResult will contain the handle to the opened key.

The RegOpenKeyEx returns a Long value of 0 if the function was successful; any other values should be treated as error codes.

The *RegQueryInfoKey* Function   The declaration that must be included in your Visual Basic application for the RegQueryInfoKey function is:

```
Declare Function RegQueryInfoKey Lib "advapi32.dll" Alias _
  "RegQueryInfoKeyA" (ByVal hKey As Long, ByVal lpClass As String, _
  lpcbClass As Long, lpReserved As Long, lpcSubKeys As Long, _
  lpcbMaxSubKeyLen As Long, lpcbMaxClassLen As Long, lpcValues As Long, _
lpcbMaxValueNameLen As Long, lpcbMaxValueLen As Long, _
  lpcbSecurityDescriptor As Long, _
  lpftLastWriteTime As FILETIME) _
  As Long
```

The RegQueryInfoKey function requires the use of the following parameters:

Parameter	Description
hKey	The handle of the open key or key access constant (refer to Table 45.5 for the valid constants).
lpClass	The class of the key is returned in the parameter.
lpcbClass	The size of the lpClass string.
lpReserved	Not used. Set to 0.
lpcSubkeys	The number of subkeys of the key specified in the hKey parameter.
lpcbMaxSubKeyLen	The length of the longest subkey of the key specified in the hKey parameter.
lpcbMaxClassLen	The length of the longest class name for the subkeys specified in the hKey parameter.
lpcValues	The number of values for this key.
lpcbMaxValueNameLen	The length of the longest name of a value for the subkeys specified in the hKey parameter.

continues

continued

Parameter	Description
lpcbMaxValueLen	The buffer size needed to store the longest value for the subkeys specified in the hKey parameter
lpcbSecurityDescriptor	The length of the key's security setting
lpftLastWriteTime	The last modification date and time for the specified key

The RegQueryInfoKey returns a Long value of 0 if the function was successful; any other values should be treated as error codes.

The *RegQueryValue* Function   The declaration that must be included in your Visual Basic application for the RegQueryValue function is:

```
Declare Function RegQueryValue Lib "advapi32.dll" Alias _
 "RegQueryValueA" (ByVal hKey As Long, _
 ByVal lpSubKey As String, ByVal lpValue As String, _
 lpcbValue As Long) As Long
```

The RegQueryValue function requires the use of the following parameters:

Parameter	Description
hKey	The handle of the open key or a key access constant (refer to Table 45.5 for the valid constants).
lpSubkey	Name of the subkey to query.
lpValue	This parameter contains the retrieved value of the subkey.
lpcbValue	The length of the lpValue parameter.

The RegQueryValue returns a Long value of 0 if the function was successful; any other values should be treated as error codes.

The *RegQueryValueEx* Function   The following declaration that must be included in your Visual Basic application for the RegQueryValueEx function is:

```
Declare Function RegQueryValueEx Lib "advapi32.dll" Alias _
 "RegQueryValueExA" (ByVal hKey As Long, _
 ByVal lpValueName As String, ByVal lpReserved As Long, _
 lpType As Long, lpData As Any, lpcbData As Long) As Long
```

The RegQueryValueEx function requires the use of the following parameters:

Parameter	Description
hKey	The handle of the open key or a key access constant (refer to Table 45.5 for the valid constants).
lpValueName	The name of the value to retrieve.
lpReserved	Not used. Set to 0.
lpType	The type of data to retrieve. Must be one of the following constants:

```
REG_BINARY = 3
REG_DWORD = 4
REG_EXPAND_SZ = 2
REG_DWORD_BIG_ENDIAN = 5
REG_DWORD_LITTLE_ENDIAN = 4
REG_LINK = 6
REG_MULTI_SZ = 7
REG_NONE = 0
REG_RESOURCE_LIST = 8
REG_SZ = 1
```

lpData	This parameter contains the value of the subkey
lpcbData	The size of the lpData variable

The RegQueryValueEx returns a Long value of 0 if the function was successful; any other values should be treated as error codes.

The *RegReplaceKey* Function   The following declaration that must be included in your Visual Basic application for the RegReplaceKey function is:

```
Declare Function RegReplaceKey Lib "advapi32.dll" Alias _
  "RegReplaceKeyA" (ByVal hKey As Long, _
  ByVal lpSubKey As String, ByVal lpNewFile As String, _
  ByVal lpOldFile As String) As Long
```

The RegReplaceKey function requires the use of the following parameters:

Parameters	Description
hKey	The handle of the open key or a key access constant (refer to Table 45.5 for the valid constants)
lpSubkey	Name of the subkey to replace
lpNewFile	The name of the file containing the Registry information to import
lpOldFile	The name of the file in which to back up the current Registry information

The RegReplaceKey returns a Long value of 0 if the function was successful; any other values should be treated as error codes.

The *RegRestoreKey* Function   The declaration that must be included in your Visual Basic application for the RegRestoreKey function is:

```
Declare Function RegRestoreKey Lib "advapi32.dll" Alias _
  "RegRestoreKeyA" (ByVal hKey As Long, _
  ByVal lpFile As String, ByVal dwFlags As Long) As Long
```

The RegRestoreKey function requires the use of the following parameters:

Parameter	Description
hKey	The handle of the open key or a key access constant (refer to Table 45.5 for the valid constants)
lpFile	The name of the file containing the Registry information to restore
dwFlags	Set to 0 for a regular Registry restore

The RegRestoreKey returns a Long value of 0 if the function was successful; any other values should be treated as error codes.

The *RegSaveKey* Function   The following declaration that must be included in your Visual Basic application for the RegSaveKey function is:

```
Declare Function RegSaveKey Lib "advapi32.dll" Alias _
 "RegSaveKeyA" (ByVal hKey As Long, _
 ByVal lpFile As String, _
 lpSecurityAttributes As SECURITY_ATTRIBUTES) As Long
```

The RegSaveKey function requires the use of the following parameters:

Parameter	Description
hKey	The handle of the open key or a key access constant (refer to Table 45.5 for the valid constants).
lpFile	The name of the file that will contain the saved Registry information.
lpSecurityAttributes	Security information of the saved key.

The RegSaveKey returns a Long value of 0 if the function was successful; any other values should be treated as error codes.

The *RegSetValue* Function   The following declaration that must be included in your Visual Basic application for the RegSetValue function is:

```
Declare Function RegSetValue Lib "advapi32.dll" Alias _
 "RegSetValueA" (ByVal hKey As Long, ByVal lpSubKey As String, _
 ByVal dwType As Long, ByVal lpData As String, _
 ByVal cbData As Long) As Long
```

The RegSetValue function requires the use of the following parameters:

Parameter	Description
hKey	The handle of the open key or a key access constant (refer to Table 45.5 for the valid constants).
lpSubkey	Name of the subkey whose value you want to set. If the subkey does not exist, it is created.
dwType	Must be set to the constant REG_SZ. (see the RegQueryValueEx definition for value of the REG_SZ constant).
lpData	The new value of the subkey.
cbData	Length of the lpData parameter.

The RegSetValue returns a Long value of 0 if the function was successful; any other values should be treated as error codes.

The *RegSetValueEx* Function   The following declaration that must be included in your Visual Basic application for the RegSetValueEx function is:

```
Declare Function RegSetValueEx Lib "advapi32.dll" Alias _
 "RegSetValueExA" (ByVal hKey As Long, _
 ByVal lpValueName As String, ByVal Reserved As Long, _
 ByVal dwType As Long, lpData As Any, ByVal cbData As Long) _
 As Long
```

The RegSetValueEx function requires the use of the following parameters:

Parameter	Description
hKey	The handle of the open key or a key access constant (refer to Table 45.5 for the valid constants).
lpValueName	The name of the Value to set.
Reserved	Not used. Set to 0.
dwType	The type of data that is to be set (see the RegQueryValueEx definition for a list of valid constants).
lpData	The value of the new key.
cbData	Length of the lpData parameter.

The RegSetValueEx returns a Long value of 0 if the function was successful; any other values should be treated as error codes.

The *RegUnLoadKey* Function   The following declaration that must be included in your Visual Basic application for the RegUnLoadKey function is:

```
Declare Function RegUnLoadKey Lib "advapi32.dll" Alias _
 "RegUnLoadKeyA" (ByVal hKey As Long, ByVal lpSubKey As String) _
 As Long
```

The RegUnLoadKey function requires the use of the following parameters:

Parameter	Description
hKey	The handle of the open key or a key access constant (refer to Table 45.5 for the Valid constants)
lpSubKey	The name of the subkey to unload (this subkey must have been previously loaded using the RegLoadKey function)

Using the Windows 95 API to Access the Registry

In this section, you create a small application that reads the contents of the Windows 95 Registry. This example provides you with access to all sections of the Registry. In addition, you can view the values that are stored in all of the keys contained in the Registry.

To create the application, perform the following steps:

1. Start Visual Basic and choose Open a New Standard EXE project.

2. Choose Project, Components and add the Microsoft Common Controls 5.0 to your project by selecting the box next to the name and clicking OK.

3. Add a standard module to the project by choosing Project, Add Module.

4. Enter Listing 45.3 into the declarations section of the newly added standard module. Alternatively, you may want to copy the listing from file exam3a.bas, which is included on the CD accompanying this book.

Listing 45.3   exam3a.bas—Registry API Declarations that Need to be Placed in *Module1*

```
Option Explicit
Option Base 1
Declare Function RegCloseKey Lib "advapi32.dll" _
 (ByVal hKey As Long) As Long
Declare Function RegEnumKey Lib "advapi32.dll" Alias _
 "RegEnumKeyA" (ByVal hKey As Long, ByVal dwIndex As Long, _
 ByVal lpName As String, ByVal cbName As Long) As Long
Declare Function RegQueryValueEx Lib "advapi32.dll" Alias _
"RegQueryValueExA" (ByVal hKey As Long, _
 ByVal lpValueName As String, ByVal lpReserved As Long, _
 lpType As Long, lpData As Any, lpcbData As Long) As Long
Declare Function RegEnumValue Lib "advapi32.dll" Alias _
"RegEnumValueA" (ByVal hKey As Long, ByVal dwIndex As Long, _
 ByVal lpValueName As String, lpcbValueName As Long, _
 lpReserved As Long, lpType As Long, lpData As Byte, _
 lpcbData As Long) As Long
Declare Function RegLoadKey Lib "advapi32.dll" Alias _
 "RegLoadKeyA" (ByVal hKey As Long, ByVal lpSubKey As String, _
 ByVal lpFile As String) As Long
Declare Function RegOpenKey Lib "advapi32.dll" Alias _
 "RegOpenKeyA" (ByVal hKey As Long, ByVal lpSubKey As String, _
 phkResult As Long) As Long
Declare Function RegOpenKeyEx Lib "advapi32.dll" Alias _
 "RegOpenKeyExA" (ByVal hKey As Long, ByVal lpSubKey As String, _
 ByVal ulOptions As Long, ByVal samDesired As Long, _
 phkResult As Long) As Long
Public Const HKEY_CLASSES_ROOT = &H80000000
Public Const HKEY_CURRENT_CONFIG = &H80000005
Public Const HKEY_CURRENT_USER = &H80000001
Public Const HKEY_DYN_DATA = &H80000006
Public Const HKEY_LOCAL_MACHINE = &H80000002
Public Const HKEY_PERFORMANCE_DATA = &H80000004
Public Const HKEY_USERS = &H80000003
Public Const KEY_QUERY_VALUE = &H1
Public Const ERROR_NO_MORE_ITEMS = 259&
Public Const REG_BINARY = 3
Public Const REG_DWORD = 4
Public Const REG_DWORD_BIG_ENDIAN = 5
Public Const REG_DWORD_LITTLE_ENDIAN = 4
Public Const REG_EXPAND_SZ = 2
Public Const REG_LINK = 6
Public Const REG_MULTI_SZ = 7
Public Const REG_NONE = 0
Public Const REG_SZ = 1
Public Const REG_RESOURCE_LIST = 8
Public Const REG_FULL_RESOURCE_DESCRIPTOR = 9
```

5. If no form is contained in the current project, choose Project, Add Form to add a form to the project.

6. Add the following controls to the form; do not change any of their properties because you can set them in the next step:

Control	Description
	One TreeView control
	One CommandButton control
	One ListBox control
	One Label control

7. Set the following properties for the TreeView control:

```
Name = treReg
Height =    3735
Left  =    360
TabIndex =    0
Top  =   0
Width =    4755
LineStyle  =   1
Style =   7
Appearance =   1
```

8. Set the following properties for the CommandButton control:

```
Name =   cmdExit
Caption =    E&xit
Height  =    300
Left  =    8820
TabIndex   =   2
Top =   3540
Width =   915
```

9. Set the following properties for the ListBox control:

```
Name  = lstValues
Height =    1620
Left =   5160
TabIndex        =   2
Top  =    480
Width  =   4575
```

10. Set the following properties for the Label control:

```
Name =   lblValue
Caption  =   Values
Height  =   315
Left  =   5340
Top              =   60
Width            =   1995
```

11. Set the following properties for the Form containing the newly added controls:

```
Name = exam3
Caption  =   Registry Explorer
Height =   3930
Left  =   2010
Top  =   1545
Width =   10065
```

12. Enter the following code into the Form_Load event. This code will retrieve all of the subkeys from the Registry and add them to the listview control:

```
Dim ntest As Long
Dim cname As String
Dim lname As Long
Dim x As Integer
Dim nodX As Node
Screen.MousePointer = vbHourglass
cname = Space$(4096)
lname = 4096
Set nodX = treReg.Nodes.Add(, , "HKEY_CLASSES_ROOT", "HKEY_CLASSES_ROOT")
Set nodX = treReg.Nodes.Add(, , "HKEY_CURRENT_USER", "HKEY_CURRENT_USER")
Set nodX = treReg.Nodes.Add(, , "HKEY_LOCAL_MACHINE", "HKEY_LOCAL_MACHINE")
Set nodX = treReg.Nodes.Add(, , "HKEY_USERS", "HKEY_USERS")
Set nodX = treReg.Nodes.Add(, , "HKEY_CURRENT_CONFIG",
"HKEY_CURRENT_CONFIG")
Set nodX = treReg.Nodes.Add(, , "HKEY_DYN_DATA", "HKEY_DYN_DATA")
x = 0
Do While ntest = 0
    ' get all of the SubKeys for HKEY_CLASSES_ROOT
    ntest = RegEnumKey(HKEY_CLASSES_ROOT, x, cname, lname)
    If ntest = 0 Then

        Set nodX = treReg.Nodes.Add("HKEY_CLASSES_ROOT", tvwChild, _
  "A" & CStr(x), cname)
          x = x + 1

    End If

Loop
x = 0
ntest = 0
Do While ntest = 0
    ' get all of the SubKeys for HKEY_CURRENT_USER
    ntest = RegEnumKey(HKEY_CURRENT_USER, x, cname, lname)
    If ntest = 0 Then

        Set nodX = treReg.Nodes.Add("HKEY_CURRENT_USER", _
  tvwChild, "B" & CStr(x), cname)
          x = x + 1

    End If

Loop
x = 0
ntest = 0
```

```
Do While ntest = 0
    ' get all of the SubKeys for HKEY_LOCAL_MACHINE
    ntest = RegEnumKey(HKEY_LOCAL_MACHINE, x, cname, lname)
    If ntest = 0 Then
        Set nodX = treReg.Nodes.Add("HKEY_LOCAL_MACHINE", _
 tvwChild, "C" & CStr(x), cname)
        x = x + 1
    End If

Loop
x = 0
ntest = 0
Do While ntest = 0
    ' get all of the SubKeys for HKEY_USERS
    ntest = RegEnumKey(HKEY_USERS, x, cname, lname)
    If ntest = 0 Then

        Set nodX = treReg.Nodes.Add("HKEY_USERS", tvwChild, _
 "D" & CStr(x), cname)
        x = x + 1

    End If

Loop
x = 0
ntest = 0
Do While ntest = 0
    ' get all of the SubKeys for HKEY_CURRENT_CONFIG
    ntest = RegEnumKey(HKEY_CURRENT_CONFIG, x, cname, lname)
    If ntest = 0 Then

        Set nodX = treReg.Nodes.Add("HKEY_CURRENT_CONFIG", tvwChild, _
 "E" & CStr(x), cname)
        x = x + 1

    End If

Loop
x = 0
ntest = 0
Do While ntest = 0
    ' get all of the SubKeys for HKEY_DYN_DATA
    ntest = RegEnumKey(HKEY_DYN_DATA, x, cname, lname)
    If ntest = 0 Then

        Set nodX = treReg.Nodes.Add("HKEY_DYN_DATA", tvwChild, _
 "F" & CStr(x), cname)
        x = x + 1

    End If

Loop

Screen.MousePointer = vbDefault
```

Listing 46.1   Continued

```
        GetWindowsVersion = strOS
'******************************************************************
'  Otherwise include the maintenance build info
'******************************************************************
    Else
        GetWindowsVersion = strOS & " " & _
            Left(strMaintBuildInfo, Len(strMaintBuildInfo) - 1)
    End If
End Function
```

This API call exhibits a common trait among many Win32 API calls in that it requires you to set the first member of the structure (dwOSVersionInfoSize) *before* calling the API. This is something new for Win32 that was not required in earlier versions of Windows. This is done so the Win32 API can be ported to future processors without requiring a new set of APIs. This means (in theory) that the Win32 code in this chapter should work unchanged in the future when the desktop computer world moves to 64-bits.

Declaring APIs

Now that you have seen how to use the GetVersionEx API call in VB, let's take a look at how you make this API available to VB. To make a function call from an external source (such as a DLL or the Win32 API), you need to write a declaration for this API in the General Declarations section. Here is what the declaration for GetVersionEx looks like:

```
Private Declare Function GetVersionEx Lib "kernel32" Alias _
"GetVersionExA" (lpVersionInformation As OSVERSIONINFO) As Long
```

Let's dissect this call to understand what it really means. The first three words, Private Declare Function, mean that we are declaring an external function for use only within the current module. The next word, GetVersionEx, when used with the Alias label means that you would like to refer to this function by using the word GetVersionEx in your VB code. When using Alias, this value could be anything. If you wanted, you could have called this MyGetWinVer.

The next two words, Lib "kernel32", tell VB which "library" (DLL—the extension is optional) contains this function. The next two words, Alias "GetVersionExA," tell VB that anytime you call "GetVersionEx" in your program, it should call the function "GetVersionExA" in Kernel32.dll. Until now, the format of this API call is typical. The function, library, and alias names will differ, but all of these items appear in most API calls.

The next part of this call contains the argument list for the function GetVersionExA. It only has one parameter of type OSVERSION info that must be passed by reference (the default). Finally, the last two words, As Long, indicate that the function GetVersionExA returns a long integer.

Calling Functions in Other DLLs

Almost every document you will ever read about using DLLs in Visual Basic is going to use the API DLLs as an example. At the end of these documents, the writer explains how you can also grab these declarations out of the API Text Viewer program. This gives you a false sense of security because you depend heavily on the API Text Viewer for your API declarations. As soon as most programmers get a DLL (or new API) that doesn't appear in the API Text Viewer, they realize that they never really learned how to write a declaration themselves. Therefore, I've created an exercise where you look at the code for a small program and try to guess the API declarations.

Listing 46.2 uses two functions from a DLL that I wrote which creates and resolves shortcuts. The function names are CreateShortcut and ResolveShortcut; they are located in a DLL called Shortcut.dll, and they both return a long value. I have retained all of the comments and source code for this program, but I've relocated the declaration statements to Listing 46.3. Your mission, should you choose to accept it, is to examine the code and figure out what the declaration statement should be. Write your declaration on a sheet of paper and compare it with the actual declarations in Listing 46.3. Good luck!

Listing 46.2   SHORTCUT.FRM—Shortcut.frm Uses a Helper DLL to Manipulate Windows Shortcuts

```
'*****************************************************************
' Shortcut.frm - Uses Ronald R. Martinsen's shortcut.dll file to
'    create and resolve Windows 95 shortcuts.
'*****************************************************************
Option Explicit
'*****************************************************************
' Constant for the path of the shortcut file used for simplicity sake.
' This isn't required.
'*****************************************************************
Private Const SHORTCUTPATH As String = "c:\Shortcut to Notepad.lnk"
'*****************************************************************
' CreateShortcut - Required function declaration to create a shortcut
' with the helper DLL.
'------------------------------------------------------------------
' strSourceFile - Filename of the target of the shortcut (can be a
'                 file, directory, or object)
' strLinkFile   - Name of the shortcut file on the disk (always use
'                 the LNK extension!!!!)
' strInitDir    - The current directory when the application starts*
' strArgs       - Command Line Arguments (i.e., filename)*
' intCmdShow    - Determines how to display the window (use Shell
'                 function constants)
' strIconPath   - The location of the DLL or EXE with the icon you
'                 wish to use.*
' intIconIndex  - The index of the icon you wish to use (only used if
'                 strIconPath was supplied)
' * = use vbNullString for the default
' RETURNS       - Zero if the call worked, otherwise a SCODE HRESULT.
'*****************************************************************
 << DECLARATION GOES HERE >>
'*****************************************************************
```

continues

Listing 46.2   Continued

```
' ResolveShortcut - Required function declaration to get the target
' path to a shortcut file.
'- - - - - - - - - - - - - - - - - - - - - - - - - - - - - - - - - - - - - - -
' hWndOfYourForm        - The handle (hWnd property) of the calling
'                          window
' strShortcutFile       - Filename of the shortcut
' strShortcutLocation - Return buffer for the path of the object the
'                          shortcut points to
' RETURNS               - Zero if the call worked, otherwise a SCODE
'                          HRESULT.
'****************************************************************
<< DECLARATION GOES HERE >>
'****************************************************************
' Create the Shortcut in c:\
'****************************************************************
Private Sub cmdCreateShortcut_Click()
    Dim strMessage As String
    '****************************************************************
    ' Get the the path to the windows directory
    '****************************************************************
    Dim strWinDir As String
    strWinDir = Environ("windir")
    '****************************************************************
    ' Try to create a shortcut to notepad.exe. Build the err string
    ' if the call failed.
    '****************************************************************
    If CreateShortcut(strWinDir & "\notepad.exe", SHORTCUTPATH, _
        "c:\", vbNullString, vbMaximizedFocus, vbNullString, 1) Then
        ' Non-zero result, so notify the user that the call failed
        strMessage = "Unable to create a shortcut to Notepad. Check "
        strMessage = strMessage & "the source code parameters and try"
        strMessage = strMessage & "again."
    '****************************************************************
    ' Otherwise, the call worked so tell the user
    '****************************************************************
    Else
        strMessage = "A shortcut to Notepad was created in c:\"
        '****************************************************************
        ' Enable the resolve button now, since the file exists
        '****************************************************************
        cmdResolveShortcut.Enabled = True
    End If
    '****************************************************************
    ' Display the success or failed message
    '****************************************************************
    MsgBox strMessage
End Sub
'****************************************************************
' Resolve the Shortcut in c:\ (created in Command1_Click)
'****************************************************************
Private Sub cmdResolveShortcut_Click()
    Dim strShortcutTargetPath As String, strTemp As String
    '****************************************************************
```

```
' Build a buffer for the return string
'*******************************************************************
strShortcutTargetPath = Space(260)
'*******************************************************************
' Make the call
'-------------------------------------------------------------------
' NOTE: If the TARGET (the return value) can't be found,
'        then Win95 will display search dialog while it
'        attempts to find it
'*******************************************************************
If ResolveShortcut(hWnd, SHORTCUTPATH, strShortcutTargetPath) Then
    '***************************************************************
    ' Non-zero result, so notify the user that the call failed
    '***************************************************************
    MsgBox "Unable to resolve your shortcut", vbCritical
Else
    '***************************************************************
    ' Trim the null terminator and display the results
    '***************************************************************
    strShortcutTargetPath = Left(strShortcutTargetPath, _
        InStr(strShortcutTargetPath, Chr(0)) - 1)
    MsgBox "Your shortcut points to " & strShortcutTargetPath, _
        vbInformation
    End If
End Sub
```

Listing 46.2 appears a bit long mainly because I've included a large number of comments. In reality, this program is rather trivial. The essential function, CreateShortcut, simply takes the same values that you would normally see in a property page when creating a shortcut. ResolveShortcut is even easier because you provide it with the path to a shortcut file, and it simply loads the strShortcutLocation with the path to the file to which the shortcut references. This code features some common techniques for working with APIs that use strings, so be sure to pay close attention to the comments.

As promised, Listing 46.3 contains the function declarations to the CreateShortcut and ResolveShortcut functions. Were your declarations the same? If so, congratulations! If not, then don't feel bad. Writing declarations can be a little tricky, especially if you've never programmed Windows in C.

Part

IX

Ch

46

Listing 46.3 SHORTCUT.FRM—Create and Resolve Shortcut Function Declarations

```
Private Declare Function CreateShortcut Lib "shortcut.dll" _
    (ByVal strSourceFile$, ByVal strLinkFile$, ByVal strInitDir$, _
    ByVal strArgs$, ByVal intCmdShow%, ByVal strIconPath$, _
    ByVal lngIconIndex As Long) As Long

Private Declare Function ResolveShortcut Lib "shortcut.dll" _
    (ByVal hWndOfYourForm As Long, ByVal strShortcutFile As String, _
    ByVal strShortcutLocation As String) As Long
```

This concludes my crash course on writing declarations. If you are interested in learning more, then there is a fantastic reference book called *The Visual Basic Programmer's Guide to the Windows API*, by Daniel Appleman, that covers this topic extensively. I encourage every VB programmer to purchase a copy of this book, as it is the only resource I know of that translates the Windows API into a form usable by Visual Basic programmers.

Using the Windows API

As with most things, learning by doing is a good way to gain some knowledge about the Windows API. I will be discussing API examples that I classify as *cool*. None of these APIs are especially difficult to use, but they all are extremely helpful to have in your sample code library. I'll start off easy and graduate up to a more complex use of the API in combination with advanced VB code techniques. Finally, I'll finish by writing the TransparentPaint function, which is almost pure API programming in VB. All of the listings in this section are rather large due to the complexity of the samples, but do not let that discourage you. Each sample is commented very well, so any intermediate programmer should be able to follow along.

Warming Up with the Memory Class

Rather than diving right in to a complicated example, I thought I'd begin by explaining the memory class. Most programmers like to include basic memory information in their About boxes, but Visual Basic does not provide any method for doing this. If you want to know how much RAM is installed on a machine, then you have to call the Windows API. Although this isn't a bad thing, it does mean that many of us have written duplicate code many different ways to accomplish the same thing. Frustrated by this, I decided to write what I believe to be a useful (and reusable) class for getting memory information.

Listing 46.4 is my interpretation of the ultimate memory class that will prevent you from having to mess with the API. This class is also structured so that you can easily add features that I omitted, should your application require them.

Listing 46.4   MEMORY.CLS—Memory.cls Demonstrates How to Wrap an API into a Reusable Class Object

```
'*********************************************************************
' Memory.cls - This class takes a snapshot of the memory status and
'    provides the user with a simple interface to get common
'    information about the current memory status.
'*********************************************************************
Option Explicit
'*********************************************************************
' Win32 required user-defined type (or struct) and declaration
'*********************************************************************
Private Type MEMORYSTATUS
        dwLength As Long
        dwMemoryLoad As Long
        dwTotalPhys As Long
```

```
                dwAvailPhys As Long
                dwTotalPageFile As Long
                dwAvailPageFile As Long
                dwTotalVirtual As Long
                dwAvailVirtual As Long
End Type

Private Declare Sub GlobalMemoryStatus Lib "kernel32" _
        (lpBuffer As MEMORYSTATUS)
'********************************************************************
' Private member variable which holds the current memory status
'********************************************************************
Private mmemMemoryStatus As MEMORYSTATUS
'********************************************************************
' Returns the number of bytes of available physical RAM (OK if zero)
'********************************************************************
Public Property Get FreeMemory() As Long
        FreeMemory = mmemMemoryStatus.dwAvailPhys
End Property
'********************************************************************
' Returns the number of bytes of RAM installed in the computer
'********************************************************************
Public Property Get TotalMemory() As Long
        TotalMemory = mmemMemoryStatus.dwTotalPhys
End Property
'********************************************************************
' Returns the number of bytes of virtual memory allocated by the
' operating system
'********************************************************************
Public Property Get TotalVirtualMemory() As Long
        TotalVirtualMemory = mmemMemoryStatus.dwTotalVirtual
End Property
'********************************************************************
' Returns the number of bytes of virtual memory available to this
' process
'********************************************************************
Public Property Get AvailableVirtualMemory() As Long
        AvailableVirtualMemory = mmemMemoryStatus.dwAvailVirtual
End Property
'********************************************************************
' Calls the operating system to find out the memory status at the
' time this object is created
'********************************************************************
Private Sub Class_Initialize()
        mmemMemoryStatus.dwLength = Len(mmemMemoryStatus)
        GlobalMemoryStatus mmemMemoryStatus
End Sub
'********************************************************************
' Updates this object with current memory status
'********************************************************************
Public Sub Refresh()
        GlobalMemoryStatus mmemMemoryStatus
End Sub
```

This class simply wraps the GlobalMemoryStatus API. When the class is created, the API call is made in the Initialize event, so this class is ready to use with no additional initialization. Your application needs only to create a new variable of this class and access the properties that satisfy your program's needs. I reluctantly included a public method called Refresh that updates mmemMemoryStatus, but I couldn't think of any good application of this method. However, it is there for the one person who will claim that he really needs this method.

Listing 46.5 uses clsMemorySnapshot the way it is designed to be used. An application should only define a variable of this class in the local sub or function where it is being used. By doing this, every time your sub or function is called, you get the current memory information. Memdemo.frm displays some of the properties from the clsMem object and includes a special note about the return value from the FreeMemory property.

Listing 46.5 MEMDEMO.FRM—Memdemo.frm Demonstrates How to Use *clsMemorySnapshot*

```
'*************************************************************************
' MemDemo.frm - Demonstrates how to use clsMemorySnapshot
'*************************************************************************
Option Explicit
'*************************************************************************
' Creates a clsMemorySnapshot object and displays the results
'*************************************************************************
Private Sub cmdGetMemoryStatus_Click()
    '*********************************************************************
    ' The efficient way to use clsMemorySnapshot is to create a new
    ' clsMemorySnapshot object every time you need to get the memory
    ' status, so that is what we will do.
    '*********************************************************************
    Dim clsMem As New clsMemorySnapshot
    '*********************************************************************
    ' Holds the current ForeColor of the form since we'll need to
    ' change it temporarily.
    '*********************************************************************
    Dim lngForeColor As Long
    '*********************************************************************
    ' Always clear the form before displaying new information
    '*********************************************************************
    Cls
    With clsMem
        '*****************************************************************
        ' Print Physical Memory Information
        '*****************************************************************
        Print "Total Installed RAM", Format(.TotalMemory \ 1024, _
            "###,###,###,###,##0") & " KB"
        Print "Free Physical RAM", Format(.FreeMemory \ 1024, _
            "###,###,###,###,##0") & " KB";
        '*****************************************************************
        ' Print a asterisk that stands out in bold red
        '*****************************************************************
        Font.Bold = True
        lngForeColor = ForeColor
```

```
                    ForeColor = RGB(255, 0, 0)
                    Print "*"
                    '******************************************************************
                    ' Restore to the default settings
                    '******************************************************************
                    ForeColor = lngForeColor
                    Font.Bold = False
                    '******************************************************************
                    ' Print Virtual Memory Information
                    '******************************************************************
                    Print "Total Virtual Memory", Format(.TotalVirtualMemory \ 1024, _
                        "###,###,###,###,##0") & " KB"
                    Print "Available Virtual Memory", Format(.AvailableVirtualMemory _
                        \ 1024, "###,###,###,###,##0") & " KB"
                End With
                '******************************************************************
                ' Print a blank space, then print a comment in bold
                '******************************************************************
                Print
                Font.Bold = True
                Print "* = It's okay (and common) for this number to be zero."
                '******************************************************************
                ' Restore the form bold value back to false
                '******************************************************************
                Font.Bold = False
        End Sub
```

By wrapping the API call in a class, I have made it as easy to use as a standard VB object in our `cmdGetMemoryStatus_Click` event. This is a great way to simplify the use of many API calls, as well as ensure the proper use of them. Not only does it make the API call easy enough to use by new VB programmers, it also promotes building an API object library that is shared among an entire programming team. I encourage you to use this technique as much as possible and try to keep your classes as simple as possible. After all, to have the best performance, you need to remember that "less is more."

Creating Your Own API Interface

Visual Basic is great because it is simple enough for an intermediate Windows user to learn how to write a Windows application. This simplicity is what attracts everyone to it, and it is what allows people to write applications in weeks that would take months (or even years) in C. However, this simplicity comes at a price. The price is that many functions in VB were written during VB 1.0 when Microsoft only envisioned VB as being a hobbyist programming language or a Windows batch language. No one really saw VB as becoming the most common programming language for Windows that it is today, so many of the 1.0 functions contain limited functionality. One such function is Dir.

While Dir is great for your fundamental needs, it falls short when you try to do something like "search for all the files with the extension BAK on your hard drive." The reason why it falls short is simple—it doesn't support nested calls. Someone at Microsoft realized this shortcoming and wrote the WinSeek sample, which uses a file and directory list box control to overcome this limitation, but this workaround is unacceptable. The spaghetti code in WinSeek is hard to follow, poorly commented, and too slow for even the most trivial tasks.

I have written the FindFile class, shown in Listing 46.6, to overcome the shortcomings of Dir and WinSeek. This class uses the previous concept of encapsulating an API into a reusable object that makes it as easy to use as a built-in VB function. FindFile also adheres to the concept of "keep it simple," by including only a minimal amount of core functionality. This allows individual users of this class to write their own algorithms for special tasks such as searching an entire drive for a specific type of file. I encourage you to review the source code and comments for this class in the following listing.

Listing 46.6   FINDFILE.CLS—FindFile.cls Provides an Interface to the Windows API Used for Finding Files

```
'******************************************************************
' FindFile.cls - Encapsulates the Win32 FindFile functions
'******************************************************************
Option Explicit
'******************************************************************
' Attribute constants which differ from VB
'******************************************************************
Private Const FILE_ATTRIBUTE_COMPRESSED = &H800
Private Const FILE_ATTRIBUTE_NORMAL = &H80
'******************************************************************
' Win32 API constants required by FindFile
'******************************************************************
Private Const MAX_PATH = 260
Private Const INVALID_HANDLE_VALUE = -1
'******************************************************************
' Win32 data types (or structs) required by FindFile
'******************************************************************
Private Type FILETIME
        dwLowDateTime As Long
        dwHighDateTime As Long
End Type

Private Type WIN32_FIND_DATA
        dwFileAttributes As Long
        ftCreationTime As FILETIME
        ftLastAccessTime As FILETIME
        ftLastWriteTime As FILETIME
        nFileSizeHigh As Long
        nFileSizeLow As Long
        dwReserved0 As Long
        dwReserved1 As Long
        cFileName As String * MAX_PATH
        cAlternate As String * 14
End Type

Private Type SYSTEMTIME
        wYear As Integer
        wMonth As Integer
```

```
            wDayOfWeek As Integer
            wDay As Integer
            wHour As Integer
            wMinute As Integer
            wSecond As Integer
            wMilliseconds As Integer
End Type
'********************************************************************
' Win32 API calls required by this class
'********************************************************************
Private Declare Function FileTimeToLocalFileTime Lib "kernel32" _
    (lpFileTime As FILETIME, lpLocalFileTime As FILETIME) As Long
Private Declare Function FileTimeToSystemTime Lib "kernel32" _
    (lpFileTime As FILETIME, lpSystemTime As SYSTEMTIME) As Long
Private Declare Function FindFirstFile Lib "kernel32" Alias _
    "FindFirstFileA" (ByVal lpFileName As String, _
    lpFindFileData As WIN32_FIND_DATA) As Long
Private Declare Function FindNextFile Lib "kernel32" Alias _
    "FindNextFileA" (ByVal hFindFile As Long, lpFindFileData As _
    WIN32_FIND_DATA) As Long
Private Declare Function FindClose& Lib "kernel32" (ByVal hFindFile&)
'********************************************************************
' clsFindFiles private member variables
'********************************************************************
Private mlngFile As Long
Private mstrDateFormat As String
Private mstrUnknownDateText As String
Private mwfdFindData As WIN32_FIND_DATA
'********************************************************************
' Public interface for setting the format string used for dates
'********************************************************************
Public Property Let DateFormat(strDateFormat As String)
    mstrDateFormat = strDateFormat
End Property
'********************************************************************
' Public interface for setting the string used when the date for a
' file is unknown
'********************************************************************
Public Property Let UnknownDateText(strUnknownDateText As String)
    mstrUnknownDateText = strUnknownDateText
End Property
'********************************************************************
' Returns the file attributes for the current file
'********************************************************************
Public Property Get FileAttributes() As Long
    If mlngFile Then FileAttributes = mwfdFindData.dwFileAttributes
End Property
'********************************************************************
' Returns true if the compress bit is set for the current file
'********************************************************************
Public Property Get IsCompressed() As Boolean
    If mlngFile Then IsCompressed = mwfdFindData.dwFileAttributes _
                                    And FILE_ATTRIBUTE_COMPRESSED

End Property
```

continues

Part

IX

Ch

46

Listing 46.6   Continued

```
'****************************************************************
' Returns the value of the Normal attribute bit for dwFileAttributes
'****************************************************************
Public Property Get NormalAttribute() As Long
    NormalAttribute = FILE_ATTRIBUTE_NORMAL
End Property
'****************************************************************
' Primary method in this class for finding the FIRST matching file in
' a directory that matches the path &¦or pattern in strFile
'****************************************************************
Public Function Find(strFile As String, Optional blnShowError _
    As Boolean) As String
    '****************************************************************
    ' If you are already searching, then end the current search
    '****************************************************************
    If mlngFile Then
        If blnShowError Then
            If MsgBox("Cancel the current search?", vbYesNo Or _
                vbQuestion) = vbNo Then Exit Function
        End If
        '****************************************************************
        ' Call cleanup routines before beginning new search
        '****************************************************************
        EndFind
    End If
    '****************************************************************
    ' Find the first file matching the search pattern in strFile
    '****************************************************************
    mlngFile = FindFirstFile(strFile, mwfdFindData)
    '****************************************************************
    ' Check to see if FindFirstFile failed
    '****************************************************************
    If mlngFile = INVALID_HANDLE_VALUE Then
        mlngFile = 0
        '****************************************************************
        ' If blnShowError, then display a default error message
        '****************************************************************
        If blnShowError Then
            MsgBox strFile & " could not be found!", vbExclamation
        '****************************************************************
        ' Otherwise raise a user-defined error with a default err msg
        '****************************************************************
        Else
            Err.Raise vbObjectError + 5000, "clsFindFile_Find", _
                strFile & " could not be found!"
        End If
        Exit Function
    End If
    '****************************************************************
    ' Return the found filename without any nulls
    '****************************************************************
    Find = Left(mwfdFindData.cFileName, _
        InStr(mwfdFindData.cFileName, Chr(0)) - 1)
```

```
End Function
'**********************************************************************
' Call this function until it returns "" to get the remaining files
'**********************************************************************
Public Function FindNext() As String
    '******************************************************************
    ' Exit if no files have been found
    '******************************************************************
    If mlngFile = 0 Then Exit Function
    '******************************************************************
    ' Be sure to clear the contents of cFileName before each call to
    ' avoid garbage characters from being returned in your string.
    '******************************************************************
    mwfdFindData.cFileName = Space(MAX_PATH)
    '******************************************************************
    ' If another file is found, then return it. Otherwise EndFind.
    '******************************************************************
    If FindNextFile(mlngFile, mwfdFindData) Then
        FindNext = Left(mwfdFindData.cFileName, _
            InStr(mwfdFindData.cFileName, Chr(0)) - 1)
    Else
        EndFind
    End If
End Function
'**********************************************************************
' A private helper method which is called internally to close the
' FindFile handle and clear mlngFile to end a FindFile operation.
'**********************************************************************
Private Sub EndFind()
    FindClose mlngFile
    mlngFile = 0
End Sub
'**********************************************************************
' Return the short name of a found file (default = long filename)
'**********************************************************************
Public Function GetShortName() As String
    Dim strShortFileName As String
    '******************************************************************
    ' If no current file, then exit
    '******************************************************************
    If mlngFile = 0 Then Exit Function
    '******************************************************************
    ' Get the short filename (without trailing nulls)
    '******************************************************************
    strShortFileName = Left(mwfdFindData.cAlternate, _
        InStr(mwfdFindData.cAlternate, Chr(0)) - 1)
    '******************************************************************
    ' If there is no short filename info, then strShortFilename will
    ' equal null (because of the (- 1) above)
    '******************************************************************
    If Len(strShortFileName) = 0 Then
        '**************************************************************
        ' If no short filename, then its already a short filename so
        ' set strShortFileName = .cFileName.
```

continues

Listing 46.6   Continued

```
'****************************************************************
            strShortFileName = Left(mwfdFindData.cFileName, _
                InStr(mwfdFindData.cFileName, Chr(0)) - 1)
        End If
'****************************************************************
        ' Return the short filename
'****************************************************************
        GetShortName = strShortFileName
End Function
'****************************************************************
' Return the date the current file was created. If the optional args
' are provided, then they will be set = to date and time values.
'****************************************************************
Public Function GetCreationDate(Optional datDate As Date, _
        Optional datTime As Date) As String

        If mlngFile = 0 Then Exit Function
'****************************************************************
        ' If dwHighDateTime, then Win32 couldn't determine the date so
        ' return the unknown string. "Unknown" is the default.  Set this
        ' value to something else by using the UnknownDateText property.
'****************************************************************
        If mwfdFindData.ftCreationTime.dwHighDateTime = 0 Then
            GetCreationDate = mstrUnknownDateText
            Exit Function
        End If
'****************************************************************
        ' Get the time (in the current local/time zone)
'****************************************************************
        With GetSystemTime(mwfdFindData.ftCreationTime)
'****************************************************************
            ' If datDate was provided, then set it to a date serial
'****************************************************************
            datDate = DateSerial(.wYear, .wMonth, .wDay)
'****************************************************************
            ' If datTime was provided, then set it to a time serial
'****************************************************************
            datTime = TimeSerial(.wHour, .wMinute, .wSecond)
'****************************************************************
            ' Use datDate and datTime as local variables (even if they
            ' weren't passed ByRef in the optional args) to create a
            ' a valid date/time value.  Return the date/time formatted
            ' using the default format of "m/d/yy h:nn:ss AM/PM" or
            ' the user-defined value which was set using the DateFormat
            ' property.
'****************************************************************
            GetCreationDate = Format(datDate + datTime, mstrDateFormat)
        End With
End Function
'****************************************************************
' Similar to GetCreationDate.  See GetCreationDate for comments.
'****************************************************************
Public Function GetLastAccessDate(Optional datDate As Date, _
```

```
        Optional datTime As Date) As String

        If mlngFile = 0 Then Exit Function

        If mwfdFindData.ftLastAccessTime.dwHighDateTime = 0 Then
            GetLastAccessDate = mstrUnknownDateText
            Exit Function
        End If

        With GetSystemTime(mwfdFindData.ftLastAccessTime)
            datDate = DateSerial(.wYear, .wMonth, .wDay)
            datTime = TimeSerial(.wHour, .wMinute, .wSecond)
            GetLastAccessDate = Format(datDate + datTime, mstrDateFormat)
        End With

End Function
'**************************************************************************
' Similar to GetCreationDate.  See GetCreationDate for comments.
'**************************************************************************
Public Function GetLastWriteDate(Optional datDate As Date, _
        Optional datTime As Date) As String

        If mlngFile = 0 Then Exit Function

        If mwfdFindData.ftLastWriteTime.dwHighDateTime = 0 Then
            GetLastWriteDate = mstrUnknownDateText
            Exit Function
        End If

        With GetSystemTime(mwfdFindData.ftLastWriteTime)
            datDate = DateSerial(.wYear, .wMonth, .wDay)
            datTime = TimeSerial(.wHour, .wMinute, .wSecond)
            GetLastWriteDate = Format(datDate + datTime, mstrDateFormat)
        End With

End Function
'**************************************************************************
' Takes a FILETIME and converts it into the local system time
'**************************************************************************
Private Function GetSystemTime(ftmFileTime As FILETIME) As SYSTEMTIME
        Dim ftmLocalTime As FILETIME
        Dim stmSystemTime As SYSTEMTIME
        FileTimeToLocalFileTime ftmFileTime, ftmLocalTime
        FileTimeToSystemTime ftmLocalTime, stmSystemTime
        GetSystemTime = stmSystemTime
End Function
'**************************************************************************
' Sets the default values for private members when this object is
' created
'**************************************************************************
Private Sub Class_Initialize()
        mstrUnknownDateText = "Unknown"
        mstrDateFormat = "m/d/yy h:nn:ss AM/PM"
End Sub
```

Part

IX

Ch

46

continues

Listing 46.6   Continued

```
'*************************************************************
' Ends any open finds, if necessary
'*************************************************************
Private Sub Class_Terminate()
    If mlngFile Then EndFind
End Sub
```

The `FindFile` class contains private declarations for everything it needs to be both an independent and complete object. What's more, it is about 60 percent faster than `WinSeek`. However, performance is not the only reason to use the `FindFile` class. It provides a wealth of information about each found file and supports searching unmapped networked drives using UNC paths.

Now that you have seen `FindFile`, let's use it. `FindFile` is similar to `Dir` in that your first call specifies the search criteria and subsequent calls retrieve the files that correspond to that search criteria. However, `FindFile` is different in that your first call is to the `Find` method, and subsequent calls are to the `FindNext` method. Your application should keep looping as long as strings are being returned from `FindNext`, or until you are ready to begin the next search by calling `Find` again.

Listing 46.7 demonstrates a simple use of the `FindFile` class. In this function, the purpose is to retrieve all of the files in the current directory that satisfy a given search criteria. All of the items found are loaded into a collection provided by the caller. Finally, this function returns the number of files that were added to the `colFiles` collection.

Listing 46.7   FINDFILE.FRM—Searching for Files in a Single Directory

```
'*************************************************************
' A simple routine that finds all of the files in a directory that
' match the given pattern, loads the results in a collection, then
' returns the number of files that are being returned.
'*************************************************************
Private Function FindFilesInSingleDir(ByVal strDir As String, _
    strPattern$, colFiles As Collection) As Integer
    '*************************************************************
    ' Create a new FindFile object every time this function is called
    '*************************************************************
    Dim clsFind As New clsFindFile
    Dim strFile As String
    '*************************************************************
    ' Make sure strSearchPath always has a trailing backslash
    '*************************************************************
    If Right(strDir, 1) <> "\" Then _
        strDir = strDir & "\"
    '*************************************************************
    ' Get the first file
    '*************************************************************
    strFile = clsFind.Find(strDir & strPattern)
```

```
'*****************************************************************
' Loop while files are being returned
'*****************************************************************
Do While Len(strFile)
    '*************************************************************
    ' If the current file found is not a directory...
    '*************************************************************
    If (clsFind.FileAttributes And vbDirectory) = 0 Then
        colFiles.Add strFile ' don't include the path
    End If
    '*************************************************************
    ' Find the next file or directory
    '*************************************************************
    strFile = clsFind.FindNext()
Loop
'*****************************************************************
' Return the number of files found
'*****************************************************************
FindFilesInSingleDir = colFiles.Count
End Function
```

This function begins by creating a new `clsFindFile` object and building the search string. The first file is then retrieved by a call to the `Find` method, and subsequent files are retrieved by looping until `FindNext` no longer returns a value. If no files are found, `FindFilesInSingleDir` returns zero, and no changes are made to the `colFiles` collection. This function is sufficient for your basic needs, but isn't much better than `Dir` because it does not support searching subdirectories. However, this limitation is due to the implementation of the `FindFile` class and not a limitation of the class itself.

Listing 46.8 goes one step further by including support for searching subdirectories. The `FindAllFiles` function overcomes the limitations of `Dir` and `FindFilesInSingleDir`, but it is slightly slower than the previous function. Your application determines if it really needs to search subdirectories and call the appropriate function. This way, the results can be obtained by using the fastest method possible.

Part IX

Ch 46

Listing 46.8   FINDFILE.FRM—*FindAllFiles* Includes Subdirectories in Its Search but It Pays a Small Performance Price

```
'*****************************************************************
' A complex routine that finds all of the files in a directory (and its
' subdirectories), loads the results in a collection, and returns the
' number of subdirectories that were searched.
'*****************************************************************
Private Function FindAllFiles(ByVal strSearchPath$, strPattern As _
    String, Optional colFiles As Collection, Optional colDirs As _
    Collection, Optional blnDirsOnly As Boolean, Optional blnBoth _
    As Boolean) As Integer
    '*************************************************************
    ' Create a new FindFile object every time this function is called
    '*************************************************************
```

continues

Listing 46.8   Continued

```
Dim clsFind As New clsFindFile
Dim strFile As String
Dim intDirsFound As Integer
'********************************************************************
' Make sure strSearchPath always has a trailing backslash
'********************************************************************
If Right(strSearchPath, 1) <> "\" Then _
    strSearchPath = strSearchPath & "\"
'********************************************************************
' Get the first file
'********************************************************************
strFile = clsFind.Find(strSearchPath & strPattern)
'********************************************************************
' Loop while files are being returned
'********************************************************************
Do While Len(strFile)
    '********************************************************************
    ' If the current file found is a directory...
    '********************************************************************
    If clsFind.FileAttributes And vbDirectory Then
        '********************************************************************
        ' Ignore . and ..
        '********************************************************************
        If Left(strFile, 1) <> "." Then
            '********************************************************************
            ' If either bln optional arg is true, then add this
            ' directory to the optional colDirs collection
            '********************************************************************
            If blnDirsOnly Or blnBoth Then
                colDirs.Add strSearchPath & strFile & "\"
            End If
            '********************************************************************
            ' Increment the number of directories found by one
            '********************************************************************
            intDirsFound = intDirsFound + 1
            '********************************************************************
            ' Recursively call this function to search for matches
            ' in subdirectories.  When the recursed function
            ' completes, intDirsFound must be incremented.
            '********************************************************************
            intDirsFound = intDirsFound + FindAllFiles( _
                strSearchPath & strFile & "\", strPattern, _
                colFiles, colDirs, blnDirsOnly)
        End If
        '********************************************************************
        ' Find the next file or directory
        '********************************************************************
        strFile = clsFind.FindNext()
    '********************************************************************
    ' ... otherwise it must be a file.
    '********************************************************************
    Else
        '********************************************************************
```

```
            ' If the caller wants files, then add them to the colFiles
            ' collection
            '*************************************************************
            If Not blnDirsOnly Or blnBoth Then
                colFiles.Add strSearchPath & strFile
            End If
            '*************************************************************
            ' Find the next file or directory
            '*************************************************************
            strFile = clsFind.FindNext()
        End If
    Loop
    '*************************************************************
    ' Return the number of directories found
    '*************************************************************
    FindAllFiles = intDirsFound
End Function
```

The main feature that allows `FindAllFiles` to search subdirectories is the fact that it recursively calls itself. It does this by checking to see if the current file is a directory. If it is, then it makes another call to `FindAllFiles` using all of the same parameters passed in by the original caller with one exception. The `strSearchPath` parameter is modified to point to the next subdirectory to search.

Now that we have our search routines written, let's look at some of the code in FindFile.frm (shown in Figure 46.1) that use this code based on requests from the user of our search dialog box. In Listing 46.9, we perform our search based on the values the user set in our search dialog box. We also play a `FindFile` video during our search, so the user has something to look at during long searches.

Part

IX

Ch

46

FIG. 46.1

FindFile.frm is our VB version of the Windows `FindFile` dialog box.

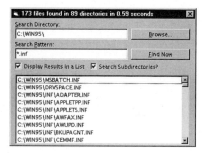

N O T E   When using this sample, the caption displays the number of files and directories found when your search is completed. This value is the correct value, but it might be different from the values returned by the MS-DOS `Dir` command and the Windows Find dialog box. Both `Dir` and the Find dialog box use a different mechanism for counting the number of "files" returned, neither of which is completely accurate. The method I use correlates to the value returned when you view the properties of a directory in the Windows Explorer. ▪

Listing 46.9 FINDFILE.FRM—Choosing the Right Search Technique

```
'*********************************************************************
' Find matching files based on the contents of the text boxes
'*********************************************************************
Private Sub cmdFind_Click()
    '*********************************************************************
    ' Prevent the user from clicking the find button twice, and
    ' hide the browse button so the AVI can be seen
    '*********************************************************************
    cmdFind.Enabled = False
    cmdBrowse.Visible = False
    '*********************************************************************
    ' Give the user a video to watch (wasteful, but cool)
    '*********************************************************************
    With aniFindFile
        .Open App.Path & "\findfile.avi"
        .Visible = True
        Refresh
        .Play
    End With
    '*********************************************************************
    ' Tell the user what you are doing and display an hourglass pointer
    '*********************************************************************
    Caption = "Searching..."
    Screen.MousePointer = vbHourglass
    '*********************************************************************
    ' Always clear before performing the operation (in case the list
    ' is already visible to the user)
    '*********************************************************************
    lstFound.Clear
    '*********************************************************************
    ' Perform the appropriate search
    '*********************************************************************
    If chkSearchSubs Then
        SearchSubDirs
    Else
        SearchCurDirOnly
    End If
    '*********************************************************************
    ' End the video, then restore the buttons and pointer
    '*********************************************************************
    aniFindFile.Stop: aniFindFile.Visible = False
    cmdFind.Enabled = True
    cmdBrowse.Visible = True
    Screen.MousePointer = vbDefault
End Sub
```

This code simply controls the user interface, but doesn't actually do any searching. Instead, it determines which helper function to call based on the default value property of the chkSearchSubs control. I chose this technique because the helper search functions are rather complex, so including it in the Click event would make this code difficult to read.

Listing 46.10 starts with the simple `SearchCurDirOnly` helper routine. This routine simply calls `FindFilesInSingleDir` and loads the results from the `colFiles` collection into a list box (if necessary). That is simple enough, but the next routine, `SearchSubDirs`, is a little more complicated. The reason is because, if the user wants to search for all the files with the extension TMP, then we must first get a list of all of the directories by calling `FindAllFiles`. After we have our list of directories, then we can search each of them for TMP files.

Listing 46.10   FINDFILE.FRM—Using the Results from Our *Find* Functions

```
'****************************************************************
' Performs a simple search in a single directory (like dir *.*)
'****************************************************************
Private Sub SearchCurDirOnly()
    Dim dblStart As Long
    Dim colFiles As New Collection
    '****************************************************************
    ' Begin timing then search
    '****************************************************************
    dblStart = Timer
    FindFilesInSingleDir txtSearchDir, txtSearchPattern, colFiles
    '****************************************************************
    ' Adding items to the list is slow, so only do it if you have to
    '****************************************************************
    If chkDisplayInList Then LoadCollectionInList colFiles
    '****************************************************************
    ' Tell the user how many files were found and how long it took
    ' to find (and load) the files
    '****************************************************************
    Caption = CStr(colFiles.Count) & " files found in" & _
        Str(Timer - dblStart) & " seconds"
End Sub
'****************************************************************
' Performs a complex search in multiple directories (like dir *.* /s)
'****************************************************************
Private Sub SearchSubDirs()
    Dim dblStart As Long
    Dim colFiles As New Collection
    Dim colDirs As New Collection
    Dim intDirsFound As Integer
    Dim vntItem As Variant
    '****************************************************************
    ' Don't forget to add the search directory to your collection
    '****************************************************************
    colDirs.Add txtSearchDir.Text
    '****************************************************************
    ' If the user searches for *.*, then the search is simple (and
    ' much faster)
    '****************************************************************
    If Trim(txtSearchPattern) = "*.*" Then
        dblStart = Timer
        intDirsFound = FindAllFiles(txtSearchDir, "*.*", colFiles, _
            colDirs, , True)
```

Part

IX

Ch

46

continues

Listing 46.10 Continued

```
'**************************************************************
' Otherwise things get sorta complicated
'**************************************************************
Else
    '**********************************************************
    ' First search to get a collection of all the directories
    '**********************************************************
    intDirsFound = FindAllFiles(txtSearchDir, "*.*", , colDirs, True)
    '**********************************************************
    ' Start timing now, since the last search was just prep work
    '**********************************************************
    dblStart = Timer
    '**********************************************************
    ' Search for the file pattern in each directory in the list
    '**********************************************************
    For Each vntItem In colDirs
        '******************************************************
        ' Display the current search directory in the caption
        '******************************************************
        Caption = vntItem
        FindAllFiles CStr(vntItem), txtSearchPattern, colFiles
    Next vntItem
End If
'**************************************************************
' Adding items to the list is slow, so only do it if you have to
'**************************************************************
If chkDisplayInList Then LoadCollectionInList colFiles
'**************************************************************
' Tell the user how many files were found in how many dirs and
' how long it took to find (and load) the files
'**************************************************************
Caption = CStr(colFiles.Count) & " files found in" & _
    Str(intDirsFound) & " directories in" & Str(Timer - dblStart) _
    & " seconds"
End Sub
```

You might notice that, when each of the two routines listed previously complete, they display some basic results in the caption. This is done so that you can experiment with the FindFile program to see that FindFile itself is very fast, but loading the items into a list can be very slow. When using the FindFile.vbp demo program, experiment with different types of searches such as searching a networked drive by using a UNC path. Try improving it to support all of the features that the Windows Find dialog box supports.

Going Graphical with the GDI API

One of the most complex features in the Win32 API are the Graphics Device Interface (GDI) APIs. Because these APIs are very complicated, tedious, and GPF-prone, Microsoft played it safe and excluded most of them from VB. While this shelters you from the complexity and makes your programs more robust, it severely limits your ability to do the cool things that many users expect. VB4 helped to relieve this problem to some extent by providing new features such as `PaintPicture` and the ImageList control, but it still fell short. This means that sometime in the near future, you are going to find yourself calling the GDI APIs from your application. This section demonstrates some of the more common GDI APIs by writing a cool function called `TransparentPaint`.

> **N O T E** Although I would like to take complete credit for the `TransparentPaint` routine, I cannot. The version you see in this chapter is my Win32 version of the `TransparentBlt` code (written by Mike Bond) that originally appeared in the Microsoft Knowledge Base KB article number Q94961. However, I have made many modifications to this code and included a wealth of new comments. ■

`TransparentPaint`, shown in Listing 46.11, is designed to treat a bitmap like an icon when you paint it on a surface. Icons allow you to designate a part of them to be transparent, but bitmaps don't. `TransparentPaint` overcomes this limitation by allowing you to make all of a single color on a bitmap transparent. To accomplish this difficult feat, it is necessary to create a series of temporary bitmaps and do some painting in memory only. Although this abstract concept can be very complicated, the comments in `TransparentPaint` try to explain what is happening at each step.

Listing 46.11   TRANSPARENT.BAS—Transparent.bas Allows You to Display Transparent Bitmaps

```
'******************************************************************
' Paints a bitmap on a given surface using the surface backcolor
' everywhere lngMaskColor appears on the picSource bitmap
'******************************************************************
Sub TransparentPaint(objDest As Object, picSource As StdPicture, _
    lngX As Long, lngY As Long, ByVal lngMaskColor As Long)
    '**************************************************************
    ' This sub uses a bunch of variables, so let's declare and explain
    ' them in advance...
    '**************************************************************
    Dim lngSrcDC As Long        'Source bitmap
    Dim lngSaveDC As Long       'Copy of Source bitmap
    Dim lngMaskDC As Long       'Monochrome Mask bitmap
    Dim lngInvDC As Long        'Monochrome Inverse of Mask bitmap
    Dim lngNewPicDC As Long     'Combination of Source & Background bmps

    Dim bmpSource As BITMAP     'Description of the Source bitmap

    Dim hResultBmp As Long      'Combination of source & background
    Dim hSaveBmp As Long        'Copy of Source bitmap
    Dim hMaskBmp As Long        'Monochrome Mask bitmap
    Dim hInvBmp As Long         'Monochrome Inverse of Mask bitmap

    Dim hSrcPrevBmp As Long     'Holds prev bitmap in source DC
    Dim hSavePrevBmp As Long    'Holds prev bitmap in saved DC
```

continues

Listing 46.11   Continued

```
Dim hDestPrevBmp As Long  'Holds prev bitmap in destination DC
Dim hMaskPrevBmp As Long  'Holds prev bitmap in the mask DC
Dim hInvPrevBmp As Long   'Holds prev bitmap in inverted mask DC

Dim lngOrigScaleMode&     'Holds the original ScaleMode
Dim lngOrigColor&         'Holds original backcolor from source DC
'*****************************************************************
' Set ScaleMode to pixels for Windows GDI
'*****************************************************************
lngOrigScaleMode = objDest.ScaleMode
objDest.ScaleMode = vbPixels
'*****************************************************************
' Load the source bitmap to get its width (bmpSource.bmWidth)
' and height (bmpSource.bmHeight)
'*****************************************************************
GetObject picSource, Len(bmpSource), bmpSource
'*****************************************************************
' Create compatible device contexts (DC's) to hold the temporary
' bitmaps used by this sub
'*****************************************************************
lngSrcDC = CreateCompatibleDC(objDest.hdc)
lngSaveDC = CreateCompatibleDC(objDest.hdc)
lngMaskDC = CreateCompatibleDC(objDest.hdc)
lngInvDC = CreateCompatibleDC(objDest.hdc)
lngNewPicDC = CreateCompatibleDC(objDest.hdc)
'*****************************************************************
' Create monochrome bitmaps for the mask-related bitmaps
'*****************************************************************
hMaskBmp = CreateBitmap(bmpSource.bmWidth, bmpSource.bmHeight, _
    1, 1, ByVal 0&)
hInvBmp = CreateBitmap(bmpSource.bmWidth, bmpSource.bmHeight, _
    1, 1, ByVal 0&)
'*****************************************************************
' Create color bitmaps for the final result and the backup copy
' of the source bitmap
'*****************************************************************
hResultBmp = CreateCompatibleBitmap(objDest.hdc, _
    bmpSource.bmWidth, bmpSource.bmHeight)
hSaveBmp = CreateCompatibleBitmap(objDest.hdc, _
    bmpSource.bmWidth, bmpSource.bmHeight)
'*****************************************************************
' Select bitmap into the device context (DC)
'*****************************************************************
hSrcPrevBmp = SelectObject(lngSrcDC, picSource)
hSavePrevBmp = SelectObject(lngSaveDC, hSaveBmp)
hMaskPrevBmp = SelectObject(lngMaskDC, hMaskBmp)
hInvPrevBmp = SelectObject(lngInvDC, hInvBmp)
hDestPrevBmp = SelectObject(lngNewPicDC, hResultBmp)
'*****************************************************************
' Make a backup of source bitmap to restore later
'*****************************************************************
BitBlt lngSaveDC, 0, 0, bmpSource.bmWidth, bmpSource.bmHeight, _
    lngSrcDC, 0, 0, vbSrcCopy
```

```
'*****************************************************************
' Create the mask by setting the background color of source to
' transparent color, then BitBlt'ing that bitmap into the mask
' device context
'*****************************************************************
lngOrigColor = SetBkColor(lngSrcDC, lngMaskColor)
BitBlt lngMaskDC, 0, 0, bmpSource.bmWidth, bmpSource.bmHeight, _
    lngSrcDC, 0, 0, vbSrcCopy
'*****************************************************************
' Restore the original backcolor in the device context
'*****************************************************************
SetBkColor lngSrcDC, lngOrigColor
'*****************************************************************
' Create an inverse of the mask to AND with the source and combine
' it with the background
'*****************************************************************
BitBlt lngInvDC, 0, 0, bmpSource.bmWidth, bmpSource.bmHeight, _
    lngMaskDC, 0, 0, vbNotSrcCopy
'*****************************************************************
' Copy the background bitmap to the new picture device context
' to begin creating the final transparent bitmap
'*****************************************************************
BitBlt lngNewPicDC, 0, 0, bmpSource.bmWidth, bmpSource.bmHeight, _
    objDest.hdc, lngX, lngY, vbSrcCopy
'*****************************************************************
' AND the mask bitmap with the result device context to create
' a cookie cutter effect in the background by painting the black
' area for the non-transparent portion of the source bitmap
'*****************************************************************
BitBlt lngNewPicDC, 0, 0, bmpSource.bmWidth, bmpSource.bmHeight, _
    lngMaskDC, 0, 0, vbSrcAnd
'*****************************************************************
' AND the inverse mask with the source bitmap to turn off the bits
' associated with transparent area of source bitmap by making it
' black
'*****************************************************************
BitBlt lngSrcDC, 0, 0, bmpSource.bmWidth, bmpSource.bmHeight, _
    lngInvDC, 0, 0, vbSrcAnd
'*****************************************************************
' XOR the result with the source bitmap to replace the mask color
' with the background color
'*****************************************************************
BitBlt lngNewPicDC, 0, 0, bmpSource.bmWidth, bmpSource.bmHeight, _
    lngSrcDC, 0, 0, vbSrcPaint
'*****************************************************************
' Paint the transparent bitmap on source surface
'*****************************************************************
BitBlt objDest.hdc, lngX, lngY, bmpSource.bmWidth, _
    bmpSource.bmHeight, lngNewPicDC, 0, 0, vbSrcCopy
'*****************************************************************
' Restore backup of bitmap
'*****************************************************************
BitBlt lngSrcDC, 0, 0, bmpSource.bmWidth, bmpSource.bmHeight, _
    lngSaveDC, 0, 0, vbSrcCopy
```

Part

IX

Ch

46

continues

Listing 46.11   Continued

```
'*********************************************************************
' Restore the original objects by selecting their original values
'*********************************************************************
SelectObject lngSrcDC, hSrcPrevBmp
SelectObject lngSaveDC, hSavePrevBmp
SelectObject lngNewPicDC, hDestPrevBmp
SelectObject lngMaskDC, hMaskPrevBmp
SelectObject lngInvDC, hInvPrevBmp
'*********************************************************************
' Free system resources created by this sub
'*********************************************************************
DeleteObject hSaveBmp
DeleteObject hMaskBmp
DeleteObject hInvBmp
DeleteObject hResultBmp
DeleteDC lngSrcDC
DeleteDC lngSaveDC
DeleteDC lngInvDC
DeleteDC lngMaskDC
DeleteDC lngNewPicDC
'*********************************************************************
' Restores the ScaleMode to its original value
'*********************************************************************
objDest.ScaleMode = lngOrigScaleMode
End Sub
```

On the CD

For simplicity's sake, I have omitted the API declarations from Listing 46.11. I could go on for pages explaining exactly what is happening during each step of TransparentPaint, but I won't because this sub contains the same comments I've made in this listing. It also would be more difficult to follow this listing if it were broken into several smaller blocks. After reading the comments for this sub, I encourage you to single-step through the TRANSPARENT.VBP project, which you can get from the book's companion CD-ROM. This will help you to visualize what is happening at each step.

Although TransparentPaint is a difficult procedure to follow, using it is easy. Listing 46.12 loads a bitmap from a resource and paints it on the upper-left corner of the form using TransparentPaint. Next, it paints it using PaintPicture. The last parameter, vbGreen, tells TransparentPaint to replace any bits in the bitmap that are green with the background color of the form. The result is shown in Figure 46.2.

Listing 46.12   TRANSPARENT.FRM—Transparent.frm Demonstrates the
***TransparentPaint* Procedure**

```
'*********************************************************************
' Transparent.frm - Demonstrates how to use basTransparent's
' TransparentPaint using a bitmap from a resource file.
'*********************************************************************
```

```
Option Explicit
'*********************************************************************
' Gets a StdPicture handle by loading a bitmap from a resource file
' and paints it transparently on the form by using Gray as the mask
' color.
'*********************************************************************
Private Sub cmdPaintTransBmp_Click()
    TransparentPaint Me, LoadResPicture(103, 0), 0, 0, QBColor(7)
End Sub
```

FIG. 46.2

TransparentPaint is a must for your multimedia applications.

Try replacing the resource file in this project with your own resource file to see how TransparentPaint works. Also, try using different mask colors as well as the images from picture boxes. Now you never again have to write an application that appears to be of inferior quality because it doesn't use transparent bitmaps.

Registry Revisited

The listing in this section, like most sections in this chapter, is long because I have included the discussion of the code in line with the code in the form of comments. Before and after each listing, I make some additional comments on the code, but the most important comments are in the listing itself. Given the sheer size of Registry.bas, I have elected to include only some of the functions from that module.

The most common interaction between VB programs and the Registry is writing and reading strings to and from a specific key. Listing 46.13 contains two functions, GetRegString and SetRegString, that accomplish this task. In addition to setting Registry strings, SetRegString also creates new keys in the Registry. If either of these functions fails, it raises a user-defined error. This way, your application can handle this error without notifying your user.

Listing 46.13 REGISTRY.BAS—*GetRegSetting* and *SetRegSetting* Read and Write Registry Strings

```
'*********************************************************************
' REGISTRY.BAS - Contains the code necessary to access the Windows
'                registration database.
'
```

continues

Part
IX

Ch
46

Listing 46.13   Continued

```
'*****************************************************************
' GetRegString takes three arguments. A HKEY constant (listed above),
' a subkey, and a value in that subkey. This function returns the
' string stored in the strValueName value in the registry.
'*****************************************************************
Public Function GetRegString(HKEY As Long, strSubKey As String, _
                             strValueName As String) As String
    Dim strSetting As String
    Dim lngDataLen As Long
    Dim hSubKey As Long
    '*****************************************************************
    ' Open the key. If success, then get the data from the key.
    '*****************************************************************
    If RegOpenKeyEx(HKEY, strSubKey, 0, KEY_ALL_ACCESS, hSubKey) = _
        ERROR_SUCCESS Then
        strSetting = Space(255)
        lngDataLen = Len(strSetting)
        '*****************************************************************
        ' Query the key for the current setting. If this call
        ' succeeds, then return the string.
        '*****************************************************************
        If RegQueryValueEx(hSubKey, strValueName, ByVal 0, _
            REG_SZ, ByVal strSetting, lngDataLen) = _
            ERROR_SUCCESS Then
            If lngDataLen > 1 Then
                GetRegString = Left(strSetting, lngDataLen - 1)
            End If
        Else
            Err.Raise ERRBASE + 1, "GetRegString", _
                "RegQueryValueEx failed!"
        End If
        '*****************************************************************
        ' ALWAYS close any keys that you open.
        '*****************************************************************
        RegCloseKey hSubKey
    End If
End Function
'*****************************************************************
' SetRegString takes four arguments. A HKEY constant (listed above),
' a subkey, a value in that subkey, and a setting for the key.
'*****************************************************************
Public Sub SetRegString(HKEY As Long, strSubKey As String, _
                        strValueName As String, strSetting _
                        As String)
    Dim hNewHandle As Long
    Dim lpdwDisposition As Long
    '*****************************************************************
    ' Create & open the key. If success, then get then write the data
    ' to the key.
    '*****************************************************************
```

```
    If RegCreateKeyEx(HKEY, strSubKey, 0, strValueName, 0, _
        KEY_ALL_ACCESS, 0&, hNewHandle, lpdwDisposition) = _
        ERROR_SUCCESS Then
        If RegSetValueEx(hNewHandle, strValueName, 0, REG_SZ, _
            ByVal strSetting, Len(strSetting)) <> ERROR_SUCCESS Then
            Err.Raise ERRBASE + 2, "SetRegString", _
                "RegSetValueEx failed!"
        End If
    Else
        Err.Raise ERRBASE + 3, "SetRegString", "RegCreateKeyEx failed!"
    End If
    '*****************************************************************
    ' ALWAYS close any keys that you open.
    '*****************************************************************
    RegCloseKey hNewHandle
End Sub
```

Although these two functions accomplish different tasks, the method they use to accomplish their task is virtually identical. The user provides a predefined long constant HKEY value (such as HKEY_CURRENT_USER), a subkey (such as "Software\Microsoft" with no leading backslash), and a value to read from or write to. Both functions (using different Registry functions) begin by opening the subkey and then reading or writing to or from it. Finally, they both end by closing the key they opened.

Listing 46.13 demonstrates a fundamental technique required during all coding with the Registry. Subkeys must be opened and closed before any values can be retrieved. The HKEY values are opened and closed by Windows, so you never have to worry about opening or closing them. This concept is repeated during every function in Registry.bas, so keep this in mind should you decide to write your own Registry functions.

Listing 46.14 demonstrates this fundamental technique again using DWORD (or Long) values. The GetRegDWord and SetRegDWord functions allow you to read and write long values to and from the Registry. Because most Registry values you'll ever use will be strings, I have included a conditional compilation argument in Registry.bas called LEAN_AND_MEAN. Because this conditional compilation constant is undefined by default, its value will be 0. This means that all of the code in the LEAN_AND_MEAN section will be included in your application by default. However, if you wanted to write an application that did not take advantage of any of the functions in the LEAN_AND_MEAN section, then you could edit your project properties and set the LEAN_AND_MEAN conditional compilation constant equal to 1. This would prevent this code from being included in your executable, thus reducing its size and memory requirements. All of the remaining code in Registry.bas that appears in this section is part of the LEAN_AND_MEAN section that may be excluded from your application.

Listing 46.14   REGISTRY.BAS—Extended Registry Functions Using Conditional Compilation

```
'*******************************************************************
' Extended registry functions begin here
'*******************************************************************
#If LEAN_AND_MEAN = 0 Then
'*******************************************************************
' Returns a DWORD value from a given registry key
'*******************************************************************
Public Function GetRegDWord(HKEY&, strSubKey$, strValueName$) As Long
    Dim lngDataLen As Long
    Dim hSubKey As Long
    Dim lngRetVal As Long
    '*************************************************************
    ' Open the key. If success, then get the data from the key.
    '*************************************************************
    If RegOpenKeyEx(HKEY, strSubKey, 0, KEY_ALL_ACCESS, hSubKey) = _
        ERROR_SUCCESS Then
        '*********************************************************
        ' Query the key for the current setting. If this call
        ' succeeds, then return the string.
        '*********************************************************
        lngDataLen = 4 'Bytes
        If RegQueryValueEx(hSubKey, strValueName, ByVal 0, _
            REG_DWORD, lngRetVal, lngDataLen) = ERROR_SUCCESS Then
            GetRegDWord = lngRetVal
        Else
            Err.Raise ERRBASE + 1, "GetRegDWord", _
                "RegQueryValueEx failed!"
        End If
        '*********************************************************
        ' ALWAYS close any keys that you open.
        '*********************************************************
        RegCloseKey hSubKey
    End If
End Function
'*******************************************************************
' Sets a registry key to a DWORD value
'*******************************************************************
Public Sub SetRegDWord(HKEY&, strSubKey$, strValueName$, lngSetting&)
    Dim hNewHandle As Long
    Dim lpdwDisposition As Long
    '*************************************************************
    ' Create & open the key. If success, then get then write the data
    ' to the key.
    '*************************************************************
    If RegCreateKeyEx(HKEY, strSubKey, 0, strValueName, 0, _
        KEY_ALL_ACCESS, 0&, hNewHandle, lpdwDisposition) = _
        ERROR_SUCCESS Then
        If RegSetValueEx(hNewHandle, strValueName, 0, REG_DWORD, _
            lngSetting, 4) <> ERROR_SUCCESS Then
            Err.Raise ERRBASE + 2, "SetRegDWord", _
                "RegSetValueEx failed!"
        End If
```

```
    Else
        Err.Raise ERRBASE + 3, "SetRegString", "RegCreateKeyEx failed!"
    End If
    '****************************************************************
    ' ALWAYS close any keys that you open.
    '****************************************************************
    RegCloseKey hNewHandle
End Sub
```

The way you read and write DWORD (or Long) values to and from the Registry are almost identical to the method you use for strings. The only difference is that, instead of passing the length of your string or buffer to `RegQueryValueEx` and `RegSetValueEx`, you pass the number of bytes of memory occupied by a Long. Because a Long holds 4 bytes, we pass in the number 4.

The last function I'm going to discuss in Registry.bas is the `GetRegKeyValues` function, shown in Listing 46.15. This function enumerates through a given subkey in the Registry and returns all of its values and settings. This function was used to load our ListView control with all of the values of the subkey selected in the TreeView control in Registry.frm. Although this function isn't extraordinarily difficult, it is long and complex given the nature of enumeration and multi-dimensional arrays.

This function is unique to most functions you've ever used or written because it returns a multi-dimensional array that contains the values in the first dimension and the settings in the second dimension. This gives the calling function the flexibility to use the values returned from this function in any manner it chooses. However, it is the responsibility of the caller to both check to make sure an array was returned (in case there were no keys) *and* to treat the results from this function as a two-dimensional array.

`GetRegKeyValues` begins like every function in Registry.bas by opening the subkey, but then it does something unique. It calls a helper function (not shown) called `QueryRegInfoKey` which returns some helpful information about the subkey. `QueryRegInfoKey` simply wraps a Registry function called `RegQueryInfoKey` that provides us with information about subkey like how many values it contains, and the length of the longest value and setting. This information helps to determine if we should begin the enumeration, the size array we will need, and how large our string buffer needs to be. After we have this information, we are ready to begin the enumeration.

Part IX
Ch 46

Listing 46.15   REGISTRY.BAS—*GetRegKeyValues* Demonstrates Registry Enumeration

```
'****************************************************************
' Returns a multi dimensional variant array of all the values and
' settings in a given registry subkey.
'****************************************************************
Public Function GetRegKeyValues(HKEY&, strSubKey$) As Variant
    Dim lngNumValues As Long      ' Number values in this key
```

continues

Listing 46.15   Continued

```
Dim strValues() As String     ' Value and return array
Dim lngMaxValSize  As Long    ' Size of longest value
Dim lngValRetBytes As Long    ' Size of current value

Dim lngMaxSettingSize As Long ' Size of longest REG_SZ in this key
Dim lngSetRetBytes As Long    ' Size of current REG_SZ

Dim lngSetting As Long        ' Used for DWORD

Dim lngType As Long           ' Type of value returned from
                              ' RegEnumValue

Dim hChildKey As Long         ' The handle of strSubKey
Dim i As Integer              ' Loop counter
'****************************************************************
' Exit if you did not successfully open the child key
'****************************************************************
If RegOpenKeyEx(HKEY, strSubKey, 0, KEY_ALL_ACCESS, hChildKey) _
    <> ERROR_SUCCESS Then
    Err.Raise ERRBASE + 4, "GetRegKeyValues", _
        "RegOpenKeyEx failed!"
    Exit Function
End If
'****************************************************************
' Find out the array and value sizes in advance
'****************************************************************
If QueryRegInfoKey(hChildKey, , , lngNumValues, lngMaxValSize, _
    lngMaxSettingSize) <> ERROR_SUCCESS Or lngNumValues = 0 Then
    Err.Raise ERRBASE + 5, "GetRegKeyValues", _
        "RegQueryInfoKey failed!"
    RegCloseKey hChildKey
    Exit Function
End If
'****************************************************************
' Resize the array to fit the return values
'****************************************************************
lngNumValues = lngNumValues - 1 ' Adjust to zero based
ReDim strValues(0 To lngNumValues, 0 To 1) As String
'****************************************************************
' Get all of the values and settings for the key
'****************************************************************
For i = 0 To lngNumValues
    '****************************************************************
    ' Make the return buffers large enough to hold the results
    '****************************************************************
    strValues(i, 0) = Space(lngMaxValSize)
    lngValRetBytes = lngMaxValSize

    strValues(i, 1) = Space(lngMaxSettingSize)
    lngSetRetBytes = lngMaxSettingSize
    '****************************************************************
    ' Get a single value and setting from the registry
    '****************************************************************
```

```
        RegEnumValue hChildKey, i, strValues(i, 0), lngValRetBytes, _
            0, lngType, ByVal strValues(i, 1), lngSetRetBytes
        '*************************************************************
        ' If the return value was a string, then trim trailing nulls
        '*************************************************************
        If lngType = REG_SZ Then
            strValues(i, 1) = Left(strValues(i, 1), lngSetRetBytes - 1)
        '*************************************************************
        ' Else if it was a DWord, call RegEnumValue again to store
        ' the return setting in a long variable
        '*************************************************************
        ElseIf lngType = REG_DWORD Then
            '*********************************************************
            ' We already know the return size of the value because
            ' we got it in the last call to RegEnumValue, so we
            ' can tell RegEnumValue that its buffer size is the
            ' length of the string already returned, plus one (for
            ' the trailing null terminator)
            '*********************************************************
            lngValRetBytes = lngValRetBytes + 1
            '*********************************************************
            ' Make the call again using a long instead of string
            '*********************************************************
            RegEnumValue hChildKey, i, strValues(i, 0), _
                lngValRetBytes, 0, lngType, lngSetting, lngSetRetBytes
            '*********************************************************
            ' Return the long as a string
            '*********************************************************
            strValues(i, 1) = CStr(lngSetting)
        '*************************************************************
        ' Otherwise let the user know that this code doesn't support
        ' the format returned (such as REG_BINARY)
        '*************************************************************
        Else
            strValues(i, 1) = REG_UNSUPPORTED
        End If
        '*************************************************************
        ' Store the return value and setting in a multi dimensional
        ' array with the value in the 0 index and the setting in
        ' the 1 index of the second dimension.
        '*************************************************************
        strValues(i, 0) = RTrim(Left(strValues(i, 0), lngValRetBytes))
        strValues(i, 1) = RTrim(strValues(i, 1))
    Next i
    '*****************************************************************
    ' ALWAYS close any keys you open
    '*****************************************************************
    RegCloseKey hChildKey
    '*****************************************************************
    ' Return the result as an array of strings
    '*****************************************************************
    GetRegKeyValues = strValues
End Function
```

During the enumeration, we set all of our string buffers in advance. Next, we attempt to retrieve the value and setting as strings. If the setting was a string, then we trim off any trailing nulls. If the setting was a DWORD, then we make the call again this time passing in a long value and 4 bytes as the buffer size. After the DWORD has been retrieved, we convert it into a string and load it into the array. If the setting was neither a string nor a DWORD, then we load the array with a special string that tells the caller the return value was in an unsupported format.

We repeat the enumeration for all of the values and settings. When completed, we close the key we opened and return the two-dimensional array by its name. The caller will get a variant return value that contains this two-dimensional array.

The remaining functions are described in detail in Registry.bas. I encourage you to read these comments and experiment with each of them. I've also included some examples that demonstrate how to use each of the functions in Registry.bas in the Form_Load event of Registry.frm. These functions are at the end of the Form_Load event and are commented out. Feel free to use them in Registry.frm, the immediate pane in VB, or in a separate application to see how each of the Registry.bas functions work.

Callbacks Revisited

By using the Windows API, you can create *callbacks* in Visual Basic. This feature allows the operating system to call a procedure in your Visual Basic program. For example, you can have Windows call a procedure in response to a Windows event. Windows knows how to call your procedure because you pass the address of it to Windows when using the API. Before version 5.0, callbacks of this type were not available in VB.

Listing 46.16 demonstrates how to use the EnumWindows API call. EnumWindows takes a function pointer and a pointer to a value that you would like passed to your function pointer. In turn, it iterates through the Windows task list, calling your callback function during each iteration. Callback.bas contains our callback function and some helper routines that allow us to print a list of visible windows on a form.

> **Listing 46.16   CALLBACK.BAS—Callback.bas Shows a Sample Callback Function**

```
'****************************************************************
' Callback.bas - Demonstrates how to do callbacks in VB
'****************************************************************
Option Explicit
'****************************************************************
' EnumWindows takes a function pointer (AddressOf your callback
' function) and a lParam argument (can be a pointer to anything you
' would like sent to your callback function)
'****************************************************************
Private Declare Function EnumWindows Lib "user32" _
    (ByVal lpfn As Long, lParam As Any) As Boolean
```

```
'*****************************************************************
' There are a lot of windows loaded that are never visible, so
' I usually use the IsWindowVisible API call to filter out only the
' top-level windows the user sees
'*****************************************************************
Private Declare Function IsWindowVisible Lib "user32" _
    (ByVal hWnd As Long) As Long
'*****************************************************************
' I use the following APIs to get the captions and classnames of the
' visible windows
'*****************************************************************
Private Declare Function GetWindowText Lib "user32" Alias _
    "GetWindowTextA" (ByVal hWnd As Long, ByVal lpString As String, _
    ByVal cch As Long) As Long

Private Declare Function GetWindowTextLength Lib "user32" Alias _
    "GetWindowTextLengthA" (ByVal hWnd As Long) As Long

Private Declare Function GetClassName Lib "user32" Alias _
    "GetClassNameA" (ByVal hWnd As Long, ByVal lpClassName$, _
    ByVal nMaxCount As Long) As Long
'*****************************************************************
' This is a callback function. Notice how the function is declared
' as Private. This private flag only applies to VB, not to Windows,
' so it is okay to declare your callback functions as Private if you
' don't want them to be accessible in external modules. Also notice
' how we used the lParam pointer to pass as a form to our callback
'*****************************************************************
Private Function CallBackFunc(ByVal hWnd As Long, _
    lParam As Form) As Long
    Dim strhWnd As String * 8
    Dim strClass As String * 20
    '*****************************************************************
    ' If the window is visible, then print some information about it
    ' on the lParam form
    '*****************************************************************
    If IsWindowVisible(hWnd) Then
        strhWnd = "&H" & Hex(hWnd)
        strClass = GetWindowClassName(hWnd)
        lParam.Print strhWnd & strClass & GetWindowCaption(hWnd)
    End If
    '*****************************************************************
    ' Only return false if you want to stop EnumWindows from calling
    ' this callback again
    '*****************************************************************
    CallBackFunc = True
End Function
'*****************************************************************
' Returns the caption of a window
'*****************************************************************
Private Function GetWindowCaption(hWnd As Long) As String
    Dim lngCaptionLen As Long
    Dim strCaption As String
    '*****************************************************************
    ' Get the length of the caption and add 1 to account for the
```

continues

Listing 46.16 Continued

```
    ' null terminator
    '****************************************************************
    lngCaptionLen = GetWindowTextLength(hWnd) + 1
    '****************************************************************
    ' Allocate your buffer to hold the caption
    '****************************************************************
    strCaption = Space(lngCaptionLen)
    '****************************************************************
    ' Get the caption, and return the characters up to (but not
    ' including) the null terminator
    '****************************************************************
    lngCaptionLen = GetWindowText(hWnd, strCaption, lngCaptionLen)
    GetWindowCaption = Left(strCaption, lngCaptionLen)
End Function
'****************************************************************
' Get the class name using the same techniques described above
'****************************************************************
Private Function GetWindowClassName(hWnd As Long) As String
    Dim strClassName As String
    Dim lngClassLen As Integer
    lngClassLen = 50
    strClassName = Space(lngClassLen)
    lngClassLen = GetClassName(hWnd, strClassName, lngClassLen)
    GetWindowClassName = Left(strClassName, lngClassLen)
End Function
'****************************************************************
' Print some headers and call EnumWindows to print the window info
'****************************************************************
Public Sub CallbackDemo(frmName As Form)
    frmName.Cls
    frmName.Print "Handle" & "  Class Name", "Window Caption"
    frmName.Print "------" & "  ----------", "--------------"
    EnumWindows AddressOf CallBackFunc, frmName
End Sub
```

CallBackFunc begins with our callback function that is declared as private. It is private, because we won't be calling this code anywhere in our VB application. However, the private qualifier has no effect on Windows capability to call this function. Each time this function is called, we check to see if the current window is visible. If it is, then we print its hwnd, class name, and window caption on the form passed in as the lParam of EnumWindows. Finally, we always return True. If, for some reason, we wanted to end the enumeration, we would return False from our callback function. You might do this if you used EnumWindows to find a specific window. After you find the window you are searching for, you can stop the enumeration.

GetWindowCaption and GetWindowClassName simply wrap a couple of APIs, so your callback routine is as simple as possible. Because both of these functions are retrieving strings from an API, they both build string buffers before the API call and trim off the null terminator after the API call.

The last, but perhaps the most important, function in Listing 46.16 is the public `CallbackDemo` method. This method is the public interface to your application that is responsible for calling `EnumWindows` and printing the results on the form you provide when you call `CallbackDemo`.

Figure 46.3 shows our callback function at work in Callback.frm. Listing 46.17 demonstrates how to build this task list. We pass in a reference to the form where we make the call by using the `Me` keyword.

FIG. 46.3

EnumWindows is great for creating a task list.

```
Callback Demo                                                    _ □ ×
Handle   Class Name          Window Caption
------   ----------          --------------

&H124    Shell_TrayWnd
&HE70    ThunderForm         Callback Demo
&HD68    ThunderMain         Callback
&HE90    IEFrame             Microsoft Corporation - Microsoft Internet Explorer
&HD64    IDEOwner            Project1 - Microsoft Visual Basic [run]
&HFB4    ExploreWClass       Exploring - C:\
&H110    Progman             Program Manager
```

Listing 46.17   CALLBACK.FRM—Callback.frm Uses Our Sample Callback Function

```
'*******************************************************************************
' Callback.frm - Demonstrates how to use basCallback
'*******************************************************************************
Option Explicit
'*******************************************************************************
' Updates the form with the current window list every time it gets
' a paint event
'*******************************************************************************
Private Sub Form_Paint()
    CallbackDemo Me
End Sub
```

Because windows are always being added and removed, I elected to put our call to `CallbackDemo` in the `Form_Paint` event. Because creating or removing windows usually causes our form to be repainted, this technique allows our form to contain the latest visible window list.

From Here...

Now that you've had a small taste of what the Win32 API can do for you, it's time to experiment on your own. Take the samples in this chapter apart and use them in your own applications. Experiment, extend, and optimize them for your own code library. You'll find that, after you get the hang of writing VB programs that leverage the power of Win32, your dependency on third-party controls will be much less. Can you think of any controls you have now that could be replaced by the code in this chapter? If so, begin reworking your program right away.

Part

IX

Ch

46

Visual Basic Resources

This book has covered a lot of material about programming in Visual Basic. You have seen how to create the interface of your programs with forms and controls, how to perform tasks using the BASIC programming language, how to handle databases, and a host of other things. Although this book provides you with a great beginning in the world of Visual Basic programming, it should not be the end of your learning experience. As a programmer in a rapidly changing world, you should be constantly learning new skills and refining old ones.

To help you in this continuous learning process, this appendix provides you with a look at some of the additional controls you might want to explore, as well as some other materials that will help you learn more about programming in Visual Basic. ■

Using Other Controls

As you have seen through the course of the book, the bulk of your Visual Basic programs are made up of controls. These controls are used to build your program the same way ignition systems, radios, and transmissions are used to build a car. Just like a car, you can add optional equipment to your development environment. This is done in the form of custom controls and add-ins. You have probably already seen how a few of these are used, as you learned about the Masked Edit control, Tabbed Dialog control, RichTextBox control, and others in earlier chapters.

Some of these controls provide an enhanced version of a standard control. This is akin to replacing the basic radio in a car with the radio/cassette/CD combination. It still handles the basic functions, but also provides you with more capabilities. Other controls provide completely new capabilities. This is like adding a sunroof to your car.

Using Other Controls You Already Have

Although we have already touched on a few of the custom controls and add-ins that are included with Visual Basic, there are a number of others that you might want to look at. The following controls and add-ins provide additional capabilities to Visual Basic that allow you to build better and more complex programs:

- PicClip control   Helps you manage picture images. This control is especially useful in helping with animation or toolbar applications.
- MSComm control   Is used to create applications that communicate directly through the serial or parallel ports of your computer.
- MAPI controls   Are used with e-mail applications.

You can find out more about these controls and others in Visual Basic's Custom Controls Help file. The Help file provides you with descriptions of the controls and their properties and methods. You will also find some usage examples.

Using Third-Party Controls

Third-party controls are one of the great benefits of using Visual Basic. Like other custom controls, these controls can allow your application to perform a variety of tasks. Typically, vendors create both "enhanced" versions of the standard controls as well as controls that give you entirely new capabilities. Two of my favorite controls are VSView by VideoSoft and Calendar Widgets by Sheridan.

VSView provides a replacement for the Printer object in Visual Basic. With VSView, you can easily create multi-column tables and handle word wrapping on the page. You also don't have to worry about keeping track of when page breaks should occur. This is handled for you. Also, one of the best features of the product is that you can easily include print preview capabilities in your code (see Figure A.1). This requires some simple code that you can obtain from the samples included with the product.

FIG. A.1

Print preview is made easy with one third-party control.

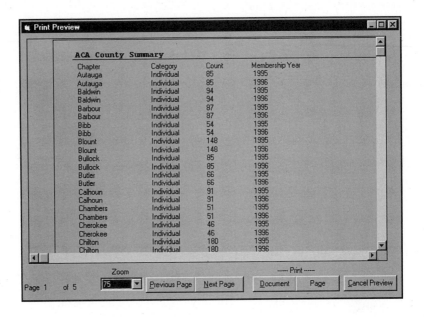

The other control, Calendar Widgets, provides you with a series of controls for handling dates. These controls make it easier for you to create programs such as appointment schedulers, to do lists, and other date dependent programs (see Figure A.2). One of the best controls in the group is the Date Combo. This control uses a drop-down calendar that allows the user to pick a date with ease (see Figure A.3). It also makes your programming job easier because you know that the dates are valid and are the correct data type. (Handling dates can be one of the greatest pains in programming.)

FIG. A.2

DayView makes quick work out of creating an appointment calendar.

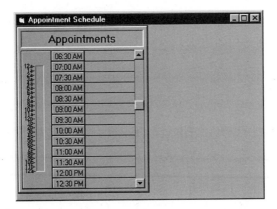

There are a number of vendors that make third-party controls for a variety of tasks. Table A.1 provides a list of some of these vendors, as well as contact information.

FIG. A.3

DateCombo makes
selecting dates as
simple as a mouse
click.

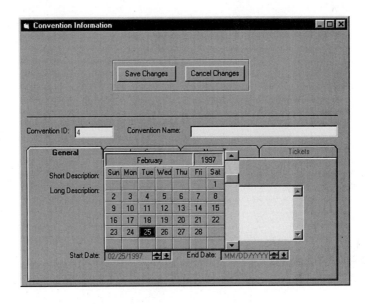

Table A.1 Vendors of Custom Controls

Vendor	Web Site	Products
Apex Software Corporation	www.apexsc.com	MyData Control, True DBGrid, VBA Companion
Crescent Division of Progress Software	www.progress.com/crescent	DBPak, PowerPak Pro, Internet Toolpak
Desaware, Inc.	www.desaware.com	SpyWorks, VersionStamper
FarPoint Technologies, Inc.	www.fpoint.com	ButtonMaker, Tab Pro, Spread
Sax Software	www.saxsoft.com	Basic Engine Pro, Setup Wizard, Webster Control
Sheridan Software Systems	www.shersoft.com	ClassAssist, Sheridan Components Suite, VBAssist
VideoSoft	www.videosoft.com	VSFlex/OCX, VS-OCX, VSView
Visual Components, Inc.	www.visualcomp.com	CodeBank, Formula One, First Impression, Visual Developers Suite Deal OCX

Using Other Print Materials

In addition to books, there are a number of [...]
These magazines provide descriptions of pr[...]
and informative columns by noted authors. [...]
with their publishers and contact numbers.

Table A.2   Magazines Covering Visu[...]

Magazine	Publisher
Visual Basic Programmer's Journal	Fawcette Tech[...] Publications
VB Tech Journal	Oakley Publis[...]
Inside Visual Basic	The Cobb Gro[...]
Access/Visual Basic Advisor	Advisor Public[...] Inc.

Using Online Resources

Finally, your best source of the most up-to-d[...]
Web sites out there that are devoted exclusi[...]
Visual Basic among their topics.

Using Web Sites   The first site is Que's Vi[...]
Figure A.6, contains information relating to [...]

- The latest books on Visual Basic
- Downloadable files containing Visual [...]
- Online Books, which are full text onli[...] Basic
- Links to other Visual Basic sites

The Visual Basic Resource center can be fo[...]

Another great site is the WINDX site maint[...]
Programmer's Journal. This site contains, a[...]
Basic products and source code for the arti[...]
at **http://www.windx.com** (see Figure A.7[...]

One final site to mention is Carl and Gary's [...]
and best known Web sites devoted to Visua[...]
latest news about VB, reviews of third-party [...]
ics, and links to other Web sites. Visit Carl [...]
www.apexwsc.com/vb/.

Finding More Information About Visual Basic

This book has provided you with a lot of the information you need to develop programs using Visual Basic. Obviously, though, there is a lot of information that could not be squeezed into this book. Fortunately for you, there are a number of other sources available to teach you about advanced programming topics.

The first source of additional information is part of the Visual Basic package itself. Visual Basic comes with an extensive set of help files that provide all the details about each control and programming command. If this is not enough for you, VB Books Online also comes with the Visual Basic package. This product provides you with additional in-depth help on a variety of programming topics. Books Online also has a good search engine that helps you find what you are looking for (see Figure A.4).

FIG. A.4
VB Books Online is a useful database of programming help and sample code.

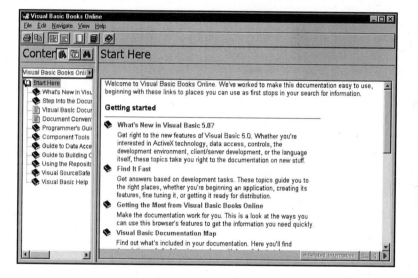

Using Microsoft Sources

As you might expect, Microsoft is a great source of additional information on Visual Basic. There are two really good sources of information available from Microsoft. One is free, and the other is available at a reasonable price.

The free resource is, of course, Microsoft's Visual Basic Web site. You can access this site at **http://www.microsoft.com/vbasic**. This site, shown in Figure A.5, provides some great information, including the following:

- Information about the latest developments in Visual Basic
- Access to the knowledge base of bug fixes and coding techniques
- Free downloads of sample programs and occasionally some product betas
- Descriptions of what some companies are doing with Visual Basic programs

FIG. A.5
Microsoft's Visual Basic Web site provides samples, Visual Basic technical articles, and access to MSDN information.

The other source available from Microsoft is the
This product is a subscription to a set of CDs. Th
provide you with the latest information on bugs,
papers from technical conferences, and a bunch
Microsoft sends out the MSDN newsletter to its
timely information about Visual Basic and other

Reading Other Books About Visual B

The first source of additional information are bo
automation and client/server programming. Oth
dia applications, the Windows API, and program

Some additional books available from Macmillan

- *Building Windows 95 Applications with Vis*
- *Building Multimedia Applications with Vis:*
- *Database Developer's Guide with Visual Ba*
- *Doing Objects in Microsoft Visual Basic*

You will also find some good books published by

- *Special Edition Using Microsoft Access 97*
- *Access 97 Expert Solutions*
- *Special Edition Using VBA for Excel*

What's on the CD

We have assembled the contents of the CD-ROM that accompanies this book to provide you with a useful resource that both supplements and extends the content of the book. On the CD you can find source code from the book that you can easily copy and paste into your own applications, and we've also included all of the applications created or used in the text. To give you more flexibility in using the content of the book, we've also supplied electronic versions of it so you can easily search for and bookmark key passages, procedures, and so forth.

Another exciting part of the CD is an ample supply of new, unique, and helpful software, shareware, and evaluation software we've included. You can use much of this software in creating your own ActiveX controls, and other software provides you with Internet, Web, and other capabilities.

This appendix outlines the basic content and structure of the CD, discusses using the CD contents, and describes the array of software included. ■

An Overview of the CD-ROM

As mentioned already, the CD provides a variety of useful contents. Here's an overview of what you can find:

- Sample code and applications from the book.
- A collection of demonstration applications, scaled-down software, and shareware.
- Full versions of programs such as Microsoft Internet Explorer 3.
- An electronic version of the book in HTML format, which can be read by using any World Wide Web browser on any platform.

The CD contains several subdirectories located off of the root directory. The directories on the CD are as follows (see Table B.1), with application, code, or chapter-specific subdirectories under each of these:

Table B.1 Directory Structure on the CD

Directory	Contents
\HTMLVER	HTML version of the online books included on the CD.
\CODE	The source code from the book. Each chapter that contains sample files, source code, and so on will be contained in a subdirectory named for the chapter it references.
\SOFTWARE	The software provided for your use and evaluation.

Sample Code and Applications

This book contains many code examples in the form of numbered listings that are referenced in the text, as in "see Listing 10.1." These listings are sample code files, provided for example, planning, and reuse purposes. The listing headings direct you to the files on the CD. For example, consider the following listing heading:

Listing 10.1 10_01.HTM—Creating the New *snarfle* Page

This heading indicates that this particular code listing (or example) is included electronically on the CD. To find it, browse to the \CODE subdirectory on the CD and select the file name that matches the one referenced in the listing header from the chapter indicated. In this example, you'd look in the Chapter 10 subdirectory and open the 10_01.HTM file.

In addition to the sample code, a variety of complete programs and controls used or created in the book are on the CD. Such files are indicated by an On the CD icon like the one in the margin next to this paragraph. You locate these files just as you do the source code files.

Using the Electronic Book

Platinum Edition Using Visual Basic 5 is available to you on the CD as an HTML document. It can be read from any World Wide Web browser that you may have currently installed on your machine (such as Internet Explorer or Netscape Navigator). If you don't have a Web browser, Microsoft's Internet Explorer is included for you.

N O T E In addition to the complete book on the CD, we have included four bonus chapters and a supplemental appendix that do not appear in the book. The bonus chapters cover the topics of graphics, Visual SourceSafe, multimedia, a SQL primer, and security. The appendixes are all found at the end of the electronic book. ▪

App

B

Reading the Electronic Book as an HTML Document

To read the electronic book as an HTML document, you need to start your Web browser and open the document file TOC.HTML located in the \HTMLVER subdirectory of the CD. Alternatively, you can browse the CD directory by using Windows Explorer or My Computer and double-clicking TOC.HTML.

After you have opened the TOC.HTML page, you can access all of the book's contents by clicking the highlighted chapter number or topic name. The electronic book works like any other Web page; when you click a hot link, a new page is opened or the browser takes you to the new location in the document. As you read through the electronic book, you will notice other highlighted words or phrases. Clicking these cross-references also takes you to a new location within the electronic book. You can always use your browser's forward or backward buttons to return to your original location.

Installing Internet Explorer

If you don't have a Web browser installed on your machine, you can use Microsoft's Internet Explorer 3.0, which is included on the CD-ROM.

Microsoft Internet Explorer can be installed from the self-extracting file in the \EXPLORER directory. Double-click MSIE30.exe, or use the Control Panel's Add/Remove Programs option and follow the instructions in the setup routine.

ON THE WEB

http://www.microsoft.com/ie   Other versions of this software can be downloaded from Microsoft's Web site.

Products and Demos from Third-Party Vendors

The rest of this appendix identifies and describes all of the third-party programs, previews, and demos included on the CD. There are some truly innovative tools on the CD. Everything from ActiveX controls to Visual Basic extensions for your site to browsers, viewers, and content creation utilities are included. Be sure to take a few minutes and browse the different toys that are available.

> **N O T E** Most of the products on the CD are demos or shareware. You could have some difficulty running them on your particular machine. If you do, feel free to contact the vendor. (A vendor would rather have you evaluate their product than ignore it.)
>
> Please note the licensing agreements and obligations for shareware and the purchasing information for registered versions when applicable. ▪

Bennet-Tec Information Systems

ALLText HT/Pro ALLText HT/Pro is a professional level edition of the popular ALLText mixed font textbox. Designed for demanding users, ALLText HT/Pro offers all the features from of the ALLText standard edition plus RTF support, Hypertext tagging, OLE Objects and Picture Support. Everything you need to make a professional HyperText or multimedia application.

MetaDraw MetaDraw is a special purpose picture box/image-editing tool. MetaDraw looks like a standard picture box within your application, but offers unique support for the creation, editing, and display of MetaFiles—an ideal graphical format for applications requiring the drawing or moving of graphical objects. MetaDraw is also specially designed to allow you to tag individual graphic objects for HyperGraphic/HotSpot applications.

TList 3/Pro TLIST3/Pro is the professional edition of the popular TList standard control. Built for users who need real power, Tlist3 Pro offers all the features from the standard edition plus a host of features to handle the most demanding job.

Black Diamond Consulting

Surround Video SDK The Surround Video SDK is a collection of tools that developers can use to add 360 degree panoramic images to an application, as well as an ActiveX control to allow the use of Surround Video images in HTML documents or Web pages. The images can either be photographed or generated via 3-D rendering software, and they allow users interactive navigation within photo-realistic environments. The Surround Video SDK supports progressive rendering, hot-spotting with URL links, and development of Internet and CD-ROM multimedia titles.

Citrix Systems

WinFrame ICA Client Work with standard Windows applications from your Internet browser using WinFrame Web Client from Citrix. WinFrame Web Client allows you to work with any 16- or 32-bit Windows-based application linked to a standard HTML Web page or embedded with an ActiveX control. For the first time, companies can enrich their Internet/intranet Web sites by seamlessly integrating off-the-shelf Windows-based applications by using WinFrame server software. WinFrame is extremely efficient over low-bandwidth connections for any PC, Mac, or UNIX client.

Data Dynamics, Limited

DynamiCube   DynamiCube facilitates data mining/analysis through instant filtering, drill-down, roll-up, and pivoting of virtually unlimited quantities of relational data. Developers can license DynamiCube and easily drop its OLAP and reporting capabilities into applications, including Web sites, with full control over which features and capabilities will be available to the end user.

ImageFX

FXPic Demo   Add the fastest, high-speed image display to your Windows applications or Web pages! With the latest, leading-edge imaging technology of Pegasus Imaging Corporation, FXPic is the exciting new way of displaying images up to eight times faster. PIC, BMP, and JPEG are displayed with over 100 professional special effects.

FractalFX Demo   FractalFX adds the highest quality display of resolution independence images with ImageFX's award-winning special effects. Choose from over 100 special effects to display FIF and BMP files. Supports color transparency, 3-D borders/bevels, hot spots, and custom cursors.

FXTools Professional Demo   FXTools 4.0, eight multimedia ActiveXs and VBXs with unmatched performance and special effects features. Display images, text, shapes, and video with 113 main, transition, and dissolve effects. Supports 10 image formats, 3-D fonts, block shadows, 3-D borders, rotated text, off-shaped hotspots, gradient styles, unlimited composition features, and more.

VectorFX Demo   VectorFX is a recent breakthrough for adding vector image support to your Windows applications and Web pages. Displays CorelDRAW, AutoCAD, and other vector images with over 100 professional special effects. Displays CDR, CGM, DRW, DXF, EPS Preview, GEM, PLT, HGL, PIC, WPG, and WMF like never before.

K L Group

Olectra Chart   Olectra Chart is the first charting OLE/ActiveX Control that is both easy to use and advanced enough to build virtually any chart, including X-Y plots, bar charts, area charts, pie charts, combination graphs, financial graphs, and logarithmic scientific charts. With two OCXs, two DLLs, and hundreds of well-structured properties, methods, and events to choose from, you can easily build and control almost any graph. End users can manipulate, tune, and adjust charts through tab-based property pages that are included with Olectra Chart.

OpenMap Software

DBMap   DBMap Control is a data bound ActiveX control targeted to developers using integrated development environments. DBMap Control enables developers to provide three main areas of functionality to users: Map and CAD drawing display; Thematic shading of points, lines, and polygons; and Database query via picked features.

ProtoView Development

Data Table Grid Control   Data Table is a high-performance grid component. With its compact size, virtual memory, and advanced data-caching schemes, Data Table is clearly designed for industrial real-world applications. Features include: editable cells, cells may have bitmaps, check boxes or combo boxes, set colors and fonts for cells, horizontal and vertical splitter windows, resize columns and rows, column sorting, region selection, built-in column searches and column totaling, 3-D effects, and more. Full message based, OWL and MFC class programming interfaces. Packaged as 16/32-bit DLL, VBX, and OCX. Source code available.

InterAct   InterAct is a software component that may be used to display complete relationships rules in an intuitive easy-to-read diagram metaphor. Choose from an assortment of shapes, bitmaps, and lines to create your diagram. Setting colors, fonts, text, and 3-D effects is easy when you use the built-in diagramming editor. Advanced features like zoom in, zoom out, and printing are standard features. Package includes OCX and DLL.

ProtoView Interface Component Set (PICS)   PICS offers sophisticated controls for date/calendar, time, and numeric input using your choice of odometer, LED readout, or normal display. Add to these a slick looking gauge control, font and point-size selection control, multidirectional spin button, stereo volume control, and fancy icon buttons. PICS also contains a powerful hierarchical list box that includes an unlimited number of bitmaps per list, over 100 functions for complete control of subtrees, selection, display, searching, and item manipulation. Full message based, OWL and MFC class programming interfaces. Packaged as 16/32-bit DLL, VBX, and OCX. Source code available.

Mabry Software

ALARM   ALARM is a custom control that lets you set multiple alarms to go off (that is, fire events) at various times during the day. This control makes it easy to schedule events. Just set the properties and wait for ALARM to notify you. You can specify such times as 9:12am, 10:45pm, every hour on the hour, every ten minutes, once per minute, and so on. ALARM even tells you when the date has changed. You can use this to remove all of the current alarms and set new ones for the day. A must if you're writing a PIM (Personal Information Manager). Includes VBX and 16- and 32-bit OCX controls.

ASOCKET   ASOCKET provides sequenced, reliable, full-duplex connection-based byte streams. Uses the Transmission Control Protocol (TCP). It also supports datagrams using the User Datagram Protocol (UDP). Includes VBX and 32-bit OCX controls. Microsoft Visual C++ v4.0 source code is available at additional cost for all controls.

BARCOD   BARCOD makes barcode display and printing really easy. Just pick the orientation, set the size, and pick the barcode style. Then set the caption to whatever you want the bars to be. BARCOD uses the Caption property to determine what to display. This control is good for inventory applications, identification systems, and any other programs that require printed computer-readable data. Samples included show you how to print barcodes using the Printer Object and how to copy a bitmap of the barcode to the Clipboard. Includes VBX and 16- and 32-bit OCX controls. Microsoft Visual C++ v4.0 source code is available at additional cost for all controls.

DFINFO   DFINFO gives you disk and file information that VB doesn't provide. It also enables you to change some aspects of a file, such as attributes, size, date, and time. The disk side of this control enables you to find out how much disk space you have and how much of it is free. You can also read volume names. The file side of this control enables you to find out all of the important information about a file (size, attribute flags, and date and time of last modification). It also enables you to change most of the attribute flags and change the size of the file as well. Includes VBX and 16- and 32-bit OCX controls. Microsoft Visual C++ v4.0 source code is available at additional cost for all controls.

FINGER   FINGER requests user information from another host. Typical information includes last date of logon, mail waiting, real name, address, and phone number. FINGER complies with RFC 1288. Includes VBX and 32-bit OCX controls. Microsoft Visual C++ v4.0 source code is available at additional cost for all controls.

FLABEL   FLABEL is a label control that lets you format the text within it. You can have different fonts, different colors, multiple paragraphs, paragraph formatting, and so forth. All this and it's bound, too. Includes VBX and 16- and 32-bit OCX controls. Microsoft Visual C++ v4.0 source code is available at additional cost for all controls.

FTP   FTP 32-bit OCX control allows you to log on to remote hosts to transfer files to and from the remote host. FTP works in conjunction with GETHST for address resolution. FTP complies with RFC 959. Microsoft Visual C++ v4.0 source code is available at additional cost for all controls.

GETHST   GETHST 32-bit OCX control allows you to translate from host name to IP address, and IP address to host name. Microsoft Visual C++ v4.0 source code is available at additional cost for all controls.

GOPHER   GOPHER 32-bit OCX control encapsulates the Gopher protocol used to provide access to documents and files, and to search databases available on the Internet. Microsoft Visual C++ v4.0 source code is available at additional cost for all controls.

HITIME   HITIME is a high-resolution timer. You use this control just like the default Timer control that comes with Visual Basic. Visual Basic's Timer control can only fire an event every 55 milliseconds (18.2 times per second). HITIME can fire events at a much higher rate. How high depends on the speed of your machine. 486D2/66s can handle more than 500 ticks per second. Includes VBX and 16- and 32-bit OCX controls. Microsoft Visual C++ v4.0 source code is available at additional cost for all controls.

INDICATOR   INDICATOR shows a gauge that looks like those found on the front of stereos (tri-color, multiple lights). This control includes horizontal and vertical versions of the indicator. Includes VBX and 16- and 32-bit OCX controls. Microsoft Visual C++ v4.0 source code is available at additional cost for all controls.

INICON   INICON makes INI file access simple. WIN.INI and private INI file access are both supported. No API calls required. Includes VBX and 16- and 32-bit OCX controls. Microsoft Visual C++ v4.0 source code is available at additional cost for all controls.

JOYSTK   JOYSTK gives your program information and events about the joystick's movement and buttons. One or two normal joysticks or one 3-D joystick are supported. JOYSTK (VBX only) comes with a joystick driver for Windows (required). This driver supports 4-button joysticks (such as the Gravis PC GamePad). Includes VBX and 16- and 32-bit OCX controls. Microsoft Visual C++ v4.0 source code is available at additional cost for all controls.

KNOB   KNOB is a knob. You can change the size, have tick marks around it, have text near the tick marks, change some of the colors, and so on. You can use KNOB to control volume, pitch, tempo, or anything else you might control with a scroll bar or slider. Includes VBX and 16- and 32-bit OCX controls. Microsoft Visual C++ v4.0 source code is available at additional cost for all controls.

LED   LED behaves like an LED. 3-D effects and colors are all user-definable. This control is useful whenever you need a passive on/off indicator (modem lights, working lights, and so forth). Includes VBX and 16- and 32-bit OCX controls. Microsoft Visual C++ v4.0 source code is available at additional cost for all controls.

MAIL   MAIL 32-bit OCX control encapsulates the Simple Mail Transfer Protocol (SMTP) and the Post Office Protocol (POP) for managing e-mail on the Internet. MAIL supports attachments. Microsoft Visual C++ v4.0 source code is available at additional cost for all controls.

MIDIFILE   MIDIFILE provides the Visual Basic programmer with an easy way to read and write MIDI files, both formats 0 (single track) and 1 (multiple tracks). By using the MIDIFILE control, you can modify existing MIDI files or create entirely new ones from scratch. You have complete control over and access to every type of MIDI message, and you can insert, delete, and modify tracks and messages at any time. Includes VBX and 16- and 32-bit OCX controls. Microsoft Visual C++ v4.0 source code is available at additional cost for all controls.

MIDI I/O   MIDI I/O is really two controls in one. The MIDIIN control handles the MIDI input and the MIDIOUT control handles the MIDI output. The MIDIIN control is used to receive MIDI messages from external MIDI devices. Messages can be retrieved using events or polling, and are time-stamped with millisecond accuracy. The MIDIIN control has an internal queueing mechanism so if messages arrive faster than your application can handle them, they will not be lost. The MIDIOUT control gives you complete control over the contents and timing of MIDI messages sent to either internal or external MIDI devices.

You can queue as many messages as you like (within the constraints of available memory) before starting output, or you can queue one or more messages prior to starting output and then add more as the output proceeds. Messages are scheduled for transmission at a time you specify relative to the time that output is started. As with the MIDIIN control, timing has millisecond resolution, giving you the ability to precisely control the timing of sent MIDI messages. Includes VBX and 16- and 32-bit OCX controls. Microsoft Visual C++ v4.0 source code is available at additional cost for all controls.

NEWS   NEWS provides easy access to Network News Transfer Protocol (NNTP) servers as specified in RFC 977. It supports user authentication protocol and is unique in providing access to non-standard server commands through READ/WRITE methods. Includes VBX and 32-bit OCX controls. Microsoft Visual C++ v4.0 source code is available at additional cost for all controls.

PERCNT   PERCNT displays a percentage bar on your form. This makes status reporting very easy. 3-D effects, fonts, and colors are all at your control. Includes VBX and 16- and 32-bit OCX controls. Microsoft Visual C++ v4.0 source code is available at additional cost for all controls.

PICBTN   PICBTN is a command button that has both text and a picture on it. The picture can be scaled and placed above, below, to the right, or to the left of the text. The text may be multi-line. Includes VBX and 16- and 32-bit OCX controls. Microsoft Visual C++ v4.0 source code is available at additional cost for all controls.

App

B

ROTEXT   ROTEXT lets you place a label on your forms at any angle or degree of rotation. This control can be bound to a data control. Includes VBX and 16- and 32-bit OCX controls. Microsoft Visual C++ v4.0 source code is available at additional cost for all controls.

SLIDER   SLIDER provides horizontal and vertical sliders. You can select from different slider styles, track styles, colors, ticks, and so forth. Includes VBX and 16- and 32-bit OCX controls. Microsoft Visual C++ v4.0 source code is available at additional cost for all controls.

SOUNDX   SOUNDX provides Soundex and Metaphone algorithms. Soundex and Metaphone convert words or names to codes that represent how they "sound." This can be really useful in a database application where users need to find names they may not know how to spell exactly. Use this control to make it easier for them. Just put in the word or name you want converted, and the appropriate codes come out. Includes VBX and 16- and 32-bit OCX controls. Microsoft Visual C++ v4.0 source code is available at additional cost for all controls.

TALK   TALK allows you to interactively communicate with users on remote hosts in order to chat. Includes 32-bit OCX control. Microsoft Visual C++ v4.0 source code is available at additional cost for all controls.

TIME   TIME encapsulates the Network Time Protocol (NTP) to allow you to retrieve the Greenwich Mean Time from supporting hosts on the Internet. The TIME control allows you to develop time synchronization applications for your system (among other things). Incorporating this control into your application allows you to request the Greenwich Mean time from any time-server that you select. Includes VBX and 32-bit OCX controls. Microsoft Visual C++ v4.0 source code is available at additional cost for all controls.

TIPS   TIPS provides Microsoft-style tool tips. Small windows pop up with bits of info when the user pauses the mouse over your controls. No code is required; just set the Tag properties. TIPS attaches itself to the hWnd property of a control. Includes VBX and 16- and 32-bit OCX controls. Microsoft Visual C++ v4.0 source code is available at additional cost for all controls.

VALIDATE   VALIDATE makes data validation much easier. This control allows you to collect all of the data validation code for a form into one event procedure. This results in smaller and more maintainable code. Validate works only with controls that have an hWnd property. Includes 16- and 32-bit OCX controls. Microsoft Visual C++ v4.0 source code is available at additional cost for all controls.

WAVE   WAVE makes it easy for you to play and get information about WAV files. Play WAV files in the background as your program performs other tasks, and add recorded speech to your applications. This is all very straightforward. Set the `Filename` property and tell it to go. That's it. WAVE requires a sound card. Includes VBX and 16- and 32-bit OCX controls. Microsoft Visual C++ v4.0 source code is available at additional cost for all controls.

WHOIS   WHOIS provides access to the WHOIS servers on the Internet. By incorporating WHOIS into your applications, you may query for information about hosts, users, and businesses who have accounts on the Internet. Includes 32-bit OCX control. Microsoft Visual C++ v4.0 source code is available at additional cost for all controls.

ZIPINF   ZIPINF gives you information about the content (directory) of a ZIP file and has many uses (file Manager replacement, drive searching, and so on). Includes VBX and 16- and 32-bit OCX controls. Microsoft Visual C++ v4.0 source code is available at additional cost for all controls.

mBED Software

mBED Control for ActiveX   mBED Software is the only open solution for Web-smart, media-rich interactivity. mBED Interactor makes authoring multimedia mbedlets quick and easy.

McRae Software International

GridWiz   GridWiz ActiveX is an incredibly flexible set of grid ActiveX controls. GridWiz support many different cell types and formatting options. Bindable to ODBC or DAO. Online documentation and sample code provided.

J. Ritmeijer

ActiveX Game of Life   The traditional game in an ActiveX control.

StatistiX   The control parses the page it's embedded in for useful statistical information and then displays it in a graph. This control is still in development.

Sax Software

Sax Webster Control   The evaluation copy of Sax Webster control contains the full-featured 32-bit OCX of their Web-browsing custom control. Webster uses your system's installed TCP/IP stack to let you browse without doing any coding. You get instant interactive access to the Web from within your program, plus support for printing, Level 3 HTML, on- or off-line browsing, and more. The Evaluation Copy can be used only for evaluation purposes.

Template Graphics Software

Visual 3Space Control   Visual 3Space control is a 3-D/VRML ActiveX control used to add 3-D functionality to Microsoft Visual C++, Visual Basic, and Internet Explorer. Delivering over 400 property and method settings, including user interface components to cameras, lights, events and geometry control, Visual 3Space control supports both intranet- and Internet-capable 3-D applications, DXF, VRML, and Open Inventor.

Tumbleweed Software

Envoy Control for ActiveX   Try one of the first controls for Internet Explorer ActiveX. Tumbleweed Envoy Control for ActiveX currently provides viewing capabilities. This demo product is also available for download free of charge from the Tumbleweed Web site: **www.tumbleweed.com/download.htm**

Vosaic

Vosaic-X   Vosaic-X permits a seamless, transparent user download of the Vosaic-X ActiveX component to view real-time video and audio streams over the Web and any IP-based network. Vosaic-X streams standards-compliant-based MPEG and H.263, and GSM audio.

Vivo Software

VivoActive Player for ActiveX   VivoActive from Vivo Software is the world's first SERVERLESS streaming video product, and users report in great numbers that they get excellent video quality even at very low bit rates. Since there's no server component, the high cost and hassle of providing streaming video are eliminated. Now, even over 28.8 modems, Web surfers can watch uninterrupted streaming audio/video content that pretty much starts to play when they click.

Microsoft

ActiveX Control Pad, VB5CCE, and Internet Explorer are all Microsoft products. There are some truly innovative tools on the CD that enable you to do some fun things with your pages. Everything from ActiveX controls to Visual Basic extensions for your site to browsers, viewers, and content creation utilities are included. Be sure to take a few minutes and browse the different toys that are available.

App
B

Index

Complete and Return this Card for a *FREE* Computer Book Catalog

Thank you for purchasing this book! You have purchased a superior computer book written expressly for your needs. To continue to provide the kind of up-to-date, pertinent coverage you've come to expect from us, we need to hear from you. Please take a minute to complete and return this self-addressed, postage-paid form. In return, we'll send you a free catalog of all our computer books on topics ranging from word processing to programming and the internet.

Mr. ☐   Mrs. ☐   Ms. ☐   Dr. ☐

Name (first) [ ] (M.I.) [ ] (last) [ ]

Address [ ]

[ ]

City [ ]   State [ ]   Zip [ ]

Phone [ ]   Fax [ ]

Company Name [ ]

E-mail address [ ]

1. Please check at least (3) influencing factors for purchasing this book.

Front or back cover information on book .... ☐
Special approach to the content .... ☐
Completeness of content .... ☐
Author's reputation .... ☐
Publisher's reputation .... ☐
Book cover design or layout .... ☐
Index or table of contents of book .... ☐
Price of book .... ☐
Special effects, graphics, illustrations .... ☐
Other (Please specify): _____

2. How did you first learn about this book?

Saw in Macmillan Computer Publishing catalog .... ☐
Recommended by store personnel .... ☐
Saw the book on bookshelf at store .... ☐
Recommended by a friend .... ☐
Received advertisement in the mail .... ☐
Saw an advertisement in: _____ ☐
Read book review in: _____ ☐
Other (Please specify): _____ ☐

3. How many computer books have you purchased in the last six months?

This book only .... ☐   3 to 5 books .... ☐
2 books .... ☐   More than 5 .... ☐

4. Where did you purchase this book?

Bookstore .... ☐
Computer Store .... ☐
Consumer Electronics Store .... ☐
Department Store .... ☐
Office Club .... ☐
Warehouse Club .... ☐
Mail Order .... ☐
Direct from Publisher .... ☐
Internet site .... ☐
Other (Please specify): _____ ☐

5. How long have you been using a computer?

☐ Less than 6 months   ☐ 6 months to a year
☐ 1 to 3 years   ☐ More than 3 years

6. What is your level of experience with personal computers and with the subject of this book?

	With PCs	With subject of book
New	☐	☐
Casual	☐	☐
Accomplished	☐	☐
Expert	☐	☐

Source Code ISBN: 0-7897-1412-4

7. Which of the following best describes your job title?

Administrative Assistant .... ☐
Coordinator .... ☐
Manager/Supervisor .... ☐
Director .... ☐
Vice President .... ☐
President/CEO/COO .... ☐
Lawyer/Doctor/Medical Professional .... ☐
Teacher/Educator/Trainer .... ☐
Engineer/Technician .... ☐
Consultant .... ☐
Not employed/Student/Retired .... ☐
Other (Please specify): _____ ☐

8. Which of the following best describes the area of the company your job title falls under?

Accounting .... ☐
Engineering .... ☐
Manufacturing .... ☐
Operations .... ☐
Marketing .... ☐
Sales .... ☐
Other (Please specify): _____ ☐

9. What is your age?

Under 20 .... ☐
21-29 .... ☐
30-39 .... ☐
40-49 .... ☐
50-59 .... ☐
60-over .... ☐

10. Are you:

Male .... ☐
Female .... ☐

11. Which computer publications do you read regularly? (Please list)

_____
_____
_____
_____
_____
_____
_____
_____
_____

Fold here and scotch-tape to mail.

Comments: _____
_____
_____

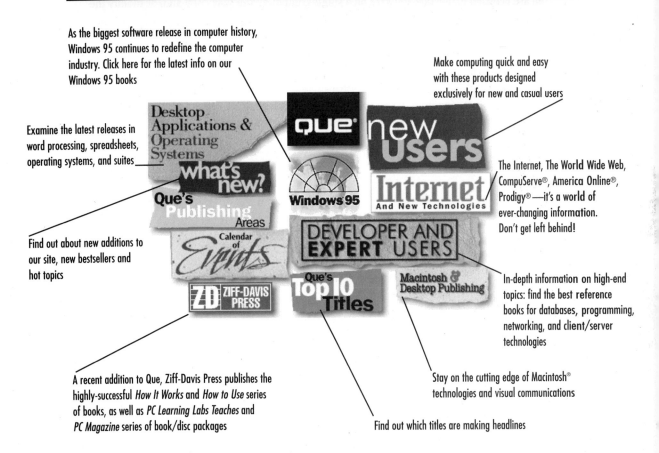